The Practical

Bible Dictionary & Concordance

- **Bible Dictionary**
- **Concordance**
- **The Treasury of Biblical Information**

Complete and Unabridged

A BARBOUR BOOK

DICTIONARY

CONCORDANCE

INFORMATION

Published by arrangement with Holman Bible Publishers by

Barbour and Company, Inc.
P.O. Box 719
Uhrichsville, Ohio 44683

EVANGELICAL CHRISTIAN PUBLISHERS ASSOCIATION  MEMBER

Trade paper 0-916441-28-8
Leatherette 0-916441-29-6
Hardbound 0-916441-30-X

Printed in the United States of America.

DICTIONARY

THE SELF-PRONOUNCING BIBLE DICTIONARY.

AN INDISPENSABLE COMPANION FOR THE CLERGY, S. S. TEACHER, AND HOME READER.

Copiously Illustrated.

WORDS SYLLABIFIED AND ACCENTED; SOUNDS DIACRITICALLY MARKED; HEBREW, GREEK AND OTHER EQUIVALENTS GIVEN IN ENGLISH; CONCISE DEFINITIONS; ABUNDANT TEXTUAL REFERENCES.

By JAMES P. BOYD, A. M.

KEY TO PRONUNCIATION: — The hyphen (-) separates unaccented syllables. The double hyphen (=) separates compound words. (′) marks the primary accent and (″) the secondary accent.
ā as in fāte; ậ in courậge; ă in hăt; â in câre; ä in fär; ȧ in lȧst; ạ in fạll; a̱ obscure as in lia̱r.
ē as in mēte; ê in rêdeem; ĕ in mĕt; ẽ obtuse as in tẽrm; ẹ obscure as in fuẹl.
ī as in pīne; ỉ in cỉtation; ĭ in pĭn; ĩ obtuse in fĩrm; ị in familịar; i̱ obscure in rui̱n.
ō as in nōte; ô in annôtate; ŏ in nŏt; ô in fôr; o̱ obscure as in valo̱r.
ū as in mūte; ŭ in tŭb; û obtuse as in hûrl; ṳ in rṳde; ụ in pụsh.
ȳ as in stȳle; y̆ in ny̆mph.
ç soft as in çent; c hard not marked; ġ soft as in ġender; ḡ hard before e, i, and y, as ḡet, Ḡideon; g hard otherwise not marked; ș as z in mușe; x̣ as *gs* in ex̣ample.

A

Ā. See ALPHA.

Aâr′on (*mountaineer or enlightener*). Son of Amram and Jochebed, and elder brother of Moses and Miriam, Num. xxvi. 59. Direct descendant of Levi by both parents. Called "the Levite," Ex. iv. 14, when chosen as the "spokesman" of Moses. Married Elisheba, daughter of the prince of Judah, and had four sons, Nadab, Abihu, Eleazar, and Ithamar, Ex. vi. 23. Eighty-three years old when introduced in the Bible. Mouthpiece and encourager of Moses before the Lord and the people of Israel, and in the Court of the Pharaoh, Ex. iv. 30; vii. 2. Miracle worker of the Exodus, Ex. vii. 19. Helped Hur to stay the weary hands of Moses in the battle with Amalek, Ex. xvii. 9-12. In a weak moment yielded to idolatry among his people and incurred the wrath of Moses, Ex. xxxii. Consecrated to the priesthood by Moses, Ex. xxix. Anointed and sanctified, with his sons, to minister in the priest's office, Ex. xl. Murmured against Moses at the instance of Miriam, but repented and joined Moses in prayer for Miriam's recovery, Num. xii. His authority in Israel vindicated by the miracle of the rod, Num. xvii. Died on Mt. Hor, at age of one hundred and twenty-three years, and was succeeded in the priesthood by his son Eleazar, Num. xx. 22-29. Office continued in his line till time of Eli. Restored to house of Eleazar by Solomon, 1 Kgs. ii. 27.

Aâr′on-ītes. Priests of the line of Aaron, 1 Chr. xii. 27, of whom Jehoiada was "chief," or "leader," in the time of King Saul, 1 Chr. xxvii. 5.

Ăb (*father*). (1) A syllable of frequent occurrence in the composition of Hebrew proper names, and signifies possession or endowment. Appears in Chaldaic form of Abba in N. T., Mark xiv. 36; Rom. viii. 15; Gal. iv. 6. (2) Eleventh month of the Jewish civil, and fifth of the sacred, year; corresponding to parts of July and August. [MONTH.]

Ăb′ā-cŭc, 2 Esdr. i. 40. [HABAKKUK.]

Ȃ-băd′don (*destroyer*). King of the locusts, and angel of the bottomless pit. The Greek equivalent is Apollyon, Rev. ix. 11.

Ăb″ă-dī′as, 1 Esdr. viii. 35. [OBADIAH.]

Ȃ-băg′thȧ (*God-given*). One of the seven chamberlains in the court of King Ahasuerus, Esth. i. 10.

Ăb′ā-na (*stony*). A river of Damascus, preferred by Naaman to the Jordan for healing purposes, 2 Kgs. v. 12. Believed to be identical with the present Barada, which rises in the Anti-Libanus range, twenty-three miles N. W. of Damascus, runs by several streams through the city, and thence across a plain into the "Meadow Lakes," where it is comparatively lost.

Ăb′ā-rim (*mountains beyond*). A range of mountains or highlands of Moab, east of and facing Jordan opposite Jericho, Num. xxvii. 12; xxxiii. 47; Deut. xxxii. 49. Ije-abarim, in Num. xxi. 11, heaps or ruins of Abarim. Nebo, Peor, and Pisgah belong to this range. "Passages," in Jer. xxii. 20.

Ăb′bȧ (*father*). Chaldaic form of Hebrew Ab. Applied to God in Mark xiv. 36; Rom. viii. 15; Gal. iv. 6.

Ăb′dȧ (*servant*). (1) Father of Adoniram, 1 Kgs. iv. 6. (2) Son of Shammua, Neh. xi. 17. Called Obadiah in 1 Chr. ix. 16.

Ăb′dẹ-el (*servant of God*). Father of Shelemiah, Jer. xxxvi. 26.

High Priest. (*See* Aaronites.)

Ăb'dī (*my servant*). (1) A Merarite, grandfather of Ethan the Singer, and father of Kishi, 1 Chr. vi. 44. (2) Father of Kish, of Levitical descent, 2 Chr. xxix. 12. (3) Son of Elam, who had married a foreign wife, in time of Ezra, Ez. x. 26.

Ăb'dī-as, 2 Esdr. i. 39. [OBADIAH.]

Ăb'dī-ĕl (*servant of God*). Father of Ahi and son of Guni. A Gadite chief of Bashan in the time of King Jotham of Judah, 1 Chr. v. 15. Milton, in "Paradise Lost," uses the name as that of a fallen angel.

Ăb'dŏn (*servile*). (1) An Ephraimite judge of Israel for eight years, Judg. xii. 13-15. Supposed to be same as Bedan in 1 Sam. xii. 11. (2) Son of Shashak, 1 Chr. viii. 23. (3) A Benjamite, son of Jehiel, of Gibeon, 1 Chr. viii. 30; ix. 36. (4) Son of Micah in Josiah's time, 2 Chr. xxxiv. 20; supposably Achbor in 2 Kgs. xxii. 12. (5) A city in tribe of Asher, assigned to the Levites, Josh. xxi. 30; 1 Chr. vi. 74; associated with modern Abdeh, 10 miles N. E. of Accho, or Acre, the Ptolemais of N. T.

Ā-bĕd'=nĕ-gō (*servant of Nego, or Nebo, name of planet Mercury worshipped as scribe and interpreter*). Name given by the prince of Chaldean eunuchs to Azariah, one of the three friends and fellow-captives at Babylon of Daniel, Dan. i. 7. He refused to bow to the golden image of Nebuchadnezzar, and was condemned to the fiery furnace, from which he miraculously escaped, Dan. iii.

Ā'bĕl (*breath, vapor*). Second son of Adam and Eve. A keeper of sheep, and murdered by his brother Cain through jealousy, Gen. iv. 2-8. *See* also Heb. xi. 4; 1 John iii. 12; Matt. xxiii. 35.

Ā'bĕl (*meadow*). A prefix for several names of towns and places. (1) The "plain of the vineyards" in Judg. xi. 33; *see* marg. (2) A city in the north of Palestine, attacked by Joab, 2 Sam. xx. 14, 15. Probably same as Abel-Beth-Maachah. "Plain of the vineyard," Judg. xi. 33, marg. note. "Great stone of," 1 Sam. vi. 18.

Ā'bĕl=bĕth=mā'ą-chah (*meadow of house of oppression*). A town in N. Palestine, near Damascus, doubtless the same as attacked by Joab, 2 Sam. xx. 14, 15; and attacked by Benhadad, 1 Kgs. xv. 20, and by Tiglath-pileser, 2 Kgs. xv. 29.

Ā'bĕl=mā'im (*meadow of waters*). Another name for Abel-beth-maachah, 2 Chr. xvi. 4.

Ā'bĕl=mĕ-hō'lah (*meadow of the dance*). A place in the Jordan valley, 1 Kgs. iv. 12, whither fled the enemy routed by Gideon, Judg. vii. 22. Home of Elisha, 1 Kgs. xix. 16.

Ā'bĕl=mĭz'ră-im (*meadow, or mourning, of Egypt*). A name given by the Canaanites to the threshing floor of Atad, where Joseph and his brethren mourned for Jacob, Gen. l. 11. Probably near Hebron.

Ā'bĕl=shĭt'tim (*meadow of the acacias*). A spot near Jordan, in Moabite plain, and last halting place of the wandering Israelites, Num. xxxiii. 49. Called Shittim in Num. xxv. 1; Josh. ii. 1.

Ā'bĕl, Stone of. Place in the field of Joshua, the Bethshemite, where the ark of the Lord was set down, 1 Sam. vi. 18.

Ā'bĕz (*lofty*). A town in the section allotted to the tribe of Issachar, Josh. xix. 20.

Ā'bī (*progenitor*). Mother of King Hezekiah and daughter of Zachariah, 2 Kgs. xviii. 2; Isa. viii. 2. Abijah in 2 Chr. xxix. 1.

Ā-bī'ȧ, Ā-bī'ah, and **Ā-bī'jah** (*the Lord is my father*), are variants of the same word. Abia in 1 Chr. iii. 10, and Matt. i. 7, is the son of Rehoboam; and in Luke i. 5, is the eighth of the twenty-four courses of priests. For division of priests *see* 1 Chr. xxiv. and particularly vs. 10.

Ā-bī'ah. (1) A son of Becher, 1 Chr. vii. 8. (2) Wife of Hezron, 1 Chr. ii. 24. (3) Second son of Samuel and associate judge with Joel in Beersheba, 1 Sam. viii. 2; 1 Chr. vi. 28.

Ā''bī=ăl'bŏn (*father of strength*). One of David's warriors, 2 Sam. xxiii. 31. Spelled Abiel in other places.

Ā-bī'ă-săph (*father of gathering*). A Levite, one of the sons of Korah, and head of a Korhite family, Ex. vi. 24. Written Ebiasaph in 1 Chr. vi. 23, 37.

Ā-bī'ą-thär (*father of abundance*). Son of Ahimelech, and fourth high priest in descent from Eli, of the line of Ithamar, younger son of Aaron, 1 Sam. xxiii. 9, only one of Ahimelech's sons who escaped the vengeance of Saul in the slaughter at Nob, 1 Sam. xxii. 19, 20. Fled to David at Keilah, and became a high priest. Deprived of the high priesthood by Solomon. For fuller history read 1 Sam. xxii. to 1 Kgs. iii.

Ā'bĭb (*green fruits*), called also Nisan. Seventh month of Jewish civil, and first of the sacred year, Ex. xii. 2. [MONTH.]

Ā-bī'dȧ and **Ā-bī'dah** (*father of knowledge*). One of the sons of Midian, 1 Chr. i. 33; Gen. xxv. 4.

Ăb'i-dăn (*father of judgment*). Chief of the tribe of Benjamin at exode, Num. i. 11; ii. 22; vii. 60; x. 24.

Ā-bī'el (*father of strength*). (1) Father of Kish and grandfather of Saul and Abner, 1 Sam. ix. 1. (2) One of David's generals, 1 Chr. xi. 32, called Abialbon in 2 Sam. xxiii. 31.

Ā''bĭ-ē'zer (*father of help*). (1) Eldest son of Gilead and head of a family in tribe of Manasseh, Josh. xvii. 2; 1 Chr. vii. 18. (2) One of David's mighty men, 2 Sam. xxiii. 27; 1 Chr. xi. 28; xxvii. 12.

Ā''bī-ĕz'rīte (*father of help*). A family descended from Abiezer, Judg. vi. 11; viii. 32.

Ăb'ī-gāil (*father of joy*). (1) Wife of Nabal of Carmel, and afterwards of David. Noted for her beauty and wisdom, 1 Sam. xxv. 3, 14-44. (2) A sister of David, married to Jether the Ishmaelite, and mother of Amasa, 2 Sam. xvii. 25; 1 Chr. ii. 17.

Ăb''i-hā'il (*father of strength*). (1) Father of Zuriel, chief of the house of the families of Marari, Num. iii. 35. (2) Wife of Abishur, 1 Chr. ii. 29. (3) Son of Huri of the tribe of Gad, 1 Chr. v. 14. (4) Wife of Rehoboam, 2 Chr. xi. 18. (5) Father of Esther and uncle of Mordecai, Esth. ii. 15; ix. 29.

Ā-bī'hū (*God is father*). Second son of Aaron and Elisheba, Num. iii. 2; Ex. vi. 23. Ascended Sinai with Moses and the elders, Ex. xxviii. 1. Set apart with his brothers for the priesthood. Consumed, with his brother Nadab, for offering strange fire before the Lord, Lev. x. 1, 2.

Ă-bī'hŭd (*father of praise*). Son of Bela and grandson of Benjamin, 1 Chr. viii. 3.

A-bī'jah and **Ă-bī'jam** (*whose father is Jehovah*). (1) A son of King Jeroboam I.; died in early life, 1 Kgs. xiv. (2) Son of Rehoboam, and his successor to the throne. A wicked king. Reign, 959-956 B. C., 2 Chr. xii. 16; xiii. Written Abijam in 1 Kgs. xv. 1. (3) A descendant of the high priest Eleazar, 1 Chr. xxiv. 10; Neh. xii. 17. The priestly course *Abia*, Luke i. 5, belonged to Zacharias, father of John the Baptist. (4) A priest who entered the covenant with Nehemiah, Neh. x. 7.

Ă-bī'jam. *See* ABIJAH (2).

Ăb-ĭ-le'nē (from Abila, *land of meadows*). A Syrian tetrarchy whose capital was Abila, situated on the eastern slopes of the Anti-Libanus range. The district was watered by the Abana, or Barada, River. Governed by Lysanias in the time of John the Baptist, Luke iii. 1.

Ă-bĭm'ă-el (*father of Mael*). A descendant of Joktan, and supposable father of the Arabic tribe of Mali, Gen. x. 28.

Ă-bĭm'ĕ-lech (*father of a king*). (1) A line of Philistine kings, like the Pharaohs and Cæsars. Kings of Gerar, Gen. xx., xxi., xxvi. 1. (2) Son of Gideon by his concubine of Shechem, Judg. viii. 31; 2 Sam. xi. 21. (3) Son of Abiathar, in David's time, 1 Chr. xviii. 16. (4) Written for the Achish of 1 Sam. xxi. 10, in title to Ps. 34.

Ă-bĭn'ă-dăb (*father of nobility*). (1) A Levite of Kirjath-jearim to whose house the ark was brought, and where it stayed for twenty years, 1 Sam. vii. 1, 2; 1 Chr. xiii. 7. (2) Second son of Jesse, and one of the three who followed Saul to battle, 1 Sam. xvi. 8; xvii. 13. (3) Son of Saul slain at Gilboa, 1 Sam. xxxi. 2. (4) Father of one of the twelve chief officers of Solomon, 1 Kgs. iv. 11.

Ăb'ĭ-nēr, Hebrew form of Abner, 1 Sam. xiv. 50, marg.

Ă-bĭn'ŏ-ăm (*gracious father*). Father of Barak, Judg. iv. 6, 12; v. 1, 12.

Ă-bī'răm (*high father*). (1) A Reubenite conspirator with Korah, Num. xvi. (2) Eldest son of Hiel, 1 Kgs. xvi. 34; written Abiron in Ecclus. xlv. 18.

Ăb-ĭ-sē'ī, or **Ăb'ĭ-shū,** son of Phinehas, 2 Esdr. i. 2. Abisum in 1 Esdr. viii. 2.

Ăb'ĭ-shag (*ignorance of the father*). The fair Shunamite, of tribe of Issachar, whom David, in his old age, introduced into his harem, 1 Kgs. i. 1-4. After David's death, Adonijah desired to marry her, but Solomon put him to death, 1 Kgs. ii. 13, etc.

Ă-bĭsh'ă-ī (*father of gift*). (1) Eldest son of David's sister Zeruiah and brother of Joab, 1 Chr. ii. 16; one of the chiefs of David's mighty men, 2 Sam. ii. 18. Counselled David to take Saul's life, 1 Sam. xxvi. 5-12. Associated with Joab in assassination of Abner, 2 Sam. iii. 30. A co-general of David's army, 2 Sam. x. 14; xviii. 2. Rescued David from the giant Ishbi-benob, 2 Sam. xxi. 16, 17.

Ă-bĭsh'a-lŏm (*father of peace*). Father-in-law of King Jeroboam, 1 Kgs. xv. 2, 10. Called Absalom in 2 Chr. xi. 20, 21.

Ă-bĭsh'ū-ă (*father of deliverance*). (1) Son of Bela, 1 Chr. viii. 4. (2) Son of Phinehas, 1 Chr. vi. 4, 5, 50; Ez. vii. 5.

Ăb'ĭ-shur (*father of the wall*). Son of Shammai, 1 Chr. ii. 28, 29.

Ăb'ĭ-tal (*father of dew*). One of David's wives, 2 Sam. iii. 4; 1 Chr. iii. 3.

Ăb'ĭ-tŭb (*father of goodness*). A Benjamite, 1 Chr. viii. 11.

A-bī'ud (*father of praise*). An ancestor of Christ, Matt. i. 13.

Ăb-lū'tion. [PURIFICATION.]

Ăb'nēr (*father of light*). (1) Son of Ner, and commander-in-chief of Saul's armies, 1 Sam. xiv. 50, 51; xvii. 57; xxvi. 5-14. Proclaimed Ishbosheth King of Israel, and went to war with David, by whom he was defeated, 2 Sam. ii. Quarrelled with Ishbosheth and espoused the cause of David, 2 Sam. iii. 7, etc. Murdered by Joab, 2 Sam. iii. 27-39. (2) Father of a Benjamite chief, 1 Chr. xxvii. 21.

Roman Standards.

Ă-bŏm-i-nā'tion (*bad omen*). A hateful or detestable thing, Gen. xlvi. 34. Used as to animals and acts in Lev. xi. 13; Deut. xxiii. 18. As to idolatry in 2 Kgs. xxiii. 13; Jer. xliv. 4. As to sins in general, Isa. lxvi. 3. The "abomination of desolation" in Dan. ix. 27; xii. 11; Matt. xxiv. 15, doubtless refers to the standards and banners of the conquering Roman armies with their idolatrous images and legends.

Absalom's Pillar. (*See* p. 4.)

Ā'bră-hăm and **Ā'brăm** (*father of a multitude*). Son of Terah, a dweller in Ur of the Chaldees, Gen.

xi. 25–31. Founder of the Jewish nation. Migrated from Chaldea to Haran. Moved thence to Canaan, to Egypt and back to Canaan, where he settled amid the oak-groves of Mamre. There confirmed in the thrice repeated promise that his seed should become a mighty nation, and his name changed from Abram to Abraham. Died, aged 175 years, and was buried in the tomb of Machpelah, Gen. xii.–xxvi.

Ăb'sa-lŏm (*father of peace*). (1) A son of David, 2 Sam. iii. 3. Killed his brother Amnon, 2 Sam. xiii. Fled to Geshur, 2 Sam. xiii. 37, 38. Returned and conspired to usurp his father's throne, 2 Sam. xiv.–xvii. Defeated at Gilead and slain by Joab, 2 Sam. xviii. (2) Father of Mattathias, 1 Macc. xi. 70.

Ăb'sa-lŏm's Pil'lar, built by Absalom in the "King's dale," or valley of Kedron, 2 Sam. xviii. 18.

Ăb'sa-lŏn. An ambassador of John to Lysias, 2 Macc. xi. 17.

Ā-bū'bŭs. Son-in-law of Simon, 1 Macc. xvi. 11–15.

Ā-cā'çĭ-å (*point*). The *Acacia seyal* of Arabia, a large tree, highly prized for its wood, is supposed to be the Shittim wood of the Bible. A smaller species (*Acacia Arabica*) yielded an aromatic gum.

Acacia.

Ăc'ă-tăn. 1 Esdr. viii. 38. [HAKKATAN.]

Ăc'căd (*fortress*). A city built by Nimrod in Shinar, Gen. x. 10.

Ăc'ca-rŏn. [EKRON.]

Ăc'chō (*heated sand*). The Ptolemais of N. T.; now Acre, on Mediterranean coast, Judg. i. 31; Acts xxi. 7.

Ăc'cŏs. Grandfather of Eupolemus, 1 Macc. viii. 17.

Ā-çĕl'da-må (*field of blood*). A field near Jerusalem purchased with Judas' betrayal money, and in which he violently died, Acts i. 19. But bought by the priests as a potters' field in Matt. xxvii. 7.

Ā-chā'ịå (*trouble*). Originally a narrow strip of country on north coast of Peloponnesus, but Achaia and Macedonia came to designate all Greece, Acts xviii. 12, 27; xix. 21; Rom. xv. 26; 2 Cor. i. 1; ix. 2; xi. 10; 1 Thess. i. 7, 8.

Ā-chā'i-cus (*of Achaia*). An Achaian friend of Paul, 1 Cor. xvi. 17.

Ā'chăn and **Ā'char** (*troubler*). The Judahite who was stoned to death for concealing the spoils of Jericho, Josh. vii. 16–26. Written ACHAR in 1 Chr. ii. 7.

Ā'chăz (*one that takes*). In Matt. i. 9 for AHAZ, King of Judah.

Ăch'bôr (*mouse*). (1) Father of Baal-hanan king of Edom, Gen. xxxvi. 38, 39. (2) A contemporary of Josiah, 2 Kgs. xxii. 12–14; Jer. xxvi. 22; xxxvi. 12. Written ABDON in 2 Chr. xxxiv. 20.

Ā''chĭ-ăch'ă-rŭs. Chief minister of Esarhaddon in Nineveh, Tobit i. 21.

Ā-chī'ăs. A progenitor of Esdras, 2 Esdr. i. 2.

Ā'chĭm. Son of Sadoc, in Christ's genealogy, Matt. i. 14.

Ā'chĭ-ôr. A general in army of Holofernes, Judith v., vii., xiii., xiv.

Ā'chĭsh (ā'kĭsh) (*serpent-charmer*). A Philistine king of Gath to whom David twice fled for safety, 1 Sam. xxi. 10–13; xxvii.–xxix.; 1 Kgs. ii. 39, 40. Called Abimelech in title to Ps. xxxiv.

Ăch'ĭ-tôb and **Ăch'ĭ-tŭb.** A priest in genealogy of Esdras, 1 Esdr. viii. 2.

Ăch'me-thå. The Median city of Ecbatana, Ez. vi. 2.

Ā'chôr, valley of. [ACHAN.]

Ăch'så and **Ăch'sah** (*anklet*). Daughter of Caleb. Given in marriage to her uncle Othniel. Josh. xv. 15–18; Judg. i. 12–15. Achsa in 1 Chr. ii. 49.

Ăch'shăph (*fascination*). A city of Asher, Josh. xi. 1; xii. 20; xix. 25.

Ăch'zĭb (*false*). (1) A town of Judah, Josh. xv. 44. (2) A town of Asher, Josh. xix. 29.

Ăc'i-phă. [HAKUPHA.] 1 Esdr. v. 31.

Ăc'i-thō. A progenitor of Judith, Judith viii. 1.

Ā-crăb'bim. [MAALEH-ACRABBIM.] Josh. xv. 3.

Acts of the Apostles. Fifth Book of N. T. Supposably compiled by Luke, shortly after A. D. 63. It carries on the Christian narrative from the ascension of Christ to first imprisonment of Paul, a period of about thirty-three years.

Ā-cū'ă. [AKKUB.] 1 Esdr. v. 30.

Ā'cŭb. [BAKBUK.] 1 Esdr. v. 31.

Ăd'ă-dah (*boundary*). A town in southern Judah, Josh. xv. 22.

Ā'dah (*beauty*). (1) One of Lamech's wives, Gen. iv. 19. (2) One of Esau's wives, Gen. xxxvi. 2, 4. Called Bashemath in Gen. xxvi. 34.

Ăd''a-ī'ah (*adorned by Jehovah*). (1) Maternal grandfather of King Josiah, 2 Kgs. xxii. 1. (2) A Levite, 1 Chr. vi. 41; called Iddo in vs. 21. (3) A Benjamite, 1 Chr. viii. 21. (4) A son of Jehoram, 1 Chr. ix. 12; Neh. xi. 12. (5) Ancestor of Maaseiah, 2 Chr. xxiii. 1. (6) A descendant of Bani, Ez. x. 29, 39. (7) A Judahite, Neh. xi. 5.

Ăd''a-lī'å (*fire-god*). Fifth son of Haman, Esth. ix. 8.

Ăd'ăm (*red earth*). A city of Reuben, on Jordan, Josh. iii. 16.

Ăd'ăm (*red earth*). Used generically for man and woman, and translated *man* in Gen. i. 26, 27; v. 1; Job xx. 29; xxi. 33; Ps. lxviii. 18; lxxvi. 10.

Ăd'ăm (*red earth*). The first man. Creative work of the sixth day. Placed in the "Garden of Eden." Tempted to eat of the forbidden fruit, fell under God's disfavor, and driven out of the Garden subject to the curse of sorrow and toil. Died at age of 930 years. Gen. i. 26, etc.; ii.–v.

Ăd'a-mah (*earth*). A fenced city of Naphtali, Josh. xix. 36.

Ăd'a-mănt (*diamond*). The original is translated "adamant" in Ezek. iii. 9; Zech. vii. 12; and "diamond" in Jer. xvii. 1. Used metaphorically. [DIAMOND.]

Ăd'a-mī (*earth*). A place on the border of Naphtali, Josh. xix. 33.

Ā'där (*height*). A boundary town of Edom and Judah, Josh. xv. 3.

Ā'där. Sixth month of Jewish civil, and twelfth of sacred, year; corresponding to parts of February and March, Esth. iii. 7.

Ăd'a-să. A place in Judea, 1 Macc. vii. 40, 45.

Ăd'bē-ĕl (*breath of God*). A son of Ishmael, Gen. xxv. 13; 1 Chr. i. 29.

Ăd'dăn (*stony*). One of the places from which Jewish captives returned, Ez. ii. 59. Addon in Neh. vii. 61.

Ăd'där (*mighty*). Son of Bela, 1 Chron. viii. 3.

Ăd'dĕr (*viper*). Used in the Bible for any poisonous snake known to the Jews, of which there were several species in Palestine. In Gen. xlix. 17, the cerastes, or horned snake, is, from its habits, supposed to be alluded to. The cockatrice of Isa. xi. 8; xiv. 29; lix. 5; Jer. viii. 17, is adder and asp in Prov. xxiii. 32; Ps. lviii. 4. In Ps. cxl. 3 and Prov. xxiii. 32, a species of viper is thought to be meant.

Ăd'dī (*adorned*). Son of Cosam in Christ's genealogy, Luke iii. 28.

Ăd'dō. [ID-DO.]

Ăd'dŏn. [ADDAN.]

Ăd'dŭs. (1) Son of the servant of Solomon, 1 Esdr. v. 34. (2) A priest in time of Ezra, 1 Esdr. v. 38.

Ā'der (*flock*). A Benjamite, 1 Chr. viii. 15. Properly EDER.

Ăd'ĭ-dȧ. A town of lower Judah, 1 Macc. xii. 38.

Ā-dī'el (*ornament of God*). (1) A prince of Simeon, 1 Chr. iv. 36. (2) A priest, 1 Chr. ix. 12. (3) An ancestor of David's treasurer, Azmaveth, 1 Chr. xxvii. 25.

Ā-dĭn (*dainty*). Head of a returned family, Ez. ii. 15; viii. 6; Neh. vii. 20; x. 16.

Ăd'ĭ-nȧ (*slender*). One of David's captains, 1 Chr. xi. 42.

Ăd'ĭ-nō. One of David's mighty men, 2 Sam. xxiii. 8. [JASHOBEAM.]

Ăd'ĭ-nŭs, 1 Esdr. ix. 48. [JAMIN.]

Ăd''ĭ-thā'im (*double ornament*). A town of Judah, Josh. xv. 36.

Ăd-jūre'. To bind under a curse, Josh. vi. 26; 1 Sam. xiv. 24. To require a declaration of truth at the peril of God's displeasure, Matt. xxvi. 63.

Ăd'la-ī (*Jehovah's justice*). Ancestor of Shaphat, 1 Chr. xxvii. 29.

Ăd'mah (*fort*). One of the cities of the plain of Siddim, Gen. x. 19; xiv. 2. Destroyed with Sodom, Deut. xxix. 23; Hos. xi. 8.

Ăd'mă thȧ (*earthy*). One of the seven Persian princes, in Esth. i. 14.

Ăd'nȧ (*pleasure*). (1) Father of a returned family, Ez. x. 30. (2) A priest in days of Joiakim, Neh. xii. 15.

Ăd'nah (*pleasure*). (1) One of Saul's captains who deserted to David, 1 Chr. xii. 20. (2) A captain in Jehoshaphat's army, 2 Chr. xvii. 14.

Ăd''ō-nā'ī (*Lord*). The Hebrews spoke this word where the word Jehovah occurred.

Ā-dŏn'ī-bē'zek (*lord of Bezek*). King of Bezek, vanquished by Judah, Judg. i. 3-7.

Ăd''ō-nī'jah (*the Lord is Jehovah*). (1) Fourth son of David, by Haggith, and rival of Solomon for the throne. Afterwards put to death by Solomon, 2 Sam. iii. 4; 1 Kgs. i., ii. (2) A Levite, 2 Chr. xvii. 8. (3) Same as Adonikam, Neh. x. 16.

Ā-dŏn'ī-kăm (*the Lord is raised*). He returned from captivity with Zerubbabel, Ezr. ii. 13; Neh. vii. 18; 1 Esdr. v. 14. Called Adonijah in Neh. x. 16.

Ăd''ō-nī'ram (*lord of heights*). Chief receiver of tribute under David, Solomon, and Rehoboam, 1 Kgs. iv. 6. Written Adoram in 2 Sam. xx. 24; 1 Kgs. xii. 18; and Hadoram in 2 Chr. x. 18.

Ā-dŏn'ī-zē'dec (*lord of justice*). The Amorite king of Jerusalem who formed a league against Joshua, and was slain, Josh. x. 1-27.

Ā-dŏp'tion (*a choosing to*). Receiving a stranger into one's family as an own child thereof, Ex. ii. 10; Esth. ii. 7. Figuratively, reception into the family of God, Rom. viii. 15-17; Gal. iv. 5; Eph. i. 5.

Ā-dō'rȧ, or **Ā'dŏr**, 1 Macc. xiii. 20. [ADORAIM.]

Ăd''ō-rā'im (*double mound*). A city of Judah, 2 Chr. xi. 9.

Ā-dō'răm. [ADONIRAM and HADORAM.]

Ăd''ō-rā'tion (*address*). The act of paying homage to God; as in bending the knee, raising hands, inclining head, prostrating the body, etc., Gen. xvii. 3; Ps. xcv. 6; Matt. xxviii. 9.

Ā-drăm'mē-lech (*fire king*). (1) An idol introduced into Samaria and worshipped with the cruel rites of Molech, 2 Kgs. xvii. 31. (2) Son and murderer of Sennacherib, king of Assyria, 2 Kgs. xix. 37; 2 Chr. xxxii. 21; Isa. xxxvii. 38.

Ăd''ra-mŷt'tĭ-ŭm (*from Adramys, brother of Crœsus*). A seaport town of Mysia in Asia, Acts xvi. 7; xxvii. 2. Now Adramyti.

Ā'drĭ-ȧ. The Adriatic Sea, Acts xxvii. 27.

Ā'drĭ-el (*flock of God*). Son-in-law of Saul, 1 Sam. xviii. 19; 2 Sam. xxi. 8.

Ā-dū'el. An ancestor of Tobit, Tob. i. 1.

Ā-dŭl'lăm (*justice of the people*). (1) A city of Canaan allotted to Judah, Gen. xxxviii. 1; Josh. xii. 15; xv. 35; 2 Chr. xi. 7. Repeopled after the captivity, Neh. xi. 30; Mich. i. 15. (2) The cave Adullam was David's hiding-place, where his friends gathered, 1 Sam. xxii. 1; 2 Sam. xxiii. 13; 1 Chr. xi. 15.

Ā-dŭl'lăm-īte. A native of Adullam, Gen. xxxviii. 1.

Ā-dŭl'ter-y (*ad*=to and *alter*, other). Under Hebrew law the crime of unchastity, wherein a man, married or single, had illicit intercourse with a married or betrothed woman, not his wife. Punished with fire, Gen. xxxviii. 24; by stoning, Deut. xxii. 22-24. In a spiritual sense, apostasy.

Ā-dŭm'mĭm (*a going up*). A steep pass on the road from Jericho to Jerusalem, Josh. xv. 7; xviii. 17; Luke x. 30-37.

Ăd'vō-cāte (*calling to*). In N. T., helper, intercessor, or comforter. Jews did not have advocates, or attorneys, till after the Roman conquest, John xiv. 16; xv. 26; xvi. 17; Acts xxiv. 1.

Æ-dī'as, Probably Elijah, 1 Esdr. ix. 27.

Æ'ne-ăs, or **Æ-nē'ăs** (*laudable*). The paralytic at Lydda, healed by Peter, Acts ix. 33, 34.

Æ'nŏn (*springs*). A place, west of Jordan, where John baptized, John iii. 23.

Ăf-fĭn'ĭ-ty. Relation by marriage and not by blood or birth, 1 Kgs. iii. 1. For preventive degrees *see* Lev. xviii. 6-17, and MARRIAGE.

Ăg'ă-bȧ, 1 Esdr. v. 30. [HAGAB.]

Ăg'ă-bŭs (*locust*). A prophet of Antioch, Acts xi. 28; xxi. 10.

Ā'găg (*flame*). General title of the kings of Amelek, Ex. xvii. 14; Num. xxiv. 7; Deut. xxv. 17; 1 Sam. xv. 8-32.

Ā-găg'īte. Subject of Agag, Esth. iii. 1-10.

Ā-găr. [HAGAR, HAGARENES, HAGARITES.]

Ag'āte (from *river Achates*). A species of precious quartz. Second stone in third row of high-priest's breastplate, Ex. xxviii. 19; xxxix. 12; Isa. liv. 12; Ezek. xxvii. 16. Original sometimes translated amethyst.

Ăg'ĕ-ē (*fugitive*). Father of one of David's mighty men, 2 Sam. xxiii. 11.

Ăg'rĭ-cul''ture (*field culture*). Patriarchal life was pastoral. After the conquest of Canaan, lands were meted and bounded, and landmarks held sacred, Deut. xix. 14. The valley soils of Palestine were fertile; natural waters abundant, Deut. viii. 7; rain plentiful, Deut. xi. 14; Jer. v. 24; James v. 7. The grains grown were wheat, barley, rye, and millet. Orchards produced the vine, olive, and fig. Gardens grew beans, fitches, pease, lettuce, endive, leeks, garlic, onions, melons, cucumbers, cabbage, etc. The implements were the plough, harrow, and hoe, but these were crude. Grains were cut with the sickle, and the sheaves were threshed by treading with oxen, usually drawing sleds; while winnowing was done in sheets before the wind. Lands rested once in seven years, Lev. xxv. 1-7. The poor were allowed to glean, Lev. xix. 9, 10; Deut. xxiv. 19.

Threshing with the Sled.

Ȧ-grĭp'pȧ. [Herod.]

Ā'gŭr (*gatherer of wisdom*). An unknown sage who compiled Prov. xxx.

Ā'hăb (*uncle*). (1) Seventh king of Israel. Reigned B. C. 919-896, 1 Kgs. xvi. 29. Married Jezebel of Tyre, who introduced the worship of Baal and Astarte. One of the most notorious of O. T. characters. Slain by a chance arrow, and the "dogs licked his blood" according to prophecy, 1 Kgs. xviii.-xxii.; 2 Chr. xviii. (2) A false prophet at Babylon, Jer. xxix. 22.

Ȧ-hăr'ah (*after the brother*). Third son of Benjamin, 1 Chr. viii. 1. [Aher and Ahiram.]

Ȧ-här'hĕl (*behind the fort*). A name in the genealogy of Judah, 1 Chr. iv. 8.

Ȧ-hăs'ă-ī (*whom Jehovah upholds*). A priest, Neh. xi. 13. Called Jahzerah in 1 Chr. ix. 12.

Ȧ-hăs'ba-ī (*trusting*). Father of one of David's thirty-seven captains, 2 Sam. xxiii. 34.

Ȧ-hăs''ū-ē'rus (*prince*). (1) King of Media, supposably Cyaxares, whose son Astyages was Darius, Dan. ix. 1. (2) A Persian king, supposed to be Cambyses, Ez. iv. 6. (3) Another Persian king, probably Xerxes. History in Esther.

Ȧ-hā'vȧ (*water*). The place on the Euphrates whence the captives started, on their second return, Ez. viii. 15-21.

Ā'hăz (*who takes*). (1) Son of Jotham, whom he succeeded, and eleventh king of Israel. Reign 742-726 B. C. Weak-minded and idolatrous, 2 Kgs. xvi.; 2 Chr. xxviii. Literally sold out his kingdom. Died dishonored, 2 Kgs. xxiii. 12; 2 Chr. xxviii. 16-27. (2) A son of Micah, 1 Chr. viii. 35, 36; ix. 42.

Ā''ha-zī'ah (*Jehovah sustains*). Son of Ahab, and his successor on the throne of Israel, as the eighth king. Reign 896-895 B. C. A weak and foolish idolater, 1 Kgs. xxii. 49-53. (2) Fifth king of Judah. Reign, B. C. 884, 2 Kgs. viii. 25-29. Killed in the rebellion of Jehu, 2 Kgs. ix. Called Azariah in 2 Chr. xxii. 6; and Jehoahaz in 2 Chr. xxi. 17.

Ah'băn (*discreet*). Son of Abishur, 1 Chr. ii. 29.

Ā'hĕr (*follower*). A title in genealogy of Benjamin, 1 Chr. vii. 12.

Ā'hī (*my brother*). (1) A Gadite chief, 1 Chr. v. 15. (2) An Asherite, 1 Chr. vii. 34.

Ȧ-hī'ah and **Ȧ-hī'jah** (*Jehovah's friend*). (1) A priest in Shiloh, 1 Sam. xiv. 3-18. (2) One of Solomon's princes, 1 Kgs. iv. 3. (3) A prophet of Shiloh, 1 Kgs. xiv. 2. His prophecies are in 1 Kgs. xi. 30-39 and 1 Kgs. xiv. 6-16. (4) Father of Baasha, 1 Kgs. xv. 27-34. (5) Name of several other Bible characters, 1 Chr. ii. 25; viii. 7; xi. 36; xxvi. 20; Neh. x. 26.

Ȧ-hī'am (*uncle*). One of David's thirty captains, 2 Sam. xxiii. 33; 1 Chr. xi. 35.

Ȧ-hī'an (*brotherly*). A Manassite, 1 Chr. vii. 19.

Ā''hī-ē'zĕr (*brother of help*). (1) A chieftain of Dan, Num. i. 12. (2) A chief of archers under David, 1 Chr. xii. 3.

Ȧ-hī'hud (*renown*). (1) A prince of Asher, Num. xxxiv. 27. (2) A chieftain of Benjamin, 1 Chr. viii. 7.

Ȧ-hī'jah. [Ahiah.]

Ȧ-hī'kam (*brother who raises*). An important court officer in reigns of Josiah and Jehoiakim, 2 Kgs. xxii. 12-14; Jer. xxvi. 24.

Ȧ-hī'lud (*brother born*). (1) Father of Jehoshaphat, the recorder of David's and Solomon's reigns, 2 Sam. viii. 16. (2) Father of Baana, 1 Kgs. iv. 12.

Ȧ-hĭm'a-ăz (*brother of wrath*). (1) Father-in-law of Saul, 1 Sam. xiv. 50. (2) Son of Zadok the high priest. Played a conspicuous part in the rebellion of Absalom, 2 Sam. xv. 24-37; xvii. 15-22; xviii. 19-33. (3) Solomon's son-in-law, 1 Kgs. iv. 15.

Ȧ-hī'măn (*brother of the right hand*). (1) One of the giant Anakim of Hebron, Num. xiii. 22, 23;

Josh. xi. 21; Judg. i. 10. (2) A gate-keeper of Levi, 1 Chr. ix. 17.

Ă-hĭm′e-lech (*my brother is king*). (1) High priest at Nob, 1 Sam. xxi. 1. Priests of Nob slain by order of Saul, 1 Sam. xxii. 11–20. (2) A Hittite friend of David, 1 Sam. xxvi. 6.

Ă-hī′mŏth (*brother of death*). A Levite, 1 Chr. vi. 25. Mahath in vs. 35, and Maath in Luke iii. 26.

Ă′hĭn-a-dăb (*noble brother*). Royal purveyor to Solomon, 1 Kgs. iv. 14.

Ă-hĭn′ō-am (*gracious*). (1) Wife of Saul, 1 Sam. xiv. 50. (2) A wife of David, 1 Sam. xxv. 43; xxvii. 3; xxx. 5, 18.

Ă-hī′ō (*brotherly*). (1) He accompanied the Ark when taken from his father's house, 2 Sam. vi. 3, 4. (2) A Benjamite, 1 Chr. viii. 14. (3) Son of Jehiel, 1 Chr. viii. 31; ix. 37.

Ă-hī′rȧ (*unlucky*). A chief of Naphtali, Num. i. 15.

Ă-hī′ram (*lofty*). Founder of the Ahiramites, Num. xxvi. 38.

Ă-hĭs′a-mach (*helper*). One of the Tabernacle architects, Ex. xxxi. 6; xxxv. 34; xxxviii. 23.

Ă-hĭsh′a-här (*brother of dawn*). A grandson of Benjamin, 1 Chr. vii. 10.

Ă-hī′shär (*singer's brother*). A controller of Solomon's household, 1 Kgs. iv. 6.

Ă-hĭth′o-phel (*brother of folly*). A privy councillor of David, 2 Sam. xv. 12; xvi. 23; xxiii. 34. Joined Absalom's conspiracy, 2 Sam. xvii. Hanged himself in despair, 2 Sam. xvii. 23.

Ă-hī′tub (*brother of goodness*). (1) Grandson of Eli, 1 Sam. xiv. 3; xxii. 9–11. (2) Father of Zadok the high priest, 1 Chr. vi. 7, 8, 11, 12; 2 Sam. viii. 17.

Ah′lăb (*fertile*). A city of Canaan, Judg. i. 31.

Ah′lāi (*ornamental*). Daughter of Sheshan and wife of his slave, Jarha, 1 Chr. ii. 31–35.

Ă-hō′ah (*brotherly*). Grandson of Benjamin, 1 Chr. viii. 4. Called Ahiah in 1 Chr. viii. 7.

Ă-hō′hīte. From Ahoah, a patronymic of some of David's mighty men, 2 Sam. xxiii. 9, 28; 1 Chr. xi. 12; xxvii. 4.

Ă-hō′lah (*her tent*). The harlot used by Ezekiel to type Samaria, Ezek. xxiii. 4, 5, 36, 44.

Ă-hō′lĭ-ab (*tent of the father*). One of the Tabernacle architects, Ex. xxxv. 31–35.

Ă-hŏl′ĭ-bah (*my tent*). The harlot used by Ezekiel to type Jerusalem, Ezek. xxiii. 4, 11, 22, 36, 44.

Ă″hō-lĭb′a-mah (*tent of the height*). (1) Wife of Esau, Gen. xxxvi. 2, 25. Called Judith in Gen. xxvi. 34. (2) A title or district in Arabia Petraea, Gen. xxxvi. 41; 1 Chr. i. 52.

Ă-hū′mȧ-ī (*cowardly*). A descendant of Judah, 1 Chr. iv. 2.

Ă-hū′zam or **Ă-hŭz′zam** (*possession*). A son of Asher, 1 Chr. iv. 6.

Ă-hŭz′zath (*possessions*). A friend of King Abimelech, Gen. xxvi. 26.

Ā′ī (*heap of ruins*). (1) An ancient city of Canaan, Gen. xii. 8, where it is spelled HA′I. Captured and destroyed by Joshua, Josh. vii. 3–5; ix. 3; x. 1; xii. 9. Written Aiath in Isa. x. 28; and Aija in Neh. xi. 31; Ezr. ii. 28. (2) A city of Heshbon, Jer. xlix. 3.

Ă-ī′ah (*vulture*). (1) Father of Saul's concubine, 2 Sam. iii. 7; xxi. 8–11. (2) Father of one of Esau's wives, 1 Chr. i. 40. Written Ajah in Gen. xxxvi. 24.

Ă-ī′ath. [AI.]

Ă-ī′jȧ. [AI.]

Ăij′a-lŏn. [AJALON.]

Ăij′e-lĕth Shā′här (*hind of the dawn*). In title to Ps. xxii. May mean a musical instrument, the argument of the Psalm, the melody, or tune name.

Ā′in (*eye*). (1) A landmark on eastern boundary of Canaan, Num. xxxiv. 11. (2) A Levitical city in south Judah and then in Simeon, Josh. xv. 32; xix. 7; xxi. 16. Ashan in 1 Chr. vi. 59.

Ă-ī′rus. A temple servant, 1 Esdr. v. 31.

Ā′jah. [AIAH.]

Ăj′a-lŏn (*place of gazelles*). (1) A Levitical city of Dan, Josh. xix. 42. Became a city of refuge, Josh. xxi. 24, where it is written Aijalon; also in 1 Sam. xiv. 31. Prominent in Philistine wars, 2 Chr. xxviii. 18. Fortified as Aijalon by Rehoboam, 2 Chr. xi. 10. Now *Yalo*, 14 miles west of Jerusalem. (2) The valley in which Joshua commanded the moon to stand still, Josh. x. 12. (3) Burial place of the Judge, Elon, Judg. xii. 12.

Ā′kan (*keen of vision*). A Horite chieftain, Gen. xxxvi. 27. Jakan in 1 Chr. i. 42.

Ă-kĕl′da-mȧ. Spelling of Aceldama in Revised Version, Acts i. 19.

Ăk′kŭb (*insidious*). (1) A descendant of Zerubbabel, 1 Chr. iii. 24. (2) A gate-keeper of the temple, 1 Chr. ix. 17. (3) A Levite who assisted Ezra, Neh. viii. 7.

Ă-krăb′bim (*scorpion*). A range forming a south boundary of Judah, Num. xxxiv. 4. Maaleh-acrabbim in Josh. xv. 3. An Amorite boundary in Judg. i. 36.

Ăl′a-băs″tẽr (*white stone*). A whitish mineral susceptible of easy carving and fine polish, much used by ancients for vases, ointment boxes, sculptures, etc., Matt. xxvi. 7; Mark xiv. 3; Luke vii. 37.

Alabaster Vases.

Ă-lăm′ē-lech (*king's oak*). A border place of Asher, Josh. xix. 26.

Ăl′a-mĕth (*covering*). A grandson of Benjamin, 1 Chr. vii. 8.

Ăl′a-mŏth. Perhaps a musical instrument or melody, 1 Chr. xv. 20; Ps. xlvi. title.

Ăl′çi-mŭs (*valiant*). A high priest, 1 Macc. vii. 9–25.

Ăl′e-mȧ. A city of Gilead, 1 Macc. v. 26.

Ăl′e-mĕth (*covering*). (1) A city of the priests in Benjamin, 1 Chr. vi. 60. Written Almon in Josh. xxi. 18. (2) A descendant of Jonathan, 1 Chr. viii. 36; ix. 42.

Ăl″ĕx-ăn′dẽr (*defender of men*). (1) King of Macedon; surnamed "The Great." Born B. C. 356. Succeeded his father Philip, B. C. 336. Subjugated Asia Minor, Syria, and Palestine. Overthrew the Persian Empire, B. C. 333. Conquered Egypt, B. C. 332. Founded Alexandria, B. C. 332. Consolidated his Persian conquests, with Babylon as capital, B. C.

324. Died, perhaps in Babylon, B. C. 323. Prefigured in Dan. ii. 39; vii. 6; viii. 5-7; xi. 3. (2) Alexander Balas, son of Antiochus IV. Usurped Syrian throne, B. C. 152. His coins are still preserved,

Alexander the Great.

1 Macc. x., xi. (3) Son of Simon, Mark xv. 21. (4) A kinsman of Annas the high priest, Acts iv. 6. (5) A Jewish convert at Ephesus, Acts xix. 33. (6) An Ephesian Christian reprobated by Paul, 1 Tim. i. 20, and perhaps the coppersmith in 2 Tim. iv. 14.

Ăl″ĕx-ăn′drĭ-ȧ (*from Alexander*). The Grecian, Roman, and Christian capital of Egypt. Founded by Alexander the Great, B. C. 332. Situated on the Mediterranean Sea, 12 miles W. of Canopic mouth of the Nile. Noted for its libraries, architecture, and commerce. Conspicuous in early church history as a Christian centre, Acts xviii. 24; xxvii. 6; xxviii. 11.

Ăl″ĕx-ăn′drĭ-ans. Inhabitants of Alexandria; but in Acts vi. 9, Jewish colonists from Alexandria, admitted to the privilege of citizenship and worship at Jerusalem.

Ăl′gŭm or **Ăl′mŭg.** Former in 2 Chr. ii. 8; ix. 10, 11; latter in 1 Kgs. x. 11, 12. Supposed to be the red sandal-wood of India. Used in temple furniture.

Ā-lī′ah. [ALVAH.]

Ā-lī′an. [ALVAN.]

Ăl′lē-gō″ry (*other speech*). That figure of speech by which a subject is set forth under the guise of some other subject, Gal. iv. 24.

Ăl″le-lū′jȧ (*Praise ye Jehovah*). Written thus in Rev. xix. 1; but HALLELUJAH, in margin of Ps. cvi., cxi., cxii., cxiii., cxvii., cxviii., cxxxv., etc. A common exclamation of joy and praise in Jewish worship.

Ăl-lī′ance (*ans*) (*binding to*). Hebrews forbidden to make alliances with surrounding nations but finally driven to them. Alliances solemnized by presents, oaths, feasts, monuments, offerings, and other pious ceremonies, Gen. xv. 10; xxvi. 30; xxxi. 51-53; Josh. ix. 15; 1 Kgs. xv. 18; v. 2-12; ix. 27. Breach of covenant severely punished, 2 Sam. xxi. 1; Ezek. xvii. 16.

Ăl′lŏm, 1 Esdr. v. 34. [AMI and AMON].

Ăl′lŏn (*oak*). (1) Ancestor of Ziza, 1 Chr. iv. 37. (2) A boundary place of Naphtali, Josh. xix. 33.

Ăl′lŏn=băch′uth (*oak of weeping*). The tree under which Deborah was buried, Gen. xxxv. 8.

Ăl-mō′dăd (*immeasurable*). Progenitor of an Arab tribe, Gen. x. 26; 1 Chr. i. 20.

Ăl′mŏn, Josh. xxi. 18. [ALEMETH.]

Ăl′mŏn=dĭb″la-thā′ĭm (*hiding of two fig cakes*). One of the last stopping places of the wandering Israelites, Num. xxxiii. 46.

Älm′ond (*hasten*). Tree resembles the peach in form, height, blossom, and fruit. Covering of fruit downy and succulent. Chiefly valuable for its nut. Gen. xliii. 11; Ex. xxv. 33, 34; xxxvii. 19, 20; Num. xvii. 8; Eccles. xii. 5; Jer. i. 11.

Älms (*pity*). Almsgiving enjoined by Mosaic law, Lev. xix. 9; Ruth ii. 2. Every third year the tithes of increase were shared with the Levite, the stranger, the fatherless and widow, Deut. xiv. 28. Receptacles for taking of alms placed in the Temple, Mark xii. 41. Almsgiving exhorted, Acts xi. 30; Rom. xv. 25-27; 1 Cor. xvi. 1-4.

Ăl′mŭg. [ALGUM.]

Ăl′oes (*ōz*). Written "Lign (*wood*) Aloes" in Num. xxiv. 6. A costly and sweet smelling wood of India, much prized in the East. Ps. xlv. 8; Prov. vii. 17; S. of Sol. iv. 14; John xix. 39.

Ā′lŏth. Solomon's ninth commissary district, 1 Kgs. iv. 16.

Ăl′phȧ. First letter of the Greek alphabet. Used with omega, the last letter, to express beginning and end, Isa. xli. 4; xliv. 6; Rev. i. 8, 11; xxi. 6; xxii. 13.

Ăl′pha-bĕt. *Alpha* and *beta*, first and second letters of Greek alphabet. Hebrew alphabet comprised twenty-two letters.

Ăl-phæ′us (*changing*). (1) Father of the apostle James the Less, Matt. x. 3; Mark iii. 18; Luke vi. 15; Acts i. 13. Called Clopas or Cleophas, in John xix. 25. (2) Father of Levi or Matthew, Mark ii. 14.

Ăl″-ta-nē′us, 1 Esdr. ix. 33. [MATTENAI.]

Altar with Horns.

Äl′tar (*high*). First altars were simple memorial piles, Gen. viii. 20; xii. 7; xxvi. 25; xxxv. 1. Afterwards to lay sacrifices upon, Ex. xvii. 15, 16, xxvii. 1-8. Usually built of earth or stone, Ex. xx. 24-26; but sacrificial altars quite elaborate, Ex. xl. 26-33. Still more elaborate in Solomon's Temple, 1 Kgs. viii. 64; 2 Chr. vii. 7. Altar fires to burn perpetually, Lev. vi. 12, 13. *Altar of Incense*, called "golden" to distinguish it from *Altar of Sacrifice*, called "brazen," Ex. xxx. 1-10; xl. 5, 1 Kgs. vii. 48; 1 Chr. xxviii. 18.

Ăl-tăs′chĭth (*destroy not*). In title to Ps. lvii., lviii., lix., and lxxv. Probably the tune is meant.

Ā′lụsh (*crowd*). Last halting-place of Israelites before Rephidim, Num. xxxiii. 13, 14.

Ăl′vah (*wickedness*). A duke of Edom, Gen. xxxvi. 40. Called Aliah in 1 Chr. i. 51.

Ăl′văn (*tall*). A Horite, Gen. xxxvi. 23. Alian in 1 Chr. i. 40.

Ā′măd (*enduring*). An unknown place in Asher, Josh. xix. 26.

Ā-măd′ạ-thȧ, Esth. xvi. 10, and Amadathus, Esth. xii. 7; Apoch. [HAMMEDATHA.]

Ā′măl (*labor*). An Asherite, 1 Chr. vii. 35.

Ăm′ạ-lĕk (*valley dweller*). An Edomite chieftain, Gen. xxxvi. 12; 1 Chr. i. 36.

Ăm′ạ-lĕk-ītes″. A nomad tribe of the Sinai wilderness, Gen. xiv. 7. Called the first of all nations in Num. xxiv. 20. Dwelt to the South, Num. xiii. 29. Smitten by Gideon, Judg. vii. 12-23; by Saul, 1 Sam. xv. 3-9; and David, 1 Sam. xxx. 18; 1 Chr. iv. 43. "Mount of Amalekites" was in Ephraim, Judg. xii. 15.

Ā′măm (*gathering place*). A city in south Judah, Josh. xv. 26.

Ā′măn (*mother*), Esther x. 7; Apoch. [HAMAN.]

Ăm′ạ-nȧ (*covenant*). Probably a mount of Anti-Libanus range, S. of Sol. iv. 8.

Ăm″ạ-rī′ah (*the Lord says*). (1) Father of Ahitub, 1 Chr. vi. 7. (2) A high priest, 2 Chr. xix. 11. (3) Head of a Kohathite family, 1 Chron. xxiii. 19; xxiv. 23. (4) Head of one of the twenty-four courses of priests, 2 Chr. xxxi. 15; Neh. x. 3. (5) A priest in Ezra's time, Ez. x. 42. (6) A priest who returned with Zerubbabel, Neh. x. 3; xii. 2, 13. (1) An ancestor of Zephaniah the prophet, Zeph. i. 1.

Ăm′-ạ-sȧ (*burden*). (1) Nephew of David, 2 Sam. xvii. 25. Rebelled with Absalom, and defeated by Joab, 2 Sam. xviii. 6. Reconciled to David, 2 Sam. xix. 13, and killed by Joab, 2 Sam. xx. 10. (2) A prince of Ephraim, 2 Chr. xxviii. 12.

Ā-măs′ạ-ī (*burdensome*). (1) A Levite, 1 Chr. vi. 25, 35. (2) A chief of captains who deserted to David, 1 Chr. xii. 18. (3) A priest who blew the trumpet before the Ark, 1 Chr. xv. 24. (4) A Kohathite, 2 Chr. xxix. 12.

Ā-măsh′ạ-ī (*burdensome*). A priest, Neh. xi. 13.

Ăm-ạ-sī′ ăh (*whom Jehovah bears*). Captain of 200,000 men in Judah, 2 Chr. xvii. 16.

Ăm″ạ-thē′ĭs, 1 Esdr. ix. 29. [ATHLAI.]

Ăm′ạ-this. A country north of Palestine, 1 Macc. xii. 25.

Ăm″ạ-zī′ah (*strength of Jehovah*). (1) Eighth king of Judah. Reign B. C. 837-809, 2 Kgs. xiv. 1-20. Rebuked by God for idolatry, 2 Chr. xxv. 1-16. Defeated by Joash and murdered at Lachish, 2 Chr. xxv. 17-28. (2) A descendant of Simeon, 1 Chr. iv. 34. (3) A Levite, 1 Chr. vi. 45. (4) An idolatrous priest of Bethel, Amos vii. 10-17.

Ăm-băs′sạ-dŏr (*servant*). A person chosen by one government to represent it at the seat of another. Earliest mention in Num. xx. 14; Josh. ix. 4; Judg. xi. 17-19. Injury to them an insult to their king, 2 Sam. x. 3-6. The term includes both messenger and message, Luke xiv. 32. Ministers called ambassadors of Christ, 2 Cor. v. 20.

Ăm′bĕr. Hardly the fossil vegetable gum of commerce, Ezek. i. 4, 27; viii. 2; but rather the yellow composition of gold and silver known as *electrum*.

Ā-mĕn′ (*true*). A final word used to fix the stamp of truth upon an assertion, Num. v. 22; Deut. xxvii. 15; Matt. vi. 13; 1 Cor. xiv. 16. Promises of God are amen, 2 Cor. i. 20. A title of Christ, Rev. iii. 14.

Ăm′ē-thyst (*not wine*). A purplish quartz, ranking among the precious stones, and forming the third stone in the third row of the high priest's breastplate, Ex. xxviii. 19; xxxix. 12. A stone in the foundations of the New Jerusalem, Rev. xxi. 20.

Ā′mī (*builder*). A returned captive, Ez. ii. 57. Amon in Neh. vii. 59.

Ā-mĭn′ạ-dab, Matt. i. 4; Luke iii. 33; for AMMINADAB.

Ā-mĭt′tạ-ī (*true*). The father of Jonah, 2 Kgs. xiv. 25; Jon. i. 1.

Ăm′mah (*head*). A hill near Gibeon to which Joab pursued Abner, 2 Sam. ii. 24.

Ăm′mī (*my people*). Applied figuratively to the Israelites, Hos. ii. i. marg.

Ăm-mĭd′ĭ-oi. A family of returned captives, 1 Esdr. v. 20.

Ăm′mĭ-el (*people of God*). (1) The spy of Dan who perished for his evil report, Num. xiii. 12. (2) Father of Machir, 2 Sam. ix. 4, 5. (3) Father of Bathsheba, 1 Chr. iii. 5; called Eliam in 2 Sam. xi. 3. (4) A door-keeper of the Temple, 1 Chr. xxvi. 5.

Ăm-mī′hŭd (*people of praise*). (1) Father of the chief of Ephraim at time of Exode, Num. i. 10; ii. 18; vii. 48, 53; x. 22; 1 Chr. vii. 26. (2) A Simeonite, Num. xxxiv. 20. (3) A Naphtalite, Num. xxxiv. 28. (4) Father of Talmai, king of Geshur, 2 Sam. xiii. 37. (5) A descendant of Pharez, 1 Chr. ix. 4.

Ăm-mĭn′ạ-dăb (*one of the prince's people*). (1) A prince of Judah, Num. i. 7; ii. 3; Ruth iv. 19, 20; 1 Chr. ii. 10. (2) Chief of the sons of Uzziel, 1 Chr. xv. 10-12. (3) Written Amminadib in S. of Sol. vi. 12.

Ăm″mĭ=shăd′dạ-ī″ (*people of the Almighty*). Father of the prince of Dan at time of the Exode, Num. i. 12; ii. 25; vii. 66; x. 25.

Ăm-mĭz′ạ-băd (*people of the giver*). Commander in David's army, 1 Chr. xxvii. 6.

Ăm′mŏn, Ăm′mŏn-ītes″, Chĭl′drĕn of Ăm′mŏn. Land of the Ammonites was east of the Dead Sea between the Arnon on the south to the Jabbok on the north, Num. xxi. 24; Deut. ii. 19, 20. People called Ammonites from their ancestor Ben-Ammi; Gen. xix. 38. Nomadic, idolatrous, incursive and cruel, 1 Sam. xi. 1-3; Amos i. 13; Judg. x. 6. Reduced to servitude by David, 2 Sam. xii. 26-31. Denounced by Jeremiah and Ezekiel, Jer. xlix. 1-6; Ezek. xxv. 2-10.

Ăm″mŏn-īt′ess. A woman of Ammon.

Ăm′mŏn=nō′. [No.]

Ăm′nŏn (*faithful*). (1) Eldest son of David, killed by his brother Absalom, 2 Sam. xiii. 1-29. (2) Son of Shimon, 1 Chr. iv. 20.

Ā′mok (*deep*). A returned priest, Neh. xii. 7, 20.

Ā′mon or **Ā′mĕn** (*mystery*). An Egyptian god worshipped at Thebes as "Amen the Sun." Written No, in Nah. iii. 8.

Ā′mon (*builder*). (1) A governor of Samaria under Ahab, 1 Kgs. xxii. 26; 2 Chr. xviii. 25. (2) Fourteenth king of Judah, B. C. 642-640. A shameless idolater, and killed in a conspiracy, 2 Kgs. xxi. 19-26. Reign pictured in Zeph. i. 4; iii. 3, 4, 11.

Ăm′ôr-ītes (*highlanders*). One of the nations of Canaan before the Hebrew conquest, Gen. x. 16; xiv. 7; Num. xiii. 29; Deut. i. 20; Josh. v. 1; x. 6; xi. 3; 1 Sam. xxiii. 29. Occupied both sides of the Jordan, Josh. xiii. 15-27; Num. xxi. 21.

Ā′mos (*weighty*). One of the lesser prophets. Lived during reigns of Uzziah and Jeroboam II., Amos i. 1-7; vii. 14-15. His book is 30th of O. T. It rebukes the sins of Israel and closes with God's promise. Book abounds in rural allusions.

Ā'moz (*strong*). Father of Isaiah, Isa. i. 1; 2 Kgs. xix. 2.

Ăm-phĭp'o-lis (*surrounded city*). A city of Macedonia, 33 miles S. W. of Philippi, Acts xvii. 1.

Ăm'plĭ-as (*large*). A Roman friend of Paul, Rom. xvi. 8.

Ăm'răm (*exalted*). (1) Father of Moses and Aaron, Ex. vi. 18–20. (2) A descendant of Seir, 1 Chr. i. 41; Hemdan in Gen. xxxvi. 26. (3) A son of Bani, Ez. x. 34.

Ăm'răm-ītes. Descendants of Amram, Num. iii. 27; 1 Chr. xxvi. 23.

Ăm'ra-phel (*keeper of gods*). A Hamite king who joined the expedition against Sodom, Gen. xiv.

Ăm'ŭ-lĕts (*charms*). Belts, rings, necklaces, ornaments, mystically inscribed or not, worn for protection against evil enchantment. Referred to in Gen. xxxv. 4; Judg. viii. 24; Isa. iii. 20; Hos. ii. 13.

Ăm'zī (*strong*). (1) A Levite, 1 Chr. vi. 46. (2) A priest, Neh. xi. 12.

Ā'nab (*grape*). Place in south Judah, Josh. xi. 21.

Ăn'a-ĕl. Tobit's brother, Tob. i. 21.

Ā'nah (*answering*). Father-in-law of Esau, Gen. xxxvi. 2–25.

Ăn''ă-hā'rath (*gorge*). A border place of Issachar and Manasseh, Josh. xix. 19.

Ăn''a-ī'ah (*whom God answers*). (1) A priest who assisted Ezra, Neh. viii. 4. (2) A co-covenanter with Nehemiah, Neh. x. 22.

Ā'năk (*collar*), Children of, Num. xiii. 22. [Anakim.]

Ăn'a-kĭm or **kĭms.** A race of giants in southern Canaan, Deut. i. 28. Defeated by Joshua, and land given to Caleb, Josh. xi. 21–22; xiv. 12–15.

Ăn'a-mĭm. A Mizraite people, not located, Gen. x. 13.

A-năm'mĕ-lech (*kingly image*). Companion god of Adrammelech, worshipped in Samaria, and representing the female power of the sun, 2 Kgs. xvii. 31.

Ā'nan (*cloud*). A co-covenanter with Nehemiah, Neh. x. 26.

Ăn-ā'nī (*covered by Jehovah*). A descendant of Judah, 1 Chr. iii. 24.

Ăn-a-nī'ah (*covered by Jehovah*). (1) A priestly assistant of Nehemiah, Neh. iii. 23. (2) A city of Benjamin, Neh. xi. 32.

Ăn''a-nī'as (*whom Jehovah has given*). (1) Five persons mentioned in 1 Esdr. ix. (2) The doubtful convert, whose tragic ending is narrated in Acts v. 1–11. (3) A Jewish disciple at Damascus, Acts ix. 10–27; xxii. 12. (4) A high priest, A. D. 48, Acts xxiii. 2–5; xxiv. 1.

A-năn'i-ĕl. A progenitor of Tobit, Tob. i. 1.

Ā'năth (*answer*). Father of Shamgar, Judg. iii. 31.

Ăn-ăth'e-mȧ (*devoted*). The devoted thing, if inanimate, fell to the priests, Num. xviii. 18; if animate, it was to be slain, Lev. xxvii. 28, 29. In N. T. a curse, Rom. ix. 3, 1 Cor. xii. 3; xvi. 22. In the latter instance Maranatha is added, the meaning being "Let him be accursed."

Ăn'a-thŏth (*answers*). (1) A descendant of Benjamin, 1 Chr. vii. 8. (2) A co-covenanter with Nehemiah, Neh. x. 19. (3) A Levitical city of Benjamin, Josh. xxi. 18; 1 Chr. vi. 60; Isa. x. 30.

Ăn'chŏr (*hook*). Anchors for holding ships to one spot were formerly cast from the stern. Acts xxvii. 29.

Ăn'drew (*manly*). An Apostle of Christ, John i. 35–40; Matt. iv. 18. Brother of Simon Peter, native of Bethsaida, and fisherman. Original disciple of John the Baptist, Mark xiii. 3; John vi. 6–13; xii. 22.

Ăn''drŏ-nī'cus (*man conqueror*). (1) A viceroy of Antiochus at Antioch, 2 Macc. iv. 31–38. (2) Another officer of Antiochus at Garizim, 2 Macc. v. 23. (3) A Christian friend of Paul's at Rome, Rom. xvi. 7.

Ā'nem (*two springs*). A Levitical city of Issachar, 1 Chr. vi. 73.

Ā'nĕr (*boy*). (1) A Levitical city in Manasseh, 1 Chr. vi. 70. (2) An Amorite chief of Hebron, Gen. xiv. 13–24.

Ăn'ĕ-thŏth-īte'', 2 Sam. xxiii. 27; **Ăn'tŏth-īte**, 1 Chr. xi. 28; xii. 3; **Ăn''ĕ-tŏth'īte**, 1 Chr. xxvii. 12. An inhabitant of Anathoth.

Ăn'gĕl (*messenger*). A messenger, 2 Sam. ii. 5; Luke vii. 24. In a spiritual sense, a messenger of God, Gen. xxiv. 7; Heb. i. 14. Nature, Matt. xviii. 10. Number, 1 Kgs. xxii. 19; Matt. xxvi. 53; Heb. xii. 22. Strength, Ps. ciii. 20; Rev. v. 2. Activity, Isa. vi. 2–6. Appearance, Matt. xxviii. 2–4; Rev. x. 1, 2. Office, Isa. vi. 1–3; Rev. vi. 11; Matt. xiii. 49; xvi. 27; xxiv. 31.

Ā'nĭ-am (*sighing of the people*). A Manassite, 1 Chr. vii. 19.

Ā'nĭm (*fountains*). A city in mountains of Judah, Josh. xv. 50.

Ăn'ise. A plant of the parsley family, producing aromatic seeds used in medicine and cookery, and with which tithes were paid, Matt. xxiii. 23.

Ănk'lĕt. Much worn in the East as ornaments for the ankles, sometimes with bells, Isa. iii. 16–20. [Bells.]

Ăn'nȧ (*gracious*). (1) Wife of Tobit, Tob. i. 9. (2) A prophetess at Jerusalem, Luke ii. 36.

Ăn'na-as, 1 Esdr. v. 23. [Senaah.]

Ăn'nas (*humble*). (1) 1 Esdr. ix. 32. Same as Harim in Ez. x. 31. (2) A Jewish high priest, A. D. 7–23. Succeeded by his son-in-law, Caiaphas, A. D. 25, John xviii. 13; Luke iii. 2.

A-noint' (*to smear on*). Anointing with oil or ointment, a common practice in East, Gen. xxviii. 18; xxxi. 13; Deut. xxviii. 40; Ruth iii. 3. A mark of respect, Luke vii. 46, Ps. xxiii. 5; or of induction to priestly office, Ex. xl. 15; Num. iii. 3; or to kingly office, 1 Sam. ix. 16; x. 1; or as an act of consecration, Ex. xxviii. 41; or as an act of healing, Mark vi. 13. Christ was anointed with the Holy Ghost, Luke iv. 18; Acts iv. 27; x. 38; Isa. lxi. 1; Ps. xlv. 7.

Ănt (*emmet*). Twice referred to in O. T.; first as to its diligence, and second as to its wisdom. Prov. vi. 6; xxx. 25.

Ăn'te-lōpe (*animal*). The word translated "fallow deer" in Deut. xiv. 5, as well as "pygarg," implies a species of antelope.

Ăn'tĭ-chrīst (*against Christ*). In 1 John ii. 18, 22; iv. 3; 2 John 7, applied to those who hold heretical opinions of the incarnation.

Ăn'tĭ-ŏch (*after Antiochus*). (1) Capital of the Greek kings of Syria, on the Orontes. First Gentile church founded there, and disciples first called Christians there; Acts xi. 19–21, 26. (2) A city of Pisidia, Acts xiii. 14. Starting point of the persecutions which followed Paul all through Asia Minor, Acts xiv.

Ăn-tī'o-chŭs (*opponent*). (1) A messenger of Jonathan to the Romans, 1 Macc. xii. 16. (2) King of Syria, B. C. 261. Prefigured as "King of the North" in Dan. xi. 6, etc. (3) Antiochus III., called "The Great," B. C. 223, Dan. xi. 14–19. (4) Antiochus IV., called Epiphanes, 1 Macc. i. (5) Antiochus V., Eupator, B. C. 164; 1 Macc. vi. 10. (6) Antiochus VI. and VII., 1 Macc. xii.–xvi.

Ăn'tĭ-păs (*like the father*). A martyr of Pergamos, Rev. ii. 13.

Ăn-tĭp'a-tĕr (*for the father*). An ambassador to Lacedemon, 1 Macc. xii. 16.

Ăn-tĭp'a-trĭs (*for his father*). Ancient Capharsaba, rebuilt and renamed by Herod; 34 miles N. W. of Jerusalem, Acts xxiii. 31.

Ăn-tō'nĭ-ȧ. A fortress on N. W. side of Temple at Jerusalem, Acts xxi. 31–40.

Ăn″to̤-thī′jah (*answers of Jehovah*). A son of Jehoram, 1 Chr. viii. 24.

Ăn′tŏth-īte. A native of Anathoth, 1 Chr. xi. 28; xii. 3.

Ȧ-pŏc′ă-lypse (*uncovered*). The Greek name for Revelation.

Ȧ-pŏc′rȳ-pha (*hidden*). That collection of 14 O. T. books not regarded as canonical. Also the rejected N. T. books.

Antelopes. (*See* p. 10.)

Ăp″ŏl-lō′nĭ-ȧ (*belonging to Apollo*). A city of Macedonia, Acts xvii. 1.

Ăp″ŏl-lō′nĭ-us. (1) A governor of Celo-Syria, 2 Macc. iv. 4. (2) A general under Antiochus, 1 Macc. iii. 10–12. (2) Several other Syrian generals of same name, 1 and 2 Macc.

Ăp″ŏl-lŏph′a̤-nē̤s. A Syrian general, 2 Macc. x. 37.

Ȧ-pŏl′lŏs (*belonging to Apollo*). A learned Jew and Christian convert of Alexandria, who became a preacher and friend of Paul, Acts xviii. 24–28; 1 Cor. iii. 6–9; Tit. iii. 13.

Ȧ pŏll′yon (*destroyer*). Greek name of Abaddon, "angel of the bottomless pit," Rev. ix. 11. [ABADDON.]

Ăp′pa̤-im (*nostrils*). Son of Nadab, 1 Chr. ii. 30, 31.

Ȧ-pŏth′ē-cā″ry (*to place away*). The apothecary's art was called for in the mixing of perfume. Ex. xxx. 35.

Ȧ-pŏs′tle (*one sent forth*). Official name of the twelve disciples. As to power and names *see* Matt. x. 1–42; John xvi. 13; Mark xvi. 20. In a broad sense, any one commissioned to preach the gospel, 2 Cor. viii. 23; Phil. ii. 25. Term applied to Christ, Heb. iii. 1.

Ăp-păr′ĕl. [CLOTHES.]

Ăp-peal′ (*drive to*). This right acknowledged by Jewish law, Deut. xvii. 8, 9. It lay to the judges, Judg. iv. 5; then to the kings; later to a special tribunal, 2 Chr. xix. 8–10; Ez. vii. 25; finally to the Sanhedrim. Paul appealed to the Roman Emperor, Acts xxv. 11.

Ā′nub (*confederate*). A descendant of Judah, 1 Chr. iv. 8.

Ā′nus, 1 Esdr. ix. 48. [BANI.]

Ăp-a′me. Daughter of Bartacus, 1 Esdr. iv. 29.

Ȧ-pĕl′lē̤s (*called*). Friend of Paul, Rom. xvi. 10.

Āpes. Were brought from the same countries which supplied ivory and peacocks, 1 Kgs. x. 22; 2 Chr. ix. 21.

Ȧ-phär′săch-ītes, Ȧ-phär′săth-chītes, Ā-phär′sītes (*rending*). Assyrian nomads settled in Samaria, Ez. iv. 9; v. 6.

Ā′phek (*strength*). (1) A royal city of the Canaanites, near Hebron, Josh. xii. 18. Probably Aphekah, Josh. xv. 53. (2) A city in the extreme north of Asher, Josh. xix. 30. Probably Aphik, Judg. i. 31. (3) A place N. W. of Jerusalem, 1 Sam. iv. 1. (4) A Philistine encampment near Jezreel, 1 Sam. xxix. 1. (5) A walled city of Syria, 1 Kgs. xx. 26.

Ȧ-phē′kah, Josh. xv. 53. [APHEK.]

Ȧ-phĕr′e̤-ma. A governor of Judea, 1 Macc. xi. 34.

Ȧ-phĕr′ra. Son of one of Solomon's servants, 1 Esdr. v. 34.

Ȧ-phī′ah (*refreshed*). A progenitor of Saul, 1 Sam. ix. 1.

Ā′phĭk, Judg. i. 31. [APHEK.]

Ăph′rah (*dust*). An uncertain place, Micah i. 10.

Ăph′sēs (*dispersion*). Chief of the 18th course of the temple service, 1 Chr. xxiv. 15.

Ăp′phĭ-ȧ (*productive*). A Christian woman addressed by Paul, Phile. 2.

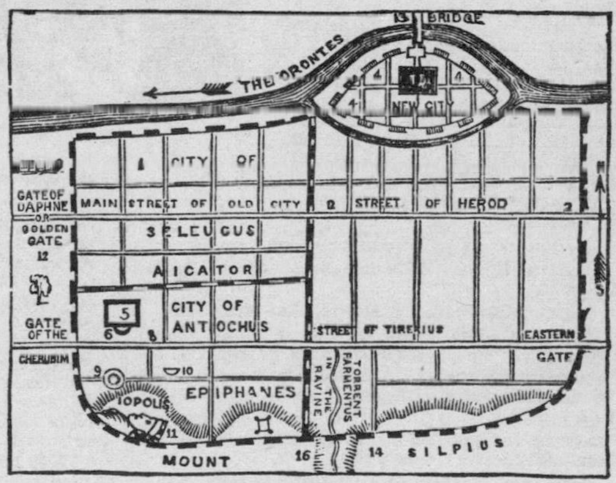

Antioch. (*See* p. 10.)

Ăp′phŭs (*wary*). Surname of Jonathan Maccabeus, 1 Macc. ii. 5.

Ăp″pĭ-ī fō′rŭm (*market-place of Appius*). A

town, 12 miles S. E. of Rome, on the Appian Way, Acts xxviii. 15.

Ăp'ple, Ăp'ple=tree (*bursting forth, in Hebrew*). The fruit is alluded to in Prov. xxv. 11; S. of Sol. ii. 5; vii. 8. Tree mentioned in S. of Sol. ii. 3; viii. 5; Joel i. 12. For figurative use *see* Prov. vii. 2; Zech. ii. 8; Ps. xvii. 8; Lam. ii. 18.

Ăq'uĭ-lȧ (*eagle*). A Jewish convert of Pontus, and valuable assistant of Paul, Acts xviii. 2; 1 Cor. xvi. 19; Rom. xvi. 3, etc.

Är, Är of Mō'ab (*city*). A chief place of Moab, Num. xxi. 28; Isa. xv. 1. Aroer in Deut. ii. 36. Used to type the Moabite people or land, Deut. ii. 9, 18, 29.

Ā'rȧ (*lion*). Head of a family of Asher, 1 Chr. vii. 38.

Ā'rab (*ambush*). A city of Hebron, Josh. xv. 52.

Ăr'a-bah (*burnt up*). A Hebrew word, Josh. xviii. 18, designating the valley of Jordan and the Dead Sea, and the depression through Arabia to the Gulf of Akabah.

Ā-rā'bĭ-ȧ (*desert*). Known in O. T. as "East Country," Gen. x. 30; xxv. 6; and "Land of the Sons of the East," Gen. xxix.; Judg. vi. 3; vii. 12. Arabia, from *Arâb* the people, in 2 Chr. ix. 14; Isa. xxi. 13; Jer. xxv. 24; Ezek. xxvii. 21. That extensive peninsula lying south of Palestine, and between the Red Sea, Indian Ocean, and Persian Gulf. Home of many nomadic races, and in close commerce and even kinship, through Ishmael, with the Hebrews, 1 Kgs. x. 15; 2 Chr. ix. 14. Paul visited it, Gal. i. 17. Often referred to by prophets, Isa. xlii. 11; Jer. xxv. 24.

Ā'răd (*wild ass*). (1) A valorous Benjamite, 1 Chr. viii. 15. (2) A royal city of the Canaanites, Num. xxi. 1; Josh. xii. 14.

Ăr'a-dus, 1 Macc. xv. 23. [Arvad.]

Ā'rah (*wandering*). (1) An Asherite, 1 Chr. vii. 39. (2) Head of a returned family, Ez. ii. 5; Neh. vii. 10.

Ā'ram (*high*). (1) Translated Mesopotamia in Gen. xxiv. 10. The high part of Syria to the N. E. of Palestine. Absorbed by Syria, with capital at Damascus, 1 Kgs. xx. 1; Isa. vii. 8; 1 Kgs. xi. 24. (2) A descendant of Nahor, Gen. xxii. 21. (3) An Asherite, 1 Chr. vii. 34. (4) An ancestor of Christ, Matt. i. 4; Luke iii. 33.

Ā'ram=nā-ha-rā'im (*highlands of two rivers*), Ps. lx. title.

Ā'ram=zō'bah [**Ā'ram**]. Ps. xl title.

Ā'ram-it''ess. A female inhabitant of Aram, 1 Chr. vii. 14.

Ā'răn (*wild goat*). A Horite, Gen. xxxvi. 28.

Ăr'ȧ-rat (*high land*). A high mountain of Armenia, and resting place of Noah's ark, Gen. viii. 4.

Ā-rau'nah (*ark*). A Jebusite prince who sold his threshing-floor to David, 2 Sam. xxiv. 18–24; 1 Chr. xxi. 25.

Är'bȧ (*one of four*). A forefather of Anak, Josh. xiv. 15; xv. 13; xxi. 11.

Är'bah. Hebron, or Kirjath-arba, Gen. xxxv. 27.

Är'băth-īte. An inhabitant of the Arabah, 2 Sam. xxiii. 31; 1 Chr. xi. 32.

Är-băt'tis. A district in Palestine, 1 Macc. v. 23.

Är'bel. Hos. x. 14. [Beth-arbel.]

Är-bē'la. A town in Galilee, 1 Macc. ix. 2.

Är'bīte. A native of Arab, 2 Sam. xxiii. 35.

Ärch-an'gel (ärk-ān'jel) (*chief angel*). 1 Thess. iv. 16; Jude 9.

Är''chĕ-lā'us (*prince of the people*). A son of Herod the Great, and ethnarch (B. C. 4–A. D. 9) of Idumea, Judea, and Samaria, Matt. ii. 22.

Ärch'e-ry (*use of the arcus, or bow*). Use of the bow and arrow, an important art in Biblical times, Gen. xxvii. 3; Isa. xxii. 6; xlix.; 2 Ps. cxxvii. 4, 5. Benjamites noted archers, Judg. xix.–xxi.

Royal Egyptian Archer.

Är'chĕ-vītes. Probably inhabitants of Erech, Ez. iv. 9.

Är'chī. A place or clan in Joseph, Josh. xvi. 2. [Archite.]

Är'chĭp'pus (*chief of stables*). A Christian teacher at Colossæ, Col. iv. 17; Phil. 2.

Är'chīte. Supposed to refer to a clan of Erech, 2 Sam. xv. 32; xvi. 16; xvii. 5–14. 1 Chr. xxvii. 33.

Är'chĭ-tec''ture (*builder's art*). Descendants of Shem were city builders, Gen. iv. 17; x. 11, 12. Hebrew ideas of architecture ripened in Egypt, and by contact with Tyre. David enlarged Jerusalem. Solomon built a palace and temple, 2 Sam. v. 11; 1 Kgs. vii. The returned captives were great builders, Ez. iii. 8–10; Neh. iii.; vi. 15.

Ärc-tū'rus (*the bear*). The constellation Ursa Major, commonly called the "Great Bear" or "Charles's Wain," Job ix. 9; xxxviii. 32.

Ärd (*fugitive*). A grandson of Benjamin, Gen. xlvi. 21; Num. xxvi. 40.

Är'dăth. A field, 2 Esdr. ix. 26.

Ărd'ites. Descendants of Ard or Addar, Num. xxvi. 40.

Är'dŏn (*fugitive*). A son of Caleb, 1 Chr. ii. 18.

Ā-rē'lī (*heroic*). A son of Gad. Children called Arelites, Num. xxvi. 17; Gen. xlvi. 16.

Är''ĕ-op'a-gīte. A member of the court of Areopagus, Acts xvii. 34.

Är''ĕ-op'a-gus (*hill of Mars*). A rocky hill near the centre of Athens, where the court of justice sat, Acts xvii. 19–34.

Ā'rēs, 1 Esdr. v. 10. [ARAH 2.]

Är'e-tas (*excellence*). (1) An Arab chief, 2 Macc. v. 8. (2) Father-in-law of Herod Antipas, 2 Cor. xi. 32.

Ā-rē'us. A Lacedæmonian king, 1 Macc. xii. 20–23.

Är'gŏb (*stony*). A country of Bashan, and one of Solomon's commissary districts, Deut. iii. 4; 1 Kgs. iv. 13.

Ā''rī-ă-rā'thes. Mithridates IV., king of Cappadocia, B. C. 163–130, 1 Macc. xv. 22.

Ā-rĭd'a-ī (*strong*). Ninth son of Haman, Esth. ix. 9.

Ā-rĭd'a-thȧ. Sixth son of Haman, Esth. ix. 8.

Ā-rī'eh (*lion*). A prince of Israel, killed by Pekah, 2 Kgs. xv. 25.

Ā-rī'el (*lion of God*). (1) A leader of returning captives, Ez. viii. 16. (2) The city of Jebus-Salem, Jerusalem, Isa. xxix. 1, 2.

Är''ī-mă-thæ'ȧ (*heights*). Home of Joseph in Judea, Matt. xxvii. 57; Mark xv. 43; Luke xxiii. 51; John xix. 38.

Ā'rī-ŏch (*venerable*). (1) A King of Elassar, Gen. xiv. 1–9. (2) Captain under Nebuchadnezzar, Dan. ii. 14, etc. (3) A king of the Elymeans, Judith i. 6.

Ā-rĭs'a-ī (*lion like*). Eighth son of Haman, Esth. ix. 9.

Är''ĭs-tär'chus (*best ruler*). A Thessalonian companion of Paul on his third missionary tour, Acts xix. 29; xx. 4; xxvii. 2; Col. iv. 10; Phil. 24.

Ă-rĭs''tŏ-bū'lus (*best counselor*). (1) A Christian and resident at Rome, Rom. xvi. 10. (2) A priest of the Egyptian Jews, 2 Macc. i. 10.

Ärk (*chest*). The vessel in which Noah and his family were saved, Gen. vi., vii., viii. Also a little boat of rushes, Ex. ii. 3.

Ärk of the Cŏv'ĕ-nănt. Built by direction, Ex. xxv. A chest of Shittim wood for tabernacle use, 3 ft. 9 in. long, by 2 ft. 3 in. wide and high, lined and covered with gold, whose lid was the mercy-seat, on either end of which were cherubs. Golden rings were on the sides, through which poles passed for carrying. Captured by Philistines, 1 Sam. iv. 10, 11; returned to Kirjath-Jearim; brought thence by David to Jerusalem, 2 Sam. vi. 1; 1 Chr. xv. 25, 28, etc.; placed in temple by Solomon, 2 Chr. v. 2–10.

Ärk'īte. A descendant of Arka, Gen. x. 17; 1 Chr. i. 15.

Armlet.

Är-ma-gĕd'don (*hill of Megiddo*). A typical battlefield between the hosts of good and evil, Rev. xvi. 16.

Är-mē'nĭ-ȧ (*Land of Aram*). The plateau of Western Asia, whence flow its great rivers Euphrates, Tigris, Araxes, etc., 2 Kgs. xix. 37; Isa. xxxvii. 38.

Ärm'-let (*for the arms*). An arm ornament in general use in the East. "Bracelet," 2 Sam. i. 10.

Är-mō'nī. A son of Saul, 2 Sam. xxi. 8.

Ärms, Är'mor. Hebrew offensive weapons were the sword, 1 Sam. xvii. 51; xxv. 13; 2 Sam. xx. 8; Judg. iii. 16; spear, 1 Sam. xvii. 7; 2 Sam. ii. 23; xxiii. 8; bow and arrow [ARCHERY]; sling, 2 Kgs. iii. 25; battle-axe, Jer. li. 20. Among defensive armor were breastplates, cuirasses, coats of mail, helmets, greaves, habergeons, shields, bucklers, 1 Sam. xvii. 5–7; 2 Chr. xxvi. 14.

Cuirass.

Är'my. Hebrew males twenty years old and upward subject to military duty, Num. i. 2, 3. Tribes formed army divisions. Numerated by hundreds and thousands, each with captains, Num. xxxi. 14. Kings had body-guards, 1 Sam. xiii. 2; xxv. 13. Later, a standing army formed, 2 Chr. xxv. 6. No cavalry till Solomon's time. War declared and exempts used as in Deut. xx. 1–14; xxiv. 5. In N. T. Roman army composed of legions, with chief captains, Acts xxi. 31; tents of legions, or cohorts, and bands, Acts x. 1; maniples, or thirds of legions; centuries, 100 men each and two to a maniple. Captain of a 100 called a Centurion, Matt. viii. 5; xxvii. 54.

Är'na. A forefather of Ezra, 2 Esdr. i. 2.

Är'nan. Head of a returned family, 1 Chr. iii. 21.

Är'nŏn (*noisy*). A stream emptying into Dead Sea from the East, and boundary between the Amorites and Moabites, Num. xxi. 13; Judg. xi. 18. Afterwards between Moab and Israel, Deut. ii. 24; Josh. xii. 1; xiii. 9; Judg. xi. 13.

Ā'rŏd (*wild ass*). Gadite founder of the **Ā'rŏd-ītes**, Num. xxvi. 17. Called **Är'ŏ-dī** in Gen. xlvi. 16.

Ā'rŏd-ītes. [AROD.]

Är'ŏ-ĕr (*ruins*). (1) A Reubenite city on the Arnon, Deut. ii. 36; Josh. xii. 1, 2; Judg. xi. 26. Later fell back to Moab, Jer. xlviii. 19, 20. (2) A town of Gad, Num. xxxii. 34; Josh. xiii. 25; 2 Sam. xxiv. 5. (3) An unidentified place, Isa. xvii. 2. (4) A town in South Judah, 1 Sam. xxx. 28.

Är'ŏ-ĕr-īte''. Designation of Hothan, 1 Chr. xi. 44.

Ā'rom. A returned family, 1 Esdr. v. 16.

Är'pad or **Är'phad** (*strong*). A city, or district, in Syria, dependent on Damascus, Isa. xxxvi. 19; xxxvii. 13; Jer. xlix. 23; 2 Kgs. xviii. 34; xix. 13.

Är-phax'ăd (*Chaldean fortress*). (1) A son of Shem, Gen. x. 22, 24; xi. 10–13; 1 Chr. i. 17, 18, 24. (2) A king of the Medes, Judith i. 1–4.

Är'rows. [Arms.]

Är"tăx-ĕrx'es (*brave warrior*). (1) A Persian king who stopped the rebuilding of the temple at Jerusalem, Ez. iv. 7, 23, 24. (2) Another Persian king, friendly to Nehemiah, Neh. ii. 1.

Är'te-măs (*gift of Artemis*). A friend of Paul, Tit. iii. 12.

Är-tĭl'lĕ-ry. The missile equipment of a Jewish soldier, lance, arrows, etc., 1 Sam. xx. 40. [Arms.]

Ärts. The tricks of magic and astrology, Acts xix. 19. [Astrologers.]

Är'u-bŏth (*windows*). The third commissary district of King Solomon, 1 Kgs. iv. 10.

Ā-ru'-mah (*height*). Residence of Abimelech, near Shechem, Judg. ix. 41.

Är'văd (*wandering*). An island, now Ruad, lying three miles off Tyre, Ezek. xxvii. 8–11.

Är'vad-īte. A native of Arvad, Gen. x. 18; 1 Chr. i. 16.

Är'zȧ. Keeper of King Elah's palace at Tirzah, 1 Kgs. xvi. 9.

Ā'sȧ (*physician*). (1) Third king of Judah, 1 Kgs. xv. 8–34; reigned B. C. 955-914; abolished idolatry; battled victoriously with Ethiopia, 2 Chr. xiv.; involved with Israel; buried with pomp, 2 Chr. xvi. (2) A Levite, 1 Chr. ix. 16.

Ăs"ā-dī'as. An ancestor of Baruch, Bar. i. 1.

Ăs'ā-el. An ancestor of Tobit, Tob. i. 1.

Ā'sa-hĕl (*creature of God*). (1) The fleet-footed nephew of David, killed by Abner, 2 Sam. ii. 18–23. (2) A Levitical legal instructor, 2 Chr. xvii. 8. (3) A Levite and tithing-man, 2 Chr. xxxi. 13. (4) A priest, Ez. x. 15.

Ā"sa-hī'ah (*the Lord made*). A learned servant of King Josiah, 2 Kgs. xxii. 12–14. Asaiah in 2 Chr. xxxiv. 20.

Ā"sa-ī'ah (*whom the Lord made*). (1) Prince of a Simeonite family, 1 Chr. iv. 36. (2) A Levite chief, 1 Chr. vi. 30; xv. 6–11. (3) A Shilonite, 1 Chr. ix. 5. Maaseiah in Neh. xi. 5. (4) Asaiah, 2 Chr. xxxiv. 20.

Ăs'a-nȧ, 1 Esdr. v. 31. [Asnah].

Ā'saph (*gatherer*). (1) Levitical leader of David's choir, 1 Chr. vi. 39; 2 Chr. xxix. 30; Neh. xii. 46. Twelve of the Psalms are attributed to him, to wit, Ps. l. and lxxiii. to lxxxiii. (2) Ancestor of Joah the chronicler, 2 Kgs. xviii. 18; Isa. xxxvi. 3, 22. (3) Keeper of royal forests under Artaxerxes, Neh. ii. 8. (4) Another conductor of the Temple choir, 1 Chr. ix. 15; Neh. xi. 17.

Ā'saph, Sons of. A school of poets and musicians founded by Asaph.

Ā-sā'rē-el (*oath bound*). A descendant of Judah, 1 Chr. iv. 16.

Ăs"ă-rē'lah (*upright*). A minstrel prophet under David, 1 Chr. xxv. 2. Jesharelah in vs. 14.

Ăs'ca-lŏn. [Ashkelon.]

Ăs-çen'sion, *see* Christ.

Ăs'e-năth (*devotee of Neith*, the Egyptian Minerva), Egyptian wife of Joseph, Gen. xli. 45–50; xlvi. 20.

Ā'sēr, Luke ii. 36; Rev. vii. 6. [Asher.]

Ăsh. Ash was not indigenous to Palestine; perhaps pine or cedar is meant, Isa. xliv. 14.

Ā'shan (*smoke*). A city in Judah, Josh. xv. 42; and Simeon, Josh. xix. 7; 1 Chr. iv. 32.

Ăsh-bē'ȧ (*I adjure*). A doubtful genealogical name, 1 Chr. iv. 21.

Ăsh'bel (*reproof*). Second son of Benjamin, Gen. xlvi. 21; Num. xxvi. 38; 1 Chr. viii. 1.

Ăsh'chĕ-naz. 1 Chr. i. 6; Jer. li. 27. [Ashkenaz.]

Ăsh'dŏd or **Ăz-ō'tus** (*stronghold*). A Philistine city between Gaza and Joppa; assigned to Judah, Josh. xv. 47; 1 Sam. v. 1. Azotus, Acts viii. 40.

Ăsh'dŏd-ītes". Dwellers in Ashdod, Neh. iv. 7.

Ăsh'dŏth-ītes. Dwellers in Ashdod, Josh. xiii. 3.

Ăsh'dŏth=pĭs'gah (*Springs of Pisgah*). Probably the "slopes of Pisgah," to the east, Deut. iii. 17; iv. 49; Josh. xii. 3; xiii. 20.

Ăsh'ĕr (*happiness*). (1) Eighth son of Jacob, Gen. xxx. 13. Aser in Apochrypha and N. T. For boundaries of his allotment *see* Josh. xix. 24–31; xvii. 10, 11; Judg. i. 31, 32. (2) A boundary town of Manasseh, Josh. xvii. 7.

Ăsh'ĕ-rah (*straight*). [Ashtaroth.]

Ăsh'ĕr-ītes. Members of the tribe of Asher. Judg. i. 32.

Ăsh'es. To sprinkle with or sit in ashes, marked humiliation, grief, and penitence, Gen. xviii. 27; 2 Sam. xiii. 19; Esth. iv. 3; Job ii. 8; Jer. vi. 26; Lam. iii. 16; Matt. xi. 21. The altar ashes, when a red heifer was sacrificed, were watered and used for purifying the unclean, Num. xix. 17–22.

Ăsh'ī-mȧ (*offence*). A Syrian god worshipped in Samaria, 2 Kgs. xvii. 30.

Ăsh'ke-lŏn, Ăs'ke-lŏn (*migration*). A Philistine city and seaport on the Mediterranean, 10 miles N. of Gaza, Josh. (Eshkalon) xiii. 3; Judg. (Askelon) i. 18; Judg. (Ashkelon) xiv. 19; 1 Sam. vi. 17. Its destruction predicted in Jer. xlvii. 5–7; Am. i. 8; Zech. ix. 5; Zeph. ii. 7.

Ăsh'ke-năz (*fire that spreads*). A grandson of Japhet, Gen. x. 3. Ashchenaz in 1 Chr. i. 6; Jer. li. 27.

Ăsh'nah (*change*). Two towns of Judah, one N. W. the other S.W. of Jerusalem, 16 miles distant, Josh. xv. 33, 43.

Ăsh'pe-naz (*horse-nose*). Master of eunuchs under Nebuchadnezzar, Dan. i. 3.

Ăsh'rī-el, 1 Chr. vii. 14. [Asriel.]

Ăsh'ta-rŏth and **Ăs'ta-rŏth** (*star*). A city of Bashan, noted for its worship of Ashtoreth, Deut. i. 4; Josh. ix. 10; xii. 4; xiii. 12.

Ăsh'tĕ-răth-īte". An inhabitant of Ashtaroth, 1 Chr. xi. 44.

Ăsh'tĕ-rŏth Kär-nā'im (*Ashteroth of two peaks*). A city of the giant Rephaim in Bashan, Gen. xiv. 5.

Ăsh'tŏ-rĕth (*star*). The principal female deity of the Phœnicians; the Ishtar of the Assyrians, and Astarte of the Greeks and Romans. Solomon introduced her worship into his kingdom, Judg. ii. 13; 1 Kgs. xi. 5, 33; 2 Kgs. xxiii. 13.

Ăsh'ŭr (*black*). Founder of Tekoa, 1 Chr. ii. 24; iv. 5.

Ăsh'ŭr-ītes. Asherites, 2 Sam. ii. 9.

Ăsh'vath. A son of Japhlet, 1 Chr. vii. 33.

Ā'si-ȧ (*eastern*). Only in N. T., and then with reference to Asia Minor, or even to western Asia Minor, with the capital at Ephesus, Acts ii. 9; vi. 9; xvi. 6; 1 Cor. xvi. 19.

Ā'si-ȧ-arch (*-ark*). Chief of the religious rites and public games of the Roman province of Asia, Acts xix. 31.

Ăs"i-bī'as, 1 Esdr. ix. 26. [Malchijah.]

Ā-sī-el (*made by God*). (1) A progenitor of Jehu, 1 Chr. iv. 35. (2) A scribe under Esdras, 2 Esdr. xiv. 24.

Ăs'ke-lŏn. [Ashkelon.]

Ăs"mō-dē'us. An evil spirit, classed with Abaddon and Apollyon, Tob. iii. 8–17.

Astarte. (*See* p. 14.)

Ăs'nah (*thorn-bush*). Father of a returned family, Ez. ii. 50.

Ăs-năp'pēr (*swift*). Leader of Cuthæan colonists into Samaria, Ez. iv. 10.

Ăsp (*viper*). The hooded venomous serpent known as the African cobra. Adder in Ps. lviii. 4; xci. 13, answers the description of asp, Deut. xxxii. 33; Job xx. 14–16; Isa. xi. 8; Rom. iii. 13.

Ăs-păl'ā-thus. A perfume, or ointment, product of Rhodian wood, Ecclus. xxiv. 15.

Ăs'pă-thȧ. Third son of Haman, Esth. ix. 7.

Ăs'phar. A pool in the wilderness of Thecoe, 1 Macc. ix. 33.

Ăs'rĭ-el (*help of God*). Founder of the Asrielites, Num. xxvi. 31; Josh. xvii. 2; Ashriel, 1 Chr. vii. 14.

Ăss. Five different Hebrew words give it name in the Bible. A patient beast of burden, and palfrey for even kings, Gen. xxii. 3; xii. 16; xxxvi. 24; 1 Chr. xxvii. 30; Job i. 3; Zech. ix. 9, which last is the prophecy of Christ's entry into Jerusalem, Matt. xxi. 1–9.

Ăs'shur. Second son of Shem, Gen. x. 22. Also Hebrew form for Assyria, Ezek. xxvii. 23.

Ăs-shu'rim (*steps*). A tribe descended from Abraham, Gen. xxv. 3.

Ăs''si-dē'ans (*pious*). A sect of orthodox Jews, bound to the external observance of the law, 1 Macc. ii. 42.

Ăs'sĭr (*prisoner*). (1) A Levite, Ex. vi. 24; 1 Chr. vi. 22. (2) A forefather of Samuel, 1 Chr. vi. 23, 37. (3) Son of Jeconiah, 1 Chr. iii. 17.

Ăs'sŏs or **Ăs'sus** (*approaching*). A Roman seaport on northern shore of Gulf of Adramyttium, Acts xx. 13, 14.

Ăs'sur, Ez. iv. 2; Ps. lxxxiii. 8. [Asshur; Assyria.]

Ăs-sўr'ĭ-ȧ (*country of Asshur*). That ancient empire on the Tigris whose capital was Nineveh, Gen. ii. 14; x. 11–22. In its splendor it embraced Susiana, Chaldea, Babylon, Media, Armenia, Assyria proper, Mesopotamia, Syria, Phœnicia, Palestine, and Idumea. Assyrian kings frequently invaded Israel, 2 Kgs. xv. 19; xvi. 7–9; xv. 29; 2 Chr. xxviii. 20. Shalmaneser destroyed Samaria, B. C. 721, and carried the people captive. Assyria was overthrown by the Medes and Babylonians, 625 B. C., after an existence of 1200 years.

Ăs'tȧ-rŏth, Deut. i. 4. [Ashtaroth.]

Ăs-tär'te. [Ashtoreth.]

Ā-sty'ă-gēs. Last king of the Medes, B. C. 500. Bel and Drag. 1.

Ā-sŭp'pim, House of (*gatherings*). Probably store-rooms in the Temple, 1 Chr. xxvi. 15, 17. "Thresholds" in Neh. xii. 25.

Ā-sўn'crĭ-tus (*incomparable*). A Christian friend of Paul, at Rome, Rom. xvi. 14.

Ā'tad, Threshing Floor of. Name changed to Abel-mizraim, which *see*, Gen. l. 10, 11.

Ăt'ȧ-rah (*crown*). Mother of Onam, 1 Chr. ii. 26.

Ā-tär'gȧ-tis (*opening*). A Syrian goddess with a woman's body and fish's tail, 2 Macc. xii. 26.

Ăt'ȧ-rŏth (*crowns*). (1) A town of Gilead, Num. xxxii. 3, 34. (2) A place on the southern boundary of Ephraim, Josh. xvi. 2, 7. (3) Perhaps same as above, 1 Chr. ii. 54.

Ā'tēr (*shut up*). Heads of two different returned families, Ez. ii. 42; Neh. vii. 21.

Ā'thăch (*stopping place*). A town in southern Judah, 1 Sam. xxx. 30.

Ăth''ȧ-ī'ah (*whom God made*). A descendant of Pharez, Neh. xi. 4. Uthai in 1 Chr. ix. 4.

Ăth''ȧ-lī'ah (*afflicted by God*). (1) Wicked wife of Jehoram, king of Judah, who introduced the worship of Baal and was slain by her own guards, 2 Kgs. xi.; 2 Chr. xxii.–xxiv. (2) A Benjamite, 1 Chr. viii. 26. (3) Head of a returned Jewish family, Ez. viii. 7.

Ā-thē'nĭ-anș. Inhabitants of Athens, Acts xvii. 21.

Ath''ĕ-nō'bĭ-us. An envoy of King Antiochus, 1 Macc. xv. 28.

Ăth'ĕnș (*city of Athena, or Minerva*). Capital of Attica and chief seat of Grecian learning and civilization. Situate in S. E. part of the Grecian Peninsula, five miles from its seaport, the Piræus. Paul preached on its Areopagus or Mars' Hill, Acts xvii. 19–22, and founded a church there.

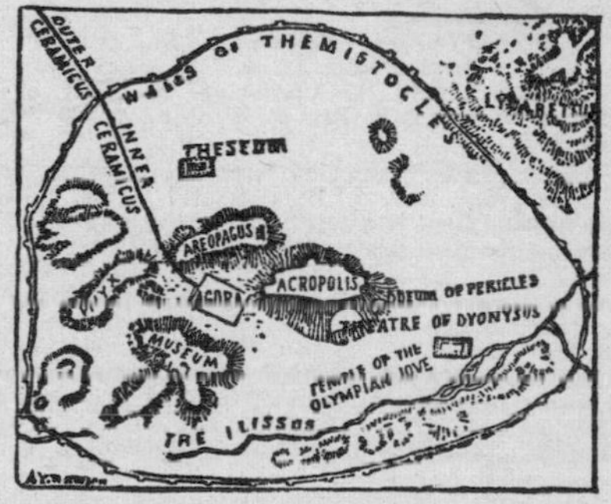

Athens.

Ăth'lāi (*whom God afflicts*). A son of Bebai, Ez. x. 28.

Ā-tōne'mĕnt (*reconciliation*). The expiation of sin and propitiation of God by the incarnation, life, suffering, and death of Christ. Day of Atonement, an annual day of Hebrew fasting and humiliation, Ex. xxx. 16; Lev. xvi.; xxiii. 27–32.

Ăt'rŏth (*crowns*). A city of Gad, Num. xxxii. 35.

Ăt'tāi (*ready*). (1) A grandson of Sheshan, 1 Chr. ii. 35, 36. (2) A lion-faced warrior of Gad, 1 Chr. xii. 11. (3) A son of King Rehoboam, 2 Chr. xi. 20.

Ăt-tȧ-lī'ȧ. A coast town of Pamphylia, Acts xiv. 25.

Ăt'tă-lus (*increased*). Names of three kings of Pergamos, 1 Macc. xv. 22.

Au-gŭs'tus (*venerable*). Caius Julius Cæsar Octavianus, grand-nephew of, and heir to, Julius Cæsar. Made first emperor of Rome B. C. 27, with title of Augustus. During his reign Christ was born, Luke ii. 1. Died A. D. 14, aged 76 years.

Au-gŭs'tus' Band, Acts xxvii. 1. [ARMY.]

Au-rā'nus. A riotous fellow at Jerusalem, 2 Macc. iv. 40.

Ā'vȧ (*ruin*). A place in Assyria, 2 Kgs. xvii. 24.

Ăv'ă-răn. Surname of Eleazer, 1 Macc. ii. 5.

Ā'ven (*nothingness*). (1) An unidentified plain, Amos i. 5. (2) Beth-aven, or Bethel, Hosea x. 8. (3) Heliopolis or city of On, Ezek. xxx. 17.

Ā-vĕnge', Ā-vĕn'ger. Exaction of just satisfaction, Luke xviii. 8; 1 Thess. iv. 6. "Avenger of Blood" was the pursuer of a slayer to avenge the blood of the slain. He must be a relative of the dead one, Deut. xix. 6.

Ā'vĭm, Ā'vĭms, Ā'vītes (*ruins*). (1) A primitive people who pushed into Palestine from the desert of Arabia, Deut. ii. 23. (2) Colonists from Ava sent to people Israel, 2 Kgs. xvii. 31.

Ā'vĭth (*ruins*). The king's city of Edom, Gen. xxxvi. 35; 1 Chr. i. 46.

Awl. Shape not known, but use expressed in Ex. xxi. 6; Deut. xv. 17.

Axe. Seven Hebrew words so translated. It was of stone or iron, crudely fastened to a handle of wood, Deut. xix. 5; 2 Kgs. vi. 5-7.

Ā'zăl. Probably a common noun, Zech. xiv. 5.

Ăz''a-lī'ah (*near Jehovah*). Father of Shaphan the scribe, 2 Kgs. xxii. 3.

Ăz''a-nī'ah (*whom God hears*). Father of Jeshua, Neh. x. 9.

Ă-zā'phĭ-on. Probably Sophereth, 1 Esdr. v. 33.

Ăz'a-rȧ. A servant of the temple, 1 Esdr. v. 35.

Ā-zăr'a-el (*whom God helps*). A Levite musician, Neh. xii. 36.

Ā-zăr'e-el (*whom God helps*). (1) A companion of David at Ziklag, 1 Chr xii. 6. (2) A Levite musician, 1 Chr. xxv. 18. (3) A prince of Dan, 1 Chr. xxvii. 22. (4) Son of Bani, Ezra x. 41. (5) A priest, Neh. xi. 13.

Ăz''a-rī'ah (*whom God helps*). (1) Grandson of Zadok, 1 Kgs. iv. 2; 1 Chr. vi. 9. (2) A chief officer under Solomon, 1 Kgs. iv. 5. (3) Tenth king of Judah, commonly called Uzziah, 2 Kgs. xiv. 21; xv. 1-27; 1 Chr. iii. 12. (4) A son of Ethan, 1 Chr. ii. 8. (5) A son of Jehu, 1 Chr. ii. 38, 39. (6) A high priest under Abijah and Asa, 1 Chr. vi. 10. (7) A wrongly inserted name, 1 Chr. vi. 13. (8) An ancestor of Samuel, vi. 36. (9) A prophet in Asa's reign, 2 Chr. xv. 1. (10) Son of King Jehoshaphat, 2 Chr. xxi. 2. (11) Another son of Jehoshaphat, 2 Chr. xxi. 2. (12) For Ahaziah, 2 Chr. xxii. 6. (13) A captain of Judah, 2 Chr. xxiii. 1. (14) High priest in reign of Uzziah, 2 Chr. xxvi. 17-20. (15) A captain of Ephraim in reign of Ahaz, 2 Chr. xxviii. 12. (16) A Levite, 2 Chr. xxix. 12. (17) Another Levite, 2 Chr. xxix. 12. (18) High priest in time of Hezekiah, 2 Chr. xxxi. 10-13. (19) One who helped to rebuild the walls of Jerusalem, Neh. iii. 23, 24. (20) Leader of a returned family, Neh. vii. 7. (21) A Levite who helped Ezra, Neh. viii. 7. (22) A co-covenanter with Nehemiah, Neh. x. 2. (23) Jer. xliii. 2, for Jezaniah. (24) Hebrew name of Abed-nego, Dan. i. 6.

Ăz''a-rī'as. A frequent name in Esdras.

Ā'zaz (*strong*). A Reubenite, 1 Chr. v. 8.

Ăz''a-zī'ah (*whom God strengthens*). (1) A Levite musician, 1 Chr. xv. 21. (2) A chief of Ephraim, 1 Chr. xxvii. 20. (3) Custodian of tithes and offerings under Hezekiah, 2 Chr. xxxi. 13.

Ăz-băz'a-rĕth. Probably Esarhaddon, 1 Esdr. v. 69.

Ăz'bŭk (*devastation*). Father of Nehemiah, Neh. iii. 16.

Ā-zē'kah (*dug over*). A town of Judah, Josh. x. 10, 11.

Ā'zel (*noble*). A descendant of Saul, 1 Chr. viii. 37, 38; ix. 43, 44.

Ā'zem (*bone*) A city of Judah and Simeon, Josh. xv. 29; xix. 3. EZEM, elsewhere.

Ā-zē'tas. A returned Hebrew family, 1 Esdr. v. 15.

Ăz'gad (*strength of fortune*). (1) Head of a large returned family, Ez. ii. 12; viii. 12; Neh. vii. 17. (2) A co-covenanter with Nehemiah, Neh. x. 15.

Ā'zĭ-el (*whom God comforts*). A Levite, 1 Chr. xv. 20; Jaaziel in vs. 18.

Ā-zī'zȧ (*strong*). A returned captive, Ez. x. 27.

Ăz'ma-vĕth (*strong unto death*). (1) One of David's mighty men, 2 Sam. xxiii. 31; 1 Chr. xi. 33. (2) A descendant of Mephibosheth, 1 Chr. viii. 36; ix. 42. (3) A Benjamite, 1 Chr. xii. 3. (4) David's treasurer, 1 Chr. xxvii. 25. (5) A place in Benjamin, Ez. ii. 24; Neh. xii. 29. The Beth-azmaveth of Neh. vii. 28.

Ăz'mŏn (*strong*). A place in southern Palestine, Num. xxxiv. 4, 5; Josh. xv. 4.

Ăz'nŏth=tā'bôr (*summits of Tabor*). A boundary of Naphtali, Josh. xix. 34.

Ā'zôr (*helper*). One of Christ's ancestors, Matt. i. 13, 14.

Ā-zō'tus. Greek form of Ashdod in Acts viii. 40. [ASHDOD.]

Ăz'rĭ-el (*help of God*). (1) Head of Manassite family, 1 Chr. v. 24. (2) A Naphtalite, 1 Chr. xxvii. 19. (3) Father of Seraiah, Jer. xxxvi. 26.

Ăz'rĭ-kam (*avenging help*). (1) A descendant of Zerubbabel, 1 Chr. iii. 23. (2) A descendant of Saul, 1 Chr. viii. 38; ix. 44. (3) A Levite, 1 Chr. ix. 14; Neh. xi. 15. (4) Prefect of King Ahaz's palace, 2 Chr. xxviii. 7.

Ā-zū'bah (*forsaken*). (1) Wife of Caleb, 1 Chr. ii. 18, 19. (2) Mother of Jehoshaphat, 1 Kgs. xxii. 42; 2 Chr. xx. 31.

Ā'zur (*helper*). (1) Father of the false prophet Hananiah, Jer. xxviii. 1. (2) Father of one of the princes against whom Ezekiel prophesied, Ezek. xi. 1.

Ăz'zah (*strong*). In Deut. ii. 23; 1 Kgs. iv. 24; Jer. xxv. 20, for GAZA.

Ăz'zan (*very strong*). A chief of Issachar, Num. xxxiv. 26.

Ăz'zur (*helper*). A co-covenanter with Nehemiah, Neh. x. 17. Azur, elsewhere.

B

Bā'al (*lord*). (1) Baal, Bel, or Belus, supreme male god of Phœnicians and Canaanites, worshipped with self-torture and human offerings, Jer. xix. 5. Even house-tops were temples, 2 Kgs. xxiii. 12, Jer. xxxii. 29. Hebrews infected with the worship, Num. xxii. 41; xxv. 3-18; Deut. iv. 16. Became the court religion, 1 Kgs. xvi. 31-33. xviii. 19-28; 2 Kgs. x. 22; xvii. 16. Bel in Isa. xlvi. 1. Baalim, plural form, in Judg. ii. 11; x. 10, and elsewhere. (2) A Reubenite, 1 Chr. v. 5. (3) Grandson of Saul, 1 Chr. viii. 30; ix. 36. (4) A town of Simeon; Bealoth and Baalath-beer, 1 Chr. iv. 33.

Bā'al-ah (*mistress*). (1) For Kirjath-jearim in Josh. xv. 9, 10; Baale, 2 Sam. vi. 2; Kirjath-baal, Josh. xv. 60; xviii. 14. (2) A town in south Judah, Josh. xv. 29. Balah in Josh. xix. 3; and Bilhah in 1 Chr. iv. 29.

Bā'al-ath (*mistress*). A town in Dan, Josh. xix. 44; 1 Kgs. ix. 18; 2 Chr. viii. 6.

Bā'al-ath=bē'ĕr (*lord of the well*). [BAAL.] (4) [BEALOTH.]

Bā'al=bē'rith (*Baal of the covenant*). Form of Baal worshipped by the Shechemites, Judg. viii. 33; ix. 4.

Bā'ā-lē of Jū'dah. Name for Kirjath-jearim. [BAALAH.]

Bā'al=gad (*troop of Baal*). Northern limit of Joshua's conquest, Josh. xi. 17; xii. 7; xiii. 5.

Bā'al=hā'mŏn (*lord of a multitude*). Solomon had a vineyard there, S. of Sol. viii. 11.

Bā'al=hā'nan (*lord of Hanan*). (1) A king of Edom, Gen. xxxvi. 38, 39; 1 Chr. i. 49, 50. (2) Superintendent of David's groves, 1 Chr. xxvii. 28.

Bā'al=hā'zôr (*village of Baal*). The shearing-place where Absalom killed Amnon, 2 Sam. xiii. 23.

Bā'al=hĕr'mŏn (*lord of Hermon*). A peak of Hermon, Judg. iii. 3; 1 Chr. v. 23.

Bā'al-ī (*my lord*). My idol! A repudiated word of endearment, Hos. ii. 16.

Bā'al-ĭm. [BAAL.]

Bā'a-lĭs (*son of exaltation*). A king of the Ammonites, Jer. xl. 14.

Bā'al=mē'on (*lord of the house*). A Reubenite town, Num. xxxii. 38; 1 Chr. v. 8; Ezek. xxv. 9.

Bā'al=pē'or (*lord of the opening*). The form of Baal worship in Peor, Num. xxv. 3–5, 18. Israelites shared in it, Deut. iv. 3; Josh. xxii. 17; Ps. cvi. 28; Hos. ix. 10.

Bā'al=pĕr'a-zĭm (*lord of divisions*). Scene of David's victory over the Philistines, 2 Sam. v. 20; 1 Chr. xiv. 11. Mount Perazim in Isa. xxviii. 21.

Bā'al=shal'ĭ-shà. An unknown place, 2 Kgs. iv. 42.

Bā'al=tā'mär (*lord of palms*). A place in Benjamin, Judg. xx. 33.

Bā'al=zē'bŭb (*god of the fly*). Form of the Baal worshipped at Ekron, 2 Kgs. i. 16.

Bā'al=zē'phon (*lord of the north*). A place on western coast of Red Sea near where the Israelites crossed, Ex. xiv. 2; Num. xxxiii. 7.

Bā'a-nà (*son of affliction*). (1) Son of Solomon's commissary in Jezreel, 1 Kgs. iv. 12. (2) Father of Zadok, Neh. iii. 4.

Bā'a-nah (*son of affliction*). (1) Co-murderer of Ish-bosheth, killed by David, 2 Sam. iv. 2–9. (2) Father of one of David's mighty men, 2 Sam. xxiii. 29; 1 Chr. xi. 30. (3) 1 Kgs. iv. 16; Baana in vs. 12. (4) One of the returned, Ez. ii. 2; Neh. vii. 7.

Bā'a-rah (*brutish*). Wife of Shaharaim, 1 Chr. viii. 8.

Bā''a-sē'jah (*work of Jehovah*). A Levite, 1 Chr. vi. 40.

Bā'a-shà (*bravery*). Third king of Israel, 1 Kgs. xv. 27–34; xvi. Warred continually with King Asa, 1 Kgs. xv. 33, and ruled wickedly for 24 years, B. C. 953 to 931. Family cut off according to prophecy, 1 Kgs. xvi. 3–11.

Bā'bel (*confusion*). One of Nimrod's cities in the plain of Shinar, Gen. x. 10. [BABYLON.]

Bā'bel, Tower of. That brick structure, built in the plain of Shinar, and intended to prevent the very confusion and dispersion it brought about, Gen. xi. 4–9.

Băb'ȳ-lon (*Greek form of Babel*). Capital city Babylonian empires. Situate on both sides of the Euphrates, 200 miles above its junction with the Tigris, Gen. x. 10; xi. 4–9; Jer. li. 58; Isa. xlv. 1–3. Once the capital of Assyria, 2 Chr. xxxiii. 11. Reached height of its splendor and strength under Nebuchadnezzar, Isa. xiii. 19; xiv. 4; xlvii. 5; Jer. li. 41. Chief home of the captive Jews. Captured by Cyrus the Persian, through his leader Darius, B. C. 539, as prophesied in Jer. li. 31, 39, and narrated in Dan. v. Its decay dates from that date. The Babylon of 1 Pet. v. 13 is conjectural. In Rev. xiv. 8; xvii. 18, Babylon types the power of Rome.

Băb''ȳ-lō'nĭ-ans. Inhabitants of Babylon, Ez. iv. 9.

Assyrian Warriors.

Băb''ȳ-lō'nish Gär'mĕnt (*robe of Shinar*). A richly embroidered robe worn in Babylon and prized by other peoples, Josh. vii. 21.

Bā'cà (*weeping*). Perhaps a figurative "valley;" but if real, probably Gehenna, Ps. lxxxiv. 6.

Băc'chĭ-dēs. A noted Syrian general, 1 Macc. vii. 8.

Băc-chū'rus. One of the "holy singers," 1 Esdr. ix. 24.

Băc'chus. [DIONYSUS.]

Bă-çē'nor. A Jewish captain, 2 Macc. xii. 35.

Băch'rites. Becherites, Num. xxvi. 35.

Bădg'ers' Skins (*striped skins*). The badger not found in Palestine. Seal, porpoise, or sheep skins may be meant, Ex. xxv. 5; xxxv. 7.

Băg (*swelling*). The bag of 2 Kgs. v. 23; xii. 10, was for holding money; that of Deut. xxv. 13–15 for carrying weights. Sack was the Hebrew grain-bag, Gen. xlii. 25. The shepherd's bag was for carrying feeble lambs, Zech. xi. 15–17. The bag of Judas was probably a small chest, John xii. 6; xiii. 29.

Bā-gō'as (*eunuch*). An attendant of Holofernes, Judith xii. 1–3.

Bā-hū'rim (*low grounds*). A village between the Jordan and Jerusalem, 2 Sam. iii. 16; xvi. 5; xvii. 18; 1 Kgs. ii. 8.

Bā'jith (*house*). Temple of the gods of Moab, Isa. xv. 2.

Băk-băk'kar (*pleasing*). A descendant of Asaph, 1 Chr. ix. 15.

Băk'bŭk (*bottle*). His children returned, Ez. ii. 51.

Băk″bŭk-ī′ah (*destruction by Jehovah*). A Levite porter, Neh. xi. 17; xii. 9, 25.

Bāke. Baking done at home and by the women, Lev. xxvi. 26; 1 Sam. viii. 13; 2 Sam. xiii. 8; Jer. vii. 18. Perhaps public bakeries in Hos. vii. 4–7.

Bā′laam (*glutton*). Son of Beor, or Bosor, Deut. xxiii. 4. A man of note and given to prophecy. Slain in battle by the Hebrews, Num. xxii.–xxiv., xxxi.; Rev. ii. 14.

Bā′lăc, Rev. ii. 14. [Balak.]

Băl′a-dăn. [Merodach-Baladan.]

Bā′lah, Josh. xix. 3. Short form of Baalah.

Bā′lăk (*destroyer*). The king of Moab who hired Balaam to curse Israel, Num. xxii.–xxiv.; Josh. xxiv. 9; Judg. xi. 25. Balac in Rev. ii. 14.

Băl′ăn-çes (*two scales*). Were in general use among the ancients for weighing gold and silver, and in traffic, Lev. xix. 36; Mic. vi. 11; Hos. xii. 7.

Băld′ness (*ball-like*). Priests forbidden to make themselves bald, Lev. xxi. 5; Deut. xiv. 1; Ezek. xliv. 20. "Bald-head" a cry of contempt, 2 Kgs. ii. 23; as indicating leprosy, Lev. xiii. 40–43. Voluntary baldness a sign of misery, Isa. iii. 24; Ezek. vii. 18; or else the conclusion of the Nazarite vow, Num. vi. 9.

Bälm (*balsam*). The Balm of Gilead, or Mecca balsam, exudes an agreeable balsamic resin, highly prized in the East as an unguent and cosmetic, as the crushed leaves were for their odor, Gen. xxxvii. 25; xliii. 11; Jer. viii. 22; xlvi. 11; Ezek. xxvii. 17.

Băl-thā′sar, Bar. i. 11, 12. [Belshazzar.]

Bā′mah (*high place*). Applied to places of idolatrous worship, Ezek. xx. 29.

Bā′mŏth, Num. xxi. 19. [Bamoth-baal.]

Bā′mŏth-bā′al (*heights of Baal*). A sanctuary of Baal in Moab, Josh. xiii. 17. Bamoth in Num. xxi. 19.

Band. Tenth part of a Roman legion; called also "cohort," Matt. xxvii. 27; Acts xxi. 31.

Bā′nī (*built*). (1) One of David's captains, 2 Sam. xxiii. 36. (2) A forefather of Ethan, 1 Chr. vi. 46. (3) A Judahite, 1 Chr. ix. 4. (4) "Children of Bani" returned, Ez. ii. 10; x. 29–34; Neh. x. 14. (5) A son of Bani, Ez. x. 38. (6) Three others, Levites, Neh. iii. 17; viii. 7; xi. 22.

Băn′ner. [Ensign.]

Băn′quet (*sitting*). A favorite part of social enjoyment and religious festivity among Hebrews. The posture was usually sitting, Gen. xxi. 8; xl. 20. Morning banquets a mark of excess, Eccles. x. 16; Isa. v. 11. Banquet incidents were foods, wines, flowers, fine robes, music vocal and instrumental, dancing, jests, riddles and merriment, Prov. ix. 2; 2 Sam. xix. 35; Neh. viii. 10; Eccl. x. 19; Isa. v. 12; xxv. 6; Matt. xxii. 11; Luke xv. 25. [Feasts.]

Băp′tism (*dipping, bathing*). The sacrament ordinance or rite commanded by Christ, Matt. xxviii. 19, in which water is used to initiate the recipient into the Christian Church. Christ did not baptize, John iv. 2. John's baptism with water, Christ's "with the Holy Ghost and with fire," Matt. iii. 1–12; Luke iii. 16. Jesus baptized by John, Matt. iii. 13–17. Outpouring of the Holy Spirit, Acts ii. John's baptized persons re-baptized, Acts xix. 1–6; xviii. 25, 26.

Bȧ-răb′bas (*son of Abba*). The prisoner at Jerusalem when Christ was condemned, Matt. xxvii. 16–28; Mark xv. 7; Luke xxiii. 18; John xviii. 40.

Băr′ă-chel (*blessed of God*). Father of Elihu, Job xxxii. 2–6.

Băr″a-chī′as, Matt. xxiii. 35. [Zecharias.]

Bā′rak (*lightning*). A Hebrew chieftain, Judg. iv.

Bär-bā′rĭ-an (*bearded*). In N. T. sense one not a Greek, Acts xxviii. 2; Rom. i. 14; 1 Cor. xiv. 11.

Bär-hū′mīte, 2 Sam. xxiii. 31; of Bahurim.

Bȧ-rī′ah (*fugitive*). Son of Shemaiah, 1 Chr. iii. 22.

Bär″=jē′sus (*son of Jesus*), Acts xiii. 6. [Elymas.]

Bär″=jō′nȧ (*son of Jonah*), Matt. xvi. 17. [Peter.]

Bär′kŏs (*painter*). "Children of Barkos" returned, Ez. ii. 53; Neh. vii. 55.

Bär′lēy. Much cultivated by the Hebrews, Ex. ix. 31; Lev. xxvii. 16; Deut. viii. 8; Ruth ii. 7. Used for bread chiefly among the poor, Judg. vii. 13; 2 Kgs. iv. 42; John vi. 9–13; and for fodder, 1 Kgs. iv. 28. Barley harvest preceded wheat harvest, Ruth i. 22; ii. 23; 2 Sam. xxi. 9, 10.

Bär′na-bās (*son of comfort*). Joseph or Joses, a convert of Cyprus, and companion of Paul, Acts iv. 36; ix. 27; xi. 25, 26; xv. 22–39.

Bă-rō′dis. Servant of Solomon, 1 Esdr. v. 34.

Bär′sa-bās. [Joseph, Judas.]

Bär′ta-cŭs. Soldier of Darius, 1 Esdr. iv. 29.

Bär-thŏl′ō-mew (*son of Tolmai*). One of the twelve apostles, Matt. x. 3; Mark iii. 18; Luke vi. 14; Acts i. 13; perhaps Nathanael in John i. 45.

Bär″ti-mæ′us (*son of Timæus*). A blind beggar of Jericho, Mark x. 46–52.

Bā′ruch (*blessed*). (1) Jeremiah's friend, amanuensis and fellow prisoner, Jer. xxxvi. 4–32; xxxii. 12; xliii. 3–7. (2) Nehemiah's assistant, Neh. iii. 20. (3) A co-covenanter, Neh. x. 6. (4) A Judahite, Neh. xi. 5. (5) Eighth Apocryphal book.

Bär-zĭl′la-ī (*strong*). (1) A Gileadite, 2 Sam. xvii. 27; xix. 32–39. (2) Father-in-law of Michal, 2 Sam. xxi. 8. (3) Son-in-law of Barzillai, Ez. ii. 61; Neh. vii. 63.

Băs′cȧ-mȧ. A place in Gilead, 1 Macc. xiii. 23.

Bā′shăn (*thin soil*). A country east of Jordan between Gilead on the south and Hermon on the north, Deut. iii. 10–13; Josh. xii. 4, 5; xiii. 12–30. Conquered by the Israelites, Num. xxi. 33, and allotted to the half tribe of Manasseh, Josh. xiii. 29, 30.

Bā′shăn=hā′voth=jā′īr (*Bashan of the villages of Jair*). Name given to Argob in Bashan, Deut. iii. 14. Havoth-Jair, Num. xxxii. 41.

Băsh′ĕ-măth (*pleasing*). Wife of Esau, Gen. xxvi. 34; xxxvi. 3, 4, 13. Mahalath, Gen. xxviii. 9.

Bā′sin. One of the smaller vessels of the tabernacle, for holding the blood of the sacrificial victims. A larger vessel in John xiii. 5.

Băs′ket. Mostly of wicker, and variously used for bread, Gen. xl. 16–19; Ex. xxix. 2, 3, 23; Lev. viii. 2; Matt. xiv. 20; xv. 37; first fruits, Deut. xxvi. 2–4; fruits, Jer. xxiv. 1, 2; bulky articles, 2 Kgs. x. 7; Ps. lxxxi. 6.

Egyptian Baskets.

Băs′măth (*pleasing*). Daughter of Solomon, 1 Kgs. iv. 15.

Băs′tărd. Not applied to one born out of wedlock, but to issue within the prohibited degrees, Deut. xxiii. 2.

Băt. An unclean beast. Same as our bat, Lev. xi. 19; Deut. xiv. 18; Isa. ii. 20.

Băth. A Jewish liquid measure, varying from 4½ to 6½ gallons.

Băth, Bā'thing. Part of the Jewish ritual of purification, Lev. xiv. 8; xv. 5, 16; xvii. 15; xxii. 6; Num. xix. 7; 2 Sam. xi. 2-4; 2 Kgs. v. 10. Customary after mourning, Ruth iii. 3; 2 Sam. xii. 20. Public bathing pools usually sheltered by porticos, 2 Kgs. xx. 20; Neh. iii. 15; Isa. xxii. 11; John v. 2; ix. 7.

Bat. (*See* p. 18.)

Băth=răb'bim (*daughter of many*). A gate of ancient Heshbon, S. of Sol. vii. 4.

Băth'=shĕ-bȧ'' (*daughter of the oath*). Wife of David, and mother of Solomon, 2 Sam. xi; 1 Kgs. i. 15; ii. 13-22. Bathshua in 1 Chr. iii. 5.

Băth'=shu-ȧ''. [BATHSHEBA.]

Băt'tĕr-ing=ram. A heavy beam of hard wood, with the end sometimes shaped like a ram, used for battering down the gates and walls of a city, Ezek. iv. 2; xxi. 22.

Băt'tle=axe. [ARMS.]

Băt'tle-ment. The barrier around the flat-roofed houses of the East, Deut. xxii. 8; Jer. v. 10.

Băv'ă-ī. A builder, Neh. iii. 18.

Bāy=tree, Ps. xxxvii. 35. The laurel, or sweet-bay (*Laurus nobilis*).

Băz'lith (*stripping*). His descendants returned, Neh. vii. 54; Ez. ii. 52.

Băz'lŭth. [BAZLITH.]

Bdĕl'li-um (*del'i-um*) (*a plant and its gum*). A fragrant gum resin. But in Gen. ii. 12 and Num. xi. 7, a precious stone.

Bea'con (*signal*). A lighted signal for warning, Isa. xxx. 17.

Bē''a-lī'ah (*Jehovah is Baal*). A friend of David, 1 Chr. xii. 5.

Bē'ă-lŏth (*mistresses*). A town of south Judah, Josh. xv. 24.

Bē'an. A Bedouin tribe, 1 Macc. v. 4.

Beans, Much cultivated in Palestine, as food for man and beast, 2 Sam. xvii. 28; Ezek. iv. 9.

Bear, Found in Syria and the mountains of Lebanon, 2 Sam. xvii. 8; 2 Kgs. ii. 24; Prov. xvii. 12.

Beard (*barbed*). Badge of manhood. Tearing, cutting, or neglecting, a sign of mourning, Ez. ix. 3; Isa. xv. 2; l. 6; Jer. xli. 5; xlviii. 37. To insult it a gross outrage, 2 Sam. x. 4. Taken hold of in salutation, 2 Sam. xx. 9. Removed in leprosy, Lev. xiv. 9.

Bĕb'ă-ī (*fatherly*). (1) Head of a returned family, Ez. ii. 11; Neh. vii. 16; x. 15. (2) Father of Zechariah, Ez. viii. 11.

Bē'chĕr (*first born*). (1) Second son of Benjamin, Gen. xlvi. 21; 1 Chr. vii. 6. (2) An Ephraimite, Num. xxvi. 35. Bered in 1 Chr. vii. 20.

Bē-chō'răth (*first fruits*). An ancestor of Saul, 1 Sam. ix. 1.

Bĕc'tī-leth. A plain, Judith ii. 21.

Bed. The Jewish bed consisted of a mattress and coverings, Gen. xlvii. 31; 1 Sam. xix. 13; Matt. ix. 6. Placed on the floor, or on a bench, 2 Kgs. i. 4; xx. 2; Ps. cxxxii. 3; Am. iii. 12; and later became ornamental and canopied, Am. vi. 4; Esth. i. 6. For bed-chamber furnishings *see* 2 Kgs. iv. 10.

Bē'dăd (*alone*). Father of Hadad, king of Edom, Gen. xxxvi. 35; 1 Chr. i. 46.

Bē'dăn (*according to judgment*). (1) A judge of Israel, 1 Sam. xii. 11. (2) A son of Gilead, 1 Chr. vii. 17.

Bē-dē'iah. A son of Bani, Ez. x. 35.

Bee. Honey bees and honey abounded in Palestine, Deut. i. 44; 1 Kgs. xiv. 3; Ps. lxxxi. 16; Isa. vii. 15, 18.

Bē''ĕl-ī'a-dȧ (*Baal knows*). A son of David, 1 Chr. xiv. 7; Eliada in 2 Sam. v. 16 and 1 Chr. iii. 8.

Bē-ĕl=tĕth'mus. An officer of Artaxerxes, 1 Esdr. ii. 16.

Bē-ĕl'ze-bŭb, properly **Bē-ĕl'ze-bŭl** (*lord of the house*). N. T. form of Baalzebub, "lord of the fly." It personified Satan, and the general sovereignty of evil spirits, Matt. x. 25; xii. 24; Mark iii. 22; Luke xi. 15.

Bē'er (*a well*). (1) A halting place of the Israelites, Num. xxi. 16-18. (2) Place to which Jotham fled, Judg. ix. 21.

Bē-ē'rȧ (*a well*). Son of Zophar, 1 Chr. vii. 37.

Bē-ē'rah (*well*). A Reubenite, 1 Chr. v. 6.

Bē-er=ē'lim (*well of Elim*), Isa. xv. 8. [BEER.]

Bē-ē'rī (*my well*). (1) Father-in-law of Esau, Gen. xxvi. 34. (2) Father of Hosea, Hos. i. 1.

Bē'er=Lă-hāi'=roi (*well of the living*). Hagar's well, Gen. xvi. 6-14; xxiv. 62; xxv. 11.

Bē-ē'rŏth (*wells*). (1) A Hivite city, Josh. ix. 17. (2) A halting place of the Israelites, Deut. x. 6. Bene-Jaakan in Num. xxxiii. 31.

Bē'er=shē'bȧ (*well of the oath*). An old place in southern Palestine; so named by Abraham, Gen. xxi. 31-33; or Isaac, Gen. xxvi. 32, 33.

Bē-ĕsh'=te-rah'' (*house of Ashterah*). A city of Manasseh, Josh. xxi. 27.

Bee'tle (*biting animal*). A species of locust is evidently meant in Lev. xi. 21, 22.

Beeves. Same as cattle, when limited to the bovine species, Lev. xxii. 19.

Bĕg'gar (*asker*). Pauperism was discouraged, Lev. xix. 10; xxv. 5, 6; Deut. xxiv. 19. Poor invited to feasts, Deut. xiv. 29; xxvi. 12. Beggars abhorred, Ps. cix. 10. In N. T. times beggars had a fixed place to beg, Mark x. 46; Acts iii. 2; Luke xvi. 20.

Bē-hē'mŏth (*water-ox*). From the poet's description a hippopotamus is meant, Job xl. 15-24.

Bē'kah. A half shekel, valued at about thirty-three cents.

Bĕl. [BAAL.]

Bē'lȧ (*destroying*). (1) A city of the plain; afterwards called Zoar, Gen. xiv. 2; xix. 22. (2) A king of Edom, Gen. xxxvi. 31-33; 1 Chr. i. 43. (3) Eldest son of Benjamin, Gen. xlvi. 21; and founder of the Belaites, Num. xxvi. 38; 1 Chr. vii. 6; viii. 1. (4) Son of Azaz, 1 Chr. v. 8.

Bē'lah. [BELA, 3.]

Bē'la-ītes, Num. xxvi. 38. [BELA, 3.]

Bē'lī-al (*lawlessness*). A vile, worthless person, reckless of God and man, Deut. xiii. 13; Judg. xix. 22; 1 Sam. ii. 12. Hence, Satan, 2 Cor. vi. 15.

Bĕl'lows (*bag, blow-skin*), though crude, did not differ in principle and use from ours, Jer. vi. 29.

Bĕlls (*bellowers*). Bells of gold were appended to priestly robes, Ex. xxviii. 33-35. Attached to anklets, Isa. iii. 16-18. Horses ornamented with bells, Zech. xiv. 20.

Bĕl-mā'im, Bĕl'men. A town of Samaria, Judith iv. 5.

Běl-shăz′zar (*prince of Bel*). Last king of Babylon; ruling at time of the great feast and handwriting on the wall, B. C. 539, Dan. v.

Běl″tę=shăz′zar (*protected by Bel*). Name given to Daniel by Nebuchadnezzar, Dan. i. 7.

Běn (*son*). A Levite, and porter, appointed to carry the ark, 1 Chr. xv. 18.

Bė-nā′ịah (*son of the Lord*). (1) Son of Jehoiada, 1 Chr. xxvii. 5; captain in David's body-guard, 2 Sam. viii. 18; and commander-in-chief of Solomon's army, 1 Kgs. i. 36; ii. 34-46. (2) One of David's mighty men, 2 Sam. xxiii. 30; 1 Chr. xi. 31; and chief of eleventh monthly course, 1 Chr. xxvii. 14. (3) A priest and trumpeter, 1 Chr. xv. 18, 20; xvi. 5. (4) A priest, 1 Chr. xv. 24; xvi. 6. (5) A Levite, 2 Chr. xx. 14. (6) A Levite, 2 Chr. xxxi. 13. (7) Prince of a family of Simeon, 1 Chr. iv. 36. (8) Four of the returned, Ez. x. 25, 30, 35, 43. (9) Father of Pelatiah, Ezek. xi. 1, 13.

Hippopotamus. (*See* Behemoth.)

Běn″=am′mī (*son of my people*). Grandson of Lot, and progenitor of the Ammonites, Gen. xix. 38.

Běn′ę=bē′răk (*sons of lightning*). A city of Dan, Josh. xix. 45.

Běn′ę=jā′a-kăn (*sons of Jaakan*). A desert tribe, Num. xxxiii. 31, 32. [BEEROTH.] Akan in Gen. xxxvi. 27.

Běn′ę=kē′dem. "People of the East," Gen. xxix. 1; Judg. vi. 3, 33; vii. 12; viii. 10; Job i. 3.

Běn=hā′dăd (*son of Hadad*). (1) King of Syria, B. C. 950, called Benhadad I. Conqueror of northern Israel, 1 Kgs. xv. 18. (2) Benhadad II., son and successor of former, 1 Kgs. xx. 1. Defeated by Jehoram, 2 Kgs. vi. 8-33. Murdered by his servants, 2 Kgs. viii. 1-15; B. C. 890. (3) Benhadad III., son and successor of Hazael on Syrian throne, about B. C. 840. Defeated by King Joash, 2 Kgs. xiii. 3-24.

Běn=hā′īl (*son of strength*). A prince in Judah, 2 Chr. xvii. 7.

Běn=hā′năn (*son of grace*). Son of Shimon, 1 Chr. iv. 20.

Běn′ī-nū (*our son*). A co-covenanter, Neh. x. 13.

Běn′ja-mīn (*son of the right hand*). (1) Youngest of Jacob's children. First named Benoni, afterwards Benjamin, Gen. xxxv. 16-18. Beloved by Jacob, Gen. xlii.; visited Egypt, Gen. xliii.; tribe distinguished as Jacob prophesied, Gen. xlix. 27; 1 Sam. xx. 20, 36; 2 Sam. i. 22; Judg. xx. 16; 1 Chr. viii. 40. Their allotment described in Josh. xviii. 11-28. Tribe awfully visited, Judg. xx., xxi. (2) Head of a Benjamite family, 1 Chr. vii. 10. (3) A returned captive, Ez. x. 32.

Bē′nō (*his son*). A Levite, 1 Chr. xxiv. 26, 27.

Běn=ō′nī (*son of my sorrow*), Gen. xxxv. 18. [BENJAMIN.]

Běn=zō′heth (*son of Zoheth*). A descendant of Judah, 1 Chr. iv. 20.

Bē′ŏn, Num. xxxii. 3. [BAAL-MEON.]

Bē′or (*burning*). (1) Father of Bela, an early king of Edom, Gen. xxxvi. 32. (2) Father of Balaam, Num. xxii. 5; xxiv. 3, 15; xxxi. 8; Deut. xxiii. 4; Josh. xiii. 22; xxiv. 9; Micah vi. 5. Bosor in N. T.

Bē′rȧ (*son of evil*). A king of Sodom, Gen. xiv. 2-22.

Běr′ă-chah (*blessing*). (1) A Benjamite, 1 Chr. xii. 3. (2) The valley in which Jehoshaphat celebrated his victory, 2 Chr. xx. 26.

Běr″a-chī′ah (*God has blessed*). Father of Asaph, 1 Chr. vi. 39.

Běr″a-ī′ah (*created by God*). A Benjamite, 1 Chr. viii. 21.

Bė-rē′ȧ (*watered*). (1) A city of Macedonia, Acts xvii. 1-15. (2) A Syrian city, now Aleppo, 2 Macc. xiii. 4. (3) A place in Judea, 1 Macc. ix. 4.

Běr″ę-chī′ah (*blessed of Jehovah*). (1) A descendant of David, 1 Chr. iii. 20. (2) A Levite, 1 Chr. ix. 16. (3) Father of Asaph, 1 Chr. xv. 17. (4) A door-keeper for the Ark, 1 Chr. xv. 23. (5) An Ephraimite, 2 Chr. xxviii. 12. (6) Father of a builder, Neh. iii. 4, 30; vi. 18. (7) Father of Zechariah, Zech. i. 1-7.

Bē′red (*hail*). (1) A place in south Palestine, Gen. xvi. 14. (2) An Ephraimite, 1 Chr. vii. 20.

Běr″ĕ-nī′çe. [BERNICE.]

Bē′rī (*well*). An Asherite, 1 Chr. vii. 36.

Bė-rī′ah (*evil*). (1) A descendant of Asher, Gen. xlvi. 17; Num. xxvi. 44, 45; 1 Chr. vii. 30, 31. (2) An Ephraimite, 1 Chr. vii. 23. (3) A chief of Benjamin, 1 Chr. viii. 13, 16. (4) A Levite, 1 Chr. xxiii. 10, 11.

Bė-rī′ītes, Num. xxvi. 44. Descendants of Beriah (1).

Bē′rītes. A people in north Palestine, 2 Sam. xx. 14.

Bē′rith (*covenant*), Judg. ix. 46. [BAAL-BERITH.]

Běr-nī′çe (*bringing victory*). Eldest daughter of Herod Agrippa, Acts xii. 1, and sister of the younger Agrippi, Acts xxv. 13-23; xxvi. 30.

Bė-rō′dăch=băl′a-dăn, 2 Kgs. xx. 12. [MERODACH-BALADAN.]

Bė-rō′thah (*of a well*). A boundary town of north Palestine, Ezek. xlvii. 16.

Běr′o-thāi (*my wells*). A city of north Palestine, 2 Sam. viii. 8.

Bē′rŏth-īte, 1 Chr. xi. 39, of Beeroth.

Běr′yl (*beril*) (*jewel*). The first stone in fourth row of a high priest's breastplate, Ex. xxviii. 20.

Bē′sāi (*sword*). His children returned, Ez. ii. 49; Neh. vii. 52.

Běs″ŏ-dē′ịah (*in the Lord's secret*). Father of an architect, Neh. iii. 6.

Bē′sŏm (*broom*). Twig broom for sweeping, Isa. xiv. 23.

Bē′sôr (*cool*). A brook in south Judah, 1 Sam. xxx. 9-21.

Bē′tah (*confidence*). A city of Zoba, 2 Sam. viii. 8. Tibhath in 1 Chr. xviii. 8.

Bět′a-nȧ. A place close to oak of Abraham, Judith i. 9.

Bē′ten (*raised*). Border city of Asher, Josh. xix. 25.

Běth (*house*). Used in combinations.

Beth″=ab′ă-rȧ (*house at the ford*). A place

beyond, or at, Jordan where John baptized Christ, John i. 28.

Bĕth″=ā′năth (*house of reply*). City of Naphtali, Judg. i. 33.

Bĕth″=ā′nŏth (*house of reply*). A mountain town of Judah, Josh. xv. 59.

Bĕth′ă-ny̆ (*house of affliction*). A village on the slope of Olivet close to Bethphage, Matt. xxi. 17; Mark xi.; Luke xix. 29; John xi. 18. Now *Lazarieh*.

Bĕth″=ăr′ă-bah (*house of the desert*). A city of Judah and Benjamin, Josh. xv. 61; xviii. 22.

Bĕth″=ā′răm, properly BETHHARAN (*house of height*). A town of Gad, Josh. xiii. 27.

Bĕth″=ăr′bel (*house of ambush*). Scene of the massacre by Shalman, Hos. x. 14.

Bĕth″=ā′ven (*house of idols*). A place in Benjamin, Josh. vii. 2; xviii. 12; 1 Sam. xiii. 5; xiv. 23. Stands for Bethel in Hos. iv. 15; v. 8; x. 5.

Bĕth″=ăz′ma-veth (*house of Azmaveth*). A town of Benjamin, Neh. vii. 28; Azmaveth and Bethsamos, elsewhere.

Bĕth″=bā′al=mē′on (*house of Baal-meon*). A place in Reuben, Josh. xiii. 17. Beon in Num. xxxii. 3; Baal-meon in xxxii. 38.

Bĕth″=bā′rah (*house of the ford*), Judg. vii. 24. [BETH-ABARA.]

Bĕth″=bā′sī. A town near Jericho, 1 Macc. ix. 62-64.

Bĕth″=bĭr′e-ī (*house of my creation*). A town in south Simeon, 1 Chr. iv. 31. Beth-lebaoth in Josh. xix. 6.

Bĕth′=cär (*house of the lamb*). A place where the Israelites' pursuit ended, 1 Sam. vii. 11.

Bĕth″=dā′gon (*house of Dagon*). (1) Town in Judah, Josh. xv. 41. (2) Town in Asher, Josh. xix. 27.

Bĕth″=dĭb″la-thā′im (*house of dried figs*). A town of Moab, Jer. xlviii. 22. [ALMON-DIBLATHAIM.]

Bĕth′=el (*house of God*). (1) City of Palestine, 12 mls. N. of Jerusalem, Gen. xii. 8; xiii. 3, 4; scene of Jacob's vision, then called Luz, Gen. xxviii. 11-19; xxxi. 13; xxxv. 1-8; Judg. i. 23; residence of "sons of the prophets" and priests, 2 Kgs. ii. 2, 3; xvii. 27, 28. Now *Beitin*. (2) A town in south Judah, Josh. xii. 16; 1 Sam. xxx. 27; Chesil in Josh. xv. 30; Bethul in xix. 4; and Bethuel in 1 Chr. iv. 30. (3) Mount Bethel, near Bethel, Josh. xvi. 1; 1 Sam. xiii. 2.

Bĕth″=ē′mĕk (*house of the valley*). A boundary of Asher, Josh. xix. 27.

Bē′thẽr. Figurative mountains, S. of Sol. ii. 17.

Bē-thĕs′dȧ (*house of mercy*). A pool near the sheep gate, Jerusalem, John v. 2.

Bĕth″=ē′zĕl (*neighbor's house*). A place in Philistia, Mic. i. 11.

Bĕth″=gā′der (*house of a wall*). A doubtful place or person, 1 Chr. ii. 51.

Bĕth″=gā′mŭl (*camel-house*). A town of Moab, Jer. xlviii. 23.

Bĕth″=gil′gal, Neh. xii. 29. [GILGAL.]

Bĕth″=hăc′çĕ-rĕm (*house of the vine*). A beacon station near Tekoa, Neh. iii. 14; Jer. vi. 1.

Bĕth″=hā′ran, Num. xxxii. 36. [BETH-ARAM.]

Bĕth″=hŏg′la, and **Hŏg′lah** (*partridge-house*). A place in boundary of Judah and Benjamin, Josh. xv. 6; xviii. 19-21.

Bĕth″=hō′rŏn (*cave-house*). A town of Benjamin, Josh. xvi. 3, 5; 1 Kgs. ix. 17; 1 Chr. vii. 24.

Bĕth″=jĕsh′ĭ-mŏth and **Jĕs′ĭ-mŏth** (*house of deserts*). A town of Moab, allotted to Reuben, Num. xxxiii. 49; Josh. xii. 3; xiii. 20.

Bĕth″=lĕb′a-ŏth (*house of lionesses*), Josh. xix. 6. [BETH-BIREI.]

Bĕth′=lĕ-hĕm, Bĕth′lĕ-hĕm (*house of bread*). (1) A town of Palestine, six miles S. of Jerusalem. First called Ephrath or Ephratah, Gen. xxxv. 16-19; xlviii. 7. Called Bethlehem-judah after the conquest, Judg. xvii. 7. Home of Ruth, Ruth i. 19. Birthplace of David, 1 Sam. xvii. 12. Here Christ was born, Matt. ii. 1, 2; Luke ii. 15-18. (2) A town in Zebulun, Josh. xix. 15.

Bĕth″=lō′mŏn, 1 Esdr. v. 17. [BETHLEHEM.]

Bĕth″mā′a-chah, 2 Sam. xx. 14, 15. Same as Abel, Abel-maim, and Abel-beth-maachah.

Bĕth″=mär′că-bŏth (*house of chariots*). A town of Simeon, Josh. xix. 5; 1 Chr. iv. 31. Madmannah in Josh. xv. 31.

Bĕth″=mē′on, Jer. xlviii. 23. Contraction of Beth-baal-meon.

Bĕth″=nim′rah (*house of leopards*). A fenced city of Gad, Num. xxxii. 36. Nimrah in vs. 3.

Bĕth″=pā′let (*house of expulsion*). A town in south Judah, Josh. xv. 27. Bethphelet in Neh. xi. 26.

Bĕth″=păz′zez (*house of dispersion*). A town of Issachar, Josh. xix. 21.

Bĕth=pē′or (*house of Peor*). A spot opposite Jericho, dedicated to Baal-peor, Deut. iii. 29; iv. 46; Josh. xiii. 20.

Bĕth′pha-ġē (*house of figs*). A place on Olivet, close to Bethany, Matt. xxi. 1; Luke xix. 29; Mark xi. 1.

Bĕth″=phē′let, Neh. xi. 26. [BETH-PALET.]

Bĕth″=rā′phȧ (*house of health*). Son of Eshton, 1 Chr. iv. 12.

Bĕth″=rē′hŏb (*house of Rehob*). A province of Aram, or Syria, 2 Sam. x. 6. Rehob in vs. 8.

Bĕth-să′ĭ-dȧ (*fishing-house*). A fishing-village on Sea of Galilee, and west of Jordan. Birthplace of Andrew, Peter and Philip, Matt. xi. 21; John i. 44; xii. 21. Bethsaida, where the five thousand were fed, Mark vi. 31-53; Luke ix. 10-17, appears to have been on eastward side of Jordan.

Bĕth″=sā′mos, 1 Esdr. v. 18. [BETH-AZMAVETH.]

Bĕth=shăn′, 1 Macc. v. 52. [BETH-SHEAN.]

Bĕth″=shē′ăn, Bĕth′=săn, Bĕth′=shăn (*house of rest*). A city of Manasseh, Josh. xvii. 11; Judg. i. 27; 1 Chr. vii. 29; Bethshan in 1 Sam. xxxi. 10-12. A commissary district of Solomon, 1 Kgs. iv. 12. Now Beisan.

Bĕth″=shē′mĕsh (*house of the sun*). (1) A Levitical town of N. Judah, Josh. xv. 10; xxi. 16. Now Ainshems. (2) A border city of Issachar, Josh. xix. 22. (3) A fenced city of Naphtali, Josh. xix. 38; Judg. i. 33. (4) Probably Heliopolis, Egypt, Jer. xliii. 13.

Bĕth″=shĭt′tah (*house of the acacia*). The place where Gideon's pursuit ended, Judg. vii. 22.

Bĕth″=sū′rȧ, 1 Macc. iv. 29. [BETH-ZUR.]

Bĕth″=tăp′pu-ah (*house of apples*). A town of Judah, near Hebron. Now Teffuh, Josh. xv. 53.

Bĕth-u′el (*filiation of God*). (1) Father of Laban and Rebekah, Gen. xxii. 22, 23; xxiv. 15, 24, 47; xxviii. 2-5. (2) [BETHUL.]

Bē′thŭl (*dweller in God*). A town of Simeon, Josh. xix. 4; Chesil in Josh. xv. 30; Bethuel in 1 Chr. iv. 30.

Bē-thu′lĭ-ȧ. Scene of Judith's exploits, Judith iv. 6; vi. 11-14.

Bĕth′=zûr (*house of rock*). Now Beit Sûr, 4 mls. N. of Hebron, Josh. xv. 58; 2 Chr. xi. 7.

Bē-tō′li-us, 1 Esdr. v. 21. [BETHEL.]

Bĕt″ō-mĕs′them. A town near Esdraelon, Judith iv. 6.

Bĕt′ō-nim (*bellies*). A town of Gad, Josh. xiii. 26.

Bē′trōth (*in promise*). To pledge troth, *i. e.*, engage to marry. A betrothed woman was regarded as the lawful wife of her spouse, and he could not break off the match without a divorce, while she, if unfaithful, would be considered an adulteress.

Beū'lah (*married*). The land of Israel when the Jewish Church is again in its true relation to God, Isa. lxii. 4.

Bē'zāi (*conqueror*). His children returned, Ez. ii. 17; Neh. vii. 23.

Bē-zăl'ĕ-el (*in the shadow of God*). (1) A Tabernacle architect, Ex. xxxi. 1–6. (2) A returned Jew, Ez. x. 30.

Bē'zek (*lightning*). (1) A place in Judah, Judg. i. 1–5. (2) Where Saul numbered Israel, 1 Sam. xi. 8.

Bē'zēr (*ore*). (1) A city of refuge east of Jordan, Deut. iv. 43; Josh. xx. 8. (2) An Asherite, 1 Chr. vii. 37.

Bē'zeth. Encampment of Bacchides, 1 Macc. vii. 19.

Bī'ble (*the book*). The term applied, not further back than the fifth century, to that collection of *biblia*, or holy books, which comprises the Old and New Testaments.

Bĭch'rī (*first-born*). A Benjamite, 2 Sam. xx. 1.

Bĭd'kär (*stabber*). One of Jehu's captains, 2 Kgs. ix. 25.

Bier (*that bears*). The frame on which a dead body was carried to the grave, Luke vii. 14; 2 Chr. xvi. 14.

Bĭg'thȧ, Bĭg'thăn, Bĭg'than-ȧ (*gift of God*). A chamberlain of King Ahasuerus, Esth. i. 10. Bigthan in ii. 21; Bigthana in vi. 2.

Bĭg'va-ī (*happy*). (1) His children returned, Ez. ii. 14; viii. 14; Neh. vii. 19. (2) A chief under Zerubbabel, Ezra ii. 2; Neh. vii. 7; x. 16.

Bĭl'dăd (*son of strife*). The Shuhite friend of Job ii. 11; viii., xviii., xxv.

Bĭl'ĕ-ăm (*foreigners*). A town of Manasseh, 1 Chr. vi. 70.

Bĭl'gah (*first-born*). (1) Head of the fifteenth temple course, 1 Chr. xxiv. 14. (2) A returned priest, Neh. xii. 5, 18. Bilgai in x. 8.

Bĭl'ga-ī, Neh. x. 8. [BILGAH.]

Bĭl'hah (*timid*). (1) Mother of Dan and Naphtali, Gen. xxix. 29; xxx. 3–8: xxxv. 25; xlvi. 25; 1 Chr. vii. 13. (2) A town of Simeon, 1 Chr. iv. 29.

Bĭl'hăn (*modest*). (1) A Horite chief, Gen. xxxvi. 27. (2) A Benjamite, 1 Chr. vii. 10.

Bĭl'shăn (*eloquent*). A returned captive, Ez. ii. 2; Neh. vii. 7.

Bĭm'hăl (*circumcised*). A son of Japhlet, 1 Chr. vii. 33.

Bĭn'e-ȧ (*fountain*). A descendant of Saul, 1 Chr. viii. 37.

Bĭn'nu-ī (*building*). Name of five returned captives, Ez. viii. 33; x. 30, 38; Neh. vii. 15; x. 9.

Bĭrds. Many birds of Palestine similar to our own. The "speckled bird" of Jer. xii. 9 means a vulture. Birds were snared, Ps. cxxiv. 7; Prov. vii. 23; Am. iii. 5. Used for curing leprosy, Lev. xiv. 2–7. List of birds not to be eaten, Lev. xi. 13-19; Deut. xiv. 11–19.

Bĭr'shȧ (*son of godliness*). A king of Gomorrah, Gen. xiv. 2.

Bĭrth'days. Observed among ancients by feasts, Gen. xl. 20; Job i. 4; Hos. vii. 5; Matt. xiv. 6–10.

Bĭrth'right. Among Jews the first-born son enjoyed the right of consecration, Ex. xxii. 29; great dignity, Gen. xlix. 3; a double portion of the paternal estate, Deut. xxi. 17; right to royal succession, 2 Chr. xxi. 3.

Bĭr'za-vĭth. An Asherite, 1 Chr. vii. 31.

Bĭsh'ŏp (*looking upon, or over*). Greek *episkopos*, overseer. An officer of the Apostolic church, identical with presbyter, or elder, Acts xx. 17, 18; 1 Tim. iii. 1–13; v. 17; Tit. i. 5–8; 1 Pet. v; 1 Thess. v. 12; James v. 14.

Bĭsh'ŏp-ric''. The jurisdiction and charge of a bishop, Acts i. 20; 1 Tim. iii. 1.

Bĭth'ī-ah (*daughter of the Lord*). Daughter of a Pharaoh, 1 Chr. iv. 18.

Bĭth'rŏn (*ravine*). A place east of Jordan, 2 Sam. ii. 29.

Bī-thȳn'ī-ȧ. A province of Asia Minor, bordering on the Euxine (Black) sea and west of Pontus, Acts xvi. 7; 1 Pet. i. 1. Capital, Nice or Nicæa.

Bĭt'ter Herbs. A part of the passover feast, Ex. xii. 8.

Bĭt'tern. A bird of the heron family, solitary in its habits, and noted for its melancholy night booming, Isa. xiv. 23; xxxiv. 11; Zeph. ii. 14.

Bĭz-jŏth'jah (*contempt*). A town of south Judah, Josh. xv. 28.

Bĭz'thȧ (*eunuch*). A eunuch, Esth. i. 10.

Blains (*boils*). The ulcerous inflammations which constituted the sixth Egyptian plague, Ex. ix. 9–11; Deut. xxviii. 27, 35.

Blăs'phē-mȳ (*injurious speaking*). Speaking evil of God, Lev. xxiv. 11; Ps. lxxiv. 18; Isa. lii. 5; Matt. xii. 32; Acts xviii. 6; Rom. ii. 24; Col. iii. 8. Royalty could be blasphemed, 1 Kgs. xxi. 10. Punished by stoning, Lev. xxiv. 11–14.

Blăs'tus (*that buds*). Chamberlain of Herod Agrippa, Acts xii. 20.

Blĕm'ish (*wound, stain*). For ceremonial blemishes *see* Lev. xxi. 18–20; xxii. 20–24.

Blīnd'ness. Blind treated with compassion, Lev. xix. 14; Deut. xxvii. 18. A punishment, Judg. xvi. 21; 1 Sam. xi. 2; 2 Kgs. xxv. 7.

Blood. The vital fluid, Gen. ix. 4. Forbidden as food, Ex. xxix. 12; Lev. vii. 26; xvii. 11–13. For N. T. atoning blood *see* Heb. ix, x.; Acts xx. 28; Rom. v. 9; Eph. i. 7; Col. i. 14; Heb. vii. 27; 1 John i. 7.

Bō''ăn-ēr'ġeṣ (*sons of thunder*). A name given by Christ to James and John, sons of Zebedee, Mark iii. 17.

Boar. Found wild in the thickets of Jordan and on the Lebanon ranges, Ps. lxxx. 13.

Wild Boar.

Bō'ăz (*lovely*). (1) The Bethlehemite who married Ruth. *See* Book of Ruth; Matt. i. 5. (2) A brazen pillar in the porch of Solomon's temple, 1 Kgs. vii. 21; 2 Chr. iii. 17; Jer. lii. 21.

Bŏch'e-ru (*young*). Son of Azel, 1 Chr. viii. 38.

Bō'chim (*weepers*). A place near Gilgal, Judg. ii. 1–5.

Bō'han (*thumb*). A Reubenite, Josh. xv. 6; xviii. 17.

Boil. Burning inflammation, Lev. xiii. 23.

Bŏnd'age. [Slave.]

Bōll'ed (*budded*). Podded, as flax, Ex. ix. 31.

Book (*beech*). Letters were at first engraved on stone, brick, or metal, Deut. xxvii. 2, 3; Job xix. 24; later, on papyrus, bark of trees, tablets of wax, cloth of linen or cotton; the latter in long rolls, or "scrolls," which were the books of the Hebrews.

Bottles.

Booth (*hut*). Temporary structures, usually of boughs, Gen. xxxiii. 17; Lev. xxiii. 42.

Boot'y (*dealt out*). Spoils of war, regulated as in Num. xxxi. 26–47; 1 Sam. xxx. 24, 25.

Bō'oz, Matt. i. 5; Luke iii. 32. [Boaz.]

Bŏs'căth, 2 Kgs. xxii. 1. [Bozkath.]

Bos'om (*buz'um*). To lean on, implied great intimacy, John xiii. 23. Figuratively, Paradise, Luke xvi. 23; xxiii. 43.

Bō'sŏr. Greek form of Beor, 2 Pet. ii. 15.

Bŏs'ŏ-rȧ. Bozrah, 1 Macc. v. 26, 28.

Bŏs'ses (*humps*). Knobs on shields and bucklers, Job xv. 26.

Bŏtch. [Blain.]

Bŏt'tle (*little boot*). Primitive bottles, either of skin or earthenware, Gen. xxi. 14; Jer. xix. 1; Matt. ix. 17; of different sizes and shapes. Tear bottles used, Ps. lvi. 8.

Bōw. Besides the bow and arrow the bow-gun was used by the ancients as an offensive weapon, 1 Macc. vi. 20. [Archery.] [Arms.]

Bŏw. The Eastern mode of salutation by kneeling on one knee and bending the head forward, Gen. xxxvii. 10; 1 Kgs. i. 53; ii. 19.

Bŏw'els. Used figuratively for the emotions, Col. iii. 12; 1 John iii. 17.

Box-tree. The evergreen, whose wood is so prized by engravers, Isa. xli. 19; lx. 13.

Bō'zĕz (*height*). Sharp rocks mentioned in 1 Sam. xiv. 4, 5.

Bŏz'kăth (*craggy*). A lowland city of Judah, Josh. xv. 39; 2 Kgs. xxii. 1.

Bŏz'rah (*strong-hold*). (1) Ancient capital of Edom, Gen. xxxvi. 33; Isa. xxxiv. 6; lxiii. 1; Jer. xlix. 13, 22. (2) A city of Moab, Jer. xlviii. 24.

Brāce'let. A wrist and arm ornament worn by both sexes, Gen. xxiv. 30; Ezek. xvi. 11. A badge of royalty, and worn above elbow, 2 Sam. i. 10.

Brăm'ble (*blackberry*). [Thorns.]

Brass. An alloy of copper and zinc, not known to the Jews. The brass of Scripture was probably copper, or a copper alloy, Gen. iv. 22; Deut. viii. 9; Judg. xvi. 21; 2 Kgs. xxv. 7; 1 Sam. xvii. 5; Job xxviii. 2; 1 Cor. xiii. 1.

Brā'zen Serpent. [Serpent.]

Breach'es (*broken*). Creeks, bays, and river-mouths; havens in case of storm, Judg. v. 17; Josh. xix. 29.

Bread (*brewed, baked*). Early used, Gen. xviii. 5, 6; Ex. xii. 34; Jer. vii. 18. Made of wheat, barley, rye, fitches, and spelt, in loaves or rolls, leavened or unleavened; the kneading being in troughs, bowls, or on flat plates, and the baking in portable ovens of earthenware, or upon heated stones, or on the coals.

Breast'plate. The breastplate of the high priest, Ex. xxviii. 15, was of embroidered stuff, some 10 inches square; its upper corners fastened with gold or lace to the ephod, its lower to the girdle, Ex. xxviii. 28. Adorned with 12 precious stones, Ex. xxviii. 12–29.

Breech'es (*broken, i. e. crotched*). Drawers or light trousers worn by priests, reaching from loins to thighs, Ex. xxviii. 42.

Brick (*fragment*). Bricks were made of clay, mixed with straw, usually larger than our bricks, and burned in a kiln or dried in the sun, Gen. xi. 3; Ex. i. 14; v. 7; 2 Sam. xii. 31; Jer. xliii. 9.

Ballista or Bow-gun.

Bride, Bridegroom [Marriage.]

Brĭg'an-dine (*brawl*), Jer. xlvi. 4; elsewhere as habergeon.

Brĭm'stone (*burn-stone*). Sulphur, Gen. xix. 24; of frequent figurative use, Job xviii. 15; Ps. xi. 6; Isa. xxxiv. 9; Rev. xxi. 8.

Bŭck'ler (*cheek*). The small round shield used to catch blows. [Armor.]

Bŭk'kī (*void*). (1) A prince of Dan, Num. xxxiv. 22. (2) Fifth from Aaron in line of high priests, 1 Chr. vi. 5, 51.

Bŭk-kī'ah (*wasting*). A Temple musician, 1 Chr. xxv. 4, 13.

Bŭl (*rain*). Marchesvan or Bul, the second month of the Hebrew civil and eighth of the sacred year, corresponding to parts of October and November, 1 Kgs. vi. 38.

Bŭl'bŭl. The Persian nightingale, common in the Jordan valley; also the titmouse, in the Latin version.

Brick Making. (*See* p. 23.)

Bull, Bullock (*bellow*). A term used generically for ox, cattle, etc., Ps. xxii. 12. Bullock in Isa. lxv. 25; cow in Ezek. iv. 15; oxen in Gen. xii. 16. The "wild bull" of Isa. li. 20, and the "wild ox" of Deut. xiv. 5, mean probably the oryx.

Bul'rush (*large rush*). The bulrush of Ex. ii. 3-5 is supposed to be the papyrus, from which paper was made, Job viii. 11.

Bū'nah (*discretion*). A descendant of Judah, 1 Chr. ii. 25.

Bŭn'ni (*built*). (1) A Levite, Neh. ix. 4. (2) A co-covenanter with Nehemiah, Neh. x. 15. (3) A Levite, Neh. xi. 15.

Bŭr'ī-al, Bŭr-ȳ (*mounding*). Place, a cave or hewn rock, Gen. xxiii. 4; xxv. 9; l. 5-13; Matt. xxvii. 60. Body washed, Acts ix. 37; swathed and spiced, Matt. xxvii. 59; Mark xv. 46; xvi. 1. Head covered separately, 2 Chr. xvi. 14; John xix. 40; pall-bearers and mourners, relatives and friends, 2 Sam. iii. 31; Luke vii. 12; sometimes hired mourners, Jer. ix. 17; Ezek. xxiv. 17; Matt. ix. 23.

Burnt offering. The offering which was wholly consumed by fire. For ceremonies *see* Lev. viii., ix., xiv., xxix.

Bush. Supposably the dwarf acacia, Ex. iii. 2-6. In Deut. xxxiii. 16, Mark xii. 26, Luke xx. 37, the reference is to the locality.

Bush'el (*little box*). Hebrew *seah*, twenty pints.

Bŭt'ler (*bottler*). Officer of a royal household in charge of the wines and drinking vessels, Gen. xl. 1-13; xli. 9; "cup-bearer," Neh. i. 11; 1 Kgs. x. 5.

Bŭt'ter (*cow-cheese*). A curd, or curded milk, is evidently meant, Gen. xviii. 8; Job xxix. 6; Judg. v. 25.

Bŭt'ter-fly. Nine Hebrew words confusedly translated locust and associated insects. Butterfly a natural incident to caterpillar life.

Bŭz (*despised*). (1) Progenitor of Elihu, Gen. xxii. 21. (2) A Gadite, 1 Chr. v. 14. (3) Land of Buz, Jer. xxv. 23.

Bŭz'ite. Elihu so called, Job xxxii. 2, 6. [ELIHU, 1.]

Bū'zī (*despised*). Father of Ezekiel, Ezek. i. 3.

C

Căb. A Jewish dry measure, about a quart, 2 Kgs. vi. 25.

Căb'bon (*understanding*). A town in lowlands of Judah, Josh. xv. 40.

Căb'ins. Cells in a dungeon, Jer. xxxvii. 16.

Cā'bŭl (*displeasing*). (1) A boundary of Asher, Josh. xix. 27. (2) The district given to Hiram by Solomon, 1 Kgs. ix. 10-14.

Căd'dis. Joannan, 1 Macc. ii. 2.

Cā'des, 1 Macc. xi. 63. [KEDESH.]

Căd'mĭ-el, 1 Esdr. v. 26. [KADMIEL.]

Çæ'şar (*hairy, or elephant*). With Julius Cæsar and Augustus Cæsar a surname, but with the latter it became official and remained so till the death of Nero. In Luke ii. 1, Augustus Cæsar is meant; in Luke iii. 1, Tiberius Cæsar; in Acts xi. 28, Claudius Cæsar; in Acts xxv. 8, Phil. iv. 22, Nero.

Çæs″a-rē'à (*for Cæsar*). Political capital of Palestine, on Mediterranean, and official residence of Herodian kings and Roman procurators; home of Philip and Cornelius, Acts viii. 40; x., xi. 1-18.

Çæs″a-rē'à Phĭ-lĭp'pī. A city of Galilee marking the northern limit of Christ's pilgrimage, and probable scene of the configuration, Matt. xvi. 13-20; xvii. 1-10; Mark viii. 27.

Cāge (*hollow*). Bird-trap in Jer. v. 27; prison in Rev. xviii. 2.

Cā'ia-phăs (*depression*). Appointed high priest by Valerius, and reappointed by Pontius Pilate; A. D. 27-36. Deposed by Vitellius, Matt. xxvi. 3-57; John xi. 49-51; xviii. 13-28; Acts iv. 6.

Bulbul. (*See* p. 23.)

Cāin (*possession*). (1) Eldest son of Adam, Gen. iv. (2) A city in lowlands of Judah, Josh. xv. 57.

Că-ī'nan (*possessor*). (1) Son of Enos, Gen. v. 9; Luke iii. 36. Kenan in 1 Chr. i. 2. (2) Son of Arphaxad, Luke iii. 36.

Cāke. [Bread.]

Cā'lah (*old age*). City of Assyria, Gen. x. 11.

Căl″ă-mŏl′ă-lus. A compound of Elam, Lod and Hadid, 1 Esdr. v. 22.

Căl'a-mus (*reed*). In Ex. xxx. 23; S. of Sol. iv. 14, Ezek. xxvii. 19, identified with the lemon-grass, or sweet-flag. "Sweet cane" in Isa. xliii. 24, Jer. vi. 20.

Căl'cŏl (*nourishment*). A Judahite, 1 Chr. ii. 6.

Căl'drŏn (*hot*). A vessel for boiling meats, 1 Sam. ii. 14; 2 Chr. xxxv. 13; Job xli. 20; Micah iii. 3.

Cā'leb (*capable*). (1) Son of Hezron, 1 Chr. ii. 18, 19, 42, 50. Chelubai in ii. 9. (2) The spy of Judah, Num. xiii. 6; Josh. xiv., xv.; 1 Sam. xxx. 14. (3) Son of Hur, 1 Chr. ii. 50. (4) Caleb's district, 1 Sam. xxx. 14.

Cälf. Fatted calf a luxury, Gen. xviii. 7; 1 Sam. xxviii. 24; Am. vi. 4; Luke xv. 23. Molten calf, Ex. xxxii. 4; 1 Kgs. xii. 28, gilded structures. Calf worship denounced, Hos. viii., x., xiii. 2. "Calves of our lips," Hos. xiv. 2, fruits of our lips.

Căl-lis'thĕ-nēs. Friend of Nicanor, 2 Macc. viii. 33.

Căl'neh, Căl'nō (*fortress*). A city of Nimrod, Gen. x. 10; Am. vi. 2; Isa. x. 9. Canneh in Ezek. xxvii. 23.

Căl'phī. A general, 1 Macc. xi. 70.

Henna Plant.

Căl'vă-rȳ (*skull*). Latin for Greek *Kranion*, "skull" (referring to shape), and Hebrew "Golgotha." Spot of crucifixion. Calvary, only in Luke xxiii. 33.

Căm'el (*carrier*). The Arabian, or one-humped camel, generally meant. Used for carriage, and source of wealth, Gen. xii. 16; Judg. vii. 12; 2 Chr. xiv. 15; Job i. 3; xlii. 12; Isa. xxx. 6. An unclean beast, Lev. xi. 4. Hair used for clothing, 2 Kgs. i. 8; Zech. xiii. 4; Matt. iii. 4. Figuratively for something beyond human power, Matt. xix. 24; xxiii. 24.

Camels.

Cā'mŏn (*straw*). Burial place of Jair, Judg. x. 5.

Cămp. [Encampment.]

Căm'phīre. The gum of the camphor-tree. But in S. of Sol. i. 14; iv. 13; the cyprus flower or henna.

Cā'nȧ (*reedy*). A town of Galilee, 7 mls. N. of Nazareth, John ii. 1-11; iv. 46; xxi. 2.

Cā'năan (*low*). (1) Fourth son of Ham, Gen. x. 6-19; 1 Chr. i. 8-13. (2) The country between the Mediterranean and Jordan, given by God to the Israelites, Ex. vi. 4; Lev. xxv. 38. "Holy Land," after the captivity, Zech. ii. 13. Palestine, from Philistia.

Cā'năan-īte. Dwellers in Canaan, and all tribes known to the Israelites at time of conquest, Gen. x. 18-20; xiii. 7; xiv. 7; xv. 20; Num. xiii. 29; Josh. xi. 3; xxiv. 11.

Căn'dă-çē (*queen of servants*). The Ethiopian queen whose servant was converted, Acts viii. 27.

Căn'dle-stĭck. The golden candlestick rather a lamp, Ex. xxv. 31-37; xxxvii. 17-24. Ten candelabra used instead, in Solomon's temple, 1 Kgs. vii. 49.

Cāne. [Calamus.]

Cănk'er-worm (*cancer-worm*). A variety of caterpillar. But in Joel i. 4; ii. 25; Nah. iii. 15, 16, probably an undeveloped locust.

Căn'neh. Ezek. xxvii. 23. [Calneh.]

Căn'on (*cane, rule*). Word first applied to the Scriptures by Amphilochius about A. D. 380, Gal. vi. 16; Phil. iii. 16. O. T. canon fixed by the Jews, and accepted by Christ and his times. N. T. canon ratified by third council of Carthage A. D. 397.

Căn'ō-pȳ (*bed with mosquito curtains*). Judith x. 21; xiii. 9; xvi. 19.

Căn'tĭ-cles (*song of songs*). The Latinized title of "The Song of Solomon."

Că-pĕr'na-ŭm (*hamlet of Nahum*). A city on N. W. shore of Sea of Galilee. Chief residence of Christ and his apostles, Matt. iv. 12-16; viii. 5; ix. 1; xvii. 24; Mark ii. 1; Luke vii. 1-5; John vi. 17.

Căph'ar (*hamlet*). Common Hebrew prefix.

Căph''ăr-săl'a-ma. A battlefield, 1 Macc. vii. 31.

Că-phĕn'a-tha. A suburb of Jerusalem, 1 Macc. xii. 37.

The Golden Candlestick. (*See* p. 25.)

Căph'tôr, Căph'tŏ-rĭm. Either Philistines or Copts of Egypt, Gen. x. 14; Deut. ii. 23; Jer. xlvii. 4; Am. ix. 7.

Căp''pa-dō'çĭ-à (*fine horses*). Largest Roman province in Asia Minor, with Cæsarea as metropolis, Acts ii. 9; 1 Pet. i. 1.

Căp'tain (*head*). Title for a leader of a band of ten, fifty, hundred or thousand, Deut. i. 15; Josh. x. 24; Judg. xi. 6, 11. Also a civic meaning, Isa. i. 10; iii. 3. Captain of the Guard," Acts xxviii. 16, was commander of the Prætorian troop of Rome. "Captain of the Temple," Acts iv. 1, was chief of the Temple watchmen.

Căp'tĭve (*taken*). Captives in war treated with great cruelty in early times, Gen. xiv. 14; Judg. i. 7; 1 Sam. xi. 2; 2 Sam. viii. 2; 2 Kgs. xxv. 7. Later, treated as servants and slaves, 1 Kgs. xx. 31–34.

Căp-tĭv'ĭ-ty. Six partial captivities mentioned in Judges. Israel had several, 2 Kgs. xv. 29; 1 Chr. v. 26, the final one being that by Shalmaneser, B. C. 721, 2 Kgs. xvii. 6. Judah was captive to Assyria B. C. 713 and finally to Nebuchadnezzar, B. C. 606–562. This captivity broken, Ez. i. 11. Last captivity was to Rome, A. D. 71.

Căr'bŭn-cle (*little coal*). A gem of deep red color, Isa. liv. 12. A stone in the high-priest's breastplate, Ex. xxviii. 17; xxxix. 10.

Căr'cas. A eunuch, Esth. i. 10.

Căr'chĕ-mĭsh (*fortress of Chemosh*). A city on the Euphrates, Isa. x. 5-9; 2 Chr. xxxv. 20–23; Jer. xlvi. 2.

Că-rē'ah (*bald*). Father of Johannan, 2 Kgs. xxv. 23. Kareah, elsewhere.

Cā'rĭ-à. Southwest province of Asia Minor. Cnidus and Miletus were in it, Acts xx. 15; xxvii. 7.

Căr'mel (*fruitful*). (1) The promontory which forms the bay of Acre, 1 Kgs. xviii.; 2 Kgs. ii. 25; iv. 25; Isa. xxxiii. 9; xxxv. 2. (2) A city of Judah, 1 Sam. xv. 12; xxv. 2–44; 2 Chr. xxvi. 10.

Căr'mī (*vine dresser*). (1) Progenitor of the Carmites, Gen. xlvi. 9; Ex. vi. 14; Num. xxvi. 6; 1 Chr. v. 3. (2) Father of Achan, Josh. vii. 1, 18; 1 Chr. ii. 7.

Căr'nă-im. City in Manasseh, 1 Macc. v. 26–44.

Căr'pĕn-tĕr (*cart-wright*). Carpentry an early art, Gen. vi. 14-16; Ex. xxv. 23; xxvii. 1–15. David and Solomon employed foreign wood-workers, 2 Sam. v. 11; 1 Kgs. v. 6. Joseph a carpenter, Matt. xiii. 55; and Christ, Mark vi. 3.

Căr'pus (*fruit*). Paul's friend, 2 Tim. iv. 13.

Căr'riage (*car*). Baggage, Judg. xviii. 21; Isa. x. 28; xlvi. 1; Acts xxi. 15.

Căr-shē'nà (*distinguished*). A Persian, Esth. i. 14.

Cărt (*carry*). A two-wheeled vehicle usually drawn by oxen, 1 Sam. vi. 7–15; Amos ii. 13.

Căr'ving (*cutting*). Carving and engraving in much request, Ex. xxxi. 5; xxxv. 33; 1 Kgs. vi. 18; 2 Chr. ii. 7–14; Ps. lxxiv. 6; Zech. iii. 9.

Cāse'ment (*house-frame*). The latticed opening of the Kiosk, or summer house, of the East, Prov. vii. 6; S. of Sol. ii. 9; Judg. v. 28.

Că-sĭph'ĭ-à (*white*). An unknown place, Ez. viii. 17.

Căs'leu, 1 Macc. i. 54. [CHISLEU.]

Căs-lu'hĭm (*fortified*). A Mizraite people, Gen. x. 14; 1 Chr. i. 12.

Căs'phor. City of Gilead, 1 Macc. v. 26.

Căs'pis, 2 Macc. xii. 13. [CASPHOR.]

Căs'sia (*that peels*). The cinnamon cassia in Ex. xxx. 24; Ezek. xxvii. 19. In Ps. xlv. 8, the shrub is unidentified.

Căs'tle (*fort*). The "Tower of Antonia," N. W. corner of the Temple at Jerusalem, Acts xxi. 34, 37; xxii. 24; xxiii. 10, 16, 32.

Căs'tŏr and **Pŏl'lux.** Two mythologic heroes; figurehead and name of Paul's ship, Acts xxviii. 11.

Prætorian Guard.

Căt′ĕr-pĭl″lar (*hairy consumer*). The larva of the butterfly, 1 Kgs. viii. 37; 2 Chr. vi. 28; Ps. lxxviii. 46; Isa. xxxiii. 4; Joel i. 4.

Căts. Only in Baruch vi. 22.

Căt′tle (*capital*). Domestic bovine animals, as oxen, cows, bulls, and calves; also any live-stock, Gen. xiii. 2; Ex. xii. 29; xxxiv. 19; Num. xx. 19; xxxii. 16; Ps. l. 10; Job. i. 3. [BULL.]

Carpenter Shop, Nazareth. (*See* p. 26.)

Cau′dȧ, Clauda in R. V.

Caul (*kŏl*) (*cap*). A net for a woman's hair, Isa. iii. 18. In Hos. xiii. 8, the membrane around the heart.

Cāve (*hollow*). Used for storage houses, dwellings, hiding and burial places, Gen. xix. 30; Josh. x. 16; Judg. vi. 2; 1 Sam. xiii. 6; xxii. 1; xxiv. 3; 2 Sam. xxiii. 13; 1 Kgs. xviii. 4; Heb. xi. 38.

Çē′dăr (*resinous*). A cone-bearing tree whose reddish fragrant wood was much prized, 1 Kgs. vii. 2; Ps. xcii. 12; S. of Sol. v. 15; Isa. ii. 13; Ezek. xxxi. 6.

Cē′drŏn (*turbid*). (1) A brook, Kedron or Kidron, below the eastern wall of Jerusalem, John xviii. 1.

Çeī′lăn. His sons returned, 1 Esdr. v. 15.

Çeil′ing (*heavens*). Hebrew temple ceilings were generally of cedar, richly carved, 1 Kgs. vi. 9-15; vii. 3; 2 Chr. iii. 5-9.

Çen′chre-a (*millet*). The eastern harbor of Corinth, Acts xviii. 18. Seat of a Christian church, Rom. xvi. 1.

Çĕn″dē-bē′us. A Syrian general, 1 Macc. xv. 38.

Çĕn′sēr (*set on fire*). A small portable vessel of copper, Num. xvi. 39; Lev. xvi. 12, or gold, 1 Kgs. vii. 50; Heb. ix. 4, for carrying the coals on which incense was burned.

Çĕn′sus (*assess*). Twelve different censuses noted in the O. T., Ex. xxxviii. 26; Num. i. 2; xxvi.; 2 Sam. xxiv. 9; 2 Chr. ii. 17, 18; 1 Kgs. xii. 21; 2 Chr. xiii. 3; xiv. 8; xvii. 14; xxv. 5, 6; xxvi. 13; Ez. ii. 64; viii. 1-14. The census in Luke ii. 1-3, was for taxation.

Çĕn-tū′rĭ-ŏn (*hundred*). A Roman officer who had command of a hundred soldiers, Matt. viii. 5; Mark xv. 39; Luke vii. 1-10; Acts x. 1.

Çē′phas (*stone*). Name given to Peter, John i. 42.

Çē′ras, 1 Esdr. v. 29. [KEROS.]

Çē′tab. A doubtful name, 1 Esdr. v. 30.

Chā′bris. Ruler of Bethulia, Judith vi. 15.

Chā′dĭ-as. Her citizens returned, 1 Esdr. v. 20.

Chaff. Was separated from the grain by throwing all into the air from sheets, or forks, the wind carrying away the chaff, Ps. i. 4; Isa. xvii. 13; Hos. xiii. 3; Zeph. ii. 2.

Chains (*links*). Used for ornament on man and beast, and for fetters, Gen. xli. 42; Judg. viii. 21; xvi. 21; 2 Sam. iii. 34; 2 Kgs. xxv. 7; Isa. iii. 19; Acts xii. 6; xxi. 33; xxviii. 20.

Chăl″çē-dō′nȳ (*from Chalcedon*). A many-colored precious stone of the agate variety, Rev. xxi. 19.

Chăl′cŏl, 1 Kgs. iv. 31. [CALCOL.]

Chăl-dē′ȧ, Chăl-dæ′ȧ (*as demons*). The country lying along the Euphrates on both sides, and between it and the Tigris, for three or four hundred miles back from their mouths, Gen. x. 10; xi. 31; Job i. 17.

Chăl-dē′ănş, Chăl′deeş. The people of that country having Babylon for its capital, Dan. i. 4; v. 15; ix. 1.

Chälk=stōnes. Possibly burnt lime, Isa. xxvii. 9.

Chām′bĕr (*vault, arched*). Sleeping apartment, Gen. xliii. 30; 2 Sam. xviii. 33; Ps. xix. 5; Dan. vi. 10; Acts ix. 37. Dining room, Mark xiv. 14; Luke xxii. 12.

Chām′bĕr-ing. Amorous intrigue, Rom. xiii. 13.

Chām′bĕr-lain (*man of the chamber*). Officer in charge of the king's chamber, 2 Kgs. xxiii. 11; Esth. i. 10, 12, 15; Dan. i. 8-11. A more dignified office, in Acts xii. 20; Rom. xvi. 23.

Chȧ-mē′lē-ŏn (*ground lion*). A species of lizard, arboreal in habit. But the word thus translated implies a frog, Lev. xi. 30.

Chăm′ois (*sham-my*) (*buck*). The chamois not known in Palestine. A wild sheep, or goat, may be meant, Deut. xiv. 5.

Chā′năan. Greek spelling of Canaan, Acts vii. 11; xiii. 19; Judith v. 3.

Chăn′çĕl-lŏr (*usher of a law-court*). A keeper of the king's seal, Ez. iv. 8.

Chăp′ĭ-ter (*head*). The ornamental head of a pillar, Ex. xxxvi. 38; xxxviii. 17; 1 Kgs. vii. 31, 38.

Chăp′man (*cheap-man*). A trader, 1 Kgs. x. 15; 2 Chr. ix. 14.

Chăr″a-ăth′ā-lar, 1 Esdr. v. 36. [CHERUB.]

Chăr′a-cȧ. An obscure place, 2 Macc. xii. 17.

Chăr′a-shĭm, Valley of (*ravine of craftsmen*). Where Joab's ancestors lived, 1 Chr. iv. 14.

Chär′chĕ-mĭsh, 2 Chr. xxxv. 20; **Chär′chă-mĭs,** 1 Esdr. i. 25. [CARCHEMISH.]

Chär′cus, 1 Esdr. v. 32. [BARKOS.]

Chär′ġer (*car*). A dish for receiving water and blood, and for presenting offerings of flour and oil, Num. vii. 13, 79; later, a large service plate, Matt. xiv. 8.

Chăr′ĭ-ot (*car*). A two-wheeled vehicle, used for travel and war, Gen. xli. 43; xlvi. 29; 1 Kgs. xviii. 44; 2 Kgs. v. 9. In use by enemies of Israel, Josh. xi. 4; Judg. iv. 3; 1 Sam. xiii. 5. Adopted for war by David and Solomon, 2 Sam. viii. 4; 1 Kgs. ix. 19; x. 26; xxii. 34; 2 Kgs. ix. 16; Isa. xxxi. 1.

Chăr′mis. Ruler of Bethulia, Judith vi. 15.

Chăr′ran, Acts vii. 2-4. [HARAN.]

Chăs′ĕ-ba, 1 Esdr. v. 31. [GAZERA.]

Chē′bär (*strength*). A river of Chaldea; seat of Ezekiel's visions, Ezek. i. 3; iii. 15, 23.

Chĕd″ŏr-lā′o-mēr (*handful of sheaves*). King of Elam, Gen. xiv. 1-24.

Chēese. The Hebrew words imply curds, or curdled milk, 1 Sam. xvii. 18; Job x. 10; 2 Sam. xvii. 29.

Chē′lăl (*perfect*). A returned captive, Ez. x. 30.

Chĕl′çĭ-as. Hilkiah, Bar. i. 7.

Chĕl′luh (*perfection*). A returned captive, Ez. x. 35.

Chĕl′lus. A place west of Jordan, Judith i. 9.

Chē′lŭb (*basket*). (1) A Judahite, 1 Chr. iv. 11. (2) Father of one of David's overseers, 1 Chr. xxvii. 26.

Chē-lū′bāi (*capable*). Caleb, 1 Chr. ii. 9.

Chĕm′a-rims (*black ones*). Sun-worshippers, Zeph. i. 4.

Chē′mosh (*subduer*). National god of Moab, and Ammon, Num. xxi. 29; Judg. xi. 23, 24; 1 Kgs. xi. 7; 2 Kgs. xxiii. 13.

Chĕ-nā′ă-nah (*merchant*). (1) Father of Zedekiah, 1 Kgs. xxii. 11. (2) A Benjamite, 1 Chr. vii. 10.

Chĕn′a-nī (*contraction of Chenaniah*). A Levite, Neh. ix. 4.

Roman Centurion. (*See* p. 27.)

Chĕn″a-nī′ah (*made by God*). A Levite, 1 Chr. xv. 22.

Chē′phăr-hă-ăm′mo-nāi. "Hamlet of the Ammonites," in Benjamin, Josh. xviii. 24.

Chē-phī′rah (*hamlet*). A Gibeonite city, Josh. ix. 17; Ez. ii. 25; Neh. vii. 29.

Chē′ran (*lyre*). A Horite, Gen. xxxvi. 26; 1 Chr. i. 41.

Chē′rē-as. A general, 2 Macc. x. 32–37.

Chĕr′ĕth-ĭms, Ezek. xxv. 16. [Cherethites.]

Chĕr′ĕth-ītes (*executioners*). A portion of David's body guard, 2 Sam. viii. 18; xv. 18; xx. 7, 23; 1 Kgs. i. 38, 44; 1 Chr. xviii. 17.

Chē′rĭth (*cutting*). The place where Elijah was fed by ravens, 1 Kgs. xvii. 3–5.

Chē′rub. A place in Babylonia, Ez. ii. 59; Neh. vii. 61.

Chĕr′ub, Chĕr′u-bĭm (*terrible*). Guards of Paradise, Gen. iii. 24; and the mercy seat, Ex. xxv. 18. Wrought in gold or wood, Ex. xxxvi. 35; xxxvii. 7–9. Of immense size in Solomon's Temple, 1 Kgs. vi. 27. Four-winged and four-faced, Ezek. i. 6; x. 14; Rev. iv. 8.

Chĕs′ă-lon (*hopes*). A landmark of Judah, Josh. xv. 10.

Chē′sed (*gain*). Fourth son of Nahor, Gen. xxii. 22.

Chē′sĭl (*fool*). A place in south Judah, Josh. xv. 30.

Chĕst (*box*). A coffin, Gen. l. 26. Treasure chest, 2 Kgs. xii. 9; 2 Chr. xxiv. 8–11. Trunk or packing-case, Ezek. xxvii. 24. In all other places, "Ark."

Chĕst′nut-tree, Gen. xxx. 37; Ezek. xxxi. 8; the plane-tree is meant.

Chē-sŭl′lŏth (*loins*). Town of Issachar, Josh. xix. 18.

Chĕt-tī′ĭm, 1 Macc. i. 1. [Chittim.]

Chē′zĭb (*lying*). Gen. xxxviii. 5. Probably Achzib.

Chī′don (*dart*). Spot where the accident befel the Ark, 1 Chr. xiii. 9–13. Nachon, 2 Sam. vi. 6.

Chief of Asia, Acts xix. 31. [Asiaarch.]

Chief Priest. [High Priest.]

Chĭl′dren. Children an honor, childlessness a misfortune, Gen. xvi. 2; Deut. vii. 14; 1 Sam. i. 6; 2 Sam. vi. 23; 2 Kgs. iv. 14; Ps. cxxvii. 3; Isa. xlvii. 9, Jer. xx. 15. Males circumcised on eighth day, Lev. xii. 3. Weaning an occasion of rejoicing, Gen. xxi. 8.

Chĭl′e-ăb (*like the father*). Son of David, 2 Sam. iii. 3.

Chĭl′ĭ-on (*sickly*). Husband of Ruth, Ruth i. 2.

Chĭl′măd (*closed*). A country on the Euphrates, Ezek. xxvii. 23.

Chĭm′ham (*longing*). A friend of David, 2 Sam. xix. 37, 38; Jer. xli. 17.

Chĭn′ne-rĕth, Chĭn′ne-rŏth. (1) A city on or near coast of Sea of Galilee, Josh. xi. 2. (2) Old name for the inland sea known as Lake Gennesareth, or Sea of Galilee, Num. xxxiv. 11; Deut. iii. 17; Josh. xiii. 27.

Chī-os (*open*). The island of Scio, Acts xx. 15.

Chĭs′lĕū. Ninth month of the Jewish sacred, and third of the civil, year, corresponding to parts of Nov. and Dec., Neh. i. 1.

Chĭs′lon (*hope*). A Benjamite, Num. xxxiv. 21.

Chĭs′lŏth-tā′bôr, Josh. xix. 12. [Chesulloth.]

Chĭt′tim, Kĭt′tim (*bruisers*). Descendants of Javan, and their country, supposably Cyprus, Gen. x. 4; Num. xxiv. 24; 1 Chr. i. 7; Isa. xxiii. 1–12.

Chī′ŭn. An Israelite idol, Am. v. 26. [Remphan.]

Chlō′ē (*green herb*). A Christian woman of Corinth, 1 Cor. i. 11.

Chameleon. (*See* p. 27.)

Chō'bȧ, Chō'bāi. A place in Bethulia, Judith vi. 4; xv. 4.

Chôr-ā'shan. A haunt of David, 1 Sam. xxx. 30.

Chō-rā'zin (*secret*). A city on the coast of the Sea of Galilee, Matt. xi. 21; Luke x. 13.

Chō'ze-bȧ. Descendants of Judah, 1 Chr. iv. 22.

Chrīst. The Anointed; the Messiah. A title of Jesus, the Saviour: at first with the article, "The Christ;" later, as part of a proper name, "Jesus Christ." [Jesus.]

Chrĭs'tian. Follower of Christ. First so called at Antioch, Syria, A. D. 43, Acts xi. 26; xxvi. 28.

Chrŏn'i-cles ("*words of days,*" *annals*). Thirteenth and fourteenth of O. T. Books. Originally one book called Paraleipomena, "things omitted." A supplement to Kings, compiled, no doubt, by Ezra. The history covers a period of 3500 years.

Chrȳs'ō-līte (*gold stone*). Evidently the yellow topaz, Rev. xxi. 20.

Chrȳs''ō-prā'sus (*golden leek*). An apple-green variety of chalcedony, Rev. xxi. 20.

Chŭb. Allies of Egypt, Ezek. xxx. 5.

Chŭn (*ready*). A city that supplied brass to Solomon, 2 Sam. viii. 8.

Chûrch (*assembly*). A congregation of religious worshippers, Acts vii. 38; Matt. xvi. 18. Visible, Acts ii.; Col. i. 24. Invisible, Heb. xii. 23.

Chûrn-ing, Prov. xxx. 33. The milk was enclosed in skin bags, which were shaken or trodden.

Chū'shan=rĭsh''a-thā'im (*great conqueror*). A king of Mesopotamia, Judg. iii. 8–10.

Chū'si. A place, Judith vii. 18.

Chū'zȧ (*seer*). Steward of Herod, Luke viii. 3; xxiv. 10.

Çi-lĭ'çia (*rolling*). A province of Asia Minor. Chief city, Tarsus, birthplace of Paul, Acts ix. 11, 30; xv. 41.

Çĭn'nă-mŏn (*dried*). Inner bark of the cinnamon-tree, Ex. xxx. 23; Rev. xviii. 13. A perfume, Prov. vii. 17.

Çĭn'ne-rŏth. A district of Naphtali, 1 Kgs. xv. 20. [Chinnereth.]

Çĭr'a-mȧ. Returned Jews, 1 Esdr. v. 20.

Çîr''cŭm-çĭ'sion (*cutting around*). Cutting off the foreskin. A rite, performed on males on eighth day after birth, Gen. xvii.; Lev. xii. 3; Ex. xii. 44; John vii. 22. Antagonized by Christianity, Acts xv.; 1 Cor. vii. 18; Gal. v. 2.

Çĭs, Acts xiii. 21. [Kish.]

Çī'sai, Esther xi. 12. [Kish.]

Çĭs'tern (*chest*). Common and necessary in the East. Sometimes synonymous with "wells," Num. xxi. 22, and "pits," Gen. xxxvii. 22; 2 Sam. xvii. 18; Eccl. xii. 6; Jer. xxxviii. 6.

Çĭt'ims, 1 Macc. viii. 5. [Chittim.]

Çĭt'i-zĕn-ship. Roman citizenship exempted from imprisonment or scourging without trial, and gave the right of appeal to the Emperor, Acts xvi. 37; xxii. 28, 29; xxv. 11.

Çĭt'ȳ (*place for citizens*). Cain and Nimrod city-builders, Gen. iv. 17; x. 9–11. "Fenced cities," fortified cities, 2 Kgs. x. 2; Isa. xxvi. 1. "City of David," Jerusalem, Bethlehem, 1 Chr. xi. 5; Luke ii. 11. "City of God," Jerusalem, Ps. xlvi. 4; Neh. xi. 1. "Cities of Refuge," six in number, Deut. xix. 7–9; Num. xxxv. 6–15.

Clau'dȧ (*lamentable*). A small island near Crete, Acts xxvii. 16.

Clau'dĭ-ȧ (*lame*). A female friend of Paul and Timothy, 2 Tim. iv. 21.

Clau'dĭ-us (*lame*). Claudius Cæsar. Fifth Roman Emperor. Reign, A. D. 41–54. Banished the Jews from Rome, Acts xviii. 2.

Clau'dĭ-us Lȳs'ĭ-as. [Lysias.]

Clāy. Used variously, Ps. xviii. 42; Isa. lvii. 20; Jer. xxxviii. 6; John ix. 6; for making pottery, Isa. xli. 25; for brick-making, 2 Sam. xii. 31; for sealing, Job xxxviii. 14; for writing tablets.

Clay Tablets from Nineveh.

Clēan and Un'clean. Words applied to personal and ceremonial conditions, and to edibility of animals, Gen. vii. 2; Lev. xi.–xv.; Num. xix.; Ex. xxii. 31; xxxiv. 15–26.

Clĕm'ent (*mild*). A co-worker with Paul, Phil. iv. 3.

Clē'o-pas (*renowned father*). One of the two disciples to whom Christ appeared, Luke xxiv. 18.

Clē'o-phas (*renowned*). Husband of Mary, John xix. 25. Called also Alphæus.

Clŏth. Skins first supplied the place of cloth. Art of weaving cloth early known, Ex. xxxv. 25. Judg. v. 30.

Clō'thing. [Dress.]

Clôud (*round mass*). A prominent feature in Oriental imagery, Prov. xvi. 15; Isa. xxv. 5; Job xxx. 15. A token of Divine presence and protection, Ex. xvi. 10; Num. xii. 5.

Clôut'ed. Worn out and patched, Josh. ix. 5.

Cnī'dus (*ni'dus*) (*age*). The peninsula of Caria, and the city upon it, Acts xxvii. 7; 1 Macc. xv. 23.

Cōal (*glow*). The coal of scripture is charcoal, or embers, Prov. xxvi. 21; John xviii. 18; xxi. 9; heated stones, 1 Kgs. xix. 6; Isa. vi. 6; metaphorical, 2 Sam. xxii. 9–13; Ps. xviii. 8, 12, 13; Rom. xii. 20.

Cōast ([illegible]). Often used as border or boundary, Judg. xi. 20; 1 Sam. v. 6; Matt. viii. 34.

Cōat (*coarse mantle*). [Dress.]

Cŏck. The crowing of the cock in Matt. xxvi. 34; Mark xiv. 30; Luke xxii. 34, indicated the third watch of the night, from midnight to daylight.

Cŏck'a-trīce (*crocodile like.*) The basilisk, Jer. viii. 17; Isa. xi. 8; xiv. 29; lix. 5; in all which some species of hissing, venomous serpent is meant.

Cŏck'le (*stinking*). A weed that grows among grain; doubtless the tare, identified as darnel, Job xxxi. 40.

Çœl'e=Sȳr'i-ȧ and Çĕl'o=Sȳr'i-ȧ (*hollow Syria*). That part of Syria lying between the Libanus and Anti-Libanus ranges, 1 Macc. x. 69.

Cŏf'fer (*basket*). A movable box hanging from the side of a cart, 1 Sam. vi. 8, 11, 15.

Cŏf'fin (*basket*). [Burial.]

Cō'hôrt (*company*). [Army.]

Cŏl-hō'zeh (*all-seeing*). A man of Judah, Neh. iii. 15; xi. 5.

Cŏ'lĭ-us, 1 Esdr. ix. 23. [Kelaiah.]

Cŏl'lar. "Collars" in Judg. viii. 26, and "chains" in Isa. iii. 19, should be "ear-drops."

Cŏl'lēge (*collected*). That part of Jerusalem north of the old city, 2 Kgs. xxii. 14.

Cŏl'lops (*tender meat*). Slices of meat, Job xv. 27.

Cŏl'ō-ny (*cultivated*). Philippi, colonized by Rome, Acts xvi. 12.

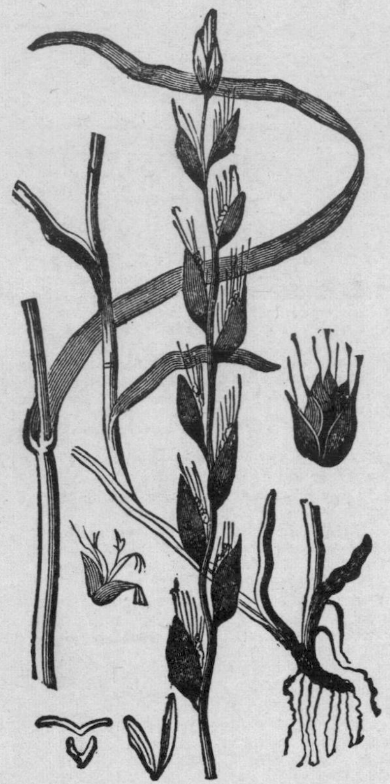

Darnel. (*See* Cockle, p. 29.)

Côl'ors (*tints*). Royal colors, purple, Judg. viii. 26; Esth. viii. 15; Luke xvi. 19; Rev. xvii. 4; blue, Ex. xxv. 4; Esth. i. 6. Vermilion used for beams, walls and ceilings, Jer. xxii. 14; Ezek. xxiii. 14.

Cŏ-lŏs'sē (*punishment*). A city of Phrygia. Paul wrote to the church there, Col. i. 2; iv. 13.

Cŏ-lŏs'sĭ-ans, Epistle to. Written by Paul from Rome, A. D. 61 or 62, and delivered by Tychicus, Acts xxviii. 16; Col. iv. 7, 8.

Cōlt (*young camel or ass*). The young of camels and asses, Gen. xxxii. 15; xlix. 11; Judg. x. 4; Job xi. 12; Matt. xxi. 2–7.

Côm'fŏrt-er (*brave together*). Defender and helper. Applied to the Holy Ghost, and Christ, John xiv. 16.

Cŏm'merce (*buying together.*) Limited among Hebrews, Gen. xiii. 2; xxiv. 22, 53. Outside enterprises a failure, 1 Kgs. xxii. 48–9. Used some foreign articles, Ez. iii. 7; Neh. xiii. 16; supplied some, 1 Kgs. v. 11; Acts xii. 20. Temple commerce led to Christ's rebuke, Matt. xxi. 12; John ii. 14.

Cŏm-mū'nion (*bound together*). Mutual love, confidence and fellowship, 1 Cor. x. 16; 2 Cor. xiii. 14; 1 John i. 3. The Lord's supper called the "holy communion."

Côm'pass (*encircle*). To make a circuit, 2 Sam. v. 23; Acts xxviii. 13.

Cŏn-a-nī'ah (*made by Jehovah*). A Levite, 2 Chr. xxxv. 9.

Cŏn-çĭ'şion (*cutting off*). A sarcastic use by Paul of the word circumcision, Phil. iii. 2.

Cŏn'cū-bine (*lying with*). In the Jewish economy, a secondary wife, betrothed according to custom, Gen. xxi. 14; xxv. 6; Ex. xxi. 7; Deut. xxi. 10–14. Concubinage repudiated in N. T., Matt. xix. 4–9; 1 Cor. vii. 2–4.

Cŏn'duit (*wit*) (*conductor*). A water pipe or aqueduct, 2 Kgs. xviii. 17; xx. 20; Isa. vii. 3; xxxvi. 2; ditch, Job xxxviii. 25.

Cō'nēy, Cō'nȳ (*rabbit*). The small rabbit-like animal known as the *Hyrax Syriacus*, Lev. xi. 5; Deut. xiv. 7; Prov. xxx. 26.

Cŏn''grē-gā'tion (*collected together*). Biblically, the Hebrew nationality, Num. xv. 15. Generally, collected Jewry, Ex. xii. 19. A popular assembly, Acts xix. 32, 39, 41. A religious assembly, or church, Acts vii. 38.

Cō-nī'ah. [Jeconiah.]

Cŏn''ŏ-nī'ah (*the Lord's appointed*). Treasurer of tithes, 2 Chr. xxxi. 12, 13.

Cŏn'sē-crāte (*together sacred*). The tribe of Levi consecrated to the priesthood, Ex. xxxii. 28, 29; Lev. vii. 37. Consecrate vessels, Josh. vi. 19; profits, Mic. iv. 13; fields, Lev. xxvii. 28; cattle, 2 Chr. xxix. 33; persons, Num. vi. 9–13; nations, Ex. xix. 6.

Cŏn''vŏ-cā'tion (*called together*). The "congregation," when called in a purely religious capacity, Ex. xii. 16; Lev. xxiii. 2; Num. xxviii. 18.

Cook'ing. Done by both sexes, Gen. xviii. 6–8; later by servantage, 1 Sam. viii. 13. Kids, lambs and calves furnished meat for guests, Gen. xviii. 7; Luke xv. 23.

Cō'ŏs (*summit*), Acts xxi. 1. [Cos.]

Cō'ping. The top and projecting layer of a wall, 1 Kgs. vii. 9.

Cŏp'per (*from Cyprus*). The "brass" of the Bible. Known to antediluvians, Gen. iv. 22. Used largely in the temple, 1 Chr. xxii. 3–14; and for vessels, ornaments and mirrors, Ex. xxxviii. 8; helmets and spears, 1 Sam. xvii. 5, 6; 2 Sam. xxi. 16.

Cŏr. [Homer.]

Cŏr'al. Used by Hebrews for beads and ornaments. Ranked among precious stones, Job xxviii. 18; Ezek. xxvii. 16.

Cŏr'ban (*offering*). The offering in fulfilment of a vow, Lev. xxvii.; Num. xxx. The plea of corban reprehended by Christ, Matt. xv. 3–9.

Cŏr'be, 1 Esdr. v. 22. [Zaccai.]

Cŏrd (*string*). Variously made and used, Isa. xix. 9; scourge, John ii. 15; ship-ropes, Acts xxvii. 32.

Cō'rē, Ecclus. xlv. 18; Jude 11. [Korah.]

Cō''ri-ăn'der (*smelling like a bed-bug*). A plant of the parsley family producing aromatic seeds. Ex. xvi. 31; Num. xi. 7.

Cŏr'inth (*ornament*). Anciently Ephyra; capital of Achaia. Destroyed by Rome, B. C. 146. Rebuilt by Julius Cæsar, B. C. 46, as a Roman colony. Paul founded a church there, Acts xviii. 1; xx. 2, 3.

Cŏr-ĭn'thĭ-ans, Epistles to. I. written by Paul at Ephesus, 1 Cor. xvi. 8; treats of church organization, social practices, holy observances, and doctrinal affairs. II. written a few months afterwards, at suggestion of Titus; largely refers to Paul's right to preach and teach, 2 Cor. vii. 5; ix. 2.

Cŏr'mō-rant (*sea raven*). A large, greedy water-bird, pronounced "unclean." Lev. xi. 17; Deut. xiv. 17. Doubtless "pelican" in Isa. xxxiv. 11; Zeph. ii. 14.

Côrn (*kernel*). In a Bible sense, grain of all kinds, except our maize, or Indian corn. Used largely in figurative speech, Gen. xli. 22; Ex. ix. 32; Deut. xi. 14; xviii. 4; xxviii. 51; 2 Chr. ii. 15; Isa. xxviii. 25; Ezek. xxvii. 17; Matt. xii. 1.

Côr'nē'li̤us (*of a horn*). A Roman centurion and first Gentile convert, Acts x. 1–33.

Côr'ner (*horned*). Grain-field corners not allowed to be wholly reaped, Lev. xix. 9; xxiii. 22. "Legal corner," one sixtieth of the field. "Length and breadth" of a country, Num. xxiv. 17; Jer. xlviii. 45. "Corner-stone," chief stone in a foundation, Job xxxviii. 6. Figuratively in Isa. xxviii. 16; Matt. xxi. 42.

Côr'net (*horn*). The curved signal horn of the Jews, usually made of the horn of a ram, ox, chamois, or wild goat, Lev. xxv. 9; Ezek. xxxiii. 4, 5; 1 Chr. xv. 28.

Cŏs, Cō'ŏs (*summit*). A small island of the Grecian archipelago, Acts xxi. 1.

Cō'sam (*diviner*). One of Christ's ancestors, Luke iii. 28.

Cōte (*cot, den*). A sheepfold, 2 Chr. xxxii. 28.

Cŏt'tage (*cot*). A rustic tent or shelter, Isa. xxiv. 20.

Cŏt'ton (*wool-plant*). Not known to Hebrews. Cotton garments mentioned on the Rosetta stone.

Cŏuch (*placed*). [BED.]

Cŏun'çil (*called together*). In N. T., (1) The Sanhedrim, Matt. xxvi. 59. (2) Lesser courts, Matt. x. 17; Mark xiii. 9. (3) A jury of councillors, Acts xxv. 12. [SANHEDRIM.]

Cōurs'es (*running*). Priests divided into twenty-four classes, courses, or orders, 1 Chr. xxiv. [ABIA.]

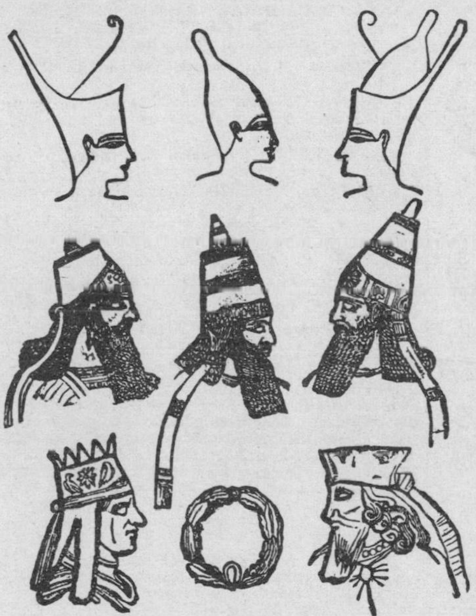

Crowns of Ancient Kings.

Cōurt (*enclosure*). The enclosed space within the limits of Oriental houses. The outer area of the tabernacle and temple, Ex. xxvii. 9; Lev. vi. 16; 2 Sam. xvii. 18; 1 Kgs. vi. 36; 2 Kgs. xxiii. 12; 2 Chr. xxxiii. 5.

Cou'tha. One of the returned, 1 Esdr. v. 32.

Côv'ē-nant (*coming together*). Ratified by eating together, oaths, witnesses, gifts, pillars, Gen. ix. 15; xxi. 30, 31; xxxi. 50–52. Covenant of the law through Moses, Ex. xx. 24; of the gospel through Christ, Gal. iii.; Heb. viii.

Egyptian Cups. (*See* p. 32.)

Côv'et (*desire*). Rightful desire, 1 Cor. xii. 31, good. Wrongful desire, sinful, Ex. xx. 17; xviii. 21; Prov. xxviii. 16; Luke xii. 15–34; 1 Tim. vi. 9, 10.

Cow. Cow and calf not to be killed on same day, Lev. xxii. 28. Symbol of plenty, Isa. vii. 21.

Cŏz (*thorn*). A Judahite, 1 Chr. iv. 8.

Cŏz'bī (*liar*). Daughter of Zur, Num. xxv. 15–18.

Crăck'nels (*that cracks*). Hard brittle cakes, 1 Kgs. xiv. 3.

Crāne. A large, long-necked, heron-like bird, of gray plumage, noisy on the wing, Isa. xxxviii. 14; Jer. viii. 7.

Crā'tes. Governor of Cyprus, 2 Macc. iv. 29.

Crē-āte', Crē-ā'tion (*make, made*). To produce out of nothing by Almighty fiat, Gen. i.; ii. The universe.

Crĕs'çens (*increasing*). Assistant of Paul, 2 Tim. iv. 10.

Crēte (*carnal*). Now Candia. One of the largest islands in the Grecian archipelago. Paul founded a church there in charge of Titus, Acts ii. 11; xxvii. 1–12; Tit. i. 5–13.

Crētes. Inhabitants of Crete, Acts ii. 11.

Crĭb. A stall for cattle, and the manger or rack for hay or straw, Job xxxix. 9; Prov. xiv. 4; Isa. i. 3.

Crĭm'son (*carmine*). A deep-red color; or a red tinged with blue, Jer. iv. 30.

Crĭsp'ing=pins (*curling pins*). Crimping pins, Isa. iii. 22.

Crĭs'pus (*curled*). Chief ruler of the synagogue at Corinth, Acts xviii. 8. Baptized by Paul, 1 Cor. i. 14.

Crŏss (*across*). A gibbet of wood of various forms, Deut. xxi. 23; John xix. 17; Gal. iii. 13. Now a sacred emblem.

Crown (*curved*). A head-dress, Ezek. xvi. 12. Head-dress of priests, kings, and queens, Ex. xxviii. 36–38; 2 Chr. xxiii. 11; Esth. ii. 17. Symbol of power, honor, and eternal life, Prov. xii. 4; Lam. v. 16; 1 Pet. v. 4.

Crŭ″cĭ-fix′ion (*fixing to the cross*). A method of death punishment by fixing to a cross, Gen xl. 19; Esth. vii. 10. Limbs sometimes broken to hasten death, John xix. 31. Sepulture denied, Deut. xxi. 22, 23, but an exception allowed in Christ's case, Matt. xxvii. 58.

Crū′cĭ-fy. [CRUCIFIXION.]

Crūse (*pot*). A bottle, flask, or jug for holding liquids, 1 Sam. xxvi. 11; 1 Kgs. xvii. 12; xix. 6.

Crȳs′tal (*frost*). A disputed original, variously translated crystal, Job xxviii. 17; frost, Gen. xxxi. 40; ice, Job xxxviii. 29.

Cū′bit (*elbow*). Distance from the elbow to end of the middle finger, or about 21.8 inches, Gen. vi. 15; 1 Sam. xvii. 4.

Cuck′oo (*crower*). A mistranslation; and perhaps the storm-petrel is meant, Lev. xi. 16; Deut. xiv. 15.

Cū′cŭm-ber (*cumberer*). Much used for food in the East, Num. xi. 5; Isa. i. 8.

Cŭm′min. An annual of the parsley family, producing aromatic seeds, Isa. xxviii. 25; Matt. xxiii. 23.

Cŭn′ning (*test*). Skilful, Gen. xxv. 27; 1 Sam. xvi. 16.

Cŭp (*coop, tub*). A drinking vessel of various designs, made of horn, clay, or metal, Gen. xliv. 2; 1 Sam. xvi. 13; 1 Kgs. vii. 26. Used figuratively in Ps. xxiii. 5; Isa. li. 17; Rev. xiv. 10; Matt. xx. 22; xxvi. 39.

Cŭp′beâr″er. [BUTLER.]

Cŭsh (*black*). (1) Oldest son of Ham, Gen. x. 6, 8; 1 Chr. i. 8–10. (2) That indefinite country translated Ethiopia in Gen. ii. 13. (3) The country settled by Ham's descendants, Gen. x. 6–8; Isa. xviii. 1; Jer. xiii. 23; Dan. xi. 43. (4) A Benjamite, Ps. vii. title.

Cu′shan (*blackness*). Hab. iii. 7. Some refer it to Cush.

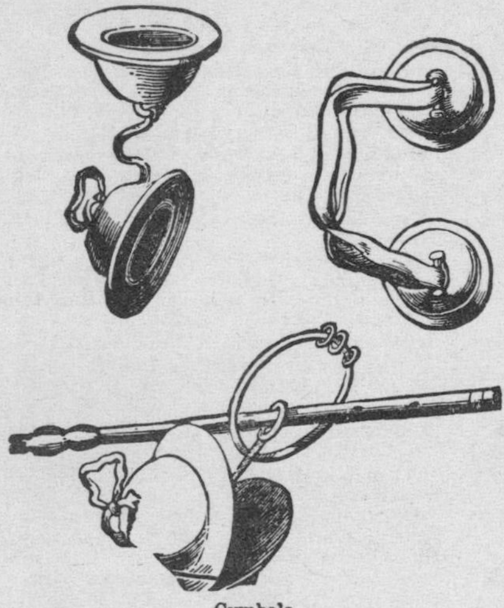

Cymbals.

Cu′shī (*Ethiopian*). (1) A foreigner in David's army, 2 Sam. xviii. 21–32. (2) An ancestor of Jehudi, Jer. xxxvi. 14. (3) Father of Zephaniah, Zeph. i. 1.

Cŭth (*burning*). The land in Persia whence colonists came into Samaria, 2 Kgs. xvii. 30. Cuthah in vs. 24.

Cyrus the Great.

Cū′thah, Cŭth-ītes, 2 Kgs. xvii. 24. [CUTH.]

Cŭt′tings, Of the flesh, forbidden by Levitical law, Lev. xix. 28; xxi. 5; Deut. xiv. 1.

Çȳ′ă-mon. A place near Carmel, Judith vii. 3.

Çȳm′bal (*hollow of a vessel*). Metallic plates, slightly concave, used as musical instruments, by striking them together, 1 Chr. xiii. 8; xvi. 5; Ps. cl. 5; 1 Cor. xiii. 1.

Çȳ′press (*from Cyprus*). Not indigenous to Palestine. Juniper may be meant, Isa. xliv. 14.

Çȳp′rĭ-an. Dweller in Cyprus, 2 Macc. iv. 29.

Çȳ′prus (*fairness*). A large island in N. E. angle of the Mediterranean. Christianity introduced quite early, Acts xi. 19. Birthplace of Barnabas, Acts iv. 36. Paul visited it, Acts xiii. 4–13.

Çȳ-rē′nē (*wall*). Capital of Cyrenaica, in northern Africa, and corresponding to Tripoli. Simon was of Cyrene, Matt. xxvii. 32; Mark xv. 21. Cyreneans present at Pentecost, Acts ii. 10; vi. 9.

Çȳ-rē′nĭ-us (*of Cyrene*). Roman governor of Syria, B. C. 4–1, and A. D. 6–11; Luke ii. 2; Acts v. 37.

Çȳ′rus (*sun*). Founder of the Persian empire, Dan. vi. 28; xi. 13; 2 Chr. xxxvi. 22. United Media to Persia. Conquered Babylon, B. C. 538, and reigned over the consolidated empire till B. C. 529. A guardian and liberator of captive Jews, Isa. xliv. 28; xlv. 1–7. Daniel was his favorite minister. *See* Dan., also Ez. i. 1–4; iii. 7; iv. 3; v. 13–17; vi. 3.

D

Dăb′a-reh, Josh. xxi. 28. [DABERATH.]

Dăb′ba-shĕth (*hump*). A boundary of Zebulun, Josh. xix. 11.

Dăb′e-răth (*pasture*). A Levitical city, Josh. xix. 12.

Dăb′rį-å. A swift scribe, 2 Esdr. xiv. 24.

Då-cō′bī, 1 Esdr. v. 28. [Akkub.]

Dagon.

Dăd-dē′us, or **Săd-dē′us,** 1 Esdr. viii. 45, 46, [Iddo.]

Dā′gŏn (*fish*). National male idol of the Philistines, 1 Chr. x. 10. Noted temples at Ashdod, 1 Sam. v. 1-7; Gaza, Judg. xvi. 23; Beth-dagon, Josh. xv. 41; and in Asher, Josh. xix. 27. Represented with human hands and face and a fish's body.

Daī′san, 1 Esdr. v. 31. [Rezin.]

Dal″ą-i′ah (*freed by God*). A Judahite, 1 Chr. iii. 24.

Dāle, the **King's.** A valley near Jerusalem, Gen. xiv. 17; 2 Sam. xviii. 18.

Dăl″ma-nū′thå. A town on Sea of Galilee, Mark viii. 10.

Dăl-mā′tī-å (*she-a*) (*deceitful*). A province of Illyricum, 2 Tim. iv. 10; Rom. xv. 19.

Dăl′phon (*swift*). Son of Haman, Esth. ix. 7.

Dăm′a-rĭs (*heifer*). An Athenian woman converted by Paul, Acts xvii. 34.

Då-măs′cus. A city of Asia, 133 miles N. E. of Jerusalem, Gen. xiv. 15; xv. 2. Adjacent region called "Syria of Damascus," 2 Sam. viii. 5. Taken by David, 2 Sam. viii. 6; and by Jeroboam, 2 Kgs. xiv. 28. Scene of Paul's conversion, Acts ix. 1-27; xxii. 1-16.

Dăm-nā′tion (*condemnation*). Consignment to everlasting perdition, Matt. xxiii. 33; Mark iii. 29; John v. 29; 2 Pet. ii. 3.

Dăn (*judge*). (1) Fifth son of Jacob, Gen. xxx. 6; xlix. 16. Allotment, Josh. xix. 40-46. Portion of the tribe moved north, Josh. xix. 47, 48; Judg. xviii. (2) Changed name of Laish, or Leshem, Josh. xix. 47; Judg. xviii. 29. (3) A place in Arabia, Ezek. xxvii. 19.

Dăn′ītes. Members of the tribe of Dan, Judg. xiii. 2; 1 Chr. xii. 35.

Dăn=jā′an (*Danite*). Probably the northern Danites, 2 Sam. xxiv. 6.

Dănce (*drag along*). (1) In Hebrew, "leaping for joy." Not a measured step, Ps. xxx. 11. Common on festal occasions, Ex. xv. 20, 21; Judg. xi. 34; 1 Sam. xviii. 6, 7; 2 Sam. vi. 14; Jer. xxxi. 4; Luke vi. 23; xv. 25; Acts iii. 8. (2) A musical instrument, Ps. cl. 3-5. "Pipe," in margin.

Dăn′įel (*judgment of God*). (1) Fourth of the greater prophets. Carried captive to Babylon, B. C. 604; and named Belteshazzar, Dan. i., ii. Made a governor under Darius, Dan. vi. 2. Last vision on the Tigris in third year of Cyrus, B. C. 534, x. 1-4. (2) Second son of David, 1 Chr. iii. 1. (3) Son of Ithamar, Ez. viii. 2. (4) A co-covenanter, Neh. x. 6.

Dăn′įel, Book of. First six chapters historic. Chapters vii.-xii. contain the earliest model of apocalyptic literature. Largely acknowledged in N. T., Matt. xxiv. 15; Luke i. 19, 26; Heb. xi. 33, 34. "The Song of the Three Holy Children," "History of Susanna," and "History of Bel and the Dragon," are apocryphal additions to Daniel's writings.

Dăn′nah (*judging*). A city of Judah, Josh. xv. 49.

Dăph′ne (*bay-tree*). Sanctuary of Apollo, near Antioch, 2 Macc. iv. 33.

Dā′rå, 1 Chr. ii. 6. [Darda.]

Där′då (*pearl of wisdom*). One of four famed for wisdom, 1 Kgs. iv. 31.

Dăr′ic (*kingly*). A Persian coin of gold and silver; former worth about five dollars; latter fifty cents. "Dram," in 1 Chr. xxix. 7; Ez. ii. 69; Neh. vii. 70-72.

Då-rī′us (*Persian "dara," king*). (1) Darius the Mede, Dan. v. 31; vi.; ix. 1; xi. 1. Captured Babylon from Belshazzar, B. C. 538. (2) Darius Hystaspes, King of Persia, B. C. 521-486. He re-

Damascus.

stored the captive Jews, Ez. iv. 5, 24; vi. 14, 15; Hag. i. 1, 15; Zech. i. 1, 7; vii. 1. (3) Darius the Persian, Neh. xii. 22. Darius Codomanus, B. C. 336–330, last king of Persia.

Därk′ness (*blackness*). Absence of light, Gen. i. 2; 9th plague, Ex. x. 20–23; State of misery, Job xviii. 6; God's dwelling, Ex. xx. 21; 1 Kgs. viii. 12; typical of national convulsion, Acts ii. 19, 20; state of the fallen, Matt. viii. 12; ignorance, John i. 5; sympathetic, Luke xxiii. 44.

Där′kon (*scatterer*). His children returned, Ez. ii. 56; Neh. vii. 58.

Dāte (*like a finger*). Fruit of the date-palm, 2 Chr. xxxi. 5, marg. [PALM.]

Date-palm and Fruit.

Dā′than (*of a spring*). A Reubenite chief and conspirator, Num. xvi.; xxvi. 9; Deut. xi. 6.

Dăth′ĕ-ma. Ramoth-gilead, 1 Macc. v. 9.

Däugh′ter (*milk*). Daughter or any female descendant, Gen. xxiv. 48; female inhabitant, Gen. vi. 2; Isa. x. 32; xxiii. 12; Luke xxiii. 28; singing birds, Eccl. xii. 4.

Dā′vid (*well-beloved*). Youngest son of Jesse, 1 Sam. xvi. 8–12, born at Bethlehem. Anointed king by Samuel, 1 Sam. xvi. 13. Re-anointed at Hebron, 2 Sam. ii. 4. United his kingdom and raised it to great strength and splendor. Died at the age of 70, B. C. 1015, after a reign of seven and a half years over Judah and thirty-three years over the entire kingdom of Israel. History told in 1 Sam. xvi. to 1 Kgs. ii.

Dā′vid, City of. [JERUSALEM.]

Dāy (*shining*). Natural Hebrew day from sunset to sunset, Gen. i. 5; Ex. xii. 18. Sabbath the only day named; others numbered, Lev. xxiii. 32. Morning, noon, and evening divisions, Ps. lv. 17. Hours introduced, Dan. iii. 6; John xi. 9. Indefinite time, Gen. ii. 4; of birth, Job iii. 1; of ruin, Hos. i. 11; of judgment, Joel i. 15; of Christ's kingdom, John viii. 56.

Dāys′man. Umpire or moderator, Job ix. 33.

Dāy′spring. Dawn, Job xxxviii. 12; Luke i. 78.

Dāy′star. Morning star, 2 Pet. i. 19.

Dēa′con (*servant*). A subordinate minister or officer in early Christian Church, Acts vi. 1–6. Qualifications in 1 Tim. iii. 8–12.

Dēa′cŏn-ess. A female officer in early Church, Rom. xvi. 1; 1 Tim. v. 10.

Dĕad Sea. Not so called until the second century. In O. T. "Salt Sea" and "Sea of the Plain." [SALT SEA.]

Dēarth. [FAMINE.]

Dē′bĭr (*oracle*). (1) A Levitical city of Judah, Josh. xxi. 15; Kirjath-sepher, Josh. xv. 15; Kirjath-sannah, xv. 49. (2) A northern boundary of Judah, Josh. xv. 7. (3) A boundary of Gad, Josh. xiii. 26. (4) A king of Eglon, Josh. x. 3–26.

Dĕb′o̯-rah (*bee*). (1) Nurse of Rebekah, Gen. xxxv. 8; xxiv. 59. (2) Prophetess and Judge, Judg. iv. 5–14; v. (3) Grandmother of Tobit, Tob. i. 8.

Dĕbt′ŏr (*ower*). Lands or the person might be taken for debt, and held till the year of jubilee, Ex. xxi. 2; Lev. xxv. 29–34; 2 Kgs. iv. 1; Neh. v. 3–5.

Dē-căp′ŏ-lis (*ten cities*). A Roman province embracing parts of Syria and Palestine, Matt. iv. 25; Mark v. 20; vii. 31.

De-çi′ṣion, Valley of. Joel iii. 14. "Valley of Jehoshaphat," "or judgment," as in verses 2 and 12.

Dē′dan (*low*). (1) Grandson of Cush, Gen. x. 7. (2) Son of Jokshan, Gen. xxv. 3. Both founders of Arabian or Idumean tribes, Isa. xxi. 13; Ezek. xxxviii. 13.

Ded′a̯-nĭm. Descendants of Dedan, Isa. xxi. 13.

Dĕd″i̯-cā′tion (*declaration*). Devoting person, place or thing to holy use, Ex. xl.; Num. vii.; 2 Sam. viii. 11; 1 Kgs. viii.; Ez. vi.; Neh. xii. 27; "Feast of Dedication" commemorated the purging of the temple, John x. 22; 1 Macc. iv. 52–59.

Dēep. Abyss, or abode, of lost spirits, Luke viii. 31; Rom. x. 7. "Bottomless pit," Rev. ix. 1, 2, 11; xi. 7.

Dēer (*wild*), Deut. xiv. 5; 1 Kgs. iv. 23. [FALLOW-DEER.]

Dē-grēe′ (*step or grade down*). Rank or station, Ps. lxii. 9; 1 Tim. iii. 13. "Song of Degrees," title to Pss. cxx.–cxxxiv.

Dê-hā′vītes. Colonists planted in Samaria, Ez. iv. 9.

Dē′kär (*lancer*). Father of one of Solomon's commissaries, 1 Kgs. iv. 9.

Del″a̯-ī′ah (*freed by God*). (1) Leader of the 23d priestly course, 1 Chr. xxiv. 18. (2) Returned Jews, Ez. ii. 60; Neh. vii. 62. (3) Father of Shemaiah, Neh. vi. 10. (4) A courtier, Jer. xxxvi. 12.

Dē-lī′lah (*longing*). A woman of Sorek, employed to discover the secret of Samson's strength, Judg. xvi. 4–20.

Dĕl′ūge (*washing away*). The usual modern word for Noah's flood, Gen. vi.–viii.

Dē′lus (*suddenly visible*). Smallest of the Cyclades islands, 1 Macc. xv. 23.

Dē′mas (*popular*). A friend of Paul at Rome, Col. iv. 14; 2 Tim. iv. 10.

Dē-mē′trĭ-us (*belonging to Ceres*). (1) A silversmith at Ephesus, Acts xix. 24–30. (2) A disciple, 3 John, 12. (3) Demetrius (I.) Soter, of Syria, 1 Macc. x. 48–50. (4) Demetrius (II.) Nicator, 1 Macc. x.

Dē-nā′rĭ-us (*ten asses*). A Roman silver coin worth about 15 cents. The "penny" of N. T., Matt. xx. 2.

Dĕp′ū-tȳ (*selected*). In N. T., a proconsul, or governor, Acts xiii. 7, 8, 12.

Dĕr′bē (*sting*). A city of Lycaonia in Asia Minor, Acts xiv. 20; xx. 4.

Dĕs′ert (*deserted*). An arid sandy plain, or wild mountainous waste, Ex. xxiii. 31; Deut. xi. 24; Ps. lxv. 12.

Dĕs′să-ū. A village, 2 Macc. xiv. 16.

Deū′el (*knowledge of God*). Father of Eliasaph, Num. i. 14. Reuel in ii. 14.

Deū″te̯-rŏn′o-mȳ. So called because it "repeats the law." Fifth book of O. T. and last of the Pentateuch. Authorship ascribed to Moses, except last chapter. Chapters i.–iv. 40, rehearse the wanderings; v.–xxvi. recapitulate the law; the others deliver the law into keeping of the Levites, and describe the death of Moses.

Dĕv′il (*slanderer*). The Hebrew Satan, "adversary," Matt. xvi. 23; Mark viii. 33; Luke xxii. 3; Rev. xx. 2. The devil of bodily possession was rather the polluting power of disease — dumbness, Matt. ix. 32; blindness, xii. 22; epilepsy, Mark ix. 17-27; insanity, Matt. viii. 28; murderous antipathy, John vii. 20.

Dew. Source of fertility, Gen. xxvii. 28; Judg. vi. 37-40; object of rich imagery, Deut. xxxii. 2; Job xxix. 19; Ps. cxxxiii. 3.

Dī'al (*daily*). An instrument for telling the time of day, 2 Kgs. xx. 11; Isa. xxxviii. 8.

Dī'a-mônd (*adamant*). Pure crystallized carbon. Third stone in second row of high-priest's breastplate, Ex. xxviii. 18; Ezek. xxviii. 13.

Dī-ăn'ȧ (*safety*). A Roman goddess. The Artemis of the Greeks. Her temple at Ephesus regarded as one of the seven wonders of the world, Acts xix. 24-28.

Diana.

Dĭb'la-ĭm (*two cakes*). Mother-in-law of Hosea, Hos. i. 3.

Dĭb'lăth. Unidentified place, Ezek. vi. 14.

Dī'bŏn (*wasting*). (1) A town of Gad, Num. xxxii. 3, 34. Dibon-gad, Num. xxxiii, 45, 46. Accounted to Reuben, Josh. xiii. 9, 17. Now Dhiban, within the gateway of which the famous Moabite stone was found in 1868. (2) A town in south Judah, Neh. xi. 25.

Dī'bon-găd. [DIBON, 1.]

Dĭb'rī (*orator.*) A Danite, Lev. xxiv. 11.

Dĭd'y̆-mus (*twin*). Surname of Thomas, John xi. 16; xx. 24; xxi. 2.

Dĭk'lah (*palm*). A son of Joktan, Gen. x. 27; 1 Chr. i. 21.

Dĭl'ĕ-an (*cucumber*). A lowland city of Judah, Josh. xv. 38.

Dĭm'nah (*dung*). A Levitical city, Josh. xxi. 35.

Dī'mon (*reddish*). A stream of Moab, Isa. xv. 9.

Dī-mō'nah (*dunghill*). A city in south Judah, Josh. xv. 22.

Dī'nah (*judged*). First daughter of Jacob and Leah, Gen. xxx. 21; xxxiv.

Dī'na-ītes. Cuthean colonists in Samaria, Ez. iv. 9.

Dĭn'hă-bah. A capital of Edom, Gen. xxxvi. 32; 1 Chr. i. 43.

Dī''ŏ-ny̆s'ĭus (*devotee of Dionysos, or Bacchus*). A member of the court of Areopagus at Athens, Acts xvii. 34.

Dī''ŏ-ny̆s'us (*Bacchus*). Bacchus, 2 Macc. xiv. 33.

Dī'os-cŏr-ĭn'thi-us (*Corinthian Jove*). A month in the Cretan calendar, 2 Macc. xi. 21.

Dī-ot'rē-phēs (*nourished by Jupiter*). A Christian, 3 John 9.

Dis-çī'ple (*learner*). Follower of Christ, Matt. x. 24; of John, Matt. ix. 14. Applied specially to the twelve, Matt. x. 1; xi. 1; xx. 17.

Dis'cus (*round plate*). The quoit, 2 Macc. iv. 14.

Dis-cov'er (*uncover*). Uncovering, making bare, Ps. xxix. 9; Isa. xxii. 8; Mic. i. 6.

Dis-ēas'es (*uneasy*). Visitations of plagues and pestilences frequent in Bible lands, Gen. vii. viii.; Ex. xii. 21-29; 2 Kgs. xix. 35; 1 Chr. xxi. 12; Acts xii. 23. Principal bodily diseases were, ophthalmia, leprosy, brain and malarial fevers, lung disorders.

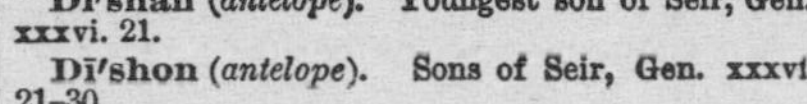

Dī'shan (*antelope*). Youngest son of Seir, Gen. xxxvi. 21.

Dī'shon (*antelope*). Sons of Seir, Gen. xxxvi. 21-30.

Dis''pĕn-sā'tion (*weighing out*), 1 Cor. ix. 17; Eph. i. 10; iii. 2; Col. i. 25. In these instances, authority to preach and teach.

Dis-pēr'sion (*scattering*). The breaking up of the Jewish kingdoms and scattering of the tribes by conquest, James i. 1; 1 Pet. i. 1.

Dis'taff (*flax-staff*). The staff around which flax was wound for spinning, Prov. xxxi. 19.

Dī'vēs (*rich*). A popular name for the rich man in Luke xvi. 19-31.

Dĭv''i-nā'tion (*belonging to a god*). In Scripture, the false use of means to discover the divine will; by rods, Hos. iv. 12; arrows, Ezek. xxi. 21; cups, Gen. xliv. 5; the liver, Ezek. xxi. 21; dreams, Deut. xiii. 3; Zech. x. 2; consulting oracles, Isa. xli. 21-24; xliv. 7. Faith in divination forbidden, Lev. xix. 26.

Di-vōrçe' (*turning asunder*). Allowed by Mosaic law, Deut. xxiv. 1-4, yet forbidden in certain cases, xxii. 19, 29. Christ regarded adultery as an only cause for divorce, Matt. v. 31, 32; xix. 9; Mark x. 11; Luke xvi. 18.

Dĭz'a-hăb (*gold region*). Scene of one of Moses addresses, Deut. i. 1.

Dŏc'tor (*teacher*). A teacher of the Law of Moses, Luke ii. 46; v. 17. Teacher of the Christian faith, 1 Cor. xii. 28.

Dō'cus. Springs near Jericho, 1 Macc. xvi. 15.

Dŏd'a-ī (*loving*). Leader of David's second military course, 1 Chr. xxvii. 4.

Dŏd'a-nĭm (*leaders*). Descendants of Javan, Gen. x. 4; 1 Chr. i. 7.

Dŏd'a-vah. Father of Eliezer, 2 Chr. xx. 37.

Dō'dō (*loving*). (1) Father of one of David's captains, 2 Sam. xxiii. 24. (2) Father of Eleazar, 2 Sam. xxiii. 9; 1 Chr. xi. 12. (3) Grandfather of Tola, Judg. x. 1.

Dō'eg (*fearful*). An overseer of Saul's herds. 1 Sam. xxi. 7; xxii. 9-22.

Dŏg. An unclean animal, Ex. xi. 7; xxii. 31; Deut. xxiii. 18; regarded with contempt, 1 Sam. xvii. 43; xxiv. 14; 2 Sam. ix. 8; 2 Kgs. viii. 13; Matt. vii. 6; Rev. xxii. 15; guards, Isa. lvi. 10; Job xxx. 1; scavengers, 1 Kgs. xiv. 11; xxi. 19-23; xxii. 38; enemies, Ps. xxii. 16-20.

Dōor (*through*). [GATE.]

Dŏph'kah (*drover*). A desert station of the Israelites, Num. xxxiii. 12.

Dôr (*dwelling*). A city on the coast north of Cæsarea, Josh. xi. 2; xii. 23; xvii. 11; Judg. i. 27; 1 Kgs. iv. 11.

Dō'rȧ, 1 Macc. xv. 11. [DOR.]

Dŏr'cas (*gazelle*). The woman of Joppa whom Peter raised from the dead, Acts ix. 36-42. [TABITHA.]

Dō-ry̆m'ĕ-nēs. Father of Ptolemy Macron, 1 Macc. iii. 38.

Dō-sĭth'ĕ-us. (1) A Jewish captain, 2 Macc. xii. 19-35. (2) A priest, Esth. xi. 1, 2.

Dō'tha-ĭm, Judith iv. 6. [DOTHAN.]

Dō'than (*two wells*). The place where Joseph was sold, Gen. xxxvii. 17; 2 Kgs. vi. 13.

Do You To Wit. To make known, 2 Cor. viii. 1.

Dove (*diver*). Clean by the law and offered as a sacrifice by the poor, Gen. xv. 9; Lev. v. 7; xii. 6-8; Luke ii. 24; symbol of innocence, Matt. x. 16; harbinger of God, Gen. viii.; emblem of Holy Spirit, Matt. iii. 16.

Dove's Dŭng. Eaten as a last resort, in time of famine, 2 Kgs. vi. 25.

Dow'ry̆ (*gift*). The consideration paid the father

of the bride by the bridegroom, Gen. xxix. 18; xxxiv. 12; 1 Sam. xviii. 25; Hos. iii. 2.

Drăch'mȧ, Drăchm (*handful*). A silver coin of Greece, corresponding to the Roman denarius, and worth about fifteen and a half cents. A piece of silver, Luke xv. 8, 9.

Drăg'on (*serpent*). An animal of the lizard species. Evidently a wild beast, as a jackal, in Job xxx. 29; Isa. xxxiv. 13; Ps. xliv. 19; Jer. ix. 11; Mic. i. 8; sea-serpent, Gen. i. 21; land-serpent, Ex. vii. 9-12; Deut. xxxii. 33; devil, Rev. xii. 3-17.

Drăg'on Well. Possibly Gihon, Neh. ii. 13.

Drăm (*handful*), 1 Chr. xxix. 7; Ez. ii. 69; Neh. vii. 70-72. [Daric.]

Drăught House. Cesspool, 2 Kgs. x. 27; Matt. xv. 17.

Drēam (*phantom*). Seriously regarded by ancients, Gen. xl. Divine method of approach, Gen. xx. 3-7; 1 Sam. xxviii. 6; Acts xxvii. 22-25. Interpretation of an exceptional gift, Gen. xl. 5-23; xli. 14-45; Dan. iv. 19-27.

Drĕss (*keeping straight*). Of leaves, Gen. iii. 7; skins, iii. 21; woolens, xxxviii. 12; Ex. xxv. 4; Lev. xiii. 47; linen, 1 Chr. iv. 21; silk, Rev. xviii. 12; mixed materials forbidden, Lev. xix. 19; colors rich, Ex. xxxv. 25; Luke xvi. 19; no sexual interchanges, Deut. xxii. 5; common inner dresses, armless shirt, second tunic, linen wrapper, Mark xiv. 51; outer, for men, woolen wrap, 2 Sam. xv. 30; Esth. vi. 12; for women, a long shawl, Ruth iii. 15; Isa. iii. 22-24; Jer. xiii. 22; girdled, Matt. xxiv. 18; Acts xii. 8; 1 Kgs. xviii. 46; poor man's bedclothes, Ex. xxii. 26, 27.

Drĭnk offering. The pouring of a small quantity of wine on the daily morning and evening sacrificial lamb, Ex. xxix. 40; Lev. xxiii. 18.

Drĭnk, Strong. Use of, not uncommon among Hebrews, Gen. ix. 21; xix. 34, 35; Ps. cvii. 27; Isa. xxiv. 20; xlix. 26; li. 17-22; John ii. 1-11; but under prohibitions, Prov. xx. 1; Isa. v. 11.

Drom'e-dā-ry (*running*). Post camel of the East, usually the one-humped species, as distinguished from the two-humped, or Bactrian, camel, 1 Kgs. iv. 28; Isa. lx. 6; Jer. ii. 23; Mic. i. 13.

Drụ-sĭl'lȧ (*watered by dew*). Daughter of Herod Agrippa I., Acts xii. 1-4, 20-23; xxiv. 24.

Dụke (*leader*). Hereditary chief or sheikh of Edom, Gen. xxxvi. 15-43.

Turtle Dove. (*See* p. 35.)

Dŭl'çi-mer (*sweet song*). The bagpipe and not the stringed dulcimer is meant, Dan. iii. 5-15.

Dụ'mah (*silence*). (1) A son of Ishmael, Gen. xxv. 14; 1 Chr. i. 30. (2) A town in Judah, Josh. xv. 52. (3) A region, Isa. xxi. 11.

Dŭng (*excrement*). Dung of cattle used for fuel, Ezek. iv. 12. Manure made from straw, Isa. xxv. 10. A fertilizer, Luke xiii. 8.

Flying Dragon.

Dŭn′geon (*tower, keep*). [PRISON.]

Du̧′râ (*circle*). A plain of Babylon, Dan. iii. 1.

Dŭst (*storm breath*). Symbol of mourning, Josh. vii. 6; Isa. xlvii. 1; feebleness, Gen. xviii. 27; Job xxx. 19; countless numbers, Gen. xiii. 16; low condition, 1 Sam. ii. 8; rage, 2 Sam. xvi. 13; Acts xxii. 23; renunciation, Matt. x. 14; Mark vi. 11; Acts xiii. 51. A sand storm, Deut. xxviii. 24.

Dwĕll′ings. [HOUSES.]

E

Ē a′gle (*dark-colored*). The eagle of Scripture is probably the griffon vulture, Mic. i. 16; Matt. xxiv. 28; Luke xvii. 37; unclean, Lev. xi. 13; Deut. xiv. 12; noted for height and rapidity of flight, Prov. xxiii. 5; 2 Sam. i. 23; Job ix. 26; Deut. xxviii. 49; Jer. iv. 13; great age, Ps. ciii. 5; care of young, Ex. xix. 4; Deut. xxxii. 11, 12; Isa. xl. 31.

Eagle.

Ē′a̧-nēs. A returned captive, 1 Esdr. ix. 21.

Ēar′ing (*plowing*). Earing time was plowing time, Gen. xlv. 6; Ex. xxxiv. 21; Deut. xxi. 4; 1 Sam. viii. 12.

Ĕarn′est (*pledge*). Pledge, Gen. xxxviii. 17; surety, Prov. xvii. 18; hostage, 2 Kgs. xiv. 14; deposit or advance, 2 Cor. i. 22; Eph. i. 14.

Ēar′rings. Included "nose-rings;" worn by both sexes; Gen. xxxv. 4; Ex. xxxii. 2; Judg. viii. 24; Job xlii. 11; offerings, Num. xxxi. 50.

Ĕarth (*producer*). The world, Gen. i. 1; dry land, i. 10; the soil, ii. 7.

Ĕarth′en-wâre. [POTTERY.]

Ĕarth′quāke (*earth-shaking*). A natural and historic phenomenon, in Am. i. 1; Zech. xiv. 5; 1 Kgs. xix. 11, 12; Matt. xxvii. 51. Token of God's wrath, Judg. v. 4; 2 Sam. xxii. 8; Ps. lxxvii. 18; xcvii. 4; civ. 32; Am. viii. 8; Hab. iii. 10.

Ēast (*dawn*). The Hebrew idea was "before" "in front of," "to the East," Gen. xxix. 1; Num. xxiii. 7; Job i. 3; Ezek. xlvii. 8; Matt. ii. 1.

Ēast′er (*Eastre, Saxon goddess*). The day commemorative of Christ's resurrection. Wrongly associated with the Saxon Eastre festival, and the Jewish Passover feast, but corrected in R. V., Acts xii. 4.

Ēast Sea. Ezek. xlvii. 18; Joel ii. 20. The Dead Sea.

Ēat. Offensive to eat or drink outside of certain limits, Gen. xliii. 32; Matt. ix. 11; John iv. 9.

Ē′bal (*stone*). (1) Son of Shobal, Gen. xxxvi. 23. (2) Son of Joktan, 1 Chr. i. 22. Obal, Gen. x. 28.

Ē′bal, Mount. The mount of curses in Samaria, Deut. xi. 29; Josh. viii. 30–35.

Ē′bed (*servant*). (1) Father of Gaal, Judg. ix. 26–35. (2) One of the returned, Ez. viii. 6.

Ē′bĕd=mē′lĕch (*king's servant*). An Ethiopian, Jer. xxxviii. 12; xxxix. 15–18.

Ĕb″en=ē′zēr (*stone of help*). A memorial stone, 1 Sam. iv. 1–5; vii. 12.

Ē′bēr (*beyond*) (1) Great-grandson of Shem, Gen. x. 24; 1 Chr. i. 19. (2) A Benjamite, 1 Chr. viii. 12. (3) A priest, Neh. xii. 20.

Ē-bī′a̧-săph (*father that adds*). A Levite, 1 Chr. vi. 23, 37.

Ĕb′ō-nȳ (*stone-like*). A hard, heavy, dark wood, used for ornamental work and musical instruments, Ezek. xxvii. 15.

Ē-brō′nah (*gateway*). A desert encampment, Num. xxxiii. 34.

Ē-cā′nus. A swift scribe, 2 Esdr. xiv. 24.

Ĕc-băt′a̧-nâ (*egress*). Greek for Achmetha, Ez. vi. 2, marg.

Ĕc-clē″si̧-ăs′tēs (*preacher*). Twenty-first book of O. T. Authorship ascribed to Solomon. An old man's confession of the vanities of life.

Ĕc-clē″si̧-ăs′ti̧-cus (*of the assembly*). The Latin name of the "Wisdom of Jesus, Son of Sirach," seventh of the Apocryphal books.

Ĕd (*witness*). A word, Josh. xxii. 34.

Ē′där (*flock*). A tower, Gen. xxxv. 21.

Ĕd-dī′as, 1 Esdr. ix. 26. [JEZIAH.]

Ē′dĕn (*pleasure*). (1) First residence of man, Gen. ii. 15. Paradise. Site not fixed. (2) A mart of Mesopotamia, 2 Kgs. xix. 12; Isa. xxxvii. 12. (3) Beth-eden, Am. i. 5. (4) A Levite, 2 Chr. xxix. 12. (5) Another Levite, 2 Chr. xxxi. 15.

Ē′dẽr (*flock*). (1) A town of Judah, Josh. xv. 21. (2) A Levite, 1 Chr. xxiii. 23; xxiv. 30.

Ē′dēs̹. 1 Esdr. ix. 35. [JADDUA.]

Ĕd′nâ. Wife of Raguel, Tob. vii. 2–16.

Ē′dom (*red*). Called also Idumea and Mount Seir. Name given to Esau, his country and people, Gen. xxxii. 3–19; xxxiii. 1–16. It lay to the south of Palestine and Moab.

Ĕd′rȩ-ī (*fortress*). (1) A capital of Bashan, Num. xxi. 33; Deut. iii. 10; Josh. xii. 4. (2) Town of northern Palestine, Josh. xix. 37.

Ĕg′lah (*heifer*). A wife of David, 2 Sam. iii. 5; 1 Chr. iii. 3.

Ĕg′la̧-ĭm (*ponds*). A place in Moab, Isa. xv. 8.

Ĕg′lŏn (*calf-like*). (1) A King of Moab, Judg. iii. 12–23. (2) A lowland town of Judah, Josh. x. 3–5; xv. 39.

Ē′ġȳpt (*Coptic land*). Northeastern country of Africa; the Hebrew "Mizraim," Gen. x. 6, and

"Land of Ham," Ps. cv. 23, 27. Bondage place of Israelites, Ex. i.-xiv. Noted for Nile river, rich soil and gigantic ruins. Ancient religion monotheistic, with sun as central object; and attributes of nature in form of trinities. Vast temples and numerous priests. Kings called Pharaohs, who perpetuated their reigns in obelisks, temples, sculptures, sphinxes, pyramids, etc. In intimate commerce with Hebrews, 1 Kgs. iii. 1. Conquered Judea, 1 Kgs. xiv. 25, 26. Frequently mentioned in Scripture.

Sphinx. (*See* Egypt.)

Ē′hī, Gen. xlvi. 21. [AHIRAM.]

Ē′hŭd (*united*). (1) Son of Bilhan, 1 Chr. vii. 10. (2) A judge of Israel, Judg. iii. 15-21.

Ē′kẽr (*tearing up*). A Judahite, 1 Chr. ii. 27.

Ĕk′rē-bel. A place in Esdraelon, Judith vii. 18.

Ĕk′rŏn (*migration*). One of the five Philistine cities, Josh. xiii. 3; xv. 45; xix. 43; 1 Sam. v. 10.

Ĕk′rŏn-ītes. Inhabitants of Ekron, Josh. xiii. 3.

Ē′lȧ, 1 Esdr. ix. 27. [ELAM.]

Ĕl′ā-dah (*eternity of God*). An Ephraimite, 1 Chr. vii. 20.

Ē′lah (*oak*). (1) Son and successor of Baasha on the throne of Israel, B. C. 928-27, 1 Kgs. xvi. 8-10. (2) Father of Hosea, 2 Kgs. xv. 30; xvii. 1. (3) A duke of Edom, Gen. xxxvi. 41. (4) Father of Solomon's commissary, 1 Kgs. iv. 18. (5) Son of Caleb, 1 Chr. iv. 15. (6) A chief of Benjamin, 1 Chr. ix. 8. (7) The valley in which David slew Goliath, 1 Sam. xvii. 2-19.

Ē′lăm (*age*). (1) Son of Shem, Gen. x. 22, and his country, xiv. 1-9; Dan. viii. 2, in Mesopotamia. (2) A chief of Benjamin, 1 Chr. viii. 24. (3) A Korhite Levite, 1 Chr. xxvi. 3. (4) Persons whose children returned, Ez. ii. 7, 31; Neh. vii. 12, 34. (5) A priest, Neh. x. 14.

Ē′lăm-ītes. Inhabitants of Elam, Ez. iv. 9.

Ĕl′a-sah (*whom God made*). (1) A priest, Ez. x. 22. (2) Son of Shaphan, Jer. xxix. 3.

Ē′lăth, E′lŏth (*oaks*). A city of Edom, Deut. ii. 8; Seat of Solomon's navy, 1 Kgs. ix. 26; 2 Chr. viii. 17.

Ĕl=bĕth′=el (*God of Bethel*). Place where God appeared to Jacob, Gen. xxxv. 7.

Ĕl′çĭ-ȧ. Progenitor of Judith, Judith viii. 1.

Ĕl′da-ah (*called of God*). Last son of Midian, Gen. xxv. 4; 1 Chr. i. 33.

Ĕl′dăd (*loved of God*). One of the seventy assistants of Moses, Num. xi. 16, 26-29.

Ĕl′dẽr (*old man*). Highest in tribal authority, Gen. xxiv. 2; l. 7; Ex. iii. 16; iv. 29; Num. xxii. 7. One of the 70 justiciars, Num. xi. 25, or Sanhedrim, Judg. ii. 7; 2 Sam. xvii. 4; Jer. xxix. 1. An official in early Christian church, like presbyter or bishop, Acts xx. 17, 28.

Ē′le-ăd (*praised of God*). An Ephraimite, 1 Chr. vii. 21.

Ē″le-ā′leh (*ascent of God*). A Moabite town, assigned to Reuben, Num. xxxii. 3, 37; Isa. xv. 4; Jer. xlviii. 34.

Ē-lē′a-sȧ. A place near Ashdod, 1 Macc. ix. 5-18.

Ē-lē′a-sah (*made by God*). (1) A Judahite, 1 Chr. ii. 39. (2) A descendant of Saul, 1 Chr. viii. 37; ix. 43.

Ē″le-ā′zar (*help of God*). (1) Third son of Aaron, Ex. vi. 23. Chief of the Levites, Num. iii. 32; and high priest, Num. xx. 28. (2) Son of Abinadab, 1 Sam. vii. 1. (3) One of David's mighty men, 2 Sam. xxiii. 9; 1 Chr. xi. 12. (4) A Levite, 1 Chr. xxiii. 21. (5) A priest, Neh. xii. 42. (6) Son of Phinehas, Ez. viii. 33. (7) Son of Parosh, Ez. x. 25. (8) Surnamed Avaran, 1 Macc. vi. 43. (9) A scribe, 2 Macc. vi. 18. (10) Father of Jason, 1 Macc. viii. 17. (11) Son of Eliud, Matt. i. 15.

Ē″le-ȧ-zū′rus, 1 Esdr. ix. 24. [ELIASHIB.]

Ē-lĕct′ (*chosen out*). One called to everlasting life; the saved collectively, Matt. xxiv. 22; Mark xiii. 27; Luke xviii. 7; Rom. viii. 33; Tit. i. 1. The "elect lady," 2 John i. 1, probably refers to the Christian church.

Ĕl=e-lō′hē=Ĭs′ra-el (*strength of the God of Israel*). Name of Jacob's altar, Gen. xxxiii. 19, 20.

Ē′leph (*ox*). A town of Benjamin, Josh. xviii. 28.

Ĕl′e-phănt (*ox*). The Hebrew *eleph* means an ox, 1 Kgs. x. 22; 2 Chr. ix. 21; Job xl. 15, margins.

Ē-leu′thĕ-rus. A Syrian river, 1 Macc. xi. 7.

Ĕl-hā′nan (*grace of God*). (1) A noted Hebrew warrior, 2 Sam. xxi. 19; 1 Chr. xx. 5. (2) One of David's body-guard, 2 Sam. xxiii. 24.

Pyramids of Gizeh. (*See* Egypt.)

Ē′lī (*going up*). A descendant of Aaron, Lev. x. 12. First of a line of high priests, 1 Sam. i. 9-17; ii. 22-36; iii. 1-14; and Judge of Israel for 40 years, iv. 14-18. Line extinguished, 1 Kgs. ii. 26, 27.

Ē′lī, Ē′lī, lā′mȧ sā-băch-thā′nī. The Lord's cry upon the cross, Matt. xxvii. 46; Mark xv. 34, "My God, my God, why hast thou forsaken me?" Ps. xxii. 1.

Ē-lī′ab (*God is father*). (1) A Chief of Zebulun,

Num. i. 9. (2) A Reubenite, Num. xxvi. 8, 9. (3) A Levite musician, 1 Chr. xv. 18-20. (4) Eldest brother of David, 1 Chr. ii. 13. (5) A Gadite leader, 1 Chr. xii. 9. (6) An ancestor of Samuel, 1 Chr. vi. 27. (7) Son of Nathaniel, Judith viii. 1.

Ē-lī'a-dȧ (*known of God*). (1) A younger son of David, 2 Sam. v. 16; 1 Chr. iii. 8. (2) A Benjamite general, 2 Chr. xvii. 17.

Ē-lī'a-dah. Father of Rezon, 1 Kgs. xi. 23-25.

Ē-lī'ah (*God the Lord*). (1) A Benjamite chief, 1 Chr. viii. 27. (2) One of the returned, Ez. x. 26.

Ē-lī'ah-bȧ (*hidden by God*). One of David's guard, 2 Sam. xxiii. 32; 1 Chr. xi. 33.

Ē-lī'a-kĭm (*raised of God*). (1) Master of Hezekiah's household, 2 Kgs. xviii. 18-37; Isa. xxxvi. 3. (2) Original name of King Jehoiakim, 2 Kgs. xxiii. 34; 2 Chr. xxxvi. 4. (3) A priest, Neh. xii. 41. (4) Forefather of Joseph, Matt. i. 13. (5) Father of Jonan, Luke iii. 30, 31.

Ē-lī'a-lī, 1 Esdr. ix. 34. [Binnui.]

Ē-lī'ăm (*God's people*). (1) Father of Bathsheba, 2 Sam. xi. 3. (2) One of David's warriors, 2 Sam. xxiii. 34.

Ē-lī'as. N. T. form of Elijah. [Elijah.]

Ē-lī'a-săph (*God increaseth*). (1) Chief of Dan, Num. i. 14, ii. 14; vii. 42; x. 20. (2) A Levite chief, Num. iii. 24.

Ē-lī'a-shib (*restored of God*). (1) Eleventh priest of "order of governors," 1 Chr. xxiv. 12. (2) A Judahite, 1 Chr. iii. 24. (3) High priest, Neh. iii. 1-21. (4) Three of the returned, Ez. x. 24, 27, 36.

Ē-lī'a-thah (*to whom God comes*). Leader of the twentieth temple course, 1 Chr. xxv. 4, 27.

Ē-lī'dad (*beloved of God*). A Benjamite, Num. xxxiv. 21.

Ē-lī'el (*God, my God*). (1) A chief of Manasseh, 1 Chr. v. 24. (2) A forefather of Samuel, 1 Chr. vi. 34. (3, 4) Two chiefs of Benjamin, 1 Chr. viii. 20, 22. (5, 6) Two heroes of David's guard, 1 Chr. xi. 46, 47. (7) A Gadite, 1 Chr. xii. 11. (8) A Levite, 1 Chr. xv. 9-11. (9) Overseer of Temple offerings, 2 Chr. xxxi. 13.

Ē'lī-ē'na-ī (*eyes toward God*). A chief of Benjamin, 1 Chr. viii. 20.

Ē'lī-ē'zĕr (*help of God*). Servant of Abraham, Gen. xv. 2, 3. (2) Second son of Moses, Ex. xviii. 4; 1 Chr. xxiii. 15-17; xxvi. 25. (3) A chief of Benjamin, 1 Chr. vii. 8. (4) A priest, 1 Chr. xv. 24. (5) A Reubenite chief, 1 Chr. xxvii. 16. (6) A prophet, 2 Chr. xx. 37. (7) Messenger of Ezra, Ez. viii. 16. (8, 9, 10) Returned Jews, Ez. x. 18, 23, 31. (11) Ancestor of Christ, Luke iii. 29.

Ĕl''i-hō-ē'nă-ī (*eyes toward God*). A returned leader, Ez. viii. 4.

Ĕl''i-hō'reph (*God his reward*). A scribe, 1 Kgs. iv. 3.

Ē-lī'hū (*God is his*). (1) A forefather of Samuel, 1 Sam. i. 1. (2) Eldest brother of David, 1 Chr. xxvii. 18. (3) A captain of Manasseh, 1 Chr. xii. 20. (4) A Levite door-keeper, 1 Chr. xxvi. 7. (5) One of Job's friends, Job xxxii. 2.

Ē-lī'jah (*God is God*). (1) The prophet; Elias in N. T., Matt. xvii. 3. A Tishbite of Gilead; appears suddenly; is fed by ravens; restores the widow's son, 1 Kgs. xvii. 1-24; invokes fire on the prophets of Baal, xviii. 17-40; anoints Hazael, Jehu, and Elisha, xix.; denounces Ahab and Jezebel, xxi. 17-24; is translated in a chariot of fire, 2 Kgs. ii.; reappears on the mount of Transfiguration, Luke ix. 28-35. (2) A son of Harim, Ez. x. 21.

Elephant. (*See* p. 38.)

Ĕl'i-kȧ (*rejected of God*). One of David's guard, 2 Sam. xxiii. 25.

Ē'lĭm (*oaks*). Second encampment of the Israelites after crossing the Red Sea, Ex. xv. 27; Num. xxxiii. 9.

Ē-lĭm'ĕ-lech (*my God is king*). Husband of Naomi, Ruth i. 1-3.

Ĕl''i-ō-ē'nă-ī (*eyes toward God*). (1) A descendant of David, 1 Chr. iii. 23, 24. (2) A Simeonite, 1 Chr. iv. 36. (3) A Levite door-keeper, 1 Chr. xxvi. 3. (4) A Benjamite, 1 Chr. vii. 8. (5) Two priests, Ez. x. 22, 27.

Ĕl-i-ō'nas, 1 Esdr. ix. 22-32. [Elioenai.]

Ĕl'ī-phal (*judged of God*). Son of Ur, 1 Chr. xi. 35. Eliphelet, 2 Sam. xxiii. 34.

Ē-lĭph'a-lĕt (*God of deliverance*). A son of David, 2 Sam. v. 16; 1 Chr. xiv. 7.

Ĕl'ī-phăz (*God his strength*). (1) A son of Esau, Gen. xxxvi. 4; 1 Chr. i. 35, 36. (2) One of Job's friends, Job iv., v., xv., xxii.

Ē'lĭph'e-leh (*who exalts God*). A harper, 1 Chr. xv. 18-21.

Ē-lĭph'e-lĕt (*God of deliverance*). (1) One of David's warriors, 2 Sam. xxiii. 34. (2) Name of two sons of David, 1 Chr. iii. 6, 8. (3) A descendant of Saul, 1 Chr. viii. 39. (4) Two of the returned, Ez. viii. 13; x. 33.

Ē-lĭs'a-bĕth (*oath of God*). Wife of Zacharias, Luke i. 36-80.

Ĕl''ī-sē'us. Greek form of Elisha, Luke iv. 27.

Ē-lī'shȧ (*God his salvation*). Anointed prophet by Elijah, 1 Kgs. xix. 16-21. Prophesied in reigns of Jehoram, Jehu, Jehoahaz and Joash, a period of sixty years. Life and works in 2 Kgs. ii.-ix.; xiii. 14-21.

Ē-lī'shah (*God saves*). Eldest son of Javan, Gen. x. 4; Ezek. xxvii. 7.

Ē-lĭsh'a-mȧ (*whom God hears*). (1) Grandfather of Joshua, Num. i. 10. (2) Two sons of David, 2 Sam. v. 16; 1 Chr. iii. 6, 8. (3) A priest, 2 Chr. xvii. 8. (4) A Judahite, 1 Chr. ii. 41. (5) Grandfather of Ishmael, 2 Kgs. xxv. 25. (6) A scribe, Jer. xxxvi. 12, 20-21. (7) A priest, 2 Chr. xvii. 8.

Ē-lĭsh'a-phăt (*whom God judges*). Captain of a hundred, 2 Chr. xxiii. 1.

Ē-lish'e-bȧ (*God her oath*). Wife of Aaron, Ex. vi. 23.

Ĕl″ĭ-shu̱′ȧ. A son of David, 2 Sam. v. 15; 1 Chr. xiv. 5. Elishama, 1 Chr. iii. 6–8.

Ē-lĭs′ĭ-mus, 1 Esdr. ix. 28. [ELIASHIB.]

Ē-lī′ū. A forefather of Judith, Judith viii. 1.

Ē-lī′ŭd (*God my praise*). Ancestor of Joseph, Matt. i. 15.

Ē-lĭz′a̱-phan (*protected of God*). (1) A Levite chief, Num. iii. 30; 1 Chr. xv. 8. Elzaphan, Ex. vi. 22; Lev. x. 4. (2) A chief of Zebulun, Num. xxxiv. 25.

Ē-lī′zŭr (*God his rock*). A prince of Reuben, Num. i. 5; ii. 10.

Ĕl′kă-nah, Ĕl′kō-nah (*provided of God*). (1) Grandson of Korah, Ex. vi. 24; 1 Chr. vi. 23. (2) Another descendant of Korah, 1 Chr. vi. 26, 35. (3) Another Levite, 1 Chr. vi. 27, 34; 1 Sam. i. 1–23; ii. 11, 20. (4) A Levite, 1 Chr. ix. 16. (5) A Korhite, 1 Chr. xii. 6. (6) An officer under Ahaz, 2 Chr. xxviii. 7.

Ĕl′kosh (*my bow is of God*). Modern Alkush on the Tigris, Nahum i. 1.

Ĕl′la̱-sär (*oak*). City of King Arioch, Gen. xiv. 1–9.

Ĕlm, Hosea iv. 13; elsewhere translated "oak."

Ĕl-mō′dăm (*measure*). Son of Er. Elmadam in R. V., Luke iii. 28.

Ĕl′na-a̱m (*God his delight*). Father of two of David's guard, 1 Chr. xi. 46.

Ĕl′na̱-than (*gift of God*). (1) Grandfather of Jehoiachin, 2 Kgs. xxiv. 8; Jer. xxvi. 22. (2) Names of three Levites, Ez. viii. 16.

Ē-lō′ī, Ē-lō′hī, Ĕl′ō-him. God. Eloi is also Aramaic form of Elias, or Elijah, Mark xv. 34.

Ē′lon (*oak*). (1) A Hittite, Gen. xxvi. 34; xxxvi. 2. (2) A son of Zebulun, Gen. xlvi. 14; Num. xxvi. 26. (3) A Zebulunite, Judg. xii. 11, 12. (4) A town of Dan, Josh. xix. 43.

Ē′lon-bĕth-hā″năn (*oak of house of grace*). Part of one of Solomon's commissary districts, 1 Kgs. iv. 9.

Ē′lŏn-ītes, Num. xxvi. 26. [ELON, 2.]

Ē′lŏth, 1 Kgs. ix. 26; 2 Chr. viii. 17; xxvi. 2. [ELATH.]

Ĕl′pă-al (*wages of God*). A Benjamite, 1 Chr. viii. 11, 12.

Ĕl′pa-let, 1 Chr. xiv. 5. [ELIPHELET, 2.]

Ĕl-pā′ran. Oak of Paran, Gen. xiv. 6. [PARAN.]

Ĕl′te̱-keh (*fear of God*). A city of Dan, Josh. xix. 44; xxi. 23.

Ĕl′te̱-kon (*founded by God*). A town in Judah, Josh. xv. 59.

Ĕl′to-lăd (*kindred of God*). A city of Judah, and Simeon, Josh. xv. 30; xix. 4; Tolad, 1 Chr. iv. 29.

Ē′lŭl (*vine*). Twelfth month of Hebrew civil, and sixth of sacred, year, corresponding to parts of September and October. Neh. vi. 15.

Ē-lū′za-ī (*God my praise*). A Benjamite warrior, 1 Chr. xii. 5.

Ĕl″y̆-mæ′ans, Judith i. 6. [ELAMITES.]

Ĕl′y̆-măs (*wise*). Arabic name of Bar-jesus, Acts xiii. 6–12.

Ĕl′za̱-băd (*gift of God*). (1) A Gadite, 1 Chr. xii. 12. (2) A Korhite Levite, 1 Chr. xxvi. 7.

Ĕl′za̱-phăn (*protected by God*). Second son of Uzziel, Ex. vi. 22; Lev. x. 4; 2 Chr. xxix. 13. Elizaphan in Num. iii. 30; 1 Chr. xv. 8.

Embroidered Robe.

Ĕm-bälm′ (*to put in balsam*). Embalming carried to great perfection by the Egyptians, whom the Jews feebly imitated, Gen. l. 2–26.

Ĕm-broi′der (*to work a border*) Ex. xxviii. 39; xxxv. 35; xxxviii. 23. Possibly nothing beyond the common weaver's art is meant. "Cunning work," Ex. xxvi. 1, implies embroidery.

Ĕm′ĕr-ăld. A bright green variety of beryl. The emerald of Ex. xxviii. 18; xxxix. 11; Ezek. xxvii. 16; xxviii. 13; Rev. iv. 3; xxi. 19, is supposably the carbuncle, a fiery garnet.

Ĕm′ē-rŏds (*flowing with blood*). Hemorrhoids or piles, Deut. xxviii. 27; 1 Sam. v. 6–12; vi. 4–11.

Ē′mĭms (*terrors*). A race of Anakim east of Dead Sea, Gen. xiv. 5; Deut. ii. 10, 11.

Ĕm-măn′ū-el, Matt. i. 23. [IMMANUEL.]

Ĕm′ma̱-us (*warm springs*). A village of Palestine, 7½ mls. from Jerusalem, Luke xxiv. 13–33.

Ĕm′mer, 1 Esdr. ix. 21. [IMMER.]

Ĕm′môr (*ass*), Acts vii. 16. [HAMOR.]

Ĕn. A fountain. Used in compounds.

Ĕn-ā′bled. Qualified, 1 Tim. i. 12.

Ē′nam (*two fountains*). A city of Judah, Josh. xv. 34.

Mummy.

Ē′nan (*eyes*). A prince of Naphtali, Num. i. 15; ii. 29; vii. 78, 83; x. 27.

Ē-năs′i̱-bus, 1 Esdr. ix. 34. [ELIASHIB.]

Ĕn-cămp′ment (*field*). Halting place of army or caravan, Ex. xiv. 19; xvi. 13; Num. ii., iii.; Josh. x. 5.

Ĕn-chănt′ment (*song-spell*). Enchantments unlawful, Lev. xix. 26; Deut. xviii. 10–12; as Egyptian trickery, Ex. vii. 11–22; viii. 7; Balaam's omens, Num. xxiv. 1; muttered spells, 2 Kgs. ix. 22; Mic. v. 12; Nah. iii. 4; serpent charming, Eccl. x. 11; magical spells, Isa. xlvii. 9–12; auguries, Jer. xxvii. 9. [DIVINATION.]

Ĕn′-dôr (*fountain of Dor*). A village of Manasseh, Josh. xvii. 11; Ps. lxxxiii. 9, 10; 1 Sam. xxviii.

Ĕn-eg′la̱-ĭm (*fountain of two calves*). An unknown place, Ezek. xlvii. 10.

Ĕn″ē-mĕs′sär. Shalmaneser, Tob. i. 2, 15.

Ē-nē′nĭ-us. A returned leader, 1 Esdr. v. 8.

Ĕn-găd′dī, Ecclus. xxiv. 14. [ENGEDI.]

Ĕn-găn′nĭm (*fount of the garden*). (1) A city of Judah, Josh. xv. 34. (2) A Levitical city, Josh. xix. 21; xxi. 29.

Ĕn-ḡē′dī (*fount of the kid*). A town on west shore of Dead Sea, Josh. xv. 62; Ezek. xlvii. 10; 1 Sam. xxiv. 1–7; S. of Sol. i. 14. Hazezon-tamar, Gen. xiv. 7; 2 Chr. xx. 2.

Ĕn′ḡĭne (*skilled product*). The ballista for throwing spears, arrows, stones, 2 Chr. xxvi. 15; the catapult, Ezek. xxvi. 9; battering ram, Ezek. iv. 2; xxi. 22.

Ĕn-grā′vĕr (*digger in*). The commandments were engraved, Ex. xxxii. 16; also stones and signets, Ex. xxviii. 11, 21, 36; Job xix. 24; Acts xvii. 29. Graven images were objects of idolatry, Ex. xx. 4; xxxii. 4.

Ĕn-hăd′dah (*fountain*). A city of Issachar, Josh. xix. 21.

Ĕn-hak′kō-rē (*fount of the caller*). Samson's fountain, Judg. xv. 19.

Ĕn-hā′zôr (*fount of Hazor*). A fenced city in Naphtali, Josh. xix. 37.

Ĕn=mish'pat (*fount of judgment*). Gen. xiv. 7. [KADESH.]

Ē'nŏch (*dedicated*). (1) A son of Cain, Gen. iv. 17. (2) Father of Methuselah, Gen. v. 18–24; Heb. xi. 5–13; Jude 14. (3) "Behemoth," 2 Esdr. vi. 49–51.

Ē'non (*springs*). John i. 28; iii. 23. [ÆNON.]

Ē'nos (*mortal*). Son of Seth, Gen. iv. 26; v. 6–11; Luke iii. 38. Enosh, 1 Chr. i. 1.

Ē'nosh, 1 Chr. i. 1. [ENOS.]

Ĕn=rĭm'mon (*fount of the pomegranate*). A settlement of returned Jews, Neh. xi. 29.

Ĕn=rō'gel (*fuller's fount*). A celebrated spring, Josh. xv. 7; xviii. 16; 2 Sam. xvii. 17; 1 Kgs. i. 9.

Ĕn=shē'mesh (*fount of the sun*). A spring, Josh. xv. 7; xviii. 17.

Ĕn'sīgn (*mark upon*). A simple device, elevated on a pole, bearing some emblem to distinguish the tribes and army divisions, Num. i. 52; S. of Sol. ii. 4; Isa. xiii. 2; xviii. 3.

Roman Standard Bearer.

Ĕn-sūe'. Pursue, 1 Pet. iii. 11.

Ĕn=tăp'pu-ah (*fount of the apple*). Tappuah in Manasseh, Josh. xvii. 7.

Ĕp'a-phrăs (*lovely*). A Roman friend of Paul, Col. i. 7; iv. 12.

Ē-pæn'ĕ-tus (*praised*). A Christian at Rome, Rom. xvi. 5.

Ē-păph"ro-dī'tus (*lovely*). Probably Epaphras, Phil. ii. 25; iv. 18.

Ē'phah (*gloomy*). (1) First son of Midian, Gen. xxv. 4; 1 Chr. i. 33; Isa. lx. 6. (2) Caleb's concubine, 1 Chr. ii. 46. (3) A Judahite, 1 Chr. ii. 47. (4) A Hebrew dry measure, estimated at 2¼ to 3¼ pecks, Ruth ii. 17; Num. v. 15. (5) A Hebrew liquid measure equal to 7½ gallons.

Ē'phāi (*gloomy*). His sons were captains left behind in Judah, Jer xl. 8.

Ē'pher (*calf*). (1) A son of Midian, Gen. xxv. 4; 1 Kgs. iv. 10. (2) A son of Ezra, 1 Chr. iv. 17. A chief of Manasseh, 1 Chr. v. 24.

Ē'phes=dam'mim (*border of blood*). A Philistine encampment, 1 Sam. xvii. 1. Pasdammim, 1 Chr. xi. 13. [ELAH.]

Ē-phē'șianș. (1) Inhabitants of Ephesus, Acts xix. 28. (2) Epistle to, written by Paul to the Christians at Ephesus, about A. D. 61 or 62, and while he was a prisoner at Rome. Forwarded by Tychicus, Eph. vi. 21. Of general import.

Ĕph'ĕ-sŭs (*desirable*). Capital of Ionia, on the Ægean Sea. Noted for its commerce, learning, and architecture. Paul visited it, Acts xviii. 1–20, and founded a church there, to which he addressed one of his best epistles, Acts xix. 1–10; xx. 17–38.

Ĕph'lăl (*judgment*). A Judahite, 1 Chr. ii. 37.

Ĕph'ŏd (*clothe*). (1) A sleeveless linen garment for priests, covering breast and back, Ex. xxviii. 4–35; 1 Sam. xxii. 18, with onyx clasp at shoulder, and breastplate at breast, crossing. Worn later by other than priests, 1 Chr. xv. 27. [BREASTPLATE.] (2) A Manassite, Num. xxxiv. 23.

Ĕph'phă-thȧ (*be opened*). Christ's utterance in Mark vii. 34.

Ē'phră-ĭm (*doubly fruitful*). (1) Second son of Joseph, Gen. xli. 52. Obtained Jacob's blessing, Gen. xlviii. 8–20. Tribe numerous, Num. i. 33; xxvi. 37. Allotment as in Josh. xvi. 1–10. (2) Site of Absalom's sheep-farm, 2 Sam. xiii. 23. (3) Place to which Christ retired, John xi. 54. (4) A gate of Jerusalem, 2 Kgs. xiv. 13; 2 Chr. xxv. 23; Neh. viii. 16; xii. 39. (5) "Mount of," in Ephraim, 1 Sam. i. 1. (6) "The wood of," east of Jordan, 2 Sam. xviii. 6.

Ē'phră-ĭm-ītes". Members of the tribe of Ephraim, Judg. xii. 5. Sometimes Ephrathites.

Ē'phră-ĭn (*doubly fruitful*). A city of Israel, 2 Chr. xiii. 19.

Ĕph'ra-tah, Ĕph'rath (*fruitful*). (1) Second wife of Caleb, 1 Chr. ii. 19, 50. (2) Ancient name of Bethlehem-judah, Gen. xxxv. 16, 19; xlviii. 7.

Ĕph'rath-ītes. (1) Inhabitants of Bethlehem, or Ephrath, Ruth i. 2. (2) Ephraimites, Judg. xii. 5; 1 Sam. i. 1; 1 Kgs. xi. 26.

Ĕph'ron (*fawn-like*). (1) A Hittite who sold Machpelah to Abraham, Gen. xxiii. 8–20; xlix. 29; l. 13. (2) Landmarks of Judah, Josh. xv. 9. (3) A city east of Jordan, 1 Macc. v. 46–52.

Ĕp"ĭ-cū-rē'anș (*followers of Epicurus*). A sect of pleasure-loving philosophers at Athens, Acts xvii. 18.

Ē-pĭph'a-nēș, 1 Macc. i. 10. [ANTIOCHUS, 4.]

Ē-pĭs'tle (*sending to*). In O. T. a letter, 2 Sam. xi. 14; 2 Kgs. v. 5, 6; 2 Chr. xxi. 12; Ez. iv. 6–11. In N. T., a formal tract containing Christian doctrine and salutary advice.

Ĕr (*watchman*). (1) First-born of Judah, Gen. xxxviii. 3–7; Num. xxvi. 19. (2) A descendant of Shelah, 1 Chr. iv. 21. (3) Son of Jose, Luke iii. 28.

Ē'răn (*watchful*). Founder of the Eranites, Num. xxvi. 36.

Ē-răs'tŭs (*beloved*). (1) A friend of Paul at Ephesus, Acts xix. 22; 2 Tim. iv. 20. (2) A Corinthian convert, Rom. xvi. 23.

Ē′rĕch (*healthy*). A city of Shinar, Gen. x. 10.

Ē′rī (*watching*). A son of Gad, Gen. xlvi. 16, and founder of the Erites, Num. xxvi. 16.

Ē-şā′ias. N. T. name of Isaiah, Matt. iii. 3.

Ē″sar-hăd′don (*conqueror*). A king of Assyria, 2 Kgs. xix. 37; 2 Chr. xxxiii. 11. He united Babylon to Assyria and reigned over both B. C. 680–667.

Ē′şau (*hairy*). Eldest son of Isaac and twin brother of Jacob, Gen. xxv. 25. Called also Edom. Sold his birthright to Jacob, Gen. xxv. 26–34; xxxvi. 1–10. Gave his name, Edom, to a country and to his descendants, Gen. xxvi., xxxvi. [EDOM.]

Ē′say, Ecclus. xlviii. 20–22. [ISAIAH.]

Eş″dra-ē′lon. Greek for Jezreel, Judith iii. 9; iv. 6.

Ĕş′dras. (1) A scribe in 1 and 2 Esdras. (2) First and second books of the Apocrypha. First a supplement to Ezra; second a series of visions.

Ē′sĕk (*strife*). A well in Gerar, Gen. xxvi. 20.

Ĕsh=bā′al (*Baal's man*). Ishbosheth, Saul's fourth son, 1 Chr. viii. 33; ix. 39.

Ĕsh′băn (*wise man*). Son of Dishon, Gen. xxxvi. 26; 1 Chr. i. 41.

Ĕsh′cŏl (*bunch of grapes*). (1) Brother of Mamre, Gen. xiv. 13–24. (2) A valley or brook near Hebron, Num. xiii. 22–27; xxxii. 9; Deut. i. 24.

Ē′shĕ-an (*slope*). A city of Judah, Josh. xv. 52.

Ē′shĕk (*oppression*). A descendant of Saul, 1 Chr. viii. 39.

Ĕsh′ka-lŏn-ītes″, Josh. xiii. 3. [ASHKELON.]

Ĕsh′tă-ŏl (*a way*). Town in Judah and Dan, Josh. xv. 33; xix. 41; burial place of Samson, Judg. xiii. 25; xvi. 31; xviii. 2–11.

Ĕsh′tă-ul-ītes″. Families of Kirjath-jearim, 1 Chr. ii. 53.

Ĕsh″te-mō′ȧ, Ĕsh′te-mōh (*bosom of a woman*). A Levitical town of Judah, Josh. xv. 50; xxi. 14; 1 Sam. xxx. 28.

Ĕsh′ton (*weak*). A Judahite, 1 Chr. iv. 11, 12.

Ĕs′lī (*reserved*). Ancestor of Joseph, Luke iii. 25.

Ē-sō′rȧ. Hazor or Zorah, Judith iv. 4.

Ĕs-pouşe′ (*promise*). [BETROTH.]

Ĕs′rom, Matt. i. 3; Luke iii. 33. [HEZRON.]

Ĕs-sēne′ (*priest*). Member of a Jewish ascetic sect, the Essenes.

Ĕs-tāte′ (*standing*). In Mark vi. 21, a class or order representing the government. The "estate of the elders," Acts xxii. 5, was a body of advisers cooperating with the Sanhedrim.

Ĕs′thẽr (*star*). Persian name of Hadassah, Mordecai's cousin, who married King Ahasuerus, and saved the lives of her countrymen. Her book, seventeenth of O. T., tells her story.

Ē′tam (*lair*). (1) A village in Simeon, 1 Chr. iv. 32. (2) Favorite resort of Solomon, 2 Chr. xi. 6; Judg. xv. 8–19. (3) A doubtful name, 1 Chr. iv. 3.

Ē′tham (*sea bound*). An Israelite encampment, Ex. xiii. 20; Num. xxxiii. 6–8.

Ē′than (*strong*). (1) One noted for wisdom, 1 Kgs. iv. 31; 1 Chr. ii. 6; title to Ps. lxxxix. (2) A Levite singer, 1 Chr. vi. 44; xv. 17–19. (3) An ancestor of Asaph, 1 Chr. vi. 42.

Ĕth′a-nīm (*flowing*). Seventh month (Tisri) of Jewish sacred, and first of civil, year; corresponding to parts of Sept. and Oct., 1 Kgs. viii. 2.

Ĕth′bā-al (*favored of Baal*). King of Sidon, 1 Kgs. xvi. 31.

Ē′thẽr (*plenty*). Town in Judah and Simeon, Josh. xv. 42; xix. 7.

Ē″thī-ō′pī-ȧ (*burnt faces*). Greek and Roman for Hebrew "Cush." The unbounded country south of Egypt, Ezek. xxix. 10; settled by Hamites, Gen. x. 6; merchants, Isa. xlv. 14; Jer. xiii. 23; Job xxviii. 19; wealthy, Acts viii. 27–37; strongly military, 2 Chr. xii. 3; xiv. 9–12; 2 Kgs. xvii. 4.

Ē″thī-ō′pī-anş. Dwellers in Ethiopia; Cushites, Num. xii. 1; 2 Chr. xiv. 9; Jer. xxxviii. 7; xxxix. 16; Acts viii. 27–37.

Ĕth′nan (*hire*). A Judahite, 1 Chr. iv. 5–7.

Ĕth′nī (*liberal*). A Levite, 1 Chr. vi. 41.

Eū-bū′lus (*prudent*). A Roman Christian, 2 Tim. iv. 21.

Eū-ẽr′gĕ-teş (*benefactor*). A common Grecian surname, and title of honor; applied especially to the Ptolemies.

Eū′nă-tan, 1 Esdr. viii. 44. [ELNATHAN.]

Eū′nīçe (*good victory*). Mother of Timothy, Acts xvi. 1; 2 Tim. i. 5.

Eū′nŭch (*couch guardian*). A castrated male. Eunuchs became court officials, 2 Kgs. ix. 32; Esth. ii. 3; Acts viii. 27; could not enter the congregation, Deut. xxiii. 1. A celibate, Matt. xix. 12.

Eū-ō′dī-as (*fragrant*). Euodia in R. V.; a Christian woman of Philippi, Phil. iv. 2.

Eū-phrā′teş (*fructifying*). A great river of western Asia, rising in Armenia and emptying into the Persian Gulf. Boundary of Eden, Gen. ii. 14; "great river," Gen. xv. 18; Deut. i. 7; eastern boundary of the promised land, Deut. xi. 24; Josh. i. 4; 1 Chr. v. 9; and of David's conquests, 2 Sam. viii. 3; 1 Chr. xviii. 3. *See* also, Jer. xiii. 4–7; xlvi. 2–10; li. 63; Ps. cxxxvii. 1; Rev. ix. 14; xvi. 12.

Eū-pŏl′e-mus. An envoy, 1 Macc. viii. 17.

Eū-rŏc′lȳ-don. A stormy northeast wind of the Levant, Acts xxvii. 14.

Eū′tȳ-chus (*fortunate*). A sleepy youth of Troas, Acts xx. 6–12.

Ē-văn′ġĕl-ĭst (*publisher of glad tidings*). One of the four writers of the gospels Matthew, Mark, Luke and John. A preacher of the gospel inferior in authority to the Apostles, Acts viii. 14–19, and apparently to the prophets, Eph. iv. 11, yet superior to the pastor and teacher, Acts xxi. 8; Eph. iv. 11; 2 Tim. iv. 5. A travelling and corresponding missionary, Acts xx. 4, 5.

Ēve (*life*). The first woman; made *of* man and *for* him, Gen. ii. 18–25; iii.–iv.

Ēve′nĭng (*decline of day*). Two evenings recognized, one before, the other after, sunset, Gen. xxiv. 63; Ex. xii. 6; Num. ix. 3; xxviii. 4.

Ē′vī (*desire*). A King of Midian, Num. xxxi. 8; Josh. xiii. 21.

Ē′vīl=mē-rō′dach (*fool of Merodach*). King of Babylon, B. C. 561–559, 2 Kgs. xxv. 27; Jer. lii. 31–34.

Ĕx″cŏm-mū″nī-cā′tion (*putting out of the community*). Threefold in Jewry. (1) Temporary suspension. (2) Further temporary suspension. (3) Final cutting off. Now rests on Matt. xvi. 19; xviii. 17; 1 Cor. v. 11; 2 Cor. ii. 5–11; 1 Cor. i. 20; Tit. iii. 10.

Ĕx″ē-cū′tion-ẽr (*a follower out*). In O. T. a position of dignity, Gen. xxxvii. 36, marg.; 1 Kgs. ii. 25, 34. Even in Mark vi. 27, the executioner belonged to the king's body-guard.

Ĕx′ō-dus (*going out*). Second Book of the Bible and Pentateuch. Written by Moses. Historic from i. to xviii. 27; legislative from xix. to end. Its history covers the period (about 142 years) of Jewish preparation to leave Egypt, the departure, the desert wanderings and the arrival at Sinai. Its legislation comprises the giving of the law at Sinai, directions for the priesthood, the establishment of the tabernacle and its service.

Ĕx′ŏr-çĭsts (*swearers out*). Those who pretended to drive out evil spirits by prayers and conjurations, Matt. xii. 27; Mark ix. 38; Acts xix. 13.

Ĕx″pī-ā′tion, Feast of. [ATONEMENT.]

Eȳe. Putting out the eye a warfare custom, especially with dangerous prisoners. Judg. xvi. 21; 1 Sam.

xi. 2; 2 Kgs. xxv. 7. Painting the eyelids a fashion, 2 Kgs. ix. 30; Jer. iv. 30; Ezek. xxiii. 40. "Eye-service," reluctant service, Col. iii. 22; Eph. vi. 6.

Ē'zär, 1 Chr. i. 38. [EZER, 1.]

Ĕz'bă-ī (*shining*). Father of one of David's mighty men, 1 Chr. xi. 37.

Ĕz'bŏn (*bright*). (1) A son of Gad, Gen. xlvi. 16; Ozni in Num. xxvi. 16. (2) A Benjamite, 1 Chr. vii. 7.

Ĕz-ē-chī'as, 2 Esdr. vii. 40. [HEZEKIAH.]

Ĕz-ē-çī'as, 1 Esdr. ix. 43. [HILKIAH.]

Ĕz-ē-kī'as, 2 Macc. xv. 22; Matt. i. 9, 10. [HEZEKIAH.]

Ē-zē'kĭ-ĕl (*strength of God*). One of the four greater prophets; carried captive to Babylon B. C. 598; entered the prophetic calling in fifth year of his captivity, Ezek. i. 1–3. Chapters i.–xxiv. of his book contain predictions before the fall of Jerusalem, and xxv.–xlviii. predictions after that event. The visions of the Temple, xl.–xlviii., are a unique feature of the book.

Ē'zĕl (*going away*). Scene of the parting of David and Jonathan, 1 Sam. xx. 19.

Ē'zĕm (*bone*). A town of Simeon, 1 Chr. iv. 29; Azem in Josh. xix. 3.

Ē'zĕr (*help*). (1) A Horite duke, Gen. xxxvi. 21, 27, 30; 1 Chr. iv. 4. (2) An Ephraimite, 1 Chr. vii. 21. (3) A Gadite, 1 Chr. xii. 9. (4) A Levite, Neh. iii. 19. (5) A priest, Neh. xii. 42.

Ĕz''ē-rī'as, Ē-zī'as, 1 Esdr. viii. 1, 2. [AZARIAH.]

Ē'zī-on=gā'bĕr, or **gē'bĕr** (*backbone of a giant*). An Israelite encampment, Num. xxxiii. 35, 36; Deut. ii. 8. Compare 1 Kgs. ix. 26; 2 Chr. viii. 17; 1 Kgs. xxii. 48.

Ĕz'nīte, 2 Sam. xxiii. 8, for Tachmonite in same verse and Hachmonite in 1 Chr. xi. 11.

Ĕz'rȧ (*help*). The famous scribe and priest, resident at Babylon, who returned to Jerusalem with his countrymen, B. C. 458, where he began instant reforms. He collected and revised the previous O. T. writings and largely settled the O. T. canon. His book, 15th of O. T., tells the story of the return and the establishment of a new order of things at Jerusalem and in Judea.

Ĕz'ra-hite''. A title applied to Ethan and Heman, 1 Kgs. iv. 31; Ps. lxxxviii. title; lxxxix. title.

Ĕz'rī (*my help*). A superintendent of David's farm laborers, 1 Chr. xxvii. 26.

F

Fā'ble (*spoken*). A narrative in which inanimate things are personalized, Judg. ix. 8–15; 2 Kgs. xiv. 9.

Fair Hā'vens. A harbor of Crete, Acts xxvii. 8–10.

Fairs (*holidays*). Wares, Ezek. xxvii. 12–33.

Făl'low=deer (*yellowish brown*). The bubalis or African deer, Deut. xiv. 5; 1 Kgs. iv. 23. Some say the Arabian wild ox.

Făl'low (*yellow*). Plowed land left to mellow. Tillage, Prov. xiii. 23. Figurative, Jer. iv. 3; Hos. x. 12. The Sabbatical, or fallow year; year of land-rest, Lev. xxv. 1–7; Deut. xxxi. 9–14.

Făm'ine (*hunger*). Generally foretold and regarded as a judgment, Gen. xii. 10; xxvi. 1; xli. 54–56; 2 Kgs. vii.

Făn (*winnower*). Winnowing shovel or fork used to throw chaff up into the wind, to separate it from the kernels, Isa. xxx. 24; Matt. iii. 12.

Fạr'thĭng. Two Roman bronze coins. One, Matt. v. 26; Mark xii. 42, worth ¼ of a cent; the other, Matt. x. 29; Luke xii. 6, worth 1½ cents.

Fȧsts (*keep*). One legal fast, the Atonement, kept by Jews, Lev. xvi. 29–34; Deut. ix. 9; Jonah iii. 5; Zech. vii. 1–7. Special fasts observed, 1 Sam. vii. 6; Jer. xxxvi. 6–10; Esth. iv. 16; Matt. ix. 14; Mark ii. 18; Luke v. 33; Acts x. 30; xiii. 3.

Făt (*fed*). Forbidden food, as belonging to God, Lev. iii. 3–17; vii. 3, 23; Neh. viii. 10; yet fatted cattle enjoyed, 1 Kgs. iv. 23; Luke xv. 23. Vat is meant in Joel ii. 24; iii. 13; Hag. ii. 16.

Fä'ther (*sire*). Source of authority, Gen. iii. 16; 1 Cor. xi. 3. Disrespect of, condemned, Ex. xxi. 15–17; xxii. 17; Lev. xx. 9; 1 Tim. i. 9. Parental obedience bears a promise, Ex. xx. 12. Father also a priest, Gen. viii. 20. Any ancestor, Deut. i. 11; Matt. xxiii. 30. A title, Judg. xvii. 10; 1 Sam. x. 12; Acts vii. 2. Protector, Ps. lxviii. 5. Author and founder, Gen. iv. 21; Rom. iv. 12. Divine appellation, Deut. xxxii. 6; Matt. vi. 4; Rom. i. 7.

Făth'om (*embrace*). Space to which a man can extend his arms; about 6 feet, Acts xxvii. 28.

Fēasts (*joyful*). Observed for joyous events, Gen. xxi. 8; xxix. 22; xl. 20; Mark vi. 21, 22. Numerous religious feasts, Ex. xii. 16; Lev. xxiii. 21–24; Jude 12.

Fēet. To wash, a sign of hospitality, Gen. xviii. 4; 1 Sam. xxv. 41; John xiii. 5, 6. To remove shoes, a reverence, Ex. iii. 5; sign of mourning, Ezek. xxiv. 17.

Fē'lix (*happy*). A procurator of Judea, Acts xxiii. 26.

Fĕnced Cities (*defenced*). Walled or palisaded cities. [CITY.]

Fĕr'ret (*thief*). A domesticated animal of the weasel family used for catching rats, Lev. xi. 30.

Fĕs'tŭs. Procurator, Acts xxiv. 27.

Fĕt'ters (*shackles*). Instruments of brass or iron for fastening feet of prisoners, Ps. cv. 18; cxlix. 8.

Fiēld. Open area beyond the enclosed gardens or vineyards, Gen. iv. 8; xxiv. 63; Deut. xxii. 25. Landmarks, sacred, Deut. xix. 14; Job xxiv. 2; Prov. xxii. 28.

Fĭg, Fĭg=tree. Common in Palestine, Deut. viii. 8; Isa. xxxiv. 4; 1 Kgs. iv. 25. Pressed figs, 1 Sam. xxv. 18. Fruit appears before leaves, Matt. xxi. 19.

Figs.

Fĩr. A tree of the pine family, 2 Sam. vi. 5; 1 Kgs. v. 8; S. of Sol. i. 17.

Fīre. Symbol of God's presence, Gen. iv. 4, 5; xv. 17; Ex. iii. 2; Judg. xiii. 19, 20. Worshipped, 2 Kgs. xvii. 17; punishment, Lev. xx. 14; xxi. 9. Christ comes in, 2 Thess. i. 8. World destroyed by, 2 Pet. iii. 7.

Fīre=pan. The censer and snuff-dish of the temple, Ex. xxv. 38; xxvii. 3; xxxvii. 23; xxxviii. 3; 2 Kgs. xxv. 15.

Fĩr'kin (*fourth*). A Greek measure equal to Hebrew bath, 4 to 6 gals., John ii. 6.

Fĩrm'ạ-ment (*made firm*). Overhead expanse, Gen. i. 17; solid, Ex. xxiv. 10; with windows and doors, Gen. vii. 11; Isa. xxiv. 18; Ps. lxxviii. 23.

Fĩrst=born. Consecrated to God, Ex. xiii. 2;

received a double portion, Deut. xxi. 17. Paid redemption money after the priesthood started, Num. iii. 12, 13; xviii. 15, 16.

Fīrst=fruits were offerings and priest's perquisites, Ex. xxii. 29; xxiii. 19; xxxiv. 26; Lev. ii. 12; xxiii. 10-12; Num. xviii. 12; Deut. xviii. 3, 4.

Flesh-hooks.

Fĭsh, Fĭsh-ing. Grand division of animal kingdom, Gen. i. 21, 22. Without scales, unclean, Lev. xi. 9-12. Plenty in waters of Palestine, Luke v. 5. Worship of, prohibited, Deut. iv. 18. Caught with nets, hooks, and spears, Hab. i. 15; Luke v. 5-7; Job xli. 7.

Fĭsh=gate. A Jerusalem gate, 2 Chr. xxxiii. 14.

Fĭsh=hooks. [Fish.]

Fĭsh=pools. Should read "pools," S. of Sol. vii. 4.

Fĭtch'es (*vetches*). "Spelt," Ezek. iv. 9. "Fennel," or black cummin, Isa. xxviii. 25-27.

Flăg (*fluttering*). Embraces many water plants, Ex. ii. 3-5; Isa. xix. 6.

Flăg'on (*flask*). Small vessel for liquids, Isa. xxii. 24; 2 Sam. vi. 19; 1 Chr. xvi. 3; S. of Sol. ii. 5.

Flăx (*flexible*). Grown and used largely in East, Ex. ix. 31; Josh. ii. 6; Isa. xix. 9. For lamp wicks, Isa. xlii. 3; Matt. xii. 20. Spinning honorable, Prov. xxxi. 13, 19, 24.

Flēa. Pests throughout the East, 1 Sam. xxiv. 14; xxvi. 20.

Flĕsh. Everything living, Gen. vi. 13-19; mankind, vi. 12; the body, Col. ii. 5; 1 Pet. iv. 6; seat of appetites, Rom. viii. 1, 5, 9; Gal. v. 17-19; Eph. ii. 3. Used much figuratively.

Flĕsh=hooks. Three-tined hooks for taking meat from a boiling vessel, Ex. xxxviii. 3; 1 Sam. ii. 13, 14.

Flĭnt. Quartz; abounds in Palestine, Ps. cxiv. 8. Types abundance, Deut. xxxii. 13; firmness, Isa. l. 7; Ezek. iii. 9.

Flōats. Rafts for floating timber, 1 Kgs. v. 9; 2 Chr. ii. 16.

Flŏck. [Sheep.]

Flood (*flow*). The Noachian deluge; "the flood," Gen. vi.-viii; Matt. xxiv. 37; 2 Pet. ii. 5; iii. 6. [Noah.]

Flōor. [Agriculture.]

Flŏur. [Bread.]

Flūte (*blow, flow*). Flute or "pipe," made of reeds or copper, and similar to those of to-day, Dan. iii. 5-15; 1 Kgs. i. 40.

Flŭx (*flow*). Violent dysentery, Acts xxviii. 8.

Fly. Of many varieties in East, and very noisome, Ex. viii. 21-31; Ps. lxxviii. 45; Eccl. x. 1; Isa. vii. 18.

Food (*feed*). Vegetable foods, soups, eggs, curds, honey, bread, etc., preferred by Hebrews to animal food, Lev. xxvi. 26; Ps. cv. 16; Ezek. iv. 16. Animal food a feature of entertainments, Gen. xviii. 7; 1 Sam. xvi. 20; Luke xv. 23. Fish used, Num. xi. 5: Matt. xiii. 47, 48; xv. 34.

Foot. Used in pumping water from Nile, Deut. xi. 10.

Foot'men. Swift runners, couriers, 1 Sam. xxii. 17; 1 Kgs. xiv. 28; 2 Kgs. xi. 4.

Foot'stool. Kings used them, 2 Chr. ix. 18. God's footstool, 1 Chr. xxviii. 2; Ps. xcix. 5.

Fŏre'hĕad. Unveiled women "hard of forehead," Gen. xxiv. 65; Ezek. iii. 7-9; Jer. iii. 3. Mark of beast on forehead, Rev. xiii. 16; God's name there, Rev. xxii. 4.

Fŏr'eign-er (*out of doors*). One not of Hebrew stock, Ex. xii. 45; Eph. ii. 12.

Fōre=knowl'edge. God's knowledge of the future, Acts ii. 23; xv. 18; 1 Pet. i. 2.

Fōre=rŭn'ner. Preparer of the way "within the vail," Heb. vi. 19, 20.

Fŏr'est. Woodland and waste land, 1 Sam. xxii. 5. "House of the Forest" was built of cedars thereof, 1 Kgs. vii. 2.

Fôrks, 1 Sam. xiii. 21. [Flesh-hooks.]

Fôr''nĭ-cā'tion (*crime under the arch*). Crime of impurity between unmarried persons. Figuratively, infidelity to God, Ezek. xvi. 2; Jer. ii. 20; Matt. v. 32.

Fôr''tū'nā'tus (*fortunate*). A Corinthian friend of Paul, 1 Cor. xvi. 17, and postscript.

Fŏun'tain (*font*). Springs of Palestine many

Frankincense. (*See* p. 45.)

but uncertain, Deut. viii. 7. They furnish many figures of speech, Ps. xxxvi. 8, 9; Isa. xlix. 10; Jer. ii. 13; John iv. 10; Rev. vii. 17.

Fowl (*flying*). The Hebrew original embraces birds in general, Gen. i. 20; 1 Kgs. iv. 23. The Greek provides the domestic limitation, Luke xii. 24.

Fŏx (*hairy*). The jackal meant, as it is gregarious and feeds on carcasses, Judg. xv. 4; Ps. lxiii. 10; S. of Sol. ii. 15; Ezek. xiii. 4; Luke ix. 58.

Frănk'ĭn-çense (*free burning*). The yellowish gum used in sacrificial fumigation, Ex. xxx. 7-9; Lev. xvi. 12, 13; Rev. viii. 3. A mixture of gums and spices in Ex. xxx. 34-38.

Frĭn'ġeş (*fibres*). The ornamental hem of the outer garment. Wearing enjoined, Num. xv. 37-40; Deut. xxii. 12; Matt. ix. 20; xiv. 36.

Frŏg. The Egyptian species akin to our own. Source of one of the plagues, Ex. viii. 2-14. Elsewhere only in Ps. lxxviii. 45; cv. 30; Rev. xvi. 13.

Egyptian Frogs.

Frŏnt'lets (*little foreheads*). Phylacteries in Greek. Parchment strips inscribed with texts, Ex. xiii. 2-17; Deut. vi. 4-22; enclosed in calf-skin case, worn at prayers on forehead or left arm, Matt. xxiii. 5; Mark vii. 3, 4; Luke v. 33.

Fu̧l'ler (*tramper on*). Fuller's art used for cleaning clothes. They were placed in vessels of water impregnated with natron or soap and trodden with the feet, Prov. xxv. 20; Jer. ii. 22; Mal. iii. 2. Chalk and fuller's earth used for bleaching, 2 Kgs. xviii. 17; Isa. vii. 3; xxxvi. 2.

Fū'nĕr-al. [Burial.]

Fŭr'long (*furrow long*). In N. T. for Greek stadium, 600 feet long, Luke xxiv. 13.

Fŭr'nace (*oven*). Oven in Gen. xv. 17; Neh. iii. 11. Smelting furnace or lime-kiln in Gen. xix. 28; Ex. ix. 8; Isa. xxxiii. 12. Refining furnace in Prov. xvii. 3. Furnace like a brick-kiln in Dan. iii. 15-27.

Fŭr'nĭ-ture (*provided*). Oriental furniture scanty, 2 Kgs. iv. 10-13. Camel's trappings in Gen. xxxi. 34. [Bed.]

Fŭr'row (*ridge*). Usual meaning, except in Hos. x. 10, where it means transgressions.

G

Gā'al (*contempt*). Son of Ebed, Judg. ix. 26-41.

Gā'ăsh (*earthquake*). The hill on which Joshua was buried, Josh. xxiv. 30; 2 Sam. xxiii. 30.

Gā'bȧ, Josh. xviii. 24; Ez. ii. 26. [Geba.]

Găb'ā-el. Ancestor of Tobit, Tob. i. 1, 14.

Găb'ba̧-ī (*gatherer*). A Benjamite family, Neh. xi. 8.

Găb'ba̧-thȧ (*elevated*). The pavement on which Christ was sentenced, John xix. 13.

Găb'dēs, 1 Esdr. v. 20. [Geba.]

Gā'brĭ-as. Brother of Tobit, Tob. i. 14; iv. 20.

Gā'brĭ-el (*man of God*). The announcing angel, Luke i. 11, 19, 26, 38; Dan. viii. 16; ix. 21.

Găd (*troop*). (1) Jacob's seventh son, Gen. xxx. 11-13; xlix. 19; Num. i. 24, 25. Tribe settled east of Jordan, and became a fierce, warlike people. Carried captive by Tiglath-pileser, 1 Chr. v. 26. (2) A prophet and David's seer, 1 Sam. xxii. 5; 1 Chr. xxi. 9-19; xxix. 29; 2 Chr. xxix. 25.

Găd'a̧-rȧ (*walled*). A city six miles S. E. of Sea of Galilee. Now Um-keis.

Găd'a̧-rēneş, Gĕr'gĕ-sēneş, Gĕr'a̧-sēneş. A people east of the Sea of Galilee, Matt. viii. 28-34; Mark v. 1-20; Luke viii. 26-40.

Găd'dī (*fortunate*). One of the spies, Num. xiii. 11.

Găd'dĭel (*fortune of God*). Another of the spies, Num. xiii. 10.

Gā'dī (*of Gad*). Father of King Menahem, 2 Kgs. xv. 15, 17.

Gā'hăm (*browned*). Son of Nahor, Gen. xxii. 24.

Gā'hăr (*hiding place*). His sons returned, Ez. ii. 47.

Gā'ịus, Cā'ịus (*lord*). (1) Of Macedonia, a friend of Paul, Acts xix. 29. (2) Of Derbe, co-worker with Paul, Acts xx. 4. (3) Of Corinth, baptized by Paul, Rom. xvi. 23; 1 Cor. i. 14. (4) John's third epistle addressed to Gaius.

Găl'a̧-ad. Greek form of Gilead.

Gā'lăl (*prominence*). Three Levites, 1 Chr. ix. 15, 16; Neh. xi. 17.

Gȧ-lā'tịȧ (*land of the Galli, Gauls*). A central province of Asia Minor, and part of Paul's missionary field, Acts xvi. 6; xviii. 23; 2 Tim. iv. 10.

Gȧ-lā'tịanş, Epistle to. Written by Paul to people of Galatia, A. D. 56 or 57, to strengthen their faith in the divinity of his mission, unfold his doctrine of justification by faith, and urge persistency in Christian work.

Găl-bā'num (*fat*). A gum-resin of yellowish color, and pungent, disagreeable odor when burning, Ex. xxx. 34.

Găl'ĕ-ed (*heap of witness*). Memorial heap of Jacob, Gen. xxxi. 47, 48.

Găl'gă-lȧ, 1 Macc. ix. 1. [Gilgal.]

Găl'ĭ-lēe (*circle*). Originally the circuit containing the 20 towns given by Solomon to Hiram, Josh. xx. 7; 1 Kgs. ix. 11; 2 Kgs. xv. 29. In time of Christ, one of the largest provinces of Palestine, in which he spent the greater part of his life and ministry. Luke xiii. 1; xxiii. 6; John i. 43-47; Acts i. 11.

Gal'ĭ-lee, Sea of. [Gennesaret.]

Gall (*yellow, bitter*). The fluid secreted by the liver. Bitter, Job xvi. 13; poison, xx. 14, 25; Deut. xxxii. 33; "hemlock" in Hos. x. 4; probably myrrh, in Matt. xxvii. 34; as in Mark xv. 23; great troubles, Jer. viii. 14; Acts viii. 23.

Găl'lĕr-ȳ (*show*). An eastern veranda or portico; but panel work in S. of Sol. i. 17; or pillared walk, Ezek. xli. 15.

Găl'ley, Isa. xxxiii. 21. [SHIP.]

Găl'līm (*heaps*). A village of Benjamin, 1 Sam. xxv. 44; Isa. x. 30.

Găl'lĭ-ō (*who lives on milk*). Roman proconsul of Achaia, A. D. 53, Acts xviii. 12–17.

Găl'lōws. [PUNISHMENT.]

Găm'ă-el, 1 Esdr. viii. 29. [DANIEL.]

Gȧ-mā'lĭ-el (*recompense of God*). (1) A prince of Manasseh, Num. i. 10; ii. 20; vii. 54; x. 23. (2) A learned president of the Sanhedrim, and Paul's legal preceptor, Acts v. 34; xxii. 3.

Gāmes (*sports*). Simple among Hebrews. Falconry, Job xli. 5; foot-racing, Ps. xix. 5; Eccl. ix. 11; bow and sling contests, 1 Sam. xx. 20; Judg. xx. 16; 1 Chr. xii. 2; dancing, Matt. xi. 16, 17; joking, Prov. xxvi. 19; Jer. xv. 17.

Găm'ma-dīms (*dwarfs*). Perhaps watchmen, Ezek. xxvii. 11.

Gā'mŭl (*weaned*). Leader of the 22d priestly course, 1 Chr. xxiv. 17.

Gär. Sons of, in 1 Esdr. v. 34.

Gär'den (*yard*). In Hebrew sense, enclosures for fruits, etc., well watered, Gen. ii. 10; xiii. 10; xxi. 33; Num. xxiv. 6; Job viii. 16; hedged, Isa. v. 5; walled, Prov. xxiv. 31; protected, Isa. i. 8; Job xxvii. 18; Mark xii. i.

Gā'rĕb (*scab*). (1) One of David's warriors, 2 Sam. xxiii. 38; 1 Chr. xi. 40. (2) A hill near Jerusalem, Jer. xxxi. 39.

Găr'ĭ-zĭm, 2 Macc. v. 23. [GERIZIM.]

Gär'lic (*spear leek*). A bulbous plant similar to an onion and leek, Num. xi. 5.

Gär'ment. [DRESS.]

Gär'mīte. A Judahite, 1 Chr. iv. 19.

Găr'rĭ-sŏn (*warning*). In Hebrew sense, a place manned, provisioned, and fortified, 1 Sam. xiii. 23; 2 Sam. xxiii. 14; 1 Chr. xi. 16; guards in 2 Chr. xvii. 2; 1 Chr. xviii. 13.

Găsh'mū, Neh. vi. 6. [GESHEM.]

Gā'tam (*burnt valley*). A duke of Edom, Gen. xxxvi. 11, 16.

Gāte (*opening*). Those of walled cities made of wood, iron, or brass, Judg. xvi. 3; Deut. iii. 5; Ps. cvii. 16; Acts xii. 10; flanked by towers, 2 Sam. xviii. 24, 33; market and judgment places near, 2 Sam. xv. 2; 2 Kgs. vii. 1; Job xxix. 7; Deut. xvii. 5; xxv. 7; Am. v. 10; Ruth iv. 1–12; symbol of power, Gen. xxii. 17; Isa. xxiv. 12; Matt. xvi. 18; the city itself, Deut. xii. 12.

Old Gate at Sidon.

Găth (*wine press*). A city of Philistia, Josh. xiii. 3; 1 Sam. vi. 17; home of Goliath, 1 Sam. xvii. 4; refuge of David, 1 Sam. xxi. 10.

Găth-hē'phĕr, Gĭt'tah-hē'phĕr (*wine press of Hepher*). A town in Zebulun, now el Meshed, Josh. xix. 13; 2 Kgs. xiv. 25.

Găth-rĭm'mon (*high wine press*). (1) A Levitical city of Dan, Josh. xxi. 24; 1 Chr. vi. 69. (2) A Levite town of Manasseh, Josh. xxi. 25. Bileam, 1 Chr. vi. 70.

Gaza.

Gā'zȧ (*strong*). Hebrew Azzah, now Ghuzzeh. A city of Philistia, Gen. x. 19; assigned to Judah, Josh. x. 41; xv. 47; Judg. i. 18; scene of Samson's exploits, Judg. xvi.; 1 Kgs. iv. 24; Acts viii. 26.

Găz'a-rȧ, 1 Macc. ix. 52. [GEZER.]

Gā'zăth-ītes. Inhabitants of Gaza, Josh. xiii. 3.

Gā'zĕr, 2 Sam. v. 25; 1 Chr. xiv. 16. [GEZER.]

Găz'ĕ-rȧ. (1) 1 Macc. iv. 15. [GEZER.] (2) His sons returned, 1 Esdr. v. 31.

Gā'zĕz (*shearer*). Son of Caleb, 1 Chr. ii. 46.

Gā'zītes. Inhabitants of Gaza, Judg. xvi. 2.

Găz'zam (*consuming*). His descendants returned, Ez. ii. 48; Neh. vii. 51.

Gē'bȧ (*hill*). Gaba in Josh. xviii. 24; now Jeba, 6 miles N. of Jerusalem. A Levitical city of Benjamin, Josh. xxi. 17; 1 Chr. vi. 60; 1 Sam. xiii. 3; 1 Kgs. xv. 22; 2 Kgs. xxiii. 8; Isa. x. 29.

Gē'bal (*mountain*). A maritime town of Phœnicia, near Tyre, Ezek. xxvii. 9. Inhabitants called Giblites, Josh. xiii. 5.

Gē'bĕr (*man*). Two of Solomon's commissaries, 1 Kgs. iv. 13, 19.

Gē'bim (*ditches*). A place near Jerusalem, Isa. x. 31.

Gĕc'ko. The fan-footed lizard of Palestine. "Ferret," in A. V., Lev. xi. 30; "Gecko" in R. V.

Gĕd''a-lī'ah (*God my greatness*). (1) A governor of Judea, 2 Kgs. xxv. 22; and friend of Jeremiah, Jer. xl. 5, 6; xli. 2. (2) A Levite harpist, 1 Chr. xxv. 3. (3) A priest, Ez. x. 18. (4) A persecutor of Jeremiah, Jer. xxxviii. 1. (5) Grandfather of Zephaniah, Zeph. i. 1.

Gĕd'dur, 1 Esdr. v. 30. [GAHAR.]

Gĕd'e-on. Greek form of Gideon, Heb. xi. 32.

Gē'dĕr (*wall*). Its king was conquered by Joshua, Josh. xii. 13.

Gē-dē'rah (*sheepfold*). A town in lowlands of Judah, Josh. xv. 36.

Gĕd'ĕ-răth-īte''. Inhabitant of Gederah, 1 Chr. xii. 4.

Gĕd'ĕ-rīte. Inhabitant of Geder, 1 Chr. xxvii. 28.

Gĕ-dē'rŏth (*sheepfolds*). A city in lowlands of Judah, Josh. xv. 41; 2 Chr. xxviii. 18.

Gĕd''ĕ-rŏth-ā'im (*two sheepfolds*). A town in lowlands of Judah, Josh. xv. 36.

Gē'dôr (*wall*). (1) A hill town of Judah, Josh. xv. 58. (2) A town of Benjamin, 1 Chr. xii. 7. (3) 1 Chr. iv. 39, probably Gerar. (4) An ancestor of Saul, 1 Chr. viii. 31.

Gē-hā'zī (*valley of vision*). Messenger of Elisha, 2 Kgs. iv. 12-37; v. 20-27; viii. 4.

Gē-hĕn'nȧ. [HINNOM.]

Gĕl'ĭ-lŏth (*circuit*). A landmark of Benjamin, Josh. xviii. 17.

Gē-măl'lī (*camel driver*). Father of Ammiel, Num. xiii. 12.

Gĕm''a-rī'ah (*perfected by God*). (1) Son of Shaphan, Jer. xxxvi. 10-27. (2) Messenger of King Hezekiah, Jer. xxix. 3, 4.

Ġĕms. [STONES, PRECIOUS.]

Ġĕn''ē-ăl'ŏ-gy (*birth record*). In Hebrew, "book of generations," Gen. v.; x.; 1 Chr. i.-viii.; ix. 1; Matt. i. 1-17; Luke iii. 23-38.

Ġĕn''ĕr-ā'tion (*begotten*). In plural, the genealogical register, Gen. ii. 4; v. 1; Matt. i. 1; family history, Gen. vi. 9; xxv. 12; men of the existing age, Lev. iii. 17; Isa. liii. 8; Matt. xxiv. 34; Acts ii. 40.

Ġĕn'ē-sĭs (*beginning*). First book of the Bible and Pentateuch. Chapters i.-xi. give history of Creation, Adam, Deluge, Noah, first inhabitants, Babel. Balance devoted to history of the patriarchs Abraham, Isaac, Jacob and Joseph. Covers a period of nearly 2500 years. Authorship attributed to Moses.

Gĕn-nĕs'a-rĕt (*garden of the prince*). (1) Land of, the small crescent country N. W. of Sea of Galilee, Matt. xiv. 34; Mark vi. 53. (2) Lake of, "Sea of Chinnereth," in O. T., Num. xxxiv. 11; Josh. xii. 3; and "Sea of Galilee," in N. T.; enlargement of Jordan river; 13 miles long, 6 wide, 700 below bed of ocean. "Lake of Gennesaret," Luke v. 1; "Sea of Tiberias," John vi. 1; "the sea," Matt. iv. 15.

Gĕn-nĕs'a-rĕth. [GENNESARET.]

Gĕn-nē'us. Father of Apollonius, 2 Macc. xii. 2.

Ġĕn'tīles (*nations*). In O. T. sense, all peoples not Jewish, Gen. x. 5; xiv. 1; Neh. v. 8. In N. T., Greeks and Romans seem to type Gentiles, Luke ii. 32; Acts xxvi. 17-20; Rom. i. 14-16; ix. 24. "Isles of the Gentiles," Gen. x. 5, supposed to embrace Asia Minor and Europe.

Gē-nū'băth (*theft*). An Edomite, 1 Kgs. xi. 20.

Gē'on, Ecclus. xxiv. 27. [GIHON.]

Gē'rȧ (*grain*). (1) A Benjamite, Gen. xlvi. 21; 1 Chr. viii. 3-7. (2) Father of Ehud, Judg. iii. 15. (3) Father of Shimei, 2 Sam. xvi. 5; xix. 16; 1 Kgs. ii. 8.

Gē'rah. One twentieth of a shekel; about 3 cents, Ex. xxx. 13.

Gē'rär (*halting place*). A town of Philistia, Gen. x. 19; xx. 1; xxvi. 26; 2 Chr. xiv. 13, 14.

Gĕr''ă-sēnes'. For Gadarenes in Luke viii. 26, R. V.

Gĕr'gĕ-sēnes, Matt. viii. 28. [GADARENES, GERASENES.]

Gĕr'ĭ-zīm (*cutters*). The mountain of blessings in Ephraim, Deut. xi. 29; xxvii. 12-26; xxviii.

Gĕr-rhē'nī-ans. Of Gerar, 2 Macc. xiii. 24.

Gĕr'shŏm (*exile*). (1) Son of Moses, Ex. ii. 22; xviii. 3. (2) A priest, Ez. viii. 2.

Gĕr'shŏn (*exile*). Eldest son of Levi, Gen. xlvi. 11; Ex. vi. 16; 1 Chr. vi. 1. Founder of the Gershonites. Given thirteen cities in Canaan, Josh. xxi. 6. Gershom in 1 Chr. vi. 62-71.

Gĕr'zītes. Dwellers south of Palestine, 1 Sam. xxvii. 8 marg.

Gē'sem, Judith i. 9. [GOSHEN.]

Gē'shăm (*filthy*). A descendant of Caleb, 1 Chr. ii. 47.

Gē'shem, Găsh'mū (*rain*). A scoffing Arabian, Neh. ii. 19; vi. 1, 2.

Gē'shŭr (*bridge*). A province of Syria peopled by Geshuri or Geshurites, Deut. iii. 14; Josh. xiii. 11; 2 Sam. iii. 3; xv. 8; 1 Chr. ii. 23.

Gĕsh'u-rī, Deut. iii. 14; Josh. xiii. 2. [GESHUR.]

Gĕsh'u-rītes. Besides above, a people of Arabia and Philistia, Josh. xiii. 11; 1 Sam. xxvii. 8.

Gē'thĕr (*fear*). Son of Aram, Gen. x. 23; 1 Chr. i. 17.

Gĕth-sĕm'a-nē (*oil press*). Scene of Christ's agony and betrayal, at the foot of Olivet, near Jerusalem, Matt. xxvi. 36-56; Mark xiv. 26-52; Luke xxii. 39-49; John xviii. 1-13.

Gē-ū'el (*majesty of God*). The Gadite spy, Num. xiii. 15.

Gē'zĕr (*steep*). Gazer, Gazara, Gazera, and Gad. A Levitical city, Josh. x. 33; xii. 12; xvi. 3; xxi. 21; whose native people remained, Judg. i. 29.

Gĕz'rītes. [GERZITES.]

Ghōst (*that terrifies*). The spirit, Matt. xxvii. 50

Gī'ah (*waterfall*). A hill near Ammah, 2 Sam. ii. 24.

Gī'ants (*sons of Gaea*). Huge men—Nephilim, Gibborim, Gen. vi. 4; Rephaim, xiv. 5; Emim, Anakim, Zuzim, etc., Num. xiii. 28-33; Deut. iii. 11; 1 Sam. xvii. 4.

Gĭb'bar (*huge*). His children returned, Ez. ii. 20.

Gĭb'be-thon (*high*). A Levitical town of Dan, Josh. xix. 44; xxi. 23; 1 Kgs. xv. 27; xvi. 17.

Gĭb'e-ȧ (*hill*). A Judahite, 1 Chr. ii. 49.

Gĭb'e-ah (*hill*). (1) A town of Judah, Josh. xv. 57. (2) Place where the ark was left, 2 Sam. vi. 3, 4. (3) A place in Benjamin, Judg. xix. 12-15; xx. 19-25; 1 Sam. xiii. 2. (4) Saul's birthplace, 1 Sam. x. 26; xi. 4; xv. 34; xxii. 6; xxiii. 19; Isa. x. 29. (5) Probably Geba, Judg. xx. 31.

Gĭb'e-ath, Josh. xviii. 28. [GIBEAH, 3.]

Gĭb'e-on (*lofty hill*). A Hivite city of Canaan, given to Levites, Josh. ix. 3-15; x. 12, 13; xxi. 17; 2 Sam. ii. 12-24; xx. 8-10. Tabernacle set up there, 1 Chr. xvi. 39; 1 Kgs. iii. 4, 5; ix. 2; 2 Chr. i. 3, 13; Jer. xli. 12-16.

Gĭb'e-on-ītes''. Inhabitants of Gibeon, 2 Sam. xxi. 1-9.

Gĭb'lītes, Josh. xiii. 5. [GEBAL.]

Gĭd-dăl'tī (*trained up*). Son of Heman, and leader of 22d musical course, 1 Chr. xxv. 4.

Gĭd'del (*great*). His children returned, Ez. ii. 47, 56.

Gĭd'e-on (*destroyer*). The powerful warrior of Manasseh, and judge of Israel for 40 years, Judges vi.-viii.

Gĭd''e-ō'nī (*destroyer*). A Benjamite, Num. i. 11.

Gī'dom (*desolation*). A place near Rimmon, Judg. xx. 45.

Ġier (*jer*) **Eagle** (*sacred eagle*). An unclean bird of prey; probably the Egyptian vulture, Lev. xi. 18; Deut. xiv. 17.

Gĭft (*given*). A common way of showing esteem and confidence and securing favors, Gen. xxxii. 13-15; xlv. 22, 23. Kings were donees, 1 Kgs. iv. 21; 2 Chr. xvii. 5. Not to give, a mark of contempt, 1 Sam. x. 27. Cattle given, Gen. xxxii. 13; garments, 2 Kgs. v. 23; money, 2 Sam. xviii. 11; perfumes, Matt. ii. 11.

Gī'hon (*stream*). (1) Second river of Paradise, Gen. ii. 13. (2) A spot, or pool, near Jerusalem, 1 Kgs. i. 33-38; 2 Chr. xxxii. 30; xxxiii. 14.

Gĭl'a-lāi (*weighty*). A musician, Neh. xii. 36.

Gĭl-bō'ȧ (*fountain*). The mountain range east of Esdraelon and overlooking Jezreel, 1 Sam. xxviii. 4; xxxi. 1; 2 Sam. i. 6.

Gĭl'e-ăd (*rocky*). (1) Mount and Land of Gilead, east of Jordan, Gen. xxxi. 21-25; Num. xxxii. 1; Josh. xvii. 6. (2) A mountain near Jezreel, Judg. vii. 3. (3) Grandson of Manasseh, Num. xxvi. 29, 30. (4) Father of Jephthah, Judg. xi. 1, 2.

Gĭl'e-ăd-ītes''. Manassites of Gilead, Num. xxvi. 29.

Mountain of Gilboa. (*See* p. 47.)

Gĭl'găl (*rolling*). (1) First encampment of Israelites west of Jordan, Josh. iv. 19, 20; v. 9, 10. Became a city and headquarters, Josh. ix. 6; xv. 7. Saul crowned there, 1 Sam. vii. 16; x. 8; xi. 14, 15. (2) Another Gilgal in Sharon plain, Josh. xii. 23. (3) Another near Bethel, 2 Kgs. iv. 38.

Gī'loh (*exile*). A town of Judah, Josh. xv. 51; 2 Sam. xv. 12.

Gī'lo-nīte. Inhabitant of Giloh, 2 Sam. xv. 12; xxiii. 34.

Gĭm'zō (*producing sycamores*). Now Jimzu, a village 2½ miles from Lydda, 2 Chr. xxviii. 18.

Ġĭn (*engine*). A bird-trap, Isa. viii. 14; Am. iii. 5.

Gī'nath (*protection*). Father of Tibni, 1 Kgs. xvi. 21, 22.

Gĭn'nĕ-thō (*gardener*). A priest, Neh. xii. 4.

Gĭn'nĕ-thon (*gardener*). A priest, Neh. x. 6; xii. 16.

Gĭr'dle (*gird*). Worn by men and women to hold the looser garments. Made of leather, 2 Kgs. i. 8; Matt. iii. 4; of linen, Jer. xiii. 1; Ezek. xvi. 10; embroidered, Dan. x. 5; Rev. i. 13; used for carrying swords and daggers, Judg. iii. 16; 2 Sam. xx. 8.

Gĭr'ga-sīte, Gĭr'ga-shītes. An original tribe of Canaan, Gen. x. 16; xv. 21; Deut. vii. 1.

Gĭs'pȧ (*fondle*). An overseer, Neh. xi. 21.

Gĭt'tah=hē'phẽr, Josh. xix. 13. [GATH-HEPHER.]

Gĭt'ta-ĭm (*two wine presses*). An unknown place, 2 Sam. iv. 3.

Gĭt'tītes. Gathite followers of David, 2 Sam. xv. 18, 19. [GATH.]

Gĭt'tith. A musical instrument or melody, Ps. viii., lxxxi., lxxxiv., titles.

Gī'zō-nīte. Hashem, 1 Chr. xi. 34.

Glȧss. Only once in O. T. as "crystal," Job xxviii. 17; N. T. "glass" mirrors were metal, 1 Cor. xiii. 12; 2 Cor. iii. 18; James i. 23; Rev. iv. 6.

Glēan'ing (*handful*). Field-gleanings were reserved for the poor, Lev. xix. 9, 10; Ruth ii. 2. [CORNER.]

Glēde (*glide*). An unclean bird of prey, Deut. xiv. 13. The European kite; but vulture in Lev. xi. 14.

Gnăt. A small insect; figuratively mentioned in Matt. xxiii. 24.

Gōad (*gad, strike*). A rod spiked at the end for driving oxen, Judg. iii. 31; and iron-shod at the other end for cleaning plows, or even for plowing, 1 Sam. xiii. 21.

Gōat. Several varieties in Palestine, both wild and tame. An important source of food, clothing, and wealth, Gen. xxvii. 9; 1 Sam. xxiv. 2; xxv. 2; Job xxxix. 1. "Scape-goat," one of the two offered on Day of Atonement, over which the priest confessed the sins of Israel, and then let it escape to the wilderness, Lev. xvi. 7-26.

Gō'ath (*lowing*). An unknown place, Jer. xxxi. 39.

Gŏb (*cistern*). A battlefield, 2 Sam. xxi. 18, 19. Gezer in 1 Chr. xx. 4.

Gŏb'let (*little cask*). A wine cup.

God (*good*). In Hebrew, Jehovah, "the self-existent and eternal," and especially the covenant God. Generally rendered Lord. The ineffable name, not pronounced by the Jews, who substituted for it Adonai, "my Lord;" or Elohim — God, the creator and moral governor — when Adonai was written with Jehovah.

God'head. The Supreme Being in all his nature and attributes, Acts xvii. 29; Rom. i. 20; Col. ii. 9.

Gŏg (*roof*). (1) A Reubenite, 1 Chr. v. 4. (2) [MAGOG.]

Gō'lan (*circuit*). A refuge city in Bashan, Deut. iv. 43; Josh. xx. 8; xxi. 27.

Gōld (*yellow*). Known early to Hebrews, Gen. ii. 11; used for ornaments, Gen. xxiv. 22; money, temple furniture and utensils, Ex. xxxvi. 34-38; 1 Kgs. vii. 48-50; emblem of purity and nobility, Job xxiii. 10; Lam. iv. 1. Obtained chiefly from Ophir, Job xxviii. 16; Parvaim, 2 Chr. iii. 6; Sheba and Raamah, Ezek. xxvii. 22.

Gŏl'gō-thȧ (*skull*). Hebrew name of the spot where Christ was crucified, Matt. xxvii. 33; Mark xv. 22; John xix. 17. [CALVARY.]

Gō-lī'ath (*splendor*). The Philistine giant who defied the army of Israel, 1 Sam. xvii. 4-54. Another Goliath in 2 Sam. xxi. 19-22.

Gō'mer (*complete*). (1) Eldest son of Japheth, Gen. x. 2, 3; 1 Chr. i. 5, 6. (2) Wife of Hosea, Hos. i. 3.

Gō-mŏr'rah (*submersion*). Gomorrha in N. T. A city of the plain destroyed by fire, Gen. xiv. 1-11; xviii. 20; xix. 24-28; Deut. xxix. 23; xxxii. 32; Matt. x. 15; Mark vi. 11.

Goat of Sinai.

Gō′pher. The unknown wood of Noah's ark, Gen. vi. 14.

Gŏr′ġĭ-as (*frightful*). A Syrian general, 1 Macc. iii. 38.

Gŏr-tȳ′na. Capital of Crete, 1 Macc. xv. 23.

Cup of the Ptolemies. (*See* Goblet, p. 48.)

Gō′shen (*drawing near*). (1) The extreme province of Egypt, northward toward Palestine; assigned to the Jews, Gen. xlv. 5–10; xlvi. 28–34; xlvii. 1–6; l. 8. (2) An undefined part of southern Palestine, Josh. x. 41; xi. 16. (3) A city of Judah, Josh. xv. 51.

Gŏs′pels (*good tidings*). The four initial books of N. T., containing the biographies of Christ.

Gŏth″ō-lī′as. One who returned, 1 Esdr. viii. 33.

Gō-thŏn′ĭ-el. Father of Chabris, Judith vi. 15.

Gōurd (*encumberer*). A large plant family, covering the melon, pumpkin, squash, calabash, etc., Jonah iv. 6–10. A poisonous apple or cucumber, 2 Kgs. iv. 39–41.

Gŏv′ẽr-nôr (*director*). Often captain, chief, or civic official; but generally the political officer in charge of a province, Gen. xlii. 6; 1 Kgs. x. 15; Ez. viii. 36; Neh. ii. 9; Matt. xxvii. 2.

Gō′zan. Place or river in Mesopotamia, 2 Kgs. xvii. 6; xviii. 11; 1 Chr. v. 26.

Grā′bȧ, 1 Esdr. v. 29. [HAGABA.]

Grāpe (*hook, grab*). Grapes of Palestine noted for size and flavor, Gen. xlix. 11; Num. xiii. 24. Used for wine and food, 1 Sam. xxv. 18; xxx. 12; 2 Sam. xvi. 1; 1 Chr. xii. 40.

Gráss (*for gnawing*). Large figurative use, Ps. xc. 5, 6; Isa. xl. 6, 8; James i. 10, 11; 1 Pet. i. 24; sometimes herbage in general, Isa. xv. 6; a fuel, Matt. vi. 30; Luke xii. 28.

Gráss′hop-per. An insect of the locust species, often translated locust, 2 Chr. vii. 13. A clean animal, Lev. xi. 22; timid, Job xxxix. 20; gregarious and destructive, Judg. vi. 5; vii. 12; Eccl. xii. 5; Jer. xlvi. 23; type of insignificance, Num. xiii. 33; Isa. xl. 22.

Grāve. [BURIAL.] [ENGRAVER.]

Grēaves (*shins*). Armor, metallic or leathern, to protect the shins from foot to knee, 1 Sam. xvii. 6.

Grēēçe, Grēēks, Grē′çians. The well known country in S. E. of Europe, called also Hellas. Javan in O. T., Gen. x. 2–5; Isa. lxvi. 19; Ezek. xxvii. 13, 19; but direct in Dan. viii. 21; x. 20; xi. 2; Joel iii. 6; Acts xx. 2. Greek the original N. T. language.

Grey′hound, Prov. xxx. 31. The original implies a "wrestler," not a quadruped.

Grīnd′ing. [MILL.]

Grōve. Except in Gen. xxi. 33, the Hebrew original means an idol; primitively set up and worshipped in groves, 1 Kgs. xviii. 19; 2 Kgs. xiii. 6.

Gŭd′go-dah, Deut. x. 7. [HOR-HAGIDGAD.]

Guĕst. [HOSPITALITY.]

Gū′nī (*painted*). (1) Son of Naphtali and founder of the Gunites, Gen. xlvi. 24; Num. xxvi. 48; 1 Chr. vii. 13. (2) A son of Gad, 1 Chr. v. 15.

Gûr (*whelp*). Spot where King Ahaziah was slain, 2 Kgs. ix. 27.

Gûr=bā′al (*abode of Baal*). A district south of Palestine, 2 Chr. xxvi. 7.

H

Hā″a hăsh′ta-rī (*runner*). Son of Ashur, 1 Chr. iv. 6.

Hȧ-bā′ịah (*God hides*). His children returned, Ez. ii. 61.

Hȧ-băk′kŭk (*embrace*). A minor prophet during reigns of Jehoiakim and Josiah. His book, thirteenth of the prophetic, denounces Chaldea, and concludes with a striking poem and prayer.

Hăb″a-zĭ-nī′ah (*God's light*). A Rechabite, Jer. xxxv. 3.

Hăb′ba-cuc, B. and D. 33–39. [HABAKKUK.]

Hăb′ẽr-ġeon (*neck protector*). Coat of mail for neck and breast, Ex. xxviii. 32.

Hā′bôr (*fertile*). A tributary of the Euphrates, 2 Kgs. xvii. 6; 1 Chr. v. 26.

Hăch″a-lī′ah (*who waits*). Father of Nehemiah, Neh. i. 1.

Hăch′ĭ-lah (*dark hill*). A hill in Ziph, 1 Sam. xxiii. 19.

Hăch′mō-nī (*wise*). A Hachmonite, 1 Chr. xi. 11; xxvii. 32.

Hā′dăd (*brave*). (1) An Ishmaelite, 1 Chr. i. 30; Hadar, Gen. xxv. 15. (2) A king of Edom, Gen. xxxvi. 35; 1 Chr. i. 46. (3) Another king of Edom, 1 Chr. i. 50; Hadar, Gen. xxxvi. 39. (4) An Edomite, 1 Kgs. xi. 14–25.

Hăd″ăd-ē′zẽr, 2 Sam. viii. 3–12. [HADAREZER.]

Hā′dăd=rĭm′mon. From two Syrian idols. Spot of mourning for Josiah, Zech. xii. 11.

Hā′dar, Gen. xxv. 15; xxxvi. 39. [HADAD.]

Hăd″ăr-ē′zẽr (*Hadad's help*). A king of Zoba, 2 Sam. viii. 3; x. 16; 1 Chr. xviii. 7; xix. 16–19.

Hăd′a-shah (*new*). Town of Judah, Josh. xv. 37.

Hȧ-dăs′sah (*myrtle*). Hebrew name of Esther, Esth. ii. 7.

Hȧ-dăt′tah (*new*). Town of Judah, Josh. xv. 25.

Hā′deṣ. Place of departed spirits. Greek equivalent of Hebrew "sheol," unseen world. Hell in A. V.; Hades in R. V., Matt. xi. 23; xvi. 18; Acts ii. 31; Rev. i. 18.

Hā′dĭd (*sharp*). Place named in Ez. ii. 33; Neh. vii. 37.

Hăd′la-ī (*restful*). An Ephraimite, 2 Chr. xxviii. 12.

Hȧ-dō′ram (*power*). (1) Son of Joktan, Gen. x. 27. (2) An ambassador to David, 1 Chr. xviii. 10. (3) 2 Chr. x. 18. [ADONIRAM.]

Hā′drăch (*dwelling*). A Syrian country, Zech. ix. 1.

Hā′găb (*locust*). His sons returned, Ez. ii. 46.

Hăg′a-bȧ, Neh. vii. 48. Hagabah, Ez. ii. 45. [HAGAB.]

Hā′gar (*flight*). Abraham's concubine, Gen. xvi. 3; mother of Ishmael, xxi. 9–21. Type of law and bondage, Gal. iv. 24, 25.

Hā′gar-ītes, Hā′gar-ēnes. Ishmaelites, 1 Chr. v. 10–20; xxvii. 31; Ps. lxxxiii. 6.

Hăg′ga-ī (*festive*). A minor prophet. His book, fifteenth of the prophetic, exhorts the Jews to crown the work of Zerubbabel.

Hăg-gē′rī (*wanderer*), 1 Chr. xi. 38. [BANI.]

Hăg′gī (*festive*). Son of Gad, Gen. xlvi. 16.

Hăg-gī′ah (*Lord's feast*). A Levite, 1 Chr. vi. 30.

Hăg′gites. Of Haggi, Num. xxvi. 15.

Hăg′gith (*dancer*). A wife of David, 2 Sam. iii. 4; 1 Kgs. i. 5.

Hā′gi-ȧ, 1 Esdr. v. 34. [HATTIL.]

Hā′ī. Ancient form of Ai, Gen. xii. 8; xiii. 3.

Hāil. The seventh plague, Ex. ix. 18–29. God's weapon, Josh. x. 11; Rev. xvi. 21.

Hâir. Worn short with elderly men, long with young men, vowed men and women, Num. vi. 5–9; 2 Sam. xiv. 26; Luke vii. 38. Lepers shorn, Lev. xiv. 8, 9.

Hăk′ka-tăn (*little*). Father of Johanan, Ez. viii. 12.

Hăk′kŏz (*thorn*). Priest of 7th course, 1 Chr. xxiv. 10.

Hȧ-kū′phȧ (*bent*). His children returned, Ez. ii. 51.

Hā′lah. Probably Habor, 2 Kgs. xvii. 6.

Hā′lăk (*smooth*). An unlocated mountain, Josh. xi. 17; xii. 7.

Greek Generals. (*See* Greece, p. 49.)

Hāle. Haul, Luke xii. 58; Acts viii. 3.

Hăl′hŭl (*trembling*). Town of Judah, Josh. xv. 58.

Hā′lī (*necklace*). Border of Asher, Josh. xix. 25.

Hăl″i-căr-năs′sus. City of Caria, 1 Macc. xv. 23.

Hăll. Court of a high priest's house, Luke xxii. 55; Matt. xxvii. 27.

Hăl″le-lū′jȧh (*ya*). [ALLELUIA.]

Hăl-lō′hesh (*enchanter*). Co-covenanter with Nehemiah, Neh. x. 24.

Hȧ-lō′hesh (*enchanter*). A builder of the wall, Neh. iii. 12.

Hăm (*hot*). Third son of Noah, Gen. v. 32; ix. 22. Father of the Hamitic races, x. 6, etc.

Hā′man (*famed*). Prime minister of Ahasuerus, Esth.

Hā′math (*fortress*). Chief city of upper Syria, Gen. x. 18; Num. xxxiv. 8. Became part of Solomon's kingdom, 1 Kgs. viii. 65; 2 Chr. viii. 3, 4. Now Hamah.

Hăm′măth (*hot springs*). A town near Tiberias, Josh. xix. 35. Hammoth-Dor, Josh. xxi. 32. Hammon, 1 Chr. vi. 76.

Hăm-mĕd′a-thȧ (*double*). Father of Haman, Esth. iii. 1.

Hăm′me-lĕch (*king*). Hardly a proper name, Jer. xxxvi. 26; xxxviii. 6.

Hăm′mĕr. Same as now, Judg. iv. 21; Isa. xliv. 12. Mighty force, Jer. xxiii. 29; l. 23.

Hăm-mŏl′e-kĕth (*queen*). Sister of Gilead, 1 Chr. vii. 17, 18.

Hăm′mŏn (*warm springs*). (1) City in Asher, Josh. xix. 28. (2) Levitical city in Naphtali, 1 Chr. vi. 76.

Hăm′moth-dôr, Josh. xxi. 32. [HAMMATH.]

Hȧ-mō′nah (*multitude*). Unknown city, Ezek. xxxix. 16.

Hā′mon-gŏg (*multitude of Gog*). Unlocated valley, Ezek. xxxix. 11–15.

Hā′mor (*ass*). Father of Shechem, Gen. xxxiii. 19; xxxiv. 26. Emmor, Acts vii. 16.

Hȧ-mū′el (*wrath*). A Simeonite, 1 Chr. iv. 26.

Hā′mŭl (*pity*). Son of Pharez, and founder of Hamulites, Gen. xlvi. 12.

Hā′mŭl-ītes, Num. xxvi. 21. [HAMUL.]

Hȧ-mū′tal (*like dew*). A wife of Josiah, 2 Kgs. xxiii. 31; Jer. lii. 1.

Hȧ-năm′e-el (*given of God*). Jeremiah's cousin, Jer. xxxii. 6–12.

Hā′nan (*merciful*). (1) A Benjamite, 1 Chr. viii. 23. (2) Descendant of Saul, 1 Chr. viii. 38. (3) One of David's guard, 1 Chr. xi. 43. (4) His sons returned, Ez. ii. 46. (5, 6, 7) Co-covenanters with Nehemiah, Neh. x. 10, 22, 26. (8) A tithe-keeper, Neh. xiii. 13. (9) One who had temple rooms, Jer. xxxv. 4.

Hȧ-năn′e-el (*given of God*). A tower on wall of Jerusalem, Neh. iii. 1; xii. 39; Jer. xxxi. 38.

Hȧ-nā′nī (*gracious*). (1) Head of the 18th temple course, 1 Chr. xxv. 4, 25. (2) A seer, 2 Chr. xvi. 7–10. (3) A priest, Ez. x. 20. (4) Brother of Nehemiah, Neh. i. 2; vii. 2.

Hăn″a-nī′ah (*given of God*). (1) Leader of 16th temple course, 1 Chr. xxv. 4, 5, 23. (2) A general, 2 Chr. xxvi. 11. (3) Father of Zedekiah, Jer. xxxvi. 12. (4) A false prophet, Jer. xxviii. (5) Grandfather of Irijah, Jer. xxxvii. 13. (6) Hebrew name of Shadrach, Dan. i. 3–19. (7) Son of Zerubbabel, 1 Chr. iii. 19. Joanna in Luke. (8) A Benjamite, 1 Chr. viii. 24. (9) One of the returned, Ez. x. 28. (10) Others, Neh. iii. 8; vii. 2, 3; x. 23; xii. 12.

Hănd. Conspicuous in Hebrew ceremonial and

other customs, Gen. xiv. 22; Deut. xxi. 6, 7; Matt. xxvii. 24; Job xxxi. 27; Isa. lxv. 2.

Hănd'breadth. Palm width; about four inches, Ex. xxv. 25.

Hănd'ĭ-craft. Though not noted for artisanship, Hebrew boys were taught trades, and reference is made to smiths, Gen. iv. 22; carpenters, Isa. xliv. 14; Matt. xiii. 55; masons, 1 Kgs. v. 18; ship-building, 1 Kgs. ix. 26; apothecaries, Ex. xxx. 25, 35; weavers, Ex. xxxv. 25, 26; dyers, Josh. ii. 18; barbers, Num. vi. 5–19; tent-makers, Acts xviii. 3; potters, Jer. xviii. 2–6; bakers, xxxvii. 21; engravers, Ex. xxviii. 9–11; tanners, Acts ix. 43.

Hănd'kĕr-chiefs. These, and napkins and aprons, signify about same as to-day, Luke xix. 20; John xi. 44; Acts xix. 12.

Hănd'stāves. Javelins, Ezek. xxxix. 9.

Hā'nēs. A city in Egypt, Isa. xxx. iv.

Här'a-dah (*fear*). An Israelite encampment, Num. xxxiii. 24, 25.

Hā'ran (*mountainous*). (1) Brother of Abraham, Gen. xi. 26–31. (2) A Levite, 1 Chr. xxiii. 9. (3) Son of Caleb, 1 Chr. ii. 46. (4) The spot in Mesopotamia where Abraham located after leaving Ur, Gen. xi. 31, 32; xxiv. 10; xxvii. 43. Charran, Acts vii. 2–4.

Hā'ra-rīte. Three of David's guard so called, 2 Sam. xxiii. 11, 33.

Här-bō'nȧ (*ass driver*). A chamberlain, Esth. i. 10. Harbonah in vii. 9.

Hâre (*leaper*). A species of rabbit, wrongly thought to chew the cud, Lev. xi. 6; Deut. xiv. 7.

Hā'reph (*plucking*). Son of Caleb, 1 Chr. ii. 51.

Hā'reth (*thicket*). A forest of Judah, 1 Sam. xxii. 5.

Stringed Instruments. (*See* Harp, p. 52.)

Hăng'ing, Hăng'ings. In strict law, culprits were strangled first, then hung, Num. xxv. 4; Deut. xxi. 22, 23. Hangings for doors and tabernacle use, quite the same as modern tapestries, Ex. xxvi. 9, 36; Num. iii. 26.

Hăn'ĭ-el (*grace of God*). An Asherite, 1 Chr. vii. 39.

Hăn'nah (*grace*). Mother of Samuel, 1 Sam. i., ii.

Hăn'na-thon (*gracious*). A city of Zebulun, Josh. xix. 14.

Hăn'nĭ-el (*grace of God*). A prince of Manasseh, Num. xxxiv. 23.

Hā'noch (*dedicated*). (1) Son of Midian, Gen. xxv. 4; Henoch, 1 Chr. i. 33. (2) A son of Reuben, and founder of Hanochites, Gen. xlvi. 9; Num. xxvi. 5.

Hā'nŭn (*gracious*). (1) A king of Ammon, 2 Sam. x. 1–6. (2) Two architects, Neh. iii. 13, 30.

Hăph-rā'im (*pits*). A city of Issachar, Josh. xix. 19.

Hā'rȧ (*hill*). No doubt Haran, 1 Chr. v. 26.

Här''hā-ī'ah (*God's anger*). Father of Uzziel, Neh. iii. 8.

Här'has (*poor*). Ancestor of Shallum, 2 Kgs. xxii. 14.

Här'hûr (*inflamed*). His children returned, Neh. vii. 53.

Hā'rim (*flat-nosed*). (1) Priestly head of third course, 1 Chr. xxiv. 8. (2) Name of several who returned, Ez. ii. 32, 39; x. 21; Neh. iii. 11; vii. 35, 42; x. 27; xii. 15.

Hā'riph (*plucking*). His children returned, Neh. vii. 24; x. 19.

Här'lot (*vagabond*). An abandoned woman, Gen. xxxviii. 15. Harlotry forbidden, Lev. xix. 29. Type of idolatry, Isa. i. 21; Ezek. xvi. Classed with publicans, Matt. xxi. 32.

Här''ma-gĕd'don. R. V. for Armageddon.

Här'ne-phĕr (*panting*). An Asherite, 1 Chr. vii. 36.

Hā'rod (*fear*). A spring near Jezreel, Judg. vii. 1.

Hā'rod-īte. Two of David's guard, so called, 2 Sam. xxiii. 25.

Hăr'ŏ-eh (*seer*). Son of Shobal, 1 Chr. ii. 52.

Hȧ-rō'sheth (*handicraft*). A city of Naphtali, Judg. iv. 2–16.

Härp (*sickle shaped*). Prominent Jewish musical instrument, invented by Jubal, Gen. iv. 21; of various shapes and sizes; different number of strings; played with fingers or plectrum (quill).

Hăr'row (*rake*). "Threshing-machine," 2 Sam. xii. 31; 1 Chr. xx. 3. Pulverizer of ground, Isa. xxviii. 24; Job xxxix. 10, and elsewhere.

Här'shȧ (*deaf*). His children returned, Ez. ii. 52; Neh. vii. 54.

The Hart.

Härt. Male of the red deer, Deut. xii. 15; xiv. 5; 1 Kgs. iv. 23; S. of Sol. ii. 9.

Hā'rum (*high*). A Judahite, 1 Chr. iv. 8.

Hȧ-ru'maph (*slit-nosed*). Father of Jedaiah, Neh. iii. 10.

Hăr'u-phīte, The. A friend of David, 1 Chr. xii. 5.

Hā'ruz (*careful*). Amon's grandfather Kgs. xxi. 19.

Här'vest. [Agriculture.]

Hăs''a-dī'ah (*loved of God*). One of David's line, 1 Chr. iii. 20.

Hăs''e-nū'ah (*hated*). A Benjamite, 1 Chr. ix. 7.

Hăsh''a-bī'ah (*regarded*). (1) Two Levites, 1 Chr. vi. 45; ix. 14. (2) Leader of twelfth course, 1 Chr. xxv. 3, 19. (3) A Hebronite, 1 Chr. xxvi. 30. (4) Other Levites, 1 Chr. xxvii. 17; 2 Chr. xxxv. 9; Ez. viii. 19, 24; Neh. iii. 17; x. 11; xi. 15, 22; xii. 24.

Hȧ-shăb'nah (*regarded*). A co-covenanter with Nehemiah, Neh. x. 25.

Hăsh''ăb-nī'ah (*regarded*). (1) His son repaired the wall, Neh. iii. 10. (2) A Levite, Neh. ix. 5.

Hăsh-băd'a-nȧ (*judge*). Assistant to Ezra, Neh. viii. 4.

Hā'shem (*fat*). His sons were of David's guard, 1 Chr. xi. 34.

Hăsh-mō'nah (*fatness*). A desert station, Num. xxxiii. 29.

Hā'shub (*informed*). (1) Hasshub, a Levite, 1 Chr. ix. 14. (2) Other Levites and builders, Neh. iii. 11, 23; x. 23.

Hȧ-shu'bah (*informed*). One of David's line, 1 Chr. iii. 20.

Hā'shum (*rich*). (1) His children returned, Ez. ii. 19. (2) Assistant to Ezra, Neh. viii. 4.

Hȧ-shū'phȧ (*stripped*). His children returned, Ez. ii. 43; Neh. vii. 46.

Hăs'rah, 2 Chr. xxxiv. 22. [Harhas.]

Hăs''sĕ-nā'ah (*thorny*). His sons built the fish-gate, Neh. iii. 3.

Hăs'shub. [Hashub.]

Hȧ-sū'phȧ. [Hashupha.]

Hā'tăch. Chamberlain of Ahasuerus, Esth. iv. 5–10.

Hā'thăth (*fear*). Son of Othniel, 1 Chr. iv. 13.

Hăt'ī-phȧ (*captive*). His sons returned, Ez. ii. 54.

Hăt'ī-tȧ (*searching*). Returned porters, Ez. ii. 42.

Hăt'til (*doubtful*). His sons returned, Ez. ii. 57.

Hăt'tŭsh (*gathered*). (1) A Judahite, 1 Chr. iii. 22; Ez. viii. 2. (2) Others of the returned, Neh. iii. 10; x. 4; xii. 2.

Hau'ran (*caves*). Present Hauran, S. of Syria in Bashan, Ezek. xlvii. 16–18.

Hăv'ī-lah (*circle*). (1) Son of Cush, Gen. x. 7. (2) Son of Joktan, x. 29. (3) An unlocated region, Gen. ii. 11; xxv. 18; 1 Sam. xv. 7.

Hā'voth=jā'ir (*villages of Jair*). Villages in Gilead or Bashan, Num. xxxii. 41; Deut. iii. 14.

Häwk (*havoc*). An unclean bird; species of falcon, Lev. xi. 16; Deut. xiv. 15; Job xxxix. 26.

Hāy (*cut*). Grass; but hardly cut and dried grass, Prov. xxvii. 25; Ps. lxxii. 6; Isa. xv. 6.

Hăz'a-el (*God sees*). A Syrian king, 1 Kgs. xix. 15; 2 Kgs. viii. 7–16; x. 32; xiii. 24.

Hȧ-zā'iah (*whom God sees*). A Judahite, Neh. xi. 5.

Hā'zar. [Hazer.]

Hā'zar=ăd'dar. [Hazer.]

Hā'zar=mā'veth. Son of Joktan, Gen. x. 26.

Hā'zel. The almond doubtless meant, Gen. xxx. 37.

Hăz''e-lĕl-pō'nī (*coming shadows*). Sister of Judahites, 1 Chr. iv. 3.

Hā'zer (*village*). In composition. (1) Hazar-addar, a landmark of Israel, Num. xxxiv. 4; Adar, Josh. xv. 3. (2) Hazar-enan, a boundary of Israel, Num. xxxiv. 9, 10. (3) Hazar-gaddah, a town of Judah, Josh. xv. 27. (4) Hazar-shual, in southern Judah, Josh. xv. 28. (5) Hazar-susah, in Judah, Josh. xix. 5; Hazar-susim, 1 Chr. iv. 31. (6) Hazar-hatticon, Ezek. xlvii. 16.

Hȧ-zē'rĭm, Deut. ii. 23. Villagers. [Hazer.]

Hȧ-zē'roth (*villages*). An Israelite encampment, Num. xi. 35; Deut. i. 1.

Hăz'e-zon=tā'mar (*felling of palms*). Old name of Engedi, Gen. xiv. 7. Hazazon-tamar, 2 Chr. xx. 2.

Hā'zĭ-el (*vision*). A Levite, 1 Chr. xxiii. 9.

Hā'zō (*vision*). Son of Nahor, Gen. xxii. 22.

Hā'zôr (*court*). (1) City of Naphtali, Josh. xi. 10; 1 Kgs. ix. 15; 2 Kgs. xv. 29. (2) Town of Judah, Josh. xv. 23–25. (3) Place in Benjamin, Neh. xi. 33.

Hĕad'dress. Sacerdotal and ornamental, Ex. xxviii. 40. Mantle or veil the usual head-dress.

Heärth (*ground*). Hot stones, Gen. xviii. 6. Pan or brazier, Jer. xxxvi. 23.

Hēath (*country*). No heath in Palestine. Evidently a desert scrub, Jer. xvii. 6; xlviii. 6.

Hēa'then (*dwellers on the heath*). All except Jews, Ps. ii. 1. Non-believer, Matt. xviii. 17.

Hĕav'en (*heaved*). Firmament, Gen. i. 1; Matt. v. 18. Abode of God, 1 Kgs. viii. 30; Dan. ii. 28; Matt. v. 45. Paradise, Luke xxiii. 43.

Hē'bĕr (*alliance*). Eber, Luke iii. 35. Others in Gen. xlvi. 17; Num. xxvi. 45; Judg. iv. 17; 1 Chr. iv. 18; v. 13; vii. 31; viii. 17, 22.

Hē'brews. "Abram the Hebrew," Gen. xiv. 13, that is, *eber*, the one who had "passed over" the Euphrates, westward. Hence, "seed" or descendants of Abraham. Among themselves, preferably,

Israelites, from Gen. xxxii. 28. Jews, *i. e.* Judahites, Judeans, after the captivity.

He'brews, Epistle to. Written probably by Paul, from Rome, A. D. 62 or 63, to overcome Hebrew favoritism for the old law.

Hē'bron (*friendship*). (1) Son of Kohath, Ex. vi. 18; Num. iii. 19, 27. (2) Person or place, 1 Chr. ii. 42. (3) Ancient city of Judah, 20 mls. S. of Jerusalem, Gen. xiii. 18; Num. xiii. 22; Arba in Josh. xxi. 11; Judg. i. 10.

Hē'bron-ītes. Kohathite Levites, Num. iii. 27; xxvi. 58.

Hědge (*haw*). In Hebrew sense, anything that encloses — wall, fence, or thorn bushes, Num. xxii. 24; Prov. xxiv. 31; Hos. ii. 6.

Hěg'a-ī, Hē'gē. Chamberlain of Ahasuerus, Esth. ii. 3, 8, 15.

Hěif'ēr (*high-bullock*). Red heifers sacrificial, Num. xix. 10. Frequent source of metaphor, Judg. xiv. 18; Isa. xv. 5; Jer. xlvi. 20; Hos. iv. 16.

Heir (*inheritor*). Eldest son became head of tribe or family with largest share of paternal estate; sons of concubines given presents; daughters, a marriage portion, Gen. xxi. 10, 14; xxiv. 36; xxv. 6; xxxi. 14; Judg. xi. 2, etc. Real estate apportioned as in Deut. xxi. 17; Num. xxvii. 4–11.

Hē'lah (*rust*). Wife of Ashur, 1 Chr. iv. 5.

Hē'lam (*fort*). A battlefield, 2 Sam. x. 16, 17.

Hěl'bah (*fertile*). Town of Asher, Judg. i. 31.

Hěl'bon (*fertile*). A Syrian city, Ezek. xxvii. 18.

Hěl-chī'ah, 1 Esdr. viii. 1. [HILKIAH.]

Hěl'da-ī (*worldly*). (1) Captain of 12th course, 1 Chr. xxvii. 15. (2) One who returned, Zech. vi. 10. Helem in vs. 14.

Hē'lěb, Hē'lěd (*passing*). One of David's guard, 2 Sam. xxiii. 29; 1 Chr. xi. 30.

Hē'lek (*portion*). Founder of Helekites, Num. xxvi. 30.

Hē'lem (*strength*). (1) An Asherite, 1 Chr. vii. 35. (2) Probably Heldai, Zech. vi. 14.

Hē'leph (*exchange*). Starting point of Naphtali's boundary, Josh. xix. 33.

Hē'lez (*strong*). (1) Captain of 7th course and one of David's guard, 2 Sam. xxiii. 26; 1 Chr. xi. 27. (2) A Judahite, 1 Chr. ii. 39.

Hē'lī (*climbing*). Eli, father of Joseph, Luke iii. 23.

Hē''lĭ-ō-dō'rus. A Syrian treasurer, 2 Macc. iii.

Hěl'ka-ī (*portion*). A priest, Neh. xii. 15.

Hěl'kăth (*part*). (1) Starting point of Asher's boundary, Josh. xix. 25. (?) Hěl'kăth hăz'zu rīm, a battlefield; 2 Sam. ii. 16.

Hěl-kī'as, 1 Esdr. i. 8. [HILKIAH.]

Hěll (*conceal*). Hebrew "sheol;" translated "grave," 1 Sam. ii. 6; "pit," Num. xvi. 30; "hell," Job xi. 8, in O. T. In N. T., Hades and Gehenna are translated hell, Acts ii. 27; Matt. v. 29. Gehenna, or Valley of Hinnom, alone implies a place of burning or torture.

Hěl'lěn-ist. A Grecian; but limited to Greek-speaking Jews in Acts vi. 1; ix. 29; xi. 20.

Hěl'met (*hide*). Armor, generally metal, for head, 1 Sam. xvii. 5; 2 Chr. xxvi. 14. [ARMOR.]

Hē'lon (*strong*). Father of Eliab, Num. i. 9; ii. 7.

Hěm (*field*). Edge, or fringe, of a garment, Num. xv. 38, 39; Matt. xxiii. 5.

Hē'mam (*driving out*). Grandson of Seir, Gen. xxxvi. 22.

Hē'man (*trusty*). (1) Son of Zerah, 1 Chr. ii. 6. (2) Grandson of Samuel, 1 Chr. vi. 33; xv. 16–22; xxv. 5.

Hē'măth (*heat*). Person or place, 1 Chr. ii. 55. Hamath, 1 Chr. xiii. 5; Am. vi. 14.

Hěm'dan (*pleasant*). Son of Dishon, Gen. xxxvi. 26. Amram, 1 Chr. i. 41.

Hěm'lock. Not the bitter, poisonous hemlock as in Hos. x. 4; Am. vi. 12, but "gall," as elsewhere.

Hěn (*rest*). (1) Son of Zephaniah, Zech. vi. 14. (2) The domestic fowl, common in Palestine, but mentioned only in Matt. xxiii. 37; Luke xiii. 34.

Hē'nä (*troubling*). A city of Mesopotamia, 2 Kgs. xviii. 34; xix. 13; Isa. xxxvii. 13.

Hěn'a-dăd (*favor of Hadad*). His sons returned, Ez. iii. 9; Neh. x. 9.

Helmets.

Hē'noch. (1) 1 Chr. i. 3. [ENOCH, 6.] (2) 1 Chr. i. 33. [HANOCH, 1.]

Hē'phēr (*pit*). (1) Founder of Hepherites, Num. xxvi. 32; Josh. xii. 17. (2) Son of Ashur, 1 Chr. iv. 6. (3) One of David's guard, 1 Chr. xi. 36. (4) A place W. of Jordan, Josh. xii. 17.

Hěph'zĭ-bah (*my delight in her*). (1) Name of restored Jerusalem, Isa. lxii. 4. (2) Wife of Hezekiah, 2 Kgs. xxi. 1.

Hēr'ăld (*army ruler*). Crier, Dan. iii. 4; preacher, as in 1 Tim. ii. 7; 2 Pet. ii. 5.

Hēr'cū-leş. The god "Melkart," 2 Macc. iv. 19.

Hērd. A collection of cattle. Herdsmen despised by Egyptians, Gen. xlvi. 34, but honored by Hebrews, 1 Sam. xi. 5; xxi. 7.

Hē'rēş (*sun*). A place in Dan, Judg. i. 35.

Hē'resh (*carpenter*). A Levite, 1 Chr. ix. 15.

Hēr'mas, Hēr'mēş (*Mercury*). Two friends of Paul, Rom. xvi. 14.

Hēr-mŏg'e-nēş (*born of Mercury*). One who deserted Paul, 2 Tim. i. 15.

Hēr'mŏn (*lofty*). Highest peak of Anti-Libanus range and northern landmark of Palestine, 10,000 ft. high, Deut. iii. 8; Josh. xi. 17.

Hēr'mon-ītes. The three peaks of Hermon, Ps. xlii. 6.

Her'od (*heroic*). (1) Herod the Great, tetrarch of Judea, B. C. 41; King of Judea, B. C. 41–4; liberal, yet tyrannical and cruel. Issued murderous edict against children of Bethlehem, Matt. ii. 16. (2) Herod Antipas, son of former; tetrarch of Galilee and Perea, B. C. 4–A. D. 39; murderer of John the Baptist, Matt. xiv. 1; Luke iii. 19; xxiii. 7–15; Acts xiii. 1. (3) Herod Philip, son of Herod the Great. Married Herodias, Matt. xiv. 3; Mark vi. 17; Luke iii. 19. Lived and died in private life. (4) Herod Philip II., son of Herod the Great, and tetrarch of Batanea, Ituræa, etc., B. C. 4–A. D. 34, Luke iii. 1. (5) Herod Agrippa I., grandson of Herod the Great; tetrarch of Galilee; king of his grandfather's realm, A. D., 37–44, Acts xii. 1–19. (6) Herod Agrippa II., son of former, and king of consolidated tetrarchies, A. D. 50–100, Acts xxv. 13–27; xxvi. 1–28.

Hē-rō'dĭ-anş. A Jewish political party who favored the Herods and Roman dependence, Matt. xxii. 16; Mark iii. 6; viii. 15.

Hē-rō'dĭ-as. Granddaughter of Herod the Great. Wife of her uncle Herod Philip and her step-uncle

She requested the head of John the Baptist, Matt. xiv. 3–6; Mark vi. 17; Luke iii. 19.

Hē-rō′dĭ-on. Kinsman of Paul, Rom. xvi. 11.

Hĕr′on. A large aquatic bird, pronounced unclean, Lev. xi. 19; Deut. xiv. 18.

Hē′sed (*kindness*). Father of one of Solomon's commissaries, 1 Kgs. iv. 10.

Hĕsh′bŏn (*device*). An Amorite capital, N. E. of Dead Sea, Num. xxi. 26; Josh. xiii. 17; Isa. xv. 4.

Hĕsh′mŏn (*fertile*). Place in south Judah, Josh. xv. 27.

Hĕs′rŏn. [Hezron.]

Hĕth (*fear*). Progenitor of the Hittites, Gen. x. 15; xxiii. 3–20; xxv. 10; xxvii. 46.

Hĕth′lŏn (*hiding place*). A mountain pass, probably Hamath, Ezek. xlvii. 15; xlviii. 1.

Hĕz′e-kī (*strong*). A Benjamite, 1 Chr. viii. 17.

Hĕz-e-kī′ah (*strength of God*). (1) Twelfth king of Judah, B. C. 726–698. Noted for abolition of idolatry and powerful resistance to neighboring nations, 2 Kgs. xviii.–xx.; 2 Chr. xxix.–xxxii. (2) Son of Neariah, 1 Chr. iii. 23. (3) [Ater.]

Coin of Herod the Great. (*See* p. 53.)

Hē′zĭ-on (*sight*). A king of Syria; probably Rezon, 1 Kgs. xv. 18; xi. 23.

Hē′zīr (*swine*). (1) Leader of 17th course, 1 Chr. xxiv. 15. (2) A co-covenanter, Neh. x. 20.

Hĕz′ra-ī (*enclosure*). One of David's guard, 2 Sam. xxiii. 35. Hezro, 1 Chr. xi. 37.

Hĕz′ron (*surrounded*). (1) A Reubenite, Gen. xlvi. 9. (2) Son of Pharez, Gen. xlvi. 12; Ruth iv. 18.

Hĕz′ron-ites. Reubenite and Judahite families, Num. xxvi. 6, 21.

Hĭd′da-ī (*joyful*). One of David's guard, 2 Sam. xxiii. 30.

Hĭd′de-kel (*rapid*). Third river of Eden, no doubt Tigris, Gen. ii. 14; Dan. x. 4.

Hī′el (*God lives*). A Bethelite who rebuilt Jericho, 1 Kgs. xvi. 34.

Hī″e-răp′o-lĭs (*holy city*). City of Phrygia, on the Meander near Colossæ, Col. iv. 13.

Hī-er′e-el, 1 Esdr. ix. 21. [Jehiel.]

Hī-er′e-moth. Jeremoth, Ramoth, in Esdr.

Hī″e-rŏn′y̆-mus (*sacred name*). A Syrian general, 2 Macc. xii. 2.

Hĭg-gā′ion (*meditation*). Musical pause for meditation, Ps. ix. 16; xix. 14, xcii. 3, marg.

High Plā′ces. Altars, temples, and dedicated places originally on high ground, Gen. xii. 8; Judg. vi. 25; Isa. lxv. 7; Jer. iii. 6. When the groves and mounts of idolatry overshadowed true worship, "high places" became a reproach.

High Priēst. Chief priest, Aaron being the first. Originally a life office, limited to a line or family, Ex. xxviii. 1; Lev. xxi. 10; Num. iii. 32; xx. 8; Deut. x. 6.

Hī′len (*caves*). A Levitical city in Judah, 1 Chr. vi. 58.

Hĭl-kī′ah (*God my portion*). (1) Father of Eliakim, 2 Kgs. xviii. 37. (2) A high priest, 2 Kgs. xxii. 8. (3) Four Levites, 1 Chr. vi. 45; xxvi. 11; Neh. viii. 4; xii. 7, 21. (4) Father of Jeremiah, Jer. i. 1. (5) Father of an ambassador, Jer. xxix. 3.

Hĭl′lel (*praise*). Father of Abdon, Judg. xii. 13, 15.

Hĭn. A Hebrew liquid measure, about 1½ gallons, Ex. xxx. 24.

Hīnd. Female of the red deer, Gen. xlix. 21; Ps. xxix. 9; Prov. v. 19.

Hĭnge (*hanged*). A pivot and socket for swinging doors, 1 Kgs. vii. 50; Prov. xxvi. 14.

Hĭn′nom (*wailing*). A narrow valley south and west of Jerusalem, Josh. xv. 8; xviii. 16, where Molech was worshipped, 1 Kgs. xi. 7; 2 Kgs. xvi. 3; hence called Tophet, "drum," noise, Isa. xxx. 33; defiled, 2 Kgs. xxiii. 10, and called ge-Hinnom, gehenna, "place of Hinnom," to type a place of eternal torment. "Hell" in N. T., Matt. v. 22, 29; x. 28; xxiii. 15; Mark ix. 43; Luke xii. 5.

Hī′rah (*noble*). An Adullamite, Gen. xxxviii. 1, 12, 20.

Hī′ram, Hū′ram (*noble*). (1) King of Tyre who furnished men and material to David and Solomon, 2 Sam. v. 11; 1 Kgs. v.; 1 Chr. xiv. 1. (2) Hiram's chief architect, 1 Kgs. vii. 13, 40.

Hĭr-cā′nus. Son of Tobias, 2 Macc. iii. 11.

Hĭt′tītes. Descendants of Heth, Gen. x. 15; xxv. 9; Josh. iii. 10; 2 Sam. xi. 3.

Hī′vītes (*villagers*). Descendants of Canaan, Gen. x. 17; located at Shechem, xxxiv. 2; noted for craft, Josh. ix.

Hĭz-kī′ah (*strength*). Ancestor of Zephaniah, Zeph. i. 1.

Hĭz-kī′jah (*strength*). A co-covenanter, Neh. x. 17.

Hō′băb (*live*). Brother-in-law of Moses, Num. x. 29–32.

Hō′bah (*hiding*). A place beyond Damascus, Gen. xiv. 15.

Hŏd (*splendor*). Son of Zophah, 1 Chr. vii. 37.

Hŏd-a-ī′ah (*praise ye*). A Judahite, 1 Chr. iii. 24.

Hŏd-a-vī′ah (*praise ye*). (1) A Manassite, 1 Chr. v. 24. (2) A Benjamite, 1 Chr. ix. 7. (3) A Levite, Ez. ii. 40.

Hō′desh (*new moon*). A Benjamite woman, 1 Chr. viii. 9.

Hō-dē′vah, Neh. vii. 43. [Hodaviah, 3.]

Hō-dī′ah (*splendor*). Wife of Ezra, 1 Chr. iv. 19. Jehudijah in vs. 18.

Hō′dī-jah (*splendor*). Three Levites, Neh. viii. 7; x. 13, 18.

Hŏg′lah (*quail*). Daughter of Zelophehad, Num. xxvi. 33.

Hō′ham (*driven*). A king of Hebron, Josh. x. 3.

Hōlm=tree. Holm-oak, Sus. 58.

Hŏl-ō-fēr′nēs. The general slain by Judith, Judith ii. 4, etc.

Hō′lŏn (*sandy*). (1) A town of Judah, Josh. xv. 51. (2) A city of Moab, Jer. xlviii. 21.

Hō′mam, 1 Chr. i. 39. [Hemam.]

Hō′mĕr. A Hebrew liquid and dry measure, from 47 to 64 gals., according to time, and 6 to 8 bush., Ezek. xlv. 14.

Hon′ey. Bees numerous and honey plentiful in Palestine. Much used, Lev. xx. 24; Deut. xxxii. 13; Matt. iii. 4.

Hooks. Various kinds. Fishing, Job xli. 2; leading, 2 Kgs. xix. 28; pruning, Isa. ii. 4; hanging meats, Ezek. xl. 43; curtains, Ex. xxvi. 32–37; lifting boiled food, 1 Sam. ii. 13.

Hŏph′nī (*fighter*). Impious son of Eli, 1 Sam. i. 3; ii. 12–17; iii. 11–14; iv. 11.

Hôr (*hill*). (1) Mount in Edom on which Aaron died, Num. xx. 22–29; xxxiii. 37. (2) A peak of Lebanon range, Num. xxxiv. 7, 8.

Hō'ram (*hill*). King of Gezer, Josh. x. 33.

Hō'reb (*desert*). [SINAI.]

Hō'rem (*offered*). A place in Naphtali, Josh. xix. 38.

Hôr-hă-gĭd'gad (*cleft mountain*). A desert station of the Israelites, Num. xxxiii. 32.

Hō'rī (*cave-dweller*). (1) Grandson of Seir, Gen. xxxvi. 22. (2) A Simeonite, Num. xiii. 5.

Hō'rītes, Hōrims. Original people of Mt. Seir, Gen. xiv. 6.

Hôr'mah (*laid waste*). A Canaanite town in southern Judah, Josh. xv. 30; 1 Sam. xxx. 30.

Hôrn. Made of horn or metal, and of various shapes, sizes, and uses. Used much figuratively, Deut. xxxiii. 17; 1 Sam. xvi. 1; Job xvi. 15; Jer. xlviii. 25.

Hôr'net (*horner*). Plenty in Palestine, Ex. xxiii. 28; Deut. vii. 20; Josh. xxiv. 12.

Hornet.

Hŏr''o-nā'im (*two caves*). City of Moab, Isa. xv. 5; Jer. xlviii. 3.

Hŏrse (*neigher*). Used chiefly for war, Ex. xiv. 9-23; 2 Chr. i. 14-17; ix. 25; Esth. vi. 8; for threshing, Isa. xxviii. 28.

Hŏrse'lēech (*adherer*). Found in stagnant waters of East, and fastens to nostrils of animals when drinking, Prov. xxx. 15.

Hō'sah (*refuge*). (1) City of Asher, Josh. xix. 29. (2) A Levite, 1 Chr. xxvi. 10.

Hō-săn'nȧ. "Save, we pray," Ps. cxviii. 25, 26. The cry when Christ entered Jerusalem, Matt. xxi. 9-15; Mark xi. 9, 10.

Hō-sē'ȧ (*help*). First of minor prophets. Prophetic career, B. C. 784-725, in Israel. Denounces the idolatries of Israel and Samaria. Style obscure.

Hŏsh''a-ī'ah (*helped by God*). (1) Nehemiah's assistant, Neh. xii. 32. (2) Jezaniah's father, Jer. xlii. 1.

Hŏsh-a'mȧ (*whom God hears*). Son of Jeconiah, 1 Chr. iii. 18.

Hō-shē'ȧ (*salvation*). (1) Nineteenth and last king of Israel, B. C. 730-721. Conquered and imprisoned by Shalmaneser, 2 Kgs. xv. 30; xvii. 1-6; Hos. xiii. 16. (2) Son of Nun, Deut. xxxii. 44. (3) An Ephraimite, 1 Chr. xxvii. 20. (4) A co-covenanter, Neh. x. 23.

Hŏs''pĭ-tăl'ĭ-ty (*guest treatment*). Regulated in Lev. xix. 33, 34; xxv. 14-17; Deut. xv. 7-11.

Hō'tham (*seal*). An Asherite, 1 Chr. vii. 32.

Hō'than (*seal*). Father of Shama, 1 Chr. xi. 44.

Hō'thir (*fulness*). Son of Heman, 1 Chr. xxv. 4, 28, and leader of 21st course.

Hough (*hok*) (*hock*). Cutting the sinews of the hind leg, hamstringing, Josh. xi. 6, 9; 2 Sam. viii. 4.

Hour (*time*). First division of Jewish day, morning, noon, evening, Ps. lv. 17. Night had three watches, Ex. xiv. 24; Judg. vii. 19; Lam. ii. 19. Later, day was, morning, heat, midday, evening. Hours introduced from Babylon, after captivity, Matt. xx. 1-10. An indefinite time, Dan. iii. 6; Matt. ix. 22.

House (*cover*). Prevailing Oriental style, low, flat roofed, with court in centre. A tent, palace, citadel, tomb, family, Gen. xii. 17; property, 1 Kgs. xiii. 8; lineage, Luke ii. 4; place of worship, Judg. xx. 18.

Hŭk'kŏk (*cut*). A border of Naphtali, Josh. xix. 34.

Hū'kŏk, 1 Chr. vi. 75. [HELKATH.]

Hūl (*circle*). Grandson of Shem, Gen. x. 23.

Hŭl'dah (*weasel*). A prophetess, 2 Kgs. xxii. 14-20; 2 Chr. xxxiv. 22.

Hŭm'tah (*place of lizards*). A city of Judah, Josh. xv. 54.

Hŭnt'ing. Hebrews not a hunting people, yet various devices mentioned for capturing wild animals, 2 Sam. xxiii. 20; Job xviii. 9, 10; Prov. xxii. 5; Isa. li. 20; Am. iii. 5.

Hū'pham (*coast-man*). Founder of Huphamites, Num. xxvi. 39.

Hŭp'pah (*covered*). Leader of 13th priestly course, 1 Chr. xxiv. 13.

Hŭp'pim (*covered*). A Benjamite, 1 Chr. vii. 12.

Hûr (*hole*). (1) The man who helped stay the hands of Moses, Ex. xvii. 10; xxiv. 14. (2) A Judahite, Ex. xxxi. 2. (3) A king of Midian, Num. xxxi. 8. (4) Father of one of Solomon's commissaries, 1 Kgs. iv. 8. (5) Father of a wall-builder, Neh. iii. 9.

Hū'rāi (*weaver*). One of David's guard, 1 Chr. xi. 32.

Hū'ram (*noble*). (1) A Benjamite, 1 Chr. viii. 5. (2) Hiram, 2 Chr. ii. 3-13; iv. 11-16.

Hū'rī (*weaver*). A Gadite, 1 Chr. v. 14.

Hū'shah (*haste*). A Judahite, 1 Chr. iv. 4.

Hū'shāi (*haste*). A friend of David, 2 Sam. xv. 32; 1 Kgs. iv. 16.

Hū'sham (*haste*). A king of Edom, Gen. xxxvi. 34, 35.

Hu'shath-ite. Two of David's guard so-called, 2 Sam. xxi. 18; xxiii. 27.

Hū'shim (*haste*). (1) Son of Dan, Gen. xlvi. 23. Shuham, Num. xxvi. 42. (2) A Benjamite, 1 Chr. vii. 12. (3) Wife of Shaharaim, 1 Chr. viii. 8, 11.

Hŭsks (*hulls*). The original means the carob, or locust bean, Luke xv. 16.

Hŭz (*strong*). Son of Nahor, Gen. xxii. 21.

Hŭz'zăb (*fixed*). A possible queen of Nineveh, Nah. ii. 7.

Hyssop.

Hȳ-ē'na (*hog*). A bristled, fierce, carnivorous animal. "Zeboim," in 1 Sam. xiii. 18; Neh. xi. 34, means hyenas. So, it is thought, the original of "speckled bird," Jer. xii. 9, should be rendered.

Hȳ-dȧs′pēs (*watery*). A river in India, Judith i. 6.

Hȳ″mĕ-næ′us (*hymeneal*). A convert and pervert, 1 Tim. i. 20; 2 Tim. ii. 17.

Hȳmn (*praise-song*). Spiritual song, Matt. xxvi. 30; Acts xvi. 25; Eph. v. 19; Col. iii. 16.

Hȳs′sop (*aromatic plant*). A bushy herb, of the mint family, Ex. xii. 22; Lev. xiv. 4, 6, 51; 1 Kgs. iv. 33; John xix. 29.

Hȳp′ŏ-crĭte (*stage-player*). Who feigns what he is not, Job viii. 13; Luke xii. 1.

I

Ĭb′här (*God's choice*). Son of David, 2 Sam. v. 15.

Ĭb′le-ăm (*destroying*). City of Manasseh, Josh. xvii. 11; Judg. i. 27.

Ĭb-nē′iah (*God builds*). A Benjamite, 1 Chr. ix. 8.

Ĭb-nī′jah (*God builds*). A Benjamite, 1 Chr. ix. 8.

Ĭb′rī (*Hebrew*). A Levite, 1 Chr. xxiv. 27.

Ĭb′zăn (*famous*). A judge of Israel, Judg. xii. 8–10.

Ī′-cha-bŏd (*inglorious*). Son of Phinehas, 1 Sam. iv. 19–22; xiv. 3.

Ī-cō′nĭ-um (*image*). City of Lycaonia, visited twice by Paul, Acts xiii. 51; xiv. 1–22; xvi. 2; 2 Tim. iii. 11.

Ī-dā′lah (*memorial*). City of Zebulun, Josh. xix. 15.

Ĭd′băsh (*stout*). A Judahite, 1 Chr. iv. 3.

Ĭd′dō (*timely*). (1) Father of Ahinadab, 1 Kgs. iv. 14. (2) A Levite, 1 Chr. vi. 21. (3) A Manassite chief, 1 Chr. xxvii. 21. (4) A seer and chronicler, 2 Chr. ix. 29; xiii. 22. (5) Grandfather of Zechariah, Zech. i. 1, 7. (6) One of the returned, Ez. viii. 17.

Ī′dol, Ī-dŏl′a-try (*apparent*). An object of worship, other than God, Gen. xxxi. 19; idolatry forbidden, Ex. xx. 3, 4; xxxiv. 13; Deut. iv. 16–19; vii. 25, 26; yet existed largely, especially under the judges and later kings, Ex. xxxii.; Judg. ii. 10–23; 1 Kgs. xi. 33; xii. 27–33; xiv. 22–24; Isa. lvii. 5–8.

Ī″du-mē′ȧ (*red*), Isa. xxxiv. 5. Idumæa, Mark iii. 8. Greek name of Edom.

Ī′găl (*redeemed*). (1) The spy of Issachar, Num. xiii. 7. (2) One of David's guard, 2 Sam. xxiii. 36.

Ĭg″da-lī′ah (*great*). "A man of God," Jer. xxxv. 4.

Ĭg′e-ăl (*redeemed*). A Judahite, 1 Chr. iii. 22.

Ī′ĭm (*heaps*). (1) Num. xxxiii. 45, Ije-abarim. (2) Town of southern Judah, Josh. xv. 29.

Ĭj″e-ăb′a-rĭm (*ruins of Abarim*). An Israelite encampment near Moab, Num. xxi. 11.

Ī′jon (*ruin*). Town of Naphtali, 1 Kgs. xv. 20; 2 Kgs. xv. 29.

Ĭk′kĕsh (*wicked*). Father of Ira, 2 Sam. xxiii. 26; 1 Chr. xi. 28; xxvii. 9.

Ī′lāi (*exalted*). One of David's guard, 1 Chr. xi. 29.

Ĭl-lȳr′ĭ-cŭm (*joy*). A country on E. shore of Adriatic, N. of Macedonia. Reached by Paul, Rom. xv. 19.

Ĭm′aġe (*likeness*). As in Gen. i. 26, 27; Col. i. 15. Also Idol.

Ĭm′lȧ (*full*). Father of Micaiah, 2 Chr. xviii. 7, 8. Imlah, 1 Kgs. xxii. 8, 9.

Ĭm-măn′ū-el (*God with us*). Name of the prophetic child, Isa. vii. 14. The Messiah, Matt. i. 23.

Ĭm′mĕr (*loquacious*). (1) A priestly family in charge of 16th course, 1 Chr. ix. 12; xxiv. 14. (2) Place in Babylonia, Ez. ii. 59; Neh. vii. 61.

Ĭm′nȧ (*lagging*). An Asherite, 1 Chr. vii. 35.

Ĭm′nah (*lagging*). (1) An Asherite, 1 Chr. vii. 30. (2) A Levite, 2 Chr. xxxi. 14.

Ĭm′rah (*stubborn*). An Asherite, 1 Chr. vii. 36.

Ĭm′rī (*talkative*). (1) A Judahite, 1 Chr. ix. 4. (2) Father of Zaccur, Neh. iii. 2.

Ĭn′çense (*set on fire*). A mixture of gums, spices, etc., Ex. xxx. 34–38, constituted the official incense. Burned morning and evening on the altar of incense, xxx. 1–10. Used also in idolatrous worship, 2 Chr. xxxiv. 25; Jer. xi. 12–17, and by angels, Rev. viii. 3.

Altar of Incense.

Ĭnd′ia (*Indus*). The indefinite country which bounded the Persian empire on the east, Esth. i. 1; viii. 9.

Ĭn-hĕr′ĭ-tance (*heirship*). [Heir.]

Ink, Ink′hôrn (*burnt in*). Ancient ink heavy and thick and carried in an ink-horn, Jer. xxxvi. 18; Ezek. ix. 2.

Ĭnn (*in*). In O. T. a halting place for caravans, Gen. xlii. 27; Ex. iv. 24. In N. T. a caravansary afforded food and shelter for man and beast, Luke x. 34, 35.

Ĭn′stant (*stand in*). Urgent, Luke vii. 4; xxiii. 23; fervent, Acts xxvi. 7; Rom. xii. 12.

Ī-ō′nia. India in 1 Macc. viii. 8.

Ĭph″e-dē′iah (*free*). A Benjamite, 1 Chr. viii. 25.

Ĭr (*city*). A Benjamite, 1 Chr. vii. 12. Iri, vs. 7.

Ī′rȧ (*watchful*). (1) "Chief ruler about David," 2 Sam. xx. 26. (2) Two of David's warriors, 2 Sam. xxiii. 38; 1 Chr. xi. 28.

Ī′răd (*fleet*). Son of Enoch, Gen. iv. 18.

Ī′ram (*citizen*). A duke of Edom, Gen. xxxvi. 43; 1 Chr. i. 54.

Ī′rī (*watchful*). A Benjamite, 1 Chr. vii. 7.

Ī-rī′jah (*seen of God*). A ward-keeper, Jer. xxxvii. 13, 14.

Ĭr-nā′hăsh (*serpent city*). Unknown person or place, 1 Chr. iv. 12.

Ī′ron (*pious*). (1) City of Naphtali, Josh. xix. 38. (2) Iron, the metal, and copper early known, Gen. iv. 22. Prepared in furnaces, 1 Kgs. viii. 51; used for tools, Deut. xxvii. 5; weapons, 1 Sam. xvii. 7; implements, 2 Sam. xii. 31; war-chariots, Josh. xvii. 16, etc.

Ĭr′pē-el (*healed*). City of Benjamin, Josh. xviii. 27.

Ĭr-shē′mĕsh (*sun city*). A Danite city, Josh. xix. 41.

Ī'ru (*watch*). Son of Caleb, 1 Chr. iv. 15.

Ī'saac (*laughter*). Son of Abraham, Gen. xvii. 17-22. Second of the patriarchs, and father of Jacob and Esau, Gen. xxi.-xxxv.

Ī-sā'iah (*salvation of Jehovah*). Son of Amoz, Isa. i. 1, and first of greater prophets. His book, 23d of O. T., covers sixty years of prophecy, Isa. i. 1, at Jerusalem. It reproves the sins of the Jews and other nations, and foreshadows the coming of Christ. Called "prince of prophets." Poetically for Israel, Am. vii. 9, 16.

Ĭs'cah (*who looks*). Sister of Lot, Gen. xi. 29.

Ĭs-căr'ĭ-ot. [JUDAS ISCARIOT.]

Ĭs'dá-el, 1 Esdr. v. 33. [GIDDEL.]

Ĭsh'bah (*praising*). A Judahite, 1 Chr. iv. 17.

Ĭsh'băk (*leaving*). Son of Abraham, and father of northern Arabians, Gen. xxv. 2; 1 Chr. i. 32.

Ĭsh-bĭ=bē'nŏb (*dweller at Nob*). A Philistine giant, 2 Sam. xxi. 16, 17.

Ĭsh=bō'sheth (*man of shame*). Son and successor of Saul. Original name, Esh-baal. Reigned two years, then defeated by David, and assassinated, 2 Sam. ii. 8-11; iii.; iv. 5-12.

Ĭsh'ī (*saving*). (1) Two Judahites, 1 Chr. ii. 31; iv. 20. (2) A Simeonite, iv. 42. (3) A Manassite, v. 24.

Ĭsh-ī'ah (*loaned*). Chief of Issachar, 1 Chr. vii. 3.

Ĭsh-ī'jah (*loaned*). A lay Israelite, Ez. x. 31.

Ĭsh'má (*ruin*). A Judahite, 1 Chr. iv. 3.

Ĭsh'ma-el (*whom God hears*). (1) Son of Abraham and Hagar, Gen. xvi. 15, 16. Banished to wilderness; became progenitor of Arabian tribes, Gen. xxi.; xxv. 9; xxxvii. 25-28. (2) Descendant of Saul, 1 Chr. viii. 38. (3) A Judahite, 2 Chr. xix. 11. (4) A Judahite captain, 2 Chr. xxiii. 1. (5) A priest, Ez. x. 22. (6) Crafty son of Nethaniah, 2 Kgs. xxv. 23-25; Jer. xli.

Ĭsh'ma-el-ītes''. Descendants of Ishmael, Judg. viii. 24. Ishmeelites, Gen. xxxvii. 25; 1 Chr. ii. 17.

Ĭsh''ma-ī'ah (*God hears*). Ruler of Zebulun, 1 Chr. xxvii. 19.

Ĭsh'mĕ-rāi (*God keeps*). A Benjamite, 1 Chr. viii. 18.

Ī'shod (*famed*). A Manassite, 1 Chr. vii. 18.

Ĭsh'păn (*bald*). A Benjamite, 1 Chr. viii. 22.

Ĭsh'=tŏb (*men of Tob*). Part of Aram, 2 Sam. x. 6-8. [TOB.]

Ĭsh'u-ah (*quiet*). An Asherite, Gen. xlvi. 17; 1 Chr. vii. 30.

Ĭsh'u-āi (*quiet*). Son of Asher, 1 Chr. vii. 30.

Ĭsh'u-ī (*quiet*). Son of Saul, 1 Sam. xiv. 49.

Isle (*island*). Habitable place, Isa. xlii. 15; island, Gen. x. 5; Isa. xi. 11; coast lands, Isa. xx. 6; xxiii. 2, 6; Ezek. xxvii. 7.

Ĭs''ma-chī'ah (*supported*). Overseer of offerings, 2 Chr. xxxi. 13.

Ĭs'ma-el, 1 Esdr. ix. 22. [ISHMAEL.]

Ĭs''ma-ī'ah (*God hears*). A chief of Gibeon, 1 Chr. xii. 4.

Ĭs'pah (*bald*). A Benjamite, 1 Chr. viii. 16.

Ĭs'ra-el (*who prevails with God*). Name given to Jacob, Gen. xxxii. 28; xxxv. 10; became national, Ex. iii. 16; narrowed to northern kingdom after the revolt of the ten tribes from Judah, 1 Sam. xi. 8; 2 Sam. xx. 1; 1 Kgs. xii. 16, with Shechem as capital, 1 Kgs. xii. 25, and Tirzah as royal residence, xiv. 17; afterwards, capital at Samaria, xvi. 24. Kingdom lasted 254 years, with 19 kings, B. C. 975-721, when it fell a prey to the Assyrians. The returned of Israel blended with those of Judah.

Ĭs'ra-ĕl-ītes''. "Children of Israel." [ISRAEL.]

Ĭs'sa-char (*rewarded*). (1) Fifth son of Jacob by Leah, Gen. xxx. 17, 18. Tribe characteristics foretold, Gen. xlix. 14, 15. Place during march at east of Tabernacle, Num. ii. 5. Allotment N. of Manasseh, from Carmel to Jordan, Josh. xix. 17-23. (2) A temple porter, 1 Chr. xxvi. 5.

Ĭs'shī-ah (*loaned*). Descendant of Levi, 1 Chr. xxiv. 21. (2) A Levite, 1 Chr. xxiv. 25.

Ĭs''tăl-cū'rus, 1 Esdr. viii. 40. [ZABBUB.]

Ĭs'u-ah, 1 Chr. vii. 30. [JESUI.]

Ĭs'u-i, Gen. xlvi. 17. [JESUI.]

Ĭt'a-ly̆ (*kingdom of Italus*). In N. T. the whole of Italy between the Alps and sea, Acts xviii. 2; xxvii. 1; Heb. xiii. 24.

Ĭth'a-ī (*with God*). A Benjamite, 1 Chr. xi. 31.

Ĭth'a-mär (*land of palms*). Son of Aaron, Ex. vi. 23; xxviii. 1-43; Num. iii. 2-4. Eli was high priest of his line, 1 Chr. xxiv. 6.

Ĭth'ī-el (*God with me*). (1) Friend of Agur, Prov. xxx. 1. (2) A Benjamite, Neh. xi. 7.

Ĭth'mah (*orphan*). One of David's guard, 1 Chr. xi. 46.

Ĭth'nan (*given*). Town in south Judah, Josh. xv. 23.

Ĭth'rá (*plenty*). David's brother-in-law, 2 Sam. xvii. 25.

Ĭth'ran (*plenty*). (1) A Horite, Gen. xxxvi. 26. (2) An Asherite, 1 Chr. vii. 37.

Ĭth're-ăm (*populous*). Son of David, 2 Sam. iii. 5.

Ĭth'rīte. Two of David's warriors so called, 2 Sam. xxiii. 38; 1 Chr. xi. 40.

Ĭt'tah=kā'zin (*hour of a prince*). A landmark of Zebulun, Josh. xix. 13.

Ĭt'ta-ī (*timely*). (1) One of David's generals, 2 Sam. xv. 19; xviii. 2-12. (2) One of David's guard, 2 Sam. xxiii. 29.

Ī''tu-ræ'á. From Jetur, Gen. xxv. 15; 1 Chr. i. 31. A small province N. W. of Palestine, now Jedur, Luke iii. 1.

Ī'vah, Ā'va. An Assyrian city, possibly Hit, 2 Kgs. xviii. 34; xix. 13.

Ī'vŏ-ry̆ (*elephant tooth*). Much used by Hebrews, 1 Kgs. x. 22; 2 Chr. ix. 17-21; Ezek. xxvii. 15.

Ĭz'e-här, Num. iii. 19. [IZHAR.]

Ĭz'här (*oil*). Uncle of Moses, Ex. vi. 18-21; Num. iii. 19. Founder of Izharites, 1 Chr. xxiv. 22.

Ĭz''ra-hī'ah (*sparkling*). Descendant of Issachar, 1 Chr. vii. 3.

Ĭz'ra-hīte. A captain of David, so called, 1 Chr. xxvii. 8.

Ĭz'rī (*created*). Leader of the 4th musical course 1 Chr. xxv. 11.

J

Jā'a-kăn, Deut. x. 6. [JAKAN.]

Jā-ăk'ŏ-bah (*supplanter*). Prince of Simeon, 1 Chr. iv. 36.

Jā-ā'lah (*wild goat*). His children returned, Ez. ii. 56. Jaala, Neh. vii. 58.

Jā-ā'lam (*hidden*). Duke of Edom, Gen. xxxvi. 5, 18.

Jā-ā'nāi (*answered*). A Gadite, 1 Chr. v. 12.

Jā-är'ĕ=ŏr'e-gĭm (*weaver's forests*). Father of Elhanan, slayer of Goliath's brother, 2 Sam. xxi. 19.

Jā'a-sau (*created*). Son of Bani, Ez. x. 37.

Jā-ā'sī-el (*created*). Son of Abner, 1 Chr. xxvii. 21.

Jā-ăz''a-nī'ah (*heard of God*). (1) A Hebrew captain, 2 Kgs. xxv. 23. (2) A denounced prince, Ezek. xi. 1. (3) Son of Jeremiah, Jer. xxxv. 3. (4) Son of Shaphan, Ezek. viii. 11.

Jā-ā'zēr, Jā'zēr (*helped*). City and province of Gilead, Num. xxi. 32; xxxii. 1; Josh. xxi. 39; 1 Chr. xxvi. 31.

Jā''a-zī'ah (*comforted*). A Levite, 1 Chr. xxiv. 26, 27.

Jā-ā'zĭ-el (*comforted*). A temple musician, 1 Chr. xv. 18.

Jā'bāl (*stream*). Son of Lamech, Gen. iv. 20.

Jăb'bok (*flowing*). A tributary of Jordan, on east side; and northern boundary of Ammon, Gen. xxxii. 22; Num. xxi. 24; Deut. ii. 37.

Jā'besh (*dry*). (1) King Shallum's father, 2 Kgs. xv. 10, 13. (2) Jabesh-gilead, a city of Gilead, Judg. xxi. 8-14; 1 Sam. xi. 1-11; xxxi. 11-13.

Jā'bĕz (*sorrow*). Persons or places, 1 Chr. ii. 55; iv. 9, 10.

Jā'bin (*observed*). (1) King of Hazor, Josh. xi. 1-14. (2) Another king of Hazor, defeated by Barak, Judg. iv. 2-24.

Jăb'nĕ-el (*building of God*). (1) Stronghold in Judah, Josh. xv. 11; Jabneh, 2 Chr. xxvi. 6. (2) Place in Naphtali, Josh. xix. 33.

Jăb'neh. [JABNEEL.]

Jā'chan (*affliction*). A Gadite, 1 Chr. v. 13.

Jā'chin (*established*). (1) A temple pillar, 1 Kgs. vii. 21; 2 Chr. iii. 17. (2) Fourth son of Simeon, Gen. xlvi. 10. (3) Head of 21st priestly course, 1 Chr. ix. 10; xxiv. 17.

Jā'chin-ītes. Descendants of Jachin, Num. xxvi. 12.

Jā'cinth (*hyacinth*). Zircon, a vari-colored gem, Rev. ix. 17; xxi. 20.

Jā'cob (*supplanter*). Son of Isaac and second born twin with Esau, Gen. xxv. 24-34. Bought Esau's birthright, fled to Padan-aram, married Rachel and Leah, wandered to Hebron, name changed to Israel, drifted to Egypt, where he died, aged 147 years, Gen. xxv.-l.

Jā-cū'bus, 1 Esdr. ix. 48. [AKKUB, 4.]

Jā'dȧ (*knowing*). A Judahite, 1 Chr. ii. 28, 32.

Jȧ-dā'u (*loving*). Son of Nebo, Ez. x. 43.

Jad-dū'ȧ (*known*). (1) A co-covenanter, Neh. x. 21. (2) High priest, and last mentioned in O. T., Neh. xii. 11, 22.

Jā'don (*judge*). Assistant wall builder, Neh. iii. 7.

Jā'el (*goat*). Heber's wife; murderess of Sisera, Judg. iv. 17-23; v.

Jā'gûr (*lodging*). Southern town of Judah, Josh. xv. 21.

Jäh. Jehovah, in poetry, Ps. lxviii. 4.

Jā'hăth (*united*). (1) A Judahite, 1 Chr. iv. 2. (2) Four Levites, 1 Chr. vi. 20; xxiii. 10, 11; xxiv. 22; 2 Chr. xxxiv. 12.

Jā'hăz (*trodden*). Place in Moab where Moses conquered the Ammonites, Num. xxi. 23, 24; Deut. ii. 32.

Jȧ-hā'zȧ, Josh. xiii. 18. [JAHAZ.]

Jȧ-hā'zah, Josh. xxi. 36. [JAHAZ.]

Jā''hȧ-zī'ah (*seen of God*). A priest, Ez. x. 15.

Jȧ-hā'zĭ-el (*seen of God*). (1) A Benjamite, 1 Chr. xii. 4. (2) A trumpeter, 1 Chr. xvi. 6. (3) A Levite, 1 Chr. xxiii. 19; xxiv. 23. (4) A Levite, 2 Chr. xx. 14. (5) His sons returned, Ez. viii. 5.

Jäh'da-ī (*directed*). A Judahite, 1 Chr. ii. 47.

Jäh'dĭ-el (*joyful*). A Manassite, 1 Chr. v. 24.

Jäh'dō (*united*). A Gadite, 1 Chr. v. 14.

Jäh'lĕ-el (*hoping*). Founder of Jahleelites, Gen. xlvi. 14; Num. xxvi. 26.

Jäh'ma-ī (*guarded*). Son of Tola, 1 Chr. vii. 2.

Jäh'zah, 1 Chr. vi. 78. [JAHAZ.]

Jäh'zĕ-el (*allotted*). Founder of the Jahzeelites, Gen. xlvi. 24; Num. xxvi. 48.

Jäh'zĕ-rah (*led back*). A priest, 1 Chr. ix. 12.

Jäh'zĭ-el, 1 Chr. vii. 13. [JAHZEEL.]

Jā'ïr (*enlightened*). (1) Conqueror of Argob and part of Gilead, Num. xxxii. 41; Deut. iii. 14. (2) A judge of Israel, Judg. x. 3-5. (3) A Benjamite, Esth. ii. 5. (4) Father of Elhanan, 1 Chr. xx. 5.

Jā'ïr-īte. Ira so called, 2 Sam. xx. 26.

Jȧ-ī'rus (*enlightened*). Ruler of a synagogue, Luke viii. 41.

Jā'kan (*thoughtful*). A Horite, 1 Chr. i. 42. [JAAKAN, AKAN.]

Jā'keh (*pious*). Father of Agur, Prov. xxx. 1.

Jā'kim (*confirmed*). (1) Head of 12th course, 1 Chr. xxiv. 12. (2) A Benjamite, 1 Chr. viii. 19.

Jā'lon (*tarrying*). A Judahite, 1 Chr. iv. 17.

Jăm'brēs. An Egyptian magician, Ex. vii. 9-13; 2 Tim. iii. 8, 9.

Jăm'brī. Supposably Ammonites, 1 Macc. ix. 36-41.

Jāmes (*Jacob*). (1) "The Greater" or "Elder," son of Zebedee and brother of John, Matt. iv. 21, 22. A fisherman of Galilee, called to the Apostolate about A. D. 28, and styled Boanerges, Matt. x. 2, 3; Mark iii. 14-18; Luke vi. 12-16; Acts i. 13. Labored at Jerusalem. Beheaded by Herod, A. D. 44. (2) "The Less," another Apostle, son of Alphæus, Matt. x. 3; Mark iii. 18; Luke vi. 15. (3) Christ's brother, or more likely cousin, and identical with James the Less, Gal. i. 19. Compare Matt. xiii. 55; Mark vi. 3; Acts xii. 17. Resident at Jerusalem and author of The Epistle of James, written before A. D. 62 to the scattered Jews, urging good works as the groundwork and evidence of faith.

Jā'min (*right hand*). (1) Founder of Jaminites, Gen. xlvi. 10; Ex. vi. 15; Num. xxvi. 12. A Judahite, 1 Chr. ii. 27. (3) Ezra's assistant, Neh. viii. 7.

Jăm'lech (*reigning*). A Simeonite chief, 1 Chr. iv. 34.

Jăm'nĭ-ȧ, 1 Macc. iv. 15. [JABNEEL.]

Jăn'nȧ (*God-given*). Ancestor of Christ, Luke iii. 24.

Jăn'nēs. An Egyptian magician, 2 Tim. iii. 8, 9; Ex. vii. 9-13.

Jȧ-nō'ah (*rest*). Town of Naphtali, 2 Kgs. xv. 29.

Jȧ-nō'hah (*rest*). Border town of Ephraim, Josh. xvi. 6, 7.

Jā'num (*sleeping*). Town of Judah, Josh. xv. 53.

Jā'pheth (*enlarged*). Son of Noah, Gen. v. 32; vi. 10; ix. 27; x. 21. His generations peopled the "isles of the Gentiles," and type the Indo-European and Caucasian races, Gen. x. 1-5.

Jȧ-phī'ȧ (*splendor*). (1) A border of Zebulun, Josh. xix. 12. (2) King of Lachish, Josh. x. 3. (3) A son of David, 2 Sam. v. 15; 1 Chr. iii. 7.

Jăph'let (*delivered*). An Asherite, 1 Chr. vii. 32, 33.

Jăph-lē'tī. Landmark of Ephraim, Josh. xvi. 3.

Jā'phō, Josh. xix. 46. [JOPPA.]

Jā'rah (*honey*). Son of Micah, 1 Chr. ix. 42.

Jā'reb (*enemy*). Unknown person or place, Hos. v. 13; x. 6.

Jā'red (*descent*). Father of Enoch, Gen. v. 15-20; Luke iii. 37.

Jăr-ĕ-sī'ah (*nourished*). A Benjamite, 1 Chr. viii. 27.

Jär'hȧ. An Egyptian servant, 1 Chr. ii. 34, 35.

Jā'rib (*enemy*). (1) A Simeonite, 1 Chr. iv. 24. (2) One who returned, Ez. viii. 16. (3) A priest, Ez. x. 18.

Jär'ĭ-moth, 1 Esdr. ix. 28. [JEREMOTH.]

Jär'mŭth (*high*). (1) Town of lower Judah, Josh. x. 3; xv. 35. (2) A Levitical city of Issachar, Josh. xxi. 29.

Jȧ-rō'ah (*moon*). A Gadite, 1 Chr. v. 14.

Jā'shen (*sleeping*). His sons were in David's guard, 2 Sam. xxiii. 32.

Jā'shēr (*upright*). Book of, wholly lost, Josh. x. 13; 2 Sam. i. 18.

Jȧ-shō'be-ăm (*turned to*). A chief of David's captains, 1 Chr. xi. 11; xii. 6; xxvii. 2. Adino, 2 Sam. xxiii. 8.

Jăsh'ŭb (*he turns*). (1) Founder of Jashubites, Num. xxvi. 24; 1 Chr. vii. 1; Job, Gen. xlvi. 13. (2) Son of Bani, Ez. x. 29.

Jăsh'u-bī-lĕ'hĕm (*turning back for food*). Person or place of Judah, 1 Chr. iv. 22.

Jā'sī-el (*created*). One of David's heroes, 1 Chr. xi. 47.

Jā'son (*healer*). (1) Son of Eleazar, 1 Macc. viii. 17. (2) Father of Antipater, xii. 16. (3) An historian, 2 Macc. ii. 23. (4) High priest, 2 Macc. iv. 7-26. (5) A friend of Paul, Acts xvii. 5-9.

Jăs'pẽr. A colored quartz. Last stone in high priest's breastplate, and first in New Jerusalem foundation, Ex. xxviii. 20; Rev. xxi. 19.

Jăth'nī-el (*God-given*). A Levite, 1 Chr. xxvi. 2.

Jăt'tīr (*prominent*). Town of south Judah, Josh. xv. 48; xxi. 14; 1 Sam. xxx. 27.

Jā'văn (*clay*). (1) Fourth son of Japheth, and type of Ionians and Grecians, Gen. x. 2-5; 1 Chr. i. 5-7. (2) An Arabian trading post, Ezek. xxvii. 13, 19.

Jăve'lĭn. A short, light spear. [ARMS.]

Jā'zär, 1 Macc. v. 8. [JAAZER.]

Jā'zẽr, Num. xxxii. 1-3; Josh. xxi. 39. [JAAZER.]

Jā'zīz (*moved*). Herdsman of David, 1 Chr. xxvii. 31.

Jē'a-rĭm (*woods*). Border mountain of Judah, Josh. xv. 10.

Jē-ăt'e-rāi (*led*). A Levite, 1 Chr. vi. 21.

Jĕ''bẽr-e-chī'ah (*blessed*). Father of Zechariah, Isa. viii. 2.

Jē'bus (*threshing floor*). Original name of Jerusalem; the "threshing floor" of the Jebushi or Jebusites, Josh. xv. 8; xviii. 16, 28; Judg. xix. 10, 11; 1 Chr. xi. 4, 5.

Jĕb'u-sīte, Jĕ-bū'si. Original people of Jebus, Deut. vii. 1; Josh. xi. 3; 2 Sam. v. 6-10; xxiv, 16-25.

Jĕc''a-mī'ah (*gathered*). One of David's line, 1 Chr. iii. 18.

Jĕch''o-lī'ah (*enabled*). Mother of King Azariah, 2 Kgs. xv. 2. Jecoliah, 2 Chr. xxvi. 3.

Jĕch''o-nī'as, Matt. i. 11, 12; Esth. xi. 4. Greek form of Jeconiah and Jehoiachin.

Jĕc''o-lī'ah, 2 Chr. xxvi. 3. [JECHOLIAH.]

Jĕc''o-nī'ah, 1 Chr. iii. 16; Jer. xxiv. 1. [JEHOIACHIN.]

Jē-dā'iah (*praise God*). (1) Head of 2d temple course, 1 Chr. xxiv. 7. (2) A priest, Zech. vi. 10-14. (3) A Simeonite, 1 Chr. iv. 37. (4) A wall-repairer, Neh. iii. 10.

Jē-dī'a-el (*known of God*). (1) A Benjamite, 1 Chr. vii. 6-11. (2) One of David's guard, 1 Chr. xi. 45. (3) A Manassite chief, 1 Chr. xii. 20. (4) A Levite, 1 Chr. xxvi. 1, 2.

Jē-dī'dah (*beloved*). Mother of King Josiah, 2 Kgs. xxii. 1.

Jĕd''ĭ-dī'ah (*beloved of God*). Name given to Solomon by Nathan, 2 Sam. xii. 25.

Jĕd'u-thŭn (*praising*). A leader of the temple choir, 1 Chr. xxv. 6; Ps. xxxix., lxii., lxxvii., title.

Jē-ē'zẽr (*father of help*). A Manassite, Num. xxvi. 30. Abiezer, elsewhere.

Jē-ē'zẽr-ītes. Descendants of above.

Jē'gar=sā-hā-dū'thȧ (*testimonial heap*). Heap of compact between Jacob and Laban, Gen. xxxi. 47.

Jē''hā-lē'le-el (*who praises*). A Judahite, 1 Chr. iv. 16.

Jē-hăl'e-lĕl (*who praises*). A Levite, 2 Chr. xxix. 12.

Jĕh-dē'iah (*made joyful*). (1) A Levite, 1 Chr. xxiv. 20. (2) David's herdsman, 1 Chr. xxvii. 30.

Jē-hĕz'e-kĕl (*made strong*). Head of the 20th priestly course, 1 Chr. xxiv. 16.

Jē-hī'ah (*God lives*). A doorkeeper of the ark, 1 Chr. xv. 24.

Jē-hī'el (*God lives*). (1) A Levite, 1 Chr. xv. 18, 20. (2) A treasurer, 1 Chr. xxiii. 8. (3) Son of Jehoshaphat, 2 Chr. xxi. 2. (4) An officer of David, 1 Chr. xxvii. 32. (5) A Levite, 2 Chr. xxix. 14. (6) Ruler of God's house, 2 Chr. xxxv. 8. (7) An overseer, 2 Chr. xxxi. 13. (8) Returned captives, Ez. viii. 9; x. 2, 21, 26.

Jē-hī'el (*treasured*). (1) Father of Gibeon, 1 Chr. ix. 35. (2) One of David's guard, 1 Chr. xi. 44.

Jē-hī'e-lī. A Levite family, 1 Chr. xxvi. 21, 22.

Jē''hĭz-kī'ah (*strengthened*). An Ephraimite, 2 Chr. xxviii. 12.

Jē-hō'a-dah (*adorned*). A descendant of Saul, 1 Chr. viii. 36.

Jē''hō-ăd'dan (*adorned*). Mother of King Amaziah, 2 Kgs. xiv. 2; 2 Chr. xxv. 1.

Jē-hō'a-hăz (*possession*). (1) Son and successor of Jehu on throne of Israel, B. C. 856-840, 2 Kgs. xiii. 1-9. Reign disastrous. (2) Son and successor of Josiah on throne of Judah. Reigned 3 months, B. C. 610. Called Shallum. Deposed and died in Egypt, Jer. xxii. 11, 12. (3) Ahaziah, Azariah, 2 Chr. xxi. 17; xxii. 1, 6.

Jē-hō'ash. [JOASH.]

Jē''hō-hā'nan (*God-given*). (1) A temple porter, 1 Chr. xxvi. 3. (2) A general of Judah, 2 Chr. xvii. 15; xxiii. 1. (3) Returned Levites, Ez. x. 28; Neh. xii. 13, 42.

Jē-hoi'a-chin (*God-appointed*). Jeconiah, 1 Chr. iii. 17; Coniah, Jer. xxii. 24; Jechonias, Matt. i. 12. Son and successor of Jehoiakim on throne of Judah. Reigned 100 days, B. C. 597; carried prisoner to Babylon; released after 36 years' captivity, 2 Kgs. xxiv. 6-16; Jer. xxix. 2; Ezek. xvii. 12.

Jē-hoi'a-dȧ (*known of God*). (1) Father of Benaiah, 2 Sam. viii. 18; 1 Kgs. i., ii. (2) An Aaronite leader, 1 Chr. xii. 27. (3) No doubt same as (1), 1 Chr. xxvii. 34. (4) High priest and religious reformer under Athaliah and Joash, 2 Kgs. xi. 4-21; xii. 1-16. (5) Second priest, or sagan, Jer. xxix. 25-29. (6) A wall-repairer, Neh. iii. 6.

Jē-hoi'a-kĭm (*God-established*). Eliakim, son of Josiah; name changed to Jehoiakim; successor to Jehoahaz, and 19th king of Judah, B. C. 609-598. Nearly entire reign one of vassalage to Egypt or Babylon, 2 Kgs. xxiii. 34-37; xxiv. 1-6; Jer. xxii. 18, 19; xxxvi. 30-32.

Jē-hoi'a-rĭb (*God-defended*). Head of 1st temple course, 1 Chr. xxiv. 7.

Jē-hŏn'a-dăb, Jŏn'a-dăb (*God-impelled*). Son of Rechab, and adherent of Jehu, 2 Kgs. x. 15-20; Jer. xxxv. 6.

Jē-hŏn'a-than (*God-given*). (1) David's storehouse keeper, 1 Chr. xxvii. 25. (2) A Levite teacher, 2 Chr. xvii. 8. (3) A priest, Neh. xii. 18.

Jē-hō'ram, Jō'ram (*God-exalted*). (1) Son of Ahab and successor to Ahaziah on throne of Israel, B. C. 896-884. Victoriously allied with Judah, but defeated and slain in Jehu's revolt. Last of Ahab's line, 1 Kgs. xxi. 21-29; xxii. 50; 2 Kgs. i. 17, 18; ii.-ix. (2) Son and successor of Jehoshaphat on throne of Judah, B. C. 893-885. Murderer and Baal worshipper. Reign calamitous. Died a terrible death, 2 Chr. xxi.

Jē''hō-shăb'e-ăth, 2 Chr. xxii. 11. [JEHOSHEBA.]

Jē-hŏsh'a-phăt (*judged of God*). (1) Recorder under David and Solomon, 2 Sam. viii. 16; 1 Kgs. iv. 3. (2) A trumpeter, 1 Chr. xv. 24. (3) Solomon's purveyor, 1 Kgs. iv. 17. (4) Father of Jehu, 2 Kgs. ix. 2-14. (5) Valley of Cedron, or else a visionary spot, Joel iii. 2-12. (6) Son and successor of Asa on throne of Judah, B. C. 914-890. A God-fearing king, in close alliance with Israel, 1 Kgs. xv. 24; 2 Kgs. viii. 16; 2 Chr. xvii.-xxi. 1.

Jĕ-hŏsh'e-bȧ (*oath of God*). Daughter of king Joram and wife of Jehoiada, the high priest, 2 Kgs. xi. 2; 2 Chr. xxii. 11.

Jĕ-hŏsh'u-ȧ. Full form of Joshua, Num. xiii. 16; Jehoshuah, 1 Chr. vii. 27.

Jĕ-hō'vah. "He that is." "I am," Ex. iii. 14. The self-existent and eternal one. Hebrew word for God, generally rendered "Lord." Not pronounced; but Adonai, "Lord," or Elohim, "God," substituted, Ex. vi. 3. [God.]

Jĕ-hō'vah=jī'reh (*God will provide*). Abraham's name for spot where Isaac was offered, Gen. xxii. 14.

Jĕ-hō'vah=nĭs'sī (*God my banner*). The altar built in honor of Joshua's victory, Ex. xvii. 15.

Jĕ-hō'vah=shā'lom (*God is peace*). Gideon's altar in Ophrah, Judg. vi. 24.

Jĕ-hŏz'a-băd (*God-given*). (1) A storekeeper and porter, 1 Chr. xxvi. 4. (2) Co-murderer of King Joash, 2 Kgs. xii. 21. (3) A Benjamite captain, 2 Chr. xvii. 18.

Jĕ-hŏz'a-dăk (*God justifies*). Captive father of Jeshua, the high priest, 1 Chr. vi. 14, 15; Ez. iii. 2.

Jē'hū (*who exists*). (1) Prophet of Judah, 1 Kgs. xvi. 1-7. (2) Tenth king of Israel, B. C. 884–856. He extirpated Ahab's line according to the prophecies, 1 Kgs. xix. 16, 17; 2 Kgs. ix., x. (3) A Judahite, 1 Chr. ii. 38. (4) A Simeonite, 1 Chr. iv. 35. (5) A Benjamite, 1 Chr. xii. 3.

Jĕ-hŭb'bah (*hidden*). An Asherite, 1 Chr. vii. 34.

Jē'hū-cal (*mighty*). Messenger to Jeremiah, Jer. xxxvii. 3.

Jē'hŭd (*famed*). Town of Dan, Josh. xix. 45.

Jĕ hū'dī (*Jew*). A messenger, Jer. xxxvi. 14-23.

Jē''hū-dī'jah (*Jewess*). Mother of Jered, 1 Chr. iv. 18.

Jē'hŭsh (*collector*). Son of Eshek, 1 Chr. viii. 39.

Jĕ-ī'el (*God's treasure*). (1) Reubenite chief, 1 Chr. v. 7. (2) Levites, 1 Chr. xv. 18; 2 Chr. xx. 14; xxvi. 11; xxix. 13; xxxv. 9; Ez. viii. 13; x. 43.

Jĕ-kăb'ze-el (*gathered*). Kabzeel, in south Judah, Neh. xi. 25; Josh. xv. 21; 2 Sam. xxiii. 20.

Jĕk''a-mē'am (*who gathers*). A Levite, 1 Chr. xxiii. 19; xxiv. 23.

Jĕk''a-mī'ah (*gathered*). A Judahite, 1 Chr. ii. 41.

Jĕ-kū'thĭ-el (*piety*). A Judahite, 1 Chr. iv. 18.

Jĕ-mī'mȧ (*dove*). Job's daughter, Job xlii. 14.

Jĕm'nă-an, Judith ii. 28. [Jabneel.]

Jĕ-mū'el (*God's day*). A Simeonite, Gen. xlvi. 10; Ex. vi. 15.

Jĕph'thă-ē, Heb. xi. 32. Greek form of Jephthah.

Jĕph'thah (*set free*). A judge of Israel, B. C. 1143-1137, Judg. xi., xii.

Jĕ-phŭn'neh (*favorably regarded*). (1) Father of Caleb the spy, Num. xiii. 6. (2) An Asherite, 1 Chr. vii. 38.

Jē'răh (*moon*). Son of Joktan, Gen. x. 26; 1 Chr. i. 20.

Jĕ-răh'me-el (*God's mercy*). (1) Son of Hezron, 1 Chr. ii. 9, 42. (2) A Levite, 1 Chr. xxiv. 29. (3) An official of Jehoiakim, Jer. xxxvi. 26.

Jĕ-răh'me-el-ītes''. Descendants of above (1), 1 Sam. xxvii. 10.

Jĕr'ĕ-cus, 1 Esdr. v. 22. [Jericho.]

Jē'rĕd (*descent*). (1) Father of Enoch, 1 Chr. i. 2. (2) A Judahite, 1 Chr. iv. 18.

Jĕr'e-māi (*mountaineer*). A layman, Ez. x. 33.

Jĕr''e-mī'ah (*exalted*). (1) Second of greater prophets. His prophecies cover reigns of Josiah, Jehoiakim, and Zedekiah, B. C. 628–586, and constitute the 24th O. T. book. Life one of vicissitude. Prophecies noted for boldness and beauty, and chiefly denunciative of Judah and her policy. Withdrew to Egypt, where he probably died. (2) Seven others in O. T., 2 Kgs. xxiii. 31; 1 Chr. xii. 4-13; v. 24; Neh. x. 2; xii. 1, 12, 34; Jer. xxxv. 3.

Jĕr''e-mī'as, Jĕr'e-mȳ. Greek form of Jeremiah, Matt. ii. 17; xvi. 14; xxvii. 9.

Jĕr'e-mŏth (*heights*). Persons in 1 Chr. viii. 14; xxiii. 23; xxv. 22; Ez. x. 26, 27.

Jĕ-rī'ah (*founded*). A chief of the house of Hebron, 1 Chr. xxiii. 19; xxiv. 23.

Jĕr'ĭ-bāi (*defended*). One of David's guard, 1 Chr. xi. 46.

Jĕr'ĭ-chō (*fragrance*). Ancient city of Canaan, 5 miles W. of Jordan and 18 from Jerusalem. Strongly fortified, and conquered by Joshua. Fell to Benjamin, Deut. xxxiv. 3; Num. xxii. 1; Josh. vi.; xvi. 7; xviii. 21; 1 Kgs. xvi. 34; Matt. xx. 29; Mark x. 46.

Jē'rĭ-el (*founded*). An Issacharite, 1 Chr. vii. 2.

Jĕ-rī'jah, 1 Chr. xxvi. 31. [Jeriah.]

Jĕr'i-mŏth (*heights*). Persons in 1 Chr. vii. 8; xii. 5; xxiv. 30; xxv. 4, 22; xxvii. 19; 2 Chr. xi. 18; xxxi. 13.

Jē'rĭ-ŏth (*curtains*). Caleb's wife, 1 Chr. ii. 18.

Jĕr'' o-bō'am (*many-peopled*). (1) First king of Israel after the division, B. C. 975–954. Plotter for Solomon's throne, 1 Kgs. xi. 26–40; fled to Egypt; returned on death of Solomon; set up kingdom of ten tribes; established idolatry; warred with Judah; defeated by Abijah; soon after died, 1 Kgs. xii.–xiv.; 2 Chr. x.–xiii. (2) Jeroboam II., 13th king of Israel. Successor to Joash. Reigned B. C. 825–784. Idolatrous, but mighty and illustrious. Raised Israel to greatest splendor, 2 Kgs. xiv. 23–29; xv. 8, 9; Am. i.; ii. 6–16.

Golden Gate, Jerusalem.

Jĕr'o-hăm (*cherished*). (1) Father of Elkanah, 1 Sam. i. 1; 1 Chr. vi. 27. (2) A Benjamite, 1 Chr. viii. 27; ix. 8. (3) Father of Adaiah, 1 Chr. ix. 12. (4) Others in 1 Chr. xii. 7; xxvii. 22; 2 Chr. xxiii. 1.

Jĕ-rŭb'ba-ăl (*contender with Baal*). Surname of Gideon, Judg. vi. 32.

Jĕ-rŭb'be-shĕth (*strife with the idol*). Another surname of Gideon, 2 Sam. xi. 21.

Jĕr'u-el (*founded*). Unknown battlefield, 2 Chr. xx. 16.

Jĕ-ru'să-lĕm (*place of peace*). Capital of Hebrew monarchy and of kingdom of Judah, 24 miles west of Jordan and 37 east of the Mediterranean. "Salem," Ps. lxxvi. 2, and perhaps, Gen. xiv. 18. "Jebus," Judg. xix. 10, 11. "Jebus-salem," Jerusalem, Josh. x. 1. "City of David," Zion, 1 Kgs. viii. 1; 2 Kgs. xiv. 20. "City of Judah," 2 Chr. xxv. 28. "City of God," Ps. xlvi. 4. "City of the great King," Ps. xlviii. 2. "The holy city," Neh. xi. 1. Captured and rebuilt by David, and made his capital, 2 Sam. v. 6-13; 1 Chr. xi. 4-9. Destroyed by Nebuchadnezzar, B. C. 588. Rebuilt by returned captives. Captured by Alexander the Great, B. C. 332; by Antiochus, B. C. 203; by Rome, B. C. 63.

Jē-ru′sā-lĕm, New. Metaphorically, the spiritual church, Rev. iii. 12; xxi.; compare Gal. iv. 26; Heb. xii. 22.

Jē-ru′shȧ (*possessed*). Daughter of Zadok, 2 Kgs. xv. 33. Jerushah, 2 Chr. xxvii. 1.

Jē-sā′iah (*saved*). (1) Grandson of Zerubbabel, 1 Chr. iii. 21. (2) A Benjamite, Neh. xi. 7.

Jē-shā′iah (*God's help*). (1) Head of 8th singing course, 1 Chr. xxv. 3, 15. (2) A Levite, 1 Chr. xxvi. 25. Isshiah, xxiv. 21. (3) Two who returned, Ez. viii. 7, 19.

Jĕsh′a-nah (*old*). Unidentified town, 2 Chr. xiii. 19.

Jē-shăr′e-lah (*right*). Head of 7th singing course, 1 Chr. xxv. 14. Asarelah, vs. 2.

Jē-shĕb′e-ăb (*father's seat*). Head of 14th priestly course, 1 Chr. xxiv. 13.

Jē′shĕr (*right*). Son of Caleb, 1 Chr. ii. 18.

Jĕsh′ī-mŏn (*waste*). Perhaps desert or plain, Num. xxi. 20; xxiii. 28.

Jē-shĭsh′a-ī (*ancient*). A Gadite, 1 Chr. v. 14.

Jĕsh″ō-ha-ī′ah (*bowed*). A Simeonite, 1 Chr. iv. 36.

Jĕsh′u-ȧ (*saviour*). (1) Joshua, Neh. viii. 17. (2) Priest of 9th course, Ez. ii. 36; Neh. vii. 39. Jeshuah, 1 Chr. xxiv. 11. (3) A Levite, 2 Chr. xxxi. 15. (4) High priest and returned captive, called also Joshua and Jesus, Zech. iii.; vi. 9-15. (5) Other Levites and returned, Ez. ii. 6, 40; viii. 33; Neh. iii. 19; viii. 7. (6) A town peopled by returned captives, Neh. xi. 26.

Jĕsh′u-rŭn (*blessed*). Symbolically, Israel, Deut. xxxii. 15; xxxiii. 5, 26. Jesurun, Isa. xliv. 2.

Jē-sī′ah (*loaned*). (1) One of David's warriors, 1 Chr. xii. 6. (2) Jeshaiah, 1 Chr. xxiii. 20.

Jē-sĭm′i-el (*set up*). A Simeonite, 1 Chr. iv. 36.

Jĕs′se (*strong*). Father of David, 1 Sam. xvi. 1-18.

Jĕs′su-e, 1 Esdr. v. 26. [JESHUA.] Jesu, viii. 63.

Jes′u-ī (*level*). Founder of Jesuites, Num. xxvi. 44. Isui, Gen. xlvi. 17. Ishuai, 1 Chr. vii. 30.

Jē′sus (*saviour*). (1) Greek form of Joshua, Jeshua, contraction of Jehoshua, Num. xiii. 16; Acts vii. 45. (2) Compiler of the Apocryphal book. Ecclesiasticus. (3) Justus, Paul's friend, Col. iv. 11,

Jē′sŭs Chrīst. Jesus the Saviour; Christ, or Messiah, the anointed. Jesus the Christ. Name given to the long promised prophet and king, Matt. xi. 3; Acts xix. 4. Only begotten of God. Born of Mary at Bethlehem, B. C. 5; reared at Nazareth, baptized at age of 30, Luke iii. 23. Ministerial career, extending over Galilee, Judea, and Perea, began A. D. 27 and ended with the crucifixion, April 7, A. D. 30. Matthew, Mark, and Luke record his Galilean ministry; John his Judean ministry. The four gospels embrace Christ's biography.

Jē′thĕr (*who excels*). (1) Son of Gideon, Judg. viii. 20. (2) Father of Amasa, 1 Chr. ii. 17. (3) Others in 1 Chr. ii. 32; iv. 17; vii. 38.

Jē′thĕth (*nail*). A duke of Edom, Gen. xxxvi. 40.

Jĕth′lah (*high*). City of Dan, Josh. xix. 42.

Jē′thrō (*his excellence*). Honorary title, Ex. iii. 1, of Reuel, Ex. ii. 18, or Raguel, Num. x. 29, the father-in-law of Moses, Ex. xviii.

Jē′tŭr, Gen. xxv. 15; 1 Chr. i. 31. [ITURÆA.]

Jē-ū′el (*treasured*). A Judahite, 1 Chr. ix. 6.

Jē′ŭsh (*assembler*). (1) Son of Esau, Gen. xxxvi. 5, 14, 18. (2) A Benjamite, 1 Chr. vii. 10. (3) A Levite, 1 Chr. xxiii. 10, 11. (4) Son of Rehoboam, 2 Chr. xi. 18, 19.

Jē′ŭz (*assembler*). A Benjamite, 1 Chr. viii. 10.

Jew. Contraction of Judah. Man of Judea, 2 Kgs. xvi. 6; xxv. 25. After captivity, Hebrews in general, Ez. iv. 12; Dan. iii. 8-12. Antithesis of Christian in N. T., John; Rom. i. 16.

Jewish High Priest.

Jew′ĕl (*joy*). Ornament, Gen. xxiv. 22; Num. xxxi. 50.

Jew′ĕss. Hebrew woman, Acts xvi. 1.

Jew′rȳ. Judah, Judea, Jewish dynasty, Dan. v. 13.

Jĕz″a-nī′ah (*heard*). A Jewish captive, Jer. xl. 7-12. Jaazaniah, 2 Kgs. xxv. 23.

Jĕz′e-bĕl (*chaste*). Idolatrous wife of Ahab, 1 Kgs. xvi. 29-33; xvii.-xxi.; 2 Kgs. ix. 30-37.

Jē-zē′lus, 1 Esdr. viii. 32-35. [JAHAZIEL.]

Jē′zēr (*help*). A Naphtalite, Gen. xlvi. 24; founder of Jezerites, Num. xxvi. 49.

Jē-zī′ah (*sprinkled*). One with a foreign wife, Ez. x. 25.

Jē′zi-el (*sprinkled*). A Benjamite, 1 Chr. xii. 3.

Jĕz-lī′ah (*preserved*). A Benjamite, 1 Chr. viii. 18.

Jĕz′o-ar (*white*). A Judahite, 1 Chr. iv. 7.

Jĕz″ra-hī′ah (*brought forth*). A Levite singer, Neh. xii. 42.

Jĕz′re-el (*seed of God*). (1) A Judahite, 1 Chr. iv. 3. (2) A city in plain of Jezreel. Ahab's royal residence, Josh. xix. 18; 1 Kgs. xxi. 1; 2 Kgs. ix. 30. (3) Valley of, stretches from Jezreel to Jordan. Greek form, Esdraelon. (4) Town of Judah,

Josh. xv. 56; 1 Sam. xxvii. 3. (5) Son of Hosea, Hos. i. 4.

Jĭb'sam (*pleasant*). An Issacharite, 1 Chr. vii. 2.

Jĭd'laph (*weeping*). Son of Nahor, Gen. xxii. 22.

Jĭm'nȧ (*prosperity*). Son of Asher and founder of Jimnites, Num. xxvi. 44. Jimnah, Gen. xlvi. 17. Imnah, 1 Chr. vii. 30.

Jĭph'tah. Lowland city of Judah, Josh. xv. 43.

Jĭph'thah=el (*God opens*). Valley between Zebulun and Asher, Josh. xix. 14, 27.

Jō'ăb (*God his father*). (1) General-in-chief of David's army, 2 Sam. ii. 18-32; iii., xviii., xx., xxiv.; 1 Kgs. ii. (2) Son of Seraiah, 1 Chr. iv. 14. (3) One who returned, Ez. ii. 6.

Jō'a-chaz, 1 Esdr. i. 34. [JEHOAHAZ.]

Jō'a-chĭm, Bar. i. 3. [JEHOIAKIM.]

Jō''a-dā'nus. Son of Jeshua, 1 Esdr. ix. 19.

Jō'ah (*God's brother*). (1) Hezekiah's recorder, 2 Kgs. xviii. 18. (2) Josiah's recorder, 2 Chr. xxxiv. 8. (3) Levites, 1 Chr. vi. 21; xxvi. 4; 2 Chr. xxix. 12.

Jō'a-hăz (*held of God*). Father of Joah, 2 Chr. xxxiv. 8.

Jō-ăn'nȧ (*God-given*). (1) An ancestor of Christ, Luke iii. 27. (2) Wife of Chusa, Luke viii. 3; xxiv. 10.

Jō'ash (*God-given*), 2 Kgs. xiii. 1. Jehoash, 2 Kgs. xii. 1. (1) Son of Ahaziah and his successor on throne of Judah, B. C. 878-839. Cruel and idolatrous. Murdered by his servants, 2 Kgs. xi., xii.; 2 Chr. xxiv. (2) Son and successor of Jehoahaz on throne of Israel, B. C. 840-825. Successful warrior, 2 Kgs. xiii. 9-25; xiv. 1-16; 2 Chr. xxv. 17-25. (3) Father of Gideon, Judg. vi. 11-31. (4) Son of Ahab, 2 Chr. xviii. 25. (5) A Judahite, 1 Chr. iv. 22. (6) One of David's heroes, 1 Chr. xii. 3. (7) Son of Becher, 1 Chr. vii. 8. (8) Officer of David, 1 Chr. xxvii. 28.

Jō'a-thăm, Matt. i. 9. [JOTHAM.]

Jōb (*persecuted*). (1) The pious and wealthy patriarch of Uz, whose poem constitutes the 18th O. T. book, and first of the poetical. It is a dramatic narrative of his life of vicissitude, the gist being, whether goodness can exist irrespective of reward. Poetry noted for its sublimity, pathos, and beauty. Authorship disputed. Oldest of sacred writings. (2) Son of Issachar, Gen. xlvi. 13. Jashub, 1 Chr. vii. 1.

Jō'băb (*desert*). (1) Son of Joktan, Gen. x. 29. (2) King of Edom, Gen. xxxvi. 33. (3) King of Madon, Josh. xi. 1. (4) Two Benjamites, 1 Chr. viii. 9, 18.

Jŏch'e-bed (*glorified*). Mother of Moses, Ex. vi. 20; Num. xxvi. 59.

Jō'dȧ, 1 Esdr. v. 58. [JUDAH.]

Jō'ed (*witnessed*). A Benjamite, Neh. xi. 7.

Jō'el (*Jehovah his God*). (1) Son of Pethuel and second of minor prophets. Probably of Judah and contemporary with Uzziah, B. C. 810-758. His book, 29th of O. T., depicts calamities, rises into exhortation, and foreshadows the Messiah. (2) Son of Samuel, 1 Sam. viii. 2. (3) Others in 1 Chr. iv. 35; v. 4, 8, 12; vi. 36; vii. 3; xi. 38; xv. 7; xxiii. 8; xxvii. 20; 2 Chr. xxix. 12; Ez. x. 43; Neh. xi. 9.

Jō-ē'lah (*helped*). A Benjamite chief, 1 Chr. xii. 7.

Jō-ē'zēr (*aided*). A Benjamite, 1 Chr. xii. 6.

Jŏg'be-hah (*high*). City of Gad, E. of Jordan, Num. xxxii. 35.

Jŏg'lī (*exiled*). A prince of Dan, Num. xxxiv. 22.

Jō'hȧ (*given life*). (1) A Benjamite, 1 Chr. viii. 16. (2) One of David's guard, 1 Chr. xi. 45.

Jō-hā'nan (*God's mercy*). (1) A Judahite captain who escaped captivity, 2 Kgs. xxv. 23, and carried Jeremiah and other Jews into Egypt, Jer. xl.-xliii. (2) Others in 1 Chr. iii. 15, 24; vi. 9, 10; xii. 4, 12; 2 Chr. xxviii. 12; Ez. viii. 12; x. 6; Neh. vi. 18.

Jŏhn (*God's gift*). Johanan, contraction of Jehohanan. (1) Kinsman of the high priest, Acts iv. 6. (2) Hebrew name of Mark, Acts xii. 25; xiii. 5; xv. 37. (3) John the Baptist, son of Zacharias. Birth foretold, Luke i. Born about six months before Christ. Retired to wilderness. Emerged to preach and baptize. Baptized Jesus, Matt. iii. Imprisoned by Herod, Luke iii. 1-22. Beheaded, Matt. xiv. 1-12. (4) John, Apostle and Evangelist; son of Zebedee, Matt. iv. 21; a fisherman of Galilee, Luke v. 1-10; a favorite apostle, noted for zeal and firmness, John xiii. 23; xix. 26; xx. 2; xxi. 7. He remained at Jerusalem till about A. D. 65, when he went to Ephesus. Banished to Patmos, and released A. D. 96. His writings, doubtless done at Ephesus, are the fourth Gospel, giving Christ's ministry in Judea; his three epistles, and Revelation. (5) A frequent name among the Maccabees, 1 Macc.

Joi'a-dȧ (*favored*). A high priest, Neh. xii. 10, 11, 22; xiii. 28.

Joi'a-kĭm (*exalted*). A high priest, Neh. xii. 10.

Joi'a-rĭb (*defended*). Two who returned, Ez. viii. 16; Neh. xii. 6, 19.

Jŏk'de-ăm (*peopled*). City of Judah, Josh. xv. 56.

Jō'kim (*exalted*). A Judahite, 1 Chr. iv. 22.

Jŏk'me-ăm (*gathered*). Levitical city in Ephraim, 1 Chr. vi. 68.

Jŏk'ne-ăm (*gathered*). Levitical city in Zebulun, Josh. xxi. 34.

Jŏk'shan (*fowler*). Son of Abraham, Gen. xxv. 2, 3; 1 Chr. i. 32.

Jŏk'tan (*small*). Son of Eber and progenitor of Joktanite Arabs, Gen. x. 25; 1 Chr. i. 19.

Jŏk'the-el (*subdued*). (1) City in Judah, Josh. xv. 38. (2) An Edomite stronghold, 2 Kgs. xiv. 7.

Jō'nȧ (*dove*). Father of Apostle Peter, Matt. xvi. 17; John i. 42.

Jŏn'a-dăb (*God-impelled*). (1) David's subtle nephew, 2 Sam. xiii. 3, 32-35. (2) Jer. xxxv. 6-19, Jehonadab.

Jō'nah (*dove*). Son of Amittai. Commissioned to denounce Nineveh. His book, 32d of O. T. and 5th of minor prophets, narrates his refusal, escape from drowning, final acceptance and successful ministry. Its lesson is God's providence over all nations.

Jō'nan (*grace*). Ancestor of Christ, Luke iii. 30.

Jō'nas. Greek form of Jonah, Matt. xii. 39-41; Luke xi. 30-32.

Jŏn'a-than (*God-given*). (1) A Levite, Judg. xvii. 7-13; xviii. (2) Eldest son of Saul, and friend of David, 1 Sam. xiii. 2, 3; xviii. 1-4; xix. 1-7; xx. Fell in battle of Gilboa. David's lament, 2 Sam. i. 17-27. (3) Others in 2 Sam. xv. 27, 36; xxi. 20, 21; xxiii. 32; 1 Chr. ii. 32, 33; xxvii. 32; Ez. viii. 6; x. 15; Neh. xii. 11, 14, 35; Jer. xxxvii. 15, 20; xl. 8.

Jŏn'a-thas, Tob. v. 13. [JONATHAN.]

Jō'nath=ē''lem=rē-chō'kim (*a dumb dove of distant places*). Title to, and probably melody of, Ps. lvi.

Jŏp'pȧ (*beauty*). Mediterranean seaport of Jerusalem; now Jaffa, 1 Kgs. v. 9; 2 Chr. ii. 16; Ez. iii. 7.

Jŏp'pē. For Joppa in Apoc.

Jō'rah (*rain*). His family returned, Ez. ii. 18.

Jō'ra-ī (*taught of God*). A Gadite chief, 1 Chr. v. 13.

Jō'ram (*exalted*). (1) Short form of Jehoram, king of Israel, 2 Kgs. viii. 16, etc.; and of Jehoram, king of Judah, 2 Kgs. viii. 21, etc.; Matt. i. 8. (2) Son of Toi, 2 Sam. viii. 10. (3) A Levite, 1 Chr. xxvi. 25.

Jôr'dan (*descender*). Chief river of Palestine, rising in the Anti-Libanus range, flowing southward, enlarging into Sea of Galilee, emptying into Dead Sea. A swift, narrow, yet fordable stream, with an entire course of about 200 miles, Gen. xiii. 10; Josh. ii. 7; Judg. iii. 28; 2 Sam. x. 17; Matt. iii. 13.

Jō'rim (*exalted*). An ancestor of Christ, Luke iii. 29.

Jŏr'ko-ăm. A person or place, 1 Chr. ii. 44.

Jŏs'a-băd (*dowered*). (1) One of David's warriors, 1 Chr. xii. 4. (2) Persons in 1 Esdr.

Jŏs'a-phăt, Matt. i. 8. [JEHOSHAPHAT.]

Jō'se. An ancestor of Christ, Luke iii. 29.

Jŏs'e-dĕch, Hag. i. 1. [JEHOZADAK.]

Jō'seph (*increase*). (1) Son of Jacob and Rachel, Gen. xxxvii. 3; sold into Egypt; promoted to high office by the Pharoah; rescued his family from famine; settled them in Goshen; died at advanced age; bones carried back to Shechem, Joshua 24:32. (2) An Issacharite, Num. xiii. 7. (3) Two who returned, Ez. x. 42; Neh. xii. 14. (4) Three of Christ's ancestors, Luke iii. 24, 26, 30. (5) Husband of Mary, and a carpenter at Nazareth, Matt. i. 19; xiii. 55; Luke iii. 23; John i. 45. (6) Of Arimathea, a member of the Sanhedrim, who acknowledged Christ, Matt. xxvii. 57-59; Mark xv. 43; Luke xxiii. 51. (7) The apostle Barsabas, substituted for Judas, Acts i. 23. (8) Frequent name in Apoc.

Jō'ses (*helped*). (1) One of Christ's brethren, Matt. xiii. 55; xxvii. 56; Mark vi. 3; xv. 40, 47. (2) Barnabas, Acts iv. 36.

Jō'shah (*dwelling*). A Simeonite chief, 1 Chr. iv. 34.

Jŏsh'a-phăt (*judged*). One of David's guard, 1 Chr. xi. 43.

Jŏsh''a-vī'ah (*dwelling*). One of David's guard, 1 Chr. xi. 46.

Jŏsh-bĕk'a-shah (*hard seat*). Head of 17th musical course, 1 Chr. xxv. 4, 24.

Jŏsh'u-ȧ (*saviour*). (1) Jehoshuah, 1 Chr. vii. 27. Oshea, Num. xiii. 8. Jesus, Acts vii. 45; Heb. iv. 8. Son of Nun, of tribe of Ephraim. The great warrior of the Israelites during the desert wanderings and conquest and apportionment of Canaan, Ex. xvii. 9-14; 1 Chr. vii. 27; Num. xiii. 8, 16; xxvii. 18-23. His book, 6th of O. T., contains the history of his conquests and governorship, B. C. 1451-1426. (2) A Beth-shemite, 1 Sam. vi. 14. (3) A governor of Jerusalem, 2 Kgs. xxiii. 8. (4) A high priest, Hag. i. 1, 14.

Jŏt. The Greek i, iota. A little thing, Matt. v. 18.

Jŏt'bah (*goodness*). Residence of Haruz, 2 Kgs. xxi. 19.

Jŏt'băth (*goodness*). Jotbathah, Num. xxxiii. 33. An Israelite encampment, Deut. x. 7.

Jō'tham (*God is upright*). (1) Youngest son of Gideon and author of the bramble fable, Judg. ix. 5-21. (2) Son and successor of Uzziah, or Azariah, on throne of Judah, B. C. 758-741. Reign prosperous, 2 Kgs. xv. 5, 6, 32-36; 2 Chr. xxvii. (3) A Judahite, 1 Chr. ii. 47.

Joûr'ney (*daily*). A day's journey, indefinite. Sabbath day's journey, 2000 paces, or ¾ of a mile from the walls of a city, Deut. i. 2; Acts i. 12.

Jŏz'a-băd (*God-given*). (1) Two Manassite chiefs, 1 Chr. xii. 20. (2) Five Levites, 2 Chr. xxxi. 13; xxxv. 9; Ez. viii. 33; x. 22; Neh. viii. 7; xi. 16.

Jŏz'a-chär (*remembered*). Zabad, 2 Chr. xxiv. 26. One of Joash's murderers, 2 Kgs. xii. 21.

Jŏz'a-dăk, Ez. iii. 2, 8, etc.; Neh. xii. 26. [JEHOZADAK.]

Jū'băl (*music*). Son of Lamech, and inventor of harp and organ, Gen. iv. 19-21.

Jū'bi-lēe (*blast of trumpets*). Year of, celebrated every fiftieth year; ushered in by blowing of trumpets; land rested; alienated lands reverted; slaves freed; outer circle of seventh or sabbatical system, year, month, and day, Lev. xxv. 8-55.

Jū'cal, Jer. xxxviii. 1. [JEHUCAL.]

Jū'dȧ (*praised*). (1) Ancestors of Christ, Luke iii. 26, 30. (2) One of Christ's brethren, Mark vi. 3. (3) The patriarch Judah, Luke iii. 33. (4) The tribe of Judah, Heb. vii. 14; Rev. v. 5.

Jū-dæ'ȧ, Jū-dē'ȧ (*from Judah*). Vaguely, Joshua's conquest, Matt. xix. 1; Mark x. 1, or Canaanite land. Limitedly, the part occupied by returned captives; the "Jewry" of Dan. v. 13; the "province" of Ez. v. 8; Neh. xi. 3. "Land of Judea" in Apoc. A Roman province jointly with Syria, with a procurator, after A. D. 6.

Jū'dah (*praise*). (1) Fourth son of Jacob, Gen. xxix. 35; xxxvii. 26-28; xliii. 3-10; xliv. 14-34. His tribe the largest, Num. i. 26, 27. Allotted the southern section of Canaan, Josh. xv. 1-63. (2) Kingdom of, formed on disruption of Solomon's empire,

Coin, commemorating Roman Conquest of Judea.

out of Judah, Benjamin, Simeon, and part of Dan, with Jerusalem as capital, B. C. 975. Had 19 kings, and lasted for 389 years, till reduced by Nebuchadnezzar, B. C. 586. Outlived its rival, Israel, some 135 years. (3) City of Jerusalem, 2 Chr. xxv. 28. (4) A town in Naphtali, Josh. xix. 34. (5) Persons in Ez. iii. 9; x. 23; Neh. xi. 9.

Jō-sī'ah (*God-healed*). (1) Son and successor of Amon on throne of Judah, B. C. 641-610. He abolished idolatry, propagated the newly discovered law, aided Assyria against Egypt, and fell in the celebrated battle of Esdraelon, 2 Kgs. xxii.-xxiii. 1-30; 2 Chr. xxxiv.-xxxv. (2) Son of Zephaniah, Zech. vi. 10.

Jō-sī'as. (1) Greek form of Josiah, 1 Esdr. i. 1; Matt. i. 10, 11. (2) 1 Esdr. viii. 33. [JESHAIAH.]

Jŏs''i-bī'ah (*dwelling*). A chief of Simeon, 1 Chr. iv. 35.

Jŏs''i-phī'ah (*increase*). His family returned, Ez. viii. 10.

Jū'das. Greek form of Judah. (1) Judah, Matt. i. 2, 3. (2) Iscariot, or of Kerioth. Betrayer of Christ, Matt. x. 4; Mark iii. 19; Luke vi. 16; John vi. 71; xii. 6; xiii. 29. (3) Man of Damascus, Acts ix. 11. (4) Barsabas, chief among the brethren, and prophet, Acts xv. 22, 32. (5) A Galilean apostate, Acts v. 37. (6) Frequent name in Apoc.

Jūde, Jude i. 1. Judas, brother of James the Less, Luke vi. 16; John xiv. 22; Acts i. 13; Matt. xiii. 55. Thaddæus, Lebbæus, Matt. x. 3; Mark iii. 18. An Apostle and author of the epistle which bears his name, 26th N. T. book. Written about A. D. 65. Place not known.

Jŭdg′es. Governors of Israel between Joshua and the kings. They were called of God, elective or usurpative. Qualification, martial or moral prowess. Rule arbitrary. Fifteen are recorded. Period, B. C. 1400-1091, about 310 years. Book of Judges, 7th of O. T., probably compiled by Samuel. Its history is that of a tumultuous period, completing Joshua's conquests and leading to legitimate kingly rule.

Jŭdg′mĕnt Hall. Pilate's residence in Jerusalem, John xviii. 28, 33; xix. 9. Prætorium or court, Acts xxiii. 35.

Jū′dith (*praised, Jewess*). (1) Wife of Esau, Gen. xxvi. 34. (2) Heroine of the 4th Apocryphal book.

Jū′el, Apoc. [JOEL.]

Jū′li̯à (*feminine of Julius*). A Christian woman at Rome, Rom. xvi. 15.

Jū′li̯us (*soft-haired*). A Roman centurion, Acts xxvii. 1-3, 43.

Jū′ni̯à (*youth*). Roman friend of Paul, Rom. xvi. 7.

Jū′nĭ-pĕr (*young producer*). Not the evergreen, but the desert broom-shrub, 1 Kgs. xix. 4, 5; Job xxx. 4; Ps. cxx. 4.

Jū′pĭ-tĕr (*father Jove*). Supreme god of Greeks and Romans, Acts xiv. 12; xix. 35.

Jū′shăb=hē′sĕd (*requited love*). Son of Zerubbabel, 1 Chr. iii. 20.

Jŭs″ti-fĭ-cā′tion. Pardon and acceptance of the just through faith, Rom. iii. 20-31; iv. 25.

Jŭs′tus (*just*). (1) Surname of Joseph, or Barsabas, Acts i. 23. (2) A Corinthian convert, Acts xviii. 7. (3) Surname of Jesus, a friend of Paul, Col. iv. 11.

Jŭt′tah (*extended*). A Levitical city in mountains of Judah; now Yutta, Josh. xv. 55; xxi. 16.

K

Kăb′ze-el (*gathered*). A city of Judah, Josh. xv. 21. Jekabzeel, Neh. xi. 25.

Kā′desh (*holy*). Halting place of Israelites near borders of Canaan, and scene of Miriam's death, Num. xiii. 26; xx. 1. Kadesh-barnea, Deut. ii. 14; Josh. xv. 3. Enmishpat, Gen. xiv. 7.

Kăd′mĭ-el (*before God*). One who returned, Ez. iii. 9; Neh. ix. 4.

Kăd′mŏn-ītes (*eastern*). Ancient Canaanites, Gen. xv. 19.

Kăl′la-ī (*runner*). A priest, Neh. xii. 20.

Kā′nah (*reedy*). (1) A boundary of Asher, Josh. xix. 28. (2) Boundary stream between Ephraim and Manasseh, Josh. xvi. 8; xvii. 9.

Kā-rē′ah (*bald*). Father of Johanan, Jer. xl. 8-16.

Kär′ka-à (*floor*). A southern boundary of Judah, Josh. xv. 3.

Kär′kôr (*foundation*). Scene of Gideon's victory, Judg. viii. 10.

Kär′tah (*city*). Levitical city in Zebulun, Josh. xxi. 34.

Kär′tan, Josh. xxi. 32. [KIRJATHAIM.]

Kăt′tath (*small*). Town of Zebulun, Josh. xix. 15.

Kē′där (*dark*). Son of Ishmael and founder of Arabic tribe, Gen. xxv. 13; Isa. xxi. 13-17; Ezek. xxvii. 21.

Kĕd′e-mah (*eastward*). Son of Ishmael, Gen. xxv. 15; 1 Chr. i. 31.

Kĕd′e-mŏth (*eastern*). Levitical town of Reuben, Josh. xiii. 18; xxi. 37; 1 Chr. vi. 79.

Kē′desh (*sacred*). (1) Josh. xv. 23. [KADESH.] (2) Levitical city in Issachar, Josh. xii. 22; 1 Chr. vi. 72. (3) City of refuge in Naphtali, Josh. xix. 37; Judg. iv. 6; 2 Kgs. xv. 29. Now Kades.

Kē′dron. [KIDRON.]

Kē-hĕl′a-thah (*assembly*). A desert encampment, Num. xxxiii. 22, 23.

Kĕi′lah (*fortress*). (1) Lowland town of Judah, Josh. xv. 44; 1 Sam. xxiii. 1-13; Neh. iii. 17, 18. (2) Person or place, 1 Chr. iv. 19.

Kē-lā′i̯ah, Ez. x. 23. [KELITA.]

Kĕl′ĭ-tà (*dwarf*). Assistant of Ezra, Neh. viii. 7.

Kē-mū′el (*helper*). (1) Son of Nahor, Gen. xxii. 21. (2) A prince of Ephraim, Num. xxxiv. 24. (3) A Levite, 1 Chr. xxvii. 17.

Kē′nan, 1 Chr. i. 2. [CAINAN.]

Kē′nath (*possession*). A city or section of Gilead, Num. xxxii. 42.

Kē′năz (*hunting*). (1) A duke of Edom, Gen. xxxvi. 15, and founder of Kenezites, Josh. xiv. 14. (2) Father of Othniel, Josh. xv. 17. (3) Grandson of Caleb, 1 Chr. iv. 15.

Kĕn′ez-īte (*hunter*). Kenizzite, Gen. xv. 19. An ancient Edomite tribe, Num. xxxii. 12; Josh. xiv. 6, 14.

Kĕn′ītes (*smiths*). A Midianite tribe allied to Israelites, Gen. xv. 19; Num. xxiv. 21, 22; Judg. iv. 11.

Kĕr′en=hăp′puch (*horn of beauty*). Third daughter of Job, Job xlii. 14.

Kē′rĭ-ŏth (*cities*). (1) A town of Judah, Josh. xv. 25. (2) A city of Moab, Jer. xlviii. 24.

Kē′ros (*crooked*). His children returned, Ez. ii. 44.

Kĕt′tle (*deep vessel*). Used for cooking and sacrifices, 1 Sam. ii. 14. Basket, Jer. xxiv. 2; caldron, 2 Chr. xxxv. 13; pot, Job xli. 20.

Kē-tū′rah (*incense*). A wife of Abraham, Gen. xxv. 1; 1 Chr. i. 32.

Kē-zī′à (*cassia*). Job's second daughter, Job xlii. 14.

Kē′ziz (*end*). A town of Benjamin, Josh. xviii. 21.

Kĭb′roth=hăt-tā′a-vah (*graves of lust*). A desert encampment of the Israelites, Num. xi. 31-35.

Kĭb′za-im (*heaps*). Levitical city in Ephraim, Josh. xxi. 22. Jokmeam, 1 Chr. vi. 68.

Kĭd. Young goat. An offering, Num. vii. 12-82. A favorite meat, Gen. xxxviii. 17; 1 Sam. xvi. 20.

Kĭd′ron (*turbid*). The brook or ravine between Jerusalem and Olivet, 2 Sam. xv. 23; 2 Kgs. xxiii. 6. Cedron, John xviii. 1.

Kī′nah (*dirge*). City of south Judah, Josh. xv. 22.

Kīne. Plural of cow, Gen. xli. 17-21.

King (*tribe*). Title of Hebrew rulers from Saul to Zedekiah, B. C. 1095-588. Other rulers, Gen. xxxvi. 31; Ex. iii. 19; Num. xxxi. 8. Supreme ruler, 1 Tim. i. 17; vi. 15.

Kings. Eleventh and twelfth O. T. books. Originally one. Compilation credited to Ezra or Jeremiah. 1 Kings gives history of Hebrew kingdoms from Solomon, B. C. 1015, to Jehoshaphat, B. C. 890. 2 Kings completes the history, B. C. 890-588.

Kĭr (*fortress*). An unlocated eastern country, 2 Kgs. xvi. 9; Am. ix. 7.

Kĭr=hăr′e-sĕth (*brick fortress*). A stronghold of Moab, 2 Kgs. iii. 25. Kirhareseth, Isa. xvi. 7. Kirharesh, Isa. xvi. 11. Kirheres, Jer. xlviii. 31, 36. Kir of Moab, Isa. xv. 1.

Kĭr″ĭ-a-thā′im, Jer. xlviii. 1, 23; Ezek. xxv. 9. [KIRJATHAIM.]

Kir″i-ath-i-ā′ri-us, 1 Esdr. v. 19. [KIRJATH-JEARIM.]

Kir′i-ŏth, Am. ii. 2. [KERIOTH.]

Kir′jath (*city*). City in Benjamin, Josh. xviii. 28.

Kir″jath-ā′im (*double city*). (1) A Moabite town, Num. xxxii. 37. (2) Levitical town in Naphtali, Josh. xiii. 19; 1 Chr. vi. 76.

Kir′jath-är′bȧ (*city of Arba*). Old name of Hebron, Gen. xxiii. 2; Josh. xiv. 15.

Kir′jath-ā′rim, Ez. ii. 25. [KIRJATH-JEARIM.]

Kir′jath-bā′al, Josh. xv. 60; xviii. 14. [KIRJATH-JEARIM.]

Kir′jath-hū′zoth (*city of streets*). City in Moab, Num. xxii. 39.

Kir′jath-jē′a-rim (*city of woods*). A Gibeonite city which fell to Judah, Josh. ix. 17; Judg. xviii. 12. Baalah, Josh. xv. 9. Kirjath-baal, xviii. 14.

Kir′jath-san′nah (*palm city*). [DEBIR.]

Kō′ȧ (*male camel*). An eastern prince, Ezek. xxiii. 23.

Kō′hath (*assembly*). Second son of Levi, and head of the house of Kohathite Levites, Gen. xlvi. 11; Ex. vi. 16, 18; Num. iii. 27; xxvi. 57; Josh. xxi. 4-42.

Kŏl″a-ī′ah (*God's voice*). (1) A Benjamite, Neh. xi. 7. (2) Father of the false prophet Ahab, Jer. xxix. 21.

Kō′rah (*baldness*). (1) Dukes of Edom, Gen. xxxvi. 5-18. (2) Son of Hebron, 1 Chr. ii. 43. (3) Leader of the rebellion against Moses, Num. xvi.; xxvi. 9-11.

Kō′rah-ītes. Descendants of Korah, 1 Chr. ix. 19. Korhites, 2 Chr. xx. 19. Korathites, Num. xxvi. 58.

Kō′rē (*quail*). (1) A Korahite, 1 Chr. ix. 19. (2) Korhites, 1 Chr. xxvi. 1-19. (3) A Levite, 2 Chr. xxxi. 14.

Lizard. (*See* p. 68.)

Kir′jath-sē′phĕr (*city of books*). [DEBIR.]

Kir of Mō′ab. [KIR-HARASETH.]

Kish (*bow*). (1) Father of Saul, 1 Sam. x. 21. (2) A Benjamite, 1 Chr. viii. 30. (3) A Levite, 1 Chr. xxiii. 21. (4) A Levite, 2 Chr. xxix. 12. (5) Ancestor of Mordecai, Esth. ii. 5.

Kish′ī (*bow*). A Levite, 1 Chr. vi. 44.

Kish′i-ŏn (*hardness*). Levitical city in Issachar, Josh. xix. 20.

Kī′shŏn (*crooked*). (1) Josh. xxi. 28. [KISHION.] (2) The brook or wady which drains the valley of Esdraelon, Judg. iv. 7-13; v. 21; 1 Kgs. xviii. 40. Kison, Ps. lxxxiii. 9.

Kī′son, Ps. lxxxiii. 9. [KISHON.]

Kiss. Form of salutation, Gen. xxix. 13; token of allegiance, 1 Sam. x. 1; pledge of Christian brotherhood, Rom. xvi. 16; 1 Pet. v. 14.

Kite (*quick of wing*). An unclean bird of the hawk species, Lev. xi. 14; Deut. xiv. 13. Vulture, Job xxviii. 7.

Kith′lish (*wall*). Lowland town in Judah, Josh. xv. 40.

Kit′rŏn (*knotty*). Town in Zebulun, Judg. i. 30.

Kit′tim, Gen. x. 4; 1 Chr. i. 7. [CHITTIM.]

Knēad′ing-troughs. Were bowls, or leather surfaces, Gen. xviii. 6; Ex. xii. 34.

Knife (*waster*). Primitively of stone or bone; later of metal. Little used at meals. For killing and cutting, Lev. viii. 20; sharpening pens, Jer. xxxvi. 23; pruning, Isa. xviii. 5; lancing, 1 Kgs. xviii. 28.

Knŏp (*knob*). Ornamental knobs, or reliefs, Ex. xxv. 31-36; 1 Kgs. vi. 18.

Kŏz (*thorn*). (1) A Judahite, 1 Chr. iv. 8. [COZ.] (2) A priest, 1 Chr. xxiv. 10. [HAKKOZ.] (3) Returned captives, Ez. ii. 61; Neh. iii. 4, 21.

Kŭsh-a′jah, 1 Chr. xv. 17. [KISHI.]

L

Lā′a-dah (*order*). A Judahite, 1 Chr. iv. 21.

Lā′a-dăn (*ordered*). (1) An Ephraimite, 1 Chr. vii. 26. (2) Son of Gershon, 1 Chr. xxiii. 7-9; xxvi. 21. Libni, elsewhere.

Lā′ban (*white*). (1) Father-in-law of Jacob, Gen. xxiv. xxx. (2) A landmark, Deut. i. 1.

Lăb′a-nȧ, 1 Esdr. v. 29. [LEBANA.]

Lăç″e-dē-mō′nĭ-ans. Inhabitants of Lacedemon. Spartans, 1 Macc. xii. 2-21.

Lā′chish (*impregnable*). An Amorite city in southern Judah, Josh. x.; 2 Kgs. xviii. 17; xix. 8; 2 Chr. xi. 9; Neh. xi. 30.

Lȧ-cū′nus. A returned captive, 1 Esdr. ix. 31.

Lā′dan, 1 Esdr. v. 37. [DELAIAH.]

Lā′el (*of God*). A Gershonite, Num. iii. 24.

Lā′hăd (*oppression*). A Judahite, 1 Chr. iv. 2.

Lȧ-hāi′-roi (*well of the living God*). Well of Hagar's relief, Gen. xxiv. 62; xxv. 11.

Läh′mam (*bread*). Lowland town of Judah, Josh. xv. 40.

Läh′mī (*warrior*). Brother of Goliath, 1 Chr. xx. 5.

Lā′ish (*lion*). (1) A northern Danite city, Judg. xviii. 7-29; Isa. x. 30. (2) Father of Phaltiel, 1 Sam. xxv. 44; 2 Sam. iii. 15. Leshem, Josh. xix. 47.

Lā'kŭm (*fortress*). A border of Naphtali, Josh. xix. 33.

Lămb. Young of sheep or goat. Favorite sacrifices, Ex. xxix. 38-41; Num. xxviii. 9-29.

Lā'mech (*strong*). (1) Father of Noah, Gen. v. 28-32. (2) Father of Jubal, inventor of the harp and organ, Gen. iv. 18-26.

Lăm"ĕn-tā'tions (*weepings*). Twenty-fifth O. T. book. An elegiac poem by Jeremiah, on the destruction of Jerusalem.

Ancient Lamp.

Lămp (*shine*). The temple candlestick, Ex. xxv. 31-40; 1 Kgs. vii. 49. Torches, Judg. vii. 16. Oriental lamps of many shapes and ornamental. Fed with oil, tallow, wax, etc., Matt. xxv. 1.

Lăn'çet (*little lance*). Light spear, 1 Kgs. xviii. 28.

Lănd'mărks, Were trees, stones, towns, mountains, streams, etc. Removal forbidden, Deut. xix. 14; Prov. xxii. 28.

Lăn'guāge (*tongue*). Originally one, Gen. xi. 1. Diversified at Babel, Gen. xi. 7-9.

Lăn'tĕrn (*shining*). Covered candle or lamp, John xviii. 3.

Lā-ŏd"ĭ-çē'ă (*just people*). Ancient Diospolis; modern Eski-hissar. A city of Phrygia, and seat of an early Christian church, Col. ii. 1; iv. 15; Rev. i. 11; iii. 14-22.

Ruins of Laodicea.

Lăp'ĭ-dŏth (*lamps*). Husband of Deborah, Judg. iv. 4.

Lăp'wĭng. An unclean bird, thought to be the beautiful migratory hoopoe, Lev. xi. 19.

Lā-sē'ă. City in Crete, Acts xxvii. 8.

Lā'shă (*cleft*). A Canaanite border, Gen. x. 19.

Lā-shâr'on (*plain*). A Canaanite town, Josh. xii. 18.

Lăs'thĕ-nēs. A Cretan, 1 Macc. xi. 31.

Lătch'et (*lace*). Sandal lacings, or fastenings, Gen. xiv. 23; Mark i. 7.

Lăt'in. Language of Latium, *i. e.* the Romans, Luke xxiii. 38; John xix. 20.

Lăt'tiçe (*lath*). Open work of wood or metal; also window, blind, or screen, Judg. v. 28; 2 Kgs. i. 2; Prov. vii. 6.

Lā'ver (*wash*). A brazen vessel holding water for priestly washings — hands, feet, and the sacrifices, Ex. xxx. 18-21; xxxviii. 8; 1 Kgs. vii. 38-40; 2 Chr. iv. 6.

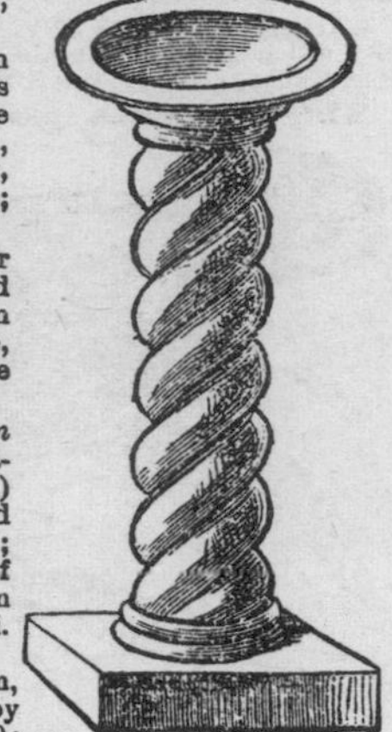

Ancient Laver.

Law (*rule*). In Scripture, reference is nearly always to the Hebrew civil, moral, and ceremonial law, Matt. v. 17; John i. 17; Acts xxv. 8.

Law'yĕr. Scribe or divine who expounded the Mosaic law in school or synagogue, Matt. xxii. 35; Luke x. 25.

Lăz'a-rus (*whom God helps*). Abbreviation of Eleazar. (1) Brother of Mary and Martha, John xi. 1; xii. 1-11. (2) Type of poverty and distress in the parable, Luke xvi. 19-31.

Lĕad. Early known, imported and used by Hebrews, Ex. xv. 10; Num. xxxi. 22; Job xix. 24; Ezek. xxvii. 12.

Lēaf. Of trees, Gen. viii. 11; Matt. xxi. 19; double doors, 1 Kgs. vi. 34; of books, Jer. xxxvi. 23; prosperity, Jer. xvii. 8; decay, Job xiii. 25.

Lē'ah (*weary*). Jacob's wife through deceit of her father, Laban, Gen. xxix., xxx., xlix. 31.

Lēas'ing (*lying*). Falsehood, Ps. iv. 2; v. 6.

Lĕath'er. Used by Hebrews, 2 Kgs. i. 8; Matt. iii. 4.

Lĕav'en (*raise*). Old fermented dough used to lighten new dough, Matt. xiii. 33. Passover bread unleavened, Ex. xii. 15-17. Corrupt doctrines, Matt. xvi. 6; evil passions, 1 Cor. v. 7, 8.

Lĕb'a-nă (*white*). His children returned, Neh. vii. 48. Lebanah, Ez. ii. 45.

Lĕb'a-non (*white*). Two mountain ranges running N. E., between which was Cœlo-Syria. The western is Libanus, or Lebanon proper. The eastern is Anti-Libanus, and skirted Palestine on the north, Deut. i. 7; Josh. i. 4. Many scripture allusions, Isa. x. 34; Jer. xxii. 23.

Lĕb'a-ŏth (*lionesses*). Boundary town of southern Judah, Josh. xv. 32.

Lĕb-bæ'us (*brave*). Thaddæus, the apostle Jude, Matt. x. 3, Mark iii. 18.

Lē-bō'nah (*incense*). Place north of Bethel, Judg. xxi. 19.

Lē'cah (*walking*). Person or place, 1 Chr. iv. 21.

Lēech. [Horse-leech.]

Lēek. Closely allied to the onion, Num. xi. 5.

Lēes (*dregs*). Sediment of liquor. Settled, pure wine, Isa. xxv. 6; sloth, Jer. xlviii. 11; extreme suffering, Ps. lxxv. 8.

Lē'gion (*gathered*). Division of Roman army; when full, 6200 men and 730 horse. N. T. use indefinite, Matt. xxvi. 53; Mark v. 9.

Lapwing or Hoopoe. (*See* p. 66.)

Lē'hă-bĭm (*flame*). A Mizraite tribe; Libyans, Gen. x. 13. Lubim, 2 Chr. xii. 3.

Lē'hī (*jawbone*). Where Samson slew the Philistines, Judg. xv. 9, 19.

Lĕm'u-el (*dedicated*). The unknown king in Prov. xxxi. 1-9.

Lĕn'tĭl (*little lens*). A podded food plant, like the pea or bean, Gen. xxv. 34; 2 Sam. xvii. 28.

Lĕop'ard (*lion-panther*). This fierce, spotted beast of the cat species once found in Jordan jungles, Jer. xiii. 23; Dan. vii. 6; S. of Sol. iv. 8.

Lĕp'ĕr (*peeled*). Who has leprosy; a loathsome, incurable skin disease, common in East, Ex. iv. 6; treatment of, Lev. xiv. 3-32; Luke xvii. 12-19.

Lē'shem, Josh. xix. 47. [LAISH.]

Lĕt'tus, 1 Esdr. viii. 29. [HATTUSH.]

Lē-tū'shim (*hammered*). Son of Dedan, and his Arabian tribe, Gen. xxv. 3.

Lē-ŭm'mim (*nations*). Son of Dedan, and his Arabian tribe, Gen. xxv. 3.

Lē'vī (*joined*). (1) Third son of Jacob, Gen. xxix. 34; avenged Dinah's wrong, xxxiv. 25-31; cursed, xlix. 5-7; went to Egypt, Ex. vi. 16; blessed, Ex. xxxii. 25-28. (2) Two of Christ's ancestors, Luke iii. 24, 29. (3) Original name of Matthew, Mark ii. 14; Luke v. 27, 29; compare Matt. ix. 9.

Lē-vī'a-than (*aquatic monster*). The crocodile is described in Job xli.; and probably meant in Ps. lxxiv. 14; civ. 26.

Lē'vītes. Descendants of Levi, Ex. vi. 16-25; Lev. xxv. 32, etc.; Num. xxxv. 2-8; Josh. xxi. 3. In above, the tribe is meant. But Levites came to mean the priestly branch, *i. e.*, descendants of Aaron, Josh. iii. 3; 1 Kgs. viii. 4; Ez. ii. 70; John i. 19. Three Levitical lines, Kohathite, Gershonite, Merarite, Num. iii. 17. Assigned 48 cities among the other tribes, Num. xxxv.

Lē-vĭt'ĭ-cus (*for Levites*). Third book of Bible and Pentateuch, containing the ceremonial law for guidance of Levites. Authorship ascribed to Moses and Aaron.

Lĭb'ă-nus. Greek form of Lebanon, 1 Esdr. iv. 48.

Lĭb'ĕr-tines (*free*). Emancipated Jewish slaves; freedmen, Acts vi. 9.

Lĭb'nah (*white*). (1) An Israelite encampment, Num. xxxiii. 20, 21. (2) Levitical city in Judah, Josh. x. 29-31; 2 Kgs. xix. 8-35; 1 Chr. vi. 57.

Lĭb'nī (*whiteness*). (1) A Levite founder of Libnites, Ex. vi. 17; Num. iii. 18-21. (2) Probably the above, 1 Chr. vi. 29.

Lĭb'ȳ-ȧ, Ezek. xxx. 5; Acts ii. 10. The African continent west of Egypt and contiguous to Mediterranean. *See* Lubim and Lehabim.

Līçe (*destroyers*). Constituted the third Egyptian plague, Ex. viii. 16-18; Ps. cv. 31.

Lieū-tĕn'ants (*place-holders*). Satraps or viceroys, Ez. viii. 36. Princes, Dan. iii. 2; vi. 1.

Līfe. Natural, Gen. iii. 17; spiritual, Rom. viii. 6; eternal, John iii. 36; Rom. vi. 23.

Līght. First gush of creation, Gen. i. 3. Frequent source of imagery, Matt. iv. 16; Luke ii. 32; John i. 7-9.

Līgn-aloes (*wood-aloes*). [ALOES.]

Lĭg'ūre (*lynx urine*). Possibly amber. First stone in third row of high priest's breastplate, Ex. xxviii. 19; xxxix. 12.

Lĭk'hī (*learned*). A Manassite, 1 Chr. vii. 19.

Lĭl'y (*pale*). Source of rich imagery, 1 Kgs. vii. 19; S. of Sol. ii. 1, 2; v. 13; Matt. vi. 28; Luke xii. 27.

Līme (*glue*). Was known and used for plaster and cement work, Deut. xxvii. 2; Isa. xxxiii. 12; Am. ii. 1.

Lĭn'en (*flax*). Used for stately robes, Gen. xli. 42; priestly vestments, Ex. xxviii. 42; Lev. vi. 10; temple veil, 2 Chr. iii. 14; choral gowns, 2 Chr. v. 12, and ordinary dress. Symbol of purity, Rev. xv. 6; of luxury, Luke xvi. 19.

Lĭn'tel (*boundary*). Support over window or door, Ex. xii. 22; 1 Kgs. vi. 31.

Lī'nus (*net*). Roman friend of Paul, 2 Tim. iv. 21.

Lī'on (*seeing*). Once found in Palestine, Judg. xiv. 5, 6; 1 Sam. xvii. 34-36; 2 Sam. xxiii. 20. Symbol of strength, Gen. xlix. 9.

Lion.

Lit'tẽr (*bed*). Covered couch or chair, carried by men or animals, Isa. lxvi. 20. "Wagons," Num. vii. 3.

Liz'ärd (*muscular*). Abundant in Palestine. Unclean, Lev. xi. 30.

Lō=ăm'mī (*not my people*). Figurative name of Hosea's son, Hos. i. 9.

Lōans. Allowed by Hebrews, but all debts cancelled in Sabbatical year, Deut. xv. 1-11. Usury not allowed, Ex. xxii. 25; Lev. xxv. 36; Deut. xv. 3-10.

Lŏck (*bar*). A bar of wood or metal for outer, and bolt for inner, doors, 1 Kgs. iv. 13; Judg. iii. 24.

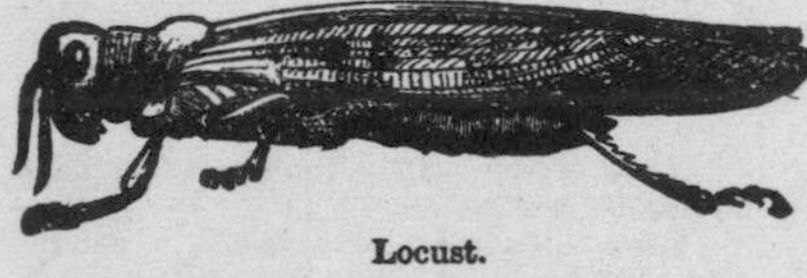

Locust.

Lō'cust (*leaping*). Confused original, supposably embracing the destructive insects, — locust, grasshopper, caterpillar, palmer-worm, etc. They constituted the eighth Egyptian plague, Ex. x. 1-15; Joel ii. 3-10.

Lŏd, 1 Chr. viii. 12; Ez. ii. 33. [LYDDA.]

Lō=dē'bär (*barren*). A place east of Jordan, 2 Sam. ix. 4; xvii. 27.

Lŏg. Hebrew liquid measure; about five sixths of a pint, Lev. xiv. 10-24.

Lō'is (*pleasing*). Timothy's grandmother, 2 Tim. i. 5.

Lily. (See p. 67.)

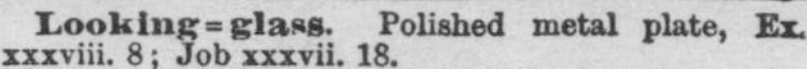

Looking=glass. Polished metal plate, Ex. xxxviii. 8; Job xxxvii. 18.

Lôrd (*loaf-guardian*). Jehovah, LORD, Gen. xv. 4; Ps. vii., c. Adonai, Lord, Christ, The Lord, Our Lord. Supreme ruler, and not the Saxon dignitary.

Lôrd's Dāy. First day of the week; resurrection day of Christ, Rev. i. 10. Sunday, after A. D. 321.

Lôrd's Sŭp'per. Substitute for the O. T. Paschal feast. Instituted by Christ the night before the crucifixion, as a reminder of his covenant with mankind, Matt. xxvi. 19; Mark xiv. 16; Luke xxii. 13. "Breaking of bread," Acts ii. 42; xx. 7. "Communion," 1 Cor. x. 16. "Lord's Supper," only in 1 Cor. xi. 20.

Lō=ru'ha-mah (*unpitied*): Hosea's daughter, Hos. i. 6.

Lŏt (*veil*). Abraham's nephew, Gen. xi. 27-31. Settled in Jordan valley, Gen. xiii. 1-13. Escaped to mountains, Gen. xix. Progenitor of Moabites and Ammonites.

Lō'tan (*hidden*). A Horite duke, Gen. xxxvi. 20-29.

Lŏth''a-sū'bus, 1 Esdr. ix. 44. [HASHUM.]

Lŏts, Feast of. [PURIM.]

Lŏts. Casting or drawing of, a usual way of settling questions. Possibly marked pebbles were used, in a bag or box. Canaan was allotted to the tribes of Israel, Num. xxvi. 55; Josh. xv., xix. Scapegoat so chosen, Lev. xvi. 8; priest's courses, 1 Chr. xxiv., xxv.; property divided, Matt. xxvii. 35.

Love Fēasts. Feasts of offerings, after the community of goods ceased, Jude 12; 2 Peter ii. 13. Forbidden by Council of Laodicea, A. D. 320.

Lu-bĭm, 2 Chr. xii. 3; xvi. 8. [LIBYA.]

Lu'cas. Luke the evangelist, Phile. 24.

Lu'çi-fẽr (*light-giver*). Types the king of Babylon, Isa. xiv. 12. Popularly, Satan.

Lu'çius (*morning born*). (1) Paul's kinsman, Rom. xvi. 21. (2) A Cyrenean convert and teacher, Acts xiii. 1.

Lŭd (*strife*). Son of Shem, Gen. x. 22.

Lu'dĭm (*strife*). A Mizraite tribe, Gen. x. 13; Isa. lxvi. 19; Ezek. xxvii. 10.

Lu'hith (*board-made*). Place in Moab, Isa. xv. 5; Jer. xlviii. 5.

Luke (*luminous*). Evangelist and physician, Col. iv. 14; 2 Tim. iv. 11. Author of third gospel and of Acts of the Apostles.

Lu'nă-tics (*moon-struck*). Epileptics are probably meant, Matt. iv. 24; xvii. 15.

Lŭz (*almond*). Site of Bethel, Gen. xxviii. 19; Josh. xvi. 2; Judg. i. 23.

Lўc''a-ō'nĭ-à (*wolf-land*). Wild district of Asia Minor, containing towns of Derbe, Lystra, and Iconium, Acts xiv. 6-11. Twice visited by Paul.

Lў'çià. A southwestern district of Asia Minor, with Myra and Patara as cities, Acts xxi. 2; xxvii. 5.

Lўd'dà (*strife*). Hebrew Lud or Lod. Now Lidd or Ludd. In Sharon plain, 9 miles east of Joppa, Acts ix. 32.

Lўd'ĭ-à (*Lydus land*). (1) A province of Asia Minor, on Mediterranean. Cities, Sardis, Thyatira, Philadelphia, 1 Macc. viii. 8. (2) Woman convert of Thyatira, Acts xvi. 14.

Lў-sā'nĭ-as (*that drives away sorrow*). Tetrarch of Abilene, Luke iii. 1.

Lўs'ias (*dissolving*). Claudius Lysias, captain of the band that rescued Paul, Acts xxi.-xxiv. 1-9. (2) Governor of southern Syria, 1 Macc. iii. 32.

Lў-sĭm'a-chus. (1) Translator of Esther, Esth. xi. 1. (2) Brother of Menelaus, 2 Macc. iv. 29-42.

Lystra.

Lȳs'trȧ (*dissolving*). City of Lycaonia, where Paul was honored, Acts xiv. 6–18; and stoned, 19–21.

M

Mā'a-can (*oppression*). (1) A wife of David, 2 Sam. iii. 3. Maachah, 1 Chr. iii. 2. (2) A petty kingdom, N. E. of Palestine, 2 Sam. x. 6–8. Syria-maachah, 1 Chr. xix. 6, 7.

Mā'a-chah (*oppression*). (1) Daughter of Nahor, Gen. xxii. 24. (2) A Gathite, 1 Kgs. ii. 39. (3) Wife of Rehoboam, 1 Kgs. xv. 2. (4) Concubine of Caleb, 1 Chr. ii. 48. (5) A Benjamitess, 1 Chr. vii. 15, 16. (6) Wife of Jehiel, 1 Chr. viii. 29. (7) Father of Hanan, 1 Chr. xi. 43. (8) A Simeonite, 1 Chr. xxvii. 16.

Mȧ-ăch'a-thī. Maachathites. People of Maacah, Deut. iii. 14; Josh. xii. 5.

Mȧ-ăd' āi (*ornament*). Son of Bani, Ez. x. 34.

Mȧ''a-dī'ah. A returned priest, Neh. xii. 5. Moadiah, vs. 17.

Mȧ-ā'ī (*merciful*). A Levite, Neh. xii. 36.

Mȧ-ăl'eh=ȧ-crăb'bim, Josh. xv. 3. Scorpion pass. [Akrabbim.]

Mȧ-ā'nī, 1 Esdr. ix. 34. [Baana.]

Mā'a-rŏth (*open*). Town in Judah, Josh. xv. 59.

Mā''a-sē'iah (*work of God*). (1) Returned Levites and captive families, Ez. x. 18, 21, 22, 30; Neh. iii. 20; viii. 4, 7; x. 25; xi. 5, 7; xii. 41, 42. (2) Father of Zephaniah, Jer. xxi. 1. (3) Father of Zedekiah, Jer. xxix. 21. (4) A porter, 1 Chr. xv. 18–20. (5) Son of Adaiah, 2 Chr. xxiii. 1. (6) Others in 2 Chr. xxvi. 11; xxviii. 7; xxxiv. 8; Jer. xxxv. 4.

Mā'ath (*small*). An ancestor of Christ, Luke iii. 26.

Mā'ăz (*wrath*). Son of Ram, 1 Chr. ii. 27.

Mā''a-zī'ah (*consolation*). Two priests, 1 Chr. xxiv. 18; Neh. x. 8.

Măb'dȧ-ī, 1 Esdr. ix. 34. [Benaiah.]

Măc'a-lon, 1 Esdr. v. 21. [Michmash.]

Măc'că-bees (*hammer*). The Asmonean princes who upheld the cause of Jewish independence, B. C. 166–40. The two Apocryphal books of Maccabees contain their history.

Măç''e-dō'nī-ȧ (*extended*). The ancient empire north of Greece proper, whose greatest kings were Philip and Alexander the Great. Often visited by Paul, who made here his first European converts, Acts xvi. 9–12; xvii. 1–15; xx. 1–6.

Măch'ba-nāi (*stout*). A Gadite chief, 1 Chr. xii. 13.

Măch'be-nah (*cloak*). Person or place, 1 Chr. ii. 49.

Mā'chī (*decrease*). Father of the Gadite spy, Num. xiii. 15.

Mā'chĭr (*sold*). (1) Eldest son of Manasseh, Num. xxxii. 39; Josh. xvii. 1. (2) Son of Ammiel, 2 Sam. ix. 4; xvii. 27.

Mā'chĭr-ītes. Descendants of Machir, Num. xxvi. 29.

Măch'mas, 1 Macc. ix. 73. [Michmash.]

Măch''nă-dē'bāi (*liberal*). Son of Bani, Ez. x. 40.

Măch-pē'lah (*double*). Abraham's burial cave at Hebron, Gen. xxiii. 17–19; xxv. 9; xlix. 29–32; l. 13.

Măd'a-ī (*middle*). Son of Japheth, and progenitor of the Medes, Gen. x. 2.

Mā'dī-an, Acts vii. 29. [Midian.]

Măd-măn'nah (*dunghill*). Town in southern Judah, near Gaza, Josh. xv. 31.

Măd'men (*dunghill*). A place in Moab, Jer. xlviii. 2.

Măd-mē'nah (*dunghill*). Town in Benjamin, Isa. x. 31.

Măd'ness. Lunacy and passionate outburst, John x. 20.

Mā'dŏn (*strife*). Ancient city of Canaan, Josh. xi. 1; xii. 19.

Măg'bish (*gathering*). Person or place, Ez. ii. 30.

Măg'da-lȧ (*tower*). Village on W. shore of Sea of Galilee, Matt. xv. 39. Magadan in R. V.

Măg'dī-el (*praise*). A duke of Edom, Gen. xxxvi. 43.

Mā'ḡĕd, 1 Macc. v. 36. [Maked.]

Mā'ġī (*priests*). Oriental priests and learned men. A Median and Persian caste of royal advisers, Jer. xxxix. 3; Matt. ii. 1–11.

Măġ'ic (*of Magi*). The magician's art. Acting through occult agencies. Potent in Oriental religions, Ex. vii., viii. Forbidden, Lev. xix. 31; xx. 6.

Mā'gŏg (*Gog's region*). (1) Second son of Japheth, and his people, Gen. x. 2. (2) Gog's land; probably Scythia, Ezek. xxxviii. 2; xxxix. 2–6. (3) Symbolical enemies, Rev. xx. 7–9.

Coin of Macedonia.

Mā'gôr=mĭs'sa-bĭb (*fear everywhere*). Pashur, who imprisoned Jeremiah, Jer. xx. 1–3.

Măg'pī-ăsh (*moth killer*). A co-covenanter, Neh. x. 20.

Mȧ-hā'lah (*sickness*). A Manassite, 1 Chr. vii. 18.

Mȧ-hā'la-lē''el (*God's praise*). (1) Son of Cainan, Gen. v. 12–17. Maleleel, Luke iii. 37. (2) A Judahite, Neh. xi. 4.

Mā'ha-lath (*harp*). (1) Wife of Esau, Gen. xxviii. 9. (2) Wife of Rehoboam, 2 Chr. xi. 18. (3) The tune or the instrument, Ps. liii., lxxxviii. titles.

Mā'ha-lī (*sick*), Ex. vi. 19. [Mahli.]

Mā''hȧ-nā'im (*two camps*). Place where Jacob met the angels, Gen. xxxii. 2. Afterwards a Levitical town in Gad, Josh. xxi. 38; 2 Sam. ii. 8–12.

Mā'hă-neh=dăn (*camp of Dan*). Located as in Judg. xiii. 25; xviii. 12.

Mȧ-hăr'a-ī (*swift*). One of David's captains, 2 Sam. xxiii. 28; 1 Chr. xi. 30; xxvii. 13.

Mā'hath (*grasping*). Two Kohathite Levites, 1 Chr. vi. 35; 2 Chr. xxix. 12.

Mā'hȧ-vīte. Designation of one of David's captains, 1 Chr. xi. 46.

Mȧ-hā'zī-ŏth (*visions*). Son of Heman, 1 Chr. xxv. 4, 30.

Mā'hĕr=shăl''al-hăsh'=băz (*speeding to the prey*). Name of Isaiah's son, symbolizing the Assyrian conquest of Damascus and Samaria, Isa. viii. 1-4.

Măh'lah (*disease*). Daughter of Zelophehad, Num. xxvii. 1-11.

Măh'lī (*sickly*). (1) A Levite, Num. iii. 20. Mahali, Ex. vi. 19. (2) Another Levite, 1 Chr. vi. 47.

Măh'lītes. Descendants of Mahli, Num. iii. 33.

Măh'lon (*sickly*). Ruth's first husband, Ruth i. 2-5; iv. 9, 10.

Mā'hol (*dancing*). Father of the four wise men, 1 Kgs. iv. 31.

Mā'kăz (*end*). Unidentified place, 1 Kgs. iv. 9.

Mā'kĕd. City of Gilead, 1 Macc. v. 26-36.

Măk-hē'loth (*meeting place*). A desert encampment, Num. xxxiii. 25.

Măk-kē'dah (*shepherd place*). An ancient Canaanite city, Josh. x. 10-30; xii. 16; xv. 41.

Măk'tesh (*mortar*). Denounced quarter of Jerusalem, Zeph. i. 11.

Măl'a-chī (*God's messenger*). Last of minor prophets. Nothing known of nativity or lineage. Contemporary with Nehemiah, B. C. 445-433. His book foretells the coming of Christ and John the Baptist.

Măl'cham (*their king*). (1) A Benjamite, 1 Chr. viii. 9. (2) The idol Molech, Zeph. i. 5.

Măl-chī'ah (*king*). (1) A Levite, 1 Chr. vi. 40. (2) Jeremiah's prison-keeper, Jer. xxxviii. 6. (3) Returned captives, Ez. x. 25, 31; Neh. iii. 14; viii. 4; xi. 12.

Măl'chī-el (*God's king*). An Asherite and founder of Malchielites, or Birzavith, Gen. xlvi. 17; Num. xxvi. 45; 1 Chr. vii. 31.

Măl-chī'jah (*king*). Priests and returned captives, 1 Chr. xxiv. 9; Ez. x. 25, 31; Neh. iii. 11; xii. 42.

Măl-chī'ram (*king of height*). Son of Jehoiachin, 1 Chr. iii. 18.

Măl'chī-shū'ȧ (*king of help*). Son of Saul, 1 Chr. ix. 39. Melchishua, 1 Sam. xiv. 49.

Măl'chus (*ruling*). The one whose ear Peter cut off, Matt. xxvi. 51; Luke xxii. 50.

Mȧ-lē'le-el, Luke iii. 37. [MAHALALEEL.]

Măl'lŏs. City in Cilicia, 2 Macc. iv. 30.

Măl'lō-thī (*fulness*). Chief of the 19th musical course, 1 Chr. xxv. 4, 26.

Măl'lōws (*soft*). Jews'-mallows of the East, used for pot-herbs, Job xxx. 4.

Măl'luch (*ruling*). Levites, 1 Chr. vi. 44; Ez. x. 29, 32; Neh. x. 4; xii. 2.

Măm'mon (*riches*). A Chaldee word used by Christ, Matt. vi. 24; Luke xvi. 9.

Măm''nī-tȧ-naī'mus. 1 Esdr. ix. 34. [MATTANIAH.]

Măm'rē (*strength*). The Amorite chief who gave his name to the plain where Abraham dwelt, Gen. xiv. 13-24. Hebron, Gen. xxiii. 19.

Mȧ-mū'chus, 1 Esdr. ix. 30. [MALLUCH.]

Măn. Adam, *ruddy*, Gen. i. 26. The human race, Gen. v. 2; viii. 21. As distinguished from woman, Deut. xxii. 5; 1 Sam. xvii. 33. Mortal, Isa. xiii. 14.

Măn'a-ĕn (*comforter*). A Christian teacher at Antioch, Acts xiii. 1.

Măn'a-hăth (*rest*). (1) A Horite progenitor of the Manahethites, Gen. xxxvi. 23; 1 Chr. ii. 52. (2) Place or person, 1 Chr. viii. 6.

Mȧ-năs'seh (*forgetting*). (1) First son of Joseph, Gen. xli. 51. The tribe divided and occupied both sides of Jordan, Josh. xvi., xvii. (2) Son and successor of Hezekiah on the throne of Judah, B. C. 698-643. Idolatrous, 2 Kgs. xxi. 1-18. Captive in Babylon; repented; restored, 2 Chr. xxxiii. 1-20. (3) Returned captives, Ez. x. 30, 33.

Mȧ-năs'sēs. (1) King Manasseh, Matt. i. 10. (2) Manasseh, Joseph's son, Rev. vii. 6.

Mȧ-năs'sītes. Descendants of Manasseh (1), Deut. iv. 43; Judg. xii. 4.

Măn'drāke (*field speaker*). A narcotic plant, resembling rhubarb, bearing a yellow, aromatic fruit, Gen. xxx. 14-16; S. of Sol. vii. 13.

Mandrake.

Mā'nĕh. The mina; a variable Hebrew weight, Ezek. xlv. 12.

Măn'ger (*eating place*). Feeding crib or trough for cattle. The stall, and even the cattleyard, Luke ii. 7-16; xiii. 15.

Mā'nī, 1 Esdr. ix. 30. [BANI.]

Măn'nȧ (*what is this?*). The bread substitute sent to the wandering Israelites, Ex. xvi. 14-36; Num. xi. 7-9; Deut. viii. 3; Josh. v. 12.

Mȧ-nō'ah (*rest*). Father of Samson, Judg. xiii. 1-23.

Măn'slāy-er. The involuntary manslayer found escape in a city of refuge, Num. xxxv. 22, 23; Deut. xix. 5.

Măn'tle (*hand-woven*). Blanket, Judg. iv. 18. Garment, 1 Sam. xv. 27. Sleeved wrapper, Isa. iii. 22. Chief outer garment, 1 Kgs. xix. 13-19.

Mā'och (*breast-bound*). A Gathite, 1 Sam. xxvii. 2.

Mā'on (*dwelling*). Town in Judah, Josh. xv. 55; 1 Sam. xxiii. 24, 25.

Mā'on-ītes. Mehunims, Judg. x. 12.

Mā'rȧ (*bitter*). Naomi so called herself, Ruth i. 20.

Mā'rah (*bitter*). The desert spring whose waters were sweetened, Ex. xv. 22-25; Num. xxxiii. 8, 9.

Măr'a-lah (*trembling*). A border of Zebulun, Josh. xix. 11.

Măr'an=ā'thȧ. "Our Lord cometh," 1 Cor. xvi. 22.

Măr'ble (*shining*). Any white or shining stone is meant, 1 Kgs. vii. 9-12; Esth. i. 6; Rev. xviii. 12.

Mär-chĕs'van. [Bul.]

Mär'cus, Col. iv. 10; Phile. 24; 1 Pet. v. 13. [Mark.]

Mär"dō-chē'us. Mordecai in Apoc.

Mā-rē'shah (*hill-top*). (1) A Hebronite, 1 Chr. ii. 42. (2) Lowland city of Judah, Josh. xv. 44; 2 Chr. xi. 8; xiv. 9-12.

Mär'ī-mŏth, 2 Esdr. i. 2. [Meraioth.]

Märk (*polite, shining*). John Mark, Acts xii. 12, 25; xv. 37. John, Acts xiii. 5, 13. Mark, Acts xv. 39. Convert of Peter, 1 Pet. v. 13. Companion of Paul, Col. iv. 10. Author of second Gospel, which was probably written in Rome.

Mā'roth (*bitter*). Town in Judah, Micah i. 12.

Măr'riage (*husbanding*). Monogamous, Gen. ii. 18-24; vii. 13. Polygamous, Gen. iv. 19; vi. 2. Forbidden within certain degrees, Lev. xviii.; Deut. xxvii.; and with foreigners, Ex. xxxiv. 16. Monogamy re-instituted, Matt. xix. 5, 6; Mark x. 5-10.

Märș' Hill, Acts xvii. 22. [Areopagus.]

Mär'se-nȧ (*worthy*). A Persian prince, Esth. i. 14.

Mär'thȧ (*lady*). Sister of Mary and Lazarus, Luke x. 38-42; John xi. 5-28.

Mär'tyr (*witness*). Matt. xviii. 16; Luke xxiv. 48. Who seals his faith with his blood, Acts xxii. 20; Rev. ii. 13; xvii. 6.

Mā'rȳ (*rebellion*). Greek form of Miriam. (1) The betrothed of Joseph and mother of Christ, Matt. i. 18-25; xii. 46; Mark vi. 3; Luke viii. 19; John ii. 1-5; xix. 26; Acts i. 14. (2) Wife of Cleophas, Matt. xxvii. 56, 61; xxviii. 1-9; Mark xvi. 1-8; Luke xxiv. 1-10. (3) Mother of John Mark, Acts xii. 12; Col. iv. 10. (4) Sister of Martha and Lazarus, Luke x. 41, 42; John xi., xii. (5) Mary Magdalene; *i. e.*, of Magdala, Matt. xxviii. 1-10; Mark xvi. 1-10; Luke xxiv. 10; John xx. 1-18. (6) A Roman convert, Rom. xvi. 6.

Măs'ā-lŏth. Place in Arbela, 1 Macc. ix. 2.

Măs'chĭl. "Didactic," or "melody." Title of thirteen Psalms.

Măsh (*drawn out*). Son of Aram, Gen. x. 23. Meshech, 1 Chr. i. 17.

Mā'shal (*entreaty*). A Levitical city in Asher, 1 Chr. vi. 74. Misheal, Josh. xix. 26. Mishal, Josh. xxi. 30.

Măs'phȧ, 1 Macc. iii. 46. [Mizpeh.]

Măs're-kah (*vineyard*). City in Edom, Gen. xxxvi. 36; 1 Chr. i. 47.

Măs'sȧ (*gift*). Son of Ishmael, Gen. xxv. 14; 1 Chr. i. 30.

Măs'sah (*temptation*). Meribah; spot of temptation, Ex. xvii. 7; Ps. xcv. 8, 9; Heb. iii. 8.

Mā-thu'sa-lȧ, Luke iii. 37. [Methuselah.]

Mā'tred (*shooting*). Mother of Mehetabel, Gen. xxxvi. 39.

Mā'trī (*rain*). A Benjamite family, 1 Sam. x. 21.

Mā'trix (*mother*). The womb, Ex. xiii 12-15.

Măt'tan (*gift*). (1) A priest of Baal, 2 Kgs. xi. 18. (2) Father of Shephatiah, Jer. xxxviii. 1.

Măt'ta-nah (*gift*). A desert encampment, Num. xxi. 18, 19.

Măt"ta-nī'ah (*God's gift*). (1) Original name of Zedekiah, 2 Kgs. xxiv. 17. (2) Levites, 1 Chr. ix. 15; xxv. 4, 16; 2 Chr. xx. 14; xxix. 13; Ez. x. 26, 27, 30, 37; Neh. xi. 17; xiii. 13.

Măt'ta-thȧ (*God's gift*). Grandson of David, Luke iii. 31.

Măt'ta-thah. One who returned, Ez. x. 33.

Măt"ta-thī'as (*God's gift*). (1) Two of Christ's progenitors, Luke iii. 25, 26. (2) Father of the Maccabees, 1 Macc. ii.

Măt"te-nā'ī. Levites, Ez. x. 33, 37; Neh. xii. 19.

Măt'than. Grandfather of Joseph, Matt. i. 15.

Măt"tha-nī'as, 1 Esdr. ix. 37. [Mattaniah.]

Măt'that, Luke iii. 24, 29. [Matthan.]

Măt'thew (*gift of God*). Contraction of Mattathias. The Apostle and Evangelist. Levi in Luke, v. 27-29. Son of Alphæus, Mark ii. 14. Tax-collector at Capernaum when called, Matt. ix. 9. His gospel is first of N. T. Its original claimed to be the Hebrew, or Syro-Chaldaic, of Palestine. Time of writing placed at A. D. 60-66. Gist, to establish Jesus as O. T. Messiah.

Măt-thī'as (*God's gift*). Apostle allotted to fill the place of Judas, Acts i. 26.

Măt"ti-thī'ah (*God's gift*). Levites, 1 Chr. ix. 31; xv. 18; xvi. 5; Ez. x. 43; Neh. viii. 4.

Măt'tŏck (*hoe*). A crude hoe, Isa. vii. 25.

Maul (*hammer*). Heavy wooden hammer, Prov. xxv. 18. Battle axe, Jer. li. 20.

Măz"i-tī'as, 1 Esdr. ix. 35. [Mattithiah.]

Măz'za-rŏth. The twelve signs of the zodiac, Job xxxviii. 32.

Mĕad'ōw (*mead*). Water-plant, flag, Gen. xli. 2. Cave, Judg. xx. 33.

Mē'ah (*hundred*). Tower in Jerusalem, Neh. iii. 1; xii. 39.

Mē-ā'rah (*cave*). Unknown place, Josh. xiii. 4.

Mĕaș'ures. Hebrew standard weights and measures provided for, Lev. xix. 35, 36; Deut. xxv. 13-15. Money passed by weight till era of coinage. For various weights and measures, *see* respective titles.

Mēat. In Bible sense, food of any kind, Gen. i. 29; Lev. ii.; vi. 14-23; Matt. xv. 37; Luke xxiv. 41.

Mēat-ŏf'fĕr-ing. Conditions in Lev. ii.; vi. 14-23.

Mē-bŭn'nāi (*building*). One of David's warriors, 2 Sam. xxiii. 27. Sibbechai, 2 Sam. xxi. 18. Sibbecai, 1 Chr. xi. 29.

Mĕch'e-rath-īte", 1 Chr. xi. 36. Maacathite. [Maacah.]

Mē'dăd (*love*). A camp prophet, Num. xi. 26, 27.

Mē'dan (*strife*). A son of Abraham, Gen. xxv. 2; 1 Chr. i. 32.

Mĕd'e-bȧ (*quiet waters*). Town in Reuben, east of Dead Sea, Num. xxi. 30; Josh. xiii. 9; 1 Macc. ix. 36.

Mēdeș. Medians, 2 Kgs. xvii. 6.

Mē'dĭ-ȧ (*middle land*). Madai, Gen. x. 2; Media, Esth. i. 3. The country northwest of Persia and south of Caspian Sea. Held early sway in Babylon. Tributary to Assyria, B. C. 880. Independent, and conquered Babylon; next, Assyria. Empire at its height, B. C. 625. Overthrown by Persian Cyrus, B. C. 558. Medo-Persian empire overthrown by Alexander the Great, B. C. 330, Isa. xiii. 17, 18; Esth. i. 19; Dan. vi. 8-12; 1 Chr. v. 26.

Mĕd'i-çine (*of a physician*). The science, as known in Egypt, was copied by Hebrews, Lev. xiii.-xv.; 2 Kgs. viii. 29; Prov. iii. 8; vi. 15.

Mē-gĭd'dō (*crowded*). A city in plain of Esdraelon, Josh. xii. 21; xvii. 11; 2 Kgs. xxiii. 29. Also the plain, or valley, itself and scene of Barak's victory over Sisera, and of Josiah's death, Judg. iv. 6-17; 2 Chr. xxxv. 20-24.

Mē-gĭd'don, Zech. xii. 11. [Megiddo.]

Mē-hĕt'a-beel. Ancestor of Shemaiah, Neh. vi. 10.

Mē-hĕt'a-bel (*God-favored*). Wife of Hadar, king of Edom, Gen. xxxvi. 39.

Mē-hī'dȧ (*famed*). His family returned, Ez. ii. 52; Neh. vii. 54.

Mē'hir (*price*). A Judahite, 1 Chr. iv. 11.

Mē-hŏl'ath-īte. Meholaite, 1 Sam. xviii. 19.

Mē-hū'ja-el (*smitten*). Son of Irad, Gen. iv. 18.

Mē'hū-man (*true*). Chamberlain of Ahasuerus, Esth. i. 10.

Mē-hū′nimş (*dwellings*). Maonites, 2 Chr. xxvi. 7; Ez. ii. 50.

Mē-jär′kŏn (*yellow waters*). Town in Dan, Josh. xix. 46.

Mĕk′o̱-nah (*pedestal*). Town in Judah, Neh. xi. 28.

Mĕl″a̱-tī′ah (*saved*). Assistant wall-builder, Neh. iii. 7.

Mĕl′chī (*king*). Two ancestors of Christ, Luke iii. 24, 28.

Mĕl-chī′ah (*royal*). A priest, Jer. xxi. 1.

Mĕl-chī′el. Governor of Bethulia, Judith vi. 15.

Mĕl-chĭş′e-dĕc. N. T. form of Melchizedek, Heb. v.-vii.

Medean Noble and Lady. (*See* p. 71.)

Mĕl″chī-shu̱′ȧ, 1 Sam. xiv. 49. [Malchishua.]

Mĕl-chĭz′e-dek (*king of justice*). King of Salem, and priest, Gen. xiv. 18–20. Prototype of Christ, Ps. cx. 4; Heb. v.-vii.

Mē′le-ȧ (*full*). Ancestor of Joseph, Luke iii. 31.

Mē′lech (*king*). Son of Micah, 1 Chr. ix. 41.

Mĕl′i-cū, Neh. xii. 14. [Malluch.]

Mĕl′i-tȧ (*honey*). The island of Malta, in Mediterranean, south of Sicily, Acts xxvii., xxviii.

Mĕl′on (*mellow apple*). Melons of Egypt prized as food, Num. xi. 5.

Mĕl′zar. Common noun—steward or tutor, Dan. i. 11, 16.

Mĕm′phis (*abode of the good*). Ancient Egyptian city, Hos. ix. 6, on west bank of Nile, near pyramids and sphinx, and 10 miles south of Cairo. Noph, Isa. xix. 13; Jer. ii. 16; Ezek. xxx. 13–16.

Mĕ-mū′can. A Persian prince, Esth. i. 14-21.

Mĕn′a-hĕm (*comforter*). Usurper of Israel's throne. Idolatrous and cruel. Reigned B. C. 772 761, 2 Kgs. xv. 14-22.

Mē′nan. Ancestor of Joseph, Luke iii. 31.

Mē′nē. First word of Belshazzar's warning. Entire, "Mene," he is numbered; "Tekel," he is weighed; "Upharsin," they are divided, Dan. v. 25-28.

Mĕn″e-lā′us. High priest, 2 Macc. iv. 23.

Mē-nĕs′the-us. Father of Apollonius, 2 Macc. iv. 21.

Mē-ŏn′e-nĭm (*enchanter*). Unlocated plain, Judg. ix. 37.

Mē-ŏn′o-thāi. A Judahite, 1 Chr. iv. 14.

Mĕph′a̱-ăth (*height*). Levitical town in Reuben, Josh. xiii. 18.

Mē-phĭb′o̱-shĕth (*idol breaker*). (1) A son of Saul, 2 Sam. xxi. 8. (2) Son of Jonathan, 2 Sam. iv. 4; ix. 6–13; xvi.; xix. 24–30.

Mē′rab (*increase*). Daughter of Saul, 1 Sam. xiv. 49; xviii. 17.

Mĕr″a̱-ī′ah (*rebellion*). A priest, Neh. xii. 12.

Mē-rā′i̱oth (*rebellious*). Three priests, 1 Chr. vi. 6; Ez. vii. 3; Neh. xii. 15.

Mē′ran, Bar. iii. 23. [Medan.]

Mē-rā′rī (*bitter*). (1) Third son of Levi, and head of family of Merarites, Gen. xlvi. 11; Ex. vi. 16; Num. iii. 17; iv. 29–33; Josh. xxi. 7-30. (2) Father of Judith, Judith viii. 1.

Mĕr″a̱-thā′im (*double rebellion*). Symbol of Chaldea, Jer. l. 21.

Mĕr-cū′rī-us (*Mercury*). Name applied to Paul in Lystra, Acts xiv. 12.

Mĕr′cy̆ Seat. Lid of the ark, Ex. xxv. 17-22; hence, covering, or atonement for sin, Heb. ix. 5.

Mē′rĕd (*rebellion*). Son of Ezra, 1 Chr. iv. 17.

Mĕr′e̱-mŏth (*heights*). Three priests, Ez. viii. 33; x. 36; Neh. x. 5.

Mē′rēş (*lofty*). One of Ahasuerus' wise men, Esth. i. 14.

Mĕr′ī-bah (*strife*). A desert encampment, where the rock was smitten, Ex. xvii. 7. Kadesh, Num. xx. 13–24.

Mĕr′ib=bā′al, 1 Chr. viii. 34; ix. 40. [Mephibosheth, 2.]

Mē-rō′dăch (*death*). A Babylonian god, and royal surname, Jer. l. 2.

Mē-rō′dăch=băl′a̱-dăn (*Baal-worshipper*). King of Babylon, B. C. 721, Isa. xxxix. 1. Berodach-baladan, 2 Kgs. xx. 12.

Mē′rom (*heights*). The lake on Jordan above Sea of Galilee, Josh. xi. 5–7.

Mē-rŏn′o̱-thīte. Designations in 1 Chr. xxvii. 30; Neh. iii. 7.

Mē′rŏz (*refuge*). Unknown place, Judg. v. 23.

Mē′sech, Mē′shech (*drawn out*). (1) Son of Japheth, Gen. x. 2; Ezek. xxvii. 13; xxxii. 26; Ps. cxx. 5. (2) 1 Chr. i. 17. [Mash.]

Mē′shȧ (*freed*). (1) A Joktanite border, Gen. x. 30. (2) A king of Moab, 2 Kgs. iii. 4. (3) Son of Caleb, 1 Chr. ii. 42. (4) A Benjamite, 1 Chr. viii. 9.

Mē′shach (*guest*). Chaldean name of Mishael, Daniel's companion, Dan i. 6, 7; iii.

Mē-shĕl″e̱-mī′ah (*rewarded*). A Levite gatekeeper, 1 Chr. ix. 21; xxvi. 1-9.

Mē-shĕz′a̱-be-el (*delivered*) Returned captives, Neh. iii. 4; x. 21; xi. 24.

Mē-shĭl′le̱-mĭth (*repaid*). A priest, 1 Chr. ix. 12.

Mē-shĭl′le̱-mŏth (*repaid*). (1) A chief of Ephraim, 2 Chr. xxviii. 12. (2) Meshillemith, Neh. xi. 13.

Mē-shŭl′lam (*friend*). (1) Ancestor of Shaphan, 2 Kgs. xxii. 3. (2) Son of Zerubbabel, 1 Chr. iii. 19. (3) A Gadite, 1 Chr. v. 13. (4) Three Benjamites, 1 Chr. viii. 17; ix. 7, 8. (5) Eleven Levites, in Ez. and Neh.

Me-shŭl'le-mĕth (*friend*). Mother of King Amon, 2 Kgs. xxi. 19.

Mĕs'o-bâ-ite''. Designation of Jasiel, 1 Chr. xi. 47.

Mĕs''o-pō-tā'mĭ-å (*between rivers*). The country between the rivers Tigris and Euphrates, Gen. xxiv. 10; Deut. xxiii. 4; Judg. iii. 8-10; Acts ii. 9; vii. 2.

Mĕs-sī'ah (*anointed*). Applied to regularly anointed priests or kings, Lev. iv. 3, 5, 16; 1 Sam. ii. 10, 35; xii. 3-5. The Greek *kristos*, "anointed," takes its place in N. T., except in John i. 41; iv. 25.

Mĕs-sī'as. Greek form of Messiah, John i. 41; iv. 25.

Mĕt'als (*mined*). Precious and useful metals, such as gold, silver, tin, lead, copper, and iron, known to Hebrews and much used, Gen. ii. 11, 12; Num. xxxi. 22.

Me-tē'rus. His family returned, 1 Esdr. v. 17.

Mē'theg-ăm'mah (*curb of the city*). A Philistine stronghold, 2 Sam. viii. 1.

Me-thu'sa-el (*man of God*). Father of Lamech, Gen. iv. 18.

Me-thu'se-lah (*dart-man*). Grandfather of Noah; oldest of antediluvians. Lived 969 years, Gen. v. 21-27.

Me-ū'nim, Neh. vii. 52. [MEHUNIMS.]

Mĕz'a-hăb (*gilded*). An Edomite, Gen. xxxvi. 39.

Mī'a-mĭn (*right hand*). Two who returned, Ez. x. 25; Neh. xii. 5.

Mĭb'har (*chosen*). One of David's heroes, 1 Chr. xi. 38.

Mĭb'sam (*odorous*). (1) An Ishmaelite, Gen. xxv. 13. (2) A Simeonite, 1 Chr. iv. 25.

Mĭb'zar (*fort*). A duke of Edom, Gen. xxxvi. 42.

Mī'cah (*God-like*). (1) The erratic Ephraimite whose story is told in Judg. xvii., xviii. (2) Sixth of the minor prophets. Prophesied B. C. 750-698. He foretells the destruction of Samaria and Jerusalem, and prefigures the Messiah. (3) A Reubenite, 1 Chr. v. 5. (4) Grandson of Jonathan, 1 Chr. viii. 34, 35. (5) A Levite, 1 Chr. xxiii. 20. (6) Father of Abdon, 2 Chr. xxxiv. 20.

Mī-cā'iah (*God-like*). A Samarian prophet, 1 Kgs. xxii. 8-38; 2 Chr. xviii. 7-27.

Mī'chå. Persons in 2 Sam. ix. 12; Neh x. 11; xi. 17, 22.

Mī'chaĕl (*God-like*). (1) Prince of angels, Dan. x. 13; xii. 1; Rev. xii. 7. (2) Characters in Num. xiii. 13; 1 Chr. v. 13, 14; vi. 40; vii. 3; viii. 16; xii. 20; xxvii. 18; 2 Chr. xxi. 2; Ez. viii. 8.

Mī'chah, 1 Chr. xxiv. 24, 25. [MICAH, 5.]

Mī-chā'iah (*God-like*). (1) Full form of Micah in 2 Chr. xxxiv. 20. (2) Same as Micha, 1 Chr. ix. 15; Neh. xii. 35. (3) A priest, Neh. xii. 41. (4) Wife of Rehoboam and mother of Abijah, king of Judah, 2 Chr. xiii. 2. (5) A prince and teacher of the law, 2 Chr. xvii. 7. (6) Son of Gemariah, Jer. xxxvi. 11-14.

Mī'chal. Daughter of Saul and wife of David, 1 Sam. xiv. 49; xxv. 44; 2 Sam. iii. 14; vi. 23.

Mi-chē'as, 2 Esdr. i. 39. [MICAH.]

Mĭch'mash (*hidden*). Noted town in Benjamin, 1 Sam. xiii. 11; Isa. x. 28. Michmas, Ez. ii. 27.

Mĭch'mĕ-thah (*stony*). Border mark of Manasseh, Josh. xvii. 7.

Mĭch'rī (*precious*). A Benjamite, 1 Chr. ix. 8.

Mĭch'tam. Musical term for six Psalms.

Mĭd'dĭn (*measures*). City in Judah, Josh. xv. 61.

Mĭd'ī-an (*strife*). Son of Abraham, and founder of Midianites, Gen. xxv. 2; Ex. iii. 1; Num. xxii. 4; Judg. vii. 13.

Mĭg'dal-ĕl (*tower of God*). Fenced city of Naphtali, Josh. xix. 38.

Mĭg'dal-găd (*tower of Gad*). Town in Judah, Josh. xv. 37.

Mĭg'dol (*tower*). Place in Egypt, Ex. xiv. 2; Num. xxxiii. 7, 8. Perhaps same in Jer. xliv. 1; xlvi. 14.

Mĭg'rŏn (*pinnacle*). Town near Gibeah, 1 Sam. xiv. 2; Isa. x. 28.

Mĭj'a-mĭn (*right hand*). (1) Chief of the 6th priestly course, 1 Chr. xxiv. 9. (2) Co-covenanters, Neh. x. 7.

Mĭk'loth (*staves*). (1) A Benjamite, 1 Chr. viii. 32; ix. 37, 38. (2) One of David's generals, 1 Chr. xxvii. 4.

Mĭk-ne'iah (*God-possessed*). A temple musician, 1 Chr. xv. 18-21.

Mĭl''a-lā'ī (*eloquent*). A priest, Neh. xii. 36.

Mĭl'cah (*queen*). (1) Wife of Nahor, Gen. xi. 29; xxiv. 15-47. (2) Daughter of Zelophehad, Num. xxvi. 33; Josh. xvii. 3.

Mĭl'com. [MOLECH.]

Mīle. Roman mile in Matt. v. 41; 1618 yards.

Mī-lē'tus, Mī-lē'tum (*red*). City in Ionia, Acts xx. 15-38; 2 Tim. iv. 20.

Mĭlk, Of cows, goats, camels, and sheep a favorite Oriental food, Gen. xxxii. 15; Deut. xxxii. 14. Symbol of fertility, Josh. v. 6; Heb. v. 12.

Mĭll (*grind*). A mortar and pestle; or, two stones, upper and nether, the former turned by hand, Job xli. 24; Isa. xlvii. 1, 2; Matt. xxiv. 41. Millstones not pawnable, Deut. xxiv. 6.

Millstones.

Mĭl'let. Here a grass; abroad a cereal, like broom-corn, Ezek. iv. 9.

Mĭl'lō (*mound*). (1) A rampart of Jerusalem, 2 Sam. v. 9; 1 Kgs. ix. 15. (2) Where Joash was murdered, 2 Kgs. xii. 20. (3) A Shechem family, Judg. ix. 6-20.

Mī'na. [MANEH.]

Mī-nī'a-mĭn. Levites, 2 Chr. xxxi. 15; Neh. xii. 17, 41.

Mĭn'is-tēr (*assistant*). Attendant, Ex. xxiv. 13; Josh. i. 1; 1 Kgs. xix. 21; Ez. viii. 17. Magistrate, Rom. xiii. 6. Preacher and teacher, 1 Cor. iv. 1; 2 Cor. iii. 6. Celestial high priest, Heb. viii. 1-3.

Mĭn'nī. Part of Armenia, Jer. li. 27.

Mĭn'nith (*division*). An Ammonite section east of Jordan, Judg. xi. 33; Ezek. xxvii. 17.

Mĭn'strel (*minister*). A musician employed, or strolling, 1 Sam. x. 5; xvi. 16; 2 Kgs. iii. 15. Professional mourners, Matt. ix. 23.

Mĭnt. An aromatic herb, varieties numerous, Matt. xxiii. 23; Luke xi. 42.

Miph'kăd. A Jerusalem gate, Neh. iii. 31.

Mĭr'a-cle (*wonderful*). In scripture, a supernatural event, Num. xxii. 28; 1 Kgs. xvii. 6; Matt. ix. 18-33; xiv. 25.

Mĭr'i-am (*rebellion*). (1) Sister of Moses and Aaron. Musician and prophetess, Ex. ii. 4-10; xv. 20, 21; Num. xii. 1-15; xx. 1; 1 Chr. vi. 3. (2) A Judahite, 1 Chr. iv. 17.

Mĭr'mȧ (*fraud*). A Benjamite, 1 Chr. viii. 10.

Mĭr'rôr (*wonder at*). Egyptian mirrors, which the Hebrew women affected, were highly polished metal plates, chiefly of copper, Ex. xxxviii. 8; Job xxxvii. 18; 1 Cor. xiii. 12.

Metal Mirror.

Mĭs'gab (*high*). Place in Moab, Jer. xlviii. 1.

Mĭsh'a-el (*what God is*). (1) Uncle of Moses, Ex. vi. 22; Lev. x. 4. (2) Ezra's assistant, Neh. viii. 4. (3) Daniel's captive companion, Dan. i. 6-19; ii. 17.

Mī'shal, Mī'she-al (*entreaty*). Levitical town in Asher, Josh. xix. 26; xxi. 30.

Mī'sham (*fleet*). A Benjamite, 1 Chr. viii. 12.

Mĭsh'mȧ (*hearing*). (1) An Ishmaelite, Gen. xxv. 14. (2) A Simeonite, 1 Chr. iv. 25.

Mĭsh-măn'nah (*fatness*). A Gadite, 1 Chr. xii. 10.

Mĭsh'ra-ītes. Colonists from Kirjath-jearim, 1 Chr. ii. 53.

Mĭs'pe-rĕth. A returned captive, Neh. vii. 7.

Mĭs're-photh=mā'im (*burning waters*). Place in northern Palestine, Josh. xi. 8; xiii. 6.

Mīte (*little*). Half a farthing, or fifth of a cent, Mark xii. 41-44; Luke xxi. 1-4.

Mĭth'cah (*sweetness*). A desert encampment, Num. xxxiii. 28.

Mĭth'nīte. A designation, 1 Chr. xi. 43.

Mĭth're-dăth (*Mithra-given*). (1) Cyrus' treasurer, Ez. i. 8. (2) Persian governor of Samaria, Ez. iv. 7.

Mĭth''rī-dā'tēs, 1 Esdr. ii. 11. [MITHREDATH.]

Mī'tre (*turban*). The priestly head-dress of linen, wrapped round the head, and bearing a frontal inscription, "Holiness to the Lord," Ex. xxviii. 4, 36-39; xxix. 6; xxxix. 28-30; Lev. viii. 9; xvi. 4.

Mĭt''y̆-lē'nē (*curtailed*). Chief town of the island of Lesbos, Acts xx. 14, 15.

Mĭxed Multitude. Camp followers, Ex. xii. 38; Num. xi. 4; Neh. xiii. 3.

Mī'zar (*little*). Unlocated hill, Ps. xlii. 6.

Mĭz'pah, Mĭz'peh (*watch tower*). (1) Jacob's covenant heap, Gen. xxxi. 47-49. (2) Mizpeh-moab, 1 Sam. xxii. 3. (3) Hivite section in northern Palestine, Josh. xi. 3-8. (4) A city in Judah. Josh. xv. 38. (5) A city of Benjamin, Josh. xviii. 26; 1 Sam. x. 17-21; 1 Kgs. xv. 22.

Mĭz'par, Ez. ii. 2. [MISPERETH.]

Mĭz'ra-ĭm (*red soil*). Son of Ham, Gen. x. 6. The O. T. word translated Egypt, Gen. xlv. 20; Isa. xi. 11.

Mĭz'zah (*fear*). Grandson of Esau, Gen. xxxvi. 13.

Mnā'son (*remembering*). A Cyprian convert, Acts xxi. 16.

Mō'ab (*of his father*). Son of Lot by his daughter, and progenitor of the Moabites. The country lay east of the Dead Sea and south of the Arnon, Num. xxi. 13-15; xxii.; Judg. xi. 18. Though idolatrous, worshipping Chemosh, they were a strong, progressive people, holding Israel subject, Judg. iii. 12-14; but finally subdued, 15-30; 2 Sam. viii. 2; Isa. xv., xvi.; Jer. xlviii.; Ruth i., ii.

Mō'ab-īte Stōne. The celebrated stone found at Dhiban (Dibon) in Moab, in A. D. 1868, on which is engraved, in Hebrew-Phœnician, the record of Mesha, king of Moab's, rebellion against Israel, 2 Kgs. iii. 4-27.

Mō''a-dī'ah, Neh. xii. 17. [MAADIAH.]

Mŏch'mur. Brook or wady, Judith vii. 18.

Mō'din. Burial ground of the Maccabees, near Lydda, 1 Macc. xiii. 25.

Mō'eth, 1 Esdr. viii. 63. [NOADIAH.]

Mŏl'a-dah (*birth*). City in south Judah, Josh. xv. 26; xix. 2; Neh. xi. 26.

Mōle (*dirt thrower*). No ground-moles in Palestine. Chameleon or lizard in Lev. xi. 30; and rat or weasel in Isa. ii. 20.

Mō'lech (*king*). Moloch, Acts vii. 43. Milcom, 1 Kgs. xi. 5. Malcham, Zeph. i. 5. Tutelary divinity (fire-god) of the Ammonites, Lev. xviii. 21; 2 Kgs. xxiii. 10.

Mō'lī, 1 Esdr. viii. 47. [MAHLI.]

Mō'lid (*begetter*). A Judahite, 1 Chr. ii. 29.

Mō'lŏch, Acts vii. 43. [MOLECH.]

Mŏm'dis, 1 Esdr. ix. 34. [MAADAI.]

Mon'ēy (*warning*). Gold and silver passed by weight among Hebrews, Gen. xvii. 13; xxiii. 16; though the ring tokens of Egypt may have been current, Gen. xx. 16; xxxvii. 28. Persian coined money (daric or dram) came into use after the captivity, Ez. ii. 69; Neh. vii. 70-72. The Maccabees first coined Jewish money, B. C. 140, — shekels and half shekels of gold and silver, with minor copper coins. The N. T. coins, Matt. xvii. 27; xxii. 19; x. 29; v. 26; Mark xii, 42, were Roman or Grecian.

Mon'ēy Chān'gers. Those who made a business of supplying the annual half-shekel offering at a premium, Ex. xxx. 13-15; Matt. xxi. 12; Mark xi. 15.

Mountains of Moab.

Month (*moon*). Hebrew month lunar, from new moon to new moon, Num. x. 10; xxviii. 11-14. Intercalary month every three years. Months named, but usually went by number, Gen. vii. 11; 2 Kgs. xxv. 3. *See* month names in place.

Moon (*measurer*). Conjointly with the sun, appointed for signs, seasons, days, months and years. Regulator of religious festivals, Gen. i. 14-18. Worship of, forbidden, Deut. iv. 19. Used largely figuratively, Isa. xiii. 10; Matt. xxiv. 29; Mark xiii. 24.

Mō′ras-thīte. Of Moresheth, Jer. xxvi. 18; Mic. i. 1.

Môr′de-cāi (*little*). A Benjamite captive at court of Ahasuerus, and deliverer of Jews from plot of Haman, Esth.

Mō′reh (*teacher*). (1) First halting place of Abram in Canaan, Gen. xii. 6. (2) Hill in valley of Jezreel, Judg. vii. 1.

Mŏr′esh-eth-găth (*possession of Gath*). Place named in Mic. i. 14.

Mō-rī′ah (*chosen*). (1) The land in which Abraham offered up Isaac, Gen. xxii. 2. (2) Site of Solomon's temple in Jerusalem, 2 Sam. xxiv. 24; 1 Chr. xxi. 24-27; 2 Chr. iii. 1, 2.

Môr′tar. (1) Hollow vessel of wood or stone, in which corn was ground with a pestle, Num. xi. 8; Prov. xxvii. 22. (2) Various cementing substances used in building, as bitumen, clay, and ordinary mixture of sand and lime, Gen. xi. 3; Ex. i. 14; Lev. xiv. 42; Isa. xli. 25.

Mō-sē′rā (*bonds*). A desert encampment, Deut. x. 6.

Moabite Stone. (*See* p. 74.)

Mō-sē′roth, Num. xxxiii. 30. [MOSERA.]

Mō′ses (*drawn out*). The great leader and lawgiver of the Hebrews. Son of Amram, a Levite. Born in Egypt, about B. C. 1571. Adopted by Pharaoh's daughter, liberally educated, fled to Midian, Ex. ii. Called to lead the Exode, Ex. iii.-xix. Promulgated the law, Ex. xx.-xl.; Lev.; Num.; Deut. Died on Nebo, aged 120 years. Reputed author of Pentateuch and Job.

Egyptian Ring Money. (*See* p. 74.)

Mō-sŏl′lam, 1 Esdr. viii. 44. [MESHULLAM.]

Mŏth. Frequent scripture references to the destructiveness of this insect, Job xiii. 28; Ps. xxxix. 11; Isa. l. 9; Matt. vi. 19.

Moth′er. Held in high respect by Hebrews, Ex. xx. 12. Often used for grandmother, or remote ancestor, Gen. iii. 20; 1 Kgs. xv. 10.

Môurn′ing. Very public and demonstrative, Gen. xxiii. 2; xxxvii. 29-35. Period, seven to seventy days, Gen. l. 3; 1 Sam. xxxi. 13. Hired mourners, Eccl. xii. 5; Matt. ix. 23. Methods, weeping, tearing clothes, wearing sackcloth, sprinkling with ashes or dust, shaving head, plucking beard, fasting, laceration, etc.

Mouse (*pilferer*). Many species in Palestine, but Bible word generic, Lev. xi. 29; 1 Sam. vi. 4; Isa. lxvi. 17.

Mōw′ing. Reaping with sickle, Ps. cxxix. 7. "King's mowings," perhaps a royal right of pasturage, Am. vii. 1.

Mō′zā (*departing*). (1) A son of Caleb, 1 Chr. ii. 46. (2) Descendant of Saul, 1 Chr. viii. 36, 37.

Mō′zah (*departing*). City in Benjamin, Josh. xviii. 26.

Mŭl′bĕr-rȳ (*dark berry*). Translation disputed, 2 Sam. v. 23, 24; 1 Chr. xiv. 14. The bacah or balsam tree is probably meant.

Mule. Mules not bred in Palestine, but imported, 2 Sam. xiii. 29; 1 Kgs. i. 33; 2 Chr. ix. 24. Warm springs meant in Gen. xxxvi. 24.

Mŭp′pim (*serpent*). A Benjamite, Gen. xlvi. 21. Shupham, Num. xxvi. 39.

Mûr′der (*death*). Punished with death, Ex. xxi. 12; Num. xxxv. 30, 31; but cities of refuge provided for the escape of the involuntary slayer, Ex. xxi. 13; Num. xxxv. 32; Deut. xix. 1-13.

Mûr′rain (*die*). The malignant cattle disease which constituted the fifth Egyptian plague, Ex. ix. 1-7.

Mū′shī (*deserted*). A son of Merari, Ex. vi. 19; Num. iii. 20.

Mū′shītes. Descendants of Mushi, Num. iii. 33; xxvi. 58.

Mū′sĭc (*muse*). Anciently known, Gen. iv. 21; xxxi. 27; Job xxi. 12. Vocal and instrumental, reached highest perfection in temple choirs, 2 Sam. vi. 5; 1 Chr. xxv. Usual instruments, harp, timbrel, psalter, trumpet, flute, pipe, etc.

Mŭs′tard (*must*). The black mustard of the East grows quite large and strong, Matt. xiii. 31, 32; xvii. 20; Mark iv. 31, 32; Luke xvii. 6.

Mŭth-lăb'ben. Enigmatical title to Ps. ix.

Mўn'dus. Town in Caria, 1 Macc. xv. 23.

Mȳ'rȧ (*weeping*). Ancient seaport of Lycia, in Asia Minor, Acts xxvii. 5.

Mўrrh (*bitter*). A gum resin much prized and variously used, Ex. xxx. 23; Esth. ii. 12; Ps. xlv. 8; Prov. vii. 17; Mark xv. 23; John xix. 39.

Field Mouse. (*See* p. 75.)

Mўr'tle. A bushy evergreen, whose flowers, leaves, and berries were much used by Hebrews for perfume, ornament, and spicery, Isa. xli. 19; lv. 13; Zech. i. 8-11.

Mўs'i̤ȧ (*beech land*). Northwestern district of Asia Minor, Acts xvi. 7, 8.

N

Nā'am (*pleasant*). Son of Caleb, 1 Chr. iv. 15.

Nā'a̤-mah (*pleasing*). (1) Sister of Tubal-cain, Gen. iv. 22. (2) A wife of Solomon and mother of King Rehoboam, 1 Kgs. xiv. 21; 2 Chr. xii. 13. (3) Town in Judah, Josh. xv. 41.

Nā'a̤-man (*pleasantness*). (1) The leprous Syrian, cured by Elisha's orders, 2 Kgs. v. (2) Founder of the Naamites, Gen. xlvi. 21; Num. xxvi. 40.

Nā'a̤-ma̤th-īte''. Designation of Job's friend, Zophar, Job ii. 11.

Nā'a-mītes, Num. xxvi. 40. [NAAMAN, 2.]

Nā'a-rah (*youth*). Wife of Ashur, 1 Chr. iv. 5, 6.

Nā'a-rāi (*youthful*). One of David's warriors, 1 Chr. xi. 37. Paarai, 2 Sam. xxiii. 35.

Nā'a-răn, 1 Chr. vii. 28. [NAARATH.]

Nā'a-răth (*youthful*). A border of Ephraim, Josh. xvi. 7.

Nȧ-ăsh'on, Ex. vi. 23. [NAHSHON.]

Nȧ-ăs'son. Greek form of Nahshon, Matt. i. 4; Luke iii. 32.

Nā'a̤-thus. Son of Addi, 1 Esdr. ix. 31.

Nā'băl (*fool*). The Carmelite shepherd who refused food to David, 1 Sam. xxv.

Năb''a̤-rī'as, 1 Esdr. ix. 44. [ZECHARIAS.]

Nā'băth-ītes, 1 Macc. v. 25. [NEBAIOTH.]

Nā'bŏth (*fruits*). The vineyardist of Jezreel whom Jezebel caused to be murdered, 1 Kgs. xxi. 1-16; 2 Kgs. ix. 26.

Năb''ū-chȯ-dŏn'ŏ-sôr. Apocryphal form of Nebuchadnezzar.

Nā'chŏn (*ready*). Owner of the threshing-floor where the over-zealous Uzzah died, 2 Sam. vi. 6, 7.

Nā'chôr, Josh. xxiv. 2; Luke iii. 34. [NAHOR.]

Nā'dăb (*liberal*). (1) Son of Aaron, Ex. vi. 23; xxiv. 1. Struck dead for offering strange fire, Lev. x. 1-3. (2) Son and successor of Jeroboam on throne of Israel, B. C. 954-953. Slain by Baasha, his successor, 1 Kgs. xv. 25-31. (3) A Judahite, 1 Chr. ii. 28. (4) Uncle of Saul, 1 Chr. viii. 30.

Nȧ-dăb'a̤-thȧ. Place east of Jordan, 1 Macc. ix. 37.

Năg'ġe (*shining*). Ancestor of Joseph, Luke iii. 25.

Nā'ha-lāl (*pasture*). Levitical city in Zebulun, Josh. xxi. 35.

Nȧ-hā'lī-el (*God's valley*). Israelite encampment in Ammon, Num. xxi. 19.

Nȧ-hăl'lăl Josh. xix. 15. [NAHALAL.]

Nā'ha̤-lŏl, Judg. i. 30. [NAHALAL.]

Nā'ham (*comforter*). Brother of Hodiah, 1 Chr. iv. 19.

Nā-hăm'a̤-nī (*compassionate*). One who returned, Neh. vii. 7.

Nā-hăr'a̤-ī (*snorer*). Joab's armor-bearer, 1 Chr. xi. 39.

Nā'ha-rī, 2 Sam. xxiii. 37. [NAHARAI.]

Nā'hăsh (*serpent*). (1) A king of Ammon, 1 Sam. xi. 1-11; 2 Sam. x. 2. (2) Father of Abigail, 2 Sam. xvii. 25.

Nā'hăth (*rest*). (1) A duke of Edom, Gen. xxxvi. 13, 17. (2) Two Levites, 1 Chr. vi. 26; 2 Chr. xxxi. 13.

Năh'bī (*secret*). The spy of Naphtali, Num. xiii. 14.

Nā'hôr (*snoring*). (1) Abraham's grandfather, Gen. xi. 22-25. (2) Abraham's brother, Gen. xi. 27-29.

Näh'shon (*enchanter*). A prince of Judah, Num. i. 7.

Nā'hum (*comforter*). Seventh of minor prophets. Probably an exile in Assyria. Approximate time of prophecy, B. C. 726-698. It relates to the fall of Nineveh. Noted for vigor and beauty.

Nā'ī-dus, 1 Esdr. ix. 31. [BENAIAH.]

Nāil (*hold, claw*). Nails of captives to be pared, Deut. xxi. 12. Ordinary metal nail, 1 Chr. xxii. 3; stylus, Jer. xvii. 1; stake, Isa. xxxiii. 20; tent-peg, wood or metal, Ex. xxvii. 19; Judg. iv. 21, 22.

Nā'in (*beauty*). A village in Galilee, now Nein, Luke vii. 11.

Nā'i̤oth (*dwellings*). Samuel's dwelling place and school in Ramah, 1 Sam. xix. 18-23; xx. 1.

Nȧ-nē'ȧ. A Persian goddess, 1 Macc. vi. 1-4.

Nȧ-ō'mī (*my delight*). Mother-in-law of Ruth, Ruth i. 2, etc.

Nā'phish (*pleasure*). Son of Ishmael, Gen. xxv. 15; 1 Chr. i. 31.

Năph'ī-sī, 1 Esdr. v. 31. [NEPHUSIM.]

Năph'ta̤-lī (*wrestling*). Fifth son of Jacob, Gen. xxx. 8. Large tribe at Sinai and Jordan, Num. i. 43; xxvi. 50. Allotment in northern Canaan, Josh. xix. 32-39. Tribe carried captive in reign of Pekah, 2 Kgs. xv. 29. For "mount Naphtali," Josh. xx. 7, read, mountains of Naphtali.

Năph'thȧr (*cleansing*). Naphtha, 2 Macc. i. 36.

Năph'tu-hīm. A Mizraite (Egyptian) tribe, Gen. x. 13.

När-çis'sus (*narcotic*). Roman friend of Paul, Rom. xvi. 11.

Närd (*smell*). [SPIKENARD.]

Năs'bās. Nephew of Tobit, Tob. xi. 18.

Nā'sith, 1 Esdr. v. 32. [NEZIAH.]

Nā'sôr, 1 Macc. xi. 67. [HAZOR.]

Nā'than (*given*). (1) Distinguished prophet, and royal adviser and biographer of David and Solomon, 2 Sam. vii. 2-17; xii. 1-22; 1 Kgs. i. 8-45; 1 Chr. xxix. 29; 2 Chr. ix. 29. (2) A son of David, 1 Chr. iii. 5; Luke iii. 31. (3) Father of one of David's warriors, 2 Sam. xxiii. 36. (4) A returned captive, Ez. viii. 16.

Nȧ-thăn'a̤-el (*gift of God*). (1) A disciple of Christ, and native of Cana in Galilee, John i. 47-51; xxi. 2. (2) Ancestor of Judith, Judith viii. 1.

Năth″a-nī′as, 1 Esdr. ix. 34. [Nathan.]

Nā′than-mē′lech. Chamberlain under King Josiah, 2 Kgs. xxiii. 11.

Nā′um (*comfort*). Father of Amos, Luke iii. 25.

Nāve. Hub of a wheel, 1 Kgs. vii. 33.

Nā′vē, Ecclus. xlvi. 1. [Nun.]

Năz′a-rēne. Inhabitant of Nazareth; Jesus so-called, Matt. ii. 23. Nazarenes, followers of Jesus, Acts xxiv. 5.

Năz′a-rĕth (*separated*). A town of Galilee, now En-nazirah. Home of Jesus, Matt. iv. 13; Mark i. 9; Luke i. 26; iv. 16, 29; John i. 45, 46.

Năz′a-rīte (*separated*). One bound by a temporary or life vow, Num. vi. 1–21; Am. ii. 11, 12; Acts xxi. 20–26.

Nē′ah (*shaking*). A Zebulun boundary mark, Josh. xix. 13.

Nē-ăp′o-lis (*new city*). Seaport in northern Greece; now Kavalla, Acts xvi. 11; xx. 1, 6.

Nē″a-rī′ah (*child of God*). (1) A Judahite, 1 Chr. iii. 22. (2) A chief of Simeon, 1 Chr. iv. 42.

Nĕb′a-ī (*budding*). A co-covenanter, Neh. x. 19.

Nē-bā′joth, Nē-bā′joth (*heights*). Son of Ishmael, Gen. xxv. 13; 1 Chr. i. 29; Isa. lx. 7.

Nē-băl′lat (*secret folly*). Re-peopled town of Benjamin, Neh. xi. 34.

Nē′băt (*view*). Father of King Jeroboam, 1 Kgs. xi. 26; xii. 2–15.

Nē′bō (*prophet*). (1) A mountain of Moab, whence Moses viewed the promised land, Deut. xxxii. 49; xxxiv. 1. (2) A Reubenite city, Num. xxxii. 3, 38; xxxiii. 47. (3) Father of returned captives, Ez. ii. 29. (4) A Chaldean god, presiding over learning. Counterpart of the Greek Hermes, Isa. xlvi. 1; Jer. xlviii. 1.

Nebo, "A Chaldean God."

Nĕb″u-chăd-nĕz′zar (*may Nebo protect*). King of Babylonish Empire, B. C. 605–561. Brought empire to greatest height of prosperity. Defeated Pharaoh-necho at Carchemish, Jer. xlvi. 2–26. Captured Jerusalem three different times, 2 Kgs. xxiv., xxv.; Dan. i.–iv.

Nĕb″u-chăd-rĕz′zar. Jeremiah so writes Nebuchadnezzar.

Nĕb″u-shăs′ban (*Nebo saves*). A chief of eunuchs under Nebuchadnezzar, Jer. xxxix. 13.

Nĕb″u-zăr′ă-dan (*whom Nebo favors*). Chief of Nebuchadnezzar's body-guard, 2 Kgs. xxv. 8–21; Jer. xxxix. 11; xl. 1–5.

Nē′chō, 2 Chr. xxxv. 20. [Pharaoh-necho.]

Nē-cō′dan, 1 Esdr. v. 37. [Nekoda.]

Nĕd″a-bī′ah (*driven*). A Judahite, 1 Chr. iii. 18.

Nĕg′ī-nah. Singular of Neginoth, Ps. lxi. title.

Nĕg′ī-nŏth. Stringed musical instruments. Title to Ps. iv., vi., liv., lv., lxvii., lxxvi.; Hab. iii. 19.

Nē-hĕl′a-mīte (*dreamer*). Designation of Shemaiah, Jer. xxix. 24–32.

Nē-he-mī′ah (*consolation*). (1) The Hebrew captive who returned, as leader of his people, to rebuild Jerusalem and administer its affairs. His book, 16th of O. T., B. C. 445–433, tells of his work. (2) Leader of returning captives, Ez. ii. 2; Neh. vii. 7. (3) An assistant wall-builder, Neh. iii. 16.

Nē″he-mī′as, 1 Esdr. v. 8, 40. [Nehemiah.]

Nē′hī-lŏth (*perforated*). The flute and similar wind instruments, Ps. v. title.

Nē′hum (*comfort*). A returned captive, Neh. vii. 7.

Nē-hŭsh′tȧ (*brazen*). Mother of King Jehoiachin, 2 Kgs. xxiv. 8.

Nē′hŭsh-tan (*little brazen thing*). Name of the preserved brazen serpent destroyed by King Hezekiah, 2 Kgs. xviii. 4.

Nē′ī-el (*God-moved*). An Asherite boundary, Josh. xix. 27.

Nē′keb (*cave*). A boundary town of Naphtali, Josh. xix. 33.

Nē-kō′dȧ (*famous*). Two fathers of returned captive families, Ez. ii. 48, 60.

Nē-mū′el (*God's day*). (1) A Reubenite, Num. xxvi. 9. (2) A Simeonite, Num. xxvi. 12; Jemuel, Gen. xlvi. 10.

Nē-mū′el-ītes″. Descendants of Nemuel (2), Num. xxvi. 12.

Nē′pheg (*sprout*). (1) Korah's brother, Ex. vi. 21. (2) Son of David, 2 Sam. v. 15.

Nĕph′ew (*grandson*). Grandchild or descendant, Job xviii. 19; Isa. xiv. 22.

Nē′phish, 1 Chr. v. 19. [Naphish.]

Nē-phĭsh′e-sĭm. His children returned, Neh. vii. 52.

Nĕph′ta-lī, Tob. i. 2–5. [Naphtali.]

Nĕph′tha-lĭm, Matt. iv. 13. [Naphtali.]

Nĕp′tha-lĭm, Rev. vii. 6. [Naphtali.]

Nĕph′to-ah (*opening*). A spring on boundary of Judah and Benjamin, Josh. xv. 9.

Nē-phū′sim, Ez. ii. 50. [Nephishesim.]

Nēr (*lamp*). Grandfather of Saul, 1 Chr. viii. 33; ix. 39. Appears as an uncle of Saul in 1 Chr. ix. 36.

Nē′re-us. A Roman Christian, Rom. xvi. 15.

Nĕr′gal (*hero*). A man-lion god of Assyria, corresponding to Mars, 2 Kgs. xvii. 30.

Nĕr′gal-shȧ-rē′zer (*fire prince*). A prince of Babylon who released Jeremiah, Jer. xxxix. 3, 13.

Nē′rī (*lamp*). Son of Melchi, Luke iii. 27.

Nē-rī′ah (*light*). Father of Baruch, Jer. xxxii. 12.

Nē-rī′as, Bar. i. 1. [Neriah.]

Nĕt. Used for hunting and fishing, Isa. xix. 8; Matt. xiii. 47. Style, manufacture, and method borrowed from Egyptians.

Nĕ-thăn′e-el (*gift of God*). Persons of this name in Num. i. 8; 1 Chr. ii. 14; xv. 24; xxiv. 6; xxvi. 4; 2 Chr. xvii. 7; xxxv. 9; Ez. x. 22; Neh. xii. 21, 36.

Nĕth″a-nī′ah (*God-given*). Persons in 2 Kgs. xxv. 23; 1 Chr. xxv. 2, 12; 2 Chr. xvii. 8; Jer. xxxvi. 14; xl. 8.

Nĕth′i-nĭm (*dedicated*). Assistant priests. A class, or order, associated with the temple service and wardship, 1 Chr. ix. 2; Ez. vii. 24; viii. 17-20.

Nĕ-tō′phah (*dropping*). Town near Bethlehem, Ez. ii. 22; Neh. vii. 26.

Nĕ-tŏph′a-thī. Netophathites. Dwellers in Netophah, 1 Chr. ii. 54; Neh. xii. 28.

Nĕt′tle (*sting*). The stinging nettle in Isa. xxxiv. 13; Hos. ix. 6. Supposably the prickly acanthus in Job xxx. 7; Prov. xxiv. 31; Zeph. ii. 9.

New Moon, 1 Sam. xx. 5. [MOON.]

New Tĕs′ta-ment. [BIBLE.]

New Year. [TRUMPETS, FEAST OF.]

Nĕ-zī′ah (*famed*). Returned Nethinim, Ez. ii. 54; Neh. vii. 56.

Nē′zib (*pedestal*). Lowland city of Judah, Josh. xv. 43.

Nĭb′hăz (*barker*). The Avite god, in form of a dog-headed man, introduced into Samaria, 2 Kgs. xvii. 31.

Nĭb′shăn (*sandy*). Town in wilderness portion of Judah, Josh. xv. 62.

Nī-cā′nor (*conqueror*). (1) A governor of Judea. 1 Macc. iii. 38. (2) One of the first seven deacons of the early church, Acts vi. 1-6.

Nĭc″o-dē′mus (*people's victor*). The Pharisee ruler and timid convert who assisted at Christ's sepulture, John iii. 1-10; vii. 50; xix. 39.

Nĭc-o-lā′i-tanes. An heretical sect condemned in Rev. ii. 6, 15.

Nĭc′o-lăs (*people's victor*). Native of Antioch. First a Jewish and then a Christian convert. One of the first seven deacons, Acts vi. 5.

Nī-cŏp′o-lĭs (*city of victory*). Many ancient cities of this name. Probably the one in Epirus is meant, Tit. iii. 12.

Nī′ger (*black*). Surname of Simeon, Acts xiii. 1.

Night. The Hebrew day, from sunset to sunset, embraced the entire night, Gen. i. 5. Death, John ix. 4; sin, 1 Thess. v. 5; sorrow, sin, and death, Rev xxi. 25; xxii. 5.

Nīght-hawk. An unclean bird, Lev. xi. 16; supposably the owl or night-jar.

Nile (*dark blue*). The great river of Egypt, worshipped as a god, famous for its annual and fertilizing overflows and its many mouths. Name not mentioned in scripture, but alluded to as "the river," Gen. xli. 1; Ex. ii. 3; vii. 21; "the river of Egypt," Gen. xv. 18; "flood of Egypt," Am. viii. 8; Sihor, "black," Josh. xiii. 3; Shihor, "dark blue," 1 Chr. xiii. 5 "Nachal of Egypt," "river of Cush," etc.

Nĭm′rah (*clear*). City in Gad, east of Jordan, Num. xxxii. 3.

Nĭm′rim (*clear*). A stream in Moab, S. E. of Dead Sea, Isa. xv. 6; Jer. xlviii. 34.

Nĭm′rŏd (*brave*). Son of Cush. A renowned hunter, city builder, empire founder in Shinar (Babylonia), Gen. x. 8-12; 1 Chr. i. 10.

Nĭm′shī (*rescued*). Father of Jehu, 1 Kgs. xix. 16; 2 Kgs. ix. 2, 14.

Nĭn′e-veh (*dwelling of Ninus*). Capital of Assyria, on river Tigris. Founded by Asshur, Gen. x. 11. At height of its wealth and splendor during time of Jonah and Nahum, and burden of their prophecies. Taken by Medes about B. C. 750, and destroyed by combined Medes and Babylonians, B. C. 606, Jonah; Nah. i.-iii; Zeph. ii. 13. Among the ruins of Nineveh, which was supposed to embrace Nimrud and other suburbs, have been discovered many palaces and temples, and a richly sculptured obelisk whose references are to Syria and Israel.

Nĭn′e-vites. Dwellers in Nineveh, Luke xi. 30.

Nī′san (*standard*). Abib, Ex. xiii. 4. First month of Hebrew sacred and seventh of civil year, corresponding to parts of March and April, Ex. xii. 2.

The Black Obelisk of Nimrud, inscribed with the names of Jehu and Hazael.

Nĭs′rŏch (*great eagle*). The eagle headed and winged Assyrian god, 2 Kgs. xix. 37; Isa. xxxvii. 38.

Nī′tre. The saltpetre of commerce. Evidently natron or washing soda is meant in Prov. xxv. 20; Jer. ii. 22.

Nō (*place*). Ancient Thebes and capital of Upper Egypt. The Diospolis of the Greeks. Situate on both banks of the Nile. Populous and splendid from B. C. 1600 to B. C. 800. Site of many imposing ruins. No-amon, "place of Amon," in marg. notes, Ezek. xxx. 14-16; Jer. xlvi. 25; Nah. iii. 8.

Nō″a-dī′ah (*met by God*). (1) A Levite, Ez. viii. 33. (2) A hostile prophetess, Neh. vi. 14.

Nō′ah (*rest*). (1) Ninth in descent from Adam, Gen. v. 28-32. Chosen to build the ark, Gen. vi. 8-22. Saved from the flood, with his three sons, Shem, Ham, and Japheth, Gen. vii., viii. Re-peopled the earth, Gen. ix., x. Died at age of 950 years. (2) A daughter of Zelophehad, Num. xxvi. 33.

Nō-ā′mon (*place of Amon*). [No.]

Nŏb (*height*). Levitical city in Benjamin, noted as scene of the massacre of the priests, 1 Sam. xxi. 1; xxii. 19-23; Neh. xi. 32.

Sculptured Gateway at Karnak (No or Thebes).

Nō'bah (*barking*). Name given by Nobah to Kenath, Num. xxxii. 42; Judg. viii. 11.

Nŏd (*fleeing*). The land to which Cain the murderer fled, Gen. iv. 16.

Nō'dăb (*noble*). An Arab tribe, 1 Chr. v. 19.

Nŏph, Isa. xix. 13; Jer. ii. 16; Ezek. xxx. 13. [MEMPHIS.]

Nō'phah (*blast*). Town in Moab, Num. xxi. 30.

Nōşe-jęw'elş. Rings worn in the nose. Still affected in the East, Isa. iii. 21.

Nŏv'ĭçe. "Newly planted." A recent convert, 1 Tim. iii. 6.

Nŭm'bērş (*distribute*). (1) Hebrews used alphabetic letters for notation. They also had preferential numbers, as "three," "seven," "ten," "seventy," etc., Gen. iv. 24; Ex. xx. 5-17; Num. vii. 13; Rev. xv. 1. (2) Fourth book of Bible and Pentateuch. Authorship ascribed to Moses. Chapters i.-x. 10 describe the departure from Sinai; x. 11-xiv. the marches to borders of Caanan; xv.-xvi. contain laws; xx.-xxxvi. describe events leading to the passage of Jordan and the conquest.

Nū-mē'nĭ-us. Jonathan's ambassador to Greece and Rome, 1 Macc. xii. 16.

Nŭn (*fish*). Father of Joshua, Ex. xxxiii. 11; 1 Chr. vii. 27.

Nûrse (*nourish*). Position of importance and honor among Hebrews, Gen. xxiv. 59; xxxv. 8; 2 Sam. iv. 4.

Nȳm'phas (*bridegroom*). A Laodicean Christian, Col. iv. 15.

O

Ōak (*strong*). Three varieties in Palestine, usually of great girth and expanse, but not noted for height, Gen. xxxv. 8; Judg. vi. 11, 19; 2 Sam. xviii. 9-14.

Ōath. Appeals to God to attest the truth of an assertion in early use, Gen. xxi. 23; xxvi. 3; Heb. vi. 16. Regulated in Ex. xx. 7; Lev. xix. 12. Forms: lifting hands, Gen. xiv. 22; placing hand under thigh, Gen. xxiv. 2; before the altar, 1 Kgs. viii. 31; laying hand on the law.

Abraham's Oak, near Hebron.

Nō'e, N. T. and Apoc. form of Noah, Matt. xxiv. 37; Luke iii. 36.

Nō-ē'bȧ, 1 Esdr. v. 31. [NEKODA.]

Nō'gah (*bright*). A son of David, 1 Chr. iii. 7.

Nō'hah (*rest*). A Benjamite, 1 Chr. viii. 2.

Nŏn. Form of Nun, 1 Chr. vii. 27.

Ō''ba-dī'ah (*servant of God*). (1) A Judahite, 1 Chr. iii. 21. (2) A chief of Issachar, 1 Chr. vii. 3. (3) Son of Azel, 1 Chr. viii. 38. (4) A Levite, 1 Chr. ix. 16. (5) A Gadite, 1 Chr. xii. 9. (6) A court officer under Ahab, 1 Kgs. xviii. 3–16. (7) A teacher of the law, 2 Chr. xvii. 7. (8) Others, in 1 Chr. xxvii. 19; 2 Chr. xxxiv. 12; Ez. viii. 9; Neh. x. 5; xii. 25. (9) Fourth of minor prophets. Prophesied after capture of Jerusalem. His book, 31st of O. T., is a denunciation of Edom. Nothing known of his history.

Ō'bal (*naked*). Son of Joktan, Gen. x. 28. Ebal in 1 Chr. i. 22.

Ŏb'dĭ-ȧ, 1 Esdr. v. 38. [Habaiah.]

Ō'bed (*servant*). (1) Son of Boaz and Ruth, Ruth iv. 17; Luke iii. 32. (2) Descendant of Sheshan, 1 Chr. ii. 37, 38. (3) One of David's warriors, 1 Chr. xi. 47. (4) A temple porter, 1 Chr. xxvi. 7. (5) Father of Azariah, 2 Chr. xxiii. 1.

Ō'bed-ē'dom (*servant of Edom*). (1) He kept the ark for three months, 2 Sam. vi. 10–12; 1 Chr. xiii. 13, 14. (2) A temple treasurer, 2 Chr. xxv. 24.

Ō'beth, 1 Esdr. viii. 32. [Ebed.]

Ō'bil (*camel-keeper*). David's camel-keeper, 1 Chr. xxvii. 30.

Ŏb-lā'tion (*spread out*). Act of offering. The offering itself, Lev. ii. 4.

Ō'both (*bottles*). An Israelite encampment, east of Moab, Num. xxi. 10; xxxiii. 43.

Fruit, Leaves and Blossoms of the Olive Tree.

Ō'chĭ-el, 1 Esdr. i. 9. [Jeiel.]

Ŏc'ran (*disturber*). An Asherite, Num. i. 13; ii. 27.

Ŏd''a-när'kēs. Chief of a nomad tribe, 1 Macc. ix. 66.

Ō'ded (*restoring*). (1) Father of Azariah, 2 Chr. xv. 1. (2) A Samaritan prophet, 2 Chr. xxviii. 9–11.

Ō-dŏl'lam. Greek form of Adullam, 2 Macc. xii. 38.

Ŏf'fĕr-ing (*bearing towards*). Either bloody, as of animals, or bloodless, as of vegetables. They embraced the burnt, sin, trespass, peace, and meat offerings, Lev. i.–ix.

Ŏg (*giant*). King of Bashan, last of the giant Rephaim, Num. xxi. 33; Deut. i. 4; iii. 3–13; Josh. ii. 10.

Ō'hăd (*strength*). Son of Simeon, Gen. xlvi. 10.

Ō'hel (*tent*). Son of Zerubbabel, 1 Chr. iii. 20.

Oil (*olive*). Used for preparing food, Ex. xxix. 2; anointing, 2 Sam. xiv. 2; illuminating, Matt. xxv. 1–13; in worship, Num. xviii. 12; in consecration, 1 Sam. x. 1; in medicine, Mark vi. 13; in burial, Matt. xxvi. 12. Types gladness, Ps. xcii. 10.

Oint'ment (*smear*). Highly prized, and made of perfumes in oil. For uses, *see* Oil.

Ŏl'īve. A tree resembling the apple in size and shape, bearing a plum-like fruit, prized for its oil, Gen. viii. 11; Deut. vi. 11; Job xxiv. 11. Olive wood used in the temple, 1 Kgs. vi. 23, 31–33.

Ŏl'īves, Ŏl'i-vĕt. The mount of Olives, or Olivet, is the ridge east of Jerusalem, beyond the brook Kidron. So named from its olive-trees. On its slopes were Gethsemane, Bethphage and Bethany, 2 Sam. xv. 30; Zech. xiv. 4; Matt. xxi. 1; Mark xi. 1; Luke xxii. 39; John viii. 1; Acts i. 12.

Ō-lỹm'pas (*heavenly*). A Roman Christian, Rom. xvi. 15.

Ō-lỹm'pĭ-us. The Grecian Zeus, or Jupiter, dwelling on Olympus, 2 Macc. vi. 2.

Ŏm''a-ē'rus, 1 Esdr. ix. 34. [Amram.]

Ō'mar (*speaker*). A duke of Edom, Gen. xxxvi. 11, 15.

Ō-mĕg'ȧ *or* **Ō-mē'gȧ** (*great or long O*). Last letter of Greek alphabet, Rev. i. 8.

Ō'mĕr. A Hebrew dry measure, equal to tenth part of an ephah, Ex. xvi. 36.

Ŏm'rī (*pupil*). (1) A general under Elah, king of Israel, and eventually king, B. C. 929–918. He built Samaria and made it the capital, 1 Kgs. xvi. 16–28. (2) A Benjamite, 1 Chr. vii. 8. (3) A Judahite, 1 Chr. ix. 4. (4) A chief of Issachar, 1 Chr. xxvii. 18.

Ŏn (*strength*). (1) Grandson of Reuben, Num. xvi. 1. (2) City of lower Egypt, Gen. xli. 45, 50. Bethshemesh or "house of the sun," Jer. xliii. 13. In Greek, Heliopolis, "city of the sun," Ezek. xxx. 17 marg. Noted for its learning, opulence, temples, shrines, monuments, sphinxes, and religious schools.

Ō'nam (*strong*). (1) Grandson of Seir, Gen. xxxvi. 23. (2) Son of Jerahmeel, 1 Chr. ii. 26.

Ō'nan (*strong*). Second son of Judah, slain for wickedness, Gen. xxxviii. 4–10; Num. xxvi. 19.

Ō-nĕs'i-mus (*useful*). Slave of Philemon, at Colosse, in whose behalf Paul wrote the epistle to Philemon, Col. iv. 9; Phile. 10, 15.

Ŏn''e-sĭph'o-rus (*profit-bearing*). Friend of Paul at Ephesus and Rome, 2 Tim. i. 16–18; iv. 19.

Ō-nī'a-rēs. Onias and Areus, 1 Macc. xii. 19.

Ō-nī'as. Name of five high priests during time of Maccabees.

On'ion (*one*). The single bulbed plant growing to perfection in the Nile valley, Num. xi. 5.

Ō'nō (*strong*). Town in Benjamin, 1 Chr. viii. 12.

Ō'nus, 1 Esdr. v. 22. [Ono.]

Ŏn'y̆-chȧ (*nail*). Incense ingredient; probably burnt seashell, Ex. xxx. 34.

Ō'nyx (*nail*). A cryptocrystalline quartz, veined and shelled, Ex. xxviii. 9–12; 1 Chr. xxix. 2.

Ō'phel (*hill*). A fortified hill in Jerusalem, 2 Chr. xxvii. 3; Neh. iii. 26; xi. 21.

Ō'phīr (*fruitful*). (1) Son of Joktan, and his country in Arabia, Gen. x. 29. (2) Place whence the

Hebrews drew gold, ivory, peacocks, and woods. Variously located, 1 Kgs. ix. 28; x. 11-22; xxii. 48; 1 Chr. xxix. 4; Job xxviii. 16; Ps. xlv. 9.

Ŏph'nī (*mouldy*). Town in Benjamin, Josh. xviii. 24.

Obelisk of On. (*See* p. 80.)

Ŏph'rah (*fawn*). (1) Town in Benjamin, Josh. xviii. 23; 1 Sam. xiii. 17. (2) Native place of Gideon, Judg. vi. 11, 24. (3) Son of Meonothai, 1 Chr. iv. 14.

Ŏr'a-cle (*speaking*). In O. T. sense, the holy place whence God declared his will, 1 Kgs. vi. 5; viii. 6. Divine revelation, Acts vii. 38; Rom. iii. 2.

Ō'reb (*raven*). (1) A Midianite chief, Judg. vii. 25. (2) The rock, "raven's crag," east of Jordan, where Oreb fell, Judg. vii. 25; Isa. x. 26.

Ō'ren (*pine*). Son of Jerahmeel, 1 Chr. ii. 25.

Ŏr'gan (*instrument*). The "pipe," or any perforated wind instrument, Gen. iv. 21; Job xxi. 12; Ps. cl. 4.

Ō-rī'on (*hunter, Orion*). The constellation, Job ix. 9; xxxviii. 31; Am. v. 8.

Ŏr'na-ments (*adornments*). Of infinite variety among Oriental peoples, Gen. xxiv. 22; Isa. iii. 16-25; Jer. ii. 32; Ezek. xvi. 11-19.

Ŏr'nan (*active*). The Jebusite prince from whom David bought the threshing-floor on which he built the altar, 1 Chr. xxi. 15-25. [ARAUNAH.]

Ŏr'pah (*fawn*). Daughter-in-law of Naomi, Ruth i. 4-14.

Ŏr-thō'sī-as. City of northern Phœnicia, 1 Macc. xv. 37.

Ō-sē'á, 2 Esdr. xiii. 40. [HOSEA.]

Ō'see. Greek form of Hosea, Rom. ix. 25.

Ō-shē'á. Original name of Joshua, Num. xiii. 8.

Ŏs'prāy (*ossifrage, bone-breaker*). An unclean bird; probably the osprey or sea-eagle, Lev. xi. 13; Deut. xiv. 12.

Ŏs'sī-frăge (*bone-breaker*). An unclean bird; the lammergeir, or bearded vulture, Lev. xi. 13; Deut. xiv. 12.

Ŏs'trĭch (*bird*). In Hebrew, "daughter of greediness." In Arabic and Greek "camel-bird." Largest of the bird species, Job xxxix. 13-18.

Ŏth'nī (*lion*). Son of Shemaiah, 1 Chr. xxvi. 7.

Ŏth'nī-el (*lion*). A judge of Israel, Josh. xv. 17; Judg. i. 13; iii. 9-11.

Ou'ches (*brooches*). Jewel settings, Ex. xxxix. 6.

Ŏv'en (*arch*). Fixed ovens, Hos. vii. 4. Portable, consisting of a large clay jar, Ex. viii. 3; Lev. xxvi. 26.

Owl (*howl*). An unclean bird and type of desolation. Five species found in Palestine, Lev. xi. 17; Deut. xiv. 16; Ps. cii. 6; Isa. xxxiv. 11-15.

Ŏx (*sprinkle*). (1) Ancestor of Judith, Judith viii. 1. (2) The male of the cow kind, and in scripture synonymous with bull. Used for plowing, Deut. xxii. 10; threshing, without muzzle, xxv. 4; draught, Num. vii. 3; burden, 1 Chr. xii. 40; beef, Deut. xiv. 4; sacrifices, 1 Kgs. i. 9.

Ō'zem (*strength*). (1) A brother of David, 1 Chr. ii. 15. (2) Son of Jerahmeel, 1 Chr. ii. 25.

Ō-zī'as. (1) Governor of Bethulia, Judith vi. 15. (2) Ancestor of Ezra, 2 Esdr. i. 2. (3) N. T. form of Uzziah, Matt. i. 8, 9.

Ō-zī'el. Ancestor of Judith, Judith viii. 1.

Ŏz'nī (*hearing*). Son of Gad, Num. xxvi. 16; Ezbon, Gen. xlvi. 16.

Ŏz'nītes. Descendants of Ozni, Num. xxvi. 16.

Ō-zō'rá, 1 Esdr. ix. 24. [SHELAMIAH.]

P

Pā'a-rāi (*opening*). One of David's warriors, 2 Sam. xxiii. 35; Naarai, 1 Chr. xi. 37.

Pā'dan (*table-land*), Gen. xlviii. 7. [PADAN-ARAM.]

Pā'dan-ā'ram (*table-land of Aram*). The

Osprey, or Fishing Eagle.

plain region of Mesopotamia, Gen. xxiv. 10; xxv. 20; xxviii. 2-7; xxxi. 18; xxxiii. 18; xxxv. 9-26; xlvi. 15.

Pā'don (*escape*). His children returned, Ez. ii. 44.

Owl. (*See* p. 81.)

Pā'gi-el (*God-allotted*). A chief of Asher, Num. i. 13; ii. 27; vii. 72, 77; x. 26.

Pā'hath-mō'ab (*ruler of Moab*). His children returned, Ez. ii. 6; viii. 4; Neh. iii. 11.

Pā'ī, 1 Chr. i. 50. [Pau.]

Pāint. Much used in East as cosmetic and beautifier, 2 Kgs. ix. 30; Jer. iv. 30. Houses, walls, beams, idols, painted, Jer. xxii. 14; Ezek. xxiii. 14. Painting as a fine art not encouraged by Hebrews.

Păl'ace. Royal residence, 1 Kgs. vii. 1-12; citadel, 1 Kgs. xvi. 18; fortress, 2 Kgs. xv. 25; entire royal court, Dan. i. 4; capital city, Esth. ix. 12. In N. T. any stately residence, Matt. xxvi. 3; Luke xi. 21.

Pā'lal (*judge*). An assistant wall-builder, Neh. iii. 25.

Păl''es-tī'nȧ, Păl'es-tīne (*land of sojourners*). Philistia, land of the Philistines, Ps. lx. 8; lxxxiii. 7. Palestina, Ex. xv. 14; Isa. xiv. 29, 31. Palestine, Joel iii. 4. Canaan, Gen. xii. 5; Ex. xv. 15. Holy Land, Zech. ii. 12. The indefinitely bounded region promised to Abraham, lying between the Mediterranean Sea and Jordan River and Dead Sea. It also embraced the Hebrew settlements beyond Jordan, Gen. xv. 18; xvii. 8; Num. xxiv. 2-12; Deut. i. 7.

Păl'lu (*famous*). Son of Reuben, Ex. vi. 14.

Păl'lu-ītes. Descendants of Pallu, Num. xxvi. 5.

Pälm'er-worm (*pilgrim-worm*). Canker-worm, or caterpillar, Joel i. 4; ii. 25; Amos iv. 9.

Pälm-tree (*hand-leaved*). The date-palm. Once grew luxuriantly in Palestine. Evergreen and stately, frequently rising to 100 feet, Ex. xv. 27; Deut. xxxiv. 3; Judg. i. 16; 1 Kgs. vi. 32; S. of Sol. vii. 7.

Pal'sy (*paralysis*). Partial or total death of muscle and nerve, 1 Kgs. xiii. 4-6; Matt. iv. 24; Luke vi. 6.

Păl'tī (*deliverance*). The Benjamite spy, Num. xiii. 9.

Păl'tī-el (*deliverance*). A prince of Issachar, Num. xxxiv. 26.

Păl'tīte. Designation of one of David's guardsmen, 2 Sam. xxiii. 26.

Păm-phy̆l'ī-ȧ (*mixture of nations*). A seacoast province of Asia Minor. Its chief town was Perga, where Paul preached, Acts xiii. 13; xiv. 24; xxvii. 5.

Păn (*open*). A flat plate for baking, and a deeper vessel for holding liquids, Lev. ii. 5; vi. 21.

Păn'năg. Disputed word. Probably a place, Ezek. xxvii. 17.

Pā'per. [Papyrus.]

Pā'phos (*hot*). Town on island of Cyprus, visited by Paul, Acts xiii. 6-13.

Pȧ-py̆'rus. The writing-paper of the Egyptians, Greeks, and Romans, made from the papyrus plant, a rush or flag growing in Egypt, Job xl. 21.

Păr'ă-ble (*comparison*). Allegorical representation of something real in nature or human affairs, whence a moral is drawn. A favorite method of Oriental teaching, 2 Sam. xii. 1-4; Isa. v. 1-7. Christ spoke over 30 parables, Matt. xiii. 3-8; 24-30, 31, 32, and elsewhere in Gospels.

Păr'ă-dīse (*pleasure ground*). "Garden of Eden;" and, figuratively, abode of happy souls — heaven, Luke xxiii. 43; 2 Cor. xii. 4; Rev. ii. 7.

Pā'rah (*place of heifers*). City in Benjamin, Josh. xviii. 23.

Pā'ran, El-pā'ran (*places of caves*). The "desert of wandering," with Canaan on the north, desert of Sinai on the south, Etham on the west, and Arabah on the east, Gen. xxi. 14-21; Num. x. 12, 33; xii. 16; xiii. 3, 26; xxxiii. 17-36.

Pā'ran, Mount of. A mount of the Sinaitic range, Deut. xxxiii. 2; Hab. iii. 3.

Palm-Tree.

Pär'bar (*suburb*). A spot between the west wall of temple at Jerusalem and the city beyond, 1 Chr. xxvi. 18.

Pärched Corn. Roasted grain, Ruth ii. 14.

Pärched Ground. Supposably the mirage frequently seen on desert tracts, Isa. xxxv. 7.

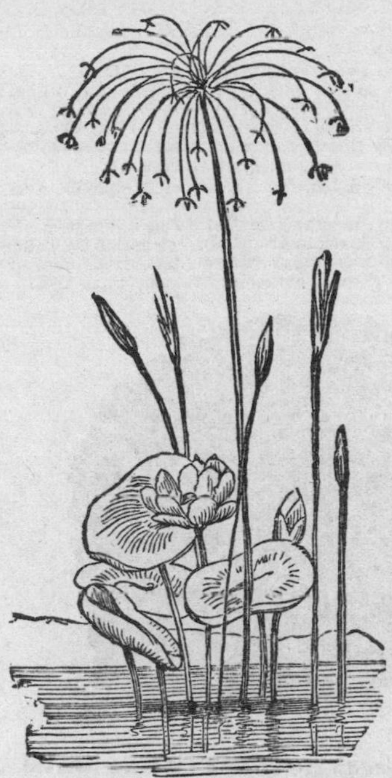

Papyrus. (*See* p. 82.)

Pärch'ment (*from Pergamum*). Skin of sheep or goats prepared for writing on, 2 Tim. iv. 13.

Pär'lor (*speaking chamber*). King's audience-chamber, Judg. iii. 20-25.

Pär-mäsh'tȧ (*stronger*). A son of Haman, Esth. ix. 9.

Pär'me-năs (*steadfast*). One of the first seven deacons, Acts vi. 5.

Pär'nach (*swift*). A Zebulunite, Num. xxxiv. 25.

Pā'rŏsh (*flea*). His children returned, Ez. ii. 3; Neh. vii. 8.

Pär-shăn'da-thȧ (*prayer-given*). Eldest son of Haman, Esth. ix. 7.

Pär'thĭ-ans. Jews settled in Parthia, that undefined country north of Media and Persia, Acts ii. 9.

Pär'trĭdge (*squatting*). Three varieties found in Palestine. Their flesh and eggs esteemed as food, 1 Sam. xxvi. 20; Jer. xvii. 11.

Păr'u-ah (*blooming*). Father of Solomon's commissary in Issachar, 1 Kgs. iv. 17.

Pär-vā'im (*eastern*). Unknown place whence Solomon shipped gold, 2 Chr. iii. 6.

Pā'sach (*cut off*) An Asherite, 1 Chr. vii. 33.

Păs-dăm'mim (*blood-border*). Spot of battles between Israel and Philistia, 1 Chr. xi. 13. Ephes-dammim, 1 Sam. xvii. 1.

Pȧ-sē'ah (*lame*). (1) A Judahite, 1 Chr. iv. 12. (2) His sons returned, Ez. ii. 49.

Păsh'ŭr (*freedom*). (1) Head of a priestly family, 1 Chr. ix. 12; Neh. xi. 12; Jer. xxi. 1. (2) Priestly governor of the house of the Lord, 1 Chr. xxiv. 14; Jer. xx. i.

Păs'sion (*suffering*). Last sufferings of Christ, Acts i. 3. Kindred feelings, Acts xiv. 15; Jas. v. 17.

Păss'ō-ver (*passing over*). First of three great Jewish feasts, instituted in honor of the "passing over" of the Hebrew households by the destroying angel, Ex. xii., xiii. 3-10; xxiii. 14-19; Lev. xxiii. 4-14. Called the "feast of unleavened bread." The Christian Passover is "The Lord's Supper," eucharist, Matt. xxvii. 62; Luke xxii. 1-20; John xix. 42.

Păs'tor (*shepherd*). Figuratively, one who keeps Christ's flocks, Eph. iv. 11.

Păt'a-rȧ (*trodden*). City on southwest coast of Lycia, Acts xxi. 1, 2.

Pāte (*flat*). Top of the head, Ps. vii. 16.

Pȧ-the'us, 1 Esdr. ix. 23. [PETHAHIAH.]

Păth'ros (*southern*). An ancient division of Upper Egypt occupied by the Pathrusim, Isa. xi. 11; Jer. xliv. 1-15; Ezek. xxix. 14.

Păth-ru'sĭm, Gen. x. 14. [PATHROS.]

Păt'mos. The rocky island in the Ægean Sea, to which John was banished, Rev. i. 9.

Pā'trĭ-arch (*father*). Father of the family and chief of its descendants. The Hebrew form of government till Moses established the theocracy, Acts ii. 29; vii. 8, 9; Heb. vii. 4.

Păt'ro-băs (*paternal*). A Roman Christian, Rom. xvi. 14.

Pȧ-trō'clus. Father of Nicanor, 2 Macc. viii. 9.

Pā'u (*bleating*). Capital of Hadar, king of Edom, Gen. xxxvi. 39. Pai, 1 Chr. i. 50.

Paul (*small*). In Hebrew, Saul. Born at Tarsus in Cilicia, of Benjamite parents, about the beginning of 1st century; a Pharisee in faith; a tent-maker by trade, Phil. iii. 5; Acts xviii. 3; xxi. 39; xxiii. 6. Studied law with Gamaliel at Jerusalem; persecuted early Christians; converted near Damascus, Acts v. 34; vii. 58; ix. 1-22. Commissioned an apostle to the Gentiles, Acts xxvi. 13-20. Carried the gospel to Asia Minor, Greece, and Rome. Author of fourteen epistles, amplifying the Christian faith. Supposably a martyr at Rome, A. D. 68.

Pāve'ment (*beaten floor*). [GABBATHA.]

Pȧ-vĭl'ion (*butterfly tent*). Movable tent or dwelling. Applied to tabernacle, booth, den, etc., 1 Kgs. xx. 16; Ps. xviii. 11; xxvii. 5; Jer. xliii. 10.

Pēa'cock (*eye-feathered cock*). An import from Tarshish, 1 Kgs. x. 22; 2 Chr. ix. 21. The peacock of Job xxxix. 13 should be ostrich.

Pẽarls (*little pears*). Stony secretions of the pearl-oyster. Reckoned as gems and highly prized as ornaments. Source of frequent metaphor, Matt. xiii. 45; 1 Tim. ii. 9; Rev. xvii. 4; xxi. 21. Pearl, in Job xxviii. 18, should be crystal.

Pĕd'a-hĕl (*saved*). A chief of Naphtali, Num. xxxiv. 28.

Pē-däh'zur (*rock-saved*). Father of Gamaliel, Num. i. 10.

Pē'dā'iah (*God-saved*). (1) Grandfather of King Jehoiakim, 2 Kgs. xxiii. 36. (2) Father of Zerubbabel, 1 Chr. iii. 18, 19. (3) A Manassite, 1 Chr. xxvii. 20. (4) Returned captives, Neh. iii. 25; viii. 4; xi. 7; xiii. 13.

Pē'kah (*open-eyed*). Murderer and successor of Pekahiah, king of Israel, B. C. 758-738. Conspired with Damascus against Judah, and perished in a conspiracy, 2 Kgs. xv. 25-31; xvi.; 2 Chr. xxviii.

Pĕk''a-hī'ah (*God opens*). Son and successor of Menahem on the throne of Israel, B. C. 760-758. Murdered and succeeded by his general, Pekah, 2 Kgs. xv. 22–26.

Pē'kŏd. The Chaldeans are so called in Jer. l. 21; Ezek. xxiii. 23.

Pĕl''a-ī'ah (*distinguished*). (1) A Judahite, 1 Chr. iii. 24. (2) A co-covenanter, Neh. viii. 7; x. 10.

Pĕl''a-lī'ah (*judged*). A returned priest, Neh. xi. 12.

Pĕl''a-tī'ah (*saved*). (1) Grandson of Zerubbabel, 1 Chr. iii. 21. (2) A Simeonite warrior, 1 Chr. iv. 42. (3) A co-covenanter, Neh. x. 22. (4) One struck dead for defying Ezekiel, Ezek. xi. 1-13.

Pē'leg (*division*). Son of Eber. His family remained in Mesopotamia, Gen. x. 25; xi. 16–19.

Pē'let (*freedom*). (1) A Judahite, 1 Chr. ii. 47. (2) An adherent of David, 1 Chr. xii. 3.

Pē'leth (*freedom*). (1) Father of the rebellious On, Num. xvi. 1. (2) Son of Jonathan, 1 Chr. ii. 33.

Pē'leth-ītes (*runners*). Retainers and messengers of David, 2 Sam. viii. 18; xv. 18; xx. 7.

Pe-lī'as, 1 Esdr. ix. 34. [BEDEIAH.]

Pe-nū'el. (1) [PENIEL.] (2) A Judahite, 1 Chr. iv. 4. (3) A Benjamite, 1 Chr. viii. 25.

Pē'or (*cleft*). (1) The mountain in Moab to which Balak brought Balaam, Num. xxiii. 28; xxv. 18; xxxi. 16. (2) [BAAL-PEOR.]

Pĕr'a-zīm (*breach*). A figurative mountain, Isa. xxviii. 21.

Pē'resh (*dung*). Son of Machir, 1 Chr. vii. 16.

Pē'rez (*rent*). An important Judahite family, 1 Chr. xxvii. 3; Neh. xi. 4–6.

Pē'rez-ŭz'zah (*breaking of Uzzah*). Where Uzzah died, 2 Sam. vi. 6–8. Perez-uzza, 1 Chr. xiii. 9–11.

Pĕr'fūme (*thorough-fume*). Perfumes largely used by Hebrews in religious rites and for toilet purposes, Ex. xxx. 35; Prov. xxvii. 9.

Pĕr'gȧ (*earthy*). A city of Pamphylia, Acts xiii. 13.

Pĕr'ga-mŏs (*heights*). Pergamum in R. V. A city of Mysia, in Asia Minor, celebrated for its library, which was transferred to Alexandria. Seat of one of the "seven churches," Rev. i. 11; ii. 12–17.

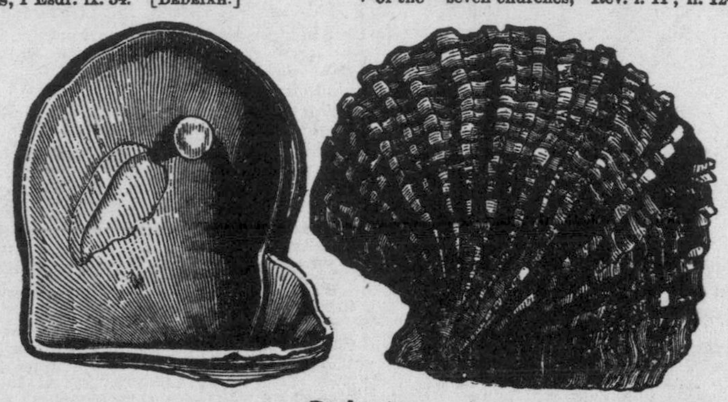

Pearl oyster.

Pĕl'ĭ-can (*axe-bill*). A voracious water-bird, large and strong-billed. The female is supplied with a pouch for supplying itself and young with water and food. Symbol of desolation. Original sometimes translated "cormorant," Lev. xi. 18; Deut. xiv. 17; Ps. cii. 6; Isa. xxxiv. 11.

Pĕl'o-nīte. Designation of two of David's warriors, 1 Chr. xi. 27, 36.

Pĕn (*feather*). Anciently, a metal graver for tracing on hard substances; the stylus, of pointed metal or bone, for writing in wax; the reed pen and hair pencil for writing on parchment and linen, Judg. v. 14; Job xix. 24; Jer. xvii. 1.

Pe-nī'el (*face of God*). Place beyond Jordan where Jacob wrestled with the angel, Gen. xxxii. 30. Penuel in Judg. viii. 17; 1 Kgs. xii. 25.

Pe-nĭn'nah (*pearl*). A wife of Elkanah, 1 Sam. i. 1-4.

Pĕn'nȳ (*cattle*). The Roman silver denarius, worth 15 to 17 cents. The Greek silver drachma was a corresponding coin, Matt. xx. 2; xxii. 19–21; Mark vi. 37; Luke xx. 24; Rev. vi. 6.

Pĕn'tȧ-teuch (*five-fold book*). Greek name for the first five O. T. books, or books of Moses. Called Torah, "the law," by Hebrews.

Pĕn'te-cŏst (*fiftieth day*). The Hebrew harvest-home festival, celebrated on fiftieth day from the Passover, or on the date of the giving of the law at Sinai, Ex. xxiii. 16; xxxiv. 22; Lev. xxiii. 15–22; Num. xxviii. In the Christian Church, Pentecost is celebrated seven weeks after Easter, to commemorate the day in Acts ii. 1–14.

Pe-rī'dȧ (*kernels*). His children returned, Neh. vii. 57.

Pĕr'ĭz-zītes (*villagers*). Original village-dwellers in Canaan, Gen. xiii. 7; Josh. xvii. 15.

Pĕr-sĕp'ō-lis (*city of Persia*). Capital of Persia. Ruins very extensive, 2 Macc. ix. 2.

Pĕr'seus (*destroyer*). Last king of Macedonia; defeated by Rome, 1 Macc. viii. 5.

Pĕr'sia (*land of Perses*). Originally the country around the head of the Persian Gulf; afterwards the great empire, including all western Asia, and parts of Europe and Africa. Reached its height under Cyrus, B. C. 486–485. Conquered by Alexander, B. C. 330, Ezek. xxxviii. 5; 2 Chr. xxxvi. 20–23; Ez. i. 8.

Pĕr'sis (*Persian*). A Christian woman at Rome, Rom. xvi. 12.

Pe-ru'dȧ, Ez. ii. 55. [PERIDA.]

Pĕs'tĭ-lence (*the plague*). In Hebrew, all distempers and calamities, Ex. ix. 14; xi. 1; 1 Kgs. viii. 37.

Pē'ter (*stone, rock*). Simon, or Simeon; son of Jonas, Matt. xvi. 17; Acts xv. 14. A fisherman, resident at Capernaum, Matt. viii. 14; called, Matt. iv. 18–20; name changed to Peter, John i. 42. Founder of Christian Church among the Jews, Acts ii.; spokesman of the apostles, Acts x.; author of two epistles; a probable martyr at Rome. His first epistle is dated from Babylon; his second is his valedictory. Both are advisory and exhortatory.

Pĕth''a-hī'ah (*freed*). (1) Head of the 19th

priestly course, 1 Chr. xxiv. 16. (2) Returned captives, Ez. x. 23; Neh. ix. 5; xi. 24.

Pē′thôr (*prophet*). Balaam's residence in Mesopotamia, Num. xxii. 5; Deut. xxiii. 4.

Pĕ-thū′el (*vision*). Father of Joel, Joel i. 1.

Pē′trȧ (*rock*). Edom. Modernly, Arabia Petræa.

Pė-ŭl′thāi (*wages*). Eighth son of Obed-edom, 1 Chr. xxvi. 5.

Phāi′sur, 1 Esdr. ix. 22. [Pashur.]

Phā′lec, Luke iii. 35. [Peleg.]

Phăl′lū, Gen. xlvi. 9. [Pallu.]

Phăl′tī (*deliverance*). The man to whom Saul gave Michal, his daughter and David's wife, 1 Sam. xxv. 44. Phaltiel, 2 Sam. iii. 15, 16.

Phăl′tĭ-el, 2 Sam. iii. 15. [Phalti.]

Phăn-ū′el (*face of God*). Father of Anna the prophetess, Luke ii. 36.

Phăr′a-cim. His sons returned, 1 Esdr. v. 31.

Phā′raōh (*sun-king*). General name of Egyptian kings. Only a few are definitely named in the Bible. Different ones alluded to are, Gen. xii. 15; xli.; Ex. i. 8; v. 1; 1 Chr. iv. 18; 1 Kgs. xi. 18-22; ix. 16; 2 Kgs. xviii. 21; Pharaoh-nechoh, 2 Kgs. xxiii. 29; Pharaoh-hophra, Jer. xxxvii. 5-8.

Sculptured Column at Persepolis.

Phā′raōh's Daugh′ter. (1) Guardian of Moses, Ex. ii. 5-10. (2) Wife of Mered, 1 Chr. iv. 18. (3) Wife of Solomon, 1 Kgs. iii. 1.

Phā′rĕs, Matt. i. 3; Luke iii. 33. [Pharez.]

Ruins of Philæ, called Pharaoh's Bed.

Phā′rĕz (*breach*). A Judahite, Gen. xxxviii. 29; xlvi. 12. Father of Pharzites, Num. xxvi. 20. Perez, Neh. xi. 4, 6. Phares, Matt. i. 3; Luke iii. 33.

Phăr′ĭ-see (*set apart*). A Jewish sect, strictly orthodox in religion, and politically opposed to foreign supremacy, Matt. xxiii. 23-33; Luke xviii. 9-14.

Phā′rŏsh, Ez. viii. 3. [Parosh.]

Phär′par (*swift*). A river of Damascus, 2 Kgs. v. 12.

Phär′zītes. Descendants of Pharez, Num. xxvi. 20.

Phȧ-sē′ah, Neh. vii. 51. [Paseah.]

Phȧ-sē′lis. A town on border of Lycia and Pamphylia, 1 Macc. xv. 23.

Phăs′ĭ-ron. An Arab chief, 1 Macc. ix. 66.

Phăs′să-ron, 1 Esdr. v. 25. [Pashur.]

Phē′bė (*shining*). A servant of the church at Cenchrea, Rom. xvi. 1, 2.

Phė-nī′çė. (1) Acts xi. 19; xv. 3. [Phœnicia.] (2) Phœnix in R. V. A seaport of Crete, Acts xxvii. 12.

Phī′col (*strong*). Chief of Abimelech's army, Gen. xxi. 22; xxvi. 26.

Phĭl″a-dĕl′phĭ-ȧ (*brotherly love*). A city of Lydia in Asia Minor, and seat of one of the seven churches of Asia, Rev. i. 11; iii. 7-13.

Phĭ-lär′chus. A cavalry leader, 2 Macc. viii. 32.

Phĭ-lē′mon (*friendship*). A Christian convert at Colosse in Phrygia, to whom Paul wrote an epistle during his captivity at Rome, in favor of Onesimus, Philemon's servant. Eighteenth N. T. book.

Phĭ-lē′tus (*amiable*). The convert whom Paul denounced for error, 2 Tim. ii. 17.

Phĭl′ĭp (*lover of horses*). (1) The apostle of Bethsaida, of whom little is known, Matt. x. 3; Mark iii. 18; Luke vi. 14; John vi. 5-9; Acts i. 13. (2) The evangelist and deacon, resident at Cæsarea, and preacher throughout Samaria, Acts vi. 5; viii. 5-13; xxi. 8-10. (3) The tetrarch. [Herod.] (4) Husband of Herodias, Matt. xiv. 3. [Herod.] (5) Governor of Jerusalem under Antiochus, and regent of Syria, 2 Macc. v. 22. (6) Philip V., king of Macedonia, 1 Macc. viii. 5. (7) King of Macedonia, B. C. 360-336, and father of Alexander the Great, 1 Macc. i. 1.

Phĭ-lĭp′pī (*city of Philip*). City in Macedonia, founded by Philip II., 12 miles from the port of Neapolis. Paul founded a vigorous church there, Acts xvi.; xx. 1-6.

Phĭ-lĭp′pĭ-anş. Dwellers in Philippi. Paul's epistle to the Christians there was written from Rome, A. D. 62 or 63. In it he sends thanks for gifts, praises their Christian walk and firmness, warns against Judaizing tendencies, and exhorts to steadfast faith.

Phĭ-lĭs′tĭȧ (*land of sojourners*). The plain and coast country on the southwest of Palestine, which imparted its name to Palestine, Ps. lx. 8; lxxxvii. 4; cviii. 9. [Palestine.]

Phĭ-lĭs′tĭneş (*villagers*). Dwellers in Philistia. Origin disputed, but associated with Cretans; also with the Caphtorim of Egypt, Jer. xlvii. 4; Am. ix. 7. Permanent settlers in time of Abraham, Gen. xxi. 32. Wealthy, energetic, and warlike, with many strong cities. Land not conquered by Joshua. Gaza, Ashkelon, Ashdod, Gath, and Ekron, their chief strongholds. Subdued by David, 2 Sam. v. 17-25; but became practically independent under the kings. Disappeared as a distinct people after the time of the Maccabees.

Phĭ-lŏl′o-gus (*learned*). A Roman Christian saluted by Paul, Rom. xvi. 15.

Phĭ-lŏs′o-phȳ (*loving wisdom*). The prominent Grecian schools of philosophy in N. T. times were the Stoic and Epicurean, Acts xvii. 18. But the most formidable enemy of early Christian thought was the tendency of the learned to engraft the speculations of Eastern Gnosticism and Greek philosophy upon the evolving doctrines of Christianity, 1 Cor. i. 18–27; 1 Tim. vi. 20; Col. ii. 8, etc.

Phĭn′e̱-es. Apocryphal form of Phinehas.

Phĭn′e̱-has (*brazen mouth*). (1) Chief of the Korhite Levites, and high priest, Ex. vi. 25; Num. xxv. 6–15; Josh. xxii. 30–32. (2) Wicked son of Eli, 1 Sam. i. 3; ii. 34; iv. 4–19; xiv. 3. (3) A Levite, Ez. viii. 33.

Phī′son. Greek form of Pison, Ecclus. xxiv. 25.

Phlē′gon (*burning*). A Roman Christian saluted by Paul, Rom. xvi. 14.

Phœ′be. [PHEBE.]

Phœ-nī′çi̱à (*land of palm-trees*). Phenicia in Acts xxi. 2. Phenice in Acts xi. 19; xv. 3. In O. T. referred to as Tyre and Sidon, or coasts of Tyre and Sidon. The small coast country north of Palestine, noted for its commercial enterprise, learning, and skill in arts. Included in the Land of Promise but never conquered, Josh. xiii. 4–6. David and Solomon employed its sailors and artisans, 2 Sam. v. 11; 1 Kgs. v.

Philadelphia. (*See* p. 85.)

Phœ-nī′çi̱ans. Dwellers in Phœnicia. In intimate commercial, political, and even religious relations with Hebrews, 1 Kgs. xvi. 31–33; xviii. 40; 1 Chr. xiv. 1; Isa. xxiii.; Ezek. xxvii. 2–8.

Phrȳġ′ĭ-à (*barren*). An undefined section of Asia Minor, out of which several Roman provinces were formed, Acts ii. 10; xvi. 6; xviii. 23.

Phŭd. Judith ii. 23. [PHUT.]

Phū′rah (*bough*). Armor-bearer of Gideon, Judg. vii. 10, 11.

Phū′rim, Esth. xi. 1. [PURIM.]

Phŭt, Pŭt (*bow*). Son of Ham, Gen. x. 6; 1 Chr. i. 8. Name is rendered Libya and Libyans, people of north Africa, in Jer. xlvi. 9; Ezek. xxx. 5; xxxviii. 5.

Phū′vah (*mouth*). Son of Issachar, Gen. xlvi. 13. Pua, Num. xxvi. 23. Puah, 1 Chr. vii. 1.

Phȳ-ġĕl′lus (*fugitive*). A Christian pervert of Asia, 2 Tim. i. 15.

Phȳ-lăc′te̱-rȳ (*safeguard*). [FRONTLET.]

Pī=bē′seth (*house of Bast*). City of Lower Egypt, on Pelusiac branch of the Nile. Bubastis of the Greeks, noted for its temple of Bast, goddess of fire, Ezek. xxx. 17.

Pĭc′tūre (*painting*), Ezek. xxiii. 14; Prov. xxv. 11. Sculptures, reliefs, or cornices, meant. Movable or hanging pictures not favored by Hebrews.

Pïēce (*part*). In O. T., "pieces of gold," "pieces of silver," may well be read shekels' weight, or shekels, of gold or silver, Gen. xx. 16; 2 Kgs. v. 5. In N. T., "pieces," Matt. xxvi. 15; xxvii. 3–9, are unknown. In Luke xv. 8, for "pieces" read drachmas.

Pĭġ′eŏn (*chirping bird*). [DOVE.]

Pī=ha-hī′roth (*place of sedges*). Last Israelite encampment before crossing the Red Sea, Ex. xiv. 2, 9; Num. xxxiii. 7, 8.

Pī′la̱te (*spear-armed*). Pontius Pilate in Matt. xxvii. 2. Sixth Roman procurator of Judea, A. D. 26–36. Official residence at Cæsarea, with judicial visits to other places. Christ was brought before him at Jerusalem for judgment. He found no guilt, but lost his moral courage in the presence of the mob. Eventually banished to Gaul, Luke xxiii. 1–7; John xviii. 27–40; xix.

Pĭl′dăsh (*flame*). Son of Nahor, Gen. xxii. 22.

Pĭl′e̱-hȧ (*worship*). A co-covenanter, Neh. x. 24.

Pĭl′lar (*pile*). Prominent in Oriental architecture, monumental evidences, and scripture metaphor, Gen. xxviii. 18; xxxv. 20; Ex. xiii. 21; Josh. xxiv. 26; Judg. xvi. 25–30; 1 Tim. iii. 15; Rev. iii. 12.

Pĭlled (*peeled*). Peeled, stripped, plundered, Gen. xxx. 37, 38; Isa. xviii. 2.

Pĭl′tāi (*saved*). A priest, Neh. xii. 17.

Pīne (*pitch*). Disputed rendering. Probably plane-tree is meant, Isa. xli. 19; lx. 13.

Pĭn′na̱-cle (*feather, edge*). Not a pinnacle, or summit, but the pinnacle, or wing, of the temple, Matt. iv. 5; Luke iv. 9.

Pī′non (*darkness*). A duke of Edom, Gen. xxxvi. 41.

Pīpe. Flute. Type of perforated wind instruments, as the harp was of stringed instruments, 1 Sam. x. 5; 1 Kgs. i. 40; Isa. v. 12.

Pī′ram (*fleet*). An Amorite king, Josh. x. 3.

Pĭr′a̱-thon (*princely*). Now Ferata, six miles southwest of Shechem, Judg. xii. 15.

Pĭr′a̱-thon-īte″. Dweller in Pirathon, Judg. xii. 13, 15; 1 Chr. xxvii. 14.

Pĭs̱′gah (*hill*). The elevation, in Moab, whence Moses viewed the Promised Land, Num. xxi. 20; Deut. iii. 27; iv. 49; xxxiv. 1.

Pi-sĭd′ĭ-ȧ (*pitchy*). A province of Asia Minor, with Antioch as its capital. Twice visited by Paul, Acts xiii. 14; xiv. 21–24.

Pī′son (*flowing*). One of the four rivers of Eden. Unlocated, Gen. ii. 11.

Pĭs′pah (*swelling*). An Asherite, 1 Chr. vii. 38.

Pĭt (*well*). Cistern or well, Gen. xxxvii. 20; grave, Ps. xxviii. 1; game-trap, Ezek. xix. 8; device, Ps. cxix. 85; Prov. xxvi. 27.

Pĭtch (*pine-resin*). The pitch of scripture was asphalt or bitumen, found in Dead Sea regions. Used for mortar, cement, calk, etc., Gen. vi. 14; xi. 3; Ex. ii. 3; Isa. xxxiv. 9.

Pĭtch′er (*goblet, wine-vessel*). A large earthen water-jar with one or two handles, Gen. xxiv. 15–20; Mark xiv. 13; Luke xxii. 10.

Pī′thom (*house of Tum*). A store-city of Egypt, built by the Israelites, Ex. i. 11.

Pī′thon (*harmless*). A son of Micah, 1 Chr. viii. 35.

Plāgue (*blow*). Pestilential disease, Lev. xiii. 2–8; xxvi. 25. Any calamitous visitation, Mark v. 29; Luke vii. 21. The judgments of God on Egypt are called plagues. They were (1) Nile changed to blood, Ex. vii. 14–25. (2) Visitation of frogs, Ex. viii. 1–15. (3) Lice, Ex. viii. 16–19. (4) Flies, Ex. viii. 20–32. (5) Murrain, Ex. ix. 1–7. (6) Boils, Ex. ix. 8–12. (7) Hail, Ex. ix. 13–35. (8) Locusts, Ex. x. 1–20. (9) Darkness, Ex. x. 21–28. (10) Smiting of the firstborn, Ex. xii. 29, 30.

Plāin (*flat*). Hebrew words so rendered have various significations. Plain, Gen. xi. 2; meadow, Judg. xi. 33; oak-grove, Gen. xiii. 18.

Plāit'ing (*folding*). Folding or pleating, as of the hair, 1 Pet. iii. 3.

Plăn'et (*wanderer*). The reference is evidently to the signs of the zodiac, as in marg. 2 Kgs. xxiii. 5.

Plås'ter (*forming on*). Used by Hebrews as wall and stone coating, Lev. xiv. 42; Deut. xxvii. 2, 4; Dan. v. 5.

Plĕdge (*holding before*). [EARNEST.] [LOAN.]

Plē'ia-dēs or **Pleī'ȧ-dēs** (*daughters of Pleione*). The "seven stars." A group of stars in the constellation Taurus, Job ix. 9; xxxviii. 31; Am. v. 8.

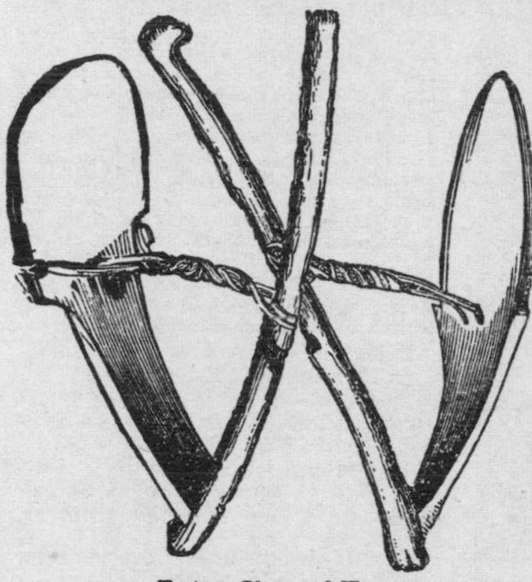

Eastern Plow and Hoe.

Plow (*plowland*). In early times, a crude implement made of a forked stick, one branch of which was shod, or shared, with iron. Drawn by oxen, camels, and asses, Gen. xlv. 6; Deut. xxii. 10; Job i. 14.

Pŏch'e-rĕth (*beguiling*). His children returned, Ez. ii. 57; Neh. vii. 59.

Pō'ĕt-rȳ (*made up*). Hebrew literature largely poetical, and of lyrical style. Job, Psalms, Proverbs, Ecclesiastes, and Song of Solomon are distinctively poetical.

Pōll (*head*). The head, Num. iii. 47. To cut the hair, 2 Sam. xiv. 26.

Pŏl'lux. [CASTOR and POLLUX.]

Pome'grăn-āte (*many-seeded fruit*). A low, straight-stemmed tree, native of Persia, Syria, and Arabia, bearing an orange-like fruit, Num. xiii. 23; Deut. viii. 8; S. of Sol. iv. 3; vi. 7; viii. 2.

Pomegranates.

Pŏm'mels (*knobs*). Globular ornaments on the capitals of pillars, 2 Chr. iv. 12, 13. Called "bowls" in 1 Kgs. vii. 41.

Pŏnds (*confined*). Egyptian ponds were pools left by subsidence of the Nile waters, Ex. vii. 19. Fish-ponds in Isa. xix. 10.

Pŏn'tĭ-us Pī'late. [PILATE.]

Pŏn'tus (*the sea*). Northeastern province of Asia Minor, bordering on the Pontus Euxinus, Euxine Sea. Empire of Mithridates, defeated by Pompey, B. C. 66. Many Jews settled there, Acts ii. 9; xviii. 2; 1 Pet. i. 1.

Pool (*hole*). Artificial reservoir for water. Very necessary in the East and sometimes built very elaborately and expensively, Eccl. ii. 6; Isa. xlii. 15.

Poor (*bare*). Poor especially cared for under Jewish dispensation, Ex. xxiii. 6; Lev. xix. 9, 10; Deut. xv. 7. Spirit continued, Luke iii. 11; xiv. 13; Acts vi. 1.

Pŏp'lär (*butterfly-leaf*). The white poplar supposed to be meant, Gen. xxx. 37; Hos. iv. 13.

Pŏr'a-thȧ (*favored*). A son of Haman, Esth. ix. 8.

Pōrch (*door*). In oriental architecture, veranda, colonnade, vestibule, Judg. iii. 23; 1 Chr. xxviii. 11; John x. 23. Any passage from street to inner hall, Matt. xxvi. 71.

Pôr'çi-us Fĕs'tus, Acts xxiv. 27. [FESTUS.]

Pōr'ters (*gate-keepers*). Keepers of city, temple, palace, and private gates and doors. The temple had 4000 of them, in classified service, 2 Sam. xviii. 26; 2 Kgs. vii. 10; 1 Chr. xxiii. 5; xxvi. 1–19; 2 Chr. xxxi. 14.

Pŏs''ĭ-dō'nĭ-as. Nicanor's envoy to Judas, 2 Macc. xiv. 19.

Pōsts (*placed*). Runners, messengers, on foot, on horses, or on dromedaries, Esth. viii. 10–14; Job ix. 25; Jer. li. 31.

Pŏt (*drinking-vessel*). Pots of various designs, sizes, and uses. Made of clay or metal, Lev. vi. 28; 1 Sam. ii. 14; 2 Kgs. iv. 2; Jer. xxxv. 5; Ezek. iv. 9.

Pŏt'ĭ-phar (*belonging to the sun*). Captain of Pharaoh's guard, Gen. xxxvii. 36; xxxix.

Pō-tĭ'=phe-rah (*belonging to the sun*). A priest of On, in Egypt, and father-in-law of Joseph, Gen. xli. 45.

Pŏt'sherd (*pot-fragment*). A piece of broken pottery, Prov. xxvi. 23.

Pŏt'tage (*pot-cooked*). A thick stew of meat or vegetables, or both, Gen. xxv. 29; 2 Kgs. iv. 39.

Pŏt'ter's Field. The burial-ground for strangers, outside of Jerusalem, bought with the betrayal money, Matt. xxvii. 7. [ACELDAMA.]

Pŏt'ter y (*pot-ware*). A very ancient art and carried to great perfection. Vessels variously moulded, and often elaborately decorated. The ceramic art furnishes many valuable contributions to ancient history, Gen. xxiv. 14; 1 Chr. iv. 23; Isa. xli. 25; Jer. xviii. 3.

Pound (*weight*). A weight; the maneh, 1 Kgs. x. 17; Ez. ii. 69; Neh. vii. 71. One sixtieth of a Grecian talent, Luke xix. 13–27.

Præ-tō'rĭ-um (*governor's headquarters*). The court, hearing-hall, and judgment-hall, of a Roman governor, wherever he might be, Matt. xxvii. 27; Mark xv. 16; John xviii. 28; Acts xxiii. 35; Phil. i. 13.

Prāy'er (*seeking favor*). Reverent petition to a divinity a universal custom. The Jews had three daily periods of prayer: 9 A. M., 12 M., 3 P. M., Ps. lv. 17; Dan. vi. 10.

Prĕs'ent. [GIFT.]

Prĭcks. [GOADS.]

Priest (*presbyter, elder*). Representative

of man in things appertaining to God. Assistants of Moses as mediator, Ex. xxiv. 5. Function of priesthood conferred on Levites, Ex. xxviii. Priests divided into regular courses, 1 Chr. xxiv. 1-19; 2 Chr. xxiii. 8; Luke i. 5.

Prĭnce (*first*). In Bible sense, patriarch, head of a family or chief of a tribe; governor or magistrate, 1 Kgs. xx. 14; satrap or ruler, Dan. vi. 1.

Prĭn″çi-păl′ĭ-ty. Territory of a prince. Seemingly an order of angels in Eph. i. 21; vi. 12; Col. i. 16; ii. 10.

Potter at Work. (*See* p. 87.)

Prĭs′cȧ (*ancient*), 2 Tim. iv. 19. [PRISCILLA.]

Prĭs-çĭl′lȧ (*little Prisca*). Wife of Aquila, Acts xviii. 2, 18, 26; Rom. xvi. 3.

Prĭ$\underset{\cdot}{s}$′on (*seizing*). Ward or lock-up, Lev. xxiv. 12; Num. xv. 34; well or pit, Gen. xxxvii. 24; Jer. xxxviii. 6-11; part of a palace, 2 Chr. xvi. 10; Jer. xxxii. 2; Acts xxiii. 10, 35.

Prŏch′o-rus (*choir leader*). One of the first seven deacons, Acts vi. 5.

Prō-cŏn′sul (*for a consul*). A Roman official, beneath a consul, who exercised authority in a province. Appointed by the senate, Acts xiii. 7; xix. 38.

Prŏc′ū-râ″tor (*caring for*). A Roman provincial officer, governor, or viceroy, appointed by the emperor, Matt. xxvii.; Acts xxiii. 24; xxvi. 30.

Prŏg-nŏs′tĭ-câ″tŏr (*knowing before*). Conjurer and fortune-teller, aided by the heavenly bodies, Isa. xlvii. 13.

Prŏph′et (*speaking beforehand*). Who tells the future under God's inspiration. The prophetic order embraced political, as well as spiritual, advisers and warners. The books of seventeen — four greater and thirteen lesser prophets — are comprised in the O. T. Christ is the prëeminent and eternal prophet, Luke xxiv. 27, 44.

Prŏs′ē-lȳte (*come to*). A convert to the Jewish faith. "Stranger" in O. T., Deut. x. 18, 19; Matt. xxiii. 15; Acts xiii. 43.

Prŏv′ērb (*for a word*). Wise utterance; enigma, Num. xxi. 27. The proverbs, collected and poetically arranged by Solomon, or by his authority, constitute the twentieth O. T. book.

Psălms (*play a stringed instrument*). In Hebrew, "Praises." The collection of one hundred and fifty lyrics which compose the nineteenth O. T. book. The liturgical hymnbook of the Hebrews, and accepted by early Christians. Authorship of seventy of them ascribed to David. The most perfect specimens of Hebrew poetry extant.

Psal′tēr-ȳ (*play on a stringed instrument*). A stringed instrument to accompany the voice, and supposed to resemble a guitar, 2 Sam. vi. 5; 2 Chr. ix. 11. The original frequently translated "viol," Isa. v. 12; xiv. 11.

Ptŏl″e-mæ′us, Ptŏl′ĕ-my. (1) The Ptolemies were a race of Egyptian kings sprung from Ptolemy Soter, who inherited that portion of the conquests of Alexander the Great. They are supposed to be alluded to in the visions of Daniel. Ptolemy I., Soter, B. C. 323-285, Dan. xi. 5. Ptolemy II., Philadelphus, B. C. 285-247, Dan. xi. 6. Ptolemy III., Euergetes, B. C. 247-222, Dan. xi. 7-9. Ptolemy IV., Philopator, B. C. 222-205, Dan. xi. 10-12. Ptolemy V., Epiphanes, B. C. 205-181, Dan. xi. 13-17. Ptolemy VI., Philometor, B. C. 181-146, Dan. xi. 25-30. Their kingdom fell under Rome. (2) Father of Lysimachus, Greek translator of Esther, Esth. xi. 1.

Ptŏl″e-mā′is, Acts xxi. 7. [ACCHO.]

Pū′ȧ, Num. xxvi. 23. [PHUVAH.]

Pū′ah (*mouth*). (1) Father of Tola, a judge of Israel, Judg. x. 1. (2) An Egyptian midwife, Ex. i. 15.

Pŭb′lĭ-can (*people's servant*). Gatherer of public revenue; tax-collector, abhorred by Jews, Matt. xviii. 17; Luke iii. 12, 13; xix. 2.

Pŭb′lĭ-us (*common*). Governor of the island of Melita, Acts xxviii. 7, 8.

Pū′den$\underset{\cdot}{s}$ (*modest*). A Roman Christian who saluted Timothy, 2 Tim. iv. 21.

Pū′hītes. A Judahite family, 1 Chr. ii. 53.

Pŭl (*lord*). (1) A possible African region, Isa. lxvi. 19. (2) A king of Assyria, 2 Kgs. xv. 19, 20.

Pŭlse (*pottage*). Peas, beans, lentils, etc., and, in a Hebrew sense, perhaps the cereals, Dan. i. 12-16.

Pŭn′ĭsh-ment (*pain*). Capital punishment was by hanging, 2 Sam. xxi. 6; stoning, Ex. xvii. 4; John x. 31; burning, Gen. xxxviii. 24; shooting, Ex. xix. 13; the sword, 1 Kgs. ii. 25; drowning, Matt. xviii. 6; sawing, 2 Sam. xii. 31; crucifixion. The death penalty was inflicted for parental reviling, blasphemy, adultery, rape, idolatry, perjury. Secondary punishments were generally those of retaliation, an "eye for an eye," etc., Ex. xxi. 23-25; Deut. xix. 18-21.

Pū′nītes. Descendants of Phuvah, or Pua, Num. xxvi. 23.

Pū′non (*darkness*). A desert encampment, Num. xxxiii. 42.

Pū″rĭ-fĭ-cā′tion (*cleansing*). A ritualistic form and sanitary precaution among Hebrews, Lev. xiv. 4-32; Mark vii. 3, 4; John xi. 55.

Pū′rim (*lots*). The Jewish festival commemorative of the preservation of the Jews in Persia. Celebrated yearly on 14th and 15th of the month Adar, Esth. iii. 7; ix. 20-32.

Pŭt, 1 Chr. i. 8. [PHUT.]

Pū-tē′o-lī (*sulphurous wells*). Now Pozzuoli, seaport of Campania, on Bay of Naples, Acts xxviii. 13.

Pŭ′tĭ-el (*afflicted*). Father-in-law of Eleazar, Ex. vi. 25.

Pȳ′garg (*white-rumped*). A species of antelope, Deut. xiv. 5.

Pўr′rhus. Father of Sopater, in R. V., Acts xx. 4.

Pў′thon (*serpent*). Pythian Apollo, Acts xvi. 16 marg.

Q

Quāils (*quackers*). Quails of the Old World species, *Coturnix coturnix*, abound in the Arabian desert, and migrate northward, in spring, in enormous flocks, Ex. xvi. 13; Num. xi. 31, 32; Ps. cv. 40.

Quăr′tus (*fourth*). A Christian at Corinth, Rom. xvi. 23.

Quă-tĕr′nĭ-on (*file of four*). A Roman guard of four soldiers, two of whom watched prisoners within the door, and two watched the door outside, Acts xii. 4-10.

dren of Ammon, in Deut. iii. 11; 2 Sam. xii. 26; xvii. 27; Jer. xlix. 2; Ezek. xxi. 20. (2) Town in Judah, Josh. xv. 60.

Răb′bath=am′mŏn. [RABBAH.]

Răb′bath=mō′ab. [AR.]

Răb′bī (*my master*). A title of respect applied to Hebrew doctors and teachers. Applied also to priests, and to Christ, Matt. xxiii. 7; Mark ix. 5; John i. 38. Rabboni in John xx. 16.

Răb′bĭth (*many*). Town in Issachar, Josh. xix. 20.

Răb-bō′nī, John xx. 16. [RABBI.]

Răb′=măg (*chief of magi*). An important office at the court of Babylonia, Jer. xxxix. 3, 13.

Răb′sa-rĭs (*chief of eunuchs*). (1) An Assyrian general, 2 Kgs. xviii. 17. (2) A Babylonian prince, Jer. xxxix. 3, 13.

Puteoli. (*See* p. 88.)

Quēen (*woman*). The three Hebrew words so rendered imply a queen-regnant, queen-consort, and queen-mother, with a dignity very like that of the present day, 1 Kgs. ii. 19; x. 1; xv. 13; Esth. i. 9; ii. 17, Jer. xiii. 18, xxix. 2.

Quēen of Heaven. The moon, worshipped as Astoreth or Astarte by idolatrous Hebrews, Jer. vii. 18; xliv. 17-25.

Quĭck′sănds. The Syrtis, greater and lesser. Two dangerous sandbanks or shoals off the north coast of Africa between Carthage and Cyrene, Acts xxvii. 17.

Quĭv′er (*cover*). Case or cover for arrows, Gen. xxvii. 3; Job xxxix. 23.

R

Rā′a-mah (*shaking*). Son of Cush, and father of a trading tribe on the Persian Gulf, Gen. x. 7; Ezek. xxvii. 22.

Rā′′a-mī′ah (*God's thunder*). A chief who returned, Neh. vii. 7. Reelaiah, Ez. ii. 2.

Ra-ăm′sēs, Ex. i. 11. [RAMESES.]

Răb′bah (*great*). (1) A strong Ammonite city east of Jordan; rebuilt by Ptolemy Philadelphus, B. C. 285-247, and called Philadelphia, Josh. xiii. 25; 2 Sam. xi. 1; xii. 27-29; 1 Chr. xx. 1. Rabbath-ammon, *i. e.*, Rabbath of the Ammonites, or of the chil-

Răb′sha-keh (*cup bearer*). An Assyrian general, 2 Kgs. xviii. 17-37; xix.; Isa. xxxvi.

Rā′cȧ (*worthless*). A Hebrew term of contempt and reproach, Matt. v. 22.

Rāce (*rush*). As a public game, not patronized by Hebrews. A favorite game with Greeks and Romans, 1 Cor. ix. 24; Heb. xii. 1.

Rā′chăb. Greek form of Rahab, Matt. i. 5.

Rā′chăl (*trade*). A town in southern Judah, 1 Sam. xxx. 29.

Rā′chel (*ewe*). Daughter of Laban, wife of Jacob, and mother of Joseph and Benjamin, Gen. xxix.-xxxv.

Răd′da-ī (*trampling*). Brother of David, 1 Chr. ii. 14.

Rā′gau. (1) Judith i. 5. [RAGES.] (2) Luke iii. 35. [REU.]

Rā′ġēs. City in Media, Tob. i. 14.

Ra-gū′el (*friend of God*). (1) A priest, or prince, of Midian, Num. x. 29. Reuel in Ex. ii. 18. (2) Father-in-law of Tobias, Tob. iii. 7.

Rā′hăb (*large*). (1) The harlot of Jericho who received the spies, and married Salmon, Josh. ii. 1-21; vi. 17-25; Ruth iv. 21; Matt. i. 5. (2) Symbolical term for Egypt, implying insolence and violence, Ps. lxxxix. 10; Isa. li. 9.

Rā′hăm (*belly*). A descendant of Caleb, 1 Chr. ii. 44.

Ra͞'hel, Jer. xxxi. 15. [RACHEL.]

Ra͞in. The early rains of Palestine fall in October, in time for seeding; the later, in April, in time for fruits. May to October is the dry season, Deut. xi. 14; Hos. vi. 3; Joel ii. 23.

Ra͞in'bo͞w. A sign of the covenant that the earth should not again be destroyed by water, Gen. ix. 12-17.

Ra͞'kem (*flower culture*). Descendant of Manasseh, 1 Chr. vii. 16.

Răk'kăth (*coast*). A fenced city in Naphtali, Josh. xix. 35.

Răk'kŏn (*void*). Town in Dan, near Joppa, Josh. xix. 46.

Răm (*high*). (1) A Judahite, 1 Chr. ii. 9. Aram, Matt. i. 3, 4; Luke iii. 33. (2) Son of Jerahmeel, 1 Chr. ii. 25. (3) Kinsman of Elihu, Job xxxii. 2.

Răm (*strong*). (1) Male of the sheep, or any ovine species, Gen. xxii. 13. (2) The battering-ram for breaking down gates and walls, Ezek. iv. 2; xxi. 22.

Quail. (*See* p. 89.)

Ra͞'må, Matt. ii. 18. [RAMAH.]

Ra͞'mah (*height*). (1) City in Benjamin, near Jerusalem, Josh. xviii. 25; 1 Kgs. xv. 17-22. Point of departure for Jewish captives, Jer. xxxix. 8-12; xl. 1. (2) Birthplace of Samuel, 1 Sam. i. 19; vii. 17. (3) A border place of Asher, Josh. xix. 29. (4) Town in Naphtali, Josh. xix. 36. (5) Ramoth-gilead, 2 Kgs. viii. 28, 29. (6) A place repeopled by returned captives, Neh. xi. 33.

Ra͞"math-a͞'im=zo͞'phim (*two watch-towers*). Full form of the town in which Samuel was born, 1 Sam. i. 1. [RAMAH, 2.]

Răm'ă-them. A part of Samaria added to Judea, 1 Macc. xi. 34.

Ra͞'math-īte. Dweller in Ramah, 1 Chr. xxvii. 27.

Ra͞'math=le͞'hī (*hill of the jaw bone*). Where Samson slew the Philistines, Judg. xv. 17.

Ra͞'math=mĭz'peh (*watch-tower hill*). A border town of Gad, Josh. xiii. 26.

Ra͞'math of the South. A border place of Simeon, Josh. xix. 8; 1 Sam. xxx. 27.

Rȧ-me͞'se͞s, Rȧ-ăm'se͞s (*sun-born*). Country and city in lower Egypt, associated with Goshen; the city being the capital, and one of the Pharaohs' store-cities, located on the Pelusiac mouth of the Nile, Gen. xlvii. 11; Ex. i. 11; xii. 37; Num. xxxiii. 3, 5.

Rȧ-mī'ah (*exaltion*). One who had taken a foreign wife, Ez. x. 25.

Ra͞'moth (*high*). A son of Bani, Ez. x. 29.

Ra͞'moth=gĭl'e-ăd (*heights of Gilead*). An ancient Amorite stronghold east of Jordan, and chief city of Gad. Both a Levitical city and city of refuge. Centre of one of Solomon's commissary districts, Deut. iv. 43; Josh. xx. 8; xxi. 38; 1 Kgs. iv. 13.

Răm's Hôrns, Josh. vi. 4-20. [CORNET.]

Ra͞'phȧ (*tall*). (1) A Benjamite, 1 Chr. viii. 2. (2) A descendant of Saul, 1 Chr. viii. 37.

Ra͞'phȧ-el (*God's healer*). One of the seven holy angels, Tob. xii. 15.

Răph'ȧ-im. An ancestor of Judith, Judith viii. 1.

Ra͞'phŏn. A city in Gilead, 1 Macc. v. 37.

Ra͞'phu (*healed*). Father of the Benjamite spy, Num. xiii. 9.

Răs'ses. A land ravaged by Holofernes, Judith ii. 23.

Rȧ-thu͞'mus, 1 Esdr. ii. 16. [REHUM.]

Ra͞'ven (*seizer*). An unclean bird of the crow (*corvus*) family. Translation much disputed, Lev. xi. 15; 1 Kgs. xvii. 6; S. of Sol. v. 11.

Ra͞'zis. An elder at Jerusalem, 2 Macc. xiv. 37-46.

Ra͞'zor (*scraper*). Known to and much used by Hebrews. Levites shaved the entire body, Lev. xiv. 8; Num. vi. 9, 18; viii. 7; Judg. xiii. 5; Acts xviii. 18.

Re͞"a-ī'ȧ (*seen of God*). A Reubenite prince, 1 Chr. v. 5.

Re͞"a-ī'ah (*seen of God*). (1) A Judahite, 1 Chr. iv. 2. (2) His children returned, Ez. ii. 47; Neh. vii. 50.

Re͞'bȧ (*fourth*). A Midianite king slain by Israel, Num. xxxi. 8; Josh. xiii. 21.

Rē-bĕc'cȧ. Greek form of Rebekah, Rom. ix. 10.

Rē-bĕk'ah (*snare*). Wife of Isaac and mother of Jacob and Esau, Gen. xxii. 23; xxiv.-xxviii.; xlix. 31.

Re͞'chăb (*horseman*). (1) Father of Jehonadab, 2 Kgs. x. 15, 23; 1 Chr. ii. 55. (2) A traitorous captain under Ishbosheth, 2 Sam. iv. 2, 5-9. (3) Father of Malchiah, an assistant wall-builder, Neh. iii. 14.

Re͞'chab-ītes. Kenite or Midianite descendants of Rechab, 1 Chr. ii. 55, who became an order or sect — said to still exist near Mecca — whose tenets were abstinence from wine, tent habitations only, freedom from agricultural labor, Jer. xxxv. 2-19.

Re͞'chah (*uttermost*). Place unknown, 1 Chr. iv. 12.

Rē-côr'der (*record keeper*). The high and responsible office of annalist and royal counselor in the Hebrew state, 2 Sam. viii. 16; xx. 24; 1 Kgs. iv. 3; 1 Chr. xviii. 15.

Rē-de͞em' (*buying back*). In O. T., buying back a forfeited estate. Metaphorically, freeing from bondage, Ex. vi. 6; Isa. xliii. 1. In N. T., rescuing or ransoming from sin and its consequences, Matt. xx. 28; Gal. iii. 13; 1 Pet. i. 18.

Rĕd Se͞a. The arm of Gulf of Aden which separates Egypt from Arabia. "The sea," Ex. xiv. 2, 9, 16, 21, 28; xv. 1-19; Josh. xxiv. 6, 7. "Egyptian sea," Isa. xi. 15. "Sea of *Suph*," *weedy* or *reedy sea*, translated "Red Sea," Ex. x. 19; xiii. 18; xv. 4; xxiii. 31; Num. xxi. 4. In N. T., the Greek "Erythrean," or Red Sea, Acts vii. 36. At its head it separates into gulfs of Akaba and Suez, the latter of which the Israelites crossed.

Reed (*rod*). Used generically for the tall grasses, sedges, flags, or rushes which grow in marshy soils. Applied to various uses by Hebrews, and source of frequent metaphor, 2 Kgs. xviii. 21; Job xl. 21; Isa. xix. 6; Ezek. xxix. 6; Matt. xi. 7; xii. 20; xxvii. 29.

Re″el-ā′iah, Ez. ii. 2. [RAAMIAH.]

Re-fi′ner (*who makes fine*). A worker in precious metals, Isa. i. 25; Jer. vi. 29; Mal. iii. 3.

Ref′uge, Cities of. The six Levitical cities set apart for the temporary escape of involuntary manslayers, Num. xxxv. 6, 11-32; Deut. xix. 7-9; Josh. xx. 2-8. [CITY.]

Re′gem (*friend*). A descendant of Caleb, 1 Chr. ii. 47.

Four-horned Ram. (*See* p. 90.)

Re′gem-me′lech (*royal friend*). A messenger sent by captive Jews to inquire about the ritual, Zech. vii. 2.

Re-gen″er-ā′tion (*begetting again*). The renovation of the world at and after the second coming of Christ, Matt. xix. 28. The new birth from the Holy Spirit, Tit. iii. 5.

Re″ha-bi′ah (*enlarged*). Only son of Eliezer, 1 Chr. xxiii. 17.

Re′hob (*breadth*). (1) Father of Hadadezer, king of Zobah, 2 Sam. viii. 3, 12. (2) A co-covenanter, Neh. x. 11. (3) Spot where the journey of the spies ended, Num. xiii. 21; 2 Sam. x. 8. Beth-rehob in 2 Sam. x. 6. (4) Place in Asher, Josh. xix. 28. (5) A Levitical town in Asher, Josh. xix. 30.

Re″ho-bo′am (*emancipator*). Son of Solomon, 1 Kgs. xi. 43; xiv. 21, and successor to his father's throne, B. C. 975-958. During his reign the ten tribes, under Jeroboam, revolted and set up the kingdom of Israel. Shishak, of Egypt, captured Jerusalem from him, 1 Kgs. xiv. 21-31.

Re-ho′both (*places*). (1) A city of Assyria founded by Asher or Nimrod, Gen. x. 11, 12. (2) A city on the Euphrates, home of Shaul or Saul, an early Edomite king, Gen. xxxvi. 37; 1 Chr. i. 48. (3) The third well dug by Isaac. It is located south of Beersheba, Gen. xxvi. 22.

Re′hum (*merciful*). Levites and returned captives, Ez. ii. 2; iv. 8, 9, 17, 23; Neh. iii. 17; x. 25; xii. 3. Nehum in Neh. vii. 7, and Harim in xii. 15.

Re′i (*friendly*). A friend of David, 1 Kgs. i. 8.

Reins (*kidneys*). Once believed to be the seat of emotions; hence coupled with the heart, Ps. vii. 9; xvi. 7; Jer. xvii. 10; xx. 12.

Re′kem (*flowered*). (1) A Midianite king slain by the Israelites, Num. xxxi. 8; Josh. xiii. 21. (2) Son of Hebron, 1 Chr. ii. 43, 44. (3) Town in Benjamin, Josh. xviii. 27.

Rem″a-li′ah (*God-exalted*). Father of Pekah, king of Israel, 2 Kgs. xv. 25-37.

Re′meth (*height*). Town in Issachar, Josh. xix. 21.

Rem′mon (*pomegranate*). Town in Simeon. Properly Rimmon, Josh. xix. 7.

Rem′mon-meth′o-ar (*Remmon to Neah*). A landmark of Zebulun, Josh. xix. 13.

Rem′phan. An idol worshipped secretly by the Israelites in the wilderness, Acts vii. 43. Rephan in R. V. Chiun, Amos v. 26.

Re′pha-el (*God-healed*). A Levite porter, 1 Chr. xxvi. 7.

Re′phah (*wealth*). An Ephraimite, 1 Chr. vii. 25.

Reph″a-i′ah (*God-healed*). (1) Descendant of David, 1 Chr. iii. 21. (2) A Simeonite chief, 1 Chr. iv. 42. (3) Descendant of Issachar, 1 Chr. vii. 2. (4) Descendant of Saul, 1 Chr. ix. 43. Rapha in viii. 37. (5) A wall-repairer and ruler of half of Jerusalem, Neh. iii. 9.

Reph′a-im (*giants*). (1) A giant race east of Jordan, and probably driven to the west side, Gen. xiv. 5; xv. 20. (2) "Valley of Rephaim" was a landmark of Judah, and supposably the valley stretching from Jerusalem to Bethlehem, Josh. xv. 8; 2 Sam. v. 18; Isa. xvii. 5.

Reph′i-dim (*rests*). Last Israelite encampment before Sinai, Ex. xvii. 1, 8-16; xix. 2.

Re′sen (*bridle*). An Assyrian city built by Asher or Nimrod, Gen. x. 12.

Re′sheph (*fire*). A descendant of Ephraim, 1 Chr. vii. 25.

Res″ur-rec′tion (*rising again*). The rising again from the dead, Ps. xvi. 10, 11; Matt. xvi. 21; xx. 19; Acts ii. 31.

Re′u (*friend*). Son of Peleg, Gen. xi. 18-21.

Reu′ben (*behold a son!*). Eldest son of Jacob and Leah, Gen. xxix. 32. Lost his birthright through crime, Gen. xxxv. 22; xlix. 3, 4. Tribe numerous and pastoral, and settled east of Jordan, Num. i. 20, 21; Josh. xiii. 15-23. Idolatrous, averse to war, carried captive by Assyria, Judg. v. 15, 16; 1 Chr. v. 26.

Reu′ben-ites. Descendants of Reuben, Num. xxvi. 7; Josh. i. 12; 1 Chr. v. 26.

Reu′el (*God's friend*). (1) A son of Esau, Gen. xxxvi. 4, 10, 13, 17. (2) Ex. ii. 18. [RAGUEL.] (3) Father of Eliasaph the Gadite leader, Num. ii. 14. (4) A Benjamite, 1 Chr. ix. 8.

Reu′mah (*lofty*). Nahor's concubine, Gen. xxii. 24.

Rev″e-lā′tion (*veil drawn back*). (1) Scripturally, revealing truth through divine agency or by supernatural means, 2 Cor. xii. 1-7. (2) Book of Revelation, or Apocalypse; last of N. T. books; written by the Apostle John, about A. D. 95-97, probably at Ephesus. It is a record of his inspired visions while a prisoner on the island of Patmos. Its aim is much disputed, but it is seemingly a prophetic panorama of church history to the end of time.

Re′zeph (*heated stone*). An unknown place, 2 Kgs. xix. 12; Isa. xxxvii. 12.

Rē-zī'á (*delight*). An Asherite, 1 Chr. vii. 39.

Rē'zin (*firm*). (1) A king of Syria or Damascus, 2 Kgs. xv. 37; xvi. 5–9; Isa. vii. 1–8; viii. 6; ix. 11. (2) His descendants returned, Ez. ii. 48; Neh. vii. 50.

Rē'zon (*prince*). A Syrian who set up a petty kingdom at Damascus, 1 Kgs. xi. 23–25.

Rhē'ġī-um (*breach*). Now Rheggio, port and capital of Calabria, southern Italy, Acts xxviii. 13.

Rhē'sȧ (*head*). One mentioned in Christ's genealogy, Luke iii. 27.

Rhō'dȧ (*rose*). A maid in the house of Mary, mother of John Mark, Acts xii. 12–15.

Rhōdes (*roses*). An Ægean island, just off the coast of Asia Minor. Noted for the splendor of its capital city, Rhodes. Paul touched there, Acts xxi. 1.

Rhŏd'o-cus. A traitorous Jew, 2 Macc. xiii. 21.

Rhō'dus, 1 Macc. xv. 23. [Rhodes.]

Rī'bāi (*pleader*). Father of Ittai, one of David's guard, 2 Sam. xxiii. 29; 1 Chr. xi. 31.

Rĭb'lah (*fertile*). An ancient strategic city on N. E. frontier of Canaan, and on military route from Palestine to Babylonia, Num. xxxiv. 11; 2 Kgs. xxiii. 33; xxv. 6–21; Jer. xxxix. 5–7.

Rĭd'dle (*counsel*). Oriental peoples fond of riddles. Hebrew riddles embraced proverbs, Prov. i. 6; oracles, Num. xii. 8; songs, Ps. xlix. 4; parables, Ezek. xvii. 2; intricate sentences, questions, and problems, Judg. xiv. 12–14; 1 Kgs. x. 1; 2 Chr. ix. 1; Dan. viii. 23.

Rĭm'mŏn (*pomegranate*). (1) Father of Ishbosheth's murderers, 2 Sam. iv. 2–9. (2) A Syrian deity worshipped at Damascus, 2 Kgs. v. 18. (3) Levitical city in Zebulun, 1 Chr. vi. 77. Remmon-methoar, Josh. xix. 13. (4) Town in Judah and Simeon, Josh. xv. 32. (5) A rock or fastness, now Rummon, 10 miles north of Jerusalem, to which the defeated Benjamites retreated, Judg. xx. 45, 47; xxi. 13.

Rĭm'mon-pā'rez (*pomegranates of the wrath*). A desert encampment, Num. xxxiii. 19.

Rĭng (*around*). Rings were indispensable articles of Jewish ornament. Worn on fingers, wrists, ankles, in ears and nostrils, Isa. iii. 20, 21; Luke xv. 22; Jas. ii. 2. Symbols of authority, Gen. xli. 42; Esth. iii. 10. Used as seals, Esth. iii. 12; Dan. vi. 17.

Rings.

Rĭn'nah (*song*). A Judahite, 1 Chr. iv. 20.

Rī'phăth (*spoken*). Son of Gomer, and founder of a northern nation, Gen. x. 3; 1 Chr. i. 6.

Rĭs'sah (*ruin*). A desert encampment of the Israelites, Num. xxxiii. 21, 22.

Rĭth'mah (*bush*). A desert encampment of the Israelites, Num. xxxiii. 18, 19.

Rĭv'ĕr (*banked*). In Hebrew sense, a large flowing stream, rivulet, ravine, valley, or wady. "River of Egypt" is the Nile, Gen. xv. 18; Num. xxxiv. 5; Josh. xv. 4, 47; 1 Kgs. viii. 65; 2 Kgs. xxiv. 7. "The river" is the Euphrates, Gen. xxxi. 21; Ex. xxiii. 31.

Rĭz'pah. Concubine of Saul, and the mother who watched over the remains of her slain sons, 2 Sam. iii. 7; xxi. 8–11.

Rōad (*ride*). In Bible sense, a path or way. For "road" in 1 Sam. xxvii. 10, read "raid" or "inroad."

Rŏb'bĕr-ȳ (*breaking, riving*). Oppression, pillage, and thievery formed almost an employment among nomad tribes, Gen. xvi. 12; Judg. ii. 14; Luke x. 30; John xviii. 40.

Ro-bō'am. Greek form of Rehoboam, Matt. i. 7.

Rŏd. Shoot or branch. Figuratively, Christ, Isa. xi. 1; root, Ps. lxxiv. 2; Jer. x. 16; support, Ps. xxiii. 4; authority, Ps. ii. 9; affliction, Job ix. 34; tithing-rod, Ezek. xx. 37.

Rōe, Rōe'bŭck (*animal*). A beautiful fleet animal, probably the roe-deer of Western Asia; but associated with antelope and gazelle, 2 Sam. ii. 18; 1 Chr. xii. 8; S. of Sol. ii. 17; viii. 14.

Rō-gē'lim (*fullers*). Home of Barzillai, in Gilead, 2 Sam. xvii. 27.

Rŏh'gah (*clamor*). A chief of Asher, 1 Chr. vii. 34.

Rōll (*little wheel*). The book of ancient times, consisting of long strips of linen, papyrus, or parchment written upon and wrapped on a stick, Isa. viii. 1; Ezek. ii. 9, 10.

Rō-măm'tī-ē'zĕr. One of Heman's fourteen sons, 1 Chr. xxv. 4, 31.

Rōme, Rō'mans. First mentioned in Bible in 1 Macc. i. 10, when Rome was pushing her conquests in Palestine and Syria. The capital, Rome, is on the Tiber, about 15 miles from the sea. Founded B. C. 752. Governed by kings till B. C. 509; then by consuls till Augustus Cæsar became emperor, B. C. 30. At the Christian era Rome was virtual mistress of the civilized world. Empire declined rapidly after removal of capital to Constantinople by Constantine, A. D. 328. Gospel early introduced among Romans, but Christians persecuted till time of Constantine. Palestine was ruled from Rome by kings, procurators, governors, or proconsuls. Paul wrote his celebrated epistle to the Romans from Corinth, about A. D. 58, to show that Jew and Gentile were alike subject to sin and in equal need of justification and sanctification.

Roof. [House.]

Room (*wide*). Frequently used in N. T. for spot, seat, place, as at table, Matt. xxiii. 6; Mark xii. 39; Luke xiv. 7; xx. 46.

Rōse (*ruddy*). Disputed translation. Some say narcissus is meant; others would simply read "flower" for "rose," S. of Sol. ii. 1; Isa. xxxv. 1.

Rŏsh (*head*). A Benjamite, Gen. xlvi. 21.

Rŏs'in (*resin*). The resin left after turpentine is distilled. But in Bible naphtha is meant, Ezek. xxvii. 17 marg.; Song of Three Children, 23.

Ru'bȳ (*red*). A ruddy, valuable gem; but the original word is thought to mean coral or pearl, Job xxviii. 18; Prov. iii. 15.

Rue (*thick-leaved*). A shrubby, medicinal plant, cultivated in the gardens of the east. Tithable, Luke xi. 42.

Ru'fus (*red*). Son of Simon of Cyrene, Mark xv. 21. Probably the same in Rom. xvi. 13.

Ru'ha-mah (*having received mercy*). A symbolical name used in Hos. ii. 1.

Ru'mah (*high*). A place, 2 Kgs. xxiii. 36, associated with Arumah and Dumah.

Rŭsh (*reed*). [Reed.]

Ruth (*beauty*). The Moabite wife of Mahlon and Boaz. The beautiful pastoral of Ruth, 8th of O. T. books, contains her life. It supplements Judges and prefaces Samuel, and traces the lineage of David. Time of writing and authorship are unknown.

Rȳe. Not an Egyptian cereal. "Spelt" is doubtless meant, it being a common Egyptian food, Ex. ix. 32; Isa. xxviii. 25. Same Hebrew word is rendered "fitches" in Ezek. iv. 9.

S

Să″băch-thā′nī (*hast thou forsaken me?*). An Aramaic, or Syro-Chaldaic, word, part of Christ's exclamation on the cross, Matt. xxvii. 46; Mark xv. 34. [Eli.]

Săb′a-ōth (*hosts*). Used usually with Jehovah, — "Lord of hosts;" — hosts being comprehensive, and signifying the powers of earth and heaven, Isa. i. 9; Rom. ix. 29; Jas. v. 4.

Roman Warriors. (*See* p. 92.)

Sā′bat (*around*). (1) His sons were returned captives, 1 Esdr. v. 34. (2) 1 Macc. xvi. 14. [Sebat.]

Săb′băth (*rest*). Rest day, or seventh of the week, Gen. ii. 2, 3. Became a Mosaic institution for rest and festal occasions, Ex. xvi. 23-30; xx. 8-11; Lev. xix. 3, 30; xxiii. 3; xxv. 4-9; Deut. v. 12-15. Day for consulting prophets, 2 Kgs. iv. 23. A day of teaching and joy, Neh. viii. 1-12; Hos. ii. 11. A whole week of time is implied in Matt. xxviii. 1; Mark xvi. 1; Luke xxiv. 1; John xx. 1; Acts xx. 7; 1 Cor. xvi. 2. Among Christians, the day after the Hebrew Sabbath, or seventh-day, gradually and till fully established, became the Sabbath, or first-day, in commemoration of the resurrection of Christ. Hence, "The Lord's Day," John xx. 26; Acts xx. 6-11; 1 Cor. xvi. 2; Rev. i. 10.

Săb′băth Day's Journey. Travel on the Sabbath was limited, Ex. xvi. 29. Custom seemed to sanction 2000 paces from the walls of a city as sufficient for all needs on the day of rest, Acts i. 12.

Săb″ba-thē′us, 1 Esdr. ix. 14. [Shabbethai.]

Săb-băt′ĭ-cal Year. By the Mosaic code, each seventh year was sacred. The land rested, the poor were entitled to what grew, and debtors were released, Ex. xxiii. 10, 11; Lev. xxv. 2-7; Deut. xv. 1-18.

Săb-bē′us, 1 Esdr. ix. 32. [Shemaiah.]

Sā-bē′ans. (1) Descendants of Sheba, son of Joktan, Joel iii. 8. (2) Evidently the descendants of Seba, son of Cush, Isa. xlv. 14. (3) Perhaps a third tribe, though it may be one of the two just mentioned. (4) A wrong translation in Ezek. xxiii. 42, "drunkards," in margin.

Sā′bī, 1 Esdr. v. 34. [Zebaim.]

Săb′tȧ, Săb′tȧh (*striking*). Third son of Cush, Gen. x. 7; 1 Chr. i. 9.

Săb′te-chȧ, Săb′te-chȧh (*striking*). Fifth son of Cush, Gen. x. 7; 1 Chr. i. 9.

Sā′car (*hire*). (1) Father of one of David's warriors, 1 Chr. xi. 35. Sharar in 2 Sam. xxiii. 33. (2) A Levite porter, 1 Chr. xxvi. 4.

Săck′bŭt (*pull and push*). A wind instrument, trombone. But in Dan. iii. 5-15, a stringed instrument of triangular shape with from four to twenty strings.

Săck′cloth (*coarse cloth*). A coarse, goat-hair cloth used for making sacks and rough garments. The latter were worn next the skin by mourners and repentants, Gen. xxxvii. 34; xlii. 25; 2 Sam. iii. 31; 1 Kgs. xxi. 27; 2 Kgs. vi. 30; Esth. iv. 1, 2; Job xvi. 15; Rev. vi. 12.

Săc′rĭ-fīçe (*making sacred*). Propitiatory, atoning or thanksgiving offering to God. An ordained rite, Lev. xvii. 4-9; Deut. xvi. 5-19. Sacrificial offerings numerous; but chiefly, the "burnt-offering," Lev. i. 1-17; "sin-offering," and "trespass-offering," Lev. vii. 1-10; "peace-offering," Lev. vii. 11-34; the latter also a "freewill" offering. Among Christians all sacrificial offerings merged in the universal offering of Christ's body, Heb. ix., x.

Săd″a-mī′as, 2 Esdr. i. 1. [Shallum.]

Sā′das, 1 Esdr. v. 13. [Iddo.]

Săd′du-çees (*disciples of Zadok*). A Jewish sect, supposably Zadokites, 1 Kgs. i. 32-45, whose chief tenets were (1) rejection of the divinity of the Mosaic oral law and traditions; (2) rejection of the later O. T. books, but acceptance of the Mosaic teachings; (3) denial of angel and spiritual existence, and consequent immortality of the soul; (4) belief in the absolute moral freedom of man. Their hatred of Christianity was as bitter as that of the Pharisees, Matt. iii. 7; Mark xii. 18; Luke xx. 27; Acts iv. 1; v. 17; xxiii. 6-10. Though composed of men of position, the sect was never very numerous nor influential, and it disappeared from history after the first century of the Christian era.

Sā′dŏc (*just*). (1) 2 Esdr. i. 1. [Zadok.] (2) One in the genealogy of Christ, Matt. i. 14.

Săf′fron (*yellow*). The fall crocus, much cultivated in the Orient for its perfume and medicinal properties, S. of Sol. iv. 14.

Sāint (*sanctified*). In O. T., a pious Jew, Ps. xvi. 3. In N. T., a Christian believer, Rom. i. 7; viii. 27; Heb. vi. 10.

Sā′lȧ, Sā′lah (*sprout*). A descendant of Shem, Gen. x. 24; xi. 12-15; Luke iii. 35. Shelah in 1 Chr. i. 18, 24.

Săl′a-mis (*shaken*). A city of the island of Cyprus, visited by Paul. It was afterwards called Constantia, Acts xiii. 5. The old city was once the capital of the island and carried on a large trade in fruit, wine, flax, and copper with adjacent continents. The Jewish population was large. Its site is now traced by masses of ruins.

Sā-lā′thĭ-el (*asked of God*). Son of Jechonias, 1 Chr. iii. 17; Matt. i. 12; Luke iii. 27. Shealtiel elsewhere.

Săl'cah, Săl'chah (*moving*). A city in Bashan which fell to Manasseh. Now Sulkhad, Deut. iii. 10; Josh. xii. 5; xiii. 11; 1 Chr. v. 11.

Sā'lem (*peace*). The place over which Melchizedek was king, supposably Jerusalem, Gen. xiv. 18; Ps. lxxvi. 2; Heb. vii. 1, 2.

Sā'lim (*peace*). The place near Ænon, where John baptized, John iii. 23.

Săl'la-ī (*basket-maker*). (1) A returned Benjamite, Neh. xi. 8. (2) A returned priest, Neh. xii. 20.

Săl'lu (*measured*). (1) A Benjamite, 1 Chr. ix. 7. (2) A priest, Neh. xi. 7; xii. 7.

Săl-lū'mus, 1 Esdr. ix. 25. [SHALLUM.]

Săl'mȧ, Săl'mŏn (*clothed*). (1) Father of Boaz and husband of Rahab, Ruth iv. 20, 21; 1 Chr. ii. 11; Matt. i. 5; Luke iii. 32. (2) One of the high hills surrounding Shechem, which afforded pasturage for Jacob's flocks, Ps. lxviii. 14. Zalmon in Judg. ix. 48.

Săl-mō'ne (*clothed*). Eastern promontory of Crete, Acts xxvii. 7.

Sā'lŏm. (1) Bar. i. 7. [SHALLUM.] (2) 1 Macc. ii. 26. [SALLU.]

Sȧ-lō'me (*clothed*). (1) Wife of Zebedee, Mark xv. 40; xvi. 1. Mentioned indirectly in Matt. xx. 20-22; xxvii. 56. (2) The daughter of Herodias, who danced before Herod, Matt. xiv. 6; Mark vi. 22.

Salt (*sea product*). Abundant in Palestine. Used with food and sacrificial offerings, Job vi. 6; Lev. ii. 13; Num. xviii. 19; Mark ix. 49. Monument of divine displeasure, Gen. xix. 26; token of indissoluble alliance, Lev. ii. 13; Num. xviii. 19; 2 Chr. xiii. 5; used to rub new-born children, Ezek. xvi. 4; type of maintenance, Ez. iv. 14 marg.; emblem of sterility, Judg. ix. 45; Jer. xvii. 6; a manure, Luke xiv. 35; emblem of holy life and conversation, Matt. v. 13; Mark ix. 50; Col. iv. 6.

Salt, City of. Fifth of the six cities of Judah, situate in the wilderness of Judah, Josh. xv. 62.

Salt Sēa. The Dead Sea. "Sea of the plain," Deut. iv. 49; 2 Kgs. xiv. 25. "Salt sea," Deut. iii. 17; Josh. iii. 16; xii. 3. "East sea," Ezek. xlvii. 18; Joel ii. 20; Zech. xiv. 8. "The sea," Ezek. xlvii. 8. "Vale of Siddim," Gen. xiv. 3. "Sodomitish sea," 1 Esdr. v. 7. Title "Dead Sea" not found among Hebrew writers, but introduced by Greek authors. Situate 16 miles E. of Jerusalem; 46 miles long by 10 wide; 1300 feet below the level of the Mediterranean; waters intensely salt; receives waters of Jordan from the north; no outlet.

Salt, Văl'ley of. Supposably the valley, or depression, of Akabah, extending from Dead Sea to Gulf of Akabah, 2 Sam. viii. 13; 2 Kgs. xiv. 7; 1 Chr. xviii. 12; 2 Chr. xxv. 11; Ps. lx. title. But many excellent authorities limit it to a section of Edom near Petra.

Sā'lu (*weighed*). Father of Zimri, a chief of Simeon, Num. xxv. 14.

Sā'lum, 1 Esdr. v. 28. [SHALLUM.]

Săl''ū-tā'tion (*good health, greeting*). Personal salutation very formal in East. The "peace be with thee," or similar expression, was accompanied by a profound bow, kiss, embrace, or other courtesy, Gen. xix. 1; 1 Sam. xxv. 23; Matt. x. 12; Luke i. 41. Epistolary salutation took the form found in the opening and closing of the epistles, Rom. i. 7; 1 Cor. i. 3; etc.

Săl-vā'tion (*deliverance*). Temporal deliverance, Ex. xiv. 13. Spiritual deliverance, 2 Cor. vii. 10; Eph. i. 13; Heb. ii. 3.

Săm''a-rā'is. Son of Ozora, 1 Esdr. ix. 34.

Sȧ-mā'rĭ-ȧ (*watch mountain*). (1) The kingdom of Samaria, synonymous with the kingdom of Israel, lay to the north of Judah. It varied in size at different times, but in general embraced the territory of the ten revolting tribes on either side of the Jordan, 1 Kgs. xiii. 32. Named from its capital, Samaria. In N. T. times, Samaria was one of the three subdivisions of Palestine, lying between Judea on the south and Galilee on the north. (2) Capital of the kingdom of Samaria or Israel, and located 30 miles north of Jerusalem. Founded by Omri, king of Israel, about B. C. 925, and called Samaria, after Shemer, from whom he bought the ground, 1 Kgs. xvi. 23, 24. It became a beautiful and strong city and remained the capital till Shalmaneser, the Assyrian, destroyed it and the empire, B. C. 721, 2 Kgs. xviii. 9-12. Herod rebuilt it and restored much of its ancient splendor, naming it Sebaste in honor of Augustus, who gave it to him. Philip preached the gospel there, Acts viii. 5-9. It is now a modest village called Sebastiyeh, which perpetuates the name Sebaste, and is noted for its many ruins, chief of which is the famous colonnade, 3000 feet in length, 100 columns of which are still standing. Respecting the city the prophecy, Mic. i. 6, has been literally fulfilled.

Sȧ-măr'ĭ-tans. Inhabitants of Samaria, 2 Kgs. xvii. 29. The planting of Assyrian colonists in Samaria, 2 Kgs. xvii. 24-34, led to a strange admixture of people, language, laws, religions, and customs, and brought the name Samaritan into reproach with Jews, Matt. x. 5; John iv. 9-26; viii. 48; Acts viii. 1; ix. 31.

Săm'găr=ne'bō (*sword of Nebo*). A general of Nebuchadnezzar at the taking of Jerusalem, Jer. xxxix. 3.

Săm'mus, 1 Esdr. ix. 43. [SHEMA.]

Săm'lah (*raiment*). A king of Edom, Gen. xxxvi. 36, 37; 1 Chr. i. 47, 48.

Sā'mos (*height*). An island of the Grecian archipelago, off the coast of Lydia. Visited by Paul on his third tour, Acts xx. 15.

Săm''o-thrā'çĭȧ (*Thracian Samos*). An island in the northern Ægean belonging to Thrace. Visited by Paul on his first tour, Acts xvi. 11.

Sămp'să-mēs. Probably Samsun, on Black Sea coast, 1 Macc. xv. 23.

Săm'son (*sunlike*). Son of Manoah, of Dan, and judge of Israel for 20 years, Judg. xiii. 3-25. Noted for his great strength, marvellous exploits, and moral weakness. Contrary to the wishes of his parents, and to the law as laid down in Ex. xxxiv. 16, Deut. vii. 3, he married a Philistine woman of Timnath, whom he deserted on account of her treachery, Judg. xiv. Wishing to return to her, and finding her given to another, he wreaked his vengeance on the Philistines by burning their crops and slaughtering great numbers of them, Judg. xv. 1-8. He was surrounded by 3000 of his enemies, while he dwelt on the rock Etam, and surrendered to them, but burst his bands, and routed them with great slaughter, Judg. xv. 9-19. Again he was surrounded by enemies in Gaza, but escaped by carrying away the gates of the city. The secret of his strength was finally detected by Delilah, and he was imprisoned and made blind. He finally killed himself and numerous enemies by pulling down the pillars of the house in which they were feasting, Judg. xvi.

Săm'u-el (*God hath heard*). Son of Elkanah and Hannah, celebrated Hebrew prophet and last of the judges, 1 Sam. i. 19-28. Educated under Eli, 1 Sam. iii. 4-14, and became his successor in the prophetic office. His sons proved so recreant that the people demanded a king, and Samuel anointed Saul, and resigned his authority to him, 1 Sam. xii. He also anointed David, Saul's successor, 1 Sam. xvi. 13. He died at Ramah, 1 Sam. xxv. 1. The two books which bear his name, the 9th and 10th of O. T., are called also First and Second Books of Kings. They were originally one book and contain the lives of Samuel, Saul, and David. The authorship is ascribed to a period subsequent to the secession of the ten tribes, and it is clearly an authorship different from Kings, for in Kings there are many references to the law, while in Samuel there are none. In Kings the Exile is alluded to; it is not so in Samuel.

The plans of the two works vary; Samuel is biographical, Kings annalistic.

Săn-băl'lat (*strong*). A Persian officer in Samaria who opposed Ezra and Nehemiah and persistently misrepresented them at court, Neh. ii. 10; iv. 1-9; xiii. 28.

Săne'tĭ-fȳ (*to make holy*). To prepare or set apart persons or things to holy use, Ex. xiii. 2. It was in allusion to the law that Christ spoke in John xvii. 19. To establish union with Christ by faith, John xvii. 17. To exercise the graces of knowledge, such as faith, love, repentance, humility, etc., toward God and man, 2 Thess. ii. 13; 1 Pet. i. 2.

Sănc'tu-ar''ȳ (*made holy*). A holy or sanctified place, Ps. xx. 2. The secret part of the temple in which the ark of the covenant was kept, and which none but the high priest might enter, and he only once a year, on the day of solemn expiation, Lev. iv. 6. Also applied to the furniture of the holy place, Num. x. 21; to the apartment where the altar of incense, table of shewbread and holy candlestick, etc., stood, 2 Chr. xxvi. 18; to the whole tabernacle or temple, Josh. xxiv. 26; 2 Chr. xx. 8. "Sanctuary of strength," because belonging to God, Dan. xi. 31. Any place of public worship of God, Ps. lxxiii. 17. Heaven, Ps. cii. 19. Place of refuge, Isa. viii. 14; Ezek. xi. 16. Land of Israel called God's sanctuary, Ex. xv. 17. "Worldly sanctuary," one of an earthly type, Heb. ix. 1.

Sănd (*whirling*). Abundant in the wastes of Palestine, Arabia, and Egypt. Used much figuratively. Innumerable multitudes, Gen. xxxii. 12; abundance, Gen. xli. 49; weight, Job vi. 3; Prov. xxvii. 3; sea boundary, Jer. v. 22; hiding place, Ex. ii. 12; Deut. xxxiii. 19.

Săn'dal (*board*). A sole of wood, leather, or plaited material, bound to the foot with straps. The shoe of the Bible. Not worn in the house nor in holy places, Ex. iii. 5; Deut. xxv. 9; Josh. v. 15.

Săn'he-drim, Săn'he-drin (*seated together*). The supreme council of the Jewish nation, whose germ was in the seventy elders, Num. xi. 16, 17, and further development in Jehoshaphat's tribunal, 2 Chr. xix. 8-11. In full power after the captivity, and lasted till A. D. 425. The "great Sanhedrim" was composed of 71 priests, scribes, and elders, and presided over by the high priest. The "lesser Sanhedrims" were provincial courts in the towns, and composed of 23 members appointed by the "great Sanhedrim." The word usually appears as "council" in N. T., Matt. v. 22; Mark xiv. 55; John xi. 47; Acts iv. 5-7. The members of the Sanhedrim embraced the three classes, priests, elders, and scribes. After the Roman conquest it had no control of the death power, but the confirmation and execution of capital sentences rested with the Roman procurator. Thus it was that while the Sanhedrim condemned Christ for blasphemy, he was not brought under the Roman judgment of death till accused by the Jews of treason, Matt. xxvi. 65, 66; John xviii. 31; xix. 12. The stoning of Stephen, Acts vii. 57-59, was either due to mob excitement, or else illegal.

Săn-săn'nah (*branch*). A town in southern Judah, Josh. xv. 31.

Săph (*giant*). A Philistine giant, 2 Sam. xxi. 18. Sippai, 1 Chr. xx. 4.

Sā'phat, 1 Esdr. v. 9. [SHEPHATIAH.]

Săph'ir (*fair*). A village addressed by Micah, Mic. i. 11.

Săp-phī'rȧ (*handsome*). Wife of Ananias, and participator in his crime and punishment, Acts v. 1-10.

Săp'phīre. A light blue gem, next to the diamond in hardness, Ex. xxiv. 10. Second stone in second row of high priest's breastplate, Ex. xxviii. 18. A foundation stone of the holy Jerusalem, Rev. xxi. 19.

Street of Columns, Samaria. (*See* p. 94.)

Sā'rȧ. (1) Daughter of Raguel, Tob. iii. 7. (2) Heb. xi. 11; 1 Pet. iii. 6. [SARAH.]

Sā'rah (*princess*). (1) Wife of Abraham and mother of Isaac, Gen. xi. 29; xxi. 2, 3. Name changed from Sarai to Sarah, Gen. xvii. 15, 16. At Abraham's request she passed herself off as his sister during their sojourn in Egypt, Gen. xii. 10-20, which angered the Pharaoh and led to their banishment. Relentless toward Hagar (whom she had given to Abraham as a concubine) when she bore Ishmael, and caused her to be banished to the desert, Gen. xvi. 5-16; deceitful when Isaac was promised, Gen. xviii. 15; cruel again toward Hagar on the occasion of Isaac's weaning, causing her to be banished finally from the household, Gen. xxi. 9-21. Commended for her faith, Heb. xi. 11; and obedience, 1 Pet. iii. 6. Died at age of 127 years and buried at Machpelah, Gen. xxiii. (2) Daughter of Asher, Num. xxvi. 46.

Sā'rāi, Gen. xi. 29. [SARAH.]

Sär'a-mel (*court*). Meeting place where Simon Maccabeus was made high priest, 1 Macc. xiv. 28.

Sā'răph (*burning*). A Judahite, 1 Chr. iv. 22.

Sär-chĕd'ō-nus, Tob. i. 21. [ESARHADDON.]

Sär'dīne, Sär'dĭ-us (*stone of Sardis*). The sard or carnelian, a blood-red or flesh-colored stone, first in first row of high priest's breastplate, Ex. xxviii. 17; Rev. iv. 3.

Sär'dis. Capital of Lydia in Asia Minor. Once noted for beauty and wealth; now the miserable village of Sert-Kalessi, Rev. iii. 1-6. It was the residence of Crœsus, renowned for riches, and Cyrus, when he conquered it, B. C. 548, is said to have captured fabulous treasure there. Alexander captured it from the Persians, and it was again sacked and captured by Antiochus, B. C. 214. It was destroyed by an earthquake, A. D. 17, but was speedily rebuilt. The art of wool-dyeing was discovered there. Seat of one of the seven churches of Asia, Rev. iii. 1.

Sär'dītes. Descendants of Sered, Num. xxvi. 26.

Sandals. (*See* p. 95.)

Sär'dō-nyx. A precious stone combining the sard and onyx varieties, whence its name, Rev. xxi. 20.

Sā'rē-ȧ. A swift scribe, 2 Esdr. xiv. 24.

Sȧ-rĕp'tȧ. Greek form of Zarephath, Luke iv. 26.

Sär'gon (*sun-prince*). An Assyrian king whom recently discovered inscriptions make the successor of Shalmaneser and father of Sennacherib, B. C. 722-705, 2 Kgs. xvii. 6; Isa. xx. 1.

Sā'rid (*survivor*). A landmark of Zebulun, Josh. xix. 10-12.

Sā'ron, Acts ix. 35. [SHARON.]

Sȧ-rō'thie. His sons returned, 1 Esdr. v. 34.

Sär-sē'chim (*master of wardrobes*). A prince of Babylon at taking of Jerusalem, Jer. xxxix. 3.

Sā'ruch, Luke iii. 35. [SERUG.]

Sā'tăn (*adversary*). In O. T. a common noun, meaning enemy or adversary in general, 1 Sam. xxix. 4; 2 Sam. xix. 22; except in Job i. 6, 12; ii. 1; Zech. iii. 1, where the word becomes a proper noun, and spiritual representative of evil. In N. T. sense, chief of the evil spirits; great adversary of man; the devil, Matt. iv. 10; xxv. 41; Rev. xx., and elsewhere. Called also "the prince of this world;" "the wicked one;" "the tempter;" and in Rev. xii. 9, the old serpent, the devil, and Satan.

Săt'ȳr. A mythical creature, half man, half goat, inhabiting woods and waste places, Isa. xiii. 21; xxxiv. 14.

Saul (*wished*). (1) An early king of Edom, Gen. xxxvi. 37, 38. Shaul in 1 Chr. i. 48, 49. (2) A Benjamite, son of Kish, and first king of Israel. Anointed by Samuel; reigned B. C. 1095-1055; slain with his sons at Gilboa. His versatile career is described in 1 Sam. ix.-xxxi. He stands in Bible history for the stature, strength, and ruggedness of character so essential to judges in times of danger or necessary reform, and for the bravery, generalship and self-confidence of one called on to institute a new empire. Of boundless ambition and erratic judgment, he usurped the priestly function, and drew the reproaches of the aged prophet Samuel, who had surrendered his line in anointing him. The announcement that royalty could not be perpetuated in his family drove him to inexcusable follies, yet with the courage of youth he fought his last despairing battle with the Philistines, and finished his course on his own sword. (3) Hebrew name of Paul, Acts xiii. 9.

Săv'a-ran, 1 Macc. vi. 43. [AVARAN.]

Sā'vī-as, 1 Esdr. viii. 2. [UZZI.]

Saw (*cutter*). Hebrew saws doubtless patterned after those of Egypt, being single-handled, with teeth inclined toward the handle, so that cutting was done by pulling. Used for sawing wood, Isa. x. 15; stone, 1 Kgs. vii. 9; torture, 2 Sam. xii. 31; 1 Chr. xx. 3; Heb. xi. 37.

Scāpe'gōat, Lev. xvi. 7-26. [GOAT.]

Scär'let (*orange-red*). A Tyrian color much prized by ancients, Ex. xxv. 4; Prov. xxxi. 21.

Sçĕp'tre (*prop*). Any rod or staff. A shepherd's crook or tithing rod, Lev. xxvii. 32; Mic. vii. 14. A symbol of royal power, Gen. xlix. 10; Num. xxiv. 17; overlaid with gold, Esth. iv. 11.

Sçē'vȧ (*fitted*). An Ephesian priest, Acts xix. 14-16.

Scôr'pī-on (*crawler*). A venomous creature allied to the spider, but resembling the lobster. Its sting is painful and often fatal, Deut. viii. 15; 1 Kgs. xii. 11; Rev. ix. 3-10. A dangerous gift, Luke xi. 12.

Scoûrġ'ing (*thonging*). A common Hebrew punishment. The scourge was made of three lashes of leather or cord. Not more than forty stripes could be administered, Deut. xxv. 1-3; Matt. x. 17; xxiii. 34. Rods or twigs were also used, 2 Cor. xi. 25.

Scrībe (*writer*). The Hebrew scribe or writer appears to have been at first a court or military official, Ex. v. 6; Judg. v. 14; then secretary or recorder, for kings, priests, and prophets, 2 Sam. viii. 17; xx. 25; finally a secretary of state, doctor, or teacher, Ez. vii. 6. Scribes became a class or guild, copyists and expounders of the law, and through their innovations fell under the same denunciations as priests and Pharisees, Matt. xxiii. 1-33; Mark vii. 5-13; Luke v. 30.

Scrĭp (*bag*). A shepherd's bag, 1 Sam. xvii. 40. A wallet for carrying food and traveller's conveniences, Matt. x. 10; Luke x. 4.

Scrĭp'ture (*written*). By way of prëeminence, the sacred writings contained in the Old and New Testaments. [BIBLE.]

Scȳth'ĭ-an (*fierce-looking*). Name applied to the fierce, nomadic nations north of the Black and Caspian seas, Col. iii. 11.

Scȳth-ŏp'ō-lis (*Scythian city*). The city of Bethshean in Palestine was for a time so called because captured and held by Scythian nomads, 2 Macc. xii. 29.

Scorpion.

Sēa. The Hebrews so designated any large body of water, whether lake, river, sea, or ocean, Gen. i. 10; Deut. xxx. 13; Job xiv. 11; Isa. xix. 5; Jer. li. 36; Ezek. xxxii. 2. (1) "Molten sea" was the immense brass laver of Solomon's temple, 1 Kgs. vii. 23-26. (2) "Sea of the Plain," Deut. iv. 49. [SALT SEA.] (3) "Great Sea," Josh. xv. 47, "uttermost sea," Deut. xi. 24, the Mediterranean, between Europe and Africa. (4) "Sea of Tiberias" [GENNESARET.] (5) "Sea of Merom" [MEROM.]

Sēal (*little mark*). Much used by ancients to authenticate documents and secure packages and doors, the impression being made in clay or wax. Seals were frequently engraved stones set in rings; Gen. xli. 42; Job xxxviii. 14; Jer. xxxii. 10; Matt. xxvii. 66.

Sē′bȧ. A son of Cush, Gen. x. 7. Mentioned as a nation or country in Ps. lxxii. 10; Isa. xliii. 3; xlv. 14, and associated with Meroe on the upper Nile.

Sē′băt, Shē′băt (*rod*). Fifth month of Jewish civil and eleventh of sacred year, corresponding to parts of February and March, Zech. i. 7.

Scribes. (*See* p. 96.)

Sĕc′a-cah (*thicket*). A city in Judah, Josh. xv. 61.

Sē′chu (*tower*). A place between Gibeah and Ramah, noted for its well, 1 Sam. xix. 22.

Sĕct (*way, school*). A party adhering to a doctrine, as the sect of Sadducees, Acts v. 17, or Pharisees, Acts xv. 5; xxvi. 5. Christians in general were for a long time called by the Jews, in a spirit of contempt, "the sect of the Nazarenes," Acts xxiv. 5. The word is also applied to a certain set of doctrines or mode of life, Acts xxiv. 14; 2 Pet. ii. 1; and to heresies proper, or perversions of Christian truth, Gal. v. 20.

Sḗ-cŭn′dus (*second*). A Thessalonian friend of Paul, Acts xx. 4.

Sĕd′′ē-çī′as (1) Ancestor of Baruch, Bar. i. 1. (2) Son of King Josiah, Bar. i. 8.

Sēed (*sowed*). Seed for sowing must not be mingled, Lev. xix. 19. Children, descendants, Gen. xvii. 12; Gal. iii. 16. Pedigree, Ez. ii. 59. The male fertilizing element, Gen. xxxviii. 9.

Sēer (*who sees*). 1 Sam. ix. 9. [PROPHET.]

Sēethe (*boil*). To boil, Ex. xvi. 23.

Sē′gub (*lifted up*). (1) A son of Hiel who rebuilt Jericho, 1 Kgs. xvi. 34. (2) A Judahite, 1 Chr. ii. 21, 22.

Sē′ĭr (*hairy*). (1) A Horite chief, Gen. xxxvi. 21; Deut. ii. 12. (2) Land or country corresponding with valley and mountains of Arabah, stretching from the Dead Sea to the Gulf of Akaba, Gen. xiv. 6; xxxii. 3; xxxiii. 14-16. The region was first occupied by the Horites, and fell into possession of Esau and his posterity, Gen. xxxvi. 8-9. Hence Seir and Edom are sometimes spoken of as identical. The Israelites, when refused permission to march through Edom to Moab, marched round the granite ranges of Seir and entered Moab by the east and north. (3) A boundary mark of Judah, Josh. xv. 10.

Sē′ĭ-răth (*hairy*). Place to which the murderer Ehud fled, Judg. iii. 26.

Sē′lȧ, Sē′lah (*rock*). A rock-founded city of Edom, the Petra of the Greeks, half way between the Dead Sea and Gulf of Akaba. Subdued by King Amaziah and called Joktheel, "subdued of God." Remarkable now for its ruins, among which are a rock-hewn temple and amphitheatre, 2 Kgs. xiv. 7; Isa. xvi. 1. The complete destruction and desolation of the place fulfils the prophecy of Jeremiah, Jer. xlix. 16, 17.

Sē′lah. A word of frequent occurrence in Psalms, and supposed to mean an interlude in vocal music, or a pianissimo of all parts, Ps. ix. 16; Hab. iii. 3, 9, 13.

Sē′lȧ-hăm′′mah-lē′koth (*rock of escapes*). Rocky stronghold in wilderness of Maon, where David escaped from Saul, 1 Sam. xxiii. 28.

Sē′led (*lifted up*). A Judahite, 1 Chr. ii. 30.

Sĕl′′ḗ-mī′ah. A swift scribe, 2 Esdr. xiv. 24.

Sḗ-leū′çĭ-ȧ (*city of Seleucus*). The seaport of Antioch in Syria, Acts xiii. 4. It was the port whence Paul and Barnabas started on their first missionary journey, and lay sixteen miles to the west of Antioch. The city was founded by Seleucus Nicator about B. C. 300, and to distinguish it from other cities of the same name was frequently called "Seleucia by the sea." The harbor is now choked with sand, and the once beautiful city is but the insignificant village of Elkalusi.

Sḗ-leū′cus. The Seleuci, or Seleucidæ, sprung from Seleucus I., a general of Alexander the Great, were a line of Syrian kings, B. C. 312-65, 2 Macc. iii. 3.

Sĕm. Greek form of Shem, Luke iii. 36.

Sĕm′′a-chī′ah (*God-sustained*). A Levite porter, 1 Chr. xxvi. 7.

Sĕm′e-ī (*distinguished*). (1) 1 Esdr. ix. 33. [SHIMEI.] (2) Father of Mattathias, Luke iii. 26. Semein in R. V.

Sē′mel, Esth. xi. 2. [SHIMEI.]

Sḗ-mĕl′lĭ-us, 1 Esdr. ii. 16. [SHIMSHAI.]

Sē-nā′ah (*brambly*). His sons were returned captives, Ez. ii. 35.

Sĕn′āte (*elders*). First body, or class, of Hebrew Sanhedrim; the other two being priests and scribes, Acts v. 21.

Sē′neh (*bramble*). One of two rocks in the pass of Michmash, 1 Sam. xiv. 4, 5.

Sē′nīr (*glistening*). Amorite name for Mount Hermon, 1 Chr. v. 23; Ezek. xxvii. 5.

Sĕn-năch′e-rĭb (*not the first-born*). Son and successor of Sargon, king of Assyria, B. C. 702-680. He extended his conquests to the Mediterranean and to Egypt, 2 Kgs. xviii. 13-37; xix. Most powerful and magnificent of eastern sovereigns, Isa. xxxvi., xxxvii. He made Nineveh his capital and adorned it with many palaces and public structures. His monuments have been found in many places, and a record of his arrival in Egypt has been unearthed close by an inscription of Rameses the Great.

Sḗ-nū′ah (*bristling*). A Benjamite, second in rule over Jerusalem after the captivity, Neh. xi. 9. Hasenuah, 1 Chr. ix. 7.

Sḗ-ō′rim (*bearded*). Head of fourth priestly course, 1 Chr. xxiv. 8.

Sē′phar (*number*). A Joktanite border in Arabia Gen. x. 30.

Sĕph'a-răd (*severed*). Unlocated place whence captive Jews would return to possess the cities of the south, Obad. 20.

Sĕph''ar-vā'im (*two Sipperas*). One of the two cities of Sippera in Syria, whence colonists were sent to Samaria, 2 Kgs. xvii. 24–34; xix. 13; Isa. xxxvii. 13.

Sĕph'ar-vītes. Inhabitants of Sepharvaim, 2 Kgs. xvii. 31.

Sennacherib. (From the ruins of Nineveh.)

Sĕp-tū'a-ġint (*seventy*). The traditional 70 or 72 translators of the Hebrew Scriptures into Greek; but especially, the Greek version of the O. T. made by 72 learned Jews at Alexandria, at command of Ptolemy Philadelphus, about B. C. 270. The beginning of active work on this, the best known of ancient Bible translations, is fixed for the years B. C. 280-285, and it covered a long period of time, the translation of the Apocryphal books having been gradually added. It was made from Egyptian Hebrew manuscripts, and in its completed form is designated by the Roman numerals LXX. It was the version used by Hebrews in Christ's time and by the Greek Fathers and early N. T. writers, and the Latin version was made from it.

Sĕp'ŭl-chre (*ker*) (*bury*), 2 Kgs. xxiii. 16; Isa. xxii. 16; Matt. xxvii. 60; Mark xvi. 2; Luke xxiii. 53. Though the Egyptians and nearly all peoples adjacent to the Hebrews have made the name of sarcophagus familiar as a stone coffin, a chest-like tomb, often ornamented and inscribed, there seems to have been nothing akin to it in all the mention of funeral customs and burial rites in the Scriptures, if we except certain titles and inscriptions over tombs such as are mentioned in 2 Kgs. xxiii. 17. [BURIAL.] [TOMB.]

Sē'rah (*lady*). A daughter of Asher, Gen. xlvi. 17; 1 Chr. vii. 30. Sarah, Num. xxvi. 46.

Sĕr''a-ī'ah (*warrior of God*). (1) David's scribe, 2 Sam. viii. 17. Sheva, 2 Sam. xx. 25. Shisha, 1 Kgs. iv. 3. Shavsha, 1 Chr. xviii. 16. (2) A high priest, slain at Riblah, 2 Kgs. xxv. 18–21. (3) One who submitted to Gedaliah, 2 Kgs. xxv. 23. (4) A Judahite, 1 Chr. iv. 13, 14. (5) A Simeonite, 1 Chr. iv. 35. (6) A returned priest, Ez. ii. 2; Neh. x. 2. (7) Ancestor of Ezra, Ez. vii. 1. (8) One of the officers who arrested Jeremiah, Jer. xxxvi. 26. (9) Jeremiah's messenger to Babylon, Jer. li. 59-64.

Sĕr'a-phĭm (*burning*). An order of celestial beings, pictured in Isaiah's vision as around the throne of God, Isa. vi. 2–7.

Sē'red (*fear*). First-born of Zebulun, Gen. xlvi. 14; Num. xxvi. 26.

Sẽr'ġĭ-us Pau'lus (*little net*). Proconsul of Cyprus at time of Paul's visit, Acts xiii. 7, 12.

Sē'ron. A Syrian general, 1 Macc. iii. 13, 23.

Sẽr'pent (*creeper*). The Hebrew original embraces the entire serpent genus. Serpents numerous and venomous in Bible lands. The word appears in Scripture under various names; adder, supposably the cerastes, Gen. xlix. 17; asp, or cobra, Deut. xxxii. 33; cockatrice, Jer. viii. 17; viper, Job xx. 16. Subtile, Gen. iii. 1; wise, Matt. x. 16; poisonous, Prov. xxiii. 32; sharp-tongued, Ps. cxl. 3; charmed, Ps. lviii. 5; emblem of wickedness, Matt. xxiii. 33; cruelty, Ps. lviii. 4; treachery, Gen. xlix. 17; the devil, Rev. xii. 9–15; fiery serpents sent as a punishment, Num. xxi. 6; sight of "brazen serpent," an antidote for poison of bite, Num. xxi. 8, 9; "fiery flying serpent," a probable allusion to dragon, Isa. xiv. 29.

Sē'rug (*branch*). Son of Reu and great-grandfather of Abraham, Gen. xi. 20-23. Saruch, Luke iii. 35.

Sẽr'vant (*server*). In a broad Bible sense, subject, assistant, person under tribute; in special sense, bondman or slave, by right of purchase, pledge for indebtedness, or indenture; which relationship was carefully guarded by Mosaic law, Lev. xxv. 39–55; Deut. xv. 12–18. [SLAVE.]

Sẽrv'i-tôr (*server*). A servant, 2 Kgs. iv. 43.

Sĕth (*pay*). Third son of Adam, Gen. iv. 25; v. 3-8.

Sē'thur (*hidden*). The Asherite spy, Num. xiii. 13.

Sĕv'en. A favorite, and often symbolic, number among Hebrews, Gen. ii. 2; vii. 2; xli. 2, 3. Used as a round number, 1 Sam. ii. 5; Matt. xii. 45. Type of abundance and completeness, Gen. iv. 15, 24; Matt. xviii. 21, 22. These references, and other places, show a seventh day and seventh year sabbath and a seven times seventh year of Jubilee; also sacrificial animals limited to seven, and the golden candlesticks. Seven priests with seven trumpets surrounded Jericho for seven days, and seven times on the seventh day. In the Apocalypse we find seven churches, seven candlesticks, seven stars, seven seals, seven trumpets, seven vials, seven plagues, seven angels.

Shā''al-ăb'bin (*place of foxes*). A boundary place of Dan, Josh. xix. 42. Shaalbim, Judg. i. 35; 1 Kgs. iv. 9.

Shā-ăl'bim. [SHAALABBIN.]

Shā-ăl'bo-nīte. One of David's heroes, so called. Place unknown, 2 Sam. xxiii. 32; 1 Chr. xi. 33.

Shā'aph (*division*). (1) A Judahite, 1 Chr. ii. 47. (2) Son of Caleb, 1 Chr. ii. 49.

Shā''a-rā'im (*two gates*). (1) Town in Judah, 1 Sam. xvii. 52. Sharaim, Josh. xv. 36. (2) Town in Simeon, 1 Chr. iv. 31.

Shā-ăsh'găz (*lover of beauty*). Keeper of concubines in palace of Xerxes, Esth. ii. 14.

Shăb-bĕth'a-ī (*my rest*). An assistant to Ezra, Ez. x. 15; Neh. viii. 7; xi. 16.

Shăch-ī'ȧ (*God-protected*). A Benjamite, 1 Chr. viii. 10.

Shăd'da-ī (*mighty*). *El-Shaddai*, "God Almighty." The name used by Hebrews for God, before "Jehovah" acquired its full significance, Gen. xvii. 1; Ex. vi. 3.

Shā'drach (*royal*). Chaldean name given to Hananiah, Dan. i. 7-21; ii.; iii.

Shā'gē (*erring*). Father of one of David's guard, 1 Chr. xi. 34.

Shā''ha-rā'im (*double morning*). A Benjamite, 1 Chr. viii. 8.

Shȧ-hăz'i-mah (*heights*). Town in Issachar, Josh. xix. 22.

Shā'lem (*peaceful*). For "to Shalem," Gen. xxxiii. 18, read "in peace to."

Shā'lim, Land of (*land of foxes*). The wild place through which Saul passed when searching for his father's asses, 1 Sam. ix. 4.

Shā'mȧ (*dutiful*). One of David's guard, 1 Chr. xi. 44.

Shăm''a-rī'ah (*God-kept*). Son of King Rehoboam, 2 Chr. xi. 19.

Shăm'bleş (*little benches*). In general, slaughterhouses, but meat-market in 1 Cor. x. 25.

Shā'med (*destroyer*). A Benjamite, 1 Chr. viii. 12.

Shāme'façed-ness. Wrong writing of shamefastness, modesty. Corrected in R. V., 1 Tim. ii. 9.

Shā'mer (*keeper*). (1) A Levite, 1 Chr. vi. 46. (2) An Asherite, 1 Chr. vii. 34. Shomer in vs. 32.

Shăm'gär (*sword*). A judge of Israel who slew 600 Philistines with an ox-goad, Judg. iii. 31; v. 6.

Shăm'huth (*destruction*). One of David's captains, 1 Chr. xxvii. 8.

Shā'mīr (*thorn*). (1) A town in the mountains of Judah, Josh. xv. 48. (2) Residence of Tola, the judge, in Mount Ephraim, Judg. x. 1, 2. (3) Son of Michah, 1 Chr. xxiv. 24.

Sarcophagus. (*See* p. 98.)

Shăl'i-shȧ, Land of (*triangular*). A wild district near Mt. Ephraim through which Saul passed, in search of his father's asses, 1 Sam. ix. 4.

Shăl'le-chĕth (*thrown down*). A westward gate of the temple at Jerusalem, 1 Chr. xxvi. 16.

Shăl'lum (*revenge*). (1) Fifteenth king of Israel, B. C. 771; slew King Zachariah, and usurped his throne; reigned one month; slain and succeeded by Menahem, 2 Kgs. xv. 10 15. (2) Husband of Huldah the prophetess, 2 Kgs. xxii. 14; 2 Chr. xxxiv. 22. (3) A descendant of Sheshan, 1 Chr. ii. 40, 41. (4) Fourth son of Josiah king of Judah, who became King Jehoahaz, B. C. 610, and reigned for three months, 1 Chr. iii. 15; Jer. xxii. 11, 12; 2 Kgs. xxiii. 30, 31; 2 Chr. xxxvi. 1-4. (5) A Simeonite, 1 Chr. iv. 25. (6) A high priest, 1 Chr. vi. 12; Ez. vii. 2. (7) Shillem, a Naphtalite, 1 Chr. vii. 13. (8) A chief of porters, 1 Chr. ix. 17; Ez. ii. 42. (9) A porter, 1 Chr. ix. 19, 31. (10) An Ephraimite, 2 Chr. xxviii. 12. (11) Uncle of Jeremiah, Jer. xxxii. 7. (12) Four Levites, Ez. x. 24, 42; Neh. iii. 12; Jer. xxxv. 4.

Shăl'lun (*revenge*). A wall-repairer and governor of part of Mizpah, Neh. iii. 15.

Shăl'ma-ī (*thanks*). His children were returned captives, Ez. ii. 46.

Shăl'man, Hos. x. 14. [SHALMANESER.]

Shăl''man-ē'şer (*Shalman is lenient*). An Assyrian king, B. C. 727-722, who twice conquered Hoshea, king of Israel, the last time capturing his capital, Samaria, 2 Kgs. xvii. 3-6; xviii. 9-12.

Shăm'mȧ (*desolation*). A chief of Asher, 1 Chr. vii. 37.

Shăm'mah (*desolation*). (1) A duke of Edom, Gen. xxxvi. 13, 17; 1 Chr. i. 37. (2) Third son of Jesse, 1 Sam. xvi. 9; xvii. 13. Called also, Shimea, Shimeah, and Shimma. (3) One of the three greatest of David's mighty men, 2 Sam. xxiii. 11-17, 33. (4) Another of David's mighty men, 2 Sam. xxiii. 25. Shammoth, 1 Chr. xi. 27. Shamhuth, 1 Chr. xxvii. 8.

Shăm'ma-ī (*desolated*). Three Judahites, 1 Chr. ii. 28, 32, 44, 45; iv. 17.

Shăm'moth, 1 Chr. xi. 27. [SHAMMAH, 4.]

Shăm-mū'ȧ, Shăm'mū-ah (*heard*). (1) The Reubenite spy, Num. xiii. 4. (2) A son of David, born in Jerusalem, 2 Sam. v. 14; 1 Chr. xiv. 4. Shimea, 1 Chr. iii. 5. (3) A Levite, Neh. xi. 17. (4) A priest representing the family of Bilgah, Neh. xii. 18.

Shăm''she-rā'ī (*hero*). A Benjamite, 1 Chr. viii. 26.

Shā'pham (*bare*). A Gadite, 1 Chr. v. 12.

Shā'phan (*rabbit*). Scribe or secretary of King Josiah, 2 Kgs. xxii. 3-14; 2 Chr. xxxiv. 8-20.

Shā'phat (*judge*). (1) The Simeonite spy, Num. xiii. 5. (2) Father of the prophet Elisha, 1 Kgs. xix. 16, 19; 2 Kgs. iii. 11; vi. 31. (3) One in the royal line of Judah, 1 Chr. iii. 22. (4) A Gadite chief, 1 Chr. v. 12. (5) A herdsman of David, 1 Chr. xxvii. 29.

Shā'pher (*bright*). A desert encampment of the Israelites, Num. xxxiii. 23.

Shăr'a-ī (*set free*). A descendant of Bani, who had married a foreign wife, Ez. x. 40.

Shăr-ā'im, Josh. xv. 36. [SHAARAIM.]

Shā'rär (*navel*). Father of one of David's warriors, 2 Sam. xxiii. 33. Sacar, 1 Chr. xi. 35.

Shā-rē'zer (*prince*). Son of Sennacherib, who helped to murder his father, 2 Kgs. xix. 37.

Shâr'on (*plain*). (1) The plain skirting the Mediterranean coast from Judah to Cæsarea. It is an extension of the "shefelah" or lowlands of Judah, and was renowned for its fertility. Called Saron in Acts ix. 35. First mentioned as Lasharon, Josh. xii. 18. David's flocks fed there, 1 Chr. xxvii. 29. Celebrated in S. of Sol. ii. 1; Isa. xxxv. 2; lxv. 10. (2) A town or district east of Jordan, and perhaps in Gilead, 1 Chr. v. 16.

Shâr'on-īte. Designation of Shitrai, one of David's herdsmen, 1 Chr. xxvii. 29.

Shâ-ru'hen (*gracious house*). A town first allotted to Judah and then to Simeon, Josh. xix. 6.

Shăsh'a-ī (*noble*). A son of Bani, who had taken a foreign wife, Ez. x. 40.

Shā'shak (*eager*). A Benjamite, 1 Chr. viii. 14, 25.

Shēar'ing-house. A spot between Jezreel and Samaria where Jehu slaughtered the royal family of Judah, 2 Kgs. x. 12-14.

Shē'är-jā'shŭb (*a remnant shall return*). Symbolical name given by Isaiah to his son, Isa. vii. 3.

Shē'bȧ (*oath*). (1) Son of Bichri, a Benjamite, who revolted from David and was beheaded, 2 Sam. xx. 1-22. (2) A Gadite chief, 1 Chr. v. 13. (3) A descendant of Ham, Gen. x. 7; 1 Chr. i. 9. (4) Son of Joktan, Gen. x. 28. (5) Son of Jokshan, Gen. xxv. 3; 1 Chr. i. 32. (6) The kingdom of Sheba, whose queen visited Solomon, 1 Kgs. x. 1-13; 2 Chr. ix. 1-12. This country has been variously located in Africa, in Arabia, on the Persian Gulf, and in Arabia, on the Red Sea. The burden of authority identifies it with Yemen or Arabia Felix, on the Red Sea, and peopled by descendants of Sheba, son of Joktan. (7) A town in Simeon, Josh. xix. 2. Probably the Shema of Josh. xv. 26.

Shē'bah (*oath*). The famous well, or series of wells, dug by the servants of Isaac, in accordance with his compact with the Philistines. It gave name to Beersheba, Gen. xxvi. 31-33.

Shē'bam (*odor*). A town east of Jordan, given to Reuben and Gad, Num. xxxii. 3. [SIBMAH.]

Egyptian Cobra. (*See* p. 98.)

Shā'ul (*asked*). (1) A son of Simeon and founder of the Shaulites, Gen. xlvi. 10; Num. xxvi. 13. (2) A king of Edom, 1 Chr. i. 48, 49. Saul in Gen. xxxvi. 37.

Shā'ul-ītes. Descendants of Shaul, Num. xxvi. 13.

Shā'veh (*plain*). The unidentified place in Palestine mentioned as the "king's dale," Gen. xiv. 17; 2 Sam. xviii. 18.

Shā'veh Kĭr''ī-a-thā'im (*plain of Kiriathaim*). Spot where the Emims dwelt when smitten by Chedorlaomer, Gen. xiv. 5. It is supposably the place that afterwards belonged to Reuben, under the name of Kirjathaim, Num. xxxii. 37; Josh. xiii. 19.

Shăv'shȧ (*God's warrior*). Royal secretary or scribe in time of King David, 1 Chr. xviii. 16. Seraiah, 2 Sam. viii. 17. Sheva, 2 Sam. xx. 25. Shisha, 1 Kgs. iv. 3.

Shā'ving. [RAZOR.]

Shawm (*pipe*). A cornet or clarionet. Only in Prayer-book version of Ps. xcviii. 6.

Shē'al (*asking*). One who had a foreign wife, Ez. x. 29.

Shē-ăl'tĭ-el (*asked of God*). Father of Zerubbabel, Ez. iii. 2, 8; v. 2; Neh. xii. 1; Hag. i. 1, 12, 14; ii. 2, 23.

Shē''a-rī'ah (*prized of God*). A descendant of Saul, 1 Chr. viii. 38; ix. 44.

Shĕb''a-nī'ah (*grown by God*). (1) A priestly trumpeter at the bringing up of the ark, 1 Chr. xv. 24. (2) Three co-covenanters with Nehemiah, Neh. ix. 5; x. 4, 10, 12; xii. 14.

Shĕb'a-rĭm (*ruins*). Place near Ai to which the defeated Israelites were pursued, Josh. vii. 5.

Shē'băt. [SEBAT.]

Shē'ber (*breaking*). A son of Caleb, 1 Chr. ii. 48.

Shĕb'nȧ (*strength*). (1) Prefect of the palace under King Hezekiah, Isa. xxii. 15-25. (2) Scribe under King Hezekiah, 2 Kgs. xviii. 18, 37; xix. 2; Isa. xxxvi. 3.

Shĕb'u-el (*captive of God*). (1) A descendant of Moses, 1 Chr. xxiii. 16; xxvi. 24. Shubael, 1 Chr. xxiv. 20. (2) A Levite minstrel, son of Heman, 1 Chr. xxv. 4. Shubael, 1 Chr. xxv. 20.

Shĕc''a-nī'ah (*dweller with God*). (1) A priest in time of David, 1 Chr. xxiv. 11. (2) A Levite, 2 Chr. xxxi. 15.

Shĕch''a-nī'ah (*dweller with God*). (1) A descendant of the royal line, 1 Chr. iii. 21, 22. (2) Levites and returned captives, in Ez. viii. 3, 5; x. 2; Neh. iii. 29; vi. 18; xii. 3.

Shē'chem (*shoulder*). (1) The Canaanite who abducted Dinah and was slain by Simeon and Levi, Gen. xxxiv. (2) An ancient and highly historic city, between mounts Ebal and Gerizim, 34 miles N. of

Jerusalem. Called also Sichem, Sychem, Sychar, later Neapolis, now Nablus. Halting place of Abraham, Gen. xii. 6. A Hivite city in time of Jacob, Gen. xxxiii. 18–20; Josh. xxiv. 32. Captured by Simeon and Levi, Gen. xxxiv. Joseph buried there, Josh. xxiv. 32. Destroyed by Abimelech, Judg. ix. Rebuilt by Rehoboam, and fortified and made capital of Israel by Jeroboam, 1 Kgs. xii. 1–19, 25; 2 Chr. x. A centre of Samaritan worship after the captivity, John iv. 5, 39–42. (3) A Manassite, of Gilead, Num. xxvi. 31. (4) A Gileadite, nephew of former, 1 Chr. vii. 19.

Broad-Tailed Sheep.

Shē′chem-ītes. The family of Shechem of Gilead, Num. xxvi. 31.

Shĕ-chī′nah (*dwelling-place*). The visible majesty of God, as in the "pillar of cloud" and the "glory" which covered the tabernacle and filled Solomon's temple. A word found only in the targums, Chaldaic version of Bible, and among early Christian writers. Alluded to in Luke ii. 9; John i. 14; Rom. ix. 4.

Shĕd′ĕ-ur (*light-sender*). Father of Elizur, chief of Reuben at time of exode, Num. i. 5; ii. 10; vii. 30, 35; x. 18.

Shēep. An important animal among Hebrews, and a main source of wealth. Shepherd's occupation highly respectable, Gen. iv. 2; Ex. iii. 1; 1 Sam. xvi. 11; Job xlii. 12, though odious to Egyptians. Used for sacrifices, Ex. xx. 24; xxix. 38; Lev. ix. 3; for food, 1 Sam. xxv. 18. Wool used for clothing, Lev. xiii. 47. Skins used for tabernacle coverings, Ex. xxv. 5. Paid as tribute, 2 Kgs. iii. 4. Sheep and shepherd employed much figuratively, 2 Chr. xviii. 16; Ps. cxix. 176; Matt. ix. 36; John x. 11; Heb. xiii. 20. The common sheep of Syria and Palestine was the broad-tailed variety.

Shēep′fold. Place for herding sheep, especially at night. Usually built strong to keep out wild animals, Num. xxxii. 16; 2 Sam. vii. 8; John x. 16. The fold, cote, or enclosure was also the place where the sheep were collected at shearing time, Jer. xxiii. 3; Zeph. ii. 6, which was a season of festivity, 1 Sam. xxv. 7–11; 2 Sam. xiii. 23. Hence "shearing-house," 2 Kgs. x. 12–14.

Shēep-gate. One of the gates of Jerusalem as rebuilt by Nehemiah, Neh. iii. 1, 32; xii. 39.

Shēep-mär′ket. Should read "sheep-gate" as above, John v. 2.

Shē″ha-rī′ah (*Jehovah dawns*). Son of Jeroham of Benjamin, 1 Chr. viii. 26.

Shĕk′el (*weight*). A weight for weighing uncoined money, of Assyrian and Babylonian origin. There seem to have been two standards, that of the sanctuary and the king, Ex. xxx. 13; 2 Sam. xiv. 26. Both approximated half an ounce, valued in silver at about 64 cents. Later, a Hebrew silver coin, with bronze half and quarter shekels. Probably the "pieces of silver" in Matt. xxvi. 15, though the "pieces of silver" in Luke xv. 8 are clearly the Greek drachmas. The first Jewish coins were struck by Simon Maccabeus, who obtained permission to coin money from Antiochus, King of Syria. His shekel showed a vase on one side, representing a pot of manna, and on the other an almond branch with flowers, representative supposably of Aaron's rod.

Shē′lah (*prayer*). (1) Youngest son of Judah and founder of Shelanites, Gen. xxxviii. 5–26; Num. xxvi. 20. (2) 1 Chr. i. 18, 24. [SALAH.]

Shē′lan-ītes. Descendants of Shelah, Num. xxvi. 20.

Shĕl″e-mī′ah (*God repays*). (1) 1 Chr. xxvi. 14. [MESHELEMIAH.] (2) Two who married foreign wives, Ez. x. 39, 41. (3) Father of Hananiah, Neh. iii. 30. (4) A priest appointed treasurer, Neh. xiii. 13. (5) Father of Jehucal, Jer. xxxvii. 3. (6) Father of one of Jeremiah's accusers, Jer. xxxviii. 1. (7) Father of the officer who arrested Jeremiah, Jer. xxxvii. 13.

Shē′leph (*drawn out*). A son of Joktan, Gen. x. 26.

Ancient Sheepfold.

Shē′lesh (*strength*). An Asherite chief, 1 Chr. vii. 35.

Shĕl′o-mi (*my peace*). An Asherite, Num. xxxiv. 27.

Shĕl'o-mīth (*my peace*). (1) Daughter of Dibri, of Dan, Lev. xxiv. 11. (2) Daughter of Zerubbabel, 1 Chr. iii. 19. (3) Two Levites, 1 Chr. xxiii. 9, 18. (4) A descendant of Eliezer, 1 Chr. xxvi. 25–28. (5) A returned captive, Ez. viii. 10.

Shĕl'o-mŏth, 1 Chr. xxiv. 22. [SHELOMITH, 3.]

Shē-lū'mī-el (*God's peace*). A prince of Simeon, Num. i. 6; ii. 12; vii. 36, 41; x. 19.

Shĕm'i-nīth (*eighth*). A musical term, variously surmised to mean the instrument, one of eight strings, the octave, the time of the piece, the part, air, pitch, or key, 1 Chr. xv. 21; Ps. vi; xii. titles.

Shē-mĭr'a-mŏth'' (*heights of heaven*). (1) A musical Levite in time of David, 1 Chr. xv. 18, 20; xvi. 5. (2) A Levite in reign of Jehoshaphat, 2 Chr. xvii. 8.

Silver Shekel. (*See* p. 101.)

Shĕm (*name*). Oldest son of Noah, preserved with his father in the ark, Gen. v. 32. Blessed by Noah for his conduct, Gen. ix. 18–27. His descendants are the Hebrews, Arameans, Persians, Assyrians, and Arabians, whose languages are called Shemitic.

Shē'mȧ (*hearing*). (1) A Judahite, 1 Chr. ii. 43, 44. (2) A Reubenite, 1 Chr. v. 8. (3) A Benjamite chief, 1 Chr. viii. 13. (4) An assistant of Ezra, Neh. viii. 4. (5) Josh. xv. 26. [SHEBA, 7.]

Shē-mā'ah (*God hears*). A Benjamite whose sons joined David at Ziklag, 1 Chr. xii. 3.

Shĕm''a-ī'ah (*God hears*). (1) Prophet and chronicler in reign of Rehoboam, 1 Kgs. xii. 22; 2 Chr. xi. 2. (2) Twenty-four others, mostly priests, Levites, and returned captives, 1 Chr. iii. 22; iv. 37; v. 4; ix. 14; ix. 16; xv. 8, 11; xxiv. 6; xxvi. 4–7; 2 Chr. xxix. 14; xvii. 8; xxxi. 15; xxxv. 9; Ez. viii. 13, 16; x. 21, 31; Neh. vi. 10; x. 8; xii. 6, 18, 34, 36, 42; Jer. xxvi. 20; xxix. 24–32; xxxvi. 12.

Shĕm''a-rī'ah (*God keeps*). (1) An adherent of David at Ziklag, 1 Chr. xii. 5. (2) Two who took foreign wives, Ez. x. 32, 41.

Shĕm'e-ber (*high flight*). King of Zeboiim, Gen. xiv. 2.

Shē'mĕr (*guarded*). Owner of the hill which King Omri bought, and on which he built Samaria, giving it the former owner's name, 1 Kgs. xvi. 24.

Shē-mī'dȧ (*wise*). A son of Gilead and founder of the Shemidaites, Num. xxvi. 32; Josh. xvii. 2. Shemidah, 1 Chr. vii. 19.

Shē-mī'dah, 1 Chr. vii. 19. [SHEMIDA.]

Shē-mī'dȧ-ītes. Descendants of Shemida, Num. xxvi. 32.

Bronze Quarter Shekel. (*See* p. 101.)

Shē-mĭt'ic. The family of languages spoken by the descendants of Shem. [SHEM.]

Shē-mū'el (*heard of God*). (1) Representative of Simeon during the apportionment of Canaan, Num. xxxiv. 20. (2) Samuel the prophet, 1 Chr. vi. 33. (3) A chief of Issachar, 1 Chr. vii. 2.

Shĕn (*tooth*). An unknown place, 1 Sam. vii. 12.

Shē-nā'zar (*ivory keeper*). A descendant of David, 1 Chr. iii. 18.

Shē'nir, Deut. iii. 9; S. of Sol. iv. 8. [SENIR.]

Shē'pham (*wild*). A landmark on eastern boundary of Promised Land, Num. xxxiv. 10.

Shĕph''a-thī'ah (*God judges*). A Benjamite, 1 Chr. ix. 8.

Shĕph''a-tī'ah (*God judges*). (1) Fifth son of David, 2 Sam. iii. 4; 1 Chr. iii. 3. (2) A Benjamite warrior, 1 Chr. xii. 5. (3) A chief of Simeon, 1 Chr. xxvii. 16. (4) Son of Jehoshaphat, 2 Chr. xxi. 2. (5) Four others in Ez. ii. 4, 57; Neh. vii. 9, 59; xi. 4; Jer. xxxviii. 1–4.

Shĕp'hērd (*herder of sheep*). A highly honorable occupation among pastoral Hebrews, engaged in by both sexes, Gen. xxix. 6; xxx. 29–35; Ex. ii. 16–22. Often arduous and dangerous employment, Gen. xxxi. 40; 1 Sam. xvii. 34. Equipment consisted of a sheepskin mantle, a scrip or wallet, a sling and crook. He led the flock to pasture in the morning, tended them by day and folded and watched them at night, Job xxx. 1; Luke ii. 8; John x. 4. The office of sheep-master or chief shepherd was one of great trust as well as honor, 2 Kgs. iii. 4; Heb. xiii. 20; 1 Pet. v. 4. It was the shepherd's duty to count the sheep daily and to tithe them, and he was held responsible for lost ones, Gen. xxxi. 38, 39; Ex. xxii. 12, 13; Lev. xxvii. 32; Jer. xxxiii. 13. Shepherd is used figuratively for Jehovah in Ps. lxxx. 1; Jer. xxxi. 10; for kings, Ezek. xxxiv. 10; in N. T. for Christ, John x. 11; Heb. xiii. 20; 1 Pet. v. 4. It is applied also to teachers in the synagogue and to those who preside over it. Hence pastor and minister of the gospel.

Shē'phī (*barren*). A descendant of Seir, 1 Chr. i. 40. Shepho, Gen. xxxvi. 23.

Shē'phō, Gen. xxxvi. 23. [SHEPHI.]

Shē-phū'phan (*serpent*). A grandson of Benjamin, 1 Chr. viii. 5. Shupham, Num. xxvi. 39. Shuppim, 1 Chr. vii. 12, 15. Muppim, Gen. xlvi. 21.

Shē'rah (*relation*). A daughter of Ephraim, 1 Chr. vii. 24.

Shĕr''e-bī'ah (*heat of God*). A co-covenanter with Nehemiah, and assistant to Ezra, Ez. viii. 18, 24; Neh. viii. 7; ix. 4; x. 12.

Shē'resh (*root*). Son of Machir, of Manasseh, 1 Chr. vii. 16.

Shē-rē'zer (*fire prince*). A messenger of the people, Zech. vii. 2.

Shĕr'iff (*shire officer*). A Babylonian official, Dan. iii. 2.

Shē'shăch (*from the goddess Shach*). Symbolical name for Babylon, Jer. xxv. 26.

Shē'shāi (*princely*). A son of Anak, slain by Caleb, Num. xiii. 22; Josh. xv. 14; Judg. i. 10.

She'shan (*princely*). A Judahite, 1 Chr. ii. 31-35.

Shĕsh-băz'zar (*fire-worshipper*). Zerubbabel's name at the Persian court, Ez. i. 8-11.

Shĕth (*tumult*). (1) 1 Chr. i. 1. [SETH.] (2) For Sheth in Num. xxiv. 17, read "tumult," as in Jer. xlviii. 45.

Shē'thăr (*star*). A Persian prince, Esth. i. 14.

She'thăr=bŏz'na-i (*star of splendor*). A Persian officer in Syria, Ez. v. 3, 6; vi. 6, 13.

Shē'vȧ. Corruption of Seraiah. (1) A son of Caleb, 1 Chr. ii. 49. (2) The scribe of David, 2 Sam. xx. 25. Shavsha, 1 Chr. xviii. 16. Shisha, 1 Kgs. iv. 3. Seraiah, 2 Sam. viii. 17.

Shew'brĕad (*showbread*). Unleavened bread baked in twelve loaves corresponding to the twelve tribes, and placed fresh every Sabbath on the golden table of the sanctuary. Eaten only by the priests, Ex. xxv. 30; Lev. xxiv. 8; 1 Sam. xxi. 1-6; Matt. xii. 3, 4. The arrangement of loaves on the table was in two rows of six loaves each. Salt and frankincense were put on each row. It was called "shewbread," "bread of the face," or "bread of the setting before," because it stood continually before the Lord. In later times it was called the "bread of ordering," 1 Chr. ix. 32 marg.; Neh. x. 33.

Shĭb'bo-lĕth (*ear of corn, stream*). Pronounced *sib'bo-leth* by Ephraimites, and *shib'bo-leth* by Gileadites. When the latter conquered the former, and held the fords of Jordan, they exacted the pronunciation of this word in order to distinguish friend from foe. Any other word beginning with *sh* would have answered the same purpose, Judg. xii. 6.

Shĭb'mah (*fragrant*). A town in Reuben, east of Jordan, Num. xxxii. 38. Shebam, Num. xxxii. 3. Sibmah, Josh. xiii. 19.

Shī'crŏn (*drunkenness*). A boundary mark of northern Judah, Josh. xv. 11.

Shiēld (*cover*). A defensive piece of armor, varying in size and shape, and made of skin or metal. Worn on left arm. Metaphorically, divine protection, Judg. v. 8; 1 Kgs. x. 17; Ps. iii. 3.

Shĭg-gā'ion (*mournful*). A word which probably designates the character of the ode, Ps. vii. title.

Shī-gī'o-noth. Plural of Shiggaion, Hab. iii. 1.

Shī'hŏn (*ruin*). A town in Issachar, Josh. xix. 19.

Shī'hŏr (*blackness*). (1) Southern boundary of David's empire, 1 Chr. xiii. 5. [SIHOR.] (2) Shihor-libnath, a boundary of Asher, and probably identical with the stream called "Blue River," which empties into the Mediterranean eight miles south of Dor, Josh. xix. 26.

Shĭl'hī (*armed*). Grandfather of King Jehoshaphat, 1 Kgs. xxii. 42; 2 Chr. xx. 31.

Shĭl'him (*armed*). A city in southern Judah, Josh. xv. 32.

Shĭl'lem (*retribution*). Son of Naphtali and founder of Shillemites, Gen. xlvi. 24; Num. xxvi. 49.

Shĭl'lem-ītes. Descendants of Shillem, Num. xxvi. 49.

Shī-lō'ah. The softly flowing waters of Siloam, Isa. viii. 6.

Shī'lōh (*peace*). (1) A disputed rendering; referred to a town and to the Messiah, Gen. xlix. 10; Isa. ix. 6. (2) A city in Ephraim, midway between Bethel and Shechem. Now Seilun. Joshua's capital and site where he apportioned his conquests. The ark remained there for three hundred years, till captured by the Philistines, Josh. xviii. 1, 8-10; Judg. xxi. 19-23. Residence of Eli and Samuel, 1 Sam. iii., and it was there that Eli received word of the capture of the ark, and died, 1 Sam. iv. The ark was not returned to Shiloh after its capture, and the tabernacle was removed to Nob and thence to Jerusalem, but the odor of sanctity clung about the venerable city for generations, and it was long a place for annual pilgrimages and religious festivals. The prophet Ahijah dwelt at Shiloh, 1 Kgs. xiv. 1-18. Jeremiah pictures Shiloh as desolate in his day, Jer. vii. 12-14; xxvi. 6-9.

Shī-lō'nī. A descendant of Shelah, Neh. xi. 5.

Shī'lo-nīte. Dweller in Shiloh, 1 Kgs. xi. 29.

Shī'lo-nītes. Members of the family of Shelah, 1 Chr. ix. 5.

Shĭl'shah (*third*). An Asherite chief, 1 Chr. vii. 37.

Shĭm'e-ȧ (*hearing*). (1) A son of David born in Jerusalem, 1 Chr. iii. 5. (2) A Levite, 1 Chr. vi. 30. (3) Another Levite, 1 Chr. vi. 39. (4) A brother of David, called also Shammah, Shimeah, and Shimma, 1 Chr. xx. 7.

Shĭm'e-ah (*hearing*). (1) Brother of David, called also Shammah, Shimma and Shimea, 2 Sam. xxi. 21. (2) A descendant of Jehiel, founder of Gibeon, 1 Chr. viii. 32.

Shĭm'e-ăm (*hearing*), 1 Chr. ix. 38. [SHIMEAH, 2.]

Shĭm'e-ăth (*hearing*). Mother of one of the murderers of King Joash, 2 Kgs. xii. 21; 2 Chr. xxiv. 26.

Shĭm'e-ath-ītes''. A family of scribes, 1 Chr. ii. 55.

Shĭm'e-ī (*famed*). (1) A son of Gershon, Num. iii. 18. Shimi, Ex. vi. 17. (2) A Benjamite who cursed David, 2 Sam. xvi. 5-13; 1 Kgs. ii. 44-46. (3) One of David's warriors, 1 Kgs. i. 8. (4) A commissary of Solomon, 1 Kgs. iv. 18. (5) Brother of Zerubbabel, 1 Chr. iii. 19. (6) A Simeonite, 1 Chr. iv. 26, 27. (7) A Reubenite, 1 Chr. v. 4. (8) A Levite, 1 Chr. vi. 42. (9) Leader of 10th musical course, 1 Chr. xxv. 17. (10) David's vineyardist, 1 Chr. xxvii. 27. (11) Ancestor of Mordecai, Esth. ii. 5. (12) Levites in 2 Chr. xxix. 14; xxxi. 12, 13; Ez. x. 23, 33, 38.

Shĭm'e-on (*hearing*). One who married a foreign wife, Ez. x. 31.

Shĭm'hī (*famed*). A Benjamite, 1 Chr. viii. 21.

Shī'mī, Ex. vi. 17. [SHIMEI, 1.]

Shĭm'ītes. Descendants of Shimei (1), Num. iii. 21.

Shĭm'mȧ (*hearing*). Third son of Jesse, 1 Chr. ii. 13.

Shī'mon (*waste*). A Judahite, 1 Chr. iv. 20.

Shĭm'rath (*watcher*). A Benjamite, 1 Chr. viii. 21.

Shĭm'rī (*vigilant*). (1) A Simeonite, 1 Chr. iv. 37. (2) Father of one of David's guard, 1 Chr. xi. 45. (3) A Levite, 2 Chr. xxix. 13.

Shĭm'rith (*vigilant*). A Moabitess, mother of Jehozabad, one of the murderers of King Joash, 2 Chr. xxiv. 26. Called Shomer in 2 Kgs. xii. 21.

Shĭm'rŏm, 1 Chr. vii. 1. [SHIMRON, 2.]

Shĭm'rŏn (*watch-place*). (1) An ancient Canaanite city allotted to Zebulun, Josh. xi. 1; xix. 15. (2) Fourth son of Issachar and founder of Shimronites, Gen. xlvi. 13; Num. xxvi. 24.

Shĭm'ron-ītes. Descendants of Shimron (2), Num. xxvi. 24.

Shĭm'ron=mē'ron, Josh. xii. 20. Probably complete name of Shimron (1).

Shĭm'shāi (*bright*). A scribe and Persian satrap in Judea. He, together with the chancellor, Rehum, wrote a letter to King Artaxerxes in opposition to the rebuilding of the temple by Zerubbabel, Ez. iv. 8, 9, 17, 23.

Shī'năb (*splendor*). A king of Admah in time of Abraham, Gen. xiv. 2.

Shī'när (*two rivers*). The alluvial plain through which the Tigris and Euphrates pass, and probably inclusive of Babylon and Mesopotamia, Gen. x. 10; xi. 1-9; Isa. xi. 11; Dan. i. 2. It was the seat of the kingdom founded by Nimrod, and which reckoned among its cities, as beginnings, Babel, Erech, Accad, and Calneh, Gen. x. 9, 10. Asshur went forth from Shinar to found Nineveh, Gen. x. 11. It was in the plain in the land of Shinar that the migrating nations undertook to build the tower of Babel, and where the confusion of tongues occurred, Gen. xi. 1-9.

Ship. Ships of Scripture dependent on oars and sails for propulsion. Hebrews not sailors. The ships of Acts, xxi. 1-6; xxvii. 6-44; xxviii. 11-13, were capable of carrying many people and much freight. Primitive ships were generally coasters. They were mounted with figure-heads and had figures painted on the sides of the bow. These composed the ship's "sign," Acts xxviii. 11. Among their furnishings were under-girders, anchors shaped like those of modern times, but without flukes, sounding-lines, rudder-bands, Acts xxvii. 40. Ancient ships, being wholly or in part propelled by oars, were properly called galleys.

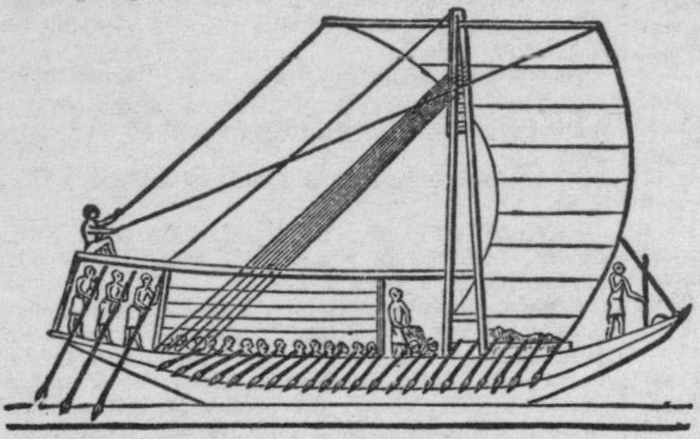

Egyptian Ship of War.

Shī'phī (*many*). A prince of Simeon, in time of Hezekiah, 1 Chr. iv. 37.

Shĭph'mīte. Probably a native of Shepham, and a designation of Zabdi, David's overseer of vineyard increase and wine cellars, 1 Chr. xxvii. 27.

Shĭph'rah (*handsome*). A Hebrew midwife in Egypt, Ex. i. 15.

Shĭph'tan (*judging*). Father of a prince of Ephraim, Num. xxxiv. 24.

Shī'shȧ (*God's strife*). Father of Solomon's scribes, 1 Kgs. iv. 3.

Shī'shăk. The king of Egypt to whom Jeroboam fled, 1 Kgs. xi. 40. He invaded Judea, B. C. 969, defeated Rehoboam, and spoiled the temple, 1 Kgs. xiv. 25, 26; 2 Chr. xii. 2-9. Inscriptions, reliefs, and statuary at Karnak, on the Nile, record his invasion of Palestine.

Shĭt'ra-ī (*scribe*). Keeper of David's herds in Sharon, 1 Chr. xxvii. 29.

Shĭt'tah, Shĭt'tim (*thorny*). (1) An Asiatic tree, a species of acacia, producing a close-grained, yellowish wood used in making the sacred furniture of the tabernacle, Ex. xxv. 10-13; xxvi. 15, 26; xxvii. 1; Isa. xli. 19. (2) Last encampment of the Israelites before crossing the Jordan. Scene of the completion of the law and farewell of Moses, Num. xxv.; xxxi. 1-12; Josh. ii. 1; iii. 1. The spies were sent out from Shittim to Jericho, and there the final preparations were made for crossing the Jordan. It was also called Abel-shittim, "meadow of acacias," and was the well-watered, fertile plain stretching from the foot of the mountains of Moab to the banks of the Jordan. (3) "Valley of Shittim," Joel iii. 18, is doubtless same as Shittim (2), which was also known as Abel-shittim.

Shī'zȧ (*loving*). Father of a Reubenite captain, 1 Chr. xi. 42.

Shō'ȧ (*fruitful*). An undetermined name or place, Ezek. xxiii. 23.

Shō'băb (*hostile*). (1) A son of David, 2 Sam. v. 14; 1 Chr. iii. 5; xiv. 4. (2) A son of Caleb, 1 Chr. ii. 18.

Shō'băch (*enlarging*). A Syrian general whom David defeated, 2 Sam. x. 15-18. Shophach, 1 Chr. xix. 16-18.

Shō'ba-ī (*captive*). A family of temple doorkeepers who returned from captivity, Ez. ii. 42; Neh. vii. 45.

Shō'bal (*current*). (1) Second son of Seir, and a Horite duke, Gen. xxxvi. 20; 1 Chr. i. 38. (2) A son of Caleb, 1 Chr. ii. 50, 52. (3) 1 Chr. iv. 1, 2, probably same as above.

Shō'bek (*forsaken*). A co-covenanter with Nehemiah, Neh. x. 24.

Shō'bī (*captive*). An Ammonite who succored David during Absalom's rebellion, 2 Sam. xvii. 27-29.

Shō'cō, Shō'chō, Shō'choh, 2 Chr. xi. 7; xxviii. 18; 1 Sam. xvii. 1. [SOCOH.]

Shoe. [SANDAL.]

Shō'hăm (*onyx*). A Levite, 1 Chr. xxiv. 27.

Shō'mer (*keeper*). (1) An Asherite, 1 Chr. vii. 32. Shamer in vs. 34. (2) Mother of Jehozabad, a co-murderer of King Joash, 2 Kgs. xii. 21. Called Shimrith in 2 Chr. xxiv. 26.

Shō'phăch, 1 Chr. xix. 16-18. [SHOBACH.]

Shō'phan (*burrow*). A fenced city east of Jordan, which fell to Gad, Num. xxxii. 35.

Shō-shăn'nim (*lilies*). Variously construed as a melody, bridal-song, and musical instrument, Ps. xlv., lxix., lxxx., titles. In the latter, *eduth*, "testimony," is added.

Shoul'der. Baring of, signified servitude, Gen. xlix. 15; withdrawing of, denoted rebellion, Neh. ix. 29; bearing upon, meant to sustain, Isa. ix. 6; xxii. 22.

Shov'el (*shove*). [FAN.] [WINNOW.]

Shu'ȧ (*wealth*). Father-in-law of Judah, 1 Chr. ii. 3. Shuah in Gen. xxxviii. 2, 12.

Shu'ah (*pit*). (1) A son of Abraham, Gen. xxv. 2; 1 Chr. i. 32. (2) Brother of Chelub, 1 Chr. iv. 11. (3) Gen. xxxviii. 2, 12. [SHUA.]

Shu'al (*fox*). (1) An Asherite, 1 Chr. vii. 36. (2) An unlocated land, 1 Sam. xiii. 17.

Shu'ba-el (*God's captive*). (1) Shebuel, son of Gershon, 1 Chr. xxiv. 20. (2) Shebuel, son of Heman the singer, and leader of the thirteenth musical course, 1 Chr. xxv. 20.

Shu'ham (*well-digger*). A son of Dan, Num. xxvi. 42. Hushim, Gen. xlvi. 23.

Shu'ham-ītes. Descendants of Shuham, Num. xxvi. 42.

Shu'hīte. Designation of Bildad, one of Job's friends; associated with *Tsukhi*, an Arabic tribe, Job ii. 11.

Shu'lam-īte. One belonging to Shulem or Shunem, S. of Sol. vi. 13.

Shu'math-ītes. One of the four families of Kirjath-jearim, 1 Chr. ii. 53.

Shu'nam-īte. A native of Shunem. The nurse of David and hostess of Elisha were so called, 1 Kgs. i. 3; 2 Kgs. iv. 12.

Shu̥′nem (*double sleeping-place*). A city of Issachar, near Jezreel. Place where the Philistines encamped before the great battle of Gilboa; home of David's nurse and wife, Abishag; residence of the woman who entertained Elisha. Now Solam, Josh. xix. 18; 1 Sam. xxviii. 4; 2 Kgs. iv. 8.

Shu̥′nī (*resting*). A son of Gad, Gen. xlvi. 16.

Shu̥′nītes. Descendants of Shuni, Num. xxvi. 15.

Shu̥′pham, Num. xxvi. 39. [Shuppim.]

Shu̥′pham-ītes. Descendants of Shupham, Num. xxvi. 39.

Shŭp′pim (*serpents*). (1) Great-grandson of Benjamin, 1 Chr. vii. 12. Shupham, Num. xxvi. 39. (2) A Levite gate-keeper, 1 Chr. xxvi. 16.

Shûr (*wall*). A desert region of Arabia, and its town, bordering on Egypt, Gen. xvi. 7; xxv. 18. "Wilderness of Etham," Num. xxxiii. 8. Inhabited by Amalekites, 1 Sam. xv. 7; xxvii. 8.

Shu̥′shan (*lily*). The Greek Susa, ancient capital of Elam, a province in Mesopotamia. A seat of wealth and power after the Persian conquest of Babylon. The events of Esther's history occurred there. Spot of Daniel's visions. Nehemiah commissioned there, Gen. x. 22; xiv. 1; Neh. i. 1; Esth.; Isa. xxi. 2; Jer. xlix. 34; Dan. viii. 2. The decline of this ancient city dates from its capture by Alexander the Great, or from its later conquest by Antigonus, B. C. 315. The site, nearly due east from Babylon and north of the Persian Gulf, is marked by ruins, some three miles in circumference, in the midst of which have been found the remains of the great palace of Darius, scene of the events narrated in the book of Esther.

Shu̥′shan=ē′duth. Abbreviated form of Shoshannim-eduth, which *see*, Ps. lx. title.

Shu̥′thal-hītes. Descendants of Shuthelah, Num. xxvi. 35.

Shu̥′the̥-lah (*discord*). Head of the Ephraimite family of Shuthalhites, Num. xxvi. 35; 1 Chr. vii. 20, 21.

Shŭt′tle (*shooter*). This weaver's device for throwing the filling thread between the warp threads is figurative of fleeting time in Job vii. 6.

Sī′à (*assembly*). His children returned from captivity, Neh. vii. 47. Siaha, Ez. ii. 44.

Sī′a̤-hà, Ez. ii. 44. [Sia.]

Sĭb′be̥-cāi, 1 Chr. xi. 29; xxvii. 11. [Sibbechai.]

Sĭb′be̥-chāi (*weaver*). One of David's guard, and eighth captain of eighth month, 2 Sam. xxi. 18; 1 Chr. xx. 4. Sibbecai, 1 Chr. xi. 29; xxvii. 11. Mebunnai, 2 Sam. xxiii. 27.

Sĭb′bo̥-lĕth, Judg. xii. 6. [Shibboleth.]

Sĭb′mah (*fragrant*). A fortified city of Reuben, east of Jordan, Josh. xiii. 19. Shebam, Num. xxxii. 3. Shibmah, Num. xxxii. 38. Noted for its grapes, Isa. xvi. 8, 9; Jer. xlviii. 32.

Sĭb′ra̤-ĭm (*twice hopeful*). A boundary mark of northern Palestine, Ezek. xlvii. 16.

Sī′chem, Gen. xii. 6. [Shechem.]

Sĭck′le (*cutter*). The reaping and mowing implement of the ancients. In its size and curvature, as represented on Egyptian monuments, it resembled the implement as known to us, Deut. xvi. 9.

Sĭç′ȳ-ŏn. A city of the Peloponnesus near the Isthmus, 1 Macc. xv. 23.

Sĭd′dim (*pitted vale*). A vale, full of slime-pits, supposably near the Dead Sea, in which the kings of the plain cities met their invaders, Gen. xiv. 1-10.

Sī′de (*trading*). A trading city in Pamphylia, 1 Macc. xv. 23.

Sī′dŏn, Gen. x. 15, 19. [Zidon.]

Sī-dō′nĭ-ans. Zidonians, Deut. iii. 9; Josh. xiii. 4, 6; Judg. iii. 3; 1 Kgs. v. 6.

Siēge (*sit*), Deut. xx. 19. [War.]

Sieve. Ancient sieves, or sifters, were crudely made of rushes, though the Gauls are credited with their manufacture from horsehair. They were used for separating the flour from the bran, or broken kernels, and what was left in the sieve was thrown back into the mill to be reground, Isa. xxx. 28.

Sī′hŏn (*rooting out*). An Amorite king, defeated by the Israelites, who occupied his country between the Arnon and Jabbok, Num. xxi. 21-31; Deut. i. 4; ii. 24-37; Josh. xiii. 15-28.

Sī′hôr (*blackness*). The Sihor, or Shihor, of Egypt, 1 Chr. xiii. 5; Isa. xxiii. 3; Jer. ii. 18, has ever been construed as "the Nile." But when unqualified, some Arabian ravine or wady may be meant.

Sī′las (*Silvanus, woody*). An eminent member of the early Christian church. Written Silvanus in Paul's epistles. Resided at Jerusalem as teacher, but accompanied Paul on his tours, and was his fellow-prisoner at Philippi. Said to have been bishop of Corinth, Acts xv. 22, 32-34, 40; xvii. 14; xviii. 5; 2 Cor. i. 19; 1 Thess. i. 1.

Sĭlk (*Seric stuff*). Silk hardly known to ancient Hebrews. In Prov. xxxi. 22; Ezek. xvi. 10, 13, some fine linen fabric is supposed to be meant. Undoubtedly known in N. T. times, Rev. xviii. 12.

Sĭl′là (*branch*). The place near which King Joash was slain, 2 Kgs. xii. 20.

Sī-lō′ah, Neh. iii. 15. [Siloam.]

Sī-lō′am (*sent*). (1) The celebrated pool, or tank, at Jerusalem, on the south side, near the opening of the Tyropheau valley into the Kidron valley. Originally a part of the water supply of the city, Neh. iii. 15; Isa. viii. 6; John ix. 7-11. (2) An unlocated tower whose fall killed eighteen men, Luke xiii. 4. Siloam still retains its ancient name under the form of the Arabic *Silwân*. It is partly hewn from rock and partly built with masonry. A flight of steps leads down to it. It is no longer a natural spring of fresh, limpid water, but is fed from the Fountain of the Virgin through a rock tunnel over 1700 feet in length. The waters are brackish and colored, and the walls and steps in ruins.

Sĭl-vā′nus (*woody*). [Silas.]

Sĭl′ver (*white*). Used by Hebrews from earliest times for money, vessels, and ornaments, but not in form of coins till after the captivity, Gen. xiii. 2; xxiv. 53; xliv. 2; Job xxviii. 1; Matt. xxvi. 15; Acts xix. 24. Silver supplied to Jerusalem from Arabia and Tarshish, 2 Chr. ix. 14, 21.

Sĭl′vĕr-lings (*little silvers*). Evidently bits of silver money, but whether by weight or coinage is not known, Isa. vii. 23.

Sī′′măl-cū′e. An Arabian chief, guardian of Antiochus, son of Balas, 1 Macc. xi. 39.

Sĭm′e̥-on (*who hears*). (1) Son of Jacob and Leah, Gen. xxix. 33. For the crime in Gen. xxxiv. 25-30 his father denounced him, Gen. xlix. 5 7. His tribe was small, Num. i. 22, 23; xxvi. 14, and their inheritance a scattered portion of Canaan, Josh. xix. 1-9. (2) Son of Judah in genealogy of Christ, Luke iii. 30. (3) Simon Peter, Acts xv. 14. (4) A venerable and pious Jew who blessed the child Jesus in the temple, Luke ii. 25-35. (5) Simeon Niger, Acts xiii. 1. [Niger.]

Sī′mon (*Simeon*). (1) Several distinguished Jews bore this name during the Maccabean period. (2) A native of Samaria and famous sorcerer, who professed Christ for mercenary purposes, Acts viii. 9-24. (3) Simon Peter, Matt. iv. 18. [Peter.] (4) Simon the Canaanite, or Simon Zelotes, was a member of the party of Zealots who advocated the Jewish ritual, and an apostle, Matt. x. 4. (5) Simon the brother of Jesus, Matt. xiii. 55; Mark vi. 3. (6) Simon the Pharisee, in whose house a woman anointed the feet of Jesus, Luke vii. 36-50. (7) Simon, the leper of Bethany, Matt. xxvi. 6. (8) Simon of Cyrene, who was compelled to bear Christ's cross, Matt. xxvii. 32; Mark xv. 21; Luke xxiii. 26. (9) The tanner of Joppa with whom Peter lodged, Acts ix. 43. (10) Simon the father of Judas Iscariot, John vi. 71; xiii. 2, 26.

Sim'ri (*alert*). A Merarite Levite in David's time, 1 Chr. xxvi. 10.

Sin (*clay*). (1) A city of Egypt identified with Pelusium, "town of clay or mud," on eastern mouth of Nile near the sea, Ezek. xxx. 15, 16. (2) A desert portion of Arabia between Gulf of Suez and Sinai, Ex. xvi. 1; xvii. 1; Num. xxxiii. 11, 12. It was in this wilderness that the Israelites were first fed with manna and quails. It skirts the eastern coast of the gulf for a distance of 25 miles.

Pool of Siloam. (*See* p. 105.)

Sin=mon'ey. Money sent from a distance to buy offerings. The surplus, if any, became a perquisite of the priest, and was called sin-money, 2 Kgs. xii. 16.

Sin=ŏf'fĕr-ing. Like the trespass-offering, the sin-offering was expiatory, but seemingly of general sins. It was presented on the great day of atonement, when one confessed the sins of the nation with his hand on the head of the scapegoat, Lev. xvi. 1–34; Num. xviii. 9.

Sī'nȧ. Greek form of Sinai, Acts vii. 30, 38.

Sī'nāi (*bushy*). The peninsula of Sinai lies between the two great arms of the Red Sea, Gulf of Akaba on the east, and Gulf of Suez on the west. This region contains the mountain system of Horeb or Sinai, on one of whose mounts, or peaks, God appeared to Moses in the burning bush, Ex. iii. 1–5, amid whose surrounding wilderness the wandering Israelites encamped, Ex. xix. 1, 2, and from whose cloud-obscured heights the law was delivered to Moses, Ex. xix. 3–25; xx.–xl.; Lev. The numbering also took place there, Num. i.–x. 1–12. The peninsula is a triangle whose base extends from the head of Suez to Akaba. This base is pierced by the plateau of Tih, the "desert of wandering," south of which are those tumultuous mountain clusters above mentioned, central among which is Mount Sinai. The coast ranges along Akaba and Suez are systematic and elevated. The region was a dependency of Egypt from earliest times, but became subject to Rome.

Sī'nim. An unidentified land mentioned in Isa. xlix. 12. Referred by some to China.

Sin'īte. A tribe descended from Canaan, Gen. x. 17; 1 Chr. i. 15.

Sī'ŏn (*lofty*). (1) An ancient name of Mount Hermon, Deut. iv. 48. (2) Greek form of Zion, Matt. xxi. 5; John xii. 15; Heb. xii. 22; Rev. xiv. 1.

Sĭph'moth (*fertile*). A haunt of David, while an outlaw, in South Judah, 1 Sam. xxx. 28.

Sĭp'pāi (*threshold*). Saph, the Philistine giant slain at Gezer, 1 Chr. xx. 4.

Sī'rach. Father of Jesus, writer of the Apocryphal book of Ecclesiasticus.

Sī'rah (*retreat*). The well, now *Ain Sarah*, from which Abner was called by Joab. It was near Hebron, 2 Sam. iii. 26.

Sĭr'ĭ-ŏn. Zidonian name of Mount Hermon, Deut. iii. 9; Ps. xxix. 6.

Sī-săm'a-ī (*famed*). A descendant of Sheshan, of Judah, 1 Chr. ii. 40.

Sĭs'e-rȧ (*ready for war*). (1) Captain of King Jabin's forces when defeated by Barak. Slain by Jael, Judg. iv.; v. (2) His children returned, Ez. ii. 53; Neh. vii. 55.

Sī-sin'nēs. Governor of Syria and Phœnicia under Darius, 1 Esdr. vi. 3.

Sĭt'nah (*strife*). Second of the two wells dug by Isaac in valley of Gerar, over which the herdsmen disputed, Gen. xxvi. 21.

Sī'van. Third month of Jewish sacred and ninth of civil year, beginning with the new moon of June, Esth. viii. 9.

Slāve (*Sclavonian*). Slavery came about under Hebrew institutions. (1) By poverty, when a man sold himself to cancel debt, Lev. xxv. 39; (2) by theft, when restitution could not be made, Ex. xxii. 3; (3) by parents selling their daughters as concubines, Ex. xxi. 7–11. It ended (1) when the debt was paid; (2) on the year of Jubilee, Lev. xxv. 40; (3) at the end of six years of service, Ex. xxi. 2; Deut. xv. 12. This as to Hebrews. As to non-Hebrew slaves, by far the most numerous class, they were purchased, Lev. xxv. 45; or captured in war, Num. xxxi. 26, 40. They were freed if ill treated, Ex. xxi. 26, 27; to slay one was murder, Lev. xxiv. 17, 22; they were circumcised and had religious privileges, Gen. xvii. 12, 13.

Slīme. The slime of Babel, and that of the pits of Siddim, and the ark of Moses, was mineral pitch or bitumen, Gen. xi. 3; xiv. 10; Ex. ii. 3.

Slĭng. The weapons of shepherds and light troops. It consisted of leather or sinew strings with a pouch at the end for the missile, Judg. xx. 16; 1 Sam. xvii. 40.

Smĭth (*smiter*). An artificer in iron, brass, or other metals, Gen. iv. 22; 1 Sam. xiii. 19–22.

Smȳr'nȧ (*myrrh*). A coast city of Ionia, Asia Minor, 40 miles north of Ephesus. Mentioned in Rev. ii. 8–11 as site of one of the seven churches of Asia. The old city of Smyrna dates back to Theseus, 1300 years B. C. Alexander the Great built the new city B. C. 320. It became subject to Rome and was noted for its beauty. Christianity got an early foothold there and the city sent a bishop to the council of Nice, A. D. 325. It is still a large city of mixed nationalities and creeds, and of considerable commercial importance.

Snāil (*snake*). In Lev. xi. 30 a lizard is meant. In Ps. lviii. 8, the common snail, slug, or slime-snake is meant. Snails abound in the Orient and are not eschewed as a food.

Snōw. Only mentioned once as actually falling,

2 Sam. xxiii. 20; but of frequent poetic and metaphoric use, Ex. iv. 6; Num. xii. 10; 2 Kgs. v. 27; Ps. li. 7; Isa. i. 18.

Snŭff-dĭsh'es. Small dishes, made of gold, for receiving the snuff from the tabernacle lamps, Ex. xxv. 38.

Snŭf'fẽrs. Scissor-like instruments, made of gold, for snuffing the wicks of the tabernacle lamps, Ex. xxxvii. 23.

Sō. A king of Egypt with whom Hoshea formed an alliance against Assyria. The discovery of this led to the imprisonment of Hoshea, the siege and capture of Samaria, and the captivity of the ten tribes of Israel, 2 Kgs. xvii. 4, 6.

Smyrna. (*See* p. 106.)

Sōap (*sap, resin*). The Hebrew word for soap implies any alkaline substance used for cleansing, Jer. ii. 22; Mal. iii. 2.

Sō'chō, 1 Chr. iv. 18. [SOCOH.]

Sō'choh, 1 Kgs. iv. 10. [SOCOH.]

Sō'coh (*brambly*). (1) A town in lowlands of Judah, Josh. xv. 35. Shocho, 2 Chr. xxviii. 18. Shoco, 2 Chr. xi. 7. Shochoh, 1 Sam. xvii. 1. (2) A town in the mountains of Judah, Josh. xv. 48.

Sō'dī (*secret*). Father of the spy from Zebulun, Num. xiii. 10.

Sŏd'om (*consuming*). Most prominent of the cities in the plain of Siddim. Destroyed by fire from heaven, Gen. x. 19; xiii. 10-13; xix. 1-29. Site of "the cities of the plain" is not known, but variously referred to the southern end, the northern end, and bottom of the Dead Sea. Sodom is often referred to in Scripture as a symbol of wickedness and warning to sinners, Deut. xxix. 23; Isa. i. 9, 10; xiii. 19; Jer. xxiii. 14; xlix. 18; Ezek. xvi. 49, 50; Matt. x. 15; xi. 23; Rev. xi. 8.

Sŏd'om-ȧ. Greek and Vulgate form of Sodom, Rom. ix. 29.

Sŏd'om-ītes. Dwellers in Sodom, or, by figure, those who practise the abominations of Sodom, Deut. xxiii. 17; 1 Kgs. xiv. 24; xv. 12.

Sŏl'o-mon (*peaceful*). Last of David's sons by Bathsheba. Named Jedidiah, "beloved of God," by Nathan, 1 Chr. iii. 5; 2 Sam. xii. 25. Placed in Nathan's care. Secured the throne according to David's pledge, 1 Kgs. i. 13-53, and much to the consternation of Adonijah, the legal successor. Reigned forty years, B. C. 1015-975. Confirmed his father's conquests, built the palace and temple, extended commerce, contracted favorable alliances, grew famous for wisdom, raised his kingdom to great wealth, splendor, and power, mingled justice with cruelty, endorsed true and false worship, encouraged literature, and wrote largely himself, fell a prey to the sensualities of his time and position, died leaving his kingdom under the eclipse of faction and on the edge of decay, 1 Kgs. ii.-xi.; 2 Chr. i.-ix.

Sŏl'o-mon's Pools. Reservoirs erected by Solomon near Bethlehem, whence water was conveyed to the distributing pools at Jerusalem. They are still in partial use, Eccl. ii. 6.

Sŏl'o-mon's Porch. The colonnade on east side of the temple, John x. 23; Acts iii. 11; v. 12.

Sŏl'o-mon's Sẽr'vants. Returned captives, and probable descendants of a class of servants favored by Solomon, Ez. ii. 55, 58; Neh. vii. 57, 60.

Sŏl'o-mon's Sŏng. [SONG OF SOLOMON.]

Son. In Hebrew sense, any descendant however remote, Gen. xxix. 5; 2 Sam. xix. 24. Applied also to pupils, adopted persons, those of kindred faith, etc., Gen. xlviii. 5; 1 Sam. iii. 6; Acts xiii. 6.

Son of God. A term applied to the angels, Job xxxviii. 7; to Adam, Luke iii. 38; to believers, Rom. viii. 14; 2 Cor. vi. 18; but preëminently to Christ, signifying his divine origin and nature, Dan. iii. 25; Matt. xi. 27; xvi. 16; John i. 18; v. 19-26; ix. 35.

Son of Man. In a limited sense, "man," Num. xxiii. 19; Job xxv. 6; Ps. viii. 4. In a broader, higher, and perhaps more generally received Hebrew sense, "the Messiah." In the N. T. sense, where the term is used some eighty times, it means Christ in incarnate form and relation, Dan. vii. 13; Matt. ix. 6; xii. 8; xviii. 11; Mark ii. 10; John i. 51; iii. 13; vi. 53.

Sŏng of Sŏl'o-mon. "Song of Songs," or "Canticles," in Latin. Twenty-second O. T. book and last of poetic. Authorship and meaning much disputed. Some make it type conjugal love; others regard it as purely allegorical; still others as literal and descriptive of Solomon's marriage to some beautiful woman.

Sooth'say-er (*truth-sayer*). One who pretends to foretell future events, Dan. ii. 27. [DIVINATION.]

Sŏp (*sip*). Bread dipped in soup, milk, wine, sauce, or other liquid, Ruth ii. 14; John xiii. 26.

Sŏp′a-tēr (*father saved*). A Berean companion of Paul, Acts xx. 4.

Sŏph′e-rĕth (*scribe*). His children were returned captives, Ez. ii. 55.

Sŏph″ō-nī′as. The prophet Zephaniah, 2 Esdr. i. 40.

Sôr′çĕr-er (*fate-worker*). [Divination.]

Sō′rek (*vine*). A valley of Philistia, where Delilah lived, Judg. xvi. 4.

Sō-sĭp′a-tēr (*Sopater*). (1) A general of Judas Maccabeus, 2 Macc. xii. 19–24. (2) A friend of Paul; probably Sopater, Rom. xvi. 21.

Sŏs′the-nēs (*saviour*). (1) A ruler of the synagogue at Corinth, who was beaten by the Greeks, Acts xviii. 17. (2) Perhaps the former, after conversion, 1 Cor. i. 1.

Sŏs′tra-tus. A Syrian general commanding in Jerusalem, 2 Macc. iv. 27.

Sō′ta-ī (*fickle*). His children were returned captives, Ez. ii. 55; Neh. vii. 57.

Sōul. The Hebrew ideal of man was threefold: (1) The body, or material part. (2) The vital part, seat of sensations, passions, etc. (3) The sentient, thinking, or spiritual part, Gen. i. 20; ii. 7; Num. xvi. 22; 1 Thess. v. 23; Heb. iv. 12.

South Rā′moth. A place in southern Judah, bordering on the desert, and one of the resorts of David during the period of his outlawry by Saul, 1 Sam. xxx. 27.

Sow. [Swine.]

Sōw′er, Sōw′ing. Cereal seeds were sown by hand, Ps. cxxvi. 6; Am. ix. 13; Mark iv. 3–29. In moist ground seeds were tramped in by cattle, Isa. xxxii. 20. Mixed seeds prohibited, Lev. xix. 19; Deut. xxii. 9.

Spāin. Anciently the whole peninsula of southwestern Europe, embracing Spain and Portugal; known to Greeks as Iberia and to Romans as Hispania. If identical with Tarshish, then known to Hebrews in Solomon's time; certainly to Phœnicians. Known to Paul, who contemplated a visit to it, Rom. xv. 24–28. Christianity early introduced there.

Spăn (*bind*). Distance from tip of thumb to that of little finger, when stretched apart; about nine inches. Also any small interval of space or time, 1 Sam. xvii. 4; Isa. xl. 12; Lam. ii. 20.

Spăr′row (*spurrer*). The Hebrew word signifies "twitterer" and is mostly rendered "bird" or "fowl." Though tree-sparrows abounded in Palestine, any small bird meets the sense in Ps. lxxxiv. 3; cii. 7. In N. T. the reference is directly to the sparrow species, used as a cheap food, Matt. x. 29; Luke xii. 6, 7.

Spēar (*spar*). In general, a wooden staff with a sharp metallic head. Some were light for throwing, others long and heavy for attack either by footmen or horsemen, 1 Sam. xiii. 22; xvii. 7; xxvi. 7; 2 Sam. ii. 23.

Spēar′men. Light-armed troops are evidently meant, Acts xxiii. 23.

Spĕck′led Bird, Jer. xii. 9. [Hyena.]

Spīce, Spī′çes (*species*). Hardly, as with us, the entire list of aromatic vegetable substances, but rather the fragrant gums, barks, etc., of ceremonial, medicinal, and toilet value, and for embalming, Gen. xxxvii. 25; xliii. 11; S. of Sol. iv. 14; Mark xvi. 1; John xix. 39, 40.

Spī′der (*spinner*). The common spider is meant in Job viii. 14; Isa. lix. 5; but the gecko, or lizard, is probably intended in Prov. xxx. 28. The lightness and frailty of the spider's web are made emblematic of visionary hopes and wicked schemes.

Spīke′närd (*pointed leaf yielding perfume*). An ancient fragrant and costly ointment made from the spikenard plant of India, S. of Sol. i. 12; iv. 13, 14; Mark xiv. 3; John xii. 3.

Spĭn′ning (*spanning, drawing*). A well-known and necessary female occupation among Hebrews. The instrument — distaff and spindle — permitted of much the same drawing and twisting process as is now employed in the East, in the absence of the more modern spinning-wheel, Ex. xxxv. 25; Prov. xxxi. 19; Matt. vi. 28.

Spĭr′it (*breath*). The breath, 2 Thess. ii. 8. The vital principle, Eccl. viii. 8. Elsewhere, the soul. [Soul.] Holy Spirit, or Ghost, is the third person in the Trinity, 2 Cor. xiii. 14; Acts xv. 28. Though Holy Spirit and Holy Ghost are synonymous in meaning, preference is given to the latter form in the Scriptures, Matt. i. 18; John i. 33; Acts ii. 4; Rom. v. 5, and elsewhere, the former being used only four times.

Spôil. Plunder seized by violence, as the spoils of an army or of bandits, 1 Sam. xxx. 19–22; but in Ex. iii. 22, the sense is that of recovery without violence of unjustly taken property. David instituted very strict regulations for the division of spoils of war among his soldiers, 1 Sam. xxx. 20–25.

Sponge. Only mentioned in N. T., though probably known to ancient Hebrews, Matt. xxvii. 48; Mark xv. 36; John xix. 29.

Spouse. [Marriage.]

Sprĭn′kling (*springing*). The blood of the sin-offering was sprinkled with the finger of the priest

Snail. (*See* p. 106.)

upon the mercy-seat of the inner sanctuary as an atonement for the holy place because of national uncleanness, Lev. xvi. 14-16. The "blood of sprinkling" or mediatorial blood of the new covenant, Heb. xii. 24, is made antithetical with the blood of vengeance, Gen. iv. 10.

Stā'chy̆s (*ear of corn*). A Roman Christian saluted by Paul, Rom. xvi. 9.

Stăc'tē (*drop*). An oriental gum or spice, one of the components of the holy incense, Ex. xxx. 34.

Stănd'ard. [Ensign.]

Stär (*strew*). All the heavenly bodies, except sun and moon, called stars by Hebrews, Gen. xv. 5; Ps. cxlvii. 4. The "star in the east," seen and followed by the "wise men," and designed to announce the birth of the Messiah, was, according to some, wholly phenomenal, and to others, natural. Stars symbolize rulers and princes, Dan. viii. 10; angels, Job xxxviii. 7; ministers, Rev. i. 16-20. Christ is "the bright and morning star," Rev. xxii. 16.

Stā'ter (*standard*). The standard gold coin of ancient Greece, worth about $4.00. Later, the silver stater, containing four drachmæ, or about sixty cents. This is thought to be the "piece of money" of Matt. xvii. 27.

Stēel. Hebrews were not acquainted with carbonized iron, or steel. Wherever the word is found in Scripture, copper is meant, Ps. xviii. 34.

Stĕph'a-năs (*crown*). One of Paul's earliest converts at Corinth, 1 Cor. i. 16; xvi. 15.

Stē'phen (*crown*). Chief of the first seven deacons, and first Christian martyr. A Greek convert of strong faith and great eloquence. Arrested and tried before the Sanhedrim, but stoned to death by an angry mob, before he had time to finish his defence. The date of his martyrdom is fixed at about A. D. 37. It was followed by the conversion of Saul, who was present at the stoning, and a bitter persecutor of early Christians at the time, Acts vi. 5-15, vii., viii. 1-3.

Stŏcks (*sticks*). Tree-trunks, Job xiv. 8; idols, Jer. ii. 27; instruments of punishment made of beams of wood which closed over the arms or ankles, Job xiii. 27; xxxiii. 11; Jer. xx. 2; Acts xvi. 24.

Stō'ĭcs (*porch scholars*). Members of a Grecian philosophical school, or sect, founded by Zeno, 308 B. C., who taught in the *stoa*, or porch, of the Agora at Athens. They held to a high morality, proud independence of spirit, fateful, in place of providential, superintendence, wisdom as the source of happiness, Acts xvii. 18. Paul encountered both Stoics and Epicureans at Athens, and, on being taken into Areopagus by them, delivered to them the oration in Acts xvii. 22-31.

Stom'ach-er. An article of dress worn over breast and stomach. Much affected in the 17th century; but whether that of Isa. iii. 24 was similar is not known.

Stōnes. Used for building, 1 Kgs. v. 17; Am. v. 11; memorial marks, Gen. xxviii. 18; xxxv. 14; knives, Ex. iv. 25; ballots, Rev. ii. 17. Symbols of hardness, 1 Sam. xxv. 37; of firmness, Gen. xlix. 24; Christian aggregation, 1 Pet. ii. 4-6. Precious stones highly prized by Hebrews and much used on priestly vestments and as ornaments. Twenty gems are mentioned in the Bible, Gen. ii. 12; Ex. xxviii. 9-21. India, Arabia, and Syria were the sources of gems used by Hebrews, Ezek. xxvii. 16-22.

Stō'ning. [Punishment.]

Stôrk (*vulture*). A large wading bird, plentiful in Palestine, gregarious, migratory, nesting in trees and noted for tenderness to its young. Unclean under the law, Lev. xi. 19; Deut. xiv. 18; Ps. civ. 17; Jer. viii. 7.

Strāin at a, Matt. xxiii. 24. "Strain out the," in R. V.

Strān'ġer (*without*). One away from his country, Gen. xxiii. 4. One not a Jew, Ex. xx. 10. One not of Aaron's family, Num. iii. 10. One not of royal blood, Matt. xvii. 25, 26. One alienated or neglected, Ps. lxix. 8. But, in general, any naturalized foreigner in the Jewish State, Deut. xvii. 15. Strangers, in Hebrew acceptation, were numerous in Israel, owing to the mixed multitudes which were permitted to follow the wanderers in the wilderness, to the fact that very many Canaanites remained in the land, and to the liberal regulations respecting captives taken in war.

Straw. Straw used for cattle fodder and litter, Gen. xxiv. 25; 1 Kgs. iv. 28; Isa. xi. 7; lxv. 25; in making bricks, Ex. v. 7, 16.

Sū'ah (*sweeping*). An Asherite, 1 Chr. vii. 36.

Sū'bȧ. His sons returned, 1 Esdr. v. 34.

Sŭc'coth (*tents*). (1) The place east of Jordan where Jacob built a house and booths, Gen. xxxiii. 17; Josh. xiii. 27; Judg. viii. 5-16. Between Succoth and Zarthan, in the plain of Jordan, lay the clay ground in which were cast the brazen utensils for the temple, 1 Kgs. vii. 46; 2 Chr. iv. 17. (2) First station of the Israelites after starting from Egypt, a day's journey from Rameses, Ex. xii. 37; xiii. 20; Num. xxxiii. 5, 6.

Sŭc'coth-bē'noth (*tents of daughters*). Some refer it to a Babylonian idol set up by colonists in Samaria, others to booths or tents in which the daughters of Babylon prostituted themselves in honor of their goddess, 2 Kgs. xvii. 30.

Sū'chath-ītes. A family of scribes at Jabez, 1 Chr. ii. 55.

Sŭd. River of Sura, probably Euphrates, Bar. i. 4.

Sŭk'kĭ-ĭms. An African people who supported Shishak when he invaded Judah, 2 Chr. xii. 3.

Stork.

Sŭn. The greater light, Gen. i. 15-18. Worshipped by idolatrous Hebrews, 2 Kgs. xxi. 3, 5; xxiii. 5; and by other nations, Job xxxi. 26, 27; Gen. xli. 45; furnishes many metaphors, Ps. lxxxiv. 11; John i. 9; Rev. i. 16.

Sûr. A place on sea-coast of Palestine, Judith ii. 28.

Sure'tȳ (*security*). Suretyship in the older sense of pledge was regulated by the Mosaic law, Gen. xliv. 32; Ex. xxii. 25, 26; Deut. xxiv. 6-17. When Solomon opened Palestine to commerce, suretyship took the forms of general law and trade, Prov. vi. 1; xi. 15; xvii. 18; xx. 16; xxii. 26. [LOANS.] [PLEDGE.]

Sụ′sȧ, Esth. xi. 3. [SHUSHAN.]

Sụ′san-chītes. Dwellers in Shushan or Susa, Ez. iv. 9.

Sụ′ṣăn′nȧ (*lily*). (1) Heroine of the story of the Judgment of Daniel, as found in "The History of Susanna," one of the Apocryphal books. (2) One of the women who ministered to Christ, Luke viii. 3.

Swallow of Palestine.

Sū′sī (*horseman*). Father of the Manassite spy, Num. xiii. 11.

Swạl′low (*throat sweller*). The common swift or swallow abounds in Palestine, and its habits, according to Bible mention, are such as we observe: building under the eaves of houses, beneath temple cornices and porticos, and in the sides of cliffs, and rapidly circling above their homes in search of their aerial food, Ps. lxxxiv. 3; Prov. xxvi. 2; Isa. xxxviii. 14; Jer. viii. 7.

Swạn. Swans rare in Palestine. Unclean, Lev. xi. 18; Deut. xiv. 16. The original seems to imply some other bird, as the ibis or water-hen.

Swear′ing. [OATH.]

Swĕat. The bloody sweat of the agony is known to medical science, and ascribed to violent mental emotion, Luke xxii. 44.

Swīne. The hog was pronounced unclean, Lev. xi. 7; Deut. xiv. 8. Priests and Arabians abstained from the meat for dietetic reasons. Swine-keeping a degrading business, Luke xv. 15; yet swine were kept, Matt. viii. 32. To cast "pearls before swine" was to waste truth on those who despised it, Matt. vii. 6.

Swôrd. A short, two-edged, dagger-like weapon, carried in a sheath or scabbard, and suspended to the girdle or belt, Gen. xxvii. 40; Judg. iii. 16; 2 Sam. xx. 8; Jer. xlvii. 6; Ezek. xxi. 9, 30.

Sy̆c′ạ-mine, Luke xvii. 6. [SYCAMORE.]

Sy̆c′ạ-mōre (*fig-mulberry*). Not our sycamore or plane-tree, but a tree of the fig species growing in Egypt and Palestine and valued for its fruit and light, soft, durable wood, 1 Kgs. x. 27; 1 Chr. xxvii. 28; Ps. lxxviii. 47; Luke xix. 4. Sycamine in Luke xvii. 6. Sycamore fruit grows singly or in clusters and in almost direct contact with the branches. It resembles the fig in shape, and though of acrid taste when first pulled soon becomes sweetish. Egyptian mummy-cases were made of the wood of the sycamore tree.

Sȳ′char, John iv. 5. [SHECHEM.]

Sȳ′chem, Acts vii. 16. [SHECHEM.]

Sȳ-ē′ne (*key*). A city of Egypt bordering on Ethiopia. Situated on the Nile below the first cataract, and noted for its quarries of syenite stone, Ezek. xxix. 10; xxx. 6. Syene was an important city during the reigns of the Hyksos, or Shepherd Kings, in Egypt. It is now represented by the Arab village of Aswan.

Sy̆n′ạ-gŏgue (*led together*). The Jewish assembly for social and religious purposes seems to have had its origin during the captivity, or to have been an outgrowth of it, Ez. viii. 15; Neh. viii. 2; ix. 1. The casual, or house, assemblages soon ran into regular congregations, with suitable buildings and stated meetings, at requisite points. These were the synagogues, often elaborate and costly, presided over by a chief, or rabbi, assisted by a council of elders, Mark v. 22, 35; Luke iv. 20; John xvi. 2; Acts xviii. 8.

Sy̆n′ty̆-chē (*fate*). A woman of the church at Philippi, Phil. iv. 2.

Sy̆r′ạ-cūse. A noted city on eastern coast of Sicily, where Paul spent three days on his voyage to Rome, Acts xxviii. 12.

Sy̆r′ị-ȧ. The Hebrew Aram. So indefinitely bounded at different times as to have been associated with Assyria (whence its name) and Babylon. More definitely the country to the north of Canaan, extending from the Tigris to the Mediterranean, and northward to the Taurus ranges. Damascus was the capital, and centre of wealth, learning, and power. Joshua subdued its petty kings, Josh. xi. 2-18; David reduced it to submission, 2 Sam. viii., x. During Solomon's reign it became independent, 1 Kgs. xi. 23-25. The earliest recorded settlers in Syria were Hittites and other Hamitic races. The Shemitic element entered it from the southeast under Abraham and Chedorlaomer. After Syria became independent it was a persistent enemy of the Jews, 1 Kgs. xv. 18-20; xx., xxii.; 2 Kgs. vi. 8-33; vii., ix. 14, 15; x. 32, 33; xiii. 3, 14-25. The attempt of the Syrian king to ally Israel with him for the

Ancient Swords.

overthrow of Judah led Ahaz to call in the help of Assyria, and Syria was soon merged into the great Assyrian empire. It was conquered by Alexander the Great, B. C. 333, and finally fell to the lot of Seleucus Nicator, who made it the central province of his empire, with the capital at Antioch. The Syriac language was closely allied to the Hebrew.

Sўr'ĭ-ac. The ancient language of Syria, an Aramean dialect. In Dan. ii. 4, the word "Syriac" should read "Aramaic," the court language of Babylon at the time.

Sycamore Figs. (*See* p. 110.)

Sўr'ĭ-ȧ=mā'ą-chah, 1 Chr. xix. 6. [SYRIA and MAACHAH.]

Sўr'ĭ-an. Inhabitant of Syria, Gen. xxv. 20, and elsewhere.

Sў'rō=phē-nĭ'çĭan. A Phœnician at the time Phœnicia was part of the Roman province of Syria; or it may mean one of half Syrian and half Phœnician blood, Mark vii. 26.

Syr'tis, in Acts xxvii. 17, R. V. The dangerous quicksands or shallows on the African coast, southwest of Crete.

T

Tā'ą-năch (*sandy*). A Canaanite city conquered by Joshua and assigned to Levites, Josh. xii. 21; xvii. 11-18; Judg. i. 27; 1 Kgs. iv. 12. Now Taanak, 4 miles from Megiddo. Tanach, Josh. xxi. 25.

Tā'ą-năth=shī'lōh (*pass to Shiloh*). A border mark of Ephraim, Josh. xvi. 6.

Tăb'bą-ōth (*rings*). Father of returned Nethinim, Ez. ii. 43; Neh. vii. 46.

Tăb'bath (*famous*). Where the fleeing Midianites stopped after Gideon's night attack, Judg. vii. 22.

Tā'bę-al (*good God*). Father of a general under Pekah, or in Rezin's Syrian army, whom it was proposed to make king of Judah, Isa. vii. 6.

Tā'bę-el (*good God*). A Persian officer in Samaria under King Artaxerxes, Ez. iv. 7.

Tȧ-bĕl'lĭ-us, 1 Esdr. ii. 15. [TABEEL.]

Tăb'ę-rah (*burning*). A place in the wilderness of Paran, where the Israelites encamped. It was so called because God there consumed the murmurers. The encampment remained there for a month, and the excessive eating of quail led to a pestilence, for which reason the place was called Kibroth-hattavah, or "graves of lust," Num. xi. 3, 34; Deut. ix. 22.

Tā'bĕr-ing. Beating upon the taber, tabret, or small drum. Word now obsolete, Nah. ii. 7.

Tăb'ĕr-nȧ-cle (*little shed or tent*). Tent of Jehovah, or movable sanctuary, which Moses was directed to erect in the wilderness, Ex. xxv. 8. Its plan, materials, and furnishings are described in Ex. xxv. 9-40; xxvi., xxvii. It could be readily taken down and set up and accompanied the Israelites during their wanderings, Ex. xl. 38. During the conquest it was stationed at Gilgal, Josh. iv. 19; ix. 6; x. 15; and at Ebal, Josh. viii. 30-35. After the conquest it was set up at Shiloh, Josh. xviii. 1, where it remained during the time of the Judges and where the ark was captured by the Philistines, 1 Sam. iv. 17, 22. Sometime after the return of the ark it was taken to Jerusalem and placed in a new tabernacle, and finally in the temple, 2 Sam. vi. 17; 1 Chr. xv. 1, but the old structure was still venerated, as long as it remained at Shiloh. It was afterwards removed to Nob, 1 Sam. xxi. 1-9, and in the reign of David to Gibeon, 1 Chr. xvi. 39; xxi. 29, where it was at the beginning of Solomon's reign. Some suppose that the tabernacle and its furniture were moved into Solomon's temple when it was completed.

Tăb'ĕr-nȧ-cle of Tĕs'ti-mō-nў. As the stone tables of the Ten Commandments were called the "tables of testimony," Ex. xxxi. 18; xxxii. 15; xxxiv. 29; and the ark which contained them was called the "ark of testimony," Ex. xxv. 22, so the tabernacle in which the ark was placed was called the "tabernacle of testimony," Ex. xxxviii. 21; Num. i. 50. Called also "the tabernacle of witness," in Num. xvii. 7, 8.

Tăb'ĕr-nȧ-cleş, Feast of. Third of the three great Hebrew feasts, celebrated from the 15th to 22d of Tisri. It commemorated the long tent life of the Israelites, and during its celebration the people dwelt in booths. Called also "feast of ingathering," Ex. xxiii. 16, because it came at end of harvest. It was closed with a holy convocation, Lev. xxiii. 36; and on Sabbatical years was similarly opened and closed, when the law was read anew, Deut. xxxi. 11-13. For law as to solemnization *see* Lev. xxiii. 34-43; Num. xxix. 12-40. Its observance is referred to in Neh. viii. 13-18; Hos. xii. 9; Zech. xiv. 16-19; John. vii. 2, 37, 38.

Tăb'ĭ-thȧ (*gazelle*). The Christian woman of Joppa whom Peter raised from the dead, Acts ix. 36-42. [DORCAS.]

Tā'ble (*board*). Primitive tables were merely leather or skins spread on the floor. After the

Syene. (*See* p. 110.)

captivity they were slightly raised. Beds or couches are meant in Mark vii. 4; writing tablet of wax in Luke i. 63. The "tables" of Matt. xxi. 12; John ii. 15, were doubtless sufficiently raised to answer the purposes of a counter for money-changing purposes. The meaning of "serve tables" in Acts vi. 2, is that duty which fell to the early Christian ministry of attending to the gathering and distributing of food to the poor, or of collecting and distributing the church funds. This duty was transferred to the deacons, Acts vi. 5, 6.

Southeast View of the Tabernacle covered by the Tent. (*See* p. 111.)

Tā′bôr (*mound*). (1) A high mountain on north side of plain of Esdraelon; landmark between Issachar and Zebulun, Josh. xix. 22; gathering place of Barak's forces, Judg. iv. 6-14; scene of murder of Gideon's brothers, Judg. viii. 18-21. (2) Levitical town in Zebulun, 1 Chr. vi. 77. (3) "Plain of Tabor," 1 Sam. x. 3, should read "oak of Tabor."

Tăb′ret (*little tabor*). A small drum or tambourine, without jingles; used to accompany pipes, 1 Sam. xviii. 6. [TIMBREL.]

Tăb′rĭ-mŏn (*Rimmon is good*). Father of Benhadad I., King of Syria in time of Asa, 1 Kgs. xv. 18.

Tăche (*tack*). Taches were hooks or clasps of gold or copper for connecting the tabernacle curtains, Ex. xxvi. 6, 11.

Tăch′mo-nīte, 2 Sam. xxiii. 8. Hachmonite, or "son of Hachmoni."

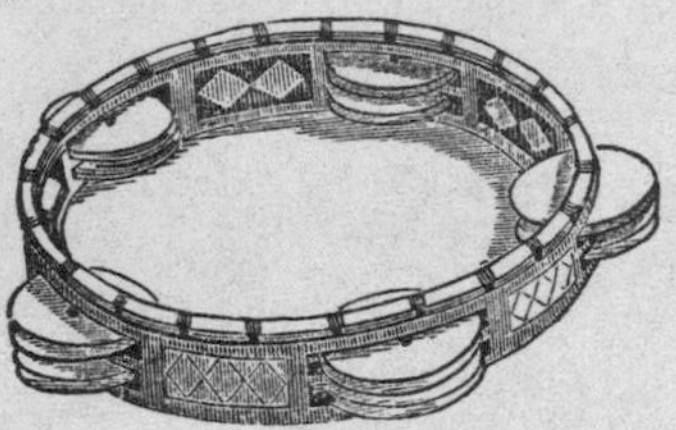

Tambourine.

Tăd′môr (*Tamar, palms*). The Palmyra of the Greeks and Romans. A city built by Solomon in Syria, toward the Euphrates, for the purpose of facilitating trade with the east. Its ruins are numerous and suggestive, 1 Kgs. ix. 18; 2 Chr. viii. 4. Tadmor, or Palmyra, reached the height of its splendor, wealth, and power under the celebrated Zenobia, "Queen of the East," who made it the capital of her empire. It fell a prey to the victorious Romans. Among its notable ruins are the Temple of the Sun, dedicated to Baal, a Street of Columns, of which 150 are still standing, and a series of magnificent tombs intended for both burial places and places of worship. The old name still exists in the form of Thadmor.

Tā′hăn (*camp*). An Ephraimite, Num. xxvi. 35; 1 Chr. vii. 25.

Tā′hăn-ītes. Descendants of Tahan, Num. xxvi. 35.

Tă-hăp′a-nēs, Jer. ii. 16. [TAHPANHES.]

Tā′hăth (*station*). (1) A desert station of the Israelites, Num. xxxiii. 26, 27. (2) A Levite, 1 Chr. vi. 24, 37. (3) Two Ephraimites, 1 Chr. vii. 20.

Tăh′pan-hēs. An ancient city of Egypt on the Tanitic mouth of the Nile. Identical with the Daphne of the Greeks. A favorite resort of exiled Jews, Jer. xliii. 7-9; xliv. 1; xlvi. 14. Jeremiah was taken thither, after the murder of Gedaliah, and the Pharaoh erected a brick palace there. The children of Noph and Tahpanhes are made to type the entire population of Egypt, Jer. ii. 16.

Tăh′pen-ēs. An Egyptian queen, wife of the Pharaoh who received Hadad, king of Edom, 1 Kgs. xi. 18-20.

Tăh-rē′ă (*cunning*). A descendant of Saul, 1 Chr. ix. 41. Tarea, 1 Chr. viii. 35.

Tăh′tim-hŏd′shī. An unknown land visited by Joab during his census tour, 2 Sam. xxiv. 6.

Tāle (*number*). A reckoning by number and not by weight, Ex. v. 8.

Tăl′ent (*weight*). A Hebrew weight and denomination for money, equal to 3,000 shekels, or 93¾ pounds of silver, and varying in value from $1,550 to $2,000, Ex. xxxviii. 25; Matt. xviii. 24. The Attic, or Greek talent, was worth about $1,200; the Roman great talent, $500; the Roman small talent, $375.

Tăl′ĭ-thă cū′mī. Two Syro-Chaldaic words spoken by Christ, and meaning "Damsel, arise," Mark v. 41.

Tăl′māi (*brave*). (1) A son of Anak, Num. xiii. 22; Josh. xv. 14; Judg. i. 10. (2) King of Geshur and father-in-law of David, 2 Sam. iii. 3.

Tăl′mon (*captive*). A temple porter, 1 Chr. ix. 17, and father of a family of returned captives, Ezr. ii. 42; Neh. vii. 45; xi. 19; xii. 25.

Tăl′mŭd (*instruction*). The body of Jewish civil and canonical law not comprised in the Pentateuch, and commonly including the *Mishna* (traditions and decisions) and *Gemara* (expositions).

Tā′mah (*mirth*). Ancestor of returned Nethinim, Neh. vii. 55. Thamah, Ez. ii. 53.

Sculptured Columns from Tadmor. (*See* p. 112.)

Tā′mar (*palm-tree*). (1) Widow of Er and Onan, of Judah, and mother of Pharez and Zarah, by Shelah, Gen. xxxviii. (2) Daughter of David and sister of Absalom, 2 Sam. xiii. 1–32. (3) Daughter of Absalom, wife of Uriel and mother of Maachah, queen of Abijah, 2 Sam. xiv. 27; 2 Chr. xiii. 2. (4) A frontier place in south Judah, a day's journey from Hebron, Ezek. xlvii. 19; xlviii. 28.

Tăm′mŭz (*sprout*). A Syrian idol corresponding to the Greek Adonis, Ezek. viii. 14.

Tā′năch, Josh. xxi. 25. [Taanach.]

Tăn′hu-mĕth (*comfort*). Father of one of Gedaliah's captains, 2 Kgs. xxv. 23; Jer. xl. 8.

Tā′nis, Ezek. xxx. 14 marg. [Zoan.]

Tăn′nĕr (*oaker*). Tanning not a reputable occupation among Hebrews. It was carried on outside of cities and towns. Peter stopped with Simon, a tanner of Joppa, Acts ix. 43.

Tā′phath (*drop*). A daughter of Solomon, 1 Kgs. iv. 11.

Tā′phŏn, 1 Macc. ix. 50. [Beth-tappuah.]

Tăp′pu-ah (*apple*). (1) A descendant of Judah, 1 Chr. ii. 43. (2) A city in the plain-country of Judah, four miles N. W of Hebron, Josh. xv. 34. (3) A border place between Ephraim and Manasseh, Josh. xvi. 8; xvii. 8.

Tā′rah (*station*). A desert encampment of the Israelites, Num. xxxiii. 27.

Tăr′a-lah (*winding*). A town in Benjamin, Josh. xviii. 27.

Tā′re-ȧ, 1 Chr. viii. 35. [Tahrea.]

Târes (*tears*). The darnel is supposed to be meant. It grows somewhat like wheat till near ripening time, and chokes the growth of cereals, Matt. xiii. 25–30.

Tär′gĕt (*shield*). A small shield is meant, and not a target or mark in a modern sense, 1 Sam. xvii. 6. In the margin it is called "gorget," which was a defensive piece of armor, in the days of chivalry, used to protect the joint or opening between the helmet and cuirass.

Tär′pel-ītes. Assyrian colonists in Samaria after the captivity, Ez. iv. 9.

Tär′shish, Thär′shish (*solid, rocky*). (1) Second son of Javan, Gen. x. 4. (2) The city with which the Phœnicians traded. Associated with Tartessus in Spain, Jer. x. 9; Ezek. xxxviii. 13. (3) Another Tarshish is inferable from the statement that Solomon's ships at Ezion-geber on the Red Sea traded with Tarshish or Tharshish, 1 Kgs. ix. 26; xxii. 48; 2 Chr. ix. 21; 2 Chr. xx. 36. But many suppose that a class of ships — "ships of Tarshish," like "East India merchantmen" — is referred to rather than a port.

Tär′sus (*wing*). Chief city of Cilicia, Asia Minor, on river Cydnus, six miles from the Mediterranean. Birthplace of Paul and rival of Athens and Alexandria in literature and fine arts, Acts ix. 11, 30; xi. 25; xxi. 39; xxii. 3. At the mouth of the Cydnus were fine docks, and Tarsus had, at one time, considerable commercial importance. Some would identify it with Tarshish. It was founded by the Assyrian, Sardanapalus, and was captured by the Romans and made a free city. It is now represented by Tersons, a mean Turkish city with a fluctuating population.

Tär′tăk (*prince of darkness*). An idol introduced into Samaria by Avite colonists, and worshipped under the form of an ass, symbolizing darkness, 2 Kgs. xvii. 31.

Tarsus.

Tär′tan. Not a proper name, but an army official, like general or commander-in-chief, 2 Kgs. xviii. 17; Isa. xx. 1.

Tăt′na-ī (*gift*). A Persian governor in Palestine, Ez. v. 3, 6; vi. 6, 13.

Tăv′ẽrns (*huts*). "Three Taverns" was a place on the Appian Way, 33 miles south of Rome, where Paul met some of his Roman brethren, Acts xxviii. 15.

Tăx′es (*touches*). First Hebrew taxes were tithes, first-fruits, redemption money, for use of the priests. Taxes amplified under the kings and became burdensome, 1 Kgs. x. 28, 29; xii. 4. Jews under heavy tribute while subject to foreign rulers, Neh. v. The tithe-tax became a poll-tax, Neh. x. 32, 33; and continued, Matt. xvii. 24. The enrollment, or census, of Luke ii. 2, and Acts v. 37, was for the purpose of Roman taxation, which was onerous, being on the head, the field-hand, the ground and the products thereof, the harbors, city-gates, and city houses.

Tears. In Ps. lvi. 8, allusion is supposed, by some, to be made to a custom of preserving the tears of mourners in a bottle and placing it in the sepulchre. Others regard the words as a bold metaphor, expressive of David's wish that God would keep in memory his many penitential tears, as the traveller stores his water, milk, or wine in leather bottles for a journey.

Tē′bah (*slaughter*). A son of Nahor, Gen. xxii. 24.

Tĕb″a-lī′ah (*purged*). Third son of Hosah the Merarite, 1 Chr. xxvi. 11.

Tē′beth (*goodness*). Tenth month of Hebrew sacred, and fourth of civil, year; commencing with new moon in January, Esth. ii. 16.

Tē-hăph′ne-hes, Ezek. xxx. 18. [TAHPANHES.]

Tē-hĭn′nah (*entreaty*). Son of Eshton and founder of Ir-nahash, city of Nahash, 1 Chr. iv. 12.

Teil-trēē (*lime-tree*). Terebinth, or oak of Palestine, Isa. vi. 13.

Tē-kō′à, Tē-kō′ah (*fort*). A town of Judah on the Hebron ridge, six miles from Bethlehem, and on the border of the wilderness, 2 Chr. xx. 20; Jer. vi. 1. Colonized by Ashur, 1 Chr. ii. 24; iv. 5; fortified by Rehoboam, 2 Chr. xi. 6. Home of the "wise woman" who interceded for Absalom, 2 Sam. xiv. 2–9. Birthplace and residence of the prophet Amos, Am. i. 1. Now Tekua.

Tē-kō′īte. Dweller in Tekoa, 2 Sam. xxiii. 26; 1 Chr. xi. 28; xxvii. 9; Neh. iii. 5, 27.

Tĕl-ā′bib (*grain-heap*). A city in Chaldea or Babylonia where captive Jews resided, Ezek. iii. 15.

Tē′lah (*strength*). An Ephraimite ancestor of Joshua, 1 Chr. vii. 25.

Tĕl′a-im (*lambs*). Place where Saul collected his forces before attacking the Amalekites, 1 Sam. xv. 4.

Te-lăs′sar, Thē-lā′sar (*Assyrian hill*). Place in western Mesopotamia, near Haran and Orfa, 2 Kgs. xix. 12; Isa. xxxvii. 12.

Tē′lem (*oppression*). (1) A city in extreme southern Judah, Josh. xv. 24. (2) A temple doorkeeper in time of Ezra, Ez. x. 24.

Tĕl-här′sà, Tĕl-ha-rē′shà (*uncultivated hill*). A place in Babylonia whence captive Jews returned, Ez. ii. 59; Neh. vii. 61.

Tĕl-mē′lah (*salt hill*). A city mentioned with the above. Identified by some with the Thelme of Ptolemy, near the Persian Gulf, Ez. ii. 59; Neh. vii. 61.

Tē′mà (*desert*). Ninth son of Ishmael, and name of his tribe and country. Referred to Teyma in Syria, on the caravan route from Damascus to Mecca, Gen. xxv. 15; 1 Chr. i. 30; Job vi. 19; Isa. xxi. 14; Jer. xxv. 23.

Tē′man (*desert*). Oldest son of Eliphaz, and grandson of Esau, Gen. xxxvi. 11. Also the tribe and country of Temani or Temanites, in Edom, Jer. xlix. 7; Ezek. xxv. 13; Am. i. 12; Obadiah 9; Hab. iii. 3.

Tĕm′a-nī, Tē′man-īte, Gen. xxxvi. 34; Job ii. 11. [TEMAN.]

Tĕm′e-nī. A son of Ashur, father of Tekoa, 1 Chr. iv. 6.

Tĕm′ple. (1) Solomon's temple erected at Jerusalem on Mount Moriah. David proposed to transform the tabernacle into a permanent temple at Jerusalem, and collected much material, but its construction was forbidden by the prophet Nathan, 1 Chr. xvii.; 2 Sam. vii. 7–29. Solomon completed the work after David's plans and with the assistance of Hiram, king of Tyre. He began to build in the fourth year of his reign, B. C. 1012, and finished and dedicated it B. C. 1005, 1 Chr. xxi., xxii., xxviii., 11–19; xxix. 4–7; 1 Kgs. vi.–viii.; 2 Chr. iii.–vii. This costly and imposing structure, for the age, was pillaged several times during the Eastern invasions, and was finally destroyed during the last siege of Jerusalem by Nebuchadnezzar, B. C. 588. (2) The temple of Zerubbabel was begun in B. C. 534, by the returned captives under the lead of Zerubbabel and the patronage of King Cyrus of Persia. Owing to discords and direct opposition it was not completed till B. C. 515. It was much inferior to the first in cost and beauty, though one third larger in dimensions. It was partially destroyed by Antiochus Epiphanes, B. C. 163, and restored by Judas Maccabeus, Ez. iii.–vi.; 2 Macc. x. 1–9. (3) Herod the Great removed the decayed temple of Zerubbabel and began the erection of a new one B. C. 17. This gorgeous and costly structure was not completed till the time of Herod Agrippa II., A. D. 64. It was of marble, after Græco-Roman designs, and was destroyed by the Romans under Titus, A. D. 70, thus verifying Mark xiii. 2.

Tĕmpt (*hold*). Ordinarily, the offering of an inducement to do wrong, Matt. iv. 1–11; Luke iv. 13; but in Gen. xxii. 1; James i. 2, 3, a trial of one's faith; trial of God's patience, Ex. xvii. 2; 1 Cor. x. 9; an effort to ensnare, Matt. xvi. 1; xix. 3; xxii. 18; Mark x. 2; Luke x. 25.

Tĕnt (*stretched*). The house of nomad and pastoral peoples. It was made of strong cloth, chiefly of goat's hair, stretched on poles, and firmly pegged to the ground, Gen. iv. 20; xviii. 1; Judg. iv. 21; Isa. xxxviii. 12.

Tē′rah (*laggard*). Father of Abraham. He was of Ur in Chaldea, started west with his family, stopped in Haran, and died there, aged 205 years. Through his sons, Abraham, Nahor, and Haran, he was the ancestor of the Israelites, Ishmaelites, Midianites, Moabites, and Ammonites, Gen. xi. 27–32.

Tĕr′a-phim (*images*). Little images kept in Eastern households for private consultation and worship. This species of idolatry or superstition was in favor with Hebrews, though often denounced, Gen. xxxi. 19, 34, 35; Judg. xviii. 17; 1 Sam. xv. 23; xix. 13, 16; 2 Kgs. xxiii. 24; Hos. iii. 4; Zech. x. 2.

Tĕr′e-bĭnth. [TEIL-TREE.]

Tē′resh (*strict*). A eunuch of Ahasuerus, whose plot to murder his master was discovered by Mordecai, Esth. ii. 21–23.

Tẽr′tius (*third*). Paul's scribe in writing his Epistle to the Romans, Rom. xvi. 22.

Tẽr-tŭl′lus (*little third*). A Roman lawyer or orator hired by the high priest and Sanhedrim to prosecute Paul before the procurator Felix, Acts xxiv. 1–9.

Tĕs′tà-ment (*witness*). One of the two volumes of the Sacred Scriptures, which treat of the old and new dispensations; distinguished as the Old Testament, treating of revelation before the Advent of Christ, and the New Testament, containing that made after the Advent, 2 Cor. iii. 6; Heb. ix. 15.

Tĕs′ti-mō-nȳ (*witness*). The entire revelation of God, Ps. cxix. 88, 99; the tables of stone, Ex. xxv. 16; the ark in which the tables were deposited, Ex. xxv. 22; the gospel of Christ, 1 Cor. i. 6; Rev. i. 2.

Tĕt′rärch (*fourth ruler*). Originally one who

governed a part of a country divided into four parts, or tetrarchies; but under Roman rule it came to mean any ruler or petty prince of the republic and empire, especially in Syria, Matt. xiv. 1; Luke iii. 1; ix. 7; Acts xiii. 1. Sometimes the tetrarch was called king, Matt. xiv. 9; Mark vi. 14, 22.

Eastern Tent. (*See* p. 114.)

Thăd-dæ′us (*wise*). Surname of the apostle Jude, and another form of Lebbæus, Matt. x. 3; Mark iii. 18. [JUDE.]

Thā′hăsh (*badger*). Son of Nahor, Gen. xxii. 24.

Thā′mah, Ez. ii. 53. [TAMAH.]

Thā′mar, Matt. i. 3. [TAMAR, 1.]

Thăm′mŭz. [TAMMUZ.]

Thăm′na-thȧ, 1 Macc. ix. 50. [TIMNATH.]

Thănk Ŏf′fẽr-ing. The peace offering of Lev. iii., as offered with thanksgiving in Lev. vii. 11-15.

Thā′rȧ, Luke iii. 34. [TERAH.]

Thăr′rȧ, Esth. xii. 1. [TERESH.]

Thăr′shish (*rocky*). (1) 1 Kgs. x. 22; xxii. 48. [TARSHISH.] (2) A Benjamite, 1 Chr. vii. 10.

Thăs′sī. Surname of Simon, son of Mattathias, 1 Macc. ii. 3.

Thē′a-trē (*sight*). A place where dramatic performances are exhibited, as in Acts xix. 29; but the spectacle or performance itself in 1 Cor. iv. 9. The introduction of the theatre by Herod the Great greatly offended the Jews.

Thēbes (*life of the god*). Classical name of No or No-amon, Jer. xlvi. 25; Nah. iii. 8; Ezek. xxx. 14, 16. [No.]

Thē′bez (*prominent*). Now Tubas, a village near Shechem, and scene of Abimelech's tragic death, Judg. ix. 50-55; 2 Sam. xi. 21.

Thē-cō′ē, 1 Macc. ix. 33. [TEKOA.]

Thĕft, Thief. Punishment of theft was severe under the Mosaic law, as in all pastoral countries where the property was chiefly in flocks, more or less exposed to persons of felonious intent. The thief was compelled to make restitution, five-fold for a stolen ox and four-fold for a sheep. To kill a thief, caught in the act, was not a capital offence. If restitution was impossible a thief could be sold, Ex. xxii. 1-4.

Thē-lā′sar, 2 Kgs. xix. 12. [TELASSAR.]

Thē-lẽr′sas, 1 Esdr. v. 36. [TELHARSA.]

Thē′man, Bar. iii. 22. [TEMAN.]

Thē-ŏd′ō-tŭs (*God-given*). Envoy of Nicanor to Judas Maccabeus, 2 Macc. xiv. 19.

Thē-ŏph′ĭ-lŭs (*lover of God*). The unknown person, probably an official, to whom Luke addressed his Gospel and his history of the Acts of the Apostles, Luke i. 3; Acts i. 1.

Thē′ras, 1 Esdr. viii. 41. [AHAVA.]

Thĕs″sa-lō′nĭ-ans. People of Thessalonica, to whom Paul addressed two epistles, 13th and 14th N. T. books. The first was written at Corinth, A. D. 52 or 53, soon after the author had founded a church at Thessalonica, and upon the strength of favorable reports from Timothy. Its design was to confirm the new converts in the faith, strengthen them against persecution, correct their errors of doctrine and work, and inculcate purity of life. The second was also written from Corinth, soon after the first, and designed to correct false impressions concerning Christ's advent, and especially to place the author right before the world as an authorized apostle and teacher.

Thĕs″sa-lō-nī′cȧ. Ancient Thermæ, "hot springs;" now Salonika. Enlarged by Cassander and called Thessalonica after his wife, daughter of Alexander the Great. An important city of Macedonia, at the head of the Gulf of Thessalonica, or Thermæ. Paul visited it during his second tour and founded a strong church there, to whose members he wrote two epistles, Acts xvii. 1-9.

Theū′das (*God's gift*). An insurgent Jew mentioned in Gamaliel's speech before the council, Acts v. 34-39.

Thīgh. Placing the hand under the thigh was form of adjuration mentioned in Gen. xxiv. 2; xlvii. 29, and supposably prevalent in patriarchal times, but only taken by inferiors, as by servants or sons, and as significant of subjection and the purpose of obedience.

Thĭm′na-thah, Josh. xix. 43. [TIMNAH.]

Thĭs′bē. A city in Bœotia, Tob. i. 2.

Thĭs′tle, Thôrn. No less than eighteen Hebrew words embrace the thistle, thorn, brier, and bramble species, which is prolific in Palestine, Gen. iii. 18. Figurative for desolation, Prov. xxiv. 31; Isa. v. 6; Hos. ii. 6; providential visitation, Num. xxxiii. 55; Judg. ii. 3; 2 Cor. xii. 7; hindrance, Prov. xv. 19; troubles, Prov. xxii. 5. "Crown of thorns," both punishment and derision, Matt. xxvii. 29.

Thŏm′as (*twin*). The cautious, susceptible, even doubtful, apostle, whose name, in Greek, was Didymus, "twin," Matt. x. 3; Mark iii. 18; Luke vi. 15; John xi. 16; xiv. 5, 6; xx. 24-29; Acts i. 13.

Thôrn. [THISTLE.]

Thrā′çĭȧ. Classic name for the country now embraced in the northern part of Turkey in Europe, 2 Macc. xii. 35.

Thrȧ-sē′us. Father of Apollonius, 2 Macc. iii. 5.

Three Tăv′ẽrns. [TAVERNS.]

Thrĕsh′ing (*thrashing*). Done anciently by treading with oxen or horses, or by drawn sleds, sometimes spiked, on earthen floors, usually on high spots of ground, Deut. xxv. 4; 1 Chr. xxi. 15-28; Isa. xxviii. 27, 28; xli. 15, 16. The flail or stick is mentioned in Ruth ii. 17.

Thrōne (*seat*). The seat of one in authority, as high priest, 1 Sam. i. 9; military chief, Jer. i. 15; but especially of a king, 2 Sam. iii. 10; 1 Kgs. ii. 12; vii. 7; x. 18-20; xxii. 10; Acts xii. 21.

Thŭm′mim, Ex. xxviii. 30. [URIM.]

Thŭn′der (*sound*). Rare in Palestine, hence regarded as God's displeasure, 1 Sam. xii. 17; Jehovah's voice, Job xxxvii. 2; Ps. xviii. 13; Isa. xxx. 30, 31; John xii. 29; symbol of divine power, Ex. xix. 16; 1 Sam. ii. 10; 2 Sam. xxii. 14; Isa. xxix. 6; Rev. viii. 5.

Thȳ″a-tī′rȧ (*burning incense*). A city of northern Lydia in Asia Minor, founded by Seleucus Nicator, much inhabited by Jews, seat of one of the seven churches of Asia, Acts xvi. 14; Rev. ii. 18-29.

Thȳ′ine-wood. Wood of the thyia, sandarac, or

pine variety, yielding a choice gum and hard, dark colored, fragrant wood. Indigenous to northern Africa, Rev. xviii. 12.

Ti-bē′rĭ-as. (1) Sea of, John vi. 1; xxi. 1. [GENNESARET.] (2) A town of Galilee on the west shore of Lake Gennesaret or Sea of Galilee, founded by Herod Antipas, A. D. 16–22, and named in honor of the emperor Tiberius. It seems to have imparted its name to the lake or sea. Once noted for its learning and architectural beauty, but now the miserable village of Tabariyeh, John vi. 1, 23; xxi. 1.

Tī-bē′rĭ-us. Tiberius Claudius Nero, second emperor of Rome, A. D. 14–37. Stepson of Augustus, a vigorous warrior, eloquent orator, and able statesman, but an indolent, despotic ruler. He is the Cæsar of Luke iii. 1; xx. 22–25; xxiii. 2; John xix. 12.

Tĭb′hath (*killing*). Capital of Hadadezer, king of Zobah, 1 Chr. xviii. 8. Betah, 2 Sam. viii. 8.

Tĭm′brel (*bell, drum*). A Hebrew musical instrument somewhat resembling the tambourine, Ex. xv. 20; Judg. xi. 34; Ps. lxviii. 25. [TABRET.]

Tĭm′nȧ, Tĭm′nah (*portion*). (1) Mother of Amalek, Gen. xxxvi. 12. (2) A duke of Edom, Gen. xxxvi. 40, who gave his name to a boundary of Judah, Josh. xv. 10. (3) A mountain town of Judah, Josh. xv. 57. Thimnathah, Josh. xix. 43.

Tĭm′năth. (1) Gen. xxxviii. 14. [TIMNA, 2.] (2) Home of Samson's wife, Judg. xiv. 1–5.

Tĭm′năth=hē′rēs, Judg. ii. 9. [TIMNATH-SERAH].

Tĭm′năth=sē′rah (*fruitful portion*). A city in Ephraim given to Joshua, and his home and burial place, Josh. xix. 50; xxiv. 30. Written Timnath-heres in Judg. ii. 9.

Tĭm′nīte. Designation of Samson's father-in-law, the Timnathite, Judg. xv. 6.

Thessalonica. (*See* p. 115.)

Tĭb′nī (*knowing*). Competitor of Omri for the throne of Israel, 1 Kgs. xvi. 21, 22.

Tī′dal (*great chief*). A chief of nomadic tribes, who joined Chedorlaomer in his attack on the cities of the plain, Gen. xiv. 1–16.

Tĭg′lath=pĭ-lē′ser (*Adar's son my help*). Second of the Assyrian kings in contact with Israel. He invaded Samaria, 2 Kgs. xv. 29, and a few years afterwards returned, taking many captives, 1 Chr. v. 26. King Ahaz, of Judah, became his vassal, 2 Kgs. xvi. 7–10. He reigned B. C. 747–739.

Tī′grĭs (*arrow*). Great eastern tributary of the Euphrates, rising in the Armenian mountains and flowing southeastwardly 1146 miles. Between it and the Euphrates lay Mesopotamia. In the Septuagint version it stands for Hiddekel, one of the rivers of Eden, Gen. ii. 14; Tob. vi. 1; Judith i. 6; Ecclus. xxiv. 25.

Tĭk′vah, Tĭk′vath (*hope*). (1) Father-in-law of Huldah the prophetess, 2 Kgs. xxii. 14; 2 Chr. xxxiv. 22. (2) Father of Jahaziah, Ez. x. 15.

Tīle (*cover*). A broad, thin slab of burnt clay, used as a shingle on Oriental houses, Ezek. iv. 1.

Tĭl′găth=pĭl-nē′ser, 1 Chr. v. 6; 2 Chr. xxviii. 20. [TIGLATH-PILESER.]

Tī′lon (*gift*). A Judahite, 1 Chr. iv. 20.

Tī-mæ′us (*honored*). Father of the blind Bartimæus, Mark 3. 46.

Tī′mon (*honorable*). One of the first seven deacons, Acts vi. 1–6.

Tĭ-mō′the-ŭs (*honoring God*). (1) An Ammonite leader defeated by Judas Maccabeus, 1 Macc. v. 6–44. (2) Acts xvi. 1; xvii. 14, etc. [TIMOTHY.]

Tĭm′o-thȳ (*honoring God*). Son of Eunice, a Jewess, by a Gentile father. Born in Derbe or Lystra, Lycaonia, Acts xvi. 1; 2 Tim. i. 5. Converted by Paul and became a close friend and valuable assistant, Rom. xvi. 21; Heb. xiii. 23. Recipient of two of Paul's epistles, 15th and 16th N. T. books. The first was written to him while at Ephesus, probably from Macedonia, and about A. D. 65. The second seems to have been written from Rome some three years later. They are called pastoral epistles, because devoted to description of church work and earnest exhortation to faithfulness.

Tĭn. A metal well known to ancients, Num. xxxi. 22; evidently dross in Isa. i. 25. Imported from Tarshish, Ezek. xxvii. 12.

Tĭph′sah (*ford*). The Greek and Roman Thapsacus, a crossing point of the Euphrates, and eastern limit of Solomon's empire, 1 Kgs. iv. 24. Smitten by Menahem, 2 Kgs. xv. 16.

Tī′ras (*longing*). Youngest son of Japheth, and supposable progenitor of the Thracians, Gen. x. 2.

Tī′rath-ītes. Designation of a family of scribes at Jabez, 1 Chr. ii. 55.

Tīre (*attire*). A head-dress, Isa. iii. 18; Ezek. xxiv. 17, 23; but the original implies any round ornament, as a necklace, worn by persons or animals, Judg. viii. 21, 26.

Tīr'ha-kah (*exalted*). A king of Ethiopia and Upper Egypt who became King Hezekiah's ally against Sennacherib, about B. C. 695, 2 Kgs. xix.; Isa. xxxvii. 9.

Tīr'ha-nah (*favor*). A son of Caleb, son of Hezron, 1 Chr. ii. 48.

Tīr'ī-ȧ (*dread*). A Judahite, 1 Chr. iv. 16.

Tīr'sha-thȧ (*governor*). Title of the governors of Judea under Persian rule, Ez. ii. 63; Neh. vii. 65, 70; viii. 9; Neh. x. 1.

Tĩr'zah (*pleasing*). (1) Youngest of the five daughters of Zelophehad, Num. xxvi. 33. (2) An ancient Canaanite city captured by Joshua, and which afterwards became the capital of the kingdom of Samaria, till Samaria, the new capital, was founded by King Omri. It was some 30 miles north of Jerusalem, and 5 miles east of Samaria, Josh. xii. 24; 1 Kgs. xiv. 17; xv. 21, 33; xvi. 6; 2 Kgs. xv. 14, 16; S. of Sol. vi. 4.

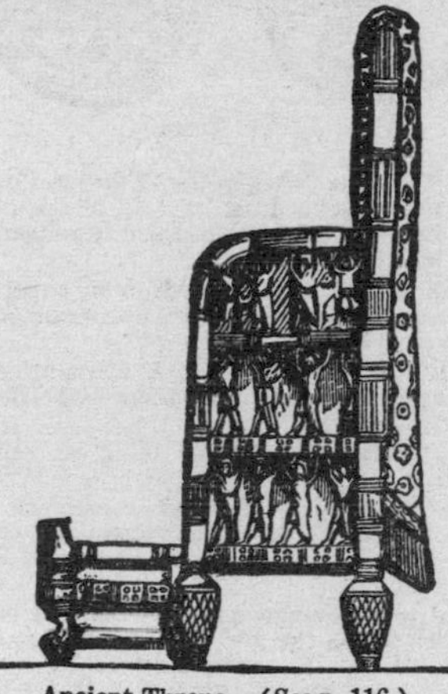

Ancient Throne. (See p. 116.)

Tĭsh'bīte. Elijah is so designated, 1 Kgs. xvii. 1; xxi. 17, 28; 2 Kgs. i. 3, 8; ix. 36. The place is generally referred to Thisbe in Naphtali, where Tobit lived, Tob. i. 2.

Tĭs'rī. Seventh month of the Jewish sacred, and first of the civil year, corresponding to parts of September and October. Called also Ethanim, 1 Kgs. viii. 2; 2 Chr. v. 3.

Tīthe (*tenth*). One tenth of all produce of lands and herds was set apart, under the Levitical law, for the support of the Levites, and a tenth of their tenth went to the priests. There were tithe regulations among other nations, Gen. xiv. 20; xxviii. 22; Lev. xxvii. 30-33; Num. xviii. 21-32; Deut. xii. 17, 18; xiv. 22-27. The Pharisees tithed their mint, anise, cummin, and rue, Matt. xxiii. 23.

Tĭt'tle (*title*). Jot; iota; any minute quantity, Matt. v. 18; Luke xvi. 17.

Tī'tus (*pleasant*). A distinguished Grecian who became a Christian convert and a companion of Paul in his trials and on his missionary tours, Tit. i. 4; Gal. ii. 3-5; 2 Cor. viii. 6, 16, 23. Entrusted with many important commissions, 2 Cor. xii. 18; 2 Tim. iv. 10; Tit. i. 5. Paul wrote an epistle to Titus, the 17th N. T. book, about A. D. 65, designed to instruct him in his ministerial duties in Crete, which were arduous, on account of the immorality of the people.

Tī'zīte. Designation of Joha, one of David's guardsmen. Place unknown, 1 Chr. xi. 45.

Tō'ah (*bent*). A Levite ancestor of Samuel, 1 Chr. vi. 34. Tohu, 1 Sam. i. 1.

Tŏb (*good*). A place or district beyond Jordan and between Gilead and the desert, to which Jephthah fled when banished from Gilead, Judg. xi. 3-5. Ish-tob, 2 Sam. x. 6, 8.

Tŏb=ăd''o-nī'jah (*my good God*). A Levite sent out by King Jehoshaphat to teach the law, 2 Chr. xvii. 8.

Tō-bī'ah (*God's goodness*). (1) His children returned with Zerubbabel, Ez. ii. 60; Neh. vii. 62. (2) An Ammonite servant of Sanballat who joined his master in opposing Nehemiah, Neh. ii. 10-20.

Tō-bī'as. Greek form of Tobiah and Tobijah. (1) Son of Tobit, and hero in his book, Tob. (2) Father of Hyrcanus, and a man of great prominence at Jerusalem, B. C. 187.

Tō'bīē, 1 Macc. v. 13. [TOB.]

Tō-bī'jah (*God's goodness*). (1) A Levite sent out by King Jehoshaphat to teach the law, 2 Chr. xvii. 8. (2) One of the captivity in whose presence Joshua was crowned high priest, Zech. vi. 10-14.

Tō'bĭt (*goodness*). Father of Tobias, and author of Tobit, the fifth Apocryphal book. It was written in Greek, with the scene in Assyria, and is a didactic narrative of Jewish social life after the captivity.

Tō'chen (*task*). An unidentified place in Simeon, 1 Chr. iv. 32.

Tō-gär'mah (*bony*). Son of Gomer, of the family of Japheth, Gen. x. 3. His descendants became horse and mule merchants, and have been associated with the ancient Armenians, Ezek. xxvii. 14.

Tō'hu, 1 Sam. i. 1. [TOAH.]

Tō'ī (*wandering*). A king of Hamath, who sent his son to congratulate David on his victory over Hadadezer, 2 Sam. viii. 9, 10. Tou, 1 Chr. xviii. 9, 10.

Tō'lȧ (*worm*). (1) First-born of Issachar, and progenitor of the Tolaites, Gen. xlvi. 13; Num. xxvi. 23; 1 Chr. vii. 1, 2. (2) Successor of Abimelech as judge of Israel for twenty-three years, Judg. x. 1, 2.

Tō'lăd (*generation*). A city in South Judah, called also El-tolad, 1 Chr. iv. 29.

Tō'lȧ-ītes. Descendants of Tola, Num. xxvi. 23.

Tŏl'ba-nēs, 1 Esdr. ix. 25. [TELEM.]

Tōll (*tell*). The Persian taxation of conquered Judea consisted of "tribute" levied on each province and collected by the authorities thereof; "custom," which could be paid in kind; "toll," which was a cash exaction for the use of bridges, fords, and highways, Ez. iv. 13; vii. 24.

Tomb. Burial places among Hebrews were caves, recesses in rocks, natural or artificial, and walled sepulchres. [SEPULCHRE.]

Tongues. "And the whole earth was of one language, and of one speech," Gen. xi. 1. Confusion of tongues and dispersion of peoples coincident, Gen. xi. 7-9. "New tongues," Mark xvi. 17, is the first notice of a gift specially characteristic of the first outpouring of the Spirit. Ten days afterward the promise was fulfilled in the Pentecostal phenomenon, Acts ii. 1-13.

Tooth. The Jewish law of retaliation permitted the deprivation of "eye for eye, tooth for tooth," Ex. xxi. 24. The principle of this law was condemned by Christ, Matt. v. 38-42. Teeth used figuratively for the inheritable quality of sin, Ezek. xviii. 2; "cleanness of teeth" a figure for famine, Am. iv. 6; "gnashing of teeth" indicative of rage and despair, Matt. viii. 12.

Tō'păz. A variously hued gem, corresponding to the modern chrysolite, which the Hebrews obtained from Ethiopia, Job xxviii. 19, and which constituted the second stone in first row of the high priest's breastplate, Ex. xxviii. 17, and a foundation stone of the New Jerusalem, Rev. xxi. 20.

Tō'phel (*mortar*). A place east of the Dead Sea near Bozrah, Deut. i. 1.

Tō'phet, Tō'pheth (*drum, noise, place of burning*). Part of the valley of Hinnom east or south of Jerusalem. Perhaps once a pleasure garden, but afterward polluted by the abominations incident to the worship of Baal and Molech, 2 Kgs. xxiii. 10; Jer. vii. 31; xix. 13, and then turned into a dumping and burning place of the city's refuse. Hence a place of judgment, Jer. xix. 6–14. [Hinnom.]

Tôr'mah, Judg. ix. 31 marg. [Arumah.]

Tôr'toise (*twisted-foot*). A faulty rendering. The Septuagint has "land-crocodile," and doubtless one of the large lizard species is meant, Lev. xi. 29.

Tō'u, 1 Chr. xviii. i. 10. [Toi.]

Tōw. The coarser part of flax, Judg. xvi. 9.

Tow'er (*shot up*). Watch-towers, or fortified posts, were frequent on frontiers and exposed places, Gen. xxxv. 21; 2 Chr. xxvi. 10; around vineyards, Isa. xxi. 5, 8, 11; Matt. xxi. 33, and for the use of shepherds, Mic. iv. 8. "Tower of Shechem," Judg. ix. 47, evidently a citadel or stronghold. Tower of Babel [Babel]. "Tower of Siloam," possibly an observatory, Luke xiii. 4.

Town Clĕrk. An official in Ephesus, who recorded the laws and decisions and read them in public, Acts xix. 35–41.

Trăch''o-nī'tis (*stony*). One of the Roman provinces into which the country north of the Jordan was divided, and generally associated with Argob, south of Damascus, Luke iii. 1.

Trănce (*going over*). The word in Num. xxiv. 4, 16, is an interjection, without a Hebrew equivalent. In Acts x. 10, xi. 5, xxii. 17, an ecstasy is implied, which carried the subject beyond the usual limits of consciousness and volition.

Trăns-fĭg''ū-rā'tion (*formed over*). The supernatural change in the appearance of Christ upon the mount — Hermon or Tabor. It served as an attestation of his Messiahship and an emblem of glorified humanity, Matt. xvii. 1–13; Mark ix. 2–13; Luke ix. 28–36.

Trĕaṣ'ûre Cĭ'tieṣ. The kings of Judah, and of other nations, kept their treasures in designated cities, called treasure-cities, and in special buildings called treasure-houses, Ex. i. 11; 1 Chr. xxvii. 25; Ez. v. 17.

Trĕas'ûr-ȳ (*place*). The place in the temple where gifts were received, 1 Chr. ix. 26; Mark xii. 41; Luke xxi. 1; John viii. 20.

Trĕnch (*cut*). In military usage, a ditch for protection, but in 1 Sam. xxvi. 5, the place where the wagons were grouped or packed.

Trĕs'păss (*passing over*). To violate the personal or property rights of another, Lev. v. 6. To violate a positive law of God, Matt. vi. 15.

Trĕs'păss Ŏf'fĕr-ing. This offering was closely allied to the sin offering, and in some cases offered with it as a distinct part of the same sacrifice, Lev. v. 15; xiv. 13–32.

Trībe (*division*). In a Roman sense, the third part of the empire, but with Hebrews any division of the people, especially that division which sprung from the twelve sons of Jacob, and was perpetuated in their descendants, Gen. xlviii. 5; Num. xxvi. 5-51; Josh. xiii. 7-33; xv.-xix. Of these tribes two, Ephraim and Manasseh, sprang from Joseph. Still there were only twelve partitions of conquered Canaan, for the tribe of Levi received no allotment of lands, but was diffused in cities among the other tribes and supported by them. Each tribe was headed by a prince, and each possessed considerable independence even under the monarchy. They waged war separately and among themselves, Judg. i. 2–4; 1 Chr. v. 18–22; 2 Sam. ii. 4–9; and finally ten of the tribes revolted and set up the separate kingdom of Israel, xix. 41–43; 1 Kgs. xii. For history of each tribe *see* its title.

Trĭb'ūte (*gift*). A payment made as a token of submission, or for sake of peace, or in pursuance of treaty, Gen. xlix. 15. The head-tax of half a shekel paid annually by Jews for the support of the temple service, Ex. xxx. 13.

Trĭp'ȯ-lis (*three cities*). The commercially linked cities of Aradus, Sidon, and Tyre, in Phœnicia, 2 Macc. xiv. 1.

Trō'ăs (*Troad*). Alexandria Troas, or in the Troad, was an important city in Mysia, Asia Minor, 6 miles south of the entrance to the Hellespont and 4 from the site of Ancient Troy. It was founded by Alexander the Great and was for many centuries the key of commerce between Europe and Asia. Paul visited it more than once, Acts xvi. 8–11; xx. 5–10; 2 Tim. iv. 13.

Coin of Troas.

Trō-ġ̇ўl'lī-um (*fruit-port*). Town and promontory on the western coast of Asia Minor, opposite Samos. Paul visited it on his third missionary tour, Acts xx. 15.

Troop, Band. These words imply small bodies of marauders in Gen. xlix. 19; 2 Sam. xxii. 30; Jer. xviii. 22; Mic. v. 1.

Trŏph'ĭ-mŭs (*fostered*). A Christian convert residing at Ephesus, and co-worker with Paul, Acts xx. 4; xxi. 29; 2 Tim. iv. 20.

Trōw (*trust*). Signifies to think or believe in, Luke xvii. 9.

Trŭm'pet (*pipe*). A wind instrument with a flaring mouth, made of horn or metal and differing but little in form and use from the cornet, Ex. xix. 16. [Cornet.]

Trŭm'pets, Feast of. The feast of the new moon which fell on the first of Tisri, Num. xxix. 1–6; Lev. xxiii. 24, 25. It was the New Year's day of the Jewish civil year, and was ushered in by the blowing of trumpets and observed by offerings.

Trȳ-phē'nȧ (*shining*). A Christian woman of Rome, saluted by Paul, Rom. xvi. 12.

Trȳ'phŏn (*effeminate*). Surname of Diodotus, who usurped the Syrian throne, 1 Macc. xii. 39.

Trȳ-phō'sȧ (*shining*). A Christian woman of Rome, saluted by Paul, Rom. xvi. 12.

Tu̧'bal (*tumult*). Fifth son of Japheth, Gen. x. 2; 1 Chr. i. 5. His descendants supposably inhabited the country between the Caspian and Euxine seas, Isa. lxvi. 19; Ezek. xxvii. 13, xxxii. 26.

Tu̧'bal=cāin. Son of Lamech the Cainite, by Zillah. He was instructor of artificers in brass and iron, Gen. iv. 22.

Tu̧''bi-ē'nī. Inhabitants of Tubion, the O. T. Tob, 2 Macc. xii. 17.

Tûr'pĕn-tīne=trēe. The terebinth, or teil-tree, Ecclus. xxiv. 16.

Tûr'tle, Tûr'tle-dove (*cooer*). The turtle embraces several species of plaintive-noted doves, Gen. xv. 9; Ps. lxxiv. 19; Isa. lix. 11. Those who could not afford the costlier sacrifices could offer two doves or pigeons, Lev. xii. 6–8; Luke ii. 24. They were migratory, S. of Sol. ii. 12; Jer. viii. 7.

Tȳch'ĭ-cŭs (*fate*). A disciple of Paul, Acts xx. 4, and his messenger and spokesman, Eph. vi. 21, 22; Col. iv. 7, 8.

Tȳ-răn′nus (*tyrant*). A Greek rhetorician at Ephesus in whose school Paul taught for two years, Acts xix. 9.

Tyre (*rock*). The celebrated commercial city of Phœnicia on the Mediterranean coast. It fell to the lot of Asher, but was never conquered, Josh. xix. 29. In intimate commercial relation with Hebrews, and King Hiram furnished the artificers and material for the temple and royal houses at Jerusalem, 2 Sam. v. 11; 1 Kgs. v. 1; vii. 13; ix. 11 14; 1 Chr. xiv. 1; 2 Chr. ii. 2-18. The city was denounced by the prophets, Isa. xxiii. 1-17; Jer. xxvii. 3; Ezek. xxvi. 3-21. It resisted the five-year siege of Shalmaneser and the thirteen-year siege of Nebuchadnezzar, but fell before that of Alexander. Referred to in N.T., Matt. xi. 21, 22; xv. 21; Mark vii. 24. Paul visited it, Acts xxi. 3, 4.

Tȳ′rus. Name for Tyre in O. T. prophecies and in Apocrypha.

U

Ū′cal (*power*). The prophecy of Agur is addressed to Ithiel and Ucal, Prov. xxx. 1. Some regard the names as symbolical, while others treat them as real.

Ū′el (*God's will*). One of the sons of Bani, Ez. x. 34. Juel in 1 Esdr. ix. 34.

Ŭk′năz. The name is made to stand for Kenaz in margin of 1 Chr. iv. 15.

Ū′la-ī (*pure water*). A river in the province of Elam, where the palace of Shushan stood, on whose banks Daniel saw the vision of the ram and the he-goat, Dan. viii. 2-16.

Ū′lam (*porch*). (1) A descendant of Manasseh, 1 Chr. vii. 16, 17. (2) Son of Eshek, a Benjamite, of the line of Saul, 1 Chr. viii. 39, 40.

Ŭl′lȧ (*yoke*). Head of an Asherite family, 1 Chr. vii. 39.

Ŭm′mah (*community*). A city in Asher, associated with modern Alma, five miles from the Mediterranean coast, Josh. xix. 30.

Ŭn″çir-cŭm-çi′ȿion (*not cut around*). In a Scriptural sense, Gentiles, Rom. ii. 25-29.

Ŭn-clēan′. A word which, with clean, was applied to personal and ceremonial conditions, as well as to the edibility of animals. The division of animals into clean and unclean existed before the Flood, Gen. vii. 2. Uncleanness and the processes of purification are particularly described in Lev. xi.-xv.; Num. xix. Unclean animals are specially mentioned in Lev. xi. 9-31; Deut. xiv. 3-20.

Ŭn″dēr-gïrd′ing. A primitive way of keeping the hull of a ship from opening by passing a cable tightly around it. The ship in which Paul sailed from Crete to Italy was undergirded, Acts xxvii. 17.

Un″der-set′terȿ. The molten projections which ornamented and supported the brazen laver in Solomon's temple, 1 Kgs. vii. 30.

Ū′ni-côrn (*one-horned*). A fabulous animal pictured as having one horn on its forehead and the body of a horse. The Hebrew word *re'em*, which is translated "unicorn," Num. xxiii. 22; xxiv. 8; Deut. xxxiii. 17; Job xxxix. 9; Ps. xxii. 21; xxix. 6; Isa. xxxiv. 7, does not refer to the one-horned creature of fable, but evidently to a two-horned animal, Deut. xxxiii. 17, possibly the now nearly extinct wild ox, auroch or urus of naturalists.

Ŭn′nī (*afflicted*). (1) A Levite appointed to play upon the psaltery, in the time of David, 1 Chr. xv. 18, 20. (2) Another Levite, who acted as watchman after the return from captivity, Neh. xii. 9.

U-phär′sin, Dan. v. 25-28. [Mene.]

Ū′phăz. Only in Jer. x. 9; Dan. x. 5, where it has been generally treated as an error for Ophir.

Ûr (*light, region*). (1) Place where Abraham lived with his father Terah and his wife Sarah, before they started for the land of Canaan, Gen. xi. 28, 31. Mentioned in Gen. xv. 7, as of the Chaldees, and Acts vii. 2, as in Mesopotamia. (2) Father of Eliphal, one of David's guard, 1 Chr. xi. 35. Called Ahasbai in 2 Sam. xxiii. 34.

Ûr′bane (*of a city, polite*). Greek form of the Latin Urbanus, a Christian disciple of Paul at Rome whom he salutes in Rom. xvi. 9. Urbanus in R. V.

Ū′rī (*fire*). (1) Father of Bezaleel, one of the architects of the tabernacle, Ex. xxxi. 2; xxxv. 30; xxxviii. 22; 1 Chr. ii. 20; 2 Chr. i. 5. (2) Father of Geber, Solomon's commissary officer in the land of Gilead, 1 Kgs. iv. 19. (3) A gate-keeper of the temple in the time of Ezra, Ez. x. 24.

U-rī′ah (*light*). (1) A Hittite, 2 Sam. xi. 3, and commander of one of the thirty divisions of David's army, 2 Sam. xxiii. 39; 1 Chr. xi. 41. He was husband of the beautiful Bathsheba whom David coveted, and with whom he had committed the crime of adultery, 2 Sam. xi. 4, 5. In order to conceal his crime and procure her for a wife, he ordered Joab, commander-in-chief, to place Uriah and his forces in the hottest part of the battle with Ammon, and then to desert him, leaving him to be overwhelmed and slain by superior numbers, 2 Sam. xi. 15-17. (2) A high priest in the reign of Ahaz, Isa. viii. 2, and probably the same as Urijah in 2 Kgs. xvi. 10-16. (3) A priest of the family of Hakkoz, in time of Ezra, and head of the seventh priestly course, Ez. viii. 33; written Urijah in Neh. iii. 4, 21.

U-rī′as. (1) Matt. i. 6. [Uriah, 1.] (2) 1 Esdr. ix. 43. [Urijah, 3.]

Ū′rī-el (*fire of God*). (1) One of the angels, 2 Esdr. iv. 1, 36. (2) A chief of the Kohathite Levites in the time of David, 1 Chr. xv. 5, 11. (3) A Kohathite Levite, son of Tahath, 1 Chr. vi. 24. (4) Father of Michaiah, or Maacha, wife of Rehoboam and mother of Abijah, 2 Chr. xiii. 2.

U-rī′jah (*light of God*). (1) A priest in the reign of Ahaz, and probably the same as Uriah (2), 2 Kgs. xvi. 10-16. (2) A priest of the family of Hakkoz or Koz, and probably same as Uriah (3), Neh. iii. 4, 21; viii. 4. (4) A prophet of Kirjath-jearim, and son of Shemaiah, who prophesied in the days of King Jehoiakim against Jerusalem and Judah according to the words of Jeremiah, and whom Jehoiakim sought to put to death. He fled to Egypt, but was pursued, caught, brought back and slain, Jer. xxvi. 20-23.

Ū′rim and Thŭm′mim (*light and perfection*). From the way these mysterious words are spoken of in Ex. xxviii. 30, and in Lev. viii. 8, compared with Ex. xxviii. 15-21, they appear to denote some material things, separate from the high priest's breastplate and its gems, and previously well known. Their purpose seems to be indicated in Num. xxvii. 21; 1 Sam. xxviii. 6, and, since they were connected with the ephod, in 1 Sam. xxii. 14, 15; xxiii. 9-12; xxx. 7, 8, it may be inferred they were consulted to ascertain the will of Jehovah, and that they were preserved in the bag of the high priest's breastplate to be borne "upon his heart before the Lord continually," Ex. xxviii. 30. Not in use after the captivity, Ez. ii. 63; Neh. vii. 65; Hos. iii. 4.

Ū′ȿu-rȳ (*use*). Exorbitant or unlawful interest for money loaned; but in a Bible sense the taking of any interest at all. The law of Moses prohibited Hebrews from exacting interest of one another on loans, though not of foreigners, Lev. xxv. 36, 37; Deut. xxiii. 19, 20. Usury is severely denounced, Neh. v. 7, 10; Ps. xv. 5; Prov. xxviii. 8; Ezek. xxii. 12.

Ū′tȧ, 1 Esdr. v. 30. [Akkub.]

Ū′tha-ī (*helpful*). (1) The son of Ammihud, of Judah, 1 Chr. ix. 4. Athaiah in Neh. xi. 4. (2) Son of Bigvai, who returned from captivity, Ez. viii. 14.

Ū′thī, 1 Esdr. viii. 40. [Uthai, 2.]

Ŭz (*fertile*). (1) The land of Uz was Job's country, Job i. 1. It was located east or southeast of Palestine, Job i. 3; adjacent to the Sabeans or Chaldeans, Job i. 15, and to the Edomites, who once occupied it as conquerors, Lam. iv. 21. It is grouped with Egypt, Philistia, and Moab, Jer. xxv. 19-21. (2) The first son of Aram, son of Shem, Gen. x. 23; 1 Chr. i. 17. (3) Son of Nahor by Milcah, Gen. xxii. 21. Huz in A. V. and probably correct name for Uz. (4) Son of Dishan and grandson of Seir, Gen. xxxvi. 28.

Ū'za-ī (*strong*). Father of Palal, who assisted in rebuilding the walls of Jerusalem, Neh. iii. 25.

Ū'zal (*wanderer*). Sixth son of Joktan, Gen. x. 27; 1 Chr. i. 21. His descendants occupied the district of Yemen in Arabia and built the city of Uzal, since changed to Sana, and still the capital.

Ŭz'zȧ (*strength*). (1) The garden attached to the house of Manasseh, king of Judah. It evidently contained the family sepulchre, 2 Kgs. xxi. 18, 26. (2) A Benjamite descendant of Ehud, 1 Chr. viii. 7. (3) One of the drivers of the cart which bore the ark from Kirjath-jearim to Jerusalem, and who was slain by the Lord for putting his hand to the cart when the oxen stumbled, 1 Chr. xiii. 7-11. Uzzah elsewhere. (4) A Merarite Levite, 1 Chr. vi. 29.

Ŭz'zah (*strength*). 2 Sam. vi. 3-8. [UZZA, 3.]

Ŭz'zen=shē'rah (*ear of Sherah*). A town built by Sherah, a daughter of Ephraim, 1 Chr. vii. 24.

Ŭz'zī (*mighty*). (1) A son of Bukki and father of Zerahiah, in the line of high priests, but never a high priest, 1 Chr. vi. 5, 6; Ez. vii. 4. (2) A son of Tola and grandson of Issachar, 1 Chr. vii. 2, 3. (3) A son of Bela, of the tribe of Benjamin, 1 Chr. vii. 7. (4) A Benjamite progenitor of several families settled in Jerusalem after the captivity, 1 Chr. ix. 8, 9. (5) A Levite, son of Bani, and overseer of the Levites at Jerusalem after the captivity, Neh. xi. 22. (6) A priest, and chief of the house of Jedaiah, in the time of the high priest Joiakim, Neh. xii. 19. (7) A priest who assisted Ezra at the dedication of the walls of Jerusalem, Neh. xii. 42.

Ŭz-zī'ȧ (*God's strength*). Designated as the Ashterathite, one of David's guard, 1 Chr. xi. 44.

Ŭz-zī'ah (*God's strength*). (1) Son and successor of Amaziah on the throne of Judah, B. C. 810-758, 2 Chr. xxvi. 1-3. He is called Azariah in 2 Kgs. xiv. 21 and elsewhere. He was a godly king, an excellent general, and renowned city builder. But for daring to enter the temple and burn incense in violation of the law, Num. xvi. 40, xviii. 7, he was stricken with leprosy and forced to live in a separate house till he died, 2 Kgs. xv. 1-7; 2 Chr. xxvi. (2) A Kohathite Levite, son of Uriel and ancestor of Samuel, 1 Chr. vi. 24. (3) Father of Jehonathan, superintendent of David's storehouses in fields, cities, villages and castles, 1 Chr. xxvii. 25. (4) A priest of the sons of Harim, Ez. x. 21. (5) A Judahite, Neh. xi. 4.

Ŭz'zī-el (*God's might*). (1) Fourth son of Kohath, son of Levi, Ex. vi. 18, 22; ancestor of the Uzzielites, Lev. x. 4; and also, through Elizaphan, of the Kohathites, Num. iii. 19, 27, 30; 1 Chr. xv. 10. (2) A captain of the sons of Simeon, 1 Chr. iv. 42, 43. (3) A son of Bela and grandson of Benjamin, 1 Chr. vii. 7; (4) A son of Heman and one of the temple musicians in time of David, 1 Chr. xxv. 4. Azareel in 1 Chr. xxv. 18. (5) A descendant of Heman, 2 Chr. xxix. 14-19. (6) An assistant wall-builder, Neh. iii. 8.

Ŭz'zī-el-ītes''. Descendants of Uzziel (1), Num. iii. 27; 1 Chr. xxvi. 23.

V

Văg'a-bŏnd (*wanderer*). In the Bible vagabond has the original meaning of fugitive or wanderer, Gen. iv. 12; Ps. cix. 10; Acts xix. 13.

Vȧ-jĕz'a-thȧ (*strong as the wind*). One of the ten sons of Haman, Esth. ix. 9.

Vāle, Văl'ley. Five Hebrew words are rendered vale or valley in the Bible, only one of which seems to imply that broad sweep of land between mountains or hills generally understood by valley. The others imply (1) a narrow ravine, gorge, or glen, Deut. xxxiv. 3, 6; (2) a wady, dry in summer but a torrent in rainy weather; (3) a plain, Josh. xi. 8, 17; xiii. 17; 2 Chr. xxxv. 22; Zech. xii. 11; (4) a stretch of sloping ground, Deut. i. 7; Josh. x. 40; 1 Kgs. x. 27; 2 Chr. i. 15; Jer. xxxiii. 13.

Vȧ-nī'ah (*praise of God*). A son of Bani, who had married a foreign wife, Ez. x. 36.

Văsh'nī (*second*). Name of Samuel's oldest son, 1 Chr. vi. 28. In 1 Sam. viii. 2, Joel appears as his firstborn son.

Văsh'tī (*beautiful*). Wife of King Ahasuerus and queen of Persia, Esth. i. 9-22.

Văt. A large vessel for holding liquids. "Fat" in Joel ii. 24; iii. 13. [WINE-FAT.]

Veil (*carry*). The veil of Gen. xxiv. 65; xxxviii. 14; Ruth iii. 15; S. of Sol. v. 7; Isa. iii. 23, was a shawl or mantle. The veil proper was worn by Hebrew women only on special occasions, as in marriage, Gen. xxiv. 65; for ornament, S. of Sol. iv. 1, 3; for concealment as in harlotry, Gen. xxxviii. 14.

Vẽr-mĭl'ion (*little worm*). A bright red color much affected by Hebrews in the painting of beams, ceilings, and conspicuous objects, Jer. xxii. 14; Ezek. xxiii. 14.

Vĕtch'es. A plant of the bean family. [FITCHES.]

Vetches.

Vī'al (*shallow cup*). In a general sense any bottle or vessel, 1 Sam. x. 1.

Vĭl'lage. In addition to the ordinary meaning, the unwalled suburbs of a walled town, Lev. xxv. 31.

Vīne (*wine*). A favorite Oriental plant of many varieties and cultivated from the earliest times, Gen. ix. 20; Num. xiii. 23. Subject of frequent metaphor, Deut. xxxii. 32; emblem of felicity and contentment, 1 Kgs. iv. 25; Ps. cxxviii. 3; Mic. iv. 4; rebellious Israel compared to "wild grapes," Isa. v. 2, "strange vine," Jer. ii. 21, "empty vine," Hos. x. 1; symbol of spiritual union, John xv. 1-5.

Vĭn'e-gär (*sharp wine*). A thin wine, Num. vi. 3; Ruth ii. 14; acid, Prov. x. 26; unpalatable, Ps. lxix. 21. The thin sour wine of the Roman soldiers was the beverage in Matt. xxvii. 48; Mark xv. 36; John xix. 29, 30.

Vĭne'yärd. Vineyards were generally on hills, Isa. v. 1; Jer. xxxi. 5; Am. ix. 13; surrounded by walls or hedges to keep out boars, Ps. lxxx. 13; jackals and foxes, Num. xxii. 24; Neh. iv. 3; S. of Sol. ii. 15; Ezek. xiii. 4; Matt. xxi. 33. Towers were erected within the vineyard for watch-houses and dwellings for the vine-keeper, Isa. i. 8; v. 2; Matt. xxi. 33.

Vint'age (*taking wine away*). The vintage season a time of joy. Town people went out and lived among the vineyards in lodges and tents, Judg. ix. 27; Isa. xvi. 10; Jer. xxv. 30. Grapes were gathered in baskets, Jer. vi. 9. [WINE-PRESS.]

Vīne of Sŏd'om, Deut. xxxii. 32. A phrase used to describe the character of Israel.

Vīne'yärds, Plain of. A place east of Jordan, beyond Aroer, Judg. xi. 33. [ABEL.]

Vī'ol (*keep holiday, sacrifice*). A stringed instrument like the psaltery, Am. vi. 5. [PSALTERY.]

Viper.

Vī'per (*bringing forth its young alive*). The Hebrew word implies a hissing and venomous serpent, as the common European viper or adder, the horned vipers of the *cerastes* genus, and the Indian vipers, Job xx. 16; Isa. xxx. 6; Acts xxviii. 1-6. A symbol of deceit and destruction, Matt. iii. 7; xii. 34; xxiii. 33; Luke iii. 7.

Vis'ion (*seeing*). An inspired dream, phantasy, or apparition, Num. xxiv. 4; Isa. vi.; Ezek. i. viii.-x.; Dan. vii., viii.; Acts xxvi. 13-19.

Vŏph'sī (*gain*). Father of Nahbi, the spy selected to represent the tribe of Naphtali, Num. xiii. 14.

Vow (*wish*). Vows were threefold, vows of devotion, abstinence, and destruction, and respecting them certain laws were laid down, Deut. xxiii. 21-23. The law in Lev. xxvii. regulated the vow of Corban, and that in Num. vi. 1-21 the Nazarite vow.

Vŭl'ture (*tearer*). A large falconoid bird, with naked head and neck, feeding mostly on carrion. The bird is pronounced unclean in Lev. xi. 14; Deut. xiv. 13; but the original implies the kite, as also in Isa. xxxiv. 15.

W

Wā'fer (*waffle*). Among Hebrews a thin cake of fine flour used in offerings. The flour was wheaten and the wafers were unleavened and anointed with oil, Ex. xvi. 31; xxix. 2, 23; Lev. ii. 4; vii. 12; viii. 26; Num. vi. 15, 19.

Wā'ġes (*pledges*). The earliest O. T. mention of wages shows that they were paid in kind and not in money, Gen. xxix. 15, 20; xxx. 28; xxxi. 7, 8, 41. Wages paid in money are mentioned in N. T., Matt. xx. 2. The Mosaic law was very strict in requiring daily payment of wages, Lev. xix. 13; Deut. xxiv. 14, 15.

Wăg'on (*mover*). Wagons of the Hebrews, like those of the ancient Egyptians, were carts, consisting of planks or at most of crude box-like bodies, supported upon axles which connected two solid wooden wheels. They were mostly drawn by oxen or kine, Num. vii. 3, 8; 1 Sam. vi. 3-14.

Walk (*move*). Walk has figurative use in the Bible to denote the behavior and spiritual character of a person, Ezek. xi. 20; Rom. viii. 1.

Wall of Pär-tĭ'tion. The allusion in Eph. ii. 14 is to the "wall of partition" which separated the holy of holies from the holy place in Solomon's temple, 1 Kgs. vi. 31, 35.

Walls (*palisades*). Solid walls limitedly used in Oriental countries for ordinary dwellings, but at times solidly laid and strongly built for palaces and temples, and as a protection to cities. They were of various materials, palisades, clay, cemented pebbles, brick, and stone. Houses were frequently erected on the walls of cities, and towers for archers and slingers, Josh. ii. 15; Ps. lxii. 3; Isa. xxx. 13; Luke vi. 48.

Wan'dēr-ings (*windings*). The wilderness wanderings of the Israelites began at Rameses, the place of rendezvous, west of the Red Sea. The time as fixed by modern Egyptologists was during the reign of the Pharaoh Menephthah, B. C. 1317, though another date, B. C. 1491, was for a long time received. After crossing into Arabia, the line of march was southerly to the wilderness of Sinai, where a long halt was made, the law given, the tabernacle built, and the people were numbered, Ex. xv. 23, 27; xvi.-xl.; Lev.; Num. i.-x. 12. From Sinai the route was northward to Kadesh near the southern border of Canaan, the time thus far consumed being two years, Num. xiii. 26. Here they were condemned to further wilderness wanderings for a period of thirty-eight years. This period was seemingly one devoted to nomadic existence like that of other Arabian tribes. When the time came for another move on Canaan, the route lay around the head of the Gulf of Akaba and thence eastward and northward to Moab and the Jordan crossing, Num. xxxiii. 48, 49.

War (*embroil*). Primitive Hebrew weapons were clubs, arrows, slings, swords, and spears. No army divisions except those indicated by the tribes. The contests of this period often hand-to-hand and brutal, 2 Sam. i. 23; ii. 18; 1 Chr. xii. 8; 2 Chr. xiii. 17. Many of the modern stratagems employed, as the double attack, Gen. xiv. 15; ambush, Josh. viii. 12; false retreat, Judg. xx. 37; night attack, 2 Kgs. vii. 12. Sometimes battles were settled by single-handed combats, 1 Sam. xvii.; 2 Sam. ii. 15, 16; 1 Chr. xi. 6. King David's army was divided into regularly disciplined and officered bands under a general-in-chief, 2 Sam. xviii. 1, 2; xxiii. 8-39; 1 Chr. xi. 25-47; xii., xxvii. He introduced the heavier weapons, such as catapults and battering-rams for siege-work and chariots for field-work, 2 Sam. viii. 4. Soldiers killed in action were plundered, 1 Sam. xxxi. 8; survivors were mutilated or killed, Judg. i. 6; ix. 45; 2 Sam. xii. 31; 2 Chr. xxv. 12; or carried into captivity, Num. xxxi. 26.

Ward (*watch*). A guard-room or lock-up, Gen. xl. 3; Acts xii. 10. A garrison or military post, Neh. xii. 25. A detachment of persons, guard, for any purpose, 1 Chr. ix. 23; Neh. xiii. 30.

Ward'rōbe (*watch-robe*). Place where the royal robes and priest's vestments were kept under watch or care, 2 Kgs. xxii. 14.

Wāres. [COMMERCE.]

Wash'ing. The custom of washing hands before meals or of feet after a journey or on entering a stranger's house was not only a polite ceremony but a religious observance, Matt. xv. 2; Mark vii. 3; Luke xi. 38. After the salutation the first act of hospitality was to proffer a basin of water to the guest for washing the feet, Gen. xviii. 4; Ex. xxx. 19, 21; Judg. xix. 21; 1 Sam. xxv. 41; Luke vii. 37, 38, 44; John xiii. 5-14.

Watch (*wake*). The Hebrew night was divided into three watches, instead of hours. The first was called "the beginning of watches," beginning at sunset and lasting till ten o'clock, Lam. ii. 19; the second, the "middle watch," from ten P. M. till two

A. M., Judg. vii. 19; the "morning watch," from two A. M. till sunrise, Ex. xiv. 24; 1 Sam xi. 11. After the captivity the Jews gradually adopted the Greek and Roman division of the night into twelve hours of four watches; "evening," 6 to 9; "midnight," 9 to 12; "cock-crowing," 12 to 3; "morning," 3 to 6, Matt. xiv. 25; Mark xiii. 35; Luke xii. 38.

Wa'ter of Jĕal'oŭs-y̆. The jealous husband brought his suspected wife before the priest, with her offering of barley meal, without oil or frankincense, in her hand. The priest took holy water in an earthen vessel in his hand and sprinkled it with the dust of the floor. Then the priest administered the oath to her. If she confessed to guilt she was compelled to drink the water, and stood accursed. If otherwise, she was allowed to go free, Num. v. 12-31.

xxviii. 4, 39; woolen garments, Lev. xiii. 47. Though the loom is not mentioned, its various parts are, as the shuttle, beam, etc., 1 Sam. xvii. 7; 2 Kgs. xxiii. 7; 1 Chr. iv. 21; Job vii. 6; Prov. xxxi. 13, 24; Isa. xxxviii. 12.

Wĕd'ding. [Marriage.]

Wĕd'ding-gär'ment. A special garment, required to be worn at marriage-suppers, seems to have been furnished by the host, Matt. xxii. 11.

Week. The division of time into weeks of seven days each dates from the earliest historic times among many and wide-apart nations. The Hebrew week began on our Sunday, their Sabbath being the seventh day or Saturday. The only day of their week they named was the Sabbath. The rest ran by numbers, as first, second, third, etc. Besides their week of

Oriental Cart. (*See* p. 121.)

Wa'ter of Sĕp"a-rā'tion. The preparation and use of the water of separation are described in Num. xix.

Wa'ter-spouts. The word translated "waterspouts" in Ps. xlii. 7 is rendered "gutter" in 2 Sam. v. 8.

Wāve-ŏf'fĕr-ing. The wave-offering, together with the heave-offering, was a part of the peace-offering. The right shoulder of the victim, which was considered the choicest part, was "heaved" or held up in the sight of the Lord, and was, therefore, to be eaten only by the priests. The breast portion was "waved" before the Lord and eaten by the worshippers. On the second day of the passover feast, a sheaf of wheat and an unblemished lamb of the first year were waved, Ex. xxix. 24-27; Lev. vii. 30-34; viii. 27; ix. 21; x. 14, 15; xxiii. 10-20; Num. vi. 20; xviii. 11-18, 26-29.

Wăx. Wax in its original sense, an animal product as of bees, is frequently used in Scripture as a means of illustration, Ps. lxviii. 2; xcvii. 5; Mic. i. 4.

Wēan (*accustom*). Weaning-time a festal occasion, and probably late, Gen. xxi. 8; 2 Chr. xxxi. 16.

Wĕap'ons. [Arms.] [War.]

Wē'sel. It is thought that "mole" would be a better translation, Lev. xi. 29.

Wēave. Most ancient nations knew the art of weaving. The Egyptians were skilled weavers, Gen. xli. 42. That the Hebrews brought the art along with them from bondage is clear from the fabrics manufactured in the wilderness: goat-hair covers, linen curtains, Ex. xxvi. 1-13; embroidered raiment, Ex.

days, Hebrews had their week of years, every seven years, and their week of seven times seven years, or year of jubilee, every fiftieth year, Gen. viii. 10; xxix. 27. The "feast of weeks" corresponded with Pentecost, Ex. xxiii. 15; xxxiv. 22; Lev. xxiii. 15-22; Num. xxviii.

Weights and Meas'ures. The standard of Hebrew weights and measures was kept in the sanctuary, Lev. xix. 35, 36. A copy of said standard was kept in the household, Deut. xxv. 13-15. The destruction of the ancient standard with the tabernacle led to the adoption of the various weights and measures of such countries as the Hebrews happened to be subject to or in commercial intercourse with. Hence the subject of Hebrew weights and measures is full of perplexity and uncertainty. *See* various weights and measures under their respective headings.

Wĕll (*boil*). Wells were of great importance in Palestine, Gen. xxiv. 11; Num. xx. 17-19; Judg. vii. 1. They were sometimes deep, John iv. 11; frequently owned in common, Gen. xxix. 2, 3; covered at times with a stone and surrounded by a low wall to protect them from drifting sand, Gen. xxix. 2-8; to stop them up an act of hostility, Gen. xxvi. 15, 16; to invade them a cause for contention, Gen. xxi. 25; water sometimes drawn by sweeps or windlasses, but generally by a bucket attached to a rope, and in some cases steps led down to them, Gen. xxi. 25-31; Judg. i. 13-15; 1 Sam. xxix. 1; emblem of blessings, Jer. ii. 13; xvii. 13.

Whāle. The Hebrew original translated "great whales" in Gen. i. 21 is used of "serpents" in Ex. vii. 9; Deut. xxxii. 33, and of the "crocodile" in Ezek.

xxix. 3; xxxii. 2. In Job vii. 12; Isa. xxvii. 1, the name belongs to sea monsters. It is thought that the shark of the Mediterranean is meant in Jonah i. 17; Matt. xii. 40.

Whēat. This well-known cereal was cultivated in the East from the earliest times, Gen. xxx. 14, and grew luxuriantly and of many varieties in Egypt, Gen. xli. 22. Syria and Palestine were both fine wheat-growing countries, Ps. lxxxi. 16; cxlvii. 14; Matt. xiii. 8. Wheat-harvest denoted a well-known season, Gen. xxx. 14.

Whīrl'wĭnd. Whirlwinds of great violence and frequency were well-known desert visitations and gave rise to many Scripture metaphors, Job xxxvii. 9; Isa. xvii. 13.

Ancient Well. (*See* p. 122.)

Whĭt'ed Sĕp'ŭl-chreṣ. Inasmuch as contact with the burial place was a cause of ceremonial defilement, Num. xix. 16, sepulchres were whitewashed that they might be seen and avoided, Matt. xxiii. 27.

Wĭd'ōw (*lack*). When a married man died without children, his brother, if still living with the family, had a right under the law to marry the widow in order to preserve the family name and inheritance, Deut. xxv. 5, 6; Matt. xxii. 23–30. Other provisions of the Mosaic law show great consideration for widows, Ex. xxii. 22; Deut. xiv. 29; xvi. 11, 14; xxiv. 19–21; xxvi. 12; xxvii. 19.

Wife. [MARRIAGE.]

Wĭl'dẽr-ness (*place of wild beasts*). Like the word desert, wilderness does not necessarily imply an absolutely arid, sandy, and uninhabitable place, but an uncultivated waste, which it was possible for pastoral tribes to occupy, and with stretches of pasturage, Josh. xv. 61; Isa. xlii. 11. The wilderness of wandering in which the Israelites spent forty years, Deut. i. 1; Josh. v. 6; Neh. ix. 19, 21; Ps. lxxviii. 40–52; cvii. 4; Jer. ii. 2, was practically the great peninsula of Sinai lying between Seir, Edom, and Gulf of Akaba on the east, and Gulf of Suez and Egypt on the west. It embraced many minor divisions or wildernesses, as those of Sin or Zin, Paran, Shur, Etham, and Sinai. [WANDERINGS.]

Will. The laws respecting realty rendered wills useless, but nuncupative disposition of personalty seems to be implied in 2 Sam. xvii. 23; 2 Kgs. xx. 1; Isa. xxxviii. 1.

Wĭl'lōw. Before the captivity the willow was an emblem of joy, Lev. xxiii. 40; Job xl. 22; Isa. xliv. 4; but in allusion to the captivity, the weeping willow of Babylonia became the poetical type of sorrow, Ps. cxxxvii. 2. The "brook of willows," Isa. xv. 7, was in the land of Moab, and is called "valley of Arabians" in margin.

Wĭm'ple. In a Bible sense, a hood or veil as in Isa. iii. 22, or a mantle or shawl as in Ruth iii. 15.

Wĭnd (*blow*). Hebrews recognized the cardinal winds in their "four winds," north, south, east, west, Ezek. xxxvii. 9; Dan. viii. 8; Zech. ii. 6; Matt. xxiv. 31. The east wind injured vegetation, Gen. xli. 6; Job i. 19; Isa. xxvii. 8. The south wind brought heat, Luke xii. 55. The southwest and north winds brought clear cool weather, Job xxxvii. 9, 22; Prov. xxv. 23. The west wind, coming from the Mediterranean, brought rain.

Wĭn'dōw (*wind-eye*). In primitive Oriental houses the windows were simply openings upon the inner or court side of houses. But on the street or public side there were frequently latticed projections both for ventilation and sitting purposes, 2 Kgs. ix. 30; Judg. v. 28; probably the casements of Prov. vii. 6; S. of Sol. ii. 9.

Wīne (*drink*). The Hebrews manufactured and used wine from earliest times, Gen. ix. 20, 21; xix. 32; xxvii. 25; xlix. 12; Job i. 18; Prov. xxiii. 30, 31; Isa. v. 11. A usual drink-offering at the daily sacrifices, Ex. xxix. 40; at the presentation of first-fruits, Lev. xxiii. 13; and at other offerings, Num. xv. 5. It was tithable, Deut. xviii. 4. Nazarites could not drink it during their vow, Num. vi. 3, nor priests before service, Lev. x. 9.

Wīne-făt, Wīne-prĕss. The Hebrew wine-fat, vat, or press, consisted of an upper and lower receptacle, the former for treading the grapes, the latter for catching the juice, Isa. lxiii. 3; Joel iii. 13; Hag. ii. 16.

Wĭn'nōw (*wind*). The process of winnowing or winding grain was that of tossing the mixed chaff and kernels into the air, on a high, windy spot, with a fork or shovel, so that the wind could carry the chaff away. The floor on which the kernels fell was usually clean and solid, and when not so, a sheet was used to catch the grains, Isa. xxx. 24; xli. 16; Matt. iii. 12. Evening was the favorite winnowing time because the breezes were then steadiest, Ruth iii. 2.

Wĭn'tẽr. Winters in Palestine are short, lasting from December till February, S. of Sol. ii. 11.

Wĭṣ'dom of Jē'ṣŭs. [ECCLESIASTICUS.]

Wĭṣ'dom of Sŏl'o-mon. Fifth of the Apocryphal books, devoted to an exposition of wisdom in its moral, philosophic, and historic aspects.

Wīṣe Mĕn, Matt. ii. 1. [MAGI.]

Wist. Same as "knew," Ex. xvi. 15; Acts xii. 9; xxiii. 5.

Wit (*know*). To become aware, learn, know, Gen. xxiv. 21; Ex. ii. 4.

Witch (*wizard*). One who pretends to deal with evil spirits in order to work a spell on persons or their belongings; conjurer, fortune-teller, exorcist, supernatural curer of diseases, Deut. xviii. 10; 1 Sam. xxviii. 3–25. The word formerly embraced both sexes, but is now applied to women. Witches were not allowed to live, Ex. xxii. 18.

Witch'craft. The occult practices of witches and wizards, 1 Sam. xv. 23. The art, the pretender, and the person deceived were alike denounced, Lev. xx. 6; Nah. iii. 4; Gal. v. 20.

Wit'ness (*see*). Under the Mosaic law at least two witnesses were required to establish a capital charge, Num. xxxv. 30; Deut. xvii. 6, 7. False swearing forbidden, Ex. xx. 16; Lev. vi. 1–7.

Wiz'ärd (*cunning*). A male witch, Lev. xx. 27.

Wolf. Wolves of Palestine were numerous and the dread of shepherds, as they were a terrible enemy to sheep, Matt. vii. 15; x. 16; John x. 12; Acts xx.

29. A wolf typed the rapacity of Benjamin, Gen. xlix. 27; and the cruelty of Israel's oppression, Ezek. xxii. 27; and the destruction of the wicked, Jer. v. 6.

Wom'an (*wife-man*). Hebrew women cared for the household, Gen. xviii. 6; carried water, Gen. xxiv. 15; tended flocks, Gen. xxix. 6; spun, Ex. xxxv. 26; made clothes, 1 Sam. ii. 19; acted as hostess and guest on social occasions, Job i. 4; John ii. 3; xii. 2; prophesied, composed, sang, and danced, Ex. xv. 20, 21; Judg. xi. 34; xxi. 21; fêted, 1 Sam. xviii. 6, 7; held public positions, Judg. iv., v.; 2 Kgs. xxii. 14; Neh. vi. 14; Luke ii. 36; acted as workers and officials in the early Christian church, Acts xviii. 18, 26; Rom. xvi. 1.

Wool. A highly prized material for clothing among Hebrews, Lev. xiii. 47; Job xxxi. 20; Prov. xxxi. 13; Ezek. xxvii. 18; xxxiv. 3. Mixed woolen and linen fabrics forbidden, Lev. xix. 19; Deut. xxii. 11.

Word. The *logos*, or Word, in John i. 1-14; 1 John i. 1; Rev. xix. 13, stands for the Son of God, the Word incarnate.

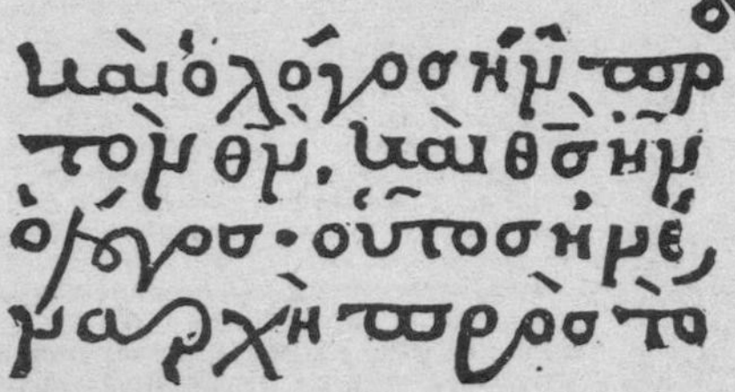
καὶ ὁ λόγος ἦν πρὸς
τὸν θν. καὶ θς ἦν
ὁ λόγος· οὗτος ἦν ἐν
ἀρχῇ πρὸς τὸ

Greek MS. A. D. 1000.— St. John i. 1, 2.

Worm. Many Hebrew words are translated worm, all indicative of something loathsome, destructive, helpless, or insignificant, as the moth, Isa. li. 8; maggot, Job xix. 26; possibly the serpent, Mic. vii. 17. The allusion in Isa. lxvi. 24; Mark ix. 44-48, is thought to be to the valley near Jerusalem where the refuse of the city constantly bred worms and where fires were kept burning to consume the collections. The helplessness of the worm affords the figures in Job xxv. 6; Ps. xxii. 6; Isa. xli. 14.

Worm'wood. A bitter plant found in Palestine, and often mentioned in Scripture in connection with gall to denote what is offensive and nauseous, Deut. xxix. 18; Prov. v. 4; Jer. ix. 15; xxiii. 15: Lam. iii. 15, 19; Am. v. 7.

Wor'ship-per, Acts xix. 35. The word should be temple-keeper as in marg. and in R. V.

Wŏt. "Wotteth not," Gen. xxxix. 8, means "knows not."

Papyrus, 1st century.

Wrī'tĭng. The first mention of writing in the Bible is in Ex. xvii. 14. The art among Hebrews was limited to persons of learning and position and to the class of scribes, Isa. xxix. 11, 12. [SCRIBE.] The oldest Semitic writings are the bricks and tablets of Nineveh and Babylon. The Hebrew alphabet was a development of the Phœnician, and it underwent many changes in the course of time. The record of Sinai was written on stone with the finger of God, Ex. xxxi. 18; xxxii. 15-19; xxxiv. 1-29. Later materials were wax, wood, metal, or plaster, Deut. xxvii. 2; Josh. viii. 32; Luke i. 63; and perhaps vellum, or fine parchment from skins, and linen were in early use for other than monumental writings, as they surely were at a later day, 2 Tim. iv. 13. Pliable substances, when written upon, were rolled on sticks, sealed and preserved as books, Ps. xl. 7; Isa. xxix. 11; Dan. xii. 4; Rev. v. 1. Hebrews doubtless knew the use of papyrus, 2 John 12. Rolls were generally written upon one side only, except in Ezek. ii. 9, 10; Rev. v. 1. Hebrew instruments of writing were the stylus and graver for hard materials, Ex. xxxii. 4; Job xix. 24; Ps. xlv. 1; Isa. viii. 1; Jer. viii. 8; xvii. 1; and for pliable materials, a reed pen, 2 Cor. iii. 3; 2 John 12; 3 John 13. Paul used an amanuensis, but authenticated his letters in a few lines with his own pen, 1 Cor. xvi. 21; Col. iv. 18; 2 Thess. iii. 17. Ancient ink was made of pulverized charcoal or burnt ivory in water to which gum had been added. It was carried in an ink-horn suspended to the girdle, Ezek. ix. 3, 4.

Y

Yärn. Though the art of spinning was well known to Hebrews, Ex. xxxv. 25; Prov. xxxi. 19; Matt. vi. 28, the spun product is only mentioned in 1 Kgs. x. 28; 2 Chr. i. 16, and in both these instances the word is rather significant of "band" as applied to a troop or drove of horses than to yarn.

Yēar. The Hebrew year was sacred and civil, with two beginnings. The sacred year began with the month Abib, April, the civil with the month Tisri, October. The months were lunar, twelve in number, with, of course, the necessary intercalary month *ve-adar* at the proper time, about every three years. As divided by seasons, the year was solar. There were two seasons, summer and winter, Ps. lxxiv. 17; Jer. xxxvi. 22; Am. iii. 15; Zech. xiv. 8.

Yēar of Jū'bi-lēe. [JUBILEE.]

Yēar, Săb-băt'ĭ-cal. [SABBATICAL.]

Yōke (*join*). This well-known means of coupling oxen for agricultural purposes was primitively laid upon the necks of the cattle, and held there by thongs which passed around their necks. A thong served also as an attachment to the cart-tongue or plow-beam. A pair of oxen yoked together were called a yoke, as to-day, 1 Sam. xi. 7; 1 Kgs. xix. 21. It would seem as if asses and mules went by pairs like oxen, Judg. xix. 10; 2 Kgs. v. 17, and even horses, camels, and chariots, Isa. xxi. 7. The word, like the Latin *jugum*, gave rise to a measurement of land, 1 Sam. xiv. 14, the amount a yoke of oxen could plow in a day. Yoke is used metaphorically for subjection, 1 Kgs. xii. 4, 9-11; Isa. ix. 4; Jer. v. 5. An unusually heavy bondage was typed by "iron yoke," Deut. xxviii. 48; Jer. xxviii. 13. Removal of the yoke implied deliverance, Gen. xxvii. 40; Jer. ii. 20; Matt. xi. 29, 30. Breaking of the yoke meant repudiation of authority, Nah. i. 13.

Z

Zā''a-nā'im (*changing*). The plain, or rather the oak, where Heber the Kenite was encamped when Sisera sought refuge in his tent, Judg. iv. 11, 17-22. It is mentioned as near Kedesh.

Zā'a-năn (*flocking-place*). A place in the lowlands of Judah, Mic. i. 11.

Zā''a-năn'nim. A border place of Naphtali, near Kedesh, and supposed to be same as Zaanaim, Josh. xix. 33.

Zā'a-văn (*disturbed*). Son of Ezer and descendant of Seir the Horite, Gen. xxxvi. 27. Zavan in 1 Chr. i. 42.

Zā'băd (*gift*). (1) A son of Nathan, 1 Chr. ii. 36, 37, and one of David's mighty men, 1 Chr. xi. 41. (2) An Ephraimite whom the Gathites slew while on a thieving expedition, 1 Chr. vii. 21. (3) Son of Shimeath, an Ammonitess, and one of the murderers of King Joash, 2 Chr. xxiv. 25, 26. Jozachar in 2 Kgs. xii. 21. (4) Three returned captives, Ez. x. 27, 33, 43.

Zăb″a-dā′ias, 1 Esdr. ix. 35. [ZABAD, 4.]

Zăb″a-dē′ans. An Arab tribe smitten by Jonathan Maccabeus, 1 Macc. xii. 31.

Zăb′bāi (*limpid*). (1) One who had taken a foreign wife, Ez. x. 28. (2) Father of Baruch, one of the repairers of the walls of Jerusalem, Neh. iii. 20.

Zăb′bud (*given*). One who returned from captivity with Ezra, Ez. viii. 14.

Zăb′dī (*gift*). (1) Son of Zerah of the tribe of Judah, and ancestor of Achan, who concealed the spoils of Jericho, Josh. vii. 1, 17, 18. (2) One of the sons of Shimhi, a Benjamite, 1 Chr. viii. 19. (3) An officer who had the care of King David's wine cellars, 1 Chr. xxvii. 27. (4) Son of Asaph the minstrel and leader of thanksgiving in prayer, Neh. xi. 17. Zaccur, Neh. xii. 35. Zichri, 1 Chr. ix. 15.

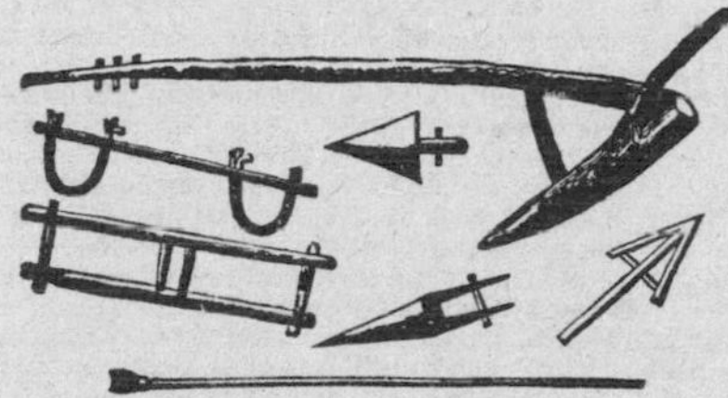

Yokes, Plow, and Goads.

Zăb′dī el (*gift of God*). (1) Father of Jashobeam, captain of first course for the first month of David's guard, 1 Chr. xxvii. 2. (2) Overseer of a returned troop of captives, Neh. xi. 14. (3) An Arabian chieftain who put Alexander Balas to death, 1 Macc. xi. 17.

Zā′bud (*given*). A friend of Solomon and his principal officer, 1 Kgs. iv. 5.

Zăb′u-lon. Greek form of Zebulun, Matt. iv. 13; Rev. vii. 8.

Zăc′ca-ī (*pure*). His descendants, 760 in number, returned with Zerubbabel, Ez. ii. 9; Neh. vii. 14.

Zăc-chæ′us (*just*). The rich chief among publicans, resident at Jericho, who climbed a tree to see Jesus pass, was invited down, became the host of Jesus, and was converted, Luke xix. 1-10.

Zăc-chē′us. An officer under Judas Maccabeus, 2 Macc. x. 19.

Zăc′chur (*mindful*). A Simeonite of the family of Mishma, 1 Chr. iv. 26.

Zăc′cur (*mindful*). (1) Father of Shammua, the spy sent out by the tribe of Reuben, Num. xiii. 4. (2) A Merarite Levite, 1 Chr. xxiv. 27. (3) A son of Asaph the minstrel, and leader of the third musical course, 1 Chr. xxv. 2, 10; Neh. xii. 35. (4) One who assisted in rebuilding the walls of Jerusalem, Neh. iii. 2. (5) One who signed the covenant with Nehemiah, Neh. x. 12. (6) Father of Hanan, whom Nehemiah made one of his treasurers, Neh. xiii. 13.

Zăch″a-rī′ah (*remembered by Jehovah*). In better Hebrew, Zechariah. (1) Son of Jeroboam II., and his successor on the throne of Israel, 2 Kgs. xiv. 29; B. C. 773-72. He reigned only six months, 2 Kgs. xv. 8-11. (2) Father of Abi, mother of Hezekiah king of Judah, 2 Kgs. xviii. 2. Written Zechariah in 2 Chr. xxix. 1.

Zăch″a-rī′as (*remembered by Jehovah*). Greek form of Zachariah. (1) The name is borne by many priests and laymen in the books of Esdras. (2) Father of John the Baptist and husband of Elizabeth. He was a priest of the course of Abia, or Abijah, 1 Chr. xxiv. 10, and probably lived at Hebron, Luke i. 5-25, 57-80. (3) Son of Barachias, who was slain between the temple and the altar, Matt. xxiii. 35; Luke xi. 51.

Zăch′a-rȳ, 2 Esdr. i. 40. [ZECHARIAH, THE PROPHET.]

Zā′cher (*testimony*). A Benjamite, one of the sons of Jehiel by Maachah, 1 Chr. viii. 29, 31.

Zā′dŏk (*just*). (1) Son of Ahitub, of the line of Eleazar. He was one of the high priests in the time of David, the other being Abiathar, 2 Sam. viii. 17. He joined David at Hebron, as a chieftain of his father's house, 1 Chr. xii. 28, remained faithful to him and subsequently anointed Solomon, 1 Kgs. i. 39. (2) A priest in the reign of King Ahaziah, 1 Chr. vi. 12. (3) Father of Jerusha, wife of Uzziah and mother of Jotham king of Judah, 2 Kgs. xv. 33. (4) Son of Baana, who helped Nehemiah to repair the walls of Jerusalem, Neh. iii. 4. (5) Another assistant wall-builder, Neh. iii. 29. (6) A co-covenanter with Nehemiah, Neh. x. 21. (7) A scribe and treasurer under Nehemiah, Neh. xiii. 13.

Zā′ham (*hateful*). A son of King Rehoboam by his wife Abihail, 2 Chr. xi. 19.

Zā′ir (*little*). A vague spot or place, where King Joram overcame the Edomites, 2 Kgs. viii. 21.

Zā′laph (*hurt*). Father of Hanun who helped to repair the walls of Jerusalem, Neh. iii. 30.

Zăl′mŏn (*shade*). (1) The Ahohite who was one of David's guard, 2 Sam. xxiii. 28. Ilai in 1 Chr. xi. 29. (2) A wooded eminence near Shechem, Judg. ix. 47-49.

Zal-mō′nah (*shady*). A desert encampment of the wandering Israelites, Num. xxxiii. 41, 42.

Zal-mŭn′nȧ (*shadow*). One of two kings of Midian captured and slain by Gideon, Judg. viii. 5-21; Ps. lxxxiii. 11.

Zăm′bĭs, 1 Esdr. ix. 34. [AMARIAH.]

Zăm′brī, 1 Macc. ii. 26. [ZIMRI.]

Zā′moth, 1 Esdr. ix. 28. [ZATTU.]

Zăm-zŭm′mims. An Ammonite name for a race of Rephaim or giants, Deut. ii. 20.

Zȧ-nō′ah (*swamp*). (1) A town in the lowlands of Judah, ten miles southwest of Jerusalem, Josh. xv. 34; 1 Chr. iv. 18. Its inhabitants helped Nehemiah to repair the walls of Jerusalem, Neh. iii. 13; xi. 30. (2) Another town of Judah in the mountains, about ten miles southwest of Hebron, Josh. xv. 56.

Zăph′nath=pā″a-nē′ah (*revealer of secrets*). A name given by the Pharaoh to Joseph upon his promotion to a high place in the royal service, Gen. xli. 45.

Zā′phŏn (*north*). An unidentified place in Gad, Josh. xiii. 27.

Zā′rȧ (*dawn*). Zarah, a son of Judah, in genealogy of Christ, Matt. i. 3.

Zăr′a-çēs. A brother of Jehoiakim, King of Judah, 1 Esdr. i. 38.

Zā′rah (*dawn*). A son of Judah by Tamar, Gen. xxxviii. 30; xlvi. 12. Called Zerah in Num. xxvi. 20, and founder of the family of Zarhites; also Zerah in Josh. vii. 1, 18; xxii. 20; 1 Chr. ii. 4, 6; ix. 6; Neh. xi. 24. Zara in Matt. i. 3.

Zăr″a-ī′as. The name stands for Zerahiah and Zebadiah in the Apocrypha, 1 Esdr. viii.

Zā′re-ah (*hornet*). Neh. xi. 29. [ZORAH, ZOREAH.]

Zā′re-ath-ītes″. Dwellers in Zareah or Zorah, 1 Chr. ii. 53.

Zā′red, Num. xxi. 12. [ZERED.]

Zăr′e-phăth (*smelting-place*). The Sarepta of Luke iv. 26. A town in Phœnicia on the Mediterranean coast between Tyre and Sidon, and about seven miles from the latter. Residence of the prophet Elijah during the great drought, 1 Kgs. xvii. 8-24.

Zăr′e-tăn, Josh. iii. 16. [ZARTHAN, 2.]

Zā'reth-shā'har (*beauty of dawn*). A town in Reuben, Josh. xiii. 19.

Zär'hītes. A branch of the tribe of Judah descended from Zerah the son of Judah, Num. xxvi. 13, 20; Josh. vii. 17; 1 Chr. xxvii. 11, 13.

Zär'ta-nah (*cooling*). A place usually identified with Zarthan, 1 Kgs. iv. 12.

Zär'than (*cooling*). (1) A town in the Jordan valley. Between it and Succoth was the clay-ground in which Solomon cast the utensils for the temple service. Now the mound called *Tell-sa-rem*, 1 Kgs. vii. 46. (2) The same place is doubtless meant by Zaretan, Josh. iii. 16, and by Zererath in Judg. vii. 22. (3) Supposably another name for the Zartanah of 1 Kgs. iv. 12. (4) Doubtless Zarthan (1) is meant by the Zeredathah of 2 Chr. iv. 17.

Zăth'o-ē, 1 Esdr. viii. 32. [Zattu.]

Zăt'thu (*branch*). One who sealed the covenant with Nehemiah, Neh. x. 14.

Zăt'tu (*branch*). The children of Zattu returned from the captivity, Ez. ii. 8; x. 27; Neh. vii. 13.

Zā'van, 1 Chr. i. 42. [Zaavan.]

Zā'zȧ (*for all*). A son of Jonathan, and descendant of Judah, 1 Chr. ii. 33.

Zĕal'ŏts (*zealous*). Name of a fanatical Jewish party, strongest from A. D. 6 to 70. It was political, having for its aim the overthrow of Roman authority; and religious, seeking a Jewish theocracy over the whole earth. In Acts v. 37 it seems to have been headed by one Judas of Galilee.

Zĕb''a-dī'ah (*portion of God*). (1) A son of Beriah, of Benjamin, 1 Chr. viii. 15. (2) A son of Elpaal of Benjamin, 1 Chr. viii. 17. (3) A son of Jeroham of Gedor, a Benjamite, 1 Chr. xii. 7. (4) A Korhite Levite, son of Meshelemiah, and one of the temple porters, 1 Chr. xxvi. 2. (5) A son of Asahel, brother of Joab, who succeeded his father as captain of the military course of the fourth month, 1 Chr. xxvii. 7. (6) A Levite sent out by King Jehoshaphat to teach the law to the people, 2 Chr. xvii. 8. (7) A son of Ishmael and ruler of the house of Judah in reign of King Jehoshaphat, 2 Chr. xix. 11. (8) One who returned with Ezra from the captivity, Ez. viii. 8. (9) A priest who had married a foreign wife, Ez. x. 20.

Zā'bah (*sacrifice*). One of the two Midianite kings slain by Gideon, Judg. viii. 5-21; Ps. lxxxiii. 11.

Zē-bā'im (*gazelles*). A disputed word, regarded as identical with Zeboim, Ez. ii. 57; Neh. vii. 59.

Zĕb'e-dee (*God's portion*). A fisherman of Galilee, husband of Salome, and father of the apostles James the Great and John, Matt. iv. 21; xxvii. 56; Mark i. 19, 20; xv. 40. His home is located at or near Bethsaida, and he appears to have been able to employ help in his occupation, Mark i. 20.

Zē-bī'nȧ (*buying*). A son of Nebo who had taken a foreign wife after the captivity, Ez. x. 43.

Zē-bō'im (*deer*). (1) One of the five cities of the plain, or circle, of Jordan, Gen. x. 19; Deut. xxix. 23; Hos. xi. 8. It is called Zeboiim in Gen. xiv. 2, 8. (2) A valley, or mountain gorge, contiguous to Michmash, 1 Sam. xiii. 18. (3) A place inhabited by Benjamites after the return from captivity, Neh. xi. 34.

Zē-bōi'īm, Gen. xiv. 2, 8. [Zeboim, 1.]

Zē-bū'dah (*given*). Wife of King Josiah and mother of King Jehoiakim, 2 Kgs. xxiii. 36.

Zē'bul (*habitation*). Ruler of the city of Shechem at the time of the contest between Abimelech and the native Canaanites, Judg. ix. 28-41.

Zĕb'u-lon-īte'', Judg. xii. 11. [Zebulunites.]

Zĕb'u-lun (*dwelling*). (1) Tenth son of Jacob, and sixth and last by Leah, Gen. xxx. 20; xxxv. 23. Three sons are ascribed to him at the time of the migration to Egypt, Gen. xlvi. 14. Zebulun was one of the six tribes stationed on Ebal to pronounce the curse, Deut. xxvii. 13. The allotment of the tribe was bounded as in Josh. xix. 10-16, and in general stretched from Acre to Jordan, taking in the plain of Esdraelon. The tribe did not expel the natives in its allotment, but associated with them and fell into easy commercial intercourse with Phœnicia on the west, Judg. i. 30. It became an idolatrous tribe, 2 Chr. xxx. 10-18, and its territory was depopulated in the captivity of Israel by Tiglath-pileser, 2 Kgs. xv. 29. (2) A boundary place of Asher, Josh. xix. 27.

Zĕb'u-lun-ītes''. Descendants of Zebulun, Num. xxvi. 27.

Zĕch''a-rī'ah (*memory of God*). Son of Berechiah, Zech. i. 1; of Iddo, Ez. v. 1. Eleventh of the minor prophets and contemporary of Haggai, born in Babylon during the captivity, returned with Zerubbabel, Ez. v. 1; vi. 14. The time of his prophecies is reckoned as between B. C. 520 and 518, during the period of building the second temple, whose completion was largely due to his energies as priest and prophet. His book, 38th of O. T., is divided into two parts. Chapters i.-viii. contain hopeful visions of the restored Hebrew state, exhortations to turn to Jehovah, warnings against God's enemies. Chapters ix.-xiv. are prophetic of the future fortunes of the theocracy, the conversion of Israel, the glorification of God's kingdom and of the coming of the Messiah. The style of the book is obscure. Many critics attribute the authorship of the second division of the book to Jeremiah. (2) A Reubenite chief, at time of the captivity by Tiglath-pileser, 1 Chr. v. 7. (3) A Korhite Levite, keeper of one of the doors of the tabernacle, 1 Chr. ix. 21. (4) A son of Jehiel, 1 Chr. ix. 37. (5) A Levite of the second order, one of the temple musicians, 1 Chr. xv. 18, 20. (6) A priest who blew the trumpet before the ark on its return, 1 Chr. xv. 24. (7) A Kohathite Levite, 1 Chr. xxiv. 25. (8) A Merarite Levite, 1 Chr. xxvi. 11. (9) A Manassite, 1 Chr. xxvii. 21. (10) A prince of Judah in reign of Jehoshaphat, 2 Chr. xvii. 7. (11) Father of Jahaziel, 2 Chr. xx. 14. (12) A son of Jehoshaphat, 2 Chr. xxi. 2. (13) Son of the high priest Jehoiada, in reign of Joash king of Judah, 2 Chr. xxiv. 20, and probably same as the Zacharias of Matt. xxiii. 35. (14) A prophet and royal counsellor in reign of Uzziah, 2 Chr. xxvi. 5. (15) Father of Abijah, mother of King Hezekiah, 2 Chr. xxix. 1. (16) A member of the family of Asaph in time of Hezekiah, 2 Chr. xxix. 13. (17) A Kohathite Levite in the reign of Josiah, 2 Chr. xxxiv. 12. (18) One of the temple rulers in reign of Josiah, 2 Chr. xxxv. 8. (19) Nine priests, Levites and returned captives in Ez. viii. 3, 11, 16; x. 26; Neh. viii. 4; xi. 4, 5, 12; xii. 16, 35, 41. (20) A witness for Isaiah, Isa. viii. 2.

Zē'dăd (*hillside*). A landmark on the northern border of Canaan, Num. xxxiv. 8; Ezek. xlvii. 15.

Zĕd''e-chī'as, 1 Esdr. i. 46. [Zedekiah.]

Zĕd''e-kī'ah (*justice of God*). (1) Last king of Judah, son of Josiah, and brother of Jehoahaz. He reigned eleven years, B. C. 598-588, 2 Kgs. xxiv. 18; 2 Chr. xxxvi. 11. He was raised to the throne by Nebuchadnezzar, who changed his name from Mattaniah to Zedekiah, 2 Kgs. xxiv. 17. In the ninth year of his reign, he revolted against Nebuchadnezzar, who thereupon completed the captivity of Judah and ended the kingdom, 2 Kgs. xxv. 1-21; 2 Chr. xxxvi. 11-21; Jer. xxi.-xxxviii.; Ezek. xvii. 15-21. (2) Son of Chenaanah, a prophet and head of the prophetic school in reign of Jehoshaphat, 1 Kgs. xxii.; 2 Chr. xviii. 10-24. (3) Son of Hananiah, and a court officer under Jehoiakim, Jer. xxxvi. 12. (4) A false prophet burnt to death by Nebuchadnezzar, Jer. xxix. 21, 22.

Zē'eb (*wolf*). A prince of Midian, slain by the Ephraimites, Judg. vii. 25; Ps. lxxxiii. 11.

Zē'eb, Wine-press of. The place where Zeeb was slain by the Ephraimites, Judg. vii. 25.

Zē'lah (*rib*). A city in Benjamin in which was

located the family tomb of Kish, father of Saul, Josh. xviii. 28; 2 Sam. xxi. 14.

Zē′lek (*chasm*). An Ammonite and one of David's guard, 2 Sam. xxiii. 37; 1 Chr. xi. 39.

Ze-lō′phe-hăd (*firstborn*). A son of Hepher, descendant of Manasseh. The law of female inheritance was changed in favor of his daughters, Num. xxvi. 33; xxvii. 1-11; Josh. xvii. 3, 4; 1 Chr. vii. 15.

Ze-lō′tes (*zealous*). A name added to that of the apostle Simon to distinguish him from Simon Peter, and to emphasize his membership of the party of Zealots, Luke vi. 15. [Simon, 4.]

Zĕl′zah (*shade*). A place in the border of Benjamin, near which was Rachel's tomb, 1 Sam. x. 2.

Zĕm″a-rā′im (*two fleeces*). (1) A town in Benjamin, four miles north of Jericho, Josh. xviii. 22. (2) Mount Zemaraim in the mountains of Ephraim, 2 Chr. xiii. 4.

Zĕm′a-rīte. An Hamitic tribe or family descended from Canaan, Gen. x. 18; 1 Chr. i. 16.

Ze-mī′rȧ (*song*). Son of Becher, a descendant of Benjamin, 1 Chr. vii. 8.

Zē′nan (*target*). A town in the lowlands of Judah, Josh. xv. 37.

Zē′nas. A Christian lawyer whom Paul wished Titus to bring along with him, Tit. iii. 13.

Zĕph″a-nī′ah (*God's secret*). (1) Ninth in order of the twelve minor prophets. Son of Cushi and a descendant of Hezekiah. He flourished during the reign of King Josiah, B. C. 641-610. His prophecy constitutes the 36th O. T. book, and denounces Judah, Nineveh, and surrounding nations, and records many cheerful promises of gospel blessings. The style is characterized by grace, strength, and dignity. (2) Son of Maaseiah and priest in the reign of Zedekiah; Jer. xxi. 1; xxix. 25-29; xxxvii. 3; lii. 24-27. (3) A Kohathite Levite, 1 Chr. vi. 36. (4) Father of Josiah and Hen, Zech. vi. 10, 14.

Zē′phath (*watchtower*). An Amorite town in the mountains near Kadesh. Called Hormah after it was conquered by the Israelites, Judg. i. 17. [Hormah.]

Zĕph′a-thah (*watchtower*). The valley near Mareshah in which King Asa marshalled his forces for battle against Zerah, 2 Chr. xiv. 9, 10.

Zē′phī, 1 Chr. i. 36. [Zepho.]

Zē′phō (*watchtower*). Zephi, 1 Chr. i. 36. One of the dukes of Edom, Gen. xxxvi. 11, 15.

Zē′phon (*watchman*). A son of Gad, Num. xxvi. 15. Called Ziphion in Gen. xlvi. 16.

Zē′phon-ītes. Descendants of Zephon, Num. xxvi. 15.

Zēr (*flint*). A city in Naphtali, Josh. xix. 35.

Zē′rah (*eastern*) (1) A grandson of Esau and one of the dukes of Edom, Gen. xxxvi. 13, 17, 33; 1 Chr. i. 37, 44. (2) Num. xxvi. 20; Josh. vii. 1, 18; xxii. 20; 1 Chr. ii. 4, 6; ix. 6; Neh. xi. 24. [Zarah.] (3) A son of Simeon and ancestor of a family of Zarhites, Num. xxvi. 13; 1 Chr. iv. 24. Called Zohar in Gen. xlvi. 10. (4) A Gershonite Levite, 1 Chr. vi. 21, 41. (5) An Ethiopian king whom Asa, king of Judah, defeated, 2 Chr. xiv. 9.

Zĕr″a-hī′ah (*rising of God*). (1) Son of Uzzi and priest of the line of Eleazar, 1 Chr. vi. 6, 51; Ez. vii. 4. (2) One whose descendants returned from captivity with Ezra, Ez. viii. 4.

Zē′red (*growth of reeds*). A brook or wady separating Moab from Edom, Deut. ii. 13, 14. Called Zared in Num. xxi. 12.

Zĕr′e-dȧ (*ambush*). Native place of Jeroboam, in the mountains of Ephraim, 1 Kgs. xi. 26.

Ze-rĕd′a-thah, 2 Chr. iv. 17. [Zarthan.]

Zĕr′e-răth, Judg. vii. 22. [Zarthan.]

Zē′resh. Wife of Haman, and his adviser in the conspiracy against Mordecai, Esth. v. 10-14.

Zē′reth (*bright*). A son of Ashur, founder of Tekoa, 1 Chr. iv. 7.

Zē′rī (*built*). A son of Jeduthun, a musician in the time of David, 1 Chr. xxv. 3.

Zē′rôr (*tied*). An ancestor of Kish, the father of Saul, 1 Sam. ix. 1.

Ze-ru′ah (*leprous*). Mother of King Jeroboam I., 1 Kgs. xi. 26.

Ze-rŭb′ba-bĕl (*born in Babylon*). He was of the family of David, and son of Shealtiel, Hag. i. 1, or Salathiel, Matt. i. 12, or Pedaiah, 1 Chr. iii. 19. Born at Babylon, commissioned governor of Judea by the Persian king, Cyrus, Neh. xii. 47; leader of the first colony of captives back to Jerusalem, B. C. 536, Ez. ii. 2; Neh. vii. 7; laid the foundation of the new temple, Zech. iv. 6-10; began the work of reconstruction, in which he was greatly hindered by Samaritan opposition, and petty Persian intrigue; finally succeeded in completing the structure, restored the order of priests according to the institution of David, Ez. vi. 14-22; Hag. i. 12, 15; ii. 2-4. Zorobabel in N. T., Matt. i. 12.

Zĕr″u-ī′ah (*bruised*). Sister of David and mother of the three leading heroes of David's army, 1 Sam. xxvi. 6; 1 Chr. ii. 16.

Zē′tham (*olive*). A Levite, son of Laadan, 1 Chr. xxiii. 8; xxvi. 22.

Zē′than (*olive*). A son of Bilhan, of Benjamin, 1 Chr. vii. 10.

Zē′thär (*star*). One of the seven chamberlains of King Ahasuerus, Esth. i. 10.

Zī′ȧ (*moving*). A Gadite, Chr. v. 13.

Zī′bȧ (*statue*). A steward of Saul, and tiller of the lands of Saul which David restored to Mephibosheth, 2 Sam. ix. 2-13; xvi. 1-4; xix. 17-29.

Zĭb′e-on (*robber*). A Horite and son of Seir, Gen. xxxvi. 2, 24, 29; 1 Chr. i. 38, 40.

Zĭb′ī-ȧ (*deer*). A Benjamite, 1 Chr. viii. 9.

Zĭb′ī-ah (*deer*). Mother of King Jehoash or Joash, 2 Kgs. xii. 1; 2 Chr. xxiv. 1.

Zĭch′rī (*remembered*). (1) A son of Izhar, son of Kohath, Ex. vi. 21. (2) A Benjamite of the sons of Shimhi, 1 Chr. viii. 19. (3) A Benjamite of the sons of Shashak, 1 Chr. viii. 23. (4) A Benjamite of the sons of Jeroham, 1 Chr. viii. 27. (5) A son of Asaph the musician, 1 Chr. ix. 15. Zabdi, Neh. xi. 17; Zaccur, Neh. xii. 35. (6) Son of Eliezer, a descendant of Moses, 1 Chr. xxvi. 25. (7) Father of Eliezer, a ruler of Reuben in reign of David, 1 Chr. xxvii. 16. (8) Father of Amasiah, a captain of 200,000 men of valor under King Jehoshaphat, 2 Chr. xvii. 16. (9) Father of Elishaphat, a captain of hundreds under Jehoiada, 2 Chr. xxiii. 1. (10) A mighty man of Ephraim in the army of Pekah, 2 Chr. xxviii. 7. (11) A Benjamite, father of Joel, overseer of Jerusalem after the captivity, Neh. xi. 9. (12) Priest of the family of Abijah, Neh. xii. 17.

Zĭd′dim (*steeps*). A fenced city of Naphtali, Josh. xix. 35.

Zī′dŏn (*fishing*). The Sidon of Gen. x. 15, 19, the N. T., and Apocrypha. An ancient and wealthy commercial city of Phœnicia on the Mediterranean coast, twenty miles north of Tyre. It was a limit of the allotment of Asher, but was never conquered, Judg. i. 31; x. 12; xviii. 7, 28. The Zidonians assisted in building the temple, 1 Kgs. v. 6; 1 Chr. xxii. 4; Ezek. xxvii. 8. Israel imported her idolatries, 1 Kgs. xi. 5, 33; 2 Kgs. xxiii. 13. Paul's ship touched at Sidon, Acts xxvii. 3.

Zī-dō′nī-ans. Dwellers in Zidon, Judg. x. 12.

Zĭf (*bloom*). Second month of Hebrew sacred and eighth of the civil year, corresponding to parts of April and May, 1 Kgs. vi. 1.

Zī′hȧ (*dried*). (1) His children returned from captivity, Ez. ii. 43; Neh. vii. 46. (2) A ruler of the Nethinims in Ophel, Neh. xi. 21.

Zĭk′lăg (*flowing, winding*). A city in southern Judah, Josh. xv. 31, afterwards assigned to Simeon, Josh. xix. 5. It became of great historic importance as the rendezvous of David when outlawed by Saul, and was then, or had just been, in the hands of the Philistines, 1 Sam. xxx. 1, 14, 26; 2 Sam. i. 1; iv. 10; 1 Chr. iv. 30; xii. 1-20.

Zĭl'lah (*shadow*). One of the wives of Lamech, and mother of Tubal-cain, Gen. iv. 19, 22, 23.

Zĭl'pah (*dropping*). A Syrian woman who became Jacob's concubine and the mother of Gad and Asher, Gen. xxix. 24; xxx. 9-13; xxxv. 26; xxxvii. 2; xlvi. 18.

Zĭl'thāi (*shadow*). (1) A Benjamite of the sons of Shimhi, 1 Chr. viii. 20. (2) A Manassite captain who deserted to David at Ziklag, 1 Chr. xii. 20.

Zĭm'mah (*wickedness*). (1) A Gershonite Levite, son of Jahath, 1 Chr. vi. 20. (2) Another Gershonite Levite, 1 Chr. vi. 42. (3) A Levite and father of Joah, 2 Chr. xxix. 12.

Zĭm'răn (*sung*). A son of Abraham by Keturah, Gen. xxv. 2; 1 Chr. i. 32.

Zĭm'rī (*sung*). (1) Son of Salu, a prince of Simeon slain by Phinehas, Num. xxv. 6-15. (2) Captain of half the chariots under Elah king of Israel. He smote his master in Tirsah, and reigned in his stead for a period of seven days, B. C. 929, 1 Kgs. xvi. 8-18. (3) A son of Zerah, of Judah, 1 Chr. ii. 6. Zabdi in Josh. vii. 1, 17, 18. (4) Son of Jehoadah and a descendant of Saul, 1 Chr. viii. 36; ix. 42. (5) An obscure name mentioned in Jer. xxv. 25.

Zĭn (*shrub*). That part of the Arabian wilderness or desert lying south of Palestine, adjacent to Judah, and bounded on the east by the Dead Sea and valley of Arabah; Num. xiii. 21, 26; xx. 1; xxvii. 14; xxxiii. 36; xxxiv. 3; Josh. xv. 1-3.

Zī'nȧ (*fruitful*). The second son of Shimei the Gershonite, 1 Chr. xxiii. 10. Zizah in vs. 11.

Zī'ŏn (*mount, sunny*). Zion or Sion in its literal and restricted sense was the celebrated mount in Jerusalem, the highest and southernmost or southwesternmost of the city. It was the original hill of the Jebusites, Josh. xv. 63. After David became king, he captured it, "the stronghold of Zion," from the Jebusites, dwelt in the fort there, and greatly enlarged and strengthened its fortifications, calling it "the city of David," 2 Sam. v. 6-9; 1 Chr. xi. 5-8. Despite David's prestige the name of Zion still clung to it, 1 Kgs. viii. 1; 2 Kgs. xix. 21, 31; 2 Chr. v. 2. The O. T. poets and prophets exalted the word Zion by frequent use and gave it a sacred turn, so that in time it came to type a sacred capital, Ps. ii. 6; holy place, Ps. lxxxvii. 2; cxlix. 2; Isa. xxx. 19; God's chosen people, Ps. li. 18; lxxxvii. 5; the Christian church, Heb. xii. 22; the heavenly city, Rev. xiv. 1.

Zī'or (*little*). A town in the mountains of Judah, Josh. xv. 54.

Zĭph (*that flows*). (1) An unidentified place in South Judah, Josh. xv. 24. (2) A town in the mountains of Judah, Josh. xv. 55. It was in the wilderness, or wastes, of Ziph that David hid himself when pursued by Saul, 1 Sam. xxiii. 14, 15, 24; xxvi. 2. (3) Son of Jehaleleel, of Judah, 1 Chr. iv. 16.

Zī'phah. A brother of the above, 1 Chr. iv. 16.

Zĭph'imș. Dwellers in Ziph, Ps. liv. title.

Zĭph'ītes. Dwellers in Ziph, 1 Sam. xxiii. 19.

Zĭph'ī-on, Gen. xlvi. 16. [ZEPHON.]

Zĭph'rŏn (*perfume*). A northern boundary of the promised land, Num. xxxiv. 9.

Zĭp'por (*little bird*). Father of Balak, king of Moab, Num. xxii. 2, 4, 10, 16; xxiii. 18.

Zĭp-pō'rah. A daughter of Reuel or Jethro, whom Moses married, Ex. ii. 16-22; iv. 25; xviii. 2-4.

Zĭth'rī (*protected*). A Kohathite Levite, son of Uzziel, Ex. vi. 22.

Zĭz (*cliff*). The cliff or pass of Ziz was that by which the Moabites and Ammonites came up from the shores of the Dead Sea to give battle to King Jehoshaphat's forces, 2 Chr. xx. 16.

Zī'zȧ (*plenty*). (1) A son of Shiphi and a prince of Simeon in the reign of Hezekiah, 1 Chr. iv. 37. (2) A son of King Rehoboam, 2 Chr. xi. 20.

Zī'zah (*plenty*), 1 Chr. xxiii. 11. [ZINA.]

Zō'an (*departure*). An ancient city of Lower Egypt, the Tanis of the Greeks and the San of modern times. It occupied a highly strategic position on the east side of the Tanitic branch of the Nile, and was built seven years before the very ancient city of Hebron, Num. xiii. 22. Isaiah mentions the "princes of Zoan," Isa. xix. 11-13; xxx. 4, and Ezekiel foretells its fate by fire, Ezek. xxx. 14.

Zō'ar (*little*). One of the most ancient cities of Canaan, mentioned as in the "plain of Jordan" and in connection with Sodom and Gomorrah, Gen. xiii. 10. It was originally called Bela, Gen. xiv. 2, 8. It was spared from the fiery destruction which came upon Sodom and the other cities of the plain, Gen. xix. 20-23. Isaiah and Jeremiah speak of Zoar as in the land of Moab, Isa. xv. 5; Jer. xlviii. 34.

Zō'bȧ, Zō'bah (*encampment*). That portion of Syria which formed a separate empire in the time of Saul, David, and Solomon. It lay to the northeast of Palestine and probably extended to the Euphrates. Though ruled by petty kings at first, it became united and strong and engaged in frequent wars with Israel, 1 Sam. xiv. 47; 2 Sam. viii. 3-8; x. 6-19; 1 Chr. xviii. 3-8; xix. 6. Hamath became the capital of Zobah, and it was captured by Solomon, 2 Chr. viii. 3.

Zō-bē'bah (*slothful*). A Judahite, 1 Chr. iv. 8.

Zō'har (*white*). (1) Father of Ephron, from whom Abraham bought the field of Machpelah, Gen. xxiii. 8; xxv. 9. (2) A son of Simeon, Gen. xlvi. 10; Ex. vi. 15. Zerah in 1 Chr. iv. 24.

Zō'hę-lĕth (*serpent*). A stone or rock by Enrogel, where Adonijah slew "sheep, oxen, and fat cattle," 1 Kgs. i. 9.

Zō'heth. A Judahite, 1 Chr. iv. 20.

Zō'phah (*viol*). An Asherite, 1 Chr. vii. 35, 36.

Zō'phāi (*honeycomb*). A Kohathite Levite, 1 Chr. vi. 26. Written Zuph in vs. 35.

Zō'phar (*little bird*). A Naamathite, and one of the three friends of Job, Job ii. 11.

Zō'phim (*watchmen*). The field on the top of Pisgah to which Balak conducted Balaam for sacrifices, Num. xxiii. 14.

Zō'rah (*hornet*). A town in the lowlands of Judah, afterwards assigned to Dan, Josh. xix. 41. Written Zoreah in Josh. xv. 33, and Zareah in Neh. xi. 29. Residence of Manoah and burial place of his son Samson, Judg. xiii. 2, 24, 25; xvi. 31.

Zō'rath-ītes. Inhabitants of Zorah; but the designation seems to be limited to the family of Judah descended from Shobal, 1 Chr. iv. 2.

Zō'rę-ah, Josh. xv. 33. [ZORAH.]

Zō'rītes. Descendants of Salma of Judah, and probably dwellers in Zorah, 1 Chr. ii. 54.

Zō-rŏb'a-bĕl. Greek form of Zerubbabel, which *see*, Matt. i. 12, 13; Luke iii. 27.

Zū'ar (*little*). Father of Nethaneel, chief of Issachar, Num. i. 8; ii. 5; vii. 18, 23; x. 15.

Zŭph (*honeycomb*). (1) The land reached by Saul while in search of his father's asses, 1 Sam. ix. 5. It was there he met Samuel the prophet, 1 Sam. ix. 6-15. (2) A Kohathite Levite, and ancestor of Elkanah and Samuel, 1 Sam. i. 1; 1 Chr. vi. 35. Called Zophai in 1 Chr. vi. 26.

Zûr (*rock*). (1) A Midianite king slain by the Israelites, Num. xxv. 15; xxxi. 8. (2) Son of Jehiel, founder of Gibeon, 1 Chr. viii. 30; ix. 36.

Zū'rī-el. (*God my rock*). Son of Abihail, and a chief of the Merarite Levites, Num. iii. 35.

Zū''rī-shăd'da-ī (*the Almighty my rock*). Father of Shelumiel, chief of the tribe of Simeon at the exodus, Num. i. 6; ii. 12; vii. 36; x. 19.

Zū'zimș. An Ammonite name for one of the races of giants, Gen. xiv. 5.

A NEW PRACTICAL, COMPARATIVE CONCORDANCE

TO THE

OLD AND NEW TESTAMENTS

Arranged in a simplified form for easy reference. It embraces the salient and ready-working features of the larger Concordances. In its Comparative feature it notes the word-changes made in the Revised Version, wherever such are of moment. Words omitted in the Revised Version are indicated by a —— (dash). The Subject Words are set in **BLACK FACE CAPITALS**, and those derived from them are shown in *italic* type. Plural Nouns are referred to under their singulars. Past tenses of Verbs and their Participles, as a rule, follow their present tenses.

ABASE, make low, &c.
Job 40. 11. every one proud *a.*
Isa. 31. 4. lion will not *a.* himself
Ezek. 21. 26. exalt him that is low and *a.* him that is high
Dan. 4. 37. those that walk in pride he is able to *a.*
Matt. 23. 12. whosoever shall exalt himself shall be *abased*
Phil. 4. 12. how to be *a.* and how to
2 Cor. 11. 7. offence in *abasing* myself
R. V. Matt. 23. 12; Luke 14. 11; 18. 14. humbled
ABATED, waters were, Gen. 8. 3.
Gen. 8. 11. so Noah knew that the waters were *a.*
Lev. 27. 18. it shall be *a.* from thy
Deut. 34. 7. his eye was not dim, nor his natural force *a.*
Judg. 8. 3. then their anger was *a.*
R. V. Gen. 8. 3. decreased
ABBA, *father*, Mark 14. 36. Rom. 8. 15. Gal. 4. 6.
ABHOR, greatly hate and loathe
Lev. 26. 11. my soul shall not *a.* you
15. if your soul *a.* my judgments
30. my soul shall *a.* you
Deut. 7. 26. utterly *a.* it
1 Sam. 27. 12. made his people to *a.* him
Job 30. 10. they *a.* me, they flee
42. 6. I *a.* myself and repent
Ps. 5. 6. Lord will *a.* the bloody
119. 163. I hate and *a.* lying
Jer. 14. 21. do not *a.* us for thy name's sake
Amos 5. 10. they *a.* him that speak.
6. 8. I *a.* the excellency of Jacob
Mic. 3. 9. ye that *a.* judgment
Rom. 12. 9. *a.* that which is evil
Ex. 5. 21. made our savour *abhorred*
Lev. 26. 43. their soul *a.* my statutes
Deut. 32. 19. when the Lord saw it he *a.*
1 Sam. 2. 17. men *a.* the offering of
Job 19. 19. all my inward friends *a.*
Ps. 22. 24. nor *a.* affliction of afflict.
78. 59. wroth and greatly *a.* Israel
89. 38. hath cast off and *a.* anoint.
106. 40. he *a.* his own inheritance
Prov. 22. 14. *a.* of the Lord shall fall
Lam. 2. 7. Lord hath *a.* his sanctuary
Ezek. 16. 25. made thy beauty to be *a.*
Rom. 2. 22. thou that *abhorrest* idols
Zech. 11. 8. their soul *abhorreth* me
Job 33. 20. his life *a.* bread
Ps. 10. 3. covetous whom the Lord *a.*
107. 18. their soul *a.* all manner of
Isa. 49. 7. him whom the nation *a.*
66. 24. be an *abhorring* to all flesh
R. V. Ps. 89. 38. rejected; Ezek. 16. 25. an abomination
ABIDE, continue, bear
Ex. 16. 29. *a.* ye every man in his
Num. 35. 25. *a.* in it unto the death
2 Sam. 11. 11. ark and Israel *a.* in tents
Ps. 15. 1. who shall *a.* in thy tabernacle
7. he shall *a.* before God for ever
Prov. 7. 11. her feet *a.* not in her house
Hos. 3. 3. shall *a.* for me many days
4. Israel shall *a.* without a king
Joel 2. 11. day of the Lord is great and very terrible; who can *a.* it
Mal. 3. 2. who may *a.* the day of his coming
Matt. 10. 11. there *a.* till ye go thence
Luke 19. 5. to-day I must *a.* at thy
John 12. 46. should not *a.* in dark.
15. 4. *a.* in me and I in you, 7.
Acts 20. 23. afflictions *a.* me.
1 Cor. 3. 14. if any man's work *a.*
7. 8. it is good for them if they *a.* even as I
20. let every man *a.* in the same calling wherein he was called
24. is called therein *a.* with God
Phil. 1. 24. to *a.* in the flesh is needful
25. know that I shall *a.* with you
1 John 2. 24. let that therefore *a.* in you
27, 28. ye shall *a.* in him
Ps. 49. 12. man in honor *abideth* not
Eccl. 1. 4. the earth *a.* for ever
John 3. 36. wrath of God *a.* on him
8. 35. servant *a.* not but the Son *a.* ever
12. 24. except it die it *a.* alone
1 Cor. 13. 13. now *a.* faith, hope
2 Tim. 2. 13. yet he *a.* faithful
1 Pet. 1. 23. word of God *a.* for ever
1 John 3. 6. whoso *a.* in him sinneth not
24. hereby we know he *a.* in us
John 5. 38. not his word *abiding* in you
1 John 3. 15. no murderer hath eternal life *a.*
John 14. 23. make our *abode* with him
R. V. Ps. 15. 1. sojourn; Hos. 11. 6. fall upon; Rom. 11. 23. continue
ABILITY, in strength, wealth, &c.
Lev. 27. 8. Ezra 2. 69. Neh. 5. 8. Dan. 1. 4.
Matt. 25. 15. to every man according to his *a.*, Acts 11. 29.
1 Pet. 4. 11. as of the *a.* God giveth
R. V. 1 Pet. 4. 11. strength
ABJECTS, *base men*, Ps. 35. 15.
ABLE men, such as fear God, Ex. 18. 21.
Lev. 14. 22. such as he is *a.* to get
Deut. 16. 17. every man give as he is *a.*
2 Chron. 20. 6. none is *a.* to withstand
Prov. 27. 4. who is *a.* to stand
Ezek. 46. 11. as he is *a.* to give
Dan. 3. 17. our God is *a.* to deliver
4. 37. walk in pride he is *a.* to abase
Matt. 3. 9. God is *a.* of these stones to raise up children, Luke 3. 8.
9. 28. believe ye that I am *a.* to
20. 22. are ye *a.* to drink of cup
Mark 4. 33. as they were *a.* to hear
John 10. 29. no man *a.* to pluck
Rom. 4. 21. promised he was *a.* to perform
14. 4. God is *a.* to make him stand
1 Cor. 3. 2. neither yet now are ye *a*
10. 13. tempted above that ye are *a.*
2 Cor. 9. 8. *a.* to make all grace abound
Eph. 3. 20. *a.* to do exceeding
2 Tim. 1. 12. *a.* to keep that committed
Heb. 2. 18. *a.* to succor the tempt.
5. 7. *a.* to save him from death
7. 25. *a.* to save to the uttermost
James 1. 21. *a.* to save your souls
4. 12. *a.* to save and to destroy
Jude 24. *a.* to keep you from fall.
R. V. Lev. 25. 26. waxen rich; Josh. 23. 9 ——; Acts 25. 5. are of power; 2 Cor. 3. 6. sufficient as; Eph. 3. 18. strong.
ABOLISHED, made to cease
Isa. 2. 18. idols he shall utterly *abolish*
Ezek. 6. 6. your works may be *a.*
2 Cor. 3. 13. to the end of that *a.*
2 Tim. 1. 10. Jesus Christ who hath *a.* death
R. V. Isa. 2. 18. pass away; 2 Cor. 3. 13. passing away.

ABOMINABLE, very hateful. Lev. 7. 21. & 11. 43. & 18. 30. Isa. 14. 19. & 65. 4. Jer. 16. 18.
1 Chron. 21. 6. king's word was *a.* to Joab
Ps. 14. 1. have done *a.* works, 53. 1.
Jer. 44. 4. do not this *a.* thing
Ezek.16 52. has committed more|*a.*
Tit. 1. 16. in works deny him being *a.*
1 Pet. 4. 3. walked in *a.* idolatries
Rev. 21. 8. unbelieving and *a.* shall

ABOMINATION, what is very filthy, hateful, and loathsome as sin, Isa. 66. 3. idols, Ex. 8. 26.
Prov. 6. 16. seven things are an *a.*
11. 1. a false balance is *a.* to the Lord. [Lord
12. 22. lying lips are *a.* to the
15. 8. the sacrifice of the wicked is an *a.* [the Lord, 3. 32.
16. 5. proud in heart is an *a.* to
20. 23. divers weights are an *a* to the Lord.
Isa. 1. 13. incense is an *a.* to me.
Dan. 11. 31. *a.* that maketh desolate. [of desolation
12. 11. Matt. 24. 15. Mark 13. 14. *a.*
Luke 16. 15. is *a.* in the sight of God [*a.*
Rev. 21. 27, whatsoever worketh
2 Kings 21. 2. *abominations* of the
Ezra 9. 14. join with the people of these *a.*
Prov. 26. 25. seven *a.* in his heart
Jer.7.10.delivered to do all these *a.*
Ezek. 16. 2. cause Jerusalem to know her *a.* 20. 4. & 23. 36.
18. 13. hath done all these *a.* shall
Dan. 9. 27. for the overspreading of *a.*
Rev. 17.5. mother of harlots and *a.*

ABOUND, become very full, large, Prov. 8. 24. Rom. 3. 7.
Prov. 28. 20. the faithful shall *a.*
Matt. 24. 12. iniquity shall *a*
Rom. 5. 20. offence might *a.* but where sin *a.* grace did much more *a.*
2 Cor. 9. 8. able to make all gr. *a.*
Phil. 1. 9. that love may *a.* more
4. 12. I know how *a.* [count
17. fruit that may *a.* to your ac-
18. I have all and *a.*
1 Thes. 3. 12. the Lord make you *a.*
2 Pet. 1. 8. if these things be in you and *a.* [us
Eph. 1. 8. hath *abounded* toward
1 Cor. 15. 58, always *abounding*
Col. 2. 7. *a.* with thanksgiving
R. V. Matt. 24. 12. multiplied.

ABOVE, higher, heaven, Ex.20.4.
John 3. 31. cometh from *a.* is *a.* all
19. 11. power given thee from *a.*
Gal. 4. 26. Jerusalem, which is *a.* is
Eph. 4. 6. one God who is *a.* all
Col. 3. 1. seek things which are *a.*
James 1. 17. every perfect gift is from *a.*

ABSENT one from another, Gen. 31. 49. 2 Cor. 10. 1. [ent
1 Cor. 5. 3. as *a.* in body but pres-
2 Cor. 5. 6. in body we are *a.* from the Lord
10. 1. being *a.* am bold toward you
Col. 2. 5. though I be *a.* in the flesh

ABSTAIN from idols, Acts 15. 20.
1 Thess. 4. 3. *a.* from fornication.
5.22. *a.* from all appearance of evil
1 Pet. 2. 11. *a.* from fleshly lusts
Abstinence from meat, Acts 27. 21.

ABUNDANCE, great fulness. and plenty. Job 22. 11. & 38. 24.
Deut. 33.19. 1 Chron. 22. 3, 4, 14, 15.
Deut. 28. 47. for the *a.* of all things
Eccl. 5. 10. he that loveth *a.* with
12. *a.* of the rich will not suffer him to sleep
Isa. 66. 11. delighted with *a.* of her glory
Matt. 12. 34, out of *a.* of the heart the mouth speaketh, Luke 6. 45.
13. 12. shall have more *a.* 25. 29.
Mark 12. 44. they did cast in of their *a.* [*a.*
Luke 12. 15. life consisteth not in
2 Cor. 8.2. *a.* of their joy abounded
12. 7. through *a.* of revelations
R. V. 2 Cor. 8. 20 bounty

ABUNDANT in goodness and truth, Ex. 34. 6. 2 Cor. 4. 15. & 9. 12.
2 Cor. 11. 23, in labors more *a.*
1 Tim. 1. 14. grace of Lord exceeding *a.*
Job 12.6. God bringeth *abundantly*
Ps. 36. 8. shall be *a.* satisfied with fatness
S. of S. 5.1. yea drink *a.* O beloved
Isa. 55. 7. he will *a.* pardon [*a.*
John 10. 10. might have life more
Eph. 3. 20. able to do exceeding *a.*
Tit. 3. 6. shed on us *a.* thro. Jesus
2 Pet. 1. 11. entrance shall be ministered unto you more *a.*
R. V. 2 Cor. 4. 15. multiplied; 1 Pet. 1. 3. great

ABUSE not my power, 1 Cor. 9. 18. 1 Cor. 7. 31. use the world as not *abusing* it [full
R.V.1 Cor. 9.18. not to us to the

ACCEPT, receive kindly in favor, Gen. 32. 20. Acts 24. 3.
Lev. 26. 41. *a.* punishment of iniquity, 43.
Deut. 33. 11. *a.* work of his hands
2 Sam. 24. 23. Lord thy God *a.* thee
Job 13. 8. will ye *a.* his person, 10.
32. 21. let me not *a.* any man's person
42. 8. servant Job, him will I *a.*
Ps. 119. 108. *a.* free-will-off. of my mouth
Ezek. 43. 27. I will *a.* you
Mal. 1. 13. should I *a.* this of your hand
Gen. 4.7.shalt thou not be *accepted*
Lev. 1. 4, shall be *a.* for atonement
Luke 4. 24. no prophet *a.* in his own country [is *a.*
Acts 10. 35. worketh righteousness
2 Cor. 5. 9. we may be *a.* of him
Eph. 1.6.made us *a.* in the beloved
Luke 20. 21. neither *acceptest* the person
Job 34. 19. him that *accepteth* not the persons of princes
Eccl. 9. 7. God now *a.* thy works
Hos. 8. 13. Lord *a.* them not
Gal. 2. 6. God *a.* no man's person
Heb. 11. 35. not *accepting* deliverance [58. 5.
Acceptable day of the Lord, Isa.
Ps. 19. 14. let the meditation of my heart be *a.*
Eccl. 12. 10. sought out *a.* words
Dan. 4. 27. let my counsel be *a.*
Rom. 12. 1. sacrifice holy *a.* to God
2. know good and *a.* will of God
Eph. 5. 10. proving what is *a.* unto the Lord [ing.
Phil. 4. 18. sacrifice *a.* well-pleas-
Heb. 12. 28. serve God *acceptably* with fear
1 Tim. 1. 15. worthy of all *acceptation* [respect
R. V. Job 13. 10; 32. 21; Ps. 82. 2.

ACCESS, admission through Christ, Rom. 5. 2. Eph. 2. 18. and 3. 12.

ACCOMPLISH, perform fully, finish, Lev. 22. 21. Job 14. 6.
Ps. 64. 6. *a.* a diligent search
Isa. 55. 11. it shall *a.* that I please
Ezek. 6. 12. thus will I *a.* my fury
Dan. 9. 2. would *a.* seventy years
Luke 9. 31. decease he should *a.* at Jerusalem
2 Chron. 36. 22. word might be *accomplished*
Prov. 13. 19. desire *a.* is sweet to soul
Isa. 40. 2. her warfare is *a.* her sin
Luke 12. 50. how am I straitened till it be *a.*
John 19. 28. all things were now *a.*
Heb. 9. 6. *accomplishing* service of God.
R. V. Jer. 25. 34. fully come; 44. 25. establish; Luke 1. 23; 2. 6, 21, 22. fulfilled

ACCORD, hearty agreement, Acts 1. 14. & 2. 1, 46. & 4. 24. & 15. 25.
Phil. 2. 2. of one *a.* of one mind
R. V. Lev. 25. 5. itself; Acts 2. 1. together

ACCOUNT, reckoning, esteem
Job 33. 13. giv. not *a.* of his matters
Ps. 144. 3. that thou mak. *a* of him
Eccl. 7. 27. one by one to find out the *a.*
Matt. 12. 36. give *a.* in the day of judgment
Luke 16. 2. give *a.* of thy stewardship
Rom. 14. 12. give *a.* of him. to God
Heb. 13. 17. as they that must give *a.*
1 Pet. 4. 5. shall give *a.* to him that is ready to judge the quick and
Ps. 22. 30. *accounted* to the Lord for a generation
Isa. 2. 22. wherein is he to be *a.* of
Luke 20. 35. shall be *a.* worthy to obtain that world
21. 36. *a.* worthy to escape
22. 24. which should be *a.* greatest
Gal. 3. 6. *a.* to him for righteousness
Heb. 11. 19. *a.* God able to raise
R. V. 2 Chr. 26. 11; Matt. 18. 23. reckoning

ACCURSED, devoted to ruin
Deut. 21. 23. hanged is *a.* of God
Josh. 6. 18. keep yourselves from the *a.* thing
Isa. 65. 20. sinner a hundred years old shall be *a.*
Rom. 9. 3. wish myself *a.* from Christ
1 Cor. 12. 3. no man by Spirit calls Jesus *a.*
Gal. 1. 8, 9. preach other gospel be *a.*
R. V. 1 Chr. 2. 7. devoted thing; Rom. 9. 3; 1 Cor. 12. 3; Gal. 1. 8. anathema.

ACCUSATION, Ezra 4. 6. Matt. 27. 37. Luke 6. 7. & 19. 8. John 18. 29. Acts 25. 18.
1 Tim. 5. 19. against an elder receive not an *a.*
2 Pet. 2. 11. bring not railing *a.*, Jude 9.
R. V. 2 Pet. 2. 11; Jude 9. judgment

ACCUSE, charge with crimes
Prov. 30. 10. *a.* not servant to master
Luke 3. 14. neither *a.* any falsely
John 5. 45. that I will *a.* you to the Father
1 Pet. 3. 16. that falsely *a.* your good conversation in Christ
Tit. 1. 6. not *accused* of riot
Rev. 12. 10. *a.* them before our God
Accuser of brethren is cast down
Acts 25. 16. have *a.* face to face
2 Tim. 3. 3. false *a.*, Tit. 2. 3.
John 5.45. there is one that *accuseth*
Rom. 2. 15. thoughts *accusing* or excusing
R. V. Prov. 30. 10. slander

ACCUSTOMED, Jer. 13. 23.

ACKNOWLEDGE, own, confess
Deut. 33. 9. neither did he *a.* his brethren
Ps. 51. 3. I *a.* my transgression
Prov. 3. 6. in all thy ways *a.* him
Isa. 33. 13. ye that are near *a.* my might
Jer. 3. 13. only *a.* thine iniquity

Hos. 5. 15. until they *a.* their offence
1 Cor. 16. 18. *a.* them that are such
Ps. 32. 5. I *a.* my sin
1 John 2. 23. that *acknowledgeth* the Son
2 Tim. 2. 25. *acknowledging* the truth
Tit. 1. 1. *a.* of the truth which is after godliness
Col. 2. 2. to the *acknowledgment* of the mystery of God
R. V. 1 John 2. 23. confesseth

ACQUAINT thyself with him, Job 22. 21.
Ps. 139. 3. *acquainted* with my ways
Isa. 53. 3. *a.* with grief
Acquaintance, familiar friends or companions, Job 19. 13. & 42. 11. Ps. 31. 11. & 55. 13. & 88. 8, 18.
R. V. Acts 24. 23. friends

ACQUIT, hold innocent, Job 10. 14.
Nah. 1. 3. will not at all *a.* the wicked

ACTS of the Lord, Deut. 11. 3, 7.
Judg. 5. 11. rehearse righteous *a.*
1 Sam. 12. 7. reason of all righteous *a.* of the Lord
Ps. 106. 2. utter mighty *a.* of Lord
145. 6. speak of thy mighty *a.*, 4.
150. 2. praise him for his mighty *a.*
Isa. 28. 21. his *a.* his strange *a.*
John 8. 4. taken in adultery in very *a.*

ACTIONS weighed, 1 Sam. 2. 3.

ACTIVITY, men of, Gen. 47. 6.

ADAMANT, Ezek. 3. 9. Zech. 7. 12.

ADD fifth part, Lev. 5. 16. & 6. 5. & 27. 13, 15, 19, 27, 31.
Deut. 4. 2. shall not *a.* unto the word
1 Kings 12. 11. I will *a.* to your yoke
Ps. 69. 27. *a.* iniquity to their iniquity
Isa. 30. 1. that they may *a.* sin to sin
Matt. 6. 27. can *a.* one cubit, Luke 12. 25.
Phil. 1. 16. to *a.* affliction to my
2 Pet. 1. 5. *a.* to your faith, virtue
Rev. 22. 18. if any man *a.* unto these things, God shall *a.* unto him
Deut. 5. 22. he *added* no more
Jer. 36. 32. were *a.* many like words
Matt. 6. 33. all these things shall be *a.* unto you, Luke 12. 31.
Acts 2. 41. same day were *a.* about three thousand souls
47. Lord *a.* to the church such
5. 14. believers were the more *a.* to
11. 24. much people was *a.* to the Lord
Prov. 10. 22. *addeth* no sorrow with

ADDER, poisonous serpent, Gen. 49. 17. Ps. 58. 4. & 91. 13. & 140. 3. Prov. 23. 32. Isa. 14. 29.

ADDICTED, gave up, 1 Cor. 16. 15.
R. V. 1 Cor. 16. 15. set.

ADJURE, to charge under pain of God's curse, 1 Kings 22. 16. 2 Chron. 18. 15. Matt. 26. 63. Mark 5. 7. Acts 19. 13. Josh. 6. 26. 1 Sam. 14. 24.

ADMINISTRATION, 1 Cor. 12. 5. 2 Cor. 9. 12. & 8. 19, 20. *administered*

ADMIRATION, high esteem, Jude 16. or wonder and amazement, Rev. 17. 6.
2 Thes. 1. 10. *admired* in them that believe
R. V. Rev. 17. 6. wonder; Jude 16. respect of persons.

ADMONISH, warn, reprove
Rom. 15. 14. able to *a.* one another
2 Thes. 3. 15. *a.* him as a brother
Eccl. 12. 12. by these be *admonished*
Jer. 42. 19. know that I have *a.* you
Acts 27. 9. Paul *a.* them
Heb. 8. 5. as Moses was *a.* of God
Col. 3. 16. *admonishing* one another in psalms and hymns
1 Cor. 10. 11. are written for our *admonition*
Tit. 3. 10. after first and second *a.* reject
R. V. Jer. 42. 19. testified unto; Heb. 8. 5. warned.

ADOPTION, putting among God's children, Jer. 3. 19. 2 Cor. 6. 18.
Rom. 8. 15. received spirit of *a.*
23. *a.* redemption of our body
Gal. 4. 5. might receive *a.* of sons
Eph. 1. 5. unto *a.* of children

ADORN, deck out, Isa. 61. 10. Jer. 31. 4.
Tit. 2. 10. *a.* the doctrine of God
Jer. 31. 4. *adorned* with thy tabrets
Luke 21. 5. *a.* with goodly stones
1 Pet. 3. 5. holy women *a.* themselves
Rev. 21. 2. as a bride *a.* for her
Isa. 61. 10. as a bride *adorneth* herself
1 Pet. 3. 3. whose *adorning* let it not
1 Tim. 2. 9. women *a.* themselves in modest apparel

ADULTERER, put to death, Lev. 20. 10.
Job 24. 15. eye of *a.* waits for twilight
Isa. 57. 3. seed of *a.* and whore
Jer. 23. 10. land is full of *adulterers*
9. 2. Hos. 7. 4. be all *a.*
Mal. 3. 5. I will be a swift witness against *a.*
1 Cor. 6. 9. neither *a.* shall inherit the kingdom of God
Heb. 13. 4. whoremongers and *a.* God will judge
James 4. 4. ye *a.* and *adulteresses*
Prov. 6. 26. *adulteress* will hunt for
32. committeth *adultery* lacks
Matt. 5. 28. committeth *a.* in his heart
2 Pet. 2. 14. having eyes full of *a.*
Matt. 15. 19. out of the heart proceed *adulteries*, fornications, Mark 7. 21.
Prov. 30. 20. way of *adulterous* woman
Matt. 12. 39. *a.* generation seeketh a sign, 16. 4. Mark 8. 38.

ADVANTAGE hath Jew, Rom. 3. 1.
2 Cor. 2. 11. lest Satan get an *a.*
Luke 9. 25. what is a man *advantaged*
R. V. Luke 9. 25. profited

ADVERSARY, opposer, enemy
Ex. 23. 22. I will be *a.* to thy *a.*
1 Kings 5. 4. is neither *a.* nor evil
Job 31. 35. my *a.* had written a book
Matt. 5. 25. agree with thine *a.*
Luke 18. 3. avenge me of mine *a.*
1 Pet. 5. 8. your *a.* the devil as a
1 Sam. 2. 10. *adversaries* of the Lord
Lam. 1. 5. her *a.* are the chief
Luke 21. 15. all your *a.* not be able
1 Cor. 16. 9. and there are many *a.*
Heb. 10. 27. shall devour the *a.*
R. V. enemy, in most O. T. texts

ADVERSITY, affliction, misery
2 Sam. 4. 9. redeem my soul from all *a.*
Ps. 10. 6. I shall never be in *a.*
35. 15. in my *a.* they rejoiced
94. 13. give rest from days of *a.*
Prov. 17. 17. brother is born for *a.*
Eccl. 7. 14. in the day of *a.* consider
Isa. 30. 20. give you the bread of *a.*
1 Sam. 10. 19. saved you out of all *a.*

ADVICE, Judg. 19. 30. 1 Sam. 25. 33. 2 Sam. 19. 43. Prov. 20. 18.

ADVOCATE with Father, 1 John 2. 1.

AFAR off, Gen. 22. 4. & 37. 18. Ps. 65. 5.
138. 6. proud he knoweth *a.*
Ps. 139. 2. understandest my thoughts *a.* off
Acts 2. 39. promise is to all *a.* and
Eph. 2. 17. preached peace to you *a.*
2 Pet. 1. 9. blind and cannot see *a.*

AFFAIRS, Ps. 112. 5. 2 Tim. 2. 4.

AFFECT, incline, move
Gal. 4. 17. they zealously *a.* you
18. good to be zealously *affected*
Lam. 3. 51. mine eye *affecteth* my heart
Rom. 1. 31. natural *affection*
Col. 3. 5. mortify inordinate *a.*
Rom. 1. 26. them up to vile *affections*
Gal. 5. 24. crucify flesh with *a.*
Rom. 12. 10. be kindly *affectioned*
1 Thes. 2. 8. *affectionately* desirous
R. V. Col. 3. 2. mind; Rom. 1. 26; Gal. 5. 24. passions

AFFINITY, relation by marriage, 1 Kings 3. 1. 2 Chron. 18. 1. Ezra 9. 14.

AFFLICT, grieve, trouble, Gen. 15. 13. Ex. 1. 11. & 22. 22.
Ezra 8. 21. that we might *a.* ourselves
Lev. 16. 29, 31. shall *a.* your souls
23. 27, 32. Num. 29. 7. & 30. 13.
Isa. 58. 5. day for a man to *a.* his soul
Lam. 3. 33. doth not *a.* willingly
2 Sam. 22. 28. *afflicted* people thou wilt save, Ps. 18. 27.
Job 6. 14. to *a.* pity should be
34. 28. heareth the cry of the *a.*
Ps. 18. 27. wilt save the *a.* people
71. it is good that I have been *a.*
107. I am *a.* very much
140. 12. wilt maintain cause of *a.*
Prov. 15. 15. all days of *a.* are evil
Isa. 49. 13. he will have mercy on *a.*
53. 4. smitten of God and *a.*
Mic. 4. 6. gather her I have *a.*
James 5. 13. is any *a.* let him pray
Ex. 3. 7. seen *affliction* of people
2 Kings 14. 26. Lord saw *a.* of
Job 5. 6. *a.* cometh not forth of
Ps. 25. 18. look on my *a.* and pain
107. 10. bound in *a.* and iron
39. brought low through *a.*
119. 50. this is my comfort in *a.*
Isa. 48. 10. chosen thee in the furnace of *a.*
63. 9. in all their *a.* he was
Hos. 5. 15. in their *a.* they will seek
Obad. 13. not have looked on their *a.*
Zech. 1. 15. helped forward the *a.*
2 Cor. 4. 17. our light *a.* which is
Phil. 4. 14. communicate with my *a.*
1 Thes. 1. 6. received word in much *a.*
James 1. 27. to visit fatherless in their *a.*
Ps. 34. 19. many are the *afflictions* of the righteous
132. 1. remember David and all his *a.*
Acts 7. 10. delivered him out of all *a.*
Col. 1. 24. which is behind of *a.* of Christ
1 Thes. 3. 3. no man moved by these *a.*
2 Tim. 1. 8. partaker of *a.* of gospel
Heb. 10. 32. endured great fight of *a.*
1 Pet. 5. 9. the same *a.* accomplished
R. V. Ez. 8. 21. humble; Ps. 55. 19. answer; Job 6. 14. ready to faint, James 5. 13. suffering

AFRAID, Lev. 26. 6. Num. 12. 8. Job 18. 11. Ps. 56. 3. & 119. 120.
Not be *afraid*, Ps. 56. 11. & 112. 7. Isa. 12. 2. Matt. 14. 27. Mark 5. 36. Luke 12. 4. 1 Pet. 3. 6, 14. Heb. 11. 23.

AFRESH, crucify Son of God, Heb. 6. 6.

AGE is as nothing before thee, Ps. 39. 5.
Job 5. 26. come to grave in full *a.*
Heb. 5. 14. strong meat to those of full *a.*
11. 11. Sarah when she was past *a.*
Tit. 2. 2, 3. *aged* men be sober
Ages Eph. 2. 7. & 3. 5, 21.
Col. 1. 26. mystery hid from *a.*
R. V. Josh. 23. 1, 2. years; Job. 11. 17. life; Job 12. 20. elders

AGONY, Christ's, in the garden, Matt. 27. 36; Luke 22. 44, &c.

AGREE, Acts 5. 9.
Matt. 5. 25. *a.* with thine adversary
1 John 5. 8. these three *a.* in one
Amos 3. 3. walk together except *agreed*
Isa. 28. 15. with hell at *agreement*

2 Cor. 6. 16. what *a.* has temple of God
R. V. 2 Kings 18. 31; Isa. 36. 16. your peace
AIR, 1 Cor. 9. 26. & 14. 9. Eph. 2. 2. 1 Thes. 4. 17. Rev. 9. 2. & 16. 17.
R. V. In Gos. and Acts, heaven
ALARM, how sounded, Num. 10. 5.
ALIEN, stranger, Ex. 18. 3. Job 19. 15.
Ps. 69. 8. heathens, Deut. 14. 21. Isa. 61. 5. Lam. 5. 2. Heb. 11. 34.
Eph. 2. 12. *a.* from commonwealth
4. 18. *alienated* from life of God
Col. 1. 21. were sometimes *a.*
R. V. Ex. 18. 3. sojourner; Deut. 14. 21. foreigner.
ALIVE, Gen. 12. 12. Num. 22. 23.
Rom. 6. 11. *a.* to God through Jesus
1 Sam. 2. 6. killeth and maketh *a.*
15. 8. he took Agag *a.*
Luke 15. 24. son was dead and is *a.*
Rom. 6. 13. as those *a.* from the dead
7. 9. I was *a.* without the law once
1 Cor. 15. 22. in Christ shall all be made *a.*
1 Thes. 4. 15, 17. we who are *a.*
Rev. 1. 18. I am *a.* for evermore
2. 8. was dead and is *a.*
R. V. Gen. 7. 23; Lev. 10. 16; 26. 36——; Num. 21. 35. remaining
ALLEGING, Acts 17. 3.
ALLEGORY, Gal. 4. 24.
ALLOW deeds of fathers, Luke 11. 48.
Acts 24. 15. which themselves *a.*
Rom. 7. 15. that which I do I *a.* not
14. 22. in that which he *alloweth.*
1 Thes. 2. 4. as we were *allowed* of God
R. V. Luke 11. 48. consent unto; Acts 24. 15. look for; Rom. 7. 15. know; Rom. 14. 22. approveth; 1 Thes. 2. 4. approved.
ALLURE, Hos. 2. 14. 2 Pet. 2. 18.
R. V. 2 Pet. 2. 18. entice.
ALL THINGS lawful, but not expedient, 1 Cor. 6. 12.
ALMIGHTY GOD, Gen. 17. 1. & 28. 3. & 35. 11. & 43. 14. & 48. 3. Ex. 6. 3. 2 Cor. 6. 18. Rev. 4. 8. & 15. 3. & 16. 14. & 19. 15. & 21. 22.
Job 21. 15. what is the Almighty that we serve
26. shall have delight in Almighty
Ps. 91. 1. under shadow of Almi.
Rev. 1. 8. is to come, the Almighty
ALMOST all things, Heb. 9. 22.
Ex. 17. 4. *a.* ready to stone me
Ps. 73. 2. my feet were *a.* gone
Prov. 5. 14. was *a.* in all evil in cong.
Acts 26. 28. *a.* persuadest me to
R. V. Ps. 94. 17. soon; Prov. 5. 14. well nigh; Acts 26. 28. with but little
ALMS, Acts 3. 2, 3. & 24. 17.
Matt. 6. 1. do not your *a.* before men
Luke 11. 41. give *a.* of such things
12. 33. sell that ye have, give *a.*
Acts 10. 2. gave much *a.* to people
4. thine *a.* are come up for memorial
9. 36. Dorcas full of *a.* deeds
R. V. Matt. 6. 1. righteousness
ALONE, Gen. 32. 24.
Gen. 2. 18. not good for man to be *a.*
Num. 23. 9. peopled well *a.*, Deut. 33. 28.
Deut. 32. 12. Lord *a.* did lead him
Ps. 136. 4. who *a.* doth great wonders
Isa. 5. 8. that they may be placed *a.*
63. 3. I have trodden wine-press *a.*
John 8. 16. I am not *a.*, 16. 32.
17. 20. neither pray I for these *a.*
Ex. 32. 10. *let me a.* that my wrath
Hos. 4. 17. Ephraim is joined to idols, let him *a.*
Matt. 15. 14. let them *a.*
R. V. Mark 4. 34. privately

ALTAR, Deut. 7. 5. & 12. 3.
altar to Lord, Gen. 8. 20. & 12. 7. & 22. 9. & 35. 1, 3. Ex. 30. 27. & 40. 10.
Judg. 6. 25. throw down *a.* of Baal
1 Kings 13. 2. cried against *a.* O *a. a.*
Ps. 26. 6. so will I compass thine *a.*
Matt. 5. 23. if thou bring thy gift to *a.*
24. leave there thy gift before the *a.*
Acts 17. 23. found *a.* with inscription
Heb. 13. 10. we have an *a.* whereof
Rev. 6. 9. saw under the *a.* souls of
8. 3. & 9. 13. the golden *a.*
R. V. Isa. 65. 3.
ALWAY, Deut. 5. 29. Job 7. 16.
Gen. 6. 3. my Spirit not *a.* strive
Deut. 14. 23. learn to fear the Lord *a.*
1 Chron. 16. 15. be mindful *a.* of covenant.
Job 27. 10. will he *a.* call on God
32. 9. great men are not *a.* wise
Ps. 9. 18. needy not *a.* be forgotten
16. 8. I set the Lord *a.* before me
103. 9. he will not *a.* chide
Prov. 5. 19. ravished *a.* with her love
28. 14. happy is the man that feareth *a.*
Isa. 57. 16. neither will I be *a.* wroth
Matt. 26. 11. have poor *a.* with you
28. 20. I am with you *a.* to the end
John 8. 29. I do *a.* things that please
Acts 10. 2. Cornelius prayed God *a.*
2 Cor. 6. 10. yet *a.* rejoicing
Eph. 6. 18. praying *a.* with all prayer
Phil. 4. 4. rejoice in the Lord *a.*
Col. 4. 6. your speech be *a.* with
I AM that I AM, Ex. 3. 14. Rev. 1. 8.
Ambassador, Prov. 13. 17. Isa. 33. 7. 2 Cor. 5. 20. Eph. 6. 20.
R. V. Job 32. 9.
AMBITION reproved, Matt. 18. 1. 20. 25. & 23. 8. Luke 22. 24.
punishment of, Prov. 17. 19. Isa. 14. 12. Ezek. 31. 10.
of Babel, Gen. 11. 4.
of Aaron and Miriam, Num. 12. 10.
Korah, Dathan, and Abiram, Num. 16. 3.
Absalom, 2 Sam. 18. 9.
Adonijah, 1 Kings 1. 5.
Babylon, Jer. 51. 53.
James and John, Matt. 20. 21.
Man of sin, 2 Thes. 2. 4.
Diotrephes, 3 John 9.
AMBUSH, Josh. 8. 4; Judg. 20. 29; 2 Chron. 13. 13; 20. 22.
AMEN, so come Lord Jesus, Rev. 22. 20.
2 Cor. 1. 20. promises in him *a.*
Rev. 3. 14. these things saith the *a.*
R. V. *A.* is omitted in Matt. 6. 13; 28. 20. and many other places in N. T.
AMEND your ways, Jer. 7. 3, 5. & 26. 13. your doings, 35. 15.
R. V. Restitution
AMIABLE thy tabernacles, Ps. 84. 1.
AMISS, 2 Chron. 6. 37. Dan. 3. 29. Luke 23. 41. James 4. 3.
ANCHOR, Acts 27. 30. Heb. 6. 19.
ANCIENT, wisdom is with, Job 12. 12.
Dan. 7. 9. the *a.* of days did sit
Ps. 119. 100. I understand more than *a.*
ANGEL, who redeemed me, Gen. 48. 16.
24. 7. send his *a.* before me
Ex. 23. 23. my *a.* shall go before thee
Angel of the Lord, Ps. 34. 7. Zech. 12. 8. Acts 5. 19. & 12. 7, 23.

Isa. 63. 9. *a.* of his presence saved.
John 5. 4. *a.* went down at a
Acts 6. 15. saw as face of an *a.*
23. 8. Sadducees say neither *a.* nor
Dan. 3. 28. sent his *a.* and delivered
6. 22. sent his *a.* and shut lions' mouths
Ps. 8. 5. a little lower than *a.*
68. 17. chariots of God thousands *a.*
78. 25. man did eat *a.* food
Matt. 4. 11. *a.* came and ministered
13. 39. reapers are the *a.*
18. 10. their *a.* always behold
36. no, not the *a.* of heaven
Mark 12. 25. are as *a.* in heaven, 13. 32.
Luke 20. 36. equal to the *a.*
Acts 7. 53. the law by disposition of *a.*
1 Cor. 6. 3. we shall judge *a.*
Col. 2. 18. beguile worshipping of *a.*
2 Thes. 1. 7. with his mighty *a.*
1 Tim. 3. 16. seen of *a.* preached unto
Heb. 2. 16. took not the nature of *a.*
12. 22. an innumerable company of *a.*
13. 2. entertained *a.* unawares
2 Pet. 2. 4. God spared not *a.* that
11. *a.* greater in power and might
Jude 6. *a.* who kept not their first
Rev. 1. 20. *a.* of seven churches
Angel of God, Gen. 28. 12. & 32. 1. Matt. 22. 30. Luke 12. 8. & 15. 10. John 1. 51.
R. V. Rev. 8. 13. eagle; Rev. 8. 7; 16. 3, 4, 8, 10, 12, 17.
ANGER of the Lord wax hot, Ex. 32. 22.
Deut. 29. 24. meaneth heat of this *a.*
Josh. 7. 26. from fierceness of *a.*
Job 9. 13. if God will not withdraw *a.*
Ps. 27. 9. put not away servant in *a.*
30. 5. his *a.* endureth but a
77. 9. hath he in *a.* shut up
78. 38. turned he his *a.* away
50. he made a way to his *a.*
90. 7. we are consumed by thine *a.*
11. who knoweth power of thine *a.*
Eccl. 7. 9. *a.* resteth in the bosom of fools
Isa. 5. 25. for all this his *a.* is not turned away, 9. 12, 17, 21. & 10. 4.
Hos. 11. 9. not execute fierceness of *a.*
Mic. 7. 18. retaineth not *a.* for ever
Nah. 1. 6. who can abide fierceness of *a.*
Eph. 4. 31. let all *a.* be put away
Col. 3. 8. put off all these; *a.* wrath
Slow to anger, Neh. 9. 17. Ps. 103. 8. Joel 2. 13. Jonah 4. 2. Nah. 1. 3. James 1. 19.
Ps. 106. 32. they *angered* him at
Gen. 18. 30. let not Lord be *angry*
Deut. 1. 37. Lord was *a.* with me
9. 20. Lord was *a.* with Aaron
1 Kings 11. 9. the Lord was *a.* with Solomon
7. 11. God is *a.* with the wicked
76. 7. who may stand when thou art *a.*
Prov. 14. 17. that is soon *a.* dealeth
22. 24. no friendship with an *a.* man
Eccl. 7. 9. be not hasty to be *a.*
S. of S. 1. 6. mother's chil. were *a.*
Isa. 12. 1. though thou wast *a.* with
Jonah 4. 9. I do well to be *a.* even
Matt. 5. 22. whoso is *a.* with brother
Eph. 4. 26. be *a.* and sin not
Tit. 1. 7. bishop must not be soon *a.*
R. V. Ps. 38. 3; 85. 4. indignation; Prov. 22. 8. wrath; Isa. 1. 4.
ANGUISH, excessive pain
Gen. 42. 21. saw the *a.* of his soul
Ex. 6. 9. hearkened not for *a.* of spirit
Ps. 119. 143. trouble and *a.* take hold
John 16. 21. remember not *a.* for joy
Rom. 2. 9. tribulation and *a.* upon
R. V. Gen. 42. 21. distress

ANOINT, rub with oil, appoint, to qualify for office of king, priest, or prophet, Ex. 28. 41.
Dan. 9. 24. to *a*. the most holy
Amos 6. 6. *a*. with chief ointments
Matt. 6. 17. when fastest *a*. thy head
Rev. 3. 18. *a*. eyes with eye salve
1 Sam. 24. 6. *anointed* of the Lord
Ps. 45. 7. *a*. thee with oil of gladness
Zech. 4. 14. two *a*. ones before the Lord
Acts 4. 27. Jesus whom thou hast *a*.
10. 38. how God *a*. Jesus of Nazareth
2 Cor. 1. 21. who hath *a*. us is God
Ps. 2. 2. Lord and his *a*., 18. 50. 2 Sam. 22. 51. 1 Sam. 2. 10. Ps. 20. 6. & 28. 8.
1 Chron. 16. 22. touch not my *a*., Ps. 105. 15. & 132. 17.
Ps. 23. 5. *anointest* my head with oil
Isa. 10. 27. because of *anointing*
1 John 2. 27. the *a*. teacheth you of all
Jas. 5. 14. *a*. him with oil
ANSWER, Gen. 41. 16. Deut. 20. 11.
Prov. 15. 1. soft *a*. turneth away
16. 1. *a*. of tongue is from the Lord
Job 19. 16. he gave me no *a*.
S. of S. 5. 6. he gave me no *a*.
Mic. 3. 7. there is no *answering* of God
Rom. 11. 4. what saith the *a*. of God
2 Tim. 4. 16. at my first *a*. no man
1 Pet. 3. 15. ready to give an *a*. to
21. the *a*. of a good conscience
Job 40. 4. what shall I *a*. thee
Ps. 102. 2. *a*. me speedily
143. 1. in thy faithfulness *a*. me
Prov. 26. 4, 5. *a*. fool according to
Isa. 50. 2. I called was none to *a*.
58. 9. shalt call and Lord shall *a*.
66. 4. when I called none did *a*.
Dan. 3. 16. not careful to *a*. thee
Matt 25. 37. then shall righteous *a*. Lord
Luke 12. 11. what thing ye shall *a*.
13. 25. he shall *a*. I know you not
21. 14. meditate not what to *a*.
2 Cor. 5. 12. have somewhat to *a*.
Col. 4. 6. know how to *a*. every man
Job 14. 15. thou shalt call and I will *a*. & 13. 22. Ps. 91. 15. Isa. 65. 24. Jer. 33. 3. Ezek. 14. 4, 7.
Ps. 18. 41. to Lord but he *answered* not
81. 7. I *a*. thee in secret place
99. 6. called on the Lord and he *a*.
Prov. 18. 23. rich *answereth* roughly
13. he that *a*. matter before hear
27. 19. as in water face *a*. to face
Eccl. 10. 19. money *a*. all things
Gal. 4. 25. *a*. to Jerusalem that now
Tit. 2. 9. not *answering* again
R. V. Acts 25. 16. to make defence; 2 Tim. 4. 16. defence; 1 Pet. 3. 21. interrogation
ANT, Prov. 6. 6. & 30. 25.
ANTICHRIST, 1 John 2. 18, 22. & 4. 3. 2 John 7.
APART, Ps. 4. 3. Zech. 12. 12. Jas. 1. 21.
R. V. Jas. 1. 21. away
APOSTATES, Deut. 13. 13; Matt. 24. 10; Luke 8. 13; John 6. 66; Heb. 3. 12; 6. 4; 2 Pet. 3. 17; 1 John 2.
their doom, Zeph. 1. 4; 2 Thes. 2. 8; 1 Tim. 4. 1; Heb. 10. 25; 2 Pet. 2. 17.
APOSTLE, minister sent by God, or Christ, infallibly to preach the gospel, and found churches, Rom. 1. 1. 1 Cor. 1. 1. & 12. 28.
Rom. 11. 13. I am *a*. of Gentiles.
1 Cor. 9. 1. am I not a free *a*.
2 Cor. 12. 12. signs of *a*. wrought
Matt. 10. 2. names of the twelve
Luke 11. 49. I will send proph. and *a*.
1 Cor. 4. 9. God hath sent forth us *a*.
15. 9. I am the least of the *a*.
2 Cor. 11. 13. such are false *a*.
Rev. 2. 2. say they are *a*. and
18. 20. holy *a*. and prophets, Eph. 3. 5.
21. 14. names of twelve *a*. of the
Acts 1. 25. part of this *apostleship*
Rom. 1. 5. received grace and *a*.
1 Cor. 9. 2. seal of my *a*. are ye
Gal. 2. 8. to *a*. of circumcision
R. V. Acts 5. 34. men
APPAREL, Isa. 63. 1. Zeph. 1. 8. 1 Tim. 2. 9. 1 Pet. 3. 3. Jas. 2. 2.
R. V. Isa. 3. 22——; Jas. 2. 2. clothing
APPEAR, Gen. 1. 9. Heb. 11. 3.
Ex. 23. 15. none shall *a*. before me empty, 34. 20. Deut. 16. 16.
2 Chron. 1. 7. did God *a*. to Solomon
Ps. 42. 2. when shall I *a*. before God
90. 16. let work *a*. to servants
Isa. 1. 12. when ye *a*. before me who
66. 5. shall *a*. to your joy, but they
Matt. 6. 16. may *a*. to men to fast
Luke 19. 11. kingdom of God immediately *a*.
Rom. 7. 13. sin that it might *a*. sin
2 Cor. 5. 10. we must all *a*. before the
Col. 3. 4. when Christ shall *a*. ye also *a*.
1 Tim. 4. 15. thy profiting *a*. to all
28. *a*. second time without sin to salvation
1 Pet. 5. 4. when the chief shepherd shall *a*.
1 John 3. 2. not yet *a*. what we shall
1 Sam. 16. 7. man looks—*appearance*
John 7. 24. judge not according to *a*.
1 Thes. 5. 22. abstain from all *a*. of
2 Tim. 1. 10. manifest by *a*. of Jesus
4. 1. judge quick and dead at his *a*.
8. all them that love his *a*.
Tit. 2. 13. look for glorious *a*. of
1 Pet. 1. 7. unto praise at *a*. of Jesus
Tit. 2. 11. grace hath *a*. to all men
Heb. 9. 26. he *a*. to put away sin
R. V. 1 Sam. 2. 27. reveal myself; S. of S. 4. 1; 6. 5. lie along the side; Acts 22. 30. come together; Rom. 7. 13. shewn to be; 2 Cor. 5. 10; 7. 12; Col. 3. 4; 1 Pet. 5. 4; 1 John 2. 28. manifested; 2 Cor. 10. 7. that are before your face; 1 Thes. 5. 22. every form; 1 Pet. 1. 7. revelation
APPETITE, Prov. 23. 2. Isa. 29. 8.
APPLE of eye, Deut. 32. 10. Ps. 17. 8. Prov. 7. 2. Lam. 2. 18. Zech. 2. 8.
Apple-trees, S. of S. 2. 3. & 8. 5.
Apples, Prov. 25. 11. S. of S. 2. 5 7. 8.
APPOINT, Gen. 30. 28.
Isa. 61. 3. *a*. to them that mourn in Zion
26. 1. salvation will God *a*. for walls
Matt. 24. 51. *a*. him portion with the hypocrites
Luke 22. 29. I *a*. unto you a kingdom
Job 7. 1. is there not an *appointed* time
14. 14. all the days of my *a*. time
30. 23. to house *a*. for all living
Ps. 79. 11. preserve those *a*. to die
Jer. 5. 24. reserve *a*. weeks for harvest
Mic. 6. 9. hear rod and him who *a*. it
Hab. 2. 3. vision is for an *a*. time
Heb. 9. 27. *a*. to men once to die
1 Pet. 2. 8. whereunto they were *a*.
R. V. Num. 35. 6. give; 2 Sam. 15. 15. choose; Ezek. 21. 22. set; 1 Sam. 19. 20. as head; 2 Chr. 34. 22. commanded; Acts 1. 23. put forward
APPLY heart to wisdom, &c. Ps. 90. 12. Prov. 2. 2. & 22. 17. & 23. 12. Eccl. 7. 25. & 8. 9, 16. Hos. 7. 6.
R. V. Eccl. 7. 25. heart was set
APPREHENDED, take fast hold of, Phil. 3. 12, 13. Acts 12. 4. 2 Cor. 11. 32.
R. V. Acts 12. 4. taken; 2 Cor. 11. 32. take
APPROACH, come near to, marry
Lev. 18. 6. *a*. to any near of kin, 20. 16.
Ps. 65. 4. blessed whom thou causest to *a*.
Jer. 30. 21. engageth heart to *a*. to
1 Tim. 6. 16. light to which none can *a*.
Isa. 58. 2. delight in *approaching* to God
Heb. 10. 25. as ye see the day *a*.
R. V. Ezek. 42. 13; 43. 19. are near
APPROVE, like, commend
Ps. 49. 13. posterity *a*. their sayings
Phil. 1. 10. may *a*. things excellent
Acts 2. 22. man *approved* of God
Rom. 14. 18. *acceptable* to God, *a*. of
16. 10. Apelles *a*. in Christ
2 Tim. 2. 15. show thyself *a*. to God
Rom. 2. 18. *approvest* things excellent
Lam. 3. 36. to subvert Lord *approveth* not
2 Cor. 6. 4. in all things *approving* ourselves
APT to teach, 1 Tim. 3. 2. 2 Tim. 2. 24.
ARE, seven years, Gen. 41. 26, 27.
1 Cor. 1. 28. bring to nought things that *a*.
30. of him *a*. ye in Christ Jesus
8. 6. of whom *a*. all things
Heb. 2. 10. for and by whom *a*. all
Rev. 1. 19. write things that *a*.
20. *a*. angels; *a*. seven churches
ARGUE, Job 6. 25. & 23. 4.
ARIGHT, set not their hearts, Ps. 78. 8.
50. 23. ordereth conversation *a*.
Prov. 15. 2. useth knowledge *a*.
Jer. 8. 6. they spake not *a*.
R. V. Prov. 23. 31. smoothly
ARISE for our help, Ps. 44. 26.
1 Chron. 22. 16. *a*. be doing
Amos 7. 2. by whom shall Jacob *a*. 5.
Mic. 7. 8. when I fall I shall *a*.
Mal. 4. 2. Son of righteousness *a*.
Ps. 112. 4. to the upright *ariseth* light
Matt. 13. 21. persecution *a*. because
ARM of flesh with him, 2 Chron. 32. 8.
Job 40. 9. hast thou an *a*. like God
Ps. 44. 3. own *a*. did not save them
Isa. 33. 2. be thou their *a*. every
51. 5. mine *a*. shall judge; on my *a*.
9. put on strength, O *a*. of Lord
52. 10. Lord made bare his holy *a*.
53. 1. *a*. of Lord revealed, John 12. 38.
63. 12. led them by his glorious *a*.
1 Pet. 4. 1. *a*. yourselves with same
His arm, Ps. 98. 1. Isa. 40. 10, 11. & 59. 16. Jer. 17. 5. Ezek. 31. 17. Zech. 11. 17. Luke 1. 51.
Stretched-out arm, Ex. 6. 6. Deut. 4. 34. & 5. 15. & 7. 19. & 11. 2. & 26. 8. 2 Chron. 6. 32. Ps. 136. 12. Jer. 27. 5. & 32. 17, 21. Ezek. 20. 33, 34.
Gen. 49. 24. *arms* of his hands made strong
Deut. 33. 27. underneath everlast.
Luke 11. 21. strong man *armed* keep
R. V. Job 31. 22. shoulder
ARMIES of living God, 1 Sam. 17. [illegible]
Job 25. 3. any number of his *a*.
Ps. 44. 9. goest not forth with our, 60. 10. & 108. 11.
S. of S. 6. 13. company of two *a*.
Rev. 19. 14. *army* in heaven followed
R. V. Gen. 26. 26; 1 Chr. 27. 34. host; Rev. 9. 16. armies.
ARMOR of light, Rom. 13. 12.
2 Cor. 6. 7. by *a*. of righteousness
Eph. 6. 7. put on whole *a*. of God
R. V. 1 Sam. 17. 38, 39. apparel
ARRAY, in order of battle, 2 Sam. 10. 9. Job 6. 4. Jer. 50. 14.
Array, to clothe, Esth. 6. 9. Job 40. 10. Jer. 43. 12. Matt. 6. 29. 1 Tim. 2. 9. Rev. 7. 13. & 17. 4. & 19. 8.
R. V. 1 Tim. 2. 9. raiment
ARROGANCY, presumptuous self-conceit, 1 Sam. 2. 3. Prov. 8. 13. Isa. 13. 11.
ARROWS of the Almighty, Job 6. 4.
Ps. 91. 5. nor for *a*. that flieth by day
Deut. 32. 23. I will spend my *a*. upon
Ps. 38. 2. thine *a*. stick fast in me
45. 5. thine *a*. are sharp in heart
Lam. 3. 12. set me as a mark for *a*.
R. V. Lam. 3. 13. shafts

ARTIFICER, Tubal-Cain the first, Gen. 4. 22.
ASCEND into hill of Lord, Ps. 24. 3.
Ps. 139. 8. if I *a.* to heaven, Rom. 10. 6.
John 20. 17. I *a.* to my Father
Ps. 68. 18. hast *ascended* on high
Prov. 30. 4. who hath *a.* into heaven
John 3. 13. no man hath *a.* up to
Rev. 8. 4. smoke of incense *a.* before God
Gen. 28. 12. angels *ascending* and descending, John 1. 51. upon Son of man
ASCRIBE greatness to God, Deut. 32. 3.
Job. 36. 3. I will *a.* righteousness to
Ps. 68. 34. *a.* strength unto God
ASHAMED and blush to lift, Ezra 9. 6.
Gen. 2. 25. man and wife naked not *a.*
Ezek. 16. 61. remember ways and be *a.*
Mark 8. 38. shall be *a.* of me
Rom. 1. 16. I am not *a.* of gospel
5. 5. hope maketh not *a.* because
Not be ashamed, Ps. 25. 2. & 119. 6, 80.
Isa. 49. 23. Rom. 9. 33. 2 Tim. 2. 15.
R. V. Job 6. 20. confounded; Luke 13. 17; Rom. 9. 33; 10. 11; 2 Cor. 7. 14; 9. 4; 10. 8; Phil. 1. 20; Heb. 11. 16; 1 Pet. 3. 16. put to shame
ASHES, Gen. 18. 27. Job 2. 8. & 13. 12. & 30. 19. & 42. 6. Ps. 102. 9. Isa. 44. 20. & 61. 3. Jer. 6. 26. Ezek. 28. 18. Mal. 4. 3.
R. V. 1 Kings 20. 38, 41. his headband
ASK the way to Zion, Jer. 50. 5.
Matt. 7. 7. *a.* and it shall be given
20. 22. ye know not what ye *a.*
Luke 12. 48. of him they will *a.* more
John 14. 13, 14. whatsoever ye *a.* in my name, & 15. 16. & 16. 23.
16. 24. *a.* and ye shall receive—*asked*
Eph. 3. 20. above all we can *a.* or
Jas. 1. 5. wisdom let him *a.* of God
6. let him *a.* in faith, not wavering
4. 2, 3. *a.* not; *a.* receive not; *a.* amiss
Isa. 65. 1. sought of—*asked* not for me
Jer. 6. 16. *a.* for good old paths
Matt. 7. 8. every one that *asketh* receiveth
ASLEEP, 1 Cor. 15. 16. 1 Thes. 4. 13.
ASP, poisonous serpent, Deut. 32. 33. Job 20. 14, 16. Isa. 11. 8. Rom. 3. 13.
ASS knows master's crib, Isa. 1. 3.
Zech. 9. 9. riding upon an ass, Matt. 21. 5. John 12. 15.
ASSEMBLY of wicked, Ps. 22. 16.
89. 7. God feared in *a.* of his saints
Heb. 12. 23. general *a.* of first-born
Eccl. 12. 11. nails fastened by masters of *a.*
Isa. 4. 5. create on her *a.* a cloud
Heb. 10. 25. forsake not *assembling*
R. V. Lev. 8. 4; Num. 8. 9; 10. 2. 3; 16. 2; 2 Chr. 30. 23. congregation; Ps. 89. 7; 111. 1; Ezek. 13. 9. council; Jas. 2. 2. synagogue
ASSUAGE, Gen. 8. 1. Job 16. 5, 6.
ASSURANCE, firm persuasion
Isa. 32. 17. effect of righteousness *a.*
1 Thes. 1. 5. gospel came in much *a.*
Heb. 6. 11. to full *a.* of hope unto end
10. 22. in full *a.* of faith
1 John 3. 19. *assure* our hearts before
R. V. Heb. 6. 11; 22. 10. fulness
ASTRAY, Ps. 119. 176. Isa. 53. 6. Matt. 18. 12. Luke 15. 4. 1 Pet. 2. 25.
ATHIRST, sore, and called, Judg. 15. 18.
Rev. 21. 6. give to him *a.* of fountain
22. 17. him that is *a.* come take of
ATONEMENT, pacifying, satisfaction for sin, Lev. 16. 11. & 24.
2 Sam. 21. 3. wherewith shall I make *a.*
Rom. 5. 11. by whom we received *a.*
R. V. Rom. 5. 11. reconciliation
ATTAIN to wise counsels, Prov. 1. 5.
Ezek. 46. 7. according as hand shall *a.*
Phil. 3. 11, 12. *a.* to resurrection not already *attained*
R. V. Acts 27. 12. could reach
ATTEND to my cry, Ps. 55. 2. & 61. 1. & 66. 19. & 86. 6. & 142. 6.
Prov. 4. 1. *a.* to know understand.
20. *a.* to my words, 7. 24.
Acts 16. 14. she *attended* to—spoken
Attendance, 1 Kings 10. 5. 1 Tim. 4. 13. Heb. 7. 13. Rom. 13. 6.
Attentive, 1 Chron. 6. 40. & 7. 15. Neh. 1. 6. & 8. 3. Ps. 130. 2. Luke 19. 48.
R. V. Ps. 86. 6. hearken; Acts 16. 14. to give heed
AUTHOR of confusion, 1 Cor. 14. 33.
Heb. 5. 9. *a.* of eternal salvation
12. 2. Jesus *a.* and finisher of our
R. V. Rom. 16. 17. turn away from; 2 Tim. 2. 23. refuse; Tit. 3. 9. shun
AUTHORITY, power to govern
Matt. 7. 29. taught as one having *a.*
John 5. 27. given him *a.* to execute
1 Cor. 15. 24. down all *a.* and power
1 Tim. 2. 2. prayer for all in *a.*
1 Pet. 3. 22. angels and *a.* subject
Rev. 13. 2. dragon gave him *a.*
R. V. 1 Tim. 2. 2. high place; 2. 12. have dominion
AVAILETH, Esth. 5. 13. Gal. 5. 6. & 6. 15. Jas. 5. 16.
AVENGE not, nor grudge, Lev. 19. 18.
Lev. 26. 25. shall *a.* quarrel of covenant
Deut. 32. 43. he will *a.* blood of
Isa. 1. 24. I will *a.* me of mine enemies
Luke 18. 7. shall not God *a.* his
Luke 18. 8. he will *a.* them speed.
Rom. 12. 19. *a.* not yourselves
Rev. 6. 10. dost thou not *a.* our blood
Rev. 18. 20. God hath *a.* you on her
Avenger, Num. 35. 12. Ps. 8. 2. & 44. 16. 1 Thes. 4. 6.
2 Sam. 22. 48. God that *avengeth* me
Judg. 5. 2. praise Lord for *avenging* Israel.
R. V. Lev. 19. 18. take vengeance; 26. 25. execute; Rev. 18. 20. judged your judgment.
AVOUCHED, Deut. 26. 17, 18.
AVOID it, pass not by it, Prov. 4. 15.
Rom. 16. 17. cause divisions, *a.*
AWAKE for thee, Job 8. 6.
Ps. 35. 23. *a.* to my judgment
139. 18. when I *a.* I am still with
1 Cor. 15. 34. *a.* to righteousness
Eph. 5. 14. *a.* thou that sleepest
Ps. 78. 65. Lord *awaked* out of sleep
73. 20. when thou *awakest* thou
AWE, stand in *a.* sin not, Ps. 4. 4.
Ps. 33. 8. would stand in *a.* of him
119. 161. heart stands in *a.* of word
AXE, Deut. 19. 5. 1 Kings 6. 7. & 2 Kings 6. 5. Isa. 10. 15. Jer. 51. 20.
Axes, 2 Sam. 12. 31. Ps. 74. 3, 6. Jer. 46. 22.
R. V. Ps. 74. 6. hatchet.

B

BABBLER, Eccl. 10. 11. Acts 17. 18.
1 Tim. 6. 20. avoid vain *babblings*, 2 Tim. 2. 16. Prov. 23. 29.
R. V. Eccl. 10. 11. charmer.
BABE leaped in womb, Luke 1. 41.
Heb. 5. 13. unskil. in words is a *b.*
Ps. 8. 2. out of mouth of *babes*
Isa. 3. 4. *b.* shall rule over them
1 Cor. 3. 1. as unto *b.* in Christ
1 Pet. 2. 2. as new-born *b.* desire
BACK to go from Samuel, 1 Sam. 10. 9.
1 Kings 14. 9. cast me behind *b.*
Prov. 26. 3. rod for the fool's *b.*
Isa. 38. 17. cast my sins behind thy *b.*
50. 6. gave my *b.* to smiters
Jer. 2. 27. turned their *b.* 32. 33.
18. 17. I will shew them *b.* not face
Ex. 33. 23. shall see my *b.* parts
Ps. 19. 13. keep *b.* thy servant from
53. 6. when God bringeth *b.* captivity
Acts 20. 20. kept *b.* nothing profit.
Neh. 9. 26. cast law behind *backs*
Backbiters, haters of God, Rom. 1. 30.
Ps. 15. 3. *backbiteth* not with his
Prov. 25. 23. *backbiting* tongue
2 Cor. 12. 20. strifes, *backbitings*
Backslider in heart, Prov. 14. 14.
Jer. 2. 19. thy *backslidings* reprove thee
3. 6, 12. return thou *b.* Israel, 14. 7. & 31. 22. & 49. 4.
14. 7. *b.* are many, we have sinned
Hos. 11. 7. my people are bent to *b.*
14. 4. I will heal their *b.*
Isa. 1. 4. they are gone away *b.*
59. 14. judgment is turned away *b.*
John 18. 6. went *b.* and fell to the ground
BAG, sack, or pouch, Deut. 25. 13. Job 14. 17. Prov. 16. 11. Mic. 6. 11. Hag. 1. 6. Luke 12. 33. John 13. 29.
R. V. Luke 12. 33. purses
BALANCE, Job 31. 6. & 6. 2. Ps. 62. 9. Isa. 40. 12, 15. & 46. 6. Dan. 5. 27.
16. 11. just weight and *b.* are
Mic. 6. 11. count pure with wick. *b.*
BALD, 2 Kings 2. 23. Jer. 16. 6. & 48. 37. Ezek. 27. 31. Mic. 1. 16.
Baldness, Lev. 21. 5. Deut. 14. 1. Isa. 3. 24. & 15. 2. & 22. 12. Ezek. 7. 18.
BALM, Gen. 37. 25. & 43. 11.
Jer. 8. 22. is there no *b.* in Gilead
46. 11. & 51. 8. Ezek. 27. 17.
BANNER, Isa. 13. 2. Ps. 20. 5.
Ps. 60. 4. *b.* to them that fear thee
S. of S. 2. 4. his *b.* over me was love
6. 4. terrible as an army with *banners*
R. V. Isa. 13. 2. ensign
BAPTISM of water, Matt. 3. 7.
Baptism of John, Matt. 21. 25. Mark 11. 30. Luke 7. 29. & 12. 50. Acts 1. 22. & 10. 37. & 18. 25. & 19. 3, 4.
Baptism of repentance, Mark 1. 4. Acts 13. 24. & 19. 4.
Baptism of suffering, Matt. 20. 22, 23. Mark 10. 38, 39. Luke 12. 50.
Rom. 6. 4. buried with him by *baptism*, Col. 2. 12.
Eph. 4. 5. one faith, one *b.*
1 Pet. 3. 21. *b.* doth now save us
Heb. 6. 2. doctrine of *baptisms*
BAPTIZE with water, with the Holy Ghost, Matt. 3. 11. Mark 1. 8. Luke 3. 16. Acts 1. 5. John 1. 26, 28, 31, 33.
Mark 1. 4. John did *b.* in wilder.
5. were all *baptized* of him, 8.
Mark 16. 16. believeth and is *b.*
Luke 3. 7. came to be *b.* 12.
7. 29, 30. publicans *b.* lawyers not *b.*
John 4. 1. Jesus *b.* more disciples
2. though Jesus himself *b.* not
Acts 2. 38. repent and be *b.* every one
8. 13. Simon believed and was *b.*
10. 47. that these should not be *b.*
48. Peter command. them to be *b.*
18. 8. believed and were *b.*
Rom. 6. 3. as many as were *b.* were
1 Cor. 1. 13. were ye *b.* in name of
15. none—*b.* in own name
10. 2. were all *b.* unto Moses
Gal. 3. 27. as have been *b.* into Christ
Matt. 28. 19. *baptizing* in name
BARE you on eagles' wings, Ex. 19. 4.
Isa. 53. 12. he *b.* the sins of many

Matt. 8. 17. himself *b.* our sicknesses
1 Pet. 2. 24. *b.* our sins in his own
BARN, Matt. 13. 30. Prov. 3. 10. Matt. 6. 26. Luke 12. 18, 24.
R. V. Job 39. 12; 2 Kings 6. 27. threshing-floor
BARREL of meal, 1 Kings 17. 14.
BARREN, Gen. 11. 30. & 25. 21. & 29. 31. Judg. 13. 2. Luke 1. 7.
Ex. 23. 26. nothing shall be *b.*
1 Sam. 2. 5. *b.* hath borne seven
S. of S. 4. 2. none is *b.* among, 6. 6.
Luke 23. 29. blessed are *b.* wombs
2 Pet. 1. 8. neither *b.* nor unfruitful
R. V. 2 Kings 2. 19. miscarrieth; Job 39. 6. salt; S. of S. 4. 2; 6. 6. bereaved; 2 Pet. 1. 8. idle
BASE in my own sight, 2 Sam. 6. 22.
1 Cor. 1. 28. *b.* things of this world
2 Cor. 10. 1. who in presence am *b.*
Ezek. 29. 14, 15. *basest* of kingdoms
BASTARD not enter, Deut. 23. 2.
Zech. 9. 6. *b.* shall dwell in Ashdod
Heb. 12. 8. without chastisement are *bastards*
BATTLE not to strong, Eccl. 9. 11.
Jer. 8. 6. as horse rusheth into *b.*
Ps. 140. 7. covered head in day of *b.*
R. V. Num. 31. 14; Josh. 22. 33; 2 Sam. 21. 18, 19, 20; 1 Cor. 14. 8; Rev. 9. 7, 9; 28. 8. war
BEAM out of timber, Hab. 2. 11.
Matt. 7. 3. considered not *b.* in own eye
S. of S. 1. 1, 17. *b.* of our house are
BEAR, Gen. 49. 15. Deut. 1. 9, 31. Prov. 9. 12. & 30. 21. Lam. 3. 27.
Gen. 4. 13. punishment greater than I can *b.*
Num. 11. 14. not able to *b.* all this people
Prov. 18. 14. wounded spirit who can *b.*
Amos 7. 10. land not able to *b.* words
Luke 14. 27. whoso doth not *b.* his
18. 7. though he *b.* long with them
John 16. 12. ye cannot *b.* them now
Rom. 15. 1. strong *b.* the infirmities
1 Cor. 3. 2. hitherto not able to *b.* it
10. 13. that may be able to *b.* it
Gal. 6. 2. *b.* ye one another's burdens
5. every man *b.* his own
17. I *b.* in my body the marks
Heb. 9. 28. offered to *b.* sins of many
Rev. 2. 2. canst not *b.* which are evil
Bear fruit, Ezek. 17. 8. Hos. 9. 16. Joel 2. 22. Matt. 13. 23. Luke 13. 9. John 15. 2, 4, 8.
Ps. 106. 4. favor thou *bearest* to
Rom. 11. 18. *b.* not root but
13. 4. *beareth* not sword in vain
1 Cor. 13. 7. charity *b.* all things
Ps. 126. 6. *bearing* precious seed
Heb. 13. 13. *b.* his reproach
BEASTS, animals without reason, Gen. 1. 24, 25. & 3. 1.—for ministers, Rev. 4. 6, 7, 8, 9. & 5. 6, 14. & 6. 1, 3. & 7. 11. & 14. 3. & 15. 7. & 19. 4.—for antichrist, Dan. 7. 11. Rev. 11. 7. & 13. 1, 11. & 15. 2. & 16. 13. & 17. 8. & 19. 19. & 20. 10.
Prov. 9. 2. wisdom killed her *b.*
Dan. 7. 17. four *b.* are four kings
1 Cor. 15. 32. I fought with *b.* at Ephesus
R. V. Ex. 11. 5; Num. 20. 8; Isa. 63. 14. cattle; in Rev. generally, living creatures
BEAT, Prov. 23. 14. Isa. 3. 15. Luke 12. 47, 48. 1 Cor. 9. 26.
R. V. Judg. 8. 17; 2 Kings 13. 25. smite; Mat. 7. 27. smote.
BEAUTY, Ex. 28. 2.
1 Chron. 16. 29. in the *b.* of holiness
Ps. 27. 4. to behold *b.* of the Lord
39. 11. makest his *b.* to consume
45. 11. king greatly desire thy *b.*
Prov. 20. 29. *b.* of old men gray head
31. 30. favor deceitful *b.* is vain
Isa. 3. 24. be burning instead of *b.*
33. 17. see the king in his *b.* and
Isa. 61. 3. give them *b.* for ashes
Zech. 11. 7. two staves, one called *b.*
Beautify, Ps. 149. 4. Isa. 60. 13
Beautiful, Eccl. 3. 11. S. of S. 6. 4. & 7. 1.
Isa. 52. 1, 7. & 64. 11. Jer. 13. 20. Ezek. 16. 12, 13. Matt. 23. 27. Acts 3. 2. Rom. 10. 15.
R. V. 2 Sam. 1. 19. glory; Job 40. 10; Lam. 1. 6. majesty; Isa. 61. 3. garland
BED, set for him, 2 Kings 4. 10.
Ps. 41. 3. make all his *b.* in sickness
S. of S. 3. 1. by night on my *b.* I
Isa. 28. 20. the *b.* is shorter than
Heb. 13. 4. marriage *b.* undefiled
Rev. 2. 22. I will cast her into a *b.*
Isa. 57. 2. rest in their *beds*
Amos 6. 4. lie on *b.* of ivory
R. V. many places in O. T., couch
BEFORE, in sight, Gen. 20. 15. & 43. 14. Ex. 22. 9. 1 Kings 17. 1. & 18. 15. 2 Kings 3. 14.—(in time or place) Gen. 31. 2. Job 3. 24. Josh. 8. 10. Luke 22. 47.
2 Chron. 13. 14.—(in dignity) 2 Sam. 6. 21. John 1. 15, 27.
Phil. 3. 13. those things which are *b.*
Col. 1. 17. he is *b.* all things and
R. V. Rev. 13. 12; 19. 20. in his sight
BEG, Ps. 109. 10. & 37. 25. Prov. 20. 4. Luke 16. 3. & 23. 52. John 9. 8.
Beggar, 1 Sam. 2. 8. Luke 16. 20, 22.
Beggarly elements, Gal. 4. 9.
R. V. Matt. 27. 58; Luke 23. 52. asked for
BEGIN at my sanctuary, Ezek. 9. 6.
Ex. 12. 2. the *beginning* of months
Gen. 49. 3. *b.* of strength, Deut. 21. 17.
Ps. 111. 10. fear of Lord is the *b.* of wisdom, Prov. 1. 7. & 9. 10.
Heb. 7. 3. neither *b.* of days nor end
2 Pet. 2. 20. latter end is worse than *b.*
Rev. 1. 8. I am Alpha and Omega, *b.* and the ending, 21. 6. & 22. 13.
3. 14. saith the *b.* of creation of
R. V. 1 Chr. 17. 9; Acts 26. 5; 2 Pet. 2. 20. first
BEGOTTEN drops of dew, Job 38. 28.
Ps. 2. 7. this day have I *b.* thee, Acts 13. 33. Heb. 1. 5, 6.
John 1. 14. only *b.* of the Father, 18.
3. 16. sent his only *b.* Son, 18.
1 Pet. 1. 3. *b.* us again to a lively
1 John 4. 9. sent his only *b.* Son
Rev. 1. 5. first *b.* of the dead
BEGUILE, Col. 2. 4, 18. Gen. 3. 13. 2 Cor. 11. 3. 2 Pet. 2. 14.
R. V. Col. 2. 4. delude; 2. 18. rob; 2 Pet. 2. 14. enticing
BEGUN to fall, Esth. 6. 13.
Gal. 3. 3. having *b.* in the spirit
Phil. 1. 6. hath *b.* a good work in
BEHAVE myself wisely, Ps. 101. 2.
Ps. 131. 2. I *b.* myself as a child
1 Tim. 3. 2. bishop of good *behavior*
Tit. 2. 3. in *b.* as becometh holiness
R. V. 1 Tim. 3. 2. orderly; Tit. 2. 3. reverent in demeanor.
BEHELD not iniquity in Jacob, Num. 23. 21.
Luke 10. 18. I *b.* Satan fall
John 1. 14. we *b.* his glory
Rev. 11. 12. their enemies *b.* them
BEHIND, Lev. 25. 51. Judg. 20. 40.
Ex. 10. 26. not an hoof left *b.*
Ps. 139. 5. beset me *b.* and before
Isa. 38. 17. cast all my sins *b.* thy
1 Cor. 1. 7. ye come *b.* in no gift
Col. 1. 24. fill up that is *b.* of afflict.
R. V. Col. 1. 24. lacking
BEHOLD with thine eyes, Deut. 3. 27.
Job 19. 27. my eyes shall *b.* and not
Ps. 11. 4. his eyes *b.* his eyelids try
7. countenance *b.* upright
17. 15. I will *b.* thy face in right.
27. 4. desired to *b.* beauty of Lord
37. 37. *b.* the upright man
113. 6. humbles himself to *b.*
Hab. 1. 13. of purer eyes than to *b.*
Matt. 18. 10. their angels *b.* face of
John 17. 24. they may *b.* my glory
19. 5. *b.* the man, 14. *b.* your king
26. *b.* thy son, 27. *b.* thy mother
1 Pet. 3. 2. *b.* your chaste conver.
Ps. 33. 13. Lord *beholdeth* all the
Jas. 1. 24. he *b.* himself and go.
Prov. 15. 3. *beholding* evil and good
Ps. 119. 37. turn eyes from *b.* vanity
Eccl. 5. 11. save *b.* of them with
Col. 2. 5. joying and *b.* your order
Jas. 1. 23. like man *b.* natural
BEING, Ps. 104. 33. & 146. 2. Acts 17. 28.
BELIAL, devil, furious and obstinate in wickedness, Deut. 13. 13. Judg. 19. 22. & 20. 13. 1 Sam. 1. 16. & 2. 12. & 10. 27. & 25. 17, 25. & 30. 22. 2 Sam. 16. 7. & 20. 1. & 23. 6. 1 Kings 21. 10, 13. 2 Chron. 13. 7. 2 Cor. 6. 15.
BELIEVE, credit as testimony, Ex. 4. 1. Num. 14. 11. & 20. 12.
Deut. 1. 32. ye did not *b.* the Lord
2 Chron. 20. 20. *b.* Lord, *b.* prophets
Isa. 7. 9. will not *b.* surely not
Matt. 9. 28. *b.* ye that I am able
Mark 1. 15. repent and *b.* the gos.
24. Lord I *b.* help my unbelief
11. 24. *b.* that ye receive them
Luke 8. 13. for a while *b.* and
24. 25. slow of heart to *b.* all
John 1. 12. even to them that *b.*
6. 29. ye *b.* on him whom he sent
69. we *b.* and are sure thou art
7. 39. they that *b.* him should
8. 24. if ye *b.* not I am he ye shall
11. 42. may *b.* thou hast sent me
13. 19. ye may *b.* that I am he
14. 1. ye *b.* in God, *b.* also in me
17. 20. pray for them who shall *b.*
20. 31. written that ye might *b.*
Acts 8. 37. I *b.* Jesus Christ is the
13. 39. all that *b.* are justified
16. 31. *b.* on the Lord Jesus and thou shalt be saved
Rom. 3. 22. on all them that *b.*
10. 9. shalt *b.* in thine heart
14. how shall they *b.* on him
2 Cor. 4. 13. we *b.* and therefore
Phil. 1. 29. not only to *b.* but suffer
1 Tim. 4. 10. especially those that *b.*
Heb. 10. 39. *b.* to saving of the soul
11. 6. cometh to God must *b.* that he is
Jas. 2. 19. devils also *b.* and
1 Pet. 2. 7. to you who *b.* he is prec.
1 John 3. 23. his command that we *b.* on Jesus Christ
Believe not, Isa. 7. 9. John 4. 48. & 8. 24. & 10. 26. & 12. 39. & 16. 9, 20, 25. Rom. 3. 3. 2 Cor. 4. 4. 2 Tim. 2. 13. 1 John 4. 1.
Gen. 15. 6. *believed* in Lord and he counted, Rom. 4. 3. Gal. 3. 6. Jas. 2. 23.
Ps. 27. 13. fainted unless I had *b.*
119. 66. I *b.* thy commandments
Isa. 53. 1. who hath *b.* our report, John 12. 38. Rom. 10. 16.
Dan. 6. 23. because he *b.* in his God
Jonah 3. 5. people of Nineveh *b.*
Matt. 8. 13. as thou hast *b.* so be it
21. 32. publicans and harlots *b.*
John 4. 53. himself *b.* and his house
17. 8. have *b.* thou didst send me
20. 29. blessed—not seen and yet *b.*
Acts 4. 32. that *b.* were of one heart
8. 13. Simon *b.* and was baptized
11. 21. great number *b.* and turned
48. as many as were ordained to eternal life *b.*
Rom. 4. 18. against hope *b.* in hope
Eph. 1. 13. after ye *b.* ye were
1 Tim. 3. 16. God was *b.* on in the
2 Tim. 1. 12. know whom I have *b.*
Believed not, Ps. 78. 22, 32. & 106. 24. Luke 24. 41. Acts 9. 26. Rom. 10. 14. 2 Thes. 2. 12. Heb. 3. 18. Jude 5.
Believers, Acts 5. 14. 1 Tim. 4. 12.
Believest, Luke 1. 20. John 1. 50. & 11. 26. & 14. 10. Jas. 2. 19.
Acts 8. 37. if thou *b.* with all thy
26. 27. *b.* thou prophets—thou *b.*
Believeth, Job 15. 22. & 39. 24.

Prov. 14. 15. simple *b.* every word
Isa. 28. 16. that *b.* — not make haste
Mark 9. 23. all things possible to—*b.*
16. 16. he that *b.* shall be saved, he that *b.* not shall be damned
John 3. 15, 16. *b.* in him should not
18. he that *b.* is not condemned
5. 24. *b.* on him that sent me
6. 35. *b.* on me shall never thirst
40. seeth the Son and *b.* may
11. 25. *b.* in me though he were d.
26. he that *b.* in me shall never d.
12. 44. *b.* on me, *b.* not on me, but
46. *b.* on me shall not abide in
Acts 10. 43. *b.* in him — receive remission
Rom. 1. 16. power of God—to every one that *b.*
3. 26. justifier of him that *b.* in
4. 5. worketh not, but *b.* on him
9. 33. *b.* on him — not ashamed, 10. 11.
10. for with the heart man *b.* unto righteousness
1 Cor. 7. 12. wife that *b.* not
13. husband that *b.* not
13. 7. charity *b.* all things
14. 24. come in one that *b.* not
2 Cor. 6. 15. he that *b.* with infidel
1 Pet. 2. 6. *b.* on him shall not be confounded
1 John 5. 1. whoso *b.* that Jesus is
5. overcom. world, but he that *b.*
10. he that *b.* on Son of God hath —*b.* not God hath made him a liar because he *b.* not record that
Matt. 21. 22. ask in prayer, *believing*
John 20. 27. be not faithless, but *b.*
31. that *b.* ye might have life
Acts 16. 34. *b.* in God with all his
Rom. 15. 13. all joy and peace in b.
1 Pet. 1. 8. yet *b.* ye rejoice with joy
2 Thes. 2. 13. *belief* of the truth
R. V. Acts 19. 9; Heb. 3. 18. disobedient

BELLOWS are burnt, Jer. 6. 29.

BELLY, on *b.* shalt go, Gen. 3. 14.
Num. 5. 21. *b.* to swell and thigh
25. 8. thrust them through the *b.*
Job 3. 11. when I came out of *b.*
15. 2. fill his *b.* with east wind
35. their *b.* prepareth deceit
20. 15. God cast them out of his *b.*
20. not feel quietness in his *b.*
Ps. 17. 14. whose *b.* thou fillest with
22. 10. art my God from mother's *b.*
Prov. 20. 27. search inw. parts of *b.*
Isa. 46. 3. borne by me from the *b.*
Jonah 1. 17. in the *b.* of the fish, Matt. 12. 40.
2. 1. prayed to God out of fish's b.
2. out of the *b.* of hell cried I
Luke 15. 16. fill his *b.* with husks
John 7. 38. out of his belly shall
Rom. 16. 18. serve their own *b.*
Phil. 3. 19. whose God is their *b.*
Rev. 10. 9. make thy *b.* bitter
Tit. 1. 12. Cretians slow *bellies*
R. V. Job 20. 20. within him; 31. 9. body; S. of S. 5. 14. body; Jer. 51. 34. maw; Tit. 1. 12. gluttons

BELONG, Lev. 27. 24. Luke 23. 7.
Gen. 40. 8. interpretations *b.* to
Deut. 29. 29. secret things *b.* to Lord, things revealed *b.* to us and to our children
Ps. 47. 9. shields of earth *b.* to God
68. 20. to God *b.* issues from death
Dan. 9. 9. to the Lord *b.* mercies
Mark 9. 41. because ye *b.* in Christ
Luke 19. 42. things that *b.* to thy
Deut. 32. 35. to me *b.* vengeance Ps. 94. 1. Heb. 10. 30. Rom. 12. 19.
Ezra 19. 4. this matter *belongeth* to
Ps. 3. 8. salvation *b.* to the Lord
62. 11. power *b.* to God, 12. *b.* mercy
Dan. 9. 7. righteousness *b.* to thee
Heb. 5. 14. strong meat *b.* to them

BELOVED — other hated, Deut. 21. 15.
Deut. 33. 12. *b.* of Lord shall dwell
Neh. 13. 26. Solomon *b.* of his God
Ps. 60. 5. thy *b.* may be delivered
127. 2. Lord giveth his *b.* sleep
S. of S. 1. 14. *my beloved*, 2. 3, 9, 16, 17. & 4. 16. & 5. 2, 6, 10, 16. & 6. 2, 3. & 7. 10, 13. Isa. 5. 1.
S. of S. 5. 9. thy *b.* more than another *b.*
Dan. 10. 11, 19. O man, greatly *b.* 9. 23.
Matt. 3. 17. my *b.* Son, 17. 5.
Rom. 9. 25. *b.* which was not *b.*
11. 28. *b.* for the Father's sake
16. 8. Amplias *b.* in the Lord
Eph. 1. 6. accepted in the *b.*
2 Pet. 3. 15. *b.* brother Paul
Rev. 20. 9. compassed *b.* city
R. V. Luke 9. 35. my chosen; Phile. 2. sister

BEMOAN, Jer. 15. 5. & 16. 5. & 22. 10. & 31. 18. & 48. 18.

BEND bow, Ps. 11. 2. & 64. 3. & 58. 7. & 7. 12. & 37. 1. Lam. 2. 4. & 3. 12. Isa. 5. 28.
Jer. 9. 3. *b.* their tongues like a bow
Isa. 60. 14. afflicted thee shall come *bending* unto thee
Hos. 11. 7. people *bent* to backslid.
Zech. 9. 13. I have *b.* Judah for me
R. V. Ps. 58. 7. aimeth

BENEATH, Prov. 15. 24. John 8. 23.

BENEFACTORS, Luke 22. 25.

BENEFITS, loaded us with, Ps. 68. 19.
Ps. 103. 2. forget not all his *b.*
116. 12. render to the Lord for all his *b.*
R. V. Phile. 14. goodness

BENEVOLENCE, due, 1 Cor. 7. 3.
R. V. 1 Cor. 7. 3. her due

BEREAVE soul of good, Eccl. 4. 8.
Jer. 15. 7. *b.* them of children, 18. 21. Gen. 42. 36. & 43. 14. Ezek. 5. 17. & 36. 12, 13, 14. Lam. 1. 20. Hos. 9. 12. & 13. 8.
R. V. Jer. 18. 21. childless

BESEECH God to be gracious, Mal. 1. 9.
2 Cor. 5. 20. as though God did b.
R. V. In O. T. mostly changed to pray; Phil. 4. 2; 1 Thes. 4. 10; Heb. 13. 22. exhort

BESET me behind and before, Ps. 139. 5.
Hos. 7. 2. own doings have *b.* them
Heb. 12. 1. sin which doth easily *b.* us

BESIDE waters, Ps. 23. 2. Isa. 32. 20.
S. of S. 1. 8. feed kids *b.* shepherd's
Isa. 56. 8. others *b.* I have gathered
R. V. Judg. 20. 36. against; Mat. 25. 20 —; Acts 26. 24. mad; 2 Pet. 1. 5. for this very cause

BESIDE SELF, Mark. 3. 21. Acts 26. 24. 2 Cor. 5. 13.

BESOM of destruction, Isa. 14. 23.

BESOUGHT the Lord, Deut. 3. 23. 2 Sam. 12. 16. 1 Kings 13. 6. 2 Kings 13. 4. 2 Chron. 33. 12. Ezra 8. 23. 2 Cor. 12. 8.

BEST estate is vanity, Ps. 39. 5.
Mic. 7. 4. *b.* of them is as a brier
Luke 15. 22. bring forth *b.* robe
1 Cor. 12. 31. covet earnestly *b.* gifts
R. V. 1 Cor. 12. 31. greater

BESTEAD, hardly, Isa. 8. 21.

BESTOW a blessing, Ex. 32. 29.
Luke 12. 17. room to *b.* my fruits
13. 3. *b.* all my goods to feed the
John 4. 38. *bestowed* no labor
1 Cor. 15. 10. his grace *b.* on me
2 Cor. 1. 11. gift *b.* on us by means
8. 1. grace of God *b.* on churches
Gal. 4. 11. lest *b.* labor in vain
1 John 3. 1. love the Father hath *b.* on us
R. V. 2 Cor. 8. 1. which hath been given in; John 4. 38. ye have not labored

BETIMES, 2 Chron. 36. 15. Job 8. 5. & 24. 5. Prov. 13. 24. Gen. 26. 31.
R. V. 2 Chron. 36. 15. early; Job 8. 5; 24. 5. diligently

BETRAY, Matt. 24. 10. & 26. 21. Mark 13. 12. & 14. 18.
R. V. In N. T. mostly, delivered up

BETROTH, Deut. 28. 30. Hos. 2. 19, 20.

BETTER than ten sons, 1 Sam. 1. 8.
Judg. 8. 2. gleanings *b.* than vintage
1 Kings 19. 4. I am not *b.* than
Prov. 15. 16. *b.* is little with the fear
17. *b.* is a dinner of herbs with love
16. 8. *b.* is a little with righteous.
16. how much *b.* to get wisdom
27. 10. *b.* is a neighbor near that
Eccl. 4. 9. two are *b.* than one
13. *b.* is a poor and wise child than
7. 1. *b.* is a good name than precious
2. *b.* to go to the house of mourning
3. *b.* is sorrow than laughter
5. *b.* to hear rebuke of the wise
9. 16. wisdom is *b.* than strength
18. wisdom is *b.* than weapons of
S. of S. 4. 10. how much *b.* is thy love than wine
Matt. 6. 26. are ye not much *b.* than
1 Cor. 9. 15. were *b.* for me to die
Phil. 1. 23. with Christ is far *b.*
2. 3. esteem others *b.* than them.
Heb. 1. 4. made so much *b.* than the angels.
6. 9. persuaded *b.* things of you
22. Jesus made surety of a *b.* testament
10. 34. a *b.* enduring substance
35. obtain a *b.* resurrection
40. provided some *b.* things
12. 24. blood speaketh *b.* than Abel
2 Pet. 2. 21. *b.* not to have known
R. V. Mat. 12. 12. of more value; Mark 9. 43; Luke 5. 39; 1 Cor. 9. 15. good

BETWEEN thy seed and her, Gen. 3. 15.
1 Kings 3. 9. discern *b.* good and
18. 21. how long halt ye *b.* two
Ezek. 22. 26. no difference *b.* holy and profane, 44. 23. & 34. 17. Lev. 10. 10.
Phil. 1. 23. in a strait *b.* two having
1 Tim. 2. 5. one mediator *b.* God

BEWARE of men, Matt. 10. 17.
Matt. 7. 15. *b.* of false prophets
16. 6. *b.* of leaven of Pharisees, 11. Mark 8. 15.
Luke 12. 15. *b.* of covetousness
Col. 2. 8. *b.* lest any man spoil you
R. V. Ex. 23. 21; Col. 2. 8. take heed; Luke 12. 15. keep yourselves from

BEYOND or defraud, 1 Thes. 4. 6.
R. V. 1 Thes. 4. 6. transgress

BIBBER, Prov. 23. 20. Matt. 11. 19.

BID, Matt. 22. 9. & 23. 3. Luke 14. 10, 24. 2 John 10, 11.

BIDE, not in unbelief, Rom. 11. 23.

BILL, Deut. 24. 1, 3. Isa. 50. 1. Jer. 3. 8. Mark 10. 4. Luke 16. 6, 7.
R. V. Luke 16. 6. bond

BILLOWS, Ps. 42. 7. Jonah 2. 3.

BIND sweet influences, Job 38. 31.
Job 31. 36. I would *b.* it as a crown
Ps. 105. 22. to *b.* his princes at
118. 27. *b.* the sacrifice with cords
Prov. 3. 3. *b.* them about thy neck
Isa. 8. 16. *b.* up testimony, seal law
Matt. 12. 29. first *b.* strong man and
13. 30. *b.* them in bundles to burn
16. 19. thou shalt *b.* on earth, 18. 18.
22. 13. *b.* him hand and foot, and
Bindeth up, Job 5. 18. Ps. 147. 3.

BIRD hasteth to snare, Prov. 7. 23.
Ps. 124. 7. escaped as a *b.* out of the
Eccl. 10. 20. *b.* of air tell the matter
Isa. 46. 11. ravenous *b.* from the east
Jer. 12. 9. heritage as a speckled *b.*
Birds, Gen. 15. 10. & 40. 17. Lev. 14. 4. 2 Sam. 21. 10. Ps. 104. 17. Eccl. 9. 12. S. of S. 2. 12. Isa. 31. 5. Jer. 5. 27. & 12. 4, 9. Matt. 8. 20.

BIRTH, 2 Kings 19. 3. Eccl. 7. 1. Isa. 66. 9. Ezek. 16. 3. Gal. 4. 19.
Birthday, Gen. 40. 20. Matt. 14. 6.
Birthright, Gen. 25. 31, 32, 33. & 27. 36. & 43. 33. 1 Chron. 5. 1. Heb. 12. 16.

BISHOP, 1 Tim. 3. 1, 2. Tit. 1. 7.
1 Pet. 2. 25. return to *b.* of souls
Phil. 1. 1. with *bishops* and deacons

BITE, Num. 21. 6, 8, 9. Eccl. 10. 8, 11. Jer. 8. 17. Amos 9. 3. Hab. 2. 7.

Mic. 3. 5. prophets *b.* with their
Gal. 5. 15. if ye *b.* and devour one another
Prov. 23. 32. at the last it *b.* like a
BITTER made their lives, Ex. 1. 14.
Ex. 12. 8. with *b.* herbs eat it, Num. 9. 11.
Deut. 32. 24. devoured with *b.* destruction
32. their grapes of gall, clusters are *b.*
2 Kings 14. 26. affliction was very *b.*
Job 3. 20. why is life given to the *b.* in soul
Ps. 64. 3. their arrows even *b.* words
Prov. 27. 7. every *b.* thing is sweet
Isa. 5. 20. woe to them put *b.* for
Jer. 2. 19. evil thing and *b.* that
Col. 3. 19. wives be not *b.* against
Rev. 10. 9. it shall make thy belly *b.*
Judg. 5. 23. curse *bitterly* inhabit.
Ruth 1. 20. Almighty dealt *b.* with
Isa. 22. 4. I will weep *b.*, 33. 7.
Hos. 12. 14. provoked him most *b.*
Matt. 26. 75. wept *b.*, Luke 22. 62.
Bitterness of soul, 1 Sam. 1. 10.
1 Sam. 15. 32. *b.* of death is past
2 Sam. 2. 26. it will be *b.* in end
Prov. 14. 10. heart knows its own *b.*
Zech. 12. 10. in *b.* for first-born
Acts 8. 23. in gall of *b.* and bond of
Rom. 3. 14. mouth full of cursing and *b.*
Heb. 12. 15. root of *b.* springing up
R. V. Job 23. 2. rebellious
BITTERN, Isa. 14. 23. & 34. 11.
BLACK, 1 Kings 18. 45. Matt. 5. 36.
S. of S. 1. 5. I am *b.* but comely, 6.
Blackness of darkness, Heb. 12. 18
Jude 13.
R. V. S. of S. 1. 6. swarthy
BLAME, Gen. 43. 9. & 44. 32. 2 Cor. 8. 20. Eph. 1. 4.
Blamed, 2 Cor. 6. 3. Gal. 2. 11.
Blameless, Gen. 44. 10. Josh. 2. 17. Judg. 15. 3. Matt. 12. 5. Phil. 3. 6. 1 Tim. 5. 7.
Luke 1. 6. in all the ordinances of the Lord *b.*
1 Cor. 1. 8. be *b.* in the day of our
1 Thes. 5. 23. be preserved *b.*
1 Tim. 3. 2. bishop must be *b.*
Tit. 1. 6, 7, 10. office of deacon found *b.*
2 Pet. 3. 14. without spot and *b.*
R. V. Eph. 1. 4. blemish; Matt. 12. 5. guiltless; 1 Tim. 3. 2; 5. 7. without reproach
BLASPHEME, revile God, &c.
Ps. 74. 10. enemy *b.* thy name
Mark 3. 29. *b.* against Holy Ghost
Acts 26. 11. compelled them to *b.*
1 Tim. 1. 20. may learn not to *b.*
Lev. 24. 11. *blasphemed* the name of the Lord
2 Kings 19. 6. servants *b.* me, Isa. 37. 6.
Isa. 52. 5. my name continually is *b.*
Rom. 2. 24. the name of God is *b.*
Tit. 2. 5. word of God be not *b.*
Rev. 16. 9, 11, 21. *b.* the God of
Lev. 24. 16. *blasphemeth* put to death
Matt. 9. 3. said this man *b.*
Luke 12. 10. to him that *b.* against the Holy Ghost
Blasphemer, 1 Tim. 1. 13. & 2 Tim. 3. 2.
Blasphemy, 2 Kings 19. 3. Isa 37. 3. Matt. 12. 31. Mark 7. 22. Col. 3. 8. Rev. 2. 9.
R. V. 2 Tim. 3. 2. railers; 2 Kings 19. 3; Isa. 37. 3. contumely; Mark 7. 22; Col. 3. 8. railing
BLAST, Ex. 15. 8. 2 Sam. 22. 16. 2 Kings 19. 7. Job 4. 9. Isa. 25. 4.
Blasting, Deut. 28. 22. 1 Kings 8. 37.
BLEMISH, without, Ex. 12. 5. & 29. 1. Lev. 1. 3, 10. & 4. 23.
Dan. 1. 4. children and no *b.*
Eph. 5. 27. church holy, and without *b.*
1 Pet. 1. 19. as a lamb without *b.*
BLESS them that *b.* thee, Gen. 12. 3.
Gen. 22. 17. in blessing I will *b.* thee
Gen. 32. 26. not let thee go except thou *b.* me
Ex. 23. 25. *b.* thy bread and water
Num. 6. 24. Lord *b.* and keep thee
Ps. 5. 12. wilt *b.* the righteous
29. 11. will *b.* his people with peace
67. 1. be merciful to us and *b.* us
115. 13. he will *b.* them that fear
Matt. 5. 44. *b.* them that curse you
Rom. 12. 14. *b.* them that persecute
Acts 3. 26. sent him to *b.* you in turning many
1 Cor. 4. 12. being reviled we *b.*
Bless the Lord, Deut. 8. 10. Judg. 5. 9. Ps. 16. 7. & 34. 1. & 103. 1, 21, 22. & 104. 1, 35. & 26. 12.
Bless thee, Ps. 63. 4. & 145. 2, 10.
Gen. 1. 22. God *blessed* them and
2. 3. God *b.* the seventh day
Ex. 20. 11. the Lord *b.* the sabbath
Ps. 33. 12, 13. *b.* whose God is the
Prov. 10. 7. memory of the just is *b.*
Matt. 13. 16. *b.* are eyes, they see, Luke 10. 23.
24. 46. *b.* is that servant when his
43. Lord cometh, Luke 12. 37, 38.
Mark 10. 16. took them in his arms and *b.* them
Luke 1. 28, 42. *b.* art thou among
48. all generations shall call me *b.*
Acts 20. 35. more *b.* to give than to
Rom. 1. 25. Creator *b.* for ever, 9. 5.
2 Cor. 11. 31. Eph. 1. 3. 1 Pet. 1. 3.
1 Tim. 1. 11. glorious gospel of *b.*
Ps. 119. 1 *b.* are the undefiled in
84. 4. *b. are they* that dwell in thy
106. 3. *b.* — that keep judgment
Prov. 8. 32. *b.* — that keep my ways
Isa. 30. 18. *b.* — that wait for him
Matt. 5. 3–11. *b.*—the poor in spirit — mourn — meek — hunger and thirst — merciful — pure in heart — peacemakers, persecuted — when men revile you, Luke 6. 21, 22.
Luke 11. 28. *b.*—that hear the word and do it
John 20. 29. *b.* — that have not seen, and yet have believed
Rom. 4. 7. *b.* — whose iniquities are forgiven
Rev. 19. 9. *b.* — called to the marriage supper
22. 14. *b.* — that do his command.
Num. 24. 9. *b.* is *he* that blesseth
Ps. 32. 1. *b.* — whose transgression is forgiven
41. 1. *b.* — that considereth the
Dan. 12. 12. *b.* — that waiteth and cometh
Matt. 11. 6. *b.* — who shall not be off
21. 9. *b.* — cometh in the name of the Lord, 23. 39. Mark 11. 19. Luke 13. 35.
Rev. 1. 3. *b.* — that readeth this
16. 15. *b.* — that watcheth and keep.
20. 6. *b.* — that hath part in the first resurrection
22. 7. *b.* — that keepeth the sayings of this book
Ps. 1. 1. *b. is the man* that walketh not in the counsel of the ungodly
34. 8. *b.* — that trusteth in him, 84. 12.
65. 4. *b.* — whom thou choosest
84. 5. *b.* — whose strength is in thee
112. 1. *b.* — that feareth the Lord
Prov. 8. 34. *b.* — that heareth me
Isa. 56. 2. *b.* — that doeth this, and
Ps. 49. 18. he *blesseth* his soul
Blessedness, Rom. 4. 6, 9. Gal. 4. 15.
Gen. 12. 2. thou shalt be a *blessing*
27. 36. he hath taken away my *b.*
28. 4. give thee *b.* of Abraham
Deut. 11. 26. set before you a *b.* and a curse, 30. 19. Jas. 3. 9, 10.
23. 5. turned curse into *b.*, Neh. 13. 2.
Neh. 9. 5. exalted above all *b.*
Job 29. 13. *b.* of him ready to perish
Ps. 3. 8. thy *b.* is upon thy people
129. 8. the *b.* of Lord be upon you
Isa. 65. 8. destroy it not for a *b.* is
Joel 2. 14. leaveth a *b.* behind him
1 Cor. 10. 16. the cup of *b.* which
Gal. 3. 14. *b.* of Abraham might
Blessings, Gen. 49. 25, 26. Josh. 8. 34. Ps. 21. 3. Prov. 10. 6. & 28. 20.
BLIND, Ex. 4. 11. Lev. 21. 18.
Job 29. 15. I was eyes to the *b.*
Ps. 146. 8. openeth the eyes of the *b.*
Isa. 42. 7. to open the *b.* eyes, 18.
19. who is *b.* but my servant ?
43. 8. bring the *b.* people that have
56. 10. his watchmen are *b.*
Matt. 11. 5. the *b.* receive sight, Luke 7. 21.
23. 16. woe to you, *b.* guides, 24.
Luke 4. 18. recovery of sight to *b.*
Rev. 3. 17. thou art *b.* and naked
John 12. 40. *blinded* their eyes
Rom. 11. 7. the rest were *b.*
2 Cor. 3. 14. their minds were *b.*
4. 4. the God of this world hath *b.* the minds
1 John 2. 11. darkness hath *b.* his
R. V. Rom. 11. 7; 2 Cor. 3. 14. hardened
BLOOD of grapes, Gen. 49. 11.
Job. 16. 18. cover not thou my *b.*
Ps. 9. 12. maketh inquisition for *b.*
72. 14. precious their *b.* in his
Isa. 26. 21. the earth shall disclose her *b.*
Ezek. 3. 18. his *b.* will I require
9. 9. the land is full of *b.*
16. 6. polluted in thine own *b.*
Hos. 4. 2. they break out, and *b.*
Mic. 3. 10. they build up Zion with *b.*
Matt. 26. 28. *b.* of New Testament
Mark 14. 24. Luke 22. 20. 1 Cor. 11. 25. & 27. 8. field of *b.*, Acts 1. 19.
25. his *b.* be on us and on our child.
Luke 13. 1. whose *b.* Pilate had
22. 44. as it were great drops of *b.*
John 1. 13. born not of *b.* nor of flesh
6. 54, 56. whoso drink. my *b.* hath
55. my *b.* is drink indeed
19. 34. out of his side came *b.* and
Acts 17. 26. made of one *b.* all
18. 6. your *b.* be upon your own
Rom. 3. 25. through faith in his *b.*
5. 9. being justified by his *b.*
1 Cor. 11. 27. guilty of body and *b.* of Christ
Col. 1. 20. made peace through the *b.* of the cross
Heb. 9. 20. this is the *b.* of the test.
22. without shedding of *b.* no
10. 19. into the holiest by the *b.* of
12. 4. ye have not yet resisted unto *b.*
24. *b.* of sprinkling that speaketh
1 Pet. 1. 2. sprinkling of the *b.* of
19. with precious *b.* of Christ
1 John 1. 7. his *b.* cleanseth from
5. 6. came by water and *b.*
Rev. 1. 5. washed us in his own *b.*
6. 10. dost thou not avenge our *b.*
7. 14. made white in the *b.* of the
8. 7. hail and fire mingled with *b.*
12. 11. overcame by the *b.* of the
16. 6. shed *b.* — given them *b.* to
17. 6. drunken with the *b.* of saints
Blood-guiltiness, Ps. 51. 14.
Bloody, Ex. 4. 25, 26. Ps. 5. 6. & 55. 23.
R. V. Ps. 5. 6; 55. 23; 59. 2; 139. 19. bloodthirsty; Acts 28. 8. dysentery
BLOSSOM, man's rod shall, Num. 17. 5.
Isa. 5. 24. their *b.* shall go up as dust
27. 6. Israel shall *b.* and bud
35. 1. the desert shall *b.* as the
Hab. 3. 17. the fig-tree shall not *b.*
Ezek. 7. 10. rod hath *blossomed* pride
R. V. Num. 17. 5. *bud.*
BLOT, Job 31. 7. Prov. 9. 7.
Ex. 32. 32, 33. *b.* me out of thy book, Num. 5. 23. Ps. 69. 28. Rev. 3. 5.
Blot out their *name* or remem. Deut. 9. 14. & 25. 19. & 29. 20. 2 Kings 14. 27. Ps. 109. 13.
Blot out sin, transgression, ini-

quity, Neh. 4. 5. Ps. 51. 1, 9. & 109. 14.
Isa. 43. 25. & 44. 22. Jer. 18. 23. Acts 3. 19.
Col. 2. 14. *blotting* out the handwriting
R. V. Job. 31. 7. spot.
BLOW on my garden, S. of S. 4. 16.
Hag. 1. 9. I did *b.* upon it
John 3. 8. wind *bloweth* where it
BLUSH to lift up my face, Ezra 9. 6.
Jer. 6. 15. neither could they *b.* 8. 12.
BOAST, Ps. 10. 3. & 34. 2. & 49. 6. & 52. 1.
Prov. 20. 14. & 25. 14. Jas. 3. 5.
Ps. 44. 8. in God we *b.* all the day
Prov. 27. 1. *b.* not of to-morrow
Boasting, Acts 5. 36. Rom. 3. 27.
Jas. 4. 16. now ye rejoice in your *b.*
Rom. 1. 30. proud *boasters*, 2 Tim. 3. 2.
R. V. Rom. 11. 18; 2 Cor. 9. 2; 10. 8. glory.
BODY of heaven, Ex. 24. 10.
Job 19. 26. though worms destroy this *b.*
Matt. 6. 22. *b.* full of light, Luke 11. 34.
10. 28. them that kill the *b.*, Luke 12. 4.
Matt. 26. 26. this is my *b.*, 1 Cor. 11. 24.
Rom. 6. 6. the *b.* of sin be destroyed
7. 4. dead to the law by the *b.* of
24. deliver me from the *b.* of this
8. 10. *b.* is dead because of sin
13. do mortify deeds of the *b.*
23. the redemption of our *b.*
1 Cor. 6. 13. *b.* is not for fornication, for the Lord; and the Lord for the *b.*
18. every sin a man doeth is without the *b.*
19. your *b.* is the temple of the Holy Ghost
7. 4. wife hath not power of her own *b.*
9. 27. I keep under my *b.* and
10. 16. communion of *b.* of Christ
11. 27. guilty of *b.* and blood of the
29. not discerning the Lord's *b.*
12. 14. the *b.* is not one member
27. ye are the *b.* of Christ
15. 35. with what *b.* do they come?
44. sown a natural *b.* raised a spiritual *b.*
Eph. 3. 6. fellow heirs of the same *b.*
5. 23. he is the Saviour of the *b.*
Phil. 3. 21. who shall change our vile *b.*
Col. 1. 18. he is the head of the *b.* the church
2. 11. putting off the *b.* of sins of
17. shadow—but the *b.* is of Christ
23. neglecting of the *b.*
1 Thes. 5. 23. spirit, soul, and *b.* be
Jas. 3. 6. able to bridle the whole *b.*
Jude 9. disputed about the *b.* of
John 2. 21. his own *b.*, 1 Cor. 6. 18. 1 Pet. 2. 24.
1 Cor. 5. 3. in the *b.*, 2 Cor. 5. 6, 10. & 12. 2. Phil. 1. 20. Heb. 13. 3.
Deut. 28. 11, 18, 53. fruit of the *b.*, 30. 9. Ps. 132. 11. Mic. 6. 7.
Rom. 8. 11. quicken your mortal *bodies*
12. 1. present your *b.* a living sacri.
1 Cor. 6. 15. your *b.* are members of
Eph. 5. 28. husbands love your wives as your own *b.*
Luke 3. 22. Holy Ghost descended in a *bodily* shape
2 Cor. 10. 10. his *b.* presence is
Col. 2. 9. dwelleth the fulness of the godhead *b.*
1 Tim. 4. 8. *b.* exercise profiteth
R. V. Isa. 51. 23. back; Matt. 14. 12; 15. 45. corpse
BOLD as a lion, Prov. 28. 1.
2 Cor. 10. 1. being absent am *b.*
11. 21. if any is *b.* I am *b.* also
Phil. 1. 14. are much more *b.* to
Mark 15. 43. went *boldly* unto Pilate
Heb. 4. 16. come *b.* to the throne of
2 Cor. 7. 4. great is my *boldness* of
Heb. 10. 19. *b.* to enter into the
1 John 4. 17. *b.* in the day of judg.
R. V. 2 Cor. 10. 1. good courage; 7. 26. openly; Eph. 6. 19 ——; Heb. 13. 6. with good courage; Eccl. 8. 1. hardness
BOND of the covenant, Ezek. 20. 37.
Acts 8. 23. in gall and *b.* of iniquity
1 Cor. 12. 13. *bond and free*, Gal. 3. 28. Eph. 6. 8. Col. 3. 11. Rev. 6. 15. & 13. 16. & 19. 18.
Ps. 116. 16. has loosed my *bonds*
Job. 12. 18. he looseth *b.* of kings
Acts 20. 23. *b.* and afflictions abide
23. 29. worthy of death or of *b.*
26. 29. such as I am except these *b.*
Eph. 6. 20. I am an ambassador in *b.*
Phil. 1. 16. to add affliction to my *b.*
2 Tim. 2. 9. suffer trouble even unto *b.*
Phile. 10. whom I have begotten in my *b.*
Heb. 10. 34. compassion in my *b.*
13. 3. remember them that are in *b.*
Ex. 13. 3. house of *bondage*, 20. 2.
1. 14. lives bitter with hard *b.*
2. 23. sighed by reason of the *b.*
Rom. 8. 15. received again the spirit of *b.*
1 Cor. 7. 15. brother or sister is not in *b.*
Gal. 4. 24. Sinai which gendereth to *b.*
5. 1. entangled with the yoke of *b.*
Bondwoman, Gen. 21. 10. Gal. 4. 23, 30.
BONDMAID, laws concerning, Lev. 19. 20. & 25. 44.
BONDMAN, laws concerning, Lev. 25. 39. Deut. 15. 12.
R. V. Ex. 1. 14; Isa. 14. 3. serve; Deut. 7. 8; Jer. 34. 13. bondage; 1 Kings 9. 22 bondservants; Gal. 4. 23, 30, 31. handmaid
BONE of my bone and flesh of my, Gen. 2. 23. & 29. 14. Judg. 9. 2. 2 Sam. 5. 1. & 19. 13. 1 Chron. 11. 11.
Ex. 12. 46. not break a *b.* of it
John 19. 36. *b.* of him shall not be
Ps. 51. 8. *b.* thou hast broken may
Eccl. 11. 5. how the *b.* grow in the
Matt. 23. 27. full of dead men's *b.*
His bones, Ps. 34. 20. Eph. 5. 30. Job 20. 11. Ezek. 32. 27. Prov. 12. 4.
Ps. 6. 2. *my bones* are vexed
22. 14. all—are out of joint
31. 10.—are consumed
38. 3. there is no rest—
102. 3.—are burnt as an hearth
5—cleave to my skin
BONNETS, of the priests, directions for making, Ex. 28. 40. & 29. 9. & 39. 28. Ezek. 44. 18. *See* MITRE.
BOOK, Gen. 5. 1. Esth. 6. 1.
Ex. 32. 32. blot me out of thy *b.*
Job 19. 23. O that they were printed in a *b.*
31. 35. mine adversary had written a *b.*
Ps. 40. 7. in the volume of the *b.*, Heb. 10. 7.
Book of life, Phil. 4. 3. Rev. 3. 5. & 13. 8. & 17. 8. & 20. 12, 15. & 21. 27. & 22. 19.
Books, Eccl. 12. 12. Dan. 7. 10. & 9. 2. John 21. 25. 2 Tim. 4. 13. Rev. 20. 12.
R. V. 1 Chr. 29. 29; 2 Chron. 9. 29; 12. 15; 20. 34. history; Jer. 32. 12.
BOOTHS, Lev. 23. 42, 43. Neh. 8. 14.
BORDER of his garment, Mark 6. 56.
BORING of the ear, Ex. 21. 6.
BORN to trouble, man is, Job 5. 7.
Job 14. 1. *b.* of a woman, 15. 14. & 25. 4. Matt. 11. 11. Luke 7. 28.
Ps. 58. 3. the wicked go astray as soon as they are *b.*
Ps. 87. 5. this and that man was *b.* in her
Prov. 17. 17. a brother is *b.* for
Eccl. 3. 2. a time to be *b.* and a time to die
Isa. 9. 6. unto us a child is *b.* a son
66. 8. shall a nation be *b.* at once
Jer. 15. 10. *borne* me a man of strife
Matt. 11. 11. among them that are *b.* of women
John 3. 4. can a man be *b.* when
5. *b.* of water and of the Spirit
Rom. 9. 11. children being not yet *b.*
1 Cor. 15. 8. one *b.* out of due time
Gal. 4. 23. *b.* after the flesh, 29.
1 Pet. 2. 2. as new *b.* babes desire sincere milk of
John 3. 3, 5, 7. *b.* again
John 1. 13. *born of God*, 1 John 3 9. & 4. 7. & 5. 1, 4, 18.
BORROW, Deut. 15. 6. & 28. 12.
Ex. 22. 14. *b.* aught of his neighbor, 3. 22. & 11. 2. & 12. 35.
Matt. 5. 42. would *b.* of thee turn
Ps. 37. 21. the wicked *borroweth* and payeth not
Prov. 22. 7. *borrower* is servant to
Isa. 24. 2. as with the lender so with *b.*
R. V. Ex. 3. 22; 11. 2; 12. 35. ask
BOSOM, Gen. 16. 5. Ex. 4. 6.
Num. 11. 12. carry them in *b.* as a
Deut. 13. 6. wife of thy *b.*, 28. 54, 56.
Ps. 35. 13. prayer returned into my own *b.*
Prov. 5. 20. why embrace the *b.* of a
6. 27. take fire in his *b.* and not be
17. 23. gift out of *b.* to pervert, 21. 14.
19. 24. hideth his hands in his *b.* 26. 15.
Isa. 40. 11. carry them in his *b.*
65. 6, 7. recompense into their *b.*
Ps. 79. 12. Jer. 32. 18.
Mic. 7. 5. her that lieth in thy *b.*
Luke 6. 38. shall men give into your *b.*
16. 22. carried into Abraham's *b.*, 23.
John 1. 18. who is in the *b.* of the Father, 13. 23. leaning on Jesus' *b.*
R. V. Prov. 19. 24; 26. 15. dish
BOTH, Gen. 2. 25. & 3. 7. & 19. 36.
Zech. 6. 13. counsel of peace between *b.*
Eph. 2. 14. our peace made *b.* one
18. we *b.* have access by one spirit
BOTTLE, Gen. 21. 14, 15, 19.
Ps. 56. 8. put my tears into thy *b.*
Jer. 13. 12. every *b.* filled with wine
Job 38. 37. who can stay *bottles* of
Matt. 9. 17. new wine into old *b.*
Mark 2. 22. new wine into new *b.* Matt. 9. 17.
R. V. generally, skins or wine skins
BOTTOMLESS pit, Rev. 9. 1. & 11. 7. & 17. 8.
Satan bound there, Rev. 20. 1, 2.
BOUGHT, Gen. 17. 12, 13. & 33. 19.
Deut. 32. 6. he thy father that *b.*
Matt. 13. 46. sold all and *b.* it
1 Cor. 6. 20. *b.* with a price, 7. 23.
2 Pet. 2. 1. denying the Lord that *b.* them
BOUND Isaac, Gen. 22. 9.
Job 36. 8. if they be *b.* in fetters
Ps. 107. 10. being *b.* in affliction
Prov. 22. 15. foolishness *b.* in heart
Matt. 16. 19. whatsoever ye bind on earth shall be *b.* in heaven, 18 18.
Acts 20. 22. I go *b.* in the spirit
21. 13. ready not to be *b.* only, but
Rom. 7. 2. wife is *b.* to her husband, 1 Cor. 7. 39.
1 Cor. 7. 27. art thou *b.* to a wife, seek
2 Tim. 2. 9. the word of God is not *b.*
Heb. 13. 3. in bonds as *b.* with them
Isa. 1. 6. closed nor *bound up*
Ezek. 30. 21. not—to be healed
34. 4. neither have ye *b.* the broken
Hos. 13. 12. iniquity of Ephraim is

BOUNTY, 1 Kings 10. 13. 2 Cor. 9. 5.
Prov. 22. 9. *bountiful* eye be blessed
Ps. 13. 6. dealt *bountifully* with me, 116. 7. & 119. 17. & 142. 7.
2 Cor. 9. 6. he that sows *b.* shall reap *b.*
BOW in the clouds, Gen. 9. 13, 14, 16.
Gen. 49. 24. his *b.* abode in strength
Josh. 24. 12. not with sword nor *b.*
2 Sam. 1. 18. teach children use of *b.*
Ps. 7. 12. he hath bent his *b.*
44. 6. I will not trust in my *b.*
78. 57. turned aside like a deceit. *b.*
Jer. 9. 3. bend tongue like a *b.* for
Lam. 2. 4. bent his *b.* like an enemy
Lam. 3. 12. bent his *b.* and set me
Hos. 1. 5. break the *b.* of Israel
17. I will not save them by *b.*
7. 16. turned like a deceitful *b.*
1 Sam. 2. 4. Ps. 37. 15. *bows*, & 64. 3. & 78. 9. Jer. 51. 56.
Bow down thine ear, 2 Kings 19. 16. Ps. 31. 2. & 86. 1. Prov. 22. 17.
Job 31. 10. let others — upon her
Ps. 95. 6. let us — and worship
Gen. 23. 12. Abraham *bowed down* himself before the people, 27. 29.
Judg. 7. 5, 6. — on their knees to
Ps. 38. 6. I am—greatly, I go mourning all the day long
Isa. 2. 11. haughtiness of men —, 17.
BOWELS did yearn, Gen. 43. 30. 1 Kings 3. 26. 2 Chron. 21. 15, 18.
Ps. 71. 6. took me out of my mother's *b.*
Isa. 63. 15. where is the sounding of thy *b.*
Jer. 4. 19. my *b.* my *b.* I am pained
31. 20. my *b.* are troubled for him, Lam. 1. 20. & 2. 11. S. of S. 5. 4.
Acts 1. 18. all his *b.* gushed out
2 Cor. 6. 12. straitened in your *b.*
Phil. 1. 8. I long after you in the *b.* of Christ
2. 1. if any comfort, if any *b.* and
Col. 3. 12. put on *b.* of mercies
1 John 3. 17. shutteth up *b.* of
R. V. Ps. 109. 18. inward parts; 2 Cor. 6. 12. affections; Phil. 1. 8; 2. 1. tender mercies; Col. 3. 12; Phile. 7. 20. heart
BOWL, Num. 7. 85. Eccl. 12. 6. Zech. 4. 2, 3. & 9. 15. & 14. 20.
R. V. Ex. 25. 31, 33, 34; 37. 17, 19, 20; 1 Kings 7. 50; 2 Kings 12. 13. cups; 2 Kings 25. 15; 1 Chr. 28. 17; Jer. 52. 18. basons
BOYS, Gen. 25. 27. Zech. 8. 5.
BRAKE the tables, Ex. 32. 19. & 34. 1. Deut. 9. 17. & 10. 2.
Judg. 16. 12. Samson *b.* the new
1 Sam. 4. 18. Eli *b.* his neck and
1 Kings 19. 11. wind *b.* in pieces the
2 Kings 11. 18. *b.* Baal's image, 10. 27.
18. 4. *b.* the images and brazen ser.
23. 14. *b.* in pieces the images, 2 Chron. 31. 1.
Job 29. 17. *b.* the jaws of the wick.
Ps. 76. 3. *b.* the arrows of the bow
105. 16. *b.* the whole staff of bread
Jer. 31. 32. my covenant they *b.*, Ezek. 17. 16.
Dan. 2. 1. his sleep *b.* from him
6. 24. *b.* all their bones to pieces
Matt. 14. 19. blessed, and *b.* and gave, 15. 36. & 26. 26. Mark 6. 41. & 8. 6. & 14. 22. Luke 9. 16. & 22. 19. & 24. 30. 1 Cor. 11. 24.
Mark 14. 3. *b.* box and poured the
Brake down images—altars of Baal, 2 Kings 10. 27. & 11. 18. 2 Chron. 14. 3. & 23. 17. & 34. 4. — wall of Jerusalem, 2 Kings 14. 13. & 25. 10. 2 Chron. 25. 23. & 36. 19. Jer. 39. 8. & 52. 14. — houses of Sodomites — high places — altars — altar of Bethel, 2 Kings 23. 7, 8, 12, 15.
BRAMBLE, Judg. 9. 14. Luke 6. 44.
R. V. Isa. 34. 13. thistles

BRANCH, with clusters of grapes, Num. 13. 23. Isa. 17. 9. &. 18. 5.
Job 15. 32. his *b.* shall not be green
Ps. 80. 15. *b.* thou madest strong
Prov. 11. 28. the right. flourish as a *b.*
Isa. 4. 2. *b.* of the Lord be beautiful
9. 14. cut off *b.* and root, 19. 15.
14. 19. cast out like an abomi. *b.*
25. 5. *b.* of terrible ones be brought
Jer. 23. 5. unto David a righteous *b.*
Ezek. 8. 17. they put *b.* to their nose
Zech. 3. 8. bring forth my servant *b.*
6. 12. behold man whose name is *b*
Mal. 4. 1. leave neither root nor *b.*
Matt. 24. 32. when his *b.* is yet ten.
John 15. 2. every *b.* in me that bear
4. *b.* cannot bear fruit of itself
Lev. 23. 40. take *branches* of palm-trees, Neh. 8. 15. John 12. 13.
Job 15. 30. flame shall dry up his *b.*
Ps. 80. 11. sent her *b.* unto the river
104. 12. fowls sing among the *b.*
Isa. 16. 8. her *b.* are stretched out
Jer. 11. 16. the *b.* of it are broken, Ezek. 17. 6, 7. & 19. 10, 14.
Dan. 4. 14. hewn down tree, cut off *b.*
Hos. 14. 6. his *b.* shall spread as
Zech. 4. 12. what be these two olive *b.*
John 15. 5. I am the vine, ye are the *b.*
Rom. 11. 6. if root be holy, so are *b.*
17. if some of the *b.* be broken off
21. God spared not natural *b.*, 24.
BRAND, Judg. 15. 5. Zech. 3. 2.
BRASS, Gen. 4. 22. Dan. 5. 4.
Num. 21. 9. made serpent of *b.*
Deut. 8. 9. out of whose hills mayest dig *b.*
28. 23. heaven over thy head shall *b.*
Job 6. 12. is my strength of *b.*—flesh
41. 27. he esteemeth *b.* as rotten
Isa. 48. 4. thy neck iron, and brow *b.*
60. 17. for wood I will bring *b.*
Dan. 2. 32. belly and thighs of *b.*
Zech. 6. 1. were mountains of *b.*
1 Cor. 13. 1. become as sounding *b.*
Rev. 1. 15. feet like fine *b.*, 2. 18.
Brazen, Num. 16. 39. 2 Kings 18. 4. & 25. 13. 2 Chron. 6. 13. Jer. 1. 18. & 15. 20. & 52. 20. Mark 7. 4.
BRAWLER, 1 Tim. 3. 3. Tit. 3. 2.
Prov. 21. 9. & 25. 24. *brawling* woman
R. V. 1 Tim. 3. 3. contentious
BRAY, Job 6. 5. Prov. 27. 22.
BREACH, be upon thee, Gen. 38. 29.
Num. 14. 34. know my *b.* of promise
Judg. 21. 15. Lord made *b.* in tribes
2 Sam. 6. 8. Lord made *b.* on Uzza, 1 Chron. 13. 11. & 15. 13.
Job 16. 14. break. me with *b.* upon *b.*
Ps. 106. 23. Moses stood in the *b.*
Isa. 30. 13. this iniq. shall be as *b.*
Lam. 2. 13. thy *b.* is great like sea
Ps. 60. 2. heal *breaches* thereof
R. V. Num. 14. 34. alienation; Judg. 5. 17. creeks; Isa. 30. 26. hurt
BREAD shall be fat, Gen. 49. 20.
Ex. 16. 4. I will rain *b.* from heaven
Lev. 21. 6. *b.* of their God they offer
Num. 14. 9. they are *b.* for us
21. 5. soul loatheth this light *b.*
Deut. 8. 3. not live by *b.* only, Matt. 4. 4.
Ruth 1. 6. visited his people giving *b.*
1 Sam. 2. 5. hired themselves for *b.*
1 Kings 18. 4. fed them with *b.* and
Neh. 5. 14. not eaten *b.* of gover., 18
9. 15. gavest them *b.* from heaven
Ps. 37. 25. nor his seed begging *b.*
78. 20. can he give *b.* also
80. 5. feedest them with *b.* of tears
102. 9. I have eaten ashes like *b.*
132. 15. satisfy her poor with *b.*
Prov. 9. 17. *b.* eaten in secret
31. 27. she eateth not *b.* of idleness

Eccl. 9. 11. nor yet *b.* to the wise
11. 1. cast thy *b.* upon the waters
Isa. 3. 1. whole stay of *b.*, 7.
30. 20. Lord give you *b.* of adversi.
55. 2. spend money for that is not *b.*
10. give seed to sower, *b.* to eater
Lam. 4. 4. the young children ask *b.*
Ezek. 18. 7. hath given *b.* to hun.
Hos. 2. 5. give me my *b.* and water
Amos 4. 6. want of *b.* in all your
Mal. 1. 7. ye offer polluted *b.* on
Matt. 4. 3. these stones be made *b.*
4. not live by *b.* alone, Luke 4. 4.
6. 11. this day our daily *b.*, Luke 11. 11.
7. 9. son ask *b.* will he give a stone
15. 26. meet to take the children's *b.*
26. 26. took *b.* and blessed it
Mark 8. 4. satisfy these men with *b.*
Luke 7. 33. neither eating *b.* nor
15. 17. servants have *b.* enough
24. 35. known in breaking of *b.*
John 6. 32. Moses gave you not that *b.*
33. the *b.* of God is he that cometh
34. evermore give us this *b.*
35. I am *b.* of life, 48. true *b.* 32.
41. I am the *b.* which came down
50. this is the *b.* that cometh down
13. 18. he that eateth *b.* with me
Acts 2. 42. breaking *b.* and in pray.
20. 7. came together to break *b.*
27. 35. he took *b.* and gave thanks
1 Cor. 10. 16. *b.* we break is it not
11. 23. night he was betrayed took *b.*
26. as often as ye eat this *b.*, 27.
Deut. 16. 3. *bread of affliction*, 1 Kings 22. 27. 2 Chron. 18. 26. Isa. 30. 20.
Gen. 3. 19. *shall eat bread*, 28. 20. Ps. 14. 4. & 127. 2. Prov. 25. 21. Eccl. 9. 7. Mark 7. 5. Luke 14. 15. 1 Cor. 11. 26. 2 Thes. 3. 12.
1 Sam. 2. 36. *piece of bread*, Prov. 6. 26. & 28. 21. Jer. 37. 21. Ezek. 13. 19.
Lev. 26. 26. *break staff of bread*, Ps. 105. 16. Ezek. 4. 16. & 5. 16. & 14. 13.
Gen. 19. 3. *unleavened bread*, Ex. 12. 8, 15. & 18. 20. & 13. 6, 7. Mark 14. 12. Luke 22. 7. Acts 12. 3. & 20. 6. 1 Cor. 5. 8.
BREAK, Gen. 19. 9. Ex. 34. 13.
Judg. 7. 19. *b.* the pitchers that were
9. 53. and all to *b.* his skull
Ezra 9. 14. should we again *b.* thy
Ps. 2. 3. let us *b.* their bands asunder
9. shalt *b.* them with a rod of iron
58. 6. *b.* their teeth in their mouth
89. 31. if they *b.* my statutes
141. 5. oil which shall not *b.* head
S. of S. 2. 17. till the day *b.* and the shadows, 4. 6.
Isa. 42. 3. bruised reed not *b.*, Matt. 12. 20.
58. 6. that ye *b.* every yoke
Jer. 14. 21. *b.* not covenant with us
15. 12. shall iron *b.* northern iron
Ezek. 4. 16. *b.* the staff of bread, 5. 16. & 14. 13. Ps. 105. 16.
17. 15. shall he *b.* covenant and be
Hos. 1. 5. *b.* the bow of Israel, 2. 18.
Zech. 11. 10. might *b.* my covenant
14. might *b.* the brotherhood
Matt. 5. 19. *b.* one of these least
Acts 21. 13. mean ye to *b.* my heart
1 Cor. 10. 16. bread which we *b.*
Ex. 23. 24. *break down*, Deut. 7. 5. Ps. 74. 6. Eccl. 3. 3. Jer. 31. 28. & 45. 4. Hos. 10. 2.
Ex. 19. 22, 24. *break forth*, Isa. 55. 8. Jer. 1. 14. Gal. 4. 27.
Isa. 14. 7. *break forth into singing*, 44. 23. & 49. 13. & 54. 1. & 55. 12. & 52. 9.
Dan. 4. 27. *break off thy sins by right.*
Ex. 22. 6. *break out*, Isa. 35. 6. Hos. 4. 2. Amos 5. 6.
Job 19. 2. *break in pieces*, 34. 24. Ps. 72. 4. & 94. 5. Isa. 45. 2. Jer. 51. 20, 21, 22. Dan. 2. 40, 44. & 7. 23.
Ex. 19. 21, 24. *break through*, and Matt. 6. 19, 20. where thieves — and
Jer. 4. 3. *break up* your fallow ground, Hos. 10. 10.

Ps. 74. 13, 14. *breakest* heads of dra.
Gen. 32. 26. let me go, for the day *breaketh*
Job 9. 17. he *b.* me with a tempest
16. 14. he *b.* me with breach
Ps. 29. 5. voice of the Lord *b.* the
119. 20. my soul *b.* for the longing
Prov. 25. 15. a soft tongue *b.* the
Eccl. 10. 8. whoso *b.* a hedge, a serpent shalt bite them
Jer. 19. 11. as one *b.* a potter's vessel
23. 29. like a hammer that *b.* rocks
Hos. 13. 13. a place of *breaking* forth of children, 1 Chron. 14. 11.
Luke 24. 35. known of them in *b.*
Acts 2. 42. *b.* of bread, 46.
Rom. 2. 23. through *b.* the law dishonorest thou
R. V. Gen. 27. 40. shake; Ex. 34. 13; Deut. 7. 5; 12. 3. dash in pieces; Job 13. 25. harass; 39. 15. trample; S. of S. 2. 17; 4. 5. be cool; Isa. 54. 3. spread; Ezek. 23. 34. gnaw; Matt. 9. 17. burst; Rom. 2. 25. transgressors; Job 41. 25. consternation; Rom. 2. 23. thy transgression of

BREASTS, Gen. 49. 25. Job 3. 12.
Job 21. 24. his *b.* are full of milk
Ps. 22. 9. I was upon my mother's *b.*
Prov. 5. 19. let her *b.* satisfy thee at
S. of S. 1. 13. shall lie all night between my *b.*
4. 5. thy *b.* are like two roes, 7. 3.
7. 7. thy *b.* to clusters of grapes, 8.
8. 1. sucked the *b.* of my mother
10. I am a wall and my *b.* like
Isa. 28. 9. weaned and drawn from *b.*
60. 16. suck the *b.* of kings, 49. 23.
Ezek. 16. 7. thy *b.* are fashioned
8. bruised the *b.* of her virginity
Hos. 2. 2. adulteries from between her *b.*
Joel 2. 16. gather those that suck *b.*
Luke 23. 48. smote *b.* and returned
Rev. 15. 6. their *b.* girded with
Ex. 28. 4. *breastplate*, Rev. 9. 9, 17.
Isa. 59. 17. put on righteousness as *b.*
Eph. 6. 14. *b.* of righteousness
1 Thes. 5. 8. *b.* of faith and love

BREATH of life, Gen. 2. 7. & 6. 17. & 7. 15, 22. Isa. 2. 22. Hab. 2. 19.
Job 12. 10. in whose hands is *b.* of all
19. 17. my *b.* is strange to my wife
Ps. 33. 6. made by *b.* of his mouth
104. 29. thou takest away their *b.*
150. 6. all that hath *b.* praise Lord
Eccl. 3. 19. they have all one *b.*
Isa. 2. 22. whose *b.* is in his nostrils
11. 4. with *b.* of his lips shall slay
Lam. 4. 20. the *b.* of our nostrils
Dan. 5. 23. in whose hand thy *b.* is
Acts 17. 25. giveth life and *b.* and all
Ps. 27. 12. *breathe* out cruelty
Ezek. 37. 9. come *b.* upon these slain
John 20. 22. he *breathed* on them
Acts 9. 1. *breathing* out slaughter
R. V. Job 4. 9. blast; 17. 1. spirit

BRETHREN, we be, Gen. 13. 8.
Gen. 49. 29. him that was separate from his *b.*, Deut. 33. 16.
Deut. 17. 20. be not lifted up above *b.*
33. 9. neither did he acknowledge his *b.*
24. let him be acceptable to his *b.*
1 Chron. 4. 9. more honorable than his *b.*
Job 6. 15. my *b.* have dealt deceit.
19. 13. put my *b.* far from me
Ps. 22. 22. declare thy name unto my *b.*
69. 8. I am become a stranger to my *b.*
Hos. 13. 15. fruitful among his *b.*
Matt. 23. 8. all ye are *b.*, Acts 7. 26.
12. 48. who are my *b.*
25. 40. the least of these my *b.*
28. 10. go tell my *b.* that they go
Mark 10. 29. left house of *b.*, Luke 18. 29.
John 7. 5. neither did his *b.* believe
20. 17. go to my *b.* and say, I ascend
Acts 11. 29. send relief to the *b.*
Rom. 8. 29. firstborn among many *b.*
9. 3. accursed from Christ for my *b.*
1 Cor. 6. 5. to judge between his *b.*
15. 6. seen of above 500 *b.* at once.
Gal. 2. 4. false *b.* unawares brought
1 Tim. 4. 6. put *b.* in remembrance
Heb. 2. 11. not ashamed to call them *b.*
1 Pet. 1. 22. unfeigned love of the *b.*
1 John 3. 14. because we love the *b.*
16. to lay down our lives for the *b.*
3 John 10. neither doth he receive *b.*
Gen. 27. 29. *thy brethren*, 48. 22. & 49. 8. Deut. 15. 7. & 18. 15. 1 Sam. 17. 18. Matt. 12. 47. Mark 3. 32. Luke 8. 20. & 14. 12. & 22. 32.
Jer. 12. 6. —have dealt treacherous.
Rev. 19. 10. I am of —, 22. 9.
1 Kings 12. 24. *your brethren*, 2 Chron. 30. 7, 9. & 35. 6.
Neh. 4. 14. fight for — your sons and
Isa. 66. 5. — that hated you
Acts 3. 22. raise up of — prophet like unto me, 7. 37. Deut. 18. 15.
Matt. 5. 47. if you salute — only
R. V. Acts 20, 32; Rom. 15. 15; 1 Cor. 11. 2 —— ; 1 John 2. 7. beloved

BRIBES, 1 Sam. 3. 8.. Amos 5. 12.
1 Sam. 12. 3. have I received any *b.*
Ps. 26. 10. right hand full of *b.*
Isa. 33. 15. hands from holding *b.*
Job 15. 34. tabernacles of *bribery*
R. V. 1 Sam. 12. 3. ransom

BRICK, Gen. 11. 3. Ex. 1. 14. & 5. 7, 8, 14, 16, 19. Isa. 65. 3. & 9. 10.
2 Sam. 12. 31. *brick-kiln*, Jer. 43. 9. Nah. 3. 14.

BRIDE, doth clothe with an orna., Isa. 49. 18.
Isa. 61. 10. as a *b.* adorneth herself
Jer. 2. 32. can a *b.* forget her attire
Joel 2. 16. *b.* go out of her closet
John 3. 29. that hath *b.* is bridegr.
Rev. 21. 2. as a *b.* adorned for her
9. I will shew thee *b.* Lamb's wife
22. 17. spirit and *b.* say, come
Matt. 9. 15. *bride-chamber*, Mark 2. 19. Luke 5. 34.

BRIDEGROOM, Joel 2. 16. John 2. 9.
Ps. 19. 5. as a *b.* coming out of
Isa. 61. 10. as a *b.* decketh himself
62. 5. as a *b.* rejoiceth over the
Jer. 7. 34. cease the voice of *b.* and bride, 16. 9. & 25. 10. & 33. 11. Rev. 18. 23.
Matt. 9. 15. as long as the *b.* is — them, Mark 2. 19, 20. Luke 5. 34.
Matt. 25. 1. went forth to meet *b.* 6.

BRIDLE for the ass, Prov. 26. 3.
Ps. 32. 9. mouth held with *b.*
Isa. 37. 29. put my *b.* in thy lips, 30. 28. 2 Kings 19. 28. Rev. 14. 20.
Jas. 3. 2. able to *b.* the whole body
1. 26. *bridleth* not his tongue

BRIERS, Judg. 8. 7, 16. Isa. 7. 23, 24, 25. & 32. 13. Heb. 6. 8. Mic. 7. 4.
Isa. 5. 6. come up *b.* and thorns
9. 18. wickedness, shall devour *b.*, 10. 17.
27. 4. set *b.* against me in battle
Ezek. 2. 6. though *b.* and thorns be
28. 24. no more a pricking *b.* unto
R. V. Heb. 6. 8. thistles

BRIGHTNESS, 2 Sam. 22. 13. Ezek. 1. 4, 27, 28. & 8. 2. & 28. 7, 17.
Job 31. 26. beheld moon walking in *b.*
Ezek. 10. 4. full of the *b.* of Lord's
Dan. 12. 3. wise shall shine as the *b.* of the firmament
Amos 5. 20. very dark and no *b.* in it.
Hab. 3. 4. his *b.* was as the light
Acts 26. 13. a light above *b.* of sun
2 Thes. 2. 8. Lord destroy with *b.*
Heb. 1. 3. being the *b.* of his glory
R. V. Heb. 1. 3. effulgence

BRIMSTONE, Gen. 19. 24. Deut. 29. 23. Job 18. 15. Ps. 11. 6. Isa. 30. 33. & 34. 9. Ezek. 38. 22. Luke 17. 29. Rev. 14. 10. & 19. 20. & 21. 8.

BRING a flood, Gen. 6. 17.
Josh. 23. 15. *b.* upon you all the evil
1 Kings 8. 32. to *b.* his way upon
Job 14. 4. who can *b.* a clean thing
Ps. 60. 9. who *b.* me into strong, 72. 10. Isa. 60. 9. & 66. 20.
72. 3. mountains *b.* peace to people
Eccl. 11. 9. God will *b.* thee into judgment, 12. 14. Job 14. 4. & 30. 23.
S. of S. 8. 2. *b.* thee to my mother's
Isa. 1. 13. *b.* no more vain oblations
43. 5. I will *b.* thy seed from east
46. 13. I *b.* near my righteousness
66. 9. shall I *b.* to the birth and
Hos. 2. 14. allure and *b.* her into
Zeph. 3. 5. every morning *b.* his
Luke 2. 10. I *b.* you good tidings
John 14. 26. *b.* all things to remem.
Acts 5. 28. intend to *b.* this man's blood
1 Cor. 1. 28. *b.* to nought things
1 Thes. 4. 14. God will *b.* with him
1 Pet. 3. 18. that he might *b.* us to
Gen. 1. 11, 20, 24. *bring forth*, 3. 16. Matt. 1. 21. Job 39. 1. Ex. 3. 10.
2 Kings 19. 3. there is not strength to —
Job 15. 35. conceive mischief and — vanity
Ps. 37. 6. he shall — thy righteous.
92. 14. still — fruit in old age
Prov. 27. 1. what a day may —
Isa. 41. 21. — your strong reasons
42. 1. — judgment to the Gentiles, 4.
66. 8. made to — in one day
Zeph. 2. 2. before the decree —
Mark 4. 20. — fruit some thirty fold
Luke 3. 8. — fruits worthy of repentance
8. 15. — fruit with patience
John 15. 2. that it may — more fruit
Ps. 1. 3. *bringeth forth* fruit in its
Hos. 10. 1. — fruit to himself
Matt. 3. 10. *b.* not forth good fruit, 7. 19. & 12. 35. Luke 6. 43.
John 12. 24. if it die it — much fruit
Jas. 1. 15. — sin — death

BROAD, Num. 16. 38, 39. Nah. 2. 4. Matt. 23. 5.
Job 36. 16. out of strait into *b.* place
Isa. 33. 21. Lord a place of *b.* rivers
Matt. 7. 13. *b.* is way to destruction
R. V. Num. 16. 38. beaten

BROIDERED work, Ezek. 16. 10.

BROKEN my covenant. Gen. 17. 14. Ps. 55. 20. Isa. 24. 5. & 33. 8. & 36. 6. Jer. 11. 10. & 33. 21.
Ps. 34. 18. nigh to them of *b.* heart
44. 19. sore *b.* us in place of drag.
17. *b.* spirit, *b.* and contrite heart
147. 3. healeth the *b.* in heart
Isa. 61. 1. to bind up the *b.* hearted
Jer. 2. 13. hewed out *b.* cisterns
Dan. 2. 42. strong and partly *b.*
Hos. 5. 11. Ephraim is *b.* in judgment
Matt. 21. 44. shall fall on stone, shall be *b.*
John 10. 35. Scripture cannot be *b.*

BROOK, Num. 15. 23. Deut. 2. 13.
Ps. 110. 7. drink of the *b.* in the way
Job 20. 17. the *b.* of honey and
Isa. 19. 6. *b.* of defence shall be
R. V. Num. 21. 14, 15. valleys

BROTHER, born for adversity, Prov. 17. 17.
Prov. 18. 19. a *b.* offended is harder
24. is a friend that sticketh closer than a *b.*
27. 10. neighbor near, than *b.* far
Jer. 9. 4. trust not in any *b.* for every *b.*
Matt. 10. 21. *b.* shall deliver up *b.* to death, Mark 13. 12. Mic. 7. 2.
1 Cor. 5. 11. *b.* be a fornicator
6. 6. but *b.* goeth to law with *b.*
7. 15. *b.* or sister is not in bondage
2 Thes. 3. 15. admonish him as a *b.*
Jas. 1. 9. let *b.* of low degree
Ps. 35. 14. *my brother*, S. of S. 8. 1. Matt. 12. 50. & 18. 21. 1 Cor. 8. 13.
Ps. 50. 20. *thy brother*, Matt. 5. 23, 24. & 18. 15. Rom. 14. 10, 15.
Gen. 45. 4. *your brother*, Rev. 1. 9.
Zech. 11. 14. *brotherhood*, 1 Pet. 2. 17.

Amos 1. 9. remember not *brotherly* covenant
Rom. 12. 10. kindly affectioned with *b.*
Heb. 13. 1. let *b.* love continue
2 Pet. 1. 7. to godliness *b.* kindness
R. V. Luke 6. 16; Acts 1. 13. son
BROUGHT me hitherto, 2 Sam. 7. 18.
Neh. 4. 15. God *b.* their counsel to
Ps. 45. 14. be *b.* unto the king in
79. 8. we are *b.* very low
107. 39. *b.* low through oppression
116. 6. I was *b.* low and he helped
Isa. 1. 2. nourished and *b.* up child.
Matt. 10. 18. *b.* before governors, Mark 13. 9. Luke 12. 12.
1 Cor. 6. 12. not be *b.* under power
Gal. 2. 4. false brethren, unawares *b.* in
1 Tim. 6. 7. *b.* nothing into this world
Ps. 107. 12. *brought down,* Matt. 11. 23.
Deut. 33. 14. *brought forth,* Ps. 18. 19.
BRUISE thy head — his heel, Gen. 3. 15.
Isa. 53. 10. it pleased Lord to *b.* him
Isa. 42. 3. *bruised* reed not break, Matt. 12. 20.
53. 5. he was *b.* for our iniquities
Ezek. 23. 3, 21. *b.* breasts, *b.* teats
R. V. Jer. 30. 12; Nah. 3. 19. hurt; Dan. 2. 40. crush; Isa. 28. 28. ground
BRUIT, report, Jer. 10. 22. Nah. 3. 19.
BRUTISH man knows not, Ps. 92. 6.
Ps. 94. 8. understand, ye *b.* among
Jer. 10. 14. man is *b.* in his knowledge, 51. 17.
BUCKLER to all that trust, Ps. 18. 30.
Ps. 18. 2. my *b.* and horn of my
91. 4. his truth shall be thy *b.*
Prov. 2. 7. a *b.* to them that walk
R. V. 2 Sam. 22. 31; Ps. 18. 2; Prov. 2. 7. shield; 1 Chron. 12. 8. spear
BUDDING of Aaron's rod, Num. 17.
BUFFETED, 2 Cor. 12. 7. Matt. 26. 67. 1 Cor. 4. 11. 1 Pet. 2. 20.
BUILD walls of Jerusalem, Ps. 51. 18.
Ps. 102. 16. Lord shall *b.* up Zion
Eccl. 3. 3. a time to *b.* up
Mic. 3. 10. *b.* up Zion with blood
Acts 20. 32. able to *b.* you up
Job 22. 23. if thou return shalt be *built* up
Ps. 89. 2. mercy shall be *b.* up for
Matt. 7. 24. *b.* his house on a rock
Eph. 2. 20. ye are *b.* on foundation
Col. 2. 7. rooted and *b.* up in him
Heb. 3. 4. he that *b.* all things is
1 Pet. 2. 5. *b.* up a spiritual house
Heb. 11. 10. *builder* and maker is
Ps. 118. 22. stone which the *b.* refused, Matt. 21. 42. Mark 12. 10. Luke 20. 17. Acts 4. 11. 1 Pet. 2. 7.
1 Cor. 3. 10. *master builder*
Josh. 6. 26. cursed that *buildeth*
Jer. 22. 13. woe to him that *b.* house
Amos 9. 6. *b.* his stories in heaven
Hab. 2. 12. *b.* a town with blood
1 Cor. 3. 10. another *b.* thereon
9. ye are God's *building*
2 Cor. 5. 1. we have a *b.* of God
Heb. 9. 11. tabernacle not of this *b.*
Jude 20. *b.* up yourselves in faith
BULLS compassed me, Ps. 22. 12.
Ps. 50. 13. will I eat the flesh of *b.*
Heb. 9. 13. if blood of *b.* and goats
Ps. 69. 31. than *bullock* with horns
Jer. 31. 18. as a *b.* unaccustomed to
Ps. 51. 19. offer *b.* on thy altar
Isa. 1. 11. delight not in blood of *b.*
R. V. Isa. 51. 20. antelope; Lev. 4. 10; 9. 18; Deut. 17. 1. ox; Jer. 31. 18. calf; Jer. 50. 11. strong horses

BULRUSHES, Ex. 2. 3. Isa. 18. 2. & 58. 5.
R. V. Isa. 58. 5. rush; 18. 2. papyrus
BULWARKS, Ps. 48. 13. Isa. 26. 1.
R. V. 2 Chr. 26. 15. battlements
BUNDLE, Gen. 42. 35. Acts 28. 3.
1 Sam. 25. 29. bound in the *b.* of
S. of S. 1. 13. *b.* of myrrh is my
Matt. 13. 30. bind tares in *bundles* to burn
BURDEN, 2 Kings 5. 17. & 8. 9.
Ex. 18. 22. shall bear the *b.* with thee, Num. 11. 17.
23. 5. ass lying under his *b.*
Deut. 1. 12. how can I bear your *b.*
2 Sam. 15. 33. thou shalt be a *b.*
2 Kings 5. 17. two mules *b.* of earth
2 Chron. 35. 3. not be *b.* on should.
Neh. 13. 19. shall be no *b.* brought in on Sabbath day, Jer. 17. 21. & 22. 24, 27.
Job 7. 20. I am a *b.* to myself
Ps. 38. 4. a *b.* too heavy for me
55. 22. cast thy *b.* upon the Lord
Eccl. 12. 5. grasshopper shall be a *b.*
Isa. 9. 4. broken the yoke of his b.
10. 27. *b.* taken from thy shoulder
Zeph. 3. 18. reproach of it was a *b.*
Zech. 12. 3. all that *b.* themselves
Matt. 11. 30. my yoke is easy, my *b.*
20. 12. borne the *b.* and heat of day
Acts 15. 28. no greater *b.* than nec.
2 Cor. 12. 16. I did not *b.* you
Gal. 6. 5. every man bear his own *b.*
Rev. 2. 24. put on you no other *b.*
Isa. 13. 1. *b.* threatening of heavy judgments, 14. 28. & 15. 1. & 17. 1. & 19. 1. & 21. 1, 11. & 22. 1. & 23. 1.
Ezek. 12. 10. Nah. 1. 1. Hab. 1. 1. Zech. 9. 1. & 12. 1.
Mal. 1. 1. *b.* of the word
2 Cor. 5. 4. we groan being *burdened*
Gen. 49. 14. *burdens,* Ex. 1. 11. & 2. 11. & 5. 4.
Isa. 58. 6. to undo the heavy *b.*
Lam. 2. 14. seen for thee false *b.*
Matt. 23. 4. bind heavy *b.,* Luke 11. 46.
Gal. 6. 2. bear one another's *b.*
Zech. 12. 3. *burdensome,* 2 Cor. 11. 9. & 12. 13, 14. 1 Thes. 2. 6.
R. V. Gen. 49. 14. sheepfolds; Amos 5. 11. exactions; 2 Cor. 8. 13. distressed
BURN upon altar, Ex. 29. 13, 18, 25. Lev. 1. 9, 15. & 2. 2. & 3. 5, 11, 16. & 5. 12. & 6. 15. & 9. 17.
Gen. 44. 18. let not thine anger *b.*
Deut. 32. 22. shall *b.* to lowest hell
Isa. 27. 4. go through them and *b.*
Mal. 4. 1. day cometh shall *b.* as an
Luke 3. 17. chaff he will *b.* with unquenchable fire
Luke 24. 32. did not our heart *b.*
1 Cor. 7. 9. it is better to marry than *b.*
Rev. 17. 6. eat her flesh and *b.* her
Ex. 3. 2. the bush *burned* with fire
Deut. 9. 15. and mount *b.* with fire
Ps. 39. 3. while I was musing fire *b.*
1 Cor. 3. 15. if any man's work shall be *b.*
13. 3. though I give my body to *b.*
Heb. 6. 8. whose end is to be *b.*
Ps. 46. 9. *burneth* the chariot in fire
97. 3. *b.* up his enemies round
Isa. 9. 18. wickedness *b.* as the fire
Rev. 21. 8. lake which *b.* with fire
Gen. 15. 17. *burning* lamp that passed between those pieces
Jer. 20. 9. his word was as *b.* fire
Hab. 3. 5. *b.* coals went forth at his
Luke 12. 35. loins girded and your lights *b.*
John 5. 35. a *b.* and a shining light
Ex. 21. 25. *b.* for *b.* wound for wou.
Deut. 28. 22. smite thee with extreme *b.*
Isa. 3. 24. *b.* instead of beauty
4. 4. by the spirit of judgment and *b.*
Amos 4. 11. firebrand plucked out of the *b.*
Isa. 33. 14. dwell with everlasting *b.*

Gen. 8. 20. *burnt-offerings,* Deut. 12. 6. 1 Sam. 15. 22. Ps. 50. 8. Isa. 1. 11. & 56. 7. Jer. 6. 20. & 7. 21, 22.
Hos. 6. 6. knowledge of God more than —
Mark 12. 33. more than all whole —
Heb. 10. 6. in — for sin and sacrifices
Ps. 74. 8. *burnt* up all synagogues
Isa. 64. 11. our beautiful house is —
Matt. 22. 7. destroyed and — their city
2 Pet. 3. 10. works that are therein be —
BURST thy bands, Jer. 2. 20.
Prov. 3. 10. presses *b.* out with new
Mark 2. 22. new wine doth *b.* the bottles, Luke 5. 37. Job 32. 19.
Acts 1. 18. *b.* asunder in the midst
R. V. Prov. 3. 10. overflow; Isa. 30. 14. pieces
BURY my dead out of my sight, Gen. 23. 4.
Gen. 49. 29. *b.* me with my fathers
Ps. 79. 3. there was none to *b.* them
Matt. 8. 21. first to go and *b.* my
Rom. 6. 4. *buried* with him by baptism into death, Col. 2. 12.
1 Cor. 15. 4. he was *b.* and rose again
Gen. 23. 4. a possession of a *burying*
47. 30. *b.* me in the *b.* place
Mark 14. 8. anoint my body to the *b.*
John 12. 7. against the day of my *b.*
2 Chron. 26. 23. *burial,* Acts 8. 2.
Eccl. 6. 3. that he have no *b.*
Isa. 14. 20. not joined with them in *b.*
Jer. 22. 19. buried with *b.* of an ass
Matt. 26. 12. she did it for my *b.*
BUSH is not burnt, Ex. 3. 2, 3, 4. Acts 7. 30. Mark 12. 26.
Deut. 33. 16. good will of him that dwelt in *b.*
R. V. Isa. 7. 19. pastures
BUSHEL, Matt. 5. 15. Luke 11. 33.
BUSHY and black, S. of S. 5. 11.
BUSINESS, Gen. 39. 11. Rom. 16. 2.
Ps. 107. 23. do *b.* in great waters
Prov. 22. 29. seest a man diligent in *b.*
Luke 2. 49. must be about Father's *b.*
Acts 6. 3. we may appoint over this *b.*
Rom. 12. 11. not slothful in *b.*
1 Thes. 4. 11. study to do your own *b.*
BUSY-BODIES censured, Prov. 20. 3. & 26. 17. 1 Thes. 4. 11. 2 Thes. 3. 11. 1 Tim. 5. 13. 1 Pet. 4. 15.
BUTTER and milk, Gen. 18. 8. Deut. 32. 14. Judg. 5. 25. 2 Sam. 17. 29. Prov. 30. 33.
Job 20. 17. brooks of honey and *b.*
Ps. 55. 21. words were smoother than *b.*
Isa. 7. 15. *b.* and honey shall he eat, 22.
BUY the truth, Prov. 23. 23.
Isa. 55. 1. *b.* and eat, yea, *b.* wine
1 Cor. 7. 30. they that *b.* as possessed
Jas. 4. 13. *b.* and sell, and get gain
Rev. 3. 18. I counsel thee *b.* gold
Prov. 20. 14. it is nought saith *buyer*
Isa. 24. 2. as with *b.* so with seller
Ezek. 7. 12. let no *b.* rejoice
Prov. 31. 16. considereth a field and *buyeth* it
Matt. 13. 44. selleth all and *b.* field
Rev. 18. 11. no man *b.* her merchan.
BY and by, Matt. 13. 21. Mark 6. 25. Luke 17. 7. & 21. 9.
By-word among all nations, Deut. 28. 37.
1 Kings 9. 7. Israel shall be a —
2 Chron. 7. 20. make this house a —
Job 17. 6. made a — of the people
30. 9. I am their song and their —
Ps. 44. 14. makest us a — among the heathen

C

CAGE, Jer. 5. 27. Rev. 18. 2.
R. V. Rev. 18. 2. hold
CAIN and Abel, Gen. 4. 1-17. Heb. 11. 4. & 12. 24. Jude 11.

CAKE of bread tumbled into host, Judg. 7. 13.
1 Kings 17. 12. I have not a *c.* but
Hos. 7. 8. Ephraim is a *c.* not turned
Cakes, Gen. 18. 6. Judg. 6. 19.
Jer. 7. 18. make *c.* to queen of
44. 19. made *c.* to worship her
R. V. 1 Chr. 23. 29. wafers
CALAMITY at hand, Deut. 32. 35.
Job 6. 2. my *c.* laid in the balance
Ps. 18. 18. prevented me in the day of my *c.*
Prov. 1. 26. I will laugh at your *c.*
6. 15. his *c.* shall come suddenly
Jer. 18. 17. the face in day of their *c.*
46. 21. day of thy *c.* is come, 48. 16. & 49. 8, 32. Ezek. 35. 5. Obad. 13.
Ps. 57. 1. till these *calamities* be overpast
Prov. 17. 5. that is glad at *c.* shall
24. 22. their *c.* shall rise suddenly
R. V. Ps. 141. 5. wickedness
CALDRON, 1 Sam. 2. 14. Job 41. 20. Ezek. 11. 3, 7, 11. Mic. 3. 3. Jer. 52. 18.
R. V. Job 41. 20. burning rushes; Jer. 52. 18, 19. pots
CALEB and Joshua, Num. 13. 30. & 14. 6, 24, 38. & 26. 65. & 32. 12.
CALF, Gen. 18. 7. Job 21. 10. Ps. 29. 6. Isa. 27. 10. Rev. 4. 7.
Ex. 32. 4. made a molten *c.*, 20. Deut. 9. 16. Neh. 9. 18. Ps. 106. 19.
Isa. 11. 6. *c.* and young lion lie
Hos. 8. 5. thy *c.* O Samaria, hath
8. 6. the *c.* of Samaria shall be
Luke 15. 23. bring hither the fatted *c.*
27. thou hast killed the fatted *c.* 30.
CALL them what he would, Gen. 2. 19.
Gen. 24. 57. we will *c.* the damsel
30. 13. daughters will *c.* me bless.
Deut. 4. 7. all that we *c.* upon him
1 Sam. 3. 6. here am I, for thou didst *c.* me
1 Kings 8. 52. in all they *c.* to thee
17. 18. to *c.* my sin to remembrance
1 Chron. 16. 8. *c.* upon his name
13. 22. *c.* thou and I will answer
27. 10. will he always *c.* upon God
Ps. 4. 1. hear me when I *c.* O God
49. 11. *c.* lands after their names
72. 17. all nations shall *c.* him
80. 18. we will *c.* on thy name
86. 5. plenteous in mercy to all that *c.*
145. 18. nigh to all them that *c.* upon
Prov. 31. 28. children rise and *c.* her
Isa. 5. 20. woe to them that *c.* evil
55. 6. *c.* upon him while he is near
65. 24. before they *c.* I will answer
Jer. 25. 29. I will *c.* for a sword upon all
Joel 2. 32. remnant whom the Lord shall *c.*
Jonah 1. 6. sleeper arise, *c.* upon
Zech. 13. 9. they shall *c.* upon my
Mal. 3. 12. all nations shall *c.* you
Matt. 9. 13. I came not to *c.* right. but sinners, Mark 2. 17.
22. 3. to *c.* them that were bidden
Luke 1. 48. all generations shall *c.*
6. 46. why *c.* ye me Lord, Lord?
John 4. 16. *c.* thy husband and
13. 13. ye *c.* me master and Lord
Acts 2. 39. as many as Lord shall *c.*
10. 15. God hath cleansed *c.* not
Rom. 9. 25. I will *c.* them my people
10. 12. rich in mercy to all that *c.* on
2 Cor. 1. 23. I *c.* God for a record
Heb. 2. 11. not ashamed to *c.* them
Jas. 5. 14. *c.* for the elders of the
1 Pet. 1. 17. if ye *c.* on the Father
Call on the name of the Lord, Gen. 4. 26. & 12. 8. & 13. 4. & 21. 33. & 26. 25. 1 Kings 18. 24. 2 Kings 5. 11. Ps. 116. 4, 13, 17. Joel 2. 32. Zeph. 3. 9. Acts 2. 21. Rom. 10. 13. 1 Cor. 1. 2.
I will call unto, or, *on the Lord*, 1 Sam. 12. 17. 2 Sam. 22. 4. Ps. 18. 3. & 55. 16. & 86. 7.
Call upon me, Ps. 50. 15. & 91. 15. Prov. 1. 28. Jer. 29. 12.

Gen. 21. 17. angel of God *called* to Hagar
22. 11. the angel of the Lord *c.* to Abraham out of heaven, 15.
Ex. 3. 4. God *c.* unto him out of the
19. 3. Lord *c.* unto him out of the
Judg. 15. 18. was athirst, and *c.* on
2 Kings 8. 1. Lord hath *c.* for a
1 Chron. 4. 10. Jabesh *c.* on God of
21. 26. David *c.* on the Lord and he
Ps. 17. 6. I have *c.* upon thee, 31. 17.
18. 6. in my distress I *c.* upon Lord
79. 6. not *c.* on thy name, Jer. 10. 25.
88. 9. I have *c.* daily upon thee
118. 5. I *c.* upon the Lord in my dis.
Prov. 1. 24. I have *c.* and ye refused
S. of S. 5. 6. I *c.* him, he gave me
Isa. 41. 2. who *c.* him to his foot
42. 6. I the Lord *c.* thee in right.
43. 1. I have *c.* thee by thy name
22. thou hast not *c.* upon me
48. 1. *c.* by the name of Israel, 44. 5.
49. 1. Lord *c.* me from the womb
50. 2. when I *c.* was none to answer
51. 2. I *c.* him alone, and blessed
61. 3. be *c.* trees of righteousness
62. 4. thou shalt be *c.* Hephzibah
Lam. 1. 19. I *c.* for my lovers they
3. 55. I *c.* upon thy name, O Lord
Hos. 11. 1. I *c.* my son out of Egypt
Amos 7. 4. Lord *c.* to contend by
Hag. 1. 11. I *c.* for a drought on
Matt. 20. 16. many be *c.* but few chosen, 22. 14.
Mark 14. 72. Peter *c.* to mind word of the Lord
Luke 15. 19. not worthy to be *c.* thy
John 1. 48. before that Philip *c.* thee
10. 35. if he *c.* them gods to whom
15. 15. I have *c.* you friends
Acts 9. 41. when he had *c.* saints
21. destroy them that *c.* on this
10. 23, 24. *c.* in — *c.* together his kinsmen
Acts 11. 26. disciples were *c.* Christians
13. 2. for work whereto I *c.* them
19. 40. we are in danger to be *c.* in question, 23. 6. & 24. 21.
20. 1. Paul *c.* to him the disciples
Rom. 1. 1. *c.* to be an apos. 1 Cor. 1. 1.
6. *c.* of Jesus Christ, 7. *c.* to be
2. 17. thou that art *c.* a Jew
8. 28. *c.* according to his purpose
30. predestinate, them he also *c.*
9. 24. whom he hath *c.* Jews also
1 Cor. 1. 9. faithful by whom ye were *c.*
26. not many wise, — noble are *c.*
5. 11. if any man *c.* a brother be
7. 18. *c.* being circumcised
21, 22. *c.* servant
24. every man wherein he is *c.*
15. 9. I am not meet to be *c.* an
Gal. 1. 6. *c.* you into the grace of
15. God who *c.* me by his grace
Eph. 2. 11. who are *c.* uncircum.
4. are *c.* in one hope of your calling
Col. 3. 15. to which ye are *c.* in one
1 Thes. 2. 12. *c.* you unto his king.
4. 7. God hath not *c.* us to unclean
2 Thes. 2. 4. above all that is *c.* God
1 Tim. 6. 12. whereunto thou art *c.*
2 Tim. 1. 9. *c.* us with a holy calling
Heb. 3. 13. exhort while it is *c.* to.
5. 4. *c.* of God, as was Aaron
10. *c.* of God a high priest
9. 15. that they who are *c.* may
11. 16. not ashamed to be *c.* their
24. refusing to be *c.* the son of Pharaoh's daughter
Jas. 2. 7. name by which ye are *c.*
1 Pet. 1. 15. as he that *c.* you is holy
21. hereunto were ye *c.*
2 Pet. 1. 3. *c.* us to glory and virtue
1 John 3. 1. we should be *c.* sons of
Jude 1. preserved in Christ Jesus and *c.*
Rev. 17. 14. with him *c.* and chosen
19. 9. are *c.* unto marriage supper
2 Chron. 7. 14. *called by my name*, Isa. 43. 7. & 65. 1. Jer. 7. 10, 11, 14, 30. & 25. 29. & 32. 34. & 34. 15. Amos 9. 12.

1 Kings 8. 43. *called by thy name*, 2 Chron. 6. 33. Isa. 4. 1. & 43. 1. & 45. 4. & 63. 19. Jer. 14. 9. & 15. 16. Dan. 9. 18, 19.
2 Kings 8. 43. to all that the stranger *calleth* for, 2 Chron. 6. 33.
Job 12. 4. who *c.* on God and he ans.
Ps. 42. 7. deep *c.* unto deep at noise
Isa. 59. 4. none *c.* for justice nor for
Hos. 7. 7. none among them that *c.*
Amos 5. 8. that *c.* for waters of sea
Luke 15. 6. *c.* together his friends, 9.
John 10. 3. he *c.* his own sheep by
Rom. 4. 17. *c.* those things which be
Gal. 5. 8. persuasion not of him that *c.*
1 Thes. 5. 24. faithful is he that *c.*
Rom. 11. 29. gifts and *calling* of God
1 Cor. 1. 26. ye see your *c.* brethren
7. 20. let every man abide in same *c.*
Eph. 1. 18. what is the hope of his *c.*
4. 4. called in one hope of your *c.*
Phil. 3. 14. prize of high *c.* of God
2 Thes. 1. 11. count you worthy of this *c.*
2 Tim. 1. 9. called with a holy *c.*
Heb. 3. 1. partakers of heavenly *c.*
2 Pet. 1. 10. make your *c.* and elect.
Isa. 41. 4. *c.* the generation from the beginning
Matt. 11. 16. sitting and *c.* their
Mark 11. 21. Peter *c.* to remembrance
Acts 7. 59. stoned Stephen *c.* upon
22. 16. *c.* upon the name of Lord
1 Pet. 3. 6. obeyed Abraham, *c.* him
CALM, Ps. 107. 29. Jonah 1. 11, 12. Matt. 8. 26. Mark 4. 39. Luke 8. 24.
CALVE (cow), Job 21. 10. (hinds) 39. 1. Ps. 29. 9. Jer. 14. 5.
1 Kings 12. 28. made two *calves* of
Hos. 14. 2. we will render *c.* of our
Mic. 6. 6. come with *c.* of a year old
Heb. 9. 12. blood of goats and *c.*, 19.
CAME, Ps. 18. 6. & 88. 17. Matt. 1. 18. & 9. 14. John 1. 7, 11. & 8. 14, 42. & 18. 37. Rom. 5. 18. & 9. 5. 1 Tim. 1. 15. 1 John 5. 6.
Came down, 2 Kings 1. 10, 12, 14. 2 Chron. 7. 1, 3. Lam. 1. 9. John 3. 13. & 6. 38, 41, 51, 58. Rev. 20. 9.
Came forth, Num. 11. 20. Judg. 14. 14. Eccl. 5. 15. Zech. 10. 4.
John 16. 28. I — from the Father
CAMEL, Gen. 24. 19. Lev. 11. 4.
Matt. 3. 4. raiment of *c.*'s hair, Mark 1. 6.
19. 24. easier for a *c.* to go through
23. 24. strain at a gnat, and swallow *c.*
CAMP, Ex. 32. 17. & 36. 6.
Ex. 14. 19. angel went before the *c.*
16. 13. quails came and covered *c.*
Num. 11. 26. they prophesied in *c.*
31. let the quails fall by the *c.*
Deut. 23. 14. Lord walketh in midst of *c.* therefore shall thy *c.* be holy
Judg. 13. 25. began to move him in *c.*
2 Kings 19. 35, smote in the *c.* of the Assyrians
Heb. 13. 13. go unto him without *c.*
Rev. 20. 9. compassed *c.* of saints
CAN we find such a one, Gen. 41. 38.
Deut. 1. 12. how *c.* I myself alone
32. 38. neither is there any *c.* deliver
2 Sam. 7. 20. what *c.* David say more
2 Chron. 1. 10. who *c.* judge this
Esth. 8. 6. how *c.* I endure to see the destruction of my people
Job 8. 11. *c.* the rush grow without
25. 4. how *c.* man be justified with
Ps. 40. 5. more than *c.* be number.
Ps. 49. 7. none *c.* redeem his brother
89. 6. who *c.* be likened unto Lord
Eccl. 4. 11. how *c.* one be warm
Isa. 49. 15. *c.* a woman forget her
Jer. 2. 32. *c.* a maid forget her orna.
Ezek. 22. 14. *c.* thy heart endure
37. 3. *c.* these dry bones live
Amos 3. 3. *c.* two walk together
Matt. 12. 34. how *c.* ye speak good
19. 25. who then *c.* be saved

Mark 2. 7. who *c.* forgive sins but
19. *c.* children of bride-chamber
10. 38. *c.* ye drink of the cup that I
John 3. 4. how *c.* man be born again
9. how *c.* these things be, Luke 1. 34.
5. 19. Son *c.* do nothing of him., 30.
6. 44. no man *c.* come to me except
9. 4. night, when no man *c.* work
15. 4. no more *c.* ye except ye abide
1 Cor. 12. 3. no man *c.* say that Jesus
2 Cor. 13. 8. *c.* do nothing against
1 Tim. 6. 7. we *c.* carry nothing out
Heb. 10. 11. *c.* never take away sins
Jas. 2. 14. *c.* faith save him
Rev. 3. 8. open door and no man *c.*
Gen. 32. 12. which *cannot* be numbered for multitude, 1 Kings 3. 8. Hos. 1. 10.
Num. 23. 20. he hath blessed; and I *c.* reverse it
Josh. 24. 19. ye *c.* serve the Lord
1 Sam. 12. 21. vain things which *c.*
1 Kings 8. 27. heaven of heavens *c.* contain thee, 2 Chron. 6. 18.
Ezra 9. 15. we *c.* stand before thee
Job 9. 3. he *c.* answer for one of a
23. 8, 9. I *c.* perceive him *c.* behold
28. 15. it *c.* be gotten for gold
36. 18. a great ransom *c.* deliver
Ps. 40. 5. they *c.* be reckoned up in
77. I am so troubled that I *c.* speak
93. 1. world establish. that it *c.* be
139. 6. too high, I *c.* attain unto it
Isa. 38. 18. the grave *c.* praise thee
44. 18. they *c.* see; they *c.* under.
20. he *c.* deliver his soul
50. 2. hand shortened that it *c.* redeem
56. 11. shepherds that *c.* understand
Jer. 4. 19. I *c.* hold my peace
6. 10. are uncircumcised, they *c.*
7. 8. ye trust in lying words that *c.*
14. 9. as a mighty man *c.* save
18. 6. *c.* I do with you as this potter
29. 17. like the vile figs that *c.* be
33. 22. the host of heaven *c.* be
Lam. 3. 7. hath hedged me, that I *c.* get
Matt. 6. 24. ye *c.* serve God and mammon, Luke 16. 13.
7. 18. a good tree *c.* bring forth evil
27. 42. himself he *c.* save, Mark 15. 31.
Luke 14. 26. *c.* be my disciple, 27. 33.
16. 26. would pass from hence to you *c.*
John 3. 3. *c.* see the kingdom of
5. he *c.* enter into the kingdom of
8. 43. because ye *c.* hear my word
10. 35. the Scripture *c.* be broken
14. 17. whom the world *c.* receive
15. 4. branch *c.* bear fruit of itself
Acts 4. 20. we *c.* but speak the things
5. 39. if it be of God ye *c.* overthrow
27. 31. except these abide in the ship, ye *c.* be saved
Rom. 8. 8. that are in flesh *c.* please God
26. groanings which *c.* be uttered
Cor. 7. 9. if they *c.* contain, let
10. 21. ye *c.* drink cup of the Lord
15. 50. flesh and blood *c.* inherit the kingdom of God
2 Cor. 12. 2. in body or out, I *c.* tell
Gal. 5. 17. ye *c.* do the things that
2 Tim. 2. 13. he *c.* deny himself
Tit. 1. 2. God who *c.* lie hath
2. 8. sound speech *c.* be condemned
Heb. 4. 15. high priest which *c.* be
9. 5. we *c.* now speak particularly
12. 27. those things which *c.* be
28. kingdom that *c.* be moved
Jas. 1. 13. God *c.* be tempted with
1 John 3. 9. he *c.* sin because born
Ex. 33. 20. *canst* not see my face
Deut. 28. 27. *c.* not be healed
Job 11. 7. *c.* thou by searching find
22. darkness that thou *c.* not see
Matt. 8. 2. if thou wilt, thou *c.*
Mark 9. 22. if *c.* do any thing have

John 3. 8. *c.* not tell whence it
13. 36. thou *c.* not follow me now
CANDLE shall be put out, Job 18. 6. & 21. 17. Prov. 24. 20.
Job 29. 3. when his *c.* shined on
Ps. 18. 28. the Lord will light my *c.*
Prov. 20. 27. spirit of man is *c.* of
31. 18. her *c.* goeth not out by
Matt. 5. 15. do men light a *c.* and — it, Mark 4. 21. Luke 8. 16. & 11. 33.
Luke 11. 36. shining of *c.* doth give
15. 8. light a *c.* and sweep house
Rev. 18. 23. light of *c.* shine no more at all, Jer. 25. 10.
Rev. 22. 5. they need no *c.* neither
Zeph. 1. 22. search Jerusalem with *candles*
Ex. 25. 31. *candlestick*, & 37. 17, 20. Lev. 24. 4. Num. 8. 2. 2 Kings 4. 10. Dan. 5. 5.
Zech. 4. 2. behold a *c.* all of gold
Matt. 5. 15. but on a *c.* and it giveth light to all, Mark 4. 21. Luke 11. 33.
Rev. 1. 20. seven *c.* are the seven
2. 5. I will remove thy *c.* out of his
R. V. Matt. 5. 15; Mark 4. 21; Luke 8. 16. stand
CANKER, 2 Tim. 2. 17. Jas. 5. 3.
CAPTAIN, Num. 2. 3. & 14. 4.
Josh. 5. 14, 15. *c.* of the Lord's host
2 Chron. 13. 12. God himself is our *c.*
Heb. 2. 10. *c.* of their salva. perfect
R. V. 1 Sam. 9. 16; 10. 1; 13. 4. prince; Jer. 51. 23, 28, 57; Dan. 3. 2, 3, 27; 6. 7. governors
CAPTIVE, Gen. 14. 14. & 34. 2.
Judg. 5. 12. lead thy captivity *c.*
Isa. 49. 24. shall the lawful *c.* be
Jer. 22. 12. die whither they led him *c.*
Amos 7. 11. Israel shall be led away *c.*
2 Tim. 2. 26. taken *c.* by him at his
Deut. 30. 3. I will turn thy *captivity*
Job 42. 10. the Lord turned the *c.*
Ps. 14. 7. Lord bringeth back the *c.*
68. 18. lead *c.* captive, Eph. 4. 8.
85. 1. brought back the *c.* of Jacob
126. 1. turned again the *c.* of Zion
Jer. 15. 2. such as are for *c.* to *c.*
29. 14. I will turn away your *c.*
30. 3. bring again *c.* of my people
Hos. 6. 11. when I returned *c.* of
Zeph. 2. 7. Lord shall turn away their *c.*
Rom. 7. 23. bringing me into *c.* of
2 Cor. 10. 5. bringing into *c.* every
Rev. 13. 10. lead into *c.* shall go into *c.*
R. V. Isa. 20. 4; 45. 13; 49. 21. exile
CARCASS, Matt. 24. 28. Luke 17. 37.
R. V. Lev. 11. 26; Judg. 14. 8. body
CARE, Luke 10. 40. 1 Cor. 7. 21.
Matt. 13. 22. *c.* of this world choke, Mark 4. 19. Luke 8. 14.
1 Cor. 9. 9. doth God take *c.* for
12. 25. have the same *c.* one for
2 Cor. 11. 28. *c.* of all the churches
1 Tim. 3. 5. how shall he take *c.* of
1 Pet. 5. 7. casting all your *c.* on
Ps. 142. 4. no man *cared* for my
John 12. 6. not that he *c.* for the
Acts 18. 17. Gallio *c.* for none of these things
Matt. 22. 16. *carest*, Mark 4. 38.
Deut. 11. 12. land thy God *careth*
John 10. 13. hireling *c.* not for
1 Cor. 7. 32, 33, 34. unmarried *c.* for things of Lord, married *c.* for things of the world
1 Pet. 5. 7. for he *c.* for you
2 Kings 4. 13. been *careful* for us
Jer. 17. 8. not be *c.* in the year of
Dan. 3. 16. not *c.* to answer thee
Luke 10. 41. art *c.* and troubled about many things
Phil. 4. 6. be *c.* for nothing; but
10. were *c.* but ye lacked opportunity
Tit. 3. 8. be *c.* to maintain good

Ezek. 12. 18, 19. *carefulness*, 1 Cor. 7. 32. 2 Cor. 7. 11.
Isa. 32. 9. *careless* daughters, 10. 11.
R. V. Ezek. 4. 16. carefulness; 1 Pet. 5. 7. anxiety; Phil. 4. 10. did take thought; Deut. 15. 5; Phil. 2. 28; Heb. 12. 17. diligently; Mic. 1. 12. anxiously; 1 Cor. 7. 32. be free from cares; 2 Cor. 7. 11. earnest care; Judg. 18. 7. in security; Ezek. 39. 6. securely
CARNAL, sold under sin, Rom. 7. 14.
Rom. 8. 7. *c.* mind is enmity against God
15. 27. minister to them in *c.*
1 Cor. 3. 1. not speak but as to *c.*
3. ye are yet *c.* — are ye not *c.*
9. 11. if we reap your *c.* things
2 Cor. 10. 4. our weapons are not *c.*
Heb. 7. 16. law of a *c.* commandment
Rom. 8. 6. to be *c.* minded is death
R. V. 1 Cor. 3. 4. men; 2 Cor. 10. 4. of the flesh; Rom. 8. 6, 7. mind of the flesh
CARPENTER, 2 Sam. 5. 11. Isa. 41. 7. Jer. 24. 1. Zech. 1. 20.
Matt. 13. 55. *carpenter's son*, Mark 6. 3.
R. V. Jer. 24. 1; 29. 2. craftsmen; Zech. 1. 20. smiths
CARRY us not up hence, Ex. 33. 15.
Num. 11. 12. *c.* them in thy bosom
Eccl. 10. 20. bird of air shall *c.*
Isa. 40. 11. *c.* lambs in his bosom
Luke 10. 4. *c.* neither purse nor scrip
1 Tim. 6. 7. can *c.* nothing out
Luke 16. 22. *carried* by angels into Abraham's bosom
Eph. 4. 14. *c.* about with every
Heb. 13. 9. *c.* about with divers
Rev. 17. 3. *c.* me away in spirit, 21. 10.
CART is pressed full, Amos 2. 13.
Isa. 5. 18. as it were with a *c.* rope
CASE, Ex. 5. 19. Ps. 144. 15.
R. V. Deut. 22. 1; 24. 13. surely
CAST law behind their backs, Neh. 9. 26.
Ps. 22. 10. *c.* upon thee from the
55. 22. *c.* thy burden on the Lord
Prov. 1. 14. *c.* in thy lot among us
Eccl. 11. 1. *c.* thy bread upon
Isa. 2. 20. a man shall *c.* his idols
Ezek. 23. 35. *c.* me behind thy back
Dan. 3. 20. *c.* them into the fiery
6. 24. *c.* them into the den of lions
Jonah 2. 4. I am *c.* out of thy sight
Mic. 7. 19. *c.* all their sins into the
Mal. 3. 11. vine shall not *c.* her fruit
Matt. 3. 10. hewn down and *c.* into the fire, 7. 19. Luke 3. 9.
5. 25. thou be *c.* into prison
7. 6. neither *c.* pearls before swine
15. 26. children's bread, and *c.* it to
22. 13. *c.* him into outer darkness
29, 30. *c.* it from *c.* into hell, 18. 8, 9.
Mark 11. 23. be thou *c.* into the sea
12. 44. she *c.* in all, Luke 21. 4.
Luke 1. 29. she *c.* in her mind what
58. lest the officer *c.* thee into prison
John 8. 7. let him first *c.* a stone at
Acts 16. 23. they *c.* them into prison
Rev. 2. 10. devil shall *c.* some of you into prison
20. 3. *c.* him into the bottomless
Lev. 26. 44. I will not *cast away*
2 Sam. 1. 21. shield is vilely —
Job 8. 20. God will not — perfect man
Ps. 2. 3. let us — their cords from us
51. 11. *c.* me not away from thy
Isa. 41. 9. I will not *c.* thee away
Ezek. 18. 31. — all your transgress.
Rom. 11. 1. hath God — his people, 2.
Heb. 10. 35. *c.* not away your confid.
1 Cor. 9. 27. myself be a —
2 Chron. 25. 8. God hath power to *cast down*

Job 22. 29. when men are — then
Ps. 37. 24. though he fall he shall not be —
42. 5. why art thou —, 11. & 43. 5.
Ps. 102. 10. lifted me up and — again
2 Cor. 4. 9. — but not destroyed
Ps. 44. 9. thou hast *cast off* and put
23. *c.* us not off for ever
71. 9. *c.* me not off in time of old
94. 14. Lord will not — his people
Jer. 31. 37. I will—all seed of Israel
Lam. 3. 31. Lord will not—for ever
Hos. 8. 3. Israel hath—thing is good
Rom. 13. 12. let us — the works of
1 Tim. 5. 12. they — their first love
Gen. 21. 10. *cast out* this bond woman and her son, Gal. 4. 30.
Ex. 34. 24. I will — the nations
Lev. 18. 24. which I — before thee
Deut. 7. 1. — many nations before
Ps. 78. 55. he—heathen before them
Prov. 22. 10.—the scorner, and contention
Isa. 14. 9. thou art — of thy grave
26. 19. the earth shall — the dead
66. 5. *c.* you out for my name's sake
Jer. 7. 15. I will *c.* out of my sight
15. 1. *c.* them out of my sight
Matt. 7. 5. *c.* beam out of thine eye
8. 12. children of kingdom shall be —
12. 24. doth not—devils but by Beelzebub
21. 12. — them that sold and
Mark 9. 28. why could not we *c.* out
16. 9. he had — seven devils
17. in my name shall they—devils
Luke 6. 22. — your name as evil
John 6. 37. that cometh will in no wise —
Rev. 12. 9. the dragon was —
Ps. 73. 18. thou *castedst* them down
Job 15. 4. thou *castest* off fear
Ps. 50. 17. *c.* my words behind thee
Job 21. 10. cow *casteth* not her calf
Ps. 147. 6. *c.* the wicked to ground
Jer. 6. 7. so she *c.* out her wicked.
Matt. 9. 34. he *c.* out devils through Beelzebub, Mark 3. 22. Luke 11. 15.
1 John 4. 18. perfect love *c.* out fear
3 John 10. *c.* them out of the
Job 6. 21. ye see my *casting* down
Rom. 11. 15. if *c.* away of them
2 Cor. 10. 5. *c.* down imaginations
1 Pet. 5. 7. *c.* all your care on him
CASTOR and Pollux, Acts 28. 11.
CATCH every man his wife, Judg. 21. 21.
Ps. 10. 9. he lieth in wait to *c.* poor
Jer. 5. 26. they set a trap, they *c.* men
Mark 12. 13. they *c.* him in his
Luke 5. 10. henceforth thou shalt *c.* men
R. V. Matt. 13. 19; John 10. 12. snatcheth
CATTLE on a thousand hills are mine, Ps. 50. 10.
104. 14. he causeth grass to grow for *c.*
Ezek. 34. 17. I judge between *c.* and *c.*
John 4. 12. drank thereof and his *c.*
R. V. Gen. 30. 40-43. flock
CAUGHT him and kissed him, Prov. 7. 13.
John 21. 3. that night they *c.* noth.
Acts 8. 39. Spirit of the Lord *c.* away Philip
2 Cor. 12. 4. he was *c.* up into para.
16. being crafty I *c.* you with guile
1 Thes. 4. 17. *c.* up together with
Rev. 12. 5. her child was *c.* up to
CAUL, Isa. 3. 18. Hos. 13. 8.
CAUSE come before judges, Ex. 22. 9.
Ex. 23. 2. not speak in a *c.* to
6. nor wrest judgment of poor in *c.*
Deut. 1. 17. *c.* that is too hard for
1 Kings 8. 45. maintained their *c.*, 49.
Job 5. 8. to God would I commit my *c.*
Ps. 9. 4. maintain my right and my *c.*
Prov. 18. 17. that is first in his own *c.*
Eccl. 7. 10. what is *c.* that former
Isa. 51. 22. pleadeth *c.* of his people
Jer. 5. 28. judge not *c.* of fatherless, 22. 16.
11. 20. to thee I revealed my *c.*, 20. 12.
Lam. 3. 36. to subvert a man in his *c.*
Matt. 19. 3. put away his wife for every *c.*
2 Cor. 4. 16. for which *c.* we faint
5. 13. if we be sober it is for your *c.*
Ex. 9. 16. *for this cause*, Matt. 19. 5. Ex. 5. 31. John 12. 27. & 18. 37. Rom. 1. 13. & 13. 6. 1 Cor. 11. 30.
1 Tim. 1. 16. — I obtained mercy
Ps. 119. 161. *without cause*, Prov. 23. 29. Matt. 5. 22. John 15. 25.
Job 6. 24. *c.* me to understand
Ps. 10. 17. wilt *c.* thine ear to hear
67. 1. *c.* his face to shine, 80. 3, 7, 19.
143. 8. *c.* me to know the way
Isa. 3. 12. lead thee, *c.* thee to err, 9. 16.
58. 14. I will *c.* thee to ride on
66. 9. and not *c.* to bring forth
Jer. 3. 12. not *c.* my anger to fall
7. 3. *c.* you to dwell in his place, 7.
15. 4. *c.* them to be removed
11. *c.* the enemy to treat thee
44. *c.* their captivity to return, 33. 7. & 34. 22. & 42. 12.
32. 37. *c.* them to dwell safely
Lam. 3. 32. though he *c.* grief, yet
Ezek. 36. 27. *c.* you to walk in my statutes
Dan. 9. 17. *c.* thy face to shine on sanctuary
Rom. 16. 17. mark them which *c.* division
Prov. 7. 21. fair speech *caused* him
Prov. 10. 5. a son *causeth*, 17. 2. & 19. 26.
Matt. 5. 32. *c.* her to commit adultery
2 Cor. 2. 14. always *c.* us to triumph
Prov. 26. 2. curse *causeless* shall not
R. V. 2 Chron. 19. 10. controversy; Prov. 31. 9. judgment; John 18. 37. to this end; Matt. 5. 32; Rev. 13. 12. maketh; 2 Cor. 9. 11. worketh
CAVE, and a stone lay on it, John 11. 41.
Gen. 19. 30. Lot dwelt in a *c.* he and
23. 19. buried Sarah his wife in *c.*
25. 9. buried him in the *c.*
49. 29. bury me with my fathers in *c.*
Josh. 10. 16. hid themselves in a *c.*
1 Kings 18. 4. hid them by 50 in a *c.*
Isa. 2. 19. go into *caves* for fear of
Ezek. 33. 27. that be in the *c.* shall die
Heb. 11. 38. wandered in *c.* of the
R. V. Job 30. 6; Heb. 11. 38. holes
CEASE not day nor night, Gen. 8. 22.
Deut. 15. 11. poor shall never *c.* out of
Neh. 6. 3. why should the work *c.*
Job 3. 17. there the wicked *c.*
Ps. 37. 8. *c.* from anger and wrath
46. 9. he maketh wars to *c.* unto
Prov. 19. 27. *c.* to hear instruction
23. 4. *c.* from thine own wisdom
Isa. 1. 16. *c.* to do evil, learn to do
1. 22. *c.* ye from man whose breath
Acts 13. 10. wilt thou not *c.* to per.
1 Cor. 13. 8. there be tongues, they *c.*
Eph. 1. 16. *c.* not to give thanks for
Col. 1. 9. *c.* not to pray for you
2 Pet. 2. 14. that cannot *c.* from sin
Ps. 12. 1. the godly man *ceaseth*
Prov. 26. 20. no talebearer, strife *c.*
1 Thes. 5. 17. pray without *ceasing*, 2. 13. 1 Sam. 12. 23. Acts 12. 5. Rom. 1. 9. 2 Tim. 1. 3.
R. V. Rom. 1. 9; 2 Tim. 1. 3. unceasingly; Acts 12. 5. earnestly
CEDAR, Lev. 14. 4. Jer. 22. 14, 15.
2 Sam. 7. 2. I dwell in a house of *c.*
2 Kings 14. 9. thistle sent to *c.* in
Ps. 29. 5. voice of Lord breaketh *c.*
92. 12. grow like a *c.* in Lebanon
S. of S. 1. 17. the beams of our house are *c.*
Isa. 9. 10. we will change them into *c.*
Ezek. 17. 22. of the high *c.*
23. goodly *c.*
Amos 2. 9. like the height of the *c.*
CELEBRATE, death cannot, Isa. 38. 18.
R. V. Lev. 23. 32. keep
CELESTIAL, 1 Cor. 15. 40.
CHAFF, wicked as, Job 21. 18. Ps. 1. 4. & 35. 5. Isa. 5. 24. & 17. 13. & 29. 5. & 41. 15. Dan. 2. 35. Hos. 13. 3. Luke 3. 17.
Isa. 33. 11. ye shall conceive *c.* ye
Jer. 23. 28. what is the *c.* to the
Zeph. 2. 2. before the day pass as the *c.*
Matt. 3. 12. burn up *c.* in unquench.
R. V. Isa. 5. 24. dry grass; Jer. 23. 28. straw
CHAIN, Gen. 41. 42. Dan. 5. 7. Ezek. 19. 4, 9. Mark 5, 3. 4.
Ps. 73. 6. pride compasseth them as a *c.*
S. of S. 4. 9. with one *c.* of thy neck
Acts 28. 20. I am bound with this *c.*
2 Tim. 1. 16. was not ashamed of my *c.*
Ps. 149. 8. bind their kings with *chains*
Prov. 1. 9. shall be a *c.* about neck
2 Pet. 2. 4. delivered into *c.* of dark.
Jude 6. reserved in everlasting *c.*
R. V. Num. 31. 50. ankle chains; S. of S. 1. 10. strings; Isa. 3. 19. pendants; Jer. 39. 7; 52. 11. fetters Ezek. 19. 4. hooks; Jude 6. bonds
CHALDEANS, Job. 1. 17. Isa. 43 14. & 48. 20. Jer. 38. 2. & 39. 8. & 40 9. & 50. 35. Ezek. 23. 14. Dan. 1. 4 & 9. 1.
CHAMBER, Ps. 19. 5. Joel 2. 16.
Job 9. 9. maketh the *chambers* of the
Ps. 104. 3. beams of *c.* in the waters
Prov. 7. 27. going down to the *c.* of
S. of S. 1. 4. king brought me into his *c.*
Isa. 26. 20. enter into *c.* and shut thy
Matt. 24. 26. he is in the secret *c.*
Rom. 13. 13. not in *chambering* and wantonness
R. V. 1 Kings 6. 6. story; Ezek. 40. 7. lodge
CHANCE, happens, 1 Sam. 6. 9. Eccl. 9. 11. 2 Sam. 1. 6. Luke 10. 31.
CHANGE of raiment, Judg. 14. 12, 13. Zech. 3. 4. Isa. 3. 22.
Job 14. 14. patiently wait till my *c.* come
Heb. 7. 12. made of necessity a *c.* of law
Job 17. 12. they *c.* the night into
Ps. 102. 26. as a vesture shalt thou *c.*
Jer. 13. 23. can Ethiopian *c.* his skin
Mal. 3. 6. I am the Lord, I *c.* not
Phil. 3. 21. who shall *c.* our vile
1 Sam. 21. 13. *changed* his behavior
Ps. 102. 26. and they shall be *c.*
Jer. 2. 11. hath a nation *c.* their gods
Rom. 1. 23. *c.* the glory of God
1 Cor. 15. 51. shall all be *c.*, 52.
2 Cor. 3. 18. *c.* into the same image
Job 10. 17. *changes* and war are against
Ps. 55. 19. they have no *c.* therefore
15. 4. sweareth and *changeth* not
Dan. 2. 21. he *c.* the times and seas.
Mark 11. 15. *money changers*, Matt. 21. 12. John 2. 14, 15.
R. V. Job 30. 18. disfigured
CHANT to sound of viol, Amos 6. 5.
CHAPEL, the king's, Amos 7. 13.
CHARGE, Gen. 26. 5. & 28. 6.
Ps. 91. 11. give his angels *c.* over
Acts 7. 60. lay not this sin to their *c.*
Rom. 8. 33. any thing to the *c.* of
S. of S. 2. 7. I *c.* you, O daughters of Jerusalem, 3. 5. & 5. 8. & 8. 4.

1 Tim. 6. 17. *c.* them that are rich
Job 1. 22. nor *charged* God foolishly
1 Thes. 2. 11. *c.* every one as a father
2 Cor. 11. 9. *chargeable*, 1 Thes. 2. 9. 2 Thes. 3. 8.
R. V. 1 Thes. 2. 9; 2 Thes. 3. 8. burden
CHARIOT, Gen. 41. 43. & 46. 29.
Ex. 14. 25. took off their *c.* wheels
2 Kings 2. 11. appeared a *c.* of fire
S. of S. 3. 9. Solomon made himself *c.*
Mic. 1. 13. bind the *c.* to swift beasts
Acts 8. 29. join thyself to this *c.*
Ps. 20. 7. some trust in *chariots*
68. 17. *c.* of God are 20,000
S. of S. 6. 12. made me like the *c.*
Hab. 3. 8. ride upon thy *c.* of salva.
R. V. S. of S. 3. 9. palanquin; Isa. 21. 7, 9. troop; 2 Sam. 8. 4 ——
CHARITY edifieth, 1 Cor. 8. 1.
13. 1. if I have not *c.* I am nothing, 2. 3.
4. *c.* suffereth long, 8. *c.* never fail.
13. now abideth faith, hope, *c.*
Col. 3. 14. above all things put on *c.*
1 Thes. 3. 6. tidings of your faith and *c.*
1 Tim. 1. 5. end of the commandment is *c.*
2. 15. if they continue in faith and *c.*
2 Tim. 2. 22. follow righteousness, faith, *c.*
2 Tim. 3. 10. know my doctrine, faith, *c.*
Tit. 2. 2. sound in faith, in *c.*, in patience
3 John 6. borne witness of thy *c.*
1 Pet. 4. 8. have fervent *c.* among yourselves
5. 14. greet one another with a kiss of *c.*
2 Pet. 1. 7. add to brotherly kindness, *c.*
Jude 12. spots in your feasts of *c.*
Rom. 14. 15. walketh not *charitably*
CHARMED, Jer. 8. 17.
Deut. 18. 11. *charmers*, Ps. 58. 5. Isa. 19. 3.
CHASTE virgin, 2 Cor. 11. 2.
Tit. 2. 5. to be discreet, *c.*, good
1 Pet. 3. 2. your *c.* conversa., with
R. V. 2 Cor. 11. 2. pure
CHASTEN with rod of men, 2 Sam. 7. 14.
Ps. 6. 1. neither *c.* me in thy, 38. 1.
Prov. 19. 18. *c.* thy son while there is
Dan. 10. 12. to *c.* thyself before thy
Rev. 3. 19. as many as I love, I *c.*
Ps. 69. 10. *chastened* my soul with
1 Cor. 11. 32. we are *c.* of the Lord
Heb. 12. 10. for a few days *c.* us
Ps. 94. 12. blessed is the man whom thou *chastenest*
Deut. 8. 5. as a man *c.* his son
Prov. 13. 24. loveth him *chasteneth* him betimes
Heb. 12. 6. whom Lord loveth he *c.*
Job 5. 17. despise not thou *chastening* of the Lord, Prov. 3. 11. Heb. 12. 5.
Isa. 26. 16. when thy *c.* was upon
11. no *c.* for present is joyous
R. V. Dan. 10. 12. humble
CHASTISE you seven times, Lev. 26. 28.
Deut. 22. 18. elders shall *c.* him
1 Kings 12. 11. I will *c.* with scorpions, 14.
Hos. 7. 12. *c.* them as their congre.
Luke 23. 16. *c.* and release him, 22.
1 Chron. 10. 11, 14. father *chastised* with whips
Ps. 94. 10. *c.* the heathen
Deut. 11. 2. not seen *chastisement* of the
Isa. 53. 5. *c.* of our peace was upon
Jer. 30. 14. with the *c.* of a cruel one
Heb. 12. 8. if ye be without *c.* then
R. V. Heb. 12. 8. chastening
CHATTER like a crane, Isa. 38. 14.
CHEEK, 1 Kings 22. 24. Job 16. 10. Isa. 50. 6. Lam. 3. 30. Mic. 5. 1. Matt. 5. 39. Luke 6. 29. Deut. 18. 3.
S. of S. 1. 10. thy *cheeks* are comely
5. 13. his *c.* are as a bed of spices
R. V. Joel 1. 6. jaw
CHEER *be of good*, Matt. 9. 2. & 14. 27. Mark 6. 50. John 16. 33. Acts 23. 11. & 27. 22, 25.
Prov. 15. 13. *cheerful*, Zech. 9. 17.
2 Cor. 9. 6. *cheerfulness*, Rom. 12. 8.
Acts 24. 10. *cheerfully* answer for my.
R. V. Zech. 9. 17. flourish
CHERISH, Eph. 5. 29. 1 Thes. 2. 7.
CHERUBIMS, between, 1 Sam. 4. 4. 2 Sam. 6. 2. 2 Kings 19. 15. 1 Chron. 13. 6. Ps. 80. 1. & 99. 1. Isa. 37. 16.
R. V. cherubim
CHICKENS, hen gathereth, Matt. 23. 37.
CHIDE, not always, Ps. 103. 9.
R. V. Ex. 17. 2. strive, strove.
CHIEF, Ezra 9. 2. Neh. 11. 3.
Matt. 20. 27. that will be *c.* among
Luke 22. 26. that is *c.* as he that ser.
Eph. 2. 20. Jesus Christ himself being *c.*
1 Tim. 1. 15. sinners,—of whom I am *c.*
S. of S. 5. 10. *chiefest* among 10,000
Rom. 3. 2. *chiefly*, Phil. 4. 22. 2 Pet. 2. 10.
R. V. In O. T. frequently, prince, head, captain; Matt. 20. 27. first; Luke 11. 15. prince; 14. 1. rulers; Acts 18. 8–17 ——; Luke 19. 47; Acts 25. 2. principal men; Mark 10. 44. first; Rom. 3. 2. first of all; Phil. 4. 22. especially
CHILD, Gen. 37. 30. 1 Cor. 13. 11.
Ex. 2. 2. saw he was a goodly *c.*
2 Sam. 12. 16. David besought God for the *c.*
Ps. 131. 2. quieted myself as a *c.* weaned
Prov. 29. 15. *c.* left to himself bring.
Eccl. 4. 8. hath neither *c.* nor brother
Isa. 3. 5. *c.* behave himself proudly
9. 6. unto us a *c.* is born
11. 6. a little *c.* shall lead them
Jer. 1. 6. cannot speak for I am a *c.*
31. 20. dear son is he a pleasant *c.*
Hos. 11. 1. when Israel was a *c.* I loved
Matt. 18. 2. Jesus called a little *c.*
Mark 9. 36. took a *c.* and set him in
10. 15. receive kingdom of God as little *c.*
2. 43. *c.* Jesus tarried behind in Jerusalem
Acts 4. 27. against thy holy *c.* Jesus
13. 10. thou *c.* of the devil, thou
1 Cor. 13. 11. when I was a *c.*
Gal. 4. 1. as long as a *c.* differs noth.
2 Tim. 3. 15. from a *c.* hast known
Rev. 12. 4. to devour her *c.* as soon
5. her *c.* was caught up to God
1 Tim. 2. 15. to be saved in *childbearing*
Eccl. 11. 10. *childhood* and youth are
1 Cor. 13. 11. put away *childish* things
Gen. 15. 2. *childless*, Jer. 22. 30.
25. 22. *children* struggled together
30. 1. give me *c.* or else I die
Ps. 17. 14. they are full of *c.* and
Prov. 17. 6. the glory of *c.* are their fathers
S. of S. 1. 6. mother's *c.* were angry
Isa. 1. 2. I brought up *c.* and they
3. 12. *c.* are their oppressors
30. 9. lying *c.*—*c.* that will not hear
Mal. 4. 6. turn hearts of fathers to *c.*
Matt. 3. 9. of these stones to raise up *c.*
15. 26. not meet to take *c.*'s bread
16. 8. *c.* of this world wiser than *c.*
Acts 3. 25. ye are *c.* of the prophets
Rom. 8. 17. if *c.* then heirs, heirs of
1 Cor. 7. 14. else were your *c.* unclean
14. 20. be not *c.* in understanding
Eph. 2. 3. are by nature *c.* of wrath
Eph. 5. 6. cometh the wrath of God upon the *c.* of disobedience. Col. 3. 6.
6. 1. *c.* obey your parents, Col. 3. 20.
Heb. 12. 5. speaketh unto you as *c.*
1 Pet. 1. 14. as obedient *c.* not fashioning
Rev. 2. 23. kill her *c.* with death
Ex. 34. 7. *children's children*, Jer. 2. 9. Ps. 103. 17. & 128. 6. Prov. 13. 22.
Prov. 17. 6.—are crown of old men
Matt. 5. 9. *children of God*, Luke 20. 36. John 11. 52. Rom. 8. 21. & 9. 8, 26. Gal. 3. 26. 1 John 3. 10. & 5. 2.
Ps. 89. 30. *his children*, 103. 13.
Luke 16. 8. *children of light*, John 12. 36. Eph. 5. 8. 1 Thes. 5. 5.
Matt. 18. 3. *little children*, 19. 14. Mark 10. 14. Luke 18. 16. John 13. 33. Gal. 4. 19. 1 John 2. 1, 12, 13. & 4. 4.
Rom. 9. 8. *children of promise*, Gal. 4. 28.
Ps. 128. 3, 6. *thy children*, 147. 13. Isa. 54. 13. Matt. 23. 37. Luke 13. 34. 2 John 4.
Ps. 115. 14. *your children*, Matt. 7. 11. Luke 11. 13. Acts 2. 39.
Job 19. 18. *young children*, Lam. 4. 4. Nah. 3. 10. Mark 10. 13.
CHOKE, Matt. 13. 7, 22. Mark 4. 7, 19. & 5. 13. Luke 8. 14, 33.
CHOOSE life, Deut. 30. 19.
Josh. 24. 15. *c.* you whom ye will
2 Sam. 24. 12. *c.* thee one of them
Ps. 25. 12. teach in the way that he shall *c.*
47. 4. *c.* our inheritance for us
Prov. 1. 29. did not *c.* the fear of
Isa. 7. 15. *c.* good and refuse evil, 16.
Phil. 1. 22. what I shall *c.* I wot not
Ps. 65. 4. man whom thou *choosest*
Heb. 11. 25. *choosing* rather to suf.
Josh. 24. 22. ye have *chosen* the Lord
1 Chron. 16. 13. children of Jacob his *c.*
Ps. 33. 12. *c.* for his own inheritance
105. 6. children of Jacob his *c.*, 43.
Prov. 16. 16. rather to be *c.* than
22. 1. a good name is rather to be *c.* than
Isa. 66. 3. have *c.* their own ways
Jer. 8. 3. death shall be *c.* rather
Matt. 20. 16. many are called, but few *c.*, 22. 14.
Mark 13. 20. elect's sake whom he hath *c.*
Luke 10. 42. Mary hath *c.* that good
John 15. 16. ye have not *c.* me
Acts 9. 15. he is a *c.* vessel to me
22. 14. God hath *c.* thee that thou
1 Cor. 1. 27. God hath *c.* the foolish
Eph. 1. 4. hath *c.* us in him before
2 Thes. 2. 13. from beginning *c.* you
1 Pet. 2. 4. *c.* of God and precious
9. ye are a *c.* generation
Rev. 17. 14. are called, and *c.* and
Isa. 41. 9. *I have chosen*, 43. 10. & 58. 6. Matt. 12. 18.
Ps. 119. 30.—the way of truth
173.—thy precepts
Isa. 44. 1, 2. Israel—Jeshurun whom
48. 10.—thee in the furnace of affli
John 13. 18. I know whom—
15. 16, 19.—you out of the world
R. V. Acts 22. 14; 2 Cor. 8. 19. appointed
CHRIST should be born, Matt. 2. 4.
16. 16. thou art *C.* son of the living
23. 8. one is your master even *C.*, 10.
Mark 9. 41. because ye belong to *C.*
Luke 24. 26. ought not *C.* to have suffered
46. it behooved *C.* to suffer and
John 4. 25. Messias which is call.
13. 34. that *C.* abideth for ever

Acts 8. 5. preached *C.* to them
Rom. 5. 6. *C.* died for the ungodly
8. while yet sinners *C.* died for us
10. if *C.* be in you the body is dead
10. 4. *C.* is the end of the law for
15. 3. *C.* pleased not himself
1 Cor. 1. 24. *C.* the power of God
3. 23. ye are *C.*'s and *C.* is God's
Gal. 2. 20. crucified with *C.* *C.* liveth
3. 13. *C.* hath redeemed us from
5. 24. that are *C*'s have crucified
Eph. 2. 12. ye were without *C.* being alienated
4. 20. ye have not so learned *C.*
5. 14. *C.* shall give thee light
23. as *C.* is the head of the church
6. 5. in singleness of heart as unto *C.*
Phil. 1. 21. to me to live is *C.*
23. I desire to dep., and be with
3. 8. that I may win *C.*
4. 13. can do all things through *C.*
Col. 1. 27. *C.* in you hope of glory
3. 4. when *C.* who is our life shall
Rom. 8. 1. to them in *Christ Jesus*
2. law of the spirit of life in—
1 Cor. 1. 30. of him are ye in—
2. 2. save—and him crucified
2 Cor. 13. 5. how that—is in you
Gal. 3. 28. ye are all one in—, 26.
Eph. 1. 1. saints and to faithful in—
2. 10. created in—unto works, 1. 1.
Phil. 2. 11. confess that—is Lord
3. 3. rejoice in—and have no confidence
12. for which I am apprehended of—
Col. 2. 6. received—the Lord, 3. 24.
1 Tim. 1. 15. that—that came into
1 Tim. 2. 5. one mediator, the man—
Heb. 13. 8. —the same yesterday
Rom. 12. 5. one body *in Christ*
16. 3, 7. were—before me, 10.
1 Cor. 15. 18. fallen asleep—are perished
19. in this life only have hope—
2 Cor. 5. 17. if any man be —he is a
19. God was—reconciling world
Gal. 1. 22. churches which were—
Phil. 1. 13. my bonds—are manifest
2. 1. if there be any consolation—
Col. 1. 2. saints and faithful breth.
1 Thes. 4. 16. the dead—shall rise
John 1. 25. *that Christ*, 6. 69.
Matt. 16. 20. *the Christ*, 26. 63. Mark 8. 29. & 14. 61. Luke 3. 15. & 9. 20. & 22. 67. John 1. 20, 41. & 3. 28. & 4. 29, 42. & 7. 41. & 10. 24. & 11. 27. & 20. 31. 1 John 2. 22. & 5. 1.
Rom. 6. 8. if we be dead *with Christ*
8. 17. heirs of God and joint heirs—
Gal. 2. 20. I am crucified—
Eph. 2. 5. quickened us together—
Col. 2. 20. if ye be dead—from the
Rev. 20. 4. reigned—1000 years
Acts 26. 28. persuadest me to be a *Christian*
1 Pet. 4. 15. suffer as a *C.* let him not be
Acts 11. 26. first called *Christians* at Antioch

CHURCH, Acts 14. 27. & 15. 3. 1 Cor. 4. 17. & 14. 4, 23. 3 John 9.
Matt. 16. 18. on this rock will I build my *c.*
18. 17. tell it to the *c.* neglect to hear the *c.*
Acts 2. 47. Lord added to *c.* daily
8. 1. great persecution against *c.*
11. 26. assembled themselves with *c.*
14. 23. ordained elders in every *c.*
1 Cor. 14. 4, 5. that *c.* may receive edifying
Eph. 1. 22. head over all things to *c.*
3. 10. known by *c.* the wisdom of
Eph. 5. 25. as Christ loved the *c.* and gave
32. concerning Christ and the *c.*
4. 15. no *c.* communic. with me
Col. 1. 18. head of the body, the *c.*
1 Tim. 5. 16. let not *c.* be charged
Heb. 12. 23. assembly and *c.* of first-born
3 John 6. witness of charity before *c.*
Acts 7. 38. *in the church*, 13. 1. 1 Cor. 6. 4. & 11. 18. & 12. 28. & 14. 19, 28, 35. Eph. 3. 21. Col. 4. 16.
Acts 20. 28. *the church of God*, 1 Cor. 1. 2. & 10. 32. & 15. 9. 2 Cor. 1. 1. Gal. 1. 13. 1 Tim. 3. 5.
9. 31. then had *churches* rest
15. 41. confirming the *c.*
16. 5. so were the *c.* established in
Rom. 16. 16. *c.* of Christ salute you
1 Cor. 7. 17. and so ordain I in all *c.*
14. 33. as in all *c.* of saints
34. women keep silence in the *c.*
1 Thes. 2. 14. became followers of *c.*
2 Thes. 1. 4. glory in you in the *c.*
Rev. 1. 4. seven *c.* in Asia, 11.
20. angels of the seven *c.* and
2. 7. hear what the Spirit saith to the *c.*, 11. 17, 29. & 3. 6, 13, 22.
2. 23. and all the *c.* shall know I
22. 16. testify these things in the *c.*

CHURL, Isa. 32. 5, 7. *Churlish*, 1 Sam. 25. 3.

CIRCUIT, 1 Sam. 7. 16. Job 22. 14. Ps. 19. 6. Eccl. 1. 6.

CIRCUMCISE the flesh, Gen. 17. 11.
Deut. 10. 16. *c.* the foreskin of your
Josh. 5. 2. *c.* again Israel
4. Joshua did *c.*
Jer. 4. 4. *c.* yourselves to the Lord
Gen. 17. 10. every male shall be *circumcised*, 14. 23, 26. Phil. 3. 5.
21. 4. Abraham *c.* his son Isaac
Josh. 5. 3. *c.* the children of Israel
Acts 15. 1. except ye be *c.* ye cannot be
Acts 16. 3. *c.* him because of the
Gal. 2. 3. neither was compelled to be *c.*
John 7. 22. Moses gave unto you *circumcision*
Acts 7. 8. God gave him the covenant of *c.*
Rom. 2. 25. *c.* profiteth if thou
29. *c.* is that of the heart in the
3. 1. what profit is there of *c.*
30. which shall justify *c.* by faith
4. 9. comes this blessedness on the *c.* only
11. he received the sign of *c.*
15. 8. Christ was minister of the *c.*
1 Cor. 7. 19. *c.* is nothing but keep.
Gal. 2. 7. gospel of the *c.* was unto
Phil. 3. 3. we are the *c.* which
Col. 2. 11. circumcised with *c.*
Tit. 1. 10. especially they of the *c.*

CIRCUMSPECT, Ex. 23. 13.
Eph. 5. 15. that ye walk *circumspectly*
R. V. take ye heed

CISTERN, Prov. 5. 15. Eccl. 12. 6.
Jer. 2. 13. hewed them out *cisterns*

CITY, Cain builded a, Gen. 4. 17.
Ps. 107. 4. found no *c.* to dwell in
7. might go to *c.* of habitation
127. 1. except the Lord keep the *c.*
S. of S. 3. 2. I will go out about the *c.* in
Isa. 1. 21. the faithful *c.* is become
33. 20. the *c.* of our solemnities
Jer. 3. 14. take one of a *c.* two of a
Amos 3. 6. shall there be evil in a *c.*
Zeph. 2. 15. this is the rejoicing *c.*
Zech. 8. 3. shall be called *c.* of truth
Matt. 5. 14. a *c.* set on a hill
Luke 10. 8. into whatsoever *c.* ye
19. 41. he beheld *c.* and wept over
Heb. 11. 10. he looked for a *c.*
12. 22. to the *c.* of the living God
Rev. 3. 12. name of the *c.* of my
Neh. 11. 1, 18, *holy city*, Isa. 48. 2.
Isa. 52. 1. Dan. 9. 24. Matt. 4. 5. & 27. 53. Rev. 11. 2. & 21. 2. & 22. 19.
Num. 35. 6. *cities of refuge*, Josh. 21. 13, 21, 27, 32, 38.
Amos 4. 8. two or three *cities* wandered unto one city
Luke 19. 17. have thou authority over ten *c.*
Acts 26. 11. persecuted unto strange *c.*
Rev. 16. 19. the *c.* of the nations
Luke 15. 15. *citizen*, & 19. 14.
Eph. 2. 19. fellow *citizens* with saints

CLAMOR, Eph. 4. 31. Prov. 9. 13.

CLAY, Job 27. 16. & 38. 14.
4. 19. them that dwell in houses of *c.*
10. 9. thou hast made me as the *c.*
Isa. 64. 8. we are the *c.* thou our potter, 45. 9. Jer. 18. 6.
Ps. 40. 2. brought me out of miry *c.*
Dan. 2. 33. part of iron, part of *c.*
Hab. 2. 6. that ladeth himself with thick *c.*

CLEAN beasts, Gen. 7. 2. & 8. 20.
Lev. 10. 10. between unclean and *c.*, 11. 47. Ezek. 22. 26. & 44. 23.
Job 14. 4. who bring *c.* thing out
15. 14. what is man that he should be *c.*
Ps. 19. 9. the fear of the Lord is *c.* enduring for ever
Prov. 16. 2. ways of man are *c.* in
Isa. 1. 16. wash ye, make you *c.* put
Jer. 13. 27. wilt thou not be made *c.*
Ezek. 36. 25. sprinkle *c.* water, ye shall be *c.*
Matt. 8. 3. I will, be thou *c.*, Luke 5. 13.
23. 25. make *c.* outside of, Luke 11. 39.
Luke 11. 41. all things are *c.* to you
John 13. 11. ye are *c.* but not all
Rev. 19. 8. fine linen, *c.* and white
Job 17. 9. *clean hands*, Ps. 24. 4.
Ps. 51. 10. *clean heart*, 73. 1.
18. 24. according to the *cleanness*
Amos 4. 6. given you *c.* of teeth in all cities
Ps. 19. 12. *cleanse* me from secret
119. 9. shall a young man *c.* his way
Jer. 33. 8. I will *c.* them fr. all sin
Ezek. 36. 25. from your idols will I *c.* you
Matt. 10. 8. heal sick, *c.* the lepers
2 Cor. 7. 1. let us *c.* ourselves from
Eph. 5. 26. *c.* it with the washing of
Jas. 4. 8. *c.* your hands, ye sinners
1 John 1. 9. *c.* us from all unright.
2 Chron. 30. 19. though not *cleansed* according
Ps. 73. 13. I have *c.* my heart in vain
Ezek. 36. 33. *c.* you from all iniqui.
Matt. 11. 5. the lepers are *c.*
Luke 17. 17. were there not ten *c.*, 9.
Acts 10. 15. what God hath *c.*, 11. 9.
1 John 1. 7. blood of Jesus Christ *c.*
R. V. Matt. 23. 25; Luke 11. 39. cleanse; Neh. 13. 22. purify; Ps. 19. 12. clear

CLEAR the guilty, Ex. 34. 7.
Ps. 51. 4. be *c.* when thou judgest
Zech. 14. 6. light shall not be *c.* nor
R. V. Zech. 14. 6. with brightness; 2 Cor. 7. 11; Rev. 21. 18. pure; 22. 1. bright; Job 33. 3. sincerely

CLEAVE to his wife, Gen. 2. 24. Matt. 19. 5. Mark 10. 7. Eph. 5. 31.
Deut. 4. 4. ye did *c.* to the Lord, 10. 20. & 11. 22. & 13. 4. & 30. 20. Josh. 22. 5. & 23. 8.
Ps. 22. 15. tongue *cleaveth* to my
119. 25. my soul *c.* unto the dust
137. 6. my tongue *c.* to the roof
Rom. 12. 9. *c.* to that which is good

CLIMB, Jer. 4. 29. Joel 2. 7, 9.
Amos 9. 2. though they *c.* up to
John 10. 1. *climbeth* some other way

CLOAK, Matt. 5. 40. Luke 6. 29.
Isa. 59. 17. clad with zeal as with *c.*
John 15. 22. have no *c.* for their sin
1 Thes. 2. 5. nor used *c.* of covetous.
1 Pet. 2. 16. liberty for *c.* of malic.

CLOSET, Joel 2. 16. Matt. 6. 6.
R. V. Luke 12. 3. inner chamber
CLOTHE, Matt. 6. 30. Luke 12. 28.
Job 10. 11. *clothed* me with skin and
Ps. 35. 26. be *c.* with shame, 132. 18.
109. 18. he *c.* himself with cursing
132. 16. *c.* her priests with salvation
Ezek. 16. 10. I *c.* thee with broid.
Zeph. 1. 8. *c.* with strange apparel
Matt. 11. 8. *c.* in soft raiment
25. 36. naked, and ye *c.* me
43. *c.* me not
2 Cor. 5. 2. desiring to be *c.* upon
1 Pet. 5. 5. be *c.* with humility
Rev. 3. 5. be *c.* with white raiment
11. 3. prophecy *c.* in sackcloth and
12. 1. a woman *c.* with the sun
19. 14. *c.* in fine linen, clean and white
Job 22. 6. *clothing*, 24. 27. Mark 12. 38. Acts 10. 30. Jas. 2. 3.
Ps. 45. 13. her *c.* is of wrought gold
Isa. 59. 17. garment of vengeance for *c.*
Matt. 7. 15. come in sheep's *c.*
11. 8. that wear soft *c.* are in
CLOUD, Gen. 9. 13. Isa. 18. 4.
Isa. 44. 22. blotted out as a *c.* and
1 Cor. 10. 1. our fathers were under *c.*
2. baptized unto Moses in the *c.*
Heb. 12. 1. so great a *c.* of witness.
Rev. 11. 12. ascended to heaven in *c.*
Hos. 6. 4. *morning cloud*, 13. 3.
Judg. 5. 4. *clouds* dropped water
2 Sam. 23. 4. as a morning without *c.*
Ps. 36. 5. faithfulness reacheth to *c.*
57. 10. thy truth unto the *c.*, 108. 4.
104. 3. who maketh *c.* his chariot
Matt. 24. 30. coming in the *c.* of heaven, 26. 64. Mark 13. 26. & 14. 62.
1 Thes. 4. 17. caught up in *c.* to meet
2 Pet. 2. 17. *c.* carried with a temp.
Jude 12. *c.* without water, carried
Rev. 1. 7. he cometh with *c.*
R. V. In Job and Ps. mostly skies
CLOVEN tongues, Acts 2. 3.
R. V. Acts 2. 3. parting asunder
COAL, 2 Sam. 14. 7. Isa. 47. 14. & 6. 6. Lam. 4. 8. Ps. 18. 8, 12. & 120. 4. & 140. 10.
Prov. 6. 28. can one go on hot *coals*
25. 22. heap *c.* of fire on head, Rom. 12. 20.
26. 21. as *c.* are to burning
S. of S. 8. 6. *c.* thereof are *c.* of fire
R. V. Prov. 26. 21. embers; S. of S. 8. 6. flashes; Hab. 3. 5. bolts
COAT, Gen. 3. 21. & 37. 3. Ex. 28. 4.
S. of S. 5. 3. put off my *c.* how put
Matt. 5. 40. if any man take away thy *c.*
R. V. 1 Sam. 2. 19. robe; Dan. 3. 21, 27. hosen
COLD, Gen. 8. 22. Job 24. 7. & 37. 9.
Matt. 24. 12. the love of many wax *c.*
Rev. 3. 15. neither *c.* nor hot, 16.
R. V. Prov. 20. 4. winter
COLLECTION, 1 Cor. 16. 1.
R. V. 2 Chron. 24. 6, 9. tax.
COME not into my secret, Gen. 49. 6.
Ex. 20. 24. I will *c.* and bless thee
1 Sam. 17. 45. I *c.* to thee in name
1 Chron. 29. 14. all things *c.* of thee, 12.
Job 22. 21. good shall *c.* unto thee
Ps. 22. 31. they shall *c.* and shall
40. 7. lo I *c.*, Heb. 10. 9.
Eccl. 9. 2. all things *c.* alike to all
S. of S. 4. 16. awake north wind, *c.* thou south
Isa. 26. 20. *c.* my people enter into
35. 4. God will *c.* and save you
Ezek. 33. 31. *c.* to thee as the people cometh
Mic. 6. 6. wherewith shall I *c.* before the Lord
Mal. 3. 1. Lord shall suddenly *c.* to
4. 6. lest I *c.* and smite the earth
Matt. 8. 11. many shall *c.* from the east and west, Luke 7. 19, 20.
11. 28. *c.* unto me all ye that labor
16. 24. if any man will *c.* after me
Luke 7. 8. I say *c.* and he cometh
Luke 14. 20. I have married a wife, I cannot *c.*
John 1. 39. *c.* and see, 46. & 4. 29.
Rev. 6. 1, 3, 5, 7, & 17. 1. & 21. 9.
John 5. 40. ye will not *c.* to me to
6. 44. no man can *c.* to me, except
7. 37. if any man thirst, let him *c.*
Acts 16. 9. *c.* over, and help us
1 Cor. 11. 26. show the Lord's death till he *c.*
2 Cor. 6. 17. *c.* out from among them
7. 25. save them that *c.* to God by
10. 37. he that shall *c.* will *c.*
Rev. 18. 4. *c.* out of her, my people
22. 7. I *c.* quickly, 12. 20.
17. Spirit and the bride say, *c.* athirst *c.*
20. amen, even so *c.* Lord Jesus
Ps. 118. 26. that *cometh* in the name
Eccl. 11. 8. all that *c.* is vanity
Matt. 3. 11. he that *c.* after me, is mightier
Luke 6. 47. whosoever *c.* to me and
John 3. 31. he that *c.* from above, is above all
6. 37. *c.* to me, I will in no wise cast
45. hath learned of Father, *c.* unto me
14. 6. no man *c.* to Father, but
Heb. 11. 6. that *c.* to God must
Jas. 1. 17. gift *c.* down from Father
Heb. 10. 1. make the *comers* perfect
Ps. 19. 5. as a bridegroom *coming*
121. 8. Lord shall preserve thy *c.* in
Mal. 3. 2. who may abide the day of his *c.*
4. 5. before the *c.* of the great day
Matt. 24. 3. what shall be sign of thy *c.*
27. so shall the *c.* of Son of man
48. my Lord delayeth his *c.*, Luke 12. 45.
John 1. 27. *c.* after me is preferred before
1 Cor. 1. 7. waiting for the *c.* of our
1 Cor. 15. 23. that are Christ's at his *c.*
1 Pet. 2. 4. to whom *c.* as to a living
2 Pet. 1. 16. the power and *c.* of
3. 12. hasting unto *c.* of day of God
1 Thes. 4. 15. *coming of the Lord*, 2 Thes. 2. 1. Jas. 5. 7, 8.
COMELY, 1 Sam. 16. 18. Job 41. 12.
Ps. 33. 1. praise is *c.* for the upright, 147. 1.
Prov. 30. 29. yea, four are *c.* in go.
S. of S. 1. 5. I am black but *c.*
10. thy cheeks are *c.* with rows
2. 14. thy countenance is *c.*
6. 4. thou art *c.* as Jerusalem
1 Cor. 7. 35. for that which is *c.*
Isa. 53. 2. no form nor *comeliness*
Ezek. 16. 14. perfect through my *c.*
R. V. Prov. 30. 29. stately; 1 Cor. 7. 35; 11. 13. seemly; Ezek. 16. 14. majesty
COMFORT in my affliction, Ps. 119. 50.
Matt. 9. 22. be of good *c.*, Mark 10. 49. Luke 8. 48. 2 Cor. 13. 11.
Acts 9. 31. walking in *c.* of the
Rom. 15. 4. patience and *c.* of the
1 Cor. 14. 3. to exhortation and *c.*
2 Cor. 7. 4. I am filled with *c.*
Col. 4. 11. have been a *c.* to me
Job 7. 13. my bed shall *c.* me
Ps. 23. 4. thy rod and staff they *c.*
119. 82. when wilt thou *c.* me
S. of S. 2. 5. *c.* me with apples, for
Isa. 40. 1. *c.* ye, *c.* ye my people
51. 3. Lord shall *c.* Zion, Zech. 1. 17.
61. 2. to *c.* all that mourn
Jer. 31. 13. I will *c.* and make them
Lam. 1. 2. none to *c.* her, 21.
2 Cor. 1. 4. be able to *c.* them — by *c.*
Eph. 6. 22. might *c.* your hearts
1 Thes. 4. 18. *c.* one another with
5. 14. *c.* the feeble minded, support
2 Thes. 2. 17. *c.* your heart and
Isa. 40. 2. *comfortably*, Hos. 2. 14. 2 Sam. 19. 7. 2 Chron. 30. 22. & 32. 6.
Gen. 24. 67. *comforted*, 37. 35.
Ps. 77. 2. my soul refused to be *c.*
119. 52. I have *c.* myself
Isa. 49. 13. God hath *c.* his people
Matt. 5. 4. that mourn, they shall be *c.*
Luke 16. 25. now is he *c.* and thou
Rom. 1. 12. I may be *c.* together
1 Cor. 14. 31. learn and all may be *c.*
2 Cor. 1. 4. wherewith we ourselves are *c.*
Col. 2. 2. that their hearts might be *c.*
1 Thes. 3. 7. were *c.* over you in all
John 14. 16, 26. *comforter*, 15. 26. & 16. 7.
Job 16. 2. *comforter*, Ps. 69. 20.
Isa. 51. 12. I am he that *comforteth*
2 Cor. 1. 4. *c.* us in all our tribula.
John 14. 18. *comfortless*
Ps. 94. 19. *comforts*, Isa. 57. 18.
R. V. Mal. 9. 22; Mark 10. 49. cheer; 1 Cor. 14. 3; Phil. 2. 1. consolation; 1 Thes. 2. 11. encouraging; 5. 11. exhort one another
COMMAND, Ex. 8. 27. & 18. 23.
Gen. 18. 19. he will *c.* his children
Lev. 25. 21. I will *c.* my blessing
Deut. 28. 8. Lord shall *c.* the bless.
Ps. 42. 8. Lord will *c.* his loving kindness
44. 4. *c.* deliverance for Jacob
Isa. 45. 11. work of my hands, *c.* ye
Matt. 4. 3. *c.* that these stones be
John 15. 14. if ye do whatsoever I *c.*
1 Cor. 7. 10. unto the unmarried I *c.*
2 Thes. 3. 4. do things which we *c.*
1 Tim. 4. 11. these things *c.* and
Ps. 68. 28. God hath *commanded* thy strength
111. 9. he hath *c.* his covenant
133. 3. *c.* blessing, even life for
Matt. 28. 20. whatsoever I have *c.* you
Heb. 12. 20. could not endure that was *c.*
Lam. 3. 37. when Lord *commandeth*
Acts 17. 30. now *c.* all men every.
Gen. 49. 33. end of *commanding* his
1 Tim. 4. 3. *c.* to abstain from meats
Num. 23. 20. receive *commandment* to bless
Ps. 119. 96. thy *c.* is exceed. broad
Prov. 6. 23. the *c.* is a lamp
Hos. 5. 11. willingly walked after *c.*
Matt. 22. 38. is the first and great *c.*
John 10. 18. this *c.* I received of
12. 49. the Father gave me a *c.*
50. his *c.* is life everlasting
13. 34. a new *c.* give I unto you
15. 12. this is my *c.* that ye love
Rom. 7. 8. sin taking occasion by *c.*
1 Tim. 1. 5. end of the *c.* is charity
Heb. 7. 16. law of a carnal *c.*
2 Pet. 2. 21. turn from the holy *c.*
1 John 2. 7. an old *c.* which ye had
Ex. 34. 28. wrote ten *commandments*, Deut. 4. 13. & 10. 4.
Ps. 111. 7. all his *c.* are sure
112. 1. delight greatly in his *c.*
119. 6. I have respect unto all thy *c.*
10. let me not wander from thy *c.*
19. hide not thy *c.* from me
21. which do not err from thy *c.*
35. make me to go in path of thy *c.*
47. I will delight myself in thy *c.*
48. thy *c.* which I have loved
66. I have believed thy *c.*
86. all thy *c.* are faithful
98. thy *c.* hath made me wiser
127. I love thy *c.*
131. longed for *c.*
143. thy *c.* are my delights
151. all thy *c.* are truth
166. I have done thy *c.*
172. all thy *c.* are righteousness
176. I do not forget thy *c.*
Matt. 15. 9. for doctrines *c.* of men
Matt. 22. 40. on these two *c.* hang all
Mark 10. 19. knowest the *c.*, Luke 18. 20.
Luke 1. 6. walking in all the *c.* of
Col. 2. 22. after the *c.* of men
1 John 3. 24. keepeth his *c.* dwelleth
2 John 6. love that walk after his *c.*
Num. 15. 40. *do all, — these, — my*

— *his c.*, Deut. 6. 25. & 15. 5. & 28. 1, 15. & 19. 9. & 27. 10. & 30. 8. 1 Chron. 28. 7. Neh. 10. 29. Ps. 103. 18, 20. & 111. 10. Rev. 22. 14.
R. V. very frequently, especially in N. T., charged or enjoined. Frequently, word, decree, precept, charge, statute.

COMMEND, Gen. 12. 15. Rom. 16. 1. 2 Cor. 3. 1. & 5. 12. & 10. 12.
Luke 23. 46. into thy hands I *c.*
Acts 20. 32. I *c.* you to God and to
14. 13. *commended* them to Lord
Luke 16. 8. Lord *c.* unjust steward
Rom. 5. 8. God *commendeth* his love
1 Cor. 8. 8. meat *c.* us not to God
2 Cor. 4. 2. *commending* ourselves to every man's conscience
6. 4. *c.* ourselves as ministers of
2 Cor. 3. 1. epistles of *commendation*
Ezra 8. 36. *commission*, Acts 26. 12.

COMMIT adultery, thou shalt not, Ex. 20. 14. Deut. 5. 18. Matt. 5. 27. & 19. 18. Rom. 13. 9. Lev. 5. 17. Luke 18. 20.
Gen. 39. 8, 22. *c.* or to *give in charge*
Job 5. 8. to God would I *c.* my cause
Ps. 31. 5. into thy hands I *c.* my
37. 5. *c.* thy way unto the Lord
Prov. 16. 3. *c.* thy works unto Lord
Luke 12. 48. *c.* things worthy of
John 2. 24. did not *c.* himself to
Rom. 1. 32. *c.* such things worthy
1 Tim. 1. 18. this charge I *c.* unto
Jer. 2. 13. *committed* two evils
Luke 12. 48. men have *c.* much
1 Tim. 1. 11. gospel *c.* to my trust, 1 Cor. 9. 17. 2 Cor. 5. 19. Tit. 1. 3. Gal. 2. 7.
6. 20. keep that which is *c.* to thee
2 Tim. 1. 12. which I have *c.* to him
1 Pet. 2. 23. *c.* himself to him that judgeth righteously
Jude 15. which they have ungodly *c.*
Ps. 10. 14. poor *committeth* himself
John 8. 34. who *c.* sin is the servant
1 John 3. 8. who *c.* sin is of the devil

COMMON, Num. 16. 29. 1 Sam. 21. 4, 5. Eccl. 6. 1. Ezek. 23. 42.
Acts 2. 44. had all things *c.*, 4. 32.
1 Cor. 10. 13. temptation *c.* to man
Tit. 1. 4. son after the *c.* faith
Jude 3. write of the *c.* salvation
Eph. 2. 12. *commonwealth* of Israel
Matt. 28. 15. *commonly*, 1 Cor. 5. 1.
R. V. Eccl. 6. 1. heavy upon; Jer. 31. 5. enjoy the fruits thereof; Acts 5. 18. public; 1 Cor. 10. 13. can bear; Matt. 28. 15. was spread abroad; 1 Cor. 5. 1. actually

COMMUNE with your own heart, Ps. 4. 4. & 77. 6. Eccl. 1. 16.
R. V. Gen. 42. 24; 43. 19; Judg. 9. 1; 1 Sam. 25. 39. spake; Zech. 1. 14. talked

COMMUNICATE to him that teacheth in all good things, Gal. 6. 6.
Phil. 4. 14. *c.* with my affliction
1 Tim. 6. 18. distribute, willing to *c.*
Heb. 13. 16. to *c.* forget not
Gal. 2. 2. *communicated* to them the
Phil. 4. 15. no church *c.* with me in
2 Kings 9. 11. *communication*
Matt. 5. 37. let your *c.* be yea, nay
Eph. 4. 29. let no corrupt *c.* proceed
Luke 24. 17. what manner of *c.* are
1 Cor. 15. 33. evil *c.* corrupt good
10. 16. *communion* of the blood of Christ — *c.* of the body of Christ
2 Cor. 6. 14. what *c.* hath light
13. 14. *c.* of the Holy Ghost be with
R. V. Gal. 2. 2. laid before them; Phil. 4. 14, 15. had fellowship; 2 Kings 9. 11. talk; Matt. 5. 37; Eph. 4. 29. speech; Col. 3. 8. speaking; Phile. 6. fellowship

COMPACT, Ps. 122. 3. Eph. 4. 16.

COMPANY, Gen. 32. 8, 21.
Ps. 55. 14. to the house of God in *c.*
Prov. 29. 3. keepeth *c.* with harlots
S. of S. 6. 13. as the *c.* of two armies
Acts 4. 23. went to their own *c.*
Rom. 15. 24. first filled with your *c.*
1 Cor. 5. 11. not to keep *c.* with
2 Thes. 3. 14. have no *c.* with him
Heb. 12. 22. innumerable *c.* of angels
Ps. 119. 63. I am a *companion* of all
Mal. 2. 14. thy *c.* and wife of cove.
Phil. 2. 25. Epaphroditus my *c.* in
Rev. 1. 9. your *c.* in tribulation
Ps. 45. 14. *companions* that follow
122. 8. for my *c.* sakes — peace be
S. of. S. 1. 7. aside by flocks of thy *c.*
Isa. 1. 23. princes *c.* of thieves
Heb. 10. 33. became *c.* of them
R. V. Num. 14. 7; 16. 16; 22. 4. congregation; Luke 5. 29; 23. 27. multitude; Acts 17. 5. crowd; Heb. 12. 22. hosts; Job 41. 6. bands of fishermen; 1 Chron. 27. 33. friend; Phil. 2. 25. fellow-worker; Rev. 1. 9. partaker with you

COMPARE, Isa. 40. 18. & 46. 5.
Ps. 89. 6. who in heaven can be *c.* to
Prov. 3. 15. not to be *c.* to wisdom, 8. 11.
S. of. S. 1. 9. I have *c.* my love to company
Rom. 8. 18. not worthy to be *c.*
1 Cor. 2. 13. *c.* spiritual things with
Judg. 8. 2. *comparison*, Hag. 2. 3. Mark 4. 30.
R. V. Mark 4. 30. set it forth

COMPASS, Ex. 27. 5. & 38. 4. 2 Sam. 5. 23. 2 Kings 3. 9. Prov. 8. 27.
Ps. 5. 12. with favor *c.* him about
Isa. 50. 11. *c.* yourselves with sparks
Jer. 31. 22. a woman shall *c.* a man
Hab. 1. 4. wicked doth *c.* about the
Matt. 23. 15. ye *c.* sea and land to
Ps. 16. 4. sorrow *compassed* me, 116. 3.
Jonah 2. 3. floods *c.* me about, 5.
Heb. 12. 1. we are *c.* about with a
Ps. 73. 6. pride *compasseth* them
Hos. 11. 12. Ephraim *c.* me about
R. V. Prov. 8. 27. circle; Isa. 44. 13. compasses; 2 Kings 3. 9; Acts 28. 13. made circuit. Frequently in O. T., turned about

COMPASSION, 1 Kings 8. 50. 2 Chron. 30. 9. 1 John 3. 17.
Matt. 9. 36. *moved with compassion*, 14. 14. & 18. 27.
Ps. 78. 38. *full of compassion*, 86. 15. & 111. 4. & 112. 4. & 145. 8.
Deut. 13. 17. *have compassion*, 33. 3. 2 Kings 13. 23. 2 Chron. 36. 15. Jer. 12. 15. Lam. 3. 32. Mic. 7. 19. Rom. 9. 15. Heb. 5. 2. & 10. 34. Jude 22.
Lam. 3. 22. his *compassions* fail not
R. V. Matt. 18. 33; Mark 5. 19; Jude 22. mercy; Heb. 5. 2. bear gently with

COMPEL them to come in, Luke 14. 23.
Esth. 1. 8. drinking, none did *c.*
2 Chron. 21. 11. *compelled* Judah
Acts 26. 11. I *c.* them to blaspheme
2 Cor. 12. 11. I am a fool, ye *c.* me
Gal. 2. 3. not *c.* to be circumcised
14. why *compellest* Gentiles to live
R. V. 1 Sam. 28. 23; Luke 14. 23. constrain

COMPLAIN, Num. 11. 11. Job 7. 11.
Lam. 3. 39. why doth a living man *c.*
Num. 11. 1. *complainers*, Jude 16.
Ps. 144. 14. *complaining* in streets
Job 21. 4. *complaint*, 23. 2. Ps. 142. 2.
R. V. Acts 25. 7. bringing charges

COMPLETE in him, Col. 2. 10.
4. 12. stand *c.* in all the will of God
R. V. Col. 2. 10. made full; 4. 12. fully assured

COMPREHEND, Job 37. 5. Eph. 3. 18. Isa. 40. 12. John 1. 4. Rom. 13. 9.
R. V. John 1. 5; Eph. 3. 18. apprehend; Rom. 3. 9. summed up

CONCEAL his blood, Gen. 37. 26.
Job 27. 11. with Almighty I will not *c.*
Job 41. 12. I will not *c.* parts nor proportion
Prov. 25. 2. glory of God to *c.* a thing
Ps. 40. 10. I have not *concealed* thy loving kindness
Prov. 12. 23. prudent man *concealeth* knowledge
R. V. Job 6. 10. denied; 4. 12. keep silence concerning

CONCEIT, own, Prov. 18. 11. & 26. 5, 12, 16. & 28. 11. Rom. 11. 25. & 12. 16.
R. V. Prov. 18. 11. imagination

CONCEIVE, Judg. 13. 3. Luke 1. 31.
Job 15. 35. they *c.* mischief, Isa. 59. 4.
Ps. 51. 6. in sin did my mother *c.*
Isa. 7. 14. a virgin shall *c.* a son
Num. 11. 12. have I *conceived* all this people
Ps. 7. 14. hath *c.* mischief — falsehood
Jer. 49. 30. *c.* a purpose against you
Acts 5. 4. why hast thou *c.* in thy heart

CONCISION, Phil. 3. 2.

CONCLUDED them all in unbelief, Rom. 11. 32.
Gal. 3. 22. Scripture *c.* all under sin
Eccl. 12. 13. *conclusion* of matter
R. V. Rom. 11. 32. shut up; Acts 21. 25. given judgment

CONCUPISCENCE, sinful lust. Rom. 7. 8. Col. 3. 5. 1 Thes. 4. 5.
R. V. Rom. 7. 8. coveting; Col. 3. 5. desire; 1 Thes. 4. 5. lust

CONDEMN wicked, Deut. 25. 1.
Job 9. 20. my own mouth shall *c.*
Ps. 37. 33. nor *c.* him when he is judged
94. 21. they *c.* innocent blood
Isa. 50. 9. Lord will help me who *c.* me
Luke 6. 37. *c.* not and ye shall not be *c.*
John 3. 17. God sent not his Son into the world to *c.* the world
1 John 3. 20. heart *c.* us, 21.
Matt. 12. 37. by words—*condemned*
John 3. 18. who believe is not *c.*
Rom. 8. 3. for sin *c.* sin in the flesh
1 Cor. 11. 32. not be *c.* with world
Tit. 2. 8. speech that cannot be *c.*
Prov. 17. 15. *condemneth* the just
Rom. 8. 34. who is he that *c.*
Luke 23. 40. same *condemnation*
John 3. 19. this is the *c.* that light
Rom. 8. 1. no *c.* to them in Christ
1 Tim. 3. 6. fall into *c.* of the devil
Jas. 3. 1. receive the greater *c.*
5. 12. swear not, lest ye fall into *c.*
R. V. Ps. 109. 31; John 3. 17. judge; John 3. 19; 5. 24; 1 Cor. 11. 34; Jas. 5. 12. judgment

CONDESCEND, Rom. 12. 16. to low

CONFESS, Lev. 5. 5. & 16. 21.
Lev. 26. 40. if they *c.* their iniquit.
Ps. 32. 5. I will *c.* my transgres.
Matt. 10. 32. shall *c.* me before men
Luke 12. 8. him will I *c.* before my
Rom. 10. 9. *c.* with thy mouth
Jas. 5. 16. *c.* your faults one to
1 John 1. 9. if we *c.* our sins, he is faithful
4. 15. *c.* Jesus is Son of God, 2. 3. 2 John 7.
Heb. 11. 13. *confessed*, Ezra 10. 1.
Prov. 28. 13. *confesseth* and forsak.
Josh. 7. 19. *confession*, 2 Chron. 30. 22. Ezra 10. 11. Dan. 9. 4.
1 Tim. 6. 13. witnessed a good *c.*

CONFIDENCE, Job 4. 6. & 31. 24.
Ps. 65. 5. *c.* of all the ends of the earth
118. 8. than to put *c.* in man
Prov. 3. 26. Lord shall be thy *c.*
Mic. 7. 5. put not *c.* in a guide,
Phil. 3. 3. have no *c.* in the flesh
Heb. 3. 6. if we hold fast the *c.*, 14.
10. 35. cast not away your *c.*
1 John 2. 28. appear we may have *c.*
Ps. 27. 2. *confident*, Prov. 14. 16.

R. V. Judg. 9. 26. trust; Acts 28. 31; Heb. 3. 6; 10. 35; 1 John 2. 28; 3. 21. boldness; 2 Cor. 5. 6, 8. of good courage
CONFIRM feeble knees, Isa. 35. 3.
Dan. 9. 27. shall *c.* the covenant
Rom. 15. 8. to *c.* the promises
1 Cor. 1. 8. shall *c.* you to the end
Isa. 44. 26. *confirmeth* word of his servant
Acts 14. 22. *confirming* souls of the
R. V. 2 Kings 14. 5; 1 Chron. 14. 2. established; Dan. 9. 27. made firm; Heb. 6. 17. interposed with
CONFLICT, Phil. 1. 30. Col. 2. 1.
CONFORMED to the image, Rom. 8. 29.
Rom. 12. 2. be not *c.* to this world
R. V. Rom. 12. 2. fashioned according
CONFOUND language, Gen. 11. 7.
Jer. 1. 17. lest I *c.* thee before them
1 Cor. 1. 27. foolish things to *c.* wise
Ps. 97. 7. *confounded* that serve
Jer. 17. 18. let not me be *c.*
Ezek. 16. 52. *c.* and bear shame, 54.
1 Pet. 2. 6. believeth shall not be *c.*
Ezra 9. 7. *confusion* of face, Dan. 9. 7, 8.
Ps. 44. 15. my *c.* is continually
1 Cor. 14. 33. God is not author of *c.*
R. V. Jer. 1. 17. dismay; 1 Cor. 1. 27. that he might put to shame; Ps. 66. 6. brought to dishonor; 83. 17; Ezek. 16. 54; Mic. 7. 16. ashamed; Jer. 10. 14; 46. 24; 50. 2. put to shame
CONGREGATION, Lev. 4. 21.
Job 15. 34. *c.* of hypocrites desolate
Ps. 1. 5. sinners in *c.* of righteous
26. 5. hated *c.* of evil doers
74. 19. forget not *c.* of thy poor
89. 5. faithfulness in *c.* of saints
Prov. 21. 16. remain in *c.* of dead
Hos. 7. 12. chastise as *c.* hath heard
Joel 2. 16. sanctify the *c.*
R. V. in O. T. generally, assembly, meeting; Acts 13. 43. synagogue
CONIES, Ps. 104. 18. Prov. 30. 26.
CONQUER, Rev. 6. 2.
Rom. 8. 37. more than *conquerors*
CONSCIENCE, John 8. 9. Acts 23. 1.
Acts 24. 16. a *c.* void of offence
Rom. 2. 15. *c.* bearing witness, 9. 1.
2 Cor. 1. 12. testimony of our *c.*
1 Tim. 3. 9. mystery of faith in
Tit. 1. 15. mind and *c.* is defiled
Heb. 9. 14. purge *c.* from dead
10. 2. worshippers no more *c.* of
Acts 23. 1. *good conscience,* 1 Tim. 1. 5. Heb. 13. 18. 1 Pet. 3. 21.
R. V. John 8. 9 ——
CONSENT, with one, Ps. 83. 5. Zeph. 3. 9. Luke 14. 18. 1 Cor. 7. 5.
Prov. 1. 10. entice thee, *c.* thou not
Rom. 7. 16. I *c.* to law that it is
Ps. 50. 18. *consentedst* to thief
Acts 8. 1. *consenting,* 22. 20.
R. V. 1 Sam. 11. 7. as one man; Dan. 1. 14. hearkened unto
CONSIDER, Lev. 13. 13. Judg. 18. 14.
Deut. 4. 39. *c.* it in thy heart
32. 29. O that—*c.* their latter end
Ps. 8. 3. when I *c.* the heavens
Eccl. 5. 1. *c.* not that they do evil
7. 13. *c.* the work of God
Isa. 1. 3. my people doth not *c.*
5. 12. neither *c.* operation of hands
Hag. 1. 5, 7. Lord *c.* your ways, 2. 15, 18.
2 Tim. 2. 7. *c.* what I say and Lord
Heb. 3. 1. *c.* apostle and high priest
10. 24. *c.* one another to provoke
12. 3. *c.* him that endured such
Job 1. 8. hast thou *considered* my
Ps. 31. 7. hast *c.* my trouble
Mark 6. 52. *c.* not miracle of loaves
Rom. 4. 19. *c.* not his own body
Matt. 7. 3. *considerest* not the beam
Ps. 41. 1. blessed *considereth* poor
Prov. 31. 16. she *c.* a field and buy.
Isa. 44. 19. none *c.* in his heart
Heb. 13. 7. *considering* end of conversation
R. V. Jer. 23. 20; 32. 24. understand; Lam. 1. 11; 2. 20; 5. 1. behold; Mark 6. 52. understood
CONSIST. Col. 1. 17. Luke 12. 15.
CONSOLATION, Acts 4. 36. & 15. 31.
Luke 2. 25. waited for *c.* of Israel
Rom. 15. 5. God of *c.* grant you be
2 Cor. 1. 5. so our *c.* aboundeth by
Phil. 2. 1. if any *c.* in Christ
2 Thes. 2. 16. given us everlasting *c.*
Heb. 6. 18. might have strong *c.*
Job 15. 11. *consolations*
R. V. Acts 4. 36. exhortation; Rom. 15. 5; 2 Cor. 1. 5; 7. 7; 2 Thes. 2. 16; Phile. 7. comfort; Heb. 6. 18. encouragement
CONSPIRACY against Christ, Matt. 26. 3; Mark 3. 6; 14. 1; Luke 22. 2; John 11. 55; 13. 18.
against Paul, Acts 23. 12.
CONSTANCY of Ruth, Ruth 1. 14.
Rom. 16. 3. of Priscilla and Aquila
CONSTRAIN, Gal. 6. 12. Acts 16. 15.
2 Cor. 5. 14. for the love of Christ *constraineth* us because we
1 Pet. 5. 2. not by *constraint*
R. V. Gal. 6. 12. compel
CONSUME, Deut. 5. 25. & 7. 16.
Ex. 33. 3. lest I *c.* thee in the way
Ps. 37. 20. they shall *c.* into smoke
78. 33. days did he *c.* in vanity
Ezek. 4. 17. *c.* away for iniquity
2 Thes. 2. 8. Lord shall *c.* with spirit
Jas. 4. 3. *c.* it upon your lusts
Ex. 3. 2. bush was not *consumed*
Ps. 90. 7. we are *c.* by thy anger
Prov. 5. 11. thy flesh and body are *c.*
Isa. 64. 7. *c.* us because of our
Lam. 3. 22. of Lord's mercy we are not *c.*
Gal. 5. 15. be not *c.* one of another
Deut. 4. 24. Lord is *consuming* fire
Lev. 26. 16. *consumption,* Deut. 28. 22. Isa. 10. 22, 23. & 28. 22.
R. V. Frequently in O. T. devour; 2 Thes. 2. 8. Jesus shall slay
CONTAIN, Ezek. 23. 32. & 45. 11.
1 Kings 8. 27. heaven of heavens cannot *c.* thee, 2 Chron. 2. 6. & 6. 18.
John 21. 25. world not *c.* the books
1 Cor. 7. 9. if they cannot *c.* let
R. V. 1 Cor. 7. 9. have not continency
CONTEMN, God, — wicked, Ps. 10. 13.
Ezek. 21. 13. if sword *c.* the rod, 10.
Ps. 15. 4. a vile person is *contemned*
Job 12. 21. pours *contempt* on prin.
Ps. 123. 3. filled with *c.*, 4.
Dan. 12. 2. some to everlasting *c.*
Mal. 1. 7. the table of the Lord is *contemptible*
2. 9. made you *c.* before all people
2 Cor. 10. 10. his speech is *c.*
R. V. Ps. 15. 4. despised
CONTEND, Deut. 2. 9. Job 9. 3.
Isa. 49. 25. I will *c.* with them that *c.*
Jer. 12. 5. how canst *c.* with horses
Amos 7. 4. Lord calleth to *c.* by fire
Jude 3. *c.* earnestly for the faith
Job 10. 2. cause why thou *contendest*
40. 2. that *contendeth* with the mighty instruct
Hab. 1. 3. *contention,* Acts 15. 39. 1. 16. 1 Thes. 2. 2.
Prov. 13. 10. by pride cometh *c.*
Jer. 15. 10. borne me a man of *c.*
Prov. 18. 18, 19. *contentions,* 19. 13. & 23. 29. & 27. 15. 1 Cor. 1. 11. Tit. 3. 9.
21. 19. *contentious,* 26. 21. & 27. 15. Rom. 2. 8. 1 Cor. 11. 16.
R. V. Prov. 29. 9. hath controversy
CONTENT, Gen. 37. 27. Luke 3. 14.
Phil. 4. 11. state therewith to be *c.*
1 Tim. 6. 8. raiment let us be *c.*
Heb. 13. 5. be *c.* with such things
3 John 10. with malicious words not *c.*
1 Tim. 6. 6. godliness with *contentment*
CONTINUAL, Ex. 29. 42. Num. 4. 7. Prov. 15. 15. Isa. 14. 6. Rom. 9. 2.
Gen. 6. 5. only evil *continually*
Ps. 34. 1. his praise *c.* in my
71. 3. I may *c.* resort
73. 23. yet I am *c.* with thee
119. 44. keep thy law *c.* for ever
Prov. 6. 21. bind them *c.* upon thy
Isa. 58. 11. Lord shall guide thee *c.*
Hos. 12. 6. wait on thy God *c.*
Acts 6. 4. give ourselves *c.* to prayer
Heb. 13. 15. sacrifice of praise to God *c.*
Deut. 28. 59. *continuance,* Ps. 139. 16. Isa. 64. 5. Rom. 2. 7.
R. V. Rom. 9. 2. unceasing; 1 Chron. 16. 11. evermore; Ps. 44. 15. all day long; 58. 7. apace; 109. 10——; Ps. 139. 16. day by day; Isa. 64. 5. them have we been of long time; Rom. 2. 7. patience
CONTINUE, Ex. 21. 21. Lev. 12. 4.
1 Sam. 12. 14. *c.* following the Lord
1 Kings 2. 4. Lord may *c.* his word
Ps. 36. 10. *c.* thy loving-kindness
John 8. 31. if ye *c.* in my word
15. 9. *c.* ye in my love, 10.
Acts 13. 43. to *c.* in grace of God
14. 22. to *c.* in the faith
Rom. 6. 1. shall we *c.* in sin that
11. 22. if thou *c.* in his goodness
Col. 1. 23. if ye *c.* in faith and not
4. 2. *c.* in prayer and watch
1 Tim. 2. 15. if they *c.* in faith
4. 16. doctrine *c.* in them
2 Tim. 3. 14. *c.* in things learned
Heb. 13. 1. let brotherly love *c.*
Rev. 13. 5. to *c.* forty-two months
Gen. 40. 4. *continued,* Neh. 5. 16.
Luke 6. 12. *c.* all night in prayer
22. 28. *c.* with me in temptations
Acts 1. 14. *c.* with one accord in
Heb. 8. 9. *c.* not in my covenant
1 John 2. 19. would have *c.* with us
Job 14. 2. shadow and *continueth* not
Gal. 3. 10. that *c.* not in all things
1 Tim. 5. 5. *c.* in supplication
Jas. 1. 25. looketh into the law and *c.*
Jer. 30. 23. *continuing,* Rom. 12. 12. Acts 2. 46. Heb. 13. 14.
R. V. John 2. 12; 8. 31; 15. 9. abide, abode; Acts 15. 35. tarried; 18. 11. dwelt; 20. 7. prolonged; in O. T. frequent changes to, abide
CONTRADICT-ING-ION, Acts 13. 45. Heb. 7. 7. & 12. 3.
R. V. Heb. 7. 7. any dispute; 12. 3. gainsaying
CONTRARY, Esth. 9. 1. Matt. 14. 24.
Lev. 26. 21. walk *c.* to, 26. 27, 30, 40, 41.
Acts 18. 13. *c.* to the law, 23. 3.
26. 9. many things *c.* to the name
Rom. 11. 24. grafted *c.* to nature
1 Thes. 2. 15. are *c.* to all men
1 Tim. 1. 10. is *c.* to sound doctrine
CONTRIBUTION, Rom. 15. 26.
CONTRITE heart, or spirit, Ps. 34. 18. & 51. 17. Isa. 57. 15, 16. & 66. 2.
CONTROVERSY, Deut. 17. 8. & 21. 5. & 25. 1. 2 Chron. 19. 8. Ezek. 44. 24.
Jer. 25. 31. Lord hath a *c.*, Isa. 34. 8.
Hos. 4. 1. & 12. 2. Mic. 6. 2.
1 Tim. 3. 16. without *c.* great is the
R. V. 2 Sam. 15. 2. suit
CONVENIENT, Jer. 40. 4, 5. Acts 24. 25.
Prov. 30. 8. feed with food *c.* for me
Rom. 1. 28. to do things — not *c.*
Phile. 8. to enjoin thee which is *c.*
R. V. Prov. 30. 8. that is needful; Rom. 1. 28. fitting; Eph. 5. 4; Phile. 8. befitting; 1 Cor. 16. 12. opportunity
CONVERSATION, Gal. 1. 13. Eph. 2. 3. & 4. 22. Heb. 13. 7. 1 Tim. 4. 12.

Ps. 37. 14. such as be of upright *c.*
50. 23. orders his *c.* aright, I will
2 Cor. 1. 12. in sincerity had our *c.*
Phil. 1. 27. let *c.* be as becometh
Heb. 13. 5. let *c.* be without covetousness
Jas. 3. 13. show out of good *c.* works
1 Pet. 1. 15. holy in all manner of *c.*
2 Pet. 2. 7. vexed with filthy *c.* of the
3. 11. in all holy *c.* and godliness
R. V. Ps. 37. 14. in the way; Gal. 1. 13; Phil. 1. 27; 1 Tim. 4. 12; 1 Pet. 3. 16. manner of life; 1 Pet. 2. 12; 3. 1. behavior; Heb. 13. 7; 2 Pet. 2. 7. life; 2 Pet. 3. 11. living

CONVERSION of Gentiles, Acts 15. 3.

CONVERT, and be healed, Isa. 6. 10.
Jas. 5. 19. err, and one *c.* him, 20.
Ps. 51. 13. sinners—*converted* to thee
Isa. 60. 5. abundance of the sea, *c.* to thee
Matt. 13. 15. should be *c.* and I heal
Luke 22. 32. when thou art *c.* strengthen
Acts 3. 19. repent and be *c.*
Ps. 19. 7. *converting* the soul
R. V. Ps. 19. 7. restoring; Isa. 60. 5. turned; Matt. 13. 15; 18. 3; Mark 4. 12; Luke 22. 32; John 12. 40; Acts 3. 19; 28. 27. turn, or turn again

CONVINCE, Tit. 1. 9. Jude 15.
Job 32. 12. *convinced*, Acts 18. 28. 1 Cor. 14. 24. Jas. 2. 9.
John 8. 46. who *convinceth* me of sin
R. V. 1 Cor. 14. 24. reproved by; Acts 18. 28. comforted; John 8. 46; Tit. 1. 9; Jas. 2. 9; Jude 15. convict

COPY of the law to be written by the king, Deut. 17. 18.

CORD, Josh. 2. 15. Mic. 2. 5.
Job 30. 11. he hath loosed my *c.*
Eccl. 4. 12. a threefold *c.* is not brok.
Isa. 54. 2. lengthen thy *c.* and strengthen
Job 36. 8. holden *in cords* of affliction
Ps. 2. 3. cast away their *c.* from us
Prov. 5. 22. holden with *c.* of his sins
Isa. 5. 18. draw iniquity with *c.* of vanity
Hos. 11. 4. drew them with *c.* of
R. V. Judg. 15. 13. ropes; Mic. 2. 5. the line

CORN, Gen. 41. 57. & 42. 2, 19.
Josh. 5. 11. eat of the old *c.* of the land, 12.
Job 5. 26. as a shock of *c.* cometh in
Ps. 65. 13. valleys covered with *c.*
72. 16. handful of *c.* in the earth
Prov. 11. 26. withholdeth *c.* people curse
Isa 62. 8. I will no more give *c.* to
Ezek. 36. 29. call for *c.* and increase
Hos. 2. 9. take away my *c.* in
10. 11. loveth to tread out the *c.*
14. 7. shall revive as *c.* and grow as
Zech. 9. 17. *c.* make young men cheer.
Matt. 12. 1. to pluck the ears of *c.*
John 12. 24. except *c.* of wheat fall
R. V. Matt. 12. 1. cornfield; John 12. 24. grain

CORNER, Prov. 7. 8, 12. Lev. 21. 5.
Prov. 21. 9. better dwell in *c.*, 25. 24.
Isa. 30. 20. teachers removed into *c.*
Zech. 10. 4. out of him came forth *c.*
Matt. 21. 42. become head of *c.*
Ps. 118. 22. *corner stone*, Isa. 28. 16. 1 Pet. 2. 6. Eph. 2. 20. Matt. 21. 42.
R. V. Ex. 25. 12; 37. 3; 1 Kings 7. 30. feet; Ex. 30. 4; 37. 27. ribs; Ex. 36. 25; 2 Kings 11. 11. side; Zech. 10. 4. corner stone

CORRECT thy son and he, Prov. 29. 17.
Ps. 39. 11. with rebuke dost *c.* man
Jer. 2. 19. own wicked. shall *c.* thee
Job 5. 17. happy is man whom God *c.*
Prov. 3. 12. whom Lord loveth he *c.*
Job 37. 13. whether for *correction*
Prov. 3. 11. but be not weary of his *c.*
23. 13. withhold not *c.* from child
Jer. 2. 30. they received not *c.*, 5. 3. & 7. 28. Zeph. 3. 2.
Hab. 1. 12. established them for *c.*
2 Tim. 3. 16. Scripture profitable for *c.*
R. V. Prov. 3. 12. reproveth; Heb. 12. 9. to chasten; Prov. 3. 11. reproof; Jer. 7. 28. instruction

CORRUPT, Job 17. 1. Ps. 38. 5.
Gen. 6. 11, 12. earth *c.* before God.
Ps. 14. 1. they are *c.*, 53. 1. & 73. 8.
Mal. 1. 14. sacrificeth to the Lord a *c.*
Matt. 7. 17, 18. a *c.* tree brings—
Eph. 4. 22. old man which is *c.*
29. let no *c.* communication
1 Tim. 6. 5. of *c.* minds, 2 Tim. 3. 8.
Matt. 6. 19. rust doth *c.*, 20.
1 Cor. 15. 33. evil communications *c.*
Gen. 6. 12. all flesh had *corrupted* his
Deut. 9. 12. thy people *c.* themsel.
Hos. 9. 9. have deeply *c.* themselves
2 Cor. 7. 2. we have *c.* no man
1 Cor. 9. 25. *corruptible*, 15. 53. 1 Pet. 1. 18, 23.
Job 17. 14. *corruption*, Ps. 16. 10. & 49. 9. Isa. 38. 17. Dan. 10. 8. John 2. 6. Acts 2. 27, 31. & 13. 34, 37. Rom. 8. 21. 1 Cor. 15. 42, 50. Gal. 6. 8. 2 Pet. 1. 4. & 2. 12, 19.
R. V. Job. 17. 4. consumed; Ps. 73. 8. scoff; Dan. 11. 32. pervert; Mal. 1. 14. blemished; Matt. 6. 19. consume; Jude 10. destroyed; Jonah 2. 6. pit; 2 Pet. 2. 12. destroying

COST, 2 Sam. 19. 42. & 24. 24. 1 Chron. 21. 24. Luke 14. 28.
R. V. John 12. 3. precious

COUNSEL, Num. 27. 21. & 31. 16.
Job 5. 13. *c.* of froward carried headlong
12. 13. he hath *c.* and understanding
21. 16. *c.* of the wicked far, 22. 18.
38. 2. who is this that darkeneth *c.* by words without knowledge, 42. 3.
Ps. 1. 1. walks not in *c.* of ungodly
33. 10. 11. *c.* of Lord stands for ever, Prov. 1 . 21. Isa. 46. 10, 11.
55. 14. we took sweet *c.* together
Prov. 1. 25. set at nought all my *c.*
8. 14. *c.* is mine and sound wisdom
11. 14. where no *c.* is people fall
20. 18. purpose established by *c.*
24. 6. by wise *c.* make war
27. 9. sweetness—by hearty *c.*
Isa. 11. 2. spirit of *c.* and might
28. 29. Lord wonderful in *c.* and
Jer. 32. 19. God great in *c.* mighty
Zech. 6. 13. *c.* of peace between them
Luke 7. 30. rejected *c.* of God against
Acts 2. 23. by determinate *c.*, 4. 28.
20. 27. to declare all the *c.* of God
Eph. 1. 11. after *c.* of his own will
Ezra 4. 5. *counsellors*, 7. 14. Job 3. 14. & 12. 17. Dan. 3. 24.
Ps. 119. 24. thy testimonies are my *c.*
Prov. 11. 14. in the multitude of *c.* is safety, 24. 26. & 15. 22.
12. 20. to *c.* of peace is joy
Isa. 9. 6. Wonderful, *C.*, the mighty
19. 11. wise *c.* of Pharaoh—brutish
R. V. Num. 27. 21; Judg. 20. 23—; Prov. 11. 14; 24. 6. guidance; Isa. 19. 17. purpose; Acts 5. 33. were minded

COUNT, Ex. 12. 4. Lev. 23. 15.
Num. 23. 10. who can *c.* the dust of
Job 31. 4. doth not he *c.* all my steps
Ps. 139. 18. if I *c.* them—more than
22. hate thee, I *c.* them my ene.
Acts 20. 24. neither *c.* I my life dear
Phil. 3. 7, 8, 9. I *c.* all things loss—dung
13. I *c.* not myself to have apprehended
Jas. 1. 2. *c.* it all joy when ye fall
5. 11. we *c.* them happy who endure
Gen. 15. 6. *counted* to him for righteousness, Ps. 106. 31. Rom. 4. 3.
Isa. 40. 17. *c.* to him less than nothing
Hos. 8. 12. of law *c.* as a strange thing
Luke 21. 36. *c.* worthy to escape
Acts 5. 41. that *c.* worthy to suffer
2 Thes. 1. 5. *c.* worthy of kingdom
1 Tim. 1. 12. he *c.* me faithful
5. 17. *c.* worthy of double honor
Heb. 3. 3. *c.* worthy of more glory
R. V. Mark 11. 32. verily held; Rom. 2. 26; 4. 3, 5; 9. 8. reckoned

COUNTENANCE, Gen. 4. 5. & 31. 2.
Num. 6. 26. lift up his *c.* on thee
1 Sam. 1. 18. her *c.* was no more sad
16. 7. look not on his *c.* nor height
Neh. 2. 2. why is thy *c.* sad
Job 29. 24. light of thy *c.* they cast
Ps. 4. 6. lift up light of thy *c.*, 80. 3, 7. 90. 8. settest secret sins in light of *c.*
S. of S. 2. 14. let me see thy *c.* comely
Matt. 6. 16. as hypocrites of a sad *c.*
Acts 2. 28. full of joy with thy *c.*
R. V. Ex. 23. 3. favor; Ps. 11. 7; 2 Cor. 3. 7. face; Ps. 21. 6. presence; S. of S. 5. 15. aspect; Matt. 28. 3. appearance

COUNTRY, far, Matt. 21. 33. & 25. 14. Mark 12. 1. Luke 15. 13. & 19. 12. & 20. 9. Prov. 25. 25.
Heb. 11. 14. declare they seek a *c.*
16. they desire a better *c.*—heavenly
2 Cor. 11. 26. *countrymen*, 1 Thes. 2. 14.
R. V. Matt. 9. 31; Acts 7. 3. land, Matt. 14. 35; Luke 3. 3; 4. 37. region; in O. T. mostly land, region, inheritance

COURAGE, Josh. 2. 11. Acts 28. 15.
Num. 13. 20. be of good *c.*, Deut. 31. 6. & 7. 23. Josh. 1. 6, 7, 9, 18. & 10. 25. & 23. 6. 2 Sam. 10. 12. & 13. 28. 1 Chron. 22. 13. & 28. 20. Ezra 10. 4. Ps. 27. 14. & 31. 24. Isa. 41. 6.

COURSE, Acts 13. 25. & 16. 11.
Acts 20. 24. finish my *c.* with joy
2 Thes. 3. 1. may have free *c.* and
2 Tim. 4. 7. I have finished my *c.*
R. V. Acts 21. 7. voyage; 1 Cor. 17. 27. in turn; 2 Thes. 3. 1. run; Jas. 3. 6. wheel

COURT, Ex. 27. 9. Isa. 34. 13.
Amos 7. 13. Bethel is king's *c.*
Ps. 65. 4. may dwell in thy *c.*
84. 10. day in thy *courts* better
92. 13. flourish in *c.* of our God
Isa. 1. 12. who required to tread my *c.*
62. 9. drink it in *c.* of my holiness
Luke 7. 25. delicate are in king's *c.*
Rev. 11. 2. *c.* without temple leave
1 Pet. 3. 8. be pitiful, *courteous*
Acts 27. 3. *courteously*, 28. 7.
R. V. 2 Kings 20. 4. part of the city; Amos 7. 13. royal house; 1 Pet. 3. 8. humble minded; Acts 27. 3. treated kindly

COVENANT, Gen. 17. 2. & 26. 28.
Gen. 9. 12. token of the *c.*, 13. 17.
17. 4. my *c.* is with thee, 7. 19.
11. a token of the *c.* betwixt
13. my *c.* shall be in the flesh
14. he hath broken my *c.*
Ex. 2. 24. God remembered his *c.*
31. 16. sabbath for a perpetual *c.*
34. 28. wrote words of *c.*
Lev. 26. 15. ye brake my *c.*
Judg. 2. 1. never brake *c.* with you
1 Chron. 16. 15. always mindful of his *c.*, Ps. 105. 8. & 111. 5.
Neh. 9. 38. we may make a sure *c.*
Job 31. 1. I made a *c.* with mine
Ps. 25. 14. Lord will show them *c.*
44. 17. not dealt falsely in thy *c.*
55. 20. broken his *c.*, Isa. 33. 8.
74. 20. have respect to the *c.*
78. 37. not steadfast in his *c.*, 10.

Ps. 78. 28. my *c.* shall stand fast, 34.
132. 12. children will keep my *c.*
Prov. 2. 17. forgetteth *c.* of her God
Isa. 28. 18. your *c.* with death
42. 6. given thee for *c.* of people
56. 4. take hold of my *c.*, 6.
Jer. 14. 21. break not *c.* with us
Ezek. 20. 37. bring into bond of *c.*
Dan. 9. 27. confirm *c.* with many
Hos. 6. 7. have transgressed the *c.*
10. 4. swearing falsely in making *c.*
Mal. 2. 14. the wife of thy *c.*
3. 1. messenger of the *c.*
Acts 3. 25. the children of the *c.*
Rom. 1. 31. *c.* breakers
Heb. 8. 6. he is the mediator of a better *c.*, 7. 9.
Gen. 9. 16. *everlasting covenant*, 17. 7, 13, 19. Lev. 24. 8. 2 Sam. 23. 5. 1 Chron. 16. 17. Ps. 105. 10. Isa. 24. 5. & 55. 3. & 61. 8. Jer. 32. 40. Ezek. 16. 60. & 37. 26. Heb. 13. 20.
Gen. 17. 9, 10. *keep, keepest, keepeth, covenant*, Ex. 19. 5. Deut. 7. 9, 12. & 29. 9. & 33. 9. 1 Kings 8. 23. & 11. 11. 2 Chron. 6. 14. Neh. 1. 5. & 9. 32. Ps. 25. 10. & 103. 18. & 132. 12. Dan. 9. 4.
Gen. 15. 18. Lord *made covenant*, Ex. 34. 27. Deut. 5. 2, 3. 2 Kings 23. 3. Job 31. 1.
Jer. 31. 31. *new covenant*, Heb. 8. 8, 13. & 12. 24.
Gen. 9. 15. *remember covenant*, Ex. 6. 5. Lev. 26. 42, 45. Ps. 105. 8. & 106. 45. Ezek. 16. 60. Amos 1. 9. Luke 1. 72.
Lev. 2. 13. *covenant of* salt, Num. 18. 19. 2 Chron. 13. 5.
Deut. 17. 2. *transgressed the covenant*, Josh. 7. 11, 15. & 23. 16. Judg. 2. 20. 2 Kings 18. 12. Jer. 34. 18. Hos. 6. 7. & 8. 1.
Rom. 9. 4. *covenants*, Gal. 4. 24.
Eph. 2. 12. *c.* of promise
R. V. Matt. 26. 15. weighed unto

COVER, Ex. 10. 5. & 40. 3.
Ex. 21. 33. dig a pit and not *c.* it
33. 22. I will *c.* thee with my hand
Deut. 33. 12. Lord shall *c.* him all
1 Sam. 24. 3. *c.* his feet, Judg. 3. 24.
Neh. 4. 5. *c.* not their iniquity
Job 16. 18. *c.* thou not my blood
Ps. 91. 4. *c.* thee with his feathers
Isa. 58. 7. naked that thou *c.* him
11. 9. as waters *c.* sea, Hab. 2. 14.
Hos. 10. 8. say to mountains, *c.* us, Luke 23. 30. Rev. 6. 16.
1 Cor. 11. 7. man ought not *c.* head
1 Pet. 4. 8. charity shall *c.* a multi.
Job 31. 33. if I *covered* my trans.
Ps. 32. 1. whose sin is *c.*, Rom. 4. 7.
85. 2. hast *c.* all their sin
Lam. 3. 44. *c.* thyself with a cloud
Matt. 10. 26. nothing *c.* that shall not
Ps. 104. 2. *coverest* thyself with
73. 6. violence *covereth* them as a
Prov. 10. 12. love *c.* all sins
Isa. 28. 20. *covering*, 1 Cor. 11. 15.
Isa. 4. 6. *covert*, 16. 4. & 32. 2. Ps. 61. 4. Jer. 25. 38.
R. V. Ex. 40. 21. screened; 1 Kings 6. 35; Prov. 26. 23. overlaid; 1 Cor. 11. 6. veiled; Ex. 35. 12; 39. 34; 40. 21. screen; Prov. 7. 16; 31. 22. carpets; Isa. 30. 22. overlaying; S. of S. 3. 10. seat

COVET, Ex. 20. 17. Mic. 2. 2.
1 Cor. 12. 31. *c.* earnestly best gifts
Acts 20. 33. *coveted*, 1 Tim. 6. 10.
Prov. 21. 26. *coveteth*, Hab. 2. 9.
Ps. 10. 3. wicked blesseth *covetous*
Luke 16. 14. Pharisees who were *c.*
1 Cor. 5. 10. or with the *c.*, 11.
6. 10. nor *c.* shall inherit kingdom
Eph. 5. 5. nor *c.* who is an idolater
1 Tim. 3. 3. bishop must not be *c.*
2 Pet. 2. 14. exercised with *c.* pract.
Ex. 18. 21. hating *covetousness*
Ps. 119. 36. to testimonies and not to *c.*
Ezek. 33. 31. heart goeth after their *c.*
Luke 12. 15. beware of *c.* for man's
Col. 3. 5. *c.* which is idolatry
Heb. 13. 5. conversation without *c.*
R. V. Hab. 2. 9. getteth; 1 Cor. 12. 31. desire; 14. 39. desire earnestly; 1 Tim. 6. 10. reaching; Luke 16. 14; 1 Tim. 3. 3; 2 Tim. 3. 2. lovers of money; Ex. 18. 21. unjust gain; Ezek. 33. 31; Hab. 2. 9. gain; Mark 7. 22. covetings; 2 Cor. 9. 5. extortions; Heb. 13. 5. free from love of money

CRAFT, Dan. 8. 25. Mark 14. 1. Acts 18. 3. & 19. 25, 27. Rev. 18. 22.
Job 5. 12. disappointeth devices of the *crafty*
15. 5. uttereth iniquity, choosest tongue of *c.*
Ps. 83. 3. taken *c.* counsel against
2 Cor. 12. 16. being *c.* I caught you with guile
Job 5. 13. *craftiness*, 1 Cor. 3. 19. Luke 20. 23. 2 Cor. 4. 2. Eph. 4. 14.
R. V. Mark 14. 1. with subtilty; Acts 18. 3; 19. 27. trade; 19. 25. business

CREATE, Gen. 1. 1, 21, 27. & 2. 3.
Ps. 51. 10. *c.* in me a clean heart
Isa. 4. 5. *c.* upon every dwelling-place
45. 7. I form light and *c.* darkness
57. 19. I *c.* the fruit of the lips, peace
65. 17. I *c.* new heavens and new earth
18. rejoice in what I *c.* I *c.* Jerusalem
Ps. 104. 30. spirit they are *created*
Isa. 43. 7. I have *c.* him for my
Jer. 31. 22. *c.* a new thing in earth
Mal. 2. 10. hath not one God *c.* us
Eph. 2. 10. *c.* in Christ Jesus unto good
3. 9. *c.* all things by Jesus Christ
Col. 1. 16. all things were *c.* by him
3. 10. image of him that *c.* him
1 Tim. 4. 3. which God *c.* to be received
Rev. 4. 11. hast *c.* all--are and were *c.*
10. 6. *c.* heaven and things therein
Amos 4. 13. *createth* the wind
Mark 10. 6. *creation*, 13. 19. Rom. 1. 20. & 8. 22. Rev. 3. 14.
Rom. 1. 25. creature — *Creator*
Eccl. 12. 1. remember thy *C.* in days
Isa. 40. 28. *C.* of ends of earth
43. 15. Lord the *C.* of Israel, your king
1 Pet. 4. 19. as to a faithful *C.*
Gen. 1. 20. *creature*, Lev. 11. 46.
Mark 16. 15. preach the gospel to every *c.*
2 Cor. 5. 17. man in Christ is a new *c.*
Gal. 6. 15. availeth but a new *c.*
Col. 1. 15. first-born of every *c.*
1 Tim. 4. 4. every *c.* of God is good
Heb. 4. 13. nor any *c.* not manifest
Isa. 13. 21. *creatures*, Jas. 1. 18.
Ezek. 1. 5, 19. *living creatures*, 3. 13. Rev. 4. 6, 9. & 5. 6, 11, 14.
R. V. Mark 16. 15. whole creation; Col. 1. 15. all creation

CREDITOR, parable of the, Luke 7. 41; of two creditors, Matt. 18. 23.

CREEP, Lev. 11. 31. Ps. 104. 20.
2 Tim. 3. 6. who *c.* into houses
Jude 4. *crept* in unawares
R. V. Gen. 8. 19; Lev. 11. 44. moveth

CRIB, Prov. 14. 4. Isa. 1. 3.

CRIME, Job 31. 11. Ezek. 7. 23.

CRIMSON, as wool, Isa. 1. 18. Jer. 4. 30. 2 Chron. 2. 7. & 3. 14.
R. V. Jer. 4. 30. scarlet

CRIPPLE healed at Lystra, Acts 14. 8.

CROOKED generation, Deut. 32. 5.
Ps. 125. 5. aside to their *c.* ways
Prov. 2. 15. whose ways are *c.* and
Eccl. 1. 15. that which is *c.* cannot
Isa. 40. 4. *c.* shall be made straight
Phil. 2. 15. in midst of *c.* generation
R. V. Job 26. 13. swift; Isa. 45. 2. rugged

CROSS, John 19. 17-31. Luke 23. 26.
Matt. 10. 38. takes not up his *c.* and follows, 16. 24. Luke 9. 23. & 14. 27.
1 Cor. 1. 17. lest the *c.* of Christ be made
18. preaching of *c.* is to them fool.
Gal. 5. 11. then is offence of the *c.* ceased
6. 12. suffer persecution for *c.* of Christ
14. glory save in *c.* of Lord Jesus
Phil. 2. 8. obedient to death of *c.*
3. 18. they are enemies of the *c.*
Col. 2. 14. took—nailing it to his *c.*
Heb. 12. 2. for joy — endured the *c.*

CROWN, Lev. 8. 9. Esth. 1. 11.
Job 31. 36. bind it as *c.* to me
Ps. 89. 39. hast profaned his *c.*
Prov. 12. 4. virtuous woman is a *c.*
14. 24. *c.* of wise is their riches
16. 31. hoary head is a *c.* of glory
17. 6. children's children are *c.* of
S. of S. 3. 11. behold king Solomon with *c.*
Isa. 28. 5. Lord of hosts for *c.* of glory
62. 3. thou shalt be a *c.* of glory
1 Cor. 9. 25. to obtain corruptible c.
Phil. 4. 1. my joy and *c.*, 1 Thes. 2. 19.
2 Tim. 4. 8. laid up—a *c.* of righte.
Jas. 1. 12. receive a *c.* of life
1 Pet. 5. 4. receive a *c.* of glory
Rev. 2. 10. give thee a *c.* of life
Ps. 8. 5. *crowned* with glory and honor
Prov. 14. 18. prudent are *c.* with knowledge
Ps. 65. 11. *crownest* the year with
103. 4. *crowneth* with loving-kind.
Zech. 6. 11, 14. *crowns*, Rev. 4. 4, 10. & 9. 7. & 12. 3. & 13. 1. & 19. 12.
R. V. Rev. 12. 3; 13. 1; 19. 12. diadems

CRUCIFY, Matt. 20. 19. & 23. 34. Luke 23. 21. John 19. 6, 15.
Acts 2. 23. *crucified* and slain, 4. 10.
Rom. 6. 6. our old man is *c.* with him
1 Cor. 1. 13. was Paul *c.*
23. Christ *c.*
2. 2. save Jesus Christ and him *c.*
Gal. 2. 20. I am *c.* with Christ nevertheless
3. 1. Christ is set forth *c.* among
6. 14. world is *c.* to me and I to
Rev. 11. 8. where also our Lord was *c.*

CRUEL, Prov. 5. 9. & 11. 17. & 27. 4.
Gen. 49. 7. cursed wrath for it was *c.*
Job 30. 21. thou art become *c.* to me
Prov. 12. 10. tender mercies of the wicked are *c.*
S. of S. 8. 6. jealousy is *c.* as grave
Isa. 13. 9. day of Lord cometh *c.* with
Jer. 6. 23. *c.* and have no mercy, 50. 42.
Heb. 11. 36. had trial of *c.* mockings

CRUELTY condemned, Ex. 23. 5. Ps. 27. 12. Prov. 11. 17. & 12. 10. Ezek. 18. 18.
of Simeon and Levi, Gen. 34. 25. & 49. 5.
of Pharaoh, Ex. 1. 8.
of Adoni-bezek, Judg. 1. 7.
of Herod, Matt. 2. 16. (Judg. 9. 5. 2 Kings 3. 27. & 10. & 15. 16.)
R. V. Heb. 11. 36 ——; Gen. 49. 5; Judg. 9. 24; Ps. 74. 20. violence; Ezek. 34. 4. rigor

CRUMBS, Matt. 15. 27. Luke 16. 21.

CRY, Ex. 5. 8. & 3. 7, 9.
Gen. 18. 21. to the *c.* that is come
Ex. 2. 23. their *c.* came up to God
22. 23. I will surely hear their *c.*
2 Sam. 22. 7. my *c.* did enter into
Job 34. 28. he hears *c.* of afflicted
Ps. 9. 12. he forgets not the *c.* of
34. 17. his ears are open to their *c.*

Ps. 145. 19. he will hear their *c*.
Jer. 7. 16. neither lift up *c*. nor prayer for them, 11. 11, 14.
Matt. 25. 6. at midnight a *c*. made
Ps. 34. 15. righteous *c*. and Lord
Isa. 40. 6. voice said *c*. — what *c*.
42. 2. not *c*. nor lift up voice
58. 1. *c*. aloud, spare not
Ezek. 9. 4. that *c*. for all the abom.
Joel 1. 19. to thee will I *c*.
Jonah 3. 8. *c*. mightily to God
Matt. 12. 19. shall not strive nor *c*.
Luke 18. 7. *c*. day and night to him
Luke 19. 40. stones would *c*. out
Rom. 8. 15. spirit *c*. Abba, Father
Ps. 22. 5. *cried* and were delivered
34. 6. this poor man *c*. and Lord
Lam. 2. 18. their heart *c*. to Lord
Prov. 2. 3. thou *criest* after know.
Gen. 4. 10. brother's blood *crieth*
Prov. 1. 20. wisdom *c*. without
Mic. 6. 9. Lord's voice *c*. to the city
Prov. 19. 18. *crying*, Zech. 4. 7. Matt. 3. 3. Heb. 5. 7. Rev. 21. 4.
R. V. Rev. 14. 18. great voice

CUBIT unto his stature, Matt. 6. 27.

CUMBER, Luke 10. 40. & 13. 7.

CUP, Gen. 40. 11. & 44. 2.
Ps. 11. 6. portion of their *c*.
23. 5. my *c*. runneth over
73. 10. waters of a full *c*. are wrung out
116. 13. take *c*. of salvation
Isa. 51. 17. *c*. of trembling, 22. Zech. 12. 2.
Jer. 16. 7. nor give *c*. of consola.
25. 15. wine *c*. of fury, 17. 28. Lam. 4. 21. Ezek. 23. 31, 32.
Hab. 2. 16. *c*. Lord's right hand, Ps. 75. 8.
Matt. 10. 42. *c*. of cold water only
20. 22. able to drink of the *c*.
26. 39. let this *c*. pass from me
John 18. 11. the *c*. which my Father hath given
1 Cor. 10. 16. *c*. of blessing which we
21. drink *c*. of the Lord and *c*. of devils
11. 25. this *c*. is new testament
26. drink this *c*., 27. 28. Luke 22. 20.
Rev. 16. 19. *c*. of his wrath, 14. 10.

CURIOUS, Ex. 35. 32. Acts 19. 19.
Ps. 139. 15. *curiously* wrought

CURSE them, Num. 5. 18, 19, 22, 24, 27.
Gen. 27. 12. bring a *c*. upon me
13. on me be thy *c*. my son
Deut. 11. 26. blessing and *c*., 30. 1.
23. 5. turned *c*. into blessing, Neh. 13. 2.
Prov. 3. 33. *c*. of the Lord in house of
26. 2. *c*. causeless shall not come
Mal. 2. 2. send a *c*. upon you
3. 9. ye are cursed with a *c*.
Isa. 65. 15. *for*, or, *to be a c*., Jer. 24. 9. & 25. 18. & 29. 18. & 42. 18. & 44. 8, 12. & 26. 6. & 49. 13.
Gen. 8. 21. I will not again *c*. the ground
12. 3. *c*. him that curseth thee
Ex. 22. 28. nor *c*. ruler of people
Lev. 19. 14. shall not *c*. the deaf
Num. 22. 6. come, *c*. me this people, 17.
Deut. 23. 4. hired Balaam to *c*., Josh. 24. 9. Neh. 13. 2.
Judg. 5. 23. *c*. ye Meroz, *c*. bitterly
Job 1. 11. he will *c*. thee to face, 2. 5.
2. 9. *c*. God and die
Ps. 109. 28. let them *c*. but bless
Prov. 11. 26. people shall *c*. him, 24. 24.
Eccl. 10. 20. *c*. not king in chamber
Jer. 15. 10. every one doth *c*. me
Mal. 2. 2. I will *c*. your blessings
Matt. 5. 44. bless them that *c*. you
Rom. 12. 14. bless and *c*. not
Gen. 49. 7. *cursed* be their anger
Job 3. 1. opened Job his mouth, and *c*. his day, 8.
5. 3. I *c*. his habitation, 24. 18.
Ps. 119. 21. proud are *c*., 37. 22.
Jer. 11. 3. *c*. be man that obeys not
17. 5. *c*. be man that trusteth in
Deut. 30. 19. *cursing*, Rom. 3. 14. Heb. 6. 8. Ps. 10. 7. & 59. 12. & 109. 17.
R. V. Josh. 6. 18. accursed; Jer. 29. 18. execration; Deut. 7. 26; 13. 17. devoted; Job 1. 5. renounced; John 7. 49. accursed; Prov. 29. 24. adjuration

CURTAINS of the tabernacle described, Ex. 26. 36.

CUSTOM, Gen. 31. 35. Rom. 13. 7. Luke 4. 16. 1 Cor. 11. 16. Jer. 10. 3.
R. V. Gen. 31. 35. manner; Ex. 3. 4. ordinance; Matt. 9. 9; Mark 2. 14; Luke 5. 27. place of toll; Matt. 17. 25. receive toll

CUT, Lev. 1. 6, 12. & 22. 24.
Zech. 11. 10. *cut asunder*, Matt. 24. 51. Luke 12. 46. Jer. 48. 2. & 50. 23. Ps. 129. 4.
Luke 13. 7, 9. *cut down*, Job 22. 16, 20.
Job 4. 7. *cut off*, 8. 14. Ps. 37. 9, 28. & 76. 12. & 90. 10. & 101. 5. Prov. 2. 22. Matt. 5. 30. & 18. 8. Rom. 11. 22. 2 Cor. 11. 12. Gal. 5. 12.
Acts 5. 33. *cut to heart*, 7. 54.
R. V. Isa. 38. 10. noontide

CUTTING the flesh forbidden, Lev. 19. 28; Deut. 14. 1; practised by prophets of Baal, 1 Kings 18. 28.

CYMBAL, Ezra 3. 10. Ps. 150. 5.
1 Cor. 13. 1. I am become a tinkling *c*.

D

DAINTY, Job 33. 20. Prov. 23. 6.
Gen. 49. 20. yield royal *dainties*
Ps. 141. 4. not eat of their *d*.
Prov. 23. 3. not desirous of his *d*.

DAMNED who believe not, Mark 16. 16. 2 Thes. 2. 12.
Rom. 14. 23. doubteth, is *d*. if he eat
2 Pet. 2. 1. *damnable* heresies
Matt. 23. 14. greater *damnation*
33. how can ye escape *d*. of hell
Mark 3. 29. in danger of eternal *d*.
John 5. 29. come forth to resurrection of *d*.
1 Cor. 11. 29. eateth and drinketh *d*.
R. V. Mark 16. 16; Rom. 14. 23. condemned; 2 Thes. 2. 12. judged; Matt. 23. 14——; 22. 33; John 5. 29; Rom. 13. 2. judgment; Mark 3. 29. sin; 12. 40; Luke 20. 47; Rom. 3. 8; 1 Tim. 5. 12. condemnation

DANCE turned to mourning, Lam. 5. 15. Ps. 30. 11. Luke 15. 25.

DANCING, as a mark of rejoicing, Ex. 15. 20. & 32. 19. Judg. 11. 34. 1 Sam. 21. 11. 2 Sam. 6. 14. Eccl. 3. 4. of Herodias's daughter pleases Herod, Matt. 14. 6; Mark 6. 22.

DANDLED on knees, Isa. 66. 12.

DANGER of the judgment, Matt. 5. 22.
Matt. 5. 21, 22. *d*. of the council—hell fire
Mark 3. 39. in *d*. of damnation
Acts 19. 27. craft in *d*.
40. we in *d*.
R. V. Mark 3. 29. guilty

DARE, 1 Cor. 6. 1. 2 Cor. 10. 12.
Rom. 5. 7. some would *d*. to die
R. V. 2 Cor. 16. 12. not bold to

DARK, Gen. 15. 17. Job 18. 6. & 24. 16.
Lev. 13. 6. if plague be *d*., 21. 26.
Num. 12. 8. speak not in *d*. speech.
2 Sam. 22. 12. *d*. waters, Ps. 18. 11.
Ps. 49. 4. *d*. sayings, 78. 2.
Dan. 8. 23. understanding *d*. sent.
2 Pet. 1. 19. light shineth in *d*.
1 Cor. 13. 12. through a glass *darkly*
Ex. 10. 15. *darkened*, Eccl. 12. 2, 3.
Ps. 69. 23. let eyes be *d*., Rom. 11. 10.
Zech. 11. 17. his right eye utterly *d*.
Rom. 1. 21. foolish heart was *d*.
Gen. 1. 2, 5, 18. *darkness*, 15. 12.
2 Sam. 22. 29. Lord will lighten my *d*.
1 Kings 8. 12. Lord dwell in thick *d*.
Job 34. 22. no *d*. where workers
Ps. 104. 20. makest *d*. and it is night
Isa. 5. 20. put *d*. for light, and light for *d*.
45. 7. I form light and create *d*.
Matt. 6. 23. whole body full of *d*.
8. 12. outer *d*., 22. 13. & 25. 30.
John 1. 5. *d*. comprehended it not
3. 19. men loved *d*. rather than lig.
Acts 26. 18. turn them from *d*. to
Rom. 13. 12. cast off works of *d*.
2 Cor. 4. 6. light to shine out of *d*.
6. 14. communion hath light with *d*.
Eph. 5. 8. were sometimes *d*. but
Col. 1. 13. delivered us from power of *d*.
1 Pet. 2. 9. called you out of *d*.
2 Pet. 2. 4. reserved in chains of *d*.
1 John 1. 5. in him is no *d*. at all
Jude 13. blackness of *d*. for ever
Deut. 28. 29. *in darkness*, 1 Sam. 2. 9. Ps. 107. 10. & 112. 4. Isa. 9. 2. & 50. 10. Matt. 4. 16. & 10. 27. John 1. 5. 1 Thes. 5. 4.
R. V. Zech. 14. 6. with gloom; Luke 23. 45. failing

DARLING, Ps. 22. 20. & 35. 17.

DARTS, fiery, of devil, Eph. 6. 16.
R. V. Job 41. 29. clubs; 2 Chron. 32. 5. weapons; Prov. 7. 23. arrow; Heb. 12. 20——

DASH, 2 Kings 8. 12. Ex. 15. 6. Isa. 13. 16, 18. Hos. 10. 14. & 13. 16. Ps. 137. 9. Jer. 13. 14.
Ps. 2. 9. *d*. them in pieces like a potter's vessel
91. 12. lest thou *d*. thy foot against a stone

DAVID, for Christ, Ps. 89. 3. Jer. 30. 9. Ezek. 34. 23, 24. & 37. 24, 25. Hos. 3. 5. Isa. 55. 3.

DAY, Gen. 1. 5. & 32. 26.
Ps. 19. 2. *d*. unto *d*. uttereth speech
84. 10. a *d*. in thy courts is better
118. 24. this is the *d*. which the Lord
Prov. 27. 1. what *d*. may bring forth
Amos 6. 3. put far away evil *d*.
Zech. 4. 10. despised the *d*. of small
Matt. 6. 34. sufficient to *d*. is the
25. 13. know neither the *d*. nor
John 8. 56. rejoiced to see my *d*.
1 Cor. 3. 13. the *d*. shall declare it
Phil. 1. 6. till *d*. of Jesus Christ
1 Thes. 5. 5. children of the *d*.
Matt. 10. 15. *day of judgment*, 11. 22, 24. & 12. 36. Mark 6. 11. 2 Pet. 2. 9. & 3. 7. 1 John 4. 17.
Isa. 2. 12. *day of the Lord*, 13. 6, 9. & 34. 8. Jer. 46. 10. Lam. 2. 22. Ezek. 30. 3. Joel 1. 15. & 2. 1, 31. & 3. 14. Amos 5. 18. Obad. 15. Zeph. 1. 8, 18. & 2. 2, 3. Zech. 1. 7. & 14. 1. Mal. 4. 5. 1 Cor. 5. 5. Rev. 1. 10. 2 Cor. 1. 14. 1 Thes. 5. 2. 2 Pet. 3. 10.
Ps. 20. 1. Lord hear thee in the *day of trouble*
50. 15. call on me in —, 91. 15.
59. 16. my defence and refuge in—
77. 2. in — I sought the Lord
Isa. 37. 3. it is a — and rebuke
Ezek. 7. 7. time is come, — is near
Hab. 3. 16. I might rest in —
Zeph. 1. 15. a — and distress, desolation
Job 8. 9. *days* on earth as a shadow
14. 1. of few *d*. and full of trouble
Ps. 90. 12. teach us to number our *d*.
Prov. 3. 16. length of *d*. is in her right
Eccl. 7. 10. former *d*. better than
11. 8. remember *d*. of darkness, many
12. 1. while evil *d*. come not
Jer. 2. 32. forgotten me *d*. without
Matt. 24. 22. except those *d*. be shortened

Gal. 4. 10. observe *d.* months, and
Eph. 5. 16. because the *d.* are evil
1 Pet. 3. 10. would see good *d.*
Gen. 49. 1. *last days*, Isa. 2. 2. Mic. 4. 1. Acts 2. 17. 2 Tim. 3. 1. Heb. 1. 2. Jas. 5. 3. 2 Pet. 3. 3.
Num. 24. 14. *latter days*, Deut. 31. 29. Jer. 23. 20. & 30. 24. Dan. 10. 14. Hos. 3. 5.
Job 10. 20. *my days*, 17. 1, 11.
7. 6. — are swifter than a shuttle
16. I loathe it, — are vanity
9. 25. — are swifter than a post
Ps. 39. 4. know measure of —
5. made — as a handbreadth
Isa. 39. 8. peace and truth in —
Jer. 20. 18. — are consumed with
Ps. 61. 8. *daily* perform my vows
Prov. 8. 34. watching *d.* at my gates
Isa. 58. 2. seek me *d.* and delight in
Acts 2. 47. added to church *d.*
Heb. 3. 13. exhort one another *d.*
Job 9. 33. *day's-man*, or umpire
38. 12. *day-spring*, Luke 1. 78.
2 Pet. 1. 19. *day-star* arise in your hearts
R. V. Matt. 27. 62; John 1. 29; Acts 14. 20; 21. 8; 25. 6. on the morrow

DEACON, Phil. 1. 1. 1 Tim. 3. 8, 10, 12, 13.

DEAD, Gen. 20. 3. & 23. 3.
Num. 16. 48. stood between *d.* and
1 Sam. 24. 14. after a *d.* dog after
Ps. 88. 10. shall *d.* praise, 115. 17.
Eccl. 9. 5. the *d.* know not any thing
10. 1. *d.* flies cause the ointment
Matt. 8. 22. let the *d.* bury their *d.*
22. 32. not God of *d.* but of living
Luke 8. 52. the maid is not *d.* but
John 5. 25. *d.* shall hear the voice
11. 25. though he were *d.* yet
Rom. 6. 8. *d.* with Christ
11. *d.* to sin
Gal. 2. 19. I through law am *d.* to law
Eph. 2. 1. who were *d.* in trespasses
Col. 2. 13. being *d.* in your sins
1 Thes. 4. 16. *d.* in Christ shall rise
2 Tim. 2. 11. *d.* with him, we shall
Heb. 11. 4. being *d.* yet speaketh
Rev. 14. 13. blessed are *d.* — in Lord
Ps. 17. 9. *deadly*, Jas. 3. 8. Rev. 13. 3.
R. V. Rev. 13. 3, 12. death stroke

DEAF, Ex. 4. 11. Ps. 38. 13. Isa. 29. 18. & 35. 5. Mic. 7. 16.
Lev. 19. 14. shalt not curse the *d.*
Isa. 42. 18. hear, ye *d.* and look, ye blind
19. who is *d.* as my messenger
43. 8. *d.* people that have ears
Matt. 11. 5. *d.* hear, dead are raised

DEAL, a measure, Ex. 29. 40. Lev. 14. 10.

DEATH, Gen. 21. 16. Ex. 10. 17.
Num. 23. 10. let me die the *d.* of the
Deut. 30. 15. set before you life and *d.*
Ps. 6. 5. in *d.* no remembrance of
33. 19. deliver soul from *d.*, 116. 8.
73. 4. have no bands in their *d.*
89. 48. liveth and shall not see *d.*
116. 15. precious — is *d.* of saints
Prov. 2. 18. her house inclines to *d.*
8. 36. they that hate me, love *d.*
18. 21. *d.* and life in power of tong.
Eccl. 7. 26. more bitter than *d.* the
8. 8. hath no power in day of *d.*
Isa. 25. 8. swallow up *d.* in victory
28. 15. made covenant with *d.*
Jer. 8. 3. *d.* chosen rather than life
21. 8. way of life, way of *d.*
Hos. 13. 14. O *d.* I will be thy plagues
Matt. 16. 28. not taste of *d.*, Luke 9. 27.
26. 38. sorrowful even unto *d.*
John 5. 24. passed from *d.* to life, 1 John 3. 14.
John 8. 51. shall never see *d.*
12. 33. what *d.* he should die, 21. 19.
Acts 2. 24. loosed the pains of *d.*
Rom. 5. 12. sin entered, and *d.* by
6. 3. baptized into his *d.*
Rom. 6. 4. buried by baptism into *d.*
5. 9. *d.* hath no more dominion
21. end of these things is *d.*
23. the wages of sin is *d.* but gift of God
8. 2. free from law of sin and *d.*
6. to be carnally minded is *d.*
38. *d.* nor life shall separate from
1 Cor. 3. 22. or life, or *d.* or things present
11. 26. ye show Lord's *d.* till he come
15. 21. by man came *d.* by man
54. *d.* is swallowed up in victory
55. O *d.* where is thy sting
56. sting of *d.* is sin, and strength
2 Cor. 1. 9. had the sentence of *d.*
10. deliver from so great a *d.*
2. 16. we are savour of *d.* unto *d.*
4. 11. delivered to *d.* for Jesus'
12. *d.* worketh in us, but life in you
Phil. 2. 8. obedient to *d.* the *d.* of
Heb. 2. 9. tasted *d.* for every man
15. through fear of *d.* are subject
11. 5. should not see *d.*, Luke 2. 26.
Jas. 1. 15. sin finished brings *d.*
5. 20. save a soul from *d.* and hide
1 Pet. 3. 18. put to *d.* in the flesh
1 John 5. 16. there is a sin unto *d.*
17. there is a sin unto *d.* I do not
Rev. 1. 18. I have the keys of hell and *d.*
2. 10. be faithful unto *d.* and I will
20. 6. second *d.* hath no power
21. 4. there shall be no more *d.*
R. V. Mark 14. 1; Luke 18. 33. kill him

DEBATE, Prov. 25. 9. Isa. 27. 8. & 58. 4. Rom. 1. 29. 2 Cor. 12. 20.
R. V. Isa. 58. 4. contention; Rom. 1. 29. strife; 2 Cor. 12. 20. should be strife; Isa. 27. 8. dost contend

DEBT, Rom. 4. 4. Matt. 6. 12, 18, 27. Ezek. 18. 7, 11. *debtor*, Gal. 5. 3. Rom. 1. 14. & 8. 12. & 15. 27. Luke 7. 41. Matt. 6. 12.
R. V. Matt. 18. 30. which was due

DECEASE, Luke 9. 31. 2 Pet. 1. 15.

DECEIT, Jer. 5. 27. & 9. 6, 8.
Ps. 72. 14. redeem their souls from *d.*
101. 7. worketh *d.* shall not dwell
Prov. 20. 17. bread of *d.* is sweet
Isa. 53. 9. any *d.* in his mouth
Jer. 8. 5. they hold fast *d.* and refuse
Col. 2. 8. spoil you through vain *d.*
Ps. 35. 20. *deceitful*, 109. 2. Prov. 11. 18. & 14. 25. & 23. 3. & 27. 6.
Ps. 5. 6. abhor bloody and *d.* man
78. 57. turn like a *d.* bow, Hos. 7. 16.
120. 2. from a *d.* tongue, 52. 4. Mic. 6. 12. Zeph. 3. 13.
Prov. 31. 30. favor is *d.* and beauty vain
Jer. 17. 9. heart is *d.* above all things
Eph. 4. 22. according to *d.* lusts
Matt. 13. 22. *deceitfulness* of riches
Ps. 24. 4. *deceitfully*, Jer. 48. 10. Job 13. 7. 2 Cor. 4. 2.
R. V. Ps. 55. 11; 72. 14. oppression; Prov. 20. 17. falsehood; 1 Thes. 2. 3. error; Prov. 27. 6. profuse; 29. 13. oppressor; Eph. 4. 22. deceit; Gen. 34. 13. with guile

DECEIVE, 2 Kings 4. 28. & 18. 29.
Prov. 24. 28. *d.* not with thy lips
Matt. 24. 4. take heed that no man *d.* you
24. if possible *d.* the very elect
1 Cor. 3. 18. let no man *d.* himself
2 Thes. 2. 10. *deceivableness*
Deut. 11. 16. heart be not *deceived*
Job 12. 16. the *d.* and the deceiver are
Isa. 44. 20. a *d.* heart hath turned
Jer. 20. 7. O Lord, thou hast *d.* me
Ezek. 14. 9. I the Lord have *d.*
Obad. 3. thy pride hath *d.* thee
Rom. 7. 11. *d.* me, and by it slew me
1 Tim. 2. 14. Adam was not *d.* but
2 Tim. 3. 13. *deceiving* and being *d.*
Gal. 27. 12. *deceiver*, Mal. 1. 14. 2 John 7. 2 Cor. 6. 8. Tit. 1. 10.
Prov. 26. 19. *deceiveth*, Rev. 12. 9.
Jas. 1. 26. *d.* his own heart, 22.
R. V. Matt. 24. 4, 5, 11, 24; Mark 13. 5, 6; 1 John 3. 7. lead astray; Rom. 16. 18; 2 Thes. 2. 3. beguile; Lev. 6. 2. oppressed; Job 31. 9. enticed; Prov. 20. 1. erreth; Luke 21. 8; John 7. 47. led astray; Rom. 7. 11. 1 Tim. 2. 14. beguiled; Jas. 1. 22. deluding

DECENTLY, 1 Cor. 14. 40.

DECLARE, Gen. 41. 24. Isa. 42. 9.
Ps. 22. 2. I will *d.* thy name unto
38. 18. I will *d.* my iniquity and
145. 4. shall *d.* thy mighty acts
Isa. 3. 9. they *d.* their sin as Sodom
53. 8. who shall *d.* his generation
Mic. 3. 8. to *d.* to Jacob his transgression
Acts 17. 23. worship, him *d.* I unto
20. 17. not shunned to *d.* all counsel
Rom. 3. 25. to *d.* his righteousness
Heb. 11. 14. say such things *d.* plain.
1 John 1. 3. seen and heard *d.* we
Rom. 1. 4. *declared* — Son of God with
2 Cor. 3. 3. manifestly *d.* to be the epistle
Amos 4. 13. *d.* to man what his thought
1 Cor. 2. 1. I *d.* to you test. of God
R. V. Ps. 2. 7; 73. 28; 75. 1; 78. 6. tell of; Eccl. 9. 1. explore; Isa. 43. 26. set forth thy cause; Matt. 13. 36. explain; Rom. 3. 25. shew; John 17. 26; Col. 4. 7. make known; 1 John 1. 5. announce; Acts 15. 4, 14. rehearsed; Rom. 9. 17. published

DECLINE, Ps. 119. 51, 157.

DECREE, Ezra 5. 13, 17. & 6. 1, 12.
Ps. 2. 7. I will declare the *d.*
Prov. 8. 15. princes *d.* justice
Isa. 10. 1. that *d.* unrighteous decr.
Zeph. 2. 2. before *d.* bring forth
Isa. 10. 22. *decreed*, 1 Cor. 7. 37.
R. V. Dan. 2. 9. law; 6. 7, 8, 9, 12, 13, 15. interdict; Esth. 9. 32. commandment

DEDICATE, Deut. 20. 5. 2 Sam. 8. 11. 1 Chron. 26. 20, 26, 27. Ezek. 44. 29.
Num. 7. 84. *dedication*, Ezra 6. 16, 17. Neh. 12. 17. John 10. 22.
R. V. 2 Kings 12. 4. hallowed; Ezek. 44. 29. devoted

DEED, Gen. 44. 15. Judg. 19. 30.
Rom. 15. 18. obedient in word and *d.*
Col. 3. 17. whatsoever ye do in word or *d.*
Neh. 13. 14. wipe not out my good *deeds*
Ps. 28. 4. give them according to their *d.*, Jer. 25. 14. Rom. 2. 6. 2 Cor. 5. 10.
John 3. 19. because their *d.* were evil
Rom. 3. 20. by *d.* of law no flesh
Jude 15. of all their ungodly *d.*
R. V. In N. T. mostly, works

DEEP, Gen. 1. 2. Job. 38. 30.
Ps. 36. 6. thy judg. are a great *d.*
42. 7. *d.* calleth unto *d.* at the noise
1 Cor. 2. 10. yea, *d.* things of God
2 Cor. 11. 25. I have been in the *d.*
Isa. 31. 6. *deeply* revolted
Hos. 9. 9. *d.* corrupted themselves
Mark 8. 17. sighed *d.* in spirit
R. V. Isa. 63. 13; Jonah 2. 3. depth; Luke 8. 31; Rom. 2. 7. abyss; Ps. 135. 6. deeps; Ezek. 32. 14; 34. 18. clear

DEFAME, 1 Cor. 4. 13. Jer. 20. 10.

DEFENCE, 2 Chron. 11. 5. Isa. 19. 6.
Num. 14. 9. their *d.* is departed
Job 22. 25. Almighty shall be thy *d.*
Ps. 7. 10. my *d.* is of God who save.
Eccl. 7. 12. wisdom is a *d.* money is a *d.*
Isa. 4. 5. on all the glory shall be *d.*
33. 16. place of *d.* the munitions
R. V. Job 22. 25. treasure; Ps. 7. 10; 89. 18. shield; 59. 9, 16; 62. 2, 6;

94. 22. high tower; Isa. 4. 5. canopy; 19. 6. Egypt; Nah. 2. 5. mantelet
DEFER, Eccl. 5. 4. Isa. 48. 9. Dan. 9. 19. Prov. 13. 12. & 19. 11.
R. V. Prov. 19. 11. maketh him slow
DEFILE, Lev. 11. 44. & 15. 31.
S. of S. 5. 3. how shall I *d*. them
Dan. 1. 8. would not *d*. himself
Matt. 15. 18. they *d*. the man, 20.
1 Cor. 3. 17. if any *d*. temple of God
Mark 7. 2. eat bread with *defiled* hands
Isa. 24. 5. earth is *d*. under inhabit.
Tit. 1. 15. are *d*. and unbelieving
Heb. 12. 15. thereby many be *d*.
Rev. 3. 4. have not *d*. their gar.
14. 4. are not *d*. with women
21. 27. any thing that *defileth*
R. V. Ex. 31. 14; Ezek. 7. 24; 28. 18. profaned; Num. 35. 33; Isa. 24. 5; Jer. 3. 9; 16. 18. polluted; Gen. 34. 2. humbled; Deut. 22. 9. forfeited; Lev. 13. 14; 15. 32; Num. 5. 2; Ezek. 4. 13; Rev. 21. 27. unclean
DEFRAUD, Lev. 19. 13. Mark 10. 19. 1 Cor. 6. 7, 8. & 7. 5. 1 Thes. 4. 6. 1 Sam. 12. 3, 4. 2 Cor. 7. 2.
R. V. Lev. 19. 13. oppress; 2 Cor. 7. 2. took advantage of; 1 Thes. 4. 6. wrong
DELAY, Ex. 22. 29. & 32. 1.
Ps. 119. 60. I *delayed* not to keep
Matt. 24. 48. my lord *delayeth* his coming
R. V. Matt. 24. 48. tarrieth
DELICATE, Deut. 28. 56. Isa. 47. 1. Jer. 6. 2. Mic. 1. 16. Jer. 51. 34.
1 Sam. 15. 32. *delicately*, Prov. 29. 21. Lam. 4. 5. Luke 7. 25.
R. V. Mic. 1. 16. of . . delight
DELIGHT, Gen. 34. 19. Num. 14. 8.
Deut. 10. 15. Lord had *d*. in fathers
1 Sam. 15. 22. hath the Lord as great *d*. in burnt offerings
Job 22. 26. have thy *d*. in Almighty
27. 10. will he *d*. himself in Almighty
Ps. 1. 2. his *d*. is in the law of God
16. 3. saints in whom is all my *d*.
37. 4. *d*. thyself in Lord, he will give
40. 8. I *d*. to do thy will, O my God
94. 19. thy comforts *d*. my soul
119. 24. thy testimonies are my *d*., 174.
Prov. 11. 20. upright are his *d*., 12. 22.
15. 8. prayer of upright is his *d*.
S. of S. 2. 3. under shadow with great *d*.
Isa. 55. 2. let your soul *d*. itself in fatness
58. 2. *d*. to know—take *d*. in approaching
13. call the sabbath a *d*. holy of
Rom. 7. 22. I *d*. in the law of God
Ps. 112. 1. *delighteth* greatly in his commandments
Prov. 3. 12. son in whom he *d*.
Isa. 42. 1. elect in whom my soul *d*.
Mic. 7. 18. because he *d*. in mercy
Ps. 119. 92. thy law hath been my *delights*, 143. Eccl. 2. 8.
Prov. 8. 31. my *d*. with sons of men
S. of S. 7. 6. how pleasant, O love, for *d*.
Mal. 3. 12. for ye shall be a *delightsome* land
R. V. Prov. 19. 10. delicate living
DELIVER, Ex. 3. 8. & 5. 18.
Job 5. 19. *d*. thee in six troubles and
10. 7. none can *d*. out of thy hand
Ps. 33. 19. to *d*. their souls from death
50. 15. I will *d*. thee, and thou, 91. 15.
56. 13. wilt thou not *d*. my feet
74. 19. *d*. not the soul of thy turtle
91. 3. *d*. thee from snare of fowler
Eccl. 8. 8. shall wickedness *d*. those
Ezek. 14. 14. should *d*. but their own
Dan. 3. 17. our God is able to *d*. us
Hos. 11. 8. how shall I *d*. thee, Israel
Rom. 7. 24. who shall *d*. from body
1 Cor. 5. 5. to *d*. such a one to Satan
2 Tim. 4. 18. the Lord shall *d*. me
Heb. 2. 15. *d*. them who thro. fear
2 Pet. 2. 9. Lord knows how to *d*.
2 Kings 5. 1. *deliverance*, 13. 17. 2 Chron. 12. 7. Esth. 4. 14. Ps. 32. 7. & 44. 4. Isa. 26. 18. Joel 2. 32. Obad. 17. Luke 4. 18. Heb. 11. 35.
Gen. 45. 7. *great deliverance*, Judg. 15. 18. 1 Chron. 11. 14. Ps. 18. 50.
Ezra 9. 13. given us such *d*. as this
Heb. 11. 35. not accepting *d*.
Prov. 11. 8. righteous is *delivered* out of trouble, and the wicked cometh, 9. 21.
28. 26. walketh wisely shall be *d*.
Isa. 38. 17. in love to soul, *d*. it
49. 24, 25. lawful captive—prey be *d*.
Jer. 7. 10. *d*. to do all abominations
Ezek. 3. 19. hast *d*. thy soul, 21. & 33. 9.
Dan. 12. 1. thy people shall be *d*.
Mic. 4. 10. Babylon, there shalt thou be *d*.
Matt. 11. 27. all things are *d*. to me
Acts 2. 23. *d*. by determinate coun.
Rom. 4. 25. who was *d*. for our offences
7. 6. we are *d*. from the law that
8. 32. God *d*. him up for us all
2 Cor. 1. 10. who *d*. us from so great
4. 11. *d*. unto death for Jesus' sake
1 Thes. 1. 10. which *d*. us from the
1 Tim. 1. 20. whom I have *d*. to
2 Pet. 2. 7. *d*. just Lot vexed with
Jude 3. faith once *d*. to the saints
R. V. Lev. 6. 4; 2 Sam. 10. 10; 1 Chron. 19. 11. committed; Deut. 5. 22. gave; Judg. 2. 16, 18; 3. 9, 31; 8. 22; 10. 12; 12. 2, 3. saved; 2 Kings 18. 30; 19. 10; Isa. 36. 15. given; 1 Chron. 11. 14. defended; Ps. 55. 18; 78. 42. redeemed; 81. 6. freed; Ezek. 6. 21; Mark 9. 31; 15. 1, 10. delivered up; Mic. 4. 10. rescued; 2 Kings 5. 1; 13. 17; 1 Chron. 11. 14. victory; Joel 2. 32; Obad. 17. those that escape; Luke 4. 18. release; Judg. 3. 9, 15. savior
DELUSION, 2 Thes. 2. 11. Isa. 66. 4.
R. V. 2 Thes. 2. 11. working of error
DEMONSTRATION, 1 Cor. 2. 4.
DEN, Judg. 6. 2. Job 37. 8. Heb. 11. 38. Rev. 6. 15. Ps. 104. 22.
Ps. 10. 9. *den of lions*, S. of S. 4. 8. Dan. 6. 7, 24. Amos 3. 4. Nah. 2. 12.
Jer. 7. 11. *den of robbers*—of thieves, Matt. 21. 13. Mark 11. 17.
Jer. 9. 11. *den of dragons*, 10. 22.
R. V. Jer. 9. 11; 10. 22. dwelling place; Job 37. 8. coverts; Rev. 6. 15. caves
DENY, 1 Kings 2. 16. Job 8. 18.
Prov. 30. 9. lest I be full and *d*. thee
Matt. 10. 33. shall *d*. me before men
26. 34. before the cock crow thou shalt *d*.
35. I will not *d*. thee, Mark 14. 31.
2 Tim. 2. 12. if we *d*. him he will *d*.
Tit. 1. 16. in works they *d*. him
1 Tim. 5. 8. hath *denied* the faith
Rev. 2. 13. hast not *d*. my faith
2 Tim. 3. 5. godliness *denying* the power
Tit. 2. 12. *d*. ungodliness and
2 Pet. 2. 1. *d*. Lord that bought th.
DEPART from, Job 21. 14. & 22. 17.
28. 28. to *d*. from evil, is understanding
Ps. 34. 14. *d*. from evil, 37. 27. Prov. 3. 7. & 13. 19. & 16. 6, 17.
Hos. 9. 12. woe to me when I *d*. from
Matt. 7. 23. *d*. from me, ye that work
Luke 2. 29. lettest thy servant *d*. in
5. 8. *d*. from me—a sinful man, O Lord
1 Tim. 4. 1. some shall *d*. from faith
2 Tim. 2. 19. name of Christ *d*. fr.
Ps. 18. 21. wickedly *departed* from
Prov. 14. 16. feareth and *departeth* from evil
Isa. 59. 15. *d*. from evil makes him.
Acts 20. 29. after my *departing*, wolves
2 Tim. 4. 6. *departure*, Ezek. 26. 18.
R. V. very largely, go, went away, withdrew
DEPTH, Job 28. 14. & 38. 16. Prov. 8. 27. Matt. 18. 6. Mark 4. 5.
Rom. 8. 39. nor *d*. separate us
11. 33. O the *d*. of riches of wisdom
Eph. 3. 18. *d*. of the love of Christ
Ex. 15. 5, 8. *depths*, Ps. 68. 22. & 71. 20. & 130. 1. Prov. 3. 20. & 9. 18.
Mic. 7. 19. cast sins into *d*. of sea
Rev. 2. 24. known *d*. of Satan
R. V. Ex. 15. 5, 8; Ps. 33. 7. deeps; Job 28. 14; 38. 16; Prov. 8. 27. deep; Mark 4. 5. deepness
DERISION, Job 30. 1. Ps. 2. 4. & 44. 13. & 59. 8. & 119. 51. Jer. 20. 7, 8.
R. V. Jer. 20. 7. laughing stock
DESCEND, Ex. 19. 18. & 33. 9.
Ps. 49. 17. glory shall not *d*. after
Isa. 5. 14. rejoiceth shall *d*. into it
Gen. 28. 12. angels of God ascending and *descending*, John 1. 51.
Matt. 3. 16. Spirit of God *d*. like dove, Mark 1. 10. John 1. 32, 33.
Rev. 21. 10. city *d*. out of heaven
R. V. Num. 34. 11; 1 Sam. 26. 10. go down; Mark 15. 32; Ps. 133. 3; Acts 24. 1; Jas. 3. 15; Rev. 21. 10. come or came down; Josh. 17. 9; 18. 13, 16, 17. went down; Heb. 7. 3, 6. genealogy
DESERT, Ex. 3. 1. & 19. 2. Num. 20. 1. Isa. 21. 1. & 35. 1. & 40. 3. & 43. 19. & 51. 3. Jer. 25. 24. & 50. 12. Ezek. 47. 8. Matt. 24. 26.
R. V. Ps. 102. 6. waste places; Ezek. 47. 8. Arabah; Ex. 3. 1; 5. 3; 19. 2; 23. 31; Num. 21. 1; 27. 14; 33. 16; 2 Chron. 26. 10; Isa. 21. 1; Jer. 25. 24; Matt. 24. 26; John 6. 31. wilderness
DESIRE, Deut. 18. 6. & 21. 11.
Gen. 3. 16. thy *d*. shall be to thy husband
4. 7. to thee shall be his *d*. and thou
Ex. 34. 24. nor any man *d*. thy land
Deut. 18. 6. with all the *d*. of his heart
2 Sam. 23. 5. this is all my *d*. though
2 Chron. 15. 15. with their whole *d*.
Job 14. 15. wilt have a *d*. to work
21. 14. we *d*. not knowledge of thy
Ps. 38. 9. all my *d*. is before thee
73. 25. none that I *d*. besides thee
145. 16. fulfil the *d*. of them that
Prov. 10. 24. *d*. of righteous shall
11. 23. *d*. of righteous is only good
21. 25. *d*. of slothful killeth him
Eccl. 12. 5. *d*. shall fall, because
Isa. 26. 8. *d*. of our soul is to thy
Ezek. 24. 16. take the *d*. of thy eyes
Hag. 2. 7. the *d*. of all nations shall
Luke 22. 15. with *d*. I have desired
Jas. 4. 2. *d*. to have and cannot
Rev. 9. 6. *d*. to die, and death shall flee
Ps. 19. 10. more to be *desired* are they
Isa. 26. 9. with my soul have I *d*. thee
Jer. 17. 16. nor have I *d*. woeful day
Ps. 37. 4. give the *desires* of heart
Eph. 2. 3. fulfilling *d*. of the flesh
Ps. 51. 6. thou *desirest* truth in
16. thou *d*. not sacrifice, else
Job 7. 2. servant earnestly *desireth*
12. what man *d*. life and
68. 16. hill which God *d*. to dwell
Prov. 12. 12. wicked *d*. not of evil
13. 4. soul of sluggard *d*. and hath
21. 10. soul of wicked *d*. evil
R. V. Job. 31. 35. signature; 2 Cor. 7. 7; Rom. 15. 23. longing; Ps. 78. 29. lusteth after; Job 20. 20. delighteth; Ps. 27. 4; Matt. 16. 1; Mark 15. 6; John 12. 21; Acts 3. 14; 7. 46; 9. 2; 13. 21, 28; 18. 20; 1 John 5. 15. asked; Hos. 6. 6; Mic. 7. 1. desire; Luke 9. 9; Acts 3. 7.

sought; 2 Cor. 8. 6; 12. 18. exhorted
DESOLATE, 2 Sam. 13. 20. Job 15. 28. & 16. 7. Ps. 25. 16. Isa. 49. 21. & 54. 1. Matt. 23. 38. Rev. 17. 16.
Isa. 49. 6. *desolations*, 61. 4. Jer. 25. 9, 12. Ezek. 35. 9. Dan. 9. 2, 18, 26.
R. V. Jer. 49. 13, 17. astonishment; Prov. 1. 27. storm; Lam. 3. 47. devastation; Job 30. 14; Ezra 9. 9; Ps. 74. 31. ruins
DESPAIR, 2 Cor. 4. 8. & 1. 8. Eccl. 2. 20.
1 Sam. 27. 1. *d. i. e.* to be past hope
Job 6. 20. *desperate*, Isa. 17. 11.
Jer. 17. 9. *desperately* wicked
DESPISE my statutes, Lev. 26. 15.
1 Sam. 2. 30. that *d.* me shall be lightly
Job 5. 17. *d.* not chastening of
Ps. 102. 17. will not *d.* their prayer
Prov. 23. 22. *d.* not mother when
Matt. 6. 24. hold to one and *d.* other
Rom. 14. 3. *d.* him that eateth not
Gen. 16. 4. mistress was *despised* in
2 Sam. 6. 16. she *d.* him in her
Prov. 12. 9. is *d.* and hath a serv.
S. of S. 8. 1. kiss thee I should not be *d.*
Isa. 53. 3. he is *d.* and rejected, Ps. 22. 6.
Zech. 4. 10. who *d.* the day of small
Luke 18. 9. righteous and *d.* others
Heb. 10. 28. that *d.* Moses' law died
Acts 13. 41. *despisers*, 2 Tim. 3. 3.
Rom. 2. 4. *despisest* thou riches of goodness
Job 36. 5. God *despiseth* not any
Prov. 11. 12. void of wisdom *d.* neighbor
13. 13. *d.* the word shall be destroyed
14. 21. that *d.* his neighbor sinneth
15. 32. refuseth instruction *d.* his
Isa. 33. 15. *d.* gain of oppression
49. 7. whom man *d.* nation abho.
Luke 10. 16. *d.* you, *d.* me, *d.* him
1 Thes. 4. 8. *d.* not man but God
Heb. 12. 2. *despising* the shame
10. 29. done *despite* to the Spirit of grace
R. V. Lev. 26. 15. reject; 26. 43; Num. 11. 20; 14. 31; Ps. 53. 5; Ezek. 20. 13, 16, 24; Amos 2. 4. rejected; Luke 18. 9; Heb. 10. 28. set at nought; Jas. 2. 6; 1 Cor. 4. 10. dishonor; Acts 19. 27. made of no account; Prov. 19. 16. careless of; Luke 10. 16; 1 Thes. 4. 8. rejecteth; 2 Tim. 3. 3. no lovers of
DESTROY, Gen. 18. 23. & 19. 13.
Ps. 101. 8. I will *d.* all wicked of the
Prov. 1. 32. the prosper. of fools *d.*
Matt. 5. 17. not come to *d.* but to fulfil
10. 28. able to *d.* both soul and body
John 2. 19. *d.* this temple, and I will raise
Rom. 14. 15. *d.* not him with thy
20. for meat *d.* not work of God
1 Cor. 3. 17. if defile temple, him God will *d.*
6. 13. God shall *d.* both it and them
Jas. 4. 12. able to save and to *d.*
1 John 3. 8. might *d.* works of devil
Hos. 4. 6. my people are *destroyed*
13. 9. Israel, thou hast *d.* thyself
2 Cor. 4. 9. cast down but not *d.*
Job 15. 21. *destroyer*, Ps. 17. 4. Prov. 28. 24. Jer. 4. 7. 1 Cor. 10. 10.
Esth. 4. 14. *shall be destroyed*, Ps. 37. 38. & 92. 7. Prov. 13. 13, 20. & 29. 1. Isa. 10. 27. Dan. 2. 44. Hos. 10. 8. Acts 3. 23. 1 Cor. 15. 26.
Deut. 7. 23. *destruction*, 32. 24.
Job 5. 22. at *d.* and famine shall laugh
18. 12. *d.* is ready at his side
Ps. 90. 3. thou turnest man to *d.*
91. 6. *d.* that wasteth at noonday
Prov. 10. 29. *d.* shall be to workers of iniquity, 21. 15. Job. 21. 30. & 31. 3.
15. 11. hell and *d.* are before the Lord
16. 18. pride goeth before *d.*
18. 12. before *d.* the heart of man
Jer. 4. 20. *d.* upon *d.* is cried, for land is spoiled
Hos. 13. 14. O grave, I will be thy *d.*
Matt. 7. 13. way that leads to *d.*
1 Cor. 5. 5. for the *d.* of the flesh
2 Cor. 10. 8. not for your *d.*, 13. 10.
1 Thes. 5. 3. peace and safety; then sudden *d.* cometh upon them
2 Thes. 1. 9. punished with everlasting *d.*
2 Pet. 2. 1. bring on themselves swift *d.*
3. 16. wrest Scriptures to their *d.*
R. V. Gen. 18. 23, 24; 1 Chron. 21. 12. consume; Ex. 23. 27; Deut. 7. 23; Ps. 144. 6. discomfit; Ex. 34. 13; Num. 24. 17; Deut. 7. 5; Ps. 28. 5. break down; Deut. 7. 24; 9. 3; 28. 51; Josh. 7. 7. perish; 2 Sam. 22. 41; Ps. 18. 40; 54. 5; 69. 4; 101. 5; 1 Kings 15. 13. cut off, or down; Ps. 5. 10. hold guilty; Prov. 15. 25. root up; Acts 9. 21; Gal. 1. 23. made havoc; Rom. 14. 20. overthrow; 1 Cor. 6. 13; Heb. 2. 14; 2 Thes. 2. 8. bring to nought; Rom. 6. 6. done away; 1 Cor. 15. 26. abolished; 1 Cor. 10. 9, 10; 2 Pet. 2. 12. perish; Acts 19. 27. despised; Jer. 50. 11. that plunder; Job 15. 21. spoiler; Ps. 17. 4. violent
DETERMINED, 2 Chron. 25. 16. Job 14. 5. Isa. 10. 23. & 28. 22. Dan. 9. 24. Acts 2. 23. & 4. 28. & 17. 26.
R. V. 2 Chron. 2. 1; Isa. 19. 17; Acts 20. 3. purposed; Dan. 9. 24. decreed; Acts 15. 37. was minded; 19. 39. settled in the regular; 15. 2. the brethren appointed
DETESTABLE, Deut. 7. 26. Jer. 16. 18. Ezek. 5. 11. & 7. 20. & 11. 18. & 37. 23. 1 Cor. 2. 2.
DEVICE, Eccl. 9. 10. Job 5. 12. Ps. 33. 10. Prov. 1. 31. & 12. 2. & 14. 17. & 19. 21. Jer. 18. 11, 12, 18. 2 Cor. 2. 11.
R. V. Ps. 33. 10. thoughts; Lam. 3. 62. imagination
DEVIL, Matt. 4. 5. & 8. 11. & 9. 32.
Matt. 4. 1. to be tempted of the *d.*
11. 18. they say he hath a *d.*
13. 39. enemy that sowed is the *d.*
25. 41. fire prepared for the *d.* and
John 6. 70. twelve, and one of you is a *d.*
7. 20. thou hast a *d.*, 8. 48.
8. 44. of your father the *d.*, 49.
13. 2. *d.* having now put it into, 27.
Acts 10. 10. thou child of the *d.*
Eph. 4. 27. neither give place to *d.*
2 Tim. 2. 26. recover out of the snare of the *d.*
Jas. 4. 7. resist *d.* and he will
1 Pet. 5. 8. your adversary the *d.* goeth
1 John 3. 8. to destroy works of *d.*
10. children of God and children of the *d.*
Jude 9. Michael contending with *d.*
Rev. 2. 10. the *d.* shall cast some
Lev. 17. 7. offer sacrifice to *devils*
Deut. 32. 17. they sacrifice to *d.*
Ps. 106. 37. sacrificed their sons to *d.*
Matt. 4. 24. possessed with *d.*, 8. 16, 28, 33. Luke 4. 41. & 8. 36.
10. 8. raise the dead, cast out *d.*
Mark 16. 9. cast out seven *d.*, Luke 8. 2.
Luke 10. 17. even *d.* are subject to
1 Cor. 10. 20. have fellowship with *d.* sacrifice to *d.*
21. cup of *d.* table of *d.*
Jas. 2. 19. *d.* believe and tremble
R. V. Lev. 17. 7; 2 Chron. 11. 15. he-goats, Deut. 32. 17; Ps. 106. 37. demons
DEVISE not evil against, Prov. 3. 29.
14. 22. do they not err that *d.* evil
16. 30. shutteth eyes to *d.* froward
Jer. 18. 18. come let us *d.* devices
Mic. 2. 1. woe to them that *d.* iniquity
DEVOTED, Lev. 27. 21, 28. Num. 18. 14.
Ps. 119. 38. servant who is *d.* to thy
Acts 17. 23. I beheld your *devotions*
DEVOUR, Gen. 49. 27. Isa. 26. 11.
Matt. 23. 14. ye *d.* widows' houses
Gal. 5. 15. if ye bite and *d.* one another
Heb. 10. 27. which shall *d.* the ad.
1 Pet. 5. 8. seeking whom he may *d.*
Isa. 1. 20. ye shall be *devoured*
Jer. 3. 24. shame hath *d.* the labor
Hos. 7. 7. *d.* judges
9. *d.* strength
Mal. 3. 11. I will rebuke *devourer*
Ex. 24. 17. *devouring fire*, Isa. 29. 6. & 30. 27, 30. & 33. 14.
Ps. 52. 4. lovest all *devouring* words
R. V. Ps. 80. 13. feed on; Isa. 42. 14. pant together; Prov. 19. 28; Hab. 1. 13. swalloweth up; Prov. 20. 25. rashly to say; Matt. 23. 14 ——
DEVOUT, Luke 2. 25. Acts 2. 5. & 10. 2. & 17. 4, 17. & 22. 12.
DEW, Gen. 27. 28. Deut. 32. 2.
Ps. 110. 3. hast the *d.* of thy youth
Isa. 26. 19. thy *d.* is as the *d.* of
Hos. 6. 4. goodness is as the early *d.*
Mic. 5. 7. Jacob — as *d.* from Lord
R. V. Ps. 133. 3 ——
DIADEM, Job 29. 14. Isa. 28. 5. & 62. 3. Ezek. 21. 26.
R. V. Ezek. 21. 26. mitre
DIE, Gen. 5. 5. & 6. 17.
Gen. 2. 17. thou shalt surely *d.*, 3. 4. & 20. 7. 1 Sam. 14. 44. & 22. 16. 1 Kings 2. 37, 42. Jer. 26. 8. Ezek. 3. 18. & 33. 8, 14.
Job 14. 14. if a man *d.* shall he live
Ps. 82. 7. ye shall *d.* like men
Prov. 23. 13. with rod he shall not *d.*
Eccl. 3. 2. there is a time to *d.*
Isa. 22. 13. to-morrow we shall *d.*
Ezek. 3. 19. *d.* in his iniquity, 33. 8.
18. 4. soul that sinneth shall *d.*
31. why will ye *d.* O house of
Jonah 4. 3. better for me to *d.* than
Matt. 26. 35. though I should *d.*
Luke 20. 36. neither can *d.* any more
John 8. 21. ye shall *d.* in your sins, 24.
11. 50. expedient that one *d.* for
Rom. 14. 8. we *d.* we *d.* unto Lord
1 Cor. 9. 15. better for me to *d.* than
15. 22. as in Adam all *d.* so in Christ
Phil. 1. 21. to live is Christ, to *d.* is gain
Heb. 9. 27. it is appointed for men to *d.*
Rev. 3. 2. that are ready to *d.*
14. 13. blessed are the dead who *d.*
Rom. 5. 6. Christ *died* for ungodly
8. while yet sinners, Christ *d.* for us
6. 9. being raised he *d.* no more
14. 9. to this end Christ *d.* and rose
1 Cor. 15. 3. Christ *d.* for our sins
2 Cor. 5. 15. he *d.* for all, that they
1 Thes. 5. 10. who *d.* for us that whether
Heb. 11. 13. these all *d.* in faith, not
Rom. 14. 7. no man *dieth* to himself
2 Cor. 4. 10. *dying*, 6. 9. Heb. 11. 21.
DIFFER, who makes, 1 Cor. 4. 7.
Phil. 1. 10. that *d.*, Rom. 2. 18.
Lev. 10. 10. *difference*, Ezra 22. 26. & 44. 23.
Acts 15. 9. no *d.*, Rom. 3. 22. & 10. 12.
R. V. Lev. 20. 25. separate; Acts 15. 9; Rom. 3. 22; 10. 12. distinction; Ezek. 22. 26. discern; 1 Cor. 12. 5. diversities; Jude 22. who are in doubt
DILIGENCE, 2 Tim. 4. 9, 21.
Prov. 4. 23. keep thy heart with all *d.*
Luke 12. 58. art in way give *d.* that

2 Pet. 1. 5. giving all *d.* add to faith
10. give *d.* to make calling and election
Jude 3. I gave all *d.* to write unto
Deut. 19. 18. *diligent*, Josh. 22. 5.
Prov. 10. 4. hand of *d.* maketh rich
12. 24. hand of *d.* shall bear rule
21. 5. thoughts of the *d.* tend to
22. 29. man *d.* in his business
2 Pet. 3. 14. be *d.* to be found of him
Ex. 15. 26. will *diligently* hearken to voice of, Deut. 11. 13. & 28. 1. Jer. 17. 24. Zech. 6. 15.
Deut. 4. 9. keep thy soul *d.*
6. 7. teach them *d.* unto thy children
17. *d.* keep the commandments, 11. 22.
24. 8. that thou observe *d.* and
Ps. 119. 4. to keep thy precepts *d.*
Heb. 11. 6. rewarder of them that *d.* seek
R. V. Cor. 8. 7. earnestness; 2 Cor. 8. 22. earnest; Tit. 3. 12; 2 Pet. 3. 14. give diligence
DIMINISH, Deut. 4. 2. Prov. 13. 11.
Rom. 11. 12. *diminishing* of them the riches of
R. V. Isa. 21. 17. few; Rom. 11. 12. their loss
DIMNESS of anguish, Isa. 8. 22. & 9. 1.
DIRECT, Eccl. 10. 10. Isa. 45. 13.
Ps. 5. 3. will I *d.* my prayer to thee
Prov. 3. 6. he shall *d.* thy paths
Isa. 61. 8. I will *d.* their work in truth
Jer. 10. 23. that walks to *d.* his steps
2 Thes. 3. 5. Lord *d.* your hearts
Isa. 40. 13. who *directed* the Spirit
Ps. 119. 5. ways were *d.* to keep
Prov. 16. 9. a man's heart deviseth, Lord *directeth* his steps
R. V. Gen. 46. 28. shew; Ps. 5. 3; Prov. 21. 29. order; Ps. 119. 5. established; Isa. 45. 13. make straight; 61. 8. give them; Num. 19. 4. toward front of
DISCERN, Eccl. 8. 5. 2 Sam. 14. 17. & 19. 35. 1 Kings 3. 9, 11. 1 Cor. 2. 14.
Mal. 3. 18. *d.* between righteous and
Heb. 5. 14. to *d.* both good and
4. 12. *discerner* of thoughts
1 Cor. 11. 29. not *discerning* Lord's body
12. 10. to another *d.* of spirits
R. V. Luke 12. 56. know how to interpret; 1 Cor. 2. 14. judge
DISCHARGE, in war, Eccl. 8. 8.
R. V. 1 Kings 5. 9. broken up
DISCIPLE, John 9. 28. & 19. 38.
Matt. 10. 24. the *d.* is not above
42. in the name of a *d.*
Luke 14. 26. ye cannot be my *d.*
John 8. 31. then are ye my *d.* ind.
Acts 21. 16. an old *d.* with whom
R. V. Matt. 26. 20; 28. 9; Mark 2. 18; Luke 9. 11; John 6. 11 ——; Acts 1. 15. brethren
DISCORD, soweth, Prov. 6. 14, 19.
DISCRETION, Ps. 112. 5. Prov. 1. 4. & 2. 11. & 3. 21. & 11. 22. & 19. 11. Isa. 28. 26. Jer. 10. 12.
R. V. Ps. 112. 5. in judgment; Isa. 28. 26. aright
DISEASE, Ps. 38. 7. & 41. 8. Eccl. 6. 2. Matt. 4. 23. & 9. 35. & 10. 1. Ex. 15. 26. Deut. 28. 60. 2 Chron. 21. 19.
Ps. 103. 3. who healeth all thy *d.*
Ezek. 34. 4. *diseased*, have ye not, 21.
R. V. 2 Kings 1. 2; 8. 8, 9; Matt. 9. 35. sickness; John 5. 4 ——; Matt. 14. 35; Mark 1. 32; John 6. 2. sick
DISFIGURE bodies, Matt. 6. 16.
DISGRACE not, Jer. 14. 21.
DISGUISES resorted to, 1 Sam. 28. 8. 1 Kings 14. 2. & 20. 38. & 22. 30. 2 Chron. 18. 29. & 35. 22.
disfiguring of face for the dead forbidden, Lev. 19. 28. Deut. 14. 1.

DISHONOR, Ps. 35. 26. Prov. 6. 33. Mic. 7. 6. son *d.* his father
Ps. 71. 13. cloth. with shame and *d.*
Rom. 1. 24. to *d.* their own bodies
1 Cor. 15. 43. it is sown in *d.* it is raised
DISOBEDIENCE, 2 Cor. 10. 6. Eph. 2. 2. & 5. 6. Col. 3. 6.
Rom. 5. 19. by one man's *d.* many
DISOBEDIENT, 1 Kings 13. 26. Neh. 9. 26.
Luke 1. 17. *d.* to wisdom of the just
Rom. 1. 30. *d.* to parents, 2 Tim. 3. 2.
Tit. 1. 16. abominable and *d.*
3. 3. *d.* deceived, serving divers lusts
1 Pet. 2. 7, 8. stumble being *d.*
R. V. 1 Pet. 2. 7. such as disbelieve
DISORDERLY, 2 Thes. 3. 6, 7, 11.
DISPENSATION, 1 Cor. 9. 17. Eph. 1. 10. & 3. 2. Col. 1. 25.
DISPERSED, Ps. 112. 9. Prov. 5. 16. Isa. 11. 12. Zeph. 3. 10. John 7. 35.
R. V. John 7. 35. Dispersion; Acts 5. 37; 2 Cor. 9. 9. scattered
DISPLEASED, Gen. 38. 10. 2 Sam. 11. 27. 1 Chron. 21. 7. Zech. 1. 2, 15. Isa. 59. 15. Mark 10. 14. 1 Kings 1. 6. Ps. 60. 1.
Deut. 9. 19. *hot* or *sore displeasure*, Ps. 2. 5. & 6. 1. & 38. 1.
R. V. Gen. 31. 35; Ps. 60. 1. angry; Gen. 38. 10. evil in sight of; Num. 11. 1. speak evil in ears of; Matt. 21. 15; Mark 10. 14, 41. moved with indignation; Judg. 15. 3. mischief
DISPOSING is of the Lord, Prov. 16. 33.
Acts 7. 53. *disposition* of angels
R. V. As if ordained by
DISPUTE, Job 23. 7. Mark 9. 33. Acts 6. 9. & 9. 29. & 17. 17. & 19. 8, 9.
Rom. 14. 1. doubtful *disputations*
Phil. 2. 14. *disputings*, 1 Tim. 6. 5.
R. V. Job 23. 7. reason; Mark 9. 33. were ye reasoning; Acts 17. 17. reasoned; Acts 15. 2. questioning; Acts 19. 8, 9. reasoning; 1 Tim. 6. 5. wranglings
DISQUIETED, Ps. 39. 6. & 42. 5, 11.
R. V. Prov. 30. 21. doth tremble
DISSEMBLE, Josh. 7. 11. Jer. 42. 20. Gal. 2. 13. Ps. 26. 4. Prov. 26. 24.
Rom. 12. 9. *dissimulation*, Gal. 2. 13.
R. V. Jer. 42. 20. dealt deceitfully; Rom. 12. 9. hypocrisy
DISSENSION, Acts 15. 2. & 23. 7, 10.
DISSOLVED, Ps. 75. 3. Isa. 24. 19. 2 Cor. 5. 1. 2 Pet. 3. 11. Job 30. 22.
R. V. Isa. 14. 31. melted away
DISTINCTLY, read law, Neh. 8. 8.
DISTRACTED, suffer terrors, Ps. 88. 15.
1 Cor. 7. 35. *distraction* without
DISTRESS, Gen. 42. 21. Deut. 2. 9, 19. Neh. 9. 37. Luke 21. 23, 25.
Gen. 35. 3. answered in day of my *d.*
2 Sam. 22. 7. in my *d.* I called on
1 Kings 1. 29. redeemed my soul out of all *d.*
2 Chron. 28. 22. in his *d.* trespassed
Ps. 4. 1. enlarged my heart in *d.*
Isa. 25. 4. strength to needy in *d.*
Zeph. 1. 15. that day is a day of *d.*, 17.
Rom. 8. 35. shall *d.* separate from Christ
1 Sam. 28. 15. *distressed*, 30. 6. 2 Sam. 1. 26.
2 Cor. 6. 4. in *distresses*, 12. 10.
Ps. 25. 17. *out of my distresses*, 107. 6, 13, 19, 28. Ezek. 30. 16. 2 Cor. 6. 4.
R. V. Ezek. 30. 16. adversaries; 1 Kings 1. 20. adversity; Neh. 2. 17. evil case; Rom. 8. 35. anguish; Deut. 2. 9, 19. vex; 2 Cor. 4. 8. straitened
DISTRIBUTE, Luke 18. 22. 1 Tim. 6. 18. 1 Cor. 7. 17. Job 21. 17. Rom. 12. 13.

Acts 4. 35. *distribution*, 2 Cor. 9. 13.
R. V. 1 Chron. 24. 3. divided; Rom. 12. 13. communicating; 2 Cor. 10. 13. apportioned
DITCH, Job 9. 31. Ps. 7. 15. Prov. 23. 27. Isa. 22. 11. Matt. 15. 14. Luke 6. 39.
R. V. 2 Kings 3. 16. trenches; Isa. 22. 11. reservoir; Matt. 15. 14; Luke 6. 39. pit
DIVERSITIES, 1 Cor. 12. 4, 6, 28.
R. V. 1 Cor. 12. 28. divers kinds
DIVIDE, Gen. 1. 6, 14. Job 27. 17.
1 Kings 3. 25. *d.* living child, 26.
Ps. 55. 9. destroy—*d.* their tongues
Isa. 53. 12. I will *d.* him a portion
Luke 12. 13. to *d.* inheritance with
2 Sam. 1. 23. in death not *divided*
Dan. 2. 41. kingdom shall be *d.*
Matt. 12. 25. kingdom, house *d.* against itself shall not stand, 26. Luke 11. 17.
12. 11. *dividing* to every man sever.
2 Tim. 2. 15. rightly *d.* the word of
Heb. 4. 12. to *d.* asunder of joints
Judg. 5. 15, 16. *divisions*, Luke 12. 51. Rom. 16. 17. 1 Cor. 1. 10. & 3. 3.
R. V. Lev. 11. 4, 7; Deut. 14. 7, 8. part; Num. 33. 54. inherit; Josh. 19. 45. distributing; 23. 4; Neh. 9. 22. allot; Matt. 25. 32. separateth; Acts 13. 19. gave them their land for an inheritance; 2 Tim. 2. 13. handling aright; Dan. 7. 25. half a; Judg. 5. 15, 16. watercourses; 1 Cor. 3. 3 ——
DIVINE sentence, Prov. 16. 10.
Heb. 9. 1. ordinance of *d.* service
2 Pet. 1. 3. his *d.* power hath given
Mic. 3. 11. prophets *d.* for money
Num. 22. 7. *divination*, 23. 23. Deut. 18. 10. Acts 16. 16.
Deut. 18. 14. *diviners*, Isa. 44. 25. Mic. 3. 6, 7. Zech. 10. 2. Jer. 29. 8.
DIVORCE, Jer. 3. 8. Lev. 21. 14. & 22. 13. Num. 30. 9. Matt. 5. 32.
Deut. 24. 1, 3. *divorcement*, Isa. 50. 1. Matt. 5. 31. & 19. 7. Mark 10. 4.
R. V. divorcement; Matt. 5. 32. put away
DO, Gen. 16. 6. & 18. 25. & 31. 16.
Matt. 7. 12. men should *d.* to you, *d.*
John 15. 5. without me ye can *d.*
Rom. 7. 15. what I would that *d.* I not
Phil. 4. 13. I can *d.* all things throu.
Heb. 4. 13. with whom we have to *d.*
Rev. 19. 10. see thou *d.* it not, 22. 9.
Rom. 2. 13. the *doers* of it shall
Jas. 1. 22. be ye *d.* of word and not
1 Chron. 22. 16. *doing*, Ps. 64. 9. & 66. 5. & 118. 23. Prov. 20. 11. Isa. 1. 16. Jer. 7. 3, 5. & 18. 11. & 26. 13. & 32. 19. Zech. 1. 4. Ezek. 36. 31. Zeph. 3. 11. Mic. 2. 7.
Rom. 2. 7. *well-doing*, Gal. 6. 9. 2 Thes. 3. 13. 1 Pet. 2. 15. & 3. 17. & 4. 19.
R. V. 2 Kings 22. 5. workmen; Ps. 101. 8. workers of iniquity; 2 Tim. 2. 9. malefactor
DOCTOR, Acts 5. 34. Luke 2. 46. & 5. 17.
Deut. 32. 2. *doctrine* shall drop as rain
Jer. 10. 8. the stock is a *d.* of vanities
Matt. 7. 28. astonished at his *d.*, 22. 33. Mark 1. 22. & 11. 18. Luke 4. 32.
Matt. 16. 12. beware of the *d.* of
Mark 1. 27. what new *d.* is this
John 7. 17. shall know of the *d.*
Acts 2. 42. apostles' *d.* and fellowship
Rom. 6. 17. form of *d.* which was
16. 17. contrary to *d.* ye have learn.
Eph. 4. 14. with every wind of *d.*
1 Tim. 5. 17. labor in word and *d.*
2 Tim. 3. 16. profitable for *d.*
Tit. 2. 7. in *d.* showing uncorrupt
10. may adorn the *d.* of God
Heb. 6. 1. principles of *d.* of Christ
Matt. 15. 9. teaching for *d.* the
Col. 2. 22. after *doctrines* of men

Heb. 13. 9. carr. about by strange *d.*
R. V. in N. T. generally, teaching
DOG, Ex. 11. 7. Deut. 23. 18.
1 Sam. 17. 43. am I a *d.*, 2 Kings 8. 13.
Prov. 26. 11. *d.* return to his vomit, 2 Pet. 2. 22.
Eccl. 9. 4. living *d.* better than
Isa. 56. 10. all dumb *dogs*
11. greedy *d.*
Matt. 7. 6. cast not that which is holy to *d.*
15. 27. *d.* eat of crumbs, Mark 7. 28.
Rev. 22. 15. without are *d.* and sorcerers
DOMINION, Gen. 27. 40. & 37. 8.
Num. 24. 19. he that shall have *d.*
Job 25. 2. *d.* and fear are with him
Ps. 8. 6. have *d.* over the works of
19. 13. not have *d.* over me, 119. 133.
49. 14. upright have *d.* over them
145. 13. thy *d.* endureth through
Isa. 26. 13. other lords had *d.* over
Dan. 4. 3. his *d.* is from generation
34.—an everlasting *d.*, 7. 14.
7. 27. all *d.* shall serve and obey
Rom. 6. 9. death has no more *d.*
14. sin shall not have *d.* over you
Col. 1. 16. thrones or *d.* or principalities
Jude 8. despise *d.* and speak evil
25. to God *d.*, 1 Pet. 4. 11. & 5. 11.
R. V. Judg. 14. 4. rule; 2 Chron. 21. 8. hand; Neh. 9. 37. power; 2 Cor. 1. 24. lordship; Matt. 20. 25. lord it
DOOR, Judg. 11. 31. & 16. 3.
Gen. 4. 7. sin lieth at the *d.*
Ps. 84. 10. *d.* keeper in the house
141. 3. keep *d.* of my lips
Prov. 26. 14. as *d.* turns on hinges
Hos. 2. 15. valley of Achor, *d.* of
John 10. 1. entereth not by the *d.* is
7. I am the *d.* of sheep
9. I am *d.*
Acts 14. 27. opened *d.* of faith
1 Cor. 16. 9. great *d.* and effectual
2 Cor. 2. 12. a *d.* was opened to me
Jas. 5. 9. judge stands before *d.*
Rev. 3. 8. I set before thee an open *d.*
20. I stand at *d.* and knock, if any
Ps. 24. 7. lift up ye everlasting *doors*
Mal. 1. 10. shut ye the *d.* for nought
Matt. 24. 33. near, even at the *d.*
R. V. Amos 9. 11. chapters; Ezek. 41. 2, 3. entrance; 41. 16. thresholds; 1 Kings 14. 17. house
DOTING, 1 Tim. 6. 4. Ezek. 23. 5, 20.
DOUBLE, Ex. 22. 4. Deut. 21. 17.
2 Kings 2. 9. *d.* portion of thy spirit
1 Chron. 12. 33. not of a *d.* heart
Job 11. 6. secrets are *d.* to that
Ps. 12. 2. with a *d.* heart do they speak
Isa. 40. 2. *d.* for all her sins, Jer. 16. 18.
Jer. 17. 18. destroy with *d.* destruct.
1 Tim. 3. 8. deacons not *d.* tongued
Jas. 1. 8. *d.* minded man, 4. 8.
Rev. 18. 6. *d.* to her, fill to her *d.*
R. V. Job 11. 6. manifold
DOUBT, Deut. 28. 66. Gal. 4. 20.
Matt. 14. 31. of little faith, why dost *d.*
21. 21. have faith and *d.* not
Mark 11. 23. and shall not *d.* in
Rom. 14. 23. he that *doubteth* is dam.
1 Tim. 2. 8. without wrath or *doubting*
Luke 12. 29. be not of *doubtful* mind
Rom. 14. 1. not to *d.* disputations
R. V. Luke 11. 20. then; 1 Cor. 9. 10. yea; Gal. 4. 20. perplexed; John 10. 24. hold us in suspense; Acts 5. 24; 10. 17; 25. 20. much perplexed; 1 Tim. 2. 8. disputing
DOUGH, Ex. 12. 34. Num. 15. 20. Neh. 10. 37. Ezek. 44. 30.
DOVE, Ps. 55. 6. & 68. 13. & 74. 19. S. of S. 1. 15. & 2. 14. & 5. 2. & 6. 9. Matt. 3. 16. Luke 3. 22. John 1. 32.
Isa. 38. 14. mourn as *d.*, 59. 11.
60. 8. fly as *d.* to their windows
Hos. 7. 11. Ephr. is like a silly *d.*
Matt. 10. 16. wise as serpents, and harmless as *d.*

DOWN sitting, Ps. 139. 2.
Isa. 37. 31. *downward*, Eccl. 3. 21.
DRAGON, Ps. 91. 13. Isa. 27. 1. & 51. 9. Jer. 51. 34. Ezek. 29. 3. Rev. 12. 3-17. & 13. 2, 4, 11. & 16. 13. & 20. 2.
Deut. 32. 33. *dragons*, Job 30. 29. Ps. 44. 19. & 74. 13. & 148. 7. Isa. 13. 22. & 34. 13. & 43. 20. Jer. 9. 11. & 14. 6. Mic. 1. 8. Mal. 1. 3.
R. V. Job 30. 29; Ps. 44. 19; Isa. 13. 22; 34. 13; 35. 7; 43. 20; Jer. 9. 11; 10. 22; 14. 6; 49. 33; 51. 37; Mic. 1. 8; Mal. 1. 3. jackals
DRAUGHTS of fishes, miraculous, Luke 5. 4, 5, 6. John 21. 6, 11.
DRAW, Gen. 24. 44. 2 Sam. 17. 13.
Job 21. 33. every man shall *d.*
Ps. 28. 3. *d.* me not away with
S. of S. 1. 4. *d.* me, we will run after
Isa. 5. 18. woe unto that *d.* iniquity
Jer. 31. 3. with loving kindness I *d.*
John 6. 44. except Father—*d.* him
12. 32. I will *d.* all men to me
Heb. 10. 38. if any man *d.* back, 39.
Ps. 73. 28. good for me to *d.* near to
Eccl. 12. 1. years *d.* nigh when say
Isa. 29. 13. *d.* near me with their
Heb. 7. 19. by which we *d.* nigh to
Jas. 4. 8. *d.* nigh to God, and he will *d.*
Ps. 18. 16. *drew* me out of many waters
Hos. 11. 4. I *d.* with cords of love
R. V. Mark 6. 53. moved; Luke 15. 1; Acts 27. 27. were drawing; Acts 19. 33. brought; Acts 14. 19; 17. 6; 21. 30. dragged
DREAD, Ex. 15. 16. Job 13. 11, 21.
Deut. 1. 29. *d.* not, nor be afraid
1 Chron. 22. 13. be strong *d.* not
Isa. 8. 13. let him be your fear and *d.*
Dan. 9. 4. great and *dreadful* God
Gen. 28. 17. how *d.* is this place
Mal. 1. 14. my name is *d.* among
4. 5. great and *d.* day of the Lord
R. V. Dan. 7. 7, 19; Mal. 1. 14; 4. 5. terrible
DREAM, Gen. 37. 5. & 40. 5. & 41. 7.
Gen. 20. 3. God came to Abimelech in a *d.*
31. 11. angel spake to Jacob in a *d.*
Num. 12. 6. speak to him in a *d.*
1 Kings 3. 5. the Lord appeared to Solomon in a *d.*
Ps. 73. 20. as *d.* when one awaketh
Eccl. 5. 3. *d.* comes through multitude
Isa. 29. 7. that fight—be as a *d.*
Dan. 2. 3. I *d.* a *d.*
4. 5. saw a *d.*
Matt. 1. 20. angel appeared in a *d.*
2. 12. Joseph warned of God in a *d.*
27. 19. suffered many things in a *d.*
Acts 2. 17. old men shall *d. dreams*, Joel 2. 28.
Job 7. 14. scarest me with *d.*
DRINK, Ex. 15. 24. & 32. 20.
Job 21. 20. *d.* of wrath of Almighty
Ps. 36. 8. *d.* of the river of thy pleasure
60. 3. *d.* wine of astonishment
80. 5. givest them tears to *d.*
Prov. 4. 17. *d.* the wine of violence
5. 15. *d.* waters out of own cistern
31. 4. it is not for kings to *d.* wine
7. *d.* and forget his poverty
S. of S. 5. 1. *d.* yea *d.* abundantly, O
Isa. 22. 13. let us eat and *d.*, 1 Cor. 15. 32.
43. 20. to give *d.* to my people
Hos. 4. 18. their *d.* is sour, committed
Amos 4. 1. say to masters, bring, and let us *d.*
Matt. 10. 42. give to *d.* to one of these little ones
20. 22. able to *d.* of cup, 23.
26. 27. *d.* ye all of it, this is my blood
29. I will not henceforth *d.* of fruit
John 6. 55. my blood is *d.* indeed
18. 11. cup Father given, shall I not *d.* it

Rom. 14. 17. king. of God is not *d.*
1 Cor. 10. 4. drink same spiritual *d.*
11. 25. as often as ye *d.* it in rem.
12. 13. all made to *d.* into one spirit
Lev. 10. 9. not *d.* wine nor *strong drink*, Judg. 13. 4, 7, 14. 1 Sam. 1. 15.
Prov. 31. 6. give—to those ready to perish
Isa. 5. 11. follow—
22. mingle—
28. 7. prophet erred through—
Mic. 2. 11. prophecy to them of—
Job 15. 16. *drinketh* iniquity like
John 6. 54. *d.* my blood hath eter.
56. that *d.* my blood dwells in me
1 Cor. 11. 29. eateth and *d.* unworth.
Heb. 6. 7. earth which *d.* in rain
Eph. 5. 18. be not *drunk* with wine
Rev. 17. 2. *d.* with wine of fornication
Deut. 21. 20. glutton and *drunkard*
Prov. 23. 21. *d.* shall come to poverty
Isa. 24. 20. earth shall reel like a *d.*
1 Cor. 5. 11. with railer and *d.* not eat
Ps. 69. 12. *drunkards*, Isa. 28. 1, 3. Joel 1. 5. Nah. 1. 10. 1 Cor. 6. 10.
Job 12. 25. stagger like a *drunken* man, Ps. 107. 27. Jer. 23. 9. Isa. 19. 14.
Isa. 29. 9. *d.* not with wine, 51. 21.
Acts 2. 15. these are not *d.* as ye suppose
1 Cor. 11. 21. one hungry another is *d.*
1 Thes. 5. 7. they that be *d.* are *d.*
Deut. 29. 19. *drunkenness*, Eccl. 10. 17. Jer. 13. 13. Ezek. 23. 33. Luke 21. 34. Rom. 13. 13. Gal. 5. 21.
DROP, Deut. 33. 28. Judg. 5. 4.
Deut. 32. 2. doctrine shall *d.* as rain
Ps. 65. 11. thy paths *d.* fatness, 12.
Prov. 5. 3. *d.* as honey-comb, S. of S. 4. 11.
Isa. 40. 15. all nations are as a *d.* of
S. of S. 5. 5. my hands *dropped* myrrh
2. locks with *drops* of the night
Luke 22. 44. sweat as it were great *d.*
DROSS, Ps. 119. 119. Isa. 1. 25. Ezek. 22. 18.
DROUGHT, Deut. 28. 24. 1 Kings 17. Hag. 1. 11.
DROWN, S. of. S. 8. 7. 1 Tim. 6. 9.
R. V. Ex. 15. 4. sunk; Amos 8. 8; 9. 5. sink again; Heb. 11. 29. swallowed up
DROWSINESS clothe, Prov. 23. 21.
DRY, Judg. 6. 37, 39. Job 13. 25. Prov. 17. 1. Isa. 44. 3. & 56. 3. Jer. 4. 11. Ezek. 17. 24. & 37. 2, 4. Hos. 9. 14.
R. V. Lev. 2. 14; Isa. 5. 13. parched; Joel 1. 12; Mark 11. 20. withered
DUE, Lev. 10. 13. Deut. 18. 3.
1 Chron. 15. 13. sought him not after *d.*
1 Chron. 16. 29. give Lord glory *d.* to his name, Ps. 29. 2. & 96. 8.
Prov. 3. 27. withhold not—whom it is *d.*
Matt. 18. 34. should pay all that was *d.*
Luke 23. 41. we received *d.* reward
Ps. 104. 27. meat in *due season*, 145. 15. Matt. 24. 45. Luke 12. 42.
Prov. 15. 23. a word spoken in—
Eccl. 10. 17. princes eat in—for strength
Gal. 6. 9. in—we shall reap, if we
Deut. 32. 35. foot shall slide in *due time*
Rom. 5. 6. in—Christ died for the
1 Cor. 15. 8. as one born out of—
1 Tim. 2. 6. to be testified in—
Tit. 1. 3. hath in—manifested
R. V. 1 Tim. 2. 6. its own; Tit. 1. 3. his own
DULL of hearing, Matt. 13. 15.
DUMB, Hab. 2. 18. Mark 9. 17.
Ex. 4. 11. who maketh *d.* or deaf
Ps. 38. 13. I was as a *d.* man

Ps. 39. 2. I was *d.* with silence, 9.
Prov. 31. 8. open thy mouth for *d.*
Isa. 35. 6. tongue of *d.* to sing
53. 7. sheep before shearers is *d.*
R. V. Luke 1. 20. silent
DUMBNESS of Zacharias, Luke 1. 20.
DUNG of solemn feasts, Mal. 2. 3.
Phil. 3. 8. I count them but *d.* to
DURABLE riches and righteousness, Prov. 8. 18.
Isa. 23. 18. merchandise for *d.* clothing
DUST thou art, and to *d.*, Gen. 3. 19.
18. 27. who am but *d.* and ashes
Job 30. 19. I am become like *d.*
Ps. 22. 15. brought me into *d.* of
30. 9. shall the *d.* praise thee
103. 14. remembereth that we are *d.*
119. 25. soul cleaveth to the *d.*
Eccl. 12. 7. then shall *d.* retu. to *d.*
Matt. 10. 14. shake off *d.* of your feet, Luke 10. 11. Acts 13. 51.
R. V. Lev. 14. 41. mortar
DUTY of marriage, Ex. 21. 10.
2 Chron. 8. 14. as the *d.* of every day
Eccl. 12. 13. this is whole *d.* of man
Luke 17. 10. which was our *d.* to do
R. V. Rom. 15. 27. owe it to them
DWARFS not to minister, Lev. 21. 20.
DWELL in thy holy hill, Ps. 15. 1.
Ps. 23. 6. I will *d.* in the house of
84. 10. than to *d.* in the tents of wickedness
120. 5. that I *d.* in tents of Kedar
133. 1. good for brethren to *d.* together
Isa. 33. 14. who shall *d.* with devouring fire—*d.* with everlasting burnings
16. he shall *d.* on high his place
Rom. 8. 9. Spirit of God *d.* in you, 11
2 Cor. 6. 16. I will *d.* in them, Ezek. 43. 7.
Col. 1. 19. in him shall all fulness *d.*
1 John 4. 13. that we *d.* in him
Rev. 21. 3. he will *d.* with them
John 6. 56. *dwelleth* in me, and I in
14. 10. Father that *d.* in me
17. he *d.* with and shall be in you
Acts 7. 48. *d.* not in temples, 17. 24.
Rom. 7. 17. sin that *d.* in me, 20.
18. in my flesh *d.* no good thing
8. 11. by his Spirit that *d.* in you
1 Cor. 3. 16. Spirit of God *d.* in you
Col. 2. 9. in him *d.* all fulness of
2 Tim. 1. 14. Holy Ghost who *d.* in
Jas. 4. 5. the Spirit which *d.* in
2 Pet. 3. 13. wherein *d.* righteous.
1 John 3. 17. how *d.* the love of God
4. 12. God *d.* in us, and his love is
16. *d.* in love, *d.* in God, and God
2 John 2. truth's sake which *d.* in
1 Tim. 6. 16. *dwelling* in light
Heb. 11. 9. *d.* in tabernacles with
2 Pet. 2. 8. righteous man *d.* among
Ps. 87. 2. more than all *d.* of Jacob
94. 17. almost *dwelt* in silence
John 1. 14. Word made flesh
Acts 13. 17. *d.* as strangers in it
2 Tim. 1. 5. faith *d.* first in grandmother
R. V. frequently in O. T., sit, sojourn

E

EAGLE stirreth up her nest, Deut. 32. 11.
Job 9. 26. as *e.* hasteth to the prey
Prov. 23. 5. fly away as *e.* towards
Jer. 49. 16. make nest as high as *e.*
Ezek. 17. 3. great *e.* with great wings
Mic. 1. 16. enlarge thy bald. as *e.*
Rev. 12. 14. to woman given wings of a great *e.*
Ex. 19. 4. bare you on *e.* wings
2 Sam. 1. 23. swifter than *eagles*
Ps. 103. 5. youth renewed like *e.*
Prov. 30. 17. young *e.* shall eat it
Isa. 40. 31. mount up with wings as *e.*
Jer. 4. 13. horses swifter than *e.*
Matt. 24. 28. there *e.* be gathered
R. V. Lev. 11. 18; Deut. 14. 17. vulture
EAR, Num. 14. 28. Ex. 9. 31.
Ex. 21. 6. bore his *e.*, Deut. 15. 17.
2 Kings 19. 16. bow down *e.*, Ps. 31. 2.
Neh. 1. 6. let thy *e.* be attentive, 11.
Job 12. 11. *e.* try words, 34. 3.
36. 10. openeth *e.* to discipline
Ps. 10. 17. cause thine *e.* to hear
Ps. 94. 9. planted the *e.* shall he not
Prov. 18. 15. *e.* of wise seek know.
20. 12. hearing *e.* and seeing eye
Eccl. 1. 8. nor *e.* filled with hearing
Isa. 50. 4. awaketh my *e.* to hear
59. 1. neither is *e.* heavy
Jer. 6. 10. their *e.* is uncircumcised
Matt. 10. 27. what ye hear in the *e.*
1 Cor. 2. 9. eye seen nor *e.* heard
Rev. 2. 7. he that hath an *e.* let him hear, 11. 17, 29. & 3. 6, 13, 22. & 13. 9. Matt. 11. 15. & 13. 9, 43.
Ex. 15. 26. *give ear*, Deut. 32. 1. Judg. 5. 3. Ps. 5. 1. & 17. 1. & 39. 12. & 49. 1. & 54. 2. & 78. 1. & 80. 1. & 84. 8. & 141. 1. Isa. 1. 2, 10. & 8. 9. & 28. 23. & 32. 9. & 42. 23. Jer. 13. 15. Hos. 5. 1. Joel 1. 2. Ps. 55. 1. & 86. 6.
Ps. 17. 6. *incline ear*, 45. 10. & 71. 2. & 88. 2. & 102. 2. & 116. 2. Isa. 37. 17. Dan. 9. 18.
49. 4. — to a parable
78. 1. — to words of my mouth
Prov. 2. 2. — to wisdom
4. 20. — to my sayings
Isa. 55. 3. — and come unto me
Jer. 11. 8. *nor inclined their ear*, 17. 23. & 25. 4. & 35. 15.
Deut. 29. 4. Lord not given *ears* to
1 Sam. 3. 11. both *e.* shall tingle, 2 Kings 21. 12. Jer. 19. 3.
2 Sam. 22. 7. cry did enter in. his *e.*
Job 33. 16. open the *e.* of men
Ps. 34. 15. his *e.* are open to their cry
40. 6. my *e.* hast thou opened
44. 1. we have heard with our *e.*
Isa. 6. 10. make their *e.* heavy, lest
35. 5. *e.* of deaf shall be unstopped
Matt. 13. 15. their *e.* dull of hearing
Luke 9. 44. these sayings sink down into your *e.*
2 Tim. 4. 4. turn away their *e.* from
2 Chron. 6. 40. *thine ears* be open to
Ps. 10. 17. cause — to hear
130. 2. let — be attentive
Prov. 23. 12. apply — to words of knowledge
Isa. 30. 21. — shall hear a word
Ezek. 3. 10. hear with —, 40. 4. & 44. 5.
Gen. 45. 6. *earing*, Ex. 34. 21.
1 Sam. 8. 12. *ear his ground*, Isa. 30. 24.
Ex. 9. 31. *in the ear*, Mark 4. 28.
Job 42. 11. gave *ear-ring* of gold
Prov. 25. 12. as an *e.* of gold so is
R. V. Gen. 24. 22, 47; 35. 4; Ex. 32. 2, 3; Job 42. 11. ring, rings; Isa. 3. 20. amulets
EARLY, Gen. 19. 2. John 18. 28. & 20. 1.
Ps. 46. 5. God shall help her, and that right *e.*
57. 8. will awake right *e.*, 108. 2.
63. 1. my God, *e.* will I seek thee
90. 14. satisfy us *e.* with mercy
Prov. 1. 28. seek me *e.* and not find
8. 17. that seek me *e.* shall find me
Isa. 26. 9. with my spir. I seek thee *e.*
Jer. 7. 13. rising up *e.*, 25. & 11. 7. & 25. 3, 4. & 26. 5. & 29. 19. & 32. 33. & 35. 14, 15. & 44. 4. 2 Chron. 36. 15.
Hos. 5. 15. in affliction will seek me *e.*
Jas. 5. 7. receive *e.* and latter rain
R. V. Judg. 7. 3; Ps. 57. 8. right early; 9. 14. in the morning; 101. 8. morning by morning; Ps. 1. 28; 8. 17. diligently; Hos. 5. 15. earnestly; Mark 16. 2. early in the morning; Acts 5. 21. about daybreak
EARNEST of Spirit given, 2 Cor. 1. 22. & 5. 5.
Eph. 1. 14. *e.* of your inheritance
Rom. 8. 19. *e.* expectation of the
2 Cor. 7. 7. told us of your *e.* desire
Heb. 2. 1. give the more *e.* heed
Job 7. 2. servant *earnestly* desireth the shadow
Jer. 11. 7. I *e.* protested to your fathers
31. 20. I do *e.* remember him still
Mic. 7. 3. do evil with both hands *e.*
Luke 22. 44. in an agony, prayed more *e.*
1 Cor. 12. 31. covet *e.* the best gifts
2 Cor. 5. 2. in this we groan *e.*
Jas. 5. 17. prayed *e.* it might not
Jude 3. *e.* contend for the faith
R. V. Mic. 7. 3. diligently; Luke 22. 56; Acts 23. 1. stedfastly; Acts 3. 12. fasten your eyes; Jas. 5. 17. fervently
EARNETH wages, Hag. 1. 6.
EARTH was corrupt, Gen. 6. 11, 12.
Gen. 6. 13. *e.* is filled with violence
11. 1. whole *e.* of one language
41. 47. *e.* brought forth by handfuls
Ex. 9. 29. *e.* is the Lord's, Deut. 10. 14. Ps. 24. 1. 1 Cor. 10. 26, 27, 28.
Num. 16. 32. *e.* opened her mouth, 26. 10. Deut. 11. 6. Ps. 106. 17.
Deut. 28. 23. *e.* under thee be iron
32. 1. O *e.* hear the words of my mouth
Judg. 5. 4. *e.* trembleth and heaven
1 Sam. 2. 8. pillars of *e.* are Lord's
2 Sam. 22. 8. *e.* shook and trembled
1 Chron. 16. 31. let *e.* rejoice, Ps. 96. 11.
Job 9. 6. shakes *e.* out of her place
24. *e.* is given into hand of wicked
11. 9. longer than *e.* broader than
16. 18. O *e.* cover not my blood
26. 7. hangeth *e.* upon nothing
28. 5. out of *e.* cometh bread and
38. 4. I laid the foundations of *e.*
Ps. 33. 5. *e.* is full of the goodness of
65. 9. visitest *e.* and waterest it
67. 6. *e.* shall yield her increase, 85. 12.
72. 19. let the whole *e.* be filled
75. 3. *e.* and inhabitants dissolved, Isa. 24. 19.
78. 69. like *e.* established for ever
97. 4. *e.* saw and trembled
104. 24. *e.* is full of thy riches, 13.
114. 7. tremble, O *e.* at presence of
115. 16. *e.* given to children of men
119. 64. *e.* is full of thy mercy
139. 15. in lowest parts of the *e.*
Prov. 25. 3. *e.* for depth is unsearchable
Isa. 6. 3. whole *e.* is full of his glory
11. 9. *e.* full of the knowledge of
24. 1. Lord maketh the *e.* empty
4. *e.* mourneth and fadeth, 33. 9.
5. *e.* is defiled under inhabitants
19. *e.* utterly broken down and
20. *e.* shall reel and stagger like a
26. 19. *e.* shall cast out her dead
Jer. 22. 29. O *e.* *e.* *e.* hear the word
Ezek. 34. 27. the *e.* shall yield her
43. 2. the whole *e.* shined with his
Hos. 2. 22. *e.* shall hear the corn
Hab. 3. 3. *e.* was full of his praise
Matt. 13. 5. stony ground had not much *e.*
John 3. 31. that is of *e.* earthly
Heb. 6. 7. *e.* which drinketh in rain
Rev. 12. 16. *e.* opened and swallowed
Ps. 67. 2. way known *upon earth*
73. 25. none — I desire besides thee
Eccl. 5. 2. God is in heaven and thou —
7. 20. there is not a just man —

Luke 5. 24. the Son of man hath power—
Col. 3. 5. mortify your members—
Lev. 6. 28. *earthen*, Jer. 19. 1. & 32. 14. Lam. 4. 2. 2 Cor. 4. 7.
John 3. 12, 31. *earthly*, 2 Cor. 5. 1. Phil. 3. 19. Jas. 3. 15.
1 Cor. 15. 47, 48, 49. *earthy*
1 Kings 19. 11, 12. *earthquake*, Isa. 29. 6. Amos 1. 1. Zech. 14. 5. Matt. 24. 7, 27, 54. & 28. 2. Acts 16. 26.
Rev. 6. 12. a great *e.*, 8. 5. & 11. 19. & 16. 18.
R. V. very frequently in O. T., land; John 3. 31. of the earth

EASE, Job 12. 5. & 16. 12. & 21. 23. Ps. 25. 13. & 123. 4. Deut. 28. 65. Isa. 32. 9, 11. Jer. 46. 27. & 48. 11. Ezek. 23. 42. Amos 6. 1. Zech. 1. 15.
Isa. 1. 24. I will *e.* me of mine adversaries
Luke 12. 19. take thine *e.* be merry
Matt. 11. 30. my yoke is *easy*, and burden light
Prov. 14. 6. knowledge is *e.* to him
1 Cor. 14. 9. words *e.* to be underst.
Jas. 3. 17. gentle, *e.* to be entreated
Matt. 9. 5. *easier*, 19. 24. Luke 16. 17.
1 Cor. 13. 5. charity is not *easily* provoked
Heb. 12. 1. sin—doth so *e.* beset us
R. V. Deut. 23. 13. sitteth down; 2 Chron. 10. 4, 9. make

EAST, Gen. 28. 14. & 29. 1. Matt. 2. 1, 2. Ps. 75. 6. & 103. 12.
Isa. 43. 5. bring thy seed from *e.*
Matt. 8. 11. many shall come from *e.*
Rev. 16. 12. way of kings of the *e.* may
Gen. 41. 6. *east wind*, Ex. 14. 21. Job 27. 21. Ps. 48. 7. Isa. 27. 8. Hos. 12. 1. & 13. 15. Hab. 1. 9.
R. V. Jer. 19. 2. Harsith; Rev. 7. 2; 16. 12. sunrising; Gen. 2. 14. in front; Num. 3. 38. toward the sunrising

EAT, Gen. 3. 5, 6, 12, 13. & 18. 8. & 19. 3.
Gen. 2. 16, 17. of every tree freely *e.*
3. 14. dust shalt thou *e.* all the
17. in sorrow thou shalt *e.* of it
Neh. 8. 10. *e.* the fat, drink the sweet
Ps. 22. 26. the meek shall *e.* and
53. 4. eat up my people as bread, 14. 4.
78. 25. man did *e.* angels' food
29. they did *e.* and were filled
Prov. 1. 31. *e.* fruit of their own way
S. of S. 5. 1. *e.* O friends; drink, yea
Isa. 1. 19. if obedient ye shall *e.*
3. 10. shall *e.* fruit of doings
55. 1. buy and *e.* yea, come buy
2. *e.* that which is good, and let
65. 13. my servants shall *e.* but ye
Dan. 4. 33. did *e.* grass as an ox
Hos. 4. 10. shall *e.* and not have enough, Hag. 1. 6. Mic. 6. 14.
Mic. 3. 3. *e.* flesh of my people
Matt. 6. 25. what shall we *e.* and
26. 26. take *e.* this is my body, Mark 14. 22. 1 Cor. 11. 24, 26, 28.
Luke 10. 8. *e.* such things as are set
15. 23. let us *e.* and be merry
17. 27. they did *e.* they drank, 28.
John 6. 26. because ye did *e.* of
53. except ye *e.* flesh of Son of man
Acts 2. 46. did *e.*—with gladness
1 Cor. 5. 11. with such, no, not to *e.*
31. whether ye *e.* or drink, do all
2 Thes. 3. 10. if not work neither *e.*
2 Tim. 2. 17. *e.* as doth a canker
Jas. 5. 3. *e.* your flesh as fire
Rev. 17. 16. shall *e.* her flesh, and
Ps. 69. 9. the zeal of thy house hath *eaten* me up, John 2. 17. Ps. 119. 139.
Prov. 9. 17. bread *e.* in secret is
S. of S. 5. 1. *e.* my honeycomb with
Hos. 10. 13. having *e.* fruit of lies
Luke 13. 26. *e.* and drunk in thy
Acts 12. 23. Herod was *e.* of worms
Judg. 14. 14. out of *eater* came meat
Isa. 55. 10. give bread to *e.* and seed
Nah. 3. 12. fall into mouth of *e.*
Eccl. 4. 5. *eateth* his own flesh
Matt. 9. 11. why *e.* your master with publicans and sinners, Luke 15. 2.
John 6. 54 whoso *e.* my flesh
57. he that *e.* me shall live by me
58. he that *e.* this bread shall live
Rom. 14. 6. he that *e. e.* to the Lord
20. evil for that man who *e.* with offence
1 Cor. 11. 29. *e.* and drinketh unworthily, *e.* and drinketh damnation, 27.
Matt. 11. 18. John came neither *eating* nor drinking, Luke 7. 33.
19. Son of man came *e.*
24. 38. were *e.* and drinking, Luke 17. 27.
Matt. 26. 26. as they were *e.* Jesus
1 Cor. 8. 4. concerning *e.* of those

EDIFY, or build up, Rom. 14. 19. 1 Thes. 5. 11. 1 Cor. 8. 1. & 10. 23. & 14. 17. Acts 9. 31.
Rom. 15. 2. please neighbor to *edification*
1 Cor. 14. 3. speak unto men to *e.*
1 Cor. 14. 12. excel to *edifying* of church
26. let all things be done to *e.*, 5. 17.
2 Cor. 12. 19. we do all for your *e.*
Eph. 4. 29. but what is good to the use of *e.*
1 Tim. 1. 4. minister questions rather than *e.*
R. V. 1 Thes. 5. 11. build each . . up; Eph. 4. 12; 4. 16. building up; 1 Tim. 1. 4. a dispensation of God; Rom. 15. 2. unto edifying; 2 Cor. 10. 8; 13. 10. building up

EFFECT, 2 Chron. 34. 22. Ezek. 12. 23.
Isa. 32. 17. *e.* of righteousness quietness
Matt. 15. 6. commandment of God *of none effect*
Mark 7. 13. making work of God—
Rom. 3. 3. make faith of God—
9. 6. not as though word hath—
1 Cor. 1. 17. lest cross of Christ—
Gal. 5. 4. Christ is become—to you
1 Cor. 16. 9. door and *effectual* is opened
2 Cor. 1. 6. which is *e.* in enduring
Eph. 3. 7. *e.* working of his power
Phile. 6. faith may become *e.*
Jas. 5. 16. *e.* fervent prayer of the righteous
Gal. 2. 8. *effectually*, 1 Thes. 2. 13.
R. V. Num. 30. 8; Matt. 15. 6; Mark 7. 13; 1 Cor. 1. 17. void; Rom. 9. 6. come to nought; Gal. 5. 4. severed from Christ; Jer. 48. 30. have wrought nothing; 2 Cor. 1. 6. worketh patient; Eph. 3. 7. according to; 4. 16. working in due measure; Jas. 5. 16. supplication; Gal. 2. 8. for; 1 Thes. 2. 13 ——

EFFEMINATE, 1 Cor. 6. 9.

EGG, Deut. 22. 6. Job 6. 6. & 39. 14. Isa. 10. 14. & 59. 5. Jer. 17. 11. Luke 11. 12.

ELDER, Gen. 10. 21. 2 John 1. 3 John 1.
Gen. 25. 23. *e.* shall serve younger, Rom. 9. 12.
1 Tim. 5. 1. rebuke not an *e.* but
2. entreat *e.* women as mothers
1 Pet. 5. 1. *elders*, I who am an *e.*
5. younger submit yourselves to *e.*
Deut. 32. 7. ask *e.* they will tell thee
Ezra 10. 8. according to counsel of *e.*
Joel 2. 16. assemble *e.*, Ps. 107. 32.
Acts 14. 23. ordain *e.* in every
15. 23. *e.* and brethren send greeting, 6.
1 Tim. 5. 17. *e.* rule well, counted worthy
Tit. 1. 5. ordain *e.* in every church
Heb. 11. 2. *e.* obtained good report
Rev. 4. 4. four and twenty *e.* sitting, 10. & 5. 6, 8, 11, 14. & 11. 16. & 19. 4. & 7. 11, 13. & 14. 3.
R. V. Joel 1. 14; 2. 16. old men; Matt. 26. 59 ——

ELECT, *chosen, choice one*
Isa. 42. 1. *e.* in whom my soul delighteth
45. 4. for Israel my *e.* I have called
65. 9. my *e.* shall inherit it
22. my *e.* shall long enjoy work
Matt. 24. 22. for *e.* sake the days are shortened
24. if possible deceive very *e.*
31. gather together his *e.* from the
Luke 18. 7. God avenge his own *e.*
Rom. 8. 33. to charge of God's *e.*
1 Tim. 5. 21. charge thee before the *e.* angels
2 Tim. 2. 10. endure all things for *e.*
Tit. 1. 1. according to the faith of God's *e.*
1 Pet. 1. 2. *e.* according to the fore.
2. 6. corner stone, *e.* precious
2 John 1. *e.* lady
13. *e.* sister
1 Pet. 5. 13. church *elected* with you
Rom. 9. 11. purpose of God according to *election*
11. 5. remnant according to the *e.* of grace
7. *e.* hath obtained it, and rest blinded
28. touching the *e.* they are beloved
1 Thes. 1. 4. knowing your *e.* of God
2 Pet. 1. 10. make calling and *e.* sure
R. V. Isa. 42. 1; 45. 4; 65. 9, 22. my chosen

ELEMENTS, Gal. 4. 3, 9. 2 Pet. 3. 10, 12.
R. V. Gal. 4. 3, 9. rudiments

ELOQUENT, Ex. 4. 10. Isa. 3. 3. Acts 18. 24.
R. V. Isa. 3. 3. skilful; Acts 18. 24. learned

EMBALMING, of Jacob, Gen. 50. 2. of Joseph, Gen. 50. 26. of Christ, John 19. 39.

EMPTY, Gen. 31. 42. & 37. 24. & 41. 27.
Ex. 23. 15. none shall appear before me *e.*, 34. 20. Deut. 16. 16.
Deut. 15. 13. not let him go away *e.*
Judg. 7. 16. with *e.* pitchers and lamps
2 Sam. 1. 22. sword of Saul returned not *e.*
Hos. 10. 1. Israel is an *e.* vine
Luke 1. 53. rich hath he sent *e.* away
Isa. 34. 11. stones of *emptiness*
R. V. Hos. 10. 1. luxuriant

EMULATION, Rom. 11. 14. Gal. 5. 20.

END of all flesh is come, Gen. 6. 13.
Deut. 32. 20. see what their *e.* shall
Ps. 37. 37. *e.* of that man is peace
39. 4. make me to know my *e.*
Prov. 5. 4. her *e.* is bitter as worm.
14. 12. *e.* thereof are ways of death
Eccl. 4. 8. no *e.* of all his labor
7. 2. that is the *e.* of all men
Isa. 9. 7. of his government shall be no *e.*
Jer. 5. 31. what will ye do in the *e.* thereof
29. 11. to give an expected *e.*
Lam. 4. 18. our *e.* is come. our *e.* is near, Ezek. 7. 2, 6. Amos 8. 2.
Ezek. 21. 25. when iniquity shall have an *e.*
Dan. 12. 8. what shall be the *e.* of these
13. go thy way till the *e.* be
Hab. 2. 3. at the *e.* it shall speak
Matt. 13. 39. harvest is *e.* of world
24. 6. but *e.* is not yet, Luke 21. 9.
Rom. 6. 21. *e.* of those things is death
10. 4. Christ is *e.* of law for righteousness
Rom. 14. 9. to this *e.* Christ both
1 Tim. 1. 5. *e.* of commandment is
Heb. 6. 8. whose *e.* is to be burned
16. oath—make an *e.* of all strife
13. 7. considering *e.* of their
Jas. 5. 11. seen the *e.* of the Lord
1 Pet. 1. 9. receiving the *e.* of your
4. 7. *e.* of all things is at hand
Rev. 21. 6. beginning and *e.*, 22. 13. & 1. 8. 1 Sam. 3. 12.

Jer. 4. 27. *make a full end*, 5. 10, 18. & 30. 11. Ezek. 11. 13.
Num. 23. 10. *last end*, Jer. 12. 4. Lam. 1. 9. & 4. 18. Dan. 8. 19. & 9. 24.
Deut. 8. 16. *latter end*, 32. 29. Job 42. 12. Prov. 19. 20. 2 Pet. 2. 20.
Ps. 119. 33. *unto the end*, Dan. 6. 26. Matt. 24. 13. & 28. 20. John 13. 1. 1 Cor. 1. 8. Heb. 3. 6, 14. & 6. 11. Rev. 2. 26.
1 Tim. 1. 4. *endless*, Heb. 7. 16.
Ps. 22. 27. all the *ends* of the world
65. 5. confidence of all *e.* of earth
67. 7. all *e.* of earth shall fear him
Prov. 17. 24. eyes of fool in *e.* of
Isa. 45. 22. be ye saved, all *e.* of the
52. 10. all *e.* of the earth shall see
Zech. 9. 10. his dominion to *e.* of
Acts 13. 47. for salvation to the *e.*
1 Cor. 10. 11. on whom *e.* of world
R. V. Josh. 15. 8; 18. 15; Isa. 13. 5; Acts 13. 47. uttermost part; Dan. 12. 8; Heb. 13. 7. issue; Luke 22. 37. hath fulfilment; Matt. 28. 1. now late on; 1 Pet. 1. 13. perfectly on; 2 Pet. 2. 20. last state . . become; Gen. 2. 2; Deut. 31. 30; 1 Kings 7. 51. finished; Ezek. 4. 8. accomplished; Luke 4. 2, 13; Acts 21. 27. completed; John 13. 2 ——

ENDOWED, Gen. 30. 20. 2 Chron. 2. 12, 13. Luke 24. 49. Jas. 3. 13.

ENDURE, Job 8. 15. & 31. 23.
Gen. 33. 14. as children are able to *e.*
Ps. 30. 5. weeping may *e.* for a night
132. 26. they perish, but thou shalt *e.*
Prov. 27. 24. doth crown *e.* to
Ezek. 22. 14. can thy heart *e.* or
Mark 4. 17. no root, and *e.* but for a
13. 13. that shall *e.* unto end shall
2 Tim. 2. 3. *e.* hardness as a soldier
10. *e.* all things for elect's sakes
4. 5. watch thou, *e.* afflictions, do
Heb. 12. 7. if ye *e.* chastening
Jas. 5. 11. we count happy who *e.*
Ps. 81. 15. should have *endured* for ever
Rom. 9. 22. *e.* with much long suffering
2 Tim. 3. 11. what persecutions I *e.*
Heb. 6. 15. had patiently *e.* he obtained
10. 32. ye *e.* a great fight of afflic.
12. 2. *e.* cross
3. *e.* contradiction
Ps. 30. 5. his anger *endureth* but a
52. 1. the goodness of God *e.* continually
100. 5. his truth *e.* to all generations
Matt. 10. 22. that *e.* to end, shall be saved, 24. 13. Mark 13. 13.
John 6. 27. meat which *e.* unto life
1 Cor. 13. 7. charity *e.* all things
Jas. 1. 12. blessed that *e.* temptation
Ps. 9. 7. *endure for ever*, the Lord, 102. 12, 26. & 104. 31. his name, Ps. 72. 17. his seed, 89. 29, 36.
1 Chron. 16. 34, 41. *endureth for ever*, his mercy, 2 Chron. 5. 13. & 7. 3, 6. & 20. 21. Ezra 3. 11. Ps. 106. 1. & 107. 1. & 118. 1, 2, 3, 4, 29. & 136. 1-26. & 138. 8. Jer. 33. 11.
Ps. 111. 3. his righteousness —, 112. 39.
10. his praise —
117. 2. truth of the Lord —
119. 160. every one of thy judgments —
135. 13. thy name —
1 Pet. 1. 25. word of Lord —
Ps. 19. 9. fear of Lord *enduring* for ever
Heb. 10. 34. in heaven *e.* substance
R. V. Gen. 33. 14. according to the pace; Job 31. 23. do nothing; Ps. 9. 7. sitteth; 30. 5. tarry; John 6. 27; 1 Pet. 1. 25. abideth; Heb. 10. 34. abiding

ENEMY, Ex. 15. 6, 9. Ps. 7. 5.
Ex. 23. 22. I will be an *e.* unto thine enemies
Deut. 32. 27. I feared wrath of the *e.*
1 Sam. 24. 19. find his *e.* will he let
Job 33. 10. counteth me for his *e.*
Ps. 7. 5. let *e.* persecute my soul
8. 2. mightest still the *e.* and
Prov. 27. 6. kisses of *e.* are deceitful
Isa. 63. 10. he turned to be their *e.*
1 Cor. 15. 26. the last *e.* destroyed
Gal. 4. 16. am I become your *e.*
2 Thes. 3. 15. count him not as *e.*
Jas. 4. 4. friend of world, *e.* of God
1 Kings 21. 20. *mine enemy*, Ps. 7. 4. Mic. 7. 8, 10. Job 16. 9. Lam. 2. 22.
Ex. 23. 4. *thy enemy*, Prov. 25. 21. Rom. 12. 20. Matt. 5. 43.
Mic. 7. 6. man's *enemies* are men of
Rom. 5. 10. if when *e.* we were reconciled
1 Cor. 15. 25. put all *e.* under his feet
Phil. 3. 18. *e.* to the cross of Christ
Col. 1. 21. *e.* in your minds by wicked
Gen. 22. 17. *his enemies*, Ps. 68. 1, 21. & 112. 8. & 132. 18. Prov. 16. 7. Isa. 59. 18. & 66. 6. Heb. 10. 13.
Deut. 32. 41. *my enemies*, Ps. 18. 17, 48. & 23. 5. & 119. 98. & 139. 22. & 143. 12. Isa. 1. 24. Luke 19. 27.
Deut. 32. 31. *our enemies*, Luke 1. 71, 74.
Ex. 23. 22. *thy enemies*, Num. 10. 35. Deut. 28. 48, 53, 55, 57. & 33. 29. Judg. 5. 31. Ps. 21. 8. & 92. 9. & 110. 1. Matt. 22. 44. Heb. 1. 13.
Gen. 3. 15. I will put *enmity* between
Rom. 8. 7. carnal mind is *e.* against God
Eph. 2. 15. abolished *e.*
16. slain *e.*
R. V. Very frequently in O. T., especially in Ps., adversary

ENGAGETH his heart, Jer. 30. 21.

ENJOIN, Phile. 8. Esth. 9. 31. Job 36. 23. Heb. 9. 20.
R. V. Heb. 9. 20. commanded to you ward

ENJOY, Num. 36. 8. Deut. 28. 41.
Lev. 26. 34. land *e.* her sabbaths, 43.
Acts 24. 2. we *e.* great quietness
1 Tim. 6. 17. giveth richly all things to *e.*
Heb. 11. 25. *e.* pleasures of sin for
R. V. Num. 36. 8; Josh. 1. 15. possess

ENLARGE, Ex. 34. 24. Mic. 1. 16.
Gen. 9. 27. God shall *e.* Japheth
Deut. 33. 20. blessed be he that *enlargeth* Gad
2 Sam. 22. 37. *enlarged* steps, Ps. 18. 36.
Ps. 4. 1. *e.* me when in distress
25. 17. troubles of my heart are *e.*
119. 32. when thou shalt *e.* my
Isa. 5. 14. hell hath *e.* herself
54. 2. *e.* the place of thy tent
Hab. 2. 5. *e.* his desires as hell
2 Cor. 6. 11. our heart is *e.*, 13.
Esth. 4. 14. *enlargement*
R. V. Ps. 4. 1. set me at large; 2 Cor. 10. 15. magnified in

ENLIGHTEN darkness, Ps. 18. 28.
Eph. 1. 18. understanding being *enlightened*
Ps. 19. 8. commandment is pure, *enlightening* the eyes
Heb. 6. 4. impossible for those once *e.*
R. V. Ps. 18. 28. lighten

ENMITY between God and man, Rom. 8. 7. Jas. 4. 4; how abolished, Eph. 2. 15. Col. 1. 20.

ENOUGH, I have, Gen. 33. 9, 11.
Gen. 45. 28. it is *e.* Joseph is alive
Ex. 36. 5. bring more than *e.*
1 Kings 19. 4. it is *e.* take away
Prov. 30. 15, 16. say not, it is *e.*
Hos. 4. 10. eat, and not *e.*, Hag. 1. 6.
Matt. 10. 25. it is *e.* for disciple
Mark 14. 41. it is *e.* the hour is
Luke 15. 17. bread *e.* and to spare
R. V. Ex. 2. 19 ——

ENQUIRE after iniquity, Job 10. 6.
Ps. 27. 4. to *e.* in his temple
78. 34. returned and *e.* early after God
Eccl. 7. 10. thou dost not *e.* wisely
Isa. 21. 12. if ye will *e. e.* ye
Ezek. 36. 37. this I will be *enquired* of by the house of Israel
Zeph. 1. 6. have not *e.* for him
Matt. 2. 7. Herod *e.* of them diligently
Judg. 20. 27. *enquired of the Lord*, 1 Sam. 23. 2, 4. & 30. 8. 2 Sam. 2. 1. & 5. 19, 23. & 21. 1. Jer. 21. 2.
Prov. 20. 25. after vows make *enquiry*
R. V. Almost always changed to inquire; Matt. 27. 7, 16. learned; 1 Pet. 1. 10. sought

ENRICHED, 1 Cor. 1. 5. 2 Cor. 9. 11.
Ps. 65. 9. thou greatly *e.* it with

ENSAMPLE, 1 Cor. 10. 11. Phil. 3. 17. 1 Thes. 1. 7. 2 Thes. 3. 9. 1 Pet. 5. 3. 2 Pet. 2. 6.
R. V. 1 Cor. 10. 11. by way of example; 2 Pet. 2. 6. example

ENSIGN, Isa. 5. 26. Zech. 9. 16.
Isa. 11. 10. stand for *e.* to people, 12.
Ps. 74. 4. set up their *e.* for signs
R. V. Zech. 9. 16. on high

ENTER, Gen. 12. 11. Num. 4. 23. Judg. 18. 9. Dan. 11. 17, 40, 41.
Job 22. 4. will he *e.* into judg.
Ps. 100. 4. *e.* into his gates with
Isa. 2. 10. *e.* into rock and hide
26. 2. open, righteous nation may *e.*
20. *e.* into thy chambers, and shut
57. 2. he shall *e.* into peace
Matt. 5. 20. in no case *e.* into the
6. 6. when thou prayest, *e.* closet
7. 13. *e.* at strait gate, Luke 13. 24.
21. shall *e.* into kingdom of heaven
18. 8. better to *e.* into life, halt
19. 23. rich man hardly *e.* into
24. than for rich man to *e.* into the kingdom of heaven, Mark 10. 25. Luke 18. 25.
25. 21. *e.* thou into joy of Lord
Mark 14. 38. watch and pray, lest ye *e.* into temptation, Luke 22. 46.
Luke 13. 24. seek to *e.* but not able
24. 26. suffered and *e.* into his glory
John 3. 4. can he *e.* the second time
5. he cannot *e.* into the kingdom
Acts 14. 22. through much tribulation *e.* kingdom of God.
Heb. 4. 3. believed, do *e.* into rest
Rev. 15. 8. no man able to *e.* into temple
21. 27. *e.* into it, any thing defileth
Rev. 22. 14. *e.* through gates into
Ps. 143. 2. *enter not into* judgment
Prov. 4. 14. *e.* not into path of
23. 10. *e.* not into the fields of the
Matt. 26. 41. that ye *e.* not into temptation
Ps. 119. 130. *entrance*, 2 Pet. 1. 11.
Luke 11. 52. ye *entered* not yoursel.
John 4. 38. ye *e.* into their labors
10. 1. that *e.* not by door, but
Rom. 5. 12. sin *e.* into the world
Heb. 4. 6. *e.* not in because of unbelief
10. that is *e.* into his rest, he ceased
Matt. 23. 13. *entering*, Luke 11. 52. Mark 4. 19. & 7. 15. 1 Thes. 1. 9. Heb. 4. 1.
R. V. Mark 5. 40; 7. 18. goeth. The same change is frequent in O. T. Ex. 35. 15. door; 2 Chron. 18. 9; 23. 13. entrance; Mark 7. 15. going; Acts 27. 2. embarking; Num. 34. 8; 1 Chron. 4. 39; 1 Thes. 2. 1. entering; 2 Chron. 12. 10. door; Ps. 119. 130. opening

ENTERTAIN strangers, Heb. 13. 2.
R. V. Show love unto
ENTICE, Ex. 20. 16. Deut. 13. 6. 2 Chron. 18. 19, 20, 21. Prov. 1. 10.
Job 31. 27. *enticed*, Jas. 1. 14.
1 Cor. 2. 4. *enticing words*, Col. 2. 4.
R. V. 1 Cor. 2. 4. persuasive; Col. 2. 4. persuasiveness of
ENVY slayeth silly one, Job 5. 2.
Prov. 3. 31. *e.* not the oppressor
14. 30. *e.* is the rottenness of bones
23. 17. let not thy heart *e.* sinners
Eccl. 9. 6. their *e.* is perished
Isa. 11. 13. *e.* of Ephraim shall depart, not *e.* Judah
Ezek. 35. 11. do according to thine *e.*
Matt. 27. 18. for *e.* they delivered
Acts 7. 9. moved with *e.*, 17. 5.
13. 45. Jews filled with *e.* spake
Rom. 1. 29. full of *e.* murder
Phil. 1. 15. preach Christ of *e.*
1 Tim. 6. 4. whereof cometh *e.*
Jas. 4. 5. spirit in us lusteth to *e.*
1 Pet. 2. 1. laying aside all *e.*
Gen. 26. 14. Philistines *envied* him
30. 1. Rachel *e.* her sister
Ps. 106. 16. they *e.* Moses in camp
Eccl. 4. 4. man is *e.* of his neigh.
Num. 11. 29. *enviest* thou for my sake
1 Cor. 13. 4. charity *envieth* not
Rom. 13. 13. not in strife and *envying*
1 Cor. 3. 3. there is among you *e.*
2 Cor. 12. 20. debates, *e.* wraths
Gal. 5. 26. *e.* one another
Jas. 3. 14. ye have bitter *e.* and
Gal. 5. 21. *envyings*, murders
Ps. 37. 1. *envious*, 73. 3. Prov. 24. 1, 19.
R. V. Isa. 26. 11. see thy zeal for the people; Job 5. 2; Prov. 27. 4; Acts 7. 9; 13. 45; 17. 5. jealousy; Rom. 13. 13; 1 Cor. 3. 3; 2 Cor. 12. 20; Jas. 3. 14, 16. jealousy
EPHOD, Ex. 39. 2. Judg. 8. 27. & 17. 5. 1 Sam. 2. 18. & 21. 9. & 23. 9. & 30. 7. 2 Sam. 6. 14. Hos. 3. 4.
EPISTLE, Acts 15. 30. & 23. 33. Rom. 16. 22. 1 Cor. 5. 9. 2 Cor. 7. 8. Col. 4. 16. 1 Thes. 5. 27. 2 Thes. 2. 15. & 3. 14, 17. 2 Pet. 3. 1.
2 Cor. 3. 2. *e.* written in our hearts
3. ye are declared the *e.* of Christ
1. *epistles*, 2 Pet. 3. 16.
R. V. Acts 23. 33. letter
EQUAL, Job 28. 17, 19. Ps. 17. 2. & 55. 13. Prov. 26. 7. Lam. 2. 13.
Isa. 40. 25. to whom shall I be *e.*
46. 5. to whom will ye make me *e.*
Ezek. 18. 25. way of Lord is not *e.*
29. & 33. 17, 20. their way is not *e.*
Matt. 20. 12. made them *e.* to us
Luke 20. 36. *e.* to the angels
John 5. 18. making himself *e.* with
Rev. 21. 16. length, breadth, and height *e.*
Gal. 1. 14. *equals*, Ps. 55. 13.
2 Cor. 8. 14. *equality*
Ps. 99. 4. dost establish *equity*
Prov. 1. 3. receive instruction of *e.*
17. 26. to strike princes for *e.*
Eccl. 2. 21. whose labor is in *e.*
Isa. 11. 4. reprove with *e.* for
59. 14. truth is fallen, and *e.* can.
Mic. 3. 9. that pervert all *e.*
Mal. 2. 6. walked with me in *e.*
R. V. Ps. 17. 2. equity; Prov. 26. 7. hang loose; Gal. 1. 14. of mine own age
ERR, 2 Chron. 33. 9. Isa. 19. 14.
Ps. 95. 10. *e.* in heart, Heb. 3. 10.
119. 21. do *e.* from thy command.
Prov. 14. 22. do they not *e.* that devise ill
Isa. 3. 12. lead — cause to *e.*, 9. 16.
63. 17. why made us to *e.* from thy
Jer. 23. 13. prophet caused to *e.* by lies, 32.
Amos 2. 4. lies caused them to *e.*
Mic. 3. 5. prophets make my people to *e.*
Matt. 22. 29. ye *e.* not knowing the
Jas. 1. 16. do not *e.* my brethren
5. 19. if any of you *e.* from truth
Num. 15. 22. if ye have *erred*
1 Sam. 26. 21. I have *e.* exceedingly
Job 6. 24. understand wherein I have *e.*
19. 4. be it that I have *e.*, my error
Ps. 119. 110. yet I *e.* not from
Isa. 28. 7. have *e.* through wine
29. 24. they that *e.* in spirit
1 Tim. 6. 10. have *e.* from the faith
21. *e.* concerning faith, 2 Tim. 2. 18.
Prov. 10. 17. *erreth*, Ezek. 45. 20.
2 Sam. 6. 7. *error*, Job 19. 4. Eccl. 5. 6. & 10. 5. Dan. 6. 4.
Isa. 32. 6. will utter *e.* against Lord
Jer. 10. 15. vanity work of *e.*, 51. 18.
Dan. 6. 4. neither was there any *e.* or fault found
Matt. 27. 64. last *e.* be worse than the first
Rom. 1. 27. recompense of their *e.*
Jas. 5. 20. sinner from *e.* of his
2 Pet. 2. 18. them who live in *e.*
1 John 4. 6. know we the spirit of *e.*
Jude 11. after the *e.* of Balaam
Ps. 19. 12. who can under. his *errors*
Heb. 9. 7. for the *e.* of the people
R. V. 1 Tim. 6. 10. been led astray; Jas. 1. 16. be not deceived; Jer. 10. 15; 51. 18. delusion
ERRAND, Judg. 3. 19. 2 Kings 9. 5.
ESCAPE, Gen. 19. 17, 22. & 32. 8.
Ezra 9. 8. leave a remnant to *e.*
Esth. 4. 13. think not that thou shalt *e.*
Job 11. 20. but the wicked shall not *e.*
Ps. 56. 7. shall they *e.* by iniquity
71. 2. deliver me and cause me to *e.*
141. 10. let wicked fall whilst I *e.*
Prov. 19. 5. he that speaks lies shall not *e.*
Eccl. 7. 26. pleaseth God, shall *e.* her
Isa. 20. 6. we flee — how shall we *e.*
Jer. 11. 11. evil — not be able to *e.*
Ezek. 17. 15. shall *e.* that doeth
Matt. 23. 33. how can ye *e.* damna.
Luke 21. 36. accounted worthy to *e.*
Rom. 2. 3. *e.* the judgment of God
1 Cor. 10. 13. with temptation make a way to *e.*
1 Thes. 5. 3. destruction they shall not *e.*
Heb. 2. 3. how shall we *e.* if neglect
12. 25. much more shall not we *e.*
Ezra 9. 15. we remain yet *escaped*
Job 1. 15, 16, 17, 19. I only am *e.* to
Ps. 124. 7. soul is *e.* we are *e.*
Isa. 45. 20. ye are *e.* of the nations
John 10. 39. he *e.* out of their hands
Heb. 12. 25. if they *e.* not who refused
2 Pet. 1. 4. *e.* corruption of the world
2. 18. those that were clean *e.*
20. have *e.* pollutions of the world
ESCHEW evil, Job 1. 8. & 2. 3. 1 Pet. 3. 11.
R. V. 1 Pet. 3. 11. turn away from
ESPECIALLY, Deut. 4. 10. Ps. 31. 11.
Gal. 6. 10. good *e.* to household of
1 Tim. 4. 10. *e.* of those that believe
5. 17. *e.* those that labor in word
R. V. Ps. 31. 11. exceedingly
ESPOUSALS, S. of S. 3. 11. Jer. 2. 2.
2 Cor. 11. 2. *espoused* to Christ
R. V. 2 Sam. 3. 14; Matt. 1. 18; Luke 1. 27. betrothed
ESPY, Josh. 14. 7. Ezek. 20. 6.
R. V. Josh. 14. 7. spy
ESTABLISH, Num. 30. 13. 1 Kings 15. 4. Deut. 28. 9. Job 36. 7.
Gen. 6. 18. *e.* my covenant, 9. 9. & 17. 7, 9, 21. Lev. 26. 9. Deut. 8. 18.
1 Sam. 1. 23. the Lord *e.* his word
2 Sam. 7. 12. I will *e.* his kingdom, 13.
25. *e.* the word for ever, and do as
2 Chron. 9. 8. God loved Israel to *e.*
7. 18. *e.* throne of kingdom
Ps. 7. 9. but *e.* the just, 48. 8.
89. 2. faithfulness shalt *e.* in heav.
4. thy seed will I *e.* for ever
99. 4. dost *e.* equity, executest
119. 38. *e.* thy word to servant
Prov. 15. 25. he will *e.* border of
Isa. 9. 7. to *e.* with judgment and
49. 8. give thee for a covenant to *e.*
62. 7. no rest till he *e.* Jerusalem
Ezek. 16. 60. I will *e.* an everlast.
Rom. 3. 31. yea, we *e.* the law
10. 3. going about to *e.* their own
1 Thes. 3. 13. may *e.* your hearts
2 Thes. 2. 17. *e.* you in every good
3. 3. Lord shall *e.* and keep you
Jas. 5. 8. patient; *e.* your hearts
1 Pet. 5. 10. God of all grace *e.* you
Gen. 41. 32. thing is *established*
Ex. 6. 4. have *e.* my covenant with
15. 17. which thy hands have *e.*
Ps. 40. 2. on rock he *e.* my goings
78. 5. he *e.* a testimony in Jacob
93. 2. thy throne is *e.* of old
112. 8. his heart is *e.* trusting
119. 90. hast *e.* the earth, and it
148. 6. hath *e.* them for ever
Prov. 3. 19. Lord hath *e.* the heav.
4. 26. let all thy ways be *e.*
12. 3. man shall not be *e.* by wickedness
16. 12. throne is *e.* by righteous.
30. 4. *e.* all the ends of the earth
Isa. 7. 9. if believe not — not be *e.*
16. 5. in mercy shall throne be *e.*
Jer. 10. 12. *e.* world by wisdom, 51. 15.
Hab. 1. 12. *e.* them for correction
Matt. 18. 16. two or three witness. *e.*
2 Cor. 13. 1. word may be *e.*
Acts 16. 5. so were the churches *e.*
Rom. 1. 11. to the end you may be *e.*
Col. 2. 7. built up — *e.* in the faith
Heb. 8. 6. *e.* upon better promises
2 Pet. 1. 12. *e.* in the present truth
Lev. 25. 30. *shall be established*, Deut. 19. 15. Ps. 89. 21. 2 Cor. 13. 1.
2 Chron. 20. 20. believe in God so ye —
Job 22. 28. shall decree a thing and it —
Ps. 102. 28. their seed—before thee
Prov. 12. 19. lip of truth —
25. 5. his throne — in righteousness, 29. 14.
Isa. 2. 2. Lord's house —, Mic. 4. 1.
54. 14. in righteousness thou —
Jer. 30. 20. their congregation —
Prov. 29. 4. king by judgment *establisheth* the land
Hab. 2. 12. woe to him that *e.* city by
2 Cor. 1. 21. who *e.* us with you is God
R. V. 2 Sam. 7. 25. confirm; Isa. 49. 8. raise up; Lev. 25. 30; 2 Sam. 7. 16. made sure; Prov. 8. 28. made firm; Zech. 5. 11. prepared; Heb. 8. 6. hath been enacted; Acts 16. 5. strengthened
ESTATE, Gen. 43. 7. Esth. 1. 7, 19.
Ps. 39. 5. man at best *e.* is vanity
Prov. 27. 23. know *e.* of thy flocks
Matt. 12. 45. last *e.* of that man is worse than the first, Luke 11. 26.
Luke 1. 48. regarded low *e.* of
Rom. 12. 16. condescend to men of low *e.*
Phil. 4. 11. in whatsoever *e.* I am — content
Jude 6. angels kept not first *e.*
R. V. Dan. 11. 7, 20, 21, 38. place; Mark 6. 21. chief men; Rom. 12. 16. things lowly; Jude 6. own principality
ESTEEM, Job 36. 19. Isa. 29. 16, 17.
Ps. 119. 128. I *e.* all thy precepts
Phil. 2. 3. *e.* each other better than
1 Thes. 5. 13. *e.* them very highly in
Deut. 32. 15. lightly *esteemed* the
1 Sam. 2. 30. despise me, lightly *e.*
Job 23. 12. I have *e.* words of his
Isa. 53. 3. despised — we *e.* him not
4. did *e.* him stricken, smitten of
Luke 16. 15. is highly *e.* among men
Rom. 14. 5. *esteemeth* one day above

another, another *e.* every day alike
Rom. 14. 14. to him that *e.* it to be unclean
Heb. 11. 26. *esteeming* the reproach
R. V. Job 23. 12. treasured up; 41. 27; Isa. 27. 17. counted; Luke 16. 15. exalted; Rom. 14. 14. accounteth; Heb. 11. 26. accounting
ESTRANGED, Job 19. 13. Jer. 19. 4.
Ps. 58. 3. wicked are *e.* from womb
78. 30. not *e.* from their lusts
Ezek. 14. 5. they are all *e.* from me
ETERNAL God thy refuge, Deut. 33. 27.
Isa. 60. 15. make thee an *e.* excell.
Mark 3. 29. in danger of *e.* damna.
Rom. 1. 20. even his *e.* power and
2 Cor. 4. 17. exceeding *e.* weight of
18. things not seen which are *e.*
5. 1. have house *e.* in the heavens
Eph. 3. 11. according to *e.* purpose
1 Tim. 1. 17. unto the King *e.* be honor
2 Tim. 2. 10. salvation with *e.* glory
Heb. 5. 9. author of *e.* salvation
6. 2. baptisms, and of *e.* judgment
9. 12. obtained *e.* redemp. for us
1 Pet. 5. 10. called us to *e.* glory
Jude 7. vengeance of *e.* fire
Matt. 19. 16. that I may have *eternal life*, Mark 10. 17. Luke 10. 25.
25.46. the righteous shall go into—
Mark 10. 30. in world to come—
John 3. 15. not perish but have—
4. 36. gathereth fruit unto—
5. 39. in Scriptures ye think ye have—
6. 54. hath—and I will raise him
68. thou hast the words of—
10. 28. I give unto them—
12. 25. shall keep it unto—
17. 2. should give—to as many
3. this is—to know only true God
Acts 13. 48. ordained to—believed
Rom. 2. 7. who seek for glory and—
5. 21. grace might reign to—
6. 23. the gift of God is—through
1 Tim. 6. 12. lay hold on—, 19.
Tit. 1. 2. in hope of—which God
3. 7. heirs according to hope of—
2. 25. promise promised us, even—
3. 15. no murderer hath—
5. 13. may know that ye have—
Jude 21. for mercy unto—
R. V. Rom. 1. 20. everlasting
ETERNITY, that inhabits, Isa. 57. 15.
EUNUCH, 2 Kings 9. 32. & 20. 18.
Isa. 56. 3. let no *e.* say, I am a dry
Matt. 19. 12. some *e.* born made *e.*
Acts 8. 27. *e.* had come to Jerusa.
R. V. Jer. 52. 35. officer
EVEN balances, Job 31. 6.
Ps. 26. 12. foot stands in *e.* place
Luke 19. 44. lay thee *e.* with ground
EVEN or **EVENING,** Gen. 1. 5, 8, 31. & 19. 1. Ex. 12. 6, 18.
1 Kings 18. 29. at *e.* sacrifice, Ezra 9. 4, 5. Ps. 141. 2. Dan. 9. 21.
Hab. 1. 8. *e.* wolves, Zeph. 3. 3.
Zech. 14. 7. at *e.* time shall be light
R. V. Mark 11. 19. every evening
EVENT, Eccl. 2. 14. & 9. 2, 3.
EVER, a long time, constantly, eternally, Josh. 4. 7. & 14. 9.
Deut. 19. 9. to walk *e.* in his way
Ps. 5. 11. let them *e.* shout for joy
25. 15. my eyes *e.* toward the Lord
51. 3. my sin is *e.* before me
Luke 15. 31. son thou art *e.* with
John 8. 35. in house son abideth *e.*
1 Thes. 4. 17. we shall be *e.* with
5. 15. *e.* follow that which is good
2 Tim. 3. 7. *e.* learning, and never
Heb. 7. 24. this man continueth *e.*
25. he *e.* liveth to make interces.
Jude 25. to God be glory now and *e.*
Gen. 3. 22. eat and live *for ever*
Deut. 32. 40. I lift up hand and live—
Josh. 4. 24. fear Lord your God—
1 Kings 10. 9. Lord loved Israel—
1 Kings 11. 39. afflict the seed of David but not—
Ps. 9. 7. Lord shall endure—
12. 7. thou wilt preserve them—
22. 26. your heart shall live—
23. 6. I will dwell in the house of the Lord—
30. 12. I will give thanks to thee—
37. 18. their inheritance shall be—
28. saints are preserved—
29. in land righteous shall dwell—
49. 9. that he should still live—
52. 9. I will praise thee—
61. 4. I will abide in tabernacle—
74. 19. forget not congregation of poor—
81. 15. their time should endure—
92. 7. that they shall be destroyed—
102. 12. but thou, O Lord, shalt endure—
103. 9. the Lord will not keep his anger—
105. 8. remember his covenant—
112. 6. righteous shall not be moved—
119. 111. testimonies as heritage—
132. 14. this is my rest—I have
146. 6. who keepeth truth—
Prov. 27. 24. riches are not—crown
Eccl. 1. 4. the earth abideth—
Isa. 26. 4. trust in Lord—for in Lord
32. 17. quietness and assurance—
40. 8. word of Lord shall stand—
59. 21. my words shall not depart—
Jer. 3. 5. will he reserve anger—, 12.
17. 4. kindled fire shall burn—
Lam. 3. 31. Lord will not cast off—
Mic. 7. 18. retaineth not his anger—
Zech. 1. 5. prophets, do they live—
John 6. 51. eateth shall live—, 58.
Rom. 1. 25. Creator who is blessed—
9. 5. over all God blessed—
2 Cor. 9. 9. his righteousness remaineth—
Heb. 13. 8. Jesus Christ, the same yesterday, and—
1 John 2. 17. doeth will of God, abideth—
Ex. 15. 18. Lord reigns *for ever and*
1 Chron. 16. 36. blessed be God—, 29. 10. Neh. 9. 5. Dan. 2. 20.
Ps. 10. 16. the Lord is king—
45. 6. thy throne, O God, is—, Heb. 1. 8.
52. 8. I will trust in God—
111. 8. command. stand fast—
119. 44. I will keep thy law—
145. 1. I will bless thy name—, 2. 21.
Dan. 12. 3. they shine as stars—
Mic. 4. 5. walk in name of God—
Gal. 1. 5. to whom be glory—, Phil. 4. 20. 1 Tim. 1. 17. 2 Tim. 4. 18. Heb. 13. 21. 1 Pet. 4. 11. & 5. 11. Rev. 1. 6. & 5. 13. & 7. 12. Rom. 11. 36. & 16. 27.
Rev. 4. 9. who liveth—, 10. & 10. 6. & 15. 7. Dan. 4. 34. & 12. 7.
22. 5. they shall reign—
EVERLASTING hills, Gen. 49. 26.
Gen. 17. 8. Canaan, an *e.* possession, 48. 4.
21. 33. called on name of *e.* God
Ex. 40. 15. *e.* priesthood, Num. 25. 13.
Lev. 16. 34. this should be an *e.* statute
Deut. 33. 27. underneath are *e.* arms
Ps. 24. 7. be lifted up ye *e.* doors
41. 13. blessed be God from *e.* to *e.*
90. 2. thou art from *e.* to *e.*, 106. 48.
100. 5. his mercy is *e.*
103. 17. mercy of Lord from *e.* to *e.*
119. 142. thy righteousness is *e.*
139. 24. lead me in the way *e.*
145. 13. *e.* kingdom, Dan. 4. 3.
Prov. 10. 25. the righteous is an *e.*
Isa. 9. 6. mighty God the *e.* Father
26. 4. in Lord Jehovah is *e.* strength
33. 14. who dwell with *e.* burnings
35. 10. shall come to Zion with songs of *e.* joy, 51. 11. & 61. 7.
40. 28. *e.* God, Creator, fainteth
54. 8. with *e.* kindness will I gather
Isa. 56. 5. an *e.* name, 63. 12, 16.
60. 19. Lord shall be an *e.* light, 20.
Jer. 10. 10. true living God, *e.* King
20. 11. *e.* confusion never forgotten
23. 40. I will bring *e.* reproach
31. 3. I loved thee with an *e.* love
Dan. 4. 34. *e.* dominion, 7. 14.
9. 24. to bring in *e.* righteousness
Mic. 5. 2. goings forth of old from *e.*
Hab. 1. 12. art thou not from *e.* my God
3. 6. *e.* mountains scattered; his ways *e.*
Matt. 18. 8. cast into *e.* fire, 25. 41.
2 Thes. 1. 9. punished with *e.* destruction
2. 16. God hath given us *e.* conso.
Luke 16. 9. receive into *e.* habita.
1 Tim. 6. 16. to whom be power *e.*
2 Pet. 1. 11. *e.* kingdom of our
Jude 6. reserved in *e.* chains of darkness
Rev. 14. 6. having the *e.* Gospel to
Dan. 12. 2. awake to *everlasting life*
Matt. 19. 29. shall inherit—
Luke 18. 30. in world to come—
John 3. 16. not perish but have—, 36.
4. 14. well springing up to—
5. 24. heareth my word hath—
6. 27. meat which endureth to—
47. that believeth on me hath—
Acts 13. 46. yourselves unworthy of—
Rom. 6. 22. ye have the end—
Gal. 6. 8. soweth to the Spirit, of the Spirit reap—
1 Tim. 1. 16. believe on him to—
R. V. 1 Chron. 16. 36; Ps. 100. 5; 119. 44. for ever; Hab. 3. 6; Matt. 18. 8; 19. 29; 25. 41, 46; Luke 16. 9; 18. 30; John 3. 16, 36; 5. 24; 6. 27, 40, 47; 12. 50; Acts 13. 46; Rom. 6. 22; 16. 26; Gal. 6. 8; 2 Thes. 1. 9; 2. 16; 1 Tim. 1. 16; 6. 16; Heb. 3. 20; 2 Pet. 1. 11. eternal
EVERMORE, Ps. 16. 11. & 105. 4. & 133. 3. John 6. 34. 2 Cor. 11. 31. 1 Thes. 5. 16. Rev. 1. 18.
R. V. 1 Thes. 5. 16. always
EVERY imagination evil, Gen. 6. 5.
Ps. 32. 6. for this *e.* one godly pray
119. 101. refrained feet from *e.* evil
104. I hate *e.* false way, 128.
Prov. 2. 9. understand *e.* good path
15. 3. eyes of Lord are in *e.* place
30. 5. *e.* word of God is pure
Eccl. 3. 1. a time to *e.* purpose
Isa. 45. 23. *e.* knee bow, and *e.* tongue, Rom. 14. 11. Phil. 2. 11.
1 Tim. 4. 4. *e.* creature of God is good
Tit. 3. 1. ready to *e.* good work
Heb. 12. 1. lay aside *e.* weight and
1 John 4. 1. believe not *e.* spirit
EVIDENCE, Jer. 32. 10. Heb. 11. 1.
Job 6. 28. *evidently*, Acts 10. 3. Gal. 3. 1, 11. Phil. 1. 28. Heb. 7. 14, 15.
R. V. Jer. 32. 10, 11, 12, 14, 16, 44. deed
EVIL, Gen. 2. 9, 17. & 3. 5, 22.
Deut. 29. 21. I will separate him to *e.*
30. 15. set before thee death and *e.*
Josh. 24. 15. if it seem *e.* to you
Job 2. 10. we receive good and not *e.*
5. 19. in trouble no *e.* touch thee
30. 26. looked for good *e.* came
Ps. 23. 4. I will fear no *e.* for thou
34. 21. *e.* shall slay the wicked
52. 3. lovest *e.* more than good
91. 10. no *e.* shall befall thee
97. 10. ye that love Lord, hate *e.*
Prov. 5. 14. I was almost in all *e.*
12. 21. no *e.* shall happen to just
31. 12. will do him good and not *e.*
Eccl. 2. 21. vanity and a great *e.*
5. 13. sore *e.* riches kept to hurt
9. 3. heart of men is full of *e.*
Isa. 5. 20. call *e.* good, and good *e.*
45. 7. I make peace and create *e.*
59. 7. feet run to *e.* and make haste
Jer. 17. 17. art my hope in day of *e.*
18. 11. I frame *e.* against you
44. 11. set my face against you for *e.*
27. I will watch over them for *e.*

Lam. 3. 38. proceedeth not *e.* and good
Ezek. 7. 5. an *e.* an only *e.* is come
Dan. 9. 12. on us a great *e.*, 13. 14.
Amos 3. 6. shall there be *e.* in a city
5. 14. seek good and not *e.* that live
15. hate *e.* love good, Mic. 3. 2.
Hab. 1. 13. of purer eyes than to behold *e.*
Matt. 5. 11. all manner of *e.* against
6. 34. sufficient to day is *e.* thereof
Rom. 2. 9. upon every soul that doeth *e.*
7. 19. *e.* I would not that I do
12. 17. recompense no man *e.* for *e.*
16. 19. simple concerning *e.*
1 Cor. 13. 5. charity thinketh no *e.*
1 Thes. 5. 15. let no man render *e.* for *e.*, 1 Pet. 3. 9.
22. abstain from all appearance of *e.*
1 Tim. 6. 10. love of money is the root of all *e.*
Tit. 3. 2. to speak *e.* of no man
Heb. 5. 14. discern both good and *e.*
Gen. 6. 5. thoughts only *e.*, 8. 21.
47. 9. few and *e.* have been the days
Prov. 14. 19. *e.* bow before the good
15. 15. all days of afflicted are *e.*
Isa. 1. 4. a seed of *e.* doers, 14. 20.
Matt. 5. 45. sun to rise on *e.* and good
7. 11. if ye being *e.* know, Luke 11. 13.
12. 34. how can ye being *e.* speak good
Luke 6. 35. kind to the unthankful and *e.*
Eph. 5. 16. because the days are *e.*
3 John 11. follow not that which is *e.*
Jude 10. speak *e.* of those things
R. V. Judg. 9. 5. wickedness; 2 Sam. 13. 16. great wrong; 1 Chron. 2. 3; 21. 17. wickedly; Ps. 40. 17. hurt; Prov. 16. 27. mischief; Jer. 24. 3, 8; 29. 17. bad; Matt. 5. 37; 6. 13; John 17. 15; 2 Thes. 3. 3. evil one; Jas. 3. 16. vile; Jas. 4. 11; 1 Pet. 3. 16 ——; Eph. 4. 31. railing

EXACT, Deut. 15. 2, 3. Ps. 89. 22. Isa. 58. 3. Luke 3. 13.
Job 39. 7. *exactor*, Isa. 60. 17.

EXALT, Dan. 11. 14, 36. Obad. 4.
Ex. 15. 2. my father's God, I will *e.*
1 Sam. 2. 10. *e.* the horn of his anointed
Ps. 34. 3. let us *e.* his name together
37. 34. *e.* thee to inherit the land
99. 5. *e.* the Lord our God for he
118. 28. my God I will *e.* thee, Isa. 25. 1.
Ezek. 21. 26. *e.* him that is low
1 Pet. 5. 6. may *e.* you in due time
Num. 24. 7. his kingdom be *exalted*
2 Sam. 22. 47. *e.* be the God of my
Neh. 9. 5. *e.* above all blessing and
Job 5. 11. *e.* to safety, 36. 7.
Ps. 89. 16. in righteousness shall be *e.*, 17.
Prov. 11. 11. by blessing of upright city is *e.*
Isa. 2. 2. Lord's house *e.* above hills
11. Lord alone shall be *e.*, 17. & 5. 16. & 30. 18. & 33. 5, 10.
40. 4. every valley shall be *e.* and
52. 13. my servant shall be *e.*
Hos. 13. 1. Eph. was *e.* in Israel, 6.
Matt. 11. 23. Capernaum which art *e.* to heaven, Luke 10. 15.
23. 12. humbleth himself shall be *e.*, Luke 14. 11. & 18. 14.
Luke 1. 52. *e.* them of low degree
Acts 2. 33. by right hand of God *e.*
5. 31. him hath God *e.* with his
2 Cor. 12. 7. I be *e.* above measure
Phil. 2. 9. God hath highly *e.* him
Jas. 1. 9. low rejoice that he is *e.*
Prov. 14. 34. righteous. *exalteth* a
Luke 14. 11. *e.* himself be abased, 18. 14.
2 Cor. 10. 5. casting down that *e.* itself
2 Thes. 2. 4. *e.* himself above all —
R. V. Job 36. 22. doeth loftily; Ps. 148. 14; Ezek. 31. 10. hath lifted up; Prov. 17. 19. raiseth high; Jas. 1. 9. his high estate

EXAMINE, Ezra 10. 16. Luke 23. 14. Acts 4. 9. & 12. 19. & 22. 24, 29. & 28. 18. 1 Cor. 9. 3.
Ps. 26. 2. *e.* me, O Lord, prove and
1 Cor. 11. 28. let a man *e.* himself
2 Cor. 13. 5. *e.* yourselves, prove
R. V. 1 Cor. 11. 28. prove; 2 Cor. 13. 5. try your own selves

EXAMPLE, 1 Thes. 1. 7. Jas. 5. 10.
Matt. 1. 19. not make her a public *e.*
John 13. 15. I have given you an *e.*
Phil. 3. 17. ye have us for an *e.*
2 Thes. 3. 9. make ourselves an *e.*
Heb. 4. 11. fall after the same *e.* of unbelief
8. 5. *e.* shadow of heavenly things
1 Pet. 2. 21. Christ leaving us an *e.*
5. 3. not lords but *e.* to the flock
2 Pet. 2. 6. making them an *e.*
Jude 7. Sodom—set forth for an *e.*
R. V. 1 Tim. 4. 12. example to those that believe; Heb. 8. 5. that which is a copy

EXCEED, Deut. 25. 3. 1 Kings 10. 7.
Matt. 5. 20. except your righteousness *e.* the righteous. of scribes
Gen. 17. 6. *exceeding* fruitful
15. 1. I am thy shield and *e.* great reward
Num. 14. 7. land is *e.* good
1 Sam. 2. 3. why talk so *e.* proudly
1 Kings 4. 29. wisdom *e.* much
1 Chron. 22. 5. house *e.* magnifical
Ps. 43. 4. I will go to God, my *e.* joy
Matt. 5. 12. rejoice and be *e.* glad
26. 38. my soul is *e.* sorrowful, to
Rom. 7. 13. sin might become *e.* sinful
2 Cor. 4. 17. work a far more *e.* weight
7. 4. I am *e.* joyful in all tribulation
Eph. 1. 19. *e.* greatness of his power
1 Tim. 1. 14. grace was *e.* abundant
1 Pet. 4. 13. rejoice, glad with *e.* joy
2 Pet. 1. 4. *e.* great and precious promise
Jude 24. present you with *e.* joy
Gen. 13. 13. sinners before the Lord *exceedingly*, 1 Sam. 26. 21. 2 Sam. 13. 15.
Ps. 68. 3. let righteous. rejoice *e.*
1 Thes. 3. 10. praying *e.* that
R. V. Job 36. 9. behave themselves proudly; 2 Chron. 14. 14 ——; 2 Cor. 7. 4. overflow with joy; 1 Tim. 1. 14. abounded exceedingly; Gen. 16. 10. greatly; Ps. 68. 3. with gladness; 2 Chron. 28. 6. waxed exceeding strong

EXCEL, Gen. 49. 4. 1 Kings 4. 30.
Prov. 31. 29. thou *excellest* them all
Eccl. 2. 13. wisdom *e.* folly, as far
1 Cor. 14. 12. seek that ye may *e.*
2 Cor. 3. 10. by reason of the glory that *e.*
Gen. 49. 3. *excellency* of dignity, and *e.*
Ex. 15. 7. in greatness of thy *e.*
Deut. 33. 26. rideth in his *e.* on sky
Job 13. 11. his *e.* make you afraid
Ps. 47. 4. *e.* of Jacob, whom he loved
Isa. 35. 2. see glory and *e.* of our God
Amos 6. 8. I abhor the *e.* of Jacob
8. 7. the Lord hath sworn by the *e.* of Jacob
1 Cor. 2. 1. not with *e.* of speech
2 Cor. 4. 7. *e.* of power may be of God
Phil. 3. 8. count all loss for the *e.* of Christ
Esth. 1. 4. *excellent* majesty, Job 37. 23.
Ps. 8. 1. how *e.* is thy name in the earth, 9.
16. 3. saints, *e.* in whom all my delight
Ps. 36. 7. how *e.* is thy lovingkind.
Prov. 12. 26. righteous is more *e.*
Isa. 12. 5. the Lord hath done *e.* things
28. 29. wonderful in counsel, *e.* in
Dan. 5. 12. an *e.* spirit in Daniel, 6. 3.
Rom. 2. 18. approvest things more *e.*
1 Cor. 12. 31. shew you a more *e.* way
Phil. 1. 10. approve things that are *e.*
Heb. 1. 4. obtained a more *e.* name
8. 6. obtained a more *e.* ministry
11. 4. offered a more *e.* sacrifice
2 Pet. 1. 17. came a voice from *e.*
R. V. 1 Chron. 15. 21. lead; Ps. 103. 20. ye mighty; 1 Cor. 14. 12. abound unto; Gen. 37. 4. majesty; Isa. 13. 19; Ezek. 24. 21. pride; Ps. 36. 7. precious; 141. 5. as upon the head; 148. 13. exalted; Prov. 17. 27. cool; 12. 26. guide to

EXCESS, Matt. 23. 25. Eph. 5. 18. 1 Pet. 4. 3, 4.
R. V. Eph. 5. 18. riot; 1 Pet. 4. 3. wine bibbings

EXCHANGE, Matt. 16. 26. Mark 8. 37.
Matt. 25. 27. *exchangers*

EXCLUDE, Rom. 3. 27. Gal. 4. 17.

EXCUSE, Luke 14. 18, 19. Rom. 1. 20. & 2. 15. 2 Cor. 12. 19.
R. V. 2 Cor. 12. 19. are excusing

EXECRATION, Jer. 42. 18. & 44. 12.

EXECUTE, Num. 5. 30. & 8. 11.
Ps. 149. 7. *e.* vengeance, Mic. 5. 15.
Rom. 13. 4. revenger to *e.* wrath
Ex. 12. 12. *execute judgment*, Deut. 10. 18. Ps. 119. 84. Isa. 16. 3. Jer. 7. 5. & 21. 12. & 22. 3. & 23. 5. Mic. 7. 9. Zech. 7. 9. & 8. 16. John 5. 27. Jude 15.
R. V. Num. 8. 11. be to do; Jer. 5. 1. doeth; Isa. 46. 11. of; Rom. 13. 4. for

EXERCISE, Ps. 131. 1. Matt. 20. 25. Acts 24. 16. 1 Tim. 4. 7, 8. Heb. 5. 14. & 12. 11. 2 Pet. 2. 14.
Jer. 9. 24. Lord *e.* lovingkindness
R. V. Matt. 20. 25; Mark 10. 42. lord it; Luke 22. 25. have

EXHORT, Acts 2. 40. & 11. 23. & 15. 32. & 27. 22. 2 Cor. 9. 5. 1 Thes. 2. 11. & 4. 1. & 5. 14. 1 Tim. 2. 1. 2 Tim. 4. 2. Tit. 1. 9. & 2. 6, 9, 15. 1 Pet. 5. 1, 12. Jude 3.
2 Thes. 3. 12. we command and *e.* by
Heb. 3. 13. *e.* one another daily
10. 25. *exhorting* one another; and
Luke 3. 18. *exhortation*, Acts 13. 15. & 20. 2. Rom. 12. 8. 1 Cor. 14. 3. 2 Cor. 8. 17. 1 Thes. 2. 3. 1 Tim. 4. 13. Heb. 12. 5. & 13. 22.
R. V. 2 Cor. 9. 5. entreat

EXPECTATION, Luke 3. 15. Acts 12. 11.
Ps. 9. 18. *e.* of the poor shall not perish
62. 5. for my *e.* is from him
Prov. 10. 28. *e.* of the wicked shall
11. 7. dieth, his *e.* shall perish
23. *e.* of the wicked is wrath
23. 18. *e.* shall not be cut off, 24. 14.
Isa. 20. 5. be ashamed of their *e.*, 6.
Rom. 8. 19. *e.* of creature waiteth
Phil. 1. 20. according to my earnest *e.*
Jer. 29. 11. give you an *expected* end
R. V. Prov. 23. 18; 24. 14. thy hope; Hope in your latter

EXPEDIENT for us that one man die for the people, John 11. 50. & 18. 14.
John 16. 7. *e.* for you that I go away
1 Cor. 6. 12. all things not *e.*, 10. 23.
2 Cor. 8. 10. this is *e.* for you
12. 1. it is not *e.* for me to glory

EXPERIENCE, Gen. 30. 27. Eccl. 1. 16. Rom. 5. 4.
2 Cor. 9. 13. by the *experiment* of
R. V. Gen. 30. 27. divined; Rom.

5. 4. probation: seeing that the proving of you by
EXPERT in war, 1 Chron. 12. 33, 35, 36. S. of S. 3. 8. Jer. 50. 9.
Acts 26. 3. know thee to be *e*. in all
EXPOUNDED, riddle, Judg. 14. 19. Mark 4. 34. Luke 24. 27. Acts 11. 4. & 18. 26. & 28. 23.
R. V. Judg. 14. 14. declare; Luke 24. 27. interpreted
EXPRESS, Heb. 1. 3. 1 Tim. 4. 1.
R. V. 1 Sam. 20. 21 ——
EXTEND mercy, Ezra 7. 28. & 9. 9. Ps. 109. 12.
Ps. 16. 2. my goodness *e*. not to thee
Isa. 66. 12. I will *e*. peace to her like a river
EXTINCT, Job 17. 1. Isa. 43. 17.
EXTOL, Ps. 30. 1. & 66. 17. & 68. 4. & 145. 1. Isa. 52. 13. Dan. 4. 37.
R. V. Ps. 68. 4. cast up a highway for; Isa. 52. 13. lifted up
EXTORTION, Ezek. 22. 12. Matt. 23. 25. Ps. 109. 11. *extortioner*, Isa. 16. 4. Luke 18. 11. 1 Cor. 5. 10, 11. & 6. 10.
R. V. Ezek. 22. 12. oppression
EXTREME, Deut. 28. 22. Job 35. 15.
R. V. neither doth he greatly regard arrogance
EYE for *e*. Ex. 21. 24. Lev. 24. 20. Matt. 5. 38.
Deut. 32. 10. as the apple of his *e*., Ps. 17. 8.
Job 24. 15. no *e*. shall see me
Ps. 33. 18. *e*. of the Lord on them that
Prov. 20. 12. the seeing *e*. Lord hath
Eccl. 1. 8. the *e*. not satisfied with
Isa. 64. 4. neither hath the *e*. seen
Matt. 6. 22. light of the body is the *e*., Luke 11. 34.
18. 9. if thine *e*. offend thee, 5. 29.
Rev. 1. 7. every *e*. shall see him
Prov. 23. 6. *evil eye*, 28. 22. Matt. 6. 23. & 20. 15. Mark 7. 22. Luke 11.34.
Job 16. 16. *eyelids*, 41. 18. Ps. 11. 4. & 132. 4. Prov. 4. 25. & 6. 4, 25. & 30. 13. Jer. 9. 18.
Rev. 3. 18. *eyesalve*
Eph. 6. 6. *eyeservice*, Col. 3. 22.
2 Sam. 22. 25. *eyesight*, Ps. 18. 24.
Luke 1. 2. *eye-witnesses*, 2 Pet. 1. 16.
Gen. 3. 5. your *eyes* shall be opened
Job 10. 4. hast thou *e*. of flesh
29. 15. I was *e*. to the blind
Ps. 15. 4. in whose *e*. a vile person
145. 15. *e*. of all things wait on thee
Eccl. 2. 14. wise man's *e*. are in his
11. 7. pleasant for *e*. to behold sun
Isa. 3. 16. walk with wanton *e*.
5. 15. the *e*. of the lofty shall be
29. 18. *e*. of the blind shall see out of obscurity
32. 3. *e*. of them that see shall
35. 5. *e*. of blind shall be opened
42. 7. to open blind *e*. and give
Jer. 5. 21. have *e*. and see not
Dan. 7. 20. horn that had *e*.
Hab. 1. 13. of purer *e*. than to beh.
Matt. 13. 16. blessed are your *e*. for
18. 9. having two *e*. to be cast into
Mark 8. 18. having *e*. see ye not
Luke 4. 20. *e*. were fastened on him
10. 23. blessed are the *e*. which see
John 9. 6. anointed *e*. of blind man
Eph. 1. 18. *e*. of your understand.
Heb. 4. 13. all things are opened unto *e*. of him
2 Pet. 2. 14. *e*. full of adultery
1 John 2. 16. lust of the *e*. and pride
Rev. 1. 14. his *e*. as a flame of fire
3. 18. anoint thine *e*.
4. 6. four beasts full of *e*., 8.
Deut. 13. 18. right in the *eyes of the Lord*, 1 Kings 15. 5, 11. & 22. 43.
Gen. 6. 8. Noah found grace in the—
1 Sam. 26. 24. life set by in—
2 Sam. 15. 25. find favor in—
2 Chron. 16. 9.—run to and fro
Ps. 34. 15.—are on righteous
Prov. 5. 21. ways of man are before—
15. 3.—are in every place behold.
Isa. 49. 5. I shall be glorious in—
Amos 9. 8.—are upon sinful king.
Zech. 4. 10.—which run to and fro
Ps. 25. 15. *my eyes* are ever towards
119. 123.—fail for thy salvation
141. 8.—are unto thee, O God
Isa. 1. 15. I will hide—from you
38. 14.—fail with looking upward
Jer. 9. 1. O that—were a fountain of
13. 17.—shall weep sore, because
14. 17.—run down with tears
Amos 9. 4. I will set—on them for evil
Luke 2. 30.—have seen thy salvation
Ps. 123. 2. so *our eyes* wait on the Lord
Matt. 20. 33. that—may be opened
1 John 1. 1. that we have seen with—
Deut. 12. 8. right *in his own eyes*, Judg. 17. 6. & 21. 25.
Job 32. 1. righteous—
Neh. 6. 16. cast down *in their own eyes*
Ps. 139. 16. *thine eyes* did see my
Prov. 23. 5. set—on that which is
S. of S. 6. 5. turn away—from me
Isa. 30. 20.—shall see thy teachers
Jer. 5. 3. are not—upon the truth
Ezek. 24.16. take away desire—, 25.
R.V. 1 Kings 16. 25; 2 Chron. 21. 6; 29. 6; Jer. 52. 2. sight; Ruth 2. 10. thy sight

F

FABLES, 1 Tim. 1. 4. & 4. 7. 2 Tim. 4. 4. Tit. 1. 14. 2 Pet. 1. 16.
FACE, Gen. 3. 19. & 16. 8.
Lev. 19. 32. honor the *f*. of old man
Num. 6. 25. Lord make his *f*.
2 Chron. 6. 42. turn not away *f*., Ps. 132. 10.
Ps. 17. 15. I will behold thy *f*.
31. 16. make thy *f*. shine, 119. 135.
67. 1. cause his *f*. to shine on, 80. 3, 7, 19.
84. 9. behold *f*. of thine anointed, 132. 10.
Ezek. 1. 10. *f*. of a man, a lion. Rev. 4. 7.
Dan. 9. 17. cause thy *f*. to shine on
Hos. 5. 5. testify to his *f*., 7. 10.
Matt. 11. 10. my messenger before thy *f*., Mark 1.2. Luke 7. 27. & 9. 52.
Acts 2. 25. set the Lord always before my *f*.
1 Cor. 13. 12. but then see *f*. to *f*.
2 Cor. 3. 18. with open *f*. beholding
Jas. 1. 23. his natural *f*. in a glass
R. V. Gen. 24. 47. nose; 46. 28. way; 1 Sam. 26. 20; Joel 2. 6. presence; 1 Kings 13. 6. favor; 20. 38, 41; 2 Kings 9.30; Jer. 4.30. eyes; Ezek. 38. 19. nostrils; 40. 15. forefront; Joel 2. 20. forepart; Deut. 14. 2; 2 Sam. 14. 7; Jer. 25. 33; Luke 22. 64 ——
FADE, we all, as a leaf, Isa. 64. 6.
Jas. 1. 11. rich man *f*. away in
1 Pet. 1. 4. inheritance that *fadeth*
5. 4. receive a crown of glory that *f*.
R. V. Ezek. 47. 12. wither
FAIL, Deut. 28. 32. Job. 11. 20.
Deut. 31. 6. Lord will not *f*. nor, 8. Josh. 1. 5. 1 Chron. 28. 20.
Ps. 12. 1. faithful *f*. from among
69. 3. my eyes *f*. while I wait for my God
Lam. 3. 22. his compassions *f*. not
Luke 16. 9. when ye *f*. they may
22. 32. prayed that thy faith *f*. not
Heb. 12. 15. lest any *f*. of the grace
S. of S. 5. 6. soul *failed* when he spake
Ps. 31. 10. my strength *faileth*, 38. 10. & 71. 9.
Ps. 40. 12. my heart *f*. me, 73. 26.
143. 7. hear me, my spirit *f*.
Luke 12. 33. lay up treasure that *f*. not
1 Cor. 13. 8. charity never *f*.
Deut. 28. 65. for *failing* of eyes
Luke 21. 26. men's hearts *f*. them
R. V. Judg. 11. 30. indeed; Gen. 47. 15. was all spent; Josh. 3. 16. wholly; Ez. 4. 22. be slack; Ps. 40. 26; 59. 15. is lacking; Isa. 19. 3. make void; 34. 16. be missing; Jer. 48. 33. cease; Luke 16. 17. fall; 1 Cor. 13. 8. be done away; Heb. 12. 15. that falleth short; Luke 21. 26. fainting
FAINT, Deut. 25. 18. Judg. 8. 4, 5.
Isa. 1. 5. head sick, whole heart is *f*.
40. 30. youths shall *f*. and be weary
Luke 18. 1. to pray always and not *f*.
2 Cor. 4. 1. received mercy we *f*. not
Heb. 12. 5. nor *f*. when rebuked of
Ps. 27. 13. I had *fainted* unless I
Rev. 2. 3. hast labored and not *f*.
Ps. 84. 2. soul *fainteth* for courts of the Lord
119. 81. my soul *f*. for thy salvation
R. V. Isa. 13. 7. feeble; Deut. 20. 8; Ezek. 21. 15. melt; Josh. 2. 9, 24. melt away; Isa. 13. 7. feeble; Jer. 45. 3; Rev. 2. 3. weary; Matt. 9. 36. distressed; Isa. 7. 4. faint; Jer. 49. 23. melted away
FAIR, Gen. 6. 2. & 24. 16.
Prov. 7. 21. *f*. speech, Rom. 16. 18.
S. of S. 1. 15. behold thou art *f*., 4. 1, 7. & 2. 10. & 6. 10. & 7. 6. Gen. 12. 11.
4. 10. how *f*. is thy love, better
Jer. 12. 6. they speak *f*. words
Acts 7. 20. Moses was exceeding *f*.
Ps. 45. 2. thou art *fairer* than the
Dan. 1. 15. their countenance appeared *f*.
R. V. Ezek. 27. 12-17. wares; Job 37. 22. golden
FAITH, Acts 3. 16. & 13. 8.
Deut. 32. 20. children in whom is no *f*.
Matt. 6. 30. O ye of little *f*., 8. 26. & 16. 8. & 14. 31. Luke 12. 28.
8. 10. not found so great *f*. no
17. 20. had *f*. as a grain of mustard
21. 21. have *f*. and doubt not
Mark 4. 40. how is it that ye have no *f*.
11. 22. Jesus saith have *f*. in God
Luke 7. 9. so great *f*. no not in Israel
17. 5. Lord increase our *f*.
Acts 3. 16. the *f*. which is by him
6. 5. Stephen, a man full of *f*.
Acts 6. 7. company of priests obedient to *f*.
14. 9. he had *f*. to be healed
27. God opened door of *f*. to
16. 5. churches established in the *f*.
20. 21. *f*. towards our Lord Jesus
Rom. 1. 5. for obedience to the *f*.
3. 3. make *f*. of God without effect
27. but by the law of *f*.
4. 5. his *f*. is counted for righteousness
12. in the steps of that *f*. of Abraham, 16.
13. through the righteousness of *f*., 9. 30. & 10. 6.
14. if of law be heirs, *f*. is made
16. of *f*. that by grace promise sure
10. 17. *f*. cometh by hearing, and
12. 3. God dealt the measure of *f*
6. according to the propor. of *f*.
14. 23. eateth not of *f*. is not of *f*. is
1 Cor. 12. 9. to another *f*. by the same spirit
13. 2. though I have all *f*. to
13. now abideth *f*. hope, charity
2 Cor. 4. 13. we have the same spirit of *f*.
Gal. 1. 23. preach the *f*. which once
3. 7. they which are of *f*., 9.
12. the law is not of *f*. but the man
23. before *f*. came. we were under
5. 6. but *f*. which worketh by love
22. fruit of the Spirit is *f*.
Eph. 4. 5. one Lord, one *f*. one

Eph. 4. 13. until we come in the unity of *f.*
6. 16. above all take shield of *f.*
23. love with *f.* from God the
Phil. 1. 25. I shall abide for your joy of *f.*
27. striving together for *f.* of gosp.
1 Thes. 1. 3. remem. your work of *f.*
5. 8. putting on breastplate of *f.*
2 Thes. 1. 11. fulfil work of *f.* with power
3. 2. for all men have not *f.*
1 Tim. 1. 5. charity out of *f.* unfeign.
14. exceeding abundantly with *f.*
19. holding *f.* and a good conscience; concerning *f.* have made shipwreck
4. 6. nourished up in the words of *f.*
5. 8. hath denied the *f.*
12. cast off their first *f.*
6. 10. erred from the *f.*
21. concerning the *f.*
12. fight the good fight of *f.*
2 Tim. 1. 5. unfeigned *f.* that is in
2. 18. overthrow *f.* of some
22. follow righteous. *f.* charity
3. 10. fully known my doctrine, life, *f.*
4. 7. fought a good fight, I have kept the *f.*
Tit. 1. 1. according to *f.* of God's elect
4. my son after the common *f.*
Heb. 4. 2. word did not profit, not being mixed with *f.*
10. 22. draw near in full assur. of *f.*
23. hold fast the profess. of our *f.*
11. 6. without *f.* it is impossible to
12. 2. Jesus the author and finisher of our *f.*
13. 7. whose *f.* follow, considering
Jas. 2. 1. have not *f.* of our Lord
14. say that he hath *f.* can *f.* save
17. *f.* if it hath not works, is dead, 26.
18. thou hast *f.* and I works; show *f.*—*f.* by my works
22. *f.* wrought with works
5. 15. prayer of *f.* shall save
2 Pet. 1. 1. like precious *f.* with us
1 John 5. 4. overcometh world, even our *f.*
Jude 3. contend earnestly for the *f.*
20. build up yourselves on holy *f.*
Rev. 2. 13. hast not denied my *f.*
19. I know thy works and *f.*
13. 10. here is the *f.* of the saints
14. 12. which keep the *f.* of Jesus
Hab. 2. 4. just shall live *by faith*, Rom. 1. 17. Gal. 3. 11. Heb. 10. 38.
Acts 15. 9. purifying their hearts—
26. 18. sanctified—that is in me
Rom. 1. 12. comforted by mutual *f.*
3. 22. righteousness which is—of Christ
28. conclude a man is justified—
5. 1. being justified—we have peace
2. have access—, Eph. 3. 12.
9. 32. sought it not—but works
2 Cor. 1. 24. of your joy for—ye stand
5. 7. we walk—and not by sight
Gal. 2. 16. not justified, but—, 3. 24.
20. I live—of the Son of God
3. 22. promise—might be given
26. ye are all children of God—in Christ Jesus.
5. 5. wait for hope of righteousness—
Eph. 3. 17. Christ may dwell in your hearts—
Phil. 3. 9. righteousness through *f.*
Heb. 11. 4.—Abel, 5.—Enoch, etc.
7 heir of righteousness which is—
Jas. 2. 24. justified by works, not—
Rom. 4. 19. not weak *in faith*
20. strong—giving glory to God
1 Cor. 16. 13. stand fast—quit you
2 Cor. 8. 7. ye abound—in utter.
Col. 1. 23. if ye continue—
2. 7. built up in him, established—

1 Tim. 1. 2. Timothy, my own son—
4. godly edifying which is—
2. 15. if they continue—and charity
3. 13. purchase great boldness—
4. 12. be an example—in purity
2 Tim. 1. 13. of sound words—and
Tit. 1. 13. they may be sound—2. 2.
Heb. 11. 13. all these died—not having
Jas. 1. 6. let him ask—nothing
1 Pet. 5. 9. whom resist, steadfast—
Matt. 9. 2. Jesus, seeing *their faith*, Mark 2. 5. Luke 5. 20.
Acts 3. 16. *through faith* in his Son
Rom. 3. 25. propitiation—in his blood
31. do we make void the law—, 30.
Eph. 2. 8. by grace ye are saved—
Col. 2. 12.—of the operation of God
2 Tim. 3. 15. salvation—which is
Heb. 6. 12.—and patience inherit
11. 3.—we understand the worlds
11.—Sarah received strength to
28.—Moses kept the passover
33.—subdued kingdoms
11. 39. obtained a good report—, 2.
1 Pet. 1. 5. kept by power of God—
Matt. 9. 22. *thy faith* hath made thee whole, Luke 8. 48. & 17. 19.
15. 28. O woman, great is—be
Luke 7. 50.—hath saved thee, 18. 42.
22. 32. I have prayed that—fail not
Jas. 2. 18. show me—without thy
Luke 8. 25. where is *your faith*
Matt. 9. 29. according to—be it to
Rom. 1. 8.—is spoken of through
1 Cor. 2. 5. that—not stand in wisdom
15. 14.—is also vain, 17.
2 Cor. 1. 24. not dominion over—
Eph. 1. 15. after I heard of—, Col. 1. 4.
Phil. 2. 17. offered upon service of—
Col. 2. 5. beholding steadfast. of—
1 Thes. 1. 8.—to God-ward is spread
3. 2. establish you, comfort you, concerning—
5. I sent to know—lest the tempter
7. comforted in affliction by—
10. perfect what is lacking in—
2 Thes. 1. 3.—groweth exceedingly
Jas. 1. 3. trying of—worketh patience
1 Pet. 1. 7. trial of—being precious
9. receiving end of—salvation
21. that—and hope might be in God
2 Pet. 1. 5. add to—virtue, knowledge
R. V. Acts 6. 8. grace; Rom. 3. 3; Gal. 5. 22. faithfulness

FAITHFUL, 1 Sam. 2. 35. & 22. 14. 2 Sam. 20. 19. Neh. 13. 13. Dan. 6. 4. 1 Tim. 6. 2. 1 Pet. 5. 12.
Num. 12. 7. *f.* in all my house
Heb. 3. 2, 5. Moses *f.* in all as a ser.
Deut. 7. 9. *f.* God which keepeth
Neh. 7. 2. a *f.* man, and feared
Ps. 12. 1. the *f.* fail from among men
31. 23. Lord preserveth the *f.*
101. 6. my eyes be upon *f.* in land
119. 86. thy commandments are *f.*
138. thy testimonies are very *f.*
Prov. 11. 13. is of a *f.* spirit, concealeth
13. 17. a *f.* ambassador is health
14. 5. a *f.* witness will not lie
20. 6. a *f.* man who can find
27. 6. *f.* are wounds of a friend
28. 20. *f.* man shall abound with
Isa. 1. 21. how *f.* city became a har.
26. city of righteousness, *f.* city
8. 2. I took *f.* witness to record
49. 7. Lord is *f.* and Holy One of
Jer. 42. 5. the Lord be a true and *f.*
Hos. 11. 12. Judah is *f.* with saints

Matt. 25. 21. well done, *f.* servant, 24. 45.
23. hast been *f.* in a few, Luke 19. 17.
Luke 12. 42. who is that *f.* steward
16. 10. *f.* 'n least is *f.* also in much
Acts 16. 15. judge me *f.* to the Lord
1 Cor. 1. 9. God is *f.* by whom ye
4. 2. required in stewards, a man *f.*
17. Timothy who is *f.* in the Lord
7. 25. obtained mercy of the Lord to be *f.*
10. 13. God is *f.* and will not suffer
Eph. 1. 1. the saints and *f.* in Christ Jesus, Col. 1. 2.
6. 21. *f.* minis., Col. 1. 7. & 4. 7, 9.
1 Thes. 5. 24. *f.* is he that calleth
2 Thes. 3. 3. the Lord is *f.* and shall
1 Tim. 1. 12. he counted me *f.*
15. this is a *f.* saying and worthy, 4. 9. 2 Tim. 2. 11. Tit. 3. 8.
3. 11. wives grave, sober, *f.* in all
2 Tim. 2. 2. heard of me, commit to *f.* men
13. he abideth *f.* cannot deny himself
Tit. 1. 6. blame. having *f.* children
9. holding fast the *f.* word as
Heb. 2. 17. might be a *f.* high priest
10. 23. *f.* is he that promised, 11. 11.
1 Pet. 4. 19. as unto a *f.* Creator
1 John 1. 9. he is *f.* to forgive all
Rev. 1. 5. *f.* and true witness, 3. 14
2. 10. be *f.* to death
13. *f.* martyr
Rev. 21. 5. words are true and *f.*, 22. 6.
1 Sam. 26. 23. render to every man his *faithfulness*
Ps. 5. 9. no *f.* in their mouth
40. 10. declared thy *f.*, 89. 1.
89. 1. make known thy *f.* to all
2. thy *f* shalt establish in heavens
5. praise thy *f.* in the great congregation
8. who like thy *f.* round about thee
24. my *f.* shall be with him
33. I will not suffer my *f.* to fail
119. 75. in *f.* thou hast afflicted me
90. thy *f.* is to all generations
143. 1. in thy *f.* answer me, and
Isa. 11. 5. *f.* is the girdle of his reins
25. 1. thy counsels of old are *f.*
Lam. 3. 23. mercies new, great thy *f.*
Hos. 2. 20. I will betroth thee to me in *f.*
Matt. 17. 17. O *faithless* and perverse generation, Mark 9. 19. Luke 9. 41.
John 20. 27. be not *f.* but believing
R. V. 1 Tim. 6. 2. believing; Tit. 1. 6. that believe who are

FALL, Num. 11. 31. & 14. 29, 32.
Gen. 45. 24. see that ye *f.* not out
2 Sam. 24. 14. let us *f.* into the
Ps. 37. 24. though he *f.* he shall not
45. 5. whereby they *f.* under thee
82. 7. *f.* like one of the princes
141. 10. let the wicked *f.* into their
145. 14. Lord upholdeth all that *f.*
Prov. 11. 5. wicked *f.* by his own
24. 16. wicked shall *f.* into mischief
26. 27. digs a pit shall *f.* into it, Eccl. 10. 8.
28. 14. hardeneth his heart shall *f.*
Eccl. 4. 10. if they *f.* one will lift
Isa. 8. 15. many shall stumble and *f.*
Dan. 11. 35. some shall *f.* to try them
Hos. 10. 8. mountains and hills *f.* on us, Luke 23. 30. Rev. 6. 16.
Mic. 7. 8. rejoice not when I *f.*
Matt. 7. 27. great was the *f.* of it
10. 29. sparrow not *f.* on ground

Matt. 15. 14. blind both *f.* into the ditch
21. 44. upon whomsoever it *f.*, Luke 20. 18.
Luke 2. 34. set for the *f.* and rising
Rom. 11. 11. stumbled that they should *f.* through their *f.* salvation is come to the Gentiles
1 Cor. 10. 12. stands, take heed lest he *f.*
1 Tim. 3. 6. *f.* into condemnation
6. 9. rich *f.* into temptation
Heb. 4. 11. *f.* after the same exam.
10. 31. fearful thing to *f.* into the hands of God
2 Pet. 1. 10. if these ye shall never *f.*
3. 17. lest ye *f.* from your steadfastness
Luke 8. 13. in time of temptation *fall away*
Heb. 6. 6. impossible if they—to renew them
Gal. 5. 4. ye are *fallen* from grace
Ps. 16. 6. *f.* to me in pleasant places
Hos. 14. 1. hast *f.* by thine iniquity
Prov. 24. 16. just *falleth* seven times
Rom. 14. 4. to his own master he *f.*
Ps. 56. 13. thou hast delivered my feet from *falling*, 116. 8.
2 Thes. 2. 3. there come a *f.* away
Jude 24. able to keep you from *f.*
R. V. Lev. 26. 37; Ps. 64. 8; Isa. 31. 3; Jer. 6. 21; 46. 16; Ezek. 36. 15; Hos. 4. 5; 5. 5; 2 Pet. 1. 10. stumble; Acts 27. 17. cast; 27. 34. perish; Isa. 34. 4. fading; Acts 27. 41. lighting upon; Jude 24. stumbling

FALLOW, Jer. 4. 3. Hos. 10. 12.
R. V. Deut. 14. 5; 1 Kings 4. 23. roebuck

FALSE, Jer. 14. 14. & 37. 14.
Ex. 23. 1. not raise a *f.* report
7. keep thee far from a *f.* matter
Ps. 119. 104. hate every *f.* way, 128.
Prov. 11. 1. *f.* balance is abomina.
Zech. 8. 17. love no *f.* oath
Matt. 24. 24. *f.* Christs, *f.* prophets
2 Cor. 11. 13, 26. *f.* apostles, *f.* brethren, Gal. 2. 4.
2 Tim. 3. 3. *f.* accusers, Tit. 2. 3.
2 Pet. 2. 1. *f.* prophets, *f.* teachers
Ps. 119. 118. their deceit is *falsehood*
144. 8. whose right hand—of *f.*
Isa. 59. 13. from heart words of *f.*
Lev. 6. 3. sweareth *falsely*, 19. 12.
Ps. 44. 17. neither dealt *f.* in coven.
Zech. 5. 4. thief and that swears *f.*
Matt. 5. 11. evil against you *f.* for
Luke 3. 14. neither accuse any *f.*
1 Pet. 3. 16. *f.* accuse your good
Acts 13. 6. *false prophet*, Rev. 16. 13. & 19. 20. & 20. 10.
Matt. 7. 15. *false prophets*, 24. 11, 24. Luke 6. 26. 2 Pet. 2. 1. 1 John 4. 1.
Ex. 20. 16. *false witness*, Deut. 5. 20. & 19. 16. Prov. 6. 19. & 12. 17. & 14. 5. & 19. 5, 9. & 21. 28. & 25. 18. Matt. 15. 19. & 19. 18. Rom. 13. 9. 1 Cor. 15. 15.
R. V. Ps. 35. 11. unrighteous; 120. 3. deceitful; Prov. 17. 4. wicked; Jer. 14. 14; 23. 32. lying; Lam. 2. 14. vanity; Matt. 26. 60——; Luke 19. 8. wrongfully; Rom. 13. 9. covet; Tit. 2. 3. slanderers; Luke 3. 14. wrongfully; 1 Pet. 3. 16——

FAMILIAR, Job. 19. 14. Ps. 41. 9.
Lev. 19. 31. & 20. 6, 27. Isa. 8. 19.
R. V. Jer. 20. 10. familiar friends

FAMILY, Gen. 10. 5. Lev. 20. 5.
Zech. 12. 12. mourn every *f.* apart
Eph. 3. 15. whole *f.* in heaven and
Ps. 68. 6. setteth solitary in *families*
107. 41. maketh him *f.* like a flock
Amos 3. 2. known of all the *f.* of
R. V. 2 Chron. 35. 5. fathers' houses

FAMINE, Gen. 12. 10. & 41. 27.
Job 5. 20. in *f.* he shall redeem thee
Ps. 33. 19. keep them alive in *f.*
Ps. 37. 19. in the days of *f.* shall be
Ezek. 5. 16. evil arrows of *f.*, 6. 11.
Amos 8. 11. not a *f.* of bread, but
R. V. Job 5. 22. dearth

FAMISH, Gen. 41. 55. Prov. 10. 3. Isa. 5. 13. Zeph. 2. 11.

FAN, Isa. 41. 16. Jer. 4. 11. & 51. 2. Matt. 3. 12. Luke 3. 17.

FAR, Ex. 8. 28. Neh. 4. 19.
Ex. 23. 7. keep *f.* from false matter
Ps. 73. 27. *f.* from thee shall perish
Amos 6. 3. put *f.* away the evil day
Mark 12. 34. not *f.* from the kingd.
Phil. 1. 23. with Christ, which is *f.*
Eph. 2. 13. sometimes *f.* off, now
R. V. Job 30. 10. aloof; Judg. 9. 17; Ps. 27. 9; Isa. 19. 6; 26. 15; Ezek. 7. 20; Mark 13. 34——; Matt. 21. 33; 25. 14; Mark 12. 1. another; 2 Cor. 4. 17. more and more

FARTHING, Matt. 5. 26. & 10. 29.

FASHION, 1 Cor. 7. 31. Phil. 2. 8.
Job 10. 8. thy hands have *fashioned* me, Ps. 119. 73.
Ps. 139. 16. in continuance were *f.*
Ezek. 16. 7. thy breasts are *f.*
Phil. 3. 21. be *f.* like his glorious
Ps. 33. 15. he *fashions* their hearts
Isa. 45. 9. the clay say to him that *fashioneth* it
1 Pet. 1. 14. not *fashioning* yourselves
R. V. Acts 7. 44. figure; Phil. 3. 21. conformed to

FAST, 2 Sam. 12. 21. Esth. 4. 16.
Isa. 58. 4. ye *f.* for strife; not *f.* as
Jer. 14. 12. when they *f.* I will not
Zech. 7. 5. did ye at all *f.* unto me
Matt. 6. 16. when ye *f.* be not as
18. appear not to men to *f.*
9. 14. why do we *f.* and thy disc.
Luke 18. 12. I *f.* twice a week
1 Kings 21. 9. proclaim a *fast*, 12.
2 Chron. 20. 3. Ezra 8. 21. Isa. 58. 3, 5, 6. Jer. 36. 9. Joel 1. 14. & 2. 15. Jonah 3. 5. Zech. 8. 19. Acts 27. 9.
Judg. 20. 26. *fasted* that day
1 Sam. 7. 6. *f.* on that day
31. 13. *f.* seven days, 1 Chron. 10. 12.
2 Sam. 1. 12. they wept and *f.* till even
1 Kings 21. 27. Ahab *f.* and lay in
Ezra 8. 23. we *f.* and besought the Lord
Isa. 58. 3. why have we *f.* and thou
Zech. 7. 5. when ye *f.* in filth and
Matt. 4. 2. when he had *f.* forty days
Acts 13. 2. ministered and *f.*
3. *f.* and prayed
Neh. 9. 1. assembled with *fasting*
Esth. 4. 3. were *f.* and weeping, 9. 31.
Ps. 35. 13. humbled soul with *f.*, 69. 10.
109. 24. my knees weak through *f.*
Jer. 36. 6. read the roll on *f.* day
Dan. 6. 18. king passed the night *f.*
9. 3. to seek by prayer with *f.*
Joel 2. 12. turn ye to me with *f.*
Matt. 15. 32. not send them away *f.*
Luke 2. 37. with *f.* and prayers
Acts 10. 30. was *f.* till this hour
14. 23. ordained elders, prayed with *f.*
1 Cor. 7. 5. give yourselves to *f.*
2 Cor. 6. 5. in *f.* often, 11. 27.

FASTENED, Job 38. 6. Eccl. 12. 11. Isa. 22. 25. Luke 4. 20.
R. V. Ex. 28. 14. shalt put; 28. 25. put on; 40. 18. laid; Judg. 4. 21. pierced through; 1 Kings 6. 6. have hold; Matt. 17. 21; Mark 9. 29——

FAT is the Lord's, Lev. 3. 16. & 4. 8.
Prov. 11. 25. liberal shall be made *f.*
13. 4. soul of the diligent shall be made *f.*
15. 30. good report maketh bones *f.*
Isa. 25. 6. *f.* things full of marrow
11. 6. *fatling*, Matt. 22. 4.
Gen. 27. 28. God give thee of *fatness* of the earth
Job 36. 16. table should be full of *f.*
Ps. 36. 8. satisfied with *f.* of house
63. 5. shall be satisfied as with *f.*
Isa. 55. 2. let your soul delight . in *f.*
Jer. 31. 14. satiate the soul with *f.*
Rom. 11. 17. root and *f.* of olive-tree
R. V. Ps. 92. 14. full of sap; Isa. 58. 11. strong; Jer. 50. 11. wanton as an; Deut. 32. 15. become sleek

FATHER, Gen. 2. 24. & 4. 20, 21.
Gen. 17. 4. be a *f.* of many nations
Job 29. 16. I was a *f.* to the poor
Ps. 68. 5. a *f.* of fatherless is God
103. 13. as a *f.* pitieth his children
Isa. 9. 6. the everlasting *F.* prince
Jer. 31. 9. I am a *F.* to Israel and
Mal. 1. 6. if I be a *F.* where is my honor
2. 10. have we not all one *F.*
John 5. 19. what he seeth the *F.* do.
20. *F.* loveth the Son, 3. 35.
22. *F.* judgeth no man but
26. *F.* hath life in himself
8. 18. *F.* beareth witness of me
44. *f.* devil is a liar and *f.* of it
16. 32. I am not alone *F.* is with
Acts 1. 4. promise of the *F.*
Rom. 4. 11. be the *f.* of all them
12. *f.* of circumcision
16. *f.* of us all
17. made thee a *f.* of many nations
1 Cor. 8. 6. the *F.* of whom are all
1 Cor. 1. 3. God and *F.* of our Lord Jesus Christ, *F.* of mer. and God of all com., Eph. 1. 3. 1 Pet. 1. 3.
6. 18. I will be a *F.* to you and
1 Tim. 5. 1. entreat him as a *f.*
Heb. 1. 5. I will be to him a *F.* and
12. 9. subjection to the *F.* of spirits
Jas. 1. 17. gift from *F.* of lights
John 5. 17. *my Father* worketh and I work
10. 30. I and my *F.* are one
14. 28. my *F.* is greater than I
Ezek. 16. 45. *your father* an Amorite
Matt. 5. 16. glorify your *F.* in heaven, 6. 1, 8, 9, 32. & 7. 11. & 45. 48.
John 8. 41. ye do deeds of your *f.*
44. ye are of your *f.* the devil
20. 17. I ascend to my *F.* and your
Ex. 15. 2. my *f.*'s God I will exalt
Neh. 9. 9, 16. *our fathers* dealt proudly
Ps. 22. 4. our *f.* trusted in thee
44. 1. our *f.* have told us, 78. 3.
Lam. 5. 7. our *f.* have sinned
Acts 15. 10. our *f.* not able to bear
Ex. 22. 22. not afflict *fatherless*
Deut. 10. 18. execute judgment of *f.*
Ps. 10. 14. thou helper of the *f.*
82. 3. defend the poor and *f.*
146. 9. Lord relieveth the *f.* and widow
Isa. 1. 17. judge *f.* plead for widow
Jas. 1. 27. visit *f.* in affliction

FAULT, Gen. 41. 9. Ex. 5. 16.
Ps. 19. 12. cleanse thou me from secret *f.*
Matt. 18. 15. if trespass, tell him his *f.*
Luke 23. 4. I find no *f.* in him, 14. John 18. 38. & 19. 4, 6.
1 Cor. 6. 7. utterly a *f.* among you
Jas. 5. 16. confess your *f.* one to
1 Pet. 2. 20. buffeted for your *f.*
Jude 24. able to present you *faultless*
R. V. Deut. 25. 2. wickedness; Mark 7. 2——; John 18. 38; 19. 4, 6. crime; 1 Cor. 6. 7. defect; Gal. 6. 1. any trespass; Jas. 5. 16. sins; Rev. 14. 5. blemish; Jude 24. blemish in

FAVOR, Gen. 39. 21. Deut. 33. 23.
1 Sam. 2. 26. Samuel in *f.* with
Job 10. 12. granted me life and *f.*
Ps. 5. 12. with *f.* wilt thou compass
106. 4. remember me with *f.* that
Prov. 31. 30. *f.* is deceitful and
Luke 2. 52. in *f.* with God and man
Ps. 41. 11. know thou *favorest* me
R. V. Ps. 112. 5. that dealeth graciously; Prov. 14. 9. good will; S. of S. 8. 10. peace; Ps. 102. 13, 14. have pity; 41. 11. delighted in

FEAR, Gen. 9. 2. Ex. 15. 16.
Ps. 53. 5. in *f.* where no *f.* was
119. 38. servant devoted to thy *f.*
120. flesh trembleth for *f.* of thee
Prov. 1. 26. mock when your *f.* cometh
Isa. 8. 12. *f.* not their *f.* nor be afraid
13. let him be your *f.*, Gen. 31. 42.
Jer. 32. 40. put my *f.* in their hearts
Mal. 1. 6. if master where is my *f.*
Rom. 13. 7. render *f.* to whom *f.*
2 Tim. 1. 7. spirit of *f.* but of power
Heb. 2. 15. who through *f.* of death
12. 28. with reverence and godly *f.*
1 Pet. 1. 17. time of sojourning here in *f.*
1 John 4. 18. no *f.* in love
Gen. 20. 11. *fear of God* not in this place
2 Sam. 23. 3. ruling in —
Neh. 5. 15. so did not I because of —
Ps. 36. 1. no — before his eyes, Rom. 3. 18.
2 Cor. 7. 1. perfecting holiness in —
Job 28. 28. *fear of the Lord*, that is wisdom
Ps. 19. 9. — is clean, enduring for ever
34. 11. children I will teach you —
Prov. 1. 29. they did not choose —
8. 13. — is to hate evil
10. 27. — prolongeth days
14. 26. in — is strong confidence
27. — is a fountain of life
15. 33. — is instruction of wisdom
22. 4. by — are riches, honor, life
23. 17. be thou in — all day long
Isa. 33. 6. — is his treasure
Acts 9. 31. walking in — and comfort
Ps. 2. 11. *with fear*, Phil. 2. 12.
Heb. 11. 7. Jude 23. save —
Deut. 4. 10. learn *to fear* me
5. 29. such a heart that would *f.* me
28. 58. mayest *f.* this glorious name
2 Kings 17. 39. Lord your God ye shall *f.*
1 Chron. 16. 30. *f.* before him all
2 Chron. 6. 31. that they may *f.* thee, 33.
Neh. 1. 11. servants, desire to *f.* thy name
Ps. 23. 4. I will *f.* no evil, for thou
31. 19. goodness laid up for those that *f.*
61. 5. heritage of those that *f.*
86. 11. incline my heart to *f.* thy name
Jer. 10. 7. who would not *f.* thee
32. 39. heart that may *f.* me for ever
Mal. 4. 2. to you that *f.* my name
Luke 12. 5. *f.* him who can cast, Matt. 10. 28.
Rom. 8. 15. not spirit of bondage again to *f.*
11. 20. be not high-minded but *f.*
Heb. 4. 1. *f.* lest a promise being left
12. 21. Moses said, I exceedingly *f.* and
Rev. 2. 10. *f.* none of these things
Gen. 42. 18. this do and live, for I *fear God*
Ex. 18. 21. such as — men of truth
Ps. 66. 16. come hear all ye that —
Eccl. 5. 7. dreams, vanities, *f.* thou God
8. 12. shall go well with them that —
12. 13. — and keep his commandments
Job 37. 24. therefore men do *fear him*
Ps. 25. 14. secret of Lord with them that —
33. 18. eye of Lord upon them that —
34. 9. there is no want to them that —
85. 9. his salvation is nigh to them that —
Ps. 103. 13. as father pitieth, so Lord them that —
111. 5. giveth meat to them that —
145. 19. fulfil the desire of them that —
Matt. 10. 28. — who is able to destroy
Luke 1. 50. his mercy on them that —
Deut. 6. 2. mightest *fear the Lord*
13. thou shalt — thy God, 10. 20.
24. — our God for our good always
10. 12. — thy God walk in his ways
14. 23. learn to — thy God, always, 17. 19. & 31. 12, 13.
Josh. 4. 24. that ye might — your
24. 14. therefore — serve in sincer.
1 Sam. 12. 14. if ye will — and serve
24. only — and serve him in truth
1 Kings 18. 12. thy servant did —, 2 Kings 4. 1.
2 Kings 17. 28. how they should —
Ps. 15. 4. he honoreth them that —
22. 23. ye that — trust in him, 115. 11.
33. 8. let all the earth —
115. 13. he will bless them that —
135. 20. ye that — bless the Lord
Prov. 3. 7. — and depart from evil
24. 21. my son — and meddle not
Jer. 5. 24. let us now — that giveth rain
26. 19. did not he — and besought
Hos. 3. 5. and shall — and his goodness
Jonah 1. 9. I — the God of heaven
Gen. 15. 1. *fear not*, I am thy shield
Num. 14. 9. Lord is with us — them
Deut. 1. 21. — neither be discour.
Ps. 56. 4. I will not *f.* what flesh can do, 118. 6. Heb. 13. 6.
Isa. 41. 10. — for I am with thee, I will help thee, 13. & 43. 5.
43. 1. — for I have redeemed thee
Jer. 5. 22. *f.* ye not me, saith the Lord
30. 10. — O my servant Jacob
Matt. 10. 28. — them that kill the body
Luke 12. 32 — little flock; for it is
Ex. 1. 17. midwives *feared* God, 21.
14. 31. people *f.* Lord and believed
1 Sam. 12. 18. all people greatly *f.* the Lord
1 Kings 18. 3. Obadiah *f.* the Lord
Neh. 7. 2. Hanani *f.* God above
Job 1. 1. one that *f.* God and
Ps. 76. 7. thou art to be *f.* who
89. 7. God is greatly to be *f.* in
96. 4. Lord is to be *f.* above all
Mal. 3. 16. they that *f.* the Lord
Acts 10. 2. one that *f.* the Lord
Heb. 5. 7. was heard in that he *f.*
Gen. 22. 12. that thou *fearest* God
Job 1. 8. that *feareth* God, 2. 3.
Ps. 25. 12. what man is he that *f.*
128. 1. every one that *f.* the Lord
Prov. 28. 14. happy is the man that *f.* alway
Isa. 50. 10. who among you *f.* Lord
Acts 10. 22. one that *f.* God and of
35. he that *f.* God and works righ.
13. 26. whosoever among you *f.* God
Ex. 15. 11. *fearful* in praises
Matt. 8. 26. why are ye *f.*, Mark 4. 40.
Heb. 10. 27. certain *f.* looking for
31. *f.* thing to fall into hands of
Rev. 21. 8. *f.* and unbelieving shall
Ps. 55. 5. *fearfulness* and trembling
Isa. 33. 14. *f.* hath surprised hypocrites
Ps. 139. 14. I am *fearfully* and
R. V. very often in O. T., terror; Luke 21. 11. terrors; Isa. 21. 4. horror hath; 33. 14. trembling
FEAST, Gen. 19. 3. & 21. 8.
Prov. 15. 15. merry heart has a continual *f.*
Eccl. 10. 9. a *f.* is made for laughter
Isa. 25. 6. Lord make to all people a *f.* of
1 Cor. 5. 8. let us keep *f.* but not
R. V. Lam. 1. 4; 2. 6, 7; Hos. 2. 11. assembly; Matt. 26. 17; Luke 23. 17; Acts 18. 21 ——
FEEBLE, Gen. 30. 42. Job 4. 4.
Ps. 105. 37. not one *f.* person among
Isa. 35. 3. confirm the *f.* knees
Zech. 12. 8. he that is *f.* shall be
1 Thes. 5. 14. comfort the *f.* minded
Heb. 12. 12. lift up the *f.* knees
R. V. 1 Sam. 2. 5. languisheth; Ps. 38. 8. faint; Isa. 16. 14. of no account; 1 Thes. 5. 14. fainthearted; Heb. 12. 12. palsied
FEED, *fed*, Gen. 25. 30. & 30. 36.
Ps. 28. 9. *f.* them and lift them up
37. 3. verily thou shalt be *f.*
49. 14. death shall *f.* on them
Prov. 10. 21. lips of righteous *f.*
Isa. 58. 14. *f.* thee with heritage of
Jer. 3. 15. pastors *f.* you with knowledge
Acts 20. 28. to *f.* the church of God
1 Cor. 13. 3. give all my goods to *f.*
3. 2. I have *f.* you with milk, and
Rev. 7. 17. Lamb in the throne *f.*
1 Kings 22. 27. *f.* him with bread
Prov. 30. 8. *f.* me with food convenient
S. of S. 1. 8. *f.* thy kids beside shepherds' tents
Mic. 7. 14. *f.* thy people with thy rod
John 21. 15. *f.* my lambs, *f.* my sheep, 16. 17.
Rom. 12. 20. if enemy hunger, *f.*
1 Pet. 5. 2. *f.* flock of God among
Isa. 44. 20. he *feedeth* on ashes
S. of S. 2. 16. he *f.* among lilies, 6. 3.
Hos. 12. 1. Ephraim *f.* on wind —
Matt. 6. 26. heavenly Father *f.* them, Luke 12. 24.
1 Cor. 9. 7. who *f.* a flock and eateth not
R. V. Gen. 46. 32. keepers of; John 21. 16; 1 Pet. 5. 2. tend; 2 Sam. 19. 33. sustain; Ps. 49. 14; Rev. 7. 17. be their shepherd; Rev. 12. 6. may nourish
FEEL, *feeling*, Gen. 27. 12. Acts 17. 27. Eph. 4. 19. Heb. 4. 15.
R. V. Job 20. 20. knew no; Eccl. 8. 5. know
FEET, Gen. 18. 4. & 19. 2. & 49. 10.
1 Sam. 2. 9. keep *f.* of his saints
Neh. 9. 21. their *f.* swelled not
Job 12. 5. is ready to slip with his *f.*
29. 15. eyes to the blind, and *f.*
Ps. 73. 2. my *f.* were almost gone
116. 8. delivered my *f.* from falling
119. 105. thy word is a lamp to my *f.*
Prov. 4. 26. ponder the path of thy *f.*
Isa. 59. 7. their *f.* run to evil, and
Luke 1. 79. guide our *f.* into way of
Eph. 6. 15. *f.* shod with the prep.
Heb. 12. 13. straight paths for your *f.*
Rev. 11. 11. they stood upon their *f.*
R. V. Isa. 3. 18; Matt. 18. 29 ——
FEIGNED, 1 Sam. 21. 13. Ps. 17. 1.
2 Pet. 2. 3. *feignedly*, Jer. 3. 10.
FELLOW, Gen. 19. 9. Ex. 2. 13.
Zech. 13. 7. man that is my *f.*
Acts 24. 5. a pestilent *f.*, 22. 22.
Rom. 16. 7. my *f.* prisoner, Col. 4. 10.
2 Cor. 8. 23. my *f.* helper, 3 John 8.
Eph. 2. 19. *f.* citizens
3. 6. *f.* heirs
Col. 1. 7. *f.* servant, 4. 7. Rev. 6. 11. & 19. 10. & 22. 9.
Phil. 4. 3. *f.* laborers, 1 Thes. 3. 2.
Ps. 45. 7. oil of gladness above *f.*, Heb. 1. 9.
94. 20. have *fellowship* with thee
Acts 2. 42. continued steadfastly in apostles' doctrine and *f.*
1 Cor. 1. 9. God by whom call. to *f.*
10. 20. should have *f.* with devils
2 Cor. 6. 14. what *f.* hath righteous.
8. 4. *f.* of ministering to saints

Gal. 2. 9. gave us right hand of *f.*
Eph. 5. 11. no *f.* with unfruitful
Phil. 1. 5. for your *f.* in the gospel
2. 1. if there be any *f.* of the Spi.
1 John 1. 3. *f.* with us, our *f.* with
R. V. Judg. 11. 37; Ezek. 37. 19; Dan. 2. 13. companions; 1 Sam. 29. 4; Matt. 12. 24; 26. 61; Luke 22. 59; 23. 2; John 9. 29; Acts 18. 13. man; Lev. 6. 2. bargain; 1 Cor. 10. 20. communion; Eph. 3. 9. dispensation

FERVENT in spirit, Acts 18. 25.
Rom. 12. 11. *f.* in spirit serving
2 Cor. 7. 7. your *f.* mind toward me
Jas. 5. 16. *f.* prayer of righteous
2 Pet. 3. 10. melt with *f.* heat, 12.
Col. 4. 12. Epaphras always laboring *fervently* for you in prayers
1 Pet. 1. 22. love one another *f.*
R. V. 2 Cor. 7. 7. zeal for; Jas. 5. 16. much in its workings; Col. 4. 12. striving

FEVER threatened for disobedience, Deut. 28. 22.
healed: Peter's wife's mother, Matt. 8. 14; nobleman's son, John 4. 52.

FEW, Gen. 29. 20. Ps. 105. 12.
Matt. 7. 14. way to life, *f.* find it
20. 16. many called, but *f.* chosen, 22. 14.
25. 21. been faithful in a *f.* things
Rev. 2. 14. I have a *f.* things

FIDELITY, all good, Tit. 2. 10.

FIERCENESS of anger, Deut. 13. 17. Josh. 7. 26. 2 Kings 23. 26. Job 4. 10. & 10. 16. & 39. 24. & 41. 10. Ps. 85. 3. Jer. 25. 38. Hos. 11. 9.

FIERY law, Deut. 33. 2.
Num. 21. 6. *f.* serpents, 8. Deut. 8. 15.
Ps. 21. 9. make them as a *f.* oven
Eph. 6. 16. quench *f.* darts of devil
Heb. 10. 27. *f.* indignation devour
1 Pet. 4. 12. not strange the *f.* trial
R. V. Heb. 10. 27. fierceness of fire

FIGHT, 1 Sam. 17. 20. Ex. 14. 14.
Acts 5. 39. found to *f.* against God
1 Cor. 9. 26. so *f.* I not as one that
2 Tim. 4. 7. I have fought a good *f.*
Heb. 10. 32. a great *f.* of afflictions
R. V. Heb. 10. 32. conflict of suffering

FIGS, Gen. 3. 7. Isa. 34. 4. & 38. 21.
Jer. 24. 2. very good *f.* naughty *f.*, 29. 17.
Matt. 7. 16. do men gather *f.* of thistles
Jas. 3. 12. can *f.* tree bear olive
Judg. 9. 10. *fig-tree*, 1 Kings 4. 25. Mic. 4. 4. Isa. 36. 16. Hos. 9. 10. Nah. 3. 12. Hab. 3. 17. Zech. 3. 10. Matt. 21. 19. & 24. 32. Luke 13. 6, 7. John 1. 48, 50. Rev. 6. 13.
R. V. Isa. 34. 4. fading leaf

FIGURE, Rom. 5. 14. 1 Cor. 4. 6. Heb. 9. 9, 24. & 11. 19. 1 Pet. 3. 21.
R. V. Heb. 9. 24. like in pattern to; 1 Pet. 3. 21. after a true likeness

FILL, Job 8. 21. & 23. 4.
Ps. 81. 10. open mouth wide, I will *f.* it
Jer. 23. 24. I *f.* heaven and earth
Rom. 15. 13. God *f.* you with all
Eph. 4. 10. ascended, might *f.* all
Col. 1. 24. I *f.* up that which is be.
Ps. 72. 19. earth *filled* with his glory
Luke 1. 53. hath *f.* hungry with
Acts 9. 17. *f.* with the Holy Ghost, 2. 4. & 4. 8, 31. & 13. 9, 52. Luke 1. 15.
Rom. 15. 14. *f.* with all knowledge
2 Cor. 7. 4. I am *f.* with comfort
Eph. 3. 19. might be *f.* with all
5. 18. not with wine but *f.* with
Phil. 1. 11. *f.* with the fruits of
Col. 1. 9. *f.* with knowledge of his
2 Tim. 1. 4. mindful of tears *f.* with
Eph. 1. 23. fulness of him that *filleth* all in all
R. V. Job 38. 39; Ezek. 32. 4. satisfy; Ps. 104. 28; Prov. 18. 20; 30. 16. satisfied, Matt. 9. 16; Mark 2. 21. should fill, Rev. 15. 1. finished; 18. 6. mingle unto; Rom. 15. 24. in some measure I shall have been satisfied

FILTH, Isa. 4. 4. 1 Cor. 4. 13.
Job 15. 16. more *filthy* is man
Ps. 14. 3. altogether become *f.*, 53. 3.
Isa. 64. 6. all our righteousness as *f.*
Col. 3. 8. put off *f.* communication
1 Tim. 3. 3. greedy of *f.* lucre, 8. Tit. 1. 7, 11. 1 Pet. 5. 2.
2 Pet. 2. 7. vexed with *f.* conver.
Jude 8. *f.* dreamers defile the flesh
Rev. 22. 11. that is *f.* let him be *f.*
Jas. 1. 21. lay apart all *filthiness*
Ezek. 36. 25. from all your *f.* I
2 Cor. 7. 1. cleanse ourselves from all *f.*
R. V. Ezra 9. 11. through the uncleanness; 2 Cor. 7. 1. defilement of; Rev. 17. 4. even the unclean things; Job 15. 16. corrupt; Isa. 64. 6. polluted; Zeph. 3. 11. rebellious; Col. 3. 8. shameful; 1 Tim. 3. 3. money; 2 Pet. 2. 7. lascivious; Jude 8 ——

FINALLY, 2 Cor. 13. 11. Eph. 6. 10. Phil. 3. 1. & 4. 8. 2 Thes. 3. 1. 1 Pet. 3. 8.

FIND, Gen. 19. 11. & 38. 22.
Num. 32. 23. your sin shall *f.* you
Job 11. 7. who by searching can *f.*
Prov. 1. 28. shall seek me and not *f.*
S. of S. 5. 6. I sought but could not *f.*
Jer. 6. 16. ye shall *f.* rest to your
29. 13. shall seek me and *f.* me
Matt. 7. 7. seek and ye shall *f.*
10. 39. *f.* life; loseth life shall *f.* it, 16. 25.
11. 29. ye shall *f.* rest to your souls
John 7. 34. seek me, and shall not *f.*
Rom. 7. 18. how to do good, I *f.* not
2 Tim. 1. 18. may *f.* mercy in that
Heb. 4. 16. may *f.* grace to help
Rev. 9. 6. seek death and shall not *f.*
Prov. 8. 35. whoso *findeth* me *f.* life
18. 22. whoso *f.* a wife, *f.* a good
Eccl. 9. 10. whatsoever thy hand *f.* to do
Matt. 7. 8. that seeketh *f.*, Luke 11. 10.
Isa. 58. 13. not *finding* thine own pl.
Rom. 11. 33. his ways past *f.* out

FINE, Job 28. 1. Isa. 3. 23. Lev. 2. 1. Ps. 81. 16. Prov. 25. 4.
R. V. Isa. 19. 9. combed; Lam. 4. 1; Dan. 10. 5. pure; Mark 15. 46. linen cloth; Rev. 1. 15; 2. 18. burnished.

FINGER of God, Ex. 8. 19. & 31. 18. Deut. 9. 10. Luke 11. 20.
1 Kings 12. 10. my little *f.* shall
Ps. 8. 3. heaven is work of thy *f.*
144. 1. he teacheth my *f.* to fight
Prov. 6. 13. he teacheth with his *f.*
Luke 11. 46. touch not with one of your *f.*
John 20. 27. reach hither thy *f.*

FINISH transgression, Dan. 9. 24.
John 17. 4. I have *f.* work
19. 30. it is *f.*
Acts 20. 24. *f.* my course with joy
2 Cor. 8. 6. would also *f.* in you
2 Tim. 4. 7. I have *f.* my course
Jas. 1. 15. sin when it is *f.* bringeth
Heb. 12. 2. author and *finisher* of
R. V. Luke 14. 28; 2 Cor. 8. 6. complete; John 3. 34, 5. 36; 17. 4. accomplish; Acts 20. 24. may accomplish, Jas. 1. 15. full-grown

FIRE, Ex. 3. 2. & 9. 23, 24. & 40. 38.
Gen. 19. 24. the Lord rained *f*
Ps. 11. 6. rain *f.* and brimstone
39. 3. while musing the *f.* burned
Prov. 6. 27. can a man take *f.*
25. 22. heap coals of *f.* on his head, Rom. 12. 20.
S. of S. 8. 6. as coals of *f.* hath vehement
Isa. 9. 18. wickedness burneth as a *f.*
10. 17. light of Israel for a *f.* for a flame
31. 9. Lord of hosts whose *f.* is in Zion
43. 2. walkest through *f.* shall not
Jer. 23. 29. is not my word like *f.*, 20. 9.
Amos 5. 6. lest Lord break out like *f.*
7. 4. Lord God called to contend by *f.*
Zech. 2. 5. I will be a wall of *f.*
3. 2. brand plucked out of *f.*, Amos 4. 11.
Mal. 3. 2. he shall be as a refiner's *f.*
Matt. 3. 10. cut down and cast into the *f.*, 7. 19.
12. burn with unquenchable *f.*, Mark 9. 43, 44, 46, 48. Luke 3. 17.
Luke 9. 54. command *f.* to come
12. 49. I am come to send *f.* on the
1 Cor. 3. 13. revealed by *f.* — *f.* try, 15.
Heb. 12. 29. our God is consuming *f.*
Jude 23. pulling them out of the *f.*
Matt. 5. 22. *hell-fire*, 18. 9. Mark 9. 47.
Lev. 10. 1. *strange fire*, Num. 3. 4. & 26. 61.
R. V. Matt. 5. 22; 18. 9. the hell of fire; Mark 9. 44, 46, 47 ——

FIRST, Matt. 10. 2. Esth. 1. 14.
Isa. 41. 4. the Lord the *f.* and the last, 44. 6. & 48. 12. Rev. 1. 11, 17. & 2. 8. & 22. 13.
Matt. 6. 33. seek *f.* the kingdom of
7. 5. *f.* cast out the beam, Luke 6. 42.
19. 30. many that be *f.* shall be last, 20. 16. Mark 10. 31.
22. 38. this is the *f.* and great
Acts 26. 23. *f.* that should rise
Rom. 11. 35. who hath *f.* given to
1 Cor. 15. 45. *f.* man Adam
47. *f.* man of the earth
2 Cor. 8. 5. *f.* gave their own selves
12. accepted, if there be *f.* willing
1 Pet. 4. 17. if judgment *f.* begin
1 John 4. 19. because he *f.* loved us
Rev. 2. 4. left thy *f.* love
5. do *f.* works
20. 5. this is the *f.* resurrection, 6.
Matt. 1. 25. *first-born*, Luke 2. 7.
Rom. 8. 29. *f.* among many breth.
Col. 1. 15. *f.* of every creature
18. *f.* from the dead
Rom. 11. 16. if *first fruit* be holy
Prov. 3. 9. honor the Lord with *f.*
Rom. 8. 23. having *first fruits*
1 Cor. 15. 20. Christ *f.* of them
Jas. 1. 18. we a kind of *f.* creatures
Rev. 14. 4. redeemed are *f.* to God

FISH, Ezek. 29. 4, 5. & 47. 9, 10.
Jer. 16. 16. *fishers*, Ezek. 47. 10. Matt. 4. 18, 19. John 21. 7. Isa. 19. 8.
R. V. Isa. 19. 10. hire; Job 41. 1; John 21. 7 ——

FLAME, Ex. 3. 2. Judg. 13. 20.
Ps. 104. 4. maketh ministers a *f.*
106. 18. *f.* burnt up wicked, Num. 16. 35.
Isa. 10. 17. the Holy One of Israel for a *f.*
2 Thes. 1. 8. in *flaming* fire taking
R. V. Judg. 20. 38, 40. cloud; Dan. 7. 11. with fire; Isa. 13. 8. faces of flame; Nah. 2. 3. flash in the steel

FLATTER, Ps. 78. 36. Prov 2. 16. & 20. 19. Job 32. 21, 22. 1 Thes. 2. 5.
R. V. Prov. 20. 19. openeth wide

FLEE, Isa. 10. 3. & 20. 6. Heb. 6. 18.
Prov. 28. 1. wicked *f.* when no
Matt. 3. 7. who warned you to *f.*
1 Cor. 6. 18. *f.* fornication
10. 14. *f.* from idolatry
1 Tim. 6. 11. man of God *f.* these
2 Tim. 2. 22. *f.* youthful lusts
Jas. 4. 7. resist the devil, he will *f.* from you
R. V. Job 30. 10. stand; 30. 3. gnaw the dry ground; Ps. 64. 8. wag the head; Jer. 48. 9. fly; Hos. 7. 13. wandered, Acts 16. 27. escaped

FLEECE, Gideon's, Judg. 6. 37.
FLESH, Gen. 2. 21. 1 Cor. 15. 39.
Gen. 2. 24. they shall be one *f.*, Matt. 19. 5. 1 Cor. 6. 16. Eph. 5. 31.
John 10. 11. clothed me with skin and *f.*
Ps. 56. 4. what *f.* can do to me
78. 39. remember that they were but *f.*
Jer. 17. 5. cursed that maketh *f.* his arm
Matt. 26. 41. spirit is willing, but *f.* weak
John 1. 14. the Word was made *f.*
6. 53. eat the *f.* of the Son of man, 52, 55, 56.
63. *f.* profiteth nothing, words are
Rom. 7. 25. serve with *f.* law of sin
8. 12. debtors not to the *f.*
9. 3. kinsmen according to the *f.*
5. of whom concerning *f.* Christ
13. 14. make not provision for *f.*
1 Cor. 1. 29. that no *f.* should glory
2 Cor. 1. 17. purpose according to *f.*
10. 2. walked according to the *f.*
Gal. 5. 17. *f.* lusts against the Spirit
24. Christ's have crucified *f.* with
Eph. 6. 5. masters according to *f.*
Heb. 12. 9. we had fathers of our *f.*
Jude 7. going after strange *f.*
23. hating garment spotted by *f.*
John 8. 15. ye judge *after the flesh*
Rom. 8. 1. walk not — but after
5. they that are — mind things of *f.*
13. if ye live — ye shall die, 12.
1 Cor. 1. 26. not many wise men —
10. 18. Israel —, Rom. 9. 8. Gal. 6. 13.
2 Cor. 5. 16. know no man — know Christ
10. 3. walk in *f.* not war —
2 Pet. 2. 10. walk — in lust of
Ps. 65. 2. to thee shall *all flesh* come
Isa. 40. 6. — is grass, 1 Pet. 1. 24.
49. 26. — shall know that I am thy
Jer. 32. 27. I am the Lord, the God of —
Joel 2. 28. I will pour my Spirit on —
Luke 3. 6. — shall see the salvation
John 17. 2. given him power over —
Rom. 7. 5. when we were *in the flesh*
8. 8. that are — cannot please God
1 Tim. 3. 16. mystery; God manifest —
1 Pet. 3. 18. he was put to death —, 4. 1.
Gen. 2. 23. *my flesh*, 29. 14. Job 19. 26.
Ps. 63. 1. & 119. 120. John 6. 51, 55, 56. Rom. 7. 18.
John 1. 13. born not of will *of the flesh*
3. 6. that which is born — is *f.*
Rom. 8. 5. after *f.* do mind things—
Gal. 5. 19. works — are manifest
6. 8. soweth to *f.* shall — reap cor.
Eph. 2. 3. lusts — desires —
1 Pet. 3. 21. not putting away filth—
1 John 2. 16. lust—of the eyes, pride
Matt. 16. 17. *flesh and blood* have
1 Cor. 15. 50. — cannot inherit the
Gal. 1. 16. I conferred not with —
Eph. 5. 30. members of his — and
6. 12. we wrestle not against — but
Heb. 2. 14. children are partakers of —
2 Cor. 1. 12. not with *fleshly* wisdom
1 Pet. 2. 11. abstain from *f.* lusts
R. V. Acts 2. 30; Rom. 8. 1; Eph. 5. 30 ——; 2 Cor. 3. 3. tables that are hearts of flesh
FLOCK, Gen. 32. 5. Ps. 77. 20. Isa. 40. 11. & 63. 11. Jer. 13. 17, 20.
Zech. 11. 4. feed *f.* of slaughter, 7.
Luke 12. 32. fear not, little *f.* for it
Acts 20. 28. take heed to all the *f.*, 29.
1 Pet. 5. 2. feed the *f.* of God
R. V. Ezek. 34. 3, 8, 10, 15, 19, 31. sheep
FLOURISH, Isa. 17. 11. & 66. 14.
Ps. 72. 7. shall the righteous *f.*, 16. & 92. 12, 13, 14. Prov. 11. 28. & 14. 11.
92. 7. when workers of iniquity *f.*
132. 18. on himself shall crown *f.*
R. V. Isa. 17. 11; Eccl. 12. 5. blossom; S. of S. 6. 11; 7. 12. budded; Phil. 4. 10. ye have revived
FOLLOW, Gen. 44. 4. Ex. 14. 4.
Ex. 23. 2. shall not *f.* a multitude
Deut. 16. 20. that is just shalt thou *f.*
Ps. 38. 20. I *f.* the thing that good is
Isa. 51. 1. my people that *f.*
Hos. 6. 3. know if we *f.* on to know
Rom. 14. 19. *f.* things that make for
1 Cor. 14. 1. *f.* after charity, desire
Phil. 3. 12. but I *f.* after that I may
1 Thes. 5. 15. ever *f.* that which is
1 Tim. 6. 11. *f.* after righteousness
2 Tim. 2. 22. *f.* righteousness, faith
Heb. 12. 14. *f.* peace with all men
13. 7. whose faith *f.* considering
1 Pet. 2. 21. example should *f.* his
3 John 11. *f.* not evil, but that whi.
Rev. 14. 13. their works do *f.* them
Ps. 23. 6. goodness and mercy shall *follow me*, Matt. 4. 19. & 9. 9. & 19. 21. Luke 5. 27. & 9. 59. John 1. 43. & 21. 19.
Matt. 16. 24. take up cross and —
Luke 18. 22. sell all that thou hast, and —
John 12. 26. if any man serve me, let him —
Num. 14. 24. hath *followed* me fully
32. 12. wholly *f.* the Lord, Deut. 1. 36. Josh. 14. 8, 9, 14.
Rom. 9. 30. *f.* not after righteousness
31. *f.* law of righteousness
Ps. 63. 8. soul *followeth* hard after
Matt. 10. 38. taketh not his cross and *f.* me
Mark 9. 38. he *f.* not us, Luke 9. 49.
R. V. Ex. 14. 17. go in after; Matt. 4. 19. come ye after; 27. 62. the day after; 2 Thes. 3. 7; Heb. 13. 7; 3 John 11. imitate; Phil. 3. 12. press on
FOLLY wrought in Israel, Gen. 34. 7. Deut. 22. 21. Josh. 7. 15. Judg. 20. 6.
Job 4. 18. angels he charged with *f.*
Ps. 49. 13. their way is their *f.*
85. 8. let them not turn again to *f.*
Prov. 26. 4, 5. answer a fool according to his *f.*
2 Tim. 3. 9. their *f.* shall be manifest
R. V. 2 Cor. 11. 1. foolishness
FOOD, Gen. 3. 6. Deut. 10. 18.
Job 23. 12. words more than necessary *f.*
Ps. 78. 25. men did eat angels' *f.*
136. 25. who giveth *f.* to all flesh
146. 7. who giveth *f.* to the hungry
Prov. 30. 8. feed me with *f.* conven.
Acts 14. 17. filling our hearts with *f.*
2 Cor. 9. 10. ministered bread for your *f.*
1 Tim. 6. 8. having *f.* and raiment
R. V. Gen. 42. 33. corn; Lev. 22. 7; 2 Sam. 9. 10. bread; Ps. 78. 25. bread of the mighty
FOOL said in his heart, Ps. 14. 1. & 53. 1.
Jer. 17. 11. at end of days shall be *f.*
Matt. 5. 22. whosoever shall say to brother, thou *f.*
Luke 12. 20. thou *f.* this night thy
1 Cor. 3. 18. let him become a *f.* that
2 Cor. 11. 16. think me a *f.*
Ps. 75. 4. *fools* deal not foolishly
94. 8. ye *f.* when will ye be wise
107. 17. *f.* because of their trans.
Prov. 1. 7. *f.* despise wisdom
22. *f.* hate knowledge
13. 20. companion of *f.* shall be
14. 8. folly of *f.* is deceitful
16. 22. instruction of *f.* is folly
Eccl. 5. 4. he hath no pleasure in *f.*
Matt. 23. 17. ye *f.* and blind, 19.
Rom. 1. 22. professing to be wise became *f.*
1 Cor. 4. 10. we are *f.* for Christ's sake
Eph. 5. 15. walk circumspectly, not as *f.*
Ps. 5. 5. *f.* shall not stand in thy sight
Ps. 73. 22. so *f.* was I and ignorant
Matt. 7. 26. on sand like to a *f.* man
25. 2. virgins, five were wise and five *f.*
Rom. 1. 21. their *f.* heart darkened
Gal. 3. 1. O *f.* Galatians, who bewitched
Eph. 5. 4. filthiness, nor *f.* talking
Tit. 3. 3. were sometimes *f.* disobe.
Gen. 31. 28. done *foolishly*, Num. 12. 11. 1 Sam. 13. 13. 2 Sam. 24. 10. 1 Chron. 21. 8. 2 Chron. 16. 9. Prov. 14. 17. 2 Cor. 11. 21.
Job 1. 22. Job sinned not, nor charged God *f.*
2 Sam. 15. 31. turn counsel into *foolishness*
Prov. 12. 23. heart of fools proclaimeth *f.*
14. 24. *f.* of fools is folly, 15. 2, 14.
22. 15. *f.* is bound in heart of child
27. 22. bray a fool, yet his *f.* will
1 Cor. 1. 18. preaching of the cross is to them that perish, *f.*
23. Christ crucified, to Greeks *f.*
25. *f.* of God is wiser than men
3. 19. wisdom of world is *f.* with God
R. V. 2 Cor. 11. 23. one beside himself; Prov. 11. 29; 12. 15; Luke 12. 20; 1 Cor. 15. 36; 2 Cor. 11. 16; 12. 6, 11. foolish; Ps. 75. 4. arrogant; Eph. 5. 15. unwise; Ps. 5. 5; 73. 3. arrogant; 73. 22. brutish; Prov. 9. 6. ye simple ones; Rom. 1. 21. senseless; 10. 19. void of understanding; Ps. 75. 4. arrogantly; Prov. 14. 24; 15. 2, 14. folly
FOOT shall not stumble, Prov. 3. 23.
Eccl. 5. 1. keep thy *f.* when thou
Isa. 58. 13. turn away *f.* from sabbath
Matt. 18. 8. if thy *f.* offend thee, cut
Heb. 10. 29. trodden under *f.* Son of God
R. V. Ex. 31. 9; 35. 16; 38. 8; 39. 39; 41. 11; Lev. 8. 11. base; Isa. 18. 7. down; Lam. 1. 15. set at nought
FORBEAR, Ex. 23. 5. 1 Cor. 9. 6.
Rom. 2. 4. goodness and *forbearance*, 3. 25.
R. V. Neh. 9. 30. bear with; Prov. 24. 11. hold not back; Ezek. 24. 17. sigh but not aloud
FORBID, Mark 10. 14. Luke 18. 16. & 6. 29. Acts 24. 23. & 28. 31.
1 Tim. 4. 3. *forbidding* to marry
1 Thes. 2. 16. *f.* us to speak to the Gentiles
R. V. Matt. 3. 14. would have hindered; Luke 6. 29. withhold not; Gal. 6. 14. far be it from me; 2 Pet. 2. 16. and stayed
FORCE, Matt. 11. 12. Heb. 9. 17.
Isa. 60. 5. *f.* of Gentiles shall come, 11.
Job 6. 25. how *forcible* right words
R. V. Deut. 20. 19. wielding; Isa. 60. 5, 11. wealth; Ezek. 35. 5. power; Dan. 11. 38. fortresses; Obad. 11. substance
FOREFATHERS, 2 Tim. 1. 3. Jer. 11. 10.
FOREHEAD, Ex. 28. 38. Lev. 13. 41.
Jer. 3. 3. thou hast a whore's *f.*
Ezek. 3. 8. thy *f.* strong against their *f.*
Rev. 7. 3. sealed in their *f.*, 9. 4.
13. 16. mark their *f.*, 14. 9. & 20. 4.
14. 1. Father's name written in *f.*, 22. 4.
R. V. Ezek. 16. 12. nose
FOREIGNERS, Ex. 12. 45. Deut. 15. 3. Obad. 11. Eph. 2. 19.
FOREKNOW, Rom. 8. 29. & 11. 2.
Acts 2. 23. *foreknowledge* of God, 1 Pet. 1. 2.
FOREORDAINED, 1 Pet. 1. 20.
FORERUNNER, Heb. 6. 20.
FORESEETH, Prov. 22. 3. & 27. 12.
R. V. Prov. 22. 3; 27. 12. seeth; Acts 2. 25. beheld

FOREWARN, Luke 12. 5.
R. V. Luke 12. 5. warn
FORGAT Lord, Judg. 3. 7. 1 Sam. 12. 9.
Ps. 78. 11. *f.* his works and wonders
106. 21. *f.* God their Saviour
Lam. 3. 17. I *f.* prosperity
Hos. 2. 13. *f.* me, saith the Lord
Deut. 9. 7. remember and *forget* not
Job 8. 13. paths of all that *f.* God
Ps. 45. 10. *f.* thy own people, and
103. 2. *f.* not all his benefits
119. 16. I will not *f.* thy words, 83, 93, 109, 141, 153, 176.
Prov. 3. 1. my son, *f.* not my law
Isa. 49. 15. can woman *f.* her sucking child
Jer. 2. 32. can a maid *f.* her orna.
Heb. 6. 10. God is not unrighteous to *f.* your
13. 16. to do good and to communicate *f.* not
Jas. 1. 25. be not a *f.* hearer
Ps. 44. 24. thou *forgettest* our afflict.
9. 12. he *f.* not the cry of humble
Prov. 2. 17. *f.* covenant of her God
Jas. 1. 24. *f.* what manner of man
Phil. 3. 13. *forgetting* those things
Ps. 10. 11. God hath *forgotten*
42. 9. why hast thou *f.* me
77. 9. hath God *f.* to be gracious
119. 61. I have not *f.* thy law
Isa. 17. 10. hast *f.* the God of thy
Jer. 2. 32. my people have *f.* me
3. 21. have *f.* their God, Deut. 32. 18.
50. 5. covenant that shall not be *f.*
Heb. 12. 5. *f.* the exhortation
FORGAVE their iniquity, Ps. 78. 38.
Matt. 18. 27. *f.* him the debt, 32.
Luke 7. 42. frankly *f.* them both
43. love most, to whom *f.* most
2 Cor. 2. 10. *f.* any thing, I *f.* it
Col. 3. 13. as Christ *f.* you, also do
Ps. 32. 5. *forgavest* the iniquity of
99. 8. thou wast a God that *f.* them
Ex. 32. 32. now *forgive* their sin
Ps. 86. 5. thou art good and ready to *f.*
Isa. 2. 9. therefore *f.* them not
Matt. 6. 12. *f.* us our debts as we
14. if ye *f.* men, 15. if you *f.* not
9. 6. Son of man hath power on earth to *f.*
Luke 6. 37. *f.* and ye shall be for.
17. 3. if he repent, *f.* him, 4.
23. 34. Father *f.* them, they know
1 John 1. 9. faithful to *f.* us
Ps. 32. 1. whose transgression is *forgiven*
85. 2. *f.* the iniquity of thy people
Isa. 33. 24. people shall be *f.* their
Matt. 9. 2. good cheer, thy sins be *f.*
12. 31. all manner of sin *f.* 32. not be *f.*
Luke 7. 47. to whom little is *f.* loveth
Rom. 4. 7. blessed whose iniquities are *f.*
Eph. 4. 32. as God hath *f.* you, Col. 3. 13.
Jas. 5. 15. if he have committed sins, they shall be *f.*
1 John 2. 12. your sins are *f.* you
Ps. 103. 3. who *forgiveth* all thy ini.
130. 4. is there *forgiveness* with thee
Dan. 9. 9. to the Lord belong mercy and *f.*
Acts 5. 31. to give repent. and *f.*
26. 18. may receive *f* of sins by faith
Eph. 1. 7. *f* of sins according to the riches
Col. 1. 14. redempt., even *f.* of sin
Ex. 34. 7. *forgiving* iniquity, transgression and sin, Num. 14. 18. Mic. 7. 18.
Eph. 4. 32. *f.* one another, Col. 3. 13.
R. V. Luke 6. 37. release; Mark 11. 26 —— ; Acts 5. 31. 13. 38; 26. 18. remission
FORM, Gen. 1. 2. 1 Sam. 28. 14.
Isa. 53. 2. hath no *f.* nor comeliness
Rom. 2. 20. hast the *f.* of knowl.
6. 17. obeyed from heart that *f.*
Phil. 2. 6. who being in *f.* of God
7. took upon him the *f.* of a ser.
2 Tim. 1. 13. hold *f.* of sound words
3. 5. having the *f.* of godliness
Isa. 45. 7. I *f.* the light and create
Deut. 32. 18. hast forgotten God that *formed* thee
Prov. 26. 10. God that *f.* all things
Isa. 27. 11. *f.* them will show no
43. 21. this people have I *f.* for myself
Rom. 9. 20. thing *f.* say to him
Gal. 4. 19. till Christ be *f.* in you
Ps. 94. 9. that *formeth* the eye
Zech. 12. 1. *f.* spirit of man within
Jer. 10. 16. he is the *former* of all things, 51. 19.
R. V. Gen. 1. 2; Jer. 4. 23. waste; Job 4. 16. appearance; Dan. 2. 31; 3. 25. aspect; 2 Tim. 1. 13. pattern; Deut. 32. 18. gave birth; Job 26. 5. tremble; 26. 13. pierced; Prov. 26. 10. wounded; Isa. 44. 10. fashioned; Zech. 14. 8. eastern; Mal. 3. 4. ancient; Job 30. 3. gloom of; Hos. 6. 3. rain that watereth; Rev. 21. 4. the first
FORNICATION, 2 Chron. 21. 11.
Isa. 23. 17. Ezek. 16. 15, 26, 29.
Matt. 5. 32. put away wife for cause of *f.*
19. 9. except it be for *f.*
John 8. 41. we be not born of *f.*
Acts 15. 20. abstain from *f.*, 29. & 21. 25.
Rom. 1. 29. filled with all *f.* wickedness
1 Cor. 5. 1. there is *f.* among you
6. 13. body not for *f.*
18. flee *f.*
7. 2. to avoid *f.* every man have his wife
2 Cor. 12. 21. not repent. of their *f.*
Gal. 5. 19. works of flesh, adult. *f.*
Eph. 5. 3. but *f.* and all uncleanness
Col. 3. 5. mortify *f.* uncleanness
1 Thes. 4. 3. should abstain from *f.*
Jude 7. giving themselves to *f.*
Rev. 2. 14. taught to commit *f.*, 20.
21. I gave her space to repent of her *f.*
9. 21. neither repented of their *f.*
17. 4. abomination and filthiness of her *f.*
19. 2. did corrupt earth with her *f.*
Ezek. 16. 15. *fornications*, Matt. 15. 19.
1 Cor. 5. 9. *fornicators*, 10. 11. & 6. 9. Heb. 12. 16.
R. V. 2 Chron. 21. 11. go a whoring; Isa. 23. 17. play the harlot; Ezek. 16. 15, 29. whoredom, Rom. 1. 29 ——
FORSAKE, Deut. 12. 19. & 31. 16.
Deut. 4. 31. Lord thy God will not *f.* thee, 31. 6, 8. 1 Chron. 28. 20. Heb. 13. 5.
Josh. 1. 5. I will not fail thee nor *f.* thee, Isa. 41. 17. & 42. 16.
1 Sam. 12. 22. Lord will not *f.* his people
1 Kings 6. 13. I will not *f.* my peo.
2 Chron. 15. 2. if ye *f.* him he will *f.*
Ps. 27. 10. father and mother *f.* me
94. 14. neither will he *f.* his inher.
Isa. 55. 7. let the wicked *f.* his way
Jer. 17. 13. they that *f.* thee shall
Jonah 2. 8. *f.* their own mercy
Ps. 71. 11. God hath *forsaken* him
22. 1. my God, why *f.* me, Matt. 27. 46.
37. 25. I have not seen the righteous *f.*
Isa. 49. 14. Lord hath *f.* my Lord
54. 7. small moment have I *f.* thee
Jer. 2. 13. *f.* me the fountain of liv.
Matt. 19. 27. we have *f.* all
29. *f.* houses or brethren or
2 Cor. 4. 9. persecuted but not *f.*
Prov. 2. 17. *forsaketh* the guide of
Prov. 28. 13. confesseth and *f.* shall find
Heb. 10. 25. not *f.* the assembling
Deut. 32. 15. he *forsook* God which
Ps. 119. 87. I *f.* not thy precepts
2 Tim. 4. 16. all men *f.* me
R. V. Deut. 4. 31. fail; Judg. 9. 11. leave; 6. 13; 2 Kings 21. 14; Jer. 23. 33, 39. cast off; Job 20. 13. will not let it go; Jer. 15. 6. rejected; 18. 14. dried up; Amos 5. 2. cast down; Matt. 19. 27; 26. 56; Mark 14. 50; Luke 5. 11. left; Luke 14. 33. renounceth
FORSAKING God, danger of, Deut. 28. 20. Judg. 10. 13. 2 Chron. 15. 2. & 24. 20. Ezra 8. 22. & 9. 10. Isa. 1. 28. Jer. 1. 16. & 5. 19. & 17. 13. Ezek. 6. 9.
FORTRESS and rock, Lord is my, 2 Sam. 22. 2. Ps. 18. 2. & 31. 3. & 71. 3. & 91. 2. & 144. 2. Jer. 16. 19.
R. V. Jer. 10. 17. siege; 16. 19. stronghold; Mic. 7. 12. Egypt
FORTY DAYS, as the flood, Gen. 7. 17.
giving of the law, Ex. 24. 18.
spying Canaan, Num. 13. 25.
Goliath's defiance, 1 Sam. 17. 16.
Elijah's journey to Horeb, 1 Kings 19. 8.
Jonah's warning to Nineveh, Jonah 3. 4.
fasting of our Lord, Matt. 4. 2. Mark 1. 13. Luke 4. 2.
Christ's appearances during, Acts 1. 3.
FORTY STRIPES, Deut. 25. 3. save one; 2 Cor. 11. 24.
FORTY YEARS, manna sent, Ex. 16. 35. Num. 14. 33. Ps. 95. 10.
of peace, Judg. 3. 11. & 5. 31. & 8. 28.
FOUND, Gen. 26. 19. & 31. 37.
Eccl. 7. 27. this have I *f.* that, 29.
28. one man among a thousand have I *f.*
S. of S. 3. 1. I *f.* him not, 4. I *f.* him
Isa. 55. 6. seek the Lord while he may be *f.*
65. 1. I am *f.* of them that sought
Ezek. 22. 30. I sought a man but *f.*
Dan. 5. 27. weighed and *f.* wanting
Phil. 3. 9. *f.* in him, not having my
2 Pet. 3. 14. may be *f.* of him in
Matt. 7. 25. *founded* on a rock, Ps. 24. 2. Prov. 3. 19. Isa. 14. 32.
Ps. 11. 3. if the *foundations* be destroyed
Job 4. 19. whose *f.* is in the dust
Prov. 10. 25. righteous is an everlasting *f.*
Rom. 15. 20. lest I build upon another man's *f.*
1 Cor. 3. 10. laid *f.*
12. build on this *f.*
Eph. 2. 20. built on *f.* of the proph.
1 Tim. 6. 19. lay up a good *f.* for
2 Tim. 2. 19. the *f.* of God stands
Heb. 11. 10. a city which hath *f.*
Rev. 21. 14. the city hath twelve *f.*
Matt. 13. 35. *foundation of the world*, 25. 34. John 17. 24. Eph. 1. 4. 1 Pet. 1. 20. Rev. 13. 8. & 17. 8. Ps. 104. 5. Prov. 8. 29. Isa. 51. 13, 16.
R. V. Luke 6. 48. because it had been well builded; Isa. 16. 7. raisin cakes; Jer. 50. 15. bulwarks
FOUNTAIN, Gen. 7. 11. Deut. 8. 7.
Deut. 33. 28. *f.* of Jacob on a land
Ps. 36. 9. with thee is *f.* of life
Prov. 5. 18. let thy *f.* be blessed
13. 14. law of wise is a *f.* of life
14. 27. fear of Lord is a *f.* of life
Eccl. 12. 6. pitcher broken at the *f.*
S. of S. 4. 12. *f.* sealed
15. *f.* of gardens
Jer. 2. 13. Lord *f.* of liv. waters, 17. 13.
9. 1. my eyes were a *f.* of tears
Rev. 21. 6. give of *f.* of life freely, 22. 17
R. V. Num. 33. 9; Prov. 8. 16 springs; Jer. 6. 7. well

FOUR living creatures, vision of, Ezek. 1. 5. & 10. 10. Rev. 4. 6. & 5. 14. & 6. 6.
kingdoms, Nebuchadnezzar's vision of, Dan. 2. 36; Daniel's vision of, Dan. 7. 3, 16.
FOURFOLD compensation, Ex. 22. 1. 2 Sam. 12. 6. Luke 19. 8.
FOXES, Judg. 15. 4. Ps. 63. 10. S. of S. 2. 15. Lam. 5. 18. Ezek. 13. 4. Matt. 8. 20. Luke 13. 32.
FRAGMENTS, Matt. 14. 20. Mark 6. 43. & 8. 19, 20. John 6. 12, 13.
FRAIL I am, Ps. 39. 4.
FRAME, Ps. 50. 19. & 94. 20. & 103. 14. Isa. 29. 16. Jer. 18. 11. Eph. 2. 21. Heb. 11. 3.
R. V. Hos. 5. 4. their doings will not suffer them
FRAUD condemned, Lev. 19. 13. Mal. 3. 5. Mark 10. 19. 1 Cor. 6. 8. 1 Thes. 4. 6. *See* DECEIT.
FREE, Ex. 21. 2. Lev. 19. 20.
2 Chron. 29. 31. as many as were of a *f.* heart
Ps. 51. 12. uphold with thy *f.* Spirit
John 8. 32. truth shall make you *f.*
36. if Son make *f.* shall be *f.*
Rom. 5. 15. so also is *f.* gift
6. 7. *f.* from sin, 18.
20. *f.* from righteousness
7. 3. *f.* from law
8. 2. *f.* from the law of sin
1 Cor. 7. 22. the Lord's *f.* man
Gal. 3. 28. neither bond nor *f.*, Col. 3. 11.
5. 1. Christ hath made us *f.* not
1 Pet. 2. 16. as *f.* and not using lib.
Hos. 14. 4. I will love them *freely*
Matt. 10. 8. *f.* ye have received, *f.*
Rom. 3. 24. justified *f.* by his grace
8. 32. with him *f.* give us all
1 Cor. 2. 12. things *f.* given us of
Rev. 21. 6. of fount. of life *f.*, 22. 17.
R. V. Ex. 21. 11. for nothing; 36. 3. free will; 2 Chron. 29. 31; Amos 4. 5. willing; Ps. 88. 5. cast off; Acts 22. 28. am a Roman; Col. 3. 11. freeman; 2 Thes. 3. 1. run; Matt. 15. 6. Mark 7. 11 ——; Rom. 6. 7. justified
FREEWILL offerings, Lev. 22. 18. Num. 15. 3. Deut. 16. 10. Ezra 3. 5.
FREEWOMAN and bondwoman, illustration of, Gal. 4. 22.
FRET, Ps. 37. 1, 7, 8. Prov. 24. 19.
Prov. 19. 3. his heart *f.* against the
Ezek. 16. 43. hast *fretted* me in all
FRIEND, Jer. 6. 21. Hos. 3. 1.
Ex. 33. 11. as a man to his *f.*
Deut. 13. 6. *f.* which is as his own
2 Sam. 16. 17. is this kind. to thy *f.*
Job 6. 14. pity should be showed from his *f.*
Prov. 17. 17. *f.* loveth at all times
18. 24. a *f.* that sticketh closer than a brother
27. 10. own *f.* and father's *f.*
S. of S. 5. 16. my beloved and *f.*
Mic. 7. 5. trust ye not in a *f.* put
John 15. 13. lay down life for his *f.*
15. 14. ye are my *f.* if
15. called you *f.*
Jas. 4. 4. *f.* of the world is enemy of God, *friendship* of the world is enmity with God
Prov. 22. 24. make no *f.* with an
18. 24. hath *f.* must show himself *friendly*
R. V. 2 Sam. 19. 6. them that love thee; Prov. 6. 1; 17. 18. neighbor; Judg. 19. 3; Ruth 2. 13. kindly; Prov. 18. 24. doeth it to his own destruction
FROWARD, Job 5. 13. 1 Pet. 2. 18.
Deut. 32. 20. a very *f.* generation
Ps. 18. 26. will show thyself *f.*
Prov. 4. 24. *f.* mouth, 6. 12. & 8. 13. 10. 31. *f.* tongue, 11. 20. *f.* heart, 17. 20.
3. 32. the *f.* is abomination to the
Isa. 57. 17. went on *frowardly*
Prov. 6. 14. *frowardness* is in him
R. V. 2 Sam. 22. 27; Ps. 18. 26; Prov. 3. 32; 11. 20. perverse; 21. 8. him that is laden with guilt is exceeding crooked
FRUIT, Gen. 4. 3. Lev. 19. 24.
2 Kings 19. 30. bear *f.* upward, Isa. 37. 31.
Ps. 92. 14. shall bring forth *f.* in old
127. 3. *f.* of womb is his reward
Prov. 11. 30. *f.* of righteous is
S. of S. 2. 3. his *f.* was sweet
4. 13. with pleasant *f.*
6. 11. to see the *f.* of the valley
Isa. 3. 10. eat the *f.* of their doings
27. 9. all the *f.* to take away sin
57. 19. create *f.* of the lips, peace
Hos. 10. 1. empty vine brings *f.*
Mic. 6. 7. *f.* of my body for sin of
Matt. 7. 17. good tree brings forth good *f.*, 21. 19.
12. 33. *f.* good; tree known by his *f.*
26. 29. not drink of *f.* of vine till
Luke 1. 42. blessed is the *f.* of thy womb
John 4. 36. gathers *f.* to eternal life
15. 2. branch beareth not *f.* he tak.
Rom. 6. 21. what *f.* had
22. *f.* to holiness
Gal. 5. 22. *f.* of Spirit is love, joy
Eph. 5. 9. *f.* of Spirit is in all good.
Phil. 4. 17. desire *f.* that may abound
Heb. 12. 11. peaceable *f.* of righteousness
Jas. 3. 18. *f.* of righteousness is
Rev. 22. 2. yielded *f.* every month
Matt. 3. 8. bring forth *fruits* meet
7. 16. shall know them by their *f.*
2 Cor. 9. 10. increase the *f.* of right.
Phil. 1. 11. filled with the *f.* of righteousness
Jas. 3. 17. full of good *f.* without
R. V. Ex. 23. 10; Deut. 22. 9. increase; Lev. 25. 15. crops; Isa. 28. 4; S. of S. 6. 11. green plant; Mic. 7. 1. fig; Amos 7. 14. trees; Luke 12. 18. corn; Jude 12. autumn trees
FRUIT TREES saved in time of war, Deut. 20. 19.
FRUSTRATE, Isa. 44. 25. Gal. 2. 21.
R. V. Gal. 2. 21. make void
FUGITIVE servant, law of, Deut. 23. 15.
FULL, Gen. 15. 16. Ex. 16. 3, 8.
Deut. 34. 9. Joshua *f.* of the spirit
Ruth 1. 21. I went out *f.* and
1 Sam. 2. 5. that were *f.* have hired
Job 5. 26. come to grave in *f.* age
14. 1. of few days and *f.* of trouble
Ps. 17. 14. they are *f.* of children
Prov. 27. 7. *f.* soul loath the honey.
Luke 4. 1. Jesus being *f.* of the Holy Ghost
John 1. 14. of God *f.* of grace and
1 Cor. 4. 8. now ye are *f.* now ye
Col. 2. 2. riches of *f.* assurance
2 Tim. 4. 5. *f.* proof of thy ministry
10. 22. draw near in *f.* assurance
Gen. 29. 27. *fulfil*, Ex. 23. 26.
Matt. 3. 15. it becometh us to *f.* all righteousness
5. 17. not to destroy the law, but *f.*
Acts 13. 22. who shall *f.* all my will
Luke 21. 24. till times of Gentiles be *f.*
Gal. 5. 14. law is *f.* in one word
16. shall not *f.* lust of the flesh
6. 2. bear burden and so *f.* law
Eph. 2. 3. *f.* the desires of flesh and
Phil. 2. 2. *f.* ye my joy, that ye be
Col. 4. 17. ministry, in the Lord, that thou *f.* it
2 Thes. 1. 11. *f.* all the good pleas.
Jas. 2. 8. if ye *f.* the royal law
Rev. 17. 17. put in their hearts to *f.*
Job 20. 22. in *fulness* of sufficiency
Ps. 16. 11. in thy presence is *f.* of
John 1. 16. of his *f.* have we receiv.
Rom. 11. 25. till *f.* of the Gent.
15. 29. *f.* of blessing of the Gospel
Gal. 4. 4. when *f.* of time was come
3. 19. ye may be filled with the *f.* of God
Col. 1. 19. in him should all *f.* dwell
2. 9. in him dwells all the *f.* of
R. V. Lev. 2. 14; 2 Kings 4. 42. fresh; 1 Cor. 10. 28 ——
FURNACE, Deut. 4. 20. Jer. 11. 4. Ps. 12. 6. Isa. 31. 9. & 48. 10. Dan. 3. 6, 11. Matt. 13. 42, 50. Rev. 1. 15.
FURNISHED, Deut. 15. 14. Prov. 9. 2.
2 Tim. 3. 17. thoroughly *f.* to all
R. V. Ps. 78. 19. prepare; Isa. 65. 11. fill up; Matt. 22. 10. filled
FURY is not in me, Isa. 27. 4.
59. 18. repay *f.* to his adversaries
Jer. 6. 11. I am full of *f.* of the
10. 25. pour out thy *f.* on heathen
Prov. 22. 24. with *furious* man not
R. V. Job 20. 23. fierceness

G

GABRIEL, Dan. 8. 16. & 9. 21. Luke 1. 19, 26.
GAIN, Prov. 3. 14. Job 22. 3.
Isa. 33. 15. despiseth the *g.* of oppre.
Phil. 1. 21. to live is Christ, to die is *g.*
3. 7. what were *g.* to me I counted
1 Tim. 6. 5. supposing *g.* is godliness
Matt. 16. 26. if he should *g.* whole
1 Cor. 9. 19. servant to all, that I might *g.*
18. 15. thou hast *gained* thy bro.
Luke 19. 16. thy pound hath *g.* ten
Tit. 1. 9. convince *gainsayers*
Acts 10. 29. *gainsaying*, Rom. 10. 21. *g.* people
Jude 11. perished in the *g.* of Core
R. V. Prov. 28. 8; Dan. 11. 39. price; Acts 19. 24. little business; 2 Cor. 12. 17, 18. take advantage; Luke 19. 16, 18. made; Acts 27. 21. gotten . . . injury
GALL, Job 16. 13. & 20. 14, 25.
Deut. 29. 18. the root bears *g.*
32. 32. their grapes are grapes of *g.*
Ps. 69. 21. gave me *g.* for drink, Matt. 27. 34.
Jer. 8. 14. given us water of *g.*, 9. 15.
Lam. 3. 19. remembering the wormwood and *g.*, 5.
Acts 8. 23. thou art in the *g.* of bit.
GAP, to stand in, Ezek. 22. 30.
GARDEN, Gen. 2. 15. & 3. 23. & 13. 10.
S. of S. 4. 12. a *g.* enclosed is my sister
16. blow on my *g.*, 5. 1. & 6. 2, 11.
Jer. 31. 12. soul as a watered *g.*, Isa. 58. 11.
GARMENT, Josh. 7. 21. Ezra 9. 3.
Job 37. 17. how thy *garments* are warm
Ps. 22. 18. parted my *g.* among
Isa. 9. 5. battle with *g.* rolled in
61. 3. *g.* of praise for the spirit
Joel 2. 13. rend your hearts and not *g.*
Matt. 21. 8. spread their *g.* in way
Acts 9. 39. showing *g.* Dorcas made
Jas. 5. 2. your *g.* are moth-eaten
Rev. 3. 4. have not defiled their *g.*
16. 15. watcheth and keepeth his *g.*
R. V. Deut. 22. 11. mingled stuff; Judg. 14. 12, 13, 19; 1 Kings 10. 25; 2 Kings 5. 22, 23; Ps. 109. 19; Dan. 11. 9. raiment; Josh. 7. 21; Zech. 13. 4. mantle; Esth. 8. 15; Mark 16. 5. robe; 1 Sam. 18. 4; 2 Sam. 20. 8; Luke 24. 4. apparel; Mark 13. 16; Luke 22. 36. cloak; Ps. 69. 11. clothing; 104. 6. vesture; Matt. 27. 31 ——
GATE, Gen. 19. 1. & 34. 20, 24.
Gen. 22. 17. possess *g.* of his ene.
28. 17. this is the house of God and the *g.* of heaven
Job 29. 7. I went to *g.* prepared
Ps. 118. 20. this *g.* of the Lord into

Matt. 7. 13. enter strait g., Luke 13. 2.
Heb. 13. 12. suffered without the g.
Ps. 9. 13. up from *gates* of death
24. 7. lift up your heads, O g., 9.
87. 2. Lord loveth g. of Zion
100. 4. enter his g. with thanks
118. 19. open for me g. of right.
Isa. 38. 10. to go to g. of the grave
Matt. 16. 18. g. of hell shall not prevail
R. V. Esth. 5. 1. entrance, Ezek. 40. 6 —; Neh. 13. 19; Isa. 45. 1, 2; S. of S. 7. 13; Luke 13. 24; Acts 4. 2. door, doors
GATHER thee from all nations, Deut. 30. 3. Neh. 1. 9. Jer. 29. 14.
Ps. 26. 9. g. not my soul with sinners
Zeph. 3. 18. g. them that are sor.
Matt. 3. 12. g. his wheat into gar.
7. 16. do men g. grapes of thorns
Eph. 1. 10. to g. in one all things
Ex. 16. 18, 21. he that *gathered* much
Matt. 23. 37. g. thy children as hen g.
John 4. 36. g. fruit unto eternal
R. V. Gen. 49. 2; Ex. 35. 1, Lev. 8. 3; Num. 8. 9; 16. 3; 19. 42; 20. 2, 8; Deut. 4. 10; 31. 12, 18; Judg. 9. 6; 20. 1; 1 Chron. 13. 5, Ezek. 38. 13; Mic. 4. 11. assembled; Ex. 9. 19. hasten in; Job 11. 10. call unto judgment; Isa. 62. 9. garnered; Jer. 6. 1. flee for safety; 51. 11. hold firm; Joel 2. 6, Nah. 2. 10. waxed pale; Eph. 1. 10. sum up
GAVE, Gen. 14. 20. Ex. 11. 3.
Job 1. 21. Lord g. and Lord taketh
Ps. 81. 12. I g. them up unto
Eccl. 12. 7. spirit return to God that g. it
Isa. 42. 24. who g. Jacob for a spoil
John 1. 12. he g. power to become
3. 16. God g. his only begotten Son
1 Cor. 3. 6. God g. the increase, 7
2 Cor. 8. 5. first g. themselves to
Gal. 1. 4. who g. himself for our
2. 20. g. himself for me, Tit. 2. 14.
Eph. 4. 8. g. gifts unto men
11. g. some apostles
1 Tim. 2. 6. g. himself a ransom
Ps. 21. 4. asked life, thou *gavest* it
John 17. 4. work thou g
22. glory thou g. me
6. the men thou g. me, 12. & 18. 9. which thou g. me, lost none
GENEALOGIES, 1 Tim. 1. 4. Tit. 3. 9.
GENERATION, Gen. 2. 4. & 6. 9.
Deut. 32. 5. they are a perverse and crooked g.
20. a very froward g. in whom
Ps. 14. 5. God is in the g. of the righteous
22. 30. accounted to Lord for a g.
24. 6. this is g. of them that seek
112. 2. g. of upright shall be
145. 4. one g. shall praise thy
Isa. 53. 8. who declare his g., Acts 8. 33.
Matt. 3. 7. ye g. of vipers, 12. 34. & 23. 33.
Luke 16. 8. g. wiser than the child
Acts 13. 36. had served his g according
1 Pet. 2. 9. chosen g. to show praises
Ps. 33. 11. thoughts to all *generations*
45. 17. to be remembered in all g.
79. 13. show forth thy praise in all g.
89. 4. build thy throne to all g.
90. 1. our dwelling place in all g
100. 5. his truth endureth to all g.
119. 90. thy faithfulness to all g.
Col. 1. 26. the mystery hid from ages and g.
R. V. Matt. 3. 7; 23. 33; 12. 34, Luke 3. 7. ye offspring, 1 Pet. 2. 9. an elect race
GENTILES, Gen. 10. 5. Jer. 4. 7.
Isa. 11. 10. to it shall the g. seek
Isa. 42. 6. a light of the g., 49. 6. Luke 2. 32. Acts 13. 47
60. 3. g. shall come to thy light
62. 2. g. shall see thy righteous.
Matt. 6. 32. after these things do the g. seek
John 7. 35. to the dispersed among the g.
Acts 13. 46. lo, we turn to the g
14. 27. opened door of faith unto g.
Rom. 2. 14. g. which have not law
3. 29. is he not also God of g. yea
15. 10. rejoice ye g. with his people
12. in his name shall the g. trust
Eph. 3. 6. g. be fellow heirs and
8. preach among g. unsearchable
1 Tim. 2. 7. a teacher of g., 2 Tim. 1. 11.
3. 16. God manifest in flesh, preached to g.
GENTLE among you, 1 Thes. 2. 7.
Tit. 3. 2. be g. showing all meek.
Jas. 3. 17. wisdom from above is g.
1 Pet. 2. 18. not only to the g. but
Ps. 18. 35. thy *gentleness* made me
2 Cor. 10. 1. beseech by the g. of
Gal. 5. 22. fruit of the Spirit is love, joy, g.
Isa. 40. 11. *gently* lead those with
R. V. Gal. 5. 22. kindness
GIFT, 1 Cor. 1. 7. & 7. 7.
Ex. 23. 8. take no g. for a g. blindeth
Prov. 17. 8. g is a preci. stone, 23.
18. 16. a man's g. maketh room for
21. 14. a g in secret pacifieth anger
Eccl. 7. 7. a g. destroyeth the heart
Matt. 5. 24. leave there thy g. and
John 4. 10. if thou knewest g. of
Rom. 6. 23. g. of God is eternal
Eph. 2. 8. through faith it is the g. of
Phil. 4. 17. not because I desire a g.
1 Tim. 4. 14. neglect not the g. that
2 Tim. 1. 6. stir up g. of God
Heb. 6. 4. tasted of heavenly g.
Jas. 1. 17 every good and perfect g.
Ps. 68. 18. received *gifts* for men
Matt. 7. 11. give good g. to your children
Rom. 11. 29. for g and calling of God
Eph. 4. 8. led captivity and gave g.
R. V. 2 Sam. 8. 2, 6 1 Chron. 18. 2, 6. presents; Ezek. 22. 12. bribes; Luke 21. 5. offerings, 2 Cor. 8. 4. this grace
GIRD with strength, Ps. 18. 32.
Ps. 30. 11. g. me with gladness
Luke 12. 35. let your loins be *girded*, 1 Pet. 1. 13.
Eph. 6. 14. having your loins g. with
Isa. 11. 5. *girdle*, Matt. 3. 4. Rev. 1. 13. & 15. 6.
R. V. Job 12. 18. bindeth, Ex. 28. 8, 27, 28; 29 5; 39 5, 20, 21; Lev. 8. 7. band
GIRL, they have sold a g. for wine, Joel 3. 3.
Zech. 8. 5. streets full of g
GIVE, Gen. 12. 7. & 30. 31.
1 Kings 3. 5. ask what I shall g.
Ps. 2. 8. I shall g. thee the heathen
29. 11. Lord will g. strength to his
37. 4. g. the desires of thy heart
109. 4. I g. myself to prayer
104. 27. mayest g. them their meat
Jer. 17. 10. to g. every man accord.
Hos. 11. 8. how shall I g. thee up
Luke 6. 38. g. and it shall be given
John 10. 28. I g. to them eternal
Acts 3. 6. such as I have g. I unto
20. 35. more blessed to g than to receive
Eph. 4. 28. that he may have to g.
1 Tim. 4. 15. g. thyself wholly to
2 Sam. 22. 50. *give thanks*, 1 Chron. 16. 8, 34, 35, 41. Neh. 12. 24. Ps. 35. 18. & 79. 13. & 92. 1 & 105. 1. & 107. 1. & 118. 1. & 136. 1
Ps. 6. 5. in grave who shall—to thee
Ps. 30. 4. — at the remembrance of
119. 62. at midnight I will rise to —
Eph. 1. 16. cease not to—, 1 Thes. 1. 2. 2 Thes. 2. 13. Col. 1. 3.
1 Thes. 5. 18. in every thing —, Phil. 4. 6.
Matt. 13. 12. to him shall be *given*
11. it is g. to you to know the mys.
Luke 12. 48. to whom much is g.
John 6. 39. of all which he hath g.
65. can come to me except it be g.
19. 11. except it were g. thee from
Rom. 11. 35. hath first g. to him
2 Cor. 9. 7 God loves the cheerful *giver*
Ps. 37. 21. shows mercy and *giveth*
Prov. 28. 27. he that g. to poor shall
Isa. 40. 29. g. power to the faint
42. 5. g. breath to people on earth
1 Tim. 6. 17. g. us richly all things
Jas. 1. 5. g. to all men liberally
1 Pet. 4. 11. of the ability that God g.
GLAD, my heart is, Ps. 16. 9.
Ps. 31. 7. I will be g. and rejoice in
64. 10. righteous shall be g. in Lord
104. 34. I will be g. in the Lord
122. 1. I was g. when they said
Luke 1. 19. *glad tidings*, & 8. 1.
Mark 6. 20. heard him *gladly*, 12. 37.
Luke 8. 40. people g. received him
Acts 2. 41. that g. received his word
2 Cor. 12. 15. I will very g. spend
Ps. 4. 7. put *gladness* in my heart
30. 11. hast girded me with g.
51. 8. make me to hear joy and g.
97. 11. g. sown for the upright
100. 2. serve the Lord with g.
Isa. 35. 10. shall obtain joy and g.
51. 3. joy and g. shall be found
Acts 2. 46. eat their meat with g.
R. V. Ps. 48. 11; 104. 34; Acts 2. 26; 1 Cor. 16. 17; 2 Cor. 13. 9; 1 Pet. 4. 13; Rev. 19. 7. rejoice; Luke 1. 19; 8. 1; Acts 13. 32. good; Luke 8. 40; Acts 2. 41 —; Ps. 105. 43. singing; 2 Sam. 6. 12; Mark 4. 16; Acts 12. 14; Phil. 2. 29. joy
GLASS, we see through, 1 Cor. 13. 12.
2 Cor. 3. 18. beholding as in a g.
Rev. 4. 6. a sea of g., 15. 2.
21. 18. the city was pure gold like clear g.
R. V. Job 37. 18. mirror; Isa. 3. 23. hand mirrors; Jas. 1. 23. mirror; Rev. 4. 6; 15. 2. glassy sea.
GLOOMINESS, Joel 2. 2. Zeph. 1. 15.
GLORY, Gen. 31. 1. Ps. 49. 16.
1 Sam. 4. 21. g. is departed from
1 Chron. 29. 11. thine the power and the g., Matt. 6. 13.
Ps. 8. 5. crowned with g. and honor.
73. 24. afterward receive me to g.
145. 11. speak of the g. of thy king.
Prov. 3. 35. the wise shall inherit g.
16. 31. hoary head is a crown of g.
20. 29. g. of young men is their str.
25. 27. to search their own g. is not g.
Isa. 4. 5. upon all the g. shall be
24. 16. heard songs, even g. to the
28. 5. Lord shall be for a crown of g.
Jer. 2. 11. chang. their g., Ps. 106. 20.
Ezek. 20. 6. the g. of all lands, 15.
Hos. 4. 7. change their g. into shame
Hag. 2. 7. I will fill this hou. with g.
9. g. of this latter house shall be
Zech. 2. 5. be the g. in the midst
Matt. 6. 2. may have g. of men
16. 27. come in g. of his Father
Luke 2. 14. g. to God in the highest
32. light of the Gentiles, g. of thy
John 1. 14. his g. the g. of the only
17. 5. *glorify* me with the g. I had
22. g. which thou gavest I have
Rom. 2. 7. seek for g. and honor
11. 36. to whom be g. for ever, 2 Tim. 4. 18. Heb. 13. 21.
16. 27. in God be g. through Christ
1 Cor. 11. 7. man is g. of God, woman is g. of man
15. 43. in dishonor, it is raised in g.
2 Cor. 3. 18. changed from g. to g.

2 Cor. 4. 17. an exceeding and eternal weight of *g.*
Eph. 1. 6. praise of *g.* of his grace
3. 21. to him be *g.* in the church
Phil. 3. 19. whose *g.* is in their shame
Col. 1. 27. Christ in you hope of *g.*
3. 4. appear with him in *g.*
1 Thes. 2. 12. hath called you to *g.*
1 Tim. 3. 16. received up into *g.*
1 Pet. 1. 8. joy unspeak., full of *g.*
4. 13. his *g.* be revealed
14. spirit of *g.*
5. 1. partaker of *g.* to be revealed
4. ye shall receive a crown of *g.*
10. called us to eternal *g.*
2 Pet. 1. 3. called us to *g.* and virtue
17. came a voice from the excellent *g.*
Rev. 4. 11. worthy to receive *g.*, 5. 12. Rom. 16. 27. 1 Tim. 1. 17. 1 Pet. 5. 11. Jude 25.
Josh. 7. 19. *give glory* to the God of Israel, 1 Sam. 6. 5. 1 Chron. 16. 29. Ps. 29. 2. & 96. 8. & 115. 1. Luke 17. 18. Rev. 14. 7.
Ps. 19. 1. *glory of God*, Prov. 25. 2. Acts 7. 55. Rom. 3. 23. & 5. 2. 1 Cor. 10. 31. & 11. 7. 2 Cor. 4. 6. Rev. 21. 11.
Ex. 16. 7. *glory of the Lord*, Num. 14. 21.
1 Kings 8. 11. Ps. 104. 31. & 138. 5. Isa. 35. 2. & 40. 5. & 60. 1. Ezek. 1. 28. & 3. 12, 23. & 43. 5. & 44. 4. Luke 2. 9. 2 Cor. 3. 18.
Ps. 29. 9. *his glory*, 49. 17. & 72. 19. & 113. 4. & 148. 13. Prov. 19. 11. Isa. 6. 3. Hab. 3. 3. Matt. 6. 29. & 19. 28. & 25. 31. John 2. 11. Rom. 9. 23. Eph. 1. 12. & 3. 16. Heb. 1. 3.
Job. 29. 20. *my glory*, Ps. 16. 9. & 30. 12. & 57. 8. & 108. 1. Isa. 42. 8. & 43. 7. & 48. 11. & 60. 7. & 66. 18. John 8. 50. & 17. 24.
Ex. 33. 18. *thy glory*, Ps. 8. 1. & 63. 2. Isa. 60. 19. & 63. 15. Jer. 14. 21.
1 Chron. 16. 10. *glory* ye in his holy
Ps. 64. 10. upright in heart shall *g.*
106. 5. I may *g.* with thy inherit.
Isa. 41. 16. shalt *g.* in Holy One of
45. 25. seed of Israel be justified, and *g.*
Jer. 9. 24. him that glorieth *g.* in this
Rom. 4. 2. hath *g.* but not bef. God
5. 3. we *g.* in tribulation
1 Cor. 1. 31. that glorieth *g.* in the
3. 21. let no man *g.* in men
2 Cor. 5. 12. to *g.* on our behalf—
11. 18. many *g.* after the flesh
12. 1. it is not exped. for me to *g.*
Gal. 6. 14. God forbid I should *g.*
Isa. 25. 5. strong people shall *glorify* thee
Matt. 5. 16. *g.* your Father in heav.
John 12. 28. Father *g.* thy name
17. 1. *g.* thy Son
21. 19. by what death he should *g.* God
1 Cor. 6. 20. *g.* God in your body
1 Pet. 2. 12. *g.* God in day of visita.
Rev. 15. 4. who shall not fear thee, and *g.* thy name
Lev. 10. 3. before all I will be *glorified*
Matt. 9. 8. they *g.* God, 15. 31.
John 7. 39. Jesus was not yet *g.*
15. 8. herein is my Father *g.*
Acts 3. 13. God of our fathers hath *g.* his
4. 21. all men *g.* God for that was
Rom. 1. 21. they *g.* him not as God
8. 30. whom he justified, them he *g.*
Gal. 1. 24. they *g.* God in me
2 Thes. 1. 10. shall come to be *g.* in
Heb. 5. 5. even Christ *g.* not him.
1 Pet. 4. 11. God in all things may be *g.*
14. on your part he is *g.*
1 Cor. 5. 6. *glorying*, 9. 15. 2 Cor. 7. 4. & 12. 11.
Ex. 15. 6. *glorious* in power
11. who is like thee, *g.* in holiness
Deut. 28. 58. fear this *g.* and fearful
1 Chron. 29. 13. praise thy *g.* name
Ps. 45. 13. king's daughter all *g.*
66. 2. make his praise *g.*
72. 19. blessed be his *g.* name
87. 3. *g.* things are spoken of
111. 3. his work is honorable and *g.*
145. 5. speak of *g.* honor of thy
12. make known his *g.* majesty
Isa. 4. 2. branch of Lord shall be *g.*
22. 23. be for a *g.* throne to his
30. 30. cause his *g.* voice to be heard
33. 21. *g.* Lord will be to us a place
49. 5. yet shall I be *g.* in eyes
60. 13. make the place of my feet *g.*
63. 1. who is this *g.* in his apparel
Jer. 17. 12. a *g.* high throne from
Rom. 8. 21. *g.* liberty of children
2 Cor. 3. 7. ministration was *g.*
4. 4. light of *g.* gospel should
Col. 1. 11. according to his *g.* power
Tit. 2. 13. looking for *g.* appearance
Ex. 15. 1. *gloriously*, Isa. 24. 23.
R. V. 1 Pet. 4. 14 —; Ps. 111. 3. majesty; Isa. 49. 5. honorable; 1 Chron. 16. 27; Job 40. 10. honor; 1 Chron. 16. 35. triumph; Ps. 89. 44. brightness; Prov. 4. 9; Isa. 62. 3. beauty; Matt. 6. 13 —; 2 Cor. 12. 11 —

GLUTTON, Deut. 21. 20. Prov. 23. 21.
Matt. 11. 19. *gluttonous*, Luke 7. 34.
R. V. Deut. 21. 20. riotous liver

GNASH, Job 16. 9. Ps. 35. 16. & 37. 12. & 112. 10. Lam. 2. 16. Mark 9. 18.
Matt. 8. 12. *gnashing of teeth*, 13. 42, 50. & 22. 13. & 24. 51. & 25. 30. Luke 13. 28.
R. V. Mark 9. 18. grindeth

GNAT, and swallow a camel, Matt. 23. 24.

GNAW, Zeph. 3. 3. Rev. 16. 10.
R. V. Zeph. 3. 3. leave nothing

GO, Judg. 6. 14. 1 Sam. 12. 21. Matt. 8. 9. Luke 10. 37. John 6. 68.
Job 10. 21. *I go*, Ps. 39. 13. & 139. 7. Matt. 21. 30. John 7. 33. & 8. 14, 21, 22. & 13. 33. & 16. 5.
Ex. 4. 23. *let my people go*, 5. 1.
Gen. 32. 26. *not let go*, Ex. 3. 19. Job 27. 6. S. of S. 3. 4.
Ex. 23. 23. *shall go*, 32. 34. & 33. 14. Acts 25. 12.
1 Sam. 12. 21. *should go*, Prov. 22. 6.
Judg. 11. 35. *go back*, Ps. 80. 18.
Num. 22. 18. *go beyond*, 1 Thes. 4. 6.
Gen. 45. 1. *go out*, Ps. 60. 10. Isa. 52. 11. & 55. 12. Jer. 51. 45. Ezek. 46. 9. Matt. 25. 6. John 10. 9. 1 Cor. 5. 10.
Deut. 4. 40. *go well* with thee, 5. 16. & 19. 13. Prov. 11. 10. & 30. 29.
Job 34. 21. seeth all his *goings*
Ps. 17. 5. hold up my *g.* in thy way
40. 2. set my feet and established my *g.*
68. 24. seen thy *g.* O God in
121. 8. Lord preserve thy *g.* out
Prov. 5. 21. he pondereth all his *g.*
Mic. 5. 2. whose *g.* are of old, from
The R. V. changes are frequent, but chiefly those relating to words before and after *go*

GOAT, Lev. 3. 12. & 16. 8, 21, 22.
Isa. 1. 11. I delight not in the blood of *goats*
Ezek. 34. 17. judge between rams and *g.*
Dan. 8. 5. he *g.*
8. rough *g.*, 21.
Matt. 25. 32, 33. set the *g.* on his
Heb. 9. 12. blood of *g.*, 13. 19. & 10. 4.

GOD, and *gods* for *men* representing God, Ex. 4. 16. & 7. 1. & 22. 28. Ps. 82. 1, 6. John 10. 34. for *idols* which are put in God's place, Deut. 32. 21. Judg. 6. 31. and 140 other places. for devil, god of this world, 2 Cor. 4. 4. and for the true God about 3120 times
Gen. 17. 1. I am Almighty *G.*, Job 36. 5. Isa. 9. 6. & 10. 21. Jer. 32. 18.
Gen. 17. 7. to be a *G.* to thee and thy seed, Ex. 6. 7, 21, 33. everlasting *G.* Ps. 90. 2. Isa. 40. 28. Rom. 16. 26.
Ex. 8. 10. none like Lord our *G.*, 1 Kings 8. 23. Ps. 35. 10. & 86. 8. & 89. 6.
18. 11. Lord is greater than all *gods*
Deut. 10. 17. *G.* of gods, Josh. 22. 22. Dan. 2. 47. Ps. 136 2.
Deut. 32. 39. there is no *g.* with me, 1 Kings 8. 23. 2 Kings 5. 15. 2 Chron. 6. 14. & 32. 15. Isa. 43. 10. & 44. 6, 8. & 45. 5, 14, 21, 22.
Job 33. 12. *G.* is greater than man, 36. 26.
Ps. 18. 31. who is *G.* save the Lord, 86. 10.
Mic. 7. 18. who is a *G.* like to thee
Matt. 6. 24. ye cannot serve *G.* and
19. 17. none good but one, that is *G.*
Mark 12. 27. not the *G.* of dead, but of the living
32. there is one *G.* and none other
John 17. 3. the only true *G.*, 1 John 5. 20.
Acts 7. 2. *G.* of glory appeared to
Rom. 8. 31. if *G.* be for us, who can
9. 5. over all *G.* blessed for ever
15. 5. *G.* of patience
13. *G.* of hope
2 Cor. 1. 3. *G.* of all comfort
1 Tim. 3. 16. *G.* manifest in flesh
1 Pet. 5. 10. *G.* of all grace, when
1 John 4. 12. no man seen *G.*, John 1. 18.
Deut. 10. 17. *great God*, 2 Sam. 7. 22. 2 Chron. 2. 5. Job 36. 26. Neh. 1. 5. Prov. 26. 10. Jer. 32. 18, 19. Dan. 9. 4. Tit. 2. 13. Rev. 19. 17.
Deut. 5. 26. *living God*, Josh. 3. 10. 1 Sam. 17. 26, 36. 2 Kings 19. 4, 16. and twenty-two other places
Ex. 34. 6. *God merciful*, Deut. 4. 31. 2 Chron. 30. 9. Neh. 9. 31. Ps. 116. 5. Jonah 4. 2.
Gen. 49. 24. *mighty God*, Deut. 7. 21. & 10. 17. Neh. 9. 32. Job 36. 5. Ps. 50. 1. & 132. 2, 5. Isa. 9. 6. & 10. 21. Jer. 32. 18. Hab. 1. 12.
2 Chron. 15. 3. *true God*, Jer. 10. 10. John 17. 3. 1 Thes. 1. 9. 1 John 5. 20.
Gen. 39. 9. do this wickedness and sin *against God*, Num. 21. 5. Ps. 78. 19. Hos. 13. 16. Acts 5. 39. & 23. 9. Rom. 8. 7. & 9. 20. Rev. 13. 6. Dan. 11. 36.
Ps. 42. 2. *before God*, 56. 13. & 61. 7. & 68. 3. Eccl. 2. 26. Luke 1. 6. Rom. 2. 13. & 3. 19. 1 Tim. 5. 21. Jas. 1. 27. Rev. 3. 2.
John 9. 16. *of God*, Acts 5. 39. Rom. 9. 16. 1 Cor. 1. 30. & 11. 12. 2 Cor. 3. 5. & 5. 18. Phil. 1. 28. 1 John 3. 10. & 4. 1, 0, 6. & 5. 10. 3 John 11.
Ex. 2. 23. *to God*, Ps. 43. 4. Eccl. 12. 7. Isa. 58. 2. Lam. 3. 41. John 13. 3. Heb. 7. 25. & 11. 6. & 12. 23. 1 Pet. 3. 18. & 4. 6. Rev. 5. 9. & 12. 5.
Gen. 5. 22. *with God*, 24. & 6. 9. & 32. 28. Ex. 19. 17. 1 Sam. 14. 45. 2 Sam. 23. 5. Job 9. 2. & 25. 4. Ps. 78. 8. Hos. 11. 12. John 5. 18. Phil. 2. 6.
Gen. 28. 21. *my God*, Ex. 15. 2. Ps. 22. 1. & 31. 14. & 91. 2. & 118. 28. Hos. 2. 23. Zech. 13. 9. John 20. 17. 28. and about 120 other places
Ex. 5. 8. *our God*, Deut. 31. 17. & 32. 3. Josh. 24. 18. 2 Sam. 22. 32. Ps. 67. 6. and 180 other places
Ex. 20. 2. *thy God*, 5, 7, 10, 12. Ps. 50. 7. & 81. 10. and about 340 other places
Ex. 6. 7. *your God*, Lev. 11. 44. & 19. 2, 3, 4. and 140 other places
Ex. 32. 11. *his God*, Lev. 4. 22. and about sixty other places
Gen. 17. 8. *their God*, Ex. 29. 45. Jer. 24. 7. & 31. 33. & 32. 38. Ezek. 11. 20. & 34. 24. & 37. 27. Zech. 8. 8. 2 Cor. 6. 16. Rev. 21. 3. and fifty other places

2 Chron. 36. 23. *God of heaven*, Ezra 5. 11. & 6. 10. & 7. 12, 23. Neh. 1. 4. & 2. 4. Ps. 136. 26. Dan. 2. 18, 19, 44. Jonah 1. 9. Rev. 11. 13. & 16. 11.
Ex. 24. 10. *God of Israel*, Num. 16. 9. Josh. 7. 19. & 13. 33. & 22. 16, 24. & 24. 23. Judg. 11. 23. Ruth 2. 12. Isa. 41. 17. Jer. 31. 1. Ezek. 8. 4. Matt. 15. 31.
Rom. 15. 33. *God of peace*, 16. 20. 2 Cor. 13. 11. 1 Thes. 5. 23. Heb. 13. 20.
Ps. 24. 5. *God of his salvation, of our salvation*, 65. 5. & 68. 19, 20. & 79. 9. & 85. 4. & 95. 1.
Acts 17. 29. *Godhead*, Rom. 1. 20. Col. 2. 9.
R. V. Rom. 1. 20. divinity

GODLY, Ps. 4. 3. & 12. 1. & 32. 6. Mal. 2. 15. 2 Pet. 2. 9. 3 John 6.
2 Cor. 1. 12. in *g.* sincerity, had our conversation
Tit. 2. 12. live soberly, righteously, and *g.*
1 Tim. 2. 2. quiet life in all *godliness*, 10. & 3. 16. & 6. 3, 5, 11. 2 Tim. 3. 5.
4. 8. *g.* is profitable to all things
6. 3. doctrine according to *g.*, Tit. 1. 1.
2 Tim. 3. 5. having a form of *g.* but
2 Pet. 1. 3. all that pertain to life and *g.*
6. add to patience *g.*
7. to *g.* brotherly kindness
R. V. 2 Cor. 1. 12. sincerity; 1 Tim. 1. 4. dispensation of God; Heb. 12. 28. awe; 3 John 6. worthily of God

GOLD, Gen. 2. 11. & 13. 2. Isa. 2. 7.
Job 23. 10. I shall come forth like *g.*
31. 24. if I made *g.* my hope or fine *g.*
Ps. 19. 10. more desired than *g.*
119. 127. love thy commandments above *g.* yea, fine *g.*, 72.
Prov. 8. 19. my fruit is better than *g.* or fine *g.*
Isa. 13. 12. man more precious than fine *g.*
Zech. 13. 9. I will try them as *g.* is
1 Tim. 2. 9. women adorn themselves in modest apparel, not with *g.*, 1 Pet. 3. 3.
1 Pet. 1. 7. trial of faith more precious than *g.*
Rev. 3. 18. buy of me *g.* tried in fire

GOLDEN CANDLESTICK, Ex. 25. 31.

GOOD, Deut. 6. 24. & 10. 13.
Gen. 1. 31. every thing he had made was very *g.*
2. 18. it is not *g.* for man to be alone
2 Kings 20. 19. *g.* is the word of the Lord, Isa. 39. 8.
Ps. 34. 8. taste and see that Lord is *g.*
73. 1. truly God is *g.* to Israel
106. 5. I may see *g.* of thy chosen
119. 68. thou art *g.* and doest *g.*
145. 9. Lord is *g.* to all, 136. 1.
Lam. 3. 25. Lord is *g.* to them that
Mic. 6. 8. he hath showed thee what is *g.*
Matt. 19. 17. why call me *g.* none
Rom. 3. 8. do evil that *g.* may come
1 Thes. 5. 15. follow that which is *g.*, 3 John 11.
Neh. 2. 18. hand for this *good work*
Matt. 26. 10. wrought a — on me
John 10. 33. for a — we stone thee not
2 Cor. 9. 8. abound to every —
Phil. 1. 6. begun a — will finish
Col. 1. 10. fruitful in every —
2 Thes. 2. 17. establish you in every —
1 Tim. 5. 10. followed every —
2 Tim. 2. 21. prepared to —, Tit. 3. 1.
Tit. 1. 16. to every — reprobate
Heb. 13. 21. perfect in every —
Matt. 5. 16. may see your *good works*
John 10. 32. many — have I showed you
Acts 9. 36. Dorcas was full of —
1 Tim. 2. 25. the — of some are manifest
Tit. 3. 8. be careful to maint. —, 14.
Heb. 10. 24. provoke to love and —
1 Pet. 2. 12. may by your — which
Ex. 33. 19. make my *goodness* pass
2 Chron. 6. 41. saints rejoice in *g.*
Neh. 9. 25. delight themselves in *g.*
35. not served thee in thy great *g.*
Ps. 16. 2. my *g.* extendeth not to
23. 6. *g.* and mercy shall follow
27. 13. believed to see *g.* of Lord
31. 19. how great is thy *g.*, Zech. 9. 17.
52. 1. the *g.* of God endureth
11. crownest the year with thy *g.*
Isa. 63. 7. great *g.* bestowed on Israel
Hos. 3. 5. fear the Lord and his *g.*
Rom. 2. 4. *g.* of God leadeth to repentance
11. 22. behold the *g.* and severity of God
Eph. 5. 9. fruit of Spirit in all *g.*, Gal. 5. 22.
R. V. changes are frequent, but nearly all based on words before or after the word *good*; 2 Sam. 7. 28; 1 Chron. 17. 26. good things; 2 Chron. 32. 32; 35. 26. good deeds; Ps. 33. 5; 144. 2. lovingkindness; Prov. 20. 6. kindness

GOSPEL, Mark 1. 1, 15. & 8. 35.
Matt. 4. 23. preaching *g.* of kingdo.
Mark 16. 15. preach the *g.* to
Acts 20. 24. *g.* of the grace of God
Rom. 1. 1. *g.* of God, 15. 16. 1 Tim. 1. 11.
1 Cor. 1. 17. but to preach the *g.*
4. 15. I have begotten you through the *g.*
2 Cor. 4. 3. if our *g.* be hid
4. glorious *g.*
11. 4. another *g.* which ye, Gal. 1. 6.
Gal. 1. 8. preach any other *g.*, 9.
Eph. 1. 13. *g.* of salvation
6. 15. *g.* of peace
Col. 1. 5. truth of *g.*, Gal. 2. 5.
23. hope of *g.*
Phil. 1. 5. fellowship in *g.*
1 Thes. 1. 5. our *g.* came in power
Heb. 4. 2. unto us was *g.* preached
1 Pet. 4. 6. *g.* was preached to dead
Rev. 14. 6. having everlasting *g.* to preach
R. V. Luke 4. 18; 7. 29; 1 Pet. 1. 25. good tidings; Rom. 10. 16. glad tidings; Rom. 10. 15——

GOVERNMENT, Isa. 9. 6, 7. & 22. 21. 1 Cor. 12. 28. 2 Pet. 2. 10
R. V. 2 Pet. 2. 10. dominion

GRACE, Ezra 9. 8. Esth. 2. 17.
Ps. 84. 11. Lord will give *g.* and glory
Prov. 3. 34. gives *g.* to the lowly
Zech. 4. 7. with shoutings, crying *g.* to it.
12. 10. spirit of *g.* and supplications
John 1. 14. of Father full of *g.* and
16. of fulness we receive *g.* for *g.*
17. *g.* and truth came by Jesus Christ
Acts 18. 27. helped them believe through *g.*
Rom. 3. 24. justified freely by his *g.*
5. 20. *g.* did much more abound
6. 14. not under law, but under *g.*
11. 5. according to the election of *g.*
2 Cor. 12. 9. my *g.* is sufficient for
Eph. 2. 5. by *g.* ye are saved, 8.
7. show exceed. riches of his *g.*, 1. 7.
4. 29. minister *g.* to hearers
Tit. 3. 7. justified by his *g.*
Heb. 4. 16. come boldly to the throne of *g.*
13. 9. heart be established with *g.*
1 Pet. 3. 7. heirs of the *g.* of life
5. 5. and giveth *g.* to the humble
2 Pet. 3. 18. grow in *g.* and in knowledge
Rom. 1. 7. *grace and peace* to you, 1 Cor. 1. 3. 2 Cor. 1. 2. Gal. 1. 3. Eph. 1. 2. Phil. 1. 2. Col. 1. 2. 1 Thes. 1. 1. 2 Thes. 1. 2. Phile. 3. 1 Pet. 1. 2. 2 Pet. 1. 2. Jude 2. Rev. 1. 4.
Luke 2. 40. *grace of God*, Acts 11. 23. & 13. 43. & 14. 3, 26. & 15. 40. & 20. 24, 32. Rom. 5. 15. 1 Cor. 1. 4. & 3. 10. & 15. 10. Eph. 3. 2, 7. Heb. 2. 9. & 12. 15.
2 Cor. 1. 12. by — we have had our conversation
6. 1. receive not — in vain
8. 1. of — bestowed on churches
9. 14. for the exceeding — in you
Gal. 2. 21. I do not frustrate —
Col. 1. 6. knew — in truth
1 Pet. 4. 10, stewards of manifold —
Jude 4. turning — into lascivious.
Acts 15. 11. *grace of our Lord Jesus Christ*, Rom. 16. 20, 24. 1 Cor. 16. 23. 2 Cor. 8. 9. & 13. 14. Gal. 6. 18. Phil. 4. 23. 1 Thes. 5. 28. 2 Thes. 3. 18. Phile. 25.
Rev. 22. 21. — be with you all
Gen. 43. 29. God be *gracious* to thee
Ex. 22. 27. I will hear for I am *g.*
33. 19. I will be *g.* to whom I will be *g.*
34. 6. Lord God merciful and *g.*
2 Chron. 30. 9. Neh. 9. 17, 31. Ps. 103. 8. & 116. 5. & 145. 8. Joel 2. 13.
Num. 6. 25. the Lord be *g.* to thee
Job 33. 24. then he is *g.* to him
Ps. 77. 9. hath God forgotten to be *g.*
86. 15. full of compassion and *g.*
Isa. 30. 18. the Lord wait that he may be *g.*
Amos 5. 15. may be, the Lord will be *g.*
Jonah 4. 2. knew that thou art a *g.* God
Mal. 1. 9. beseech God to be *g.*, Isa. 33. 2.
Gen. 33. 5. *graciously*, 11. Ps. 119. 29.
Hos. 14. 2. receive us *g.*
R. V. 2 Sam. 16. 4. favor; Rom. 11. 6; 16. 24——; Jer. 22. 23. to be pitied; Hos. 14. 2. accept . . . good

GRAFTED, Rom. 11. 17, 19, 23, 24

GRANT, Job 10. 12. Ps. 140. 8. Prov. 10. 24. Rom. 15. 5. Eph. 3. 16. 2 Tim. 1. 18. Rev. 3. 21.
R. V. 1 Chron. 21. 22; Rev. 3. 21. give; Matt. 20. 21. command; Rev. 19. 8. given unto

GRAPES, of gall, Deut. 32. 32.
S. of S. 2. 13. the tender *g.*, 15.
7. 7. clusters of *g.*
Isa. 5. 4. wild *g.*
Ezek. 18. 2. sour *g.*
Mic. 7. 1. soul desireth firstripe *g.*
R. V. Lev. 19. 10. fallen fruit; S. of S. 2. 13; 7. 12. in blossom

GRASS, Ps. 37. 2. & 90. 5. & 92. 7. & 102. 4, 11. Isa. 44. 4. & 51. 12.
Ps. 103. 15. man's days are like *g.*
Isa. 40. 6. all flesh is *g.*, 7. 8. 1 Pet. 1. 24. Jas. 1. 10, 11.
Matt. 6. 30. if God so clothe the *g.*
Rev. 8. 7. green *g.*
9. 4. not hurt *g.*
R. V. Isa. 15. 6. hay; Jer. 14. 6. herbage; Jer. 50. 11. treadeth out the corn

GRAVE, 1 Kings 2. 9. & 14. 13.
1 Sam. 2. 6. Lord brings down to *g.*
Job 5. 26. come to thy *g.* in full
14. 13. hide me in the *g.*, 17. 1, 13.
Ps. 6. 5. in *g.* who shall give thanks
Prov. 1. 12. swallow them up alive, as the *g.*
Isa. 38. 18. *g.* cannot praise thee
Hos. 13. 14. the power of the *g.* O *g.* I will be thy destruction
1 Cor. 15. 55. O *g.* where is thy vic.
Zech. 3. 9. I will *engrave* the graving

Job 19. 24. *graven* with an iron pen
Isa. 49. 16. I have *g.* thee upon
Jer. 17. 1. sin *g.* upon table of their
1 Tim. 3. 4, 8, 11. *grave*, Tit. 2. 2, 7.
R. V. Job 33. 22. pit; Matt. 27. 52; Luke 11. 44; John 5. 28; 11. 17, 31; Rev. 11. 9. tombs; 1 Cor. 15. 55. death; Isa. 14. 19. sepulchre; Job 30. 24. ruinous heap; Job 7. 9; 17. 13; Ps. 6. 5; 30. 3; 31. 17; 49. 14, 15; 88. 3; 89. 48; Prov. 1. 12; Hos. 13. 14. Sheol

GRAY, Ps. 71.18. Prov. 20.29. Hos. 7. 9.
R. V. Prov. 20. 29. hoary

GREAT, Gen. 12. 2. & 30. 8.
Deut. 29. 24. *g.* anger, 2 Chron. 34. 21,
1 Sam. 6. 9. *great evil*, Neh. 13. 27. Eccl. 2. 21. Jer. 44. 7. Dan. 9. 12.
Ps. 47. 2. *great king*, 48. 2. & 95. 3. Mal. 1. 14. Matt. 5. 35.
Job 32. 9. *great men*, Jer. 5. 5.
Ex. 32. 11. *great power*, Neh. 1. 10. Job 23. 6. Ps. 147. 5. Nah. 1. 3. Acts 4. 33. & 8. 10. Rev. 11. 17.
Ex. 32. 21. *so great*, Deut. 4. 7, 8. 1 Kings 3. 9. Ps. 77. 13. & 103. 11. Matt. 8. 10. & 15. 33. 2 Cor. 1. 10. Heb. 2. 3. & 12. 1. Rev. 16. 18. & 18. 17.
Job 5. 9. *great things*, 9. 10. & 37. 5. Jer. 45. 5. Hos. 8. 12. Luke 1. 49.
Gen. 6. 5. *great wickedness*, 39. 9. Job 22. 5. Joel 3. 13. 2 Chron. 28. 13.
Job 33. 12. God is *greater* than man
Matt. 12. 42. *g.* than Solomon is here
John 1. 50. see *g.* things than these
4. 12. art thou *g.* than, 8. 53.
14. 28. my Father is *g.* than I
1 Cor. 14. 5. *g.* is he that prophe.
1 John 4. 4. *g.* is he that is in you, 3. 20.
5. 9. witness of God is *g.*
1 Sam. 30. 6. David was *greatly* distressed
2 Sam. 24. 10. I have sinned *g.* in
1 Kings 8. 3. Obadiah feared the Lord *g.*
1 Chron. 16. 25. great is the Lord and *g.* to be praised, Ps. 48. 1. & 96. 4. & 145. 3.
2 Chron. 33. 12. humbled himself *g.* before God
Job 3. 25. thing I *g.* feared is come
Ps. 28. 7. my heart *g.* rejoiceth
47. 9. God is *g.* exalted
Dan. 9. 23. O man *g.* beloved, 10. 11, 19.
Mark 12. 27. ye do *g.* err
Ex. 15. 7. *greatness* of thy excellency
Num. 14. 19. pardon according to *g.*
Deut. 32. 3. ascribe ye *g.* to our God
1 Chron. 29. 11. thine is the *g.*
Neh. 13. 22. spare according to the *g.* of thy mercy
Ps. 66. 3. *g.* of thy power, 79. 11. Eph. 1. 19.
145. 3. his *g.* is unsearchable, 6.
Isa. 63. 1. travelling in the *g.* of his strength
The R. V. changes, which are frequent, mostly turn on antecedent and consequent words

GREEDY of gain, Prov. 1. 19. & 15. 27.
Isa. 56. 11. they are *g.* dogs, never
Eph. 4. 19. work uncleanness with *greediness*

GRIEF, Isa. 53. 3, 4, 10. Heb. 13. 17.
Gen. 6. 6. *grieved* him at his heart
Judg. 10. 16. his soul was *g.* for
Ps. 95. 10. forty years long was I *g.*
Isa. 54. 6. woman forsaken and *g.*
Jer. 5. 3. hast stricken them, they have not *g.*
Lam. 3. 33. nor *g.* children of men
Amos 6. 6. not *g.* for the affliction of Joseph
Mark 3. 5. being *g.* for hardness of heart
10. 22. went away *g.* for he had
Rom. 14. 15. if brother be *g.* at thy meat
Ps. 10. 5. his ways are always *grievous*
Matt. 23. 4. burdens *g.* to be borne
Acts 20. 29. shall *g.* wolves enter
Matt. 8. 6. *grievously* tormented, 15. 22.
R. V. 1 Sam. 1. 16. provocation; 2 Chron. 6. 29; Ps. 31. 10; 69. 29; Jer. 45. 3; 2 Cor. 2. 5. sorrow; Job 6, 2. vexation; Jer. 6. 7. sickness; Jonah 4. 6. evil case; 1 Sam. 15. 11. was wroth; 1 Chron. 4. 10. not to my sorrow; Prov. 26.15. wearieth; Isa. 57. 10. faint; Mark 10. 22. sorrowful; Acts 4. 2; 16. 18. sore troubled; 2 Cor. 2. 4. made sorry; 2. 5. caused sorrow; Heb. 3. 10, 17. displeased; Gen. 12. 10. sore; Ps. 10. 5. firm; 31. 18. insolently; Isa. 15. 4. trembleth within; Jer. 23. 19. whirling; Phil. 3. 1. perilous; Isa. 9. 1. hath made it glorious; Jer. 23. 19. burst; Ezek. 14. 13. committing a trespass

GRIND the faces of the poor, Isa. 3. 15.
Matt. 21. 44. it will *g.* him to powder
Eccl. 12. 3. *grinders* cease because few, 4.
R. V. Lam. 5. 13. young men bare the mill; Matt. 21. 44; Luke 20. 18. scatter

GROAN earnestly, 2 Cor. 5. 2, 4.
John 11. 33. Jesus *groaned* in spirit
Rom. 8. 22. whole creation *groaneth*
Ps. 6. 6. weary with my *groaning*
Rom. 8. 26. *g.* that cannot be uttered

GROUNDED, or *correcting* staff, Isa. 30. 32.
Eph. 3. 17. rooted and *g.* in love
Col. 1. 23. if continue in the faith *g.*
R. V. Isa. 30. 32. appointed

GROW, Gen. 48. 16. 2 Sam. 23. 5.
Ps. 92. 12. *g.* like cedar in Lebanon
Hos. 14. 5. shall *g.* as a lily
7. *g.* as the vine
Mal. 4. 2. shall *g.* up as calves of
Eph. 2. 21. *g.* unto a holy temple
1 Pet. 2. 2. sincere milk that ye may *g.*
2 Pet. 3. 18. *g.* in grace and knowl.
R. V. Lev. 13. 39. hath broken out; Job 14. 19. overflowings; 18. 18. spring; 38. 38. runneth; Isa. 11. 1. bear fruit; Hos. 14. 5, 7. blossom; Mal. 4. 2. gambol; Matt. 21. 19. no fruit from

GRUDGE, Lev. 19. 18. Jas. 5. 9.
1 Pet. 4. 9. *grudging*, 2 Cor. 9. 7.
R. V. Ps. 59. 15. tarry all night; Jas. 5. 9; 1 Pet. 4. 9. murmur

GUIDE unto death, Ps. 48. 14.
Ps. 73. 24. shall *g.* me with thy counsel
Prov. 2. 17. forsaketh the *g.* of her youth
Isa. 58. 11. Lord shall *g.* thee con.
Jer. 3. 4. my Father thou art *g.* of
Luke 1. 79. *g.* our feet into way
John 16. 13. *g.* you into all truth
1 Tim. 5. 14. bear children, *g.* house
R. V. Ps. 55. 13. companion; Prov. 2. 17. friend; 6. 7. chief; Ps. 32. 8. counsel; 112. 5. shall maintain; 1 Tim. 5. 14. rule

GUILE, Ex. 21.14. Ps. 55.11. 2 Cor. 12. 16. 1 Thes. 2. 3.
Ps. 32. 2. in whose spirit is no *g.*
34.13. keep thy lips from *g.*, 1 Pet. 3. 10.
John 1. 47. Israelite in whom there is no *g.*
22. neither was *g.* found in mouth
R. V. Rev. 14. 5. lie

GUILTY, Lev. 4. 13. & 22. 27.
Ex. 34.7. by no means clear the *g.* Num. 14. 18. Gen. 42. 21.
Rom. 3. 19. all world *g.* before
1 Cor. 11. 27. *g.* of body and blood of Lord
Jas. 2. 10. offend in one point, is *g.* of all
Ex. 20. 7. not hold him *guiltless*
R. V. Num. 5. 31. free; Matt. 23. 18. debtor; 26. 66; Mark 14. 64. worthy; Rom. 3. 19. brought under judgment of

GULF, fixed, Luke 16. 26.

H

HABITABLE part, Prov. 8. 31.

HABITATION, 2 Chron. 6. 2. & 29. 6.
Deut. 26. 15. look down from thy holy *h.*, Ps. 68. 5. Jer. 25. 30. Zech. 2. 13.
Ps. 26. 8. have loved the *h.* of thy
74. 20. earth full of *h.* of cruelty
89. 14. are *h.* of thy throne, 97. 2.
91. 9. hast made Most High thy *h.*
Prov. 3. 33. he blesseth *h.* of the just
Isa. 33. 20. see Jerusalem a quiet *h.*
Jer. 31. 23. the Lord bless thee, O *h.* of justice
Luke 16. 9. receive you into everlasting *h.*
Jude 6. angels which left their own *h.*
Rev. 18. 2. Babylon is become *h.* of
R. V. Gen. 49. 5. their swords; Ex. 15. 2. praise him; Lev. 13. 46. dwelling; 1 Chron. 4. 41. Meunim (Mehunim); Job 5. 24; Jer. 25. 30, 37. fold; 41. 17. Geruth; Ps. 89. 14; 97. 2. foundation; Jer. 9. 10; 50.19; Amos 1.2. pasture; Luke 16. 9. eternal tabernacles

HAIL, Isa. 28. 2, 17. Rev. 8. 7. & 16. 21.

HAIR, Job 4. 15. S. of S. 4. 1.
Ps. 40. 12. more than the *h.* of my head, 69. 4.
Hos. 7. 9. gray *h.* are here and there
Matt. 5. 36. make one *h.* white or
10. 30. *h.* of your head are numbered, Luke 12. 7.
1 Cor. 11. 14. if man have long *h.*
1 Pet. 3. 3. not of plaiting the *h.*

HALT, between two, 1 Kings 18. 21.
Mic. 4. 6. will I assemble her that *halteth*
Jer. 20. 10. watched for thy *halting*
R. V. Luke 14. 21. lame

HAND, Gen. 3. 22. & 16. 12.
Deut. 33. 3. all his saints are in thy *h.*
Ezra 7. 9. the good *h.* of his God is upon him
8. 22. *h.* of our God is upon them
Job 12. 6. into whose *h.* God bring.
Prov. 10. 4. *h.* of diligent maketh
11. 21. though *h.* join in *h.*, 16. 5.
Isa. 1. 12. who required this at your *h.*
Matt. 22. 13. bind him *h.* and foot
John 13. 3. given all things into his *h.*
1 Pet. 5. 6. humble yourselves under the mighty *h.* of God
Num. 11. 23. *Lord's hand* waxed
2 Sam. 24. 14. let us fall into—not man
Job 2. 10. received good at—and not evil
12. 9.—hath wrought all this, Isa. 41. 20.
Isa. 40. 2. received of the—double
59. 1.—is not shortened that cannot
Ps. 16. 8. he is at my *right hand*, I shall not
11. at thy—are pleasures for ever
18. 35. thy—hath holden me up

Ps. 73. 23. hast holden me by my—
137. 5. let my—forget her cunning
139. 10. thy *h.* lead and thy—hold
Prov. 3. 16. length of days is in her—
Eccl. 10. 2. wise man's heart is at his—
9. 1. wise and their works are in the *h.* of God
S. of S. 2. 6. his—doth embrace me, 8. 3.
Matt. 5. 30. if thy—offend thee, cut it off
6. 3. left *h.* know what thy—doeth
20. 21. one on the—and the other on the left
25. 33. sheep on his—goats on the left, 34. 41.
Mark 14. 62. sitting on—of power
16. 19. sat on—of God, Rom. 8. 34. Col. 3. 1. Heb. 1. 3. & 8. 1. & 10. 12. 1 Pet. 3. 22. Acts 2. 33. & 7. 55, 56.
Ps. 31. 5. into *thy hand* I commit
Prov. 30. 32. lay—upon thy mouth
Eccl. 9. 10. whatsoever—findeth to
Isa. 26. 11. when—is lifted up, they
Matt. 18. 8. if—or thy foot offend
Gen. 27. 22. *hands* are the *h.* of Esau
Ex. 17. 12. Moses' *h.* were heavy
Job 17. 9. hath clean *h.* shall be stronger
Ps. 24. 4. hath clean *h.* and a pure
76. 5. men of might found their *h.*
Prov. 31. 20. reacheth forth *h.* to the needy
31. give her of the fruit of her *h.*
Isa. 1. 15. spread forth your *h.* I will hide
Mic. 7. 3. do evil with both *h.* earn.
Matt. 18. 8. having two *h.* or feet
Luke 1. 74. delivered out of the *h.*
9. 44. delivered into *h.* of men
John 13. 9. but also my *h.* and head
2 Cor. 5. 1. house not made with *h.*
Eph. 4. 28. working with his *h.*
1 Tim. 2. 8. every where lifting up holy *h.*
Heb. 9. 11. tabernacle, not made with *h.*
10. 31. fearful thing to fall into the *h.* of the living God
Jas. 4. 8. cleanse your *h.* ye sinners
Col. 2. 14. *handwriting* of ordinances

HANDLE me and see, Luke 24. 39.
Col. 2. 21. touch not, taste not, *h.*
2 Cor. 4. 2. not *h.* the word of God

HANDMAID, Ps. 86. 16. & 116. 16. Prov. 30. 23. Luke 1. 38, 48.
R. V. 1 Sam. 1. 18; 25. 27; 2 Sam. 14. 15. servant

HANG, Ps. 137. 2. Josh. 8. 29.
Deut. 21. 33. *h.* is accursed of God, Gal. 3. 13.
Job 26. 7. he *h.* the earth on nothing
Matt. 18. 6. millstone *h.* about neck
22. 40. on these *h.* all the law and
Heb. 12. 12. hands which *h.* down

HAPPEN, Jer. 44. 23. Rom. 11. 25.
Prov. 12. 21. no evil shall *h.* to just, 1 Pet. 4. 12.
Eccl. 2. 14. one event *h.* to them all
8. 14. *h.* according to work of
1 Cor. 10. 11. these *h.* for ensamples
R. V. Rom. 11. 25. hath befallen

HAPPY am I, for the daughters, Gen. 30. 13.
Deut. 33. 29. *h.* art thou, O Israel
1 Kings 10. 8. *h.* are thy men, *h.* these
Job 5. 17. *h.* is the man whom God correcteth
Ps. 127. 5. *h.* is the man who hath his quiver full
137. 8. *h.* that rewards thee, 9.
144. 15. *h.* that people whose God is the Lord
Jer. 12. 1. why are they *h.* that deal treacherously
Prov. 3. 13. *h.* is the man that findeth wisdom, 18.
14. 21. he that hath mercy on poor, *h.* is
Prov. 16. 20. whoso trusteth in the Lord *h.* is he
29. 18. he that keepeth the law, *h.* is he
Mal. 3. 15. we call the proud *h.* that
John 13. 17. *h.* are ye, if ye do them
Rom. 14. 22. *h.* he that conde. not
Jas. 5. 11. count them *h.* which endure
1 Pet. 3. 14. suffer for righteousness' sake, *h.* are ye
1 Cor. 7. 40. *happier* if she so abide
R. V. Jer. 12. 1. at ease; John 13. 17; Jas. 5. 11; 1 Pet. 3. 14; 4. 14. blessed

HARD, Gen. 35. 16, 17. Ex. 1. 14. & 18. 26. 2 Sam. 13. 2. Ps. 88. 7.
Gen. 18. 14. is any thing too *h.* for the Lord
2 Sam. 3. 39. sons of Zeruiah be too *h.* for me
2 Kings 2. 10. thou askest a *h.* thing
Ps. 60. 3. hast showed thy people *h.* things
Prov. 13. 15. the way of transgressors is *h.*
Matt. 25. 24. that thou art a *h.* man
Mark 10. 24. how *h.* is it for them
John 6. 60. this is a *h.* saying; who
Acts 9. 5. *h.* for thee to kick, 26. 14.
Jude 15. of all their *h.* speeches
R. V. Job 41. 24. firm; Ps. 94. 4. arrogantly; Prov. 13. 15. rugged; Acts 9. 5——

HARDEN, Ex. 4. 21. Deut. 15. 7. Josh. 11. 20. Job 6. 10. & 39. 16.
Heb. 3. 8. *h.* not your hearts as in the provocation, 15. & 4. 7. Ps. 95. 8.
Prov. 21. 29. *h.* his face
28. 14. *h.* his heart
29. 1. *h.* his neck shall be destroyed
Job 9. 4. hath *hardened* himself against
Isa. 63. 17. *h.* our heart from thy fear
Mark 6. 52. their heart was *h.*, 3. 5.
Rom. 9. 18. whom he will, he *hardeneth*
Prov. 18. 19. a brother offended is *harder*
Jer. 5. 3. made faces *h.* than a rock
Ezek. 3. 9. *h.* than a flint thy fore.
Matt. 19. 8. because of *hardness* of your hearts
Mark 3. 5. grieved for the *h.* of their
2 Tim. 2. 3. endure *h.* as a good soldier
R. V. Job 6. 10. exult; Ex. 7. 14; 9. 7. stubborn; Jer. 7. 26; 19. 15. made stiff

HARLOT, Gen. 34. 31. Josh. 2. 1. Judg. 11. 1. Prov. 7. 10. Isa. 1. 21. & 23. 15.
Jer. 2. 20. play the *h.*, 3. 1, 6, 8. Ezek. 16. 15, 16, 41. Hos. 2. 5. & 4. 15.
Matt. 21. 31. *h.* go into the kingdom
1 Cor. 6. 16. joined to *h.* is one body
Jas. 2. 25. was not Rahab the *h.* justified
Rev. 17. 5. mother of *h.* and abominations

HARM, Gen. 31. 52. Acts 28. 5.
1 Chron. 16. 22. do my prophets no *h.*, Ps. 105. 15. Prov. 3. 30. Jer. 39. 12.
1 Pet. 3. 13. who is he that will *h.*
Matt. 10. 16. *harmless*, Phil. 2. 15.
Heb. 7. 26. holy, *h.* undefiled
R. V. Acts 27. 21. injury; 28. 6. nothing amiss; Heb. 7. 26. guileless

HARVEST, Gen. 8. 22. & 30. 14.
Ex. 34. 21. in *h.* thou shalt rest
Isa. 9. 3. joy before thee according to joy of *h.*
Jer. 5. 24. reserved appointed weeks of *h.*
8. 20. the *h.* is past, the summer
51. 33. time of *h.* shall come, Joel 3. 13.
Matt. 9. 37. *h.* plenteous
38. pray ye the Lord of the *h.*
Rev. 14. 15. *h.* of earth is ripe, Joel 3. 13.

HASTE, Ex. 12. 11, 33. Isa. 52. 12.
Ps. 31. 22. I said in my *h.*, 116. 11.
Ps. 38. 22. make *h.* help me, 40. 13. & 70. 1, 5. & 71. 12. & 141. 1.
119. 60. I made *h.* and delayed not
S. of S. 8. 14. make *h.* my beloved
Isa. 28. 16. believ. shall not make *h.*
49. 17. thy children shall make *h.*
Ps. 16. 4. *hasten* after another god
Isa. 5. 19. let him *h.* his work that
60. 22. I the Lord will *h.* it in his time
Jer. 1. 12. I will *h.* my word to
Prov. 14. 29. *hasty* of spirit, Eccl. 7. 9.
20. 21. inheritance gotten *hastily*
R. V. Job 9. 26. swoopeth; 40. 23. trembleth; John 11. 31. quickly; Isa. 28. 4. first ripe; Dan. 2. 15. urgent

HATE, Gen. 24. 60. Deut. 21. 15.
Lev. 19. 17. shall not *h.* thy brother
Deut. 7. 10. repayeth them that *h.*
1 Kings 22. 8. I *h.* him for he doth not
Ps. 68. 1. let them that *h.* him flee
97. 10. ye that love Lord, *h.* evil
139. 21. do not I *h.* them that *h.*
Prov. 8. 13. fear of Lord is to *h.* evil
36. all they that *h.* me love death
Jer. 44. 4. abominable thing that I *h.*
Amos 5. 10. they *h.* him that rebuketh
15. *h.* the evil, and love the good
Mic. 3. 2. who *h.* the good and love
Luke 14. 26. and *h.* not his father
John 7. 7. world cannot *h.* you, but
15. 18. if the world *h.* you it hated
Rom. 7. 15. what I *h.* that do I
1 John 3. 13. marvel not if world *h.*
Rev. 2. 6. hatest the deeds, which I also *h.*, 15.
17. 16. these shall *h.* the whore
Prov. 1. 29. for that they *hated* knowledge
5. 12. and say how have I *h.* instruction
Isa. 66. 5. your brother that *h.* you
Mal. 1. 3. I *h.* Esau, Rom. 9. 13.
Matt. 10. 22. shall be *h.* of all men, Mark 13. 13. Luke 21. 17.
Luke 19. 14. his citizens *h.* him
John 15. 24. *h.* me and my father, 18.
Eph. 5. 29. no man ever *h.* his own
Rom. 1. 30. backbiters, *haters* of God
2 Sam. 19. 6. *hatest* friends and lovest thine enemies
Ps. 5. 5. *h.* all workers of iniquity
Ex. 23. 5. ask of him that *hateth* thee
Prov. 13. 24. spareth rod, *h.* his son
John 12. 25. *h.* his life in this world
Ex. 18. 21. men of truth *hating* covetousness
Tit. 3. 3. *hateful* and *h.* one another
Jude 23. *h.* garment spotted by flesh
R. V. Gen. 49. 23; Ps. 55. 3. persecute; Matt. 5. 44——

HAUGHTY, my heart is not, Ps. 131. 1.
Prov. 16. 18. *h.* spirit before fall, 18. 12.
21. 24. proud and *h.* scorner dealeth
Zeph. 3. 11. no more be *h.* because
Isa. 2. 11. *haughtiness*, 17. & 13. 11. & 16. 6.
R. V. Isa. 16. 6. arrogancy; Isa. 10. 33; 24. 4. lofty

HEAD, Gen. 2. 10. & 40. 13.
Gen. 3. 15. it shall bruise thy *h.*
49. 26. blessings on *h.* of him
Ezra 9. 6. iniquity increased over our *h.*
Prov. 16. 31. hoary *h.* is a crown of
20. 29. beauty of old men is gray *h.*
Eccl. 2. 14. wise men's eyes are in *h.*
Ps. 38. 4. iniquity gone over my *h.*
S. of S. 5. 2. my *h.* is filled with
Isa. 1. 5. whole *h.* is sick and heart
6. from sole of foot even unto *h.*
Jer. 9. 1. O that my *h.* were waters
Ezek. 9. 10. their way on *h.*, 16. 4.
Dan. 2. 28. visions of thy *h.* on

Zech. 4. 7. bring forth *h.* stone thereof
Matt. 8. 20. not where to lay his *h.*
14. 8. give me *h.* of John Baptist
Rom. 12. 20. coals of fire on his *h.*, Prov. 25. 22.
1 Cor. 11. 3. *h.* of man is Christ, *h.* of woman is man, *h.* of Christ is God
Eph. 1. 22. gave him to be *h.* over
Col. 1. 18. he is *h.* of the body, 2. 19.
Rev. 19. 12. on his *h.* many crowns
Ps. 24. 7. lift up your *heads*, O ye gates, 9.
Isa. 35. 10. everlasting joy on their *h.*, 51. 11.
Luke 21. 28. lift up your *h.* for a
Rev. 13. 1. seven *h.* and ten horns
Job 5. 13. *headlong*, Luke 4. 29. Acts 1. 18.
2 Tim. 3. 4. *heady*, high-minded

HEAL her now, O God, Num. 12. 13.
Deut. 32. 39. I wound, I *h.* and I
2 Chron. 7. 14. I will *h.* their land
Ps. 6. 2. *h.* me, for my bones are
60. 2. *h.* breaches for land shaketh
Isa. 57. 18. I have seen his way and will *h.* him
Jer. 3. 22. I will *h.* your backsliding, Hos. 14. 4.
17. 14. *h.* me, and I shall be *h.*
Hos. 6. 1. hath torn and he will *h.*
Luke 4. 18. *h.* the broken-hearted
John 12. 40. convert. and I should *h.*
2 Chron. 30. 20. Lord *healed* the
Ps. 30. 2. I cried and thou hast *h.*
Isa. 6. 10. convert and be *h.*, Acts 28. 27.
53. 5. with his stripes we are *h.*, 1 Pet. 2. 24.
Jer. 6. 14. *h.* the hurt of the daughter of, 8. 11.
Hos. 7. 1. when I would have *h.* Israel
Matt. 4. 24. he *h.* them all, 12. 15. & 14. 14.
Heb. 12. 13. let it rather be *h.*
Jas. 5. 16. pray that ye may be *h.*
Rev. 13. 3. his deadly wound was *h.*
Ex. 15. 26. I am the Lord that *healeth* thee
Ps. 103. 3. who *h.* all thy diseases
147. 3. he *h.* the broken in heart
Isa. 30. 26. Lord *h.* stroke of their
Jer. 14. 19. looked for time of *healing*
30. 13. thou hast no *h.* medicine
Mal. 4. 2. with *h.* in his wings
Matt. 4. 23. *h.* all manner of sick.
1 Cor. 12. 9. to another the gifts of *h.*
Rev. 22. 2. leaves were for *h.* nations
Ps. 42. 11. *health* of my countenance, 43. 5.
Prov. 3. 8. shall be *h.* to thy navel
Jer. 8. 15. looked for a time of *h.*
30. 17. I will restore *h.* and heal
R. V. Mark 5. 23; Luke 8. 36; Acts 14. 9. made whole; 28. 9. cured; Nah. 3. 19. assuaging; 2 Sam. 20. 9. is it well with thee

HEAP coals, Prov. 25. 22. Rom. 12. 20.
Deut. 32. 23. I will *h.* mischiefs
Job 36. 13. hypocrites in heart *h.*
2 Tim. 4. 3. *h.* to themselves teach.
Ps. 39. 6. he *heapeth* up riches, and
Jas. 5. 3. ye have *heaped* treasures
Judg. 15. 16. *heaps* upon *h.* with the
R. V. Isa. 17. 11. fleeth away; Jer. 31. 21. guide posts

HEAR, Gen. 21. 6. & 23. 6.
Deut. 30. 17. if heart turn away, so that thou wilt not *h.*
1 Kings 8. 30. *h.* thou in heaven thy dwelling place
2 Kings 19. 16. bow down thine ear, and *h.*
2 Chron. 6. 21. *h.* from thy dwelling
Job 5. 27. *h.* it and know it for
Ps. 4. 1. *h.* my prayer, 39. 12. & 54. 2. & 51. 8. & 84. 8. & 102. 1. & 143. 1. Dan. 9. 17, 19.
Ps. 4. 3. Lord will *h.*, 17. 6. & 145. 19. Zech. 10. 6.
51. 8. make me to *h.* joy and
59. 7. who, say they, doth *h.*, 10.
66. 16. come and *h.* all ye that
115. 6. they have ears, but *h.* not
Prov. 19. 27. cease to *h.* instruction
Eccl. 5. 1. be more ready to *h.* than
S. of S. 2. 14. let me *h.* thy voice, 8. 13.
Isa. 1. 2. *h.* O heavens, and give
6. 10. lest they *h.* with ears, Deut. 29. 4.
Matt. 10. 27. what ye *h.* in the ear
13. 17. to *h.* those things ye *h.*
17. 5. this is my beloved Son, *h.* ye
Mark 4. 24. take heed what ye *h.*
33. spake the word as they were able to *h.* it
Luke 8. 18. take heed how ye *h.*
16. 29. Moses and the prophets, let them *h.* them
John 5. 25. they that *h.* shall live
Acts 10. 33. to *h.* all things that
Jas. 1. 19. every man be swift to *h.*
Rev. 2. 7. let him *h.* what the Spirit saith to the churches, 3. 6, 13, 22. & 11. 17, 29.
3. 20. if any *h.* my voice, and open
Ex. 2. 24. God *heard* their groaning
Ps. 6. 9. Lord hath *h.* my supplica.
10. 17. hast *h.* desire of humble, 34. 6.
34. 4. I sought the Lord, and he *h.*
61. 5. thou hast *h.* my vows, 116. 1.
120. 1. I cried to Lord and he *h.*
Isa. 40. 28. hast thou not *h.* that God
64. 4. from beginning men have not *h.*
Jer. 8. 6. I hearkened and *h.* but
Jonah 2. 2. I cried to Lord and he *h.*
Mal. 3. 16. Lord hearkened and *h.*
Matt. 6. 7. be *h.* for much speaking
Luke 1. 13. thy prayer is *h.* and thy
John 3. 32. what he hath seen and *h.*
Rom. 10. 14. of whom they have not *h.*
1 Cor. 2. 9. eye hath not seen nor ear *h.*
Phil. 4. 9. what *h.* and seen in me
Heb. 4. 2. with faith in them that *h.*
Jas. 5. 11. ye have *h.* of patience of Job
Ex. 3. 7. *I have heard* their cry
6. 5. — the groaning, Acts 7. 34.
16. 12. — the murmurings, Num. 14. 27.
1 Kings 9. 3. — thy prayer and supplication, 2 Kings 19. 20. & 20. 5. & 22. 19.
Job 42. 5. — of thee by the hearing
Isa. 49. 8. in an acceptable time —
Ps. 65. 2. thou that *hearest* prayer
John 11. 42. I knew thou *h.* me
1 Sam. 3. 9. speak, Lord, thy servant *heareth*
Prov. 8. 34. blessed is man that *h.*
Matt. 7. 24. whoso *h.* these sayings
Luke 10. 16. he that *h.* you *h.* me
John 9. 31. God *h.* not sinners, but
Rev. 22. 17. let him that *h.* say come
Rom. 2. 13. not *hearers* but doers
Eph. 4. 29. minister grace to the *h.*
Jas. 1. 22. be doers of the word and not *h.*
Job 42. 5. of thee by *hearing* of ear
Prov. 20. 12. the *h.* ear, and seeing
28. 9. turneth away his ear from *h.*
Matt. 13. 14. *h.* they hear not, Acts 28. 27.
Rom. 10. 17. faith cometh by *h.* and *h.* by
Heb. 5. 11. seeing ye are dull of *h.*
2 Pet. 2. 8. in seeing and *h.* vexed his
R. V. The O. T. changes, which are numerous, are chiefly to *answer*

HEARKEN unto the voice of, Deut. 28. 15.
Deut. 28. 1. if thou *h.* diligently, 30. 10.
1 Sam. 15. 22. to *h.* better than the fat of rams
Ps. 103. 20. angels *h.* to voice of
Isa. 46. 12. *h.* unto me, ye stout

HEART, Ex. 28. 30. & 35. 5.
1 Sam. 1. 13. she spake in her *h.* only
16. 7. but Lord looketh on *h.*
24. 5. David's *h.* smote him after
1 Chron. 16. 10. let the *h.* of them rejoice that seek the Lord, Ps. 105. 3.
22. 19. set your *h.* to seek the Lord your God
2 Chron. 17. 6. his *h.* was lifted up
30. 19. prepareth his *h.* to seek God
Ps. 22. 26. your *h.* shall live for ever, 69. 32.
37. 31. law of his God is in his *h.*
51. 17. a broken and a contrite *h.*, Isa. 66. 2.
64. 6. inward thought, and *h.* is
Prov. 4. 23. keep thy *h.* with dili.
10. 20. *h.* of wicked is little worth
16. 9. a man's *h.* deviseth his way
27. 19. *h.* of man answereth to man
Eccl. 7. 4. *h.* of wise is in house
10. 2. wise man's *h.* is at his right hand, but a fool's *h.* is at his left
S. of S. 3. 11. in the day of gladness of his *h.*
Isa. 6. 10. make *h.* of this people fat
Jer. 11. 20. triest the reins and the *h.*, 17. 10.
12. 11. no man layeth it to *h.*, Isa. 42. 25.
17. 9. *h.* is deceitful above all
24. 7. I will give them a *h.* to know
32. 39. I will give them one *h.*, Ezra 11. 19.
Lam. 3. 41. lift up our *h.* with our
Ezek. 11. 19. take stony *h.* give *h.* of flesh
36. 26. new *h.* take stony *h.* give *h.*
Joel 2. 13. rend your *h.* not your
Mal. 4. 6. turn *h.* of fathers to
Matt. 6. 21. there will your *h.* be
12. 34. out of abundance of the *h.* the mouth speaketh
Luke 2. 19. pondered them in her *h.*, 51.
24. 25. O fools, and slow of *h.* to
32. did not our *h.* burn within us
John 14. 1. let not your *h.* be troubled, 27.
Acts 5. 33. were cut to the *h.*, 7. 54.
11. 23. with purpose of *h.* cleave to the Lord
13. 22. found man after mine own *h.*
Rom. 10. 10. with *h.* man believeth
1 Cor. 2. 9. nor entered into *h.* of man
2 Cor. 3. 3. in fleshly tables of the *h.*
1 Pet. 3. 4. in the hidden man of the *h.*
1 John 3. 20. if *h.* condemn us, God
Deut. 11. 13. serve him *with all heart*, Josh. 22. 5. 1 Sam. 12. 20.
13. 3. love Lord your God —, 30. 6. Matt. 22. 37. Mark 12. 30, 33. Luke 10. 27.
Deut. 26. 16. keep and do them —
30. 2. turn to the Lord — and soul, 10. 2 Kings 23. 25. Joel 2. 12.
1 Kings 2. 4. walk before me in truth —
8. 23, 48. return to thee —, 2 Chron. 6. 38.
2 Chron. 15. 12. seek the God of their fathers —
15. sworn —
Prov. 3. 5. trust in Lord — and be
Jer. 29. 13. search for me —
Zeph. 3. 14. sing, be glad, rejoice —
Acts 8. 37. if thou believest —
Ps. 86. 12. I will praise thee *with all my heart*
45. 1. *my heart* is inditing a
57. 7. — is fixed, O God, — is fixed
61. 2. what time — is overwhelmed
84. 2. my flesh and — crieth for

Ps. 109. 22. — is wounded within me
131. 1. Lord — is not haughty
S. of S. 5. 2. I sleep, but — waketh
Hos. 11. 8. — is turned within me
1 Kings 8. 61. *heart perfect* with the Lord, 11. 4. & 15. 3, 14. 2 Chron. 15. 17.
2 Kings 20. 3. and with —, 2 Chron. 19. 9.
1 Chron. 28. 9. serve him with —, 29. 9.
2 Chron. 16. 9. in behalf of them whose —
Ps. 101. 2. I will walk within my house with a —
24. 4. clean hands and *pure heart*
Matt. 5. 8. blessed are the pure in *h.*
1 Tim. 1. 5. charity out of a —
2 Tim. 2. 22. call on Lord out of —
1 Pet. 1. 22. love with — fervently
Ps. 9. 1. praise him *with my whole heart*
119. 2. seek him —
Jer. 3. 10. not turned with her whole *h.*
Col. 3. 23. do it *heartily* as to Lord
R. V. 2 Sam. 3. 21; Ezek. 25. 15; 27. 31; Lam. 3. 51. soul; Job 38. 36; Jer. 7. 31. mind

HEATH, Jer. 17. 16. & 48. 6.

HEATHEN, Lev. 25. 44. & 26. 45.
Ps. 2. 1. why do the *h.* rage
2. 8. give them the *h.* for
Matt. 18. 17. let him be as a *h.* man
Gal. 3. 8. justify the *h.* through faith

HEAVEN of *h.* cannot contain, 1 Kings 8. 27. 2 Chron. 2. 6. & 6. 18.
Ps. 103. 11. as *h.* is high above the
Prov. 25. 3. *h.* for height, and earth
Isa. 66. 1. *h.* is my throne, Acts 7. 49.
Jer. 31. 37. if *h.* above can be
Hag. 1. 10. *h.* over you is stayed
Matt. 5. 18. till *h.* and earth pass
Luke 15. 18. sinned against *h.*, 21.
John 1. 51. see *h.* open and angels
Ps. 73. 25. whom have I *in heaven*
Eccl. 5. 2. God is — and thou upon
Heb. 10. 34. have — a better sub.
1 Pet. 1. 4. inheritance reserved — for you
Ps. 8. 3. consider *the heavens*, the
19. 1. — declare the glory of God
89. 11. — are thine, and earth also
Isa. 65. 17. I create new *h.* and
Acts 3. 21. *h.* must receive him till
2 Cor. 5. 1. house eternal in the *h.*
Eph. 4. 10. ascend far above all *h.*
Matt. 6. 14. *heavenly* Father, 26. 32. & 15. 13. & 18. 35. Luke 11. 13.
John 3. 12. if I tell you of *h.* things
1 Cor. 15. 48. as is *h.* such are the *h.*
Eph. 1. 3. in *h.* places, 20. & 2. 6.
2 Tim. 4. 18. unto his *h.* kingdom
Heb. 3. 1. partak. of the *h.* calling
R.V. Mark 11. 26; Luke 11. 2; Heb. 10. 34; 1 John 5. 7; Rev. 16. 17 ——

HEAVE OFFERING, Ex. 29. 27. Num. 15. 19. & 18. 8, 28, 29.

HEAVY, Num. 11. 14. Job 33. 7.
Ps. 38. 4. as a *h.* burden too *h.* for
Prov. 31. 6. wine to those of *h.* hearts
Isa. 6. 10. make their ears *h.* lest
58. 6. to undo the *h.* burden
Matt. 11. 28. labor and are *h.* laden
23. 4. bind *h.* burdens and griev.
Ps. 69. 20. I am full of *heaviness*
119. 28. my soul melteth for *h.*
Prov. 12. 25. *h.* in the heart
14. 13. the end of that mirth is *h.*
Rom. 9. 2. I have great *h.* and
1 Pet. 1. 6. in *h.* through
R. V. Ezra 9. 5. humiliation; Job 9. 27. sad countenance; Isa. 29. 2. mourning; 2 Cor. 2. 1. with sorrow; Phil. 2. 26. sore troubled; 1 Pet. 1. 6. have been put to grief; Prov. 31. 6. bitter; Isa. 30. 27. rising smoke; 46. 1. made a load; 58. 6. bands of the yoke; Matt. 26. 37; Mark 14. 33. troubled

HEDGE, Job 1. 10. Prov. 15. 19. Isa. 5. 5. Hos. 2. 6. Job 3. 23. Lam. 3. 7.
R. V. 1 Chron. 4. 23. Gederah; Ps. 80. 12; Eccl. 10. 8; Jer. 49. 3. fences; Lam. 3. 7. fenced; Matt. 21. 33. set a hedge about

HEED, 2 Sam. 20. 10. 2 Kings 10. 31.
Deut. 2. 4. take good *h.* to yoursel.
Josh. 22. 5. take diligent *h.* to do
Ps. 119. 9. by taking *h.* thereto
Eccl. 12. 9. he gave good *h.* sought
Jer. 18. 18. not give *h.* to any of his
R. V. Deut. 27. 9. silence; 2 Chron. 19. 6. consider; 33. 8. observe; Eccl. 12. 9. pondered; Matt. 18. 10. see; Luke 11. 35. look; Acts 8. 11. regard; 22. 26; Rom. 11. 21 ——

HEEL, his, thou shalt bruise
Ps. 41. 9. lifted up his *h.* against
Hos. 12. 3. he took his brother by *h.*

HEIFER, Num. 19. 2. Jer. 46. 20. & 48. 34. Hos. 4. 16. & 10. 11. Heb. 9. 13.

HEIR, Gen. 15. 4. & 21. 10.
Prov. 30. 23. handmaid *h.* to her
Jer. 49. 1. hath Israel no sons, hath he no *h.*
Matt. 21. 38. this is the *h.* let us
Rom. 4. 13. Abraham should be *h.*
8. 17. if children, *h.* of God, joint *h.* with Christ
Gal. 3. 29. children *h.* according
4. 7. if a son, then an *h.* of God
Eph. 3. 6. Gentiles should be fellow *h.*
Heb. 1. 2. God hath appointed *h.* of
6. 17. might show to *h.* of promise
21. 7. became *h.* of righteousness
1 Pet. 3. 7. *h.* together of grace of
R. V. Jer. 49. 2; Mic. 1. 15. possess; Gal. 4. 30. inherit

HELD, Ps. 94. 18. S. of S. 3. 4.

HELL, Matt. 18. 9. Mark 9. 43, 45.
Deut. 32. 22. shall burn to lowest *h.*
2 Sam. 22. 6. the sorrows of *h.*
Job 11. 8. it is deeper than *h.*
26. 6. *h.* is naked before him and
Ps. 9. 17. wicked be turned into *h.*
16. 10. not leave my soul in *h.*
116. 3. pains of *h.* gat hold on me
139. 8. make my bed in *h.* thou art
Prov. 5. 5. her steps take hold of *h.*
7. 27. her house is the way to *h.*
9. 18. her guests are in depths of *h.*
15. 11. *h.* and destruction are
24. that he may depart from *h.*
23. 14. shalt deliver his soul from *h.*
27. 20. *h.* and destruction are
Isa. 5. 14. *h.* hath enlarged herself
14. 9. *h.* from beneath is moved to
28. 15. with *h.* are we at agree.
57. 9. debase thyself even to *h.*, Ezek. 31. 16, 17. & 32. 21, 27.
Amos 9. 2. though they dig into *h.*
Jonah 2. 2. out of belly of *h.* cried I
Hab. 2. 5. enlarged his desire as *h.*
Matt. 5. 22. be in danger of *h.* fire
29. body be cast into *h.*, 30. & 18. 9. Mark 9. 43, 45, 47.
10. 28. destroy both soul and body in *h.*
11. 23. brought down to *h.*, Luke 10. 15.
16. 18. the gates of *h.* shall not
23. 15. twofold more the child of *h.*
Luke 12. 5. power to cast into *h.*
16. 23. in *h.* he lifted up his eyes
Acts 2. 31. his soul not left in *h.*, 27.
Jas. 3. 6. tongue set on fire of *h.*
2 Pet. 2. 4. cast them down to *h.*
Rev. 1. 18. having keys of *h.* and
6. 8. death and *h.* followed with
20. 13. death and *h.* delivered up
14. death and *h.* were cast into
R. V. 2 Sam. 22. 6; Job 11. 8; 26. 6; Ps. 16. 10; 18. 5; 116. 3; 139. 8; Prov. 5. 5; 7. 27; 9. 18; 15. 11, 24; 23. 14; 27. 30. Sheol; Matt. 11. 23; 16. 18; Luke 10. 15; 16. 23; Acts 2. 27, 31; Rev. 1. 18; 6. 8; 20. 13, 14. Hades; Matt. 5. 22; 18. 9. hell of fire

HELMET, 1 Sam. 17. 5. 2 Chron. 26. 14.
Isa. 59. 17. a *h.* of salvation on head
Eph. 6. 17. take the *h.* of salvation
1 Thes. 5. 8. for a *h.* the hope of sal.

HELP meet for him, Gen. 2. 18.
Deut. 33. 29. Lord shield of thy *h.*
Judg. 5. 23. came not to the *h.* of
Ps. 27. 9. thou hast been my *h.*
33. 20. he is our *h.* and shield
40. 17. my *h.* and deliverer, 70. 5.
46. 1. God is a very present *h.* in trouble
60. 11. vain is *h.* of man, 108. 12.
71. 12. O my God, make haste for my *h.*
89. 19. laid *h.* upon one that is
115. 9. Lord is their *h.* and shield, 10. 11.
124. 8. our *h.* is in name of Lord
Hos. 13. 9. but in me is thy *h.*
Acts 26. 22. having obtained *h.* of God
1 Cor. 12. 28. *helps*, governments
2 Chron. 14. 11. nothing with thee to *h.*
Ps. 40. 13. make haste to *h.* me, 70. 1.
Isa. 41. 10. I will *h.* thee
63. 5. there was none to *h.*
Acts 16. 9. come unto Macedonia, and *h.* us
Heb. 4. 16. find grace to *h.* in time
1 Sam. 7. 12. hitherto hath the Lord *helped* us
Ps. 118. 13. I might fall; but Lord *h.* me
Isa. 49. 8. in day of salvation I *h.*
Zech. 1. 15. they *h.* forward afflicted
Acts 18. 27. *h.* them much who had
Rev. 12. 16. the earth *h.* the woman
Rom. 8. 26. Spirit *helpeth* our infirmities
Ps. 10. 14. thou art the *helper*
54. 4. God is my *h.*, Heb. 13. 6.
Job 9. 13. proud *helpers* do stoop
2 Cor. 1. 24. we are *h.* of your joy
3 John 8. fellow *h.* to the truth
R. V. 1 Sam. 11. 9. deliverance; 1 Chron. 18. 5. succor; 2 Chron. 20. 9. save; Job 8. 20. uphold; Ps. 116. 6. saved; Eccl. 4. 10. lift

HEM, Matt. 9. 20. & 14. 36.
R. V. Ex. 28. 33, 34; 39. 24, 25, 26. skirts; Matt. 9. 20; 14. 36. border

HEN, Matt. 23. 37. Luke 13. 34.

HERESY, Acts 24. 14. 1 Cor. 11. 19. Gal. 5. 20. 2 Pet. 2. 1.
Tit. 3. 10. a man that is a *heretic*
R. V. Acts 24. 14. a sect

HERITAGE appointed by God, Job 20. 29.
Ps. 16. 5. I have a goodly *h.*
61. 5. given me the *h.* of those
127. 3. lo, children are a *h.* of Lord
Isa. 54. 17. this is *h.* of servants
Jer. 3. 19. goodly *h.* of the host
Joel 2. 17. give not thy *h.* to rep.
1 Pet. 5. 3. not as lords over God's *h.*
R. V. 1 Pet. 5. 3. charge allotted

HEW tables of stone, Ex. 34. 1. Deut. 12. 3.
Jer. 2. 13. *hewed* them out cisterns
Hos. 6. 5. therefore have I *h.* them
Matt. 3. 10. *hewn* down, 7. 19.
R. V. 1 Kings 5. 18. fashion; 1 Sam. 11. 7. cut

HID themselves, Adam and wife, Gen. 3. 8.
Ps. 119. 11. word have I *h.* in heart
Zeph. 2. 3. it may be, ye shall be *h.*
Matt. 10. 26. nor *h.* that shall not be
11. 25. *h.* these things from wise
2 Cor. 4. 3. if Gospel be *h.* it is *h.*

Col. 2. 3. in whom are *h.* all treas.
3. 3. your life is *h.* with Christ
Ps. 83. 3. and consulted against thy *hidden* ones
1 Cor. 4. 5. bring to light *h.* things of
1 Pet. 3. 4. the *h.* man of heart
Rev. 2. 17. give to eat the *h.* manna
Gen. 18. 17. shall I *hide* from Abra.
Job 33. 17. may *h.* pride from man
Ps. 17. 8. *h.* me under the shadow
27. 5. in time of trouble he shall *h.*
30. 7. didst *h.* thy face and I
31. 20. shalt *h.* them in secret
Ps. 51. 9. *h.* thy face from my sin
143. 9. I flee to thee to *h.* me, 7.
Isa. 26. 20. *h.* thyself for a moment
Jas. 5. 20. *h.* a multitude of sins
Rev. 6. 16. *h.* us from the face of
Job 13. 24. why *hidest* thou thy face, Ps. 30. 7. & 44. 24. & 88. 14. & 143. 7.
Isa. 45. 15. thou art a God that *h.*
Job 34. 29. when he *hideth* his face
42. 3. who is he that *h.* counsel
Ps. 139. 12. darkness *h.* not from
Isa. 8. 17. I will wait on Lord that *h.*
Hab. 3. 4. *hiding* of his power
Ps. 32. 7. *h.* place, 119. 114.
R. V. Deut. 30. 11. too hard for; Job 15. 20; 20. 26; 24. 1; Prov. 2. 1. laid up; Prov. 19. 24; 26. 15. burieth; 27. 16. restraineth; Jer. 16. 17; Luke 9. 45. concealed; Luke 8. 17. secret; 2 Cor. 4. 3, 13. is veiled; Jas. 5. 20. cover

HID TREASURE, parable, Matt. 13. 44.

HIGH, Deut. 3. 5, 12. & 28. 43.
Deut. 26. 19. make thee *h.* above all
1 Kings 9. 8. house which is *h.*
1 Chron. 17. 17. man of *h.* degree
Job 11. 8. as *h.* as heaven, what
Ps. 49. 2. both low and *h.* rich and
89. 13. strong arm, and *h.* is right
97. 9. thou Lord art *h.* above all
103. 11. as heaven is *h.* above earth
131. 1. not in things too *h.* for me
Prov. 21. 4. a *h.* look and proud
Eccl. 12. 5. afraid of that which is *h.*
Isa. 57. 15. I dwell in the *h.* and
Ezek. 21. 26. abase him that is *h.*
Rom. 12. 16. mind not *h.* things
2 Cor. 10. 5. every *h.* thing that
Phil. 3. 14. for the prize of the *h.* calling of God
Num. 24. 16. *Most High*, Deut. 32. 8. 2 Sam. 22. 14. Ps. 7. 17. & 9. 2. & 21. 7. & 46. 4. & 50. 14. & 56. 2.
Ps. 47. 2. the Lord — is terrible
83. 18. Jehovah art — over all earth
92. 8. thou art — for evermore
Isa. 14. 14. I will ascend and be like the —
Acts 7. 48. — dwelleth not in temples
Job 5. 11. set up *on high* those that
Ps. 107. 41. setteth the poor from
113. 5. like our God who dwelleth —
Isa. 26. 5. bring down those that dwell —
Luke 24. 49. be endued with power from —
Eccl. 5. 8. there be *higher* than they
Isa. 55. 9. heaven *h.* than earth
Heb. 7. 26. made *h.* than the heavens
Ps. 18. 13. *Highest* gave his voice
87. 5. *H.* himself shall establish
Eccl. 5. 8. he that is higher than *h.*
Luke 1. 35. power of the *H.* shall
2. 14. glory to God in the *h.*, 19. 38.
6. 35. children of the *H.*
14. 8. sit not down in the *h.* room
1. 28. thou that art *highly* favored
16. 15. which is *h.* esteemed
Rom. 12. 3. not think of himself more *h.*
1 Thes. 5. 13. esteem them very *h.*
2 Tim. 3. 4. heady, *high-minded*
Rom. 11. 20. be not — but fear
1 Tim. 6. 17. rich, that they be not —
Job 22. 12. *height*, Rom. 8. 39. Eph. 3. 18.
R. V. 2 Tim. 3. 4. puffed up

HILL, Ex. 24. 4. Ps. 68. 15, 16.
Ps. 2. 6. set my King on holy *h.* of Zion, 3. 4. & 15. 1. & 43. 3. & 68. 15. & 99. 9.
Gen. 7. 19. all high *h.* under heaven
Num. 23. 9. from the *h.* I behold
Ps. 65. 12. little *h.* rejoice on every
68. 16. why leap ye, high *h.*
98. 8. let *h.* be joyful together
Hos. 10. 8. to the *h.* fall on us, Luke 23. 30.
Hab. 3. 6. the perpetual *h.* did bow
R. V. Ex. 24. 4; 1 Kings 11. 7. mount; Gen. 7. 19; Num. 14. 44, 45; Deut. 1. 41, 43; Josh. 15. 9; 18. 13, 14; 24. 30; Judg. 2. 9; 16. 3; 1 Sam. 25. 20; 26. 13; 2 Sam. 21. 9; 1 Kings 22. 17; Ps. 18. 7; 68. 15, 16; 80. 10; 95. 4; 97. 5; 104. 10, 13, 18, 32; 121. 1; Luke 9. 37. mountain, or mountains; Deut. 1. 7; Josh. 9. 1; 11. 16; 17. 6. hill country; 1 Sam. 9. 11; 2 Sam. 16. 1. ascent; Acts 17. 22. the Areopagus

HIND, 2 Sam. 22. 34. Ps. 29. 9. Prov. 5. 19. S. of S. 2. 7. & 3. 5. Hab. 3. 19.

HIRE, Deut. 24. 15. Isa. 23. 18. Mic. 1. 7. & 3. 11. Luke 10. 7. Jas. 5. 4.
Job 7. 1. a *hireling*, John 10. 12, 13.
R. V. Gen. 31. 8. wages

HITHERTO Lord helped us, 1 Sam. 7. 12.
Job 38. 11. *h.* shalt thou come, but
John 16. 24. *h.* ye asked nothing
1 Cor. 3. 2. *h.* ye were not able to
R. V. 1 Sam. 7. 18; 1 Chron. 17. 16. thus far; 2 Sam. 15. 34. in time past; Isa. 18. 2, 7. onward; Dan. 7. 28. here; John 5. 17. even until now; 1 Cor. 3. 2. yet

HOLD, Gen. 21. 18. Ex. 9. 2. & 20. 7.
Judg. 9. 46. a *h.* of the house
Job 17. 9. righteous shall *h.* on way
Isa. 41. 13. God will *h.* thy right
62. 1. for Zion's sake will I not *h.*
Jer. 2. 13. cisterns that can *h.* no
Matt. 6. 24. *h.* to one and despise the
Rom. 1. 18. *h.* truth in unrighteous.
Phil. 2. 29. *h.* such in reputation
Heb. 3. 14. if we *h.* beginning of
1 Thes. 5. 21. prove all, *hold fast* that which is good
2 Tim. 1. 13. — form of sound words
Heb. 3. 6. if we — the confidence of hope
Heb. 4. 14. let us — our profession
Rev. 2. 25. what ye have — till I
3. 11. — that thou hast that no man
Ps. 77. 4. *holdest* my eyes waking
Rev. 2. 13. *h.* fast my name and
Job 2. 3. still he *holdeth* fast
Ps. 66. 9. which *h.* our soul in life
Prov. 17. 28. a fool, when he *h.*
Jer. 6. 11. I am weary with *holding*
Phil. 2. 16. *h.* forth the word of life
Col. 2. 19. not *h.* the head, from
1 Tim. 1. 19. *h.* faith and a good
3. 9. *h.* mystery of faith in
Tit. 1. 9. *h.* fast the faithful word
R. V. Jer. 51. 30. strongholds; Dan. 11. 39; Nah. 3. 12, 14. fortresses; Acts. 4. 3. ward
The R. V. changes are based on words before and after *hold*

HOLY ground, Ex. 3. 5.
Ex. 16. 23. *h.* sabbath, & 31. 14, 15.
19. 6. *h.* nation, 1 Pet. 2. 9.
29. 6. *h.* crown; 30. 25. *h.* ointment
Lev. 16. 33. *h.* sanctuary
27. 14. house to be *h.*; 30. *h.* tithes
Num. 5. 17. *h.* water; 31. 6. *h.* instruments
Lev. 11. 45. be ye *h.* for I am *h.*, 20. 7.
1 Sam. 2. 2. there is none *h.* as Lord
21. 5. vessels of young men are *h.*
Ps. 22. 3. thou art *h.* that inhabitest
99. 5. worship at his footstool, for he is *h.*
145. 17. Lord is *h.* in all his works
Prov. 20. 25. a snare to devour that which is *h.*
Isa. 6. 3. *h. h. h.* Lord God of hosts
Ezek. 22. 26. difference between *h.*
Matt. 7. 6. give not that which is *h.*
Luke 1. 35. *h.* thing which shall be
Acts 4. 27. thy *h.* child Jesus, 30.
Rom. 7. 12. law *h.* commandment *h.*
12. 1. sacrifice *h.* acceptable to God
1 Cor. 7. 14. children unclean, but now *h.*
Eph. 1. 4. be *h.* and without blame
2 Tim. 1. 9. called us with *h.* calling
3. 15. hast known the *h.* Scriptures
Tit. 1. 8. sober, just, *h.*, temperate
1 Pet. 1. 15. be ye *h.* in all manner
2. 5. a *h.* priesthood, 9. *h.* nation
2 Pet. 1. 21. *h.* men of God spake as
3. 11. *h.* in all conversation and
Rev. 3. 7. saith he that is *h.* and
4. 8. *h. h. h.* Lord God Almighty
15. 4. fear thee for thou only art *h.*
20. 6. blessed and *h.* is he that hath
22. 11. he that is *h.* let him be *h.*
Ex. 26. 33. *most holy place*, 34. & 29. 37. & 40. 10. 1 Kings 6. 16. & 7. 50. & 8. 6. Ezek. 44. 13. & 45. 3.
Lev. 6. 25. *most holy offering*, 7. 1, 6. & 10. 17. & 14. 13. Num. 18. 9, 10. Ezek. 48. 12.
21. 22. bread of his God most *h.*
27. 28. *most holy things*, Num. 4. 4, 19. 1 Chron. 6. 49. & 23. 13. 2 Chron. 31. 14.
Ezek. 43. 12. the whole limit shall be most *h.*
Jude 20. building up on your most *h.* faith
Ps. 42. 4. with multitude that kept *holy day*, Isa. 58. 13. Col. 2. 16. Ex. 25. 2.
Matt. 1. 18. with child of *Holy Ghost*
20. that is conceived in her is of —
3. 11. baptize you —, Mark 1. 8. John 1. 33. Acts 1. 5. & 11. 16.
12. 31. blasphemy against —, 32. Mark 3. 29.
Mark 12. 36. David said by —, Acts 1. 16.
13. 11. not ye that speak, but the —
Luke 1. 35. — shall come upon thee
2. 15 — was upon him
3. 22. — descended in bodily shape
12. 12. — shall teach you in that same
John 7. 39. for — was not yet given
14. 26. Comforter which is — whom
20. 22. receive ye the —
Acts 1. 2. though — had given
8. after that the — is come upon
2. 33. receive promise of the —
38. receive gift of —, 10. 45.
7. 51. ye do always resist the —
8. 15. receive —, 19.
18. — given
9. 31. walking in the fear of Lord and in the comfort of the —
10. 38. anointed Jesus with the —
44. — fell on all them, 11. 15.
47. received the —, 8. 17.
19. 2. be any —, 6.
13. 2. the — said, separate me Saul
4. they being sent forth by the —
15. 28. it seemed good to — and us
16. 6. forbidden of — to preach in
20. 23. save that — witnesseth
21. 11. thus saith — so shall the Jews
28. 25. well spake the — by Esaias
Rom. 5. 5. love of God shed abroad by —
14. 17. righteousness, peace, and joy in —
15. 13. abound in hope through power of —
16. offering of Gentiles sanctified by —
1 Cor. 2. 13. in words which the — teacheth
6. 19. temple of — which is in you
12. 3. can say Jesus is Lord but by the —
2 Cor. 6. 6. by — by love unfeigned
13. 14. communion of — be with you
1 Thes. 1. 5. in — much assurance
2 Tim. 1. 14. keep by — which dwell
Tit. 3. 5. not by works, but by the renewing of —
Heb. 2. 4. miracles and gifts of —

Heb. 3. 7. wherefore, as — saith
6. 4. made partakers of —
9. 8.—this signifying that the way
10. 15. whereof — is a witness to
1 Pet. 1. 12. preach unto you—sent
2 Pet. 1. 21. holy men of God moved by —
1 John 5. 7. Father, Word, and — are
Jude 20. building up . . praying in —
Luke 1. 15. *filled with*, or *full of the Holy Ghost*, 41. 67. Acts 2. 4. & 4. 8. & 6. 3, 5. & 9. 17. & 11. 24. & 13. 9, 52.
Ps. 51. 11. take not thy *Holy Spirit* from me
Isa. 63. 10. rebell. and vexed his —
Luke 11. 13. give — to them that
Eph. 1. 13. ye were sealed with — of promise
4. 30. grieve not the — of God
Ps. 87. 1. *holy mountain*, Isa. 11. 9. & 56. 6. & 57. 13. & 65. 11, 25. & 66. 20. Dan. 9. 16. & 11. 45. Joel 2. 1. & 3. 17. Obad. 16. Zeph. 3. 11. Zech. 8. 3.
Lev. 20. 3. *holy name*, & 22. 2, 33. 1 Chron. 16. 10, 35. Ps. 33. 21. & 103. 1. & 111. 9. & 145. 21. Isa. 57. 15. Ezek. 36. 20, 21.
Deut. 33. 8. *Holy One*, Job 6. 10. Ps. 16. 10. & 89. 19. Isa. 10. 17. & 29. 23. & 40. 25. & 43. 15. & 49. 7. Hab. 1. 12. & 3. 3. Mark 1. 24. Acts 3. 14. & 4. 27, 30. 1 John 2. 20.
2 Kings 19. 22. *Holy One of Israel*, Ps. 71. 22. & 78. 41. & 89. 18. Isa. 1. 4. & 5. 19, 24. & 10. 20. & 12. 6. & 17. 7. & 29. 19. & 30. 11, 12. & 31. 1. & 41. 14. & 45. 11. & 47. 4. & 49. 7. & 55. 5. & 60. 9, 14. Jer. 50. 29. & 51. 5.
Deut. 7. 6. *holy people*, 14. 2, 21. & 26. 19. & 28. 9. Isa. 62. 12. Dan. 8. 24. & 12. 7.
Ex. 28. 29. *holy place*, Lev. 6. 16. & 10. 17. Eccl. 8. 10. and about thirty other texts
Ps. 5. 7. *holy temple*, 11. 4. & 65. 4. & 79. 1. & 138. 2. Jonah 2. 4. Mic. 1. 2. Hab. 2. 20. Eph. 2. 21.
Isa. 65. 5. I am *holier* than thou
Heb. 9. 3. the *holiest* of all, 8.
1 Thes. 2. 10. how *holily* and justly
Ex. 15. 11. glorious in *holiness*
28. 36. *h.* to Lord, 39. 30. Isa. 23. 18.
1 Chron. 16. 29. in beauty of *h.*, Ps. 29. 2. & 96. 9. & 110. 3. 2 Chron. 20. 21.
2 Chron. 31. 18. sanctified themselves in *h.*
Ps. 30. 4. at remembrance of his *h.*
47. 8. God sits on throne of his *h.*
48. 1. in mountain of his *h.*
89. 35. I have sworn by my *h.*
93. 5. *h.* becometh thy house
Isa. 23. 18. her hire shall be *h.* to
35. 8. it shall be called the way of *h.*
63. 15. habitation of thy *h.*
18. people of *h.*
Jer. 2. 3. Israel was *h.* to the Lord
Amos 4. 2. Lord hath sworn by his *h.*
Obad. 17. on mount Zion there shall be *h.*
Zech. 14. 20. on horse bells, *h.* to
Mal. 2. 11. Judah hath profaned *h.*
Luke 1. 75. in *h.* and righteousness
Acts 3. 12. as though by our own *h.*
Rom. 1. 4. Son of God according to the Spirit of *h.*
6. 19. yield members servants to righteousness unto *h.*
22. fruit unto *h* and end everlast.
2 Cor. 7. 1. perfecting *h.* in the fear
Eph. 4. 24. created in righteousness and true *h.*
1 Thes. 3. 13. unblameable in *h.*
4. 7. called not to uncleanness but to *h.*
1 Tim. 2. 15. in faith, love, *h.*
Tit. 2. 3. in behavi. as becometh *h.*
Heb. 12. 10. partakers of his *h.*
14. *h.* without which no man shall
R. V. Ex. 38. 24; Lev. 10. 17, 18; 14. 13; Ps. 68. 17; Ezek. 21. 2. sanctuary; Matt. 12. 31, 32; Mark 3. 29; Luke 2. 25, 26; John 1. 33; 7. 39; Acts 2. 4; 6. 5; 1 Cor. 2. 13. Holy Spirit

HOME, Gen. 39. 16. & 43. 16.
Ps. 68. 12. that tarried at *h.* divided
Eccl. 12. 5. man goeth to his long *h.*
2 Cor. 5. 6. while we are at *h.* in
Tit. 2. 5. obedient, keepers at *h.*
R. V. Gen. 43. 16; Josh. 2. 18; 1 Sam. 10. 26; Matt. 8. 6; Mark 5. 19. house; Luke 9. 61——; 1 Tim. 5. 4. family

HONEST and good heart, Luke 8. 15.
Acts 6. 3. men of *h.* report, full of
Rom. 12. 17. provide things *h.* in
2 Cor. 8. 21. providing for *h.* things
Phil. 4. 8. whatsoever things are *h.*
1 Pet. 2. 12. have your conversation *h.*
Rom. 13. 13. walk *honestly* as in day
1 Thes. 4. 12. walk *h.* towards them
Heb. 13. 18. in all things willing to live *h.*
1 Tim. 2. 2 in all godliness and *honesty*
R. V. Acts 6. 3. good; Rom. 12. 17; 1 Cor. 8. 21; 2 Cor. 13. 7; Phil. 4. 8. honorable; 1 Pet. 2. 12. behavior seemly

HONEY, Gen. 43. 11. Lev. 2. 11. Judg. 14. 8, 18. 1 Sam. 14. 26, 29.
Ps. 19. 10. sweeter than *h.* and
Prov. 25. 27. it is not good to eat much *h.*
S. of S. 4. 11. *h.* and milk are under
Isa. 7. 15. butter and *h.* shall he eat
Matt. 3. 4. his meat was locusts and wild *h.*
Rev. 10. 9. in mouth sweet as *h.*, 10.
1 Sam. 14. 27. dipt in *honeycomb*, Prov. 5. 3, 16, 24. & 24. 13. & 27. 7. S. of S. 4. 11. & 5. 1. Luke 24. 42.

HONOR, be not thou united
1 Chron. 29. 12. both riches and *h.*
Ps. 7. 5. lay mine *h.* in the dust
8. 5. crown. him with glory and *h.*
26. 8. place where thine *h.* dwell.
49. 12. man being in *h.* abideth not
20. man that is in *h.* and under.
Prov. 3. 16. in her left hand riches and *h.*
15. 33. before *h.* is humility
26. 1. *h.* is not seemly for a fool
29. 23. *h.* shall uphold the humble
Mal. 1. 6. if I be a father where is mine *h.*
Matt. 13. 57. prophet is not without *h.*
John 5. 41. I receive not *h.* from men
Rom. 2. 7. seek for glory and *h.* and immortality
12. 10. in *h.* preferring one another
13. 7. give *h.* to whom *h.* is due
2 Cor. 6. 8. by *h.* and dishonor
2 Tim. 2. 20. some to *h.* and some to
Heb. 5. 4. taketh this *h.* to himself
1 Pet. 1. 7. be found unto praise and *h.*
Ex. 20. 12. *h.* thy father and mother
1 Sam. 2. 30. that *h.* me I will *h.*
Prov. 3. 9. *h.* Lord with substance
Isa. 29. 13. with their lips do *h.* me
John 5. 23. should *h.* the Son as *h.*
12. 26. if any man serve me him will my Father *h.*
1 Pet. 2. 17. *h.* all men, love
Ps. 15. 4. he *honoreth* them that
Mal. 1. 6. a son *h.* his father
Matt. 15. 8. *h.* me with their lips
Heb. 13. 4. marriage is *honorable* in
R. V. Gen. 49. 6; Ps. 7. 5; 26. 8; 66. 2; Prov. 14. 28; 25. 2; Dan. 4. 30; John 5. 41, 44; 8. 54; 2 Cor. 6. 8. glory; Ps. 31. 25. dignity; Dan. 4. 36. majesty; Rev. 19. 1; 21. 24——; John 8. 54. glorify

HOOF, Ex. 10. 26. Lev. 11. 3-7.

HOOK, Ex. 26. 32. Ezek. 29. 4. & 38. 4.
Isa. 2. 4. *pruning hooks*, 18. 5. Mic. 4. 3.
R. V. Job 41. 1. fishhook; 2. rope

HOPE in Israel concerning this, Ezra 10. 2.
Job 8. 13. hypocrite's *h.* shall perish
27. 8. what is the *h.* of hypocrite
Ps. 78. 7. might set their *h.* in God
146. 5. whose *h.* is in Lord his God
Prov. 10. 28. *h.* of righteous shall
11. 7. the *h.* of unjust men perish.
14. 32. righteous hath *h.* in death
19. 18. chasten thy son while there is *h.*
Isa. 57. 10. saidst thou there is no *h.*, Jer. 2. 25. & 18. 12. Ezek. 37. 11.
Jer. 14. 8. O the *h.* of Israel, 17. 13. & 50. 7.
17. 7. blessed is the man that trusteth in the Lord, and whose *h.* the Lord is
Lam. 3. 29. if so be there may be *h.*
Hos. 2. 15 valley of Achor for door of *h.*
Joel 3. 16. Lord will be the *h.* of
Zech. 9. 12. turn to the strong hold ye prisoners of *h.*
Acts 24. 15. have *h.* towards God
Rom. 5. 4. experience *h.*
5. *h.* maketh not ashamed
8. 24. we are saved by *h.* but *h.* that is seen is not *h.*
15. 4. comfort of Scriptures, might have *h.*
1 Cor. 9. 10. husbandman partaker of his *h.*
13. 13. now abideth faith, *h.* and
15. 19. if in this life only, *h.*
Gal. 5. 5. wait for *h.* of righteous.
Eph. 2. 12. having no *h.* and with.
Col. 1. 23. not moved away from *h.*
1 Thes. 4. 13. sorrow not as others that have no *h.*
5. 8. for a helmet, the *h.* of salva.
1 Tim. 1. 1. Jesus Christ who is our *h.*
Tit. 2. 13. looking for that blessed *h.*
3. 7. according to the *h.* of eternal
Heb. 6. 11. to the full assurance of *h.*
19. which *h.* we have as an anchor
1 Pet. 1. 3. begotten us again to a lively *h.*
21. that your faith and *h.* might be
3. 15. asketh a reason of *h.* in you
1 John 3. 3. man that has his *h.* in
Ps. 16. 9. my flesh also shall rest *in hope*
Rom. 4. 18, against *h.* believed —
5. 2. rejoice — of glory of God, 12. 12.
Tit. 1. 2. — eternal life of which
Ps. 39. 7. *my hope* is in thee
71. 5. thou art —, Jer. 17. 17.
22. 9. didst make me *hope* when I
42. 5. *h.* thou in God, for, 11.
119. 49. thou hast caused me to *h.*
81. I *h.* in thy word, 114.
130. 7. let Israel *h.* in the Lord
147. 11. those that *h.* in his mercy
Lam. 3. 26. good that man should *h.*
Rom. 8. 25. if we *h.* for that we see
1 Pet. 1. 13. be sober and *h.* to end
Ps. 119. 43. I have *hoped* in thy
74. I have *h.* in thy word, 147.
166. I have *h.* in thy salvation
Heb. 11. 1. faith is the substance of things *h.* for
1 Cor. 13. 7. charity *hopeth* all
Luke 6. 35. lend, *hoping* for nothing
R. V. Job 8. 14. confidence; Ps. 16. 9. safety; Jer. 17. 17. refuge; Lam. 3. 18. expectation; Jer. 3. 23. look.

HORN of my salvation, Ps. 18. 2.
Ps. 75. 4. lift not up the *h.*, 5. 10.
92. 10. my *h.* shalt thou exalt as the *h.* of the unicorn
148. 14. he exalted the *h.* of his
Luke 1. 69. raised up *h.* of salva.
Mic. 4. 13. I will make thy *h.* iron
Dan. 8. 20. having two *horns*
Hab. 3. 4. *h.* coming out of his hand
Rev. 13. 1. beast having ten *h.*

Rev. 13. 11. had two *h.* like a lamb
5. 6. lamb having seven *h.*
R. V Ex. 21. 29 —— ; Hab. 3. 4. rays

HORRIBLE, Ps. 11. 6. & 40. 2. Jer. 5. 30. & 18. 13. & 23. 14. Hos. 6. 10. Jer. 2. 12. Ezek. 32. 10.
R. V. Ps. 11. 6. burning

HORROR, Gen. 15. 12. Job 18. 20. Ps. 55. 5. & 119. 53. Ezek. 7. 18.
R. V. Ps. 119. 53. hot indignation

HORSE and rider thrown, Ex. 15. 21.
Ps. 32. 9. be ye not as *h.* or mule
33. 17. *h.* is a vain thing for safety
Prov. 21. 31. *h.* is prepared for the
Eccl. 10. 7. I have seen serv. on *h.*
Jer. 8. 6. as *h.* rusheth into battle
12. 5. canst thou contend with *h.*
Hos. 14. 3. we will not ride upon *h.*
Zech. 1. 8. & 6. 2, 3, 6. *h.* red, white, black, Rev. 6. 2, 4, 5, 8. & 9. 17.
Rev. 6. 2. and behold a white *h.*

HOSPITALITY, Rom. 12. 13. 1 Tim. 3. 2. Tit. 1. 8. 1 Pet. 4. 9.

HOST, Luke 10. 35. Rom. 16. 23. Ps. 27. 3. & 33. 16. & 103. 21. & 108. 11. & 148. 2. Isa. 40. 26. Luke 2. 13. Ps. 103. 21. Jer. 3. 19.
R. V. Ex. 16. 13; Deut. 2. 14, 15; Josh. 1. 11; 3. 2; 18. 9; Judg. 7. 8, 10, 13, 15; 1 Sam. 11. 11; 14. 15, 19; 1 Chron. 9. 19. camp; 2 Kings 18. 17; 25. 1; 2 Chron. 14. 9; 24. 23; 26. 11. army

HOT, Ps. 38. 1. & 39. 3. Prov. 6. 28. Hos. 7. 7. 1 Tim. 4. 2. Rev. 3. 15.
R. V. Judg. 2. 14; 3. 8; 6. 39; 10. 7. kindled

HOUR, Dan. 3. 6, 15. & 4. 33.
Matt. 10. 19. shall be given you in the same *h.*
24. 36. of that day and *h.* knoweth
25. 13. ye know neither day nor *h.*
Luke 12. 12. Holy Ghost shall teach you that same *h.*
22. 53. this is your *h.* and power of darkness
John 2. 4. my *h.* is not yet come
4. 23. the *h.* cometh and now is
12. 27. save me from this *h.*
Rev. 3. 3. not know what *h.* I come
10. will keep thee from the *h.* of
17. 12. power as kings one *h.* with
18. 10. in one *h.* is thy judgment
R. V. Matt. 24. 42. on what day; 1 Cor. 8. 7. until now

HOUSE, Ex. 20. 17. Lev. 14. 36.
Ex. 12. 30. not a *h.* where not one
Job 21. 28. where is the *h.* of prince
30. 23. *h.* appointed for all living
Prov. 3. 33. curse of the Lord is in *h.*
12. 7. *h.* of righteous shall stand
19. 14. *h.* and riches are inherit.
Eccl. 7. 2. go to the *h.* of mourn.
12. 3. when keepers of *h.* tremble
S. of S. 2. 4. brought me to the banqueting *h.*
Isa. 5. 8. woe to them that join *h.* to *h.*
60. 7. I will glorify the *h.* of my
64. 11. our holy and beautiful *h.*
Matt. 10. 13. *h.* worthy
23. 38. *h.* left desolate, Luke 11. 17.
Luke 12. 3. proclaimed on *h.* tops
John 14. 2. in my father's *h.* are
Rom. 16. 5. church in their *h.*, 1 Cor. 16. 19. Col. 4. 15. Phile. 2.
2 Cor. 5. 1. earthly *h. . . h.* of God not made with hands
2 Tim. 1. 16. give mercy to the *h.*
Heb. 3. 3. built *h.* hath more honor than the *h.*
2 John 10. receive him not into *h.*
Ps. 105. 21. made him Lord of all *his house*
112. 3. wealth and riches shall be in —
Acts 10. 2. feared God with all —
16. 34. believed in God with all —
Heb. 3. 2. faithful in all —, 5. 6.
John 4. 53. his *whole house* believed
1 Tim. 5. 8. especially for those of his own *h.*
Josh. 24. 15. as for me and *my house*
2 Sam. 23. 5. though — be not so
Ps. 101. 2. will walk within — with
Isa. 56. 7. joyful in — of prayer, Matt. 21. 13. Mark 11. 7. Luke 19. 46.
Matt. 12. 44. will return to —, Luke 11. 24.
Acts 16. 15. judged me faithful, come into —
Deut. 6. 7. when sittest in *thy house*
Ps. 26. 8. I loved habitation of —
Isa. 38. 1. set — in order, for thou
Acts 11. 14. thou and all — saved, 16. 31.
Gen. 28. 17. *house of God* or Lord, Ps. 42. 4. & 55. 14. & 23. 6. & 27. 4. Eccl. 5. 1. Isa. 2. 3. Mic. 4. 2. 1 Tim. 3. 15. 1 Pet. 4. 17. Ex. 23. 19. Josh. 6. 24. and about one hundred other places
Job 4. 19. dwell in *houses* of clay
Ps. 49. 11. *h.* shall continue for
Matt. 11. 8. in soft linen sit in kings' *h.*
19. 29. forsaken *h.* or lands
23. 14. devour widows' *h.*
Luke 16. 4. may receive me into *h.*
1 Cor. 11. 22. have ye not *h.* to eat
1 Tim. 3. 12. ruling their own *h.*
2 Tim. 3. 6. creep into *h.* and lead
Tit. 1. 11. subvert whole *h.* teach.
Acts 16. 15. baptized and her whole *household*
Gal. 6. 10. *h.* of faith
Eph. 2. 19. *h.* of God
Matt. 13. 52. like *householder*, 20. 1.
R. V. Ex. 12. 3; 2 Kings 7. 11; 10. 5, 12; 15. 5; Isa. 36. 3; 1 Cor. 1. 11; 1 Tim. 5. 14. household; 2 Cor. 5. 2. habitation; Deut. 6. 22; 1 Sam. 25. 17; 2 Sam. 6. 11; 17. 23; 1 Kings 11. 20; 2 Tim. 4. 19. house

HOW long, Ps. 6. 3. & 13. 1. & 74. 9. & 79. 5. & 80. 4. & 89. 46. Isa. 6. 11. Jer. 4. 14. Dan. 8. 13. & 12. 6. Matt. 17. 17. Luke 9. 41. Rev. 6. 10.
Job 15. 16. *how much more*, Prov. 21. 27. Matt. 7. 11. Luke 12. 24, 28. Heb. 9. 14.
Matt. 18. 21. & 23. 37. *how oft*, Luke 13. 34. Job 21. 17. Ps. 78. 40.

HOWL, Isa. 13. 6. & 14. 31. Jer. 4. 8. Joel 1. 5, 11, 13. Jas. 5. 1. Hos. 7. 14. Deut. 32. 10. Amos 8. 3.

HUMBLE person shall save, Job 22. 29.
Ps. 9. 12. forgett. not the cry of *h.*
10. 12. forget not the *h.*
17. desire of the *h.*
34. 2. *h.* shall hear of it, and be
69. 32. *h.* shall see this, and be
Prov. 16. 19. to be of an *h.* spirit
29. 23. honor shall uphold *h.* in
Isa. 57. 15. of contrite and *h.* spirit
Jas. 4. 6. giveth grace to the *h.*
Ex. 10. 3. thou refuse to *h.* thyself
Deut. 8. 2. to *h.* thee, and to prove
2 Chron. 7. 14. shall *h.* themselves
34. 27. because didst *h.* thyself
Prov. 6. 3. ,.. thyself, and make
Jer. 13. 18. *h.* yourselves, sit down
Matt. 18. 4. whoso *h.* himself shall
2 Cor. 12. 21. my God will *h.* me
Jas. 4. 10. *h.* yourselves in sight
1 Pet. 5. 6. *h.* yourselves therefore
Lev. 26. 41. if uncircumcised hearts be *humbled*
2 Kings 22. 19. hast *h.* thyself
2 Chron. 12. 6. princes and kings *h.* themselves
33. 12, 23. *h.* not himself before the Lord, 36. 12.
Ps. 35. 13. I *h.* my soul with fasting
113. 6. Lord who *h.* himself to
Isa. 2. 11. lofty looks shall be *h.*
10. 33. high and haughty shall be *h.*
Jer. 44. 10. are not *h.* unto this day
Lam. 3. 20. my soul is *h.* in me
Dan. 5. 22. hast not *h.* thy heart
Phil. 2. 8. *h.* himself and became
Deut. 21. 14. *humbled her*, 22. 24, 29. Ezek. 22. 10, 11.
Col. 3. 12. put on *humbleness* of
Mic. 6. 8. walk *humbly* with thy God
Prov. 22. 4. by *humility* are riches
Acts 20. 19. serv. Lord with all *h.*
Col. 2. 18. in a voluntary *h.*, 23.
1 Pet. 5. 5. be clothed with *h.*
R. V. Ps. 9. 12; 10. 12. poor; Ps. 10. 17; 34. 2; 69. 32; Prov. 16. 19; 29. 23. lowly; Ps. 35. 13. afflicted; Isa. 2. 11; 10. 33. brought low; Lam. 3. 20. brought down; 2 Sam. 16. 4. do; Acts 20. 19. lowliness

HUNGER, Ex. 16. 3. Deut. 28. 48.
Ps. 34. 10. young lions suffer *h.*
Prov. 19. 15. idle soul shall suffer *h.*
Jer. 42. 14. no war nor have *h.* of
Lam. 4. 9. sword better than slain with *h.*
Deut. 8. 3. suffered thee to *h.*
Isa. 49. 10. shall not *h.* nor thirst
Matt. 5. 6. blessed are they that *h.*
Luke 6. 21. blessed are ye that *h.*
John 6. 35. that cometh to me shall never *h.*
Rom. 12. 20. if thine enemy *h.* feed
1 Cor. 4. 11. we both *h.* and thirst
11. 34. if any man *h.* let him eat
Ps. 107. 9. fill the *hungry* with goodness
146. 7. God giveth food to the *h.*
Prov. 25. 21. if enemy be *h.* give
27. 7. to the *h.* every bitter thing
Isa. 58. 7. is it not to deal thy bread to the *h.*
10. if thou draw out thy soul to *h.*
65. 13. shall eat; but ye shall be *h.*
Ezek. 18. 7. hath given his bread to the *h.*, 16.
Luke 1. 53. filled the *h.* with good
Phil. 4. 12. how to be full and to be *h.*
R. V. Jer. 38. 9; Ezek. 34. 29; Rev. 6. 8. famine

HUNT, 1 Sam. 26. 20. Job 38. 39.
Ps. 140. 11. evil doth *h.* the violent
Prov. 6. 26. adulteress will *h.* for precious
Ezek. 13. 18. ye *h.* the souls of my people
Job 10. 16. thou *huntest* me as

HURT, Gen. 4. 23. & 26. 29.
Josh. 24. 20. will turn and do you *h.*
Ps. 15. 4. sweareth to his *h.* and
Eccl. 5. 13. riches kept for owners to their *h.*
Jer. 6. 14. healed *h.* of the daugh.
Rev. 2. 11. shall not be *h.* of
6. 6. *h.* not the oil and wine
Ezra 4. 15. *hurtful*, Ps. 144. 10.
1 Tim. 6. 9. fall into foolish and *h.*
R. V. Josh. 24. 20. evil; Acts 27. 10. injury; Acts 18. 10. harm

HUSBAND, Gen. 3. 6, 16. & 29. 32.
Ex. 4. 25. bloody *h.* art thou to me
Isa. 54. 5. thy Maker is thy *h.* Lord
Jer. 31. 32. though I was a *h.* to
Mark 10. 12. if a woman put away her *h.*
John 4. 17. I have no *h.*
1 Cor. 7. 14. unbelieving *h.* is sanc.
34. careth how she may please *h.*
14. 35. let them ask *h.* at home
2 Cor. 11. 2. espoused you to one *h.*
Eph. 5. 22. wives submit to your *h.*
23. the *h.* is the head of wife, 24.
25. *h.* love your wives, as Christ
Eph. 5. 33. the wife see that she reverence her *h.*
Col. 3. 18. wives submit to your *h.*
1 Pet. 3. 1. subject to their own *h.*
7. ye *h.* dwell with them, accord.
R. V. 1 Cor. 7. 14. brother

HUSBANDMAN, my Father is. John 15. 1.
1 Tim. 2. 6. *h.* that labors must be
Jas. 5. 7. *h.* waiteth for precious
1 Cor. 3. 9. ye are God's *husbandry*

HYMN, Matt. 26. 30. Eph. 5. 19 Col. 3. 16.

HYPOCRISY, Isa. 32. 6. Matt. 23. 28. Mark 12.15. Luke 12.1. 1 Tim. 4. 2. Jas. 3. 17. 1 Pet. 2. 1.
Matt. 7. 5. *hypocrite*, Luke 6. 42. & 13. 15.
Matt. 24. 51. appoint him portion with *h.*
Job 20. 5. joy of *h.* is but for a moment
27. 8. what is the hope of the *h.*
36. 13. *h.* in heart heap up wrath
Isa. 9. 17. every one is a *h.* and evil
33. 14. fearful. hath surprised *h.*
Matt. 6. 2. *hypocrites*, 6. 16. & 15. 7. & 16. 3. & 23. 13, 14, 15, 23.
Job 8. 13. the *h.* hope shall perish
15. 34. congregation of *h.* shall
R. V. Isa. 32. 6. profaneness; Job 8. 13; 13. 16; 17. 8; 20. 5; 27. 8; 34. 30; 36. 13; Prov. 11. 9; Isa. 33. 14. godless; Isa. 9. 17. profane; Matt. 16. 3; 23. 14; Luke 11. 44 ——

I

IDLE, they be, Ex. 5. 8, 17.
Prov. 19. 15. an *i.* soul shall suffer
Matt. 12. 36. every *i.* word give
20. 3. standing *i.*
6. why stand ye *i.*
Luke 24. 11. words seemed as *i.* tales
1 Tim. 5. 13. they learn to be *i.*
Prov. 31. 27. *idleness*, Eccl. 10. 18. Ezek. 16. 49.
R. V. Matt. 20. 6 ——; Ezek. 16. 49. ease

IDOL, 2 Chron. 15. 16. & 33. 7.
Isa. 66. 3. as if he blessed an *i.*
Zech. 11. 17. who to the *i.* shepherd
1 Cor. 8. 4. an *i.* is nothing in world
Ps. 96. 5. gods of nations are *idols*
Isa. 2. 8. land is full of *i.* they wor.
Jer. 50. 38. they are mad upon *i.*
Hos. 4. 17. Ephraim is joined to *i.*
Acts 15. 20. abstain from pollu. of *i.*
Rom. 2. 22. thou that abhorrest *i.*
1 Cor. 8. 1. touch. things offered to *i.*
2 Cor. 6. 16. temple of God with *i.*
1 John 5. 21. keep yourselves from *i.*
Rev. 2. 14. eat things sacrificed to *i.*
9. 20. worship devils and *i.* of gold
1 Cor. 5. 10, 11. *idolater*, 6. 9. & 10. 7. Eph. 5. 5. Rev. 21. 8. & 22. 15.
1 Sam. 15. 23. stubbornness as iniquity and *idolatry*
Acts 17. 16. city wholly given to *i.*
1 Cor. 10. 14. dearly beloved, flee *i.*
Gal. 5. 20. *i.* witchcraft, hatred
Col. 3. 5. covetousness, which is *i.*
1 Pet. 4. 3. walked in abominable *idolatries*
R. V. 1 Kings 15. 13; 2 Chron. 15. 16; Jer. 50. 2. image, and images; 2 Chron. 15. 18. abominations; Isa. 57. 5. among oaks; Jer. 22. 28. vessel; Zech. 2. 10. teraphim; 11. 17. worthless; 1 Cor. 12. 28 ——; 1 Sam. 15. 23. teraphim; Acts 17. 16. full of idols
2 Chron. 34. 7. hewed down all the *sun-images* throughout all the land of Israel

IGNORANCE, sin through, Lev. 4. 2, 13, 22, 27. Num. 15. 24, 25. Acts 3. 15.
Acts 17. 30. the times of this *i.*
Eph. 4. 18. alienated through *i.* in
Ps. 73. 22. so foolish was I and *ignorant*
Isa. 63. 16. though Abraham be *i.* of
Rom. 10. 3. being *i.* of God's righteousness
1 Cor. 14. 38. if any man be *i.* let
Heb. 5. 2. who can have compassion on *i.*
Acts 17. 23. *ignorantly*, 1 Tim. 1. 13.
R. V. Lev. 4. 2, 22, 27; 5. 18; Num. 15. 24, 26, 27, 28, 29. unwittingly; Lev. 4. 13. shall err; Num. 15. 25. was an error; Isa. 56. 10. without knowledge; 63. 16. knoweth not; Num. 15. 28. erreth; Deut. 19. 4. unawares

ILLUMINATED, Heb. 10. 32.

IMAGE, Lev. 26. 1. Dan. 2. 31.
Gen. 1. 26. let us make man in our own *i.*, 27. & 5. 1. & 9. 6. Col. 3. 10.
Gen. 5. 3. Adam begat a son after his *i.*
Ps. 73. 20. Lord, thou shalt despise their *i.*
Matt. 22. 20. whose *i.* is this, Luke 20. 24.
Rom. 8. 29. conformed to *i.* of Son
1 Cor. 15. 49. have borne the *i.* of the earthly we shall also bear *i.* of the heavenly
4. 4. Christ who is the *i.* of God
2 Cor. 3. 18. into same *i.* from glory
Heb. 1. 3. express *i.* of his person
Rev. 13. 14. make an *i.* to the beast
Ex. 23. 24. break down *images*, 34. 13.
R. V. Lev. 26. 1. figured stones; Ex. 23. 24; 34. 13; Lev. 26. 1; Deut. 7. 5; 16. 22; 1 Kings 14. 23; 2 Kings 17. 10; 18. 4; 23. 14; 2 Chron. 14. 3; 31. 1; Jer. 43. 13; Hos. 1. 2; Mic. 5. 13. pillar, and pillars; Job 4. 16. form; Rom. 11. 4 ——

IMAGINE, Ps. 2. 1. Nah. 1. 9. Zech. 7. 10. & 8. 17. Acts 4. 25.
Gen. 6. 5. every *imagination* of the thoughts was evil, 8. 21. Prov. 6. 18. Lam. 3. 60, 61. Rom. 1. 21. 2 Cor. 10. 5.
R. V. Lam. 3. 60, 61. devices; Rom. 1. 21. reasonings; Gen. 11. 6. purpose

IMMEDIATELY, Mark 4. 15. Acts 12. 23.

IMMORTAL, invisible, 1 Tim. 1. 17.
Rom. 2. 7. seek for *immortality*
1 Cor. 15. 53. this mortal must put on *i.*
1 Tim. 6. 16. who only hath *i.* in
2 Tim. 1. 10. brought *i.* to light
R. V. *incorruption*
Rom. 2. 7. seek for glory . . and *i.*

IMMUTABLE, Heb. 6. 17, 18.

IMPART, Luke 3. 11. Rom. 1. 11. 1 Thes. 2. 8.

IMPENITENT heart, Rom. 2. 5.

IMPERIOUS whorish woman, Ezek. 16. 30.

IMPLACABLE, unmerciful, Rom. 1. 31.
R. V. Rom. 1. 31 ——

IMPORTUNITY, Luke 11. 8.

IMPOSSIBLE, Matt. 17. 20. & 19. 26.
Luke 1. 37. with God nothing is *i.*
17. 1. it is *i.* but offences will come
Heb. 6. 4. it is *i.* for those once
18. in two things it is *i.* for God to
11. 6. without faith it is *i.* to please
R. V. Luke 1. 37. void of power; Heb. 6. 4. as touching

IMPUDENT, Prov. 7. 13. Ezek. 2. 4.
R. V. Ezek. 3. 7. of hard forehead

IMPUTE, 1 Sam. 22. 15. Lev. 7. 18. & 3. 7.
Ps. 32. 2. to whom Lord *i.* not iniq.
Rom. 4. 6. *i.* righteousness without
8. blessed to whom Lord will not *i.*
22. *i.* to him for righteousness
2 Cor. 5. 19. not *i.* their trespasses
Jas. 2. 23. *i.* to him for righteous.
R. V. Hab. 1. 11. even; Rom. 4. 6, 8, 11, 22, 23, 24. reckon; 2 Cor. 5. 19. reckoning; Jas. 2. 23. reckoned

IN Christ, Acts 24. 24. Rom. 12. 5. 1 Cor. 1. 2, 30. & 3. 1. & 15. 18, 22. 2 Cor. 1. 21. & 2. 14. & 3. 14. & 5. 17, 19. & 12. 2. Gal. 1. 22. Eph. 1. 1, 3, 10, 12, 20. & 2. 6, 10, 13. Phil. 1. 1, 13. & 2. 1, 5. & 3. 14. Col. 1. 2, 4.
1 Thes. 1. 1. *in God*, 4. 16. John 3. 21. Col. 3. 3.
Gen. 15. 16. *in the Lord*, Ps. 4. 5. & 31. 24. & 34. 2. & 35. 9. & 37. 4, 7. Isa. 45. 17, 24, 25. Jer. 3. 23. Zech. 12. 5. 1 Cor. 1. 31. & 4. 17. & 7. 22, 39. Eph. 2. 21. & 6. 10. Phil. 4. 2, 4. Col. 3. 18. & 4. 7, 17. 1 Thes. 5. 12. Phile. 16, 20. Rev. 14. 13.

INCEST condemned, Lev. 18. & 20. 17. Deut. 22. 30. & 27. 20. Ezek. 22. 11. Amos 2. 7. cases of, Gen. 19. 33. & 35. 22. & 38. 18. 2 Sam. 13. & 16. 21. Mark 6. 17. 1 Cor. 5. 1.

INCHANTMENT, Lev. 19. 26. Num. 23. 23. Eccl. 10. 11. Isa. 47. 9.

INCLINE heart, Josh. 24. 23. Judg. 9. 3. 1 Kings 8. 58. Ps. 119. 36, 112. & 141. 4.
Ps. 78. 1. *incline*, 40. 1. & 116. 2. Prov. 2. 2. & 5. 13. Jer. 7. 24, 26. & 11. 8. & 17. 23. & 25. 4. & 34. 14. & 35. 15. & 44. 5. Isa. 55. 3.
R. V. Ps. 71. 2. bow down

INCLOSED, Ps. 17. 10. & 22. 16. S. of S. 4. 12. & 8. 9. Lam. 3. 9.
R. V. S. of S. 4. 12. shut up; Lam. 3. 9. fenced up

INCONTINENT, 1 Cor. 7. 5. 2 Tim. 3. 3.

INCORRUPTIBLE God, Rom. 1. 23.
1 Cor. 9. 25. to obtain an *i.* crown
15. 52. dead shall be raised *i.*
1 Pet. 1. 4. begotten to inheritance *i.*
23. born not of corruptible seed, but of *i.*
1 Cor. 15. 42, 50, 53, 54. *incorruption*

INCREASE, Lev. 19. 25. & 25. 7.
Lev. 25. 36. take no usury nor *i.*, 37.
Deut. 16. 15. bless thee in all thine *i.*
Ps. 67. 6. earth yield her *i.*, 85. 12.
Prov. 3. 9. with first fruits of all *i.*
Isa. 9. 7. of the *i.* of his govern.
1 Cor. 3. 6. I planted; but God gave the *i.*, 7.
Col. 2. 19. increaseth with *i.* of God
Ps. 62. 10. if riches *i.* set not heart
Prov. 1. 5. wise man will *i.* learn.
Isa. 29. 19. meek shall *i.* their joy
Luke 17. 5. Lord, *i.* our faith
John 3. 30. he must *i.* but I decrease
1 Thes. 3. 12. Lord make you to *i.* in
2 Tim. 2. 16. will *i.* to more ungod.
Ezra 9. 6. iniquities are *increased*
Isa. 9. 3. multi. nation, not *i.* joy
Luke 2. 52. Jesus *i.* in wisdom and
Acts 6. 7. the word of God *i.* and the
Rev. 3. 17. am rich and *i.* with goods
Eccl. 1. 18. *increaseth* knowledge
Isa. 40. 29. have no might, he *i.*
Col. 2. 19. whole body *i.* with the
1 Chron. 11. 9. David went on *increasing*
Col. 1. 10. *i.* in knowledge of God
R. V. Gen. 47. 34. ingathering; Job 10. 16. exalteth; Prov. 28. 8. augmenteth; Ps. 7. 23. ascendeth; Isa. 52. 1. made many; Lam. 2. 5, Ezek. 16. 26; Hos. 4. 7; 10. 1; 12. 1. multiplied; Luke 2. 52. advanced; 2 Cor. 2. 15. groweth; Rev. 3. 17. have gotten

INCREDIBLE thing, Acts 26. 8.

INCURABLE wound, Job 34. 6. Jer. 15. 18.
Mic. 1. 9. *i.* bruise, Jer. 30. 12, 15.

INDEED, 1 Kings 8. 27. 1 Chron. 4. 10. Matt. 3. 11. Luke 4. 24. John 1. 47. & 4. 42. & 6. 55. & 8. 31, 36. 1 Tim. 5. 3, 5. 1 Pet. 2. 4.

INDIGNATION, Neh. 4. 1. Esth. 5. 9. Ps. 69. 24. & 78. 49. & 102. 10.
Isa. 10. 5. staff in their hand is my *i.*
26. 20. hide thee until *i.* be over.
Mic. 7. 9. I will bear the *i.* of Lord
Nah. 1. 6. who can stand before his *i.*
Matt. 20. 24. moved with *i.*
Rom. 2. 8. *i.* and wrath, tribulation
2 Cor. 7. 11. yea, what *i.* yea, what
Heb. 10. 27. fiery *i.* which shall
Rev. 14. 10. poured into cup of his *i.*
R. V. 2 Kings 3. 27; Esth. 5. 9. wrath; Acts 5. 17. jealousy; Heb. 10. 27. fierceness of fire; Rev. 14. 10. anger

INDITING a good matter, Ps. 45. 1.

INDUSTRY, Gen. 2. 15. & 3. 23. Prov. 6. 6. & 10. 4. & 12. 24. & 13. 4. & 21. 5. & 22. 29. & 27. 23. Eph. 4. 28. 1 Thes.

4. 11. 2 Thes. 3. 12. Tit. 3. 14; rewarded, Prov. 13. 11. & 31. 13.
INEXCUSABLE, O man, Rom. 2. 1.
INFALLIBLE proofs, many, Acts 1. 3.
INFANT, 1 Sam. 15. 3. Job 3. 16. Isa. 65. 20. Hos. 13. 16. Luke 18. 15.
R. V. Luke 18. 15. their babes
INFIDEL, 2 Cor. 6. 15. 1 Tim. 5. 8.
INFINITE iniquities, Job 22. 5.
Ps. 147. 5. his understanding is *i.*
Nah. 3. 9. her strength, and it was *i.*
R. V. Job 22. 5. end
INFIRMITY, this is my *i.*, Ps. 77. 10.
Prov. 18. 14. the spirit of a man will sustain his *i.*
Matt. 8. 17. himself took our *infirmities*
Rom. 8. 26. the Spirit also helpeth our *i.*
15. 1. strong ought to bear the *i.*
2 Cor. 12. 9. glory in my *i.*
10. pleasure in *i.*
1 Tim. 5. 23. drink wine for thine often *i.*
Heb. 4. 15. with the feeling of our *i.*
R. V. Lev. 12. 2. her sickness; Luke 7. 21; 2 Cor. 12. 5, 9, 10. weaknesses
INFLAME them, wine, Isa. 5. 11. & 57. 5.
INFLICTED punishment, 2 Cor. 2. 6.
INFLUENCES of Pleiades, Job 38. 31.
INGATHERING, feast of, Ex. 23. 16. & 34. 22.
INGRAFTED word, receive, Jas. 1. 21.
INGRATITUDE to God, Rom. 1. 21.
INHABIT, Prov. 10. 30. Isa. 65. 21, 22.
Ps. 22. 3. thou that *inhabitest* the praises of Israel
Isa. 57. 15. lofty One that *inhabiteth*
R. V. Prov. 10. 30; Jer. 48. 18. dwell in; Lev. 16. 22. solitary land; 1 Chron. 5. 9; Zech. 12. 6; 14. 10, 11. dwell
INHERIT, Gen. 15. 8. Ps. 82. 8.
1 Sam. 2. 8. to make them *i.* throne
Ps. 25. 13. his seed shall *i.* earth
37. 11. the meek shall *i.* the earth, Matt. 5. 5.
Ps. 37. 29. the righteous shall *i.* the land, Isa. 60. 21.
Prov. 3. 35. wise shall *i.* glory; but
Matt. 19. 29. hath forsaken, shall *i.* everlasting life
25. 34. *i.* king. prepared for you
Mark 10. 17. what shall I do that I may *i.* eternal life, Luke 10. 25. & 18. 18.
1 Cor. 6. 9. unrighteous not *i.* the kingdom of God, 10.
Gal. 5. 21. do such things not *i.* the kingdom of God
Heb. 6. 12. through faith *i.* prom.
1 Pet. 3. 9. that ye should *i.* bless.
Rev. 21. 7. overcometh shall *i.* all
Num. 18. 20. I the Lord am thy *inheritance*, Deut. 10. 9. & 18. 2. Ezek. 44. 28.
Deut. 4. 20. a people of *i.*, 9. 20, 29. & 32. 9. 1 Kings 8. 5. Ps. 28. 9. & 33. 12. & 68. 9. & 74. 2. & 78. 62, 71. & 79. 1. & 94. 14. & 106. 5, 40. Isa. 19. 25. Jer. 10. 16. & 51. 19.
Ps. 16. 5. Lord is portion of mine *i.*
Prov. 19. 14. riches are *i.* of fathers
Eccl. 7. 11. wisdom is good with an *i.*
Acts 20. 32. *i.* among the sanctified
Eph. 1. 11. among whom he obtained an *i.*
14. earnest of our *i.* and purchased
5. 5. hath an *i.* in the kingdom
Col. 1. 12. partakers of *i.* of saints
3. 24. shall receive the reward of *i.*
Heb. 9. 15. receive the promise of eternal *i.*
1 Pet. 1. 4. to an *i.* incorruptible

R. V. Isa. 54. 3; Jer. 8. 10; 49. 1. possess; Josh. 13. 15, 24, 32 ——; Job 31. 2; Eph. 1. 11. heritage; Ezek. 22. 16. be profaned
INIQUITY, Gen. 15. 16. & 19. 15.
Ex. 20. 5. visiting *i.* of the fathers
34. 7. forgiving *i.* transgression
Lev. 26. 41. accept the punishment of their *i.*, 43.
Num. 23. 21. hath not beheld *i.*
Deut. 32. 4. a God of truth, without *i.*
Job 4. 8. they that plough *i.* reap
11. 6. less than thine *i.* deserveth
15. 16. man drinketh in *i.* like
22. 23. put away *i.* far from thee
34. 32. if I have done *i.* I will do
Ps. 32. 5. mine *i.* have I not hid
39. 11. with rebukes correct man for *i.*
51. 5. behold I was shapen in *i.*
66. 18. if I regard *i.* in my heart
119. 3. they also do not *i.* they walk
Prov. 22. 8. that soweth *i.* shall
Eccl. 3. 16. place of righteousness *i.* was there
Isa. 1. 4. a people laden with *i.*
5. 18. woe to them that draw *i.*
27. 9. by this shall *i.* of Jacob
33. 24. people shall be forgiven their *i.*
53. 6. Lord laid on him the *i.* of us
57. 17. for *i.* of his covetousness
59. 3. defiled your fingers with *i.*
Jer. 2. 5. what *i.* have your
3. 13. only acknowledge thine *i.*
31. 30. every one shall die for *i.*
50. 20. *i.* of Israel be sought for
Ezek. 3. 18. he shall die in his *i.*
18. 30. so *i.* shall not be your ruin
Dan. 9. 24. makes reconcilia. for *i.*
Hos. 14. 2. take away all *i.* and
Mic. 7. 18. a God like thee, that pardoneth *i.*
Hab. 1. 13. Holy One canst not look on *i.*
Matt. 7. 23. depart from me ye that work *i.*
Acts 8. 23. in gall of bitterness and bond of *i.*
Rom. 6. 19. servants to uncleanness and to *i.* unto *i.*
1 Cor. 13. 6. charity rejoic. not in *i.*
2 Thes. 2. 7. mystery of *i.* already
2 Tim. 2. 19. that nameth Christ depart from *i.*
Tit. 2. 14. he might redeem us from all *i.*
Jas. 3. 6. tongue is a fire, a world of *i.*
Ps. 18. 23. *my iniquity*, 25. 11. & 32. 5. & 38. 18. & 51. 2.
Job 34. 22. *workers of iniquity*, Ps. 5. 5. & 6. 8. & 14. 4. & 92. 7. Prov. 10. 29. & 21. 15. Luke 13. 27.
Lev. 16. 21. confess over him all *iniquities*
26. 39. pine in their *i.* and *i.* of
Ezra 9. 6. our *i.* are increased
Neh. 9. 2. confessed the *i.* of
Job 13. 26. to possess *i.* of my youth
Ps. 38. 4. mine *i.* are gone over my
40. 12. mine *i.* have taken hold
51. 9. hide from my sins, blot out my *i.*
79. 8. remember not against us former *i.*
90. 8. thou hast set our *i.* before
103. 3. who forgiveth all thine *i.*
10. not rewarded us accord. to *i.*
130. 3. if thou, Lord, shouldest mark *i.*
8. he shall redeem Israel from all *i.*
Prov. 5. 22. his own *i.* shall take
Isa. 43. 24. hast wearied me with *i.*
53. 5. he was wounded, bruised for *i.*
Jer. 14. 7. though our *i.* testify
Dan. 4. 27. break off thy *i.* by show.
Mic. 7. 19. he will subdue our *i.*
Acts 3. 26. bless you in turning from *i.*
Rom. 4. 7. blessed are they whose *i.*

Rev. 18. 5. God hath remem. her *i.*
Isa. 53. 11. he shall bear *their iniquities*
Jer. 33. 8. I will cleanse them from all — and I will pardon all —
Ezek. 43. 10. may be ashamed of —
Heb. 8. 12. their sins, and — will I
Num. 14. 34. shall ye bear *your iniquities*
Isa. 50. 1. for — have ye sold
59. 2. — have separated between you and God
Jer. 5. 25. — turned away these things
Ezek. 24. 23. ye shall pine away for —
36. 31. loathe yourselves . . for —
33. I shall have cleansed you from all —
Amos 3. 2. I will punish you for all —
R. V. 1 Sam. 15. 23. idolatry; Job 6. 29, 30. injustice; Job 22. 23; 36. 23; Ps. 37. 1; 119. 13; Jer. 2. 5; Ezek. 28. 15, 18; Mal. 2. 6; 1 Cor. 13. 6; 2 Tim. 2. 19. unrighteousness; Ps. 94. 20; Eccl. 3. 16. wickedness; Dan. 9. 5. perversely; Hab. 1. 13. perverseness; 2 Thes. 2. 7. lawlessness; Heb. 8. 12 ——; 2 Pet. 2. 16. transgression
INJURED me, ye have not, Gal. 4. 12.
1 Tim. 1. 13. was a persecutor and *injurious*
INJUSTICE, Ex. 22. 21. & 23. 6. Lev. 19. 15. Deut. 16. 19. & 24. 17. Job 31. 13. Ps. 82. 2. Prov. 22. 16. & 29. 7. Jer. 22. 3. Luke 16. 10.
results of, Prov. 11. 7. & 28. 8. Mic. 6. 10. Amos 5. 11. & 8. 5. 1 Thes. 4. 6. 2 Pet. 2. 9.
INK, 2 John 12. 3 John 13.
INNER, 1 Kings 6. 27. Eph. 3. 16.
R. V. Eph. 3. 16. inward
INNOCENT, Ps. 19. 13. Prov. 28. 20.
Gen. 20. 5. in *innocency* of hands
Ps. 6. 6. wash my hands in *i.*, 73. 13.
Dan. 6. 22. before him *i.* was
Hos. 8. 5. how long ere they at. *i.*
R. V. Ps. 19. 3. clear; Prov. 6. 29; 28. 20. unpunished
INNUMERABLE, Job 21. 33. Ps. 40. 12. Luke 12. 1. Heb. 11. 12. & 12. 22.
INORDINATE, Ezek. 23. 11. Col. 3. 5.
R. V. *passion;* Col. 3. 5. uncleanness, *i.* affection
INQUISITION, Deut. 19. 18. Ps. 9. 12.
INSCRIPTION to unknown God, Acts 17. 23.
INSPIRATION, Job 32. 8. 2 Tim. 3. 16.
R. V. Job 32. 8. breath; 2 Tim. 3. 16. inspired
INSTANT, Isa. 29. 5. & 30. 13. Jer. 18. 7. Rom. 12. 12. 2 Tim. 4. 2. Acts 12. 5.
Luke 7. 4. besought him *instantly*
Acts 26. 7. *i.* serving God day and
R. V. Luke 2. 38. very hour; Rom. 12. 12. earnestly
INSTRUCT, Deut. 4. 36. & 32. 10.
Neh. 9. 20. thy good Spirit to *i.* them
Job 40. 2. contendeth with the Almighty *i.*
16. 7. my reins *i.* me in the night
32. 8. I will *i.* thee, and teach
S. of S. 8. 2. moth. who would *i.* me
Isa. 28. 26. his God doth *i.* him
Dan. 11. 33. that under. shall *i.*
1 Cor. 2. 16. Lord that he may *i.* him
Isa. 8. 11. Lord *instructed* me
Ps. 2. 10. be *i.* ye judges of earth
Matt. 13. 52. every scribe, *i.* unto
Phil. 4. 12. in all things I am *i.* both
2 Tim. 2. 25. in meekness *i.* those
Rom. 2. 20. an *instructor* of foolish
1 Cor. 4. 15. have ten thousand *i.*
Job 33. 16. sealeth their *instruction*
Ps. 50. 17. hatest *i.* and castest my

Prov. 4. 13. take fast hold of *i*. keep
5. 12. how have I hated *i*.
19. 27. cease to hear *i*. that causeth
23. 12. apply thy heart to *i*. and
2 Tim. 3. 16. profitable for *i*. in
R. V. Deut. 32. 10. cared for;-
2 Chron. 3. 3. laid; Job 40. 2. contend with Almighty; Matt. 13. 52. hath been made a disciple; 14. 8. put forward by; Phil. 4. 12. learned the secret; 2 Tim. 2. 25. correcting; Prov. 10. 17; 12. 1; 13. 18; 15. 5, 32; 16. 22; Zeph. 3. 7. correction
INSTRUMENTS of cruelty, Gen. 49. 5.
Ps. 7. 13. prepared for him *i*. of
Rom. 6. 13. neither yield members *i*. of unrighteousness; but *i*. of righteousness to God
Isa. 32. 7. the *i*. of the churl are
R. V. Gen. 49. 5; Isa. 54. 16. weapon; Ex. 25. 9; Num. 3. 8; 7. 1; 2 Sam. 24. 22. furniture; Num. 4. 12; 31. 6; 1 Chron. 9. 20; 28. 14; 2 Chron. 4. 16; 5. 1. vessels; Ps. 68. 25. minstrels; 87. 7. that dance; 33. 2; 144. 9 ——
INTANGLE, Matt. 22. 15. Gal. 5. 1. 2 Tim. 2. 4. 2 Pet. 2. 20.
INTEGRITY of my heart, Gen. 20. 5.
Job 2. 3. still he holdeth fast his *i*.
27. 5. I will not remove mine *i*.
Ps. 7. 8. according to my *i*. that is
25. 21. let *i*. and uprightness
26. 1. I have walked in mine *i*.
Prov. 11. 3. *i*. of upright shall guide
INTERCESSION, Jer. 7. 16. & 27. 18.
Isa. 53. 12. made *i*. for transgress.
Rom. 8. 26. Spirit maketh *i*. for us, 27.
34. who also maketh *i*. for
11. 2. Elias maketh *i*. to God
1 Tim. 2. 1. prayers and *i*. be made
Heb. 7. 25. he ever liveth to make *i*.
Isa. 59. 16. wondered there was no *intercessor*
R. V. Rom. 11. 2. pleadeth with
INTERMEDDLE, Prov. 14. 10. & 18. 1.
R. V. Prov. 18. 1. rageth against
INTERPRETATION, Gen. 40. 5. & 41. 11. Judg. 7. 15. Dan. 2. 4, 7, 36. 1 Cor. 12. 10. & 14. 26. 2 Pet. 1. 20.
Job 33. 23. *interpreter* one among
R. V. 1. 6. a figure
INTREAT, Gen. 12. 16. & 23. 8. Ex. 8. 8. & 9. 28. & 10. 17. Jer. 15. 11.
1 Sam. 2. 25. man sin, who shall *i*.
1 Cor. 4. 13. we suffer; being defamed we *i*.
1 Tim. 5. 1. but *i*. him as a father
Jas. 3. 17. gentle and easy to be *intreated*
Prov. 18. 23. the poor useth *intreaties*
2 Cor. 8. 4. praying us with much *i*.
R. V. Job 19. 17. my supplication; Phil. 4. 3. beseech; 1 Tim. 5. 1. exhort
INTRUDING into those things, Col. 2. 18.
INVENT, Amos 6. 5. Rom. 1. 30.
Ps. 99. 8. tookest vengeance of their *inventions*
106. 28. provoked him with their *i*.
Prov. 8. 12. find out knowledge of witty *i*.
Eccl. 7. 29. men have sought many *i*.
R. V. Ps. 99. 8; 106. 29, 39. doings; Prov. 8. 12. and discretion
INVISIBLE, Rom. 1. 20. Col. 1. 15, 16. 1 Tim. 1. 17. Heb. 11. 27.
INWARD friends abhorred me, Job 19. 19.
Ps. 5. 9. *inward part*, 51. 6. Prov. 20. 27. Jer. 31. 33. Luke 11. 39.
Rom. 7. 22. *inward man*, 2 Cor. 4. 16.
2 Cor. 7. 15. *inward affection* is
Ps. 62. 4. curse *inwardly*

Matt. 7. 15. *i*. wolves
Rom. 2. 29. he is a Jew that is one *i*.
IRON sharpeneth iron, Prov. 27. 17.
Eccl. 10. 10. if the *i*. be blunt, put
Isa. 48. 4. neck is an *i*. sinew, and
Jer. 15. 12. shall *i*. break northern *i*.
Dan. 2. 33. legs of *i*. his feet *i*. and
4. 23. even with a band of *i*. and
1 Tim. 4. 2. conscience seared with hot *i*.
ISSUES from death, Ps. 68. 20.
Prov. 4. 23. out of the heart are the *i*. of life
R. V. Lev. 12. 7. fountain; Matt. 22. 23. seed
ITCHING ears, 2 Tim. 4. 3.
IVORY, 1 Kings 10. 18. & 22. 39. Ps. 45. 8. S. of S. 5. 14. & 7. 4. Ezek. 27. 6. Amos 3. 15. & 6. 4. Rev. 18. 12.

J

JAW-BONE of an ass, Samson uses, Judg. 15. 15; water flows from, 15. 19.
JEALOUS God, I am a, Ex. 20. 5. & 34. 14. Deut. 5. 9. & 6. 15. Josh. 24. 19.
1 Kings 19. 10. I have been very *j*.
Ezek. 39. 25. be *j*. for my holy
Joel 2. 18. will Lord be *j*. for land
Nah. 1. 2. God is *j*. and the Lord
Zech. 1. 14. I am *j*. for Jerusalem
2 Cor. 11. 2. *j*. over you with godly *jealousy*
Deut. 29. 20. Lord's *j*. shall smoke
Ps. 79. 5. shall thy *j*. burn like fire
Prov. 6. 34. *j*. is the rage of a man
S. of S. 8. 6. *j*. is cruel as the grave
Rom. 10. 19. provoke you to *j*.
1 Cor. 10. 22. do we provoke Lord to *j*.
JEHOVAH, Ex. 6. 3. Ps. 83. 18. Isa. 12. 2. & 26. 4. Gen. 22. 14. Ex. 17. 15. Judg. 6. 24. it is about 2000 times translated Lord, in capitals
JERUSALEM, for the church, Isa. 24. 23. & 62. 1. & 66. 10, 13. Jer. 3. 17. Joel 2. 32. & 3. 16, 17. Zech. 12. 10. & 8. 22. Gal. 4. 25, 26. Heb. 12. 22. Rev. 3. 12. & 21. 2.
JESHURUN, i. e. Israel, Deut. 32. 15. & 33. 5, 26. Isa. 44. 2.
JESTING, evil, censured, Eph. 5. 4.
JESUS, or Joshua, Acts 7. 45. Heb. 4. 8.
JESUS the Saviour of men, Matt. 1. 21. & 2. 1. & 8. 29. & 14. 1. & 27. 37. 1 Cor. 12. 3. 2 Cor. 4. 5. Eph. 4. 21. Heb. 2. 9. & 12. 2. Rev. 22. 16. and in about 650 other places
JEWELS, I make up my, Mal. 3. 17.
R. V. 2 Chron. 32. 27. vessels; S. of S. 1. 10. hair; Ezek. 16. 12. ring
JEWS first, and also Greeks, Rom. 1. 16. & 2. 9, 10, 28. not a *J*. which is one outwardly, but is a *J*. which is one inwardly, 29.
Rom. 10. 12. no difference between *J*. and Greek
1 Cor. 9. 20. to *J*. I became as a *J*. to gain *J*.
Gal. 3. 28. neither *J*. nor Greek
Rev. 2. 9. say they are *J*. and are
JOIN, Ex. 1. 10. Ezra 9. 14.
Prov. 11. 21. though hand *j*. in
Isa. 5. 8. woe to them that *j*. house
Jer. 50. 5. let us *j*. ourselves to Lord
Acts 5. 13. of the rest durst no man *j*. himself
9. 26. assayed to *j*. himself to the
Hos. 4. 17. Ephraim is *joined* to idols
Num. 25. 3. Israel *j*. himself to Ba.
Eccl. 9. 4. *j*. to all living there is
Zech. 2. 11. many nat. shall be *j*.
Matt. 19. 6. what God hath *j*. let not

1 Cor. 1. 10. be perfectly *j*. together
6. 17. he that is *j*. to the Lord is
Eph. 5. 31. shall be *j*. to his wife
Col. 2. 19. all the body by *joints* and bands
Heb. 4. 12. dividing asunder of *j*.
R. V. Ex. 4. 12. repaired; Isa. 9. 11. stir up; Gen. 14. 8. set in array; Ezra 4. 12. repaired; Job 3. 6. rejoice; Ezek. 46. 22. inclosed; 1 Cor. 1. 10. perfected; Eph. 4. 16. framed; 5. 31. cleave to; Gen. 32. 25. strained
JOURNEY, Num. 9. 13. Rom. 1. 10.
R. V. Num. 33. 12; Deut. 10. 6. journeyed; Mark 13. 34. sojourning in another country; Rom. 1. 10 ——
JOY, 1 Chron. 12. 40. 2 Chron. 20. 27.
Neh. 8. 10. *j*. of Lord is your strength
Esth. 8. 17. the Jews had *j*. and
Job 20. 5. *j*. of the hypocrite is
Ps. 16. 11. in thy presence is fulness of *j*.
30. 5. but *j*. cometh in the morn.
51. 8. make me hear *j*. and glad.
12. restore to me *j*. of thy salva.
126. 5. who sow in tears shall reap in *j*.
Eccl. 9. 7. eat thy bread with *j*.
Isa. 9. 3. hast not increased the *j*.
12. 3. with *j*. shall draw water out
35. 10. with songs and everlast. *j*.
61. 3. give them the oil of *j*. for
7. everlasting *j*. shall be to them
66. 5. shall appear to your *j*.
Zeph. 3. 17. the Lord will *j*. over
Matt. 2. 10. rejoiced with exceeding great *j*.
13. 20. hear the word and with *j*.
25. 21. enter into *j*. of thy Lord
Luke 1. 44. babe leaped in my womb for *j*.
15. 7. *j*. shall be in heaven over
24. 41. while they believe not for *j*.
John 15. 11. that your *j*. might be
16. 20. your sorrow be turn. into *j*.
22. your *j*. no man taketh from
Acts 20. 24. finish my course with *j*.
Rom. 14. 17. righteousness and peace and *j*. in the Holy Ghost
2 Cor. 1. 24. we are help. of your *j*.
Gal. 5. 22. fruit of the Spirit is love, *j*.
Phil. 4. 1. brethren, my *j*. and crown
1 Thes. 1. 6. receive word with *j*. of
Heb. 12. 12. who for the *j*. set be.
Jas. 1. 2. count it all *j*. when ye
1 Pet. 1. 8. rejoice with *j*. unspeak.
4. 13. rejoice, be glad with exceeding *j*.
1 John 1. 4. we write that your *j*.
Col. 2. 5. *joying* and beholding
Heb. 12. 11. no chastening is *joyous*
Ezra 6. 22. the Lord hath made them *joyful*
Ps. 35. 9. my soul shall be *j*. in Lord
63. 5. I will praise thee with *j*. lips
89. 15. blessed they that know *j*.
Eccl. 7. 14. in day of prosper. be *j*.
Isa. 56. 7. make them *j*. in my
61. 10. my soul shall be *j*. in God
2 Cor. 7. 4. exceeding *j*. in all our tribulations
Deut. 28. 47. servedst not the Lord with *joyfulness*
Col. 1. 11. patience and long suffering with *j*.
Eccl. 9. 9. live *joyfully* with the wife
R. V. Job 41. 22. terror danceth; Jer. 48. 27. the head; Acts 2. 28. gladness; Rom. 5. 11. rejoice; Ps. 96. 12; 149. 5. exult; 98. 8. sing for; Col. 1. 11. joy
JUDGE, Deut. 17. 9. & 25. 2.
Gen. 18. 25. shall not the *J*. of earth
Ex. 2. 14. who made thee a *j*.
Judg. 11. 27. Lord the *J*. be *j*. this

1 Sam. 2. 25. the *j*. shall *j*. him;
Isa. 33. 22. Lord is our *j*. and our
Ps. 68. 5. father of fatherless and *j*.
75. 7. God is the *j*. he putteth
Luke 12. 14. who made me a *j*. over
Acts 10. 42. to be the *J*. of quick
2 Tim. 4. 8. Lord the righteous *J*.
Heb. 12. 23. are come to God the *J*.
Jas. 5. 9. the *J*. standeth before
Gen. 16. 5. Lord *j*. between me and
Deut. 32. 36. the Lord shall *j*. his people, Ps. 135. 14. Heb. 10. 30.
Ps. 7. 8. Lord shall *j*. the people
9. 8. the Lord shall *j*. the world in righteous. 96. 13. & 98. 9. Acts 17. 31.
Mic. 3. 11. heads thereof *j*. for re.
Matt. 7. 1. *j*. not that ye be not jud.
John 5. 30. as I hear I *j*. and my
12. 47. I came not to *j*. the world
Acts 23. 3. sittest thou to *j*. me
Rom. 2. 16. when God shall *j*. the
3. 6. then how shall God *j*. the world
14. 10. why dost thou *j*. thy brother
1 Cor. 4. 3. I *j*. not mine own self
5. *j*. nothing before the time, until
11. 31. if we would *j*. ourselves, we
14. 29. let the prophets speak, and others *j*.
Col. 2. 16. let no man *j*. you in meat
2 Tim. 4. 1. who shall *j*. the quick
Jas. 4. 11. if ye *j*. the law
Ps. 51. 4. *judgest*, Rom. 14. 4. Jas. 4. 12.
7. 11. God *judgeth* the righteous
John 5. 22. the Father *j*. no man
1 Cor. 2. 15. he that is spiritual *j*.
Matt. 19. 28. *judging* twelve tribes
Deut. 1. 17. the *judgment* is God's
32. 4. all his ways are *j*. a God of
Ps. 1. 5. the ungodly shall not stand in the *j*.
9. 16. the Lord is known by the *j*.
101. 1. I will sing of mercy and *j*.
119. 66. teach me good *j*. for
143. 2. enter not into *j*. with thy
Prov. 21. 15. it is joy to just to do *j*.
29. 26. every man's *j*. cometh from
Eccl. 11. 9. God will bring into *j*.
Isa. 1. 27. Zion shall be redeemed with *j*.
28. 17. *j*. also will I lay to the line
30. 18. Lord is a God of *j*.
42. 1. shall bring forth *j*. to the
53. 8. was taken from prison and *j*.
61. 8. I the Lord love *j*. and hate
Jer. 5. 1. if there be any that executeth *j*.
8. 7. they know not the *j*. of Lord
Dan. 4. 37. all whose ways are *j*.
7. 22. *j*. was given to the saints
Hos. 12. 6. keep mercy and *j*. wait
Amos 5. 7. who turn *j*. to worm.
24. let *j*. run down as waters, and
Matt. 5. 21. be in danger of the *j*.
12. 20. till he send forth *j*. unto victory
John 5. 22. Father committed all *j*.
27. given him author. to execute *j*.
9. 39. for *j*. I am come into the
16. 8. he will reprove the world of sin and *j*.
Acts 24. 25. he reasoned of *j*. to come
Rom. 5. 18. *j*. came on all men to
14. 10. must all stand before *j*. seat
Heb. 9. 27. all men once to die, but after this the *j*.
1 Pet. 4. 17. *j*. must begin at house
Jude 15. to execute *j*. upon all
Rev. 17. 1. show thee *j*. of great
Ps. 19. 9. *judgments* of Lord are
36. 6. thy *j*. are a great deep
119. 75. I know that thy *j*. are
108. O Lord, teach me thy *j*.
Isa. 26. 8. in the way of thy *j*. we
9. when thy *j*. are in the earth
Jer. 12. 1. let me talk with thee of *j*.
Rom. 11. 33. how unsearchable are his *j*.
R. V. 1 Sam. 2. 25. God; Job 9. 15. mine adversary; 1 Sam. 24. 15. give sentence; Jer. 5. 28. plead; Ezek. 28. 23. fall; 1 Cor. 6. 5. decide; 11. 31; 14. 29. discern; Heb. 11. 11. counted; Acts 24. 6; Jas. 4. 12—; Job 29. 14. justice; Ps. 76. 8; Acts 25. 15; 2 Pet. 2. 3. sentence; Judg. 5. 10. on rich carpets; Phil. 1. 9. discernment; Mark 6. 11 —

JUST man was Noah, Gen. 6. 9.
Lev. 19. 36. *j*. balance, *j*. weights
Deut. 16. 20. that which is *j*. shalt
32. 4. a God of truth, *j*. and right
2 Sam. 23. 3. ruleth over men must be *j*.
Neh. 9. 33. *j*. in all that is brought
Job 4. 17. shall man be more *j*. than
9. 2. how should man be *j*. with
Prov. 4. 18. path of *j*. is as shining
10. 6. blessings are on head of *j*.
11. 1. but a *j*. weight is his delight
12. 21. no evil shall happen to *j*.
17. 26. to punish the *j*. is not good
20. 7. a *j*. man walketh in integrity
21. 15. it is joy to *j*. to do judgment
24. 16. *j*. man falleth seven times
Eccl. 7. 15. *j*. man that perisheth in
20. there is not a *j*. man on earth
Isa. 26. 7. way of the *j*. is upright.
45. 21. none beside me; a *j*. God
Ezek. 18. 9. he is *j*. he shall surely
Hab. 2. 4. *j*. shall live by his faith
Zeph. 3. 5. the *j*. Lord is in the
Zech. 9. 9. he is *j*. and having sal.
Matt. 1. 19. Joseph being a *j*. man
5. 45. sendeth rain on the *j*. and
Luke 15. 7. more than over ninety-nine *j*. persons
John 5. 30. my judgment is *j*.
Acts 7. 52. showed coming of *j*. one
24. 15. resurrection both of *j*. and
Rom. 2. 13. not the hearers of the law are *j*.
3. 26. he might be *j*. and justifier
7. 12. commandment holy, *j*. and
Phil. 4. 8. whatsoever things are true, *j*. pure
Col. 4. 1. give that which is *j*. and
Heb. 2. 2. received a *j*. recompense
12. 23. the spirits of *j*. men made
1 John 1. 9. he is faithful and *j*. to
Rev. 15. 3. *j*. and true are thy ways
Mic. 6. 8. to do *justly*, and love
Luke 23. 41. we indeed *j*. for we
1 Thes. 2. 10. how *j*. we behaved
Gen. 18. 19. to do *justice* and
Ps. 89. 14. *j*. and judgment are the
Prov. 8. 15. by me princes decree *j*.
Jer. 31. 23. O habitation of *j*.
Ezek. 45. 9. execute judg. and *j*.
R. V. For most part, righteous; Ps. 89. 14; Isa. 9. 7; 56. 1; 59. 9, 14. righteousness; 1 Thes. 2. 10. righteously

JUSTIFY not the wicked, Ex. 23. 7.
Deut. 25. 1. they shall *j*. righteous
Job 9. 20. if I *j*. myself, my mouth
27. 5. God forbid that I should *j*.
33. 32. speak, for I desire to *j*. thee
Isa. 5. 23. woe to them that *j*. the
Luke 10. 29. he, willing to *j*. himself
16. 15. ye are they which *j*. your.
Rom. 3. 30. God shall *j*. circumci.
Gal. 3. 8. God would *j*. heathen
Job 11. 2. should a man full of talk be *justified*
13. 18. I know I shall be *j*.
25. 4. can a man be *j*. with God
Ps. 51. 4. mightest be *j*. when thou
143. 2. in thy sight shall no man living be *j*.
Isa. 43. 9. that they may be *j*., 26.
Jer. 3. 11. hath *j*. herself more
Ezek. 16. 51. *j*. thy sisters in all
Matt. 11. 19. wisdom is *j*. of child.
12. 37. by thy words thou shalt be *j*.
Luke 7. 29. *j*. God, being baptized
18. 14. went away *j*. rather than
Acts 13. 39. are *j*. from all things
Rom. 2. 13. doers of law shall be *j*.
3. 4. might be *j*. in thy sayings
20. there shall no flesh be *j*. in his
24. being *j*. freely by his grace
28. man is *j*. by faith without
4. 2. if Abraham were *j*. by works
5. 1. being *j*. by faith, we have
9. being *j*. by his blood, be saved
Rom. 8. 30. whom he *j*. them he also
1 Cor. 4. 4. yet am I not hereby *j*.
6. 11. ye are *j*. in name of the Lord
Gal. 2. 16. not *j*. by works of law
3. 11. no man is *j*. by the law
24. that we might be *j*. by faith
1 Tim. 3. 16. God manifest in flesh, *j*. in Spirit
Tit. 3. 7. that being *j*. by his grace
Jas. 2. 21. was not Abraham *j*. by
24. by works a man is *j*. not faith
25. was not Rahab *j*. by works
Prov. 17. 15. he that *justifieth* the wicked
Isa. 50. 8. he is near, that *j*. me
Rom. 4. 5. God that *j*. the ungodly
8. 33. it is God that *j*. who is he
3. 26. the *justifier* of him that
1 Kings 8. 32. condemning the wicked and *justifying* the righteous, 2 Chron. 6. 23.
Rom. 4. 25. raised for our *justification*
5. 16. gift is of many offences unto *j*.
18. free gift came on all men, to *j*.
R. V. Job 13. 18. am righteous; 25. 4. just; Job 9. 20; 13. 18. righteous

K

KEEP, Gen. 2. 15. & 33. 9.
Gen. 18. 19. they shall *k*. the way
28. 15. I am with thee and will *k*.
Ex. 23. 7. *k*. thee far from a false
20. I send an angel to *k*. thee in
Num. 6. 24. the Lord bless thee, and *k*. thee
Deut. 23. 9. *k*. thee from every
29. 9. *k*. words of this covenant
1 Sam. 2. 9. he will *k*. the feet of
1 Chron. 4. 10. thou wouldst *k*. me
Ps. 17. 8. *k*. me as the apple of the eye
25. 10. to such as *k*. his covenant
20. *k*. my soul
89. 28. my mercy will I *k*. for
91. 11. angels to *k*. thee in all
103. 9. not chide nor *k*. his anger
119. 2. *k*. his testimonies, 88, 129, 146; *k*. thy precepts, 4, 63, 69, 100; *k*. his statutes, 119. 33; *k*. his word and law, 17, 34, 57, 106, 136.
127. 1. except the Lord *k*. the city
140. 4. *k*. me, O Lord, from the
141. 3. *k*. the door of my lips
Eccl. 5. 1. *k*. thy foot when thou
Isa. 26. 3. Lord will *k*. him in per.
27. 3. I the Lord *k*. it; I will *k*. it
Jer. 3. 12. I will not *k*. anger for
Hos. 12. 6. *k*. mercy and judgment
Mic. 7. 5. *k*. the door of thy mouth
Mal. 2. 7. priest's lips *k*. knowledge
Luke 11. 28. hear the word of God and *k*. it
John 12. 25. he that hateth his life shall *k*. it
14. 23. if man love me, will *k*. my
17. 11. holy Father, *k*. through
15. thou shouldest *k*. them from
1 Cor. 5. 8. let us *k*. the feast, not
11. not to *k*. company with such
9. 27. I *k*. under my body, and
Phil. 4. 7. peace of God shall *k*.
1 Tim. 5. 22. *k*. thyself pure
6. 20. *k*. that is committed to thy
2 Tim. 1. 12. able to *k*. that which is
Jas. 1. 27. *k*. himself unspotted
Jude 21. *k*. yoursel. in love of God
24. who is able to *k*. you from
Rev. 1. 3. blessed are they that hear and *k*.
3. 10. I will *k*. thee from the hour
22. 9. thy brethren which *k*. say.
Lev. 26. 3. if ye *keep* my *commandments*
Deut. 6. 7. diligently—always
13. 4. —his—and obey his voice
Ps. 119. 60. I delayed not to—thy—
Prov. 4. 4. —my—and live, 7. 2.
Eccl. 12. 13. fear God and—his—

Matt. 19. 17. if ye will enter into life — the —
John 14. 15. if ye love me — my —
1 John 2. 3. we know him, if we — his —
5. 3. this is the love of God that we — his —
Rev. 14. 12. here are they that — the —
Judg. 3. 19. *keep silence*, Ps. 35. 22. & 50. 3, 21. & 83. 1. Eccl. 3. 7. Isa. 41. 1. & 62. 6. & 65. 6. Lam. 2. 10. Amos 5. 13. Hab. 2. 20. 1 Cor. 14. 28, 34.
1 Kings 8. 23. who *keepest* covenant and mer., 2 Chron. 6.14. Neh. 9. 32.
Deut. 7. 9. which *keepeth* covenant
Ps. 121. 3. he that *k.* thee will not
146. 6. which *k.* truth for ever
Prov. 13. 3. he that *k.* his mouth *k.*
29. 18. he that *k.* the law, happy
1 John 5. 18. that is of God *k.* him.
Rev. 16. 15. blessed is he that *k.*
22. 7. blessed is he that *k.* his
Ex. 34. 7. *keeping* mercy for thous.
Ps. 19. 11. in *k.* of them there is
Dan. 9. 4. *k.* the covenant and mercy
1 Pet. 4. 19. commit the *k.* of their
Ps. 121. 5. the Lord is thy *keeper*
Eccl. 12. 3. when *k.* of house shall
S. of S. 1. 6. made me *k.* of vine.
5. 7. *k.* took away my veil from me
Tit. 2. 5. chaste, *k.* at home, good
Deut. 32. 10. *k.* them as the apple
33. 9. they *kept* thy covenant
Josh. 14. 10. Lord hath *k.* me alive
2 Sam. 22. 22. *k.* ways of the Lord
23. *k.* myself from mine iniquity
Job 23. 11. his ways have I *k.* and
Ps. 17. 4. *k.* me from paths of the
30. 3. *k.* me alive, that I go not
S. of S. 1. 6. mine own vineyard have I not *k.*
Matt. 19. 20. these have I *k.* from
Luke 2. 19. Mary *k.* all these things
John 15. 20. if they have *k.* my say.
17. 6. they have *k.* thy word
12. all thou gavest me, I have *k.*
Rom. 16. 25. *k.* secret since the world
2 Tim. 4. 7. I have *k.* the faith
1 Pet. 1. 5. *k.* by the power of God
Rev. 3. 8. hast *k.* my word, and not
R. V. Deut. 5. 1, 12; 23. 23; 1 Chron. 28. 8; Ps. 105. 45; 119. 5, 8, 44, 57, 60, 63, 88. observe; Acts 12. 4; Phil. 4. 7; 2 Thes. 3. 3; 1 Tim. 6. 20; 2 Tim. 1. 12; 1 John 5. 21; Jude 24. guard; Matt. 28. 4. watchers; Acts 12. 6; 12. 19. guards; 16. 27. jailor; Tit. 2. 5. workers

KERCHIEFS, woe respecting, Ezek. 13. 18.

KEY of house of David, Isa. 22. 22. Rev. 3. 7.
Matt. 16. 19. *k.* of the kingdom of
Luke 11. 52. taken away the *k.* of
Rev. 1. 18. I have *k.* of hell
9. 1. *k.* of the bottomless pit

KICK, Deut. 32. 15. 1 Sam. 2. 29. Acts 9. 5. & 26. 14.

KID, Isa. 11. 6. Luke 15. 29.
S. of S. 1. 8. feed *k.* beside sheph.
R. V. In Gen. Lev. Num. and Ezek. mostly he-goat, or goat

KIDNEYS, for sacrifices, burnt, Ex. 29. 13. Lev. 3. 4.
— of wheat, fat of, Deut. 32. 14.

KILL, thou shalt not, Ex. 20. 13.
Deut. 32. 39. I *k.* and I make alive
2 Kings 5. 7. I am God to *k.* and to
Eccl. 3. 3. time to *k.* and to heal
Matt. 10. 28. fear not them which *k.* the body, but are not able to *k.*
Mark 3. 4. lawful to save life, or *k.*
Acts 10. 13. rise, Peter, *k.* and eat
1 Kings 21. 19. hast thou *killed* and
Ps. 44. 22. we are *k.* all day long
Luke 12. 5. after he hath *k.* hath
Acts 3. 15. *k.* the Prince of Life
2 Cor. 6. 9. we are chast. and not *k.*
1 Thes. 2. 15. both *k.* the Lord
Rev. 13. 10. that *k.* with the sword
Matt. 23. 37. thou that *killest* the prophets, Luke 13. 34.
1 Sam. 2. 6. the Lord *killeth*, and
John 16. 2. who *k.* you will think
2 Cor. 3. 6. letter *k.* but spirit
R. V. Ex. 20. 13; Deut. 5. 17; Matt. 19. 18. do no murder; Num. 35. 27; 1 Sam. 19. 1; 2 Kings 11. 15; Acts 23. 15; Rev. 6. 4. slay; Mark 14. 12; Luke 22. 7. sacrificed

KIND, Gen. 1. 11. 2 Chron. 10. 7.
Luke 6. 35. he is *k.* to unthankful
1 Cor. 13. 4. charity suff. long . is *k.*
Eph. 4. 32. be *k.* to one another
1 Sam. 20. 14. show me the *kindness*
2 Sam. 9. 3. may show the *k.* of God
16. 17. is this thy *k.* to thy friend
Neh. 9. 17. a God slow to anger and of great *k.*
Ps. 117. 2. his merciful *k.* is great
Prov. 19. 22. the des. of man is his *k.*
31. 26. in her tongue is law of *k.*
Isa. 54. 8. with everlasting *k.* will
10. my *k.* shall not depart from
Jer. 2. 2. I remember thee, the *k.*
Joel 2. 13. God is of great *k.*
Col. 3. 12. put on bowels of mer., *k.*
2 Pet. 1. 7. to godliness, brother. *k.*
Ps. 25. 6. remember thy *loving kindness*
36. 7. how excellent is thy —
63. 3. thy — is better than life
103. 4. who crowneth thee with —
Isa. 63. 7. I will mention the — of
Jer. 9. 24. I am the Lord which exercise —
32. 18. thou showest — to thous.
Hos. 2. 19. I will betroth thee in —
R. V. Matt. 17. 21 ——

KINDLE, Prov. 26. 21. Isa. 10. 16.
Isa. 30. 33. breath of Lord doth *k.* it
Hos. 11. 8. my repentings are *kindled*
2 Sam. 22. 9. coals *k.* by it, Ps. 18. 8.
Ps. 2. 12. when his wrath is *k.* but a
Isa. 50. 11. walk in light of sparks ye have *k.*
Luke 12. 49. fire on earth, what if it be already *k.*
R. V. Prov. 26. 21. inflame; Jer. 33. 18. burn; Jas. 3. 5. much wood is kindled by how small a fire

KING, Gen. 14. 18. & 36. 31.
Job 18. 14. bring him to *k.* of ter.
34. 18. is it fit to say to a *k.* thou
Ps. 10. 16. Lord is *K.* for ever and
24. 7. the *K.* of glory shall come
33. 16. no *k.* saved by multitude
47. 7. God is *K.* of all the earth
74. 12. God is my *k.*, 5. 2. & 44. 4.
Prov. 30. 31. a *k.* against whom is
Eccl. 5. 9. *k.* himself is served by
8. 4. where word of *k.* is there
S. of S. 1. 4. the *k.* brought me into
12. while the *k.* sitteth at his table
7. 5. the *k.* is held in the galleries
Isa. 32. 1. a *k.* shall reign in
33. 22. the Lord is our lawgiver and our *k.*
43. 15. Creator of Israel, your *K.*
Jer. 10. 10. Lord is true God, and everlasting *K.*
23. 5. a *K.* shall reign and prosper
46. 18. saith the *K.* whose name
Hos. 3. 5. seek the Lord and David their *k.*
7. 5. in day of our *k.* the princes
13. 11. I gave them a *k.* in anger
Matt. 25. 34. then shall the *K.* say
Luke 23. 2. he himself is Christ, a *k.*
John 6. 15. come by force to make him *k.*
19. 14. behold your *k.*
15. no *k.* but Cæsar
1 Tim. 1. 17. to the *K.* eternal
6. 15. *K.* of kings, and Lord of lords, Rev. 16. 16. & 17. 14.
1 Pet. 2. 17. fear God, honor *k.*, 13.
Rev. 15. 3. just and true, thou *K.*
Ps. 76. 12. terrible to *kings* of the earth, 72. 11.
102. 15. *k.* of the earth see thy glory
144. 10. that giveth salva. to *k.*
149. 8. to bind their *k.* with fetters
Prov. 8. 15. by me *k.* reign, and
Hos. 8. 4. they set up *k.* but not by
Matt. 11. 8. soft clothing are in *k.* houses
Luke 22. 25. *k.* of Gentiles exercise
1 Cor. 4. 8. reigned as *k.* without us
1 Tim. 2. 2. give thanks for *k.* and
Rev. 1. 6. made us *k.* and priests
16. 12. that way of *k.* of the east
Ex. 19. 6. be a *kingdom* of priests
1 Sam. 10. 25. Samuel told man. of *k.*
1 Chron. 29. 11. thine is the *k.* O Lord, Matt. 6. 13.
Ps. 22. 28. for the *k.* is the Lord's
Dan. 2. 44. in last days shall God set up a *k.*
7. 27. whose *k.* is everlasting *k.*, 14.
Matt. 12. 25. every *k.* divided
38. good seed are the children of *k.*
25. 34. inherit *k.* prepared for you
Mark 11. 10. blessed be the *k.* of
Luke 12. 32. Father's pleasure to give you the *k.*
19. 12. to receive for himself a *k.*
John 18. 36. *k.* is not of this world
1 Cor. 15. 24. shall have delivered up the *k.*
Col. 1. 13. translated us into the *k.*
2 Tim. 4. 18. preserve me to his heavenly *k.*
Heb. 12. 28. we receiving a *k.* not to
Jas. 2. 5. rich in faith, heirs of *k.*
2 Pet. 1. 11. into everlasting *k.* of
Rev. 1. 9. in *k.* and patience of
11. 15. the *k.* of this world are *k.*
17. 17. to give their *k.* to the beast
Matt. 6. 33. *kingdom of God*, 12. 28. & 21. 43. Mark 1. 15. & 10. 14, 15. & 12. 34. & 15. 43. Luke 4. 43. & 6. 20. & 9. 62. & 10. 9, 11. & 13. 29. & 17. 20, 21. & 18. 16, 17, 29. & 21. 16.
John 3. 3. except born again, cannot see —, 5.
Rom. 14. 17. — is not meat and drink
1 Cor. 4. 20. — is not in word, but
6. 9. unright. shall not inherit —
15. 50. flesh and blood cannot inherit —
Eph. 5. 5. hath any inheritance in —
2 Thes. 1. 5. be counted worthy of —
Rev. 12. 10. now is come — and power
Matt. 3. 2. *kingdom of heaven*, 4. 17. & 10. 7. & 5. 3, 10, 19, 20. & 7. 21. & 8. 11. & 11. 11, 12. & 13. 11, 24, 31, 52. & 16. 19. & 18. 1, 3, 23. & 20. 1. & 22. 2. & 23. 13. & 25. 1, 14.

KISS the Son, lest he be angry, Ps. 2. 12.
S. of S. 1. 2. let him *k.* me with the *k.*
Rom. 16. 16. salute with a holy *k.*
1 Pet. 5. 14. greet with *k.* of charity
Ps. 85. 10. righteousness and peace have *kissed*
Luke 7. 38. *k.* his feet and anointed
Prov. 27. 6. *kisses* from an enemy

KNEELING in prayer, 2 Chron. 6. 13. Ezra 9. 5. Ps. 95. 6. Dan. 6. 10. Acts 7. 60. & 9. 40. & 21. 5. Eph. 3. 14.

KNEES, Gen. 30. 3. & 41. 43.
Job 4. 4. feeble *k.*, Isa. 35. 3. Heb. 12. 12.
Isa. 45. 23. to God every *k.* shall bow, Rom. 14. 11. Phil. 2. 10. Matt. 27. 29. Eph. 3. 14.
Nah. 2. 10. the *k.* smite together

KNIFE, Prov. 23. 2. & 30. 14.
R. V. Ezek. 5. 1, 2. sword

KNIT, 1 Sam. 18. 1. Col. 2. 2, 19.

KNEW, Gen. 3. 7. & 4. 1. & 42. 7.
Gen. 28. 16. God is in this place, I *k.* it not
Deut. 34. 10. whom Lord *k.* face to
Jer. 1. 5. before I formed thee, I *k.*
Matt. 7. 23. depart ye, I never *k.*
John 4. 10. if you *k.* the gift of God
Rom. 1. 21. when they *k.* God, they
2 Cor. 5. 21. made him to be sin who *k.* no sin
Deut. 8. 2. to *know* what was in thy
Josh. 22. 22. God knoweth, and Israel he shall *k.*
1 Sam. 3. 7. Samuel did not yet *k.*
1 Kings 8. 38. man shall *k.* plague

1 Chron. 28. 9. k. thou the God of
Job. 5. 27. k. thou it for thy good
13. 23. make me to k. my trans.
22. 13. how doth God k., Ps. 73. 11.
Ps. 4. 3. k. the Lord hath set apart
9. 10. that k. thy name will trust in
46. 10. be still, and k. that I am God
51. 6. God shall make me to k.
139. 23. k. my heart; and k. my
Eccl. 11. 9. k. that for all these
Isa. 58. 2. they seek and delight to k.
Jer. 17. 9. heart is dece. who can k.
22. 16. was not this to k. me
24. 7. I will give them a heart to k.
31. 34. saying, k. the Lord
Ezek. 2. 5. shall k. that a prophet hath, 33. 33.
Hos. 2. 20. in faithfulness thou shalt k. the Lord
Mic. 3. 1. is it not for you to k.
Matt. 6. 3. let not left hand k. what
7. 11. k. how to give good gifts
13. 11. given you to k. mystery
John 4. 42. we k. this is indeed
7. 17. he shall k. of the doctrine
10. 4. sheep follow him, for they k.
14. I k. my sheep and am known
13. 7. k. not now, but shalt k.
17. if ye k. these things, happy are
35. by this men k. ye are my
Acts 1. 7. it is not for you to k. the
Rom. 10. 19. did not Israel k. yes
1 Cor. 2. 14. neither can ye k. them
4. 19. I will k. not the speech
8. 2. k. any thing, k. nothing as he
Eph. 3. 19. to k. love of Christ
1 Thes. 5. 12. to k. them who labor
Tit. 1. 16. they profess that they k.
Ex. 4. 14. *I know*, Job 9. 2, 28.
Gen. 18. 19. — him that he will
22. 12. now — that thou fearest God
2 Kings 19. 27. — thy abode and thy
Job 19. 25. — that my Redeemer liveth
Ps. 41. 11. by this — that thou fav.
Jer. 10. 23. — that the way of man
Matt. 25. 12. — you not, Luke 13. 25.
John 13. 18. — whom I have chosen
Acts 26. 27. — that thou believest
Rom. 7. 18. — that in me
1 Cor. 4. 4. though — nothing by
13. 12. now — in part; but then
Phil. 4. 12. — how to be abased
2 Tim. 1. 12. — whom I have believed
1 John 2. 4. he that saith — him, is
Rev. 2. 2. — thy works, 9. 13, 19. & 3. 1, 3, 15.
Hos. 6. 3. *we know*, 8. 2. John 4. 22.
1 Cor. 2. 12. 1 John 2. 3, 5.
John 16. 30. *thou knowest* all things
21. 17. — all things — that I love thee
Ps. 1. 6. Lord *knoweth* the way of
94. 11. Lord k. thoughts of man
103. 14. he k. our frame, that we
139. 14. my soul k. right well
Eccl. 9. 1. no man k. either love or
Isa. 1. 3. ox k. his owner, and ass
Jer. 8. 7. stork k. appointed times
9. 24. understandeth and k. me to
Zeph. 3. 5. the unjust k. no shame
Matt. 6. 8. k. what things ye have
24. 36. of that day and hour k. no
1 Cor. 8. 2. k. any thing, he k. nothing yet
2 Tim. 2. 19. the Lord k. them that
Jas. 4. 17. that k. to do good doeth
2 Pet. 2. 9. Lord k. how to deliver
Rev. 2. 17. a name which no man k.
Ps. 9. 16. Lord is *known* by the
31. 7. hast k. my soul in adversity
67. 2. thy way may be k. on earth
Isa. 45. 4. thou hast not k. me, 5.
Amos 3. 2. you only have I k. of all
Matt. 10. 26. there is nothing hid that shall not be k., Luke 8. 17. & 12. 2.
Luke 19. 42. if thou hadst k. in this
Acts 15. 18. k. unto God are all his
Rom. 1. 19. that which may be k.
7. 7. I had not k. sin but by the
1 Cor. 8. 3. the same is k. of him
Gal. 4. 9. k. God, or rather are k. of
Rev. 2. 24. have not k. the depths of
Gen. 2. 17. *knowledge* of good and
1 Sam. 2. 3. the Lord is a God of k.
Ps. 19. 2. night unto night show. k.
73. 11. is there k. in the Most High
94. 10. he that teacheth men k.
139. 6. such k. is too wonderful
Prov. 8. 12. I find out k. of witty
14. 6. k. is easy to him that understandeth
19. 2. the soul be without k. is not
30. 3. I have not the k. of the holy
Eccl. 9. 10. there is no device nor k.
Isa. 28. 9. whom shall he teach k.
Jer. 3. 15. pastors shall feed you with k.
Dan. 12. 4. run to and fro, and k. be
Hos. 4. 6. are destroy. for lack of k.
Hab. 2. 14. earth filled with k. of the Lord, Isa. 11. 9.
Mal. 2. 7. priest's lips should keep k.
Rom. 2. 20. a teacher hast form of k.
3. 20. for by the law is k. of sin
10. 2. zeal for God not accord. to k.
1 Cor. 8. 1. all have k. k. puffeth up
Eph. 3. 19. the love of Christ which passeth k.
Phil. 3. 8. loss for excellency of the k.
Col. 2. 3. are hid treasures of wisdom and k.
3. 10. renewed in k. after image of
1 Pet. 3. 7. dwell with them according to k.
2 Pet. 1. 5. add to virtue k. and to k.
3. 18. grow in grace and in the k. of Jesus Christ
R. V. Many changes to, perceive, understand, learn, discern, etc., but none affecting general meaning. Prov. 2. 3. discernment; Eph. 3. 4. understanding
KNOCK, Matt. 7. 7. Rev. 3. 20.

L

LABOR, Gen. 31. 42. & 35. 16.
Ps. 90. 10. yet is their strength l.
104. 23. man goeth to his l. until eve
128. 2. thou shalt eat the l. of thine
Prov. 14. 23. in all l. there is profit
Eccl. 1. 8. all things are full of l.
4. 8. yet is there no end of all his l.
Isa. 55. 2. ye spend your l. for that
Hab. 3. 17. though l. of the olive
1 Cor. 15. 58. your l. is not in vain
1 Thes. 1. 3. work of faith, and l.
Heb. 6. 10. God will not forget your l. of
Rev. 14. 13. dead may rest from l.
Prov. 23. 4. l. not to be rich; cease
Matt. 11. 28. come all ye that l. and
John 6. 27. l. not for the meat
1 Thes. 5. 12. know them which l.
1 Tim. 5. 17. honor those who l.
Heb. 4. 11. let us l. to enter into
Isa. 49. 4. I have *labored* in vain
John 4. 38. other men l. and ye
1 Cor. 15. 10. I l. more abundantly
Phil. 2. 16. not run, nor l. in vain
Prov. 16. 26. he that *laboreth*, l.
Eccl. 5. 12. sleep of the *laboring* man is sweet
Col. 4. 12. Epaphras l. fervently
Luke 10. 7. the *laborer* is worthy
Matt. 9. 37. but *laborers* are few, Luke 10. 2.
1 Cor. 3. 9. we are l. toge. with God
R. V. Deut. 26. 7; Rev. 2. 2. toil; Eccl. 1. 8. weariness; Phil. 1. 22. work; Josh. 7. 3; 1 Cor. 4. 12. toil; Neh. 4. 21. wrought; Lam. 5. 5. are weary; 2 Cor. 5. 9. make it our aim; Col. 4. 12. striving; 1 Thes. 2. 9. working; Heb. 4. 11. give diligence; Rev. 2. 3 —
LACK, Hos. 4. 6. Matt. 19. 20, 21.
2 Cor. 11. 9. 1 Thes. 3. 10. Jas. 1. 5.
R. V. 1 Thes. 4. 12. need
LADEN with iniquity, Isa. 1. 4.
Matt. 11. 28. labor and heavy l.
2 Tim. 3. 6. silly women, l. with
LADDER, Jacob's, Gen. 28. 12.
LADY of kingdoms, Isa. 47. 5.
Isa. 47. 7. I shall be a l. for ever
2 John 1. unto the elect l.
Esth. 1. 18. *ladies* of Persia
Judg. 5. 29. her wise l. answered
R. V. Esth. 1. 18. princesses
LAMB, Gen. 22. 7, 8. Ex. 12. 3.
2 Sam. 12. 3. man had nothing save one ewe l.
Isa. 11. 6. wolf shall dwell with l.
53. 7. he is brought as a l. to the
John 1. 29. behold the L. of God
1 Pet. 1. 19. as a l. without blem.
Rev. 5. 12. worthy is the L. that
6. 16. fall on us and hide us from the face of the L.
7. 14. robes made white in blood of the L., 12. 11.
17. L. in the midst of the throne shall feed them
13. 8. L. slain from the foundation of the world
R. V. In Num., he-lamb
LAME, Lev. 21. 18. Mal. 1. 8, 13.
Job 29. 15. eyes to the blind and feet to the l.
Prov. 26. 7. legs of the l. are not
Isa. 35. 6. the l. man shall leap
Heb. 12. 13. lest the l. be turned
LAMP, Gen. 15. 17. Ex. 27. 20.
1 Kings 15. 4. Matt. 25. 1, 3, 4, 7, 8.
2 Sam. 22. 29. thou art my l. O Lord
Ps. 119. 105. thy word a l. to my
132. 17. I have ordained a l. for
Prov. 6. 23. the command. is a l.
13. 9. l. of wicked shall be put out
Isa. 62. 1. salvation as a l. that
Ex. 25. 37. *seven lamps*, 37. 23. Num. 8. 2. Zech. 4. 2. Rev. 4. 5.
R. V. Gen. 15. 17; Rev. 8. 10. torch; Judg. 7. 16, 20; Job 41. 19; Ezek. 1. 13. torches
LAND, Eccl. 10. 16, 17. Isa. 5. 30.
Deut. 19. 14. remove *landmark*, 27. 17. Job 24. 2. Prov. 22. 28. & 23. 10.
R. V. Many changes in O. T. to earth, ground, country, etc.
LANGUAGE, Gen. 11. 1. Neh. 13. 24.
Ps. 81. 5. Isa. 19. 18. Zeph. 3. 9.
LANGUISH, Isa. 24. 4. Ps. 41. 3.
LASCIVIOUSNESS, Mark 7. 22.
2 Cor. 12. 21. Gal. 5. 19. Eph. 4. 19. 1 Pet. 4. 3.
Jude 4. turning grace of God into l.
LAST end be like his, Num. 23. 10.
Lam. 1. 9. she remembered not her l. end
Luke 11. 26. l. state is worse than
1 Pet. 1. 5. *last time*, 20. 1 John 2. 18.
Jude 18. should be mockers in the —
R. V. Gen. 49. 1; Isa. 2. 2; Jer. 12. 4; Lam. 1. 9; Dan. 8. 19; Mic. 4. 1. latter; Matt. 21. 37; Luke 20. 32. afterward
LATTER day, Job 19. 25; l. end, Prov. 19. 20; l. house, Hag. 2. 9; l. time, 1 Tim. 4. 1. 2 Tim. 3. 1.
LAUGH, Gen. 17. 17. & 18. 12, 15.
2 Chron. 30. 10. but they l. them
Job 5. 22. at destruction and famine thou shalt l.
Ps. 2. 4. he that sitteth in the heavens shall l.
37. 13. the Lord shall l. at him
52. 6. righteous. shall see and l.
59. 8. thou, O Lord, shall l. at
Prov. 1. 26. I will l. at your calam.
Luke 6. 21. blessed that weep, for ye shall l.
Job 8. 21. he fill thy mouth with *laughing*
Ps. 126. 2. our mouth was filled with *laughter*
Prov. 14. 13. even in l. heart is sor.
Eccl. 7. 3. sorrow is better than l.
Jas. 4. 9. let your l. be turned
LAW, Gen. 47. 26. Prov. 28. 4.
Deut. 33. 2. from his right hand went a fiery l.

Neh. 8. 7. caused people to understand the *l.*
10. 28. separated from people to *l.*
Ps. 1. 2. his delight is in the *l.*
19. 7. *l.* of the Lord is perfect
37. 31. *l.* of his God is in his heart
119. 72. *l.* of thy mouth is better
Prov. 6. 23. *l.* is light
7. 2. keep my *l.* as apple of eye
28. 9. turns away from hearing *l.*
29. 18. keepeth the *l.* happy is he
Isa. 2. 2. shall go forth the *l.*
8. 16. seal the *l.* among my dis.
20. to the *l.* and the testimony
42. 21. magnify the *l.* and make
51. 7. peo. in whose heart is my *l.*
Jer. 18. 18. *l.* shall not perish from
31. 33. I will put my *l.* in inward
Ezek. 7. 26. *l.* shall perish from
Hos. 8. 12. writ. great things of my *l.*
Mal. 2. 7. people seek *l.* at his
Luke 16. 16. *l.* and prophets till
John 1. 17. *l.* was given by Moses
19. 7. we have a *l.* and by our *l.*
Acts 13. 39. not justified by the *l.*
Rom. 2. 12. sinned without *l.*
13. not hearers of *l.* but doers of *l.*
3. 20. by deeds of *l.* shall no flesh
27. boasting by what *l.* by *l.* of
31. do we make void the *l.*
5. 13. sin is not imput. where no *l.*
7. 7. had not known sin but by *l.*
8. for without the *l.* sin was dead
12. the *l.* is holy, just, and good
14. *l.* is spiritual, but I am carnal
22. I delight in the *l.* of God
23. *l.* in my members against *l.*
8. 2. *l.* of Spirit made free from *l.*
10. 4. Christ is end of the *l.* for
5. righteousness of *l.*, 9. 31, 32.
1 Cor. 6. 1. dare any of you go to *l.*
Gal. 2. 16. man not justified by works of the *l.*
3. 10. of works of the *l.* are under
12. the *l.* is not of faith, but the
13. Christ redeemed us from the curse of the *l.*
5. 23. love, faith, against such there is no *l.*
1 Tim. 1. 8. the *l.* is good if we use
9. that *l.* is not made for right.
Heb. 7. 19. *l.* made nothing perfect
Jas. 1. 25. whoso looketh into the perfect *l.*
1 John 3. 4. sin transgresseth the *l.* sin is transgression of *l.*
Neh. 9. 26. cast *thy law* behind their backs
Ps. 40. 8. — is within my heart
94. 12. whom thou teach. out of —
119. 70. I delight in —, 77. 92, 174.
18. wondrous things out of —
97. how I love —, 113. 163.
Ezek. 18. 5. do that which is *lawful* and right, 33. 14, 19.
1 Cor. 6. 12. all things are *l.* to
Isa. 33. 22. Lord is *lawgiver*
R. V. Gen. 47. 26; 1 Chron. 16. 17; Ps. 94. 20; 105. 10. statute; Acts 15. 24; 24. 6; Rom. 9. 32; 1 Cor. 7. 39; 9. 20 ——; Acts 19. 39. regular; Gen. 49. 10. ruler's staff; Num. 21. 18; Ps. 60. 7; 108. 8. sceptre
LAY, Gen. 19. 33, 35. Job 29. 19.
Eccl. 7. 2. the living will *l.* it to
Isa. 28. 16. I *l.* in Zion a tried
Mal. 2. 2. I cursed, ye do not *l.*
Matt. 8. 20. hath not where to *l.*
Acts 7. 60. *l.* not this sin to their
15. 28. *l.* on you no greater bur.
Heb. 12. 1. *l.* aside every weight
Jas. 1. 21. *l.* apart all filthiness
John 10. 15. *lay down life*, 13. 37. & 15. 13.
1 Tim. 5. 22. *lay hands*, Heb. 6. 2.
6. 12. *lay hold* on eternal life
Heb. 6. 18. — on hope set before us
Matt. 6. 20. *lay up* for yourselves
Ps. 62. 9. to be *laid* in the balance
89. 19. I *l.* help on one that is
Isa. 53. 6. Lord *l.* on him iniquities
Matt. 3. 10. axe *l.* to root of trees
1 Cor. 3. 10. I have *l.* foundation
Heb. 6. 1. not *l.* again foundation

1 Sam. 21. 12. David *laid up* these
Ps. 31. 19. thy goodness — for them
Luke 1. 66. — in their hearts
Col. 1. 5. hope which is — for you
2 Tim. 4. 8. — for me a crown of
Job 21. 19. God *layeth* up his iniq.
24. 12. yet God *l.* not folly to them
Prov. 2. 7. *l.* up wisdom
26. 24. *l.* up deceit
Isa. 56. 2. blessed is the man that *l.* hold on
57. 1. no man *l.* to heart, 42. 25.
R. V. The frequent changes do not modify general meaning. *See* also the *v. i.* **Lie, lay, lain.**
LEAD, Ex. 15. 10. Job 19. 24. Zech. 5. 7, 8. Gen. 33. 14. Ex. 13. 21.
Ps. 5. 8. *lead me* in thy righteous.
25. 5. — in thy truth
27. 11. — in a plain path
61. 2. — to rock higher than I
24. — in the way everlasting
Isa. 11. 6. a little child shall *l.* them
40. 11. gently *l.* those with young
Matt. 15. 14. if blind *l.* the blind, Luke 6. 39.
1 Tim. 2. 2. may *l.* a quiet and
Rev. 7. 17. Lamb shall *l.* them to
Ps. 23. 2. *leadeth* me beside still
48. 17. God which *l.* thee by way
Matt. 7. 13. gate *l.* to destruction
John 10. 3. calleth sheep and *l.*
Rom. 2. 4. goodness of God *l.*
Gen. 24. 27. *Lord led*, 48. Ex. 13. 18. & 15. 13. Deut. 8. 2. & 29. 5. & 32. 10, 12. Neh. 9. 12. Ps. 77. 20. & 80. 1. & 78. 14, 53. & 106. 9. & 136. 16. & 107. 7.
Isa. 48. 2. & 63. 13, 14. Jer. 26. 17.
Rom. 8. 14. *led by Spirit*, Gal. 5. 18.
Isa. 55. 4. *leader* to people, 9. 16.
R. V. Ps. 25. 5; Matt. 15. 14; Luke 6. 39; Rev. 7. 17. guide
LEAF, Job 13. 25. Ezek. 47. 12. Rev. 22. 2.
LEAGUE with stones of field, Job 5. 23.
R. V. Josh. 9. 6, 7, 11, 15, 16; Judg. 2. 2; 2 Sam. 3. 21; 5. 3. covenant
LEAN not to own understanding, Prov. 3. 5.
Job 8. 15. he shall *l.* upon his
S. of S. 8. 5. that *l.* on her beloved
Mic. 3. 11. yet will they *l.* on Lord
John 13. 23. *l.* on Jesus' bosom
R. V. John 13. 23. reclining
LEANNESS, Job 16. 8. Ps. 106. 15. Isa. 10. 16. & 24. 16. my *l.* my *l.*
R. V. Isa. 24. 16. I pine away
LEAP, S. of S. 2. 8. Isa. 35. 6. Zeph. 1. 9.
Luke 1. 41. & 6. 23. rejoice and *l.* for
LEARN to fear me, Deut. 4. 10. & 5. 1. & 14. 23. & 31. 12, 13.
Ps. 119. 71. might *l.* thy statutes
Prov. 22. 25. lest thou *l.* his ways
Isa. 1. 17. *l.* to do well, seek
26. 10. yet will he not *l.* righteous.
Jer. 10. 2. *l.* not way of the heathen
Matt. 9. 13. *l.* what that means
11. 29. *l.* of me, for I am meek
1 Tim. 2. 11. let woman *l.* in silence
Tit. 3. 14. let ours *l.* to maintain
Rev. 14. 3. no man could *l.* that
Ps. 106. 35. *learned* their works
Isa. 50. 4. Lord God hath given me the tongue of the *l.*
John 6. 45. hath *l.* of Father cometh
Acts 7. 22. Moses was *l.* in all wis.
Eph. 4. 20. ye have not so *l.* Christ
Phil. 4. 11. I have *l.* in whatsoever
Heb. 5. 8. though a son, yet *l.* he
Prov. 1. 5. wise will incre. *learning*
Acts 26. 24. much *l.* doth make
Rom. 15. 4. was written for our *l.*
2 Tim. 3. 7. ever *l.* never come
R. V. Isa. 50. 4. are taught; Acts 7. 22. instructed
LEAST of thy mercies, Gen. 32. 10.
Jer. 31. 34. shall know me from *l.* to
Matt. 11. 11. *l.* in kingdom of God
Luke 16. 10. faithful in *l.* is faithful
1 Cor. 6. 4. judge who are *l.* esteemed

1 Cor. 15. 9. I am *l.* of all the apostles
Eph. 3. 8. less than the *l.* of all
R. V. 1 Sam. 21. 4. only; Matt. 13. 22. less than; 11. 11; Luke 7. 28. but little; Luke 16. 10. a very little; 1 Cor. 6. 4. of no account
LEAVE father and mother and cleave to his wife, Gen. 2. 24. Matt. 15. 9. Eph. 5. 31.
1 Kings 8. 57. let him not *l.* us, nor
Ps. 16. 10. not *l.* my soul in hell
27. 9. *l.* me not, neither forsake me
Matt. 5. 24. *l.* there thy gift before
23. 23. and not to *l.* other undone
John 14. 18. I will not *l.* you com.
27. peace I *l.* with you, my peace
Heb. 13. 5. I will never *l.* nor
Acts 14. 17. *left*, Rom. 9. 29. Heb. 4. 1. Jude 6. Rev. 2. 4.
R. V. Changes frequent, but usual meanings retained
LEAVEN, Ex. 12. 15. Lev. 2. 11.
Matt. 13. 33. the kingdom of heaven is like *l.*
16. 6. beware of *l.* of Pharisees
1 Cor. 5. 7. purge out the old *l.*
6. a little *l.* leaveneth lump
LEES, Isa. 25. 6. Jer. 48. 11. Zeph. 1. 12.
LEFT-HANDED slingers, Judg. 20. 16.
LEGS, Ps. 147. 10. Prov. 26. 7.
R. V. Isa. 47. 2. train
LEND, Ex. 22. 25. Deut. 23. 19, 20.
Jer. 15. 10. neither *l.* on usury
Luke 6. 35. do good and *l.* hoping
Ps. 37. 26. ever merci. and *lendeth*
Prov. 19. 17. giveth to the poor *l.*
22. 7. borrower is servant to *lender*
1 Sam. 1. 28. I have *lent* him to Lord
R. V. Lev. 25. 37. give; 1 Sam. 1. 28. granted
LEOPARD, S. of S. 4. 8. Isa. 11. 6. Jer. 5. 6. & 13. 23. Hos. 13. 7. Hab. 1. 8.
LEPROSY, in a house, Lev. 14. 33; of Miriam, Num. 12. 10; of Naaman and Gehazi, 2 Kings 5; of Uzziah, 2 Chron. 26. 19; symptoms of, Lev. 13; observances on healing, Lev. 14. & 22. 4. Deut. 24. 8; cured by Christ, Matt. 8. 3. Mark 1. 41. Luke 5. 12. & 17. 12.
LESS, Ezra 9. 13. Job 11. 6. Isa. 40. 17. Heb. 7. 9. Eph. 3. 8. Gen. 32. 10.
LETTER, Rom. 7. 2. 2 Cor. 3. 6.
R. V. 2 Cor. 7. 8; 2 Thes. 2. 2. epistle; Luke 23. 38; 2 Cor. 3. 1; Heb. 13. 22 ——
LETTEST, Luke 2. 29. 2 Thes. 2. 7.
LEVIATHAN, Job 41. 1. Ps. 74. 14.
LIBERAL, Prov. 11. 25. Isa. 32. 5, 8. 2 Cor. 9. 13.
1 Cor. 16. 3. *liberality*, 2 Cor. 8. 2.
Jas. 1. 5. God giveth to all men *liberally*
R. V. 1 Cor. 16. 3. bounty
LIBERTINES, the, Acts 6. 9.
LIBERTY, Lev. 25. 10. Jer. 34. 8.
Ps. 119. 45. I will walk at *l.* for I
Isa. 61. 1. anoint. me to proclaim *l*
Luke 4. 18. sent me to set at *l.*
Rom. 8. 21. into glorious *l.* of the
2 Cor. 3. 17. where Spirit of Lord is there is *l.*
Gal. 5. 1. stand fast in *l.*
13. use not *l.* for an occasion to the
Jas. 1. 25. whoso looketh into the law of *l.*
2. 12. be judged by the law of *l.*
1 Pet. 2. 16. not using your *l.*
R. V. Acts 27. 3. leave; 1 Cor. 7. 39. free; Gal. 5. 13. freedom
LIE, Lev. 6. 3. & 19. 11. Job 11. 3.
Ps. 58. 3. wicked go astray speak ing *l.*
62. 9. men of high degree are a *l.*
101. 7. that telleth a *l.* shall not
Hos. 11. 12. compasseth me about with *l.*
2 Thes. 2. 11. that they should believe a *l.*
1 Tim. 4. 2. speaking *l.* in hypocrisy
Rev. 22. 15. loveth and maketh a *l.*

Num. 23. 19. God is not a man, that he should *l.*
Isa. 63. 8. children that will not *l.*
Hab. 2. 3. at the end it shall speak and not *l.*
Col. 3. 9. *l.* not one to another
Tit. 1. 2. God that cannot *l.* hath
Heb. 6. 18. impossible for God to *l.*
Ps. 116. 11. I said, all men are *liars*
Tit. 1. 12. the Cretians are always *l.*
Rev. 2. 2. hast tried and found them *l.*
21. 8. all *l.* shall have their part
John 8. 44. he is a *liar* and the
Rom. 3. 4. God be true, and every man a *l.*
1 John 1. 10. we make him a *l.*
2. 4. keepeth not the command ments is a *l.*
Ps. 119. 29. remove from me the way of *lying*
163. I abhor *l.* but love thy law
Prov. 12. 19. *l.* tongue but for a
Jer. 7. 4. trust not in *l.* words
Hos. 4. 2. by stealing and *l.* the,
Jonah 2. 8. observe *l.* vanities
R. V. Job 11. 3; Jer. 48. 30. boastings; Ezek. 24. 12. toil; Ps. 101. 7; Prov. 29. 12; Jer. 9. 3; Hos. 11. 12. falsehood; Gen. 4. 7; 49. 25. coucheth

LIFE, Gen. 2. 7, 9. & 42. 15. & 44. 30.
Deut. 30. 15. set before you *l.* and
1 Sam. 25. 29. bound in bundle of *l.*
Ps. 16. 11. thou wilt show me the path of *l.*
21. 4. asked *l.* of thee and thou gavest
36. 9. with thee is the fountain of *l.*
63. 3. loving-kind. better than *l.*
66. 9. God holdeth our soul in *l.*
Prov. 8. 35. whoso findeth me findeth *l.*
15. 24. way of *l.* is above to wise
18. 21. death and *l.* are in power
Isa. 57. 10. hast found *l.* of thy
Matt. 6. 25. take no thought for *l.*
Luke 12. 15. man's *l.* consists not in
John 1. 4. in him was *l.* and the *l.*
3. 36. believ. on Son hath ever. *l.*
5. 40. not come, that ye might have *l.*
6. 35. I am the bread of *l.*, 48. 40, 47, 54.
51. my flesh I give for *l.* of world
63. words I speak are spirit and *l.*
8. 12. followeth me shall have light of *l.*
10. 10. I am come that they might have *l.*
11. 25. I am the resurrection and *l.*
14. 6. I am the way, truth, and *l.*
Rom. 5. 17. reign in *l.* by Jesus
8. 2. law of Spirit of *l.* in Christ Jesus
6. to be spiritually minded is *l.*
2 Cor. 2. 16. the savor of *l.* unto *l.*
3. 6. the letter killeth, but the spirit giveth *l.*
4. 11. *l.* of Jesus might be mani.
Gal. 2. 20. the *l.* I now live in flesh
Eph. 4. 18. being alienated from *l.*
Col. 3. 3. your *l.* is hid with Christ
1 Tim. 2. 2. lead a peaceful *l.*
4. 8. having promise of the *l.* that
2 Tim. 1. 10. brought *l.* and immor.
2 Pet. 1. 3. that pertain to *l.* and
1 John 5. 12. he that hath the Son hath *l.* he that hath not the Son hath not *l.*
Job 2. 4. all that a man hath will he give for *his life*
Prov. 13. 3. keepeth his mouth, keepeth —
Matt. 20. 28. Son of man gave — a ransom
Rom. 5. 10. much more saved by —
1 Kings 19. 4. to take away *my life*
Ps. 26. 9. gather not — with bloody men
27. 1. the Lord is strength of
Jonah 2. 6. brought up — from cor.
John 10. 15. I lay down — for sheep
Acts 20. 24. neither count I — dear
Ps. 17. 14. *this life*, Luke 8. 14. & 21. 34. Acts 5. 20. 1 Cor. 15. 19. & 6. 3.
Deut. 30. 23. he is *thy life*, and
Ps. 103. 4. redeem — from destruc.
Jer. 39. 18.—shall be for a prey, 45. 5.
Prov. 10. 16. tends *to life*, 11. 19. & 19. 23. Matt. 7. 14. John 5. 24. Acts 11. 18. Rom. 7. 10. Heb. 11. 35. 1 John 3. 14.

LIFT *up* his countenance on thee, Num. 6. 26.
1 Sam. 2. 7. Lord brings low—again
2 Kings 19. 4. — prayer for remnant
2 Chron. 17. 6. heart — in ways of
Ps. 4. 6. Lord—light of thy counte.
7. 6. Lord — thyself because
24. 7. — ye gates, — ye doors, and
25. 1. to thee I — my soul, 86. 4.
75. 4. — not the horn, 5.
83. 2. — the head
102. 10. thou — me and castest me
121. 1. — mine eyes, 123. 1.
147. 6. Lord — the meek, but casts
Prov. 2. 3. — thy voice for under.
Eccl. 4. 10. one will — his fellow
Isa. 26. 11. Lord when thy hand is —
33. 10. I will be exalted; now I — myself
42. 2. he shall not cry, nor — voice
Jer. 7. 16. nor — a prayer for them
Lam. 3. 14. let us—our hearts with
Hab. 2. 4. his soul which is — is
Luke 21. 28. — your heads for day of redemption
John 3. 14. so must the Son of man be —, 12. 34.
8. 28. when ye have — Son of man
12. 32. if I be — I will draw all men
Heb. 12. 12. — hands which hang
Jas. 4. 10. the Lord shall *l.* you up
Ps. 3. 3. my glory and *lifter up* of
141. 2. *lifting* up of hands, 1 Tim. 2. 8.
R. V. Ps. 30. 1; Mark 1. 31; 9. 27; Acts 3. 7; 9. 41. raised

LIGHT, Num. 21. 5. Deut. 27. 16. Judg. 9. 4. 1 Kings 16. 31. Ezek. 8. 17. & 22. 7.
Isa. 49. 6. it is a *l.* thing to be my
Zeph. 3. 4. her prophets *l.* and
Matt. 11. 30. my yoke is easy and my burden *l.*
2 Cor. 4. 17. *l.* affliction endureth
Ps. 62. 9. man is *lighter* than vanity
Jer. 3. 9. *lightness* of whoredoms
Gen. 1. 3. let there be *light*, 4, 5, 16. & 44. 3.
Job 18. 5. *l.* of wicked men shall
33. 30. enlightened with *l.* of living
Ps. 4. 6. lift up *l.* of thy countenance
36. 9. in thy *l.* shall we see *l.*
43. 3. O send out thy *l.* and truth
90. 8. set secret sins in the *l.* of
97. 11. *l.* is sown for the righteous
104. 2. coverest thyself with *l.*
112. 4. to the upright ariseth *l.* in
119. 105. thy word is *l.* to my path
139. 12. darkness and *l.* are both
Prov. 4. 18. path of the just is as the shining *l.*
6. 23. law is *l.* and reproofs are way
13. 9. *l.* of the righteous rejoiceth
15. 30. *l.* of the eyes rejoiceth the
Eccl. 11. 7. *l.* is sweet and a pleasant
Isa. 5. 20. darkness for *l.* and *l.* for
8. 20. because there is no *l.* in them
9. 2. walked in darkness, have seen a great *l.*
30. 26. *l.* of moon as *l.* of sun
42. 6. keep thee, and give thee for a *l.* of the Gentiles
50. 10. walketh in darkness and hath no *l.*
11. walk ye in the *l.* of your fire
58. 8. shall thy *l.* break forth as
60. 1. arise, shine; for thy *l.* is
Zech. 14. 6. *l.* shall not be clear nor
7. evening time it shall be *l.*
Matt. 5. 14. ye are the *l.* of the world
16. let your *l.* so shine before men
6. 22. the *l.* of the body is the eye
Luke 2. 32. a *l.* to lighten Gentiles
John 1. 4. the life was the *l.* of men
John 1. 7. John came to bear witness of *l.*
9. true *l.* that lighteth every man
3. 19. men loved darkness rather than *l.*
20. cometh not to the *l.*
21. cometh to the *l.*
5. 35. John burn. and a shining *l.*
8. 12. I am the *l.* of the world
12. 35, 36. walk while ye have the *l.*
Acts 13. 47. I have set thee for a *l.*
26. 18. turn them from dark. to *l.*
Rom. 13. 12. put on the armor of *l.*
1 Cor. 4. 5. bring to *l.* hidden
2 Cor. 4. 4. lest the *l.* of the Gospel
6. 14. what communion hath *l.* with
Eph. 5. 8. walk as children of *l.*
14. awake, and Christ shall give thee *l.*
1 Thes. 5. 5. ye are the children of *l.*
1 Pet. 2. 9. called to his marvell. *l.*
1 John 1. 5. God is *l.* and in him is
Rev. 21. 23. the Lamb is the *l.* thereof
Ps. 136. 7. *lights*, Ezek. 32. 8. Luke 12. 35. Phil. 2. 15. Jas. 1. 17.
2 Sam. 22. 29. *lighten*, Ezra 9. 8. Ps. 13. 3. & 35. 5. Rev. 21. 23.
Ex. 19. 16. *lightning*, Ps. 18. 14. Matt. 28. 3. & 24. 27. Luke 10. 18.
R. V. Jer. 23. 32. vain boasting; 2 Cor. 1. 17. fickleness; 2 Sam. 21. 17; 1 Kings 11. 36; 2 Kings 8. 19; 2 Chron. 21. 7; Matt. 6. 22; Luke 11. 34. lamp

LIKE men, quit you, 1 Cor. 16. 13.
Heb. 2. 17. to be made *l.* his breth.
1 John 3. 2. he appears we shall be *l.*
Phil. 2. 2. *like-minded*
20. no man —
Gen. 1. 26. after our *likeness*
5. 3. Adam begat a son in his own *l.*
Ps. 17. 15. I shall be sat. with thy *l.*
Rom. 6. 5. been planted in *l.* of his
8. 3. in *l.* of sinful flesh, Phil. 2. 7.
R. V. Rom. 1. 28. refused. Frequent changes to, as

LILY, S. of S. 2. 1, 2, 16. & 4. 5. & 5. 13. & 6. 2, 3. & 7. 2. Hos. 14. 5. Matt. 6. 28.

LINE upon *l.* *l.* upon *l.* Isa. 28. 10, 13.
28. 17. judgment will I lay to the *l.*
34. 11. stretch on it *l.* of confusion
2 Cor. 10. 16. not boast in another man's *l.*
Ps. 16. 6. *l.* are fallen in pleasant
R. V. Isa. 44. 13. pencil; 2 Cor. 10. 16. province

LINGER, Gen. 19. 16. 2 Pet. 2. 3.

LION, Gen. 49. 9. Judg. 14. 5, 18. Job 4. 10, 11. & 10. 16. & 28. 8. Ps. 7. 2. & 17. 12. & 10. 9. & 22. 13. Isa. 38. 13.
Prov. 22. 13. there is a *l.* without, 26. 13.
28. 1. righteous are bold as a *l.*
Eccl. 9. 4. living dog is better than a dead *l.*
Isa. 11. 6. calf and young *l.*
35. 9. no *l.* shall be there, nor
Ezek. 1. 10. face as a *l.*, 10. 14.
Hos. 5. 14. be as a young *l.*
Mic. 5. 8. rem. of Jacob be as a *l.*
2 Tim. 4. 17. delivered out of mouth of the *l.*
1 Pet. 5. 8. the devil as a roaring *l.*
Rev. 5. 5. *L.* of the tribe of Juda
R. V. Gen. 49. 9; Num. 23. 24; 24. 9; Deut. 33. 20; Job 38. 39. lioness

LIPS, Ex. 6. 12, 30. Prov. 16. 10.
Ps. 12. 3. all flattering *l.*
17. 1. not feigned *l.*
31. 18. lying *l.*, 120. 2. Prov. 10. 18. & 12. 22. & 17. 4, 7. Isa. 59. 3.
Ps. 63. 5. I will praise thee with joyful *l.*
Prov. 10. 21. the *l.* of the righteous
26. 23. burning *l.* and wicked heart
S. of S. 7. 9. *l.* of those that are asleep
Isa. 6. 5. man of unclean *l.* people
57. 19. create the fruit of the *l.*
Hos. 14. 2. render calves of our *l.*
Mal. 2. 7. priest's *l.* should keep
Ps. 51. 15. open thou *my lips*; and
63. 3. — shall praise thee, 71. 23.

Ps. 141. 3. keep the door of —
17. 4. *thy lips*, 34. 13. & 45. 2.
LITTLE, Ezra 9. 8. Neh. 9. 32.
Ps. 2. 12. when his wrath is kindled but a *l.*
8. 5. a *l.* lower than the angels
37. 16. a *l.* that a righteous man
Prov. 6. 10. a *l.* sleep, a *l.* slumber
10. 20. heart of wicked is *l.* worth
15. 16. better is *l.* with fear of the
Isa. 28. 10. here a *l.* and there a *l.*
54. 8. in a *l.* wrath I hid my face
Ezek. 11. 16. I will be as a *l.* sanc.
Zech. 1. 15. I was but a *l.* displeased
Matt. 6. 30. of *l.* faith, 8. 26. & 14. 31.
Luke 12. 32. fear not *l.* flock, it is
19. 17. thou hast been faithful in a very *l.*
1 Tim. 4. 8. bod. exercise profit. *l.*
Rev. 3. 8. hast *l.* strength, and kept
LIVE, Gen. 3. 22. & 17. 18.
Lev. 18. 5. if a man do, he shall *l.*, Neh. 9. 29. Ezek. 3. 21. & 18. 9. & 33. 13, 15, 16, 19. Rom. 10. 5. Gal. 3. 12.
Deut. 32. 40. *live for ever*, 1 Kings 1. 31. Neh. 2. 3. Ps. 22. 26. & 49. 9. Dan. 2. 4. & 3. 9. & 5. 10. & 6. 21. Zech. 1. 5. John 6. 51, 58. Rev. 4. 9. & 5. 14. & 10. 6. & 15. 7.
Job 14. 14. if a man die, shall he *l.*
Ps. 55. 23. bloody men not *l.* out
118. 17. I shall not die, but *l.* and
Isa. 38. 16. by these men *l.* and
55. 3. hear, and your soul shall *l.*
Ezek. 16. 6. said, when thou wast in thy blood, *L.*
18. 32. turn yourselves and *l.*
Hab. 2. 4. just shall *l.* by faith
Matt. 4. 4. man not *l.* by bread
John 14. 19. because I *l.* ye shall *l.*
Acts 17. 28. in him we *l.* and move
Rom. 8. 13. if *l.* after the flesh, ye
41. whether we *l.* we *l.* to Lord
2 Cor. 5. 15. who *l.* should not *l.* to
6. 9. as dying, and behold we *l.*
13. 11. be of one mind, *l.* in peace
Gal. 12. 20. I *l.* yet not I, but Christ
5. 25. if we *l.* in Spirit, walk in
Phil. 1. 21. to *l.* is Christ, 22.
2 Tim. 3. 12. all that will *l.* godly in
Tit. 2. 12. *l.* soberly, righteously
Heb. 13. 18. willing to *l.* honestly
1 Pet. 2. 24. should *l.* to righteous.
1 John 4. 9. that we might *l.*
Acts 23. 1. I *lived* in all good con.
Jas. 5. 5. ye have *l.* in pleasure
Rev. 18. 9. *l.* deliciously
20. 4. they *l.* and reigned with
Job 19. 25. I know that my Redeemer *liveth*
Rom. 6. 10. in that he *l.* he *l.* to God
14. 7. none *l.* to himself or dieth
1 Tim. 5. 6. *l.* in pleasure, dead
Heb. 7. 25. *l.* to make intercession
Rev. 1. 18. I am he that *l.* and was
3. 1. I know that thou *l.* and art
Acts 7. 38. received *lively* oracles
1 Pet. 1. 3. bego. again to a *l.* hope
2. 5. ye, as *l.* stones, are built up a
1 John 3. 16. *lives*, Rev. 12. 11.
Eccl. 7. 2. *living* will lay it to heart
Isa. 38. 19. the *l.* the *l.* shall praise
Jer. 2. 13. Lord fountain of *l.* waters
Matt. 22. 32. not the God of the dead, but of the *l.*
Mark 12. 44. cast in all her *l.*
John 4. 10. would have given thee *l.* water
7. 38. flow rivers of *l.* water
Rom. 12. 1. present your bodies a *l.* sacrifice
14. 9. Lord both of dead and *l.*
1 Cor. 15. 45. the first Adam was made a *l.* soul
Heb. 10. 20. by a new and *l.* way
1 Pet. 2. 4. coming as to a *l.* stone
Rev. 7. 17. lead them to *l.* fountains
R. V. 1 Cor. 9. 13. eat; Rev. 18. 7. waxed
LOAD, Ps. 68. 19. Isa. 46. 1.
LOATHE themselves for evil, Ezek. 6. 9. & 16. 5. & 20. 43. & 36. 31.
Jer. 14. 19. *loathed* Zion, Zech. 11. 8.
Num. 21. 5. soul *loatheth*, Prov. 27. 7.
Ps. 38. 7. *loathsome* disease
R. V. Job 7. 5. out afresh; Ps. 38. 7. burning
LOAVES, miraculous multiplication of, Matt. 14. 17. & 15. 32. Mark 6. 35. Luke 9. 12. John 6. 5.
LOFTY eyes, Ps. 131. 1. Prov. 30. 13.
Isa. 2. 11. *l.* looks humbled, 5. 15.
57. 15. *l.* One that inhabiteth
R. V. Isa. 2. 12. haughty; 57. 7. high
LOINS girt, Prov. 31. 17. Isa. 11. 5. Luke 12. 35. Eph. 6. 14. 1 Pet. 1. 13.
LONG, Ps. 91. 16. Eccl. 12. 5. Matt. 23. 14. Luke 18. 7. Jas. 5. 7.
Ex. 34. 6. Lord God, *long-suffering*, Num. 14. 18. Ps. 86. 15. Jer. 15. 15. Rom. 2. 4. & 9. 22. 1 Tim. 1. 16. 1 Pet. 3. 20. 2 Pet. 3. 9, 15.
Gal. 5. 22. fruit of Spirit is *l.*, Eph. 4. 2. Col. 1. 11. & 3. 12. 2 Tim. 3. 10. & 4. 2.
Ps. 63. 1. my flesh *longeth* for thee
84. 2. my soul *l.* for courts of
119. 40. *I have longed* after thy
131. — for thy commandments
174. — for thy salvation
20. my soul breaketh for *longing*
107. 9. he satisfieth the *l.* soul
R. V. Num. 9. 19; Deut. 28. 32; Ps. 94. 4; Matt. 23. 14; Mark 16. 5; Luke 1. 20——; Ex. 34. 6; Num. 14. 18; Ps. 86. 15. slow to anger
LOOK, Gen. 13. 14. Ex. 10. 10.
Ps. 5. 3. direct my prayer and I will *l.* up
Isa. 8. 17. wait upon the Lord, and *l.* for
45. 22. *l.* unto me and be saved
66. 2. to this man will I *l.* that is
Mic. 7. 7. I will *l.* unto the Lord
Luke 7. 19. do we *l.* for another
2 Cor. 4. 18. we *l.* at things not seen
Phil. 2. 4. *l.* not every one on own
3. 20. heaven, from whence we *l.*
Heb. 9. 28. to them that *l.* for him
1 Pet. 1. 12. angels desire to *l.* into
3. 14. seeing we *l.* for such things
Gen. 29. 32. the Lord *looked* on my affliction, Ex. 2. 25. & 3. 7. & 4. 31. Deut. 26. 7.
Ps. 34. 5. they *l.* to him and were
Isa. 5. 7. he *l.* for judgment, behold
22. 11. hath not *l.* to the maker
Jer. 8. 15. we *l.* for peace, but, 14. 19.
Obad. 13. not have *l.* on affliction
Hag. 1. 9. ye *l.* for much, and it
Luke 2. 38. *l.* for redemption in
22. 61. the Lord *l.* on Peter and
Heb. 11. 10. *l.* for a city whose
1 John 1. 1. which we have seen and *l.* on
1 Sam. 16. 7. man *looketh* on the outward appearance, but the Lord *l.* on the heart
S. of S. 2. 9. he *l.* forth at the win.
Matt. 5. 28. *l.* on a woman to lust
24. 50. come in a day he *l.* not for
Jas. 1. 25. *l.* into perfect law of
Ps. 18. 27. thou wilt bring down high *looks*
Isa. 38. 14. mine eyes fail with *looking* upward
Luke 9. 62. no man *l.* back is fit for
Tit. 2. 13. *l.* for that blessed hope
Heb. 10. 27. a fearful *l.* of judg.
12. 2. *l.* to Jesus, the author and
15. *l.* diligently, lest any fail
2 Pet. 3. 12. *l.* for and hasting
Jude 21. *l.* for the mercy of our
R. V. The changes are chiefly those brought about by subsequent words, and do not affect meanings
LOOSE, Deut. 25. 9. Josh. 5. 15
Ps. 146. 7. the Lord *l.* the prisoners
102. 20. to *l.* those appointed to
Isa. 58. 6. fast chosen to *l.* bands
Eccl. 12. 6. before the silver cord be *loosed*
Matt. 16. 19. *l.* on earth, *l.* in heav.
Acts 2. 24. having *l.* pains of death
1 Cor. 7. 27. bound to a wife, seek not to be *l.* art thou *l.* seek not a
R. V. Judg. 15. 14. dropped; Matt. 18. 27. released; Acts 13. 13; 16. 11; 27. 21. set sail; 27. 13. weighed anchor; Rom. 7. 2. discharged
LORD, ascribed to man, Gen. 18. 12. & 23. 11. Isa. 26. 13. 1 Cor. 8. 5. 1 Pet. 5. 3. and in about fourteen other places; and to God, Gen. 28. 16. Ex. 5. 2. 1 Cor. 12. 5. and in about three hundred other texts
Ex. 34. 6. the *L.* the *L.* God mer.
Deut. 4. 35. *L.* is God, 39. 1 Kings 18. 39.
6. 4. *L.* our God is one *L.*, 10.
17. *L.* of *l.*, Dan. 2. 47. 1 Tim. 6. 15. Rev. 17. 14. & 19. 16.
Neh. 9. 6. art *L.* alone, Isa. 37. 20.
Ps. 118. 27. God is the *L.*, 100. 3.
Zech. 14. 9. one *L.* and his name
Mark 2. 28. the Son of man is *L.* of
Acts 2. 36. made him *L.* and Christ
Rom. 10. 12. same *L.* over all
14. 9. *L.* of the dead and of the
1 Cor. 2. 8. *L.* of glory
15. 47. *L.* from heaven
8. 6. one God, one *L.* Jesus Christ
Eph. 4. 5. one *L.* one faith, one
Gen. 15. 6. and he believed *in the Lord*
1 Sam. 2. 1. heart rejoiceth —, Ps. 32. 11. & 33. 1. & 35. 9. & 97. 12. & 104. 34. Isa. 41. 16. & 61. 10. Joel 2. 13. Hab. 3. 18. Zech. 10. 7. Phil. 3. 1. & 4. 4.
1 Kings 18. 5. trust —, Ps. 4. 5. & 11. 1. & 31. 6. & 32. 10. & 37. 3. & 115. 9, 10, 11. & 118. 8. & 125. 1. Prov. 3. 5. & 16. 20. & 28. 25. & 29. 25. Isa. 26. 4. Zeph. 3. 2.
Ps. 31. 24. hope —, 130. 7. & 131. 3.
34. 2. soul make her boast —
37. 4. delight thyself —, 7. rest —
Isa. 45. 17. Israel shall be saved —
24. — have I righteousness and
42. 25. — shall all the seed of Israel
Rom. 16. 12. labor —, 1 Cor. 15. 58.
Eph. 6. 10. be strong — and power
1 Thes. 5. 12. over you —, Col. 4. 7, 17.
Rev. 14. 13. blessed are the dead which die —
LORD'S PRAYER, Matt. 6. 9.
LOSE, Eccl. 3. 6. Matt. 10. 39, 42. & 16. 26. John 6. 39. 2 John 8. Prov. 23. 8.
1 Cor. 3. 15. *loss*, Phil. 3. 7, 8.
Ps. 119. 176. astray like *lost* sheep
Ezek. 37. 11. our hope is *l.* we
Matt. 5. 13. if salt have *l.* its savor
10. 6. to the *l.* sheep of Israel
18. 11. save that was *l.*, Luke 19. 10.
Luke 15. 32. thy brother was *l.* and
John 18. 9. them thou gavest me, I have *l.* none
2 Cor. 4. 3. the Gospel be hid it is to them that are *l.*
R. V. Matt. 16. 26; Mark 8. 36. forfeit: John 17. 12. perished
LOT, Lev. 16. 8, 9, 10. Josh. 1. 6.
1 Sam. 14. 41. Saul said, give us a perfect *l.*, 42.
Ps. 16. 5. thou maintainest my *l.*
125. 3. rod of wicked not rest on *l.*
Prov. 16. 33. the *l.* is cast into lap
Acts 1. 26. the *l.* fell on Matthias
8. 21. hast neither *l.* nor part in
Ps. 22. 18. on my vesture they did cast *lots*
R. V. Matt. 27. 35 ——
LOVE, Gen. 27. 4. 2 Sam. 13. 15.
2 Sam. 1. 26. passing the *l.* of wo.
Eccl. 9. 1. no man knoweth either *l.*
S. of S. 2. 5. I am sick of *l.*, 5. 8.
7. 12. there I will give thee my *loves*
8. 6. *l.* is strong as death, jealous
Isa. 38. 17. thou hast in *l.* to my
Jer. 2. 2. remember the *l.* of
31. 3. loved thee with everlast. *l.*
Ezek. 16. 8. thy time was time of *l.*

Hos. 11. 4. draw them with bands of *l.*
Matt. 24. 12. the *l.* of many shall
John 15. 9. continue ye in my *l.*
13. greater *l.* hath no man than
Rom. 8. 35. who shall separate us from the *l.* of Christ, 39.
12. 9. let *l.* be without dissimula.
13. 10. *l.* is the fulfill. of the law
15. 30. for Christ's sake, and *l.*
2 Cor. 5. 14. *l.* of Christ constrain.
Gal. 5. 6. faith which worketh by *l.*
13. by *l.* serve one another
22. fruit of the Spirit is *l.* joy and
1 Thes. 1. 3. your labor of *l.*
5. 8. putting on breastplate of faith and *l.*
2 Thes. 2. 10. received not the *l.*
Heb. 13. 1. let brotherly *l.* continue
1 John 3. 1. what manner of *l.* the Father bestowed on us
4. 7. *l.* is of God
4. 9. manifest the *l.* of God
11. we ought to *l.* one another
18. perfect *l.* casteth out fear
21. who loveth God *l.* his brother
Rev. 2. 4. thou hast left thy first *l.*
Eph. 1. 4. without blame before God *in love*
4. 15. speaking truth —, 16.
5. 2. walk — as Christ hath loved
Col. 2. 2. knit together — and
1 Thes. 3. 12. abound —
5. 13. esteem —
Luke 11. 42. *love of God*, John 5. 42.
Rom. 5. 5. — is shed abroad in our
2 Cor. 3. 14. — be with you all
2 Thes. 3. 5. direct your hearts into —
1 John 2. 5. in him is — perfected
3. 16. perceive we —
17. dwelleth — in him
4. 9. in this was manifested — towards
5. 3. this is — keep his command.
Deut. 7. 7. his *love*, Zeph. 3. 17. Ps. 91. 14. Isa. 63. 9. John 15. 10. Rom. 5. 8.
Lev. 19. 18. thou shalt *l.* thy neighbor as thyself, 34. Matt. 19. 19. & 22. 39. Rom. 13. 8. Gal. 5. 14. Jas. 2. 8.
Deut. 6. 5. shalt *l.* the Lord thy God with all thy heart, Matt. 22. 37. Luke 10. 27.
Deut. 10. 12. to fear the Lord and to *l.*
Ps. 31. 23. O *l.* the Lord, all ye his
97. 10. ye that *l.* the Lord hate
145. 20. the Lord preserveth them that *l.* him
S. of S. 1. 4. the upright *l.* thee
Mic. 6. 8. to do justly, and *l.* mercy
Zech. 8. 19. *l.* the truth and peace
Matt. 5. 44. *l.* your enemies, bless
John 13. 34. *l.* one another, 15. 12, 17. Rom. 13. 8. 1 John 3. 11, 23. & 4. 7, 11, 12. 1 Pet. 1. 22.
14. 23. if a man *l.* me, my Father will *l.* him
1 Cor. 16. 22. if any man *l.* not Lord
Eph. 5. 25. *l.* your wives, Col. 3. 19.
2 Tim. 4. 8. to all them that *l.* his
1 Pet. 1. 8. whom having not seen, ye *l.*
2. 17. *l.* the brotherhood, 3. 8.
1 John 2. 15. *l.* not world nor
4. 19. we *l.* him because he first *loved* us
Ps. 116. 1. *I love* the Lord because, 18. 1.
119. 97. how — thy law, 113. 119, 127, 159, 163, 167. & 26. 8. Isa. 43. 1.
John 21. 15. *lovest* thou me — thee, 16. 17.
2 John 1. whom — in the truth
Rev. 3. 19. as many as — I rebuke
Deut. 7. 8. because the Lord *loved*
1 Sam. 18. 1. *l.* David as his own
2 Sam. 12. 24. called Solomon, and Lord *l.* him
1 Kings 3. 3. Solomon *l.* the Lord
10. 3. the Lord *l.* Israel
Hos. 11. 1. Israel was a child, then I *l.* him
Mark 10. 21. Jesus behold. him, *l.*
Luke 7. 47. sins are forgiven, she *l.*
2 Tim. 4. 10. having *l.* this present
Heb. 1. 9. hast *l.* righteousness
John 3. 16. God so *l.* the world
3. 19. men *l.* darkness rather
11. 36. behold how he *l.* him
12. 43. *l.* the praise of men more
13. 1. having *l.* his own, he *l.*
23. one of his disciples whom Jesus *l.*, 19. 26. & 20. 2. & 21. 7, 20.
14. 21. *l.* me, be *l.* of my Father
28. if ye *l.* me, ye would rejoice
15. 9. as my Father *l.* me, so have
16. 27. Father *loveth* you because
17. 23. I *l.* them as thou hast *l.* me
26. 1. wherewith thou hast *l.* them
Rom. 8. 37. conquerors through him that *l.* us
9. 13. Jacob I *l.* Esau I hated
Gal. 1. 20. Son of God, who *l.* me
Eph. 2. 4. great love where. he *l.* us
5. 2. as Christ *l.* us
25. as Christ *l.* church
2 Thes. 2. 16. God our Father *l.* us
2 Pet. 2.15. *l.* wages of unrighteous.
1 John 4. 10. not that we *l.* God but
Rev. 1. 5. that *l.* us and washed
12. 11. *l.* not their lives unto death
Ps. 11. 7. the righteous Lord *l.*
146. 8. the Lord *l.* the righteous
Prov. 3. 12. whom the Lord *l.* he
17. 17. a friend *l.* at all times
21. 17. he who *l.* pleasure, shall
S. of S. 1. 7. whom my soul *l.*, 3. 1, 4.
Matt. 10. 37. *l.* father or mother
John 3. 35. Father *l.* the Son, 15. 20.
16. 27. Father himself *l.* you
2 Cor. 9. 7. God *l.* a cheerful giver
3 John 9. *l.* to have preeminence
Rev. 22. 15. whoso *l.* and mak. a lie
2 Sam. 1. 23. *lovely*, S. of S. 5. 16. Ezek. 33. 32. Phile. 4. 8.
Ps. 88. 18. *lover*, Tit. 1. 8. Ps. 38. 11. Hos. 2. 5. 2 Tim. 3. 2, 4.
R. V. Tit. 1. 8. given to

LOW, Deut. 28. 43. Ezek. 17. 24.
1 Sam. 2. 7. Lord brings *l.* and lifts
Job 40. 12. look on every one that is proud and bring him *l.*
Ps. 49. 2. both high and *l.* rich and
136. 23. remem. us in our *l.* estate
Isa. 26. 5. lofty city he layeth it *l.*
32. 19. city shall be *l.* in a *l.* place
Luke 1. 48. he regard. the *l.* estate
52. he exalted them of *l.* degree, Job 5. 11. Ezek. 21. 26. Jas. 1. 9, 10.
Luke 3. 5. every mountain and hill be made *l.*
Rom. 12. 16. condescend to men of *l.* estate
Ps. 63. 9. *lower* parts of the earth, 139. 15. Isa. 44. 23. Eph. 4. 9.
138. 6. Lord hath respect to *lowly*
Prov. 3. 34. he giveth grace unto *l.*
11. 2. with the *l.* is wisdom
Matt. 11. 29. learn of me, for I am meek and *l.*
Eph. 4. 2. *lowliness*, Phil. 2. 3.
R. V. 2 Chron. 26. 10; 28. 18. lowland; Ps. 107. 39. bowed down; Ezek. 26. 20. nether

LUCRE, filthy, 1 Tim. 3. 3, 8. Tit. 1. 7. 1 Pet. 5. 2.

LUKEWARM, thou art, Rev. 3. 16.

LUMP, Isa. 38. 21. Rom. 9. 21. & 11. 16. 1 Cor. 5. 6, 7. Gal. 5. 9.
R. V. 2 Kings 20. 7; Isa. 38. 21. cake

LUST, Ex. 15. 9. Ps. 78. 18. Jas. 4. 2.
Ps. 81. 12. gave them up to their own hearts' *l.*
Matt. 5. 28. looketh on a woman to *l.*
Rom. 7. 7. not known *l.* except law
1 Cor. 10. 6. not *l.* after evil things
Gal. 5. 16. shall not fulfil *l.* of flesh
1 Thes. 4. 5. not in the *l.* of
Jas. 1. 15. when *l.* is conceived, it
1 John 2. 16. *l.* of the flesh, and *l.*
Mark 4. 19. *lusts* of other things
John 8. 44. *l.* of your father ye will
Rom. 6. 12. should obey it in the *l.*
Rom. 13. 14. for the flesh, to fulfil the *l.*
Gal. 5. 17. flesh *l.* against Spirit
24. crucified flesh with affec. and *l.*
Eph. 2. 3. *l.* of our flesh, and mind
1 Tim. 6. 9. foolish and hurtful *l.*
2 Tim. 2. 22. flee youthful *l.* follow
3. 6. laden with sins, led away with divers *l.*
Tit. 2. 12. denying ungodliness and worldly *l.*
3. 3. divers *l.* and pleasures
Jas. 4. 3. consume it on your *l.*
1 Pet. 2. 11. abstain from fleshly *l.*
2 Pet. 3. 3. walk after their own *l.*
R. V. Ps. 81. 12. stubbornness; Rom. 7. 7. coveting; Jas. 4. 1, 3. pleasures; Deut. 14. 26. desireth; Jas. 4. 5. long

M

MAD, Deut. 28. 34. 1 Sam. 21. 13.
Eccl. 2. 2. I said of laughter it is *m.*
Jer. 50. 38. they are *m.* upon idols
Hos. 9. 7. the prophet is a fool, the spiritual man is *m.*
John 10. 20. he hath a dev. and is *m.*
Acts 26. 11. exceedingly *m.* against
24. learning doth make thee *m.*
Deut. 28. 28. *madness*, Eccl. 1. 17. & 2. 12. & 9. 3. & 10. 13. Zech. 12. 4. Luke 6. 11. 2 Pet. 2. 16.
R. V. Eccl. 7. 7. foolish

MADE, Ex. 2. 14. 2 Sam. 13. 6.
Ps. 104. 24. thy works in wisdom hast thou *m.*
Prov. 16. 14. Lord *m.* all things
John 1. 3. all things were *m.* by him
Rom. 1. 3. Christ *m.* of the seed of David
1 Cor. 1. 30. Christ who of God is *m.*
9. 22. *m.* all things to all men
Gal. 4. 4. *m.* of a woman, *m.* under
Phil. 2. 7. *m.* in the likeness of men
R. V. The changes are mostly to such words as, created, wrought, become, manifested, etc.
See also MAKE.

MAGISTRATES, Ezra 7. 25; to be obeyed, Ex. 22. 8. Rom. 13. Tit. 3. 1. 1 Pet. 2. 14.

MAGNIFY, Josh. 3. 7. 1 Chron. 29. 25.
Job 7. 17. what is man that thou shouldst *m.* him
36. 24. remember to *m.* his work
Ps. 34. 3. *m.* the Lord with me
Isa. 42. 21. *m.* the law, and make
Luke 1. 46. my soul doth *m.* Lord
Acts 10. 46. spake with tongues and *m.* God
Gen. 19. 19. thou hast *magnified* thy
2 Sam. 7. 26. let thy name be *m.* for
Ps. 35. 27. let the Lord be *m.*
138. 2. hast *m.* thy word above
Acts 19. 17. the name of the Lord was *m.*
Phil. 1. 20. Christ shall be *m.* in
R. V. 2 Chron. 32. 23. exalted; Rom. 11. 13. glorify my ministry

MAID, Gen. 16. 2. Deut. 22. 14. Job 31. 1. Jer. 2. 32. Amos 2. 7. Zech. 9. 17.
R. V. Gen. 16. 2; 29. 24; 30. 7; Ex. 2. 5. handmaid; Matt. 9. 24. dam.

MAIMED healed by Christ, Matt. 15. 30.
animal, unfit for sacri. Lev. 22. 22.

MAINTAIN my cause, 1 Kings 8. 45. Ps. 9. 4. & 140. 12. Job 13. 15.
Tit. 3. 8. care. to *m.* good works, 14.
Ps. 16. 5. thou *maintainest* my lot
R. V. 1 Chron. 26. 27. repair

MAJESTY, Dan. 4. 30, 36. & 5. 18, 19. Job 40. 10. Ps. 21. 5. & 45. 3, 4.
1 Chron. 29. 11. thine, O Lord, is *m.*
Job 37. 22. with God is terrible *m.*
Ps. 29. 4. voice of Lord is full of *m.*
93. 1. the Lord is clothed with *m.*
145. 5. glorious honor of thy *m.*
12. glorious *m.* of his kingdom

Isa. 2. 19. hide for fear of the glory of his *m.*
Heb. 1. 3. right hand of *M.* on high
8. 1. of the throne of the *M.*
2 Pet. 1. 16. eyewitnesses of his *m.*
Jude 25. to the only wise God be glory and *m.*
R. V. Dan. 4. 36; 5. 18, 19. greatness
MAKE, Gen. 1. 26. & 3. 6, 21. Deut. 32. 35. 1 Cor. 4. 15. 1 Sam. 20. 38.
Job 4. 17. shall man be purer than his *Maker*
32. 22. my *M.* would soon take me
35. 10. where is God my *M.*
36. 3. I will ascribe righ. to my *M.*
Ps. 95. 6. kneel before Lord our *M.*
Prov. 14.31. reproach. his *M.*, 17. 5.
22. 2. Lord is the *M.* of them all
Isa. 17. 7. that day shall man look to his *M.*
51. 13. forgettest the Lord thy *M.*
54. 5. thy *M.* is thy husband; the
Heb. 11. 10. whose builder and *m.*
MALE or female, Gen. 1. 27. Num. 5. 3. Mal. 1. 14. Matt. 19. 4. Gal. 3. 28.
MALEFACTORS, execution of, Deut. 21. 22.
crucified with Christ, Luke 23. 32.
MALICE, leaven of, 1 Cor. 5. 8.
1 Cor. 14. 20. in *m.* be children, in
Eph. 4. 31. put away with all *m.*, Col. 3. 8. 1 Pet. 2. 1.
Tit. 3. 3. living in *m.* and envy
Rom. 1.29. filled with all *maliciousness;* full of envy, 1 Pet. 2. 1.
R. V. 1 Pet. 2. 1. wickedness
MAMMON, Matt. 6. 24. Luke 16. 9.
MAN, Gen. 1. 26, 27. 2 Kings 9. 11.
Job 4. 17. shall *m.* be more just
5. 7. *m.* is born to trouble, 14. 1.
7. 17. what is *m.* that thou
9. 2. how shall *m.* be just with God
14. 1. *m.* born of woman, is of
15. 14. what is *m.* that he should
6. *m.* is a worm
28. 28. unto *m.* he said, depart
Ps. 8. 4. what is *m.* that thou art
10. 18. *m.* of earth no more oppress
90. 3. thou turnest *m.* to destruc.
104. 23. *m.* goeth forth to his work
118. 6. not fear; what can *m.* do
144. 3. what is *m.* that thou takest
Prov. 20. 24. *m's* goings are of Lord
Eccl. 6. 10. it is known that it is *m.*
7. 29. God made *m.* upright, but
12. 5. *m.* goeth to his long home
Isa. 2. 22. cease ye from *m.* whose
Jer. 17. 5. cursed be the *m.* that
Zech. 13. 7. awake against the *m.* that is my fellow
Matt. 4. 4. *m.* shall not live by
26. 72. I know not the *m.*
John 7. 46. nev. *m.* spake like this *m.*
Rom. 6. 6. old *m.* crucified with
1 Cor. 2. 11. what *m.* knoweth the things of a *m.* save the spirit of *m.* in him
14. natural *m.* receiveth not things
11. 8. *m.* not of woman, but woman of *m.*
15. 47. first *m.* is earthy; second *m.*
2 Cor. 4. 16. though outward *m.* perish, yet inward *m.* is renewed
Eph. 4. 22. put off the old *m.* which
24. put on new *m.* renewed
1 Pet. 3. 4. be the hidden *m.* of heart
Ex. 15. 3. Lord is *a man* of war
Num. 23. 19. God is not — that he
Isa. 47. 3. I will not meet thee as —
53. 3.— of sorrows and acquainted
Jer. 15. 10. borne me — of strife
Matt. 8. 9. I am — under authority
16. 26. what shall — give in ex.
John 3. 3. except — be born again
Acts 10. 26. I myself also am —
2 Cor. 12. 2. I knew — in Christ, 3.
Phil. 2. 8. in fashion as — he hum.
1 Tim. 2. 5. one Meditator the *m.* Christ Jesus
Prov. 30. 2. *if any man*, Matt. 16. 24. John 6. 51. & 7. 17, 37. Rom. 8. 9. 2 Cor. 5.17. Gal. 1. 9. Rev. 22.19.

Ps. 39. 5. *every man*, Prov. 19. 6. Mic. 4. 4. & 7. 2. Gal. 6. 4, 5. Col. 1. 28. Heb. 2. 9.
Ps. 87. 4. *this man*, Isa. 66. 2. Mic. 5. 5. Luke 19. 14. John 7. 46. Jas. 1. 26.
Prov. 1. 5. *a wise man* will hear
9. 8. rebuke — and he will love thee
17. 10. reproof enters into — more
Eccl. 2. 14. — eyes are in his head
10. 2. — heart is at his right hand
Jer. 9. 23. let not — glory in wisdom
Jas. 3. 13. who is — among you
Deut. 33. 1. *man of God*, Judg. 13. 6, 8. 2 Kings 1. 9, 13. 1 Tim. 6. 11. 2 Tim. 3. 17.
R. V. Numerous changes in N. T. to one
MANDRAKES, Gen. 30. 14. S. of S. 7. 13.
MANIFEST, Eccl. 3. 18. 1 Cor. 15. 27.
Mark 4. 22. nothing hid which shall not be *m.*
John 14. 21. I will *m.* myself
2. 11. *m.* forth his glory to dis.
17. 6. I have *m.* thy name unto
1 Cor. 4. 5. make *m.* counsels
Gal. 5. 19. works of the flesh are *m.*
2 Thes. 1. 5. a *m.* token of right.
1 Tim. 3. 16. God was *m.* in the flesh
Heb. 4. 13. any creature not *m.* in
1 John 3. 5. he was *m.* to take
10. in this children of God are *m.*
4. 9. in this was *m.* the love of God
Luke 8. 17. *made manifest*, John 3. 21. 1 Cor. 3. 13. 2 Cor. 4. 10. & 5. 11. Eph. 5. 13.
Rom. 8. 19. *manifestation* of sons
1 Cor. 12. 7. *m.* of the Spirit is given
2 Cor. 4. 2. but by *m.* of the truth
R. V. 1 Cor. 15. 27; 1 Tim. 5. 25; 2 Tim. 3. 9. evident; Rom. 8. 19. revealing
MANIFOLD mercies, Neh. 9. 19, 27.
Ps. 104. 24. how *m.* are thy works
Amos 5. 12. I know your *m.* trans.
Luke 18. 30. *m.* more in this pre.
Eph. 3. 10. known *m.* wisdom of
1 Pet. 1. 6. in heaviness through *m.* temptations
MANNA, Ex. 16. 15. Num. 11. 6. Deut. 8. 3, 16. Josh. 5. 12. Neh. 9. 20. Ps. 78. 24. John 6. 31, 49, 58.
Rev. 2. 17. give to eat of hidden *m.*
R. V. Ex. 16. 15. what is it; John 6. 58 —
MANNER, 1 Sam. 8. 9, 11. Isa. 5. 17. Jer. 22. 21. 1 Thes. 1. 5, 9. 1 John 3. 1.
2 Kings 17. 34. *manners*, Acts 13. 18. 1 Cor. 15. 33. Lev. 20. 23. Heb. 1. 1.
R. V. Numerous changes to custom, ordinance, form, etc.; and frequent omissions of the word
MANSIONS in my Father's house, John 14. 2.
MAN-STEALING, Ex. 21. 16. Deut. 24. 7.
MARK, set me as a, Job 7. 20. & 16. 12.
Lam. 3. 12. Gal. 6. 17. bear *marks*
Ezek. 9. 4. set a *m.* upon the foreheads, Rev. 13.16,17. & 14.9.& 19.20.
Phil. 3. 14. I press toward the *m.*
Ps. 37. 37. *m.* the perfect man
130. 3. if thou shouldest *m.* iniquity, Job 10. 14. Jer. 2. 22.
Rom. 16. 17. *m.* them which cause
Phil. 3. 17. *m.* them which walk
R. V. Gen. 4. 15. sign; Phil. 3. 14. goal; Rev. 15.2 —; Job 18. 2. consider; 22. 15. keep; 24. 16. shut themselves up
MARRIAGE, Gen. 38. 8. Deut. 25. 5.

Matt. 22. 2. king made a *m.* for son
25. 10. that were ready went into the *m.*
Heb. 13. 4. *m.* is honorable in all
Rev. 19. 7. the *m.* of the Lamb
Jer. 3. 14. I am *m.* to you, saith Lord
Luke 14. 20. I have *m.* a wife, and
17. 27. they drank, *m.* and
Isa. 62. 5. as a man *m.* a virgin
1 Cor. 7. 9. better to *m.* than to burn
1 Tim. 4. 3. forbidding to *m.* and
5. 14. that younger women *m.* and
R. V. Matt. 22. 2, 4, 9; 25. 10. marriage feast
MARROW, to bones, Prov. 3. 8. Job 21. 24.
Ps. 63. 5. soul is satis. as with *m.*
Isa. 25. 6. feast of fat things full of *m.*
Heb. 4. 12. dividing asunder joints and *m.*
MARTYR, Acts 22. 20. Rev. 2. 13. & 17. 6.
MARVEL not, Eccl. 5. 8. John 5. 28. Acts 3. 12. 1 John 3. 13.
Ps. 48. 5. they *marvelled*, Matt. 8. 27. & 9. 8, 33. & 21. 20. & 22. 22. Luke 1. 63. Acts 2. 7. & 4. 13.
Matt. 8. 10. Jesus *m.*, Mark 6. 6.
Job 5. 9. doeth *marvellous* things
10. 16. showed thyself *m.* against
Ps. 17. 7. show me thy *m.* kind.
98. 1. done *m.* things, Mic. 7. 15.
118. 23. it is *m.* in our eyes
1 Chron. 16. 12. remember his *m.* works, Ps. 105. 5. & 9. 1.
Ps. 139. 14. *m.* are thy works, Rev. 15. 3.
R. V. Ps. 48. 5. amazed; Matt. 9. 8. were afraid; Rev. 17. 7. wonder; Ps. 139. 14. wonderful; John 9. 30. the marvel
MASTER, Isa. 24. 2. Mal. 1. 6. & 2. 12.
Matt. 23. 10. one is your *M.*
Mark 10. 17. good *M.* what shall I
John 3. 10. art thou a *m.* in Israel
13. 13. ye call me *M.* and say well
14. if I your *M.* have washed
Rom. 14. 4. to his own *m.* he stands
Eccl. 12. 11. *masters* of assemblies
Matt. 6. 24. no man can serve two *m.*
23. 10. neither be ye called *m.*, Jas. 3. 1.
Col. 4. 1. *m.* give your servants
1 Cor. 3. 10. I as a *master builder*
R. V. 1 Sam. 24. 6; 26. 16; 29. 4, 10; 2 Sam. 2. 7; Amos 4. 1; Mark 13. 39; Rom. 14. 4; 2 Pet. 2. 1. lord; Matt. 26. 25, 49; Mark 9. 5; 11. 21; 14. 45; John 4. 31; 9. 2; 11. 8. Rabbi; Matt. 23. 8; John 3. 10; Jas. 3. 1. teacher
MATTER, Ex. 18. 22. & 23. 7. 1 Sam. 10. 16. Job 19. 28. & 32. 18. Ps. 45. 1. Dan. 7. 28. 2 Cor. 9. 5.
Acts 8. 21. part nor lot in this *m.*
Job 33. 13. account of any of his *matters*
Ps. 131. 1. exerc. myself in great *m.*
Matt. 23. 23. omitted the weight. *m.*
1 Pet. 4. 15. a busybody in other men's *m.*
R. V. Job 32. 18; Ps. 35. 20. words; 1 Sam. 16. 18. speech; Ps. 64. 5. purpose; Dan. 4. 17. sentence; Jas. 3. 5. much wood
MEAN, what, Ex. 12. 26. Deut. 6. 20, 24. Josh. 4. 6, 21. Ezek. 17. 12. Acts 17. 20. & 21. 13. Ezek. 37. 18. Jonah 1. 6.
Gen. 50. 20. ye thought ill; God *meant* good
Ps. 49. 7. *by any means*, Jer. 5. 31. 1 Cor. 9. 22. Phil. 3. 11. 1 Thes. 3. 15.
R. V. Acts 21. 13. do; 2 Cor. 8. 13. say not this; Acts 27. 2. which was about; Luke 15. 26. might be; Prov. 6. 26. on account; Luke 5

18 ——; 8. 36; John 9. 21. how; Luke 10. 19; 2 Thes. 2. 3. in any wise; Judg. 5. 22; Rev. 13. 14. reason

MEASURE, Lev. 19. 35. Deut. 25. 15.
Job 11. 9. the *m.* is longer than
Ps. 39. 4. make me know the *m.*
Isa. 27. 8. in *m.* when it shooteth
Matt. 7. 2. with what *m.* ye mete
23. 32. fill up the *m.* of your
John 3. 34. giveth not Spirit by *m.*
Rom. 12. 3. gives to every man *m.*
2 Cor. 1. 8. were pressed out of *m.*
12. 7. I should be exalt. above *m.*
Eph. 4. 7. according to *m.* of the
13. to the *m.* of fulness of Christ
Rev. 11. 1. *m.* the temple of God
R. V. Mark 10. 26; 2 Cor. 1. 8. exceedingly; Mark 6. 51; Rev. 21. 15 ——; 2 Cor. 10. 14; 12. 7. over much

MEAT, Job 6. 7. Ps. 42. 3. & 69. 21.
Ps. 104. 27. give *m.* in due season
111. 5. giveth *m.* to them that
Prov. 6. 8. provided *m.* in summer
Hos. 11. 4. I laid *m.* unto them
Hab. 1. 16. portion is fat and *m.*
3. 17. the fields shall yield no *m.*
Mal. 1. 12. that say his *m.* is con.
Matt. 6. 25. is not life more than *m.*
10. 10. workman worthy of his *m.*
John 4. 32. I have *m.* to eat ye
34. my *m.* is to do the will
6. 55. my flesh is *m.* indeed
Rom. 14. 15. destroy not him with thy *m.*
17. kingdom of God is not *m.* and drink
1 Cor. 6. 13. *m.* for belly, belly for
8. 8. *m.* commend. us not to God
10. 3. did all eat same spirit. *m.*
R. V. very frequent changes to food, meal, etc.

MEDDLE, 2 Kings 14. 10. Prov. 17. 14. & 20. 3, 19. & 24. 21. & 26. 17.
R. V. Deut. 2. 5, 19. contend; Prov. 17. 4; 20. 3. quarrelling; 26. 17. vexeth himself

MEDIATOR, is not *m.* of one, Gal. 3. 20.
Gal. 3. 19. ordained by angels in the hand of a *m.*
1 Tim. 2. 5. one *m.* between God
Heb. 8. 6. he is the *m.* of a better
9. 15. *m.* of New Testament
12. 24. *m.* of new covenant

MEDICINE, Prov. 17. 22. Jer. 30. 13. & 46. 11. Ezek. 47. 12.
R. V. Ezek. 47. 12. healing

MEDITATE, Isaac went to, Gen. 24. 63.
Josh. 1. 8. *m.* in thy law day and night, Ps. 1. 2. & 119. 15, 23, 48, 78, 148.
Ps. 63. 6. *m.* on thee in the night
77. 12. I will *m.* of thy works
Isa. 33. 18. thy heart shall *m.* terror
Luke 21. 14. not *m.* before what
1 Tim. 4. 15. *m.* upon these things
Ps. 5. 1. consider my *meditation*
19. 14. let the *m.* of my heart
49. 3. *m.* of my heart shall be
104. 34. my *m.* of him shall be sweet
119. 97. thy law is my *m.* all the day
99. thy testimonies are my *m.*
R. V. Isa. 33. 18. muse; 1 Tim. 4. 15. be diligent in

MEEK, Moses was very, Num. 12. 3.
Ps. 22. 26. the *m.* shall eat and be
25. 9. *m.* will he guide in judg.
37. 11. *m.* shall inherit the earth
76. 9. Lord rose to save all *m.* of
147. 6. the Lord lifteth up the *m.*
149. 4. he will beautify the *m.*
Isa. 11. 4. reprove for *m.* of the earth
29. 19. *m.* shall increase their joy
61. 1. preach good tidings to *m.*
Amos 2. 7. that turn aside way of *m.*
Zeph. 2. 3. seek the Lord all *m.*
Matt. 5. 5. blessed are *m.* for they
11. 29. I am *m.* and lowly in heart
21. 5. thy king cometh *m.* sitting
1 Pet. 3. 4. ornament of *m.* and
Zeph. 2. 3. seek righteousness, seek *meekness*
Ps. 45. 4. ride prosperously because of *m.*
1 Cor. 4. 21. come in the spirit of *m.*
2 Cor. 10. 1. I beseech you by the *m.* of Christ
Gal. 5. 23. faith, *m.* against such
6. 1. restore him in spirit of *m.*
Eph. 4. 2. walk with all lowliness and *m.*
Col. 3. 12. put on *m.* long-suffering
1 Tim. 6. 11. follow after faith, love, *m.*
2 Tim. 2. 25. in *m.* instructing those
Tit. 3. 2. showing all *m.* to all men
Jas. 1. 21. receive with *m.*
3. 13. show his works with *m.* of wisdom
1 Pet. 3. 15. of hope in you with *m.*

MEET, help, for him, Gen. 2. 18.
Job 34. 31. it is *m.* to be said to God
Matt. 3. 8. fruits *m.* for repent.
1 Cor. 15. 9. not *m.* to be called
Col. 1. 12. *m.* to be partakers of the
2 Tim. 2. 21. vessel *m.* for the master's use
Heb. 6. 7. *m.* for them by whom
Prov. 22. 2. rich and poor *m.*
Isa. 47. 3. I will not *m.* thee as a
64. 5. thou *m.* him that rejoiceth
Hos. 13. 8. I will *m.* them as a bear
Amos 4. 12. prepare to *m.* thy God
1 Thes. 4. 17. caught up to *m.* Lord
R. V. Deut. 3. 18. men of valor; Jer. 26. 14; 27. 5; Phil. 1. 7; 2 Pet. 1. 13. right; Judg. 5. 30. on; Ezek. 15. 4. profitable; Matt. 3. 8; Acts 26. 20. worthy of; Rom. 1. 27. due; Josh. 2. 16. light upon

MELODY in heart to the Lord, Eph. 5. 19.

MEMBER, body not one, 1 Cor. 12. 14.
Jas. 3. 5. tongue is a little *m.*
Ps. 139. 16. and in thy book all my *members*
Matt. 5. 29. one of thy *m.* perish
Rom. 6. 13. yield your *m.* as
7. 23. I see another law in my *m.*
12. 5. every one *m.* one of another
1 Cor. 6. 15. your bodies are *m.*
12. 12. the body is one, and hath many *m.*
Eph. 4. 25. we are *m.* one of anoth.
5. 30. *m.* of his body, his flesh
Col. 3. 5. mortify your *m.* on earth
R. V. 1 Cor. 12. 23. parts

MEMORY cut off, Ps. 109. 15.
Ps. 145. 7. utter the *m.* of thy
Prov. 10. 7. *m.* of the just is blessed
Eccl. 9. 5. *m.* of them is forgotten
Isa. 26. 14. made their *m.* to perish
1 Cor. 15. 2. if ye keep in *m.* what I
Ex. 3. 15. my *memorial* to all
13. 9. be for *m.* between thine eyes
17. 14. write this for a *m.* in book
Ps. 135. 13. thy *m.* through all
Hos. 12. 5. Lord of hosts; the Lord is his *m.*
Matt. 26. 13. be told for a *m.* of her
Acts 10. 4. come up for a *m.* before

MEN, Gen. 32. 28. & 42. 11.
Ps. 9. 20. know themselves to be but *m.*
17. 14. *m.* of thy hand; *m.* of
62. 9. *m.* of low degree are vanity
82. 7. ye shall die like *m.* and fall
Eccl. 12. 3. strong *m.* shall bow
Isa. 31. 3. Egyptians are *m.* not God
46. 8. remember this; show yourselves *m.*
Hos. 6. 7. they like *m.* transgress.
Rom. 1. 27. *m.* with *m.* working
Eph. 6. 6. *m.* pleasers, Col. 3. 22.
1 Thes. 2. 4.

MENSTRUOUS, Isa. 30. 22. Lam. 1. 17.
Ezek. 18. 6. neither come near a *m.* woman
R. V. Lam. 1. 17; Isa. 30. 22. unclean thing

MENTION, Ex. 23. 13. Job 28. 18.
Ps. 17. 16. I will make *m.* of thy
Isa. 26. 13. by thee only make *m.* of
62. 6. ye that make *m.* of the Lord
Rom. 1. 9. make *m.* of you in my prayers, Eph. 1. 16. 1 Thes. 1. 2. Phile. 4.
R. V. 2 Chron. 20. 34. inserted; Ezek. 18. 22, 24; 33. 16. remember.

MERCHANT, Hos. 12. 7. Matt. 13. 45.
Isa. 23. 18. *merchandise* be holiness, Matt. 22. 5. John 2. 16. 2 Pet. 2. 3.
R. V. Deut. 21. 14; 24. 7. deal with; Ezek. 27. 15. mart; 28. 16. traffic; Isa. 23. 11. concerning Canaan; 47. 15. that trafficked with thee; Ezek. 27. 20; Hos. 12. 7. trafficker; Ezek. 27. 13, 15, 17; 22. 23, 24. traffickers

MERCY, Gen. 19. 19. & 39. 21.
Ex. 34. 7. keep *m.* for thousands, Deut. 7. 9. 1 Kings 8. 23. Neh. 1. 5. & 9. 32. Dan. 9. 4.
Num. 14. 18. Lord is of great *m.*
Ps. 23. 6. goodness and *m.* shall
25. 10. all paths of the Lord are *m.*
33. 18. fear him and hope in his *m.*
52. 8. I trust in the *m.* of God for
57. 3. God shall send forth his *m.*
66. 20. not turned away his *m.*
86. 5. plenteous in *m.* to all, 103. 8.
101. 1. I will sing of *m.* and
103. 11. great is his *m.* to them
17. *m.* of the Lord is from ever.
106. 1. his *m.* endureth for ever, 107. 1. & 118. 1. & 136. 1-26. 1 Chron. 16. 34, 41. 2 Chron. 5. 13. & 7. 3, 6. & 20. 21. Ezra 3. 11. Jer. 33. 11.
Prov. 16. 6. by *m.* and truth, iniq.
20. 28. *m.* and truth preserve
Isa. 27. 11. he that made them will not have *m.*
Hos. 6. 6. I desired *m.* and not sacrifice
10. 12. reap in *m.*
12. 6. keep *m.*
14. 3. in thee fatherless findeth *m.*
Jonah 2. 8. they for. their own *m.*
Mic. 6. 8. what doth God require, but to love *m.*
20. *m.* to Abraham
Hab. 3. 2. in wrath remember *m.*
Luke 1. 50. his *m.* is on them that
78. through tender *m.* of our God
Rom. 9. 23. on vessels of *m.* pre.
15. *m.* on whom he will have *m.*
11. 31. through your *m.* they obtain *m.*
15. 9. may glorify God for his *m.*
2 Cor. 4. 1. as we have received *m.*
1 Tim. 1. 13. I obtained *m.* because I did it ignorantly
2. grace, *m.* and peace, Tit. 1. 4. 2 John 3. Jude 2.
2 Tim. 1. 18. grant may find *m.* in
Tit. 3. 5. according to his *m.* saved
Jas. 2. 13. shall have judgment without *m.* that showed no *m.* and *m.*
Heb. 4. 16. we may obtain *m.* and
Jas. 3. 17. full of *m.* and good
5. 11. Lord is pitiful and of tend. *m.*
Jude 21. looking for the *m.* of our
Gen. 32. 10. not worthy of the least of thy *mercies*
1 Chron. 21. 13. great are his *m.*
Ps. 69. 13. in multitude of thy *m.*
Isa. 55. 3. the sure *m.* of David
Lam. 3. 22. of Lord's *m.* we are
Dan. 9. 9. to the Lord belong *m.*
Rom. 12. 1. I beseech you by the *m.*
2 Cor. 1. 3. Father of *m.* and God of
Col. 3. 12. put on bowels of *m.*
Ps. 25. 6. *tender mercies*, 40. 11. & 51. 1. & 77. 9. & 79. 8. & 103. 4. & 119. 77, 156. & 145. 9.

Prov. 12. 10. —of wicked are cruel
Gen. 19. 19. *thy mercy*, Num. 14. 19.
Neh. 13. 22. Ps. 5. 7. & 6. 4. & 13. 5.
& 25. 7. & 31. 7, 16. & 33. 22. & 36. 5.
& 44. 26. & 85. 7. & 86. 13. & 90. 14.
& 94. 18. & 108. 4. & 57. 10. & 119.
64. & 143. 12.
Ex. 34. 6. Lord God *merciful* and
gracious, 2 Chron. 30. 9. Neh. 9.
17, 31. Ps. 103. 8. Joel 2. 13. Jonah
4. 2.
Ps. 18. 25. with *m.* show thyself *m.*
37. 26. he is ever *m.* and lendeth
117. 2. his *m.* kindness is great to
Prov. 11. 17. *m.* man doeth good
Isa. 57. 1. *m.* men are taken away
Jer. 3. 12. I am *m.* and will not
Matt. 5. 7. blessed are *m.* they
Luke 6. 36. be *m.* as your Father is
m.
Heb. 2. 17. might be a *m.* high priest
8. 12. I will be *m.* to their
R. V. Ex. 34. 6; Neh. 9. 17; Ps. 103.
8; Joel 2. 13; Jonah 4. 2. full of
compassion; Ps. 41. 4; 41. 10; 119.
132. have mercy; 37. 26. dealeth
graciously; Gen. 39. 21; 2 Sam. 22.
51; 1 Kings 3. 6; 2 Chron. 1. 8; Ps.
5. 7; 18. 50; 21. 7; 25. 7, 10; 36. 5; 61.
7; 143. 12; Isa. 16. 5. kindness, or
lovingkindness; Prov. 14. 21. pity;
Isa. 9. 17; 14. 1; 27. 11; 49. 13; Jer.
13. 14; 30. 18; Heb. 10. 28. compassion

MERRY, be, Luke 12. 19. & 15. 23,
24, 29, 32.
Jas. 5. 13. is any *m.* let him sing
Prov. 15. 13. *merry-hearted*, 17. 22.
Eccl. 9. 7. Isa. 24. 7.
R. V. Judg. 9. 27. festival; Prov.
15. 15; Jas. 5. 13. cheerful; 2 Chron.
7. 10. joyful· Eccl. 10. 19. glad in
life

MESSAGE from God, Judg. 3. 20.
Hag. 1. 13. 1 John 1. 5. & 3. 11.
Job 33. 23. if there be a *messenger*
Isa. 14. 32. what shall one answer
the *m.*
42. 19. who is blind or deaf, as *m.*
44. 26. that performeth counsel of
his *m.*
Mal. 2. 7. he is the *m.* of the Lord
3. 1. I send my *m.* even the *m.* of
R. V. Luke 19. 14. ambassage; Gen.
50. 16. message; 1 Sam. 4. 17. that
brought tidings; Job 33. 23. angel;
Isa. 57. 9. ambassador

MESSIAH, Dan. 9. 25, 26. John 1.
41. & 4. 25.

MICE, golden, 1 Sam. 6. 11.

MIDNIGHT, Egyptians smitten
at, Ex. 12. 29.
prayer at, Ps. 119. 62. Acts 16. 25.
& 20. 7.
bridegroom cometh at, Matt. 25. 6.
master of house cometh at, Mark
13. 35.

MIDST, Ps. 22. 14. & 46. 5. & 110. 2.
Prov. 4. 21. Isa. 4. 4. & 41. 18. Ezek.
43. 7, 9. & 6. 10. Joel 2. 27. Zeph. 3.
5, 12, 15, 17. Phil. 2. 15. Rev. 1. 13.
& 5. 6. & 7. 17. Lamb in *m.* of the
throne

MIDWIVES of Egypt, Ex. 1. 16, 20.

MIGHT, Gen. 49. 3. Num. 14. 13.
Deut. 6. 5. love Lord with all thy
m.
2 Kings 23. 25. turned to Lord with
all his *m.*
2 Chron. 20. 12. no *m.* against
Ps. 76. 5. none of men of *m.* found
145. 6. men speak of the *m.* of thy
Eccl. 9. 10. findeth to do, do it
with thy *m.*
Isa. 40. 29. that have no *m.* he
Zech. 4. 6. not by *m.* but by Spirit
Eph. 3. 16. his glory, to be strengthened with *m.*
6. 10. be strong in power of his *m.*
Col. 1. 11. strengthened with all *m.*
Deut. 7. 23. with *mighty* destruc.
10. 17. a great God, a *m.* and a
Ps. 24. 8. the Lord strong and *m.*
the Lord *m.* in battle

Ps. 89. 10. I have laid help on one
that is *m.*
Isa. 5. 22. *m.* to drink wine, men
of
Jer. 32. 19. great in counsel, *m.* in
work
1 Cor. 1. 20. not many *m.* are called
2 Cor. 10. 4. warfare not carnal
but *m.*
Ps. 93. 4. Lord on high is *mightier*
Acts 18. 28. *mightily*, Col. 1. 29.
19. 20. so *m.* grew word of God
R. V. changes chiefly to great,
strong, etc.

MILK, Gen. 18. 8. & 49. 12.
Job 10. 10. hast poured me out as *m.*
S. of S. 4. 11. honey and *m.* under
Isa. 55. 1. buy wine and *m.* without
Joel 3. 18. the hills shall flow with
m.
Heb. 5. 12. become such as have
need of *m.*
1 Pet. 2. 2. desire sincere *m.* of
word

MILLSTONES, Ex. 11. 5. Matt.
24. 41. Rev. 18. 21.

MIND, Gen. 26. 35. Lev. 24. 12.
1 Chron. 28. 9. serve him with willing *m.*
Neh. 4. 6. people had a *m.* to work
Job 23. 13. he is of one *m.* who can
Isa. 26. 3. whose *m.* is stayed on
thee
Luke 12. 29. be ye not of doubtful
m.
Acts 17. 11. receive the word with
readiness of *m.*
20. 19. serving the Lord with all
humility of *m.*
Rom. 7. 25. with the *m.* I serve law
8. 7. carnal *m.* is enmity against
11. 34. who hath known the *m.* of
12. 16. be of same *m.* one
1 Cor. 1. 10. joined together in the
same *m.*
2 Cor. 8. 12. be first a willing *m.* it
is
13. 11. be of one *m.* live in peace,
Phil. 1. 27. & 2. 2. & 4. 2. 1 Pet. 3. 8.
2 Tim. 1. 7. spirit of love and of a
sound *m.*
Tit. 1. 15. their *m.* and conscience
Rom. 8. 5. of flesh, do *m.* things of
12. 16. *m.* not high things
Phil. 3. 16. *m.* same thing
19. *m.* earthly things
2 Cor. 3. 14. *minds* were blinded
Phil. 4. 7. God keep your hearts
and *m.*
Heb. 10. 16. in their *m.* I will write
1 Pet. 3. 1. stir up your pure *m.* by
Rom. 8. 6. to be carnally *minded*
11. 20. be not high *m.* but fear
15. 5. God of patience grant you
to be like *m.*
Tit. 2. 6. exhort young men to be
sober *m.*
Jas. 1. 8. a double *m.* man, 4. 8.
Ps. 111. 5. ever *mindful* of his covenant, 1 Chron. 16. 15. Ps. 105. 8.
115. 12. Lord hath been *m.* of us
R. V. Acts 20. 13. intending

MINISTER, Josh. 1. 1. Luke 4. 20.
Matt. 20. 26. let him be your *m.*
Acts 26. 16. to make thee a *m.* and
Rom. 13. 4. he is *m.* of God to thee
15. 8. Christ was a *m.* of the
16. I be the *m.* of Jesus Christ to
Eph. 3. 7. was made a *m.* according
4. 29. may *m.* grace unto hearers
Rom. 15. 25. to *m.* unto the saints
15. 27. *m.* to them in carnal
1 Cor. 9. 13. they who *m.* about
2 Cor. 9. 10. *m.* seed to sower and
1 Pet. 4. 11. if any man *m.* let him
1 Tim. 4. 6. shall be a good *m.* of
Heb. 8. 2. *m.* of the sanctuary
Ps. 103. 21. *ministers* of his that do
104. 4. his *m.* a flaming fire
Isa. 61. 6. men call you the *m.* of
Luke 1. 2. from beginning, *m.* of
Rom. 13. 6. they are God's *m.*
1 Cor. 3. 5. *m.* by whom ye believed
4. 1. account of us as *m.* of Christ

2 Cor. 3. 6. made us able *m.* of
6. 4. approved ourselves as *m.* of
11. 23. are they *m.* of Christ, so
Matt. 4. 11. *ministered*, Luke 8. 3.
Gal. 3. 5. Heb. 6. 10. 2 Pet. 1. 11.
Luke 1. 23. *ministration*, Acts 6. 1.
2 Cor. 3. 7, 8. & 9. 1, 13.
Heb. 1. 14. all *ministering* spirits
Rom. 15. 16. *m.* the gospel of God
Acts 6. 4. give ourselves to *ministry*
20. 24. I might finish the *m.* I have
2 Cor. 4. 1. seeing we have this *m.*
5. 18. given to us the *m.* of recon.
6. 3. that the *m.* be not blamed
Col. 4. 17. take heed to *m.* that thou
1 Tim. 1. 12. putting me into the *m.*
2 Tim. 4. 5. full proof of thy *m.*
Heb. 8. 6. obtained more excell. *m.*
R. V. Ezra 7. 24. servants; Luke 4. 24.
attendant; 1 Chron. 28. 1. served;
2 Cor. 9. 10; Gal. 3. 5. supplieth;
1 Chron. 9. 28. vessels of service;
Rom. 12. 7. ministry; Acts 12. 25;
2 Cor. 6. 3. ministration; Eph. 4.
12; 2 Tim. 4. 11. ministering;
1 Tim. 1. 12. his service

MIRACLE, Mark 6. 52. & 9. 39.
Luke 23. 8. John 2. 11. & 6. 26. &
10. 41. & 11. 47. Acts 2. 22. & 4. 16.
& 6. 8. & 19. 11. 1 Cor. 12. 10, 28, 29.
Gal. 3. 5. Heb. 2. 4.
R. V. Heb. 2. 4. manifold powers.
Elsewhere, for most part,
changed to sign or signs

MIRTH, Prov. 14. 13. Eccl. 2. 2. &
7. 4. Isa. 24. 8, 11. Jer. 7. 34. & 16.
9. & 25. 10. Hos. 2. 11. Ezek. 21. 10.

MISCHIEF, Gen. 42. 4. & 44. 29.
Job 15. 35. they conceive *m.* bring
Ps. 10. 14. thou beholdest *m.* and
28. 3. *m.* is in their hearts, 10. 7.
36. 4. he deviseth *m.* upon his bed
94. 20. which frameth *m.* by a law
Prov. 10. 23. sport to a fool to do *m.*
11. 27. he that seeketh *m.* it shall
24. 16. wicked shall fall into *m.*
Acts 13. 10. full of all sub., and *m.*
R. V. Ex. 32. 12; Prov. 6. 14; 13. 17.
evil; Ps. 52. 2; 119. 150; Prov. 10.
23. wickedness; 2 Kings 7. 9. punishment; Ps. 36. 4. iniquity; Prov.
24. 16. calamity; Acts 13. 10. villany

MISERY, Job 3. 20. Lam. 3. 19.
Judg. 10. 16. soul grieved for *m.*
Prov. 31. 7. drink and remember *m.*
Eccl. 8. 6. the *m.* of man is great
Rom. 3. 16. destruction and *m.*
Job 16. 2. *miserable* comforters are
1 Cor. 15. 19. are of all men most *m.*
Rev. 3. 17. knowest not thou art *m.*
R. V. 1 Cor. 15. 19. pitiable

MOCK when fear cometh
Prov. 14. 9. fools make a *m.* at sin
1 Kings 18. 27. Elijah *mocked* and
2 Chron. 36. 16. they *m.* the mes.
Prov. 17. 5. whoso *mocketh* the poor
30. 17. eye that *m.* at his father
20. 1. wine is a *mocker* and strong
Isa. 28. 22. be not *mockers*, lest
Jude 18. there should be *m.* in last
R. V. Job 13. 9. deceiveth; 12. 4.
laughing stock; Isa. 28. 22. scorners; Jer. 15. 17. them that made
merry

MODERATION known to all,
Phil. 4. 5.

MODEST apparel, 1 Tim. 2. 9.

MOMENT, Ex. 33. 5. Isa. 27. 3.
Num. 16. 21. consume them in a *m.*
Job 7. 18. try him every *m.*
20. 5. joy of hypocrite is for a *m.*
Ps. 30. 5. his anger endureth but
for a little *m.*
Isa. 26. 20. hide thee, as it were,
for a little *m.*
54. 7. for a small *m.* have I for.
1 Cor. 15. 52. in a *m.* in the twink.
2 Cor. 4. 17. affliction is but for a
m.

MONEY, Gen. 23. 9. & 31. 15.
Eccl. 7. 12. wisdom is def. and *m.*
10. 19. *m.* answereth all things
Isa. 55. 1. he that hath no *m.* come
2. wherefore spend *m.* for that

Mic. 3. 11. the prophets divine for *m.*
Acts 8. 20. thy *m.* perish with thee
1 Tim. 6. 10. love of *m.* is the root
R. V. Gen. 23. 9. 13; Ex. 21. 35. price of; Ex. 21. 30. ransom; Matt. 17. 24. half-shekel; 17. 27. shekel; Acts 7. 16. price in silver; 8. 20. silver
MORROW, Ex. 8. 23. & 16. 23.
Prov. 27. 1. boast not thy. of to *m.*
Isa. 22. 13. to *m.* we shall die
56. 12. to *m.* shall be as this day
Matt. 6. 34. take no thought for *m.*
Jas. 4. 14. know not what shall be on the *m.*
MORTAL man be just, Job 4. 17.
Rom. 6. 12. let not sin reign in *m.* body
8. 11. raised Christ, quicken *m.* body
1 Cor. 15. 53. this *m.* put on immor.
2 Cor. 5. 4. *mortality* be swallowed
Rom. 8. 13. *mortify* deeds of body
Col. 3. 5. *m.* your members on earth
MORTGAGES, Neh. 5. 3.
MOTE, Matt. 7. 3, 4, 5. Luke 6. 41.
MOTH, Job 4. 19. & 27. 18. Ps. 39. 11. Isa. 50. 9. & 51. 8. Hos. 5. 12. Matt. 6. 19, 20. Luke 12. 33.
MOTHER, Gen. 3. 20. & 21. 21. Judg. 5. 7. 2 Sam. 20. 19. 1 Kings 3. 27. Gal. 4. 26.
Job 17. 14. worm, thou art my *m.*
Ps. 27. 10. when father and *m.* for.
71. 6. took me out of my *m.'s* bowels
Matt. 12. 49. behold my *m.* and my
R. V. Luke 2. 43. his parents
MOUNT to be cast against Jerusalem, Jer. 6. 6.
MOURN, Neh. 8. 9. Job 5. 11.
Isa. 61. 2. to comfort all that *m.*
Matt. 5. 4. blessed are they that *m.*
Jas. 4. 9. be afflicted and *m.* and
Matt. 11. 17. we have *mourned*
1 Cor. 5. 2. are puffed up and have not rather *m.*
Eccl. 12. 5. *mourners* go about the
Isa. 57. 18. restore comfort to him and his *m.*
Ps. 30. 11. turned *mourning* into
Isa. 22. 12. Lord did call to weeping and *m.*
61. 3. to give the oil of joy for *m.*
Jer. 9. 17. call for the *m.* women
31. 13. I will turn their *m.* into joy
Joel 2. 12. turn to me with fasting and *m.*
Jas. 4. 9. let laughter be turned into *m.*
R. V. Gen. 50. 3; Num. 20. 29. wept; 2 Sam. 11. 26. made lamentation; Job 2. 11. bemoan; Gen. 50. 10; Isa. 19. 8. lament; Ps. 35. 14. bewaileth; 55. 2. am restless; 88. 9. wasteth away; Prov. 29. 2. sigh; Ezek. 24. 23. moan; Matt. 11. 17; Luke 7. 32. wailed; Job 3. 8. leviathan; Isa. 51. 11. sighing; Mic. 1. 11. wailing
MOUTH of babes and sucklings, Ps. 8. 2.
Ps. 37. 30. *m.* of righteous speaketh
Prov. 10. 14. *m.* of fools is near
10. 31. *m.* of the just bringeth
12. 6. *m.* of upright shall deliver
14. 3. in *m.* of fools is a rod of pride
15. 2. the *m.* of fools poureth out
18. 7. a fool's *m.* is his destruction
22. 14. *m.* of strange women is a
Lam. 3. 38. out of *m.* of the Most
Matt. 12. 34. out of abundance of the heart the *m.* speaketh
Luke 21. 15. will give you a *m.* and
Rom. 10. 10. with the *m.* confession
15. 6 with one mind and *m.* glorify
Prov. 13. 3. keepeth *his mouth*, keep.
Lam 3. 29. putteth — in dust if
Mal. 2. 7. they shall seek law at —
Ps. 17. 3. *my mouth* shall not transgress
39. 1. I will keep — with a bridle
49. 3. — shall speak of wisdom
Ps. 51. 15. — shall show forth thy
71. 15 — shall show forth thy
Eph. 6. 19. that I may open — boldly
Ps. 81. 10. open *thy mouth* wide
103. 5. who satisfieth — with good
Prov. 31. 8. open — for the dumb in
Eccl. 5. 6. suffer not — to cause flesh
R. V. Job 12. 11; 34. 3. palate; Ps. 32. 9. trappings; Isa. 19. 7. brink; Matt. 15. 8 —
MOVE, Ex. 11. 7. Judg. 13. 25.
Acts 17. 28. in him we live and *m.*
20. 24. none of these things *m.* me
Ps. 15. 5. shall never be *moved*, 21. 7. & 26. 5. & 55. 22. & 62. 2, 6. & 66. 9. & 112. 6. & 121. 3. Prov. 12. 3.
Col. 1. 23. be not *m.* away from hope
1 Thes. 3. 3. no man be *m.* by these
Heb. 12. 28. a kingdom which cannot be *m.*
2 Pet. 1. 21. spake as *m.* by the Holy Ghost
Rom. 7. 5. *motions*
Prov. 5. 6. *moveable*
R. V. Gen. 9. 2. teemeth; 2 Kings 21. 8. wander; Ps. 23. 31. goeth down smoothly; Jer. 25. 16. reel to and fro; 46. 7, 8. toss themselves; 49. 21; 50. 46. trembleth; Ezek. 47. 9. swarmeth; Mic. 7. 17. trembling; Matt. 14. 14; Mark 6. 34. he had . . on; Matt. 21. 10; Mark 15. 11. stirred; Acts 20. 24 ——; Heb. 12. 28. shaken
MULTITUDE, Gen. 16. 10. & 28. 3. Ex. 12. 38. & 23. 2. Num. 11. 4.
Job 32. 7. *m.* of years should teach
Ps. 5. 7. *m.* of mercies
10. *m.* of transgressions
33. 16. no king saved by the *m.* of
51. 1. according unto the *m.* of thy
94. 19. in the *m.* of my thoughts
Prov. 10. 19. *m.* of words wanteth
11. 14. in the *m.* of counsellors
Eccl. 5. 3. *m.* of business, *m.* words
Jas. 5. 20. hide *m.* of sins, 1 Pet. 4. 8.
R. V. Gen. 28. 3; 48. 4; Luke 23. 1. company; Job. 39. 7; Jer. 3. 23; 10. 13; 51. 16. tumult; 46. 25. Amon; Ps. 42. 4. throng; Prov. 20. 15. abundance; Isa. 17. 12. ah, the uproar; Jer. 12. 6. aloud; Ezek. 31. 5; Matt. 12. 15. many; Mark 3. 9; Acts 21. 34. crowd; Luke 8. 37. all the people; Acts 23. 7. assembly; Job 33. 19; Acts 21. 22 ——
MURDER, Rom. 1. 29. Matt. 15. 19. Gal. 5. 21. Rev. 9. 21.
Job 24. 14. *murderer* rising with light
John 8. 44. devil was a *m.* from the
Hos. 9. 13. bring forth children to *m.*
1 Pet. 4. 15. none of you suffer as a *m.*
1 John 3. 15. who hateth his brother is a *m.* and no *m.* hath eternal life
R. V. Matt. 19. 18. not kill; Gal. 5. 21 ——; Num. 35. 16, 17, 18, 21. manslayer; Hos. 9. 13. slayer; Acts 21. 38. assassins
MURMUR, Deut. 1. 27. Ps. 106. 25. Jude 16. Ex. 16. 7. Phil. 2. 14.
MUSE, Ps. 39. 3. & 143. 5.
R. V. Luke 3. 15. reasoned
MUSIC, Lam. 3. 63. Amos 6. 5.
R. V. Lam. 3. 63. song
MUSTARD seed, Matt. 13. 31. & 17. 20.
MUZZLE, Deut. 25. 4. 1 Cor. 9. 9.
MYSTERY of the kingdom, Mark 4. 11.
Rom. 11. 25. not be ignorant of *m.*
16. 25. according to revelation of the *m.*
1 Cor. 2. 7. speak the wisdom of God in a *m.*
4. 1. stewards of the *m.* of God
13. 2. prophesy and understand *m.*
14. 2. in the Spirit he speaketh *m.*
15. 51. I show you a *m.* we shall
Eph. 1. 9. made known *m.* of his
3. 4. my knowledge in *m.*
5. 32. this is a great *m.* of Christ
Eph. 6. 19. make known *m.* of gospel
Col. 1. 2. *m.* which hath been hid
1. 27. glory of this *m.* among Gen.
2. 2. acknowledg. of *m.* of God
4. 3. open a door to speak *m.* of
2 Thes. 2. 7. *m.* of iniquity doth
1 Tim. 3. 9. holding *m.* of the faith
16. great is the *m.* of godliness
Rev. 1. 20. write the *m.* of seven
10. 7. *m.* of God should be finish.
17. 5. her name, *m.* Babylon the

N

NAIL, Judg. 4. 21. & 5. 26.
Ezra 9. 8. give us a *n.* in his
Eccl. 12. 11. *n.* fastened by the masters
Isa. 22. 23. fastened as a *n.* in a sure
Zech. 10. 4. out of him came the *n.*
R. V. Judg. 4. 21, 22. tent pin
NAKED, Gen. 2. 25. & 3. 7, 11.
Ex. 32. 25. when the people were *n.*
2 Chron. 28. 19. he made Judah *n.*
Job 1. 21. *n.* came I out of
Matt. 25. 26. I was *n.* and ye cloth.
1 Cor. 4. 11. we hunger and thirst and are *n.*
2 Cor. 5. 3. clothed may not be *n.*
Heb. 4. 13. all things are *n.* and
Rev. 3. 17. misera., poor, blind, *n.*
16. 15. keepeth his garments lest he walk *n.*
R. V. Ex. 32. 25. broken loose, let them loose for derision; 2 Chron. 28. 19. dealt wantonly; Hab. 3. 9. bare
NAME, Ex. 34. 14. Lev. 18. 21.
Ps. 20. 1. the *n.* of God of Jacob
109. 13. let their *n.* be blotted
Prov. 10. 7. *n.* of the wicked shall
22. 1. good *n.* is rather to be chos.
Eccl. 7. 1. a good *n.* is better than
Isa. 55. 13. shall be to the Lord for *n.*
56. 5. a *n.* better than of sons and
62. 2. thou shalt be call. by new *n.*
Jer. 13. 11. for a people, for a *n.* and
32. 20. made thee *n.* as at this day
33. 9. shall be to me a *n.* of joy, a
Mic. 4. 5. we will walk in the *n.* of
Matt. 10. 41. receive a prophet in *n.*
Luke 6. 22. cast out your *n.* as evil
Acts 4. 12. is none other *n.*
Rom. 2. 24. *n.* of God is blasphem.
Col. 3. 17. do all in the *n.* of Lord
2 Tim. 2. 19. that nameth *n.* of Ch.
Heb. 1. 4. obtained more excell. *n.*
1 Pet. 4. 14. if ye be reproached for the *n.* of Christ
1 John 3. 23. should believe on the *n.* of his Son
5. 13. that we believe on the *n.*
Rev. 2. 17. *n.* written, which no man
3. 1. I know thy works, that thou hast a *n.*
12. write on him *n.* of my God
14. 1. Father's *n.* on their fore.
Eph. 1. 21. every *n.* that is *named*, Phil. 2. 9.
Ps. 76. 1. *his name* is great in Israel
72. 17. — shall endure for ever
106. 8. he saved them for — sake
Prov. 30. 4. what is — and what
Isa. 9. 6. — shall be called Wonder.
Zech. 14. 9. shall be one Lord and — one
John 20. 31. might have life thro. —
Rev. 3. 5. I will confess — before
13. 17. the name of the beast, or the number of —, 15. 2.
Ex. 23. 21. *my name* is in him
3. 15. this is — for ever, and my
Judg. 13. 18. askest after —, Gen. 32. 29.
Isa. 48. 9. for — sake I will defer
Ezek. 20. 9. wrought for — sake
Mal. 1. 14. — is dreadful among the
2. 2. lay it to heart to give glory to —
Matt. 10. 22. hated of all for — sake
19. 29. forsaken houses for — sake

John 14. 13. ask in —, 15. 16. & 16. 23, 26.
16. 24. asked nothing in —
Acts 9. 15. he is a chosen vessel to bear —
Rev. 2. 3. for — hast labored, and
13. holdest fast—
3. 8. hast not denied my —
2 Chron. 14. 11. in *thy name* we go
Ps. 8. 1. how excellent is — in all
9. 10. that know — will put their
48. 10. according to — so is thy
75. 1.— is near, thy works declare
138. 2. magnified thy word above all —
S. of S. 1. 3.— is as ointment pour.
Isa. 26. 8. desire of our souls is to—
64. 7. none that calleth on —
Jer. 14. 7. do it for—sake, 21. Dan. 9. 6. Josh. 7. 9. Ps. 79. 9.
Mic. 6. 9. man of wisdom shall see —
John 17. 12. I kept them in —, 26.
Ex. 23. 13. make no mention of the *names* of other gods, Deut. 12. 3. Ps. 16. 4.
Ex. 28. 12. Aaron bear their *n*.
Ps. 49. 11. call lands after their *n*.
147. 4. stars he calleth by their *n*.
Luke 10. 20. *n*. written in heaven
Rev. 3. 4. hast a few *n*. in Sardis
R. V. Mark 9. 41; 11. 10; 1 John 5. 13 ——; Luke 24. 18; Acts 7. 58; 28. 7. named; Matt. 9. 9; Mark 15. 7; Luke 19. 2. called; John 11. 1——; John 11. 49; Acts 24. 1. one; 1 Cor. 5. 1. even

NARROW, 1 Kings 6. 4. Prov. 23. 27. Isa. 28. 20. & 49. 19. Matt. 7. 14.
R. V. 1 Kings 6. 4. fixed; Ezek. 40. 16; 41. 16, 26. closed; Matt. 7. 14. straitened

NATION, Gen. 15. 14. & 21. 13.
Gen. 20. 4. wilt thou slay a righteous *n*.
Num. 14. 12. make of thee a great *n*.
2 Sam. 7. 23. what *n*. is like thy
Ps. 33. 12. blessed is the *n*. whose
147. 20. not dealt so with any *n*.
Isa. 1. 4. ah sinful *n*. a people laden
2. 4. *n*. shall not lift up sword
49. 7. him whom the *n*. abhorreth
66. 8. shall a *n*. be born at once
Matt. 24. 7. *n*. shall rise against *n*.
Luke 7. 5. he loveth our *n*. and
Acts 10. 35. in every *n*. he that fear.
Rom. 10. 19. by a foolish *n*. I will
Phil. 2. 15. in midst of a crooked *n*.
1 Pet. 2. 9. ye are a holy *n*.
Rev. 5. 9. redeemed us out of every *n*.
Gen. 10. 32. *nations*, 17. 4, 6, 16.
Deut. 26. 19. high above all *n*., 28. 1.
Ps. 9. 20. *n*. may know themselves
113. 4. Lord is high above all *n*.
Isa. 2. 2. all *n*. shall flow unto it
40. 17. *n*. before him are as noth.
55. 5. *n*. that knew thee not shall
Jer. 4. 2. *n*. shall bless themselves
Zech. 2. 11. many *n*. be joined
Matt. 25. 32. before him be gathered all *n*.
Acts 14. 16. suffered all *n*. to walk
Rev. 21. 24. the *n*. of them that
R. V. Gen. 14. 1, 9; Josh. 12. 23. Goiim; Lev. 18. 26. homeborn; Ex. 2. 18; Deut. 2. 25; 4. 6, 19, 27; 14. 2; 28. 37; 30. 3; 1 Chron. 16. 24; 2 Chron. 7. 20; 13. 9; Neh. 1. 8; 19. 22; Ps. 96. 5; 106. 34; Ezek. 38. 8. peoples; Isa. 37. 18. countries; Mark 7. 26. race; Gal. 1. 14. countrymen; Phil. 2. 15. generation

NATURE, Rom. 2. 27. Jas. 3. 6.
Rom. 1. 26. that which is against *n*.
2. 14. do by *n*. things contained in
11. 24. olive wild by *n*. contr. to *n*.
1 Cor. 11. 14. doth not *n*. itself teach
Gal. 2. 16. are Jews by *n*. and
4. 8. served them which by *n*. are
Eph. 2. 3. were by *n*. the children
Heb. 2. 16. took not *n*. of angels
2 Pet. 1. 4. partakers of divine *n*.
Deut. 34. 7. *natural*, Rom. 1. 26, 27, 31. & 11. 21, 24. 1 Cor. 2. 14. & 15. 44, 46. 2 Tim. 3. 3. Jas. 1. 23. 2 Pet. 2. 12. Phil. 2. 20. Jude 10.
R. V. 2 Pet. 2. 12. creatures without reason

NAUGHT, it is, saith the buyer, Prov. 20. 14.
Jas. 1. 21. filthiness and superfluity of *naughtiness*
R. V. Prov. 11. 6. mischief; Jas. 1. 21. wickedness

NAVY of Solomon, 1 Kings 9. 26. 2 Chron. 8. 17.
of Jehoshaphat, 1 Kings 22. 48.

NEAR, nigh, Ps. 119. 151. & 148. 14.
Isa. 55. 6. & 57. 19. Jer. 12. 2.
R. V. frequent changes to at, nigh, ——, etc.

NECESSARY, Job 23. 12. Acts 13. 46. & 15. 28. Tit. 3. 14. Heb. 9. 23.
Rom. 12. 13. *necessity*, Acts 20. 34. 1 Cor. 9. 16. 2 Cor. 6. 4. & 9. 7. & 12. 20. Phile. 14. Heb. 9. 16.
R. V. Acts 28. 10. we needed; Luke 23. 17——; Heb. 8. 3. necessary; Phil. 4. 16. need

NECK, S. of S. 1. 10. Isa. 48. 4. Rom. 16. 4.
Acts 15. 10. put a yoke on *n*. of
2 Kings 17. 14. hardened their *necks*, Neh. 9. 16, 17, 29. Jer. 7. 26. & 19. 15.

NEED of all these things, Matt. 6. 32.
Matt. 9. 12. they that are whole *n*.
Luke 15. 7. the righteous *n*. no
Heb. 4. 16. find grace to help in time of *n*.
1 John 2. 27. *n*. not that any
Rev. 3. 17. rich, and have *n*. of
21. 23. no *n*. of sun
22. 5. *n*. no candle
Eph. 4. 28. give to him that *needeth*
2 Tim. 2. 15. *n*. not be ashamed of
Luke 10. 42. one thing is *needful*
Ps. 9. 18. *needy* not always be for.
72. 12. he shall deliver the *n*. and
82. 3. do justice to afflicted and *n*.
Isa. 14. 30. *n*. shall lie down in saf.
Jer. 22. 16. he judgeth cause of *n*.
R. V. Jude 3. was constrained

NEGLECT to hear, Matt. 18. 17.
1 Tim. 4. 14. *n*. not the gift that is
Heb. 2. 3. if we *n*. so great salva.
R. V. Matt. 18. 17. refuse; Col. 2. 23. severity of.

NEIGH. Jer. 5. 8. & 8. 16. & 13. 27.

NEIGHBOR, Ex. 3. 22. & 11. 2.
Ex. 20. 16. not bear false witness against thy *n*.
Lev. 19. 13. thou shalt not defr. *n*.
17. thou shalt rebuke thy *n*.
18. thou shalt love thy *n*. as thyself, Matt. 19. 19. & 22. 39. Rom. 13. 9. Gal. 5. 14. Jas. 2. 8. Matt. 7. 12. Heb. 13. 3.
Ps. 15. 3. nor doeth evil to his *n*.
Prov. 27. 10. better is a *n*. near
Jer. 22. 13. useth *n*.'s servant
31. 24. teach no more his *n*.
Luke 10. 29. who is my *n*., 36.
Rom. 13. 10. love worketh no ill to his *n*.
15. 2. let every one please his *n*.
R. V. 1 Kings 20. 35. fellow; Ps. 15. 3; Prov. 19. 4. friend; Heb. 8. 11. fellow-citizen

NEST, Job 20. 18. Ps. 84. 3. Prov. 27. 8. Isa. 10. 14. Hab. 2. 9. Matt. 8. 20.

NET, Job 18. 8. & 19. 6. Ps. 9. 15. & 25. 15. & 31. 4. & 35. 7, 8. & 57. 6. & 66. 11. Isa. 51. 20. Hab. 1. 15, 16. Matt. 13. 47. Ps. 141. 10. Eccl. 7. 20.

NEW, Lord make a *n*. thing, Num. 16. 30.
Judg. 5. 8. they chose *n*. gods, Deut. 32. 17.
Eccl. 1. 9. no *n*. thing under sun, 10.
Isa. 65. 17. *n*. heavens and a *n*. earth, 66. 22. 2 Pet. 3. 13. Rev. 21. 1.
Jer. 31. 22. created a *n*. thing in earth
Lam. 3. 23. his mercies are *n*.
Ezek. 11. 19. I will put a *n*. spirit
18. 31. make you a *n*. heart and *n*. spirit
36. 26. *n*. heart I will give, and a *n*. spirit
Matt. 9. 16. putteth *n*. cloth on old
17. neither put *n*. wine in old bot.
13. 52. bringeth forth things *n*.
Mark 1. 27. what *n*. doctrine is this, Acts 17. 19.
John 13. 34. a *n*. commandment I give unto you, 1 John 2. 7, 8.
Acts 17. 21. to tell or hear some *n*. thing
1 Cor. 5. 7. that ye may be a *n*.
2 Cor. 5. 17. if any man be in Christ, he is a *n*. creature
Gal. 6. 15. neither circumcision nor uncircumcision, but a *n*. creature
Eph. 4. 24. that ye put on *n*. man
1 Pet. 2. 2. as *n*. born babes desire
Rev. 2. 17. a *n*. name written
5. 9. sung a *n*. song, 14. 3.
Rom. 6. 4. should walk in *newness*
7. 6. we should serve in *n*. of spirit
R. V. Joel 1. 5; 3. 18. sweet; Matt. 9. 16; Mark 2. 21; Luke 5. 38. fresh; Matt. 9. 16; Mark 2. 21. undressed; Neh. 10. 39; Matt. 26. 28; Mark 2. 22; 14. 24——

NIGH, Lev. 25. 49. Num. 24. 17
Deut. 4. 7. who hath God so *n*.
Ps. 34. 18. Lord is *n*. them of brok.
85. 9. salvation is *n*. them that
145. 18. Lord is *n*. them that call
Matt. 15. 8. draweth *n*. with mouth
Eph. 2. 13. made *n*. by blood of
R. V. Gen. 47. 29; Ex. 24. 2; Lev. 21. 3; Luke 7. 12. near; Luke 21. 20; John 6. 4; Jas. 5. 8. at hand; Matt. 15. 8. honoreth

NIGHT, Gen. 1. 5, 14. & 26. 24.
Ex. 12. 42. this is that *n*. of Lord
Ps. 19. 2. *n*. unto *n*. showeth know.
30. 5. weeping may endure for a *n*.
Isa. 21. 11. what of the *n*.
Jer. 14. 8. as wayfaring man to tarry for a *n*.
Luke 6. 12. continued all *n*. in pray.
12. 20. this *n*. shall thy soul be
John 9. 4. *n*. cometh when no man
Rom. 13. 12. *n*. is far spent; day is
1 Thes. 5. 5. children not of *n*. nor
Rev. 21. 25. shall be no *n*. there
Ps. 134. 1. *by night*, S. of S. 3. 1. John 3. 2. & 7. 50. & 19. 39.
Job 35. 10. who giveth songs *in the night*
Ps. 16. 7. instruct me — seasons
42. 8. — his song shall be with me
77. 6. I call to remembrance my song —
119. 55. I have remem. thy name—
Isa. 26. 9. my soul desired thee —
59. 10. stumble at noon day as —
John 11. 10. if a man walk — he
1 Thes. 5. 7. sleep— and are drunk—
Ps. 63. 6. *night watches*, 119. 148.
R. V. Lev. 6. 20. evening; Isa. 21. 4; 59. 10. twi.; Judg. 19. 13; Matt. 27. 64; Mark 14. 27; 2 Pet. 3. 10——

NOBLE, Esth. 6. 9. Jer. 2. 21. Luke 19. 12. Acts 17. 11. Ex. 24. 11. Num. 21. 12.
1 Cor. 1. 26. not many *n*. are called
Col. 3. 5. *nobles* put not their necks
13. 17. I contended with the *n*. of
Ps. 149. 8. bind their *n*. with fetters
Prov. 8. 16. by me princes rule, and *n*.
Eccl. 13. 17. when thy king is the son of *n*.
R. V. Isa. 43. 14. as fugitives; Jer. 30. 21. prince; Nah. 3. 18. worthless; Acts 24. 3; 26. 25. excellent

NOISOME, Ps. 91. 3. Rev. 16. 2.

NOSE, Prov. 30. 33. Isa. 65. 5.
Isa. 2. 22. breath in *nostrils*, Lam. 4. 20.
R. V. S. of S. 7. 8. breath; Ezek. 39. 11. them that pass through; Job 4. 9. anger; 39. 20. snorting

NOTHING, Gen. 11. 6. Ex. 9. 4. &

12. 10. Num. 6. 4. & 16. 26. Josh. 11. 15.
2 Sam. 24. 24. offer that which costs me *n.*
1 Kings 8. 9. *n.* in ark save the two
Neh. 8. 10. send to them from whom *n.* is prepared
Job 6. 21. ye are *n.*
8. 9. of yesterday, and know *n.*
26. 7. hangeth earth on *n.*
34. 9. it profiteth *n.*
Ps. 17. 3. thou hast tried me and shalt find *n.*
39. 5. my age is as *n.* before thee
49. 17. when he dieth, shall carry *n.*
119. 165. *n.* shall offend them
Prov. 13. 4. the sluggard desireth and hath *n.*
7. that make. him.rich, yet hath *n.*
Isa. 40. 17. all nations before him are as *n.*
Jer. 10. 24. lest thou bring me to *n.*
Lam. 1. 12. is it *n.* to you, all ye
Hag. 2. 3. is it not in your eyes in comparison of it as *n.*
Luke 1. 37. with God *n.* shall be
John 8. 28. I do *n.* of myself
14. 30. prince of this world hath *n.* in me
15. 5. without me ye can do *n.*
1 Cor. 1. 19. bring to *n.* the under.
13. 2. I am *n.*
2 Cor. 12. 11. having *n.* yet possessing all, 2 Cor. 6. 10.
1 Tim. 6. 7. we brought *n.* into world

NOUGHT, Gen. 29. 15. Deut. 13. 17.
Isa. 41. 12. shall be as a thing of *n.*
49. 4. I have spent my strength for *n.*
52. 3. sold yourselves for *n.*
Amos 6. 13. rejoice in a thing of *n.*
Luke 23. 11. Herod and men set him at *n.*
Acts 19. 27. Diana in danger to be set at *n.*
Rom. 14. 10. why set at *n.* brother

NOVICE, not a, lest, 1 Tim. 3. 6.

NUMBER our days, teach us to, Ps. 90. 12.
Isa. 65. 12. I will *n.* you to the sword
Rev. 7. 9. multitude which no man could *n.*
Isa. 53. 12. was *numbered* with transgressors
Dan. 5. 26. God hath *n.* thy kingdom
Job 14. 16. thou *numberest* my steps
Ps. 71. 15. I know not the *numbers*
Rev. 13. 17. the *n.* of his name, 18.
R. V. Mark 10. 46; Acts 1. 15. multitude; 2 Sam. 24. 2. sum; Josh. 8. 10; 1 Kings 20. 15, 26, 27; 2 Kings 3. 6. mustered; 1 Tim. 5. 9. enrolled

NUMBERING of the people, by Moses, Num. 1. 26; by David, 2 Sam. 24. 1 Chron. 21. of the Levites, Num. 3. 14. & 4. 34.

NURSE, 1 Thes. 2. 7. Isa. 49. 23.

O

OATH, Gen. 24. 8. & 26. 3, 28.
1 Sam. 14. 26. people feared the *o.*
2 Sam. 21. 7. Lord's *o.* was between
2 Chron. 15. 15. Israel rejoiced at *o.*
Eccl. 8. 2. keep in regard of *o* of God
9. 2. that feareth and sweareth an *o.*
Ezek. 16. 59. despised the *o.*
Luke 1. 73. *o.* which he sware to
Heb. 6. 16. *o.* for confirmat. is end
Jas. 5. 12. swear not by heaven neither by any other *o.*

OBEY, Gen. 27. 8. Ex. 5. 2.
Deut. 11. 27. a blessing if ye *o.*
13. 4. walk after the Lord and *o.*
Josh. 24. 24. his voice will we *o.*
1 Sam. 12. 14. fear the Lord and *o.*
15. 22. to *o.* is better than sacrifice
Jer. 7. 23. *o.* my voice and I will
26. 13. amend your ways, and *o.*
Acts 5. 29. ought to *o.* God rather
Rom. 2. 8. contenti., and do not *o.*
6. 16. his servants ye are to whom ye *o.*
Eph. 6. 1. children *o.* your parents
Col. 3. 22. servants *o.* in all things
2 Thes. 1. 8. that *o.* not the Gospel
3. 14. if any man *o.* not your word
Tit. 3. 1. put them in mind to *o.*
Heb. 5. 9. salvation to all who *o.*
13. 17. *o.* them that have rule over
1 Pet. 3. 1. if any *o.* not the word
Rom. 6. 17. *obeyed* from heart that
1 Pet. 3. 6. Sarah *o.* Abraham
4. 17. the end of them that *o.* not
Isa. 50. 10. *obeyeth* voice, Jer. 11. 3.
1 Pet. 1. 22. purified in *obeying* truth
Rom. 1. 5. received grace for *obedience*
15. 19. by the *o.* of one many
6. 16. yield *o.* unto righteousness
16. 19. your *o.* is come abroad
26. made known for *o.* of faith
1 Cor. 14. 34. women to be under *o.*
2 Cor. 7. 15. remember the *o.* of you
10. 5. every thought to *o.* of Christ
Heb. 5. 8. learned he *o.* by things
1 Pet. 1. 2. sanctifi. of Spirit unto *o.*
Ex. 24. 7. will we do and be *obedient*
Num. 27. 20. children of Israel may be *o.*
Deut. 3. 30. turn and be *o.* to voice
8. 20. perish because not *o.* to Lord
2 Sam. 22. 45. strangers shall be *o.*
Isa. 1. 19. if ye be *o.* ye shall eat
42. 24. they were not *o.* to his law
Acts 6. 7. priests were *o.* to the faith
Rom. 15. 18. Gentiles *o.* by word
2 Cor. 2. 9. whether ye be *o.* in all
Eph. 6. 5. servants be *o.* to masters
Phil. 2. 8. he became *o.* unto death
Tit. 2. 5. discreet, *o.* to your hus.
1 Pet. 1. 14. as *o.* children, not
R. V. Ex. 5. 2; 23. 21, 22; Deut. 11. 27, 28; 28. 62; Josh. 24. 24; 1 Sam. 8. 19; 12. 14, 15; Job 36. 11, 12; Jer. 7. 23; Rom. 10. 16. hearken; Josh. 5. 6; 22. 2; Judg. 2. 2; 6. 10; 1 Sam. 28. 21; Jer. 17. 23, 28; 2 Chron. 11. 4. hearkened; Jer. 11. 3; 12. 17. hear; Gal. 3. 1 ——; 1 Cor. 14. 34. subjection; Deut. 8. 20; Dan. 4. 30. hearken; Num. 27. 20; 2 Sam. 22. 45. obey; Tit. 2. 5, 9. subjection; 1 Pet. 1. 22. obedience

OBSCURITY, Isa. 29. 18. & 58. 10.
R. V. 58. 10; 59. 9. darkness

OBSERVE, Ex. 12. 17. & 34. 11.
Ps. 107. 43. who is wise and will *o.*
119. 34. *o.* it with my whole heart
Prov. 23. 26. let thine eyes *o.* my
Jonah 2. 8. that *o.* lying vanities
Matt. 28. 20. teaching them to *o.*
Gal. 4. 10. ye *o.* days months and
Gen. 37. 11. his father *observed* the
Ex. 12. 42. a night to be much *o.*
Mark 6. 20. Herod fear. John and *o.*
10. 20. all these have I *o.* from my
Luke 17. 20. cometh not with *observation*
R. V. Lev. 19. 26; 2 Kings 21. 6; 2 Chron. 33. 6. practise; Deut. 16. 13; 2 Chron. 7. 17; Neh. 1. 5; Ps. 105. 45. keep; Prov. 23. 26. delight in; Hos. 14. 8; John 2. 8. regard; Gen. 37. 11; Mark 6. 20. kept; Ps. 107. 43. give heed; Hos. 13. 7. watch; Matt. 23. 3; Acts 21. 25 ——

OBSTINATE, Deut. 2. 30. Isa. 48. 4.

OBTAIN favor of Lord, Prov. 8. 35.
Isa. 35. 10. shall *o.* joy and gladness
Luke 20. 35. worthy to *o.* that world
1 Cor. 9. 24. so run, that ye may *o.*
Heb. 4. 16. may *o.* mercy and find
11. 35. might *o.* better resurrection
Hos. 2. 23. her that had not *obtained* mercy
Acts 26. 22. having *o.* help of God
Rom. 11. 7. the election hath *o.* it
Eph. 1. 11. in whom we have *o.* an
1 Tim. 1. 13. I *o.* mercy, because
Heb. 1. 4. *o.* a more excellent
6. 15. endured, he *o.* the promises
Heb. 9. 12. *o.* eternal redemption for us
R. V. Luke 20. 35; 1 Cor. 9. 24. attain; 1 Cor. 9. 25; Heb. 4. 16; Acts 1. 17. receive; Neh. 13. 6. asked

OCCASION, Gen. 43. 18. Judg. 14. 4.
2 Sam. 12. 14. given *o.* to enemies
Job 33. 10. he findeth *o.* against me
Jer. 2. 24. in her *o.* who can turn
Dan. 6. 4. could find none *o.*, 5.
Rom. 7. 8. sin taking *o.* by the
14. 13. *o.* to fall in brother's way
2 Cor. 11. 12. cut off *o.* from the
Gal. 5. 13. use not for *o.* to the flesh
1 Tim. 5. 14. give none *o.* to adver.
1 John 2. 10. none *o.* of stumbling

OCCUPY, Luke 19. 13. Heb. 13. 9.
R. V. Ex. 38. 24. used; Ezek. 27. 16, 19, 22. Luke 19. 13. trade, or traded; 1 Cor. 14. 16. filleth

ODOR, Phil. 4. 18. Rev. 5. 8.
R. V. Jer. 34. 5. make burning; Rev. 5. 8; 18. 13. incense

OFFENCE, 1 Sam. 25. 31. Isa. 8. 14.
Eccl. 10. 4. yield. pacifieth great *o.*
Hos. 5. 15. acknowledge their *o.*
Acts 24. 16. conscience void of *o.*
Rom. 4. 25. delivered for our *o.* and
Matt. 16. 23. thou art an *o.* unto me
18. 7. woe to the world because of *o.* for *o.* must come
Rom. 5. 15. not as *o.* so is free gift
16. the free gift is of many *o.*
17. by one man's *o.* death came
9. 33. rock of *o.*, 1 Pet. 2. 8. Isa. 8. 14.
14. 20. is evil for him that eateth with *o.*
16. 17. cause divisions and *o.*
1 Cor. 10. 32. give none *o.* neither
2 Cor. 6. 3. giving no *o.* in any
11. 7. committed an *o.* in abasing
Gal 5. 11. then is the *o.* of the
Phil. 1. 10. without *o.* till day of Christ
R. V. Matt. 16. 23; Gal. 5. 11. stumbling block; Matt. 18. 7. occasion; Rom. 4. 25; 5. 15-18. trespass; Matt. 18. 7; Luke 17. 1; Rom. 16. 17; 2 Cor. 6. 3. occasion for stum.

OFFEND, I will not any more, Job 34. 31.
Ps. 73. 15. *o.* against generation
119. 165. nothing shall *o.* them
Jer. 2. 3. all that devour him shall *o.*
50. 7. we *o.* not because we have
Matt. 5. 29. if thy right eye *o.* thee
13. 41. gather out of his kingdom all that *o.*
17. 27. yet lest we should *o.* go
18. 6. whoso shall *o.* one of these
1 Cor. 8. 13. if meat make thy brother to *o.*
Jas. 2. 10. *o.* in one point is guilty
3. 2. in many things we *o.* all
Prov. 18. 19. brother *offended* is harder to be won
Matt. 11. 6. blessed who is not *o.*
26. 33. though all be *o.* I will
Mark 4. 17. immediate. they are *o.*
Rom. 14. 21. *o.* or is made weak
2 Cor. 11. 29. who is *o.* and I burn
Isa. 29. 21. make a man *offender* for
R. V. Gen. 20. 9; Jer. 37. 18; Acts 25. 8. sinned; Jer. 2. 3; Hab. 1. 11. guilty; Rom. 14. 21 ——. In most of the above references under the head of *Stumble*, the word stumble, stumbling or stumbleth has been introduced into R. V. text; Acts 21. 11. wrong doer

OFFER, Gen. 31. 54. Lev. 1. 3.
Matt. 5. 24. then come and *o.* thy gift
Heb. 13. 15. let us *o.* the sacrifice
Rev. 8. 3. *o.* it with prayers of
Mal. 1. 11. incense *offered* to my
Phil. 2. 17. *o.* upon sacrifice and service
2 Tim. 4. 6. I am now ready to be *o.*
Heb. 9. 14. *o.* himself without spot
28. Christ was once *o.* to bear

Heb. 11. 4. by faith Abel *o.* to God a
17. Abraham *o.* up Isaac
Ps. 50. 14. *o.* to God thanksgiving
23. whoso *offereth* praise glori.
Eph. 5. 2. *offering* a sacrifice to God
Heb. 10. 5. sacrifice and *o.* thou
14. by one *o.* hath perfected for
R. V. Frequent changes to sacrifice, present, bring or brought, especially in O. T. Frequent changes in Lev. and Num. to oblation

OFFSCOURING, Lam. 3. 45. 1 Cor. 4. 16.

OFFSPRING, Acts 17. 28. Rev. 22. 16.
R. V. Job 31. 8. produce

OFTEN reproved hardeneth, Prov. 29. 1.
Mal. 3. 16. spake *o.* one to another
Matt. 23. 37. how *o.* would I have
1 Cor. 11. 26. *o.* as ye eat this
Phil. 3. 18. of whom I have told you *o.*
Heb. 9. 25. needed not offer himself *o.*

OIL, Gen. 28. 18. Ex. 25. 6.
Ps. 45. 7. with *o.* of gladness
89. 20. with my holy *o.* I have
92. 10. be anointed with fresh *o.*
104. 15. *o.* to make his face shine
141. 5. *o.* which shall not break
Isa. 61. 3. *o.* of joy for mourning
Matt. 25. 3. took no *o.* in lamps
8. give us of your *o.* for our lamps
Luke 10. 34. pouring in wine and *o.*

OINTMENT, Ps. 133. 2. Prov. 27. 9, 16. Eccl. 7. 1. & 10. 1. S. of S. 1. 3. Isa. 1. 6. Amos 6. 6. Matt. 26. 7. Luke 7. 37.
R. V. Ex. 30. 25. perfume; 2 Kings 20. 13; Ps. 123. 2; Isa. 1. 6; 39. 2. oil

OLD, Gen. 5. 32. & 18. 12, 13.
Ps. 37. 25. been young, and now am *o.*
71. 18. when I am *o.* and gray.
Prov. 22. 6. when he is *o.* he will
Jer. 6. 16. ask for the *o.* paths and
Acts 21. 16. Mnason an *o.* disciple
1 Cor. 5. 7. purge out the *o.* leaven
2 Cor. 5. 17. *o.* things are passed
2 Pet. 1. 9. purged from his *o.* sins
Gen. 25. 8. *old age,* Judg. 8. 32. Job 30. 2. Ps. 71. 9. & 92. 14. Isa. 46. 4.
Rom. 6. 6. *old man,* Eph. 4. 22. Col. 3. 9.
Prov. 17. 6. of *old men,* 20. 29.

OLD PROPHET, the, 1 Kings 13. 11.

OMEGA, Alpha and, Rev. 1. 8, 11. & 21. 6. & 22. 13.
R. V. Rev. 1. 11 ——

ONE, Gen. 2. 24. Matt. 19. 5.
Jer. 3. 14. *o.* of a city, and two of
Zech. 14. 9. shall be *o.* Lord and
Matt. 19. 17. none good but *o.*
1 Cor. 8. 4. none other God but *o.*
10. 17. we being many are *o.* bread
Gal. 3. 20. mediator not of *o.* but
1 John 5. 7. these three are *o.*
Josh. 23. 14. not *one thing* hath failed
Ps. 27. 4. — have I desired of Lord
Mark 10. 21. — thou lackest, go sell
Luke 10. 42. but — is needful
Phil. 3. 13. this — I do, forgetting

OPEN thou my lips, Ps. 51. 15.
Ps. 81. 10. *o.* thy mouth wide
119. 18. *o.* thou mine eyes, that I
Prov. 31. 8. *o.* thy mouth for dumb
S. of S. 5. 2. *o.* to me, my sister, my
Isa. 22. 22. shall *o.* and none shall
42. 7. to *o.* blind eyes, Ps. 146. 8.
Ezek. 16. 63. never *o.* thy mouth
Matt. 25. 11. Lord *o.* to us
Acts 26. 18. to *o.* their eyes, and
Col. 4. 3. *o.* to us door of utterance
Rev. 5. 2. who is worthy to *o.*
Gen. 3. 7. eyes of them both were *opened*
Isa. 35. 5. eyes of the blind shall be *o.*
53. 7. he *o.* not his mouth
Matt. 7. 7. knock and it shall be *o.*
Luke 24. 45. then *o.* he their
Acts 14. 27. *o.* the door of faith
16. 14. Lydia whose heart Lord *o.*
1 Cor. 16. 9. a great door and effectual is *o.*
2 Cor. 2. 12. a door was *o.* to me of
Heb. 4. 13. naked and *o.* to eyes of
Ps. 104. 28. *openest* thy hand, 145. 16.
R. V. Gen. 38. 14. gate of Enaim; 2 Cor. 3. 18. unveiled; 1 Tim. 5. 24. evident; Job 38. 17; Jer. 20. 12. revealed; Mark 1. 10. rent asunder

OPERATION, Ps. 28. 5. Isa. 5. 12. Col. 3. 12. 1 Cor. 12. 6.
R. V. 1 Cor. 12. 6. workings; Col. 2. 12. in the working

OPINION, Job 32. 6, 10. 1 Kings 18. 21.

OPPORTUNITY, Matt. 26. 16. Gal. 6. 10. Phil. 4. 10. Heb. 11. 15.

OPPOSE, 2 Tim. 2. 25. 2 Thes. 2. 4.
R. V. Job 30. 21. persecutest

OPPRESS, Ex. 3. 9. Judg. 10. 12.
Ex. 22. 21. *o.* not a stranger, 23. 9.
Lev. 25. 14. *o.* not one another, 17.
Deut. 24. 14. shall not *o.* a hired
Ps. 10. 18. that man may no more *o.*
Prov. 22. 22. neither *o.* afflicted in
Zech. 7. 10. *o.* not the widow or
Mal. 3. 5. a witness against those that *o.*
Jas. 2. 6. do not rich men *o.* you
Ps. 9. 9. the Lord will be a refuge for the *oppressed*
10. 18. judge the fatherless and *o.*
Eccl. 4. 1. tears of such as were *o.*
Isa. 1. 17. relieve the *o.*, 58. 6.
38. 14. I am *o.* undertake for me
53. 7. he was *o.* and afflicted
Ezek. 18. 7. hath not *o.* any
Acts 10. 38. Jesus healed all *o.* of
Prov. 22. 16. *oppresseth,* 14. 31. & 28. 3.
Deut. 27. 7. Lord looked on our *oppression*
2 Kings 13. 4. the Lord saw the *o.*
Ps. 12. 5. for *o.* of poor and sighing
62. 10. trust not in *o.* and become
Eccl. 7. 7. *o.* maketh a wise man
Isa. 5. 7. looked for judgment but behold *o.*
33. 15. he that despiseth gain of *o.*
Ps. 72. 4. *oppressor,* 54. 3. & 119. 121. Prov. 3. 31. & 28. 16. Eccl. 4. 1. Isa. 3. 12. & 14. 4. & 51. 13.
R. V. Lev. 25. 14, 17. wrong; Job 35. 9. cry out; Ezek. 18. 7, 12, 16. wronged; Ps. 12. 5. spoiling; Eccl. 7. 7. extortion; Ezek. 46. 18 ——; Job 3. 18. taskmaster; Ps. 54. 3. violent man; Zech. 10. 4. exactor

ORACLES of God, Acts 7. 38. Rom. 3. 2. Heb. 5. 12. 1 Pet. 4. 11.

ORDAIN, Isa. 26. 12. Tit. 1. 5.
Ps. 8. 2. hast *ordained* strength
132. 17. *o.* a lamp for mine anoint.
Isa. 30. 33. Tophet is *o.* of old, for
Jer. 1. 5. *o.* thee a prophet
Hab. 1. 12. thou hast *o.* them
Acts 13. 48. as were *o.* to eternal
14. 23. *o.* elders in every church
17. 31. judge by that man whom he hath *o.*
Rom. 7. 10. commandment which was *o.*
1 Cor. 9. 14. Lord *o.* that they
Gal. 3. 19. *o.* by angels in hand
Eph. 2. 10. God before *o.* we
1 Tim. 2. 7. *o.* a preacher and an
Heb. 5. 1. *o.* for men in things
Jude 4. *o.* to this condemnation
R. V. 1 Chron. 17. 9; Tit. 1. 5. appoint; Ps. 8. 2. established; 7. 13. maketh; Isa. 30. 33; Eph. 2. 10; Heb. 9. 6. prepared; 1 Cor. 2. 7. foreordained; 2 Chron. 11. 15; Ps. 81. 5; Jer. 1. 5; Dan. 2. 24; Mark 3. 14; John 15. 16; Acts 14. 23; 1 Tim. 2. 7; Heb. 5. 1; 8. 3. appointed

ORDER, Gen. 22. 9. Job 33. 5.
Job 23. 4. *o.* my cause before
Ps. 40. 5. be reckoned up in *o.*
50. 21. sins set them in *o.* before
119. 133. *o.* my steps in thy word
1 Cor. 14. 40. all things be done decently and in *o.*
Col. 2. 5. joying and beholding your *o.*
Tit. 1. 5. set in *o.* things wanting
2 Sam. 23. 5. everlasting covenant, *ordered* in all things
Ps. 37. 23. steps of a good man are *o.* by the Lord
50. 23. that *ordereth* his conversation aright
R. V. Ex. 40. 4; Luke 1. 1; Heb. 7. 21 ——; Ex. 26. 17. joined; 1 Chron. 15. 13; 23. 31; 2 Chron. 8. 14. ordinance; 1 Kings 20. 14. begin; Ps. 37. 23; Isa. 9. 7. establish

ORDINANCE of God, Isa. 58. 2. Rom. 13. 2.
1 Pet. 2. 13. submit to every *o.* of man
Neh. 10. 32. make *ordinances* for us
Isa. 58. 2. ask of me the *o.* of justice
Jer. 31. 35. *o.* of the moon and of
Ezek. 11. 20. keep mine *o.* and do them, Lev. 18. 4, 30. & 22. 9. 1 Cor. 11. 2.
Luke 1. 6. walking in all *o.* of Lord
Eph. 2. 15. law contained in *o.*
Col. 2. 14. handwriting of *o.* against
20. why are ye subject to *o.*
Heb. 9. 1. had *o.* of divine service
R. V. Lev. 18. 30; 22. 9; Mal. 3. 14. charge; Ex. 18. 20; Lev. 18. 3, 4, 30; 22. 9; Num. 9. 12, 14; 10. 8; 15. 15; 19. 2; 31. 21; Ps. 99. 7. statute, or statutes; Ezra 3. 10. order; Ezek. 45. 14. portion; 1 Cor. 11. 2. traditions

ORNAMENTS, Ex. 33. 5. Prov. 1. 9. & 25. 12. Isa. 49. 18. & 61. 10. Jer. 2. 32. Ezek. 16. 7, 11. 1 Pet. 3. 4.
R. V. Judg. 8. 21, 26. crescents; Prov. 1. 9; 4. 3. chaplet; Isa. 30. 22. plating; 61. 10. garland; 3. 20. ankle chains; 3. 18. anklets; 1 Pet. 3. 4. apparel

OSTENTATION condemned, Prov. 25. 14; 27. 2; Matt. 6. 1.

OUGHT ye to do, Matt. 23. 23. Jas. 3. 10.

OURS, Gen. 26. 20. Num. 32. 32.
Mark 12. 7. inheritance shall be *o.*, Luke 20. 14.
1 Cor. 1. 2. Christ our Lord both theirs and *o.*
Tit. 3. 14. let *o.* learn to maintain good works

OUTCASTS of Israel, Ps. 147. 2. Isa. 11. 12. & 16. 3. & 56. 8.
Isa. 16. 14. let mine *o.* dwell

OUTER, Ezek. 46. 21. & 47. 2. Matt. 8. 12. & 22. 13. & 25. 30.

OUTGOINGS, Josh. 17. 9. Ps. 65. 8.
R. V. In Josh. goings out

OUTRAGEOUS, Prov. 27. 4.

OUTSIDE, Ezek. 40. 5. Matt. 23. 25.

OUTSTRETCHED arm, Deut. 26. 8. Jer. 21. 5. & 27. 5.

OUTWARD, 1 Sam. 16. 7. Rom. 2. 28. 2 Cor. 4. 16. & 10. 7. 1 Pet. 3. 3.
Matt. 23. 28. *outwardly,* Rom. 2. 28.

OVEN, Ps. 21. 9. Hos. 7. 4. Mal. 4. 1.
R. V. Ps. 21. 9; Mal. 4. 1. furnace

OVERCHARGE, Luke 21. 31. 2 Cor. 2. 5.

OVERCOME, Gen. 49. 19. Num. 13. 30.
S. of S. 6. 5. thine eyes have *o.* me
John 16. 33. I have *o.* the world
Rom. 12. 21. be not *o.* of evil

1 John 2. 13. ye have *o*. the wick.
4. 4. ye are of God, and have *o*.
Rev. 17. 14. Lamb shall *o*. them
1 John 5. 4. born of God *overcometh*
Rev. 2. 7. to him that *o*. I will give
26. he that *o*. will I give power
3. 5. he that *o*. shall be clothed
12. him that *o*. will I make a pillar
21. him that *o*. will I grant to sit
21. 7. he that *o*. shall inherit all
R. V. Acts 19. 16. mastered
OVERMUCH, Eccl. 7. 16, 17. 2 Cor. 2. 7.
OVERPAST, Ps. 57. 1. Isa. 26. 20. Jer. 5. 28.
OVERSEER, Prov. 6. 7. Acts 20. 28.
R. V. Acts 20. 28. bishops
OVERSIGHT, Gen. 43. 12. 1 Pet. 5. 2.
R. V. Num. 4. 16. charge; Neh. 13. 4. who was appointed
OVERTAKE, Ex. 15. 9. Amos 9. 13. Hos. 2. 7. Gal. 6. 1. 1 Thes. 5. 4.
OVERTHROW, Deut. 12. 3. & 29. 23. Job 12. 19. Ps. 140. 4, 11. Prov. 13. 6. & 21. 12. Amos 4. 11. Acts 5. 39. 2 Tim. 2. 18.
R. V. Deut. 12. 3. break down; Ps. 140. 4. thrust aside; Prov. 18. 5. turn aside; 2 Sam. 17. 9. fallen; Job 19. 6. subverted
OVERTURN, Ezek. 21. 27. Job 9. 5. & 12. 15. & 28. 9. & 34. 25.
OVERWHELMED, Ps. 55. 5. & 61. 2. & 77. 3. & 124. 4. & 142. 3. & 143. 4.
R. V. Job 6. 27. cast lots upon
OVERWISE, neither make self, Eccl. 7. 16.
OWE, Rom. 13. 8. Matt. 18. 24, 28.
OWL, Job 30. 29. Ps. 102. 6. Isa. 13. 21. & 34. 11, 15. & 43. 20. Mic. 1. 8.
R. V. Lev. 11. 16; Deut. 14. 15; Job 30. 29; Isa. 13. 21; 34. 13; 43. 20; Jer. 50. 39; Mic. 1. 8. ostrich, or ostriches; Isa. 34. 14. night monster; 34. 15. arrowsnake
OWN, Deut. 24. 16. Judg. 7. 2.
John 1. 11. his *o*. and his *o*. receiv.
1 Cor. 6. 19. ye are not your *o*.
10. 24. let no man seek his *o*.
Phil. 2. 4. look not on his *o*. things
21. all seek their *o*. not of Jesus
R. V. In very many instances, the word is omitted.
OX knoweth his owner, Isa. 1. 3. & 11. 7. Ps. 7. 22. & 14. 4. & 15. 17.
Ps. 144. 14, *oxen*, Isa. 22. 13. Matt. 22. 4. Luke 14. 19. John 2. 14. 1 Cor. 9. 9.
R. V. Gen. 34. 28; Ex. 9. 3. herds; Num. 23. 1. bullocks; Deut. 14. 5. antelope; 1 Sam. 14. 14. half furrow's length; Jer. 11. 19 —

P

PACIFY, Esth. 7. 10. Prov. 16. 14.
Ezek. 16. 63. when I am *pacified*
Prov. 21. 14. gift in secret *pacifieth* anger
Eccl. 10. 4. yield. *p*. great offences
R. V. Eccl. 10. 4. allayeth; Ezek. 16. 63. have forgiven
PAIN, Isa. 21. 3. & 26. 18. & 66. 7. Jer. 6. 24. Mic. 4. 10. Rev. 21. 4.
Ps. 116. 3. *pains* of hell gat hold
Acts 2. 24. loosed the *p*. of death
Ps. 55. 4. my heart is sore *pained*, Isa. 23. 5. Jer. 4. 19. Joel 2. 6.
Rev. 12. 2. travail. in birth and *p*.
Ps. 73. 16. *painful*, 2 Cor. 11. 27.
R. V. Nah. 2. 10. anguish; Acts 2. 24. pangs; Joel 2. 6. anguish
PAINTED, 2 Kings 9. 30. Jer. 4. 30. & 22. 14. Ezek. 23. 40.
PALACE, 1 Chron. 29. 19. Ps. 45. 8, 15. S. of S. 8. 9. Isa. 25. 2. Phil. 1. 13.
R. V 1 Kings 16. 18; 2 Kings 15. 25; Neh. 2. 8; 7. 2; Hos. 8. 14. castle; Ps. 78. 69. heights; 2 Chron. 9. 11. house; S. of S. 8. 9. turret; Amos 4. 3. Harmon; Matt. 26. 3, 29, 58; Mark 14. 54, 66; Luke 18. 21; John 18. 15. court; John 18. 28. judgment hall; Phil. 1. 13. prætorian guard; Ezek. 25. 14. encampments
PALM tree, Ps. 92. 12. S. of S. 7. 7.
PANT, Amos 2. 7. Ps. 38. 10. & 42. 1. & 119. 131. Isa. 21. 4.
R. V. Ps. 38. 10. throbbeth
PAPER REEDS of Egypt, Isa. 19. 7.
PARABLE, Ps. 49. 4. & 78. 2. Prov. 26. 7, 9. Ezek. 20. 49. Mic. 2. 4. Matt. 13. 3. Luke 5. 36. & 13. 6. & 21. 29.
PARADISE, Gen. 2. 15. Luke 23. 43. 2 Cor. 12. 4. Rev. 2. 7.
PARCHMENTS, 2 Tim. 4. 13.
PARDON our iniquity, Ex. 34. 9.
Ex. 23. 21. he will not *p*. your
Num. 14. 19. *p*. iniquity of people
1 Sam. 15. 25. *p*. my sin, 2 Kings 5. 18.
2 Kings 24. 4. which the Lord would not *p*.
2 Chron. 30. 18. the good Lord *p*.
Neh. 9. 17. a God ready to *p*.
Job 7. 21. why dost not *p*. my
Ps. 25. 11. for name's sake *p*.
Isa. 55. 7. our God, he will abundantly *p*.
Jer. 5. 7. how shall I *p*. thee for
33. 8. I will *p*. all their iniquities
Isa. 40. 2. cry that her iniquity is *pardoned*
Lam. 3. 42. we transgressed thou hast not *p*.
Mic. 7. 18. a God like thee that *p*.
PARENTS, Luke 2. 27. & 8. 56.
Matt. 10. 21. children rise up against their *p*.
Luke 18. 29. no man hath left house or *p*.
John 9. 2. who did sin, this man or his *p*.
Rom. 1. 30. disobedient to *p*.
2 Cor. 12. 14. children ought not to lay up for *p*. but *p*. for children
1 Tim. 5. 4. learn to requite their *p*.
PART, it shall be thy, Ex. 29. 26.
Num. 18. 20. I am thy *p*. and
Ps. 5. 9. their inward *p*. is very
51. 6. in hidden *p*. make me know
Luke 10. 42. hath chos. that good *p*.
John 13. 8. if I wash thee not, thou hast no *p*.
Acts 8. 21. neither *p*. nor lot in this
1 Cor. 13. 9. know in *p*. and proph.
10. that which is in *p*. shall be done
R. V. Frequent changes to portion; and many omissions of word. Also many changes due to preceding word
PARTAKER with adulterers, Ps. 50. 18.
Rom. 15. 27. *p*. of their spiritual
1 Cor. 9. 10. *p*. of this hope
13. *p*. with altar
10. 17. *p*. of one bread
21. *p*. of Lord's table
30. if I by grace be a *p*. why am
1 Pet. 5. 1. a *p*. of the glory reveal.
2 John 11. is *p*. of his evil deeds
Eph. 5. 7. be not *partakers* with
1 Tim. 5. 22. be not *p*. of other
Heb. 3. 14. *p*. of Christ
6. 4. *p*. of the Holy Ghost
12. 10. might be *p*. of his holiness
R. V. 1 Cor. 9. 14. have their portion; Heb. 2. 14. sharers in
PARTIAL, Mal. 2. 9. Jas. 2. 4.
1 Tim. 5. 21. *partiality*, Jas. 3. 17.
R. V. *divided in own mind*; Jas. 2. 4. Are ye not *p*. in yourselves; Jas. 3. 17. variance
PASS, Ex. 33. 19. Ezek. 20. 37. Zeph. 2. 2. Zech. 3. 4. 2 Pet. 3. 10.
Mark 14. 35. the hour might *p*. from
Luke 16. 17. easier for heaven and earth to *p*.
1 Pet. 1. 17. *p*. the time of sojourn.
John 5. 24. is *passed* from death to
Isa. 43. 2. when thou *passest* throu.
Mic. 7. 18. *passeth* by transgression
1 Cor. 7. 31. fashion of this world *p*.
Eph. 3. 19. love of Christ which *p*.
Phil. 4. 7. peace of God which *p*.
1 John 2. 17. world *p*. away and lusts
PASSION, Acts 1. 3. & 14. 15.
PASSOVER, Ex. 12. 11. Deut. 16. 2. Josh. 5. 11. 2 Chron. 30. 15. & 35. 1, 11. Heb. 11. 28.
1 Cor. 5. 7. Christ our *p*. is sacri.
PASTORS, Jer. 3. 15. & 17. 16. Eph. 4. 11.
Ps. 74. 1. sheep of thy *pasture*, 79. 13. & 95. 7. & 23. 2. & 100. 3. Isa. 30. 23. & 49. 9. Ezek. 34. 14, 18. John 10. 9.
R. V. Jer. 2. 8. rulers; 3. 15; 10. 21; 12. 10; 17. 16; 22. 22; 23. 1, 2. shepherds; Isa. 49. 9. all bare heights
PASTURE, spiritual, Ps. 23. 2. & 74. 1. & 79. 13. & 95. 7. & 100. Ezek. 34. 14. John 10. 9.
PATH, Num. 22. 24. Job 28. 7.
Ps. 16. 11. wilt show me *p*. of life
27. 11. lead me in a plain *p*.
119. 35. go in *p*. of thy
Prov. 4. 18. *p*. of the just is as
26. ponder the *p*. of thy feet
5. 6. lest thou ponder the *p*. of life
Isa. 26. 7. thou dost weigh *p*. of just
Ps. 17. 4. keep me from *paths* of
25. 4. show thy ways; teach me *p*.
10. all *p*. of the Lord are mercy
Prov. 3. 17. all her *p*. are peace
Isa. 59. 7. destruc. are in their *p*.
8. they have made them crook. *p*.
Jer. 6. 16. ask for old *p*. the good
Hos. 2. 6. shall not find her *p*.
Matt. 3. 3. make his *p*. straight
Heb. 12. 13. make straight *p*. for
R. V. Num. 22. 34. hollow way; Ps. 17. 4. ways; Jer. 18. 15. by paths
PATIENCE with me, Matt. 18. 26, 29.
Luke 8. 15. bring forth fruit with *p*.
21. 19. in your *p*. possess your souls
Rom. 5. 3. tribulation worketh *p*.
15. 4. that we through *p*. might have hope
2 Cor. 6. 4. as minist. of God, in *p*.
Col. 1. 11. strengthened unto all *p*.
1 Thes. 1. 3. *p*. of hope in our Lord
2 Thes. 1. 4. for your *p*. and faith
1 Tim. 6. 11. follow after *p*. meek.
2 Tim. 3. 10. my doctr., charity, *p*.
Tit. 2. 2. sound in faith, charity, *p*.
Heb. 6. 12. through *p*. inherit the
10. 36. have need of *p*. that after
12. 1. run with *p*. race set bef. us
Jas. 1. 3. trying of your faith worketh *p*.
4. let *p*. have her perfect work
5. 7. long *p*. for it till he receive
10. prophets for an example of *p*.
11. ye have heard of the *p*. of Job
2 Pet. 1. 6. to temperance *p*. to *p*.
Rev. 1. 9. brother in the *p*. of Jesus
2. 2. I know thy *p*., 19.
Eccl. 7. 8. the *patient* in spirit
Rom. 2. 7. by *p*. continuance in
12. 12. *p*. in tribulation, instant in
1 Thes. 5. 14. be *p*. towards all men
2 Thes. 3. 5. *p*. waiting for Christ
1 Tim. 3. 3. not gree. of lucre but *p*.
2 Tim. 2. 24. gentle, apt to teach, *p*.
Jas. 5. 7. *p*. unto coming of Lord
8. be ye also *p*. establish your
Ps. 37. 7. wait *patiently* for the Lord
Heb. 6. 15. after he had *p*. endured
1 Pet. 2. 20. ye be buffeted for your faults take it *p*.
R. V. 1 Thes. 5. 14. long suffering; 1 Tim. 3. 3. gentle; 2 Tim. 2. 24. forbearing
PATRIARCH, Acts 2. 29. & 7. 8, Heb. 7. 4.
PATRIMONY, his, Deut. 18. 8.
PATTERN, 1 Tim. 1. 16. Tit. 2. 7. Ezek. 43. 10. Heb. 8. 5. & 9. 23.

R. V. 1 Tim. 1. 16; Tit. 2. 7. ensample; Heb. 9. 23. copies
PAVILION, Ps. 27. 5. & 31. 20. & 18. 11. 1 Kings 20. 12, 16. Jer. 43. 10.
PAY, Matt. 18. 28. Ps. 37. 21.
R. V. Num. 20. 19. give price; 2 Chron. 27. 5. render
PEACE, Lev. 26. 6. Num. 6. 26.
Job 22. 21. acquaint thyself with God, and be at *p*.
Ps. 34. 14. seek *p*. and pursue it
37. 37. the end of that man is *p*.
85.10. righteousness and *p*. kissed
119. 165. great *p*. have they that
122. 6. pray for *p*. of Jerusalem
125. 5. *p*. shall be upon Israel
Prov. 16. 7. his enemies to be at *p*.
Isa. 9. 6. everl. Father, Prince of *p*.
26. 3. keep him in perfect *p*.
27.5. that he may make *p*. with me
45. 7. I make *p*. and create evil
48. 18. had thy *p*. been as a river
22. there is no *p*. to the wicked
57. 2. enter into *p*. shall rest in
19. *p*. *p*. to him that is far off
59. 8. way of *p*. they know not
63. 17. will make thy officers *p*.
66. 12. I will extend *p*. to her
Jer. 6. 14. saying, *p*. *p*. when there is no *p*., 8. 11. Ezek. 13. 10. 2 Kings 9. 18, 22.
Jer. 8. 15. looked for *p*. but no
29. 7. seek *p*. of the city, for in
11. thoughts of *p*. and not of evil
Mic. 5. 5. this man shall be the *p*.
Zech. 8. 19. love the truth and *p*.
Matt. 10. 34. I came not to send *p*.
Mark 9. 50. have *p*. one with another
Luke 1. 79. guide our feet in the way of *p*.
2. 14. on earth *p*. good will towards
29. lettest thy servant depart in *p*.
John 14. 27. *p*. I leave; my *p*. I give
16. 33. in me ye might have *p*.
Rom. 5. 1. we have *p*. with God
8. 6. spiritual. minded is life and *p*.
15. 13. fill you with all *p*. and joy
1 Cor. 7. 15. God hath call. us to *p*.
2 Cor. 13. 11. live in *p*. and the God of *p*. shall
Gal. 5. 22. fruit of Spirit is love, *p*.
Eph. 2. 14. he is our *p*.
15. making *p*.
Phil. 4. 7. the *p*. of God, Col. 3. 15.
1 Thes. 5. 13. at *p*. among your.
Heb. 12. 14. follow *p*. with all men
Jas. 3. 18. sown in *p*. of them
1 Pet. 3. 11. let him seek *p*. and
2 Pet. 3. 14. found of him in *p*.
1 Tim. 2. 2. lead a *peaceable* life in
Heb. 12. 11. yielding *p*. fruit of
Jas. 3. 17. is first pure, then *p*.
Rom. 12. 18. live *peaceably* with all
Matt. 5. 9. blessed are the *peacemakers*
R. V. 1 Cor. 14. 30. silence; Rom. 10. 15——; Dan. 11. 21, 24. time of security; Rom. 12. 18. at peace
PEACE OFFERINGS, laws pertaining to, Ex. 20. 24. & 24. 5. Lev. 3. 6. & 7. 11. & 19. 5.
PEARL of great price, Matt. 13. 46.
Matt. 7. 6. cast not *pearls* before
1 Tim. 2. 9. gold, or *p*. or costly array
Rev. 21. 21. gates were twelve *p*
R. V. Job 28. 18. crystal
PECULIAR treasure, Ex. 19. 5. Ps. 135. 4.
Eccl. 2. 8. *p*. treasure of provinces
Deut. 14. 2. *p*. people. 26. 18. Tit. 2. 14. 1 Pet. 2. 9.
PEN of iron, Job 19. 24. Jer. 17. 1.
Ps. 45. 1. tongue is as the *p*. of a ready writer
R. V. Tit. 2. 14; 1 Pet. 2. 9. own possession
PENURY, Prov. 14. 23. Luke 21. 4.
R. V. Luke 21. 4. want
PEOPLE, Gen. 27. 29. Ex. 6. 7.
Ps. 144. 15. happy is the *p*. whose
148. 14. Israel is a *p*. near unto him
Isa. 1. 4. sinful nation, a *p*. laden
10. 6. against the *p*. of my wrath
34. 5. upon the *p*. of my curse
Hos. 4. 9. like *p*. like priest
1 Pet. 2. 10. in time past were not *p*.
Ps. 73. 10. *his people* return hither
100. 3. we are—and sheep of his
Matt. 1. 21. Jesus shall save—from
Rom. 11. 2. God hath not cast away—
Ps. 50. 7. hear, O *my people*, and I will speak
81. 11.—would not hearken, 8. 13.
Isa. 19. 25. blessed be Egypt—and
63. 8. surely they are—that will
Jer. 30. 22. ye shall be—and I will be your God, 31. 33. & 24. 7. & 32. 38. Ezek. 11. 20. & 36. 38. & 37. 27. Zech. 2. 11. & 8. 8. & 13. 9. 2 Cor. 6. 16.
Hos. 1. 9. ye are not—
10. say to them which were not—thou art—
Heb. 11. 25. *p*. of God, 1 Pet. 2. 10.
R. V. Very frequent changes to peoples, multitude, multitudes, etc.
PERCEIVE, Deut. 29. 4. 1 John 3. 16.
R. V. Deut. 29. 4; Josh. 22. 31; 1 Sam. 12. 17; 1 John 3. 16. know; Judg. 6. 22; 1 Kings 22. 33; 2 Chron. 18. 32; Eccl. 3. 22; Luke 9. 27. saw; Neh. 6. 12; Prov. 1. 2. discern; Acts 8. 23; 14. 9; 2 Cor. 7. 8. see and seeing; Luke 6. 41. considereth; Mark 12. 28. knowing; John 12. 19. behold; Acts 23. 29. found
PERDITION, John 17. 12. Phil. 1. 28. 2 Thes. 2. 3. 1 Tim. 6. 9. Heb. 10. 39. 2 Pet. 3. 7. Rev. 17. 3, 11.
R. V. 2 Pet. 3. 7. destruction
PERFECT, Deut. 25. 15. Ps. 18. 32.
Gen. 6. 9. Noah was a just man and *p*.
17. 1. walk before me, and be *p*.
Deut. 18. 13. shalt be *p*. with God
32. 4. this work is *p*., just, and right
2 Sam. 22. 31. his way is *p*.
Job 1. 1. man was *p*. and upright
Ps. 19. 7. law of the Lord is *p*. con.
37. 37. mark the *p*. man and
Ezek. 16. 14. it was *p*. through my
Matt. 5. 48. *p*. as your Father is *p*.
19. 21. if thou wilt be *p*. go and
1 Cor. 2. 6. wisdom among them that are *p*.
2 Cor. 12. 9. strength is made *p*. in
13. 11. be *p*. be of good comfort
Eph. 4. 13. to a *p*. man unto the
Phil. 3. 12. not as though I were already *p*.
15. as many as be *p*. thus minded
Col. 1. 28. present every man *p*.
4. 12. may stand *p*. and complete
2 Tim. 3. 17. man of God may be *p*.
Heb. 2. 10. captain of salvation *p*.
12. 23. spirits of just men made *p*.
13. 21. make you *p*. in every good
Jas. 1. 4. be *p*. and entire
17. *p*. gift
1 Pet. 5. 10. make you *p*. establish
1 John 4. 18. *p*. love casteth out fear
Rev. 3. 2. not found thy works *p*.
2 Cor. 7. 1. *perfecting* holiness in
Eph. 4. 12. for the *p*. of the saints
Job 11. 7. find out the Almighty *perfection*
Ps. 119. 96. have seen end of all *p*
Luke 8. 14. bring no fruit to *p*.
2 Cor. 13. 9. we wish, even your *p*.
Heb. 6. 1. let us go on unto *p*.
Col. 3. 14. charity the bond of *perfectness*
R. V. Isa. 42. 16. at peace; Acts 22. 3. strict; 24. 22. exact; Eph. 4. 13. full grown; 2 Tim. 3. 17. complete; Job 28. 3. furtherest bound; Isa. 47. 9. full measure
PERFORM, Gen. 26. 3. Ruth 3. 13.
Job 5. 12. hands cannot *p*. their
Ps. 119. 106. I have sworn and I will *p*. it
112. inclined my heart to *p*. thy
Isa. 9. 7. zeal of Lord of hosts will *p*.
44. 28. shall *p*. all my pleasure
Rom. 4. 21. promis., was able to *p*.
7. 18. how to *p*. that which is good
Phil. 1. 6. he will *p*. it unto day of
1 Kings 8. 20. Lord hath *performed*
Neh. 9. 8. hast *p*. thy words
Isa. 10. 12. Lord hath *p*. his whole
Jer. 51. 29. every purpose of Lord shall be *p*.
Ps. 57. 2. God that *performeth* all things
Isa. 44. 26. *p*. counsel of messengers
R. V. Gen. 26. 3; Deut. 9. 5; 1 Kings 6. 12; 8. 20; 12. 15; 2 Chron. 10. 15; Jer. 11. 5. establish, or established; Num. 4. 23. wait upon Deut. 23. 23; Esth. 1. 15; Rom. 7. 18. do or done; 2 Kings 23. 3, 4; Ps. 119. 106. confirm; Num. 15. 38; Luke 2. 39; Rom. 15. 28. accomplish; 2 Cor. 8. 11. complete; Phil. 1. 6. perfect
PERILOUS times, 2 Tim. 3. 1.
PERISH, Gen. 41. 36. Lev. 26. 38.
Num. 17. 12. we die, we *p*. we all *p*.
Esth. 4. 16. I will go in, if I *p*. I *p*.
Ps. 2. 12. ye *p*. from the way, when
119. 92. have *p*. in my affliction
Prov. 29. 18. where no vision is, the people *p*.
Matt. 8. 25. Lord save us, or we *p*.
John 3. 15. believeth should not *p*.
10. 28. I give eternal life, they shall never *p*.
1 Cor. 8. 11. through thy knowledge the weak *p*.
2 Pet. 3. 9. not willing that any *p*.
R. V. Num. 17. 12; Jer. 48. 46. undone; 2 Cor. 4. 16. is decaying
PERJURY condemned, Ex. 20. 16. Lev. 6. 3. & 19. 12. Deut. 5. 20. Ezek. 17. 16. Zech. 5. 4. & 8. 17. 1 Tim. 1. 10.
PERMIT, if Lord, 1 Cor. 16. 7. Heb. 6. 3.
1 Cor. 7. 6. by *permission*, not of commandment
PERNICIOUS ways, 2 Pet. 2. 2.
PERPETUAL, Jer. 50. 5. & 51. 39, 57.
R. V. Ps. 9. 6. forever; Jer. 50. 5; Hab. 3. 6. everlasting
PERPLEXED, 2 Cor. 4. 8. Isa. 22. 5.
PERSECUTE me, Ps. 7. 1. & 31. 15.
Job 19. 22. why *p*. me as God, 28.
Ps. 10. 2. wicked doth *p*. the poor
35. 6. let angel of the Lord *p*. them
71. 11. *p*. and take him; is none
83. 15. *p*. them with thy tempest
Lam. 3. 66. *p*. and destroy them in
Matt. 5. 11. blessed are ye when men *p*. you
44. pray for them that *p*. you
Rom. 12. 14. bless them which *p*.
Ps. 109. 16. *persecuted* the poor and
119. 161. princes *p*. me without
143. 3. the enemy hath *p*. my soul
John 15. 20. if they *p*. me they
Acts 9. 4. why *p*. thou me, 22. 7.
22. 4. I *p*. this way to death, 7. 8.
26. 11. I *p*. them to strange cities
1 Cor. 4. 12. being *p*. we suffer it
15. 9. because I *p*. the church of
2 Cor. 4. 9. *p*. but not forsaken, cast
Gal. 1. 13. beyond measure I *p*. the
4. 29. *p*. him born after the Spirit
1 Thes. 2. 15. have *p*. us and please
1 Tim. 1. 13. who was before a *persecutor*
2 Tim. 3. 12. live godly, shall suffer *persecution*
R. V. Ps. 7. 1, 5; 35. 3, 6; 71. 11; 83. 15; Jer. 29. 18; Lam. 3. 43, 66; 2 Cor. 4. 9. pursue, or pursued; 1 Thes. 2. 15. drave out; Acts 11. 19. tribulation; Neh. 9. 11; Lam. 4. 19. pursuers; Ps. 7. 13. fiery shafts
PERSEVERANCE, watching, Eph. 6. 18.
PERSON, Lev. 19. 15.
Mal. 1. 8. will he accept thy *p*.
Matt. 22. 16. regardest not *p*. of
Acts 10. 34. God is no respecter of

p., Deut. 10. 16. Gal. 2. 6. Eph. 6. 9. Col. 3. 25. 1 Pet. 3. 17.
Heb. 1. 3. express image of his *p.*
12. 16. fornicator or profane *p.* as
2 Pet. 3. 11. what manner of *p.*
Jude 16. men's *p.* in admiration
R. V. Gen. 36. 6; Num. 5. 6. soul; Deut. 15. 22; Ps. 49. 10 ——; Judg. 9. 4. fellows; Jer. 52. 25. face; Matt. 27. 24. man; Heb. 1. 3. substance

PERSUADE we men, 2 Cor. 5. 11.
Gal. 1. 10. do I *p.* men, or God
Acts 13. 43. *persuaded* them to
21. 14. when we would not be *p.*
Rom. 8. 38. I am *p.* that neither death
Heb. 6. 9. we are *p.* better things
11. 13. having seen them, were *p.*
Acts 26. 28. almost thou *persuadest* me to be a Christian
Gal. 5. 8. this *persuasion* cometh
R. V. 1 Kings 22. 20, 21, 22. entice; 2 Chron. 18. 2. moved; Acts 13. 43. urged; Rom. 4. 21; 14. 5. assumed; Heb. 11. 13. greeted

PERTAIN, Lev. 7. 29. 1 Cor. 6. 3, 4. Rom. 9. 4. Heb. 2. 17. & 5. 1. & 9. 9. 2 Pet. 1. 3.
Acts 1. 3. *pertaining*
R. V. Num. 4. 16. shall be; 31. 43. congregation's half; Josh. 24. 33; 1 Chron. 11. 31. of; 2 Sam. 2. 15. and for; 1 Kings 7. 48. were in; Acts 1. 3. concerning; Rom. 4. 1. according; 9. 4. whose is; Heb. 7. 13. belongeth; 9. 9. touching

PERVERSE, Num. 22. 32. Deut. 32. 5. Job 6. 30. Prov. 4. 24. & 12. 8. & 14. 2. & 17. 20. Isa. 19. 14. Matt. 17. 17. Acts 20. 30. Phil. 2. 15. 1 Tim. 6. 5.
R. V. Job 6. 30. mischievous; Prov. 23. 33. froward; 1 Tim. 6. 5. wranglings

PERVERT judgment, Deut. 24. 17. & 16. 19. 1 Sam. 8. 3. Job 8. 3. & 34. 12. Prov. 17. 23. & 31. 5. Mic. 3. 9.
Acts 13. 10. not cease to *p.* right
Gal. 1. 7. would *p.* Gospel of Christ
Job 33. 27. *perverted* that which
Jer. 3. 21. they have *p.* their way
Prov. 19. 3. foolishness of man *p.*
Luke 23. 2. this fellow *p.* the nation
R. V. Deut. 24. 17; 27. 19. wrest; Prov. 19. 3. subverteth; Eccl. 5. 8. taking away

PESTILENCE, 2 Sam. 24. 15. 1 Kings 8. 37. Ps. 78. 50. & 91. 3. Jer. 14. 12. Ezek. 5. 12. Amos 4. 10. Hab. 3. 5. Matt. 24. 7.
Acts 24. 5. found this man a *pestilent* fellow
R. V. Matt. 24. 7 ——

PETITION, 2 Sam. 1. 17. Esth. 5. 6. Ps. 20. 5. *petitions*, 1 John 5. 15.

PHILOSOPHY, Col. 2. 8.

PHYLACTERIES, Matt. 23. 5.

PHYSICIAN of no value, Job 13. 4.
Jer. 8. 22. is there no *p.* there
Matt. 9. 12. that be whole need not *p.*
Luke 4. 23. say to me, *p.* heal thyself
Col. 4. 14. Luke the beloved *p.*

PIECE of bread. Prov. 6. 26. & 28. 21.
Matt. 9. 16. no man putteth a *p.*
Luke 14. 18. bought a *p.* of ground

PIERCE, Num. 24. 8. 2 Kings 18. 21.
Luke 2. 35. sword shall *p.*
Ps. 22. 16. they *pierced* my hands
Zech. 12. 10. on me whom they *p.*
1 Tim. 6. 10. *p.* themselves through
Rev. 1. 7. they also which *p.* him
Heb. 4. 12. *piercing* even to divid.
R. V. Num. 24. 8. smite; Isa. 27. 1. swift

PIETY at home, 1 Tim. 5. 4.

PILGRIMS, Heb. 11. 13. 1 Pet. 2. 11.
Gen. 47. 9. *pilgrimage*, Ex. 6. 4. Ps. 119. 54.
R. V. Ex. 6. 4. sojournings

PILLAR of salt, Gen. 19. 26.
Ex. 13. 21. by day in *p.* of cloud; and by night in a *p.* of fire, Num. 12. 5. & 14. 14. Deut. 31. 15. Neh. 9. 12. Ps. 99. 7.
Isa. 19. 19. a *p.* at the border
Jer. 1. 18. I have made thee iron *p.*
1 Tim. 3. 15. *p.* and ground of truth
Rev. 3. 12. in temple I will make him a *p.*
Job 9. 6. *pillars* thereof tremble
26. 11. the *p.* of heaven tremble
Ps. 75. 3. I bear up the *p.* of it
Prov. 9. 1. hewn out her seven *p.*
S. of S. 3. 6. *p.* of smoke
5. 15. *p.* of marble
3. 10. *p.* of silver
Rev. 10. 1. *p.* of fire

PILLOW, Gen. 28. 11. Ezek. 13. 18.
R. V. Gen. 28. 11, 18. under his head; Mark 4. 38. cushion

PINE, Lev. 26. 39. Ezek. 24. 23.

PINE TREE, Isa. 41. 19. & 60. 13.

PIPE, Zech. 4. 2, 12. Matt. 11. 17.
R. V. Zech. 4. 12. spouts

PIT, Gen. 14. 10. & 37. 20.
Ex. 21. 33. if a man dig a *p.*, 34.
Num. 16. 30. they go down quick into the *p.*
Job 33. 24. deliver him from going to the *p.*
Ps. 9. 15. sunk in *p.* they had made
28. 1. go down to the *p.*, 30. 3. & 88. 4. & 143. 7. Prov. 1. 12. Isa. 38. 18.
Ps. 40. 2. horrible *p.*
119. 85. proud digged a *p.* for me
Prov. 22. 14. strange wom. a deep *p.*
28. 10. fall into his own *p.*, Eccl. 10. 8.
Isa. 38. 17. delivered it from the *p.*
51. 1. hole of *p.* whence he digged
Jer. 14. 13. come to *p.* and found
Zech. 9. 11. sent prison. out of *p.*
Rev. 9. 1. key of bottomless *p.*, 20. 1.
R. V. Job 6. 27. make merchandise; 17. 16. Sheol; Isa. 30. 4. abyss; Luke 14. 5. well; Rev. 9. 1, 2, 11; 11. 7; 17. 8; 20. 1, 3. abyss

PITY, Deut. 7. 16. & 13. 8. & 19. 13.
Job 6. 14. to the afflicted *p.* should
19. 21. have *p.* on me, have *p.*
Prov. 19. 17. hath *p.* on poor, lend.
Isa. 63. 9. in his *p.* he redeemed
Ezek. 36. 21. I had *p.* for my
Matt. 18. 33. even as I had *p.* on
Ps. 103. 13. as a father *pitieth* his children, so the Lord *p.* them
Jas. 5. 11. *pitiful*, 1 Pet. 3. 8.
R. V. 1 Pet. 3. 8. tenderhearted; Job 6. 14. kindness; Matt. 18. 33. mercy

PLACE, Ex. 3. 5. Deut. 12. 5, 14.
Ps. 26. 8. *p.* where thine honor
32. 7. art my hiding *p.*, 119. 114.
90. 1. hast been our dwelling *p.*
Prov. 15. 3. eyes of the Lord are in every *p.*
Isa. 66. 1. where is the *p.* of my
Hos. 5. 15. go and return to my *p.*
John 8. 37. my word hath no *p.* in
Rom. 12. 19. aven. not, but give *p.*
1 Cor. 4. 11. no certain dwelling *p.*
11. 20. ye come together in one *p.*
Eph. 4. 27. neither give *p.* to devil
2 Pet. 1. 19. a light that shineth in a dark *p.*
Rev. 12. 6. hath *p.* prepared of God
Job 7. 10. neither shall *his place*
Ps. 37. 10. diligently consider —
Isa. 26. 21. Lord cometh out of —
Acts 1. 25. that he might go to —
Ps. 16. 6. lines fallen in pleasant *places*
Isa. 40. 4. rough *p.* shall be made
Eph. 1. 3. in *heavenly p.*, 20. & 2. 6. & 3. 10.
6. 12. *high p.*, Hab. 3. 19. Amos 4. 13. Hos. 10. 8. Prov. 8. 2. & 9. 14.
R. V. Frequent changes, mostly dependent on antecedent and consequent words

PLAGUE, 1 Kings 8. 37, 38. Ps. 89. 23. Hos. 13. 14. *plagues*, Rev. 16. 9. & 18. 4, 8. & 22. 18.
R. V. Ex. 32. 35. smote; Ps. 89. 23. smite

PLAIN man, Jacob was a, Gen. 25. 27.
Ps. 27. 11. lead me in a *p.* path
Prov. 8. 9. words are all *p.* to him
Zech. 4. 7. before Zerubbabel thou shalt become *p.*
John 16. 29. now speakest *plainly*
2 Cor. 3. 12. we use great *plainness*
R. V. Gen. 12. 6; 13. 18; 14. 13; Judg. 4. 11; 9. 6; 1 Sam. 10. 3. oak, or oaks; Obad. 19; Zech. 7. 7. lowland; 2 Sam. 15. 28. fords; Luke 6. 17. level place; 1 Sam. 2. 27. reveal; Heb. 11. 14. make manifest

PLAISTER, Lev. 14. 42. Isa. 38. 21.

PLAIT, Matt. 27. 29. 1 Pet. 3. 3.

PLANT, Gen. 2. 5. Job 14. 9.
Isa. 53. 2. will grow up as a tend. *p.*
Jer. 2. 21. turned into degener. *p.*
24. 6. *p.* them, and not pluck
Ezek. 34. 29. raise for them a *p.*
Ps. 128. 3. children like olive *plants*
1. 3. like a tree *planted* by river
92. 13. *p.* in the house of the Lord
94. 9. that *p.* ear, shall he not hear
Isa. 40. 24. yea, they shall not be *p.*
Jer. 2. 21. I *p.* thee a noble vine
17. 8. as a tree *p.* by the waters
Matt. 15. 13. my Father hath not *p.*
21. 33. *p.* a vine, and let it out
Rom. 6. 5. *p.* together in likeness
1 Cor. 3. 6. I have *p.* Apollos
9. 7. who *planteth* a vineyard
Isa. 60. 21. my *planting*
61. 3. *p.* of the Lord

PLAY, Ex. 32. 6. 2 Sam. 2. 14. & 10. 12. Ezek. 33. 32. 1 Cor. 10. 7.
R. V. S. of S. 4. 13. shoots; Jer. 48. 32. branches; Ezek. 31. 4; 34. 29. plantation; 1 Chron. 4. 23. inhabitants of Netaim

PLEAD for Baal, Judg. 6. 31.
Job 13. 19. who will *p.* with me
16. 21. might *p.* for me with God
23. 6. will he *p.* against me with
Isa. 1. 17. *p.* for the widow
43. 26. let us *p.*
66. 16. by fire and sword will Lord *p.*
Jer. 2. 9. I will *p.* with you and
29. wherefore will ye *p.* with me
25. 31. he will *p.* with all flesh
Hos. 2. 2. *p.* with your mother, *p.*
Joel 3. 2. I will *p.* with them for
R. V. Job 16. 21. maintain right; 23. 6. contend with; Ps. 35. 1. strive; Prov. 31. 9. minister judg.

PLEADING of God with Israel, Isa. 1. & 3. 13. & 43. 26. & Jer. 2-6. & 13. Ezek. 17. 20. & 20. 36. & 22. Hos. 2. &c. Joel 3. 2. Micah 2; of Job with God, Job 9. 19. & 16. 21.

PLEASE, 2 Sam. 7. 29. Job 6. 9.
Ps. 69. 31. this also shall *p.* Lord
Prov. 16. 7. when a man's ways *p.*
Isa. 55. 11. accomp. that which I *p.*
56. 4. choose the things that *p.* me
Rom. 8. 8. that in flesh cannot *p.* God
15. 1. bear with weak and not *p.*
2. let every one *p.* his neighbor
1 Cor. 7. 32. how *p.* the Lord
33. *p.* his wife
10. 33. I *p.* men, in all things
Gal. 1. 10. do I seek to *p.* men
1 Thes. 4. 1. walk, and to *p.* God
Heb. 11. 6. without faith impossible to *p.* God
Ps. 51. 19. thou be *pleased* with sacrifices
115. 3. hath done whatsoever he *p.*
Isa. 42. 21. Lord is well *p.* for his
53. 10. it *p.* the Lord to bruise him
Mic. 6. 7. will the Lord be *p.*
Matt. 3. 17. beloved Son, in whom he is well *p.*, 17. 5.
Rom. 15. 3. Christ *p.* not himself
Col. 1. 19. *p.* the Father that in him

Heb. 13. 16. with such sacrifices God is well *p.*
Eccl. 7. 26. *p.* God, shall escape
8. 3. he doeth whatever *p.* him
Phil. 4. 18. a sacrifice well *pleasing*
Col. 1. 10. worth. of Lord unto all *p.*
3. 20. obey parents is well *p.* to
1 Thes. 2. 4. not as *p.* men, Eph. 6. 6. Col. 3. 22.
Heb. 13. 21. working in you, that is well *p.*
1 John 3. 22. do things *p.* in his
Gen. 2. 9. *pleasant*, 3. 6. Mic. 2. 9.
2 Sam. 1. 23. Saul and Jonathan were *p.*
Ps. 16. 6. lines fallen to me in *p.*
133. 1. how *p.* for brethren to
Prov. 2. 10. knowledge is *p.* to soul
9. 17. bread eaten in secret is *p.*
Eccl. 11. 7. *p.* for eyes to behold
S. of S. 1. 16. thou art fair, yea, *p.*
4. 13. *p.* fruits, 16. & 7. 13.
7. 6. how *p.* art thou, O love
Isa. 5. 7. men of Judah, his *p.* plant
Jer. 31. 20. Ephraim, is he a *p.* child
Dan. 8. 9. *p.* land, Jer. 3. 19. Zech. 7. 14.
Prov. 3. 17. her ways are ways of *pleasantness*
Gen. 18. 12. shall I have *pleasure*
1 Chron. 29. 17. *p.* in uprightness
Ps. 5. 4. not a God that hath *p.* in
35. 27. hath *p.* in prosperity of
51. 18. do good in good *p.* to Zion
102. 14. servants take *p.* in stones
103. 21. ministers that do his *p.*
147. 11. Lord taketh *p.* in them
Prov. 21. 17. he that loveth *p.* shall
Eccl. 5. 4. he hath no *p.* in fools
12. 1. say, I have no *p.* in them
Isa. 44. 28. shall perform all my *p.*
53. 10. *p.* of Lord shall prosper in
58. 13. not finding thy own *p.*
Jer. 22. 28. vessel wherein is no *p.*
Ezek. 18. 32. have no *p.* in death
Mal. 1. 10. I have no *p.* in you
Luke 12. 32. fear not, it is your Father's good *p.*
2 Cor. 12. 10. I take *p.* in infirmi.
Eph. 1. 5. according to the good *p.*
Phil. 2. 13. and to do of his good *p.*
2 Thes. 1. 11. fulfil all good *p.* of
Heb. 10. 38. soul shall have no *p.*
12. 10. chastened us after their *p.*
Rev. 4. 11. for thy *p.* they are cre.
Ps. 16. 11. at thy right hand are *pleasures* evermore
36. 8. drink of the river of thy *p.*
2 Tim. 3. 4. lovers of *p.* more than
Tit. 3. 3. serv. divers lusts and *p.*
Heb. 11. 25. than to enjoy *p.* of sin
R. V. Gen. 3. 6. a delight; S. of S. 4. 13; 7. 13. precious; Dan. 8. 9. glorious; Jer. 23. 10. pastures; Gen. 16. 6. good in eyes; 2 Chron. 3. 4. right in eyes; Ps. 51. 19. delight in; Rom. 15. 26, 27; 1 Cor. 1. 21; Gal. 1. 15; Col. 1. 19. good pleasure; Gal. 1. 10; Heb. 11. 5. pleasing; 1 Cor. 7. 12. content; Acts 15. 22. seemed good; Acts 15. 34——; Job 21. 25. good; Jer. 2. 24; 2 Thes. 1. 11. desire; Acts 24. 27; 25. 9. gain favor; Jas. 5. 5. delicately

PLEDGE, Ex. 22. 26. Deut. 24. 6.

PLEIADES, Job 9. 9. & 38. 31.

PLENTY, Job 37. 23. Prov. 3. 10.
Ps. 86. 5. *plenteous* in mercy, 103. 8.
130. 7. with him is *p.* redemption
Matt. 9. 37. harvest is *p.* but
R. V. Lev. 1. 36. gathering; Job 22. 25. precious; 37. 23. plenteous

PLOUGH, Deut. 22. 10. Prov. 20. 4.
Job 4. 8. they that *p.* iniquity, and
Isa. 28. 24. doth ploughman *p.* all
Luke 9. 62. hav. put his hand to *p.*
Judg. 14. 18. if ye had not *ploughed*
Ps. 129. 3. ploughers *p.* on my back
Jer. 26. 18. Zion shall be *p.* as a
Hos. 10. 13. ye have *p.* wickedness
Prov. 21. 4. *ploughing* of wicked is
1 Cor. 9. 10. *plougheth* should *p.*
Amos 9. 13. *ploughman*, Isa. 61. 5.
Isa. 2. 4. *ploughshares*, Joel 3. 10. Mic. 4. 3.

PLUCK out, Ps. 25. 15. & 52. 5. & 74. 11. Amos 4. 11. Zech. 3. 2. Matt. 5. 29. & 18. 9. John 10. 28, 29. Gal. 4. 15.
2 Chron. 7. 20. *pluck up*, Jer. 12. 17. & 18. 7. & 31. 28, 40. Dan. 11. 4. Jude 12.
Ezra 9. 3. *pluck off*, Job 29. 17. Isa. 50. 6. Ezra 23. 34. Mic. 3. 2.
R. V. Ex. 4. 7. took; Lev. 1. 16. take; Num. 33. 52. demolish; Ruth 4. 7. drew; Ezek. 23. 34. tear; Luke 17. 6. root up; Mark 5. 4. rent; 9. 7. cast; John 10. 28, 29. snatch

PLUMBLINE and plummet, 2 Kings 21. 13. Isa. 28. 17. Amos 7. 8. Zech. 4. 10.

POISON, Deut. 32. 24, 33. Job 6. 4. & 20. 16. Ps. 58. 4. & 140. 3. Rom. 3. 13. Jas. 3. 8.

POLLUTE, Num. 18. 32. Ezek. 7. 21. Mic. 2. 10. Zeph. 3. 1. Mal. 1. 7, 12.
Acts 15. 20. *pollutions*, 2 Pet. 2. 20.
R. V. Jer. 7. 30. defile; Num. 18. 23; Ezek. 7. 21, 22; 13. 19; 20. 39; 39. 7; 44. 7; Dan. 11. 31. profane, or profaned; Isa. 47. 6; 48. 11; Jer. 34. 16; Lam. 2. 2; Ezek. 20. 9, 13, 14, 16, 21, 22, 24. profaned; Ezek. 16. 6, 22. weltering; 2 Kings 23. 16; Jer. 2. 23; Ezek. 14. 11; 36. 18; Acts 21. 28. defiled; Hos. 6. 8. stained; Amos 7. 17. unclean; Mic. 2. 10. uncleanness; 2 Pet. 2. 20. defilements

PONDER path of thy feet, Prov. 4. 26.
Luke 2. 19. *pondered* them in heart
Prov. 5. 21. *pondereth* all his goings
21. 2. Lord *p.* the hearts, 24. 12.
R. V. Prov. 4. 26; 5. 6; 5. 21. level, and make level; 21. 2; 24. 12. weigheth

POOR may eat, Ex. 23. 11.
Ex. 30. 15. the *p.* shall not give less
Lev. 19. 15. not respect person of *p.*
Deut. 15. 4. there shall be no *p.*
1 Sam. 2. 7. Lord maketh *p.* and
8. raiseth *p.* out of dust, Ps. 113. 7.
Job 5. 16. the *p.* hath hope
36. 15. delivereth *p.* in affliction
Ps. 10. 14. *p.* committeth himself
69. 33. the Lord heareth the *p.* and
72. 2. he shall judge thy *p.*, 4. 13.
132. 15. satisfy her *p.* with bread
Prov. 13. 7. there is that maketh himself *p.*
14. 20. *p.* is hated of his neighbor
31. oppresseth *p.* reproacheth
19. 4. the *p.* is separated from
7. all brethren of the *p.* do hate
22. 2. rich and the *p.* meet together
22. rob not the *p.* because he is *p.*
30. 9. lest I be *p.* and steal
Isa. 14. 32. *p.* of his people shall
29. 19. *p.* among men shall rejoice
41. 17. when the *p.* and needy
58. 7. bring *p.* that are cast into
66. 2. that is *p.* and of a contrite
Jer. 5. 4. surely these are *p.* they
Amos 2. 6. sold *p.* for a pair of
Zeph. 3. 12. an afflicted and *p.* peo.
Zech. 11. 11. *p.* of flock waited on
Matt. 5. 3. blessed are the *p.* in spi.
11. 5. *p.* have Gospel preached to
26. 11. have *p.* with you, John 12. 8.
Luke 6. 20. blessed be ye *p.* for
14. 13. call the *p.* maimed and the
2 Cor. 6. 10. as *p.* yet making rich
8. 9. for your sakes he became *p.*
9. 9. he hath given to *p.*, Ps. 112. 9.
Gal. 2. 10. that we should remember the *p.*
Jas. 2. 5. God hath chosen *p.* of
Rev. 3. 17. knowest not that thou art *p.*
R. V. In O. T., frequent changes to needy

PORTION, Deut. 21. 17. & 33. 21.
Deut. 32. 9. Lord's *p.* is his people
2 Kings 2. 9. double *p.* of thy spir.
Job 20. 29. the *p.* of a wicked man
26. 14. how little a *p.* is heard
31. 2. what *p.* of God is there
Ps. 16. 5. the Lord is the *p.* of my
17. 14. have their *p.* in this life
63. 10. shall be a *p.* for foxes
3. 26. God is my *p.* for ever, 119. 57.
142. 5. art my *p.* in land of living
Eccl. 11. 2. give *p.* to seven and to
Isa. 53. 12. divide him a *p.* with the
61. 7. they shall rejoice in their *p.*
Jer. 10. 16. the *p.* of Jacob not
Lam. 3. 24. Lord is my *p.* saith my
Hab. 1. 16. by them their *p.* is fat
Zech. 2. 12. the Lord shall inherit Judah his *p.*
Matt. 24. 51. appoint him his *p.*
Neh. 8. 10. send *portions*, Esth. 9. 19, 22.
R. V. Josh. 17. 14; 19. 9. part; Job 26. 14. whisper; Prov. 31. 15. task; Hos. 5. 7. fields; Ezek. 45. 7; 48. 18——

POSSESS, Gen. 22. 17. Judg. 11. 24.
Job 7. 3. I am made to *p.* months
13. 26. makest *p.* iniquities of
Luke 21. 9. in patience *p.* your souls
1 Thes. 4. 4. know how to *p.* vessel
Ps. 139. 13. hast *possessed* my reins
Prov. 8. 22. Lord *p.* me in beginning
Isa. 63. 18. people of thy holiness *p.*
Dan. 7. 22. saints *p.* kingdom, 18.
1 Cor. 7. 30. as though they *p.* not
2 Cor. 6. 10. having nothing yet *p.* all things
Eph. 1. 14. redemption of purchased *possession*
Gen. 14. 9. God *possessor* of heaven
R. V. Job 13. 26; Zeph. 2. 9; Zech. 8. 12. inherit; Num. 26. 56; Josh. 22. 7. inheritance

POSSIBLE, all things with God, Matt. 19. 26.
Matt. 24. 24. if *p.* shall deceive elect
Mark 9. 23. all things *p.* to him
14. 36. Father, all things are *p.* to
Luke 18. 27. impossible with men, *p.* with God
Rom. 12. 18. if *p.* much as in you
Heb. 10. 4. not *p.* that blood of bulls

POSTERITY, Gen. 45. 7. Ps. 49. 13.

POT, Ex. 16. 33. Ps. 68. 13. & 81. 6. Jer. 1. 13. Zech. 14. 21.
Job 2. 8. *potsherd*, Ps. 22. 15. Prov. 26. 23. Isa. 45. 9. Rev. 2. 27.
Isa. 29. 16. *potter*, 64. 8. Jer. 18. 6. Lam. 4. 2. Rom. 9. 21.
R. V. Lev. 6. 28. vessel; Job 41. 31; Mark 7. 8——; Ps. 68. 13. sheepfolds; 81. 6. basket; Jer. 1. 13. caldron; 35. 5. bowls; Prov. 26. 23. earthen vessel

POTENTATE, blessed, 1 Tim. 6. 15.

POUND, Luke 19. 13. John 19. 39.

POUR, Job 36. 27. Lev. 14. 18, 41.
Ps. 62. 8. *p.* out your heart
79. 6. *p.* out thy wrath on the heathen, 69. 24. Jer. 10. 25. Zeph. 3. 8.
Prov. 1. 23. I will *p.* out my Spirit
Isa. 44. 3. *p.* water on the thirsty; *p.* my Spirit
Joel 2. 28. *p.* my Spirit on all flesh
Job 10. 10. *poured* me out as milk
12. 21. *p.* contempt on princes
16. 20. mine eye *p.* out tears to
30. 16. my soul *p.* out in me
Ps. 45. 2. grace is *p.* into thy lips
S. of S. 1. 3. name is as ointment *p.*
Isa. 26. 16. in trouble *p.* out a pray.
53. 12. *p.* out his soul unto death
Jer. 7. 20. my fury shall be *p.* out, 42. 18. & 44. 6. Isa. 42. 25. Ezek. 7. 8. & 14. 19. & 20. 8, 13, 21. & 30. 15.
Rev. 16. 1-17. *p.* out vials of God's wrath

POVERTY, Gen. 45. 11. Prov. 11. 24.
Prov. 6. 11. so shall thy *p.* come, 24. 34.
10.15. destruction of the poor is *p.*
20. 13. love not sleep lest thou come to *p.*
23. 21. drunkard and glutton shall come to *p.*
30. 8. give me neither *p.* nor rich.
2 Cor. 8. 2. their deep *p.* abounded
9. ye through his *p.* might be rich
Rev. 2. 9. I know thy works and *p.*
R. V. Prov. 11. 24; 28. 22. want
POWDER, Ex. 32. 20. Deut. 28. 24. 2 Kings 23. 15. S. of S. 3. 6. Matt. 21. 44.
R. V. Matt. 21. 44; Luke 20. 18. dust
POWER, with God as a prince, Gen. 32. 28.
Gen. 49. 3. excell. of dignity and *p.*
Lev. 26. 19. I will break the pride of your *p.*
Deut. 8. 18. giveth *p.* to get wealth
2 Sam. 22. 33. God is my strength and *p.*
1 Chron. 29. 11. thine is the *p.* and
Ezra 8. 22. *p.* and wrath is against
Job 26. 2. him that is without *p.*
14. thunder of his *p.* who can
Ps. 62. 11. *p.* belongeth unto God
90. 11. knoweth *p.* of thy anger
Prov. 3. 27. when it is in the *p.* of
18. 21. death and life are in *p.*
Isa. 40. 29. he giveth *p.* to the faint
Eccl. 8. 4. where word of king is there is *p.*
Jer. 10.12. made the earth by his *p.*
Hos. 12. 3. by his strength had *p.*
Mic. 3. 8. I am full of *p.* by the
Hab. 1. 11. imputing his *p.* to God
Zech. 4. 6. not by might, nor by *p.*
Matt. 9. 6. *p.* on earth to forgive
8. glorified God who had given *p.*
22. 29. not knowing the *p.* of God
28. 18. *p.* is given to me in heaven
Mark 9. 1. kingdom of God come with *p.*
Luke 1. 35. *p.* of the Highest
4. 32. astonished, for his word was with *p.*
5. 17. *p.* of the Lord to heal them
22. 53. this is your hour and *p.* of
24. 49. till ye be endued with *p.*
John 1. 12. gave he *p.* to become
10. 18. *p.* to lay it down and *p.*
17. 2. given him *p.* over all flesh
19. 10. *p.* to crucify, *p.* to release
Acts 26. 18. turn them from the *p.*
Rom. 1. 16. Gospel is *p.* of God to
20. his eternal *p.* and Godhead, 4.
9. 22. to make his *p.* known
13. 1. there is no *p.* but of God
1 Cor. 1. 24. Christ, the *p.* of God, 18.
2. 4. demonstra. of Spirit and *p.*
4. 19. speech of them, but the *p.*
5.4. gathered together with the *p.*
9. 4. have we not *p.* to eat and
2 Cor. 4. 7. excellency of *p.* may be
13. 10. according to *p.* Lord
Eph. 1. 19. exceed. greatness of *p.*
2. 2. prince of the *p.* of the air
6. 12. principalities and *p.*, 1. 21.
Phil. 3. 10. know *p.* of his resur.
Col. 1. 11. according to his glorious
13. delivered from *p.* of darkness
1 Thes. 1. 5. Gospel not in word, but in *p.*
2 Thes. 1. 9. the glory of his *p.*
11. fulfil the work of faith with *p.*
2 Tim. 1. 7. Spirit of *p.* and of love
3. 5. form of godliness, deny. *p.*
Heb. 1. 3. upholding all things by word of his *p.*
6. 5. tasted word of God and *p.* of
1 Pet. 1. 5. *p.* of God through faith
2 Pet. 1. 3. his divine *p.* hath given
Rev. 2. 26. to him will I give *p.*
4. 11. worthy to receive *p.*, 5. 13. & 7. 12. & 19. 1. 1 Tim. 6. 16. Jude 25.
Rev. 11. 3. *p.* to my two witnesses
17. taken to thee thy great *p.*
12. 10. now is come *p.* of his Chri.
Rev. 16. 9. had *p.* over these plagues
Ex. 15. 6. *in power*, Job 37. 23. Nah. 1. 3. 1 Cor. 4. 20. & 15. 43. Eph. 6. 10.
Ps. 63. 2. *thy power*, 110. 3. & 145. 11.
29. 4. *powerful*, Heb. 4. 12.
R. V. 1 Sam. 9. 1. valor; Esth. 9. 1. rule; Job 41. 12; Ps. 59. 16; Dan. 11. 6; 2 Cor. 12. 9; Eph. 6. 10. strength; Ps. 66. 7; 71. 8; 2 Thes. 1. 19. might; Hab. 2. 9. hand; Matt. 10. 1; 28. 18; Mark 3. 15; 6. 7; Luke 4. 6, 32; 10. 19; John 17. 2; Acts 1. 7; 1 Cor. 11. 10; 2 Cor. 13. 10; Eph. 1. 21; Rev. 2. 26; 6. 8; 8. 1; 12. 10; 13. 4, 7, 12, 15; 17. 12. authority; Luke 9. 43. majesty; Rom. 9. 21; 1 Cor. 9. 4, 5, 6, 12; 2 Thes. 3. 9. a right; Rev. 5. 13. dominion; Matt. 6. 13; Rev. 11. 3——; 2 Cor. 10. 10. strong; Heb. 4. 12. active
PRAISE, Judg. 5. 3. Ps. 7. 17.
Deut. 10. 21. he is thy *p.* and thy
Neh. 9. 5. above all blessing and *p.*
Ps. 22. 25. my *p.* shall be of thee
33. 1. *p.* is comely for upright
34. 1. his *p.* is continually in
50. 23. who offers *p.* glorifies me
65. 1. *p.* waiteth for thee, O God
109. 1. hold not thy peace, God of my *p.*
Isa. 60.18. walls Salvation, gates *P.*
62. 7. Jerusalem a *p.* in the earth
Jer. 13. 11. for a *p.* and for a glory
17. 14. art my *p.*
26. sacrifice of *p.*
Hab. 3. 3. earth was full of his *p.*
John 12. 43. loved the *p.* of men
Rom. 2. 29. whose *p.* is not of men
2 Cor. 8. 18. whose *p.* is in Gospel
Eph. 1. 6. *p.* of glory of his grace
Phil. 4. 8. if there be any *p.* think
Heb. 13. 15. offer sacrifice of *p.*
1 Pet. 2. 14. *p.* of them that do well
Ex. 15. 11. *praises*, Ps. 22. 3. & 78. 4. & 149. 6. Isa. 60. 6. & 63. 7. 1 Pet. 2. 9.
Ps. 30. 9. shall dust *praise* thee
42. 5. I shall *p.* him for help
63. 3. my lips shall *p.* thee
88. 10. shall the dead arise and *p.*
119. 164. seven times a day will I *p.*
Prov. 27. 2. let another *p.* thee, not
31. 31. let her own works *p.* her
Isa. 38. 18. the grave cannot *p.* thee
19. the living shall *p.* thee as I do
Dan. 2. 23. I thank thee, and *p.* thee
Joel 2. 26. eat in plenty, and *p.* Lord
Ps. 9. 1. *I will praise thee*, 111. 1. & 138. 1. & 35. 18. & 52. 9. & 56. 4. & 118. 21. & 119. 7. & 139. 14. Isa. 12. 1.
2 Sam. 22. 4. worthy to be *praised*
1 Chron. 16. 25. greatly to be *p.*, Ps. 48. 1. & 96. 4. & 145. 3. & 72. 15.
2 Chron. 5. 13. *praising*, Ezra 3. 11. Ps. 34. 4. Luke 2. 13, 20. Acts 2. 46.
R. V. A few changes to thanksgiving. Many changes, especially in Ps., to give thanks
PRATING, Prov. 10. 8, 10. 3 John 10.
PRAY for thee and shalt live, Gen. 20. 7.
1 Sam. 7. 5. I will *p.* for you to
2 Sam. 7. 27. found in heart to *p.*
Job 21. 15. profit have we if we *p.*
42. 8. my servant Job shall *p.* for
Ps. 5. 2. my God, to thee will I *p.*
55. 17. evening and morning and noon I will *p.*
Jer. 7. 16. *p.* not for this people, 11. 14. & 14. 11.
Zech. 8. 22. seek Lord and *p.* before
Matt. 5. 44. *p.* for them that desp.
26. 41. watch and *p.* that ye enter
Mark 11. 24. things ye desire when ye *p.*
13. 33. watch and *p.* ye know not
Luke 11. 1. teach us to *p.* as John
18. 1. men ought always to *p.*
21. 36. watch ye and *p.* always
John 16. 26. I will *p.* the Father for
20. neither *p.* I for these alone
Acts 8. 22. *p.* God, if perhaps the
Acts 8.24. *p.* ye to the Lord for me
10. 9. Peter went on housetop to *p.*
Rom. 8. 26. we know not what we should *p.* for
1 Cor. 14. 15. I will *p.* with Spirit
2 Cor. 5. 20. *p.* you in Christ's stead
Col. 1. 9. do not cease to *p.* for you
1 Thes. 5. 17. *p.* without ceasing
25. *p.* for us, 2 Thes. 3. 1. Heb. 13. 18.
Jas. 5. 13. any afflicted let him *p.*
16. *p.* for one another, Eph. 6. 18.
Luke 22. 32. I have *prayed* for thee
Acts 10. 2. gave alms and *p.* to God
20. 36. Paul *p.* with them all
Jas. 5. 17. he *p.* earnestly that it
Acts 9. 11. behold he *prayeth*
Dan. 9. 20. *praying*, 1 Cor. 11. 4.
1 Thes. 3. 10. night and day *p.* ex.
Jude 20. building up faith, *p.* in
1 Kings 8. 45. hear in heaven their *prayer*
2 Sam. 7. 27. found in his heart to pray this *p.*
1 Kings 8. 28. respect to *p.* of serv.
38. what *p.* and supplication
2 Chron. 30. 27. *p.* came up to God
Neh. 1. 6. mayest hear *p.* of servant
4. 9. we made our *p.* to our God
Job 15. 4. restrainest *p.* before God
Ps. 65. 2. thou that hearest *p.* to
102. 17. he will regard the *p.* of
109. 4. I give myself to *p.*
Prov. 15. 8. *p.* of the upright is his
29. Lord heareth *p.* of righteous
Isa. 26. 16. poured out a *p.* when
56. 7. an house of *p.* for all people
Jer. 7. 16. lift up cry, nor *p.* for
Lam. 3. 44. our *p.* should not pass
Dan. 9. 3. by *p.* and supplication
Matt. 17. 21. not come out but by *p.*
Acts 3. 1. to temple at hour of *p.*
6. 4. give ourselves continu. to *p.*
12. 5. *p.* was made without ceasing
1 Cor. 7. 5. give yourselves to fasting and *p.*
2 Cor. 1. 11. helping together by *p.*
Eph. 6. 18. *praying* alw. with all *p.*
Phil. 4. 6. in every thing by *p.* and
1 Tim. 4. 5. sanctifi. by word and *p.*
Jas. 5. 15. *p.* of faith shall save
16. effectual fervent *p.* of right.
1 Pet. 4. 7. watch unto *p.*, Col. 4. 2.
Luke 6. 12. continued *in prayer*, Acts 1. 14. Rom. 12. 12. Col. 4. 2.
Job 16. 17. *my prayer*, Ps. 5. 3. & 6. 9. & 17. 1. & 35. 13. & 66. 20. & 88. 2. Lam. 3. 8. Jonah 2. 7.
Job 22. 27. *thy prayer*, Isa. 37. 4 Luke 1. 13. Acts 10. 31.
Ps. 72. 20. *prayers* of David ended
Isa. 1. 15. when ye make many *p.*
Matt. 23. 14. make long *p.*
Acts 10. 4. thy *p.* and thine alms
1 Tim. 2. 1. first of all that *p.* and
1 Pet. 3. 7. your *p.* be not hindered
12. his ears are open to their *p.*
Rev. 5. 8. which are *p.* of saints
R. V. But few changes, and mostly to beseech, intreat. Job 15. 4. devotion; Ps. 64. 1. complaint, Luke 1. 13; 2. 37; 5. 33; Rom. 10. 1; 2 Cor. 1. 11; 9. 14; Phil. 1. 4, 19; 2 Tim. 1. 3; Jas. 5. 16; 1 Pet. 3. 12. supplication; Matt. 17. 21; 23 14——
PREACH at Jerusalem, Neh. 6. 7.
Isa. 61. 1. anointed to *p.* good
Jonah 3. 2. *p.* to it preaching I bid
Matt. 4. 17. Jesus began to *p.*
10. 27. what ye hear in ear, *p.* on
Mark 1. 4. *p.* baptism of repent.
Luke 4. 18. *p.* liberty to captives
9. 60. go and *p.* kingdom of God
Acts 10. 42. commanded to *p.* to
Rom. 10. 8. word of faith we *p.*
15. how shall they *p.* except they
1 Cor. 1. 23. we *p.* Christ crucified
15. 11. so we *p.* and so ye believed
2 Cor. 4. 5. we *p.* not ourselves but
Phil. 1. 15. some *p.* Christ of envy
Col. 1. 28. whom we *p.* warning
2 Tim. 4. 2. *p.* the word; be instant
Ps. 40. 9. I *preached* righteousness

Mark 2. 2. he *p.* the word unto them
6. 12. he *p.* that men should rep.
16. 20. *p.* every where, the Lord
Luke 4. 44. he *p.* in the synagogues
24. 47. remission of sins be *p.* in
Acts 8. 5. Philip *p.* Christ, 40.
9. 20. Saul *p.* Christ in synagogues
1 Cor. 9. 27. when I have *p.* to
15. 7. Gospel which I *p.* unto you
2. keep in memory what I *p.*
12. if Christ be *p.* that he rose
2 Cor. 11. 4. *p.* another Jesus whom
Gal. 1. 23. *p.* faith he once destroyed
Eph. 2. 17. *p.* peace to you, which
Col. 1. 23. which was *p.* to every
Heb. 4. 2. the word *p.* did not profit
1 Pet. 3. 19. *p.* to the spirits in
Eccl. 1. 1. *preacher*, 2. 12. & 12. 8, 9.
Rom. 10. 14. how shall they hear without a *p.*
1 Tim. 2. 7. I am ordained a *p.*
2 Pet. 2. 5. saved Noah a *p.* of
Acts 10. 36. *preaching* peace, by
11. 19. *p.* word to none but Jews
1 Cor. 1. 18. *p.* of the cross to them
21. by foolishness of *p.* to save
2. 4. my *p.* was not with enticing
15. 14. then is our *p.* vain, and faith
R. V. Ps. 40. 9; Luke 6. 90. published; Matt. 10. 27; Luke 4. 18, 19; Acts 4. 2; 8. 5; 9. 20; 13. 5, 38; 15. 36; 17. 13; 1 Cor. 9. 14; Phil. 1. 16, 18; Col. 1. 28. proclaim, or proclaimed; Mark 2. 2; Acts 16. 6. speak or spake; Acts 20. 7. discoursed; Acts 11. 19. speaking; 1 Cor. 1.18. word; Tit. 1.3; 2 Tim. 4. 17. message; 2 Cor. 10. 14——

PRECEPTS, Neh. 9. 14. Jer. 35. 18.
Ps. 119. 4. commanded us to keep *p.*
15. I will meditate in thy *p.*, 78.
40. long after thy *p.*
56. I kept thy *p.*, 63, 69, 100, 134.
110. I erred not from thy *p.*
141. I do not forget thy *p.*, 93.
159. I love thy *p.*
173. chosen thy *p.*
Isa. 28. 10. *p.* upon *p.*, *p.* upon *p.*
29. 14. fear is taught by *p.* of men
R. V. Isa. 29. 13; Neh. 9. 14; Mark 10. 5; Heb. 9. 19. commandment

PRECIOUS things, Deut. 33. 13–16.
1 Sam. 3. 1. word of the Lord *p.* in
26. 21. my soul was *p.* in thine eyes
Ps. 49. 8. redemption of soul is *p.*
72. 14. *p.* shall their blood be in
116. 16. p. in sight of the Lord
126. 6. goeth forth, bearing *p.* seed
139. 17. how *p.* are thy thoughts
Eccl. 7. 1. good name is better than *p.* ointment
Isa. 13. 12. a man more *p.* than
28. 16. foundation *p.* corner stone
Jer. 15. 19. if thou take forth *p.*
Lam. 4. 2. *p.* sons of Zion are as
Jas. 5. 7. husbandman waiteth for *p.* fruit
1 Pet. 1. 7. tri. of your faith more *p.*
19. redeemed with *p.* blood of
2. 4. stone chosen of God and *p.*, 6.
7. unto them who believe he is *p.*
2 Pet. 1. 1. obtained the like *p.* faith
4. exceeding great and *p.* promis.
R. V. Ps. 49. 8; Mark 14. 3; 1 Cor. 3. 12. costly; Isa. 13. 12. rare; Dan. 11. 8. goodly

PREDESTINATE, Rom. 8. 29, 30.
Eph. 1. 5. *predestinated*, 11.

PREEMINENCE, man hath no, Eccl. 3. 19. Col. 1. 18. 3 John 9.

PREFER, Ps. 137. 6. John 1. 15, 27, 30.
Rom. 12. 10. *preferring*, 1 Tim. 5. 21.
R. V. Esth. 2. 9. removed; Dan. 6. 3. distinguished; John 1. 15, 30. become: 1 Tim. 5. 21. prejudice

PREMEDITATE not, Mark 13. 11.

PREPARE, Ex. 15. 2. & 16. 5.
1 Sam. 7. 3. *p.* your hearts to Lord
1 Chron. 29. 18. *p.* hearts unto thee
2 Chron. 35. 6. *p.* your brethren
Job 11. 13. if thou *p.* thy heart and
Ps. 10. 17. thou wilt *p.* their heart
Prov. 24. 27. *p.* thy work without
Isa. 40. 3. *p.* ye the way of the Lord
Amos 4. 12. *p.* to meet thy God, O
Mic. 3. 5. they *p.* war against him
Matt. 11. 10. shall *p.* thy way
John 14. 2. I go to *p.* a place for you
2 Chron. 19. 3. hast *prepared* heart
27. 6. *p.* his ways before the Lord
30. 19. every one that *p.*
Ezra 7. 10. Ezra had *p.* his heart to
Neh. 8. 10. for whom nothing is *p.*
Ps. 23.5. thou hast *p.* a table before
68. 10. *p.* goodness
147. 8. who *p.* rain for the earth
Isa. 64. 4. what God *p.* for, 1 Cor. 2. 9.
Hos. 6. 3. his going forth is *p.*
Matt. 20. 23. given to them for whom it is *p.*
22. 4. I have *p.* my dinner; my
25. 34. inherit the kingdom *p.* for
Luke 1.17. ready people *p.* for Lord
12. 47. knew Lord's will, and *p.*
Rom. 9. 23. vessels of mercy *p.* to
2 Tim. 2. 21. *p.* to every good work
Heb. 10. 5. a body hast thou *p.* me
11. 7. *p.* ark to save his house
16. God hath *p.* for them a city
Rev. 12. 6. into the wilderness, a place *p.* of God
21. 2. new Jerusalem *p.* as a bride
Prov. 16. 1. *preparations* of heart
Mark 15. 42. it was the *p.* the day
Eph. 6. 15. shod with *p.* of Gospel
R. V. Many changes to make ready, establish, etc.

PRESBYTERY, 1 Tim. 4. 14.

PRESENT help in troub., Ps. 46. 1.
Acts 10. 33. all here *p.* before God
Rom. 7. 18. to will is *p.*
8. 38. nor things *p.* nor, 1 Cor. 3. 22.
1 Cor. 5. 3. absent in body, *p.* in
2 Cor. 5. 8. to be *p.* with the Lord
9. whether *p.* or absent, we may
2 Tim. 4. 10. having loved *p.* world
Heb. 12. 11. chastening for the *p.*
2 Pet. 1. 12. established in *p.* truth
Rom. 12. 1. *p.* your bodies a living
2 Cor. 11. 2. *p.* you as a chaste
Col. 1. 22. to *p.* you holy and
28. *p.* every man perfect in Christ
Jude 24. *p.* you faultless before
Gen. 3. 8. hide themselves from the *presence* of the Lord
4. 16. Cain went from *p.* of Lord
Job 1. 12. & 2. 7. Ps. 114. 7. Jer. 4. 26. Jonah 1. 3, 10. Zech. 1. 7. Jude 24.
Job 23. 15. I am troubled at his *p.*
Ps. 16. 11. in thy *p.* is fulness
31.20. hide them in secret of thy *p.*
100. 2. before his *p.* with singing
114.7. tremble, earth, at *p.* of Lord
139. 7. whither shall I flee from *p.*
140. 13. upright shall dwell in thy *p.*
Isa. 63. 9. angel of his *p.* saved
Jer. 5. 22. will ye not tremble at my *p.*
Luke 13. 26. eaten and drunk. in *p.*
Acts 3. 19. blotted out from *p.* of Lord
1 Cor. 1. 29. no flesh glory in his *p.*
2 Cor. 10. 1. in *p.* am base among
2 Thes. 1. 9. punished from *p.* of
Rev. 14. 10. *p.* of holy angels
R. V. Few changes to before; Matt. 21. 19. immediately; 26. 53. even now: Phil. 2. 23. forthwith

PRESERVE, Gen. 45. 7. Ps. 12. 7.
Ps. 16. 1. *p.* me, O God, for I trust
25. 21. let integrity and truth *p.*
32. 7. thou shalt *p.* me from
61. 7. mercy and truth *p.* him
64. 1. *p.* life from fear of enemies
86. 2. *p.* my soul, for I am holy
121. 7. Lord shall *p.* thee from evil
140. 1. *p.* me from the violent man
Prov. 2.11. discretion shall *p.* thee
Luke 17. 33. will lose his life, *p.* it
2 Tim. 4. 18. will *p.* to his heaven.
Josh. 24. 17. *preserved* us in all the
2 Sam. 8. 6. Lord *p.* David
Job 10. 12. thy visitation *p.* my
1 Thes. 5. 23. soul and body be *p.*
Jude 1. *p.* in Christ Jesus, and
Ps. 36. 6. Lord thou *preservest* man
29. 10. he *preserveth* the souls of
116. 6. Lord *p.* the simple
145. 20. Lord *p.* all that love him
Prov. 2. 8. he *p.* way of his saints
Job 7. 20. O thou *Preserver* of men
R. V. 2 Sam. 8. 6, 14; 1 Chron. 18. 6, 13. gave victory; Job 29. 2; Prov. 2. 11. watch over; Ps. 121. 7. keep; 2 Tim. 4. 18. save; Jude 1. kept; Luke 5. 38——

PRESS, Gen. 40. 11. Judg. 16. 16.
Phil. 3. 14. I *p.* towards the mark
Ps. 38. 2. thy hand *presseth* me sore
Luke 16. 16. kingdom of God every man *p.* unto
Amos 2. 13. *pressed* as a cart is *p.*
Luke 6. 38. good measure, *p.* down
Acts 18. 5. Paul was *p.* in spirit
R. V. Joel 3. 13. winepress; Mark 2. 4; 5. 27, 30; Luke 8. 19; 19. 3. crowd; 8. 45. crush; Gen. 19. 3. urged; Acts 18. 5. constrained; 2 Cor. 1. 8. weighed down; Luke 16. 16. entereth violently

PRESUMPTION of Israelites, Num. 14. 44. Deut. 1. 43; prophets, Deut. 18. 20; builders of Babel, Gen. 11; Korah, &c., Num. 16; Beth-shemites, 1 Sam. 6.19; Hiel, the Bethelite, 1 Kings 16. 34; Uzzah, 2 Sam. 6. 6; Uzziah, 2 Chron. 26. 16; Jewish exorcists, Acts 19. 13; Diotrephes, 3 John 9.

PRESUMPTUOUS, Ps. 19. 13. 2 Pet. 2. 10. Num. 15. 30. Deut. 17. 12, 13.
R. V. 2 Pet. 2. 10. daring

PRETENCE, Matt. 23. 14. Phil. 1. 18.
R. V. Matt. 23. 14——

PREVAIL, Gen. 7. 20. Judg. 16. 5.
1 Sam. 2. 9. by strength, shall no man *p.*
Ps. 9. 19. O Lord, let not man *p.*
65. 3. iniquities *p.* against me
Eccl. 4. 12. if one *p.* against him
Matt. 16. 18. gates of hell not *p.*
Gen. 32. 28. power with God and hast *prevailed*
Ex. 17. 11. Moses held up hand, Israel *p.*
Hos. 12. 4. pow. over angels, and *p.*
Acts 19. 20. word of God grew, and *p.*
Job 14. 20. thou *prevailest* for ever
R. V. Gen. 47. 20; 2 Kings 25. 3. was sore upon; Job 18. 9. lay hold on; Isa. 42. 13. do mightily; Rev. 5. 5. overcome

PREVENT, Job 3. 12. Ps. 59. 10. & 79. 8. & 88. 13. & 119. 148. Amos 9. 10. 1 Thes. 4. 15.
2 Sam. 22. 6. *prevented*, 19. Job 30. 27. & 41. 11. Ps. 18. 5, 18. & 21. 3. & 119. 147. Isa. 21. 14. Matt. 17. 25.
R. V. Job 3. 12. receive; Ps. 88. 13. come before: 2 Sam. 22. 6, 19; Job 30. 27; Ps. 18. 5, 18. came upon; Matt. 17. 25. spake first to

PREY, Gen. 49. 9, 27. Esth. 9. 15, 16.
Isa. 49. 24. *p.* be taken from mighty
Jer. 21. 9. life for a *p.*, 38. 2 & 39. 18. & 45. 5.
Ps. 124. 6. not given us a *p.* to their
R. V. Judg. 5. 30; 8. 24, 25, Esth. 9. 15, 16; Isa. 10. 2; Jer. 50. 10. spoil; Job 24. 5. meat; Prov. 23. 28. robber

PRICE, Lev. 25. 16. Deut. 23. 18.
Job 28. 13. man knoweth not the *p.*
Ps. 44. 12. not increase wealth, by their *p.*
Prov. 17. 16. a *p.* in the hand of
Isa. 55. 1. wine and milk without *p.*
Matt. 13. 46. pearl of great *p.*
Acts 5. 2. kept back part of the *p.*
1 Cor. 6. 20. bought with a *p.*, 7. 23.
1 Pet. 3. 4. sight of God of great *p.*
R. V. Deut. 23. 18. wages; Zech. 11. 12. hire

PRICKS, kick against, Acts 9. 5. & 26. 14.
Ps. 73. 21. *pricked*, Acts 2. 37.
R. V. Acts 9. 5 ——; 26. 14. goad
PRIDE of heart, 2 Chron. 32. 26. Ps. 10. 4.
Job 33. 17. he may hide *p.* from
Ps. 10. 2. wicked in *p.* doth per.
31. 20. hide them from *p.* of man
73. 6. *p.* compasseth them about
Prov. 8. 13. *p.* and arrogance I hate
13. 10. by *p.* cometh contention
16. 18. *p.* goeth before destruction
Isa. 23. 9. Lord purposed it, to stain *p.*
Jer. 13. 17. weep in secr. for your *p.*
Ezek. 7. 10. rod hath blossomed, *p.*
16. 49. iniquity of Sodom, *p.* and
Dan. 4. 37. those that walk in *p.*
Hos. 5. 5. *p.* of Israel testify
Obad. 3. *p.* of thy heart deceived
Mark 7. 22. blasphemy, *p.* foolish.
1 Tim. 3. 6. lifted up with *p.* he fall
1 John 2. 16. lust of eyes, *p.* of life
R. V. Ps. 31. 20. plottings; 1 John 2. 16. vainglory. A few other changes due to the context
PRIEST, Gen. 14. 18. Ex. 2. 16. Lev. 6. 20, 26. & 5. 6. & 6. 7. & 12. 8.
Isa. 24. 2. with peop., so with the *p.*
28. 7. *p.* and prophet have erred
Jer. 23. 11. prophet and *p.* profane
Ezek. 7. 26. law shall perish from *p.*
Hos. 4. 4. those that strive with *p.*
9. like people, like *p.*
Mal. 2. 7. *p.* lips should keep
Heb. 5. 6. a *p.* for ever, 7. 17, 21.
Lev. 21. 10. *high priest*, Heb. 2. 17. & 3. 1. & 4. 14, 15. & 5. 1, 10. & 6. 20. & 7. 26. & 8. 1, 3. & 9. 11. & 10. 21.
Ps. 132. 9. let thy *priests* be clothed
16. clothe her *p.* with salvation
Isa. 61. 6. ye be named *p.* of
Jer. 5. 31. *p.* bear rule by their
31. 14. satisfy soul of *p.* with
Ezek. 22. 26. *p.* have violated my
Joel 1. 9. *p.* Lord's ministers, 2. 17.
Mic. 3. 11. the *p.* teach for hire
Matt. 12. 5. *p.* in the temple
Acts 6. 7. company of *p.* obedient
Rev. 1. 6. kings and *p.* to God
Ex. 40. 15. everlasting *priesthood*
Heb. 7. 24. an unchangeable *p.*
1 Pet. 2. 5. ye are a holy *p.*
PRINCE, Gen. 23. 6. & 34. 2.
Gen. 32. 28. as a *p.* hast power with
Ex. 2. 14. who made thee a *p.* over
2 Sam. 3. 38. *p.* and great man
Job 31. 47. as a *p.* would I go
Isa. 9. 6. everlasting Father, *p.* of
Ezek. 34. 24. my servant David, a *p.* among them, 37. 24, 25. & 44. 3. & 45. 7. & 46. 10, 16. Dan. 9. 25.
Dan. 10. 21. Michael your *p.*
Hos. 3. 4. many days without a *p.*
John 12. 31. now shall *p.* of world
14. 30. *p.* of world cometh and
16. 11. *p.* of this world judged
Acts 3. 15. ye killed the *p.* of life
5. 31. to be a *P.* and a Saviour
Eph. 2. 2. *p.* of the power of air
Rev. 1. 5. Jesus *p.* of kings of earth
Job 12. 19. leads *princes* away
21. pours contem. on *p.*, Ps. 107. 40.
Job 34. 18. is it fit to say to *p.*
Ps. 45. 16. thou makest *p.* in earth
82. 7. shall fall like one of the *p.*
118. 9. than to put confidence in *p.*
161. *p.* persecuted me without
146. 3. put not trust in *p.* nor man
Prov. 8. 15. by me *p.* decree jus.
17. 26. not good to strike *p.* for
31. 4. not for *p.* to drink strong
Eccl. 10. 7. seen *p.* walk on earth
Isa. 3. 4. give children to be their *p.*
Hos. 7. 5. *p.* made the king sick
Matt. 20. 25. *p.* of Gentiles exer.
1 Cor. 2. 6. wisdom of *p.* of world
8. none of *p.* of this world knew
Prov. 4. 7. wisdom is the *principal*
Eph. 1. 21. *principality* and power, Col. 2. 10. Jer. 13. 18. Rom. 8. 38. Eph. 6. 12. Col. 2. 15. Tit. 3. 1.
Heb. 5. 12. *principles*, 6. 1.
R. V. Frequent changes in Kings and Chron. to captains; in Dan. to satraps; in N. T. to rulers; Ex. 30. 23; Neh. 11. 17. chief; 2 Kings 25. 19; Jer. 52. 25. captain; Jer. 13. 18. headtires; Eph. 1. 21. rule; Tit. 3. 1. rulers
PRISON, Gen. 39. 20. Eccl. 4. 14.
Isa. 42. 7. bring out prison. from *p.*
58. 8. he was taken from *p.* and
61. 1. opening of the *p.* to them
Matt. 5. 25. and thou be cast into *p.*
18. 30. cast into *p.* till he should
25. 36. I was in *p.* and ye came
1 Pet. 3. 19. preach. to spirits in *p.*
Rev. 2. 10. devil cast some into *p.*
Luke 21. 12. *prisons*, 2 Cor. 11. 23.
Ps. 79. 11. sighing of *prisoner* come
102. 20. to hear the groaning of *p.*
Eph. 4. 1. I the *p.* of the Lord
Job 3. 18. there the *prisoners* rest
Ps. 69. 33. Lord despiseth not his *p.*
146. 7. the Lord looseth the *p.*
Zech. 9. 11. sent forth thy *p.* out
R. V. Gen. 42. 16. bound; Neh. 3. 25; Jer. 32. 2, 8, 12; 33. 1; 37. 21; 38. 6, 13, 28; 39. 14, 15. guard; Isa. 42. 7. dungeon; Acts 12. 7. cell; Num. 21. 1; Isa. 20. 4. captive; Acts 28. 16 ——
PRIVATE, 2 Pet. 1. 20. Gal. 2. 2.
PRIVY, Deut. 23. 1. Acts 5. 2.
Ps. 10. 8. *privily*, 11. 2. & 101. 5. Acts 16. 37. Gal. 2. 4. 2 Pet. 2. 1.
R. V. Ezek. 21. 14 ——; Judg. 9. 31. craftily; Ps. 11. 2. darkness
PRIZE, 1 Cor. 9. 24. Phil. 3. 14.
PROCEED, 2 Sam. 7. 12. Jer. 30. 21.
Job 40. 5. twice spoken; I will *p.*
Isa. 29. 14. I will *p.* to do a marvel.
51. 4. a law shall *p.* from me
Jer. 9. 3. they *p.* from evil to evil.
Matt. 15. 19. out of heart *p.* evil
Eph. 4. 29. no corrupt communication *p.* out of your mouth
2 Tim. 3. 9. they shall *p.* no further
Luke 4. 22. the gracious words that *proceeded* out of his mouth
John 8. 42. I *p.* and came from God
Gen. 24. 50. thing *proceedeth* from
Deut. 8. 3. by every word that *p.*
1 Sam. 24. 13. wickedness *p.* from
Lam. 3. 38. out of the mouth of the Lord *p.* not evil
John 15. 26. Spirit of tru. which *p.*
Jas. 3. 10. out of the same mouth *p.* blessing
Rev. 11. 5. fire *p.* out of their mouth
PROCLAIM, Lev. 23. 2. Deut. 20. 10.
Ex. 33. 19. I will *p.* the name of the Lord, 34. 6.
Prov. 20. 6. most men will *p.* their
Isa. 61. 1. *p.* liberty to the captives
2. to *p.* the acceptable year of Lord
Prov. 12. 23. the heart of fools *proclaimeth* foolishness
PROCURED, Jer. 2. 17. & 4. 18.
R. V. Prov. 11. 27. seeketh; Jer. 26. 19. commit
PRODIGAL son, parable of, Luke 15. 11.
PROFANE not the name of Lord, Lev. 18. 21. & 19. 12. & 20. 3. & 21. 6. & 22. 9, 15.
Neh. 13. 17. *p.* sabbath, Matt. 12. 5.
Ezek. 22. 26. put no difference between holy and *p.*
Amos 2. 7. to *p.* my holy name
1 Tim. 1. 9. law is for unholy and *p.*
4. 7. refuse *p.* and old wives' fa.
Heb. 12. 16. fornicator or *p.* person
Ps. 89. 39. hast *profaned* his crown
Ezek. 22. 8. thou hast *p.* my sabb.
Mal. 1. 11. Judah hath *p.* the holi.
2. 10. by *profaning* the covenant
R. V. Ezek. 21. 25. deadly wounded; 22. 26; 44. 23. common
PROFESS, Deut. 26. 3. Tit. 1. 16.
1 Tim. 6. 12. *profession*, 13. Heb. 3. 1. & 4. 14. & 19. 23.
R. V. 1 Tim. 6. 12. confess; Heb. 3. 1; 4. 14; 10. 23. confession
PROFIT, Prov. 14. 23. Eccl. 7. 11. Jer. 16. 19. 2 Tim. 2. 14. Heb. 12. 10.
1 Sam. 12. 21. *not profit*, Job 33. 27. & 34. 9. Prov. 10. 2. & 11. 4. Isa. 30. 5. & 44. 9, 10. & 57. 12. Jer. 2. 8, 11. & 7. 8. & 23. 32. John 6. 63. 1 Cor. 13. 3. Gal. 5. 2. Heb. 4. 2. Jas. 2. 14.
Job 22. 2. *profitable*, Eccl. 10. 10. Acts 20. 20. 1 Tim. 4. 8. 2 Tim. 3. 16. Tit. 3. 8. Phile. 11.
1 Tim. 4. 15. thy *profiting* appear
PROLONG thy days, Deut. 4. 26, 40. & 5. 16, 33. & 6. 2. & 11. 9. & 17. 20. & 22. 7. & 30. 18. & 32. 47. Prov. 10. 27. & 28. 16. Eccl. 8. 13. Isa. 53. 10.
R. V. Job 6. 11. be patient; Ezek. 12. 25, 28. deferred
PROMISE, Num. 14. 34. Neh. 5. 12
Ps. 77. 8. doth his *p.* fail for ever
105. 42. he remember. his holy *p.*
Luke 24. 49. the *p.* of my Father
Acts 1. 4. wait for *p.* of the Father
2. 39. *p.* is to you, and your child.
Rom. 4. 16. *p.* might be sure to all
9. 8. children of *p.*, 9. Gal. 4. 28.
Eph. 1. 13. holy Spirit of *p.*
2. 12. covenant of *p.* having no
6. 2. commandment with *p.*
1 Tim. 4. 8. *p.* of the life, 2 Tim. 1. 1.
Heb. 4. 1. lest a *p.* being left us of
6. 17. heirs of his *p.*, 11. 9.
9. 15. receive *p.* of eternal life
2 Pet. 3. 4. where is the *p.* of com.
1 John 2. 25. *p.* he *promised* eternal life, Luke 1. 72. Rom. 1. 2. & 4. 21. Tit. 1. 2. Heb. 10. 23. & 11. 11. & 12. 26.
Rom. 9. 4. pertain the *promises*
15. 8. confirm *p.* made to fathers
2 Cor. 1. 20. all *p.* of God are yea
7. 1. having these *p.* let us
Gal. 3. 21. is the law against the *p.*
Heb. 6. 12. patience inherit *p.*
11. 17. he that had received *p.*
2 Pet. 1. 4. great and precious *p.*
R. V. Deut. 10. 9; Josh. 9. 21; 22. 4; 23. 5, 10, 15. spake unto; Luke 1. 72. shew mercy; 22. 6. consented
PROMOTION, Ps. 75. 6. Prov. 3. 35.
PROOF, Acts 1. 3. 2 Cor. 2. 9. & 8. 24.
PROPER, 1 Chron. 29. 3. Heb. 11. 23.
R. V. 1 Cor. 7. 7. own gift from
PROPHECY, 1 Cor. 12. 10. 1 Tim. 4. 14. & 1. 18. 2 Pet. 1. 19, 20. Rev. 1. 3. & 11. 6. & 19. 10. & 22. 7, 10, 18, 19.
1 Kings 22. 8. not *prophesy* good, 18.
Isa. 30. 10. speak smooth things, *p.* deceits
Jer. 14. 14. prophets *p.* lies in my
Joel 2. 28. your sons and your daughters shall *p.*
Amos 2. 12. *p.* not
1 Cor. 13. 9. we *p.* in part
14. 1. but rather that ye may *p.*
39. covet to *p.* and forbid not to
Rev. 10. 11. thou must *p.* again
Num. 11. 25. they *prophesied*
Jer. 23. 21. not spoken yet they *p.*
Matt. 7. 22. we have *p.* in thy
11. 13. the prophets *p.* until John
John 11. 51. *p.* that Jesus should
1 Pet. 1. 10. prophets *p.* of the grace
Jude 14. Enoch also *p.* of these
Ezra 6. 14. *prophesying*, 1 Cor. 11. 4. & 14. 6, 22. 1 Thes. 5. 20.
Gen. 20. 7. he is a *prophet*, and
Ex. 7. 1. Aaron thy brother shall be thy *p.*
Deut. 18. 15. raise up un. thee a *p.*

1 Kings 5. 13. if the *p.* had bid
Ps. 74. 9. there is no more any *p.*
Ezek. 33. 33. then shall they know that a *p.* hath been among them
Hos. 9. 7. *p.* is a fool, spiritual man
12. 13. by a *p.* was he preserved
Amos 7. 14. no *p.* neither a *p.'s* son
Matt. 10. 41. he that receiveth a *p.*
11. 9. see a *p.* and more than a *p.*
13. 57. a *p.* is not without honor
Luke 7. 28. there is not a greater *p.*
24. 19. *p.* mighty in deed and
John 7. 40. this is the *p.*, 1. 21. & 6. 14.
52. out of Galilee ariseth no *p.*
Acts 3. 22. a *p.* shall the Lord raise
23. will not hear that *p.* shall
Tit. 1. 12. a *p.* of their own, said
1 Pet. 2. 16. madness of the *p.*
Num. 11. 29. all the Lord's people *prophets*
1 Sam. 10. 12. is Saul among the *p.*
Ps. 105. 15. do my *p.* no harm
Jer. 5. 13. the *p.* shall become
23. 26. are *p.* of the deceit of
Lam. 2. 14. *p.* have seen vain
Hos. 6. 5. I hewed them by the *p.*
Zeph. 3. 4. her *p.* are treacherous
Zech. 1. 5. *p.* do they live for ever
Matt. 5. 17. not come to destroy law, or the *p.*
7. 12. this is the law and the *p.*
13. 17. many *p.* have desired
22. 40. on these hang all the law and the *p.*
23. 34. I send you *p.* and wise men
Luke 1. 70. spake by mouth of holy *p.*, 2 Pet. 1. 20.
6. 23. so did their fathers to *p.*
16. 29. they have Moses and the *p.*
31. if they hear not Moses and *p.*
24. 25. to believe all that *p.*
John 8. 52. Abraham is dead, and *p.*
Acts 3. 25. ye are children of the *p.*
10. 43. to him give all the *p.*
13. 27. knew not voices of the *p.*
26. 27. believest thou the *p.*
22. things which the *p.* and Moses
Rom. 1. 2. which he had promised afore by his *p.* in Holy Scriptures
1 Cor. 12. 28. God hath set some in the church, first apostles; secondarily *p.*
Eph. 2. 20. are built upon the foundation of the apostles and *p.*
1 Cor. 14. 32. spirit of *p.* sub. to *p.*
1 Thes. 2. 15. who kill. their own *p.*
Heb. 1. 1. God spake to fath. by *p.*
Jas. 5. 10. take *p.* for example
1 Pet. 1. 10. of which salva. the *p.*
Rev. 18. 20. rejoice over her, ye apostles and *p.*
22. 6. Lord God of holy *p.* sent his
9. and of the brethren the *p.*
R. V. Prov. 30. 1. oracle

PROPHETESSES, Anna, Luke 2. 36; Deborah, Judg. 4. 4; Huldah, 2 Kings, 22. 14; Miriam, Ex. 15. 20; Noadiah, Neh. 6. 14.

PROPITIATION, Rom. 3. 25. 1 John 2. 2. & 4. 10.

PROPORTION of faith, Rom. 12. 6.
R. V. 1 Kings 7. 36. space

PROSELYTE, Matt. 23. 15. Acts 2. 10. & 6. 5. & 13. 43.

PROSPER, Gen. 24. 40. Neh. 1. 11.
Gen. 39. 3. Lord made all to *p.*
Deut. 29. 9. may *p.* in all ye do
2 Chron. 20. 20. believe prophets, so shall ye *p.*
Job 12. 6. tabernacles of robbers *p.*
Ps. 1. 3. whatsoever he doeth, it shall *p.*
122. 6. they shall *p.* that love thee
Isa. 53. 10. pleasure of Lord shall *p.*
54. 17. no weapon formed against thee shall *p.*
55. 11. shall *p.* in the thing whereto
Jer. 12. 1. wherefore doth the way of the wicked *p.*
1 Cor. 16. 2. God hath *prospered* him
3 John 2. *p.* as thy soul *prospereth*
Job 36. 11. spend their days in *prosperity*
1 Kings 10. 7. thy wisdom and *p.* exceedeth
Ps. 30. 6. in my *p.* I shall never
73. 3. when I saw *p.* of the wicked
122. 7. *p.* be within thy palaces
Prov. 1. 32. *p.* of fools shall destroy
Eccl. 7. 14. in day of *p.* be joyful
Jer. 22. 21. I spake to thee in thy *p.*
Gen. 24. 21. journey *prosperous*, Josh. 1. 8. Ps. 45. 4. Rom. 1. 10.
R. V. Ps. 73. 12. being at ease; Jer. 20. 11; 23. 5. deal wisely; Jer. 33. 9. peace

PROTEST, Gen. 43. 3. 1 Sam. 8. 9. Jer. 11. 7; Zech. 3. 6. 1 Cor. 15. 31.

PROUD, Job 9. 13. & 26. 12. & 38. 11. & 40. 11, 12. Ps. 12. 3.
Ps. 40. 4. respecteth not the *p.* nor
101. 5. a *p.* heart I will not suffer
Prov. 6. 17. *p.* look and lying tongue
21. 4. high look and *p.* heart
Eccl. 7. 8. patient is better than *p.*
Mal. 3. 15. we call the *p.* happy
Luke 1. 51. the *p.* in imagination
1 Tim. 6. 4. is *p.* knowing nothing
Jas. 4. 6. God resisteth *p.*, 1 Pet. 5. 5.
Ex. 18. 11. wherein dealt *proudly*
1 Sam. 2. 3. no more so exceeding *p.*
Neh. 9. 10. knowest they dealt *p.*, 16.
Ps. 17. 10. they spake *p.*, 31. 18.
Isa. 3. 5. child shall behave *p.* against
R. V. Job 26. 12. Rahab; Ps. 12. 3; Ps. 138. 6; Prov. 6. 17; Hab. 2. 5; Rom. 1. 30; 2 Tim. 3. 2. haughty; 1 Tim. 6. 4. puffed up

PROVE them, Ex. 16. 4. Deut. 8. 16.
Ex. 20. 20. God is come up to *p.* you
Deut. 13. 3. the Lord *p.* you
33. 8. Holy One thou didst *p.* at
1 Kings 10. 1. she came to *p.* him
Job 9. 20. mouth shall *p.* me
Ps. 26. 2. examine me, O Lord, *p.*
Rom. 12. 2. *p.* what is will of God
2 Cor. 8. 8. to *p.* the sincerity of
13. 5. *p.* your own selves, know
Gal. 6. 4. let every man *p.* his work
1 Thes. 5. 21. *p.* all things; hold fast
Ps. 17. 3. thou hast *proved* my heart
66. 10. thou, O God, hast *p.* us as
Acts 9. 22. *proving*, Eph. 5. 10.

PROVERB and a by-word, Deut. 28. 37. 1 Kings 9. 7. Jer. 24. 9. Ezek. 14. 8.
Ps. 69. 11. I became a *p.* to them
Eccl. 12. 9. he set in order many *p.*, 1 Kings 4. 32. Prov. 1. 1. & 10. 1. & 25. 1.
Isa. 14. 4. thou shalt take up this *p.* against, Luke 4. 23.
John 16. 25. I have spoken in *p.*
2 Pet. 2. 22. according to true *p.*
R. V. Isa. 14. 4; Luke 4. 23. parable

PROVIDE, Ex. 18. 21. Acts 23. 24.
Gen. 22. 8. God will *p.* himself a
Ps. 78. 20. can he *p.* flesh for people
Matt. 10. 9. *p.* neither gold nor
Rom. 12. 17. *p.* things honest in
Job 38. 41. *provideth* raven his food
Prov. 6. 8. *p.* her meat in summer
1 Tim. 5. 8. if any *p.* not for his
Ps. 132. 15. *provision*, Rom. 13. 14.
R. V. Ps. 65. 9. prepared; Matt. 10. 9. get you no; Luke 12. 33. make for; Rom. 12. 17; 2 Cor. 8. 21. take thought for

PROVIDENCE of God, Gen. 8. 22. Josh. 7. 14. 1 Sam. 6. 7. Ps. 36. 6. 104. & 136. & 145. & 147. Prov. 16. & 19. & 20. & 33. Matt. 6. 26. & 10. 29, 30. Luke 21. 18. Acts 1. 26. & 17. 26.

PROVOKE him not, Ex. 23. 21.
Num. 14. 11. how long will ye *p.*
Deut. 31. 20. *p.* me, and break my
Job 12. 6. that *p.* God are secure
Ps. 78. 40. how oft did they *p.* him
Isa. 3. 8. to *p.* the eyes of his glory
Jer. 7. 19. do they *p.* me to anger
44. 8. ye *p.* me to wrath with your
Luke 11. 53. to *p.* him to speak of
Rom. 10. 19. *p.* you to jealousy
1 Cor. 10. 22. do we *p.* the Lord to
Eph. 6. 4. fathers *p.* not children
Heb. 3. 16. when they heard did *p.*
10. 24. to *p.* unto love and good
Num. 16. 30. these have *provoked*
14. 23. neither any which *p.* me
Deut. 9. 8. ye *p.* Lord to wrath
1 Sam. 1. 6. adversary *p.* her sore
1 Kings 14. 22. *p.* him to jealousy
2 Kings 23. 26. because Manasseh *p.*
1 Chron. 21. 1. Satan *p.* David to
Ezra 5. 12. our fathers had *p.* God
Ps. 78. 56. and *p.* the Most High
106. 7. *p.* him at the Red sea
Zech. 8. 14. when your fathers *p.*
1 Cor. 13. 5. not easily *p.* thinketh
2 Cor. 9. 2. your zeal hath *p.* many
Deut. 32. 19. *provoking*, 1 Kings 14. 15. & 16. 7. Ps. 78. 17. Gal. 5. 26.
R. V. Num. 14. 11, 23; 16. 30; Deut. 31. 20; Isa. 1. 4. despise; Deut. 32. 16; 1 Chron. 22. 1. moved; Ps. 78. 40, 56. rebel against; Ps. 106. 7, 33, 43. were rebellious; 2 Cor. 9. 2. stirred up

PRUDENT in matters, 1 Sam. 16. 18.
Prov. 12. 16. a *p.* man covereth
23. *p.* man concealeth knowledge
13. 16. every *p.* man dealeth with
14. 8. wisdom of the *p.* is to
15. the *p.* man looketh well to his
15. 5. he that regard. reproof is *p.*
16. 21. wise in heart shall be call. *p.*
18. 15. heart of *p.* getteth knowl.
22. 3. a *p.* man foreseeth the evil
Isa. 5. 21. woe to them that are *p.* in
Jer. 49. 7. is counsel perish. from *p.*
Hos. 14. 9. who is *p.* and he shall
Amos 5. 13. *p.* shall keep silent in
Matt. 11. 25. hid these things from the wise and *p.*
1 Cor. 1. 19. I will bring to nothing the understanding of the *p.*
Isa. 52. 13. my servant shall deal *prudently*
2 Chron. 2. 12. endued with *prudence* and understanding, Prov. 8. 12. Eph. 1. 8.
R. V. 2 Chron. 2. 12. discretion; Prov. 8. 12. subtlety; Isa. 3. 2. diviner; Matt. 11. 25; Luke 10. 21; Acts 13. 7. understanding

PSALM, 1 Chron. 16. 7. Ps. 81. 2. & 98. 5. Acts 13. 33. 1 Cor. 14. 26.
1 Chron. 16. 9. sing *psalms* unto him, Ps. 105. 2.
Ps. 95. 2. a joyful noise with *p.*
Eph. 5. 19. speaking to your. in *p.*
Col. 3. 16. admon. one another in *p.*
Jas. 5. 13. merry, let him sing *p.*
R. V. 1 Chron. 16. 9; Ps. 105. 2; Jas. 5. 13. praises

PSALMODY, singing, service of song, Jewish, Ex. 15. 1. 1 Chron. 6. 31. & 13. 8. 2 Chron. 5. 13. & 20. 22. & 29. 30. Neh. 12. 27; Christian, Matt. 26. 30. Mark 14. 26. Jas. 5. 13; spiritual songs, Eph. 5. 19. Col. 3. 16.

PUBLICAN, Matt. 18. 17; Luke 18. 13.
Matt. 5. 46. even the *p.* the same, 47
11. 19. a friend of *p.* and sinners
Luke 3. 12. came also *publicans* to
7. 29. the *p.* justified God
R. V. Matt. 5. 47. Gentiles

PUBLISH name of the Lord, Deut. 32. 3.
2 Sam. 1. 20. *p.* it not in the streets
Ps. 26. 7. *p.* with voice of thanks.
Isa. 52. 7. feet of him that *publisheth* peace
Jer. 4. 15. a voice *p.* affliction
Mark 13. 10. the Gospel must first be *published*
Acts 13. 49. word of the Lord was *p.*
R. V. Deut. 32. 3. proclaim; 1 Sam. 31. 9. carry tidings; Ps. 26. 7. make to be heard; Mark 13. 10.

preached; Acts 13. 49. spread abroad
PUFFED up, 1 Cor. 4. 6, 19. & 5. 2. & 8. 1. & 13. 4. Col. 2. 18.
PULL out, Ps. 31. 4. Jer. 12. 3. Matt. 7. 4. Luke 14. 5. Jude 23.
Isa. 22. 19. *pull down*, Jer. 1. 10. & 18. 7. & 24. 6. & 42. 10. Luke 12. 18. 2 Cor. 10. 4.
Lam. 3. 11. *pull in pieces*, Acts 23. 10.
Ezek. 17. 9. *pull up*, Amos 9. 15.
Zech. 7. 11. they *pulled* away the
R. V. Gen. 8. 9; 19. 10. brought; 1 Kings 13. 4; Luke 14. 5. draw; Ps. 31. 4; Amos 9. 15. pluck; Jer. 1. 10; 18. 7. break; Mic. 2. 8. strip; Matt. 7. 4; Luke 6. 42. cast; Acts 23. 10. torn; 2 Cor. 10. 4. casting; Jude 23. snatching.
PULPIT of wood, Neh. 8. 4.
PUNISH, seven times, Lev. 26. 18.
Prov. 17. 26. to *p.* the just is not
Isa. 10. 12. *p.* fruit of the stout
13. 11. I will *p.* the world for their
Jer. 9. 25. *p.* all circumcised with
Hos. 4. 14. I will not *p.* daughters
Ezra 9. 13. *p.* us less than we
2 Thes. 1. 9. be *p.* with destruction
2 Pet. 2. 9. reserve unjust to be *p.*
Gen. 4. 13. my *punishment* is great.
Lev. 26. 41. accept *p.* of their iniq.
Job. 31. 3. a strange *p.* to workers
Lam. 3. 39. complain for *p.* of sins
Amos 1. 3. not turn away the *p.*
Matt. 25. 46. go into everlasting *p.*
2 Cor. 2. 6. suffi. to such is this *p.*
Heb. 10. 29. of how much sorer *p.*
1 Pet. 2. 14. sent by him, for the *p.*
R. V. Ex. 21. 22. fined; Lev. 26. 18. chastise; 26. 24. smite; Prov. 22. 3; 27. 12. suffer for it; Jer. 41. 44. do judgment; Amos 3. 2. visit upon you; Zech. 8. 14. do evil unto; Prov. 19. 19. penalty; Lam. 4. 6; Ezek. 14. 10——; Ezek. 14. 10. iniquity; Job 31. 3. disaster; 1 Pet. 2. 14. vengeance
PURCHASED, Ps. 74. 2. Acts 8. 20. & 20. 28. Eph. 1. 14. 1 Tim. 3. 13.
R. V. Lev. 25. 33. redeem; Acts 1. 18; 8. 20. obtain
PURCHASES, Gen. 23. Ruth 4. Jer. 32. 6.
PURE, Ex. 27. 20. & 30. 23, 34.
2 Sam. 22. 27. with the *p.* thou wilt
Job 4. 17. can man be more *p.* than
25. 5. stars are not *p.* in his sight
Ps. 12. 6. words of the Lord are *p.*
19. 8. commandment of Lord is *p.*
24. 4. clean hands and a *p.* heart
Prov. 15. 26. words of *p.* are pleas.
30. 5. every word of God is *p.*
12. a generation *p.* in
Zeph. 3. 9. turn to the people a *p.*
Acts 20. 26. I am *p.* from blood of
Rom. 14. 20. all things indeed are *p.*
Phil. 4. 8. whatsoever things are *p.*
1 Tim. 3. 9. mystery of faith in a *p.* conscience
5. 22. of other men's sins keep thyself *p.*
Tit. 1. 15. to the *p.* all things are *p.*
Heb. 10. 22. washed with *p.* water
Jas. 1. 27. *p.* religion and undefiled
3. 17. wis. from above is first *p.*
2 Pet. 3. 1. stir up your *p.* minds
Isa. 1. 25. *purely* purge away dross
Job 22. 30. by *pureness*, 2 Cor. 6. 6.
1 Tim. 4. 12. *purity*, 5. 2.
Hab. 1. 13. of *purer* eyes than to
R. V. Ex. 30. 23. flowing; Ps. 21. 3. fine; Prov. 30. 5. tried; Rom. 14. 20. clean; 2 Pet. 3. 1. sincere; Rev. 22. 1——
PURGE me with hyssop, Ps. 51. 7.
Ps. 65. 3. our transgressions, thou shalt *p.* them away
79. 9. *p.* away our sins for thy
Mal. 3. 3. purify and *p.* them as
Matt. 3. 12. thoroughly *p.* his floor
1 Cor. 5. 7. *p.* the old leaven
2 Tim. 2. 21. if a man *p.* himself
Heb. 9. 14. *p.* your conscience from
Prov. 16. 6. by mercy iniquity is *purged*
Isa. 6. 7. iniqu. is taken, and sin *p.*
Ezek. 24. 13. because I *p.* thee
Heb. 1. 3. had by himself *p.* our
2 Pet. 1. 9. he was *p.* from sins
John 15. 2. he *purgeth* that it may
R. V. Ezek. 43. 20. make atonement; Dan. 11. 35. purify, Matt. 3. 12; Mark 7. 19; Luke 3. 17; John 15. 2; Heb. 9. 14, 22; 10. 2; 2 Pet. 1. 9. cleanse, cleansed, clean
PURIFY sons of Levi, Mal. 3. 3.
Jas. 4. 8. *p.* your hearts, ye double
Ps. 12. 6. silver *purified* seven
Dan. 12. 10. many shall be *p.*
1 Pet. 1. 22. *p.* your souls in obey.
Mal. 3. 3. sit as *purifier* of silver
1 John 3. 3. *purifieth* himself as he
Acts 15. 9. *purifying* their hearts
Tit. 2. 14. *p.* to himself a peculiar
Heb. 9. 13. sanctifieth to *p.* of flesh
R. V. Job. 41. 25. are beside; Heb. 9. 23. cleansed; Num. 8. 7. expiation, Acts 15. 9. cleansing
PURPOSE, Jer. 6. 20. & 49. 30.
Job 33. 17. withdraw man from *p.*
Prov. 20. 18. every *p.* is established
Eccl. 3. 17. a time to every *p.*, 8. 6.
Isa. 14. 26. the *p.* that is purposed
Jer. 51. 29. *p.* of Lord shall stand
Acts 11. 23. with *p.* of heart cleave
Rom. 8. 28. according to his *p.*
Eph. 1. 11. according to *p.* of him
3. 11. the eternal *p.* which he *p.*
2 Tim. 1. 9. according to his own *p.*
1 John 3. 8. for this *p.* he was
R. V. Acts 26. 18; 1 John 3. 8. to this end. Acts 20. 3. determined
PURSE, Prov. 1. 14. Matt. 10. 9.
PURSUE, Gen. 35. 5. Deut. 28. 22.
Ex. 15. 9. the enemy said, I will *p.*
Job 13. 25. wilt thou *p.* dry stubble
Ps. 34. 14. seek peace and *p.* it
Prov. 11. 19. that *pursueth* evil, *p.* it
28. 1. wicked flee when none *p.*
R. V. Judg. 20. 45. followed; Job 30. 15; Lam. 4. 19. chase
PUT, Gen. 2. 8. & 3. 15, 22.
Neh. 2. 12. what God *p.* in my heart, 7. 5. Ezra 7. 27. Rev. 17. 17.
Neh. 3. 5. nobles *p.* not their necks
Job 4. 18. he *p.* no trust in servants
38. 36. hath *p.* wisdom in inward
Ps. 4. 7. hast *p.* gladness in heart
8. 6. *p.* all things under his feet
Eccl. 10. 10. *p.* to more strength
S. of S. 5. 3. *p.* off my coat, how shall
Isa. 5. 20. woe to them that *p.* dark.
42. 1. I will *p.* my Spirit upon
53. 10. Lord hath *p.* him to grief
63. 11. who *p.* his Holy Spirit in
Jer. 31. 33. *p.* law in inward parts
32. 40. I will *p.* my fear in hearts
Ezek. 11. 19. *p.* a new spirit within
36. 27. I will *p.* my Spirit within
Mic. 7. 5. *p.* not confidence in guide
Matt. 5. 15. *p.* it under a bushel
19. 6. what God joined, let no man *p.* asunder
Luke 1. 52. *p.* down mighty from
Acts 1. 7. which Father *p.* in his
13. 46. seeing you *p.* the Gospel
15. 9. *p.* no difference between us
Eph. 4. 22. *p.* off the old man
2 Pet. 1. 14. I must *p.* off this
Gen. 28. 20. God will give raiment to *put on*
Job 29. 14. I—righteousness and it
Isa. 51. 9. awake, arm of Lord,—strength
59. 15. for he—righteousness as a breastplate
Matt. 6. 25. nor for body what ye—
Rom. 13. 12.—armor of light
14.—Lord Jesus Christ
Gal. 3. 27. baptized into Christ have—Christ
Eph. 4. 24.—the new man, Col. 3. 10.
6. 11.—whole armor of God
Col. 3. 12.—bowels of mercies
1 Chron. 5. 20. *put trust* in, Ps. 4. 5. & 7. 1. & 9. 10. & 56. 4. & 146. 3.
Prov. 28. 25. & 29. 25. Isa. 57. 13. Jer. 39. 18. Hab. 2. 13.
Num. 22. 38. word that God *putteth*
Job 15. 15. he *p.* no trust in saints
Ps. 15. 5. that *p.* not out money
75. 7. God *p.* down one, and set.
S. of S. 2. 13. *p.* forth green figs
Lam. 3. 29. he *p.* his mouth in
Mic. 3. 5. that *p.* not into their
Mal. 2. 16. he hateth *putting* away
Eph. 4. 25. *p.* away lying, speak
Col. 2. 11 in *p.* off the body of sins
1 Thes. 5. 8. *p.* on the breastplate
2 Tim. 1. 6. gift given thee by *p.*
1 Pet. 3. 3. wearing of gold or *p.* on
R. V. Many changes, but chiefly due to context

Q

QUAILS, Ex. 16. 13. Num. 11. 31.
QUAKE, Ex. 19. 18. Matt. 27. 51.
Ezek. 12. 18. *quaking*, Dan. 10. 7.
QUARREL, Lev. 26. 25. Col. 3. 13.
R. V. Lev. 26. 25. execute vengeance, Mark 6. 19. set herself; Col. 3. 13. complain
QUEEN, 1 Kings 10. 1. & 15. 13. Ps. 45. 9. S. of S. 6. 8. Jer. 44. 17, 24. Rev. 18. 7.
Matt. 12. 42. *q.* of the south rise
Isa. 49. 23. *q.* their nursing moth.
R. V. Jer. 13. 18; 29. 12. queen-mother
QUENCH my coal, 2 Sam. 14. 7.
2 Sam. 21. 17. that thou *q.* not
S. of S. 8. 7. waters cannot *q.* love
Isa. 42. 3. flax he will not *q.*
Eph. 6. 16. to *q.* fiery darts of dev.
1 Thes. 5. 19. *q.* not the Spirit
Mark 9. 43. fire that never shall be *quenched*, 44. 46, 48.
R. V. Num. 11. 2. abated; Mark 9. 44, 45, 46——
QUESTION, Mark 12. 34. 1 Cor. 10. 25.
1 Kings 10. 1. *questions*, Luke 2. 46.
1 Tim. 1. 4. & 6. 4. 2 Tim. 2. 23.
R. V. 1 Tim. 1. 4; 6. 4; 2 Tim. 2. 23; Tit. 3. 9. questionings
QUICK, Num. 16. 30. Ps. 55. 15.
Ps. 124. 3. had swallowed us up *q.*
Isa. 11. 3. of *q.* understanding
Acts 10. 42. Judge of *q.* and dead
2 Tim. 4. 1. who shall judge the *q.*
Ps. 71. 20. *quicken* me again and
80. 18. *q.* us and we will call
119. 25. *q.* me according to word
40. *q.* me in thy righteousness
149. *q.* me according to judgment
Rom. 8. 11. *q.* your mortal bodies
Eph. 2. 5. *q.* us together with
Ps. 119. 50. for thy word hath *quickened* me
Eph. 2. 1. you he *q.* who were
1 Pet. 3. 18. but *q.* by the Spirit
John 5. 21. Son *quickeneth* whom he
1 Cor. 15. 45. last Adam be made a *quickening* Spirit
R. V. Num. 16. 30; Ps. 55. 15; 124. 3. alive; Isa. 11. 3. his delight shall be; Heb. 4. 12. living; 1 Cor. 15. 45. become a life giving
QUICKLY, Ex. 32. 8. Deut. 11. 17.
Eccl. 4. 12. cord is not *q.* broken
Matt. 5. 25. agree with adversary *q.*
Rev. 3. 11. behold I come *q.*, 22. 7.
R. V. Mark 16. 8; Rev. 2. 5——
QUIET, Judg. 18. 27. Job 3. 13, 26.
Eccl. 9. 17. the words of the wise are heard in *q.*
Isa. 7. 4. take heed and be *q.* fear
33. 20. shall see Jerusalem a *q.*
1 Thes. 4. 11. study to be *q.* and to
1 Tim. 2. 2. lead a *q.* and peaceable
1 Pet. 3. 4. ornament of a meek and *q.* spirit
1 Chron. 22. 9. *quietness*, Job 20. 20.
Job 34. 29. when he giveth *q.* who
Prov. 17. 1. better is dry morsel and *q.*
Eccl. 4. 6. better is a hand. with *q.*

Isa. 30. 15. in *q*. shall be strength
32. 17. the effect of righteousness shall be *q*.
2 Thes. 3. 12. exhort with *q*. they
R. V. Nah. 1. 12. in full strength; Judg. 8. 28. had rest; Acts 24. 2. much peace

QUIT you like men, 1 Sam. 4. 9. 1 Cor. 16. 13.
R. V. Josh. 2. 20. guiltless

QUIVER full of them, Ps. 127. 5.
Isa. 49. 2. in his *q*. hath he hid me
Jer. 5. 16. *q*. is an open sepulchre

R

RABBI, Matt. 23. 7, 8. John 20. 16.
R. V. Matt. 23. 7 ——

RACE, Ps. 19. 5. Eccl. 9. 11. 1 Cor. 9. 24. Heb. 12. 1.
R. V. Ps. 19. 5. course

RAGE, 2 Kings 5. 12. 2 Chron. 16. 10.
2 Chron. 28. 9. ye have slain them in a *r*.
Ps. 2. 1. why do the heathen *r*.
Prov. 6. 34. jealousy is *r*. of a man
29. 9. whether he *r*. or laugh is no
Ps. 46. 6. the heathen *raged*
Prov. 14. 16. the fool *rageth*
Ps. 89. 9. rulest the *raging* of sea
Prov. 20. 1. wine is a mocker, strong drink is *r*.
Jude 13. *r*. waves of sea, foaming
R. V. Job 40. 11. overflowings; Prov. 29. 9. be angry; 14. 16. beareth himself insolently; Prov. 20. 1. a brawler

RAGS, Prov. 23. 21. Isa. 64. 6.

RAILER, or drunkard, 1 Cor. 5. 11.
1 Tim. 6. 4. *railing*, 1 Pet. 3. 9.
2 Pet. 2. 11. *r*. accusation, Jude 9.
R. V. 1 Pet. 3. 9. reviling

RAIMENT to put on, Gen. 28. 20.
Ex. 21. 10. food and *r*. not dimin.
Deut. 8. 4. thy *r*. waxed not old
Zech. 3. 4. clothe thee with change of *r*.
Matt. 6. 26. body more than *r*., 28.
11. 8. man clothed in soft *r*.
17. 2. his *r*. was white as the light
1 Tim. 6. 8. having food and *r*. let
Rev. 3. 5. clothed in white *r*., 18.
R. V. Ex. 22. 26, 27; Deut. 22. 3; 24. 13; Num. 31. 20; Matt. 17. 2; 27. 31; Mark 9. 3; Luke 23. 34; John 19. 24; Acts 22. 20; Rev. 3. 5, 18; 4. 4. garment or garments; Ps. 45. 14. broidered work; Zech. 3. 4. apparel; 1 Tim. 6. 8. covering; Jas. 2. 2. clothing; Luke 10. 30 ——

RAIN in due season, Lev. 26. 4. Deut. 11. 14. & 28. 12.
Deut. 32. 2. my doctrine drop as *r*.
2 Sam. 23. 4. clear shining after *r*.
1 Kings 8. 35. no *r*. because sinned
2 Chron. 7. 13. that there be no *r*.
Job 5. 10. giveth *r*. on the earth
38. 28. hath the *r*. a father
Ps. 68. 9. didst send a plentiful *r*.
72. 6. he shall come down like *r*.
147. 8. who prepareth *r*. for earth
Prov. 16. 15. king's favor is like the latter *r*.
Eccl. 12. 2. nor clouds ret. after *r*.
S. of S. 2. 11. winter is past; *r*. is over
Isa. 4. 6. covert from storm and *r*.
30. 23. shall give the *r*. of thy
55. 10. as *r*. cometh down from
Jer. 5. 24. fear Lord who giveth *r*.
14. 22. vanities of the Gentiles that can *r*.
Amos 4. 7. withholden *r*. from you
Zech. 10. 1. ask of the Lord *r*. in
14. 17. upon them shall be no *r*.
Matt. 5. 45. sendeth *r*. on the just
Heb. 6. 7. earth which drink. in *r*.
Jas. 5. 18. he prayed, and heaven gave *r*.
Job 38. 26. cause it to *r*. on the earth
Ps. 11. 6. on the wicked he shall *r*.
Hos. 10. 12. till he *r*. righteousness
Ps. 78. 27. had *rained* upon them
Ezek. 22. 24. land not cleansed nor *r*. upon
Prov. 27. 15. continual dropping in a *rainy* day

RAISE, Deut. 18. 15, 18. 2 Sam. 12. 11.
Isa. 44. 26. *r*. up decayed places
58. 12. *r*. up foundations of
Hos. 6. 2. third day he will *r*. us
Amos 9. 11. I will *r*. up tabernacle
Luke 1. 69. *r*. up a horn of salva.
John 6. 40. I will *r*. him up at
Ex. 9. 16. I *raised* thee up to show
Matt. 11. 5. deaf hear, dead are *r*.
Rom. 4. 25. *r*. again for justifica.
6. 4. as Christ was *r*. by glory of
1 Cor. 6. 14. God hath *r*. up the
2 Cor. 4. 14. he that *r*. up the
Eph. 2. 6. hath *r*. us up together
1 Sam. 2. 8. he *raiseth* up the poor
Ps. 113. 7. he *r*. up poor out of
145. 14. *r*. up those that be
R. V. Job 3. 8; 14. 12. roused; S. of S. 8. 5. awakened; Job 50. 9; Ezek. 1. 5; Jer. 6. 22; 50. 41; 51. 11; Joel 3. 7; Zech. 9. 13; Acts 13. 50. stir or stirred

RANSOM of life, Ex. 21. 30.
Ex. 30. 12. give every man a *r*. for
Job 33. 24. deliver him, I have found *r*.
36. 18. great *r*. cannot deliver
Ps. 49. 7. nor give to God a *r*. for
Prov. 6. 35. will not regard any *r*.
13. 8. *r*. of man's life are his
21. 18. wicked ar a *r*. for right.
Isa. 43. 3. I gave Egypt for thy *r*.
Hos. 13. 14. *r*. them from power
Matt. 20. 28. to give his life a *r*. for
1 Tim. 2. 6. gave himself a *r*. for
Isa. 35. 10. *ransomed*, 51. 10. Jer. 31. 11.
R. V. Ex. 21. 30. redemption; Isa. 51. 10. redeemed

RASH, Eccl. 5. 2. Isa. 32. 4.

RAVISHED, Prov. 5. 19. S. of S. 4. 9.

REACH, Gen. 11. 4. John 20. 27.
Ps. 36. 5. faithfulness *reacheth* to
Phil. 3. 13. *reaching* forth to those
R. V. Ex. 26. 28. pass through; Phil. 3. 13. stretching forward

READ in audience, Ex. 24. 7.
Deut. 17. 19. *r*. therein all his life
Neh. 13. 1. *r*. in the book of Moses
Luke 4. 16. as his custom was, stood up to *r*.
Acts 15. 21. *r*. in synagogue
2 Cor. 3. 2. known and *r*. of all
Acts 8. 30. understandest thou what thou *readest*
Rev. 1. 3. blessed is he that *readeth*
Neh. 8. 8. *reading*, 1 Tim. 4. 13.

READY to pardon, God, Neh. 9. 17.
Ps. 45. 1. tongue is as a pen of a *r*. writer
86. 5. thou, Lord, art good, and *r*. to forgive
Eccl. 5. 1. more *r*. to hear, than
Matt. 24. 44. be ye also *r*.
Mark 14. 38. spirit is *r*. but the
Acts 21. 13. *r*. not to be bound
1 Tim. 6. 18. do good *r*. to distrib.
2 Tim. 4. 6. now *r*. to be offered
Tit. 3. 1. *r*. to every good work
1 Pet. 5. 2. willingly of a *r*. mind
Rev. 3. 2. strengthen things *r*. to
Acts 17. 11. *readiness*, 2 Cor. 10. 6.
R. V. 2 Chron. 35. 14; 2 Cor. 9. 2, 3. prepared; 1 Chron. 12. 23, 24. armed for; Mark 14. 38. willing; Acts 20. 7. intending; Heb. 8. 13. nigh; Rev. 12. 4. about

REAP, Lev. 19. 9.
Hos. 10. 12. *r*. in mercy
1 Cor. 9. 11. a great thing if we *r*.
Gal. 6. 9. shall *r*. if we faint not
Hos. 10. 13. ploughed wickedness, ye have *reaped* iniquity
Rev. 14. 16. the earth was *r*., 15.
Matt. 13. 39. *reapers* are angels, 30.
John 4. 36. he that *reapeth* receiv.
R. V. Lev. 23. 22 ——; Jas. 5. 4. mowed

REASON, Prov. 26. 16. Dan. 4. 36.
Isa. 41. 21. bring forth your strong *r*.
1 Pet. 3. 15. asketh a *r*. of the hope
Acts 24. 25. as he *reasoned* of
Rom. 12. 1. your *reasonable* service

REBEL not against Lord, Num. 14. 9. Josh. 22. 19.
Job 24. 13. of those that *r*. against
Neh. 9. 26. they *rebelled* against thee
Isa. 63. 10. they *r*. and vexed his
1 Sam. 15. 23. *rebellion*, the sin
Num. 20. 10. hear now, ye *rebels*
Ezek. 20. 38. purge out the *r*. from
Deut. 9. 7. been *rebellious* against
Ps. 68. 18. received gifts for men, for the *r*. also
Isa. 30. 9. this a *r*. people, lying
50. 5. I was not *r*. nor turned
Jer. 4. 17. hath been *r*.
Ezek. 2. 3, 5, 8. *r*. house, 3. 9, 26. & 12. 2, 3. & 17. 12. & 24. 3. & 44. 6.

REBUKE thy neighbor, Lev. 19. 17.
2 Kings 19. 3. a day of *r*.
Ps. 6. 1. *r*. me not in anger, nor
Prov. 9. 8. *r*. a wise man, he will
27. 5. open *r*. is better than secret
Zech. 3. 2. the Lord said to Satan, the Lord *r*. thee
Matt. 16. 22. Peter began to *r*. him
Luke 17. 3. if thy brother trespass, *r*. him
Phil. 2. 15. sons of God without *r*.
1 Tim. 5. 1. *r*. not an elder, entreat
20. them that sin *r*. before all
Tit. 1. 13. *r*. them sharply, that
3. 15. exhort and *r*. with author.
Heb. 12. 5. not faint, when *rebuked*
Prov. 28. 23. he that *rebuked*, shall
Amos 5. 10. hate him that *r*. in
R. V. Phil. 2. 15. blemish; Jer. 15. 15. reproach; Prov. 9. 7, 8; Amos 5. 10; 1 Tim. 5. 20; Tit. 2. 15; Rev. 3. 19. reprove or reproveth

RECEIVE good and not evil, Job 2. 10.
Job 22. 22. *r*. the law from his
Ps. 6. 9. the Lord will *r*. my prayer
73. 24. guide me and afterwards *r*.
75. 2. when I shall *r*. congregation
Hos. 14. 2. take away iniqu., *r*. us
Matt. 10. 41. *r*. a prophet's reward
18. 5. *r*. little child in my name
19. 11. all men cannot *r*. this
21. 22. ask, believing, ye shall *r*.
Mark 4. 16. hear the word, and *r*.
11. 24. believe that ye *r*. and ye
Luke 16. 9. may *r*. into everlast.
John 3. 27. man can *r*. nothing
5. 44. which *r*. honor one of
Acts 2. 38. shall *r*. gift of Holy Ghost
7. 59. Lord Jesus *r*. my spirit
13. 43. he that believeth shall *r*.
20. 35. more bless. to give than *r*.
26. 18. may *r*. forgiveness of sins
Rom. 14. 1. that is weak in faith *r*.
1 Cor. 3. 8. every man *r*. his reward
2 Cor. 5. 10. may *r*. things done
6. 1. *r*. not grace of God in vain
Gal. 3. 14. *r*. promise of the
4. 5. might *r*. the adoption of
Eph. 6. 8. same shall he *r*. of
Col. 3. 24. *r*. reward of inheritance
Jas. 1. 21. *r*. with meekness
3. 1. *r*. greater condemnation
1 Pet. 5. 4. shall *r*. a crown of glory
1 John 3. 22. whatso. we ask, we *r*
2 John 8. look that we *r*. a full
Job 4. 12. mine ear *received* a little
Ps. 68. 18. thou hast *r*. gifts for
Jer. 2. 30. *r*. no correction
Matt. 10. 8. freely ye have *r*. freely
Luke 6. 24. have *r*. your consola.
16. 25. hast *r*. thy good things
John 1. 11. own *r*. him not
16. of his fulness have we all *r*.
Acts 8. 17. they *r*. the Holy Ghost
17. 11. *r*. the word

Acts 20. 24. which I *r.* of Lord
Rom. 5. 11. Christ by whom we have *r.* atonement
14. 3. judge him not, for God hath *r.* him
15. 7. *r.* one anoth. as Christ *r.* us
1 Tim. 3. 16. *r.* up into glory
4. 3. to be *r.* with thanksgiving
Heb. 11. 13. not having *r.* promises
Jer. 7. 28. nor *receiveth* correction
Matt. 7. 8. every one that asketh *r.*
10. 40. he that *r.* you, *r.* me
13. 20. hears the word, and anon *r.*
John 3. 32. no man *r.* his testimony
12. 48. rejecteth me, *r.* not my
1 Cor. 2. 14. natural man *r.* not
Phil. 4. 15. in giving and *receiving*
Heb. 12. 28. we *r.* a kingdom
1 Pet. 1. 9. *r.* the end of your faith
R. V. Ex. 29. 25; 1 Sam. 12. 3; 2 Kings 12. 7, 8; John 16. 14; Heb. 7. 6. take; Hos. 14. 2; Mark 4. 20; 1 Thes. 2. 13. accept; Luke 9. 11; 3 John 8. welcome; many other changes due to context

RECKONED, Ps. 40. 5. Isa. 38. 13. Luke 22. 37. Rom. 4. 4, 9, 10. & 6. 11. & 8. 18.

RECOMPENSE, Prov. 12. 14. Isa. 35. 4.
Deut. 32. 35. to me belongeth *r.*
Job 15. 31. vanity shall be his *r.*
Prov. 20. 22. say not thou I will *r.* evil
Jer. 25. 14. I will *r.* your iniquities
Luke 14. 14. they cannot *r.* thee
Rom. 12. 17. *r.* to no man evil for
Isa. 34. 8. it is the year of *r.* for
66. 6. render *r.* to his enemies
Jer. 51. 56. the Lord God of *r.*
Hos. 9. 7. the days of *r.* are come
Luke 14. 12. lest a *r.* be made thee
Heb. 2. 2. received just *r.* of reward
11. 26. he had respect unto *r.* of
Num. 5. 8. trespass be *recompensed*
2 Sam. 22. 21. according to righteousness he *r.* me
Prov. 11. 31. righteous shall be *r.*
Jer. 18. 20. shall evil be *r.* for good
Rom. 11. 35. it shall be *r.* to him
R. V. Num. 5. 7, 8. restitution; Ezek. 7. 3, 4, 9; 11. 21; 16. 34; 17. 19; 22. 31; 2 Chron. 6. 23; bring or brought; Rom. 12. 17. render

RECONCILE with blood, Lev. 6. 30.
Eph. 2. 16. *r.* both to God into one
Col. 1. 20. to *r.* all things to him.
2 Cor. 5. 19. God in Christ *reconciling* the world
Matt. 5. 24. be *reconciled* to brother
Rom. 5. 10. when enemies we were *r.*
2 Cor. 5. 18. he hath *r.* us to
20. be ye *r.* to God
Lev. 8. 15. to make *reconciliation*, 2 Chron. 29. 24. Ezek. 45. 15, 17. Dan. 8. 24. Heb. 2. 17.
2 Cor. 5. 18. given to us ministry of *r.*
19. committ. to us the word of *r.*
R. V. Lev. 6. 30; Ezek. 45. 20. make atonement; Lev. 8. 15; 16. 20; Ezek. 45. 15, 17. atonement; 2 Chron. 29. 24. sin offering; Heb. 2. 17. propitiation

RECORD my name, Ex. 20. 24.
Deut. 30. 19. I call heaven and earth to *r.* against, 31. 28.
Job 16. 19. my witness and my *r.*
John 1. 32. bare *r.*, 8. 13, 14. & 12. 17. & 19. 35. Rom. 10. 2. Gal. 4. 15.
2 Cor. 1. 23. I call God for a *r.*
1 John 5. 7. three bear *r.* in heaven
11. this is the *r.* God hath given
Rev. 1. 2. bare *r.* of the word of
R. V. Very general change to witness; Deut. 30. 19. witness; 1 Chron. 16. 4. celebrate; Acts 20. 26. testify

RECOVER strength, Ps. 39. 13.
Hos. 2. 9. I will *r.* my wool and
2 Tim. 2. 26. may *r.* themselves
Jer. 8. 22. is not health of my people *recovered*
Luke 4. 18. *recovering* of sight to
R. V. 1 Sam. 30. 19. brought back; Hos. 2. 9. pluck away

RED, Ps. 75. 8. Isa. 1. 18. & 27. 2. & 63. 2. Zech. 1. 8. & 6. 2. Rev. 6. 4. & 12. 3.
R. V. Ps. 75. 8. foameth

RED DRAGON, Rev. 12. 3.

RED HORSE, vision of, Zech. 1. 8. & 6. 2. Rev. 6. 4.

REDEEM with outstretched arm, Ex. 6. 6.
2 Sam. 7. 23. Israel whom God went to *r.*
Job 5. 20. in famine he shall *r.* thee
Ps. 44. 26. *r.* us for thy mercies' sake
130. 8. shall *r.* Israel from
Hos. 13. 14. I will *r.* them from
Tit. 2. 14. might *r.* us from iniquity
Gen. 48. 16. angel which *redeemed*
2 Sam. 4. 9. hath *r.* my soul out
Ps. 136. 24. hath *r.* us from our
Isa. 1. 27. Zion shall be *r.* with
51. 11. *r.* of the Lord shall return
52. 3. shall be *r.* without money
63. 9. in his love and pity he *r.*
Luke 1. 68. visited and *r.* his peo.
24. 21. he that should have *r.*
Gal. 3. 13. Christ hath *r.* us from
1 Pet. 1. 18. not *r.* with corrupti.
Rev. 5. 9. hast *r.* us to God, by
14. 4. these were *r.* from among
Ps. 34. 22. Lord *redeemeth* the soul
103. 4. who *r.* thy life from de.
Eph. 5. 16. *redeeming* the time
Job 19. 25. I know that my *Redeemer* liveth
Ps. 19. 14. my strength and my *R.*
Prov. 23. 11. their *R.* is mighty
Isa. 63. 16. our Father and *R.*
Jer. 50. 34. their *R.* is strong
Lev. 25. 34. *redemption*, Num. 3. 49.
Ps. 49. 8. *r.* of their soul is pre.
130. 7. with him is plenteous *r.*
Luke 2. 38. looked for *r.* in Jerusalem
21. 28. your *r.* draweth nigh
Rom. 3. 24. through *r.* in Christ
8. 23. waiting for the *r.* of our body
1 Cor. 1. 30. made unto us wisdom, and righteousness, and *r.*
Eph. 1. 7. in whom we have *r.*
14. until *r.* of the purchased
4. 30. sealed unto the day of *r.*
Heb. 9. 12. obtain. eternal *r.* for us
R. V. Lev. 25. 29; 27. 27; Isa. 5. 11; Jer. 31. 11. ransom; Lev. 25. 29; Num. 3. 51; Ruth 4. 6. redemption; Ps. 136. 24. delivered; Rev. 5. 9; 14. 3, 4. purchased

REFINE, Isa. 25. 6. & 48. 10. Zech 13. 9. Mal. 3. 2, 3.

REFORMATION, Heb. 9. 10.

REFRAIN, Prov. 1. 15. 1 Pet. 3. 10.
Prov. 10. 29. he that *refraineth* his lips is wise

REFRESHING, Isa. 28. 12. Acts 3. 19.

REFUGE, Num. 35. 13. Josh. 20. 3.
Deut. 33. 27. eternal God is thy *r.*
Ps. 9. 9. the Lord also will be a *r.* for the oppressed, 14. 6. Isa. 4. 6. & 25. 4.
Ps. 57. 1. God is my *r.* and, 59. 16. & 62. 7. & 71. 7. & 142. 5. Jer. 16. 19.
Ps. 46. 1. God is our *r.*, 7. 11. & 62. 8.
Isa. 28. 15. have made lies our *r.*
Heb. 6. 18. fled for *r.* to lay hold on
R. V. Deut. 33. 27. dwelling place; Ps. 9. 9. high tower

REFUSE, Lam. 3. 45. Amos 8. 6.
Neh. 9. 17. *refused* to obey, neither
Ps. 77. 2. my soul *r.* to be comforted
118. 22. the stone which builders *r.*
Prov. 1. 24. I have called, and ye *r.*
Jer. 31. 15. Rachel *r.* to be com.
Hos. 11. 5. because they *r.* to return
1 Tim. 4. 4. good and noth. to be *r.*
Jer. 3. 3. *refusedst* to be ashamed
15. 18. *refuseth* to be healed
Heb. 12. 25. *r.* not him that speak.
R. V. 1 Sam. 16. 7; Ps. 118. 22; Ezek. 5. 6; 1 Tim. 4. 4. reject or rejected; Prov. 10. 17. forsaketh; Isa. 54. 6. cast off

REGARD not works of the Lord, Ps. 28. 5.
Ps. 66. 18. if I *r.* iniquity in heart
102. 17. will *r.* prayer of destitute
Isa. 5. 12. that *r.* not work of Lord
Prov. 1. 24. no man *regarded*
Ps. 106. 44. he *r.* their affliction
Luke 1. 48. *r.* low estate of his
Heb. 8. 9. not in my covenant I *r.* them not
Deut. 10. 17. God *regardeth* not
Job 34. 19. nor *r.* rich more than
Prov. 12. 10. righteous *r.* life of
15. 5. he that *r.* reproof is prudent
Eccl. 5. 8. he that is higher than the highest *r.*
Rom. 14. 6. he that *r.* the day, *r.* it
Matt. 22. 16. *regardest* not person
R. V. *gave heed*; 2 Sam. 13. 20. take thing to heart; Job 39. 7. heareth; Ps. 94. 7. consider; Prov. 5. 2. preserve; Mal. 1. 9. accept; Luke 1. 48. looked upon; Acts 8. 11. gave heed; Phil. 2. 30. hazarding; Rom. 14. 6; Gal. 6. 4 ——

REGENERATION, Matt. 19. 28. Tit. 3. 5.

REIGN, Gen. 37. 8. Lev. 26. 17.
Ex. 15. 18. Lord shall *r.* for ever, Ps. 146. 10.
Prov. 8. 15. by me kings *r.* and
Isa. 32. 1. a king shall *r.* in right.
Jer. 23. 5. a king shall *r.* and pros.
Luke 19. 14. not have this man to *r.*
Rom. 5. 17. shall *r.* in life by one
1 Cor. 4. 8. would to God ye did *r.*
2 Tim. 2. 12. if we suffer, we shall *r.*
Rev. 5. 10. we shall *r.* on the earth
22. 5. they shall *r.* for ever and
Rom. 5. 14. death *reigned* from
21. that as sin *r.* unto death so
Rev. 20. 4. they lived and *r.* with
1 Chron. 20. 12. thou *reignest* over
Ps. 93. 1. Lord *reigneth*, 97. 1. & 99. 1.
Isa. 52. 7. saith unto Zion, thy God *r.*
Rev. 19. 6. Alleluia, Lord God omnipotent *r.*
R. V. Lev. 26. 17; Deut. 15. 6; Josh. 12. 5; Judg. 9. 2; 1 Kings 4. 21; Rom. 15. 12. rule or ruled

REINS, Job 16. 13. & 19. 27.
Ps. 7. 9. God trieth hearts and *r.*, Jer. 17. 10. & 20. 12. Rev. 2. 23.
Ps. 16. 7. my *r.* instruct me in
73. 21. I was pricked in my *r.*
139. 13. thou hast possessed my *r.*
Prov. 23. 16. my *r.* shall rejoice
Jer. 12. 2. thou art far from their *r.*

REJECT, Mark 6. 26. Gal. 4. 14.
Mark 7. 9. ye *r.* command. of God
Tit. 3. 10. after first and second admonition *r.*
1 Sam. 8. 7. have not *rejected* thee
Isa. 53. 3. is despised and *r.* of men
Jer. 2. 37. Lord hath *r.* confidences
6. 30. Lord *r.* them, 7. 29. & 14. 19.
2 Kings 17. 20. Lam. 5. 22.
Jer. 8. 9. *r.* word of the Lord
Hos. 4. 6. hast *r.* knowledge
Luke 7. 30. *r.* the counsel of God
Heb. 12. 17. was *r.* for he found no
John 12. 48. he that *rejecteth* me

REJOICE, Ex. 18. 9. Deut. 12. 7.
Deut. 28. 63. Lord will *r.* over you
1 Sam. 2. 1. because I *r.* in thy
2 Chron. 6. 41. let thy saints *r.* in
20. 27. the Lord made them to *r.*
Neh. 12. 43. God made them *r.* with
Ps. 2. 11. serve God and *r.* with
5. 11. let those that trust in thee *r.*
9. 14. I will *r.* in thy salvation

Ps. 58. 10. righteous will *r.* when he
63. 7. in the shadow of thy wings
I will *r.*
65. 8. thou makest the morning
and the evening to *r.*
68. 3. let righteous *r.* before God
86. 4. *r.* the soul of thy servant
104. 31. Lord shall *r.* in his works
119. 162. I *r.* at thy word as one
Prov. 5. 18. *r.* with wife of thy
24. 17. *r.* not when enemy falleth
Eccl. 11. 9. *r.* O young man, in thy
Isa. 29. 19. poor among men shall *r.*
62. 5. thy God shall *r.* over thee
Jer. 32. 41. I will *r.* over them to do
Zeph. 3. 17. *r.* over thee with joy
Luke 6. 23. *r.* ye in that day; leap
10. 20. rather *r.* that your names
John 5. 35. willing to *r.* in his light
14. 28. if ye loved me ye would *r.*
Rom. 5. 2. *r.* in hope of glory of God
12. 15. *r.* with them that do *r.*
1 Cor. 7. 30. that *r.* as though *r.* not
Phil. 3. 3. worship God and *r.* in
Col. 1. 24. *r.* in my sufferings for
1 Thes. 5. 16. *r.* evermore
Jas. 1. 9. brother of low degree *r.*
1 Pet. 1. 8. *r.* with joy unspeakable
Ps. 33. 1. *rejoice in the Lord*, 97. 12.
Isa. 41. 16. & 61. 10. Joel 2. 23. Hab.
3. 18. Zech. 10. 7. Phil. 3. 1. & 4. 4.
Ps. 119. 14. I have *rejoiced* in way
Luke 1. 47. my spirit *r.* in God my
10. 21. Jesus *r.* in spirit and said
John 8. 56. Abraham *r.* to see my
1 Cor. 7. 30. as though they *r.* not
Ps. 16. 9. my heart is glad, my
glory *rejoiceth*
28. 7. Lord my heart greatly *r.*
Prov. 13. 9. the light of righteous *r.*
Isa. 62. 5. bridegroom *r.* over bride
64. 5. thou meetest him that *r.*
1 Cor. 13. 6. *r.* not in iniquity
Jas. 2. 13. mercy *r.* against
Ps. 19. 8. the statutes of the Lord
rejoicing the heart
119. 111. are the *r.* of my heart
Prov. 8. 31. *r.* in the habitable
Isa. 65. 18. I create Jerusalem a *r.*
Jer. 13. 15, 16. thy word was the *r.*
Acts 5. 41. *r.* that they were
counted
8. 39. eunuch went on his way *r.*
Rom. 12. 12. *r.* in hope, 5. 2, 3.
2 Cor. 1. 12. our *r.* is the testimony
Gal. 6. 4. he shall have *r.* in him.
Heb. 3. 6. *r.* of hope, firm to the
R. V. 1 Sam. 2. 1; 1 Chron. 16. 32;
Ps. 9. 2; 60. 6; 68. 3, 4; 108. 7; Isa.
13. 3. exult; Ps. 20. 5; Prov. 28. 12.
triumph; Ps. 96. 12; 98. 4. sing for
joy; Ps. 96. 11; 107. 42; Prov. 23.
15; Zech. 10. 7; Acts 2. 26. be glad;
Prov. 31. 25. laugheth; Phil. 2. 16;
3. 3; Jas. 1. 9; 2. 13; 4. 16. glory;
Job 8. 21. shouting; Ps. 107. 22.
singing; 126. 6. joy; 1 Cor. 15. 31;
2 Cor. 1. 12, 14; Gal. 6. 4; Phil. 1.
26; 1 Thes. 2. 19; Heb. 3. 6; Jas. 4.
16. glorying

RELEASE, year of, Ex. 21. 2.
Deut. 15. 1. & 31. 10. Jer. 34. 14.

RELIEVE, Lev. 25. 35. Isa. 1. 17.
Ps. 146. 9. Acts 11. 29. 1 Tim. 5. 16.
R. V. Lev. 25. 35; Ps. 146. 9. uphold;
Lam. 1. 11, 16, 19. refresh

RELIGION, Acts 26. 5. Gal. 1. 13,
14. Jas. 1. 26, 27.
Acts 13. 43. *religious*, Jas. 1. 26.

REMAINDER, 1 Thes. 4. 13. Rev.
3. 2. Eccl. 2. 9. Lam. 5. 19. John 1.
33.
John 9. 41. your sin *remaineth*
2 Cor. 9. 9. righteousness *r.* for
Heb. 4. 9. *r.* a rest for people of God
10. 26. there *r.* no more sacrifice
1 John 3. 9. his seed *r.* in him
Ps. 76. 10. *remainder* of wrath
R. V. Several changes, chiefly to
abide, or to a sense of settling,
rest; Lev. 6. 16. is left; Ps. 76. 10.
residue

REMEDY, 2 Chron. 36. 16. Prov. 6.
15. & 29. 1.

REMEMBER, Gen. 40. 23. Neh. 1.
8.
Gen. 9. 16. look upon it that I may *r.*
Ex. 13. 3. *r.* this day ye came out
Deut. 5. 15. *r.* thou wast a servant
8. 8. thou shalt *r.* Lord thy God
9. 7. *r.* and forget not how
32. 7. *r.* days of old, consider
2 Kings 20. 3. *r.* how I walked
Ps. 20. 7. we will *r.* name of Lord
74. 2. *r.* thy congregation, 18.
79. 8. *r.* not against us former, Isa.
64. 9. Jer. 14. 10. Hos. 8. 13.
89. 47. *r.* how short my time is
132. 1. *r.* David and his afflictions
Eccl. 12. 1. *r.* thy Creator in days
S. of S. 1. 4. we will *r.* thy love
Isa. 43. 25. I will not *r.* thy sins
46. 8. *r.* this, show yourselves
Jer. 31. 20. I do earnestly *r.* him
Ezek. 16. 61. shall *r.* thy ways
63. mayest *r.* and be confounded
36. 31. shall *r.* your own evil
Mic. 6. 5. *r.* what Balak consulted
Hab. 3. 2. in wrath *r.* mercy
Luke 1. 72. to *r.* his holy covenant
17. 32. *r.* Lot's wife, Gen. 19. 26.
Gal. 2. 10. that we should *r.* the
Col. 4. 18. *r.* my bonds
Heb. 8. 12. iniquity I will *r.* no
13. 3. *r.* them that are in bonds
Neh. 13. 14. *r.* me, 22. 31. Ps. 25. 7.
& 106. 4. Luke 23. 43.
Ps. 63. 6. *I remember*, 143. 5.
Jer. 2. 2. for—kindness of thy
Lev. 26. 43. *I will remember* my
covenant, 45. Ezek. 16. 60.
Ps. 79. 11—the works of the Lord
Jer. 31. 34.—their sin no more
Gen. 8. 1. God *remembered* Noah
30. 22. God *r.* Rachel, 1 Sam. 1. 19.
Ex. 2. 24. God *r.* his covenant
Num. 10. 9. shall be *r.* before Lord
Ps. 77. 3. I *r.* God and was troubled
78. 39. he *r.* they were but flesh
98. 3. hath *r.* his mercy and truth
119. 52. I *r.* thy judgments of old
136. 23. who *r.* us in our low estate
137. 1. we wept when we *r.* Zion
Matt. 26. 35. Peter *r.* words of
Luke 24. 8. they *r.* his words, and
John 2. 17. his disciples *r.* that it
Rev. 18. 5. God hath *r.* her iniqui.
Ps. 103. 14. he *r.* we are but dust
Lam. 1. 9. she *r.* not her last end
3. 19. *remembering*, 1 Thes. 1. 3.
1 Kings 17. 18. call my sin to *re-
membrance*
Ps. 6. 5. in death there is no *r.* of
Isa. 26. 8. *r.* of thee
Lam. 3. 20. my soul hath them in *r.*
Mal. 3. 16. in a book of *r.* was
Luke 1. 54. he hath holpen Israel
in *r.* of his mercy
22. 19. this do in *r.* of me
John 14. 26. bring all things to
your *r.*
Acts 10. 31. thy alms are had in *r.*
2 Tim. 1. 6. put in *r.*, 2. 14. 2 Pet. 1.
12. & 3. 1. Jude 5.
Rev. 16. 19. Babylon came in *r.*
R. V. Ps. 20. 7; 77. 11; S. of S. 1. 4;
Hos. 2. 17. mention; Job 32. 12.
memorable sayings; Isa. 57. 8.
memorial; 1 Tim. 4. 6. mind

REMIT sins, they shall, John 20. 23.
Matt. 26. 28. *remission of sins*, Mark
1. 4. Luke 1. 77. & 3. 3. & 24. 47.
Acts 2. 38. & 10. 43. Rom. 3. 25. Heb.
9. 22. & 10. 18.

REMNANT, Lev. 2. 3. Deut. 3. 11.
2 Kings 19. 4. lift up thy prayer
for *r.*
Ezra 9. 8. leave us a *r.* to escape
Isa. 1. 9. Lord left us a small *r.*
10. 21. a *r.* shall return, 22.
Jer. 15. 11. it shall be well with thy
r.
23. 3. I will gather *r.* of my flock
Ezek. 6. 8. yet will I leave a *r.*
Rom. 9. 27. a *r.* shall be saved, 11. 5.
R. V. Lev. 2. 3. which is left; Ex.
2. 12. overhanging part; 2 Kings
25. 11; Jer. 39. 9; Ezek. 23. 25; Mic.
5. 3. residue; Lev. 14. 18; 1 Kings
12. 23; 1 Chron. 6. 70; Ezra 3. 8;
Matt. 22. 6; Rev. 11. 13; 12. 17; 19.
21. rest

REMOVE thy stroke from me, Ps.
39. 10.
Ps. 119. 22. *r.* from me reproach
29. *r.* from me the way of lying
Prov. 4. 27. *r.* thy foot from evil
30. 8. *r.* far from me vanity
Eccl. 11. 10. *r.* sorrow from thy
Matt. 17. 20. *r.* hence, and it shall *r.*
Luke 22. 42. if willing *r.* this cup
Rev. 2. 5. I will *r.* thy candlestick
Ps. 103. 12. so far he *removed* our
Prov. 10. 30. the righteous shall
never be *r.*
Isa. 30. 20. teachers not be *r.*
Ezek. 36. 17. as uncleanness of a *r.*
woman
Gal. 1. 6. so soon *r.* for him that
R. V. Gen. 13. 18; Ps. 104. 5; 125. 1;
Isa. 24. 20. moved; Ex. 20. 18.
trembled; Num. (in all places)
journeyed; 2 Sam. 20. 12; 2 Kings
17. 26; 1 Chron. 8. 6, 7; Isa. 38. 12.
carried; 1 Kings 15. 14; 2 Kings
15. 4, 35. taken away; Job 19. 10;
Isa. 33. 20. plucked up; Isa. 10. 31.
fugitive; Lam. 1. 8; Ezek. 7. 19.
unclean; Deut. 28. 25; Jer. 15. 4;
24. 9; 29. 18; 34. 17; Ezek. 23. 46.
tossed to and fro; Matt. 21. 21;
Mark 11. 23. taken up; other
changes of minor moment

REND heav. and come, Isa. 64. 1.
Joel 2. 13. *r.* hearts and not gar.
Jer. 4. 30. though thou *rendest* face
R. V. Gen. 37. 33; Mark 9. 26. torn;
Jer. 4. 30. enlargest

RENDER vengeance, Deut. 32.
41, 43.
2 Chron. 6. 30. *r.* to every man
Job 33. 26. he will *r.* to man his
34. 11. work of a man shall he *r.* to
Ps. 116. 12. what shall I *r.* to Lord
Prov. 26. 16. men that can *r.* a
Hos. 14. 2. *r.* the calves of our lips
Matt. 22. 21. *r.* to Cesar the things
Rom. 13. 7. *r.* to all their dues
1 Thes. 5. 15. that none *r.* evil, 3. 9.
2 Chron. 30. 25. Hezekiah *rendered*
R. V. Judg. 9. 56, 57. requite; Job
33. 26. restoreth

RENDING the clothes, Gen. 37.
34. 2 Sam. 13. 19. 2 Chron. 34. 27.
Ezra 9. 5. Job 1. 20. & 2. 12. Joel 2.
13; by the high priest, Matt. 26.
65. Mark 14. 63.

RENEW right spirit within me,
Ps. 51. 10.
Isa. 40. 31. wait on Lord shall *r.*
Heb. 6. 6. *r.* them again to repent.
Ps. 103. 5. thy youth is *renewed* like
2 Cor. 4. 16. inward man is *r.* day
Eph. 4. 23. be *r.* in spirit of mind
Col. 3. 10. *r.* in knowledge, image
Ps. 104. 30. *renewest* face of earth
Rom. 12. 2. *renewing*, Tit. 3. 5.

RENOUNCED hidden things of,
1 Cor. 4. 2.

RENOWN, Ezek. 34. 29. & 39. 13.
Isa. 14. 20. *renowned*, Ezek. 23. 23.
R. V. Num. 1. 16. called; Isa. 14.
20. named

REPAIRER of breach., Isa. 58. 12.
R. V. 2 Chron. 24. 27. rebuilding

REPAY, Job 21. 31. & 41. 11.
Deut. 7. 10. he will *r.* him to his
Isa. 59. 18. according to deeds he *r.*
Rom. 12. 19. vengeance is mine, I
will *r.*
Prov. 13. 21. to the righteous good
be *repaid*
R. V. Prov. 13. 21; Rom. 12. 19.
recompense

REPENT of this evil, Ex. 32. 12.
Num. 23. 19. not the son of man
that he should *r.*
Deut. 32. 36. Lord shall *r.* himself
1 Sam. 15. 29. not man that he
should *r.*
1 Kings 8. 47. *r.* and make suppli.
Job 42. 6. I abhor and *r.* in dust

Ps. 90. 13. let it *r.* thee concerning
135. 14. will *r.* himself concerning
Jer. 18. 8. I will *r.* of evil I
Ezek. 14. 6. *r.* and return, 18. 30.
Joel 2. 14. if he will *r.* and
Jonah 3. 9. can tell if God will turn and *r.*
Matt. 3. 2. *r.* for kingdom of
Mark 1. 15. *r.* and believe Gospel
6. 12. preached that men should *r.*
Luke 13. 3. except ye *r.* ye shall
17. 3. if he *r.* forgive him, 4.
Acts 2. 38. *r.* and be baptized
3. 19. *r.* and be converted, that
17. 30. commandeth all men to *r.*
26. 30. should *r.* and turn to God
Rev. 2. 5. rem. whence fall. and *r.*
16. *r.* or I will come unto thee
21. I gave her space to *r.* of her
3. 19. be zealous and *r.*
Gen. 6. 6. *repented* the Lord, Ex. 32. 14. Judg. 2. 18. 2 Sam. 24. 16. Joel 2. 13.
Jer. 8. 6. no man *r.* of his wicked.
Matt. 21. 29. afterward *r.* and went
27. 3. Judas *r.* himself, and
Luke 15. 7. one sin. that *repenteth*
Jer. 15. 6. *repenting*, Hos. 11. 8.
Hos. 13. 14. *repentance* hid from
Matt. 3. 8. fruits meet for *r.*
11. baptiz. you with water unto *r.*
9. 13. not righte. but sinners to *r.*
Mark 1. 4. baptism of *r.*, Luke 3. 3.
Luke 15. 7. just persons need no *r.*
24. 47. that *r.* and remission be
Acts 5. 31. give *r.* to Israel and
11. 18. God to Gentiles granted *r.*
20. 21. testifying *r.* towards God
Rom. 2. 4. goodness of God leadeth thee to *r.*
2 Cor. 7. 10. sorrow worketh *r.*
Heb. 6. 1. not laying foundation of *r.*
12. 17. found no place of *r.*
2 Pet. 3. 9. all should come to *r.*
R. V. 1 Kings 8. 47. turn again; Ezek. 14. 6; 18. 30. return ye; 2 Cor. 7. 8. regret; Matt. 9. 13; Mark 2. 17 —— ; *compassions;* Hos. 11. 8. my *c.* are kindled together

REPETITIONS, vain, Matt. 6. 7.

REPLIEST against God, Rom. 9. 20.

REPORT, evil, Gen. 37. 2. Num. 13. 32. & 14. 37. Neh. 6. 13.
Ex. 23. 1. should not raise a false *r.*
Prov. 15. 30. good *r.* maketh bones
Isa. 53. 1. who hath believed our *r.*, John 12. 38. Rom. 10. 16.
2 Cor. 6. 8. by evil *r.* and good *r.*
1 Tim. 3. 7. a good *r.* of them who
Heb. 11. 2. obtained a good *r.*
R. V. Isa. 28. 19. message; Jer. 50. 43. fame; Prov. 15. 30. good tidings; 1 Tim. 3. 7. testimony; Heb. 11. 2, 39; 3 John 12. witness; Neh. 6. 19 spake of; 1 Pet. 1. 12. announced; Matt. 28. 15. spread abroad

REPROACH, Josh. 5. 9. Neh. 1. 3. Ps. 69. 7. Prov. 18. 3. Isa. 54. 4. Jer. 31. 19. Heb. 13. 13. Gen. 30. 23. Luke 1. 25.
Job 27. 6. my heart shall not *r.* me
Ps. 15. 3. up a *r.* against neighbor
20. *r.* hath broken my heart
Prov. 14. 34. sin is a *r.* to any peo.
Isa. 51. 7. fear ye not the *r.* of men
Zeph. 3. 18. to whom *r.* of it
Heb. 11. 26. esteeming the *r.* of Christ
Ps. 69. 9. *r.* of them that *reproached*
2 Cor. 12. 10. I take pleasure in *reproaches*
Prov. 14. 31. *reproacheth* his Maker
1 Pet. 4. 14. if *reproached* for name
R. V. Prov. 22. 10. ignominy; Job 20. 3. reproof; 2 Cor. 11. 21. disparagement; 12. 10. injuries; Isa. 43. 28. a reviling; Num. 15. 30. blasphemeth

REPROBATE, Jer. 6. 30. Rom. 1. 28. 1 Cor. 13. 5, 6, 7. 2 Tim. 3. 8. Tit. 1. 16.
R. V. Jer. 6. 30. refuse

REPROOF, astonished at, Job 26. 11.
Prov. 1. 23. turn ye at my *r.* I will
10. 17. he that refuseth *r.* erreth
13. 18. he that regardeth *r.* shall be honored
15. 5. he that regardeth *r.* is
10. he that hateth *r.* shall die
31. heareth *r.* abideth among wise
17. 10. *r.* entereth more into a wise
29. 15. the rod and *r.* give wisdom
2 Tim. 3. 16. Scripture profitable for *r.*
Ps. 38. 14. *reproofs*, Prov. 6. 23.
Ps. 50. 21. I will *reprove* thee, and
Prov. 9. 8. *r.* not a scorner, lest he
Hos. 4. 4. let no man strive nor *r.*
John 16. 8. *r.* world of sin
Eph. 5. 11. works of dark. but *r.*
Ps. 105. 14. he *reproved* kings
Prov. 29. 1. he that being often *r.*
John 3. 20. deeds should be *r.*
Eph. 5. 13. things that are *r.* are
Isa. 29. 21. snare from him that *reproveth* in the gate
Prov. 9. 7. that *r.* a scorner, getteth
15. 12. loveth not one that *r.* him
25. 12. *reprover*, Ezek. 3. 26.
R. V. Job 26. 11; Prov. 17. 10. rebuke; 2 Kings 19. 4; Isa. 37. 4; Jer. 29. 27. rebuke; John 16. 8. convict

REPUTATION, Eccl. 10. 1. Acts 5. 34. Gal. 2. 2. Phil. 2. 7, 29.
R. V. Eccl. 10. 1. outweigh; Acts 5. 34. honor of; Gal. 2. 2. repute; Phil. 2. 7. emptied himself

REQUEST, Ps. 106. 15. Phil. 4. 6.
R. V. Phil. 1. 4. supplication

REQUIRE, Gen. 9. 5. & 42. 22. Ezek. 3. 18, 20. & 33. 8.
Deut. 10. 12. what doth the Lord *r.*
18. 19. speak in my name, I will *r.*
1 Kings 8. 59. maintain as matter shall *r.*
Prov. 30. 7. two things I *required*
Isa. 1. 12. who *r.* this at your
Luke 12. 20. shall thy soul be *r.*
48. of him shall much be *r.*
1 Cor. 4. 2. it is *r.* of stewards to be
R. V. Neh. 5. 18. demanded; Ex. 12. 36; Prov. 30. 7; Luke 23. 23, 25. ask; Ruth 3. 11. sayest; Eccl. 3. 15. seeketh again

REQUITE, Gen. 50. 15. 2 Sam. 16. 12.
Deut. 32. 6. do ye thus *r.* the Lord
1 Tim. 5. 4. learn to *r.* their parents
2 Chron. 6. 23. by *requiting* wicked
R. V. 1 Sam. 25. 21. returned; Ps. 10. 14. take

RERE-WARD, Isa. 52. 12. & 58. 8.

RESERVE, Jer. 50. 20. 2 Pet. 2. 9.
Jer. 3. 5. will he *r.* his anger for ever
Job 21. 30. wicked is *reserved* to
1 Pet. 1. 4. inheritance *r.* in heav.
Jude 6. *r.* in everlasting chains
Jer. 5. 24. he *reserveth* the appoin.
Nah. 1. 2. *r.* wrath for his enemies
R. V. Deut. 33. 21. seated; Judg. 21. 22. took; Ruth 2. 18; Rom. 11. 4. left; Acts 25. 21; Jude 6. kept

RESIDE, Zeph. 2. 9. Matt. 1. 15.

RESIST not evil, Matt. 5. 39.
Zech. 3. 1. Satan at his right hand to *r.* him
Acts 7. 51. ye do always *r.* the Holy
2 Tim. 3. 8. so do these *r.* the truth
Jas. 4. 7. *r.* the devil and he
1 Pet. 5. 9. whom *r.* steadfast in
Rom. 9. 19. who hath *resisted* will
Heb. 12. 4. have not yet *r.* to blood
Rom. 13. 2. that *resisteth* shall
Jas. 4. 6. God *r.* proud, 1 Pet. 5. 5.
R. V. Luke 21. 15; Acts 6. 10; Rom. 9. 19; 13. 2; 2 Tim. 3. 8; 1 Pet. 5. 9. withstand; Zech. 3. 11. be adversary

RESPECT to Abel, Lord had, Gen. 4. 4. Ex. 2. 25. Lev. 26. 9. 2 Kings 13. 23.
Deut. 1. 17. ye shall not *r.* persons
2 Chron. 19. 7. nor *r.* of persons, Rom. 2. 11. Eph. 6. 9. Col. 3. 25. Acts 10. 34. Job 37. 24. 1 Pet. 1. 17.
Ps. 40. 4. *r.* not the proud
119. 6. *r.* to all thy commandments
138. 6. *r.* the lowly
Prov. 24. 23. not good to have *r.* of persons, 28. 21. Lev. 19. 15. Jas. 2. 1, 3, 9.
Heb. 11. 26. he had *r.* to recom.
R. V. Ex. 2. 25. took knowledge; Heb. 11. 26. looked; Jas. 2. 3. regard; Job 37. 24. regardeth

REST, Ex. 16. 23. & 33. 14. Deut. 12. 9.
Ps. 95. 11. not enter into my *r.*
116. 7. return to thy *r.* O my soul
132. 14. this is my *r.* here I will
Isa. 11. 10. his *r.* shall be glorious
28. 12. this is the *r.* and refreshing
62. 7. him no *r.* till he establish
Jer. 6. 16. shall find *r.* for your
Mic. 2. 10. this is not your *r.* it is
Matt. 11. 28, 29. I will give *r.* to
Acts 9. 31. had the churches *r.*
2 Thes. 1. 7. who are troubled *r.*
Heb. 4. 9. *r.* for the people of God
10. enter into his *r.*
11. enter into that *r.* lest any
Rev. 14. 11. they have no *r.* day not
Ps. 16. 9. my flesh shall *r.* in hope
37. 7. *r.* in the Lord and wait
Isa. 57. 2. in peace *r.* on their beds
20. wicked are like the troubled sea when it cannot *r.*
Hab. 3. 16. I might *r.* in the
Zeph. 3. 17. he will *r.* in his love
Rev. 14. 13. dead in the Lord, *r.*
Rom. 2. 17. art a Jew, and *restest*
Prov. 14. 33. wisdom *resteth*
Eccl. 7. 9. anger *r.* in bosom
1 Pet. 4. 14. Spirit of God *r.* upon
Num. 10. 33. *resting place*, 2 Chron. 6. 41. Prov. 24. 15. Isa. 32. 18. Jer. 50. 6.
R. V. Several changes, but none of moment

RESTORE, Ps. 51. 12. & 23. 3. & 69. 4. Isa. 58. 12. Luke 19. 8. Gal. 6. 1.
Ex. 22. 3. *restitution*, Acts 3. 21.
R. V. Job 20. 18. hath gotten; Acts 3. 21. restoration; Ex. 22. 1. pay; Lev. 24. 21. make good; 25. 28. get it back; 2 Chron. 8. 2. given

RESTRAIN, 1 Sam. 3. 13. Job 15. 4. Ps. 76. 10. Isa. 63. 15.
R. V. Gen. 11. 6. withholden

RESURRECTION, Matt. 22. 23, 28, 30. Acts 23. 8. 1 Cor. 15. 12. Heb. 6. 2.
Luke 20. 36. children of God being children of the *r.*
John 5. 29. done good to *r.* of life
11. 25. I am the *r.* and the life
Acts 17. 18. preached Jesus and *r.*
Rom. 6. 5. in likeness of his *r.*
Phil. 3. 10. power of *r.*
11. attain unto the *r.* of the dead
1 Tim. 2. 18. erred, say. that *r.* is
Heb. 11. 35 might obtain better *r.*
Rev. 20. 5. this is the first *r.*, 6.

RETAIN, Job 2. 9. John 20. 23. Prov. 3. 18. & 11. 16. Eccl. 8. 8. Rom. 1. 28.
Mic. 7. 18. *retaineth* not his anger
R. V. Job 2. 9. hold fast; Rom. 1. 28. have; Phile. 13. fain have kept

RETURN to the ground, Gen. 3. 19. *r.* to dust
1 Kings 8. 48. *r.* to thee with all
Job 1. 21. naked shall I *r.* thither
Ps. 73. 10. his people *r.* hither
116. 7. *r.* unto thy rest, O my soul
Eccl. 12. 7. dust shall *r.* to the
S. of S. 6. 13. *r.* *r.* O Shulamite
Isa. 10. 21. remnant shall *r.* to
35. 10. the ransomed of the Lord shall *r.*, 51. 11.
55. 11. my word shall not *r.* void
Jer. 3. 12. *r.* backsliding Israel
4. 1. if thou wilt *r.* *r.* unto me
Hos. 2. 7. *r.* to my first husband
5. 15. I will go and *r.* to my place
7. 16. they *r.* but not to Most High
11. 9. not *r.* to destroy Ephraim

Mal. 3. 7. *r.* to me, and I will *r.* to
Ps. 35. 13. my prayer *returned*
78. 34. they *r.* and inquired early
Amos 4. 6. ye *r.* not to me, 8-11.
1 Pet. 2. 25. are *r.* unto Shepherd
Isa. 30. 15. in *returning* and rest
Jer. 5. 3. they refused to *return*
Deut. 30. 2. *return to the Lord*, 1 Sam. 7. 3. Isa. 55. 7. Hos. 6. 1. & 3. 5. & 7. 10. & 14. 1, 7.
R. V. Several unimportant changes, chiefly to sense of turned, came, or bring back
REVEAL, Prov. 11. 13. Dan. 2. 19.
Job 20. 27. heaven shall *r.* his ini.
Gal. 1. 16. pleased God to *r.* his
Phil. 3. 15. God shall *r.* even this
Deut. 29. 29. those things which are *revealed*
Isa. 22. 14. it was *r.* in mine ears
53. 1. to whom is arm of Lord *r.*
Matt. 10. 26. covered that shall not be *r.*
11. 25. hid from wise, and *r.*
16. 17. flesh and blood hath not *r.*
Rom. 1. 17. righteous. of God *r.*
1 Cor. 2. 10. God hath *r.* them to us
2 Thes. 1. 7. when the Lord Jesus shall be *r.*
2. 3. fall. away, man of sin be *r.*
Prov. 20. 19. a tale-bearer *revealeth*
Amos 3. 7. *r.* his secret to servants
Rom. 2. 5. *revelation*, 16. 25. Gal. 1. 12. Eph. 1. 17. & 3. 3. 1 Pet. 1. 13. 2 Cor. 12. 1. Rev. 1. 1.
R. V. 1 Cor. 14. 30; 2 Thes. 1. 7; 1 Pet. 4. 13. revelation
REVELLINGS, Gal. 5. 21. 1 Pet. 4. 3.
REVENGE, Jer. 15. 15. 2 Cor. 7. 11. & 10. 6. Nah. 1. 2.
Ps. 79. 10. by *revenging* blood
Num. 35. 19. *revenger*, Rom. 13. 4.
R. V. Deut. 32. 42. leaders; 2 Cor. 7. 11. avenging; Jer. 15. 15; 2 Cor. 10. 6. avenge
REVERENCE my sanctuary, Lev. 19. 30.
Ps. 89. 7. to be had in *r.* of all
Eph. 5. 33. see that she *r.* her
Heb. 12. 28. serve God acceptably with *r.*
Ps. 111. 9. and *reverend* is his name
R. V. 2 Sam. 9. 6; 1 Kings 1. 31. obeisance; Ps. 89. 7. feared above; Eph. 5. 33. fear
REVILE, Ex. 22. 28. Matt. 5. 11.
1 Cor. 4. 12. being *reviled* we bless
1 Pet. 2. 23. when he was *r.* *r.* not
1 Cor. 6. 10. nor *revilers* inherit
Isa. 51. 7. *revilings*, Zeph. 2. 8.
R. V. Matt. 27. 39. railed on; Mark 15. 32. reproached
REVIVE us again, Ps. 85. 6.
Isa. 57. 15. to *r.* the spirit of the
Hos. 6. 2. after two days will *r.* us
14. 7. they shall *r.* as the corn
Hab. 3. 2. *r.* thy work in midst of
Rom. 7. 9. sin *revived* and I died
14. 9. Christ died, and rose, and *r.*
Ezra 9. 8. give us a little *reviving*
R. V. Ps. 85. 6. quicken; Rom. 14. 9. lived again
REVOLT more and more, Isa. 1. 5.
Isa. 31. 6. children of Israel have deeply *revolted*
Jer. 5. 23. this people hath a *revolting heart*
6. 28. *revolters*, Hos. 5. 2. & 9. 5.
REWARD, exceeding great, Gen. 15. 1.
Deut. 10. 17. God taketh not *r.*
Ps. 19. 11. keeping them is great *r.*
58. 11. there is a *r.* for righteous
Prov. 11. 18. that soweth righteousness sure *r.*
Isa. 3. 11. the *r.* of his hands
5. 23. who justify wicked for a *r.*
Mic. 7. 3. the judge asketh for a *r.*
Matt. 5. 12. great is your *r.* in
6. 2. verily they have their *r.*
10. 41. shall receive a prophet's *r.*

Rom. 4. 4. *r.* is not reckoned of
1 Cor. 3. 8. shall receive his own *r.*
Col. 2. 18 man beguile you of *r.*
1 Tim. 5. 18. labor. is worthy of *r.*
Heb. 2. 2. just recompense of *r.*
2 John 8. we may receive a full *r.*
Matt. 6. 4. Father shall *r.* openly
2 Tim. 4. 14. Lord *r.* him accord.
Rev. 22. 12. I come and my *r.* is with
18. 6. *r.* her as she *rewarded* you
Ps. 103. 10. nor *r.* us according
Isa. 3. 9. *r.* evil unto themselves
Ps. 31. 23. plentifully *rewardeth*
Heb. 11. 6. *rewarder* of them that
R. V. Job 6. 22; Prov. 21. 14; Jer. 40. 5. present; Job 7. 2. wages; Ps. 40. 15; 70. 3. by reason; 94. 2. desert; Ezek. 16. 34; Hos. 2. 12; 9. 1; 1 Tim. 5. 18; 2 Pet. 2. 13; Jude 11. hire; Obad. 15. dealing; Col. 2. 18. prize by; 3. 24. recompense; 1 Sam. 24. 17; Matt. 16. 27; 2 Tim. 4. 14; Rev. 18. 6. render; Deut. 32. 41; Matt. 6. 4, 6, 18. recompense; Ps. 54. 5. requite
RICH, Gen. 13. 2. & 14. 23. Ex. 30. 15.
Prov. 10. 4. hand of diligent maketh *r.*
22. bless. of the Lord maketh *r.*
13. 7. maketh himself *r.* yet
14. 20. *r.* man hath many friends
18. 11. *r.* man's wealth is
23. the *r.* answereth roughly
22. 2. *r.* and poor meet together
23. 4. labor not to be *r.*
28. 11. *r.* man is wise in his
Eccl. 5. 12. abundance of the *r.*
10. 20. curse not the *r.* in thy
Jer. 9. 23. let not *r.* man glory in
Matt. 19. 23. *r.* man hardly enter
Luke 1. 53. *r.* he sent empty away
6. 24. woe unto you that are *r.*
12. 21. layeth up, and is not *r.*
16. 1. certain *r.* man which had
18. 23. sorrow. for he was very *r.*
2 Cor. 6. 10. yet making many *r.*
8. 9. Jesus, though he was *r.*
Eph. 2. 4. God who is *r.* in mercy
1 Tim. 6. 9. they that will be *r.*
18. they that be *r.* in good works
Jas. 2. 5. poor of this world, *r.*
Rev. 2. 9. I know thy poverty, but thou art *r.*
3. 17. sayest, I am *r.*
18. mayest be *r.*
1 Chron. 29. 12. *riches* and honor
Ps. 39. 6. he heapeth up *r.* and
52. 7. trust. in abundance of his *r.*
62. 10. if *r.* increase, set not
104. 24. the earth is full of thy *r.*
112. 3. wealth and *r.* shall be
119. 14. rejoic. as much as in all *r.*
Prov. 3. 16. in her left hand *r.*
11. 4. *r.* profit not in day of
13. 8. ransom of man's life are his *r.*
23. 5. *r.* make themselves wings
27. 24. *r.* are not for ever, nor the
30. 8. give me neither pover. nor *r.*
Jer. 17. 11. so he that getteth *r.*
Matt. 13. 22. deceitfulness of *r.*
Luke 16. 11. your trust the true *r.*
Rom. 2. 4. despisest thou *r.* of his
9. 23. known the *r.* of his glory
2 Cor. 8. 2. abounded unto *r.* of
Eph. 1. 7. according to the *r.* of
2. 7. show exceeding *r.* of grace
Phil. 4. 19. according to his *r.* in
Col. 2. 2. unto all *r.* of the full
1 Tim. 6. 17. trust in uncertain *r.*
Heb. 11. 26. the reproach of Christ greater *r.*
Jas. 5. 2. your *r.* are corrupted
Col. 3. 16. word of God dwell *richly*
1 Tim. 6. 17. giveth us *r.* all things
R. V. Gen. 36. 7; Dan. 11. 13, 24, 28. substance; Josh. 22. 8; Isa. 61. 6. wealth; Ps. 37. 16; Jer. 48. 36. abundance; Prov. 22. 16. gain
RIDE, Ps. 45. 4. & 66. 12. Hab. 3. 8.
Deut. 33. 26. *rideth*, Ps. 68. 4, 33. Isa. 19. 1.
RIGHT, Num. 27. 7. Deut. 21. 17.

Gen. 18. 25. shall not the Judge of the earth do *r.*
Ezra 8. 21. seek of him a *r.* way for
Job 34. 23. lay on man more than *r.*
Ps. 19. 8. statu. of the Lord are *r.*
51. 10. renew a *r.* spirit within
119. 128. I esteem all thy precepts to be *r.*
Prov. 4. 11. I have led thee in *r.* paths
8. 9. all *r.* to them that find
12. 5. thoughts of righteous are *r.*
14. 12. a way which seemeth *r.* to
21. 2. way of man is *r.* in own
Isa. 30. 10. prophesy not unto us *r.*
Ezek. 18. 5. be just and do lawful and *r.*
Hos. 14. 9. ways of the Lord are *r.*
Amos 3. 10. know not to do *r.*
Mark 5. 15. and in his *r.* mind
Luke 12. 57. jud. ye not what is *r.*
Acts 4. 19. whether it be *r.* in sight
8. 21. thy heart is not *r.* in sight
13. 10. not cease to pervert *r.* ways
Eph. 6. 1. children obey your parents; this is *r.*
2 Pet. 2. 15. forsaken the *r.* way
Rev. 22. 14. have *r.* to tree
2 Tim. 2. 15. *rightly* dividing word
Gen. 7. 1. seen thee *righteous* be.
18. 23. wilt thou destroy *r.*
Num. 23. 10. let me die death of *r.*
Deut. 25. 1. justify *r.* and condemn
1 Kings 8. 32. justifying the *r.* to
Job 4. 7. where were the *r.* cut off
17. 9. the *r.* shall hold on his way
Ps. 1. 6. Lord knoweth way of *r.*
5. 12. wilt bless the *r.* with favor
7. 11. God judgeth the *r.*
11. 5. Lord trieth *r.* but wicked
32. 11. rejoice in the Lord ye *r.*
34. 17. *r.* cry, and Lord heareth
37. 17. the Lord upholdeth the *r.*
25. I have not seen the *r.* forsaken
29. the *r.* shall inherit the land
55. 22. shall never suffer the *r.*
58. 11 there is a reward for the *r.*
64. 10. *r.* shall be glad in the Lord
68. 3. let the *r.* be glad and rejoice
92. 12. the *r.* shall flourish like
97. 11. light is sown for the *r.*
112. 6. the *r.* shall be in everlast.
141. 5 let *r.* smite me; it shall be
Ps. 145. 17. Lord is *r.*, Lam. 1. 18. Dan. 9. 14.
146. 8. the Lord loveth the *r.*
Prov. 3. 22. his secret is with the *r.*
10. 3. will not suffer the soul of *r.*
16. labor of the *r.* tendeth to life
21. the lips of the *r.* feed many
24. desire of the *r.* shall be grant.
25. *r.* is an everlasting foundation
28. the hope of *r.* shall be glad.
30. the *r.* shall never be removed
32. the lips of the *r.* know what
11. 8. *r.* is delivered out of
21. seed of *r.* shall be delivered
28. the *r.* shall flourish as a
30. fruit of the *r.* is a tree of life
12. 3. root of *r.* shall not be
5. the thoughts of the *r.* are *r.*
7. the house of the *r.* shall
10. a *r.* man regardeth life of
12. root of *r.* yieldeth fruit
13. 9. the light of the *r.* rejoiceth
25. *r.* eateth to satisfying of soul
14. 32. *r.* hath hope in his death
15. 6. in house of *r.* is much
29. Lord heareth the prayer of *r.*
18. 10. *r.* runneth into it and is
28. 1. the *r.* are bold as a lion
Eccl. 7. 16. be not *r.* overmuch, nor
Isa. 3. 10. say to *r.* it shall be well
41. 2. raised up *r.* man from east
57. 1. the *r.* perisheth and are
60. 21. thy people also shall be *r.*
Ezek. 3. 20. when a *r.* man turneth
Mal. 3. 18. discern between *r.* and
Matt. 9. 13. not come to call *r.* but
10. 41. shall receive *r.* man's rew.
25. 46. *r.* shall go into life eternal
Luke 1. 6. were both *r.* before God
18. 9. trusted that they were *r.*

Rom. 3. 10. there is none *r.* no not
5. 7. scarcely for a *r.* man will one
19. by the ob. of one many made *r.*
2 Thes. 1. 5. a manifest token of *r.* judgment
1 Tim. 1. 9. law is not made for a *r.*
Jas. 5. 16. fervent prayer of *r.* man
1 Pet. 4. 18. the *r.* scarcely be saved
1 John 3. 7. he that doeth righteousness is *r.* even as he is *r.*
Rev. 22. 11. he that is *r.* let him be *r.*
Tit. 2. 12. live soberly, *righteously*
Deut. 6. 25. it shall be our *righteousness*
33. 19. offer sacrifice of *r.*
Job 29. 14. I put on *r.* and it cloth.
36. 3. I will ascribe *r.* to my Maker
Ps. 11. 7. righteous Lord loveth *r.*
15. 2. walk. upright. and work. *r.*
97. 2. *r.* and judgment are habita.
106. 3. he that doeth *r.* at all
Prov. 10. 2. *r.* delivereth from
11. 5. *r.* of perfect shall direct way
6. *r.* of upright shall deliver them
18. to him that soweth *r.* a sure
19. *r.* tendeth to life; so evil to
12. 28. in the way of *r.* is life
13. 6. *r.* keepeth the upright in
14. 34. *r.* exalteth a nation, but sin
15. 9. he loveth him that followeth after *r.*
16. 8. better is a little with *r.* than
12. his throne is established by *r.*
Isa. 11. 5. *r.* shall be girdle of his
26. 9. inhabitants of the world will learn *r.*
28. 17. judgment to line and *r.* to
32. 17. work of *r.* shall be peace
45. 24. in the Lord have I *r.* and
46. 12. far from *r.*
13. I bring near my *r.*
54. 17. their *r.* is of me, saith Lord
61. 3. trees of *r.* planting of Lord
10. covered me with robes of *r.*
62. 1. till the *r.* thereof go forth
64. 5. that rejoiceth and work. *r.*
Jer. 23. 6. be called Lord our *r.*
Dan. 4. 27. break off thy sins by *r.*
9. 7. O Lord *r.* belongeth unto thee
12. 3. that turn many to *r.* shine
Zeph. 2. 3. seek *r.* seek meekness
Mal. 4. 2. Sun of *r.* arise with
Matt. 3. 15. it becom. to fulfil all *r.*
5. 6. hunger and thirst after *r.*
20. except your *r.* exceed the *r.* of
21. 32. John came in the way of *r.*
Luke 1. 75. in holiness and *r.* before
John 16. 8. reprove world of sin, *r.*
Acts 10. 35. he that worketh *r.* is
13. 10. thou enemy of all *r.*
24. 25. as he reasoned of *r.*
Rom. 1. 17. therein is the *r.* of God
3. 22. even *r.* of God by faith
4. 6. man to whom God imput. *r.*
11. a seal of the *r.* of faith
5. 18. by *r.* of one free gift came
21. grace reign through *r.* unto
6. 13. membe. as instruments of *r.*
18. servants of *r.* to holiness, 19.
8. 4. that the *r.* of the law might
9. 30. Gentiles who followed not after *r.* have attained to *r.* even *r.* of faith, 31.
10. 3. ignorant of *r.* of God, establish their own *r.* have not submitted to *r.* of God
5. *r.* of law
6. *r.* which is of faith
9, 10. with the heart man beli. to *r.*
14. 17. kingdom of God is *r.* peace
1 Cor. 1. 30. made unto us wisdom and *r.*
15. 34. awake to *r.* and sin not
2 Cor. 5. 21. the *r.* of God in him
6. 7. armor of *r.*
14. what fellowship hath *r.*
9. 10. increase the fruits of your *r.*
11. 15. ministers as ministers of *r.*
Gal. 2. 21. if *r.* come by the law
Eph. 6. 14. having on the breastplate of *r.*
Phil. 1. 11. being filled with fruits of *r.*
3. 6. touching *r.* of law blameless

1 Tim. 6. 11. follow *r.*, 2 Tim. 2. 22.
Tit. 3. 5. not by works of *r.* we
Heb. 12. 11. peaceable fruits of *r.*
Jas. 1. 20. man worketh not the *r.* of God
3. 18. fruit of *r.* is sown in peace
1 Pet. 3. 14. if ye suffer for *r.* happy
2 Pet. 1. 1. through the *r.* of God
2. 5. Noah a preacher of *r.*
3. 13. wherein dwelleth *r.*
1 John 2. 29. that doeth *r.* is born
3. 7. he that doeth *r.* is righteous
Rev. 19. 8. fine linen is the *r.* of saints
Gen. 15. 6. counted to him for *righteousness*, Ps. 106. 31. Rom. 4. 3, 5, 9, 22. Gal. 3. 6.
1 Kings 8. 32. *his righteousness*, Job 33. 26. Ps. 50. 6. Ezek. 3. 20. Matt. 6. 33. Rom. 3. 25. 2 Cor. 9. 9.
Ps. 17. 15. *in righteousness*, Hos. 10. 12. Acts 17. 31. Ps. 96. 13. & 98. 9. Eph. 4. 24. Rev. 19. 11.
Deut. 9. 5. *thy righteousness*, Job 35. 8. Ps. 35. 28. & 40. 10. & 51. 14. & 89. 16. & 119. 142. Isa. 57. 12. & 58. 8. & 62. 2.
Isa. 64. 6. *all our righteousness*, Ezek. 33. 13. Dan. 9. 18.
R. V. Many changes, chiefly due to context. Many changes in Job, Ps., and Prov. to upright; Ps. 67. 4; 96. 10. with equity; Rom. 2. 26; 8. 4. ordinance; Rom. 9. 28; 10. 3——

RIGOR, Ex. 1. 13. Lev. 25. 43, 53.

RIOT, Tit. 1. 6. 1 Pet. 4. 4.
2 Pet. 2. 13. *rioting*, Rom. 13. 13.
Prov. 23. 20. *riotous*, 28. 7. Luke 15. 13.
R. V. Rom. 13. 13. revelling; 2 Pet. 2. 13. revel; Prov. 23. 20; 28. 7. gluttonous

RIPE fruit, Ex. 22. 29. Num. 18. 13. Mic. 7.1. Jer. 24. 2; *r.* figs, Hos. 9. 10. Nah. 3. 12.
Gen. 40. 10. *ripe grapes*, Num. 13. 20.
Joel 3. 13. harvest is *r.*, Rev. 14. 15.

RISE, S. of S. 3. 2. Isa. 14. 21. & 24. 20. & 26. 14. & 33. 10. & 43. 17. & 54. 17. & 58. 10. 1 Thes. 4. 16.
Prov. 30. 31. *rising*, Luke 2. 34.
R. V. Many changes to arise; oth. frequent but suiting context

RIVER, Ex. 1. 22. & 4. 9. Job 40. 23. Ps. 36. 8. & 46. 4. & 65. 9. Isa. 48. 18. & 66. 12. Rev. 22. 1, 2.
Job 20. 17. *rivers*, 29. 9. Ps. 119. 136. Prov. 5. 16. & 21. 1. Isa. 32. 2. & 33. 21. Mic. 6. 7. John 7. 38.
R. V. Num. 34. 5; Deut. 10. 7; Josh. 15. 4, 47; 16. 8; 17. 9; 19. 11; 1 Kings 8. 65; 2 Kings 24. 7; 2 Chron. 7. 8; S. of S. 5. 12; Ezek. 47. 19; Amos 6. 14; Joel 3. 18. brook or brooks; Ezek. 6. 3; 31. 12; 32. 6; 34. 13; 35. 8; 36. 4, 6; Prov. 21. 1. water courses; Deut. 2. 24, 36; 3. 8, 12; 4. 48; Josh. 12. 1, 2; 13. 9, 16; 2 Sam. 24. 5; 2 Kings 10. 33. valley; Ex. 8. 5; Ps. 1. 3. streams; Isa. 23. 3, 10; Zech. 10. 11. Nile; Job 28. 10; Ezek. 31. 4. channels

ROAR, Isa. 42. 13. Jer. 25. 30. Hos. 11. 10. Joel 3. 16. Amos 1. 2.
R. V. Isa. 42. 13. shout aloud

ROB, Lev. 19. 13. Prov. 22. 22.
Mal. 3. 8. will a man *r.* God
Isa. 42. 22. a people *robbed* and
2 Cor. 11. 8. I *r.* other churches
Job 5. 5. the *robber* swalloweth up
John 10. 1. that climbeth up is a thief and a *r.*
Ps. 62. 10. *robbery*, Prov. 21. 7. Isa. 61. 8. Amos 3. 10. Phil. 2. 6.
R. V. Ps. 119. 61. wrapped me round; Job 5. 5; 18. 9. snare; Dan. 11. 14. children of the violent; Prov. 21. 7. violence; Nah. 3. 1. rapine

ROBE, Isa. 61. 10. Rev. 7. 9, 13, 14.
R. V. Luke 23. 11. apparel; John 19. 2. garment; Rev. 22. 14. do his commandments

ROCK, Ex. 17. 6. Num. 20. 8, 11. Deut. 32. 4, 13, 15, 18, 30, 31.
Ps. 18. 2. Lord is my *r.* and, 92. 15.
31. 3. thou art my *r.* and fortress
61. 2. lead me to the *r.* higher
62. 2. he only is my *r.* and, 6.
71. 3. thou art my *r.* and fortress
89. 26. my Father and *r.* of my
94. 22. God is the *r.* of my refuge
Matt. 7. 24. wise man built his house on a *r.*
16. 18. on this *r.* will I build
1 Cor. 10. 4. that *r.* was Christ
Rev. 6. 16. said to *rocks*, fall on us
R. V. Judg. 6. 26. stronghold; 1 Sam. 14. 4. crag; Isa. 42. 11. Sela; Luke 6. 48. well builded; Acts 27. 29. rocky ground

ROD, Ex. 4. 4, 20. Num. 17. 2, 8.
Ps. 23. 4. thy *r.* and staff comfort
125. 3. *r.* of wicked shall not rest
Prov. 13. 24. spareth *r.* hateth his
22. 15. *r.* of correction shall drive
29. 15. *r.* and reproof give wisdom
Isa. 10. 5. *r.* of my anger, staff of
Ezek. 20. 37. cause to pass under *r.*
Mic. 6. 9. hear the *r.*
Rev. 12. 5. rule with *r.* of iron, 19.
R. V. Ps. 125. 3. sceptre; Isa. 11. 1. shoot; Jer. 10. 16; 51. 19. tribe

ROOM, Prov. 18. 6. Luke 14. 22.
R. V. 2 Kings 15. 25; 1 Chron. 4. 41. stead; Ps. 31. 8; Luke 14. 9, 10; 20. 46; 1 Cor. 14. 16. place; Matt. 23. 6; Mark 12. 39. chief place; Luke 14. 7. 8. chief seat; Acts 1. 13. chamber

ROOT, Job 5. 3. & 31. 12. Ps. 52. 5. Deut. 29. 18. a *r.* that beareth gall
Job 19. 28. seeing *r.* of the matter
Prov. 12. 3. *r.* of the righteous
Isa. 11. 10. there shall be *r.*
Matt. 3. 10. axe is laid to *r.* of tree
13. 6. because it had no *r.* it
Rom. 11. 16. if *r.* be holy, so are
1 Tim. 6. 10. love of money is *r.* of
Heb. 12. 15. lest *r.* of bitterness
Matt. 15. 13. plant Father hath not planted shall be *rooted* up
Eph. 3. 17. being *r.* and grounded
Col. 2. 7. *r.* and built up in him

ROSE, S. of S. 2. 1. Isa. 35. 1.

ROYAL diadem in hand of God, Isa. 62. 3.
Jas. 2. 8. if ye fulfil *r.* law
1 Pet. 2. 9. ye are a *r.* priesthood

RUBIES, price of wisdom is above, Job 28. 18. Prov. 3. 15. & 8. 11. & 31. 10.

RUDDY, S. of S. 5. 10. Lam. 4. 7.

RUDIMENTS, Col. 2. 8, 20.

RULE, Esth. 9. 1. Prov. 17. 2.
Prov. 25. 28. no *r.* over own spirit
Gal. 6. 16. walk according to this *r.*
Phil. 3. 16. let us walk by same *r.*
Heb. 13. 7. which have *r.* over you
Col. 3. 15. let the peace of God *r.*
1 Tim. 3. 5. how to *r.* his own house
5. 17. let the elders that *r.*
Rev. 12. 5. man child was to *r.* all
2 Sam. 23. 3. *ruleth* over men
Ps. 103. 19. his kingdom *r.* over all
Prov. 16. 32. he that *r.* his spirit
Hos. 11. 12. Judah yet *r.* with God
Mic. 5. 2. is to be *ruler* in Israel
Matt. 25. 21. make thee *r.* over
Acts 23. 5. not speak evil of *r.*
Rom. 13. 3. *rulers* are not a terror
Eph. 6. 12. *r.* of darkness of world
R. V. 1 Kings 22. 31. command; Prov. 25. 26. restraint; Isa. 44. 13. line; 2 Cor. 10. 13, 15. province; Ezek. 22. 33. be king; Matt. 2. 6. be shepherd; Ruth 1. 1. judged; Gen. 43. 16. steward; Num. 13. 2; 1 Sam. 25. 30; 2 Sam. 6. 21; 7. 8; 1 Kings 1. 35; 1 Chron. 2. 12; 5. 2; 11. 2; 17. 7; 28. 4; 2 Chron. 6. 5; 11. 22; 29. 20; Ezra 10. 14; Neh. 11. 1; Esth. 3. 12; 8. 9; 9. 3. prince or princes; 1 Kings 11. 28; Neh. 7. 2. charge; 2 Kings 25. 22; Mark 13. 9; Luke 21. 12. governor; 2 Chron. 26. 11. officer; 2 Sam. 8. 18; 20. 26. priest; Gen. 41. 43; Matt. 24. 45, 47; 25. 21.

23. set; Deut. 1. 13; Isa. 29. 10. heads; 1 Chron. 26. 32. overseers; Jer. 51. 23, 28, 57. deputies
RUN, Gen. 49. 22. Lev. 15. 3. 1 Sam. 8. 11. Ps. 19. 5. Eccl. 1. 7. Heb. 6. 20. 2 Chron. 16. 9. eyes of the Lord *r.*
Ps. 119. 32. I will *r.* in way
S. of S. 1. 4. draw me, we will *r.*
Isa. 40. 31. shall *r.* and not be
Dan. 12. 4. many shall *r.* to and
1 Cor. 9. 24. *r.* so that we may
Gal. 2. 2. *r.* in vain
5. 7. did *r.* well
Heb. 12. 1. *r.* with patience the race
1 Pet. 4. 4. *r.* not to same excess of
Ps. 23. 5. my cup *runneth* over
Prov. 18. 10. righteous *r.* into it
Rom. 9. 16. it is not of him that *r.*
R. V. Judg. 18. 25. fall; 1 Sam. 17. 17. carry quickly; Amos 5. 24. roll; Joel 2. 9. leap upon; Matt. 9. 17. is spilled

S

SABBATH holy, Ex. 16. 23, 29. & 20. 8-11. & 31. 14. Acts 13. 42. & 18. 4.
Lev. 23. 3. seventh day is *s.* of rest
Neh. 9. 14. madest known thy *s.*
13. 18. bring wrath by profan. *s.*
Isa. 56. 2. keepeth *s.* from pollut.
58. 13. call *s.* a delight, holy
Matt. 12. 5. priests profane *s.* and
28. 1. end of *s.* as it began to dawn
Lev. 19. 3. *my sabbaths*, 30. & 26. 2. Isa. 56. 4. Ezek. 20. 12, 13. & 22. 8, 26. & 23. 38. & 44. 24. & 46. 3.
Deut. 5. 12. *sabbath day*, Neh. 13. 22. Jer. 17. 21. Acts 15. 21. Col. 2. 16.
R. V. Lev. 23. 24, 39. solemn rest; Lam. 1. 7. desolations
SACKCLOTH, Gen. 37. 34. Job 16. 15. Ps. 30. 11. & 35. 13. Isa. 22. 12. Rev. 11. 3.
SACRIFICE, Gen. 31. 54. Ex. 8. 25.
1 Sam. 2. 29. wherefore kick ye at my *s.*
3. 14. Eli's house not purg. with *s.*
15. 22. to obey is better than *s.*
Ps. 4. 5. offer *s.* of righteousness
40. 6. *s.* and offering thou
51. 16. desirest not *s.* else I would
17. *s.* of God are a broken spirit
107. 22. *s.* the *s.* of thanksgiving
141. 2. lifting up hands as even. *s.*
Prov. 15. 8. *s.* of wicked is abomination
21. 3. to do justice more acceptable than *s.*
Eccl. 5. 1. than to give *s.* of fools
Dan. 8. 11. daily *s.* was taken away
9. 27. cause *s.* and oblation to cease
11. 31. take away daily *s.*, 12. 11.
Hos. 6. 6. mercy and not *s.*
Mark 9. 49. every *s.* be salted
Rom. 12. 1. present bodies a liv. *s.*
1 Cor. 5. 7. Christ our passover is *s.*
Eph. 5. 2. *s.* to God for a sweet
Phil. 2. 17. offered on *s.* of your
4. 18. a *s.* acceptable to God
Heb. 9. 26. put away sin by *s.* of
13. 15. *s.* of praise
1 Pet. 2. 5. priesthood to offer spiritual *s.*
R. V. In O. T. frequent changes to offering, oblation
SACRILEGE, commit, Rom. 2. 22.
SAD, 1 Sam. 1. 18. Ezek. 13. 22. Mark 10. 22.
Eccl. 7. 3. by *sadness* the heart is
R. V. Ezek. 13. 22. grieved; Mark 10. 22. countenance fell
SAFE, Ps. 119. 117. Prov. 18. 10. & 29. 25.
Job 5. 4. *safety*, 11. Ps. 4. 8. & 12. 5. & 33. 17. Prov. 11. 14. & 21. 31.
R. V. Ezek. 34. 27. secure; 2 Sam. 18. 29, 32. well with; Job 3. 26. ease; 24. 23. security; Prov. 21. 31. victory
SAINTS, Ps. 52. 9. & 79. 2. & 89. 5.
Deut. 33. 2. came with ten thousands of *s.*, Jude 14.
Deut. 33. 3. all his *s.* are in thy
1 Sam. 2. 9. keep feet of his *s.*
2 Chron. 6. 41. let thy *s.* rejoice
Job 15. 15. he putteth no trust in *s.*
Ps. 16. 3. goodness extendeth to *s.*
37. 28. Lord forsaketh not his *s.*
50. 5. gather my *s.* together
97. 10. Lord preserveth souls of *s.*
106. 16. envied Aaron *s.* of Lord
116. 15. precious in the sight of the Lord is death of *s.*
149. 9. this honor have all his *s.*
Prov. 2. 8. preserv. way of his *s.*
Hos. 11. 12. Judah is faith. with *s.*
Zech. 14. 5. shall come and all *s.*
Rom. 1. 7. called to be *s.*, 1 Cor. 1. 2. 2 Cor. 1. 1. Eph. 1. 1. Col. 1. 2, 4, 12, 26.
Rom. 8. 27. intercession for *s.*
12. 13. necessity of *s.*
15. 25. minister to *s.*, 26. 31. 1 Cor. 16. 1. 2 Cor. 8. 4. & 9. 1. Heb. 6. 10.
1 Cor. 6. 2. *s.* shall judge the world
Eph. 3. 8. less than the least of all *s.*
4. 12. for perfecting the *s.* for
1 Thes. 3. 13. coming of Jesus with all his *s.*
2 Thes. 1. 10. come to be glorified in his *s.*
Rev. 5. 8. prayers of the *s.*, 8. 3, 4.
11. 18. reward of *s.*
14. 11. patience of *s.*
15. 3. King of *s.*
16. 16. blood of *s.*, 17. 6. & 18. 24.
19. 8. righteousness of *s.*
R. V. Deut. 33. 2; 1 Sam. 2. 9; Job 5. 11; 15. 15; Ps. 89. 5, 7; Dan. 8. 13; Hos. 11. 12; Zech. 14. 5; Jude 14. holy one, or ones; Rev. 15. 3. ages
SALT, Gen. 19. 26. Lev. 2. 13. Matt. 5. 13. Mark 9. 49, 50. Col. 4. 6.
R. V. Mark 9. 49 ——
SALVATION, Ps. 14. 7. & 53. 6.
Ex. 14. 13. stand still and see the *s.*
Ps. 3. 8. *s.* belongeth only to Lord
50. 23. I will show him the *s.* of
68. 20. God is the God of *s.*, 65. 5.
85. 9. his *s.* is nigh them that
98. 2. made known his *s.*
119. 155. *s.* is far from the wicked
149. 4. Lord will beautify the meek with *s.*
Isa. 25. 9. we will rejoice in his *s.*
26. 1. *s.* will God appoint for walls
33. 2. our *s.* also in the
46. 13. I will place *s.* in Zion for
52. 7. him that publisheth *s.*
59. 16. arm brought *s.* unto me
17. for a helmet of *s.*, Eph. 6. 17.
Ps. 60. 18. call thy walls *s.* thy
62. 1 [illegible] as a lamp
Jer. 3. 23. in vain is *s.* hoped for
Lam. 3. 26. quietly wait for *s.*
Jonah 2. 9. *s.* is of the Lord
Hab. 3. 8. ride on thy char. of *s.*
Zech. 9. 9. king cometh having *s.*
Luke 19. 9. *s.* is come to thy house
John 4. 22. *s.* is of the Jews
Acts 4. 12. neither is there *s.* in
13. 26. word of *s.* sent
Rom. 1. 16. Gospel is the power of God to *s.*
11. 11. through their fall *s.* is come
2 Cor. 1. 6. for your *s.*
Eph. 1. 13. the Gospel of your *s.*
Phil. 2. 12. work out your own *s.*
1 Thes. 5. 8. hope of *s.*
2 Thes. 2. 13. hath chosen you to *s.*
2 Tim. 2 10. to obtain *s.* with eter.
3. 15. scriptures able to make wise unto *s.*
Tit. 2. 11. grace of God bringeth *s.*
Heb. 1. 14. who shall be heirs of *s.*
2. 3. how escape if we neglect so great *s.*
10. make Captain of our *s.* perfect
6. 9. things that accompany *s.*
9. 28. appear without sin unto *s.*
1 Pet. 1. 5. kept through faith to *s.*
Jude 3. write unto you of com. *s.*
Rev. 7. 10. *s.* to our God, 12. 10. & 19. 1.
Ex. 15. 2. God is become *my salvation*, Job 13. 16. Ps. 18. 2. & 25. 5. & 27. 1. & 38. 22. & 51. 14. & 62. 7. & 88. 1. & 118. 14. Isa. 12. 2. Mic. 7. 7. Hab. 3. 18.
Ps. 89. 26. rock of —
140. 7. strength of —
2 Sam. 23. 5. thy covenant is all —
Isa. 46. 13. — shall not tarry, 49. 6. & 51. 5, 6, 8. & 56. 1.
Gen. 49. 18. *thy salvation*, 1 Sam. 2. 1. Ps. 9. 14. & 13. 5. & 20. 5. & 18. 35. & 21. 1, 5. & 35. 3. & 40. 10, 16. & 51. 12. & 69. 13, 29. & 70. 4. & 71. 15. & 85. 7. & 106. 4. & 119. 41, 81, 123, 166, 174. Isa. 17. 10. & 62. 11. Luke 2. 30.
R. V. 1 Sam. 11. 13; 2 Sam. 22. 51; Ps. 68. 20. deliverance; 1 Sam. 19. 5. victory; Jer. 3. 23. help; 2 Cor. 1. 6 ——
SAME, Ps. 102. 27. Heb. 13. 8. Rom. 10. 2. 1 Cor. 12. 4, 5, 6. Eph. 4. 10.
SANCTIFY, Ex. 13. 2. & 19. 10.
Ex. 31. 13. I am Lord that doth *s.*
Lev. 20. 7. *s.* yourselves and be holy
Num. 20. 12. believed me not, to *s.*
Isa. 8. 13. *s.* the Lord of hosts
Ezek. 28. 23. I will *s.* myself
Joel 1. 14. *s.* a fast
John 17. 17. *s.* them through truth
19. for their sakes I *s.* myself
Eph. 5. 26. might *s.* and cleanse it
1 Thes. 5. 23. God of peace *s.* you
Heb. 13. 12. that he might *s.* people
1 Pet. 3. 15. *s.* the Lord God in
Gen. 2. 3. blessed the seventh day and *sanctified* it
Lev. 10. 3. I will be *s.* in them
Deut. 32. 51. ye *s.* me not in midst
Job 1. 5. Job sent and *s.* them
Isa. 5. 16. God that is holy shall be *s.*
13. 3. commanded my *s.* ones
Jer. 1. 5. before thou camest I *s.*
Ezek. 20. 41. be *s.* in you before the heathen, 28. 22, 25. & 38. 16. & 39. 27.
John 10. 36. whom Father hath *s.*
Acts 20. 32. inheritance among all them which are *s.*, 26. 18.
Rom. 15. 16. offering of Gent. *s.*
1 Cor. 1. 2. *s.* in Christ Jesus
7. 14. unbelieving husband is *s.*
1 Tim. 4. 5. *s.* by word and
2 Tim. 2. 21. *s.* and meet for mas.
Heb. 2. 11. they who are *s.* all
Matt. 23. 17. temple that *sanctifieth*
1 Cor. 1. 30. *sanctification*, 1 Thes. 4. 3, 4. 2 Thes. 2. 13. 1 Pet. 1. 2.
R. V. Gen. 2. 3; 2 Chron. 7. 16, 20. hallowed: Deut. 5. 12. keep it holy; 1 Sam. 21. 5. be holy; Isa. 13. 3. consecrated; Jude 1. beloved
SANCTUARY, Ps. 63. 2. & 73. 17. Isa. 8. 14 Ezek. 11. 16. Dan. 9. 17. Heb. 9. 2.
R. V. Ezek. 45. 2; Heb. 9. 2; 13. 11. holy place
SAND, Gen. 22. 17. & 32. 12. Job 6. 3. & 29. 18. Isa. 10. 22. Matt. 7. 26.
SATAN provoked David, 1 Chron 21. 1.
Job 1. 6. *s.* came also among
Ps. 109. 6. let *s.* stand at his right
Matt. 4. 10. get thee hence *s.*
Luke 10. 18. I beheld *s.* as light.
22. 31. *s.* hath desired to

Acts 26. 18. turn from power of *s.*
Rom. 16. 20. God shall bruise *s.*
1 Cor. 5. 5. deliver such a one to *s.*
7. 5. that *s.* tempt you not for
2 Cor. 2. 11. lest *s.* get advantage
11. 14. *s.* is transformed into angel
12. 7. messenger of *s.* to
1 Tim. 1. 20. I have delivered to *s.*
Rev. 2. 9. synagogue of *s.*
24. depth of *s.*
SATIATE, Jer. 31. 14, 25. & 46. 10.
SATISFY, Job 38. 27. Prov. 6. 30.
Ps. 90. 14. O *s.* us early with mercy
91. 16. with long life I will *s.* him
103. 5. who *s.* thy mouth with
107. 9. he *s.* the longing soul
132. 15. will *s.* her poor with
Prov. 5. 19. breasts *s.* thee at all
Isa. 55. 2. that which *s.* not
Ps. 17. 15. *satisfied* with thy like.
22. 26. meek shall eat and be *s.*
63. 5. soul shall be *s.* as with
65. 4. *s.* with goodness of house
Prov. 14. 14. good man *s.* from
27. 20. eyes of man are never *s.*
30. 15. are three things never *s.*
Eccl. 5. 10. that loveth silver shall not be *s.*
Isa. 9. 20. shall eat and not be *s.*
66. 11. be *s.* with breasts of her
Jer. 31. 14. my people be *s.* with
Ezek. 16. 28. couldest not be *s.*
Amos 4. 8. they were not *s.*
Hab. 2. 5. his desire cannot be *s.*
Num. 35. 31. shall take no *satisfaction*, 32.
R. V. Prov. 12. 11. have plenty; 18. 20. filled
SAVE your lives, preserve and, Gen. 45. 7.
Gen. 50. 20. for good to *s.* much
Job 22. 29. he shall *s.* the humble
Ps. 18. 27. wilt *s.* afflicted people
28. 9. *s.* thy people and lift them
69. 35. God will *s.* Zion
72. 4. *s.* children of needy
13. *s.* souls of needy
86. 2. *s.* thy servant
109. 31. poor to *s.* him
118. 25. *s.* now; send prosperity
Prov. 20. 22. he shall *s.* thee
Isa. 35. 4. God will come and *s.*
45. 25. cannot *s.*, 59. 1. Jer. 9. 14.
Isa. 49. 25. I will *s.* thy children
Ezek. 18. 27. shall *s.* his soul
36. 29. I will *s.* from all unclean.
Hos. 1. 7. I will *s.* them by Lord
Zeph. 3. 17. he will *s.*
19. *s.* her that halteth
Zech. 8. 7. I will *s.* my people
Matt. 1. 21. *s.* his people from sins
16. 25. who will *s.* his life shall
8. 11. Son of man is come to *s.* that which was lost, Luke 19. 10.
Mark 3. 4. Is it lawful to *s.* life or
John 12. 47. not to judge but to *s.*
Acts 2. 40. *s.* yourselves from this
1 Cor. 1. 21. by foolishness of preaching to *s.*
9. 22. became all, that I might *s.*
1 Tim. 1. 15. to *s.* sinners, of whom
Heb. 7. 25. able to *s.* to the utter.
Jas. 1. 21. word able to *s.*
2. 14. faith *s.*
5. 15. faith shall *s.* sick
20. converts a sinner shall *s.* soul
Jude 23. others *s.* with fear
Ps. 6. 4. *save me*, 55. 16. & 57. 3. & 119. 94. Jer. 17. 14. John 12. 27.
Isa. 25. 9. *save us*, 33. 22. & 37. 20. Hos. 14. 3. Matt. 8. 25. 1 Pet. 3. 21.
Ps. 44. 7. thou hast *saved* us from
106. 8. *s.* them for his name's sake
Isa. 45. 22. look . . and be ye *s.*
Jer. 4. 14. mayest be *s.*
8. 20. we are not *s.*
Matt. 19. 25. who then can be *s.*, Luke 18. 29.
Luke 1. 71. be *s.* from our enemies
7. 50. thy faith hath *s.* thee
13. 23. are few *s.*
23. 35. he *s.* others
John 3. 17. through him be *s.*
Acts 2. 47. added to church such as should be *s.*
4. 12. name whereby be *s.*
16. 30. what must I do to be *s.*
Rom. 8. 24. we are *s.* by hope
10. 1. prayer for Israel that they may be *s.*
1 Cor. 1. 18. to us who are *s.* it is
Eph. 2. 5. by grace ye are *s.*, 8.
1 Tim. 2. 4. all men to be *s.*
Tit. 3. 5. according to his mercy *s.*
1 Pet. 4. 18. righteous scarcely be *s.*
Rev. 21. 24. nations which are *s.*
Ps. 80. 3. *shall be saved*, 7. 19. Isa. 45. 17. & 64. 5. Jer. 23. 6. & 30. 7. Matt. 10. 22. & 24. 13. Mark 16. 16. Acts 16. 31. Rom. 5. 10, 11, 26. 1 Tim. 2. 15.
2 Sam. 22. 3. God my refuge and my *Saviour*
2 Kings 13. 5. Lord gave Israel a *S.*
Ps. 106. 21. forgat God their *S.*
Isa. 43. 3. I am thy *S.*, 49. 26.
11. besides me is no *S.*, Hos. 13. 4.
45. 15. of Israel, the *S.*, Jer. 14. 8.
Obad. 21. *S.* shall come up on
Luke 1. 47. rejoiced in God my *S.*
2. 11. to you is born a *S.* which is
Acts 5. 31. him hath God exalted to be a *S.*
Eph. 5. 23. Christ is head and *S.*
1 Tim. 4. 10. who is the *S.* of all men, 1. 1; God our *S.*, Tit. 1. 4. & 2. 10, 13. & 3. 4, 6. 2 Pet. 1. 1, 11. Jude 25.
2 Pet. 2. 20. knowledge of our *S.*
SAVOR, sweet, Gen. 8. 21. Ex. 29. 18. Lev. 1. 9. & 2. 9. & 3. 16.
S. of S. 1. 3. of *s.* of thy good oint.
2 Cor. 2. 14. the *s.* of his knowledge
15. are to God a sweet *s.* of Christ
16. to one *s.* of death
Eph. 5. 2. sacrifice to God of sweet smelling *s.*
Matt. 16. 23. *savorest* not things of God
SAY, Matt. 3. 9. & 5. 22, 28, 32, 34, 39, 44. & 7. 22. & 23. 3. 1 Cor. 12. 3.
R. V. Frequent changes to speak, tell, etc.
SCAB, Lev. 13. 1; Deut. 28. 27; Isa. 3. 17.
SCARCELY, Rom. 5. 7. 1 Pet. 4. 18.
SCATTER them in Israel, Gen. 49. 7.
Num. 10. 35. let thine enemies be *scattered*
Matt. 9. 36. *s.* abroad as sheep
Luke 1. 51. *s.* proud in imagination
Prov. 11. 24. that *scattereth* and yet
SCEPTRE not depart from Judah, Gen. 49. 10.
Num. 24. 17. a *s.* shall rise out of
Ps. 45. 6. the *s.* of thy kingdom is
Zech. 10. 11. *s.* of Egypt shall de.
R. V. 2 Sam. 10. 0, Job 37. 1. spread; Ps. 60. 1. broken down; Prov. 20. 26. winnoweth; Isa. 18. 2 tall; 30. 30. a blast; Dan. 12. 7. breaking in pieces; Ezek. 12. 15; Acts 5. 36. disperse; Jas. 1. 1; 1 Pet. 1. 1. the Dispersion
SCHISM, 1 Cor. 1. 10. &. 12. 25.
SCHOLAR, 1 Chron. 25. 8. Mal. 2. 12.
Gal. 3. 24. the law was our *schoolmaster*
R. V. Mal. 2. 12. that answereth
SCOFFERS, Hab. 1. 10. 2 Pet. 3. 3.
R. V. Mal. 2. 12. that answereth
SCORN, Job 16. 20. Ps. 44. 13.
Prov. 9. 8. reprove not a *scorner*
14. 6. a *s.* seeketh wisdom and
1. 22. *scorners* delight in scorning
3. 34. he *scorneth* the *s.* but giveth
9. 12. if thou *scornest* thou
Ps. 1. 1. *scornful*, Prov. 29. 8. Isa. 28. 14.
R. V. Job 12. 4. laughing-stock; Hab. 1. 10. derision; Prov. 19. 28. mocketh at
SCORPIONS, 2 Chron. 10. 11. Ezek. 2. 6.
SCOURGE of the tongue, Job 5. 21.
Isa. 28. 15. overflowing *s.*, 18.
Heb. 12. 6. Lord *scourgeth* every
R. V. Lev. 19. 20. punished
SCRIPTURE of truth, Dan. 10. 21.
Matt. 22. 29. err, not knowing *s.*
John 5. 39. search *s.*, Acts 17. 11. & 18. 24.
Rom. 15. 4. through comfort of *s.*
2 Tim. 3. 15. from a child known *s.*
16. all *s.* is given by inspiration
2 Pet. 1. 20. no prophecy of *s.* is of private interpretation
R. V. Dan. 10. 21. writing; 2 Tim 3. 15. holy writing; Mark 15. 28 ——
SCROLL, the heavens compared to, Isa. 34. 4; Rev. 6. 14.
SEA, Ps. 35. 7. & 72. 8. Prov. 8. 29. Isa. 48. 18. & 57. 20. Zech. 9. 10. Rev. 4. 6. & 10. 2. & 15. 2. & 21. 1.
SEAL upon thine heart, S. of S. 8. 6.
John 3. 33. set to his *s.* that God is
Rom. 4. 11. *s.* of the righteousness
1 Cor. 9. 2. *s.* of my apostleship
2 Tim. 2. 19. having *s.* Lord know.
Rev. 7. 2. angel having *s.* of living
Deut. 32. 34. *sealed* up among
Job 14. 17. my transgression is *s.*
S. of S. 4. 12. spring shut up, fountain *s.*
John 6. 27. hath God the Father *s.*
2 Cor. 1. 22. who hath *s.* us and
Eph. 1. 13. ye were *s.* with the
Rev. 5. 1. a book *s.* with seven
7. 3. *s.* the servants of our God
4. were *s.* a hundred and forty
R. V. Rev. 7. 5-8 ——
SEARCH out resting place, Num. 10. 33.
Ps. 139. 23. *s.* me, O God, and
Prov. 25. 27. men to *s.* own glory
Jer. 17. 10. I the Lord *s.* the heart
29. 13. when ye shall *s.* with me
Lam. 3. 40. *s.* and try our ways
Zeph. 1. 12. *s.* Jerusalem with
Acts 17. 11. *s.* Scriptures, John 5. 39.
1 Chron. 28. 9. the Lord *searcheth* all hearts
1 Cor. 2. 10. Spirit *s.* deep things
Rev. 2. 23. I am he that *s.* the
Job 10. 6. that *searchest* after my
Prov. 2. 4. *s.* for her as for hidden
Judg. 5. 16. great *searchings* of
R. V. Job 38. 16. recesses; Gen. 31. 34, 37. felt about; Num. 10. 33; Deut. 1. 33. seek; Num. 13. 2, 21, 32; 14. 6, 7, 34, 36, 38; Deut. 1. 24. spy or spied out; Acts 17. 11. examining; Num. 13. 25. spying out
SEARED, with hot iron, 1 Tim. 4. 2.
SEASON, Gen. 40. 4. Ex. 13. 10.
Ps. 1. 3. bring. forth fruit in his *s.*
Eccl. 3. 1. to . . thing there is a *s.*
Isa. 50. 4. to speak a word in *s.*
Luke 4. 13. depart. from him for *s.*
John 5. 35. willing for a *s.* to re.
Acts 1. 7. know the times and *s.*
14. 17. gave us rain and fruitful *s.*
1 Thes. 5. 1. of times and *s.* ye
2 Tim. 4. 2. instant in *s.* and out
Heb. 11. 25. pleasures of sin for a *s.*
1 Pet. 1. 6. for a *s.* ye are in heav.
Col. 4. 6. let speech be *seasoned*
R. V. Josh. 24. 7. days; 1 Chron. 21. 29; Luke 23. 8; Acts 20. 18; Rev. 6. 11; 20. 3. time; Acts 19. 22; 1 Pet. 1. 6. while; John 5. 4 ——
SECOND COMING, Christ's, Acts 1. 11.
SECOND DEATH, Rev. 20. 14.
SECRET, Gen. 49. 6. Job 40. 13.
Job 11. 6. show thee *s.* of wisdom
29. 4. *s.* of God on my tabernacle
Ps. 25. 14. *s.* of Lord is with them
31. 20. hide them in *s.* presence
Prov. 3. 32. his *s.* is with righteous
9. 17. bread eaten in *s.* is pleasant
11. 13. talebearer revealeth *s.*
25. 9. discover not *s.* to another
Dan. 2. 28. a God that revealeth *s.*
Amos 3. 7. revealeth his *s.* unto
Matt. 6. 4. alms in *s.* Father seeth in *s.*

John 18. 20. in s. have I said no.
19. 38. *secretly* for fear of Jews
Rom. 2. 16. when God shall judge *secrets* of men
R. V. Gen. 49. 6. council; Judg. 13. 18. wonderful; Job 40. 13; Ps. 19. 12; Prov. 27. 5; Eccl. 12. 14; Matt. 13. 35. hidden; Ps. 10. 8; 27. 5; 31. 20; S. of S. 2. 14. covert; Ps. 18. 11. hiding; Job 20. 26. treasures; Matt. 24. 26. inner; Luke 11. 33. cellar; 1 Sam. 23. 9——; Ps. 10. 9. the covert
SECT, Acts 24. 5. & 26. 5. & 28. 22.
SEDITION, Gal. 5. 20; 2 Pet. 2. 19.
SEDUCE, Ezek. 13. 10. Mark 13. 22.
2 Tim. 3. 13. *seducers*, 1 Tim. 4. 1.
R. V. Isa. 19. 13; Mark 13. 22; 1 John 2. 26. go or lead astray
SEE, Ps. 34. 8. Matt. 5. 8. John 16. 22. 1 John 3. 2. Rev. 1. 7. & 22. 4.
Matt. 6. 1. before men to be *seen* of
13. 17. to see and have not s.
23. 5. their works to be s.
John 1. 18. no man hath s. God
14. 9. he that hath s. me hath s. the Father
20. 29. thou hast s. and believed
2 Cor. 4. 18. look not at things s.
1 Tim. 6. 16. no man hath s.
Heb. 11. 1. evidence of things not s.
1 Pet. 1. 8. having not s. ye love
1 John 1. 1. that which we have s.
12. no man hath s. God at any
Job 10. 4. seest thou as man *seeth*
John 12. 17. because it s. him not
12. 45. he that s. me, s. him that
SEED, Gen. 1. 11. & 17. 7. & 38. 9.
Ps. 126. 6. bearing precious s.
Eccl. 11. 6. in morning sow thy s
Isa. 55. 10. give s. to the sower
Matt. 13. 38. good s. are children
Luke 8. 11. good s. is word of God
1 Pet. 1. 23. born again not of corruptible s.
1 John 3. 9. his s. remaineth in
Ps. 37. 28. s. of wicked shall be
69. 36. s. of his servants
Prov. 11. 21. s. of righteous
Isa. 1. 4. sinful nation s. of evil
14. 20. the s. of evil doers
45. 5. all s. of Israel be justified
Mal. 2. 15. might seek a godly s.
Rom. 9. 8. children are count. for s.
Gal. 3. 16. not to *seeds* but to thy s.
SEEK, Ezra 8. 21. Job 5. 8. Ps. 10. 15.
Deut. 4. 29. if thou s. him with all the heart, 1 Chron. 28. 9. 2 Chron. 15. 2. Jer. 29. 13.
2 Chron. 19. 3. prepare heart to s. God, 30. 19.
Ezra 8. 22. them for good that s.
Ps. 9. 10. forsake them that s.
63. 1. God, early will I s. thee
69. 32. heart . live that s. God
119. 2. bless. are they that s. him
Prov. 8. 17. that s. me early
S. of S. 3. 2. s. him whom soul lov.
Isa. 26. 9. my spirit will I s. thee
45. 19. I said not s. me in vain
Jer. 29. 13. he shall s. me and
Amos 5. 4. s. me and ye shall live
Zeph. 2. 3. s. Lord, s. righteous.
Mal. 2. 7. s. the law
Matt. 6. 33. s. first kingdom of God
7. 7. s. and ye shall find
Luke 13. 24. many will s. to enter
19. 10. to s. and to save that which is lost, Matt. 18. 11.
John 8. 21. shall s. me and not
Rom. 2. 7. s. for glory, honor
1 Cor. 10. 24. let no man s. own
13. 5. charity s. not her own
Phil. 2. 21. all s. their own, not
Col. 3. 1. s. things which are above
1 Pet. 3. 11. s. peace and ensue it
Lam. 3. 25. to soul that *seeketh*
John 4. 23. the Father s. such
1 Pet. 5. 8. *seeking* whom he may
SEEM, Gen. 27. 12. Deut. 25. 3.
1 Cor. 11. 16. if any man s. conten.
Heb. 4. 1. lest any s. to come short
Jas. 1. 26. if any s. to be religious
Luke 8. 18. taken that he *seemeth*
1 Cor. 3. 18. if any man s. wise
Heb. 12. 11. no chastening s. joyous
SELF-DENIAL, Prov. 23. 2. Jer. 35. Luke 3. 11. & 14. 33. Acts 2. 45. Rom. 6. 12. & 8. 13. & 14. 20. & 15. 1. 1 Cor. 10. 23. & 13. 5. & 24. 33. Gal. 5. 24. Phil. 2. 4. Tit. 2. 12. 1 Pet. 2. 11.
Christ an example of, Matt. 4. 8. & 8. 20. Rom. 15. 3. Phil. 2. 6.
incumbent on His followers, Matt. 10. 38. & 16. 24. Mark 8. 34. Luke 9. 23.
SELF-EXAMINATION enjoined, Lam. 3. 40. Ps. 4. 4. 1 Cor. 11. 28. 2 Cor. 13. 5.
SELFISHNESS, Isa. 56. 11. Rom. 15. 1. 1 Cor. 10. 24. 2 Cor. 5. 15. Phil. 2. 4, 21. 2 Tim. 3. 2. Jas. 2. 8.
SELF-WILL, Ps. 75. 5. Tit. 1. 7. 2 Pet. 2. 10.
SELL me thy birthright, Gen. 25. 31.
Prov. 23. 23. buy truth and s. it
Matt. 19. 21. go s. that thou hast
25. 9. go to them that s. and buy
13. 44. he *selleth* all and buyeth
R. V. Jas. 4. 13. trade
SENATORS, Ps. 105. 22.
SEND help from the sanctuary, Ps. 20. 2.
Ps. 43. 3. O s. out thy light and
57. 3. he shall s. from heaven
Matt. 9. 38. s. forth laborers into
John 14. 26. the Father will s.
16. 7. if I depart I will s. him
2 Thes. 2. 11. s. them strong delus.
R. V. Gen. 12. 20. brought; Judg. 5. 15. rushed forth; other changes of slight moment, and chiefly dependent on antecedent or consequent word
SENSE, Neh. 8. 8. Heb. 5. 14.
Jas. 3. 15. *sensual*, Jude 19.
SENTENCE, Deut. 17. 9. Dan. 12.
Prov. 16. 10. a divine s. is in lips
2 Cor. 1. 9. we had s. of death in
R. V. Jer. 4. 12; Acts 15. 19. judgment
SEPARATE, Gen. 13. 9. Ex. 33. 16.
Gen. 49. 6. head of him that was s. from his brethren, Deut. 33. 16.
Deut. 29. 21. Lord shall s. him
Isa. 59. 2. iniquities have *separated*
Acts 13. 2. s. me Saul and Barna.
19. 9. departed and s. the disciples
Rom. 8. 35. who s. us from Christ
2 Cor. 6. 17. come out, be ye s.
Gal. 1. 15. who s. me from moth.
Heb. 7. 26. holy, harmless, s. from
R. V. Num. 6. 2. make special; Jer. 37. 12. receive his portion; Hos. 4. 14. go apart; 9. 10. consecrated
SERAPHIMS, Isa. 6. 2, 6.
SERMON on the mount, Matt. 5-7. Luke 6. 20. *See* CHRIST.
SERPENT, Gen. 3. 1, 13. & 49. 17.
Num. 21. 6. Lord sent fiery s., 8. 9.
Prov. 23. 32. it biteth like a s.
Eccl. 10. 11. s. will bite without
Matt. 7. 10. will he give him a s.
10. 16. be wise as s. harmless as
John 3. 14. as Moses lifted up s.
2 Cor. 11. 3. as the s. beguiled Eve
Rev. 12. 9. that old s. called devil
R. V. Deut. 32. 24. crawling things; Jas. 3. 7. creeping things
SERVE the Lord with all thy heart, Deut. 10. 12, 20. & 11. 13. Josh. 22. 5. 1 Sam. 12. 20.
Deut. 13. 4. shall s. him, and cleave
Josh. 24. 14. fear the Lord, s. him
15. choose this day whom ye will s. . . me and my house, we will s. the Lord
1 Sam. 12. 24. fear the Lord, s. him
Job 21. 15. what is the Almighty that we should s. him
Ps. 2. 11. s. Lord with fear, rejoice
Isa. 43. 24. made me to s. with sins
Matt. 6. 24. no man can s. two masters; ye cannot s. God and mam.
Luke 1. 74. s. him in holiness
12. 37. will come forth and s.
John 12. 26. if any man s. me let
Acts 6. 2. leave word of God and s. tables
27. 23. whose I am, and whom I s.
Rom. 1. 9. whom I s. with my spirit
6. 6. henceforth should not s. sin
7. 25. s. law of God
Col. 3. 24. s. Lord Jesus Christ
Gal. 5. 13. by love s. one another
1 Thes. 1. 9. to s. living God
Heb. 12. 28. may s. God accept.
Rev. 7. 15. s. him day and night
Prov. 29. 19. a *servant* will not be
Isa. 24. 2. with s. so with his mas.
42. 1. behold my s., 49. 3. & 52. 13.
Matt. 20. 27. be chief, let him be s.
25. 21. well done, good and faithful s., 23.
John 8. 34. committeth sin is s.
13. 16. s. is not greater than his
1 Cor. 7. 21. called, being a s.
9. 19. I made myself s. to
Gal. 1. 10. pleased men, not s.
Phil. 2. 7. took on him form of a s.
2 Tim. 2. 24. s. of Lord must not
Ezra 5. 11. *servants* of the God of heaven, Dan. 3. 26. Acts 16. 17. 1 Pet. 2. 16. Rev. 7. 3.
Rom. 6. 16. yield yourselves s. to obey, his s. ye are, whom ye obey
19. members s. to uncleanness
1 Cor. 7. 23. ye the s. of men
Phil. 1. 1. s. of Christ
2 Pet. 2. 19. s. of corruption
Rev. 22. 3. his s. shall serve him
Rom. 12. 1. reasonable *service*
Luke 10. 40. cumbered about much *serving*
Acts 20. 19. s. Lord with all humil.
26. 7. tribes instantly s. God
Rom. 12. 11. fervent in spirit s. Lord
Tit. 3. 3. s. divers lusts and pleas.
R. V. Gen. 26. 14. household; 44. 10, 16, 17. bondmen; Gen. 14. 14. 1 Sam. 24. 7. men; 1 Sam. 16. 18; 25. 19; 2 Sam. 21. 2. young men; Ex. 33. 11; Num. 11. 28; Mark 9. 35. minister; Deut. 15. 18. hireling; 2 Kings 10. 19. worshippers; Ezra 2. 65; Eccl. 2. 7. menservants; Matt. 26. 58; Mark 14. 54. officers; John 8. 34, 35; 1 Cor. 7. 21, 22, 23; Gal. 4. 1, 7; 1 Pet. 2. 16; 2 Pet. 2. 19. bondservant; Gen. 39. 4; 40. 4; 2 Chron. 29. 11; Esth. 1. 10; Ps. 101. 6, Isa. 56. 6. minister; 19. 23. worship; Jer. 40. 10; 52. 12. stand before; Ezek. 48. 18, 19. labor in; Ex. 35. 19; 39. 1, 41; 1 Chron. 9. 28. ministering; Num. 4. 47, & 24. work; Rom. 15. 31. ministration; Gal. 4. 8. bondage; Rev. 2. 19. ministry; 2 Cor. 11. 8. minister unto
SERVILE work forbidden on holy days, Lev. 23. 7. Num. 28. 18 & 29. 1.
SET, Ps. 2. 6. & 4. 3. & 12. 5. & 16. 8. & 54. 8. & 75. 7. & 113. 8. Prov. 1. 25. S. of S. 8. 6. Rom. 3. 25. Col. 3. 2.
R. V. Frequent changes, chiefly due to antecedent and consequent words
SETTLE, Luke 21. 14. 1 Pet. 5. 10.
Col. 1. 23. if ye continue in faith, *settled*
R. V. Ezek. 36. 11. cause to be inhabited; 1 Pet. 5. 10 ——
SEVENTY elders, the, Ex. 18. 25. Num. 11. 16.
years' captivity foretold, Jer. 25. 11.
weeks, Daniel's prophecy concerning, Dan. 9. 24.
disciples, Christ's charge to, Luke 10.
SEVERITY, goodness and, Rom. 11. 22.
SHADE, Lord is thy, Ps. 121. 5.

SHADOW, our days are as a, 1 Chron. 29. 15. Eccl. 8. 13. & 6. 12. Job 8. 9. Ps. 107. 11. & 109. 23. & 144. 4.
Ps. 17. 8. hide me under the *s.* of thy wings, 36. 7. & 57. 1. & 63. 7.
S. of S. 2. 3. I sat under his *s.*
Isa. 4. 6. for a *s.* from heat
49. 2. in *s.* of his hand hath he
Jer. 6. 4. *s.* of evening are stretch.
Acts 5. 15. *s.* of Peter might
Col. 2. 17. *s.* of things to come
Jas. 1. 17. no variableness nor *s.*
SHAKE heaven and earth, Hag. 2. 6, 21.
Hag. 2. 7. I will *s.* all nations
Matt. 10. 14. *s.* off the dust of feet
11. 7. a reed *shaken* with the wind
Luke 6. 38. good measure *s.* toget.
2 Thes. 2. 2. be not soon *s.* in mind
Ps. 44. 14. *shaking*, Isa. 17. 6. & 24. 13. & 30. 32. Ezek. 37. 7. & 38. 19.
R. V. Lev. 26. 36. driven; Job 16. 12. dashed; Isa. 13. 13; Heb. 12. 26. make tremble; Matt. 28. 4. quake; Job 41. 29. rushing; Ezek. 37. 7. an earthquake
SHAME, 1 Sam. 20. 34. 2 Sam. 13. 13.
Ps. 119. 31. put me not to *s.*, 69. 7.
Prov. 3. 35. *s.* shall be the promotion of fools, 9. 7. & 10. 5. & 11. 2. & 13. 5, 18. & 14. 35. & 17. 2. & 18. 13. & 19. 26. & 25. 8. & 29. 15. Isa. 22. 18.
Isa. 50. 6. hid not my face from *s.*
Dan. 12. 2. some to life, some to *s.*
Hos. 4. 7. change glory into *s.*
Zeph. 3. 5. unjust knoweth no *s.*
Acts 5. 41. worthy to suffer *s.* for
Phil. 3. 19. glory is in their *s.*
Heb. 12. 2. endured the cross, despising the *s.*
Rev. 3. 18. *s.* of thy nakedness
1 Tim. 2. 9. *shamefacedness*
R. V. Ex. 32. 25. derision; Ps. 4. 2; 35. 4; 40. 14; 44. 9; 109. 29; Acts 5. 41; 1 Cor. 11. 14. dishonor; Ps. 83. 16. confusion; 83. 17. confounded; Prov. 25. 10. revile; Jer. 3. 24; Hos. 9. 10; 1 Cor. 14. 35. shameful; Mic. 2. 6. reproaches
SHAPE, Luke 3. 22. John 5. 37. Ps. 51. 5.
R. V. Luke 3. 22; John 5. 37. form
SHARP, Isa. 41. 15. & 49. 2. Rev. 1. 16.
Job 16. 9. *sharpeneth*, Prov. 27. 17.
Mic. 7. 14. *sharper* than, Heb. 4. 12.
Judg. 8. 1. *sharply*, Tit. 1. 13.
2 Cor. 13. 10. should use *sharpness*
R. V. Josh. 5. 2, 3. flint; 1 Sam. 14. 4. rocky; Job 41. 30. threshing wain; Ex. 4. 25 —; Mic. 7. 4. worse
SHEARING sheep, rejoicing at, 1 Sam. 25. 4. 2 Sam. 13. 23.
SHEAVES of corn, Joseph's dream, Gen. 37. 7.
sheaf of the firstfruits of harvest, Lev. 23. 10-12.
forgotten, to be left in the field, Deut. 24. 19. Job 24. 10.
typical, Ps. 126. 6. Mic. 4. 12. Matt. 13. 30.
SHED for many, for remission, Matt. 26. 28.
Rom. 5. 5. love of God is *s.* abroad
Tit. 3. 6. Holy Ghost be *s.* on us
R. V. Ex. 22. 2, 3; 1 Sam. 25. 26, 33. bloodguiltiness; Ezek. 35. 5. given over to; Ezek. 36. 18; Luke 22. 20; Acts 2. 33; Tit. 3. 6; Rev. 16. 6. poured out
SHEEP, Ps. 49. 14. & 74. 1. & 78. 52.
Ps. 44. 22, 23. *s.* for the slaughter
79. 13. *s.* of thy pasture, 100. 3.
119. 176. gone astray like lost *s.*
Isa. 53. 6. like *s.* have gone astray
Ezek. 34. 12. *s.* that are scattered
Matt. 9. 36. as *s.* having no shep.
10. 6. to lost *s.* of house of
18. 12. hundred *s.* and one of
25. 32. divideth the *s.* from goats
John 10. 2-7. the *s.*
27. my *s.*
21. 15-17. feed lambs, feed my *s.*
1 Pet. 2. 25. were as *s.* going astray
R. V. Gen. 31. 28; Ex. 9. 3; Lev. 22. 21; Num. 31. 28; Deut. 7. 13; 15. 19; 28. 4, 18, 51; 1 Sam. 8. 17; Ps. 49. 17. flock or flocks; S. of S. 4. 2; 6. 6. ewes; John 10. 4. his own; 10. 14. mine own
SHEPHERD, Gen. 46. 34. & 49. 24. Ex. 2. 17, 19.
Num. 17. 17. sheep that have no *s.*, 1 Kings 22. 17. Mark 6. 34.
Ps. 23. 1. the Lord is my *s.*
S. of S. 1. 8. feed thy kids before the *s.* tents
Ezek. 34. 2. prophesy against *s.*, woe to the *s.*
5. scattered because no *s.*
12. *s.* seeketh out his flock
23. set up one *s.* even David
37. 24. all shall have one *s.*
Mic. 5. 5. against him seven *s.*
John 10. 11. I am the good *s.*
16. one fold and one *s.*, Eccl. 12. 11.
Heb. 13. 20. Jesus, that great *s.*
1 Pet. 2. 25. returned to *s.* of souls
5. 4. when the chief *s.* shall ap.
SHIELD and great reward, Gen. 15. 1.
Deut. 33. 29. Lord the *s.* of thy help
Ps. 3. 3. Lord is a *s.* for me, 28. 7.
33. 20. Lord our *s.*, 59. 11. & 84. 9.
84. 11. God is a sun and a *s.*
115. 9. their help and their *s.*
Prov. 30. 5. a *s.* unto them that
Eph. 6. 16. taking the *s.* of faith
SHINE, Job 22. 28. & 36. 32. & 37. 15.
Num. 6. 25. make his face to *s.*
Job 10. 3. *s.* on counsel of wicked
Ps. 31. 16. thy face to *s.* on thy
Eccl. 8. 1. man's wisdom maketh his face *s.*
Dan. 12. 3. wise shall *s.* as firma.
Matt. 5. 16. let your light so *s.*
13. 43. righteous *s.* forth as the
2 Cor. 4. 6. commanded light to *s.*
Phil. 2. 15. among whom ye *s.* as
R. V. Matt. 24. 27. is seen; Job 25. 25. no brightness
SHIPWRECK, 1 Tim. 1. 19.
SHORT, is the Lord's hand waxed, Num. 11. 23.
Ps. 89. 47. remember how *s.* time
Rom. 3. 23. and come *s.* of glory
Ps. 102. 23. he *shortened* my days
Isa. 50. 2. is my hand *s.*, 59. 1.
Matt. 24. 22. except the days be *s.*
SHOUT, Num. 23. 21. Isa. 12. 6. & 42. 11. & 44. 23. Zeph. 3. 14. Zech. 9. 9.
Ps. 47. 5. God is gone up with a *s.*
1 Thes. 4. 16. the Lord shall descend with a *s.*
SHOW, Ps. 39. 6. Luke 20. 47. Col. 2. 23.
Ps. 4. 6. who will *s.* us any good
16. 11. wilt *s.* me path of life
91. 16. I will *s.* him my salvation
1 Cor. 11. 26. *s.* forth Lord's death
Tit. 2. 7. *s.* thyself a pattern
1 Pet. 2. 9. *s.* forth the praise
Rev. 22. 6. sent his angel to *s.*
John 5. 20. loved Son, and *showeth*
R. V. frequent changes, chiefly to tell, declare, manifest, etc.
SHRINES, Acts 19. 24.
SHUT up or left, Deut. 32. 36.
Matt. 23. 13. ye *s.* up the kingdom
Gal. 3. 23. *s.* up to the faith which
Rev. 3. 7. that openeth, and no man *shutteth*, Isa. 22. 22.
R. V. Deut. 32. 30. delivered
SICK of love, S. of S. 2. 5. & 5. 8.
Isa. 1. 5. whole head is *s.* and
John 11. 1. a certain man was *s.*
Jas. 5. 14. is any *s.* call the
15. faith shall save the *s.*
1 Cor. 11. 30. are weak and *sickly*
Ps. 41. 3. make his bed in *sickness*
Ex. 23. 25. I will take *s.* away
Matt. 8. 17. bare our *sicknesses*
R. V. Prov. 23. 35. hurt; Mic. 6. 13. wound; Luke 7. 10 —; 5. 24; Acts 9. 33. palsied; Matt. 8. 17. diseases; Mark 3. 15 —
SIFT, Isa. 30. 28. Amos 9. 9. Luke 22. 31.
SIGHT, Ex. 3. 3. 2 Cor. 5. 7.
R. V. Many changes to eyes, presence, appearance, etc.
SIGN, Gen. 9. 12, 13. & 17. 11. Ex. 4. 17. Isa. 8. 18. Rom. 15. 19.
Rom. 4. 11. received the *s.* of cir.
Jer. 22. 24. *signet*, Hag. 2. 23.
SILENT in darkness, 1 Sam. 2. 9.
Ps. 21. 1. be not *s.* to me, 30. 12.
Zech. 2. 13. be *s.* O all flesh before
Ps. 31. 18. *silence*, 32. 3. & 35. 22. & 50. 3. 21. & 83. 1. & 94. 17. Jer. 8. 14. Amos 5. 13. & 8. 3. 1 Cor. 14. 34, 1 Tim. 2. 11, 12. 1 Pet. 2. 15. Rev. 8. 1.
R. V. Ps. 31. 18. dumb; Isa. 15. 1. nought; 62. 6. take no rest; Acts 22. 2. quiet; 1 Tim. 2. 11, 12. quietness; Ps. 28. 1. deaf unto
SILLY, Job 5. 2. 2 Tim. 3. 6.
SIMPLE, Prov. 1. 4, 22, 32. & 7. 7 & 8. 5. & 9. 4, 13. & 19. 25. & 21. 11.
Ps. 19. 7. testimony sure, making wise the *s.*
116. 16. Lord preserveth the *s.*
119. 130. understanding to the *s.*
Prov. 14. 15. the *s.* believeth
22. 3. *s.* pass on and are punished
Rom. 16. 19. but *s.* concerning evil
R. V. Rom. 16. 18. innocent
SIN lieth at the door, Gen. 4. 7.
Job 10. 6. searchest after my *s.*
Ps. 4. 4. stand in awe and *s.* not
32. 1. blessed is he whose *s.* is covered
38. 18. I will be sorry for my *s.*
51. 3. my *s.* is ever before me
119. 11. that I might not *s.* against
Prov. 14. 34. *s.* is a reproach to
Isa. 30. 1. counsel to add *s.* to *s.*
53. 10. offering for *s.*
John 1. 29. take. away *s.* of world
5. 14. *s.* no more lest a worse
Rom. 5. 12. by one *s.* entered
6. 14. *s.* shall not have dominion
7. 13. *s.* might appear *s.*
17. *s.* that dwelleth in me
8. 2. free from the law of *s.*
1 Cor. 15. 34. awake to righteousness and *s.* not
2 Cor. 5. 21. made *s.* for us, who
Eph. 4. 26. be angry, and *s.* not
Jas. 1. 15. lust bringeth forth *s.* and *s.* death
1 Pet. 2. 22. who did no *s.* neither
1 John 1. 8. say we have no *s.*
2. 1. ye *s.* not; if any man *s.* we have an advocate
5. 10. there is a *s.* unto death
Ps. 19. 13. keep me from presumptuous *sins*
Isa. 43. 25. not remember *s.*
Ezek. 33. 16. none of his *s.* shall
Dan. 9. 24. transgression, make end of *s.*
1 Tim. 5. 22. partaker of other men's *s.*
2 Tim. 3. 6. women laden with *s.*
1 John 2. 2. propitiation for *s.* of
Ps. 69. 5. *my sins*, 51. 9. Isa. 38. 17. 79. 9. *our sins*, 90. 8. & 103. 10. Isa. 59. 12. Dan. 9. 16. Gal. 1. 4. 1 Cor. 15. 3. Heb. 1. 3. 1 Pet. 2. 24. Rev. 1. 5.
Matt. 1. 21. *their sins*, Rom. 11. 27. Heb. 8. 12. & 10. 17. Num. 16. 26.
Isa. 59. 2. *your sins*, Jer. 5. 25. John 8. 21. 1 Cor. 15. 17. Josh. 24. 19.
Ex. 32. 33. who hath *sinned*, I
Job 1. 22. in all this Job *s.* not
Lam. 1. 8. Jerusalem grievously *s.*
Rom. 2. 12. many as *s.* without
3. 23. all have *s.* and come short
1 John 1. 10. say we have not *s.*
Ex. 9. 27. *I have sinned*, Num. 22. 34. Josh. 7. 20. 1 Sam. 15. 24, 30. 2 Sam. 12. 13. & 24. 10. Job 7. 20. &

33. 27. Ps. 41. 4. & 51. 4. Mic. 7. 9. Matt. 27. 4. Luke 15. 18, 21.
Judg. 10. 10. *we have sinned*, 1 Sam. 7. 6. Ps. 106. 6. Isa. 42. 24. & 64. 5. Jer. 3. 25. & 8. 14. & 14. 7, 20. Lam. 5. 16. Dan. 9. 5, 8, 11, 15.
1 Kings 8. 46. man that *sinneth*
Prov. 8. 36. *s.* against me wrong
Eccl. 7. 20. doeth good, and *s.* not
Ezek. 18. 4. soul that *s.* it shall die
1 John 5. 18. is born of God *s.* not
Eccl. 7. 26. the *sinner* shall be
9. 18. *s.* destroyeth much good
Isa. 65. 20. *s.* a hundred years
Luke 15. 7. joy over one *s.* that repenteth
18. 13. be merciful to me a *s.*
Jas. 5. 20. convert a *s.* from
1 Pet. 4. 18. where shall *s.* appear
Gen. 13. 13. *sinners* before the
Ps. 1. 1. standeth in way of *s.*
51. 13. *s.* shall be converted to thee
Isa. 33. 14. *s.* in Zion are afraid
Matt. 9. 13. call *s.* to repentance
John 9. 31. God heareth not *s.*
Rom. 5. 8. that while we were yet *s.* Christ died for us
19. by disobedi. many made *s.*
Gal. 2. 15. are Jews and not *s.*
1 Tim. 1. 15. Jesus came to save *s.*
Heb. 7. 26. holy, separate from *s.*
Jude 15. ungodly *s.* have spoken
Num. 32. 14. *sinful*, Isa. 1. 4. Luke 5. 8. Rom. 7. 13. & 8. 3.
R. V. Prov. 10. 12, 19; 28. 13. transgression; 14. 9. Jer. 51. 5. guilt; 2 Chron. 28. 10; Eph. 1. 7; 2. 5; Col. 2. 13. trespasses; Col. 2. 11; 1 John 2. 2 ——; Lev. 4. 13. err

SINCERE, Phil. 1. 10, 16. 1 Pet. 2. 2.
Josh. 24. 14. serve him in *sincerity*
1 Cor. 5. 8. unleavened bread of *s.*
2 Cor. 1. 12. in godly *s.* we have
2. 17. as of *s.* in the sight of God
8. 8. prove the *s.* of your love
Eph. 6. 24. love Lord Jesus in *s.*
Tit. 2. 7. showing gravity, *s.*
R. V. 1 Pet. 2. 2. spiritual; Eph. 6. 24. uncorruptness; Tit. 2. 7 ——

SINEW, Isa. 48. 4. Job 10. 11.
R. V. Job 30. 17. gnaw

SING to the Lord, Ex. 15. 21. 1 Chron. 16. 23. Ps. 30. 4. & 68. 32. & 81. 1. & 95. 1. & 96. 1, 2. & 98. 1. & 147. 7. & 149. 1. Isa. 12. 5. & 52. 9. Eph. 5. 19.
Ex. 15. 1. I will *s.*, Judg. 5. 3. Ps. 13. 6. & 57. 7, 9. & 59. 16, 17. & 101. 1. & 104. 33. & 144. 9. Isa. 5. 1. 1 Cor. 14. 15.
Job 29. 13. *s.* for joy, Isa. 65. 14.
Ps. 9. 11. *s.* praise, 18. 49. & 27. 6. & 30. 12. & 47. 6, 7. & 68. 4. & 75. 9. & 92. 1. & 108. 1, 3. & 135. 3. & 146. 2. & 147. 1. & 149. 3.
Ps. 145. 7. *s.* of thy righteousness
Prov. 29. 6. righteous doth *s.*
Isa. 35. 6. shall tongue of dumb *s.*
1 Cor. 14. 15. I will *s.* with the spirit
R. V. Ps. 30. 4; 33. 2; 57. 9; 71. 22, 23; 98. 5; 101. 1. sing praises; Isa. 24. 14. shout; Hos. 2. 15. make answer

SINGLE eye, Matt. 6. 22. Luke 11. 34.
Acts 2. 46. *singleness* of heart, Eph. 6. 5. Col. 3. 22.

SINK, Ps. 69. 2, 14. Luke 9. 44.

SISTER, S. of S. 4. 9. & 5. 1. & 8. 8.
R. V. 1 Chron. 7. 15; 1 Cor. 9. 15. wife; Col. 4. 10. cousin

SITUATION, 2 Kings 2. 19. Ps. 48. 2.
R. V. Ps. 48. 2. elevation

SKIN for skin, Job 2. 4. & 10. 11. & 19. 26. Jer. 13. 23. Heb. 11. 37.
R. V. Ex. 16. 10; 36. 19; Num. 4. 6, 8, 10, 11, 12, 14, 25; Ezek. 16. 10. sealskin; Job 18. 13. body; Ps. 102. 5. flesh; Mark 1. 6. leathern girdle

SKIP, Ps. 29. 6. & 114. 4. S. of S. 2. 8.
R. V. Jer. 48. 27. waggest the head

SLACK, Deut. 7. 10. Prov. 10. 4. Hab. 1. 4. Zeph. 3. 16. 2 Pet. 3. 9.

SLANDER, Ex. 23. 1; Ps. 15. 3; 31. 13; 34. 13. (1 Pet. 3. 10.); 50. 20; 64. 3; 101. 5; Prov. 10. 18; Jer. 6. 28; 9. 4; Eph. 4. 31; Tit. 3. 2.
effects of, and conduct under, Prov. 16. 28; 17. 9; 18. 8; 26. 20, 22; Jer. 38. 4; Ezek. 22. 9; Matt. 5. 11; 26. 59; Acts 6. 11; 17. 7; 24. 5; 1 Cor. 4. 12.

SLANDEROUSLY reported, Rom. 3. 8.

SLAY, Job 13. 15. Ps. 139. 19. Lev. 14. 13.
Eph. 2. 16. having *slain* the enmi.
Rev. 5. 9. wast *s.* and hast redeem.
6. 9. were *s.* for word of God
13. 8. Lamb *s.* from foundation
R. V. Lev. 26. 17; Deut. 1. 1. smitten. Many changes to kill, smote, put to death, etc.

SLAYING unpremeditatedly, Num. 35. 11. Deut. 4. 42. & 19. 3. Josh. 20. 3.

SLEEP, deep, Gen. 2. 21. & 15. 12. 1 Sam. 26. 12. Job 4. 13. Ps. 76. 6. Prov. 19. 15. Isa. 29. 10.
Ps. 90. 5. as a *s.* in morning
127. 2. he giveth his beloved *s.*
Prov. 3. 24. thy *s.* shall be sweet
6. 10. a little *s.* a little slumber
20. 13. love not *s.* lest thou
Eccl. 5. 12. *s.* of a laboring man
Jer. 31. 26. my *s.* was sweet to me
Luke 9. 32. were heavy with *s.*
Rom. 13. 11. time to wake out of *s.*
Esth. 6. 1. night king could not *s.*
Eccl. 5. 12. the abundance of the rich will not suffer him to *s.*
S. of S. 5. 2. I *s.* but my heart wak.
1 Cor. 11. 30. for this cause many *s.*
15. 51. we shall not all *s.* but
1 Thes. 4. 14. them which *s.* in Jesus
5. 6. let us not *s.* as others; but
Ps. 3. 5. laid me down and *slept*
76. 5. they have *s.* their sleep
1 Cor. 15. 20. the firstfruits of them that *s.*
Eph. 5. 14. awake, thou that *sleepest*
R. V. Isa. 56. 10. dreaming

SLIDE, Deut. 32. 35. Ps. 26. 1. & 37. 31. Jer. 8. 5. Hos. 4. 16.
R. V. Ps. 26. 1. without wavering; Hos. 4. 16. behaved stubbornly

SLIGHTLY, Jer. 6. 14. & 8. 11.

SLING, 1 Sam. 25. 29. Jer. 10. 18.

SLIP, Ps. 17. 5. & 18. 36. & 38. 16. & 94. 18. Heb. 2. 1.
Ps. 35. 6. *slippery*, 73. 18. Jer. 23. 12.
R. V Heb. 2. 1. drift away

SLOTHFUL are under tribute, Prov. 12. 24.
Prov. 12. 27. *s.* roasteth not which
18. 9. *s.* is brother to great waster
19. 24. *s.* hideth hand in bosom
24. 30. by the field of the *s.*
26. 14. door on hinges so doth *s.*
Rom. 12. 11. not *s.* in business
Heb. 6. 12. be not *s.* but followers
Prov. 19. 15. *slothfulness* casteth in a deep sleep
R. V. Prov. 15. 19; 19. 24; 22. 13; 26. 13, 14, 15. sluggard; 18. 9. slack; Heb. 6. 12. sluggish

SLOW to anger, Neh. 9. 17.
Luke 24. 25. fools, *s.* of heart to
Jas. 1. 19. *s.* to speak, *s.* to wrath, Prov. 14. 29.
R. V. Tit. 1. 12. idle

SLUGGARD, go to ant, Prov. 6. 6.
Prov. 6. 9. how long wilt sleep, O *s.*
20. 4. *s.* will not plough by reason
26. 16. *s.* is wiser in his own conceit

SLUMBER, Ps. 132. 4. Rom. 11. 8.
Ps. 121. 3. he that keepeth thee will not *s.*, 4.
Matt. 25. 5. they all *slumbered* and
2 Pet. 2. 3. their damnation *slumbereth* not
R. V. Rom. 11. 8. stupor

SMITE, Lord shall, Deut. 28. 22.
Ps. 141. 5. let the righteous *s.* me
Zech. 13. 7. *s.* the shepherd
Matt. 5. 39. *s.* thee on thy right
John 18. 23. why *smitest* thou me
Isa. 53. 4. him *smitten* of God
Hos. 6. 1. hath *s.* and he will bind
R. V. 1 Sam. 23. 5. slew · 2 Sam. 10. 15, 19. put to the worse; 2 Chron 22. 5. wounded; Matt. 24 49; Luke 12. 63. beat; Matt. 26. 51; Luke 22 64; John 18. 10; 19. 3. struck

SMOKE, Gen. 19. 28. Ex. 19. 18.
Deut. 29. 20. anger of Lord shall *s.*
Ps. 74. 1. why doth thy anger *s.*
102. 3. as *s.*, Prov. 10. 26. Isa. 65. 5
Rev. 14. 11. *s.* of torment ascend.
Isa. 42 3. *smoking* flax, Matt. 12. 20.

SMOOTH, Gen. 27. 11, 16. Isa. 30. 10.
Ps. 55. 21. *smoother*, Prov. 5. 3.

SNARE, Ex. 23. 33. Judg. 2. 3.
Ps. 69. 22. table become a *s.*
91. 3. deliver thee from the *s.*
119. 110. wicked laid a *s.* for me
Prov. 29. 25. fear of man bringeth a *s.*
1 Tim. 6. 9. they that will be rich fall into a *s.*
2 Tim. 2. 26. out of the *s.* of devil
Ps. 11. 6. on the wicked he will rain *snares*
Prov. 13. 14. depart from *s.* of dea.
Ps. 9. 16. *snared*, Prov. 6. 2. & 12. 13. Eccl. 9. 12. Isa. 8. 15. & 28. 13. & 47. 22.
R. V. Job 18. 8. toils; 18. 10. noose; Prov. 29. 8. flame; Lam. 3. 47. pit; Jer. 5. 26. lie in wait

SNOW, as, Ps. 51. 7. & 68. 14. Isa. 1. 18. Dan. 7. 9. Matt. 28. 3. Rev. 1. 14.

SNUFFED, Mal. 1. 13. Jer. 2. 24.

SOAP, Jer. 2. 22. Mal. 3. 2.

SOBER for your cause, 2 Cor. 5. 13.
1 Thes. 5. 6. watch and be *s.*
1 Tim. 3. 2. bishop must be vigilant, *s.*
11. wives not slanderers, *s.*
Tit. 1. 8. *s.* just, holy, temperate
2. 4. teach young women to be *s.*
1 Pet. 1. 13. gird up your loins, be *s.*
4. 7. be *s.* and watch unto prayer
5. 8. be *s.* be vigilant, for your
Rom. 12. 3. not to think highly, but *soberly*
Tit. 2. 12. teaching us to live *s.*
Acts 26. 25. words of *soberness*
1 Tim. 2. 9. *sobriety*, 15.
R. V. 2 Cor. 5. 13; 2 Tim. 3. 2; Tit. 1. 8. soberminded; 1 Tim. 3. 11; Tit. 2. 2. temperate; 1 Pet. 4. 7. of sound mind; Tit. 2. 4 ——

SOFT, God maketh my heart, Job 23. 16.
Prov. 15. 1. *s.* answer turneth
25. 15. *s.* tongue breaketh the
Matt. 11. 8. man clothed in *s.* rai.
R. V. Job 23. 16. faint

SOJOURN, Gen. 12. 10. Ps. 120. 5. Lev. 25. 23. *sojourners* with me, 1 Chron. 29. 15. Ps. 39. 12.
Ex. 12. 40. *sojourning*, 1 Pet. 1. 17.

SOLD thyself to work evil, 1 Kings 21. 20.
Rom. 7. 14. I am carnal, *s.* under sin

SOLDIER of Jesus Christ, 2 Tim. 2. 3, 4.
R. V. 1 Chron. 7. 4. host; 2 Chron 25. 13; Isa. 15. 4. men; 1 Chron. 7. 11; Matt. 27. 27 ——

SON, 2 Sam. 18. 33. & 19. 4.
Ps. 2. 12. kiss the *S.* lest he be
Prov. 10. 1. a wise *s.* maketh a glad father, 15. 20.
Mal. 3. 17. as a man spareth his *s.*
Matt. 11. 27. no man know. the *S.*
17. 5. this is my beloved *S.*, 3. 17.

Luke 10. 6. if *s*. of peace be there
John 1. 18. only begotten *S*., 3. 16.
5. 21. *S*. quickeneth whom he will
8. 35. *S*. abideth ever
36. the *S*. maketh free
Rom. 8. 3. sent his own *S*. in the
Gal. 4. 7. if *s*. then an heir of God
2 Thes. 2. 3. man of sin, *s*. of per.
Heb. 5. 8. though a *S*. yet learned
1 John 2. 22. denieth the *S*. denieth
5. 12. that hath *S*. hath life
Matt. 21. 37. *his son*, Acts 3. 13. Rom. 1. 3, 9. & 5. 10. & 8. 29, 32. 1 Cor. 1. 9. Gal. 1. 16. & 4. 4, 6. 1 Thes. 1. 10. Heb. 1. 2. 1 John 1. 7. & 2. 23. & 3. 23. & 4. 9, 10, 14. & 5. 9, 10, 11, 20.
Luke 15. 19. *thy son*, John 17. 1. & 19. 26.
Dan. 3. 25. *the son of God*, Matt. 4. 3. & 16. 16. and forty-one other places
Num. 23. 19. *Son of man*, Job 25. 6. Ps. 8. 4. & 80. 17. & 144. 3. Dan. 7. 13. Ezekiel is so called about ninety and Christ about eighty-four times
Ps. 144. 12. that our *sons* may be as
S. of S. 2. 3. is my beloved among *s*.
Isa. 60. 10. *s*. of strangers, 61. 5. & 62. 8.
Mal. 3. 3. purify *s*. of Levi
Mark 3. 17. Boanerges, *s*. of thun.
1 Cor. 4. 14. as my beloved *s*. I
Gal. 4. 6. because ye are *s*. God sent forth the Spirit of his Son
Heb. 2. 10. bring many *s*. to glory
12. 7. God dealeth with you as *s*.
Gen. 6. 2. *sons of God*, Job 1. 6. & 2. 1. & 38. 7. Hos. 1. 10. John 1. 12. Rom. 8. 14, 19. Phil. 2. 15. 1 John 3. 1, 2.
R. V. Gen. 23. 3, 16, 20; 25. 10; 32. 22; Num. 2. 14, 18, 22; Deut. 4. 1; 2 Chron. 21. 7; Mark 13. 12; John 1. 12; 1 Cor. 4. 14, 17; Col. 3. 6; Phil. 2. 15, 22; 1 Tim. 1. 18; 2 Tim. 1. 2; 2. 1; Tit. 1. 4; Phile. 10; 1 John 3. 1, 2. child or children; Num. 1. 20; 26. 5. firstborn; 2 Sam. 23. 6. ungodly; Acts 3. 13, 26. Servant; Col. 4. 10. cousin; Gen. 36. 15; Isa. 56. 3, 6; Matt. 18. 11; 24. 36; 25. 13; Luke 9. 56; John 12. 4; Acts 8. 37; 1 John 5. 13——

SONG to the Lord, Ex. 15. 1. Num. 21. 17.
Ex. 15. 2. Lord is my *s*., Ps. 118. 14. Isa. 12. 2.
Job 30. 9. I am their *s*., Ps. 69. 12.
35. 10. giveth *s*. in the night, Ps. 42. 8. & 77. 6. Isa. 30. 29.
Ps. 32. 7. compass with *s*. of deliv.
119. 54. *s*. in house of pilgrimage
Ezek. 33. 32. as a very lovely *s*.
Eph. 5. 19. speak to yourselves in spiritual *s*.
Rev. 14. 3. could learn that *s*.
15. 3. sing *s*. of Moses and of Lamb
Ps. 33. 3. sing a *new song*, 40. 3. & 96. 1. & 144. 9. & 149. 1. Isa. 42. 10. Rev. 5. 9.
R. V. 1 Chron. 25. 7; Isa. 35. 10. singing

SOON as they be born, Ps. 58. 3.
Ps. 106. 13. *s*. forget his works
Prov. 14. 17. *s*. angry dealeth fool.
Gal. 1. 6. *s*. removed to another
R. V. Ps. 68. 31. haste to; Matt. 21. 20. immediately; Gal. 1. 6; 2 Thes. 2. 2. quickly; Josh. 3. 13; 2 Sam. 6. 18; Mark 14. 45; Luke 1. 44; 15. 30; 23. 7; John 16. 21; Acts 10. 29; Rev. 10. 10; 12. 4. when

SORCERER, Acts 13. 6, 8. & 8. 9, 11.
Jer. 27. 9. *sorcerers*, Mal. 3. 5. Rev. 21. 8.

SORE, 2 Chron. 6. 28. Job 5. 18.
Heb. 10. 29. much *sorer* punish.
Isa. 1. 6. and putrefying *sores*
R. V. Lev. 13. 42, 43; 2 Chron. 6. 28, 29; Ps. 38. 11. plague

SORRY, Ps. 38. 18. 2 Cor. 2. 2. & 7. 8.
Ps. 90. 10. labor and *sorrow*
Prov. 15. 13. by *s*. of heart the
Eccl. 1. 18. knowledge increaseth *s*.
7. 3. *s*. is better than laughter
Isa. 35. 10. *s*. and sighing flee, 51. 11.
Lam. 1. 12. be any *s*. like unto my
John 16. 6. *s*. hath filled your
20. *s*. shall be turned into joy
2 Cor. 7. 10. godly *s*. worketh repentance to salvation, but *s*. of world, 9.
Phil. 2. 27. should have *s*. upon *s*.
1 Thes. 4. 13. *s*. not as others
Rev. 21. 4. no more death, neither *s*.
Ps. 18. 5. the *s*. of hell
116. 3. the *s*. of death
Isa. 53. 3. man of *s*.
4. carried our *s*.
Matt. 24. 8. beginning of *sorrows*
1 Tim. 6. 10. pierced through with many *s*.
2 Cor. 7. 9. *sorrowed*, Jer. 31. 12.
1 Sam. 1. 15. woman of *sorrowful* spirit
Prov. 14. 13. in laughter heart is *s*.
Jer. 31. 25. replenished *s*. soul
Matt. 19. 22. man went away *s*.
26. 22, 38. my soul is exceeding *s*.
2 Cor. 6. 10. *s*. yet always rejoicing
Luke 2. 48. *sorrowing*, Acts 20. 38.
R. V. Gen. 3. 17; Ps. 127. 2. toil; Ex. 15. 14. pangs; Deut. 28. 65. pining; Job 3. 10. trouble; 41. 22. terror; Job 6. 10; Jer. 30. 15; 45. 3; 51. 29; Rom. 9. 2. pain; 2 Sam. 22. 6; Ps. 18. 4, 5; 116. 3. cords; Ps. 55. 10. mischief; Isa. 5. 30. distress; Isa. 29. 2. lamentation; Matt. 24. 8; Mark 13. 8. travail; Rev. 18. 7; 21. 4. mourning; Neh. 8. 10; Matt. 14. 9. grieved; Isa. 51. 19. bemoaned

SORT, 2 Cor. 7. 11. 3 John 6.
R. V. Deut. 22. 11. mingled stuff; Ps. 78. 45; 105. 31. swarms; Dan. 1. 10. own age; Acts 17. 5. rabble; Rom. 15. 15. measure

SOUGHT the Lord, Ex. 33. 7. 2 Chron. 14. 7.
Ps. 34. 4. I *s*. Lord, and he heard
119. 10. with my whole heart I *s*.
Eccl. 7. 29. *s*. out many inventions
Isa. 62. 12. be called *s*. out, a city
65. 1. found of them that *s*. me
Rom. 9. 32. *s*. it not by faith, but
Heb. 12. 17. though he *s*. it care.
2 Chron. 16. 12. *s*. not Lord
1 Chron. 15. 13. *sought him*, 2 Chron. 14. 7. & 15. 4. Ps. 78. 34. S. of S. 3. 1, 2. & 5. 6. Jer. 8. 2. & 26. 21.

SOUL abhor my judgments, Lev. 26. 15, 43.
Gen. 2. 7. man became a living *s*.
Deut. 11. 13. serve him with all *s*.
13. 3. love the Lord with all thy *s*., Josh. 22. 5. 1 Kings 2. 4. Mark 12. 33.
1 Sam. 18. 1. *s*. of Jonathan knit
1 Kings 8. 48. with all their *s*.
1 Chron. 22. 19. set your *s*. to seek
Job 16. 4. if your *s*. were in my *s*.'s stead
Ps. 19. 7. law is perfect, convert. *s*.
49. 8. redemption of *s*. is precious
107. 9. filleth the hungry *s*. with
Prov. 10. 3. not suffer *s*. of right.
18. 2. *s*. be without knowledge
27. 17. full *s*. loatheth honey-comb
Isa. 55. 2. let your *s* delight
58. 10. I will satisfy the afflicted *s*.
Jer. 31. 25. have satiated weary *s*.
38. 16. the Lord made us this *s*.
Ezek. 18. 4. *s*. that sinneth, it
Matt. 10. 28. are not able to kill *s*.
Rom. 13. 1. let every *s*. be subject
1 Thes. 5. 23. spirit, *s*. and body
Heb. 4. 12. piercing to divid. of *s*.
10. 39. believe to saving of the *s*.
Ex. 30. 12. ransom for *his soul*
Judg. 10. 16. —was grieved for
2 Kings 23. 25. turned to Lord with all—
Job 27. 8. God taketh away—
Hab. 2. 4. —lifted up, is not
Matt. 16. 26. lose—; what in exchange for—
Ps. 16. 10. not leave *my soul* in
35. 3. say to—I am thy salvation
42. 5, 11. why cast down, O—
62. 1. —waiteth upon God, 5.
63. 1. —thirsteth for thee, my flesh
Isa. 26. 9. with—have I desired thee, 8.
61. 10. shall be joyful in my God
Luke 1. 46. —doth magnify the
John 12. 27. now is—troubled, Matt. 26. 38.
Ps. 33. 20. *our soul*, 44. 25. & 66. 9. & 123. 4. & 124. 4. Isa. 26. 8.
Deut. 13. 6. *own soul*, 1 Sam. 18. 1. & 20. 17. Ps. 22. 29. Prov. 8. 36. & 11. 17. & 15. 32. & 19. 8, 16. & 6. 32. & 20. 2. & 29. 24. Mark 8. 36. Luke 2. 35.
Deut. 4. 9. *with all thy soul*, 6. 5. & 10. 12. & 30. 6. Matt. 22. 37.
Ezek. 3. 19. deliver *thy soul*, 21. & 33. 9.
Luke 12. 20. this night—shall be required of thee
3 John 2. prosper—as prospereth
Ps. 72. 13. save *souls* of the
Prov. 11. 30. winneth *s*. is wise
Isa. 57. 16. spirit fail, and *s*.
Ezek. 14. 14. should but deliver *s*.
1 Pet. 3. 20. few, i. e. eight *s*. saved
2 Pet. 2. 14. beguiling unstable *s*.
Rev. 6. 9. *s*. of slain and behead.
Luke 21. 19. *your souls*, Josh. 23. 14. Jer. 6. 16. & 26. 19. Matt. 11. 29. Heb. 13. 17. 1 Pet. 1. 9, 22. & 2. 25.
R. V. Lev. 17. 11; Num. 16. 38; 1 Sam. 26. 21; Job 31. 30; Prov. 22. 23; Matt. 16. 26; Mark 8. 36, 37. life or lives; Lev. 4. 2; 5. 1, 2, 4, 15, 17. 6. 2; 7. 21. any one; Num. 15. 27. one person; Job 30. 15. honor; Prov. 19. 18. heart; Hos. 9. 4. appetite; Ps. 16. 2; Jer. 5. 41; Mark 12. 23——

SOUND, dreadful, Job 15. 21.
Ps. 47. 5. God is gone up with *s*.
119. 80. let my heart be *s*.
Prov. 2. 7. *s*. wisdom, 3. 21.
Eccl. 12. 4. *s*. of the grinding is
Amos 6. 5. that chant to *s*. of viol
Rom. 10. 18. *s*. went into all the
1 Tim. 1. 10. contrary to *s*. doc.
2 Tim. 1. 7. *s*. mind
13. of *s*. words
Tit. 1. 9. *s*. doctrine, *s*. in faith
2. 8. *s*. speech that cannot
Isa. 63. 15. *sounding* of bowels, 16. 11.
Ps. 38. 3, 7. no *soundness*, Isa. 1. 6.
R. V. Job 39. 24; John 3. 8; 1 Cor. 14. 7, 8; Rev. 1. 15; 18. 22. voice; Ps. 119. 80. perfect; 2 Tim. 1. 7. discipline; Isa. 63. 15. yearning; Ezek. 7. 7. joyful shouting

SOUR GRAPES, proverb concerning, Jer. 31. 29. Ezek. 18. 2.

SOUTH, the king of, Dan. 11.
—queen of, Matt. 12. 42.

SOW that was washed, 2 Pet. 2. 22.

SOW wickedness reap the same, Job 4. 8.
Ps. 126. 5. *s*. in tears, reap in joy
Isa. 32. 20. blessed that *s*. beside
Jer. 4. 3. *s*. not among thorns
Hos. 10. 12. *s*. in righteousness
Mic. 6. 15. thou shalt *s*. and not
Matt. 13. 3. sower went out to *s*.
Luke 12. 24. the ravens neither *s*.
Ps. 97. 11. light is *sown* for right.
Hos. 8. 7. *s*. wind, reap whirlwind
1 Cor. 9. 11. have *s*. to you spiritual
15. 42. it is *s*. in corruption
2 Cor. 9. 10. multiply your seed *s*.
Jas. 3. 18. fruit of righteousness is *s*. in peace
Prov. 11. 18. that *soweth* righteous
22. 8. *s*. iniquity, shall reap van.
John 4. 37. one *s*. another reapeth
2 Cor. 9. 6. *s*. sparingly, *s*. bounti.
Gal. 6. 7. what a man *s*. that shall
Isa. 55. 10. seed to *sower*, 2 Cor. 9. 10.
R. V. Prov. 16. 28. scattereth

SPARE all the place, Gen. 18. 16.
Neh. 13. 22. *s*. me according to

Ps. 39. 13. *s.* me that I may
Prov. 19. 18. let not thy soul *s.* for
Joel 2. 17. *s.* thy people and give
Mal. 3. 17. I will *s.* them, as
Rom. 8. 32. *spared* not his own Son
11. 21. if God *s.* not the natural
2 Pet. 2. 4. God *s.* not angels that
Prov. 13. 24. he that *spareth* rod
R. V. Ps. 72. 13; Jonah 4. 11. have pity on; Prov. 21. 26. withholdeth
SPARKS, Job 5. 7. Isa. 50. 11.
R. V. Isa. 50. 11. firebrands
SPARROW, Ps. 102. 7. Matt. 10. 29.
SPEAK against Moses, Num. 12. 8.
Gen. 18. 27. taken on me to *s.*
Ex. 4. 14. Aaron thy brother can *s.*
34. 35. went in to *s.* to the Lord
1 Sam. 3. 9. *s.* Lord, thy servant
Ps. 85. 8. Lord will *s.* peace to peo.
Isa. 8. 20. if *s.* not according to
Jer. 18. 7. at what instant I *s.*, 9.
Hab. 2. 3. at end it shall *s.* and
Matt. 10. 19. what ye shall *s.*
Luke 6. 26. when all men *s.* well
John 3. 11. we *s.* that we do know
Acts 4. 20. cannot but *s.* things
1 Cor. 1. 10. ye all *s.* the same
Tit. 3. 2. to *s.* evil of no man
Jas. 1. 19. swift to hear, slow to *s.*
2 Pet. 2. 10. *s.* evil of dignities
Jude 10. *s.* evil of things which
Matt. 12. 32. *speaketh* against Son
34. out of the abundance of the heart the mouth *s.*
Heb. 11. 4. he being dead yet *s.*
12. 24. *s.* better things than
1 Pet. 2. 12. *s.* against you as evil
Isa. 45. 19. *I speak*, 63. 1. John 4. 26. & 7. 17. & 8. 26, 28, 38. & 12. 50. Rom. 3. 5. & 6. 19. 1 Tim. 2. 7.
Isa. 58. 13. nor *speaking* own
65. 24. while they are *s.* I will
Dan. 9. 20. while I was *s.* and
Matt. 6. 7. heard for much *s.*
Eph. 4. 15. *s.* the truth in love
31. evil *s.* be put away
5. 19. *s.* to yourselves in psalms
1 Tim. 4. 2. *s.* lies in hypocrisy
Rev. 13. 5. a mouth *s.* great
Gen. 11. 1. earth was of one *speech*
Deut. 32. 2. my *s.* shall distil
Matt. 26. 73. thy *s.* bewrayeth
1 Cor. 2. 1. with excellency of *s.*
2 Cor. 3. 12. great plainness of *s.*
Col. 4. 6. let your *s.* be with grace
Tit. 2. 8. sound *s.* that cannot
Jude 15. all their hard *speeches*
Rom. 16. 18. by fair *s.* deceive
Matt. 22. 12. he was *speechless*
R. V. Many changes, chiefly to say, said, answered, spoken, utter; 2 Sam. 14. 20. matter; 2 Chron. 32. 18. language; S. of S. 4. 3. mouth; Ezek. 1. 24. tumult; Hab. 3. 2. report; 1 Cor. 4. 19. word; Jude 15. things; Luke 1. 22. dumb
SPECTACLE to angels, 1 Cor. 4. 9.
SPEED, Gen. 24. 12. 2 John 10. 11.
Ezra 7. 21. *speedily*, 26. Ps. 31. 2. & 79. 8. Ex. 8. 11. Luke 18. 8.
R. V. Ezek. 6. 12. all diligence; 2 John 10. 11. greeting; Gen. 44. 11. hasted; 2 Sam. 17. 16. in any wise; 2 Chron. 35. 13. quickly; Ezek. 6. 13; 7. 17, 21, 26. with diligence; Ps. 143. 7. make haste
SPEND their days in wealth, Job 21. 13.
Ps. 90. 9. *s.* our years as a tale
Isa. 55. 2. *s.* money for that is
49. 4. have *spent* my strength
Rom. 13. 12. night is far *s.* day
2 Cor. 12. 15. spend and be *s.*
R. V. Ps. 90. 9. bring to an end; Prov. 21. 20. swalloweth; 29. 3. wasteth
SPICES, S. of S. 4. 10, 14, 16. & 8. 14.
R. V. Gen. 43. 11. spicery; 1 Kings 10. 15 ——; Ezek. 24. 10. make thick the broth
SPIDER, Prov. 30. 28. Job 8. 14. Isa. 59. 5.

Prov. 30. 28. *s.* take hold with hands
R. V. *lizard*
SPIES sent into Canaan by Moses, Num. 13. 3, 17, 26. & 14. 36. Deut. 1. 22. Heb. 3. 17.
sent to Jericho by Joshua, Josh. 2. 1, 4, 17, 23. & 6. 17, 23.
SPIKENARD, S. of S. 1. 12. & 4. 13, 14.
SPIRIT made willing, Ex. 35. 21.
Num. 11. 17. take of *s.* which is
2 Kings 2. 9. portion of thy *s.*
Ezra 1. 5. whose *s.* God raised
Neh. 9. 20. gavest good *s.* to instr.
Job 26. 13. by his *s.* he garnished
Ps. 31. 5. into thy hand I commit *s.*
32. 2. in whose *s.* there is no guile
51. 10. renew a right *s.* within me
12. uphold me with thy free *s.*
17. a broken *s.* and contrite, 34. 18. Prov. 15. 13. & 17. 22. Isa. 57. 15. & 66. 2.
Ps. 76. 12. will cut off *s.* of princes
104. 30. sendest forth thy *s.*
139. 7. whither should I go from *s.*
142. 3. my *s.* was overwhelmed
143. 7. *s.* faileth
10. thy *s.* is good
Prov. 14. 29. hasty of *s.* exalteth
15. 13. sorrow of heart the *s.*
16. 18. a haughty *s.* before a fall
18. 14. a wounded *s.* who can bear
Eccl. 3. 21. who knoweth *s.* of man
8. 8. no power over *s.* to retain *s.*
12. 7. the *s.* shall return to God
Isa. 32. 15. until *s.* be poured on us
Mic. 2. 11. walking in *s.* and false.
Zech. 12. 1. formeth *s.* of man within
Mal. 2. 15. take heed to your *s.*
Matt. 22. 43. doth David in *s.* call
26. 41. *s.* is willing, but flesh
Luke 1. 80. John waxed strong in *s.*
8. 55. *s.* came again and she arose
9. 55. what kind of *s.* ye are
24. 39. *s.* hath not flesh and
John 3. 5. born of water and of *s.*
34. God giveth not *s.* by measure
4. 24. God is a *s.* worship him
6. 63. it is the *s.* that quickeneth
Acts 6. 10. not able to resist the *s.*
16. 7. the *s.* suffered them not
17. 16. Paul's *s.* was stirred in
Rom. 8. 1. not after flesh, but *s.*
2. *s.* of life in Christ Jesus made
9. if any have not *s.* of Christ
8. 13. if ye through *s.* mortify
26. the *s.* helpeth our infirmi.
1 Cor. 2. 10. *s.* searcheth all things
5. 3. present in *s.*
5. *s.* may be saved
6. 17. joined unto the Lord is one *s.*, 12. 13.
2 Cor. 3. 3. written with *s.* of liv.
17. *s.* of Lord is, there is liberty
Gal. 3. 3. begun in *s.* are now per.
4. 6. sent forth *s.* of Son into
5. 16. walk in the *s.*
18. if led by *s.* are not under law
22. fruit of *s.* is love, joy, peace
25. if we live in the *s.* let us walk
6. 18. grace be with your *s.*
Eph. 1. 13. with holy *s.* of promise
4. 4. one body and one *s.*
23. renewed in *s.* of your mind
5. 9. fruit of *s.* is in all godliness
Col. 2. 5. I am with you in the *s.*
1 Thes. 5. 23. whole *s.* soul and
Heb. 4. 12. dividing asunder of soul and *s.*
9. 14. through eternal *s.* offered
Jas. 4. 5. *s.* that dwelleth in us
1 Pet. 3. 4. ornament of a meek and quiet *s.*
4. 6. live according to God in the *s.*
1 John 4. 1. believe not every *s.* but try *s.*
Rev. 1. 10. I was in *s.* on Lord's
11. 11. *s.* of life from God entered
14. 13. yea, saith the *s.* that they
Gen. 6. 3. *my spirit*, Job 10. 12. Ps. 31. 5. & 77. 6. Isa. 38. 16. Ezek. 36. 27. Zech. 4. 6. Luke 1. 47. & 23. 46. Acts 7. 59. Rom. 1. 9. 1 Cor. 14. 14.

Gen. 1. 2. *Spirit of God*, Ex. 31. 3. 2 Chron. 15. 1. Job 33. 4. Ezek. 11. 24. Matt. 3. 16. & 12. 28. Rom. 8. 9, 14. & 15. 19. 1 Cor. 2. 11, 14. & 3. 16. & 6. 11. & 12. 3. 2 Cor. 3. 3. Eph. 4. 30. 1 Pet. 4. 14. 1 John 4. 2.
Isa. 11. 2. *s.* of wisdom, Eph. 1, 17.
Zech. 13. 2. unclean *s.*, Matt. 12. 43.
Ps. 104. 4. maketh angels *spirits*
Prov. 16. 2. Lord weigheth the *s.*
Matt. 10. 1. *unclean spirits*, Acts 5. 16. & 8. 7. Rev. 16. 13, 14.
Luke 10. 20. the *s.* are subject
1 Cor. 14. 32. *s.* of the prophets
Heb. 12. 23. to *s.* of just men made
1 Pet. 3. 19. preached to *s.* in prison
1 John 4. 1. try *s.* whether they be
Hos. 9. 7. the *spiritual* man is mad
Rom. 1. 11. impart some *s.* gift
7. 14. law is *s.* but I am carnal
15. 27. partakers of their *s.* things
1 Cor. 2. 13. comparing *s.* things
15. he that is *s.* judgeth all things
9. 11. sown to you *s.* things
10. 3. eat *s.* meat
15. 44. it is raised a *s.* body
Gal. 6. 1. ye which are *s.* restore
Eph. 1. 3. blessed us with *s.* bless.
5. 19. speaking in *s.* songs
6. 12. wrestle against *s.* wicked.
Col. 1. 9. filled with *s.* understand.
1 Pet. 2. 5. built us *s.* house; offer
Rom. 8. 6. to be *spiritually* minded
1 Cor. 2. 14. because *s.* discerned
Rev. 11. 8. *s.* is called Sodom and
R. V. Ps. 104. 4; Eccl. 1. 14, 17; 2. 11, 17, 26; 4. 4, 6, 16; 6. 9; 11. 5; Zech. 6. 5; Heb. 1. 7. wind or winds; Isa. 40. 7; 59. 19; 2 Thes. 2. 8; Rev. 11. 1. breath; Matt. 14. 26; Mark 6. 49. apparition; Acts 18. 5. by word; Eph. 5. 9. light; Luke 2. 40; 9. 55; Rom. 8. 1; 1 Cor. 6. 20; 1 Tim. 4. 12; 1 Pet. 1. 22——
SPITE, Ps. 10. 14. Matt. 22. 6.
SPITTING, Isa. 50. 6. Luke 18. 32.
SPOIL, Gen. 49. 27. Ps. 68. 12.
Ps. 119. 162. that finds great *s.*
Matt. 12. 29. he will *s.* his house
Col. 2. 8. lest any *s.* you through
Ex. 12. 36. *spoiled* the Egyptians
Col. 2. 15. having *s.* principalities
Heb. 10. 34. took joyfully *spoiling*
R. V. Num. 31. 53; 2 Chron. 14. 13. booty; Job 29. 17. prey; Prov. 31. 11. gain; Isa. 25. 11. craft; Hab. 2. 17. destruction; Ps. 35. 12. bereaving
SPOT, without, Num. 19. 2. & 28. 3, 9. Job 11. 19. 2 Tim. 6. 14. Heb. 9. 14. 1 Pet. 1. 19. 2 Pet. 3. 14.
S. of S. 4. 7. there is no *s.* in thee
Eph. 5. 27. not having *s.* or wrinkle
Jer. 13. 33. *spots*, Jude 12, 23.
R. V. Num. 28. 3, 9, 11; 29. 17, 26; Deut. 32. 5; Heb. 9. 14. blemish; Lev. 13. 39. tetter; Jude 12. hidden rocks
SPREAD, Job 9. 8. Isa. 25. 11. & 37. 14. Jer. 4. 3. Lam. 1. 17. Ezek. 16. 8.
R. V. 2 Sam. 17. 19. strewed; 1 Chron. 14. 9. made raid; Job 9. 8. stretcheth; Mark 1. 28. went out; 6. 14. become known; 1 Thes. 1. 8. gone forth
SPRING, Ps. 85. 11. Matt. 13. 5, 7.
Ps. 65. 10. *springing*, John 4. 14. Heb. 12. 15.
Ps. 87. 7. all my *springs* are in thee
R. V. Deut. 4. 49; Josh. 10. 40; 12. 8. slopes; Ps. 87. 7; Jer. 51. 36. fountains; Lev. 13. 42. breaking out; Matt. 13. 7; Luke 8. 6, 7, 8. grew; Mark 4. 8. growing
SPRINKLE, Lev. 14. 7. & 16. 14.
Isa. 52. 15. he shall *s.* many nations
Ezek. 36. 25. I will *s.* clean water
Heb. 10. 22. having hearts *sprinkled* from an evil conscience
12. 24. to blood of *sprinkling*
1 Pet. 1. 2. through *s.* of the blood
SPUE thee out of my mouth, Rev.

3. 16. Hab. 2. 16. Lev. 18. 28. Jer. 25. 27.
R. V. Lev. 18. 28; 20. 22. vomit
SPY, Num. 13. 16. Josh. 2. 1. Gal. 2. 4.
STABILITY of times, Isa. 33. 6.
STAFF, Gen. 32. 10. Zech. 11. 10.
Ps. 23. 4. thy rod and *s.* comfort
Isa. 3. 1. stay and *s.* of bread
10. 5. *s.* in their hand is my
STAGGER, Ps. 107. 27. Rom. 4. 20.
STAIN, Isa. 23. 9. & 63. 3.
R. V. Job 3. 5. claim it
STAKES, Isa. 33. 20. & 54. 2.
STAMMER, Isa. 28. 11. & 33. 19. & 32. 4.
STAND, Ezek. 29. 7. Ex. 9. 11.
Job 19. 25. *s.* at latter day on earth
Ps. 76. 7. who may *s.* in thy sight
130. 3. if Lord mark iniquities who shall *s.*
Isa. 46. 10. my counsel shall *s.*
Mal. 3. 2. who shall *s.* when he
Matt. 12. 25. house divided against itself shall not *s.*
Rom. 5. 2. this grace wherein we *s.*
14. 4. God is able to make him *s.*
2 Cor. 1. 24. by faith ye *s.*
Eph. 6. 13. having done all to *s.*
1 Pet. 5. 12. grace of God wherein ye *s.*
Rev. 3. 20. I *s.* at the door and
Nah. 1. 6. *stand before*, 1 Sam. 6. 20. Luke 21. 36. Rom. 14. 10. Rev. 20. 12.
1 Cor. 16. 13. *stand fast* in the faith
Gal. 5. 1. — in the liberty where.
Phil. 1. 27. — in one spirit
4. 1. — in the Lord
1 Thes. 3. 8. live, if ye — in Lord
2 Thes. 2. 15. — and hold traditions
Ps. 1. 5. *stand in*, 4. 4. & 24. 3.
Ex. 14. 13. *stand still*, see salvation, 2 Chron. 20. 17. Josh. 10. 12. Zech. 11. 16.
Ps. 1. 1. *standeth*, 26. 12. & 33. 11. Prov. 8. 2. S. of S. 2. 9. Isa. 3. 13.
Ps. 119. 161. my heart *s.* in awe of
1 Cor. 10. 12. thinketh he *s.* take
2 Tim. 2. 19. foundation of God *s.*
Jas. 5. 9. the Judge *s.* at the door
R. V. Several changes, but chiefly due to words before and after
STAR, Num. 24. 17. Matt. 2. 2.
Judg. 5. 20. *stars* in their courses
Job 25. 5. *s.* are not pure in his
Dan. 12. 3. shall shine as *s.* for
Jude 13. wandering *s.* to whom is
Rev. 12. 1. a crown of twelve *s.*
R. V. Amos 5. 8. Pleiades
STATURE, Matt. 6. 27. Eph. 4. 13.
STATUTES and laws, Neh. 9. 14.
Ps. 19. 8. *s.* of the Lord are right
Ezek. 20. 25. *s.* not good
Ex. 15. 26. *his statutes*, Deut. 6. 17. 2 Kings 17. 15. Ps. 18. 22. & 105. 45.
1 Chron. 29. 19. *thy statutes*, Ps. 119. 12, 16, 23, 26, 33, 54, 64, 68, 71, 117.
STAVES for the tabernacle, Ex. 25. 13. & 37. 15. & 40. 20. Num. 4. 6.
STAY, Ps. 18. 18. S. of S. 2. 5. Isa. 10. 20. & 26. 3. & 27. 8. & 48. 2. & 50. 10.
R. V. 1 Sam. 24. 7. checked; Job 38. 37. pour out
STEAD, Gen. 4. 25. & 22. 13.
Job 16. 4. if your soul were in my soul's *s.*
2 Cor. 5. 20. pray you in Christ's *s.*
R. V. Phile. 13. behalf
STEADFAST, Job 11. 15. Dan. 6. 26.
Ps. 78. 8. spirit not *s.* with God
Acts 2. 42. continued *s.* in apos.
1 Cor. 15. 58. be ye *s.*, immovable
Heb. 3. 14. hold confidence *s.* to
Col. 2. 5. *steadfastness*, 2 Pet. 3. 17.
R. V. Ps. 78. 37. faithful; Heb. 3. 14. firm
STEAL, Ex. 20. 15. Lev. 19. 11.
Prov. 6. 30. if he *s.* to satisfy his
30. 9. lest I be poor and *s.* and
Matt. 6. 19. thieves break through and *s.*
Matt. 27. 64. disciples come by night and *s.* him away
Eph. 4. 28. that *stole*, steal no more
Prov. 9. 17. *stolen* waters are sweet
STEALING, Ex. 20. 15. & 21. 16. Lev. 19. 11. Deut. 5. 19. & 24. 7. Ps. 50. 18. Zech. 5. 4. Matt. 19. 18. Rom. 13. 9. Eph. 4. 28. 1 Pet. 4. 15.
restoration inculcated, Ex. 22. 1. Lev. 6. 4. Prov. 6. 30, 31.
STEPS, Ex. 20. 26. Ps. 18. 36.
Ps. 37. 23. *s.* of good men ordered
44. 18. neither our *s.* declined
Prov. 16. 9. Lord directeth his *s.*
Jer. 10. 23. man to direct his *s.*
Rom. 4. 12. walk in *s.* of that faith
1 Pet. 2. 21. should follow his *s.*
R. V. Ps. 27. 23. goings; 85. 13. footsteps
STEWARD, Luke 12. 42. & 16. 2. 1 Cor. 4. 1. Tit. 1. 7. 1 Pet. 4. 10.
R. V. 1 Chron. 28. 1. rulers
STIFF neck, Deut. 31. 27. Jer. 17. 23.
Ex. 32. 9. *stiff-necked* people, 33. 3, 5. & 34. 9. Deut. 9. 6, 13. & 10. 16.
Acts 7. 51. — ye do always resist
2 Chron. 36. 13. he *stiffened* his neck
STILL, Ex. 15. 16. Ps. 8. 2. & 139. 18.
Ps. 4. 4. be *s.*, Jer. 47. 6. Mark 4. 39.
46. 10. be *s.* and know that I am
Isa. 30. 7. their strength is to sit *s.*
Rev. 22. 11. unjust *s.* filthy *s.*
Ps. 65. 7. *stilleth* noise of the sea, 89. 9.
STING, 1 Cor. 15. 55, 56. Rev. 9. 10.
Prov. 23. 32. it *stings* like an adder
STINK, Ps. 38. 5. Isa. 3. 24.
R. V. Isa. 3. 24. rottenness
STIR up, Num. 24. 9. Job 17. 8.
Ps. 35. 23. *s.* up thyself, awake
78. 38. did not *s.* up all his wrath
S. of S. 2. 7. that ye *s.* not up
2 Tim. 1. 6. *s.* up gift of God that
2 Pet. 1. 13. think it meet to *s.* you
R. V. Isa. 22. 2. shoutings; Num. 24. 9. rouse; 1 Kings 11. 14, 23. raised; Dan. 11. 10. war; Acts 13. 50. urged on; 17. 16. provoked
STONE of Israel, Gen. 49. 24.
Ps. 118. 22. *s.* which the builders refused
Isa. 8. 14. a *s.* of stumbling
28. 16. a tried *s.* a precious cor. *s.*
Hab. 2. 11. *s.* shall cry out of wall
Matt. 3. 9. of *s.* to raise up children unto Abraham
7. 9. bread, will he give him *s.*
1 Pet. 2. 4. as unto a living *s.*
6. lay in Sion a chief corner *s.*
Ezek. 11. 19. *stony*, Matt. 13. 5.
R. V. Ex. 4. 25. flint; Job 40. 17. thighs; Ps. 137. 9. rock; Isa. 34. 11. plummet; Mark 12. 4. —; John 1. 42. Peter; Matt. 13. 5, 20; Mark 4. 5, 16. rocky
STOOP, Job 9. 10. Prov. 12. 25. Mark 1. 7.
R. V. 1 Sam. 24. 8; 28. 14. bowed
STORE, 1 Cor. 16. 2. 1 Tim. 6. 19.
Luke 12. 24. *storehouse*, Ps. 33. 7.
R. V. Deut. 28. 5, 17. kneading-trough
STORM, Ps. 55. 8. & 83. 15.
Ps. 107. 29. maketh the *s.* a calm
Isa. 4. 6. covert from the *s.*
Mark 4. 37. a great *s.*, Luke 8. 23.
Ps. 148. 8. *stormy* wind fulfilling
R. V. Isa. 29. 6. whirlwind
STOUT hearted, Ps. 76. 5. Isa. 46. 12.
Isa. 10. 12. punish fruit of *s.* heart
Mal. 3. 13. words have been *s.*
Isa. 9. 9. say to pride and *stoutness*
STRAIGHT, Josh. 6. 5. Jer. 31. 9.
Ps. 5. 8. thy way *s.* before my
Isa. 40. 3. make *s.* a highway
4. crooked he made *s.*, 43. 16. Luke 3. 5.
Luke 3. 4. way of the Lord, make his paths *s.*
Heb. 12. 13. make *s.* paths for feet
R. V. Isa. 45. 2. plain
STRAIN at a gnat, Matt. 23. 24.
STRAIT, 2 Sam. 24. 14. Job 20. 22. & 36. 16. Isa. 49. 20. Phil. 1. 23.
Matt. 7. 13. enter in at the *s.* gate
Job 18. 7. steps *straitened*
Mic. 2. 7. spirit of the Lord *s.*
Luke 12. 50. how am I *s.* till it be
2 Cor. 6. 12. not *s.* in us, *s.* in your
R. V. Job 36. 16. distress; Matt. 7. 13, 14; Luke 13. 24. narrow
STRANGE, Ex. 21. 8. & 30. 9. Lev. 10. 1. Ps. 81. 9. Jer. 2. 21. Luke 5. 26. Heb. 11. 9. 1 Pet. 4. 12. Jude 7.
Job 31. 3. is not a *s.* punishment
Isa. 28. 21. do his *s.* work bring
Hos. 8. 12. counted as a *s.* thing
Zeph. 1. 8. clothed with *s.* apparel
Heb. 13. 9. about with *s.* doctrines
Judg. 11. 2. *strange women*, Prov. 2. 16. & 5. 3, 20. & 6. 24. & 20. 16. & 23. 27. & 27. 13. Ezra 10. 2, 11.
Gen. 23. 4. *stranger* and sojourner, Ps. 39. 12. & 119. 19. 1 Chron. 29. 15.
Prov. 14. 10. a *s.* doth not meddle
Jer. 14. 8. should. thou be as a *s.*
Matt. 25. 35. I was a *s.* and ye
Luke 17. 18. to give God glory save this *s.*
John 10. 5. a *s.* will they not follow
Ps. 105. 12. very few and *strangers*
146. 9. Lord preserveth the *s.*
Eph. 2. 12. *s.* from the covenant
Heb. 11. 13. confessed they were *s.*
13. 2. not forgetful to entertain *s.*
1 Pet. 2. 11. beseech you as *s.*
R. V. Job 31. 3. disaster; 19. 13. hardly with; Prov. 21. 8. crooked; Judg. 11. 2. another; Zeph. 1. 8; Acts 26. 11. foreign; Heb. 11. 9. not his own; Gen. 17. 8; 28. 4; 36. 7; 37. 1. sojournings; Ex. 12. 43; Prov. 5. 10; Ezek. 44. 7, 9. alien; Ex. 2. 22; 12. 19; Lev. 25. 47; 1 Chron. 16. 19; Ps. 105. 12; 119. 19; Jer. 14. 8; Acts 2. 10; 7. 29; 1 Pet. 2. 11. sojourner; Deut. 17. 15; 23. 20; 29. 22. foreigner; Isa. 5. 17. wanderers; 29. 5. foes; Obad. 12. of his disaster
STRANGLED, Acts 15. 20, 29. & 21. 25.
Job 7. 15. soul chooseth *strangling*
STREAM, Isa. 30. 33. & 66. 12. Dan. 7. 10. Amos 5. 24. Luke 6. 48.
Ps. 46. 4. *streams*, 126. 4. S. of S. 4. 15. Isa. 30. 25. & 33. 21. & 35. 6.
R. V. Ex. 7. 19; 8. 5. rivers; Num. 21. 15. slope; Job 6. 15. channel; Isa. 27. 12. brook; 57. 6. valley
STREET, Rev. 11. 8. & 21. 21. & 22. 2.
Prov. 1. 20. *streets*, S. of S. 3. 2. Luke 14. 21.
R. V. 2 Chron. 29. 4; 32. 6; Ezra 10. 9; Neh. 8. 1, 3, 16; Esth. 4. 6; Prov. 1. 20; 7. 12; Isa. 15. 3; Amos 5. 10. broad place or way; Ps. 144. 13. fields; Mark 6. 56. market place
STRENGTH, Gen. 49. 24. Ex. 13. 3.
Ex. 15. 2. the Lord is my *s.* and my song, Ps. 18. 2. & 28. 7. & 118. 14. Isa. 12. 2.
Judg. 5. 21. soul thou hast trodden down *s.*
1 Sam. 2. 9. by *s.* shall no man
Job 9. 19. if I speak of *s.* lo, he
Ps. 18. 32. girded me with *s.*, 39.
27. 1. the Lord is the *s.* of my life
29. 11. Lord will give *s.* to his
33. 16. mighty not delivered by *s.*
39. 13. spare me that I recover *s.*
46. 1. God is our refuge and *s.*
73. 26. God is *s.* of my heart
84. 5. blessed whose *s.* is in thee
93. 1. the Lord is clothed with *s.*
96. 6. *s.* and beauty are in his
140. 7. Lord, the *s.* of my salvation
Prov. 10. 29. Lord is *s.* to the up.
Eccl. 9. 16. wisd. is better than *s.*
Isa. 25. 4. *s.* to poor and *s.* to needy
26. 4. in Jehovah is everlasting *s.*
Joel 3. 16. Lord is the *s.* of child.
Luke 1. 51. shewed *s.* with his

Rom. 5. 6. we were without *s*.
1 Cor. 15. 56. *s*. of sin is the law
Rev. 3. 8. thou hast a little *s*. and
5. 12. worthy is the Lamb to receive *s*.
17. 13. give their *s*. to beast
1 Chron. 16. 11. *his strength*, Ps. 33. 17. Isa. 61. 1. Hos. 7. 9. & 12. 3.
Gen. 49. 24. *in strength*, Job 9. 4. & 36. 5. Ps. 71. 16. & 103. 20. & 147. 10. Isa. 33. 6.
Gen. 49. 3. *my strength*, Ex. 15. 2. 2 Sam. 22. 33. Job 6. 12. Ps. 8. 1, 2. & 19. 14. & 28. 7. & 38. 10. & 43. 2. & 59. 17. & 62. 7. & 71. 9. & 99. 4. & 102. 23. & 118. 14. & 144. 1. Isa. 12. 2. & 27. 5. & 49. 4, 5. Jer. 16. 19. Hab. 3. 19. 2 Cor. 12. 9.
Ps. 37. 39. *their strength*, 89. 17. Prov. 20. 29. Isa. 30. 7. & 40. 31.
Ps. 8. 2. *thy strength*, 86. 16. & 110. 2. Prov. 24. 10. & 31. 3. Isa. 17. 10. & 63. 15. Mark 14. 32. Deut. 33. 25.
Neh. 8. 10. *your strength*, Isa. 23. 14. & 30. 15. Ezek. 24. 21. Lev. 26. 20.
Ps. 20. 2. Lord *strengthen* thee
27. 14. the Lord, he shall *s*. your
31. 24. he shall *s*. your heart
41. 3. *s*. him on bed of languish.
Isa. 35. 3. *s*. ye the weak hands
Dan. 11. 1. stood to confirm and *s*.
Zech. 10. 12. I will *s*. them in Lord
Luke 22. 32. when converted *s*. thy brethren
Rev. 3. 2. *s*. the things that rema.
1 Sam. 23. 16. *strengthened* his hand in God
Ezek. 34. 4. diseased have ye not *s*.
Eph. 3. 16. *s*. with might, Col. 1. 11.
2 Tim. 4. 17. the Lord stood with me and *s*. me
Ps. 138. 3. *s*. me with *s*. in my soul
104. 15. bread which *strengtheneth*
Phil. 4. 13. Christ who *s*. me
R. V. Job 12. 13; 39. 19; Ps. 80. 2; Prov. 8. 14; 24. 5; Rev. 5. 12. might; Ps. 18. 2; 144. 1; Isa. 26. 4. rock; Ps. 60. 7; 108. 8. defence; Ps. 31. 4; 37. 39; Prov. 10. 29; Isa. 23. 4, 14; 25. 4; Ezek. 30. 15; Nah. 3. 11. strong hold; Ps. 33. 17; Ezek. 24. 21; 30. 18; 33. 28; 1 Cor. 15. 56; 2 Cor. 12. 9; Heb. 11. 11; Rev. 3. 8; 12. 10. power; Ps. 41. 3. support; Ezek. 30. 25. hold up; Luke 22. 32; Acts 18. 23; Rev. 3. 2. stablish

STRETCH thy hands, Job 11. 13.
Amos 6. 4. *s*. themselves on couch.
Matt. 12. 13. *s*. forth thy hand
John 21. 18. thou shalt *s*. forth
Gen. 22. 10. *stretched* forth his
1 Kings 17. 21. *s*. himself upon
1 Chron. 21. 16. drawn sword *s*.
Isa. 5. 25. hand is *s*. out still
Job 15. 25. he *stretcheth* out hand
Prov. 31. 20. she *s*. out hand to
Isa. 40. 22. *s*. out the heavens as a curtain, 42. 5. & 44. 24. & 45. 12. & 51. 13. Jer. 10. 12. & 51. 15. Zech. 12. 1.
R. V. Ex. 3. 20; 9. 15; 1 Sam. 24. 6; 26. 9, 11, 23; 2 Sam. 1. 14; Job 30. 24; Acts 12. 1. put; Ex. 25. 20; Ps. 44. 20; 88. 9; 136. 6; 143. 6; Prov. 31. 20; Isa. 16. 8; Rom. 10. 21. spread, or spread forth

STRIFE between me, Gen. 13. 8.
Ps. 80. 6. us a *s*. to our neighbors
Prov. 10. 12. hatred stirreth up *s*.
16. 28. froward man soweth *s*.
20. 3. an honor to cease from *s*.
28. 25. proud heart stirreth up *s*.
Isa. 58. 4. ye fast for *s*. and debate
Luke 22. 24. was a *s*. among them
Rom. 13. 13. not in *s*. and envying
Gal. 5. 20. wrath, *s*., sedition
Phil. 1. 15. preach Christ of *s*. and
2 Tim. 2. 23. gender *s*., 2 Cor. 12. 20.
Jas. 3. 14. bitter envying and *s*.. 16.
R. V. Ps. 106. 32. Meribah; Prov. 15. 18; 26. 20; Luke 22. 24. contention; 2 Cor. 12. 20; Gal. 5. 20; Phil. 2. 3; Jas. 3. 14, 16. faction: 1 Tim. 6. 4. disputes

STRIKE hands, Job 17. 3. Prov. 6. 1.
Prov. 17. 26. *s*. princes for equity
Isa. 1. 5. why be *stricken* any more
53. 4. esteem him *s*. of God
1 Tim. 3. 3. a bishop, no *striker*
R. V. Ex. 12. 7. put; Deut. 21. 4. break; 2 Kings 5. 11. wave; Hab. 3. 14. pierce; Mark 14. 65. received blows; 2 Chron. 13. 20; Matt. 26. 51. smote; Luke 22. 64 ——

STRIPES, Isa. 53. 5. 1 Pet. 2. 24.
Prov. 17. 10. & 20. 30. Luke 12. 47, 48.
R. V. Prov. 20. 30. strokes

STRIVE, Ex. 21. 18, 22. Job 33. 13.
Gen. 6. 3. Spirit shall not alw. *s*.
Prov. 8. 30. *s*. not without cause
Hos. 4. 4. let no man *s*. nor reprove
Matt. 12. 19. he shall not *s*. nor
Luke 13. 24. *s*. to enter in at strait
Isa. 45. 9. that *striveth* with Maker
Phil. 1. 27. *striving* together for
Heb. 12. 4. resisted unto blood *s*.
R. V. Ex. 21. 18; 2 Tim. 2. 5. contend; Rom. 15. 20. making it my aim

STRONG this day, Josh. 14. 11.
Ps. 24 8. Lord is *s*. and mighty
30. 7. made mountain to stand *s*.
31. 2. be thou my *s*. rock
71. 7. thou art my *s*. refuge, 3.
Prov. 10. 15. rich man's wealth is his *s*. city
18. 10. name of Lord is a *s*. tower
24. 5. a wise man is *s*. and
Eccl. 9. 11. battle is not to the *s*.
S. of S. 8. 6. love is *s*. as death
Isa. 1. 31. *s*. shall be as tow and
35. 4. be *s*. fear not, behold your
53. 12. divide the spoil with *s*.
Jer. 50. 34. their Redeemer is *s*.
Joel 3. 10. the weak say I am *s*.
Luke 11. 21. *s*. man armed keepeth
Rom. 4. 20. *s*. in faith, giving glory
15. 1. we that are *s* ought to bear the infirmities of the weak
Heb. 11. 34. weakness made *s*.
1 John 2. 14. because ye are *s*.
Isa. 35. 4. *be strong*, Hag. 2. 4. 1 Cor. 16. 13. Eph. 6. 10. 2 Tim. 2. 1.
1 Cor. 1. 25. *stronger* than men
Job 17. 9. clean hands shall be *s*.
Jer. 20. 7. thou art *s*. than I
R. V. Few changes to mighty, valiant, etc.

STUBBLE, Job 13. 25. & 21. 18. Ps. 83. 13. Isa. 33. 11. Mal. 4. 1. 1 Cor. 3. 12.

STUBBORN, Deut. 21. 18. Ps. 78. 8.
1 Sam. 15. 23. *stubbornness*, Deut. 9. 27.
R. V. Prov. 7. 11. wilful

STUDY, Eccl. 12. 12. 1 Thes. 4. 11. 2 Tim. 2. 15. Prov. 15. 28. & 24. 2.
R. V. 2 Tim. 2. 15. give diligence

STUMBLE, foot shall not, Prov. 3. 23.
Prov. 4. 12. runnest, shalt not *s*.
Isa. 5. 27. shall be weary nor *s*.
8. 15. many shall *s*. and fall
Mal. 2. 8. cause many to *s*. at law
1 Pet. 2. 8. which *s*. at the word
Rom. 9. 32. they *stumbled* at that
John 11. 9. day he *stumbleth* not
Rom. 14. 21. whereby thy brother *s*.
Isa. 8. 14. *stumbling*, 1 John 2. 10.
Lev. 19. 14. *stumbling-block*, Isa. 8. 14. & 57. 14. Jer. 6. 21. Ezek. 3. 20. & 7. 19. & 14. 3, 4, 7. Rom. 9. 32, 33. & 11. 9. & 14. 13. 1 Cor. 1. 23. & 8. 9. Rev. 2. 14.
R. V. Prov. 24. 17. is overthrown

SUBDUE our iniquities, Mic. 7. 9.
Ps. 81. 14. soon *s*. their enemies
Phil. 3. 21. able to *s*. all things
Heb. 11. 33. through faith *subdued*
R. V. Deut. 20. 20. fall; Dan. 7. 24. put down; Mic. 7. 19. tread under foot; Zech. 9. 15. tread down; 1 Cor. 15. 28; Phil. 3. 21. subject

SUBJECT, devils are, Luke 10. 17, 20.
Rom. 8. 7. not *s*. to law of God
13. 1. every soul be *s*. to higher
1 Cor. 14. 32. spirit of prophets *s*.
15. 28. Son shall be *s*. to him that
Eph. 5. 24. as church is *s*. to Christ
Tit. 3. 1. to be *s*. to principalities
Heb. 2. 15. all lifetime *s*. to bond.
Jas. 5. 17. Elias, a man *s*. to
1 Pet. 2. 18. servants be *s*. to mas.
3. 22. angels and powers made *s*.
5. 5. all ye be *s*. one to another
1 Cor. 9. 27. *subjection*, 1 Tim. 2. 11. & 3. 4. Heb. 2. 5, 8. & 12. 9. 1 Pet. 3. 1, 5.
R. V. Rom. 13. 5; Tit. 3. 1; 1 Pet. 2. 18. in subjection; 1 Cor. 9. 27. bondage; 2 Cor. 9. 13. obedience

SUBMIT, Gen. 16. 9. Ps. 18. 44. & 66. 3. & 68. 30. & 81. 15.
1 Cor. 16. 16. *submit yourselves*, Eph. 5. 21, 22. Col. 3. 18. Heb. 13. 17. Jas. 4. 7. 1 Pet. 2. 13. & 5. 5.
Rom. 10. 3. have not *submitted* to righteousness
R. V. Rom. 10. 3; Eph. 5. 21, 22; 1 Cor. 16. 16; Col. 3. 18; Jas. 4. 7; 1 Pet. 2. 13; 5. 5. be subject or subjection

SUBSCRIBE, Isa. 44. 5. Jer. 32. 44.

SUBSTANCE, Gen. 7. 4. & 15. 14.
Deut. 33. 11. bless Lord, his *s*.
Job 30. 22. thou dissolvest my *s*
Ps. 139. 15. my *s*. was not hid
Prov. 3. 9. honor Lord with thy *s*.
Hos. 12. 8. I have found me out *s*.
Luke 8. 3. ministered to him of *s*.
Heb. 10. 34. a more enduring *s*.
11. 1. faith is *s*. of things hoped
R. V. Gen. 7. 4. thing; Deut. 11. 6. living thing; Gen. 36. 6; Heb. 10. 34. possession; Ps. 139. 15. frame; Prov. 10. 3. desire; Isa. 6. 13. stock; Hos. 12. 8. wealth; Heb. 11. 1. assurance

SUBTIL, Gen. 3. 1. Prov. 7. 10.
Acts 13. 10. *subtilty*, 2 Cor. 11. 3. Prov. 1. 4.
R. V. Prov. 7. 10. wily

SUBVERT, Lam. 3. 36. Tit. 1. 11. & 3. 11.
Acts 13. 24. *subverting* souls, 2 Tim. 2. 14.
R. V. Tit. 1. 11. overthrow; 3. 11. perverted

SUCK, Gen. 21. 7. Deut. 32. 13. & 33. 19.
Job 20. 16. *s*. poison of asps and
Isa. 60. 16. *s*. milk of Gentiles
66. 11. *s*. and be satisfied, 12.
Matt. 24. 19. to them that give *s*.
Luke 23. 29. blessed are paps which never gave *s*.
11. 27. blessed are paps thou hast *sucked*
Isa. 11. 8. *sucking* child, 49. 15.
Ps. 8. 2. *suckling*, Lam. 2. 11. & 4. 4.
R. V. Ezek. 23. 34. drain

SUDDEN, Prov. 3. 25. 1 Thes. 5. 3.

SUFFER, Ex. 12. 23. Lev. 19. 17.
Ps. 55. 22. never *s*. righteous
89. 33. nor *s*. my faithfulness
121. 3. *s*. thy foot to be moved
Prov. 10. 3. *s*. soul of righteous
Matt. 16. 21. must *s*. many things
17. 17. how long shall I *s*. you
19. 14. *s*. little children to come
1 Cor. 4. 12. being persecuted, we *s*.
Phil. 1. 29. also to *s*. for his sake
2 Tim. 2. 12. if we *s*. we shall reign
Heb. 11. 25. rather to *s*. affliction
13. 3. them who *s*. adversity
1 Pet. 4. 15. none *s*. as a murderer
Ps. 105. 14. he *suffered* no man
Acts 14. 16. *s*. all to walk in his
16. 7. the Spirit *s*. them not
Phil. 3. 8. for whom I *s*. loss of all
Heb. 5. 8. learned obedience by the things he *s*.
1 Pet. 2. 21. *s*. for us leaving us
3. 18. Christ hath *s*. once for sins

Matt. 11. 12. *suffereth*, 1 Cor. 13. 4.
Rom. 8. 18. *sufferings*, 2 Cor. 1. 5, 6. Phil. 3. 10. Col. 1. 24. Heb. 2. 10. 1 Pet. 1. 11. & 4. 13. & 5. 1.
R. V. Lev. 22. 16. cause; Lev. 19. 17; Prov. 19. 19; Matt. 17. 17; Mark 9. 19; Luke 9. 41; 1 Cor. 9. 12; 2 Cor. 11. 19, 20; Heb. 13. 22. bear, or bear with; Luke 8. 32. give leave; 12. 39. left; 1 Cor. 4. 12; 2 Tim. 2. 12. endure; 1 Tim. 2. 12. permit; 4. 10. strive
SUFFICE, 1 Pet. 4. 3. John 14. 8.
Matt. 6. 34. *sufficient* to-day is evil
2 Cor. 2. 16. who is *s*. for these
3. 5. we are not *s*. of ourselves
12. 9. my grace is *s*. for thee
Job 20. 22. *sufficiency*, 2 Cor. 3. 5. & 9. 8.
SUM, Ps. 139. 17. Ezek. 28. 12. Heb. 8. 1.
R. V. Ex. 21. 30. ransom; Acts 7. 16. price; Heb. 8. 1. chief point
SUMMER and winter not cease, Gen. 8. 22.
Ps. 74. 17. hast made *s*. and winter
Prov. 6. 8. provideth her meat in *s*.
10. 5. gathereth in *s*. is a wise
Isa. 18. 6. fowls shall *s*. and winter
Jer. 8. 20. harvest past and *s*. ended
Zech. 14. 3. living waters in *s*.
SUMPTUOUSLY, fared, Luke 16. 19.
SUN, stand thou still, Josh. 10. 12.
Ps. 19. 4. he set a tabernacle for *s*.
104. 19. *s*. knoweth his going
121. 6. *s*. not smite thee by day
136. 8. *s*. to rule day, Gen. 1. 16.
Eccl. 12. 2. while *s*. or stars be not darkened
S. of S. 1. 6. because the *s*. hath
Isa. 30. 26. light of the *s*. shall
60. 19. *s*. no more thy light by
Jer. 31. 35. giveth *s*. for a light by
Mal. 4. 2. *S*. of righteousness arise
Matt. 5. 45. his *s*. to rise on evil
13. 43. shine as *s*. in the kingdom
1 Cor. 15. 41. there is one glory of *s*.
Eph. 4. 26. let not *s*. go down on
Rev. 7. 16. neither *s*. light on them
10. 1. his face as *s*., 1. 16.
21. 23. city had no need of the *s*., 22. 5.
SUP, Luke 17. 8. Rev. 3. 20. Hab. 1. 9.
Luke 14. 16. certain man made a great *supper*
1 Cor. 11. 20. to eat Lord's *s*., Luke 22. 20.
Rev. 19. 9. to marriage *s*.
R. V. Hab. 1. 9. set eagerly
SUPERFLUITY of naughtiness, Jas. 1. 21.
SUPERSTITION, Acts 25. 19. & 17. 22.
SUPPLICATION, 1 Kings 8. 28. & 9. 3. Job 8. 5. & 9. 15. Ps. 6. 9. & 30. 8. & 55. 1. & 142. 1. & 119. 170. Dan. 6. 11. & 9. 20. Hos. 12. 4. Zech. 12. 10. Eph. 6. 18. Phil. 4. 6. 1 Tim. 2. 1. & 5. 5. Heb. 5. 7.
SUPPLY spirit of Jesus Christ, Phil. 1. 19.
Phil. 4. 19. God shall *s*. all need
2 Cor. 9. 12. *supplieth*, Eph. 4. 16.
R. V. 2 Cor. 9. 12. filleth measure
SUPPORT the weak, Acts 20. 35. 1 Thes. 5. 14.
R. V. Acts 20. 35. help
SUPREME, 1 Pet. 2. 13.
SURE, Gen. 23. 17. 1 Sam. 25. 28.
Neh. 9. 38. we make a *s*. covenant
Ps. 19. 7. testimo. of the Lord is *s*.
111. 7. his commandments are *s*.
Prov. 11. 15. hateth suretiship is *s*.
18. righteous. shall be *s*. reward
Isa. 22. 23, 25. *s*. place
28. 16. *s*. foundation
55. 3. *s*. mercies of David
John 6. 69. we believe and are *s*.
Rom. 4. 16. promise might be *s*.
2 Tim. 2. 19. the foundation of God standeth *s*.

2 Pet. 1. 10. calling and election *s*.
R. V. Prov. 6. 3. importune; Ex. 3. 19; 1 Sam. 20. 7; Luke 10. 11; John 6. 69; 16. 30; Rom. 2. 2; 15. 29. know; 2 Tim. 2. 19. firm
SURETY for servant, Ps. 119. 122.
Heb. 7. 22. Jesus made *s*. of better
R. V. Acts 12. 11. truth
SURETYSHIP, evils of, Prov. 6. 1. & 11. 15. & 17. 18. & 20. 16. & 22. 26. & 27. 13.
SURFEITING and drunkenness, Luke 21. 34.
SURPRISED hypocrites, Isa. 33. 14.
SUSTAIN, Ps. 55. 22. Prov. 18. 14.
Ps. 3. 5. *sustained*, Isa. 59. 16.
R. V. Isa. 59. 16. upheld
SWALLOW, Ps. 84. 3. Jer. 8. 7.
Isa. 25. 8. will *s*. up death in vic.
Matt. 23. 24. gnat, and *s*. a camel
Ex. 15. 12. earth *swallowed* them
Ps. 124. 3. they had *s*. us up quick
2 Cor. 2. 7. be *s*. up with overmuch sorrow
5. 4. mortality be *s*. up of life
R. V. Job 5. 5. gapeth for; Hab. 1. 13. devoureth
SWEAR, Num. 30. 2. Deut. 6. 13.
Isa. 45. 23. every tongue shall *s*.
65. 16. shall *s*. by the God of truth
Jer. 4. 2. shalt *s*. Lord liveth in
Zeph. 1. 5. *s*. by Lord, and *s*.
Matt. 5. 34. *s*. not at all
Ps. 15. 4. *sweareth* to his own hurt
Eccl. 9. 2. *s*. as he that feareth
Zech. 5. 3. every one that *s*. shall
Jer. 23. 10. because of *swearing*
Hos. 4. 2. by *s*. and lying they
10. 4. *s*. falsely in making a cov.
Mal. 3. 5. I will be a witness against false *s*.
R. V. Ex. 6. 8. lifted up my hand; Lev. 5. 1. adjuration
SWEAT, Gen. 3. 19. Luke 22. 44.
SWEET, Job 20. 12. Ps. 55. 14.
Ps. 104. 34. meditation of him be *s*.
119. 103. how *s*. thy words to my
Prov. 3. 24. thy sleep shall be *s*.
9. 17. stolen waters are *s*.
27. 7. to hungry bitter thing is *s*.
Eccl. 5. 12. sleep of labor. man *s*.
S. of S. 2. 8. his fruit was *s*. to my
14. *s*. is thy voice and thy counte.
Isa. 5. 20. put bitter for *s*. and *s*.
Phil. 4. 18. odor of a *s*. smell
Rev. 10. 9. in thy mouth *s*. as hon.
Ps. 19. 10. *sweeter* than honey
Judg. 14. 14. *sweetness*, Prov. 16. 21. & 27. 9.
R. V. Jer. 6. 20. pleasing; Mark 16. 1——
SWELLING, Jer. 12. 5. 2 Pet. 2. 18.
R. V. Jer. 12. 5; 49. 19; 50. 44. pride
SWIFT, Deut. 28. 49. Job 9. 26.
Eccl. 9. 11. race is not to the *s*.
Rom. 3. 15. feet are *s*. to shed
Jas. 1. 19. *s*. to hear, slow to
2 Pet. 2. 1. bring on themselves *s*. destruction
Job 7. 6. days *swifter* than a shut.
Ps. 147. 15. *swiftly*, Joel 3. 4.
SWIM, 2 Kings 6. 6. Ps. 6. 6. Ezek. 47. 5.
SWORD, Ex. 32. 27. Lev. 26. 24.
Deut. 32. 29. *s*. of thy excellency
Judg. 7. 20. *s*. of Lord and Gideon
2 Sam. 12. 10. *s*. shall never depart
Ps. 17. 13. wicked which is thy *s*.
149. 6. two-edged *s*. in their hands
S. of S. 3. 8. man hath his *s*. on
Jer. 9. 16. send a *s*. after them
Ezek. 21. 13. if *s*. contemn rod
Zech. 11. 17. *s*. shall be upon his
13. 7. awake, O *s*., against shep.
Matt. 10. 34. not send peace, but *s*.
Luke 2. 35. a *s*. shall pierce through
Rom. 13. 4. beareth not *s*. in vain
Eph. 6. 17. *s*. of the Spirit, which
Heb. 4. 12. word is sharper than any two-edged *s*.
Rev. 1. 16. a sharp two-edged *s*.
Ps. 55. 21. *swords*, 59. 7. Prov. 30. 14. Isa. 2. 4. Ezek. 32. 27. Joel 3. 10.

R. V. Job 2. 25. point; Joel 2. 8. weapons
SWORN by myself, Gen. 22. 16.
Ps. 24. 4. that hath not *s*. deceit.
119. 106. I have *s*. and will per.
SYNAGOGUE, Ps. 74. 8. Matt. 6. 5. & 23. 6. Luke 7. 5. John 9. 22. & 18. 20. Acts 15. 21. Rev. 2. 9. & 3. 9.
R. V. Acts 13. 42——

T

TABERNACLE, Ex. 26. 1. & 29. 43.
Job 5. 24. thy *t*. shall be in peace
Ps. 15. 1. who shall abide in thy *t*.
27. 5. in secret of his *t*. shall hide
Prov. 14. 11. *t*. of the upright shall
Isa. 33. 20. a *t*. shall not be taken
Amos 9. 11. raise up *t*. of David
2 Cor. 5. 1. earthly house of this *t*.
Heb. 8. 2. minister of the true *t*.
2 Pet. 1. 13. I am in this *t*.
Rev. 21. 3. *t*. of God is with men
Job 12. 6. *tabernacles* of robbers
Ps. 84. 1. how amiable are thy *t*.
118. 15. salvation is in the *t*. of the
Heb. 11. 9. dwell in *t*. with Isaac
R. V. In O. T. nearly always tent or tents; Luke 16. 9; Acts 7. 46. habitation
TABLE, Ex. 25. 23. Job 36. 16.
Ps. 23. 5. prepared a *t*. before me
69. 22. let their *t*. become a snare
Prov. 3. 3. write them on *t*. of heart
S. of S. 1. 12. king sitteth at his *t*.
Mal. 1. 7. *t*. of Lord is contempt.
Matt. 15. 27. crumbs from mast. *t*.
1 Cor. 10. 21. partakers of Lord's *t*.
Deut. 10. 4. *tables*, 5. Heb. 9. 4. 2 Chron. 4. 8, 19. Isa. 28. 8. Ezek. 40. 41.
Hab. 2. 2. make it plain upon *t*.
Acts 6. 2. leave . . God and serve *t*.
2 Cor. 3. 3. not in *t*. of stone, but
R. V. Isa. 30. 8; Luke 1. 63. tablet; Mark 7. 4——; John 12. 2. meat
TAKE you for a people, Ex. 6. 7
Ex. 20. 7. not *t*. name of the Lord
34. 9. *t*. us for thine inheritance
Ps. 27. 12. the Lord will *t*. me up
116. 12. I will *t*. cup of salvation
119. 43. *t*. not the word of truth
Hos. 14. 2. *t*. with you words; say *t*.
Matt. 16. 24. *t*. up his cross and
18. 16. *t*. with thee one or two
20. 14. *t*. that thine is, and go thy
26. 26. said *t*. eat, this is my body, 1 Cor. 11. 24.
Luke 12. 19. *t*. thine ease, eat
Eph. 6. 13. *t*. the whole armor of
Rev. 3. 11. no man *t*. thy crown
Ex. 23. 25. *take away*, Josh. 7. 13. 2 Sam. 24. 10. 1 Chron. 17. 13. Job 7. 21. & 32. 22. & 36. 1. Ps. 58. 9. Isa. 58. 9. Jer. 15. 15. Hos. 1. 6. & 4. 11. & 14. 2. Amos 4. 2. Mal. 2. 3. Luke 17. 31. John 1. 29. 1 John 3. 5. Rev. 22. 19.
Deut. 4. 9. *take heed*, 11. 16. & 27. 9. 2 Chron. 19. 6. Ps. 39. 1. Isa. 7. 4. Mal. 2. 15. Matt. 6. 1. & 16. 6. & 18. 10. & 24. 4. Mark 4. 24. & 13. 33. Luke 8. 18. & 12. 15. 1 Cor. 10. 12. Col. 4. 17. Heb. 3. 12. 2 Pet. 1. 19.
Deut. 32. 41. *take hold*, Ps. 69. 24. Isa. 27. 5. & 56. 4. & 64. 7. Zech. 1. 6.
Ps. 83. 3. *taken* crafty counsel
119. 111. testimony have I *t*.
Isa. 53. 8. he was *t*. from prison
Lam. 4. 20. the anointed was *t*. in
Matt. 21. 43. kingdom of God *t*.
24. 40. one shall be *t*. the other
Mark 4. 25. be *t*. that which he hath
Acts 1. 9. *t*. up into heaven
2 Tim. 2. 26. *t*. captive by him
Isa. 6. 7. thy iniquity is *taken away*
57. 1. merciful men are—
Luke 10. 42. good part not be—from
2 Cor. 3. 16. return to Lord, veil—
Ps. 40. 12. my iniquities *taken hold*
Prov. 1. 19. *taketh away*, John 1. 29 & 10. 18. & 15. 2; *taketh from*. 16. 22

Ps. 119. 9. by *taking* heed thereto
Matt. 6. 27. who by *t.* thought can
Rom. 7. 8. sin *t.* occasion deceived
Eph. 6. 16. above all *t.* shield of
R. V. The frequent changes are mostly due to context; as, Matt. 6. 25. take no thought, becomes, be not anxious, etc.

TALE, Ps. 90. 9. Ezek. 22. 29. Luke 24. 11.
Lev. 19. 16. *tale-bearer*, Prov. 11. 13. & 18. 8. & 20. 19. & 26. 20, 22.
R. V. Luke 24. 11. talk

TALENTS, Matt. 18. 24. & 25. 15, 25.

TALK of them when thou sittest, Deut. 6. 7.
1 Sam. 2. 3. *t.* no more so proudly
Job. 13. 7. and *t.* deceitfully for
Ps. 71. 24. my tongue shall *t.*
77. 12. I will *t.* of thy doings
105. 2. *t.* ye of his wondrous works
145. 11. speak of glory and *t.* of
Jer. 12. 1. *t.* with thee of judgment
John 14. 30. I will not *t.* much
Ps. 37. 30. his tongue *talketh* of
Eph. 5. 4. nor foolish *talking*
Tit. 1. 10. unruly and vain *talkers*
R. V. Several changes and nearly all to speak or spake; 1 Kings 18. 27. musing

TAME, Mark 5. 4. Jas. 3. 7, 8.

TARRY, 1 Chron. 19. 5. 2 Kings 14. 10.
Prov. 23. 30. that *t.* long at wine
Isa. 46. 13. my salvation shall not *t.*
Hab. 2. 3. though it *t.* wait for it
Matt. 26. 38. *t.* ye here and watch
John 21. 22. that he *t.* till I come
1 Cor. 11. 33. come to eat *t.* for one
Ps. 68. 12. she that *tarried* at home
Matt. 25. 5. the bridegroom *t.* all
Luke 2. 43. child Jesus *t.* behind in
Acts 22. 16. why *tarriest* thou
Ps. 40. 17. make no *tarrying*, 70. 5.
R. V. Lev. 14. 8. dwell; 1 Sam. 14. 2; 2 Sam. 15. 29; 2 Kings 14. 10; Matt. 26. 38; Mark 14. 34; Luke 24. 29; John 4. 40; Acts 9. 43; 18. 20. abide or abode; Ps. 101. 7. be established; Hab. 2. 3. delay; Acts 20. 5; 27. 33; 1 Cor. 11. 38. wait or waiting, Acts 15. 33. spent time; Acts 20. 15 ——

TASKMASTERS, Ex. 1. 11. & 5. 6.

TASTE, Ex. 16. 31. 1 Sam. 14. 43.
Job 6. 6. *t.* in white of an egg
Ps. 34. 8. *t.* and see Lord is good
119. 103. sweet are thy words to *t.*
S. of S. 2. 3. fruit was sweet to *t.*
Jer. 48. 11. *t.* remained in him
Matt. 16. 28. not *t.* of death
Luke 14. 24. *t.* of my supper
John 8. 52. keep my saying, never *t.* death
Col. 2. 21. touch not, *t.* not, handle
Heb. 2. 9. *t.* death for every man
6. 4. *t.* heavenly gift
5. *t.* good word of God
1 Pet. 2. 3. if ye have *tasted* that

TATTLERS, 1 Tim. 5. 13.

TAXATION of all the world, under Cæsar Augustus, Luke 2. 1.

TEACH, Ex. 4. 12. Lev. 10. 11.
Deut. 4. 9. *t.* them thy sons, 6. 7.
33. 10. shall *t.* Jacob thy judg.
1 Sam. 12. 23. *t.* good way
2 Chron. 17. 7. to *t.* in cities of
Job 21. 22. shall any *t.* God
Ps. 25. 8. *t.* sinners in the way
34. 11. *t.* you fear of Lord
51. 13. *t.* transgressors thy way
90. 12. *t.* us to number our days
Isa. 2. 3. he will *t.* us of his ways
Jer. 31. 34. *t.* no more every man
Matt. 28. 19. go and *t.* all nations
John 9. 34. dost thou *t.* us
14. 26. Holy Ghost shall *t.* you all
1 Cor. 4. 17. as I *t.* in every church
1 Tim. 3. 2. given to hospitality, apt to *t.*
2 Tim. 2. 2. faithful men able to *t.*
Heb. 5. 12. need that one *t.* you
Job 34. 32. what I see not, *teach me*
Ps. 25. 4. —thy paths, 5. & 27. 11.—thy way, 86. 11. & 119. 12.—thy statutes, 26. 64, 66, 68, 124, 135.—good judgment, 108.—thy judgments, 143. 10.—to do thy will
2 Chron. 32. 22. *taught* good knowl.
Ps. 71. 17. hast *t.* me from my
119. 171. hast *t.* me thy statutes
Eccl. 12. 9. he *t.* people knowledge
Isa. 29. 13. *t.* by precepts of men
John 6. 45. shall be all *t.* of God
Acts 20. 20. *t.* you publicly and
Gal. 6. 6. let him that is *t.* in word
1 Thes. 4. 9. yourselves are *t.* of God
Ps. 94. 12. *teachest* him out of law
Matt. 22. 16. *t.* way of God in
Rom. 2. 21. *t.* another, *t.* not thy.
Job 36. 22. who *teacheth* like him
Ps. 18. 34. *t.* my hands to war
94. 10. he that *t.* man knowledge
Isa. 48. 17. Lord thy God *t.* thee to
1 Cor. 2. 13. words which man's wisdom *t.* but which the Holy Ghost *t.*
1 John 2. 27. anointing *t.* you
Hab. 2. 18. *teacher*, John 3. 2. Rom. 2. 20. 1 Tim. 2. 7. 2 Tim. 1. 11.
Ps. 119. 99. *teachers*, Isa. 30. 20.
2 Tim. 4. 3. heap to themselves *t.*
Tit. 2. 3. be *t.* of good things
Heb. 5. 12. ought to be *t.* ye have
2 Chron. 15. 3. a *teaching* priest
Matt. 15. 9. *t.* for doctrines the
28. 20. *t.* them to observe all things
Col. 1. 28. *t.* every man in all wis.
Tit. 2. 12. *t.* us that denying
R. V. 1 Sam. 12. 23; Ps. 25. 8, 12; Acts 22. 3; 1 Cor. 14. 19. instruct; Jer. 28. 16; 29. 32. spoken; Matt. 28. 19. make disciples; Acts 16. 21. set forth; Tit. 2. 4. train; Isa. 43. 27. interpreters

TEAR, Ps. 50. 22. Hos. 5. 14. Job 16. 9.
R. V. 2 Sam. 13. 31. rent; Jer. 16. 17. break bread; Mark 9. 18. dasheth down; Isa. 5. 25. refuse; Mal. 1. 13. taken by violence

TEARS, Job 16. 20. Ps. 6. 6. Isa. 38. 5.
Ps. 56. 8. put *t.* in thy bottle
126. 5. they that sow in *t.* shall
Isa. 25. 8. wipe away all *t.* from off
Jer. 9. 1. eyes were a fountain of *t.*
Luke 7. 38. to wash his feet with *t.*
Acts 20. 19. *t.* and temptations, 31.
2 Cor. 2. 4. wrote with many *t.*
2 Tim. 1. 4. being mindful of thy *t.*
Heb. 5. 7. with strong crying and *t.*
Rev. 7. 17. wipe all *t.* from their
R. V. Mark 9. 24 ——

TEATS, Isa. 32. 12. Ezek. 23. 3, 21.

TEETH white with milk, Gen. 49. 12.
Job 4. 10. *t.* broken, Ps. 3. 7. & 58. 6.
S. of S. 4. 2. *t.* are like a flock of
Jer. 31. 29. children's *t.* set on
Amos 4. 6. cleanness of *t.* in all
Matt. 8. 12. weeping and gnashing of *t.*, 22. 13. & 24. 51. & 25. 30. Ps. 112. 10.

TEKEL, Dan. 5. 25.

TELL it not in Gath, 2 Sam. 1. 20.
Ps. 48. 13. *t.* it to the generation
Prov. 30. 4. name, if thou canst *t.*
Matt. 8. 4. see thou *t.* no man
18. 15. *t.* him his fault
John 3. 8. not *t.* whence it cometh
4. 25. he is come he will *t.*
8. 14. ye cannot *t.* whence I come
2 Cor. 12. 2. out of body I cannot *t.*
Gal. 4. 16. I *t.* you the truth
Phil. 3. 18. *t.* you even weeping
Ps. 56. 8. *tellest* all my wanderings
R. V. Frequent changes to speak, say, shew, etc.

TEMPERANCE, Acts 24. 25. Gal. 5. 23. 2 Pet. 1. 6.
1 Cor. 9. 25. *temperate*, Tit. 1. 8. & 2. 2.

TEMPLE, 1 Sam. 1. 9. 1 Kings 6. 5.
Ps. 29. 9. in *t.* doth every one speak
Jer. 7. 4. *t.* of the Lord, *t.* of Lord
Mal. 3. 1. suddenly come to his *t.*
Matt. 12. 6. greater than the *t.* is
John 2. 19. destroy this *t.* and in
21. he spake of the *t.* of his body
1 Cor. 3. 16. ye are the *t.* of God
6. 19. body is *t.* of Holy Ghost
2 Cor. 6. 16. what agreement hath the *t.* of God with idols, for ye are the *t.* of the living God
Rev. 7. 15. serve him in his *t.*
11. 19. *t.* of God was opened in
S. of S. 4. 3. thy *temples*, 6. 7.
Acts 7. 48. Most High dwel. not in *t.*
R. V. 1 Kings 11. 10, 11, 13; 1 Chron. 6. 10; 10. 10; 2 Chron. 23. 10; Acts 7. 48. house or houses; Hos. 8. 14. palaces; Matt. 23. 35; 27. 5; Luke 11. 51. sanctuary

TEMPORAL, 2 Cor. 4. 18.

TEMPT Abraham, God did, Gen. 22. 1.
Ex. 17. 2. wherefore do ye *t.* Lord
Deut. 6. 16. shall not *t.* the Lord
Isa. 7. 12. ask, nor will I *t.* Lord
Matt. 4. 7. shalt not *t.* the Lord
22. 18. why *t.* ye me, show
Acts 5. 9. agreed together to *t.*
1 Cor. 7. 5. that Satan *t.* you not
Ex. 17. 7. they *tempted* Lord
Num. 14. 22. *t.* me now ten times
Ps. 78. 18. *t.* God in their heart
95. 9. when your fathers *t.* me
Matt. 4. 1. wilderness, to be *t.*
Luke 10. 25. lawyer *t.* him, saying
1 Cor. 10. 13. suffer you to be *t.*
Gal. 6. 1. lest thou also be *t.*
Heb. 2. 18. he is able to succor them that are *t.*
4. 15. in all points *t.* as we are
Jas. 1. 13. I am *t.* of God
14. every man is *t.* when drawn
Matt. 16. 1. *tempting* him, 19. 3. & 22. 35. Luke 11. 16. John 8. 6.
Ps. 95. 8. as in day of *temptation*
Matt. 6. 13. lead us not into *t.*
Luke 4. 13. devil had ended all *t.*
8. 13. in time of *t.* fall away
1 Cor. 10. 13. no *t.* taken you
Gal. 4. 14. my *t.* in flesh despised
1 Tim. 6. 9. rich fall into *t.* and
Heb. 3. 8. in day of *t.* in wilderness
Jas. 1. 12. blessed is he that endureth *t.*
Deut. 4. 34. *temptations*, 7. 19. Luke 22. 28. Acts 20. 19. Jas. 1. 2. 1 Pet. 1. 6. 2 Pet. 2. 9.
Matt. 4. 3. *tempter*, 1 Thes. 3. 5.
R. V. Luke 20. 23 ——; Ps. 95. 8. Massah; Acts 20. 19; Rev. 3. 10. trial

TENDER, thy heart was, 2 Kings 22. 19. Eph. 4. 32.
Luke 1. 78. *t.* mercy, Jas. 5. 11.
R. V. S. of S. 2. 13, 15; 7. 12. in blossom; Dan. 1. 9. compassion; Jas. 5. 11. merciful

TENDETH, Prov. 10. 16. & 11. 19. & 19. 23. & 11. 24. & 14. 23. & 21. 5.

TENTS of Shem, dwell in, Gen. 9. 27.
1 Kings 12. 16. to your *t.* O Israel, 2 Sam. 20. 1.
Ps. 84. 10. dwell in *t.* of wickedness
S. of S. 1. 8. kids besi. shepherds' *t.*
R. V. Gen. 26. 17; 33. 18; Num. 9. 17, 18, 20-23; Ezra 8. 15. encamped: Num. 25. 8. pavilion; Num. 13. 19: 1 Sam. 17. 53; 2 Kings 7. 16: 2 Chron. 31. 2. camp or camps: 2 Sam. 11. 11. booths

TERRESTRIAL, 1 Cor. 15. 40.

TERRIBLE, Ex. 34. 10. Deut. 1. 19.
Deut. 7. 21. a mighty God and *t.*, 10. 17. Neh. 1. 5. & 4. 14. & 9. 32. Jer. 20. 11.
Deut. 10. 21. done *t.* things
Job 37. 22. with God is *t.* majesty
Ps. 45. 4. hand shall teach *t.*
47. 2. Lord most high is *t.*
65. 5. *t.* things wilt thou answer
66. 3. how *t.* art thou in thy
76. 12. he is *t.* to kings of the
99. 3. praise thy great and *t.*
S. of S. 6. 4. *t.* as army with ban.
Isa. 64. 3. *t.* things we looked not
Joel 2. 11. day of the Lord is *t.*
Zeph. 2. 11.
Heb. 12. 21. so *t.* was the sight

1 Chron. 17. 21. *terribleness*, Jer. 49. 16.
Job 7. 14. *terrifiest*, Phil. 1. 28.
R. V. Lam. 5. 10. burning; Dan. 7. 7. powerful; Heb. 12. 21. fearful
TERROR, Gen. 35. 5. Deut. 32. 25.
Job 31. 23. destr. from God was a *t.*
Isa. 33. 18. heart shall meditate *t.*
Jer. 17. 17. be not a *t.* unto me
20. 4. a *t.* to thyself, and all
Rom. 13. 3. rulers are not a *t.* to
2 Cor. 5. 11. know. *t.* of the Lord
1 Pet. 3. 14. be not afraid of their *t.*
Job 6. 4. *terrors*, 18. 11, 14. & 27. 20.
Ps. 55. 4. & 73. 19. & 88. 15, 16.
R. V. 2 Cor. 5, 11; 1 Pet. 3. 14. fear
TESTAMENT, Matt. 26. 28. Luke 22. 20. 1 Cor. 11. 25. 2 Cor. 3. 6, 14. Gal. 3. 15. Heb. 7. 22. & 9. 15, 16, 17, 18. Rev. 11. 19.
Heb. 9. 16. death of the *testator*
TESTIFY, Deut. 8. 19. & 32. 46. Neh. 9. 26, 34. Ps. 50. 7. & 81. 8.
Num. 35. 30. witness shall not *t.*
Isa. 59. 12. our sins *t.* against us
Hos. 5. 5. pride of Israel *t.* to his
John 3. 11. *t.* that we have seen
5. 39. search the Scriptures, they *t.* of me, 15. 26.
Acts 20. 24. *t.* the Gospel of grace
1 John 4. 14. *t.* that the Father
2 Chron. 24. 19. *testified*, Neh. 13. 15. Acts 23. 11. 1 Tim. 2. 6. 1 John 5. 9.
Heb. 11. 4. *testifying*, 1 Pet. 5. 12.
2 Kings 11. 12. gave him the *testimony*
Ps. 78. 5. established a *t.* in Jacob
Isa. 8. 16. bind up the *t.*, seal the law
Matt. 10. 18. for a *t.* against them
John 3. 32. no man receiveth his *t.*
Acts 14. 3. *t.* to word of his grace
2 Cor. 1. 12. the *t.* of our conscience
Rev. 1. 9. *t.* of Jesus Christ
11. 7. have finished their *t.*
Ps. 25. 10. keep his *testimonies*, 93. 5; *thy testimonies*, 119. 14, 24, 31, 46, 59, 95, 111, 129, 144.
R. V. John 2. 25; 3. 11, 39; 5. 39; 15. 26; 21. 24; Heb. 11. 14; 1 John 4. bear witness; 1 Cor. 15. 15; Heb. 7. 17. witnessed; Ruth 4. 7. attestation; John 3. 32, 33; 8. 17; 21. 24. witness; Acts 13. 22; 14. 3; Heb. 11. 5. bear witness; 1 Cor. 2. 1. mystery
THANK, 1 Chron. 16. 4. & 29. 13. Matt. 11. 25, 26. Luke 6. 32, 33. & 17. 9. & 18. 11. John 11. 41. Rom. 1. 8. & 7. 25. 1 Cor. 1. 4. 2 Thes. 2. 13. 1 Tim. 1. 12.
Ps. 100. 4. be *thankful*, Acts 24. 3. Rom. 1. 21. Col. 3. 15.
1 Pet. 2. 19. this is *thankworthy*
Dan. 6. 10. gave *thanks*, Matt. 26. 27. Mark 8. 6. Luke 22. 17. Rom. 14. 6.
2 Cor. 9. 15. *t.* to God for his unspeakable gift, 2. 14. & 8. 16. 1 Cor. 15. 57.
Eph. 5. 4. *giving of thanks*, 20. 1. Tit. 2. 1. Heb. 13. 15.
1 Thes. 3. 9. what *t.* can we render
Lev. 7. 12. *thanksgiving*, Neh. 11. 17. Ps. 26. 7. & 50. 14. & 100. 4. & 107. 22. & 116. 17. Isa. 51. 3. Phil. 4. 6. 1 Tim. 4. 3. Rev. 7. 12.
R. V. Heb. 13. 15. confession; Ps. 100. 4; Rom. 1. 21. give thanks
THEATRE, Acts 19. 29.
THINE is the day and night, Ps. 74. 16.
Ps. 119. 94. I am *t.*, save me
Isa. 63. 19. we are *t.* thou never
Matt. 20. 14. take that *t.* is and go
John 17. 6. *t.* they were, and thou
10. all mine are *t.* and *t.* are mine
R. V. Many changes to thy
THINGS devoted, Lev. 27. Num. 18. 14. Ezek. 44. 29; not to be redeemed, Lev. 27. 33; abuse of (Corban), Matt. 15. 5. Mark 7. 11.
THINK on me for good, Neh. 5. 19.
Job 31. 1. should I *t.* on a maid
Jer. 29. 11. I know that I *t.* toward
Rom. 12. 3. not to *t.* more highly
1 Cor. 8. 2. if any *t.* that he know.
Gal. 6. 3. *t.* himself to be some.
Eph. 3. 20. above all we ask or *t.*
Phil. 4. 8. *t.* on these things
Gen. 50. 20. *thought* evil against
Ps. 48. 9. we have *t.* of thy loving
119. 59. I *t.* on my ways and
Matt. 3. 16. that *t.* on his name
Mark 14. 72. he *t.* thereon wept
1 Cor. 13. 11. I *t.* as a child, spake
Phil. 2. 6. *t.* it not robbery to be
Ps. 139. 2. understandest my *t.*
Prov. 24. 9. the *t.* of foolishness
Eccl. 10. 20. curse not king in thy *t.*
Matt. 6. 25. take no *t.* for life
6. 34. take no *t.* for the morrow
Mark 13. 11. take no *t.* beforehand
2 Cor. 10. 5. every *t.* into captivity
Ps. 50. 21. thou *thoughtest* I was
Gen. 6. 5. imagination of *thoughts*
Judg. 5. 15. were great *t.* of heart
Ps. 10. 4. God is not in all his *t.*
33. 11. the *t.* of his heart to all
94. 11. Lord know. the *t.* of man
19. in multitude of my *t.* within
119. 113. hate vain *t.* but thy law
139. 17. how precious are thy *t.*
139. 23. try me and know my *t.*
Prov. 12. 5. *t.* of righte. are right
15. 26. the *t.* of the wicked are
16. 3. thy *t.* shall be established
Isa. 55. 7. let the unrighteous man forsake his *t.*
8. my *t.* are not your *t.*
Jer. 4. 14. how long shall vain *t.*
29. 11. *t.* I think toward you are *t.*
Mic. 4. 12. know not *t.* of the Lord
Matt. 15. 19. out of the heart proceed evil *t.*
Luke 2. 35. the *t.* of many hearts
24. 38. do *t.* arise in your hearts
Rom. 2. 15. their *t.* accusing, or
1 Cor. 3. 20. Lord knoweth the *t.*
Heb. 4. 12. a discerner of the *t.*
Jas. 2. 4. become judges of evil *t.*
R. V. Gen. 50. 10. meant; Ex. 32. 14; Esth. 6. 6. said; 2 Sam. 14. 13; Ezek. 38. 10. devise; 2 Chron. 11. 32. was minded; Neh. 5. 19. remember; Job 31. 1. look; 42. 2. purpose; Ezek. 38. 10. device; Luke 9. 47; 12. 7. reasoned; Luke 19. 11; Acts 13. 25. suppose; Acts 26. 8, Heb. 10. 29. judged; Rom. 2. 3. reckon; 2 Cor. 3. 5; 12. 16. account; 10. 7. consider; 10. 11. reckon
THIRST, Deut. 28. 48. & 29. 19.
Isa. 49. 10. shall not hunger nor *t.*
Matt. 5. 6. blessed are they which hunger and *t.* after righteousness
John 4. 14. shall never *t.*, 6. 35.
7. 37. if any *t.* let him come
Rom. 12. 20. if he *t.* give him drink
Rev. 7. 16. hunger nor *t.* any more
Ps. 42. 2. my soul *thirsteth* for God
Isa. 55. 1. ho, every one that *t.*
THORNS in your sides, Num. 33. 55. Judg. 2. 3. Gen. 3. 18.
Josh. 23. 13. be *t.* in your eyes
2 Sam. 23. 6. as *t.* thrust away
Jer. 4. 3. sow not among *t.*
Hos. 2. 6. hedge up thy way with *t.*
Matt. 7. 16. gather grapes of *t.*
13. 7. some fell among *t.*, 22.
Heb. 6. 8. that which beareth *t.*
R. V. 2 Chron. 33. 11. in chains; Job 41. 2. hook
THREATENING, Eph. 6. 9. Acts 4. 29. & 9. 1. 1 Pet. 2. 23.
THREE, 2 Sam. 24. 12. Prov. 30. 15, 18, 21, 29. Amos 1. 3, 13. & 2. 1. 1 Cor. 14. 27. 1 John 5. 7, 8. Rev. 16. 13.
THRESH, Isa. 21. 10. & 41. 15. Jer. 51. 33. Mic. 4. 13 Hab. 3. 12. 1 Cor. 9. 10.
Lev. 26. 5. and your *threshing* shall reach unto the vintage
2 Sam. 24. 18. *threshing-floor*, 21. 24.
R. V. Judg. 6. 11. beating out; Jer. 51. 33. trodden
THROAT is an open sepulchre, Ps. 5. 9.
Ps. 69. 3. weary of crying, my *t.*
Prov. 23. 2. put a knife to thy *t.*
THRONE, Lord is in heaven, Ps. 11. 4.
Ps. 94. 20. *t.* of iniquity have fel.
Prov. 25. 5. *t.* is established by
Isa. 66. 1. heaven is my *t.*
Jer. 14. 21. not disgrace *t.* of glory
Lam. 5. 19. *t.* from generation to
Dan. 7. 9. *t.* was like fiery flame
Matt. 19. 28. sit in *t.* of his glory, ye shall sit on twelve *thrones*
Col. 1. 16. whether they be *t.* or
Heb. 4. 16. boldly to the *t.* of grace
Rev. 3. 21. sit on my *t.* with my Father on his *t.*
22. 3. *t.* of God and Lamb shall be
Job 26. 9. *his throne*, Ps. 89. 14, 29, 44. & 97. 2. & 103. 19. Prov. 20. 28. & 25. 5. Dan. 7. 9. Zech. 6. 13.
Ps. 45. 6. *thy throne*, 99. 4. Heb. 1. 8.
Isa. 22. 33. *glorious throne*, Jer. 17. 12.
THRUST, Ex. 11. 1. Job 32. 13. Luke 13. 28. John 20. 25. Acts 16. 37.
R. V. Deut. 13. 5, 10. draw; Judg. 6. 38. pressed; 9. 41; 11. 2. drave; Job 32. 13. vanquished; 1 Sam. 11. 2; Luke 5. 3; John 20. 25, 27. put; Luke 4. 29; Acts 16. 24, 37; Rev. 14. 19. cast; Luke 10. 15. brought; Acts 27. 39. drive; Heb. 12. 20——; Rev. 14. 15, 18. send forth
THUNDER, Job 26. 14. & 40. 9. Ps. 29. 3. & 81. 7. Mark 3. 17.
Rev. 4. 5. *thunderings*, 8. 5. & 10. 3. & 11. 19. & 16. 18. & 19. 6.
R. V. Job 39. 19. quivering mane
TIDINGS, evil, Ex. 33. 4. Ps. 112. 7.
Luke 1. 19. show the glad *t.*, 8. 1. Acts 13. 32. Rom. 10. 15.
R. V. 1 Sam. 11. 4, 5, 6. word; Acts 11. 22. report
TIME when thou mayest be found, Ps. 32. 6.
Ps. 37. 19. evil *t.*
41. 1. *t.* of trouble
69. 13. acceptable *t.*, Isa. 49. 8. 2 Cor. 6. 2.
Ps. 89. 47. how short my *t.*
Eccl. 3. 1-8. *a time* to every purpose—to be born—to die—to plant—to pluck up—to love—to hate—of war—of peace
9. 11. *t.* and chance happen.
Ezek. 16. 8. *t.* was the *t.* of love
Dan. 7. 25. till a *t.* and times, div.
Amos 5. 13. evil *t.*, Mic. 2. 3.
Luke 19. 44. knew. not *t.* of thy
John 7. 6. my *t.* is not yet come
Acts 17. 21. spent *t.* in nothing
Rom. 13. 11. high *t.* to awake out
1 Cor. 7. 29. the *t.* is short, it rem.
2 Cor. 6. 2. accepted *t.* the day of
Eph. 5. 16. redeeming the *t.*
1 Pet. 1. 17. past *t.* of your sojourn.
Rev. 10. 6. *t.* shall be no longer
Ps. 31. 15. my *times* are in thy
Luke 21. 24. till *t.* of the Gentiles
Acts 1. 7. for you to know the *t.*
17. 26. determined the *t.* before
1 Tim. 4. 1. in latter *t.* some shall
2 Tim. 3. 1. in last days perilous *t.*
Ps. 34. 1. bless the Lord *at all times*
106. 3. blessed is he that doeth righteousness—
Prov. 5. 19. her breasts satisfy—
17. 17. a friend loveth—
R. V. Many changes to day, season, hour. So, many to suit context, as Matt. 4. 6. at any time to haply
TIN, Num. 31. 22. Isa. 1. 25. Ezek. 22. 18.
TITHES, Gen. 14. 20. Mal. 3. 8. Amos 4. 4. Matt. 23. 23. Luke 18. 12.
TITTLE or jot pass from the law, Matt. 5. 18.
R. V. 2 Kings 23. 17. monument
TOGETHER, Ps. 2. 2. Prov. 22. 2. Rom. 8. 28. all things work *t.* for
1 Cor. 3. 9. laborers *t.* with God

2 Cor. 6. 1. as workers *t.* with him
Eph. 2. 5. quickened us *t.* with
6. raised us up *t.* made us sit *t.*
TOKEN of covenant, Gen. 9. 12, 13. & 17. 11.
Ps. 86. 17. show me a *t.* for good
Phil. 1. 28. evident *t.* of perdition
2 Thes. 1. 5. manifest *t.* of right.
Job 21. 29. not know their *tokens*
Ps. 65. 8. they are afraid at thy *t.*
135. 9. who sent *t.* and wonders
Isa. 44. 25. frustrated the *t.* of liars
R. V. Ex. 13. 16; Ps. 135. 9. sign
TONGUE, Ex. 11. 7. Josh. 10. 21.
Job 5. 21. hid from scourge of *t.*
Ps. 34. 13. keep thy *t.* from evil
Prov. 10. 20. *t.* of the just is as
12. 18. *t.* of wise is health
15. 4. wholesome *t.* is a tree of
21. 6. get. treasure by a lying *t.*
25. 15. soft *t.* breaketh the bone
Isa. 30. 27. *t.* as a devouring fire
Jer. 9. 5. taught their *t.* to speak
18. 18. smite him with the *t.*
Jas. 1. 26. be religious and bridleth not his *t.*
3. 8. the *t.* can no man tame, 5.
1 Pet. 3. 10. refrain his *t.* from evil
1 John 3. 18. love in *t.* but deed
Ps. 35. 28. *my tongue*, 39. 1. & 45. 1. & 51. 14. & 71. 24. & 119. 172. & 137. 6. & 139. 4. Acts 2. 26.
Ps. 31. 26. *tongues*, 55. 9. Mark 16. 17. Acts 19. 6. 1 Cor. 12. 10, 28. & 14. 23.
TOOK out of the womb, Ps. 22. 9.
Phil. 2. 7. *t.* on him form of ser.
Heb. 10. 34. *t.* joyfully the spoiling
R. V. Ezra 4. 17; Esth. 7. 4; Job 6. 24; 13. 19; Amos 6. 10. peace; Acts 2. 8; 21. 40; 22. 2; 26. 14. language; Rev. 9. 11; 16. 16 —
TOPHET, Isa. 30. 33. Jer. 7. 31, 32.
TORCH, Zech. 12. 6. Nah. 2. 3, 4.
R. V. Nah. 2. 3. flash with steel
TORMENT us before the time, Matt. 8. 29.
Luke 16. 28. to this place of *t.*
Rev. 18. 7. so much *t.* and sorrow
Luke 16. 24. am *tormented* in this
25. he is comforted, thou art *t.*
Heb. 11. 37. destitute, afflicted, *t.*
R. V. 1 John 4. 18. punishment; Luke 16. 24, 25. in anguish; Heb. 11. 37. evil entreated
TORN, Hos. 6. 1. Mal. 1. 13. Mark 1. 26.
TOSS, Isa. 22. 18. Jer. 5. 22. Jas. 1. 6.
Ps. 109. 23. I am *tossed* up and
Isa. 54. 11. *t.* with a tempest
Eph. 4. 14. children *t.* to and fro
R. V. Prov. 21. 6. driven; Matt. 14. 24. distressed; Acts 27. 18. labored
TOUCH not mine anointed, Ps. 105. 15.
Job 5. 19. in seven shall no evil *t.*
Isa. 52. 11. *t.* no unclean thing
Matt. 9. 21. but *t.* his garment
14. 36. only *t.* hem of his garment
Mark 10. 13. chil. that he should *t.*
Luke 11. 46. *t.* not the burdens
John 20. 17. *t.* me not, for I am
2 Cor. 6. 17. *t.* not the unclean
Col. 2. 21. *t.* not, taste not, handle
1 Sam. 10. 26. whose heart God had *touched*
Job 19. 21. hand of God hath *t.*
Luke 8. 45. who *t.* me
Zech. 2. 8. *toucheth* you, *t.* apple
1 John 5. 18. wicked one *t.* him
TOWER, God is a high, Ps. 18. 2. & 144. 2.
Ps. 61. 3. strong *t.*, Prov. 18. 10.
S. of S. 4. 4. *t.* of David
7. 4. *t.* of ivory; *t.* of Lebanon
Isa. 5. 2. built a *t.*, Matt. 21. 33.
R. V. 2 Kings 5. 24. hill; Zeph. 1. 16; 3. 6. battlements
TRADERS in Tyre, Ezek. 27.
TRADITION, Matt. 15. 3. Gal. 1. 14. Col. 2. 8. 2 Thes. 2. 15. & 3. 6. 1 Pet. 1. 18.
R. V. 1 Pet. 1. 18. handed down
TRAIN, Prov. 22. 6. Isa. 6. 1.
TRAITOR, Luke 6. 16. 2 Tim. 3. 4.
TRAMPLE, Isa. 63. 3. Matt. 7. 6.
TRANCE, Num. 24. 4. Acts 10. 10. & 11. 5. & 22. 17.
R. V. Num. 24. 4, 16. down
TRANQUILLITY, Dan. 4. 27.
TRANSFIGURED, Matt. 17. 2. Mark 9. 2.
TRANSFORMED, Rom. 12. 2. 2 Cor. 11. 14, 15.
R. V. 2 Cor. 11. 13, 14, 15. fashion
TRANSGRESS the commandment of the Lord, Num. 14. 41.
1 Sam. 2. 24. ye make the Lord's people to *t.*
2 Chron. 24. 20. why *t.* ye the
Neh. 1. 8. if ye *t.* I will scatter
Ps. 17. 3. mouth shall not *t.*
25. 3. ashamed that *t.* without
Prov. 28. 21. for piece of bread man will *t.*
Amos 4. 4. come to Bethel and *t.*
Matt. 15. 2. why do thy disciples *t.*
3. why do ye *t.* the command.
Rom. 2. 27. by circumcision dost *t.*
Deut. 26. 13. not *transgressed* thy
Josh. 7. 11. have *t.* my covenant
Isa. 43. 27. teachers have *t.* against
Jer. 2. 8. pastors also *t.* against
Lam. 3. 42. have *t.* and rebelled
Ezek. 2. 3. and their fathers *t.*
Dan. 9. 11. all Israel have *t.* thy
Hos. 6. 7. men have *t.* the covenant
Hab. 2. 5. *transgresseth* by wine
1 John 3. 4. committeth sin, *t.*
Ex. 34. 7. forgiving iniquity, *transgression*, and sin, Num. 14. 18.
1 Chron. 10. 13. Saul died for his *t.*
Ezra 10. 6. mourned because of *t.*
Job 13. 23. make me to know my *t.*
Ps. 32. 1. blessed is he whose *t.* is forgiven
89. 32. visit their *t.* with rod
Prov. 17. 9. he that covereth *t.* seek.
Isa. 53. 8. for *t.* of my people
58. 1. show my people their *t.*
Dan. 9. 24. to finish *t.* and make
Amos 4. 4. at Gilgal multiply *t.*
Mic. 3. 8. declare to Jacob his *t.*
Rom. 4. 15. no law is, there is no *t.*
1 John 3. 4. sin is the *t.* of the
Ex. 23. 21. pardon *transgressions*
Lev. 16. 21. all their *t.* in all their
Josh. 24. 19. not forgive your *t.*
Job 31. 33. covered my *t.* as Adam
Ps. 25. 7. remember not my *t.*
39. 8. deliver me from all my *t.*
51. 1. blot out my *t.*
65. 3. our *t.* thou shalt purge
103. 12. so far removed our *t.*
Isa. 43. 25. he that blotteth out *t.*
44. 22. out as a thick cloud, thy *t.*
53. 5. he was wounded for our *t.*
Ezek. 18. 31. cast away all your *t.*
Heb. 9. 15. the redemption of *t.*
Isa. 48. 8. wast a *transgressor* from
Jas. 2. 11. if thou kill, thou art become a *t.* of the law
Ps. 51. 13. teach *transgressors* thy
59. 5. be not merciful to wicked *t.*
119. 158. I beheld the *t.* and
Prov. 13. 15. the way of *t.* is hard
Isa. 53. 12. was numbered with *t.* and made intercession for *t.*, Mark 15. 28.
Hos. 14. 9. the *t.* shall fall therein
R. V. 1 Chron. 2. 7; 5. 25; 2 Chron. 12. 2; 26. 16; 28. 19; 36. 14; Ezra 10. 10; Neh. 1. 8; 13. 27; Hos. 7. 13. trespass; 1 Sam. 14. 33; Ps. 25. 3; Hab. 2. 5. deal treacherously; Jer. 2. 20. serve; 1 John 3. 4. doeth lawlessness; 2 John 9. goeth onward; Josh. 22. 22; 1 Chron. 10. 13; Ezra 9. 14; 10. 6; 2 Chron. 29. 19. trespass; 1 John 3. 4. lawlessness; Prov. 2. 22; 11. 3, 6; 13. 2, 15; 21. 18; 22. 12; 23. 28. treacherous; 26. 10. that pass by
TRANSLATION, of Enoch, Gen. 5. 24. Heb. 11. 5; of Elijah, 2 Kings 2
TRAVAIL, Isa. 53. 11. Gal. 4. 19, 27.
Job 15. 20. the wicked *travaileth*
Ps. 7. 14. he *t.* with iniquity
Isa. 66. 7. before she *travailed*, 8.
42. 14. *travailing* woman, Hos. 13. 13. Isa. 13. 8. & 21. 3. Jer. 31. 8. Rev. 12. 2.
R. V. Eccl. 4. 4. labor; 5. 14. adventure
TRAVEL, Eccl. 1. 13. & 2. 23, 26. & 4. 4, 6, 8. & 5. 14. 2 Thes. 3. 8.
Job 15. 20. *travelleth*, Prov. 6. 11. & 24. 34.
Isa. 21. 13. *travelling*, 63. 1.
R. V. Prov. 6. 11; 24. 34. a robber; Isa. 63. 1. marching; Matt. 25. 14. going
TREACHEROUS, Isa. 21. 2. & 24. 16.
Jer. 9. 2. an assembly of *t.* men
Isa. 21. 2. *treacherously*, 24. 16. & 33. 1.
48. 8. knew thou wouldst deal *t.*
Jer. 3. 20. as a wife *t.* departeth
12. 1. all happy that deal *t.*
Hos. 5. 7. dealt *t.* against Lord
Mal. 2. 15. none deal *t.* against
TREACHERY, instances of, Gen. 34. 13. Judg. 9. 1 Sam. 21. 7. & 22. 9. (Ps. 52.) 2 Sam. 3. 27. & 11. 14. & 16. & 20. 9. 1 Kings 21. 5. 2 Kings 10. 18. Esth. 3. Matt. 26. 47. Mark 14. 43. Luke 22. 47. John 18. 3.
TREAD down wicked in place, Job 40. 12.
Ps. 7. 5. let him *t.* down my life
Isa. 1. 12. required this to *t.* my
63. 3. *t.* them in mine anger, 6.
Hos. 10. 11. Ephraim loveth to *t.*
Rev. 11. 2. city shall be *t.* under
Deut. 25. 4. not muzzle the ox that *treadeth* out the corn, 1 Cor. 9. 9. 1 Tim. 5. 18.
Isa. 22. 5. *treading*, Amos 5. 11.
R. V. Isa. 1. 12; Amos 5. 11. trample
TREASON, instances, 2 Sam. 15-18. & 20. 1 Kings 1. & 16. 10. 2 Kings 11. & 15. 10. 2 Chron. 22. 10. Esth. 2. 21.
TREASURE, Prov. 15. 6, 16. & 21. 20.
Ex. 19. 5. peculiar *t.*, Ps. 135. 4.
Isa. 33. 6. fear of the Lord is his *t.*
Matt. 6. 21. where your *t.* is there
12. 35. good man out of good *t.*
13. 52. bringeth forth out of his *t.*
19. 21. shalt have *t.* in heaven
Luke 12. 21. layeth up *t.* for him.
2 Cor. 4. 7. this *t.* in earthen ves.
Deut. 32. 34. sealed up among my *treasures*
Ps. 17. 14. fillest with thy hid *t.*
Prov. 2. 4. search. for her as hid *t.*
10. 2. *t.* of wickedness profit no.
Matt. 6. 19. lay not up *t.* on earth
20. lay up for yourselves *t.* in
Col. 2. 3. in whom are hid all the *t.* of wisdom
Rom. 2. 5. *treasurest* up unto thy.
R. V. 1 Chron. 26. 20, 22, 24, 26; 27. 25; Job 38. 22; Prov. 8. 21; Jer. 10. 3; 51. 16. treasuries; Jer. 41. 8. stores hidden
TREE, Gen. 2. 16, 17. & 3. 22.
Ps. 1. 3. like a *t.* planted by rivers
52. 8. I am like a green olive *t.*
Prov. 3. 18. she is a *t.* of life to
11. 30. fruit of righteous. is *t.* of
Isa. 6. 13. be eaten as a teil *t.*
56. 3. eunuch say, I am a dry *t.*
Jer. 17. 8. a *t.* planted by the wat.
Matt. 3. 10. *t.* that bringeth not
7. 17. good *t.* bringeth forth
12. 33. make the *t.* good; or else
1 Pet. 2. 24. in his own body on *t.*
Rev. 2. 7. give to eat of *t.* of life
22. 2. midst of city was *t.* of life
14. have right to the *t.* of life
Ps. 104. 16. the *trees* of the Lord
Isa. 61. 3. called *t.* of righteous.
Ezek. 47. 12. grow all *t.* for meat
Mark 8. 24. I see men as *t.* walk.
Jude 12. *t.* whose fruit withereth

TREMBLE at the commandment of our God, Ezra 10. 3.
Ps. 99. 1. Lord reign., let people *t.*
Isa. 66. 5. ye that *t.* at his word
Jer. 5. 22. not *t.* at my presence
10. 10. at his wrath earth shall *t.*
Dan. 6. 26. men *t.* before the God
Jas. 2. 19. devils believe and *t.*
1 Sam. 4. 13. heart *trembled* for ark
Ezra 9. 4. every one that *t.* at
Acts 24. 25. he reasoned, Felix *t.*
Job 37. 1. *trembleth*, Ps. 119. 120. Isa. 66. 2.
1 Sam. 13. 7. followed *trembling*
Deut. 28. 65. give thee a *t.* heart
Ezra 10. 9. people sat *t.* because
Ps. 2. 11. serve God and rejoice *t.*
Ezek. 12. 18. drink thy water with *t.*, 26. 16.
Hos. 13. 1. Ephraim spake *t.*
1 Cor. 2. 3. fear and in much *t.*
Eph. 6. 5. fear and *t.* in singleness
Phil. 2. 12. work out your sal. with *t.*
R. V. Hab. 3. 10. were afraid; Acts 24. 25. was terrified; Job 21. 6. horror; Isa. 51. 17, 22. staggering; Zech. 12. 2. reeling

TRESPASS, Lev. 26. 40. Ezra 9. 6. 1 Kings 8. 31. Matt. 18. 15. Luke 17. 3.
Ezra 9. 15. *trespasses*, Ezek. 39. 26.
Ps. 68. 21. goeth on still in his *t.*
Matt. 6. 14. forgive men their *t.*
18. 35. if ye forgive not every one his brother their *t.*
Eph. 2. 1. dead in *t.* and sins
Col. 2. 13. forgiven you all *t.*
R. V. Gen. 50. 17. transgression; Num. 5. 7, 8; Lev. 6. 5; 22. 16; 1 Chron. 21. 3; 2 Chron. 19. 10; Ezra 9. 7, 13; 10. 10, 19. guilt or guilty; 2 Chron. 24. 18; Ezra 6. 15; 9. 6, 15; Ps. 68. 21. guiltiness; Matt. 8.35; Mark 11. 26 ——; 2 Chron. 19. 10. be guilty; 1 Kings 8. 31; Matt. 18. 5; Luke 17. 3, 4. sin

TRIAL, Job 9. 23. Ezek. 21. 13. 2 Cor. 8. 2. Heb. 11. 36. 1 Pet. 1. 7. & 4. 12.
R. V. 2 Cor. 8. 2; 1 Pet. 1. 7. proof

TRIBES, Num. 24. 2.
Ps. 105. 37. one feeble among *t.*
122. 4. whither *t.* go up, *t.* of
Matt. 24. 30. all the *t.* of earth
Acts 26. 7. promise our twelve *t.*

TRIBULATION, art in, Deut. 4. 30.
Judg. 10. 14. deliver you in *t.*
Matt. 13. 21. when *t.* or persecu.
24. 21. then shall be great *t.* such
29. immediately after the *t.*
John 16. 33. ye shall have *t.*
Acts 14. 22. through much *t.*
Rom. 2. 9. *t.* and anguish on every
5. 3. knowing *t.* worketh patience
12. 12. in hope, patient in *t.*
2 Cor. 1. 4. comfort. us in all our *t.*
1 Thes. 3. 4. we should suffer *t.*
2 Thes. 1. 6. to recompense *t.* to
Rev. 1. 9. and companion in *t.*
2. 9. I know thy works and *t.*
22. cast into great *t.* except
7. 14. have come out of great *t.*
Rom. 5. 3. glory in *tribulations*
1 Sam. 10. 19. save. you out of all *t.*
Eph. 3. 13. faint not at my *t.* for
2 Thes. 1. 4. patience in all *t.*
R. V. Judg. 10. 14; 1 Sam. 10. 19. distress; 2 Cor. 1. 4; 7. 4; 1 Thes. 1. 4; 3. 4; 2 Thes. 1. 6. affliction

TRIBUTE, Gen. 49. 15. Num. 31. 28.
Matt. 17. 24. doth not your Master pay *t.*
22. 17. is it lawful to give *t.* to Cæsar
Rom. 13. 7. *t.* to whom *t.* is due
R. V. Gen. 49. 15; Josh. 16. 10; 17. 13; Judg. 1. 28; Prov. 12. 24. task work; 1 Kings 4. 6; 9. 21; 12. 18; 2 Chron. 10. 18. levy; 2 Chron. 8. 8. bond servants; Matt. 17. 24. half shekel

TRIMMED, Jer. 2. 33. Matt. 25. 7.

TRIUMPH, 2 Sam. 1. 20. Ps. 25. 2.
Ps. 92. 4. *t.* in works of thy hands
2 Cor. 2. 14. always cause. us to *t.*
Ex. 15. 1. *triumphed* gloriously
Job 20. 5. *triumphing*, Col. 2. 15.
R. V. Ps. 60. 8; 108. 9. shout

TRODDEN down strength, Judg. 5. 21.
Ps. 119. 118. *t.* down all them
Isa. 63. 3. have *t.* winepress alone
Luke 21. 24. Jerusalem shall be *t.*
Heb. 10. 29. *t.* under foot Son of

TROUBLE, 2 Chron. 15. 4. Neh. 9. 32.
Job 5. 6. neither doth *t.* spring
14. 1. man is of few days and full of *t.*
Ps. 9. 9. refuge in times of *t.*
22. 11. *t.* is near; there is none
27. 5. in time of *t.* he shall hide
46. 1. God is a present help in *t.*
91. 15. I will be with him in *t.*
143. 11. bring my soul out of *t.*
Prov. 11. 8. the righteous is delivered out of *t.*
Isa. 26. 16. Lord, in *t.* have they
33. 2. our salvation in time of *t.*
Jer. 8. 15. looked for health, and behold *t.*
14. 8. and Saviour in time of *t.*
Dan. 12. 1. shall be a time of *t.*
Cor. 7. 28. have *t.* in the flesh
Ps. 25. 17. the *troubles* of my heart
34. 17. deliver them out of all *t.*
88. 3. my soul is full of *t.*
Ex. 14. 24. Lord *troubled* the host
Ps. 30. 7. and I was *t.*
Isa. 57. 20. wic. are like the *t.* sea
John 12. 27. now is my soul *t.*
14. 1. let not your hearts be *t.*
2 Cor. 4. 8. *t.* on every side, 7. 5.
2 Thes. 1. 7. to you who are *t.* rest
Job 23. 16. Almighty *troubleth* me
1 Kings 18. 17. he that *t.* Israel
Prov. 11. 17. cruel *t.* his own flesh
29. he that *t.* his own house
Luke 18. 5. because this widow *t.*
Gal. 5. 10. he that *t.* you shall
Job 3. 17. *troubling*, John 5. 4.
R. V. 1 Chron. 22. 14; Ps. 9. 13; 31. 7, 9; 2 Cor. 1. 4, 8. affliction; 2 Chron. 15. 4; Job 15. 24; Ps. 59. 16; 66. 14, 17; 102. 2; Isa. 8. 22. distress; 2 Chron. 29. 8. tossed to and fro; Neh. 9. 32. travail; Job 34. 29. condemn; Ps. 41. 1. evil; Ps. 78. 33; Isa. 17. 14. terror; Ps. 3. 1; 13. 4; 60. 11. adversaries; Isa. 22. 5. discomfiture; 65. 23. calamity; Jer. 8. 15; 14. 19. dismay; Ezek. 7. 7. tumult; Acts 20. 10. make no ado; 1 Cor. 7. 28. tribulation; 2 Tim. 2. 9. hardship; Mark 13. 8 ——; Ex. 14. 24. discomfited; Job 34. 20. shaken; Ps. 38. 5. pained; 77. 3. disquieted; 77. 16. trembled; 48. 5; 83. 17; Ezek. 26. 18. dismayed; Zech. 10. 2; 2 Thes. 1. 7. afflicted; John 5. 4 ——

TRUCE breakers, 2 Tim. 3. 3.

TRUE, Gen. 42. 11. 2 Sam. 7. 28.
Ps. 19. 9. judgments of Lord are *t.*
119. 160. thy word is *t.*
Prov. 14. 25. *t.* witness delivereth
Jer. 42. 5. be *t.* and faithful wit.
Ezek. 18. 8. *t.* judgment, Zech. 7. 9.
Matt. 22. 16. we know thou art *t.*
Luke 16. 11. *t.* riches
John 1. 9. *t.* light
4. 23. *t.* worshippers
6. 32. *t.* bread from heaven
15. 1. I am the *t.* vine
2 Cor. 1. 18. as God is *t.* our word
6. 8. as deceivers and yet *t.*
Phil. 4. 8. what. things are *t.*
1 John 5. 20. know him that is *t.*
Rev. 3. 7. saith he that is *t.*
19. 11. was called faithful and *t.*
R. V. 2 Cor. 1. 18; 1 Tim. 3. 1. faithful

TRUMP. 1 Cor. 15. 52. 1 Thes. 16. 4.

TRUMPET, Ex. 19. 16. Ps. 81. 3.
Isa. 27. 13. great *t.* shall be blown
Isa. 58. 1. lift up thy voice like a *t.*
Matt. 6. 2. not sound a *t.* before
Num. 10. 2. *trumpets*, Josh. 6. 4. Ps. 98. 6. Rev. 8. 9.

TRUST in him, 1 Chron. 5. 20.
Job 4. 18. put no *t.* in servants
8. 14. his *t.* is a spider's web
Ps. 4. 5. put your *t.* in the Lord
40. 4. maketh the Lord his *t.*
71. 5. art my *t.* from my youth
Prov. 22. 19. thy *t.* may be in Lord
Job 13. 15. though he slay me I will *t.*
Ps. 37. 3. *t.* in Lord, and do good
5. *t.* in him; he will bring it to
55. 23. I will *t.* in thee
62. 8. *t.* in him at all times, ye
115. 8, 9, 10, 11. *t.* in the Lord
118. 8. it is better to *t.* in Lord, 9.
119. 42. for I *t.* in thy word
Prov. 3. 5. *t.* in the Lord with all
Isa. 26. 4. *t.* ye in the Lord for ever
Jer. 7. 4. *t.* not in lying words
9. 4. *t.* not in any brother
Mic. 7. 5. *t.* ye not in a friend
Mark 10. 24. them that *t.* in riches
2 Cor. 1. 9. not *t.* in ourselves
Phil. 3. 4. whereof to *t.* in flesh
1 Tim. 6. 20. committed to thy *t.*
Ps. 22. 4. our fathers *trusted* in
52. 7. *t.* in abundance of his
Luke 18. 9. *t.* in themselves
Eph. 1. 12. who first *t.* in Christ
Ps. 32. 10. *trusteth* in Lord's
34. 8. blessed is man that *t.* in
86. 2. save servant that *t.* in thee
Jer. 17. 5. cursed be the man that *t.* in man
1 Tim. 5. 5. desolate *t.* in God
Ps. 112. 7. heart is fixed *trusting*
R. V. Ruth 2. 12; Ps. 36. 7; 37. 40; 61. 4; 91. 4; Isa. 14. 32. take refuge; Matt. 12. 21; Luke 24. 21; Rom. 15. 12, 24; 1 Cor. 16. 7; 2 Cor. 1. 10, 13; 5. 11; 13. 6; Eph. 1. 12; Phil. 2. 19; 1 Tim. 4. 10; 6. 17; Phile. 22; 2 John 12; 3 John 14. hope or hoped; 2 Cor. 3. 4; Phil. 3. 4. confidence; Heb. 13. 18. persuaded

TRUTH, Gen. 24. 27. Ex. 18. 21.
Deut. 34. 4. a God of *t.* and with.
Ps. 15. 2. speaketh *t.* in his heart
25. 10. the paths of the Lord are mercy and *t.*
91. 4. his *t.* shall be thy shield
117. 2. his *t.* endureth for ever
119. 30. chosen the way of *t.*
Prov. 12. 19. lip of *t.* shall be
16. 6. by mercy and *t.* iniquity
23. 23. buy the *t.* and sell it not
Isa. 59. 14. *t.* is fallen in the streets
Jer. 4. 2. swear Lord liveth in *t.*
Dan. 4. 37. all whose ways are *t.*
Zech. 8. 16. speak every man *t.* to his neighbor
Mal. 2. 6. law of *t.* was in his mouth
John 1. 14. full of grace and *t.*
8. 32. know the *t.* and the *t.* shall make you free
14. 6. the way, the *t.* and life
17. 17. sanctify them through *t.*
18. 37. bear witness to *t.*
Acts 26. 25. words of *t.* and sober.
Rom. 1. 18. hold *t.* in unrighteous.
2. 2. judg. of God is accord. to *t.*
1 Cor. 5. 8. the unleavened bread of sincerity and *t.*
2 Cor. 13. 8. do nothing against *t.*
Gal. 3. 1. should not obey the *t.*
Eph. 4. 15. speaking *t.* in love
5. 9. fruit of the Spirit is in all *t.*
6. 14. loins girt about with *t.*
2 Thes. 2. 10. receiv. not love of *t.*
1 Tim. 3. 15. pillar and ground of *t.*
6. 5. corrupt, destitute of the *t.*
2 Tim. 2. 18. who concerning the *t.*
25. acknowledging of the *t.*
3. 7. come to the knowl. of the *t.*
4. 4. turn away their ears from *t.*
Jas. 3. 14. nor lie against *t.*
2 Pet. 1. 12. establish. in present *t.*
1 John 1. 8. *t.* is not in us
5. 6. Spirit is *t.*

Josh. 24. 14. *in truth*, 1 Sam. 12. 24. Ps. 145. 18. Jer. 4. 2. John 4. 24. 1 Thes. 2. 13. 1 John 3. 18. 2 John 4.
Ps. 25. 5. *thy truth*, 26. 3. & 43. 3. & 108. 4. John 17. 17.
R. V. Deut. 32. 4; Ps. 33. 4; 89. 49; 98. 3; 119. 30. faithfulness

TRY, Judg. 7. 4. Job 12. 11. Jer. 6. 27.
2 Chron. 32. 31. God left him to *t.*
Job 7. 18. visit him and *t.* him
Ps. 11. 4. eyelids *t.* the children
26. 2. *t.* my reins and my heart
Jer. 9. 7. melt them, and *t.* them
Lam. 3. 40. search and *t.* our ways
Dan. 11. 35. shall fall to *t.* them
Zech. 13. 9. *t.* them as gold is tried
1 Cor. 3. 13. fire shall *t.* every
1 Pet. 4. 12. fiery trial which is to *t.*
1 John 4. 1. *t.* the spirits whether
Rev. 3. 10. to *t.* them that dwell
2 Sam. 22. 31. word of Lord is *tried*, Ps. 18. 30.
Ps. 12. 6. word is pure as silver *t.*
66. 10. *t.* us as silver is *t.*
105. 19. word of the Lord *t.* him
Jer. 12. 3. *t.* mine heart towards
Dan. 12. 10. be purified and *t.*
Jas. 1. 12. when he is *t.* he shall receive the crown of life
Rev. 2. 2. hast *t.* them and found
3. 18. buy of me gold, *t.* in the
1 Chron. 29. 17. I know thou *triest*
Jer. 11. 20. that *t.* the reins and
20. 12. thou that *t.* the righteous
Ps. 7. 9. the righteous God *trieth*
11. 5. the Lord *t.* the righteous
1 Thes. 2. 4. pleasing God, who *t.*
Jas. 1. 3. *trying* of your faith
R. V. Dan. 11. 35. refine; 1 Cor. 3. 13; 1 Pet. 4. 12; 1 John 4. 1. prove

TUMULT, Ps. 65. 7. 2 Cor. 12. 20.
R. V. 2 Kings 19. 28; Isa. 37. 29. arrogancy; Acts 21. 34. uproar

TURN, from their sin, 1 Kings 8. 35.
2 Kings 17. 13. *t.* from your evil
Job 23. 13. who can *t.* him
Prov. 1. 23. *t.* you at my reproof
S. of S. 2. 17. *t.* my belov., be thou
Isa. 31. 6. *t.* ye unto him, from
Jer. 18. 8. if *t.* from their evil; I
31. 18. *t.* thou me and I shall
Lam. 5. 21. *t.* us unto thee, O Lord
Ezek. 3. 19. *t.* not from his wicked.
18. 30. *t.* yourselves from your
32. *t.* yourselves and live, 33. 9. Hos. 12. 6. Joel 2. 12. Zech. 9. 12.
Zech. 1. 3. *t.* to me, and I will *t.*
Mal. 4. 6. *t.* hearts of fathers to
Acts 26. 18. *t.* them from darkness
20. should repent, and *t.* to God
2 Pet. 2. 21. to *t.* from holy com.
2 Chron. 30. 6. *turn again*, Ps. 60. 1. & 80. 3, 7, 19. & 85. 8. Lam. 3. 40. Mic. 7. 19. Zech. 10. 9. Gal. 4. 9.
1 Sam. 12. 20. *turn aside*, Ps. 40. 4. Isa. 30. 11. Lam. 3. 35. Amos 2. 7. & 5. 12.
Ps. 119. 37. *turn away*, 39. S. of S. 6. 5. Isa. 58. 13. 1 Tim. 3. 5. Heb. 12. 25.
Deut. 4. 20. *turn to the Lord*, 20. 10. 2 Chron. 15. 4. Ps. 4. 22, 27. Lam. 3. 40. Hos. 14. 2. Joel 2. 13. Luke 1. 16. 2 Cor. 3. 16.
Ps. 9. 17. wicked shall be *turned*
30. 11. *t.* my mourning into danc.
119. 5. *t.* my feet to thy testimo.
Isa. 53. 6. *t.* every one to own
63. 10. was *t.* to be their enemy
Jer. 2. 27. *t.* their back to me
8. 6. every one *t.* to his own
Hos. 7. 8. Ephraim is a cake not *t.*
John 6. 20. sorrow shall be *t.* to
1 Thes. 1. 9. *t.* to God from idols
Jas. 4. 9. laughter be *t.* to mourn.
2 Pet. 2. 22. dog is *t.* to his vomit
Deut. 9. 12. *turned aside*, Ps. 78. 57. Isa. 44. 20. 2 Tim. 1. 6. & 5 15.
1 Kings 11. 3. *turned away*, Ps. 66. 20. & 78. 38. Isa. 5. 25. & 9. 12. & 10. 4. Jer. 5. 25.
Ps. 44. 18. *turned back*, 78. 9, 41. Isa. 42. 17. Jer. 4. 8. Zeph. 1. 6.
Job 15. 13. *turnest*, Ps. 90. 3.
Ps. 146. 9. wicked he *turneth*
Prov. 15. 1. soft answer *t.* away
21. 1. he *t.* it whithersoever he
Isa. 9. 13. the people *t.* not unto
Jer. 14. 8. *t.* aside to tarry for a
Jas. 1. 17. no shadow of *turning*
Jude 4. *t.* grace of God into
R. V. Changes are chiefly to return, change, and other words dependent on context

TURTLE, Lev. 1. 14. & 5. 7, 11. & 12. 6. Ps. 74. 19. S. of S. 2. 12. Jer. 8. 7.

TUTORS, Gal. 4. 2.

TWAIN, Matt. 5. 41. & 19. 5. Eph. 2. 15.

TWELVE, the, ordained, Mark 3. 14.

TWICE, Gen. 41. 32. Ex. 16. 22. Num. 20. 11. 1 Kings 11. 9. Job 33. 14. & 40. 5. Ps. 62. 11. Mark 14. 30. Luke 18. 12. *t.* dead, Jude 12.

TWINKLING, 1 Cor. 15. 52.

TYPES of Christ. *See* CHRIST

TYRANNY, instances of, Ex. 1. & 5. 1 Sam. 22. 9. 1 Kings 12. 4. & 21. Jer. 26. 20. Matt. 2. Acts 12.

U

UNACCUSTOMED, Jer. 31. 18.

UNADVISEDLY, Ps. 106. 33.

UNAWARES, Deut. 4. 42. Ps. 35. 8. Luke 21. 34. Heb. 13. 2. Jude 4.
R. V. Num. 35. 11, 15; Josh. 20. 3, 9. unwittingly; Luke 21. 34. suddenly; Gal. 2. 4; Jude 4. privily

UNBELIEF, did not many mighty works there bec. of, Matt. 13. 58.
Mark 6. 6. marvelled because of *u.*
9. 24. help thou mine *u.*
Rom. 4. 20. stagger. not through *u.*
11. 20. because of *u.* were broken
1 Tim. 1. 13. ignorantly in *u.*
Heb. 3. 12. an evil heart of *u.*
19. not enter in because of *u.*
R. V. Matt. 17. 20. little faith; Rom. 11. 30, 32; Heb. 4. 6, 11. disobedience; Rom. 3. 3. want of faith

UNBELIEVERS, Luke 12. 46. 2 Cor. 6. 14.
R. V. Luke 12. 46. unfaithful

UNBELIEVING, Acts 14. 2. 1 Cor. 7. 14, 15. Tit. 1. 15. Rev. 21. 8.
R. V. Acts 14. 2. disobedient

UNBLAMABLE, Col. 1. 22. 1 Thes. 3. 13.
1 Thes. 2. 10. *unblamably* behaving
R. V. Col. 1. 22. without blemish

UNCERTAIN, 1 Cor. 14. 8. 1 Tim. 6. 17.

UNCIRCUMCISED, Ex. 6. 12, 30. Jer. 6. 10. & 9. 25, 26. Acts 7. 51.

UNCIRCUMCISION, Rom. 2. 25, 26, 27. & 3. 30. & 4. 10. 1 Cor. 7. 18, 19. Gal. 2. 7. & 5. 6. & 6. 15. Col. 2. 13. & 3. 11.

UNCLEAN, Lev. 5. 11, 13, 15. Num. 19. 19.
Lev. 10. 10. difference between *u.*
Isa. 6. 5. I am a man of *u.* lips
Lam. 4. 15. depart ye; it is *u.*
Ezek. 44. 23. discern between *u.*
Hag. 2. 13. if one *u.* touch
Acts 10. 28. not call any man common or *u.*, 14.
Rom. 14. 14. is nothing *u.* of itself
1 Cor. 7. 14. else were children *u.*
Eph. 5. 5. nor *u.* person hath any
Num. 5. 19. *uncleanness*, Ezra 9. 11.
Zech. 13. 1. fountain for sin and *u.*
Matt. 23. 27. are with. full of all *u.*
Eph. 4. 19. all *u.* with greediness
5. 3. all *u.* let it not once be
1 Thes. 4. 7. not called us to *u.*
Ezek. 36. 29. save you from all *u.*
R. V. 2 Pet. 2. 10. defilement

UNCLEAN SPIRITS, Matt. 10. 1. & 12. 43, 45. Acts 5. 16. Rev. 16. 13.
—animals, Lev. 11. & 20. 25. Deut. 14. 3.

UNCLOTHED, 2 Cor. 5. 4.

UNCOMELY, 1 Cor. 7. 36. & 12. 23.

UNCONDEMNED, Acts 16. 37. & 22. 25.

UNCORRUPTNESS, Tit. 2. 7.

UNCOVER, Lev. 18. 18. 1 Cor. 11. 5, 13.
R. V. Lev. 21. 6, 10; Num. 5. 18. let hair go loose; Isa. 47. 2. remove; Hab. 2. 16. circumcised; Zeph. 2. 14. laid bare; 1 Cor. 11. 5, 13. unveiled

UNCTION, 1 John 2. 20, 27.

UNDEFILED in way, Ps. 119. 1.
S. of S. 5. 2. my dove, my *u.*, 6. 9.
Heb. 7. 26. holy, harmless, *u.*
Jas. 1. 27. pure religion and *u.*
R. V. Ps. 119. 1. perfect

UNDER their God, Hos. 4. 12.
Rom. 3. 9. all *u.* sin, 7. 14. Gal. 3. 22; *u.* law, Rom. 6. 15. 1 Cor. 9. 20. Gal. 3. 23. & 4. 4.
1 Cor. 9. 27. I keep *u.* my body

UNDERSTAND not, one another's speech, Gen. 11. 7.
Neh. 8. 7. caused people to *u.*
Ps. 19. 12. who can *u.* his errors
107. 43. shall *u.* loving kindness
119. 100. I *u.* more than ancients
Prov. 2. 5. shalt thou *u.* fear of
8. 5. *u.* wisdom
19. 25. *u.* knowledge
Isa. 32. 4. heart of the rash shall *u.*
1 Cor. 13. 2. to *u.* all mysteries
Ps. 139. 2. thou *understandest* my thoughts
Acts 8. 30. *u.* thou what thou
1 Chron. 28. 9. *understandeth* all the imaginations
Ps. 49. 20. man that *u.* not, is like
Prov. 8. 9. plain to him that *u.*
Jer. 9. 24. glory in this, that he *u.*
Matt. 13. 19. hear. word and *u.* not
Ex. 31. 3. wis. and *understanding*
Deut. 4. 6. is your wisdom and *u.*
1 Kings 3. 11. asked for thyself *u.*
4. 29. Solomon wisdom and *u.*
7. 14. filled with wisdom and *u.*
1 Chron. 12. 32. men that had *u.* of
Job 12. 13. he hath counsel and *u.*
17. 4. hid their heart from *u.*
28. 12. where is the place of *u.*
28. to depart from evil is *u.*
38. 36. who hath given *u.* to heart
Ps. 47. 7. sing ye praise with *u.*
49. 3. the meditations of my heart shall be of *u.*
119. 34. give me *u.* and I shall keep
130. giveth *u.* unto the simple
147. 5. his *u.* is infinite
Prov. 2. 2. apply thine heart to *u.*
11. *u.* shall keep thee; to deliver
8. 5. lean not to thine own *u.*
13. the man that getteth *u.*
8. 1. doth not *u.* cry
9. 6. go in the way of *u.*
14. 29. slow to wrath is of great *u.*
19. 8. keepeth *u.* shall find good
21. 30. no *u.* nor counsel against
23. 23. buy truth, wisdom and *u.*
30. 2. I have not the *u.* of a man
Eccl. 9. 11. nor riches to men of *u.*
Isa. 11. 2. spirit of wisdom and *u.*
3. make him of quick *u.* in the
27. 11. it is a people of no *u.*
Jer. 51. 15. stretched out heaven by his *u.*
Matt. 15. 16. also without *u.*
Mark 12. 33. love him with all the heart and with all the *u.*
Luke 2. 47. astonished at his *u.*
Rom. 1. 31. without *u.* unthankful
1 Cor. 1. 19. bring to nothing the *u.* of the prudent
14. 14. my *u.* unfruitful
15. pray with the *u.* also
Eph. 1. 18. eyes of *u.* enlightened
4. 18. having the *u.* darkened
Phil. 4. 7. the peace of God, which passeth all *u.*

Col. 1. 9. filled with all spiritual *u.*
2 Tim. 2. 7. give thee *u.* in all
1 John 5. 20. given us *u.* to know
Ps. 111. 10. *good understanding*, Prov. 3. 4. & 13. 15.
Prov. 1. 5. *a man of understanding*, 10. 23. & 11. 12. & 15. 21. & 17. 27.
Deut. 32. 29. O that they *understood*
Ps. 73. 17. then *u.* I their end
Dan. 9. 2. *u.* by books number
Matt. 13. 51. have ye *u.* all these
John 12. 16. these things *u.* not
1 Cor. 13. 11. when a child I *u.*
2 Pet. 3. 16. things hard to be *u.*
R. V. Gen. 41. 15. hearest; Deut. 9. 3, 6. know; Neh. 8. 13. give attention; Ps. 19. 12; Dan. 9. 25. discern; 11. 33. be wise; Ps. 73. 17; 94. 8; 107. 43; Isa. 44. 18. consider; Ps. 81. 5; 1 Cor. 13. 2; Phil. 1. 12. know or knew; Matt. 15. 17; 26. 10; John 8. 27; 12. 40; Rom. 1. 20; Eph. 3. 14. perceive; Acts 23. 27. learned; 1 Cor. 13. 11. felt; Ezra 8. 16. teachers; 8. 18. discretion; Prov. 17. 28. prudent; 10. 13. discernment; Dan. 11. 35. wise; Luke 1. 3. accurately; 24. 45; 1 Cor. 14. 20. mind; Eph. 1. 18. heart
UNDERTAKE for me, Isa. 38. 14.
R. V. Isa. 38. 14. be surety
UNDONE, Isa. 6. 5. Matt. 23. 23.
UNEQUAL, your ways are, Ezek. 18. 25.
2 Cor. 6. 14. not *unequally* yoked
UNFAITHFUL, Prov. 25. 19. Ps. 78. 57.
R. V. Ps. 78. 57. treacherously
UNFEIGNED, 2 Cor. 6. 6. 1 Tim. 1. 5. 2 Tim. 1. 5. 1 Pet. 1. 22.
UNFRUITFUL, Matt. 13. 22. 1 Cor. 14. 14. Eph. 5. 11. Tit. 3. 14. 2 Pet. 1. 8.
UNGODLY men, 2 Sam. 22. 5.
2 Chron. 19. 2. should. help the *u.*
Job 16. 11. delivered me to the *u.*
34. 18. say to princes ye are *u.*
Ps. 1. 1. walketh not in counsel of *u.*
6. way of *u.* men shall perish
3. 7. hast broken the teeth of *u.*
73. 12. these are *u.* that prosper
Prov. 16. 27. *u.* man diggeth up
19. 28. an *u.* witness scorneth
Rom. 4. 5. God that justifi. the *u.*
5. 6. in due time Christ died for *u.*
1 Tim. 1. 9. law not for righteous, but for the *u.*
1 Pet. 4. 18. where shall *u.* appear
2 Pet. 2. 5. bring a flood on world of the *u.*
3. 7. day of perdition of *u.* men
Jude 4. *u.* men turning grace
15. convince all that are *u.* of
10. mockers walk after *u.* lusts
Rom. 1. 18. wrath revealed against *ungodliness*
2 Tim. 2. 16. increase to more *u.*
Tit. 2. 12. denying *u.* and worldly
R. V. Prov. 16. 27; 19. 28. worthless; 2 Chron. 19. 2; Job 34. 18; Ps. 1. 1, 4, 5, 6; 3. 7; 78. 12. wicked
UNHOLY, Lev. 10. 10. 1 Tim. 1 9. 2 Tim. 3. 2. Heb. 10. 29.
R. V. Lev. 10. 10. the common
UNION in worship and prayer, Ps. 34. 3. & 55. & 14. & 122. Rom. 15. 30. 2 Cor. 1. 11. Eph. 6. 18. Col. 1. 3. & 3. 16. Heb. 10. 25.
UNITE, Ps. 86. 11. Gen. 49. 6.
Ps. 133. 1. brethren to dwell together in *unity*
Eph. 4. 3. keep the *u.* of the Spirit
13. till we all come in *u.* of faith
UNJUST, deliver from, Ps. 43. 1.
Prov. 11. 7. hope of the *u.* perish.
29. 27. *u.* man is abomination
Zeph. 3. 5. the *u.* knoweth no
Matt. 5. 45. rain on the just and *u.*
Luke 16. 8. Lord commended the *u.* steward
10. he that is *u.* in least, is
18. 6. hear what the *u.* judge
Acts 24. 15. resurrection both of just and *u.*
1 Cor. 6. 1. go to law before the *u.*
1 Pet. 3. 18. suffered, just for *u.*
2 Pet. 2. 9. reserve the *u.* to day
Rev. 22. 11. that is *u.* let him be *u.*
Ps. 82. 2. will ye judge *unjustly*
Isa. 26. 10. will he deal *u.*
R. V. Prov. 28. 8 ——; 11. 7. iniquity; Luke 16. 8, 10; 18. 6; 1 Cor. 6. 1; 1 Pet. 3. 18; 2 Pet. 2. 9; Rev. 22. 11. unrighteous
UNKNOWN God, Acts 17. 23. Gal. 1. 22.
1 Cor. 14. 2. speak in an *u.* tongue, 4. 27.
2 Cor. 6. 9. as *u.* and yet well
UNLAWFUL, Acts 10. 28. 2 Pet. 2. 8.
R. V. 2 Pet. 2. 8. lawless
UNLEARNED, Acts 4. 13. 1 Cor. 14. 16, 23, 24. 2 Tim. 2. 23. 2 Pet. 3. 16.
R. V. 2 Tim. 2. 23; 2 Pet. 3. 16. ignorant
UNLEAVENED, Ex. 12. 39. 1 Cor. 5. 7.
UNMARRIED (virgins), Paul's exhortation to, 1 Cor. 7. 8, 11, 25, 32.
UNMERCIFUL, Rom. 1. 31.
UNMINDFUL, Deut. 32. 8.
UNMOVABLE, 1 Cor. 15. 58.
UNPERFECT, Ps. 139. 16.
UNPREPARED, 2 Cor. 9. 4.
UNPROFITABLE talk, Job 15. 3.
Matt. 25. 30. cast the *u.* servant
Luke 17. 10. are all *u.* servants
Rom. 3. 12. altogether become *u.*
Tit. 3. 9. they are *u.* and vain
Phile. 11. was to thee *u.* but
Heb. 13. 17. for that is *u.* for you
UNPUNISHED, Prov. 11. 21. & 16. 5. & 17. 5. & 19. 5, 9. Jer. 25. 29. & 30. 11. & 46. 28. & 49. 12.
UNQUENCHABLE, Matt. 3. 12. Luke 3. 17.
UNREASONABLE, Acts 25. 27. 2 Thes. 3. 2.
UNREBUKABLE, 1 Tim. 6. 14.
UNREPROVABLE, Col. 1. 22.
UNRIGHTEOUS decrees, Isa. 10. 1.
Isa. 55. 7. *u.* man forsake his
Rom. 3. 5. is God *u.* who taketh
1 Cor. 6. 9. *u.* shall not inherit
Heb. 6. 10. God is not *u.* to forget
Lev. 19. 15. do no *unrighteousness*
Ps. 92. 15. there is no *u.* in him
Luke 16. 9. mammon of *u.*
John 7. 18. true, and no *u.* in him
Rom. 1. 18. hold the truth in *u.*
6. 13. members instruments of *u.*
9. 14. is there *u.* with God? God
2 Cor. 6. 14. fellowship hath righteousness with *u.*
2 Thes. 2. 10. all deceivable. of *u.*
Heb. 8. 12. be merciful to their *u.*
1 John 1. 9. cleanse us from all *u.*
5. 17. all *u.* is sin
R. V. 2 Cor. 6. 14; Heb. 8. 12. iniquity; 2 Pet. 2. 13, 15. wrong doing
UNRULY, 1 Thes. 5. 14. Tit. 1. 6, 10. Jas. 3. 8.
R. V. 1 Thes. 5. 14. disorderly; Jas. 3. 8. restless
UNSAVORY, Job 6. 6. Jer. 23. 13.
UNSEARCHABLE things, Job 5. 9.
Ps. 145. 3. his greatness is *u.*
Prov. 25. 3. heart of kings is *u.*
Rom. 11. 33. *u.* are his judgments
Eph. 3. 8. preach *u.* riches of
UNSEEMLY, Rom. 1. 27. 1 Cor. 13. 5.
UNSKILFUL in word, Heb. 5. 13.
UNSPEAKABLE, 2 Cor. 9. 15. & 12. 4. 1 Pet. 1. 8.
UNSPOTTED, Jas. 1. 27.
UNSTABLE, Gen. 49. 4. Jas. 1. 8.
2 Pet. 2. 14. *u.* souls
3. 16. unlearned and *u.*
R. V. 2 Pet. 2. 14; 3. 16. unstedfast
UNTHANKFUL, Luke 6. 35. 2 Tim. 3. 2.
UNTOWARD, Acts 2. 40.
UNWASHEN, Matt. 15. 20. Mark 7. 2, 5.
R. V. Mark 7. 5. defiled
UNWISE, Deut. 32. 6. Hos. 13. 13. Rom. 1. 14. Eph. 5. 17.
R. V. Rom. 1. 14. Eph. 5. 17. foolish
UNWORTHY, Acts 13. 46. 1 Cor. 6. 2.
1 Cor. 11. 27. drinketh *unworthily*
UPBRAID, Judg. 8. 15. Matt. 11. 20. Mark 16. 14. Jas. 1. 5.
UPHOLD me with thy Spirit, Ps. 51. 12.
Ps. 119. 116. *u.* me according to
Prov. 29. 23. honor shall *u.* humble
Isa. 41. 10. I will *u.* thee with the right hand of my righteousness
42. 1. my servant whom I *u.*
63. 5. my fury it *upheld* me
57. 17. Lord *upholdeth* righteous
145. 14. Lord *u.* all that fall
41. 12. thou *upholdest* me in
Heb. 1. 3. *upholding* all by word
UPRIGHT in heart, Ps. 7. 10.
Ps. 11. 7. his countenance doth behold the *u.*
18. 23. I was also *u.* before him
25. with *u.* wilt show thyself *u.*
25. 8. good and *u.* is the Lord
37. 37. mark the perfect man and behold the *u.*
64. 10. all *u.* in heart shall glory
112. 4. to *u.* light ariseth in dark.
140. 13. the *u.* shall dwell in
Prov. 2. 21. *u.* shall dwell in the
11. 3. integrity of *u.* shall guide
20. *u.* in their way, are his de.
12. 6. mouth of *u.* shall deliver
13. 6. righteous. keepeth the *u.*
15. 8. prayer of *u.* is his delight
21. 18. the transgressor for the *u.*
28. 10. *u.* shall have good things
Eccl. 7. 29. God hath made man *u.*
S. of S. 1. 4. the *u.* love thee
Hab. 2. 4. his soul is not *u.* in him
Ps. 15. 2. that walketh *uprightly*, 84. 11. Prov. 2. 7. & 10. 9. & 15. 21. & 29. 18. Mic. 2. 7. Gal. 2. 14.
Ps. 58. 1. do ye judge *u.*, 75. 2.
Isa. 33. 15. he that speaketh *u.*
Deut. 9. 5. not for the *uprightness* of thy heart
Job 33. 23. to show unto man his *u.*
Ps. 25. 21. let integrity and *u.* preserve me
Isa. 26. 7. way of the just is *u.*
10. land of *u.* will he deal unjustly
R. V. 2 Sam. 22. 24, 26; Job 12. 4; Ps. 18. 23, 25; 19. 13; 37. 18; Prov. 11. 20; 28. 10; 29. 10. perfect; Prov. 2. 7; Job 4. 6; Prov. 28. 6. integrity
URIM and Thummim, Ex. 28. 30. Lev. 88. Num. 27. 21. 1 Sam. 28. 6. Ezra 2. 63. Neh. 7. 65.
US, Gen. 1. 26. & 3. 22. & 11. 7. Isa. 6. 8. & 9. 6. Rom. 4. 24. 2 Cor. 5. 21. Gal. 3. 13. 1 Thes. 5. 10. Heb. 6. 20. 1 Pet. 2. 21. & 4. 1. 1 John 5. 11.
USE, Rom. 1. 26. Eph. 4. 29. Heb. 5. 14.
1 Cor. 7. 31. *u.* world as not abus.
Gal. 5. 13. *u.* not liberty for occa.
1 Tim. 1. 8. law is good if a man *u.*
1 Cor. 9. 15. I have *used* none of
Jer. 22. 13. *useth* his neighbor's
Tit. 3. 14. learn good works for necessary *uses*
Ps. 119. 132. as thou *usest* to do to
Col. 2. 22. *using*, 1 Pet. 2. 16.
R. V. 2 Sam. 1. 18. song
USURP, 1 Tim. 2. 12.
USURY, Ex. 22. 25. Lev. 25. 36, 37. Deut. 23. 19, 20. Neh. 5. 7, 10. Ps. 15. 5. Prov. 28. 8. Isa. 24. 2. Jer. 15. 10. Ezek. 18. 8, 13, 17. & 22. 12. Matt. 25. 27. Luke 19. 23.
R. V. Matt. 25. 27; Luke 19. 23. interest
UTTER, Ps. 78. 2. & 94. 4.

Ps. 106. 2. who can *u.* mighty acts
2 Cor. 12. 4. lawful for a man to *u.*
Rom. 8. 26. groanings that cannot be *uttered*
Heb. 5. 11. things hard to be *u.*
Ps. 19. 2. day unto day *uttereth*
Acts 2. 4. as the spirit gave them *utterance*
Eph. 6. 19. that *u.* may be given
Deut. 7. 2. *utterly*, Ps. 89. 33. & 119. 8, 43. S. of S. 8. 7. Jer. 14. 9.
1 Thes. 2. 16. *uttermost*, Heb. 7. 25.
R. V. *outer*, Ezek. 40. 31. arches were toward *u.* court; 42. 1; 44. 19; 46. 20; 47. 2; Ex. 26. 4; 36. 11, 17; 2 Kings 7. 5, 8. outmost; Deut. 11. 24. hinder; Josh. 15. 5. end; Matt. 5. 26. last

V

VAIL (of women), Gen. 24. 65. Ruth 3. 15. 1 Cor. 11. 10.
of Moses, Ex. 34. 33. 2 Cor. 3. 13.
of the tabernacle and temple, Ex. 26. 31. & 36. 35. 2 Cor. 3. 14. *See* Heb. 6. 19. & 9. 3. & 10. 20.
of temple rent at crucifixion, Matt. 27. 51. Mark 15. 38. Luke 23. 45.

VAIN, Ex. 5. 9. & 20, 7.
Deut. 32. 47. it is not a *v.* thing
1 Sam. 12. 21. turn not after *v.*
Ps. 39. 6. every man walketh in a *v.* shew, and they are disquiet. in *v.*
Job 11. 12. *v.* man would be wise
Ps. 60. 11. *v.* is help of man
119. 113. I hate *v.* thoughts, but
Jer. 4. 14. long shall *v.* thoughts
Mal. 3. 14. it is *v.* to serve God
Matt. 6. 7. use not *v.* repetitions
Rom. 1. 21. they glorified not God, but became *v.* in their imagina.
1 Cor. 3. 20. thoughts of wise are *v.*
Eph. 5. 6. deceive you with *v.*
Col. 2. 8. through *v.* philosophy
1 Pet. 1. 18. from *v.* conversation
Ps. 73. 13. cleansed my heart *in vain*
89. 47. why hast thou made all men —
127. 1. labor —; walketh —
Isa. 45. 19. seek ye me —
Jer. 3. 23 — is salvation hoped
Matt. 15. 9. — do they worship me
Rom. 13. 4. bear not the sword —
1 Cor. 15. 58. your labor is not —
2 Cor. 6. 1. receive not grace of God —
Phil. 2. 16. not run — nor labored —
2 Kings 17. 15. followed *vanity*
Job 7. 3. possess months of *v.*
16. let me alone; my days are *v.*
Ps. 12. 2. speak *v.* every one
24. 4. nor lifted up his soul to *v.*
11. surely every man is *v.*
62. 9. men of low degree are *v.*
119. 37. turn mine eyes from beholding *v.*
Prov. 22. 8. that soweth iniquity shall reap *v.*
Eccl. 1. 2. *v.* of vanities, all is *v.*, 14. & 3. 19. & 2. 1. & 4. 8. & 12. 8.
Isa. 5. 18. iniquity with cords of *v.*
40. 17. less than nothing and *v.*
Hab. 2. 13. weary themselves for *v.*
Rom. 8. 20. the creature was made subject to *v.*
Eph. 4. 17. walk in *v.* of their
2 Pet. 2. 18. swelling words of *v.*
Ps. 31. 6. I hate them that regard lying *vanities*
Jer. 10. 8. a doctrine of *v.*
Jonah 2. 8. that observe lying *v.*
Acts 14. 15. turn from these *v.*
R. V. Ex. 5. 9. lying; Job 35. 16; Ps. 89. 47; Isa. 49. 4; Jer. 10. 3; 23. 15; 51. 58; Lam. 2. 14; Isa. 49. 4. vanity; Jer. 4. 14. evil; Isa. 45. 18. waste; Eph. 5. 6. empty; Gal. 2. 21. nought; 1 Tim. 6. 20; 2 Tim. 2. 16 —

VALIANT, S. of S. 3. 7. Isa. 10. 13.
Jer. 9. 3. not *v.* for the truth
Heb. 11. 34. faith waxed *v.*
Ps. 60. 12. *valiantly*, 108. 13. & 118. 15, 16. Num. 24. 18.
R. V. 1 Kings 1. 42; 1 Chron. 7. 2, 5; 11. 26; 28. 1; S. of S. 3. 7; Heb. 11. 34. mighty; Jer. 46. 15. strong

VALUE, Job 13. 4. Matt. 10. 31.

VAPOR, Jer. 10. 13. Jas. 4. 14.

VARIABLENESS, Jas. 1. 17.

VARIANCE, Matt. 10. 35. Gal. 5. 29.
R. V. Gal. 5. 20. strife

VAUNT, Judg. 7. 2. 1 Cor. 13. 4.

VEHEMENT, S. of S. 8. 6. 2 Cor. 7. 11.
R. V. 2 Cor. 7. 11 —

VEIL, Gen. 24. 65. S. of S. 5. 7.
Isa. 25. 7. destroy the *v.* spread
Matt. 27. 51. *v.* was rent from top
2 Cor. 3. 13. Moses put a *v.* over
15. *v.* is upon their heart
Heb. 6. 19. into that within *v.*

VENGEANCE taken, Gen 4. 15.
Deut. 32. 35. to me belongeth *v.*, Ps. 94. 1. Rom. 12. 19. Heb. 10. 30.
Ps. 58. 10. rejoice when he seeth *v.*
99. 8. tookest *v.* of their inven.
Isa. 34. 8. day of the Lord's *v.*
Jer. 11. 20. let me see thy *v.*
51. 6. time of the Lord's *v.*, 11.
Luke 21. 22. these be days of *v.*
2 Thes. 1. 8. fire taking *v.*
Jude 7. suffering *v.* of eternal fire
R. V. Acts 28. 4. justice; Jude 7. punishment

VENISON, Gen. 25. 28. & 27. 3.

VERILY, Gen. 42. 21. Jer. 15. 11. It is often used by Christ, as well as *verily, verily*, John 1. 51. & 3. 3, 5, 11. & 5. 19, 24, 25. & 6. 26.

VERITY, Ps. 111. 7. 1 Tim. 2. 7.

VERY, Prov. 17. 9. Matt. 24. 24. John 7. 26. & 14. 11. 1 Thes. 5. 23.

VESSEL, Ps. 2. 9. & 31. 12. Jer. 18. 4.
Jer. 22. 28. *v.* wherein is no pleas.
48. 11. emptied from *v.* to *v.*
Acts 9. 15. he is a chosen *v.* unto
Rom. 9. 21. one *v.* to honor and
1 Thes. 4. 4. possess his *v.* in sanc.
2 Tim. 2. 21. be a *v.* unto honor
1 Pet. 3. 7. honor to wife as the weaker *v.*
Rom. 9. 21. *vessels* of wrath fitted
2 Cor. 4. 7. treasure in earthen *v.*
R. V. Ex. 27. 19; 39. 40; Num. 3. 36. instruments; Ex. 40. 9; Num. 1. 50; 4. 15, 16; 1 Chron. 9. 29. furniture

VESTURE, lots cast for Christ's, Matt. 27. 35; John 19. 24. *See* Ps. 22. 18. Rev. 19. 13.

VEXED, Job 27. 2. Ps. 6. 2, 3, 10.
Isa. 63. 10. and *v.* his Holy Spirit
2 Pet. 2. 7. Lot *v.* with filthy con.
R. V. Neh. 9. 27; 2 Pet. 2. 7. distressed; Isa. 63. 10. grieved; Ezek. 22. 7. wronged; Luke 6. 18. troubled

VIAL, Rev. 5. 8. & 16. 1. & 21. 9.
R. V. In Rev. bowl or bowls

VICTORY is thine, O Lord, 1 Chron. 29. 11.
Ps. 98. 1. hand and arm gotten him the *v.*
Isa. 25. 8. swallow up death in *v.*
Matt. 20. 12. judgment unto *v.*
1 Cor. 15. 54. death is swallowed up in *v.*
55. O grave, where is thy *v.*
57. God who giveth us *v.*
1 John 5. 4. *v.* that overcometh

VIGILANT, 1 Tim. 3. 2. 1 Pet. 5. 8.
R. V. 1 Tim. 3. 2. temperate; 1 Pet. 5. 8. watchful

VILE, thy brother seem, Deut. 25. 3.
1 Sam. 3. 13. made themselves *v.*
2 Sam. 6. 22. I will yet be more *v.*
Job 40. 4. I am *v.*; what shall I an.
Ps. 15. 4. whose eyes a *v.* person
Isa. 32. 6. *v.* person will speak vill.
Rom. 1. 26. up to *v.* affections
Phil. 3. 21. change our *v.* body
R. V. Judg. 19. 24. folly; Job 18. 3. unclean; 40. 4. small account; Ps. 15. 4. reprobate; Dan. 11. 21. contemptible; Phil. 3. 21. humiliation

VINE, 1 Kings 4. 25. Mic. 4. 4.
Deut. 32. 32. *v.* is the *v.* of Sodom
Ps. 128. 3. thy wife shall be as a fruitful *v.*
Jer. 2. 21. planted thee a noble *v.*
Hos. 10. 1. Israel is an empty *v.*
14. 7. they shall grow as the *v.*
Matt. 26. 29. drink of fruit of *v.*
John 15. 1. I am the true *v.* and my Father is the husbandman
5. I am the *v.* ye are the branch.
Ps. 80. 15. *vineyard*, Prov. 24. 30. S of S. 1. 6. Isa. 5. 1, 7. Matt. 20. 1. & 21. 33. Luke 13. 6. 1 Cor. 9. 7. S. of S. 8. 11, 12.
R. V. Rev. 14. 19. vintage

VIOLENCE, Lev. 6. 2. 2 Sam. 22. 3.
Gen. 6. 11. earth was filled with *v.*
Hab. 1. 2. cry out unto thee of *v.*
Matt. 11. 12. the kingdom of heaven suffereth *v.*
Luke 3. 14. do *v.* to no man, and
Heb. 11. 34. quenched the *v.* of
R. V. Lev. 6. 2. robbery; Mic. 2. 2. seize; Acts 24. 7 —; Heb. 11. 34. power; Rev. 18. 21. mighty fall

VIRGIN, Isa. 7. 14. 2 Cor. 11. 2. S. of S. 1. 3. *virgins*, Rev. 14. 4.

VIRTUE, Mark 5. 30. Luke 6. 19.
2 Pet. 1. 3. call. us to glory and *v.*
5. to faith *v.* and to *v.* knowledge
Phil. 4. 8. if there be any *v.* think
Prov. 12. 4. *virtuous* woman, 31. 10
R. V. Mark 5. 30; Luke 6. 19; 8. 46. power

VISAGE, Isa. 52. 14. Lam. 4. 8.

VISIBLE and invisible, Col. 1. 16.

VISION, 1 Sam. 3. 1. Ps. 89. 19. Matt. 17. 9. Acts 10. 19. & 16. 9.
Hab. 2. 2. write the *v.*
3. the *v.* is for a time
Ezek. 13. 16. see *visions* of peace
Hos. 12. 10. I have multiplied *v.*
Joel 2. 28. young men shall see *v.*
2 Cor. 12. 1. I will come to *v.* and
R. V. Ezek. 8. 4. appearance; Acts 9. 12 —

VISIT you, Gen. 50. 24, 25. Ex. 13. 19.
Job 7. 18. shouldest *v.* him every
Ps. 106. 4. *v.* me with thy salvation
Jer. 5. 9. shall I not *v.* you for
Lam. 4. 22. *v.* iniquity, Jer. 14. 10. & 23. 2. Hos. 2. 13. & 8. 13.
Acts 7. 23. *v.* his brethren, 15. 36.
15. 14. God did *v.* the Gentiles
Jas. 1. 27. to *v.* the fatherless
Ex. 3. 16. I have surely *visited*
Ps. 17. 3. thou hast *v.* me in night
Isa. 26. 16. in trouble have they *v.*
Matt. 25. 36. I was sick and ye *v.*
Luke 1. 68. *v.* and redeem. people
Ps. 8. 4. *visitest*, 65. 9. Heb. 2. 6.
Ex. 20. 5. *visiting* the iniquity of the fathers upon the children, 34. 7.

VOCATION, worthy of, Eph. 4. 1.

VOICE is *v.* of Jacob, Gen. 27. 22
Gen. 4. 10. *v.* of brother's blood
Ex. 5. 2. who is the Lord that I should obey his *v.*
Ps. 5. 3. my *v.* shalt thou hear
18. 13. the Highest gave his *v.*
95. 7. to-day, if ye will hear his *v.*
Eccl. 12. 4. rise up at the *v.* of
S. of S. 2. 14. let me hear thy *v.*
Isa. 30. 19. gracious at *v.* of thy
Ezek. 33. 32. hath a pleasant *v.*
John 5. 25. dead shall hear the *v.*
10. 3. sheep hear his *v.*, 4. 16, 27.
Gal. 4. 20. I desire to change my *v.*
1 Thes. 4. 16. with *v.* of archangel
Rev. 3. 20. if any man hear my *v.*
Acts 13. 27. *voices*, Rev. 4. 5. & 11. 19.

VOID of counsel, Deut. 32. 28.
Ps. 30. 39. made *v.* the covenant
Isa. 55. 11. shall not return *v.*
Acts 24. 16. conscience *v.* of offence
Rom. 3. 31. do we make *v.* the law
1 Cor. 9. 15. make my glorying *v.*
VOLUME, Ps. 40. 7. Heb. 10. 17.
VOMIT, Job 20. 15. Prov. 23. 8. & 26. 11. Isa. 19. 14. 2 Pet. 2. 22.
VOW, Jacob vowed a, Gen. 28. 20. & 31. 13. Num. 6. 2. & 21. 2. & 30. 1 Sam. 1. 11. 2 Sam. 15. 7, 8.
Ps. 65. 1. to thee shall the *v.* be
76. 11. *v.* and pay unto the
Eccl. 5. 4. a *v.* defer not to pay, 5.
Isa. 19. 21. shall *v.* a *v.* to the Lord
Jonah 2. 9. pay that I have *vowed*
Job 22. 27. shall pay thy *vows*
Ps. 22. 25. I will pay my *v.* before
56. 12. thy *v.* O God are upon
61. 5. heard my *v.*
Prov. 20. 25. after *v.* to make enqu.
31. 2. son of my *v.*, 1 Sam. 1. 11.
Jonah 1. 16. offer. sacri. and made *v.*
VOYAGE, Paul's, Acts 27. & 28.

W

WAGES, Lev. 19. 13. Ezek. 29. 18.
Jer. 22. 13. neighbor's service without *w.*
Hag. 1. 6. earneth *w.* to put it
Mal. 3. 5. oppress hirel. in his *w.*
Luke 3. 14. be conte. with your *w.*
Rom. 6. 23. the *w.* of sin is death
R. V. 2 Pet. 2. 15. hire
WAIT till my change come, Job 14. 14.
Ps. 25. 5. on thee do I *w.* all the day
27. 14. *w.* on the Lord; *w.* I say
37. 34. *w.* on the Lord and keep
62. 5. *w.* thou only upon God
130. 5. I *w.* for the Lord, my
145. 15. eyes of all *w.* upon thee
Prov. 20. 22. *w.* on the Lord and
Isa. 8. 17. I will *w.* upon the Lord
30. 18. will the Lord *w.* blessed
40. 31. that *w.* on the Lord shall renew their strength
Lam. 3. 25. good to them that *w.*
26. quietly *w.* for salvation of
Hos. 12. 6. *w.* on thy God contin.
Mic. 7. 7. I will *w.* for God of my
Hab. 2. 3. *w.* for it, it will surely
Zeph. 3. 8. *w.* ye on me, I will rise
Luke 12. 36. men that *w.* for their
Gal. 5. 5. through the Spirit *w.*
1 Thes. 1. 10. *w.* for his Son from
Gen. 49. 18. *waited* for thy salva.
Ps. 40. 1. I *w.* patiently for the
Isa. 25. 9. our God, we have *w.* for
Zech. 11. 11. poor of flock that *w.*
Mark 15. 43. *w.* for kingdom of God
1 Pet. 3. 20. long suffering of God *w.*
Ps. 33. 20. our soul *waiteth* for
65. 1. praise *w.* for thee, in Zion
130. 6. my soul *w.* for Lord more
Isa. 64. 4. prepared for him that *w.*
Prov. 8. 34. *waiting* at the posts
Luke 2. 25. *w.* for the consolation
Rom. 8. 23. *w.* for the adoption
1 Cor. 1. 7. *w.* for coming of Lord
2 Thes. 3. 5. to a patient *w.* for
R. V. Job 17. 13; Isa. 59. 9; Ps. 128. 2; Luke 12. 36. look; Ps. 71. 10; Jer. 5. 26. watch; Judg. 9. 35. ambush
WAKETH, Ps. 127. 1. S. of S. 5. 2.
Ps. 77. 4. holdest my eyes *waking*
Isa. 50. 4. *wakeneth*, Joel 3. 12.
WALK in my law, Ex. 16. 4.
Gen. 17. 1. *w.* before me and be per.
24. 40. before whom I *w.*
Lev. 26. 12. I will *w.* among
24. will I *w.* contrary unto you
Deut. 5. 33. *w.* in the ways of the Lord, 8. 6. & 10. 12. & 11. 22. & 13. 5. & 28. 9.
13. 4. shall *w.* after the Lord
Ps. 23. 4. though I *w.* through valley of death
Ps. 84. 11. no good thing from them that *w.* uprightly
Eccl. 11. 9. *w.* in way of thy heart
Isa. 2. 3. will *w.* in his paths
30. 21. this is the way, *w.* ye in
40. 31. shall *w.* and not faint
Dan. 4. 37. that *w.* in pride he is
Hos. 14. 9. just shall *w.* in them
Mic. 6. 8. *w.* humbly with thy
Amos 3. 3. how can two *w.* to.
Zech. 10. 12. *w.* up and down in
Luke 13. 33. I must *w.* to-day and
John 8. 12. followeth me, not *w.*
11. 9. *w.* in day, he stumbleth not
Rom. 4. 12. *w.* in steps of that faith
8. 1. *w.* not after the flesh, 4.
2 Cor. 5. 7. we *w.* by faith, not
10. 3. though *w.* in the flesh, we
Gal. 6. 16. as many as *w.* accord.
Eph. 2. 10. ordained that we *w.*
5. 15. *w.* circumspectly, not as
Phil. 3. 17. mark them who *w.* so
Col. 1. 10. that ye might *w.* worthy
1 Thes. 2. 12. ye would *w.* worthy
4. 1. how ought ye to *w.* and
1 John 1. 7. if we *w.* in the light
2. 6. ought so to *w.* as he walked
Rev. 3. 4. *w.* with me in white
16. 15. lest he *w.* naked and see
21. 24. nations shall *w.* in light
John 12. 35. *w.* in light while ye
Rom. 13. 13. let us *w.* honestly as
Gal. 5. 16. *w.* in Spirit, and not ful.
25. if we live in Spirit, let us *w.*
Eph. 5. 2. *w.* in love as Christ
8. *w.* as children of light
Phil. 3. 16. let us *w.* by the same
Gen. 6. 9. Noah *walked* with God
5. 22. Enoch *w.* with God, 24.
Ps. 55. 14. we *w.* unto the house
81. 12. *w.* in their own counsels
Isa. 9. 2. people that *w.* in darkness
2 Cor. 10. 2. as if we *w.* accord.
12. 18. *w.* we not in same spirit
Gal. 2. 14. they *w.* not uprightly
Eph. 2. 2. in time past we *w.*
1 Pet. 4. 3. we *w.* in lasciviousness
Isa. 43. 2. when thou *walkest* through the fire
Rom. 14. 15. *w.* thou not charitably
Ps. 15. 2. he that *walketh* uprightly
39. 6. every man *w.* in a vain
Prov. 10. 9. he that *w.* uprightly
13. 20. *w.* with wise men shall
Isa. 50. 10. *w.* in darkness, and
Jer. 10. 23. not in man that *w.* to direct his steps
Mic. 2. 7. him that *w.* uprightly
2 Thes. 3. 6. from brother that *w.* disorderly
1 Pet. 5. 8. *w.* about seeking
Rev. 2. 1. *w.* in midst of the
Gen. 3. 8. voice of Lord *walking* in
Isa. 57. 2. *w.* in his own upright.
Jer. 6. 28. revolters *w.* with sland.
Mic. 2. 11. if man *w.* in falsehood
Luke 1. 6. *w.* in all command.
Acts 9. 31. *w.* in the fear of the
2 Cor. 4. 2. not *w.* in craftiness
2 Pet. 3. 3. *w.* after their own
2 John 4. thy children *w.* in truth
WALL, Ps. 62. 3. Prov. 18. 11. S. of S. 2. 9. & 8. 9, 10. Isa. 26. 1. & 60. 18.
R. V. Gen. 49. 6. ox; Num. 13. 28; 22. 24; Deut. 1. 28; Isa. 5. 5; Hos. 2. 6. fence or fenced; 1 Kings 21. 23. rampart
WANDER, Num. 14. 33. Ps. 119. 10.
Lam. 4. 14. *wandered*, Heb. 11. 37.
Prov. 21. 16. *wandereth*, 27. 8.
1 Tim. 5. 13. *wandering*, Jude 13.
Ps. 56. 8. tellest my *wanderings*
WANT, Deut. 28. 48. Job 31. 19.
Ps. 23. 1. the Lord is my shepherd, I shall not *w.*
34. 9. no *w.* to them that fear
Prov. 6. 11. thy *w.* come as an
2 Cor. 8. 14. a supply for your *w.*
Phil. 4. 11. speak in respect of *w.*
Jas. 1. 4. perfect and entire, *wanting*
R. V. Prov. 10. 21. lack; Phil. 2. 25 need; Prov. 28. 16; Eccl. 6. 2; Jas. 1. 4. lack or lacking
WANTONNESS, Rom. 13. 13. 2 Pet. 2. 18.
R. V. 2 Pet. 2. 18. lasciviousness
WAR, Ex. 13. 17. & 17. 16. Ps. 27. 3.
Job 10. 17. changes and *w.* are
Ps. 18. 34. teacheth my hands to *w.*
120. 7. I am for peace, they for *w.*
Prov. 20. 18. good advice make *w.*
Eccl. 8. 8. discharge in this *w.*
Isa. 2. 4. not learn *w.* any more
Mic. 3. 5. prepare *w.* against him
2 Cor. 10. 3. do not *w.* after flesh
1 Tim. 1. 18. mightest *w.* a good warfare
Rev. 11. 7. beast shall make *w.*
12. 7. there was *w.* in heaven
Num. 21. 14. in the book of the *wars* of the Lord
Ps. 46. 9. he maketh *w.* to cease
Matt. 24. 6. hear of *w.* and rumors of *w.*
Jas. 4. 1. whence come *w.* and
2 Tim. 2. 4. no man that *warreth*
Isa. 37. 8. *warring*, Rom. 7. 23.
R. V. Deut. 21. 10; Judg. 21. 22; 2 Chron. 6. 34; Jer. 6. 23. battle
WARFARE, Isa. 40. 2. 1 Cor. 9. 7. 2 Cor. 10. 4. 1 Tim. 1. 18.
WARN, 2 Chron. 19. 10. Acts 10. 22.
Ezek. 3. 19. if thou *w.* the wicked
33. 3. blow the trumpet and *w.*
Acts 20. 31. I ceased not to *w.* every one night and day
1 Cor. 4. 14. my beloved sons I *w.*
1 Thes. 5. 14. *w.* them that are un.
Ps. 19. 11. by them is thy servant *warned*
Matt. 3. 7. who hath *w.* you to flee
Heb. 11. 7. Noah being *w.* of God
Jer. 6. 10. to whom I give *warning*
Col. 1. 28. teaching every man, *w.*
R. V. Acts 20. 31; 1 Cor. 4. 14; 1 Thes. 5. 14. admonish
WASH, Lev. 6. 27. & 14. 15, 16.
Job 9. 30. if I *w.* myself in snow
Ps. 26. 6. *w.* my hands in innocen.
51. 7. *w.* me and I shall be whiter
58. 10. shall *w.* his feet in blood
Isa. 1. 16. *w.* you, make you clean
Jer. 2. 22. *w.* thee with nitre
Luke 7. 8. *w.* his feet with tears
John 13. 5. *w.* disciples' feet
8. I *w.* thee not, thou hast no
14. *w.* one another's feet
Acts 22. 16. baptized and *w.* away
Job 29. 6. I *washed* my steps
S. of S. 5. 3. I have *w.* my feet
Isa. 4. 4. *w.* away the filth
Ezek. 16. 4. neither wast thou *w.*
16. 9. I thoroughly *w.* away blood
1 Cor. 6. 11. we are *w.* justified
Heb. 10. 22. *w.* with pure water
Rev. 1. 5. *w.* us from sins in his
7. 14. *w.* robes, and made white in
Eph. 5. 26. *washing*, Tit. 3. 5.
R. V. Ex. 2. 5; Lev. 14. 8, 9; 15. 16 16. 4, 24; 22. 6; Deut. 23. 11; 2 Sam. 11. 2; John 13. 10. bathe; Luke 7. 38, 44. wet; Rev. 1. 5. loosed
WASTE, Ps. 80. 13. Matt. 26. 8.
Luke 15. 11. *wasted*, 36. 1. Gal. 1. 13.
Job 14. 10. *wasteth*, Prov. 19. 26.
Prov. 18. 9. *waster*, Isa. 54. 16.
Isa. 59. 7. *wasting* and destruction, 60. 18.
R. V. Prov. 18. 9. destroyer
WATCH, Neh. 4. 9. Job 7. 12.
Job 14. 15. dost thou not *w.* over
Ps. 102. 7. I *w.* and am as a sparrow
141. 3. set a *w.* before my mouth
Jer. 44. 27. *w.* over them for evil
Matt. 24. 42. *w.* for ye know not
26. 41. *w.* and pray that ye enter
Mark 13. 33. take heed, *w.* and
1 Cor. 16. 13. *w.* ye, stand fast in
1 Thes. 5. 6. let us *w.* and be sober
2 Tim. 4. 5. *w.* thou in all things
Heb. 13. 17. they *w.* for your souls
1 Pet. 4. 7. be sober, *w.* unto prayer

Jer. 31. 28. like as I *watched* over
Matt. 24. 43. he would have *w.*
Ps. 37. 32. the wicked *watcheth*
Ezek. 7. 6. the end is come; it *w.*
Rev. 16. 15. blessed is he that *w.*
Dan. 4. 13. a *watcher* and holy
Ps. 63. 6. *watches*, 119. 148. Lam. 2. 19.
Rev. 3. 2. be *watchful*
Prov. 8. 34. *watching* daily at gates
Luke 12. 37. blessed whom the Lord shall find *w.*
2 Cor. 6. 5. in *watchings*, 11. 27.
Isa. 21. 11. *watchman*, Ezek. 3. 17. & 33. 7.
S. of S. 3. 3. *watchmen*, 5. 7. Isa. 52. 8. & 56. 10. & 62. 6. Jer. 31. 6.
WATER, Gen. 49. 4. Ex. 12. 9. & 17. 6.
2 Sam. 14. 14. we are as *w.* spilt
Job 15. 16. drink. iniquity like *w.*
Ps. 22. 14. I am poured out like *w.*
Isa. 12. 3. draw *w.* out of the wells of salvation
30. 20. give you *w.* of affliction
58. 11. shalt be like a spring of *w.*
Lam. 1. 16. mine eye runneth down with *w.*, 3. 48.
Ezek. 36. 25. sprinkle clean *w.* on
Amos 8. 11. nor a thirst for *w.*
Matt. 3. 11. I baptize you with *w.*
10. 42. cup of cold *w.* in name of
Luke 16. 24. tip of his finger in *w.*
John 3. 5. man be born of *w.*
4. 14. shall be in him a well of *w.*
7. 38. flow rivers of living *w.*
19. 34. there out blood and *w.*
Acts 8. 38. went down into the *w.*
Eph. 5. 26. cleanse it with the washing of *w.*
1 John 5. 6. he that came by *w.*
8. three bear witness, Spirit, *w.*
Jude 12. clouds they are without *w.*
Rev. 7. 17. lead them to living fountains of *w.*
21. 6. fountain of *w.* of life
22. 17. take the *w.* of life freely
Ps. 23. 2. leadeth me beside the still *waters*
Prov. 5. 15. drink *w.* out of thine
9. 17. stolen *w.* are sweet
Eccl. 11. 1. cast thy bread upon *w.*
S. of S. 4. 15. a well of living *w.*
Isa. 32. 20. blessed are ye that sow beside all *w.*
35. 6. in wilderness shall *w.* break
55. 1. come ye to *w.* buy and eat
58. 11. whose *w.* fail not
Jer 2. 13. fountain of living *w.*
9. 1. O that my head were *w.*
Hab. 2. 14. as *w.* cover the sea
Zech. 14. 8. living *w.* shall go out
Rev. 1. 15. his voice as the sound of many *w.*, 14. 2. & 19. 6.
Prov. 11. 25. he that *watereth* shall be *watered*
Isa. 58. 11. be like a *w.* garden
1 Cor. 3. 6. I planted, Apollos *w.*
Ps. 42. 7. noise of thy *waterspouts*
WAVERING, Heb. 10. 23. Jas. 1. 6.
R. V. Jas. 1. 6. doubteth
WAX, Ex. 32. 10, 11, 22. Ps. 22. 14. & 68. 2. & 97. 5. Matt. 24. 12. Luke 12. 33. 1 Tim. 5. 11. 2 Tim. 3. 13.
R. V. Gen. 41. 56; Josh. 23. 1. was; Acts 13. 46. spake out
WAY, Ex. 13. 21. & 23. 20. & 32. 8.
1 Sam. 12. 23. teach you good and right *w.*
1 Kings 2. 2. *w.* of all the earth
Ezra 8. 21. seek of him a right *w.*
Ps. 1. 6. the Lord knoweth the *w.* of the righteous
49. 13. their *w.* is their folly
67. 2. thy *w.* may be known
119. 30. chosen *w.* of truth
104. I hate every false *w.*
Prov. 2. 8. Lord preserveth the *w.* of his saints
10. 29. *w.* of the Lord is strength
14. 12. a *w.* that seemeth right
Eccl. 11. 5. thou knowest not what is the *w.* of the spirit
Isa. 26. 7. *w.* of just is upright.
30. 21. this is the *w.* walk ye in
35. 8. a high *w.* and a *w.* called
40. 3. prepare the *w.* of the
43. 19. a *w.* in the wilderness
59. 8. *w.* of peace they know not
Jer. 6. 16. where is a good *w.* and
21. 8. set before you the *w.* of life
32. 39. give them one heart and *w.*
Amos 2. 7. turn aside *w.* of the
Mal. 3. 1. prepare the *w.* before
Matt. 7. 13. broad is *w.* to destruc.
14. narrow is *w.* that leadeth to
22. 16. teacheth *w.* of God in
John 1. 23. straight the *w.* of Lord
14. 4. *w.* ye know
6. I am the *w.*
Acts 16. 17. which show unto us the *w.* of salvation
1 Cor. 10. 13. make a *w.* to escape
12. 31. show you more excellent *w.*
2 Pet. 2. 2. the *w.* of truth be evil
1 Kings 8. 32. bring *his way* on his head
Job 17. 9. right. shall hold on —
Ps. 18. 30. as for God — is perfect
37. 23. delight in —
34. and keep —
119. 9. young man cleanse —
Prov. 14. 8. prudent to understand —
Isa. 55. 7. let the wicked forsake —
Ps. 25. 8. teach sinners *in the way*
119. 14. I rejoiced — of testimo.
139. 24. lead me — everlasting
Isa. 26. 8. — of thy judgments we
Matt. 5. 25. agree with adversary —
21. 32. John came — of righteous.
Luke 1. 79. guide your feet —
Job 40. 19. he is chief of *ways* of
Ps. 84. 5. in whose heart are *w.*
Prov. 3. 17. *w.* are *w.* of pleasant.
5. 21. *w.* of man are before Lord
16. 7. a man's *w.* please
Jer. 7. 3. amend your *w.* and doings
Lam. 1. 4. the *w.* of Zion do mourn
Deut. 32. 4. *his ways*, Ps. 145. 17. Isa. 2. 3. Mic. 4. 2. Rom. 11. 33.
Ps. 119. 5. *my ways*, 15. 26, 59, 168. & 139. 3. & 39. 1. Prov. 23. 26. Isa. 55. 8. & 49. 11.
Prov. 14. 14. *own ways*, Isa. 53. 6. & 58. 13. & 66. 3. Ezek. 36. 31, 32.
Job 21. 14. *thy ways*, Ps. 25. 4. & 91. 11. Prov. 3. 6. & 4. 26. Isa. 63. 17. Ezek. 16. 61. Dan. 5. 23. Rev. 15. 3.
Isa. 35. 8. *wayfaring*, Jer. 14. 8.
WEAK, 2 Chron. 15. 7. Job 4. 3. Ps. 6. 2.
Isa. 35. 3. strengthen ye *w.* hands
Ezek. 16. 30. how *w.* is thy heart
Matt. 26. 41. spirit is willing but the flesh is *w.*
Rom. 4. 19. not *w.* in faith
14. 1. him that is *w.* in faith receive
1 Cor. 4. 10. we are *w.* but ye
2 Cor. 11. 29. who is *w.* and I not *w.*
12. 10. I am *w.* then am I strong
1 Thes. 5. 13. support the *w.* be
Isa. 14. 12. *weaken*, Ps. 102. 23. Job 12. 21.
2 Sam. 3. 1. *weaker*, 1 Pet. 3. 7.
1 Cor. 1. 25. *weakness*, 2. 3. & 15. 43. 2 Cor. 12. 9. & 13. 4. Heb. 11. 34.
R. V. Job 12. 21. looseth; Isa. 14. 12. lay low
WEALTH, Gen. 34. 29. Deut. 8. 17.
Deut. 8. 18. give. power to get *w.*
Job. 21. 13. spend their days in *w.*
Ps. 49. 6. that trust in their *w.*
112. 3. *w.* and riches are in his
Prov. 10. 15. the rich man's *w.* is
13. 11. *w.* gotten by vanity
22. *w.* of sinners is laid up for
19. 4. *w.* maketh many friends
1 Cor. 10. 24. seek another's *w.*
R. V. Ezra 9. 12; Job 21. 13. prosperity; Esth. 10. 3; 1 Cor. 10. 24. good; Prov. 5. 10. strength
WEANED, Ps. 131. 2. Isa. 11. 8. & 28. 9.
WEAPON. Isa. 13. 5. & 54. 17. 2 Cor. 10. 4.
WEAR, Deut. 22. 5, 11. Dan. 7. 25. Matt. 11. 8. Jas. 2. 3. 1 Pet. 3. 3.
WEARY of my life, Gen. 27. 46.
Job 3. 17. there the *w.* be at rest
10. 1. soul is *w.* of life, Jer. 4. 31.
Prov. 3. 11. neither be *w.* of his
Isa. 7. 13. *w.* men, but will ye *w.*
40. 31. shall run and not be *w.*
43. 22. hast been *w.* of me, O
Jer. 6. 11. *w.* with holding in
9. 5. *w.* themselves to commit
15. 6. I am *w.* with repenting
Gal. 6. 9. *w.* in well doing
Isa. 43. 24. *wearied*, 57. 10. Jer. 12. 5. Ezek. 24. 12. Mic. 6. 3. Mal. 2. 17. John 4. 7. Heb. 12. 3.
Eccl. 12. 12. *weariness*, Mal. 1. 13.
Job 7. 3. *wearisome* nights
R. V. Job 37. 11. ladeth
WEB, Job 8. 14. Isa. 59. 5, 6.
WEDDING, Matt. 22. 3, 8, 11. Luke 14. 8.
WEEK, Dan. 9. 27. Matt. 28. 1. Luke 18. 12. Acts 20. 7. 1 Cor. 16. 2.
Jer. 5. 24. *weeks*, Dan. 9. 24-26. & 10. 2.
WEEP, Job 30. 25. Isa. 30. 19. & 33. 7. Jer. 9. 1. & 13. 17. Joel 2. 17.
Luke 6. 21. blessed are ye that *w.*
Acts 21. 13. what mean ye to *w.*
Rom. 12. 15. *w.* with them that *w.*
1 Cor. 7. 30. that *w.* as though *wept*
Jas. 5. 1. rich men *w.* and howl
Ps. 126. 6. *weepeth*, Lam. 1. 2.
1 Sam. 1. 8. why *weepest*, John 20. 13, 15.
Ps. 30. 5. *weeping* may endure for
Isa. 22. 12. Lord call to *w.* and
Jer. 31. 9. they shall come with *w.*
Joel 2. 12. turn to me with *w.*
Matt. 8. 12. *w.* and gnashing of teeth, 22. 13. & 24. 51. & 25. 30.
WEIGH the paths of the just, Isa. 26. 7.
Prov. 16. 2. Lord *weigheth* spirits
Job 31. 6. me be *weighed* in balances
Dan. 5. 27. art *w.* in the balances
Prov. 11. 1. just *weight* is his de.
2 Cor. 4. 17. eternal *w.* of glory
Heb. 12. 1. laying aside every *w.*
Lev. 19. 36. just *weights*
Deut. 55. 13. divers *w.*, Prov. 20. 10, 23.
Matt. 23. 23. omit *weightier* matters
WELL, Ps. 84. 6. Prov. 5. 15. & 10. 11. S. of S. 4. 15. Isa. 12. 3. John 4. 14. 2 Pet. 2. 17.
Gen. 4. 7. if thou doest *well*, shalt
Ex. 1. 20. God dealt *w.* with mid.
Ps. 119. 65. hast dealt *w.* with thy
Eccl. 8. 12. it shall be *w.* with them
Isa. 3. 10. shall be *w.* with him
Rom. 2. 7. *well doing*, Gal. 6. 9. 2 Thes. 3. 13. 1 Pet. 2. 15. & 3. 17. & 4. 19.
R. V. Gen. 24. 13, 16, 29, 30, 42, 43; 49. 22; Josh. 18. 15; 2 Kings 3. 19, 25; Prov. 10. 11. fountain or fountains; Ex. 15. 27; Judg. 7. 1; Ps. 84. 6; 2 Pet. 2. 17. spring or springs; Deut. 6. 11; 2 Kings 26. 10; Neh. 9. 25. cisterns
WENT, Ps. 42. 4. & 119. 67. Matt. 21. 30.
WEPT, Neh. 1. 4. Ps. 69. 10. Hos. 12. 4. Matt. 26. 75. Luke 19. 41. John 11. 35.
WHEAT, Ps. 81. 16. Prov. 27. 22. S. of S. 7. 2.
Jer. 12. 13. have sown *w.* but reap
23. 28. what is the chaff to the *w.*
Matt. 3. 12. gather his *w.* into the
Luke 22. 31. may sift you as *w.*
John 12. 24. except a corn of *w.* fall
R. V. Num. 18. 12. corn; Prov. 27. 22. bruised corn
WHEEL, Ps. 83. 13. Prov. 20. 26.
Ezek. 1. 16. a *w.* in the midst of a *w.*
Ex. 14. 25. *wheels*, Judg. 5. 28. Dan. 7. 9. Nah. 3. 2.
R. V. Ps. 83. 13. whirling dust; Ezek. 23. 24; 26. 10. wagons
WHELPS (lions'), parable of, Ezek. 19. Nah. 2. 12

WHET, Deut. 32. 41. Ps. 7. 12. & 64. 3.
WHISPERER, Prov. 16. 28.
WHIT, John 7. 23. & 12. 10. 2 Cor. 11. 5.
WHITE, Lev. 13. 3, 4. Num. 12. 10.
Job 6. 6. in the *w.* of an egg
Ps. 68. 14. *w.* as snow, Dan. 7. 9.
Eccl. 9. 8. garments be always *w.*
S. of S. 5. 10. my beloved is *w.* and
Isa. 1. 18. sins shall be *w.* as snow
Dan. 11. 35. fall . . to make them *w.*
Matt. 17. 2. his raiment was *w.*
Rev. 2. 17. gave him a *w.* stone
3. 4. walk with me in *w.* raiment, 5. 18. & 4. 4. & 7. 9, 13. & 15. 16. & 19. 8, 14.
Matt. 23. 27. *whited*, Acts 23. 3.
Ps. 51. 7. *whiter* than snow
WHITE HORSE, Rev. 6. 2. & 19. 11 ; cloud, Rev. 14. 14.
WHITE THRONE, Rev. 20. 11.
WHOLE, Ps. 9. 1. & 119. 10. Isa. 54. 5. Mic. 4. 13. Zech. 4. 14. Matt. 6. 26. Eph. 6. 11. 1 John 2. 2. & 5. 19.
Job 5. 18. his hands make *w.*
Matt. 9. 12. those that are *w.* need not a physician, Luke 5. 31.
Mark 5. 34. faith hath made thee *w.*, 10. 52. Luke 8. 48. & 17. 19.
John 5. 4. *w.* of whatsoever dis.
Acts 9. 34. Christ maketh thee *w.*
Jer. 46. 28. *wholly*, 1 Thes. 5. 23. 1 Tim. 4. 15.
Prov. 15. 4. *wholesome*, 1 Tim. 6. 3.
WHORE, Lev. 19. 29. & 21. 7, 9. Deut. 22. 21. & 23. 17, 18. Prov. 23. 27. Ezek. 16. 28. Rev. 17. 1, 16.
Jer. 3. 9. *whoredom*, Ezek. 16. Hos. 2. 2, 4. & 4. 11, 12. & 5. 3, 4.
Eph. 5. 5. *whoremonger*, 1 Tim. 1. 10. Heb. 13. 4. Rev. 21. 8. & 22. 15.
R. V. Lev. 19. 29; 21. 7, 9; Deut. 22. 21; 23. 17; Judg. 19. 2; Ezek. 16. 28, 33; Rev. 17. 1, 15, 16; 19. 2. harlot
WICKED, Ex. 23. 7. Deut. 15. 9. & 25. 1.
Gen. 18. 25. destroy right. with *w.*
1 Sam. 2. 9. *w.* shall be silent
Job 21. 30. *w.* is reserved till the
34. 18. is it fit to say to king thou art *w.*
Ps. 7. 11. God is angry with the *w.*
9. 17. *w.* shall be turned into
11. 6. on *w.* he will rain snares
119. 155. salvation is far from *w.*
145. 20. all the *w.* shall he destroy
Prov. 11. 5. *w.* shall fall by his
21. *w.* shall not be unpunished
21. 12. God overthroweth the *w.*
28. 1. the *w.* flee when no man
Eccl. 7. 17. be not overmuch *w.*
Isa. 55. 7. let the *w.* forsake his
57. 20. *w.* are like the troubled
Jer. 17. 9. heart is desperately *w.*
Ezek. 3. 18. warn the *w.*, 33. 8, 9.
Dan. 12. 10. *w.* shall do *wickedly*
Gen. 19. 7. do not so *w.*, Neh. 9. 33.
1 Sam. 12. 25. if ye shall do *w.*
Job 13. 7. will ye speak *w.* for God
Ps. 18. 21. have not *w.* departed
Gen. 6. 5. God saw that *wickedness*
39. 9. how can I do this great *w.*
1 Sam. 24. 13. *w.* proceedeth from
Job 4. 8. that sow *w.* shall reap
Ps. 7. 9. *w.* of wicked come to end
Prov. 8. 7. *w.* is abomination to
13. 6. *w.* overthroweth sinners
Eccl. 8. 8. neither shall *w.* deliver
Isa. 9. 18. *w.* burneth as the fire
Jer. 2. 19. thine own *w.* shall cor.
14. 20. we acknowledge our *w.*
Hos. 10. 13. ye have ploughed *w.*
Acts 8. 22. repent of this thy *w.*
1 John 5. 19. world lieth in *w.*
R. V. Frequent changes to evil, unrighteous, etc.
WIDE, Deut. 15. 8, 11. Ps. 35. 2. & 81. 10. Prov. 13. 3. Matt. 7. 13.
WIDOW, Mark 12. 42. 1 Tim. 5. 5. Deut. 10. 18. Ps. 146. 9. Luke 18. 3, 5.
Ps. 68. 5. *widows*, Jer. 49. 11. Matt. 23. 14. 1 Tim. 5. 3. Jas. 1. 27.

WIFE, Ex. 20. 17. Lev. 21. 13.
Prov. 5. 18. rejoice with *w.* of
18. 22. findeth a *w.* findeth a good
Eccl. 9. 9. live joyfully with thy *w.*
Hos. 12. 12. Israel served for a *w.*
Mal. 2. 15. against *w.* of thy youth
Luke 17. 32. remember Lot's *w.*
Eph. 5. 33. every man love his *w.*
Rev. 19. 7. his *w.* made herself
21. 9. the bride, the Lamb's *w.*
1 Cor. 7. 29. *wives*, Eph. 5. 25, 28, 33. Col. 3. 18, 19. 1 Tim. 3. 11. 1 Pet. 3. 1, 7.
R. V. Ex. 19. 15; Lev. 21. 7; Judg. 21. 14; Ezra 10. 2, 10, 11, 14, 17, 18; Neh. 12. 43; 13. 23, 27; 1 Tim. 3. 11; 1 Pet. 3. 7. woman or women; Matt. 19. 29; 22. 25; Mark 10. 29; Luke 17. 27; 20. 30 —
WILDERNESS, Deut. 32. 10. Prov. 21. 19. S. of S. 3. 6. & 8. 5. Isa. 35. 1, 6. & 41. 18, 19. & 42. 11. & 43. 19, 20. Rev. 12. 6.
R. V. Job 30. 3. dry ground; Ps. 107. 40. waste; Amos 6. 14. Arabah; Ps. 78. 17; Prov. 21. 19; Isa. 33. 9; Jer. 51. 43; Matt. 15. 43; Mark 8. 14; Luke 5. 16; 8. 29. desert, or desert place
WILES, Num. 25. 18. Eph. 6. 11.
WILL, Lev. 1. 3. & 19. 5. & 22. 19.
Deut 33. 16. the good *w.* of him that dwelt in the bush
Matt. 7. 21. doeth *w.* of my Father
Luke 2. 14. good *w.* towards men
John 1. 13. *w.* of flesh, nor
3. 34. my meat is to do *w.* of him
6. 40. this is the *w.* of him that
Acts 21. 14. *w.* of the Lord be done
Eph. 5. 17. understandeth what the *w.* of the Lord is
Acts 22. 14. *his will*, John 7. 17. Rom. 2. 18. Eph. 1. 5, 9. Col. 1. 9. 2 Tim. 2. 26. Heb. 13. 21. 1 John 5. 14. Rev. 17. 17.
Luke 23. 42. *my will*, Acts 13. 22.
John 5. 30. *own will*, 6. 38. Eph. 1. 11. Heb. 2. 4. Jas. 1. 18.
Ps. 40. 8. *thy will*, 143. 10. Matt. 6. 10. & 26. 42. Heb. 10. 7, 9.
Ezra 7. 18. *will of God*, Mark 3. 35. Rom. 1. 10. & 8. 27. & 12. 2. 1 Cor. 1. 1. 2 Cor. 8. 5. Gal. 1. 4. Eph. 1. 1. & 6. 6. Col. 1. 1. & 4. 12. 1 Thes. 4. 3. Heb. 10. 36. 1 Pet. 4. 2, 19. 1 John 2. 17.
Matt. 26. 39. not as *I will*, but as
John 15. 7. ask what ye *w.* and it
17. 24. I *w.* that those thou hast
Rom. 7. 18. to *w.* is present with
Phil. 2. 13. worketh to *w.* and to
Rev. 22. 17. whosoever *w.* let him
Rom. 9. 16. of him that *willeth*
Heb. 10. 26. if we sin *wilfully*
Ex. 35. 5. whoso is of a *willing* heart
1 Chron. 28. 9. with a perfect heart and *w.* mind
Ps. 110. 3. people shall be *w.* in the
Isa. 1. 19. be *w.* and obedient
Matt. 26. 41. Spirit is *w.* but the
Luke 22. 42. if thou be *w.* remove
John 5. 35. *w.* for a season to rej.
2 Cor. 5. 8. *w.* rather to be absent
1 Tim. 6. 18. be *w.* to communicate
Heb. 13. 18. *w.* in all things to
2 Pet. 3. 9. not *w.* any should per.
Judg. 5. 2. *willingly* offered them.
1 Chron. 29. 9. heart offered *w.*
Lam. 3. 33. Lord doth not afflict *w.*
Hos. 5. 11. he *w.* walked after the
Col. 2. 23. wisdom in *will worship*
R. V. Changes of the pure auxiliary are to would, should, shall, etc. Ex. 35. 29. free will; Job 39. 9. content; Mark 15. 15; 2 Pet. 3. 9. wishing; Luke 10. 29; 23. 20; Acts 24. 27; 25. 9; 27. 43; Heb. 13. 18. desiring; 1 Thes. 2. 8. well pleased; Heb. 6. 17. being minded
WILLOWS, Lev. 23. 40. Isa. 44. 4.
WIN, Phil. 3. 8.
Prov. 11. 30. *winneth*
R. V. Phil. 3. 8. gain

WIND, Job 7. 7. & 30. 15. Ps. 103. 16.
Prov. 11. 29. inherit *w.*
30. 4. gathereth the *w.*
Eccl. 11. 4. that observeth the *w.*
Isa. 26. 18. have brought forth *w.*
Jer. 5. 13. prophets shall become *w.*
10. 13. bring *w.* out of his treas.
Hos. 8. 7. sown *w.*
John 3. 8. *w.* bloweth where it
Eph. 4. 14. about with every *w.*
2 Kings 2. 11. *whirlwind*, Prov. 1. 27. & 10. 25. Isa. 66. 15. Hos. 8. 7. & 13. 3. Nah. 1. 3. Hab. 3. 14. Zech. 7. 14. & 9. 14.
Ezek. 37. 9. *winds*, Matt. 8. 26. Luke 8. 25.
R. V. Isa. 27. 8. blast; Jer. 14. 6. air; Hos. 13. 15. breath; Ezek. 41. 7. encompass
WINDOWS, Gen. 7. 11. Eccl. 12. 3. S. of S. 2. 9. Isa. 60. 8. Jer. 9. 21.
R. V. Gen. 6. 16. light; 1 Kings 7. 4, 5. prospects; Isa. 54. 12. pinnacles
WINE maketh glad the heart, Ps. 104. 15.
Prov. 20. 1. *w.* is a mocker
21. 17. loveth *w.* and oil shall
23. 30. that tarry long at *w.* that
31. look not upon *w.* when it is
S. of S. 1. 2. love is better than *w.*
Isa. 5. 11. till *w.* inflame them
25. 6. *w.* on the lees well refined
55. 1. buy *w.* and milk
Hos. 2. 9. take away my *w.* in
4. 11. *w.* take away the heart
Hab. 2. 5. transgresseth by *w.*
Eph. 5. 18. not drunk with *w.*
1 Tim. 3. 3. not given to *w.*, 8.
5. 23. a little *w.* for stomach's
Prov. 23. 20. *wine-bibber*, Matt. 11. 19.
R. V. Num. 18. 12; Mic. 6. 15. vintage; Num. 28. 7. drink; 2 Sam. 6. 19; 1 Chron. 16. 3; Hos. 3. 1. raisins
WINGS of the God of Israel, Ruth 2. 12.
Ps. 17. 8. hide under shadow of *w.*, 36. 7. & 57. 1. & 61. 4. & 91. 4.
18. 10. on *w.* of the wind, 2 Sam. 22. 11.
Prov. 23. 5. riches make themselves *w.* and fly away
Isa. 6. 2. seraphims; each had six *w.*
Mal. 4. 2. with healing in his *w.*
R. V. Deut. 32. 11. pinions
WINK, Job 15. 12. Ps. 35. 19. Prov. 6. 13. & 10. 10. Acts 17. 30.
R. V. *overlook*, Acts 17. 30. ignorance God *w.* at
WINTER, S. of S. 2. 11. Zech. 14. 8.
WIPE, 2 Kings 21. 13. Neh. 13. 14. Prov. 6. 33. Isa. 25. 8. Rev. 7. 17. & 21. 4.
WISE, Gen. 41. 39. Ex. 23. 8. Deut. 16. 19.
Deut. 4. 6. this great nation is a *w.* people
Job 5. 13. taketh the *w.* in their
11. 12. vain man would be *w.*
32. 9. great men are not always *w.*
Ps. 2. 10. be *w.* O kings, be taught
29. 7. making the simple *w.*
Prov. 3. 7. be not *w.* in own eyes
35. the *w.* shall inherit glory
26. 12. a man *w.* in his own conceit
Eccl. 7. 4. heart of *w.* in house
9. 1. the *w.* are in the hand of God
Isa. 5. 21. are *w.* in their own eyes
Jer. 4. 22. they are *w.* to do evil
Dan. 12. 3. *w.* shall shine as stars
Hos. 14. 9. who is *w.* and he shall
Matt. 10. 16. be ye *w.* as serpents
Rom. 1. 22. professing themselves to be *w.*
16. 19. be *w.* to that which is good
1 Cor. 3. 18. seem. *w.* in this world
4. 10. but ye are *w.* in Christ
Eph. 5. 15. not as fools but as *w.*
2 Tim. 3. 15. is able to make thee *w.*

Matt. 10. 42. *in no wise* lose his
Luke 18. 17. shall—enter therein
John 6. 37. cometh, I will—cast out
Rev. 21. 27. shall—enter into it
Deut. 4. 6. this is your *wisdom*
1 Kings 4. 29. God gave Solomon *w.*, 5. 12.
Job 28. 28. fear of Lord, that is *w.*
Prov. 4. 5. get *w.* get understand.
7. *w.* is the principal thing, 8.
16. 16. better to get *w.* than gold
19. 8. he that getteth *w.* loveth his own soul
Eccl. 1. 18. in much *w.* is much grief
8. 1. a man's *w.* maketh his face
Matt. 11. 19. *w.* is justified of her
1 Cor. 1. 30. who of God is made unto us *w.*
2. 6. we speak *w.* among perfect
3. 19. *w.* of this world is foolish.
2 Cor. 1. 12. not with fleshly *w.*
Col. 1. 9. might be filled with all *w.*
4. 5. walk in *w.* towards them that
Jas. 1. 5. if any lack *w.* ask it of
3. 17. *w.* from above is pure
Rev. 5. 12. worthy is the Lamb to receive *w.*
13. 18. here is *w.* let him that hath, 17. 9.
Ps. 111. 10. *of wisdom*, Prov. 9. 10. & 10. 21. Mic. 6. 9. Col. 2. 3. Jas. 3. 13.
64. 9. *wisely*, 101. 2. Eccl. 7. 10.
1 Kings 4. 31. *wiser*, Job 35. 11. Ps. 119. 98. Luke 16. 8. 1 Cor. 1. 25.
R. V. 1 Chron. 26. 14. discreet; Prov. 1. 5. sound; 1 Tim. 1. 17; Jude 25——; Lev. 19. 17; Deut. 21. 23. surely; Rom. 10. 6. thus; 1 Chron. 22. 12. discretion; Job 36. 5; Ps. 136. 5; Prov. 10. 21; Eccl. 10. 3. understanding; Prov. 1. 3. wise dealing; 8. 5. subtilty; 8. 14. knowledge; Dan. 2. 14. prudence

WITCH, Ex. 22. 18. Deut. 18. 10.
1 Sam. 15. 23. *witchcraft*, Gal. 5. 20.

WITHDRAW, Job 9. 13. & 33. 17. Prov. 25. 17. S. of S. 5. 6. 2 Thes. 3. 6. 1 Tim. 6. 5.

WITHERED hand of Jeroboam healed, 1 Kings 13.
——hand healed by Christ, Matt. 12. 10. Mark 3. Luke 6. 6.

WITHHOLD not thy mercies, Ps. 40. 11.
Ps. 84. 11. no good thing will he *w.*
Prov. 3. 27. *w.* not good from them
23. 13. *w.* not correction from child
Gen. 20. 6. *withheld*, 22. 12. Job 31. 16.
Job 42. 2. *withholden*, Jer. 5. 25.
Prov. 11. 24. *withholdeth*, 26. 2 Thes. 2. 6.
R. V. Job 42. 2; 2 Thes. 2. 6. restrain

WITHIN, Ps. 40. 8. & 45. 13. Matt. 3. 9. & 23. 26. Mark 7. 21. 2 Cor. 7. 5. Rev. 5. 1.

WITHOUT, Prov. 1. 20. & 24. 27. 1 Cor. 5. 12. 2 Cor. 7. 5. Col. 4. 5. Rev. 22. 15.

WITHSTAND, Eccl. 4. 12. Eph. 6. 13.
Acts 11. 17. what was I, that I could *w.* God
Gal. 2. 11. *withstood*, 2 Tim. 4. 15.

WITNESS, Gen. 31. 44, 48. Lev. 5. 1.
Num. 35. 30. one *w.* shall not testify against him, Deut. 17. 6. & 19. 15. 2 Cor. 13. 1.
Judg. 11. 10. Lord be *w.*, 1 Sam. 12. 5. Jer. 42. 5. & 29. 23. Mic. 1. 2.
Ps. 89. 37. as a faithful *w.* in heaven
Prov. 14. 5. a faithful *w.* will not lie
Isa. 55. 4. him for a *w.* to the people
Mal. 3. 5. I will be a swift *w.* again.
John 3. 11. ye receive not our *w.*
Acts 14. 17. left not himself without *w.*
1 John 5. 10. believeth him hath *w.*
Rev. 1. 5. is the faithful *w.*, 3. 14.
20. 4. beheaded for *w.* of Jesus
Deut. 17. 6. two or three *witnesses*, 19. 15. 2 Cor. 13. 1. Matt. 18. 16. Heb. 10. 28. 1 Tim. 5. 19. Num. 35. 30.
Josh. 24. 22. ye are *w.* against
Isa. 43. 10. ye are my *w.* saith the Lord, 12. & 44. 8.
1 Thes. 2. 10. ye are *w.* and God
6. 12. before many *w.*
Heb. 12. 1. so great a cloud of *w.*
Rev. 11. 3. power unto my two *w.*

WIVES, their duties to husbands, Gen. 3. 16. Ex. 20. 14. Rom. 7. 2. 1 Cor. 7. 3. & 14. 34. Eph. 5. 22, 33. Tit. 2. 4. 1 Pet. 3. 1.
good, Prov. 12. 4. & 18. 22. & 19. 14. & 31. 10.
Levitical laws concerning, Ex. 21. 3, 22. & 22. 16. Num. 5. 12. & 30. Deut. 21. 10, 15. & 24. 1. Jer. 3. 1. Matt. 19. 3.
the wife a type of the church, Eph. 5. 23. Rev. 19. 7. & 21. 9.

WIZARDS, Lev. 19. 31. & 20. 6. Isa. 8. 19.

WOES against wickedness, etc., Isa. 5. 8. & 10. 1. & 29. 15. & 31. 1. & 45. 9. Jer. 22. 13. Amos 6. 1. Mic. 2. 1. Hab. 2. 6. Zeph. 3. 1. Zech. 11. 17. Matt. 26. 24. Luke 6. 24. Jude 11. Rev. 8. 13. & 9. 12. & 11. 14.
against unbelief, Matt. 11. 21. & 23. 13. Luke 10. 13. & 11. 42.

WOLF, Isa. 11. 6. & 65. 25. Jer. 5. 6. Ezek. 22. 27. *wolves*, Hab. 1. 8. Zeph. 3. 3. Matt. 7. 15. & 10. 16. Acts 20. 29.

WOMAN, Gen. 2. 23. & 3. 15. Lev. 18. 22, 23. & 20. 13. Num. 30. 3.
Prov. 11. 16. gracious *w.* retaineth honor
Ps. 48. 6. pain as of a *w.* in travail
Prov. 12. 4. a virtuous *w.* is a crown
14. 1. every wise *w.* buildeth her
31. 10. a virtuous *w.* who can find
30. *w.* that feareth the Lord shall
Eccl. 7. 26. *w.* whose heart is snares
28. *w.* among all I have not found
Isa. 49. 15. can a *w.* forget her suckl-
54. 6. called thee as a *w.* forsaken
Jer. 31. 22. *w.* shall compass a man
Matt. 5. 28. looketh on a *w.* to lust
15. 28. O *w.* great is thy faith
John 2. 4. *w.* what have I to do with
8. 3. brought *w.* taken in adultery
19. 26. *w.* behold thy son
Rom. 1. 27. the natural use of *w.*
1 Cor. 11. 7. *w.* is the glory of man
Gal. 4. 4. sent his Son made of a *w.*
1 Tim. 2. 12. I suffer not *w.* to teach
14. *w.* being deceived was in the
Rev. 12. 1. *w.* clothed with the sun, 6. 16.
17. 18. *w.* thou sawest is that city
Judg. 5. 24. blessed above *women* shall Jael be
Prov. 31. 3. give not thy strength to *w.*
S. of S. 1. 8. fairest among *w.*, 5. 9. & 6. 1.
Jer. 9. 17. call for the mourning *w.*
Lam. 4. 10. *w.* had sodden children
Matt. 11. 11. among them born of *w.*
Luke 1. 28. blessed art thou among *w.*
Rom. 1. 26. *w.* did change their
1 Cor. 14. 34. let *w.* keep silence
1 Tim. 2. 9. let *w.* adorn themselves
11. let *w.* learn in silence with
5. 14. that the younger *w.* marry
1 Pet. 3. 5. after this manner holy *w.*
Rev. 14. 4. are not defiled with *w.*

WOMB, Gen. 25. 23. & 29. 31.
Gen. 49. 25. blessings of the *w.* and
1 Sam. 1. 5. Lord hath shut her *w.*
Ps. 22. 9. took me out of the *w.*
10. I was cast upon thee from *w.*
139. 13. covered me in mother's *w.*
Eccl. 11. 5. how bones grow in *w.*
Isa. 44. 2. the Lord that formed thee from the *w.*
Hos. 9. 14. give them miscarrying *w.*
Luke 1. 42. blessed is fruit of thy *w.*
11. 27. blessed is *w.* that bare thee
23. 29. blessed are *w.* that never
R. V. Deut. 7. 13. body

WONDER, Deut. 13. 1. & 28. 46. Ps. 71. 7. Isa. 29. 14. Rev. 12. 1.
Acts 13. 41. *w.* and perish, Hab. 1. 5.
Ex. 3. 20. *wonders*, 7. 3. & 15. 11.
1 Chron. 16. 12. remember his *w.*, Ps. 105. 5.
Job 9. 10. God doeth *w.*, Ps. 77. 11, 14.
Ps. 88. 11. wilt thou show *w.* to the dead
Dan. 12. 6. how long to the end of these *w.*
John 4. 48. except they see signs and *w.*
Acts 2. 43. many *w.* were done, 6. 8.
Rom. 15. 19. mighty signs and *w.*
2 Thes. 2. 9. and signs and lying *w.*
Rev. 13. 13. he doeth great *w.*
Zech. 3. 8. they are men *wondered*
Isa. 59. 16. *w.* there was no inter.
Luke 4. 22. *w.* at the gracious words
Rev. 13. 3. all the world *w.* after
17. 6. I *w.* with great admiration
Job 37. 14. *wondrous* works, Ps. 26. 7. & 75. 1. & 105. 2. & 119. 27. & 145. 5. & 71. 17. & 78. 32. & 106. 22.
Ps. 72. 18. *w.* things, 86. 10. & 119. 18.
Judg. 13. 19. *wondrously*, Joel 2. 26.
Deut. 28. 59. thy plagues *wonderful*
Ps. 119. 129. thy testimonies are *w.*
Prov. 30. 18. three things too *w.* for
Isa. 9. 6. his name shall be called *W.*
Jer. 5. 30. a *w.* thing is committed
Ps. 139. 14. *wonderfully*, Lam. 1. 9.
R. V. Rev. 12. 1, 3. sign; Gen. 24. 21. looked stedfastly; Mark 6. 51. ——; Luke 8. 25; 11. 14. marvelled; Acts 8. 13. amazed; Ps. 78. 4. wondrous; Matt. 7. 22; Acts 2. 21. mighty; 1 Chron. 16. 9; Ps. 105. 2. marvellous

WOOD, hay, stubble, 1 Cor. 3. 12.
2 Tim. 2. 20. also vessels of *w.* and
R. V. Deut. 19. 5; Josh. 17. 18; 1 Sam. 14. 25, 26; Ps. 83. 14; Eccl. 2. 6; Isa. 7. 2; Mic. 7. 14. forest; 1 Chron. 22. 4. trees; Ex. 26. 32, 37; 36. 36; Ps. 141. 7——

WORD, Num. 23. 5. Deut. 4. 2.
Deut. 8. 3. every *w.* of God, Matt. 4. 4.
30. 14. *w.* is very nigh, Rom. 10. 8.
Ps. 68. 11. the Lord gave the *w.*
Prov. 15. 23. *w.* spoken in due season
25. 11. a *w.* fitly spoken is like apples of gold
Isa. 29. 21. man an offender for a *w.*
50. 4. how to speak a *w.* in season
Jer. 5. 13. the *w.* is not in them
Matt. 8. 8. speak the *w.* only and my servant shall be healed
12. 36. every idle *w.* that men
Luke 4. 36. what a *w.* is this
John 1. 1. in the beginning was the *W.* and the *W.* was with God
14. the *W.* was made flesh
15. 3. ye are clean through the *w.*
Acts 13. 15. any *w.* of exhortation
26. to you is *w.* of salvation sent
17. 11. the *w.* with all readiness
20. 32. and to the *w.* of his grace
1 Cor. 4. 20. kingdom of God is not in *w.*
Gal. 6. 6. taught in *w.* communicate
Eph. 5. 26. washing of water by *w.*
Col. 3. 16. let *w.* of Christ dwell in
17. whatsoever ye do in *w.* or deed
1 Thes. 1. 5. Gospel came not in *w.*
2 Thes. 2. 17. stablish you in every good *w.*
3. 14. if any obey not our *w.* note
1 Tim. 5. 17. labor in *w.* and
2 Tim. 4. 2. preach *w.* be instant in
Tit. 1. 9. holding fast the faithful *w.*
Heb. 4. 2. the *w.* preached did not
5. 13. is unskilful in *w.* of right.
13. 22. suffer the *w.* of exhortation
Jas. 1. 21. receive the engrafted *w.*
22. be doers of the *w.*
3. 2. offend not in *w.*
1 Pet. 3. 1. if any obey not the *w.*
2 Pet. 1. 19. sure *w.* of prophecy
1 John 1. 1. hands handled of the *w.*

1 John 5. 7. Father, *W.* and Holy Ghost
Rev. 3. 10. kept *w.* of my patience
12. 11. overcame by *w.* of their testimony
Ps. 130. 5. in *his word* do I hope, 119. 81.
Jer. 20. 9.—was in my heart as fire
John 5. 38. have not—abiding in you
Acts 2. 41. that gladly received—were baptized
John 8. 37. *my word*, 43. Rev. 3. 8.
Isa. 8. 20. *this word*, Rom. 9. 9.
Ps. 119. 11. *thy word* have I hid in mine heart
105.—is a lamp unto my feet
140.—is very pure
160.—is true from the beginning
Jer. 15. 16.—was unto me joy and
John 17. 6. I kept—
17.—is truth
Prov. 30. 5. *word of God*, Isa. 40. 8. Mark 7. 13. Rom. 10. 17. 1 Thes. 2. 13. Heb. 4. 12. & 6. 5. 1 Pet. 1. 23. Rev. 19. 13.
2 Kings 20. 19. *word of the Lord*, Ps. 18. 30. & 33. 4. 2 Thes. 3. 1. 1 Pet. 1. 25.
Ps. 119. 43. *word of truth*, 2 Cor. 6. 7. Eph. 1. 13. Col. 1. 5. 2 Tim. 2. 15. Jas. 1. 18.
Job 23. 12. esteemed *words* of
Prov. 15. 26. *w.* of pure are pleas.
22. 17. bow down thine ear, hear *w.*
Eccl. 10. 12. the *w.* of a wise man
11. *w.* of the wise are as goads
Jer. 7. 4. trust ye not in lying *w.*
Dan. 7. 25. speak great *w.* against
Hos. 6. 5. slain by *w.* of my mouth
Zech. 1. 13. good *w.* comfortable *w.*
Matt. 26. 44. prayed, saying same *w.*
Luke 4. 22. the gracious *w.* that
John 6. 63. *w.* I speak are Spirit and
68. thou hast the *w.* of eternal life
17. 8. given unto them *w.* which
Acts 7. 22. Moses mighty in *w.* and
15. 24. troubled you with *w.*, 18. 15.
20. 35. remember the *w.* of Lord
26. 25. speak the *w.* of truth and
1 Cor. 2. 4. not with enticing *w.* of
2 Tim. 1. 13. hold fast the form of sound *w.*
2. 14. strive not about *w.* to no
Rev. 1. 3. hear *w.* of this prophecy, 22. 18.
Ps. 50. 17. *my words*, Isa. 51. 16. & 59. 21. Jer. 5. 14. Mic. 2. 7. Mark 8. 38. & 13. 31. John 5. 47. & 15. 7.
1 Thes. 4. 18. *these words*, Rev. 21. 5.
Ps. 119. 103. *thy words*, 130. & 139. Prov. 23. 8. Eccl. 5. 2. Ezek. 33. 31. Matt. 12. 37.
R. V. Num. 4. 45; Josh. 19. 50; 22. 9. commandment; Deut. 8. 3; 2 Kings 23. 16; John 7. 9; 8. 30; 9. 22, 40; 17. 1. thing; 2 Sam. 19. 14; 1 Kings 2. 42; Luke 20. 26; John 12. 47, 48. saying; 1 Kings 13. 26. mouth; 1 Chron. 21. 12. answer; Jonah 3. 6. tidings; Matt. 2. 13. tell; Luke 4. 4; Acts 28. 29; 1 John 5. 7

WORK, Gen. 2. 3. Ex. 20. 10. & 31. 14.
Deut. 33. 11. accept *w.* of his hands
Job 1. 10. thou hast blessed the *w.*
10. 3. despise the *w.* of thy hands
36. 9. he showeth them their *w.*
Ps. 19. 1. the firmament sheweth his handy-*w.*
101. 3. I hate the *w.* of them that
143. 5. muse on *w.* of thy hands
Eccl. 8. 14. according to *w.* of wicked
17. I beheld all the *w.* of God
12. 14. God shall bring every *w.* into judgment
Isa. 10. 12. performed his whole *w.*
64. 8. we are called *w.* of thy hands
Jer. 10. 15. vanity and *w.* of error
18. 3. potter wrought a *w.* on the
Hab. 1. 5. a *w.* in your days, Acts 13. 41.
Mark 6. 5. could do no mighty *w.*
John 17. 4. finished *w.* thou gavest
Acts 5. 38. if this *w.* be of men
13. 2. for the *w.* whereto I called
Rom. 2. 15. show *w.* of law written
11. 6. otherwise *w.* is no more *w.*
1 Cor. 3. 13. every man's *w.* made
9. 1. are not ye my *w.* in the Lord
Eph. 4. 12. for *w.* of the ministry
2 Thes. 1. 11. *w.* of faith with pow.
2. 17. stablish you in every good *w.*
2 Tim. 4. 5. do *w.* of an evangelist
Jas. 1. 4. let patience have perfect *w.*
25. doer of the *w.* shall be blessed
1 Pet. 1. 17. judgeth every man's *w.*
Ps. 104. 23. *his work*, 62. 12. & 111. 3. Prov. 24. 29. Isa. 40. 10. Job 36. 24.
Ps. 90. 16. *thy work*, 92. 4. Prov. 24. 27. Jer. 31. 16. Hab. 3. 2.
Ex. 32. 16. *work of God*, Ps. 64. 9. Eccl. 7. 13. & 8. 17. John 6. 29. Rom. 14. 20.
Ps. 28. 5. *work of the Lord*, Isa. 5. 12. Jer. 48. 10. 1 Cor. 15. 58. & 16. 10.
Ps. 17. 4. concerning *works* of men
92. 4. triumph in *w.* of thy hands
138. 8. forsake not *w.* of thy hands
Prov. 31. 31. let her own *w.* praise
Isa. 26. 12. wrought all our *w.* in us
Dan. 4. 37. all whose *w.* are truth
John 5. 20. show him greater *w.*
10. 32. of those *w.* do ye stone me
38. believe the *w.* that I do
Acts 26. 20. *w.* meet for repent.
Rom. 3. 27. by what law? of *w.*
4. 6. God imputeth righteousness without *w.*
9. 32. sought it as by *w.* of the law
11. 6. then it is no more of *w.*
13. 12. us cast off *w.* of darkness
Gal. 2. 16. by *w.* of law no flesh be
3. 2. received ye spirit by *w.* of law
10. as many as are *w.* of the law
5. 19. *w.* of the flesh are manifest
Eph. 2. 9. not of *w.*
10. to good *w.* which God
5. 11. unfruitful *w.* of darkness
Col. 1. 21. enemies in mind by wicked *w.*
1 Thes. 5. 13. love them for their *w.*
2 Tim. 1. 9. not according to our *w.*
Tit. 1. 16. in *w.* they deny him
3. 5. not by *w.* of righteousness
Heb. 6. 1. repentance from dead *w.*
9. 14. conscience from dead *w.*
Jas. 2. 14. and have not *w.* can
20. faith without *w.* is dead, 17. 26.
21. justified by *w.*, 24. 25.
22. by *w.* was faith made perfect
1 John 3. 8. he might destroy *w.* of
Rev. 9. 20. repented not of the *w.* of
18. 6. according to her *w.*, 20. 12, 13.
Ps. 33. 4. *his works*, 78. 11. & 103. 22. 104. 31. & 106. 13. & 107. 22. & 145. 9, 17. Dan. 9. 14. Acts 15. 18. Heb. 4. 10.
Ps. 106. 35. *their works*, Isa. 66. 18. Jonah 3. 10. Matt. 23. 3, 5. 2 Cor. 11. 15. Rev. 14. 13. & 20. 12, 13.
Deut. 15. 10. *thy works*, Ps. 66. 3. & 73. 28. & 92. 5. & 104. 24. & 143. 5. Prov. 16. 3. Eccl. 9. 7. Rev. 2. 3.
Ps. 40. 5. *wonderful works*, 78. 4. & 107. 8. & 111. 4. Matt. 7. 22. Acts 2. 11.
Job 37. 14. *works of God*, Ps. 66. 5. & 78. 7. Eccl. 11. 5. John 6. 28. & 9. 3.
Ps. 46. 8. *w.* of the Lord, 111. 2.
1 Sam. 14. 6. may be the Lord will *work* for us
Isa. 43. 13. I will *w.* and who
Matt. 7. 23. depart from me ye that *w.* iniquity
John 6. 28. might *w.* works of God
9. 4. I must *w.* the works of him
Phil. 2. 12. *w.* out your salvation
2 Thes. 2. 7. iniquity doth already *w.*
3. 10. if any *w.* not, neither should
Prov. 11. 18. the wicked *worketh* a deceitful *w.*
Isa. 64. 5. meet. him that *w.* right.
John 5. 17. my Father *w.* and I *w.*
Acts 10. 35. that *w.* righteousness is accepted
2 Cor. 4. 17. *w.* for us a far more
Gal. 5. 6. faith which *w.* by love
Phil. 2. 13. it is God that *w.* in you
1 Thes. 2. 13. effectually *w.* in you
Mark 16. 20. the Lord *w.* with them
Rom. 7. 13. sin *w.* death in me
Eph. 1. 10. accord. to *w.* of mighty
3. 7. by effectual *w.* of his power
4. 28. *w.* with his hands the thing
Phil. 3. 21. accord. to *w.* whereby
2 Thes. 3. 11. *w.* not at all, but are
Heb. 13. 21. *w.* in you that which
2 Cor. 6. 1. *workers*, 11. 13. Phil. 3. 2.
Job 31. 3. *workers of iniquity*, 34. 8, 22. Ps. 5. 5. & 6. 8. & 28. 3. & 125. 5. & 141. 9. Prov. 10. 29. & 21. 15.
Matt. 10. 10. *workman*, 2 Tim. 2. 15.
Ex. 31. 3. *workmanship*, Eph. 2. 10.
R. V. Ex. 35. 33, 35. workmanship; Prov. 11. 18. wages; Isa. 40. 10; 49. 4; 61. 8; 62. 11. recompense; Ps. 77. 11; 141. 4; Matt. 16. 27. deeds; Rom. 11. 6. grace; Heb. 13. 21. thing

WORLD, 1 Sam. 2. 8. 1 Chron. 16. 30.
Ps. 17. 14. from men of the *w.*
24. 1. *w.* is the Lord's, 9. 8. Nah. 1. 5.
Ps. 50. 12. *w.* is mine and the ful.
Eccl. 3. 11. hath set *w.* in his heart
Isa. 26. 9. the inhabitants of the *w.* learn righteousness
Jer. 10. 12. established the *w.* by his wisdom, 51. 15. Ps. 93. 1. & 96. 10.
Matt. 16. 26. what is a man profited if he shall gain the whole *w.* and lose his own soul, Mark 8. 36.
18. 7. woe to the *w.* because
Mark 16. 15. go into all the *w.* and
Luke 20. 35. worthy to obtain that *w.*
John 1. 10. *w.* was made by him, and *w.* knew him not
29. Lamb of God taketh away sin of the *w.*
3. 16. God so loved the *w.* he gave
17. *w.* through him might be saved
7. 7. the *w.* cannot hate you, but
14. 17. whom *w.* cannot receive
19. *w.* seeth me no more; but ye
15. 18. if the *w.* hate you
19. chosen you out of the *w.* therefore the *w.* hateth you
17. 9. I pray not for the *w.*
11. I am no more in the *w.*
16. not of *w.* even as I am not of *w*
23. *w.* may know thou hast sent
Rom. 3. 19. all the *w.* become guilty
1 Cor. 1. 21. *w.* by wisdom knew not
Gal. 6. 14. *w.* is crucified unto me
Col. 1. 6. as in all *w.* and bringeth
Tit. 1. 2. promised before *w.* began
Heb. 2. 5. *w.* to come, 6. 5.
11. 38. the *w.* was not worthy
1 John 2. 2. a propitiation for sins of the whole *w.*
2. 15. love not the *w.* nor things in the *w.*
16. all that is in the *w.* is of the *w.*
3. 1. the *w.* knoweth us not
4. 5. they are of the *w.* they speak of the *w.* and the *w.* heareth them
Rev. 3. 10. temptation come on all *w.*
13. 3. all *w.* wondered after beast
Matt. 12. 32. *this world*, John 8. 23. & 13. 36. Rom. 12. 2. 1 Tim. 6. 7.
Heb. 1. 2. he made the *worlds*
11. 3. the *w.* were framed by him

R. V. Ps. 22. 27; Isa. 62. 11; Rev. 13. 13. earth; 1 Cor. 10. 11; Eph. 3. 9; Heb. 6. 5; 9. 26. age or ages; Isa. 60. 4. of old; Matt. 12. 32. that which is; Rom. 16. 25; 2 Tim. 1. 9; Tit. 1. 2. time eternal; John 17. 12 ——

WORM, Ex. 16. 20. Isa. 51. 8.
Job 25. 6. man that is a *w.*
Isa. 41. 14. fear not, thou *w.* Jacob
66. 24. their *w.* shall not die, Mark 9. 44, 48.
Job 19. 26. *worms* destroy my body, Acts 12. 23.
Deut. 29. 18. *wormwood*, Prov. 5. 4. Lam. 3. 15, 19. Amos 5. 7. Rev. 8. 11.
R. V. Mic. 7. 17. crawling thing; Job 19. 26; Mark 9. 44, 46 ——

WORSE, Matt. 12. 45. John 5. 14. 1 Cor. 8. 8. & 11. 17. 2 Tim. 3. 13. 2 Pet. 2. 20.

WORSHIP the Lord in beauty of holiness, 1 Chron. 16. 29. Ps. 29. 2. & 66. 4. & 96. 9. & 45. 11. & 95. 6. & 99. 5. Matt. 4. 10.
Matt. 15. 9. in vain do they *w.* me
John 4. 24. *w.* him must *w.* in truth
Acts 17. 23. whom ye ignorantly *w.*
24. 14. so *w.* I the God of my
Rev. 3. 9. *w.* before thy feet
19. 10. to *w.* God, 22. 9.
Ex. 4. 31. *worshipped*, 32. 8. Jer. 1. 16. 1 Chron. 29. 20. Rom. 1. 25. 2 Thes. 2. 4. Rev. 5. 14. & 7. 11. & 11. 16. & 13. 4.
R. V. 2 Kings 17. 36. bow; Luke 14. 10. glory; Acts 7. 42; 17. 25; 24. 14. serve

WORTH, Job 24. 25. Prov. 10. 20.
Gen. 32. 10. I am not *worthy* of least
Matt. 8. 8. I am not *w.* thou shouldest
10. 10. workman is *w.* of his meat
13. if house be *w.* let your peace
22. 8. that were bidden were not *w.*
Luke 3. 8. fruits *w.* of repentance
7. 4. *w.* for whom he should do this
10. 7. laborer is *w.* of his hire
15. 19. no more *w.* to be called
Acts 5. 41. counted *w.* to suffer
Rom. 8. 18. not *w.* to be compared
Eph. 4. 1. walk *w.* of the vocation
Col. 1. 10. walk *w.* of the Lord being
1 Thes. 2. 12. walk *w.* of God who
2 Thes. 1. 5. be counted *w.* of the
11. God count you *w.* of this calling
1 Tim. 1. 15. *w.* of all acceptation, 4. 9.
5. 17. elders *w.* of double honor
18. laborer is *w.* of reward
6. 1. counted masters *w.* of honor
Heb. 11. 38. of whom world was not *w.*
Rev. 3. 4. walk in white, they are *w.*
5. 12. *w.* is the Lamb that was slain
16. 6. blood to drink; for they are *w.*

WOULD God, Ex. 16. 3. Num. 11. 29. Acts 26. 29. 1 Cor. 4. 8. 2 Cor. 11. 1.
Neh. 9. 30. *would not*, Isa. 30. 15. Matt. 18. 30. & 23. 30, 37. Rom. 11. 25.
Prov. 1. 25. *w.* none of my reproof
30. they *w.* none of my counsel
Matt. 7. 12. whatsoever ye *w.* that men should do unto you
Rev. 3. 15. I *w.* thou wert cold or hot
R. V. Many changes to did, could, may, should, might, etc.

WOUND, Ex. 21. 25. Prov. 6. 33. Jer. 10. 19. & 15. 18. & 30. 12, 14. Mic. 1. 9.
Prov. 27. 6. *wounds*, Isa. 1. 6. Jer. 30. 17.
Deut. 32. 39. I *wound* and I heal
1 Cor. 8. 12. *w.* their weak conscience
Rev. 13. 3. his deadly *w.* was healed, 14.
Ps. 69. 26. *wounded*, 109. 22. S. of S. 5. 7.
Prov. 18. 14. a *w.* spirit who can bear
Isa. 53. 5. *w.* for our transgressions
Job 5. 18. he *woundeth* and his hands
R. V. Prov. 18. 8; 26. 22. dainty morsels; Obad. 7. snare; Rev. 13. 3, 12. death stroke; 2 Sam. 22. 39; Ps. 18. 38; 32. 39; 110. 6; Rev. 13. 13. smite or smitten through; 1 Sam. 31. 3; 1 Chron. 10. 3. distressed; Isa. 51. 9. pierced; Luke 10. 30. beat

WRATH, Gen. 49. 7. Ex. 32. 10, 11.
Num. 16. 46. *w.* gone out from
Deut. 32. 27. feared *w.* of the enemy
Neh. 13. 18. bring more *w.* on Israel
Job 5. 2. *w.* killeth the foolish man
Prov. 16. 14. *w.* of a king is as mes.
Isa. 54. 8. in a little *w.* I hid my face
Matt. 3. 7. flee from *w.* to come
Rom. 2. 5. treasure up *w.* against
5. 9. saved from *w.* through him
12. 19. give place unto *w.*
Eph. 2. 3. by nature children of *w.*
4. 26. let not the sun go down on your *w.*
1 Thes. 1. 10. delivered from the *w.*
2. 16. *w.* is come on them to the
1 Tim. 2. 8. holy hands without *w.*
Heb. 11. 27. not fearing *w.* of king
Jas. 1. 19. slow to speak, slow to *w.*
20. *w.* of man worketh not right.
Rev. 6. 16. from *w.* of the Lamb
12. 12. having great *w.* because
14. 8. wine of *w.* of her fornication, 18. 3.
Ezra 8. 22. *his wrath*, Ps. 2. 5, 12. & 78. 38. Jer. 7. 29. & 10. 10. Rev. 6. 17.
Num. 25. 11. *my wrath*, Ps. 95. 11. Isa. 10. 6. & 60. 10. Ezek. 7. 14. Hos. 5. 10.
Ps. 38. 1. *thy wrath*, 85. 3. & 88. 7, 16. & 9. 46. & 90. 9, 11. & 102. 10. 89. 38. *wroth*, Isa. 54. 9. & 57. 17.
R. V. Num. 11. 33; Deut. 11. 17; 2 Chron. 29. 10; 30. 8; Job 36. 13; 40. 11; Ps. 55. 3; 78. 31; Prov. 14. 29; Jer. 44. 8. anger; Deut. 32. 27. provocation; Job 5. 2; Prov. 12. 16; 27. 3. vexation; Ps. 58. 9. burning

WREST, Ex. 23. 2. 2 Pet. 3. 16.

WRESTLE, Gen. 32. 24, 25. Eph. 6. 12.

WRETCHED, Rom. 7. 24. Rev. 3. 17.

WRINKLE, Job 16. 8. Eph. 5. 27.

WRITE, Ex. 34. 1, 27. Deut. 27. 3. Isa. 3. 8. Jer. 30. 2. Hab. 2. 2.
Deut. 6. 9. *w.* them upon the posts
Prov. 3. 3. *w.* them on the table of thine heart, 7. 3.
Jer. 31. 33. I will *w.* it in their hearts
Ps. 102. 18. be *written* for the generation
Prov. 22. 20. have not I *w.* to thee
Eccl. 12. 10. that which was *w.*
Dan. 12. 1. shall be found *w.* in book
1 Cor. 10. 11. *w.* for our admonition
2 Cor. 3. 3. ministered by us, *w.* not with ink, but with the Spirit
Heb. 12. 23. are *w.* in heaven, Luke 10. 20.
R. V. Few changes, and chiefly to wrote

WRONG, Ps. 105. 14. Jer. 22. 3, 13.
Matt. 20. 13. I do thee no *w.* didst
1 Cor. 6. 7. why not rather take *w.*, 8.
Col. 3. 25. that doeth *w.* shall receive
2 Cor. 7. 2. *wronged*, Phile. 18.
Prov. 8. 36. *wrongeth* his own soul
R. V. Jer. 22. 13. injustice; Hab. 1. 4. perverted

WROUGHT, 1 Sam. 6. 6. & 14. 45.
Ps. 139. 15. curiously *w.* in lowest
Ezek. 20. 9. I *w.* for my name's sake, 22.
John 3. 21. his works are *w.* in God
2 Cor. 5. 5. that hath *w.* us for the selfsame thing is God
Eph. 1. 20. which he *w.* in Christ
1 Pet. 4. 3. have *w.* will of Gentiles
R. V. Ex. 26. 36; 27. 16; 36. 1. work; Deut. 17. 2. doeth; 1 Kings 16. 25; 2 Kings 3. 2; 2 Chron. 21. 6; 34. 13. did; 2 Sam. 18. 13. dealt; Jonah 1. 11. grow; Ps. 78. 43. set; Matt. 20. 12. spent; 2 Thes. 3. 8. working

Y

YARN, Solomon brought out of East, 1 Kings 10. 28.
2 Chron. 1. 16. merchants received linen *y.*
R. V. 1 Kings 10. 28; 2 Chron. 1. 16. droves

YE, wherefore look so sadly, Gen. 40. 7.
Matt. 5. 13. *y.* are the salt of earth

YEA, yea, nay, nay, Matt. 5. 37.
2 Cor. 1. 18. *y.* and nay
20. *y.* and amen

YEAR, Gen. 1. 14. & 47. 9.
Ex. 7. 7. Moses was fourscore *y.* old
Lev. 12. 6. sh. bring lamb of first *y.*
Num. 1. 3. from twenty *y.* old and upward
Deut. 8. 2. God led thee forty *y.* in
Josh. 5. 6. chil. of Is. walk. forty *y.*
Judg. 3. 11. land had rest forty *y.*
Ruth 1. 1. dwelt there about ten *y.*
1 Sam. 1. 7. he did so *y.* by *y.* when
2 Sam. 14. 28. A. dw. two *y.* in Jer.
1 Kings 5. 11. Solomon gave to Hiram *y.* by *y.*
2 Kings 1. 17. in second *y.* of Jehoram
1 Chron. 21. 12. either three *y.* famine, or
2 Chron. 8. 13. three times in *y.*; or
Ezra 1. 1. in first *y.* of Cyrus of Persia
Neh. 1. 1. twent *y.*, I was in Shus.
Esth. 1. 3. third *y.* he ma. a decree
Job 10. 5. are thy *y.* as man's days
Ps. 90. 4. thousand *y.* in thy sight are but as yesterday
10. our *y.* are threescore and
Prov. 10. 27. *y.* of the wicked shall be shortened
Eccl. 6. 3. so that his *y.* be many
Isa. 6. 1. In *y.* Uz. died I saw Lord
Jer. 17. 8. not care. in *y.* of drought
Ezek. 1. 2. fifth *y.* of King Jehoiac.
Dan. 1. 5. so nourish. them three *y.*
Joel 2. 2. ev. to *y.* of many genera.
Amos 1. 1. two *y.* before the earth.
Mic. 6. 6. come with calves of a *y.* old?
Hab. 3. 2. thy work in midst of *y.*
Hag. 1. 1. in second *y.* of Da. came
Zech. 14. 16. go up *y.* to *y.* to wor.
Mal. 3. 4. offerings, as in former *y.*
Matt. 9. 20. an issue of bl. twenty *y.*
Mark 5. 42. she was age of twelve *y.*
Luke 4. 19. to preach accep. *y.* of Lord
John 2. 20. forty and six *y.* was the temple in building
Acts 4. 22. the man was ab. fort. *y*
Rom. 15. 23. hav. gr. desire many *y.*
2 Cor. 8. 10. but to be forward a *y.*
Gal. 1. 18. aft. three *y.* went to Jer.
1 Tim. 5. 9. to num. und. threesc. *y.*

Heb. 1. 12. and thy *y.* shall not fail
2 Pet. 3. 8. and thous. *y.* as one day
Rev. 20. 2. Sa., bound him thous. *y.*
YESTERDAY, Job 8. 9. Hab. 13. 8.
YIELD, fruit after his kind, Gen. 1. 11.
Lev. 25. 19. land shall *y.* her fr., and
Num. 17. 8. rod of Aa. *y.* almonds
Deut. 11. 17. land *y.* not her fruit
2 Chron. 30. 8. *y.* yourselves unto Lord
Neh. 9. 37. it *y.* increase to kings
Ps. 67. 6. shall earth *y.* her increase
Prov. 12. 12. root of right. *y.* fruit
Eccl. 10. 4. *y.* pacifi. great offences
Isa. 5. 10. ten acres sh. *y.* one bath
Jer. 17. 8. nei. shall cease fr. *y.* fruit
Ezek. 34. 27. earth sh. *y.* her incre.
Hos. 8. 7. the bud shall *y.* no meal
Joel 2. 22. fig tree and vi. *y.* stren.
Hab. 3. 17. altho. fields *y.* no meat
Matt. 27. 50. Jesus *y.* up the ghost
Mark 4. 7. choked it, it *y.* no fruit
Acts 23. 21. do not thou *y.* to them
Rom. 6. 13. but *y.* yourselves unto God
Heb. 12. 11. it *y.* peaceable fruit
Jas. 3. 12. no fount. bo. *y.* salt wat.
Rev. 22. 2. tree of life *y.* her fruit
R. V. Num. 17. 8. bare; Acts 5. 10. gave; Rom. 16. 19. presented
YOKE, break from thy neck, Gen. 27. 40.
Lev. 26. 13. brok. bands of your *y.*
Num. 19. 2. on which nev. came *y.*
Deut. 28. 48. put *y.* of iron on thy n.
1 Sam. 11. 7. they took a *y.* of oxen
14. 14. a *y.* of oxen might plow
1 Kings 12. 4. thy father made our *y.* grievous
2 Chron. 10. 11. I will put more to your *y.*
Job 1. 3. J. had fiv. hun. *y.* of oxen
Isa. 9. 4. hast brok. *y.* of his burd.
Jer. 2. 20. of old I ha. broken thy *y.*
Lam. 1. 14. *y.* of my trans. is bound
Ezek. 30. 18. break there *y.* of Egy.
Hos. 11. 4. as they had taken off *y.*
Nah. 1. 13. now will I break his *y.*
Matt. 11. 30. for my *y.* is easy, and
Luke 14. 19. I bought five *y.* of oxen
Acts 15. 10. put *y.* on disciples' neck
Gal. 5. 1. be not entangled with *y.*
1 Tim. 6. 1. as many as under *y.*
R. V. Jer. 27. 2; 28. 10, 12, 13. bar or bars; 1 Sam. 14. 14 —
YOU only have I known, Amos 3. 2.
Luke 10. 16. heareth *y.* heareth me
13. 28. and *y.* yourselves thrust out
2 Cor. 12. 14. I seek not *yours* but *y.*
Eph. 2. 1. *y.* hath he quickened
Col. 1. 21. *y.* that were sometime
Luke 6. 20. *y.* is the kingdom of God
1 Cor. 3. 22. all are *y.* and ye are Christ's, 23.
YOUNG, I have been, Ps. 37. 25.
Isa. 40. 11. gently lead those with *y.*
1 Tim. 5. 1. entreat the *younger*
14. I will that *y.* women marry
1 Pet. 5. 5. ye *y.* submit to elder
Gen. 8. 21. the imagination of man is evil from his *youth*
1 Kings 18. 12. the Lord from my *y.*
Job 13. 26. possess iniquities of my *y.*
Ps. 25. 7. sins of my *y.*
103. 5. thy *y.* is renewed as eagle's
Eccl. 11. 9. O young man, in thy *y.*
10. childhood and *y.* are vanity
Jer. 2. 2. the kindness of thy *y.*
1 Tim. 4. 12. man despise thy *y.*
Prov. 7. 7. *youths*, Isa. 40. 30.
2 Tim. 2. 22. flee *youthful* lusts
R. V. 1 Sam. 20. 22. boy; Mark 7. 25; 10. 13. little; Acts 20. 12. lad; Job 29. 4. ripeness; 30. 12. rabble

Z

ZEAL for Lord, 2 Kings 10. 16.
Ps. 69. 9. the *z.* of thine house hath
119. 139. my *z.* hath consumed me
Isa. 9. 7. *z.* of the Lord will perform
59. 17. I was clad with *z.* as a cloak
63. 15. where is thy *z.* and stren.
Rom. 10. 2. they have a *z.* for God
2 Cor. 7. 11. *z.* yea, what revenge
Phil. 3. 6. concerning *z.* persecut.
Num. 25. 13. was *zealous* for his God
Acts 22. 3. I was *z.* towards God as
Tit. 2. 14. people *z.* of good works
Rev. 3. 19. therefore be *z.* and repent
Gal. 4. 18. good to be *zealously* affected in a good thing
R. V. Num. 25. 11, 13. jealous
ZION, 2 Sam. 5. 7. 1 Kings 8. 1. for Jerusalem, temple, or church, 2 Kings 19. 31. Ps. 2. 6. & 9. 11. & 14. 7. & 48. 2, 11, 12. & 146. 10. & 147. 12. Isa. 1. 27. & 2. 3. & 60. 14. & 62. 1. and in about seventy other places

---

CURIOUS FACTS AND INTERESTING INFORMATION ABOUT THE BIBLE

The 66 Books or sub-divisions comprising the Old and New Testaments contain: 1,189 Chapters, 31,093 Verses, 773,692 Words, 3,586,489 Letters.

The Shortest Verse in the Bible is the 35th in the 11th Chapter of St. John.
The Longest Verse in the Bible is the 9th in the 8th Chapter of Esther.
The Middle Verse in the Bible is the 8th in the 118th Chapter of Psalms.

The 21st Verse of the 7th Chapter of Ezra contains all the letters of the Alphabet except "j."
The 8th, 15th, 21st, and 31st Verses of the 107th Psalm are alike.

Every Verse in the 136th Psalm has the same ending.
The Longest Chapter is the 119th Psalm.
The Shortest Chapter is the 117th Psalm.

The word "Lord" occurs 7736 times in the Old and New Testaments.
The word "God" occurs 4370 times in the Old and New Testaments.
The words "Boy" and "Boys" are mentioned 3 times as follows: Gen. 25. 27; Joel 3. 3; Zech. 8. 5.
The words "Girl" and "Girls" are mentioned 2 times as follows: Joel 3. 3; Zech. 8. 5.
The name of "God" is not mentioned in the Book of Esther, or in the Song of Solomon (A. V.).
The 19th Chapter of II. Kings and the 37th Chapter of Isaiah are practically alike.

TREASURY OF BIBLICAL INFORMATION

A COMPENDIUM OF INFORMATION ESSENTIAL TO THE MORE INTELLIGENT STUDY AND CLEARER UNDERSTANDING OF THE BIBLE.

ARRANGED IN THE MOST HELPFUL
AND ATTRACTIVE FORMS

BY

REV. F. N. PELOUBET, D.D.
Author of Select Notes on the International Lessons, etc., etc.

TABLE OF CONTENTS

OLD TESTAMENT CHRONOLOGY.

I. FROM "THE BEGINNING" TO THE DELUGE.

SUBJECTS.	EVENTS.	USSHER'S DATES.
CREATION and EARLIEST MAN.	The Creation of the world.	B.C.
	The formation of lands and seas.	
	The Creation of plants and animals.	4004
	The Creation of Man.	
MAN in his EARLIEST HOME.	The Garden of Eden, in the region of the Tigris and the Euphrates; ancient Mesopotamia and Babylonia.	4004
	The first sin.	
	Expulsion of Adam and Eve from Eden.	
CAIN and ABEL.	Cain born, perhaps in	4002
	Abel born, perhaps in	4001
	Cultivation of the soil, and keeping of flocks begun.	
	Abel murdered by his brother Cain	3875
From the DEATH of ABEL to the DELUGE.	Seth born, Adam being 130 years old	3874
	Enoch born	3382
	Methuselah born	3317
	Adam dies, being 930 years old	3074
	Enoch translated, being 365 years old	3017
	Seth dies, aged 912 years	2962
	Noah born	2948
	Methuselah dies, aged 969 years	2348
THE DELUGE.	Noah enters into the ark, being 600 years old	2348
	Noah leaves the ark, after dry land appears	2347
	Traditions of the Deluge are found among all races.	
	The Babylonian story of the Deluge was found, written on clay tablets, in the ruins of Nineveh. It differs little in its main points from that in the Bible.	
THE NEW START.	The Covenant with Noah, immediately following the Deluge	2347

NOTE: There is great uncertainty among Bible scholars as to the dates in this period. The dates we have given here are those found in the margins of many of our Bibles. They were calculated by Archbishop Ussher, of Armagh, in A.D. 1650–1654, and first put into the Bible in 1701. While they are based on the statements in the Bible they are not a part of the inspired word.

II. FROM THE DELUGE TO THE EXODUS.

Events in Scripture History.	Places.	Dates. Beecher.	Dates. Ussher. B.C.	Dates. Others.
The Deluge		?	2348	or long before
The confusion of tongues	Babylonia		2247	
Death of Noah	Arabia		1998	
Abram, Birth of, at Ur	Chaldea	(2003)	1996	
Abram moves from Ur to Haran	Mesopotamia		1926	
The call of Abram	"	1928	1921	2250 to 1906
Abram and Lot move to Canaan	Canaan	1928	1921	
Abram and Lot separate	"	1924	1918	
Lot captured by Chedorlaomer	Sodom	1921	1913	
The Covenant with Abraham	Hebron	1920	1912	
Birth of Ishmael	"	1917	1910	
Renewal of Covenant. Change of Abram's name to Abraham	"	1904	1897	
Destruction of *Sodom*	Sodom	1904	1897	
Isaac, Birth of	Moab	1903	1896	
Ishmael sent away		1901(?)	1892	
Covenant with Abimelech		1900(?)	1891	
Moab and Ammon born		1899(?)	1897	
Ishmael marries an Egyptian		1895(?)		
Sacrifice of Isaac	Moriah	1879	1871	
Death of Sarah	Hebron	1866	1860	
Abraham marries Keturah		1865(?)		
Marriage of Isaac and Rebekah	Lahai-roi	1864	1857	
Jacob and Esau, Birth of	Beersheba	1844	1837	These dates are all only approximate.
Death of Abraham	"	1828(?)	1822	
Esau sells his birthright	Lahai-roi	1827(?)	1804	
Isaac forbidden to enter Egypt goes to.	Gerar	1826(?)	1804	
Esau marries Hittite wives		1805	1796	
Jacob obtains birthright blessing	Beersheba	1784(?)	1760	
Jacob goes to Padan-aram. His vision at Bethel		1784(?)	1760	
Esau's Ishmaelite marriages		1783(?)	1760	
Death of Ishmael		1781(?)	1773	
Jacob marries Leah and Rachel	Padan-aram	1776(?)	1753	
Birth of Jacob's children (except Benjamin)	"	1775-1752	1752-1739	
Joseph, Birth of	"	1752	1739	
Jacob returns to Canaan		1747		
Jacob wrestles with the angel	Peniel	1747	1739	
Birth of Benjamin and death of Rachel	Bethlehem	1747	1729	
Joseph sold into Egypt from	Dothan	1736	1718	
Joseph put in prison	Egypt	1725	1718	
Death of Isaac	Hebron	1724	1716	
Joseph interprets Pharaoh's dream	Egypt	1723	1716	
Joseph made prime minister	"	1723	1716	
The seven years of plenty begin			1716	
Birth of Manasseh and Ephraim	Egypt			
The seven years of famine begin			1709	
Jacob and his family move to	Goshen in Egypt	1715	1706	
Death of Jacob	"	1698	1689	1300 to 1208
Death of Joseph	"	1643	1635	
Beginning of oppression of Israel	"	1599(?)	1573	
Moses, Birth of	"	1578	1571	
Exile of Moses begins	Arabia	1539	1531	
Call of Moses. Burning bush	"	1499	1492	
Plagues of Egypt	Egypt	1499-8	1492-1	
The first Passover	"	1498	1491	
The Exodus in April		1498	1491	

Other Historical Events.

Seventh ruler of China died 2257.

Nineveh built 2218 (?).

Zoroaster 2115 (?).

Celts in Europe about 2000.

Hyksos in Egypt in time of Abraham, probably. Dates vary from 2100-1675.

Sesostris I, Egypt, 1980-1935 (?).

Hammurabi (Amraphel of Gen. 14:1), and his code, contemporary with Abraham. The dates vary from 2300 B.C. to 1900. His Monument discovered at Susa, (Shushan) of Persia (in A.D. 1901, 2) contains the earliest known writing on stone, with laws something like those in Leviticus.

Tel-el-Amarna letters, 15th century or earlier, 300 letters inscribed on clay tablets 2 by 3 inches, and sent between Palestine and Amarna in Egypt showing a general prevalence of dissatisfaction with the rule of Egypt.

The Israelites were shepherds in the fertile land of Goshen for 116 years, 1715-1599. Then they were slaves of the Egyptians for 100 years, 1599-1498.

Others make the slavery in Egypt to continue much longer and the date of the Exodus to be between 1300 and 1200 B.C.

NOTE. The dates in this period are still more or less uncertain, The *New Encyc. Britannica* calls its dates only approximate. For instance, the 19th dynasty in which this period ends, begins in 1490, or 1320 according to different authorities.

The date of the Exodus depends partly on whether the Pharaoh of the Oppression was Thotmes III, or Rameses II. Most modern authorities incline to Rameses II, and a date for the Exodus about 200 years later. Beecher, in his *Dated Events* reconciles the history by giving Rameses the earlier date, but still making him the "Pharaoh of the Oppression." He puts an interrogation point after all these dates.

On the whole there is not better authority than Beecher in this book. He does not differ much from Ussher. We give other authorities in another column.

III. FROM EGYPT TO PALESTINE. — *40 years.*

Persons.	Events.	Places.	Dates. Beecher.	Ussher.	Others.
	The Exodus, in April				1300 or 1200
	The Pillar of fire	Arabia	1498	1491	
	The giving of the manna	"	1498	1491	
MOSES.	The giving of the law	Mt. Sinai	1498	1491	Most scholars incline to these later dates and Rameses II as the Pharaoh of the Oppression.
	The golden calf	"	1498	1491	
	The Tabernacle set up	"	1497	1490	
AARON.	The ceremonial law given	"	1497	1490	
	Nadab and Abihu	Wilderness of Arabia			
	Wandering for 40 years in Wilderness.	Between branches of Red Sea	1498–1459	1491–1451	
CALEB.	New start for Canaan from	Kadesh			
	Waters from the rock	Meribah	1459	1452	
JOSHUA.	Death of Aaron on	Mt. Hor	1459	1452	
	Brazen serpent	The Arabah	1459	1452	
	Balaam's blessing	Moab	1459	1452	
	Death of Moses	Nebo-Pisgah	1459	1451	

IV. THE CONQUEST OF PALESTINE.

Persons.	Events.	Places.	Beecher.	Ussher.	Others.
	Passing over Jordan opposite	Jericho	1458	1451	See above.
	The Fall of Jericho	"	1458	1451	
JOSHUA.	Defeat at Ai	Near Jericho	1458	1451	
	Law read from Ebal and Gerizim	Shechem	1458	1451	
CALEB.	Conquest of Canaan		1458–1449	1451–1443	
	Cities of Refuge appointed		1453	1444	
	Joshua renews the covenant	Shechem	1451 (?)	1427	
	Death of Joshua	Timnath-serah	1450 (?)	1427	

V. THE PERIOD OF THE JUDGES.

See Notes below.

Judges and Events.	Places.	Years of Oppression.	Years of Peace.	Years B. C. from Beecher.
Oppression of Chushan-Rishathaim, from Mesopotamia (during the last years of Joshua).	Palestine	8		1441–1434
I. **OTHNIEL**, Son-in-law of Caleb, Deliverer. Judge 14 years	Near Hebron			1434
Peace and Prosperity			37	1434–1397
Oppression by Eglon of Moab	So. Palestine	18		1397–1380
II. **EHUD** of Benjamin	Near Jericho			1380
Peace and Prosperity			10	1380–1370
Oppression by Jabin of Canaan	Northern tribes }	{ 20		1370–1351
Oppression by the Philistines, during the last 3 years of Jabin's oppression	Southern tribes }			1353–1351
III. **DEBORAH** of Ephraim, IV. **BALAK** of Naphtali } deliverers from Jabin	No. Palestine			1351
V. **SHAMGAR** of Judah, delivers from Philistines	S. W. Palestine			1351
Peace and Prosperity			22	1351–1329
Oppression by Midianites	So. Galilee	7		1329–1323
VI. **GIDEON** of Manasseh, Deliverer and Judge	So. Galilee			1323
Peace and Prosperity			24	1323–1299
VII. **ABIMELECH**, Prince of Israel for 3 years	Shechem		3	1298–1296
VIII. **TOLA** of hill country of	Ephraim		23	1295–1273
Oppression by Philistines begun	S. W. Israel			1283
IX. **JAIR** was a judge of Israel E. of Jordan	Gilead		22	1272–1251
X. **SAMSON** — exploits as judge	S. W. Israel		20	1250–1231
Oppression by Ammonites beyond Jordan	East Israel	18		1230–1213
XI. **JEPHTHAH**, judge 6 years beyond Jordan	Gilead		6	1212–1207
XII. **IBZAN**, judge from Bethlehem 7 m. N. W. of Nazareth	Galilee		7	1206–1200
XIII. **ELON** of Zebulun, a part of	Galilee		10	1199–1190
XIV. **ABDON**, a judge for 8 years in	Ephraim		8	1189–1182
Oppression by Philistines began again	W. Israel			1182
XV. **ELI**, the high priest acts as judge. Shiloh	Benjamin		40	1182–1142
XVI. **SAMUEL** called to be prophet	Shiloh			1160?
Judge of Israel, or chief citizen	Israel			1141–1065?

NOTE I. The dates given here are from Prof. Willis J. Beecher's *Dated Events of the Old Testament*, and for the most part do not vary very largely from those given by Ussher in many of our Bibles.

The tendency of scholars is to shorten this period, and to make the earlier dates much later than those given above. No definite and certain chronology is possible.

NOTE II. It is entirely probable that many of the Oppressions and Deliverances were not successive, but took place at the same time in different parts of the country. Prof. Moore in *Int. Crit. Com.* is right when he says "They were, in fact, without exception, local struggles; and it is not only conceivable, but highly probable, that while one part of the land was enjoying security under its judge, other tribes were groaning under the foreign yoke." Hence the mere adding together of the figures given in the book would not give the correct length of the period.

VI. THE UNITED KINGDOM.

Period 120 years { 1103 or 983 / 1057 or 937 }

EVENTS IN SCRIPTURE HISTORY.	PLACES.	DATES. Beecher.	Ussher.	Revised from Assyrian Records.	OTHER EVENTS.
Saul's Kingdom.					
Israel asks for a king............	....	1103(?)	1095	......	Chow dynasty in China brings us to historic ground, 1123–255.
SAUL chosen and made king	Gilgal	1102	1095	1057	
Saul's victory over Ammon.........	....	1102	1095	......	
Birth of David..............	Bethlehem	1092	1085	1047	
Saul's final rejection and break with Samuel..............	....	1078(?)	1079	......	
Private anointing of David..........	Bethlehem	1077(?)	1065	......	
David becomes Saul's minstrel.....	....	1074(?)	1063	......	
David and Goliath	Ephes-dammim	1073(?)	1063	......	
David's marriage to Michal	....	1071(?)	1062	......	
David's outlaw life, 7 years..........	....	1068–1063	1062–1055	......	
David spares Saul's life (skirt)	Engedi..........	1066(?)	1060	......	
Death of Samuel...............	Ramah........	1065(?)	1060	......	
David and Nabal...............	Carmel	1065(?)	1059	......	
The spear and the cruse incident....	....	1065(?)	1058	......	
David among the Philistines	Ziklag.	1064	1057	......	
Death of Saul and Jonathan.........	Gilboa.........	1063	1056	......	
David's Kingdom.					
DAVID becomes king in Judah	Hebron.........	1063	1056	1017	Hiram, King of Tyre. contemporary of David and Solomon.
War between David and *Ish-bosheth*.	....	1063–1056	1056–1048	......	
David king over all Israel...........	....	1055	1048	......	
Jerusalem becomes capital.					
Period of war	....	1055–1043	1048–1042	......	
Ark brought to Jerusalem...........	....	1042(?)	1042	1003	
The great promise to David..........	Jerusalem......	1041(?)	1042	......	Homer thought by some to be contemporary with David.
Birth of Solomon	"	1041(?)	1033	......	
Preparation for building the temple.	"	....	....	......	
Absalom's rebellion............	....	1023	1023	......	
Solomon anointed and proclaimed. .	Jerusalem......	1022	1015	......	
Death of David	"	1022	1015	977	
Solomon's Kingdom.					
SOLOMON becomes real king.........	Jerusalem......	1022	1015	977	Homer, 1000(?)
Temple foundations laid............	"	1019	1012	......	Zoroaster, 1000(?)
Temple dedicated..............	"	1011	1004	966	
Visit of Queen of Sheba to Solomon.	"	995(?)	995	......	Shishak in Egypt, who invades Israel.
Jeroboam flees to Shishak in Egypt.	....	986(?)	980	......	
Death of Solomon....	Jerusalem......	983	975	937	

NOTE ON THE DIVIDED KINGDOM.

The dates are given according to Prof. Willis J. Beecher in his *Dated Events of the Old Testament History*, the most thorough and scholarly study of the subject including the Assyrian Canon. There are also given the dates of Arbp. Ussher, as in many Bibles; and of Hastings' and other Bible Dictionaries, as they interpret the Assyrian Canon, and make the division of the kingdom to begin at various dates from 939 to 931.

THE MOVEMENT OF THE HISTORY. FIVE GREAT PERIODS.

I. **The United Kingdom.** Three kings. 120 years, 1102–982.

II. **The Divided Kingdom.** { JUDAH. One dynasty. 11 kings, 1 queen / ISRAEL. Nine dynasties. 19 kings. } 260 years to 720.

III. **Judah. Alone.** 8 kings, David's dynasty 136 years, 722–586.

IV. **The Exile.** 70 years, 605–536.

V. **The Return. The New Nation.** 536–400 and on.

Judah. One dynasty (David's). 11 kings and one queen.

VII. THE DIVIDED KINGDOMS OF JUDAH AND ISRAEL.

Periods: **Judah** nearly 400 years. **Israel** about 260 years. **Judah** alone 136 years.

Israel. 9 Dynasties. 19 kings.

Judah: Prophets.	Judah: Kings and Events.	Judah: Years of Reign.	Dates: Beecher.	Dates: Hastings B.D.	Dates: Ussher.	Dates: Assyr. Eponym.	Israel: Years of Reign.	Israel: Kings and Events.	Israel: Prophets.	Contemporary History.
	Rehoboam, 17 years	1	982	939	975	931	1	**Jeroboam I,** 22 years.	Ahijah.	
	Influx of Levites, etc., from Israel							Semi-idolatry established.		
	Rehoboam forsakes Jehovah	3	980	936	......	930	3	Exodus of religious people to Judah.		
	Invasion by Shishak	5	978	934	......	927	5			Shishak monument.
	Abijam, 3 years	17 1	965	922	957	914	18			
		3	962	919	955	911	21			
	Asa, 41 years	1	961	918	954	910	1 22	**Nadab,** parts of 2 years.		
	Land at rest 10 years									
	Invasion by Zerah the Ethiopian	3	960	917	953	909	2 1	**Baasha,** 24 years.		
		14	949	......	941	898	12			
	Great revival and reformation	15	948	......	941	897	13			
	War with Israel	16	947	......	......	......	14	Civil war with Judah.		
		26	937	894	930	886	1 24	**Elah.** Parts of 2 years.		
								Zimri, 7 days.		
		27	936	893	929	885	2 1	**Omri,** 12 years. Great enlargement of kingdom.		Moabite stone naming Omri.
	Decline.	38	925	882	918	874	1 12	**Ahab,** 22 years.		
								Marries Jezebel.	Elijah.	
	Jehoshaphat, 25 years	41 1	921	878	917	870	5	Idolatry introduced.		Shalmanezer II, Assyria.
	Wide extended revival.							Religious persecution.		
	Outward prosperity.	16	905	862	854	854	21 1	**Ahaziah.** Co-regnant, 2 years.		Battle of Karkar, 854, Assyr.
	Decline through alliance with Jezebel.	17	904	861	853	853	22 2	**Jehoram,** 12 years.	Elisha.	
	Jehoram. Co-regnant, 4 years	1 22	900	857	893	849	1 5			
son of Jehoiada.	Alone, 4 years	4 25	897	854	......	846	8			
		5						Mesha of Moab revolts.		
	Ahaziah. Part of one year	8 1	893	850	885	842	12			
	Athaliah, 6 years	2	892	849	884	841	1	**Jehu,** 28 years.		*Black Obelisk,* with name of Jehu.
	Murder of seed-royal.	1						Zealous reformer.		907 (?) Homer, Hesiod.
	Baal worship.							Destroys house of Ahab.		884 Lycurgus.
	Temple desecrated.	6								878 (?) } Carthage founded.
	Joash, 40 years	1	886	843	878	835	7	Tributary to Assyria.		858 (?) }

Prophets	Judah	Year					Year	Israel	Prophets	Contemporary History
Zechariah,	Temple and its worship restored.	23	864	821	856	813	28 / 1	**Jehoahaz**, 17 years.		
		37	850	807	842	799	1 / 15	*Jehoash.* Co-regnant, 3 years.		Sheshonk III, Egypt. 820 (?) Lycurgus, Sparta. 814 Macedonia founded.
							17	Hazael's expedition.		
	Amaziah	40	847	......	......	......		**Jehoash**, sole ruler 16 years.		
	Defeat of Edom	1	846	803	840	795	1	Death of Elisha.		
	Conquest by Jehoash of Israel.									
								Victories over Damascus.		814 (?) Carthage founded.
	Nominal ruler under suzerainty of Israel	14	833	......	......	......	15	Conquest of Judah.		
		15	832	804	825	782	16 / 1	**Jeroboam II**, 41 years.	Amos. Hosea. Jonah.	797. Damascus taken by Assyrians.
Amos.	Death of Amaziah	29	818	......	......	767	15	Suzerain of all peoples from Mediterranean to Euphrates.		
	INTERREGNUM for 11 years	1								
		11								
	Uzziah, 52 years. Also called Azariah.	1	806	801	811	......	27			Blank in Assyrian history. Confusion in Egyptian.
		15	792	......	......	741	41	Death of Jeroboam.		First Olympiad, 776 B. C.
							1	INTERREGNUM, 22 years.		
	Succeeds Jeroboam as suzerain of region	16	791	......	......	......				
Isaiah.		38	769	763	773	741		**Zechariah**, 6 months.		The Jewish Cyclopedia gives 2 reigns of Jeroboam II, 825–799 and 788–773; Israel being under Syria 799 to 788.
	Leprosy of Uzziah (?)	39	768	763	772	......		**Shallum**, 1 month.		
	Jotham regent 23 years	40	767	762	772	741	22	**Menahem**, 10 years.		Rome founded 753. Draco.
		1					1			
	Eclipse of sun by which Assyrian dates are determined. June 15, 763 B. C.	44	763	763	......	738	5			
		49	758	752	761	737	10	**Pekahiah**, 2 years.		Expedition of Pul or Tiglath-pileser of Assyria, captures Damascus and Samaria. 733 (?)
							1 / 2			
		52	755	750	759	736	1	**Pekah**, 20 years.		The Jewish Cycl. gives 2 reigns for Pekah, 759–744, and 735–730. Time between Israel under Menahem II, under Assyria.
Micah.	**Jotham** sole king 16 years	23 / 1	754	749	742	......	2			
	Invasion by Israel and Rezin of Damascus	15	740	......	......	......	16	Invasion of Judah.		
	Ahaz, 16 years	16	739	......	......	735	17			
		1	738	741	742	......	18	Deportation by Tiglath-pileser. Death of Pekah.		
	Tributary to Assyria.	3	736	......	......	734	20	*Hoshea*, governor.		
		13	726	730	730	734	1	**Hoshea**, king 9 years.		*Taylor Cylinder.*
		16	723	727	726	......	4			
	Hezekiah, 29 years	1								
	Great Passover	2	722	......	......	......	5			

VII. THE DIVIDED KINGDOMS OF JUDAH AND ISRAEL (*Continued*).

JUDAH. Prophets.	JUDAH. Kings and Events.	JUDAH. Years of Reign.	DATES. Beecher.	DATES. Hastings B.D.	DATES. Ussher.	DATES. Assyr. Eponym.	ISRAEL. Years of Reign.	ISRAEL. Kings and Events.	ISRAEL. Prophets.	Contemporary History.
Isaiah.		4	720	......	......	......	7	First siege and capture of Samaria.		Year in Rome begun with January, 713.
		6	718	722 } 721 }	......	722	9	{ Final FALL OF SAMARIA. { End of Kingdom of Israel.		Sargon I, Assyria, 722. Sennacherib, Assyria, 705.
	First invasion of Sennacherib.	14	710	......	......	......				First Mikado in Japan, 660-585.
	Hezekiah's sickness.									
	Second invasion of Sennacherib.	23	701	......	......	......				Esarhaddon, Assyria, 681.
	Manasseh, 55 years	29 / 1	694	......	697	......				Second Messenian war, 685-668.
	Death of Isaiah (?)	16	679	Authorities are practically agreed on these dates.	......	......				Byzantium founded, 659.
	Manasseh carried to Babylon (?)	47	648		......	......				Scythian invasion.
Nahum.	Manasseh's return and reformation	48 / 55	647		......	......				Median Empire independent, 640.
	Amon, 2 years	1 / 2	639		642	......				Draco's legislation, 624 [621 ?]
Zephaniah. Joel.	**Josiah,** 31 years	1	638		640	......				"Buddha," India, 623-543. Public beginning, July, 594.
	Josiah begins reforms	12	627		......	......				
Jeremiah.		13	626		......	......				Expedition of Pharaoh Necho, 608.
	Josiah's great reformation } Reformation passover }	17	622		......	......				Destruction of Nineveh, 606.
	Jehoahaz, 3 months	31 / 1	608		609	......				Nebuchadnezzar, 604.
Daniel.	**Jehoiakim,** 11 years. *First captivity begins.*	1	607		609	......				Carchemish, 603. Daniel in exile, 605.
Habakkuk.	First deportation	3	605		606	......				Expounds King's dream, 603.
	Second deportation	10	598		......	......				
	Jehoiachin, 3 months	11	597		598	......				
Ezekiel.	The great deportation. **Zedekiah,** 11 years	1 / 1	597		598	......				Phœnicians circumnavigate Africa, 604.
	Siege of Jerusalem	1 / 9	588		588	......				Solon's legislation, 594.
	Destruction of Jerusalem and the Temple	11	586		586	......				Seven wise men in Greece, 593.
	Beginning of great captivity	11	586		586	......				Pythian games begin, 588.

VIII. THE CAPTIVITY TO THE END OF THE OLD TESTAMENT.

Period about 200 years.

Prophets.	Jewish Events.	Dates. Beecher.	Hastings.	Usher.	Contemporary History.
Jeremiah. Ezekiel.	*First* captivity	605		606	
	Second captivity	597			
	Final captivity	586	586	586	Nebuchadnezzar besieges Tyre, 585.
					Æsop.
Daniel.	Last of Ezekiel's prophecies			571	Evil Merodach, Babylon, 562.
Obadiah.	Jehoiachin released	561			Temple of Diana, Ephesus, 552.
					Public library at Athens, 544.
					Babylon taken by Cyrus, 539.
	Belshazzar's feast	539		538	First year of Cyrus, 538.
	Daniel in den of lions	538		538	Pythagoras, 540–510.
	The decree for the return	538	538	536	
	End of first reckoning of 70 years				Pisistratus, Athens, 560–527.
Zechariah.	**First return.** 50,000 under Zerubbabel.	538	538–7		Nabonidus, Babylon, 556.
	Foundation of Temple laid	537–6	536		Darius in Babylon, 521.
Haggai.	Long delay				
	Building of Temple resumed	520	520		Beginning of Roman republic, 510.
	TEMPLE DEDICATED	516	516	516	Marathon, 490.
	End of second reckoning of 70 years				Xerxes (Ahasuerus), 489.
Malachi.	No knowledge of events until				Invasion of Greece, 480.
	Feast of Ahasuerus (Xerxes)	483			Herodotus, Socrates.
	Esther becomes queen	479			Xenophon, Plato.
	Haman's plot	474			First decemvirate, Rome, 451.
	Second return under Ezra	458	458		Pericles, Athens, 444.
	Return under Nehemiah				Parthenon, Athens, 443–438.
	Wall of Jerusalem rebuilt	444	445		First Peloponnesian war, 431.
	Reforms				Xenophon's retreat, 401.
	Death of Nehemiah. After	391			

NOTE. It will perhaps be easier to understand the double reckoning of the 70 years' captivity by the following diagram showing how it is reckoned as beginning at different points, and closing at equi-different points.

70 Years.

First Captivity began 605
Second Captivity began 597
Third Captivity and Temple Destroyed, 586

The Seventy Years of Exile foretold by Jeremiah.

537,6 First Return.
516 { Second Temple Completed.

IX. PERIOD BETWEEN THE TESTAMENTS.

B.C.	Jewish History.	Contemporary History.
350	Jaddua, High Priest	Egypt a Persian Province.
359		Philip II of Macedon.
336		Darius Codomannus, king of Persia.
		Alexander the Great.
332	Alexander visits Jerusalem.	Alexandria in Egypt founded.
331	Jews settle in Alexandria.	Battle of Arbela.
330	Onias I, High Priest.	End of Persian Empire.
320	Ptolemy takes Jerusalem.	Ptolemy I, Soter.
312	Seleucidæ in Syria.	Seleucus I, Nicator.
301	Palestine under Egypt.	Battle of Ipsus.
284	Septuagint.	
264		First Punic War: Rome.
261		Manetho, in Egypt.
219	Beginning of War of Antiochus and Ptolemy.	Second Punic War: Rome.
198	Antiochus the Great master of Palestine.	
170	Tyranny of Antiochus Epiphanes.	
167	Revolt of Maccabees.	
166	Judas Maccabeus.	
165	Rededication of Temple.	

B.C.	Jewish History (*continued*).	Contemporary History.
149		Third Punic War: Rome.
146		Greece a Roman Province.
141	Deliverance of Judea complete.	
109	Pharisees and Sadducees first mentioned.	
107	Aristobulus "king."	
63	Pompey captures Jerusalem.	Judea annexed to Rome.
		Conspiracy of Catiline.
58	Herod in Palestine.	Cæsar in Gaul
54	Crassus plunders Temple.	
48		Battle of Pharsalia.
47	Antipater procurator. Herod governor of Galilee.	Cæsar dictator at Rome.
44		Cæsar assassinated.
40	Herod king of Judea.	
37	Herod takes Jerusalem.	
31	Earthquake in Judea.	Battle of Actium.
30		Egypt a Roman Province.
29		Temple of Janus closed.
27		Augustus made Emperor.
19	Herod begins rebuilding the Temple.	
4	Herod dies at Jericho.	

DATE OF THE BIRTH OF CHRIST.

Many people are greatly perplexed by the statement that Jesus was born four years before the time from which we count his birth, or on December 25, B.C. 5. The reason is that no one began to reckon dates generally from the birth of Christ till centuries had passed. The general method was from the founding of Rome (A.U.C.) and not till after Rome ceased to be the mistress of the world would people begin to think seriously of a change. Finally, in A.D. 526, a monk, Dionysius Exiguus, made the calculations, but made an error of four years. He placed the birth of Christ in the year of Rome 754. But Herod the Great, who slew the innocents of Bethlehem, died in April of the year of Rome 750: so that Jesus must have been born several months before. The date, December 25th, is generally accepted, but we cannot be sure of that. Since it is manifestly impossible to rectify the dates in all books and records throughout the world, we simply apply the true dates to the life of Christ, and say he was five years old at the close of A.D. 1.

The following table may aid in making the matter clear.

Year of Rome (*Anno Urbis Conditæ* = A.U.C.)	749	750	751	752	753	754	755	756
Year of Our Lord (*Anno Domini* = A.D.)	B.C. 5	B.C. 4	B.C. 3	B.C. 2	B.C. 1	A.D. 1	A.D. 2	A.D. 3
Age of Jesus	birth	1st year	2d year	3d year	4th year	5th year	6th year	7th year

HARMONY OF THE LIFE OF CHRIST.

John the Baptist.	Ministry of Jesus: Divisions.	Ministry of Jesus: Years.	Events.	Places.	Dates.	Matt.	Mark.	Luke.	John.
Birth.			Pre-existence						1: 1-14
			Genealogies			1:1-17		3:23-28	
Early Life.	Training for his Work. A.D. 26-30 years — B.C. 4.	Birth B.C. 4. Youth B.C. 4 to A.D. 26.	Birth of John the Baptist foretold	Jerusalem	Sept., B.C. 6			1: 5-23	
			Annunciation to Mary	Nazareth	Mar., B.C. 5			1:24-38	
			Birth of John the Baptist	Judea	June, B.C. 5			1:57-80	
			Birth of Jesus	Bethlehem	Dec. 25, B.C. 5	1:18-25		2: 1-20	
			Presentation in the Temple at	Jerusalem	Feb. 2, B.C. 4			2:22-39	
			Visit of the Magi	Bethlehem	Early Feb., B.C. 4	2: 1-12			
			Flight into Egypt		Feb., B.C. 4	2:13-23			
			Childhood and youth	Nazareth	B.C. 2-A.D. 26	2:23		2:39-52	
A.D. 26.			First passover he attended	Jerusalem	April, A.D. 8			2:41-50	
Public Ministry.		Special Preparations A.D. 26.	Ministry of John the Baptist	Wilderness of Judea	Summer A.D. 26 to Mar. A.D. 28	3: 1-12	1: 1-8	3: 1-18	1:19-28
			Baptism of Jesus	Jordan	Jan. A.D. 27	3:13-17	1: 9-11	3:21-23	1:29-34
			Temptation of Jesus	Wilderness of Judea	Jan.-Feb.	4: 1-11	1:12,13	4: 1-13	
	Judean Ministry.	First Year A.D. 27. Year of Beginnings.	First disciples won	Bethabara	*A.D. 27.* February				1:35-51
			First miracle: Wedding at Cana	Cana	"				2: 1-12
			First cleansing of the Temple	Jerusalem	April 11-17				2:13-25
			First recorded discourse: Nicodemus	"	"				3: 1-21
			First ministry in Judea begun	Judea	Summer				3:22-36
			First converts in Samaria: Jacob's Well	Sychar	December				4: 1-42
			Healing of the nobleman's son	Capernaum	"				4:43-54

John. Public Ministry. — March A.D. 28. — At Macherus (one year). John the Baptist in Prison. — Martyred March A.D. 29.

The Great Galilean Ministry. — One Year and Nine Months.

Period	Event	Place	Time	Matthew	Mark	Luke	John
SECOND YEAR A.D. 28.			*A.D. 28.*				
	Passover	....	March or April	....	....	....	5: 1
	Imprisonment of John the Baptist	Macherus	March	14: 3-5	6:17-18	3:19-20	....
	Beginning of Great Galilean Ministry	Galilee	April	4:12	1:14,15	4:14,15	....
	[First (?) rejection at Nazareth	Nazareth	"	....	....	4:16-30]	....
	Takes up residence at Capernaum	Capernaum	"	4:13-17	....	4:31	....
	Calls first disciples to follow him	"	April, May	4:18-22	1:16-20	5: 1-11	....
	Cure of demoniac in Synagogue	"	"	....	1:21-28	4:31-37	....
	Many miracles of healing	Capernaum and Galilee	April and May	4:23-25; 8:14-17	1:29-39	4:38-44	....
	Cure of a leper	Galilee	May	8: 2-4	1:40-45	5:12-16	....
	Healing a paralytic	Capernaum	May, June	9: 2-8	2: 1-12	5:17-26	....
	Call of Matthew: His feast	"	"	9: 9-17	2:13-22	5:27-39	....
	Healing at Pool of Bethesda	Jerusalem	....	....	....	....	5: 2-47
	Man with withered hand	Capernaum	....	12: 1-14	2:23-3:6	6: 1-11	....
YEAR OF FUNDAMENTAL PRINCIPLES.	Appointing of the twelve Apostles	Horns of Hattin	Midsummer	10: 2-4	3:13-19	6:12-19	....
	The Sermon on the Mount	"	"	Chs. 5-7	....	6:20-49	....
	Healing of the Centurion's servant	Capernaum	"	8: 5-13	....	7: 1-10	....
	Raising of the widow's son	Nain	"	....	....	7:11-17	....
	John the Baptist sends messengers to Jesus.	Galilee	"	11: 2-19	....	7:18-35	....
	Warnings and Invitations (later?)	....	....	11:20-30	....	....	....
	Anointing of Jesus by the penitent woman.	....	....	....	....	7:36-50	....
	Another tour of Galilee	Galilee	Autumn	....	....	8: 1-3	....
	Blind and dumb demoniac	Capernaum	"	12:22-45	3:22-30	11:14-36	....
	Visit of his mother and brethren	"	"	12:46-50	3:31-35	8:19-21	....
	Eight parables by the seaside	"	"	13: 1-53	4: 1-34	8: 4-18	....
	Stilling of the tempest	Sea of Galilee	"	8:18-27	4:35-41	8:22-25	....
	Restoration of the demoniac	Gergesa	"	8:28-34	5: 1-20	8:26-39	....
	Jairus' daughter raised: Woman cured	Capernaum	"	9:18-26	5:21-43	8:40-56	....
	Cure of two blind and one dumb	"	"	9:27-34	....	....	....
THIRD YEAR A.D. 29.			*A.D. 29.*				
	Second (?) rejection at Nazareth	Nazareth	Winter	13:53-58	6: 1-6	(4:16-30)	....
	The twelve sent out to preach	Galilee	"	9:35-11:1	6: 6-13	9: 1-6	....
	Death of John the Baptist	Macherus	March	14: 1-12	6:14-29	9: 7-9	....
	Feeding of the 5,000	Bethsaida	April	14:13-21	6:30-46	9:10-17	6: 1-15
	Jesus walks on the water	Sea of Galilee	"	14:22-33	6:47-52	....	6:16-21
	Heals many sick	Gennesaret	"	14:34,35	6:53-56	....	....
YEAR OF DEVELOPMENT.	Discourse on the Bread of Life	Capernaum	"	....	....	....	6:22-71
	Eating with unwashed hands	"	"	15: 1-20	7: 1-23	....	....
	Heals daughter of Syrophenician woman.	Phœnicia	Summer	15:21-28	7:24-30	....	....
	Miracles of healing in Decapolis	Decapolis	"	15:29-31	7:31-37	....	....
	Feeding the 4,000	"	"	15:32-39	8: 1-10	....	....
	Demand for a sign from heaven	Capernaum	"	16: 1-12	8:11-21	....	....
GREAT DEEDS AMID GREAT OPPOSITION.	Blind man healed	Bethsaida	"	....	8:22-26	....	....
	Peter's great confession of faith	Near Cæsarea-Philippi	"	16:13-20	8:27-30	9:18-21	....
	Jesus for the first time foretells his death.	"	"	16:21-28	8:31-9:1	9:22-27	....
	The Transfiguration	"	"	17: 1-13	9: 2-13	9:28-36	....
	Healing of the demoniac boy	"	"	17:14-21	9:14-29	9:37-43	....
	Jesus again foretells his death	Galilee	"	17:22,23	9:30-32	9:43-45	....
	Jesus and the children	Capernaum	"	18: 1-14	9:33-50	9:46-50	....
	Unmerciful servant	"	"	18:15-35	....	....	....

HARMONY OF THE LIFE OF CHRIST (*Continued*).

Divisions.	Years.	Events.	Place.	Date.	Matt.	Mark.	Luke.	John.
Close of the Galilean Ministry.	THIRD YEAR. A.D. 29.			*A.D. 29.*				
		At the Feast of Tabernacles	Jerusalem	Autumn				7:1-10:21
		The water of Life	"	Oct. 11–18				7:37–39
		Officers sent to arrest him	"	"				7:44–53
		Discourse on light and freedom	"	"				8:12–59
		Healing of man born blind	"	"				9: 1–39
		The Good Shepherd	"	"				10: 1–21
	YEAR OF DEVELOPMENT.	Returns to Galilee; final departure		Nov.–Dec.	19:1	10:1	9:51	
		Repulse by the Samaritans	Samaria	"			9:51–62	
		The mission of the Seventy	Perea	"			10: 1–24	
		Parable of the Good Samaritan	"	"			10:25–37	
		Discourse on prayer	"	"			11: 1–13	
		Answers attack of Pharisees	"	"			11:14–54	
Dec. A.D. 29.	GREAT DEEDS AMID GREAT OPPOSITION.	The Rich Fool; the Watchful Servant, etc.	"	"			12: 1–59	
		Discourses: Galileans slain by Pilate; Healing on Sabbath; Parables of mustard seed and leaven; the strait gate; lament over Jerusalem		"			13: 1–35	
		Jesus the guest of Mary and Martha	Bethany	"			10:38–42	
		Feast of Dedication. Discourses	Jerusalem	Dec. 20–27				10:22–39
PEREAN MINISTRY (Four or five months).	A.D. 30. THREE MONTHS.			*A.D. 30.*				
		Jesus retires beyond Jordan into	Perea	January				10:40–42
		Dines with a Pharisee	"	"			14: 1–14	
		Parable of the Great Supper,	"	"			14:15–24	
		Counting the cost of discipleship	"	"			14:25–35	
		Parables of lost sheep and lost coin	"	"			15: 1–10	
		Parable of prodigal son	"	"			15:11–32	
		Parable of the unjust steward	"	"			16: 1–13	
		Parable of the rich man and Lazarus	"	"			16:14–31	
		Teachings on forgiveness	"	"			17: 1–10	
		Raising of Lazarus	Bethany	February				11: 1–46
		Retreat to Ephraim	Ephraim	Feb., March				11:47–57
		The healing of the ten lepers	Samaria	March			17:11–19	
		On the coming of the kingdom	Perea	"			17:20–37	
		Parable of the importunate widow	"	"			18: 1–8	
		Parable of the Pharisee and publican	"	"			18: 9–14	
	CULMINATION OF MIRACLES AND TEACHING.	Discourse about divorce	"	"	19: 2–12	10: 2–12		
		Christ blesses little children	"	"	19:13–15	10:13–16	18:15–17	
		The rich young man	"	"	19:16–30	10:17–31	18:18–30	
		The laborers in the vineyard	"	"	20: 1–16			
March A.D. 30.		Jesus again predicts his death	"	"	20:17–19	10:32–34	18:31–34	
		Ambitious request of James and John	"	"	20:20–28	10:35–45		
		Healing two blind men (one being Bartimeus)	Jericho	"	20:29–34	10:46–52	18:35–43	
		Visit to Zaccheus the publican	"	"			19: 1–10	
		Parable of the pounds (Minæ)	"	"			19:11–28	

The Last Week. March 31-to April 7.

A. D. 30.			A.D. 30.				
Fri. Mar. 31.	Jesus arrives at Bethany	Bethany	Friday, Mar. 31				12: 1
Sat. Apr. 1.	Anointing by Mary	Bethany	Sat. Apr. 1	26: 6-13	14: 3-9		12: 2-11
Sun. Apr. 2.	Triumphal Entry. Visit to Temple. Return to Bethany	Jerusalem	Sun. Apr. 2	21: 1-11	11: 1-11	19:29-44	12:12-19
Mon. Apr. 3.	Cursing of barren fig-tree	Mt. of Olives	Mon. Apr. 3	21:18-19	11:12-14		
	Cleansing of the temple and return to Bethany	Jerusalem	"	21:12-17	11:15-19	19:45-48; 21:37, 38	
Tues. Apr. 4. The Last Day of Public Teaching.	The fig-tree withered. Lesson on faith	Mt. of Olives	Tues. Apr. 4	21:20-22	11:20-26		
	Christ's authority challenged	The Temple	"	21:23-27	11:27-33	20: 1-8	
	Three parables of warning:						
	The Two Sons	"	"	21:28-32			
	The Wicked Husbandman	"	"	21:33-46	12: 1-12	20: 9-19	
	Marriage of the king's son	"	"	22: 1-14			
	Three Questions by Jewish rulers	"	"	22:15-40	12:13-34	20:20-40	
	Christ's unanswerable question	"	"	22:41-46	12:35-37	20:41-44	
	Woes against Scribes and Pharisees	"	"	23: 1-36	12:38-40	20:45-47	
	Lamentation over Jerusalem	"	"	23:37-39			
	The Widow's two mites	"	"		12:41-44	21: 1-4	
	Greeks seeking Jesus	"	"				12:20-36
	Prophecy of the end of the age	Mt. of Olives	"	24: 1-51	13: 1-37	21: 5-36	
	Parable of the ten virgins	"	"	25: 1-13			
	Parable of the talents	"	"	25:14-30			
	The last judgment	"	"	25:31-46			
	Conspiracy between the rulers and Judas	Jerusalem	"	26: 1-5, 14-16	14: 1, 2, 10-11	22: 1-6	
Wed. Apr. 5.	Jesus in retirement	Bethany	Wed. Apr. 5				
Thurs. Apr. 6. The Last Day with His Disciples.	Preparation for the Passover	Jerusalem	Thurs. Apr. 6	26:17-20	14:12-17	22: 7-14	
	Strife for precedence	"	"			22:24-30	
	Jesus washes the disciples' feet	"	"				13: 1-20
	The last supper	"	"			22:15-18	
	Jesus declares the betrayer. Judas goes out	"	"	26:21-25	14:18-21	22:21-23	13:21-35
	Institution of the Lord's Supper	"	"	26:26-30	14:22-25	22:19, 20	(1Cor.11)
	Jesus foretells the fall of Peter	"	"			22:31-38	13:36-38
	Christ's farewell Discourses	"	"				Chs. 14-16
	Prayer of Jesus for the disciples	"	"				17: 1-26
	Jesus goes forth. Peter's confidence	"	"	26:30-35	14:26-31	22:39	18: 1-3
	The Agony in the Garden of Gethsemane	Mt. of Olives	"	26:36-46	14:32-42	22:40-46	

HARMONY OF THE LIFE OF CHRIST (*Continued*).

THE LAST DAY. Hours.	Friday, Apr. 7.	Events.	Place.	Date.	Matt.	Mark.	Luke.	John.
1–5 A.M.	THE ARREST.	Betrayal by Judas	....	Friday, April 7 Midnight	26:47–50	14:43–45	22:47, 48	18: 4–9
		The arrest	....	"	26:50–56	14:46–52	22:49–53	18:10–12
	THE JEWISH TRIAL.	The trial before Annas	Jerusalem	1–5 A. M.	....	....	....	18:13–15
		Before Caiaphas	"	"	26:57, 58	14:53, 54	22:54, 55	18:19–24
		Before the Sanhedrin	"	"	26:59–66	14:55–64	....	....
		Denials by Peter	"	....	26:69–75	14:66–72	22:56–62	18:15–18, 25–27
5–6 A.M.		Mockery by enemies	"	....	26:67, 68	14:65	22:63–65	....
		Legal meeting of Sanhedrin; Jesus condemned for blasphemy	"	5–6 A. M.	27: 1, 2	15:1	22:66–71; 23:1	....
		Death of Judas	"	....	27: 3–10	....	(Acts 1: 18, 19)	....
6–9 A.M.	THE ROMAN TRIAL.	Jesus before Pilate	"	6–9 A. M.	27:11–14	15: 2–5	23: 2–5	18:28–38
		Jesus sent to Herod	"	"	....	....	23: 6–12	....
		Pilate seeks to release Jesus; people demand Barabbas	"	"	27:15–23	15: 6–14	23:13–23	18:38–40
		Jesus condemned, scourged and mocked	"	"	27:26–30	15:15–19	23:24, 25	19: 1–3
		"Ecce Homo." Other attempts by Pilate to release Jesus	"	....	27:24, 25	....	....	19: 4–16
9 A.M. to 3 P.M.	THE CRUCIFIXION.	Jesus led away to be crucified	"	9 A. M.	27:31–34, 38	15:20, 23, 25, 27, 28	23:26–32	19:16–18
		The superscription	"	"	27:37	15:26	23:38	19:19–22
		First word from the cross: "*Father, forgive them*," etc.	"	"	....	....	23:33, 34	....
		Soldiers cast lots for garments	"	"	27:35, 36	15:24	23:34	19:23, 24
		Jews mock at Jesus on the cross	"	"	27:39–44	15:29–32	23:35–37	....
		Second word from the cross: to the penitent thief	"	"	....	....	23:39–43	....
		Third word: "*Woman, behold thy son.*"	"	"	....	....	....	19:25–27
		Darkness covers the land	"	12 M.	27:45	15:33	23:44, 45	....
		Fourth word: cry of distress to God	"	"	27:46, 47	15:34, 35	....	....
		Fifth word: "*I thirst*"	"	"	27:48, 49	15:36	....	19:28, 29
		Sixth word: "*It is finished*"	"	"	....	....	....	19:30
		Seventh word: "*Into thy hands*," etc.	"	"	....	....	23:46	....
		Jesus dies. Veil rent. Earthquake	"	3 P. M.	27:50–56	15:37–41	23:45–49	19:30
		Jesus is pierced in the side	"	"	....	....	....	19:31–37
3–6 P.M.	THE BURIAL.	The burial	....	3–6 P. M.	27:57–61	15:42–47	23:50–56	19:38–42

RESURRECTION DAYS A.D. 30.

Parts of April 7, 8, 9.	THREE DAYS IN THE TOMB.	The watch at the tomb	Jerusalem	Sat., April 8	27:62–66			
April 9 to May 18.	40 RESURRECTION DAYS.	The morning of the resurrection	"	Sunday, April 9	28: 2–4			
		Women come to the tomb	"	"	28:1	16: 1–4	24: 1, 2	20:1
		Mary Magdalene calls Peter and John	"	"				20:2
		The women at the tomb	"	"	28: 5–8	16: 5–8	24: 3–8	
		Peter and John at the tomb	"	"			24:12	20: 3–10
		Jesus appears to Mary Magdalene	"	"		16: 9–11		20:11–18
		Jesus appears to the women	"	"	28: 9, 10		24: 9–11	
		The guards report to the priests	"	"	28:11–15			
		The walk to Emmaus	Emmaus	"		16:12, 13	24:13–35	
		Jesus appears to Peter	Jerusalem	"	(1Cor. 15:5)		24:34	
		Jesus appears to the Apostles except Thomas	"		(1Cor. 15:5)	16:14	24:36–48	20:19–23
		Jesus appears to all the Apostles, including Thomas	"					20:24–29
		Jesus appears to seven in Galilee	Sea of Galilee	April				21: 1–23
		Appears to over 500 at once	"	April, May	28:16–20	16:15–18	(1 Cor. 15:6)	
		Jesus appears to James	"				(1 Cor. 15:7)	
		Jesus appears to the apostles	Jerusalem				24:49	Acts 1:1–18
May 18.	THE ASCENSION.	Jesus ascends to heaven	Bethany, Mt. of Olives	Thurs., May 18		16:19	24:50–53	Acts 1:9–12
		The conclusions of Mark and John				16:20		20:30, 31; 21:24, 25
May 28.	BIRTH OF THE CHURCH.	Holy Spirit given at Pentecost	Jerusalem				Acts 2:1–11	
	CONTINUED LIFE OF JESUS.	Jesus appears to Paul	Damascus	A.D. 36			(Acts 22:6–16)	
		Jesus appears to John	Patmos	A.D. 68 or 96				(Rev. 1:9–20)

CHART OF THE LIFE OF JESUS CHRIST.

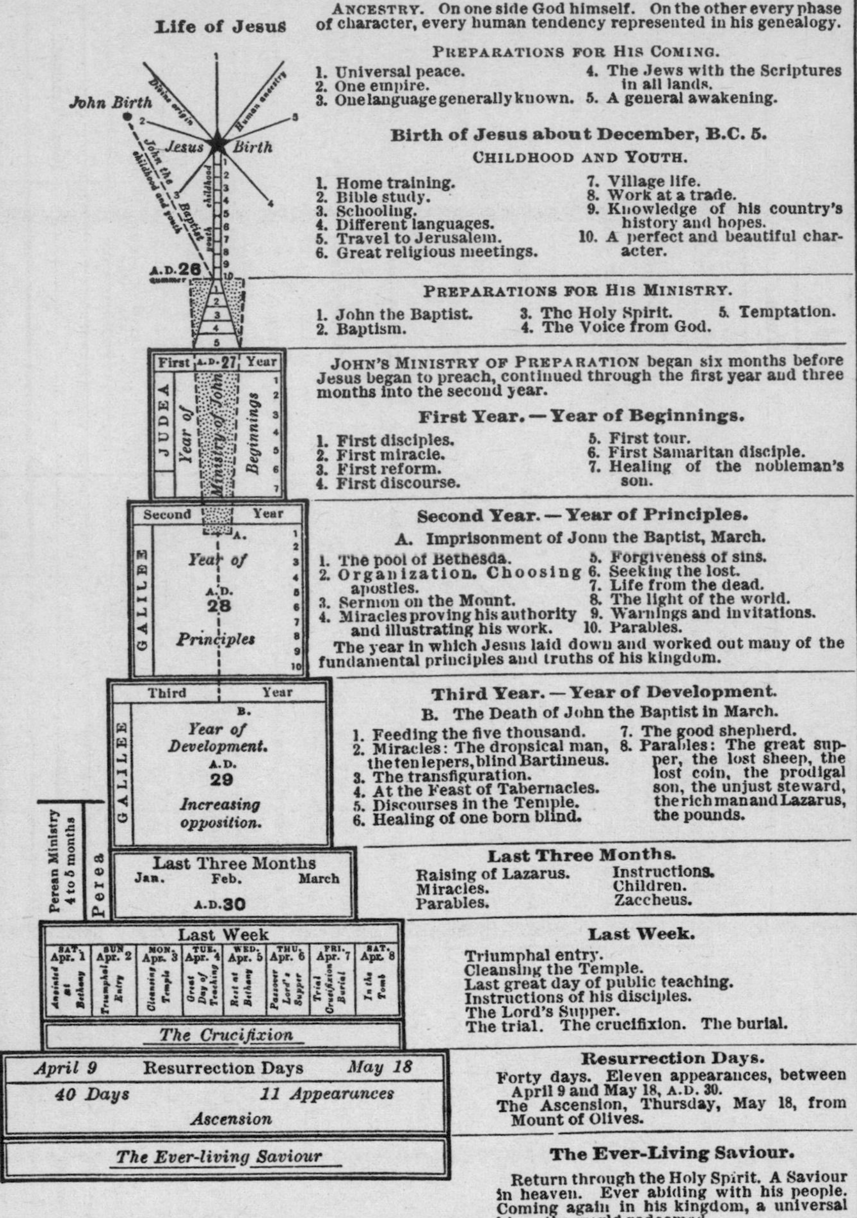

ANCESTRY. On one side God himself. On the other every phase of character, every human tendency represented in his genealogy.

PREPARATIONS FOR HIS COMING.

1. Universal peace.
2. One empire.
3. One language generally known.
4. The Jews with the Scriptures in all lands.
5. A general awakening.

Birth of Jesus about December, B.C. 5.

CHILDHOOD AND YOUTH.

1. Home training.
2. Bible study.
3. Schooling.
4. Different languages.
5. Travel to Jerusalem.
6. Great religious meetings.
7. Village life.
8. Work at a trade.
9. Knowledge of his country's history and hopes.
10. A perfect and beautiful character.

PREPARATIONS FOR HIS MINISTRY.

1. John the Baptist.
2. Baptism.
3. The Holy Spirit.
4. The Voice from God.
5. Temptation.

JOHN'S MINISTRY OF PREPARATION began six months before Jesus began to preach, continued through the first year and three months into the second year.

First Year. — Year of Beginnings.

1. First disciples.
2. First miracle.
3. First reform.
4. First discourse.
5. First tour.
6. First Samaritan disciple.
7. Healing of the nobleman's son.

Second Year. — Year of Principles.

A. Imprisonment of John the Baptist, March.

1. The pool of Bethesda.
2. Organization. Choosing apostles.
3. Sermon on the Mount.
4. Miracles proving his authority and illustrating his work.
5. Forgiveness of sins.
6. Seeking the lost.
7. Life from the dead.
8. The light of the world.
9. Warnings and invitations.
10. Parables.

The year in which Jesus laid down and worked out many of the fundamental principles and truths of his kingdom.

Third Year. — Year of Development.

B. The Death of John the Baptist in March.

1. Feeding the five thousand.
2. Miracles: The dropsical man, the ten lepers, blind Bartimeus.
3. The transfiguration.
4. At the Feast of Tabernacles.
5. Discourses in the Temple.
6. Healing of one born blind.
7. The good shepherd.
8. Parables: The great supper, the lost sheep, the lost coin, the prodigal son, the unjust steward, the rich man and Lazarus, the pounds.

Last Three Months.

Raising of Lazarus.
Miracles.
Parables.
Instructions.
Children.
Zaccheus.

Last Week.

Triumphal entry.
Cleansing the Temple.
Last great day of public teaching.
Instructions of his disciples.
The Lord's Supper.
The trial. The crucifixion. The burial.

Resurrection Days.

Forty days. Eleven appearances, between April 9 and May 18, A.D. 30.
The Ascension, Thursday, May 18, from Mount of Olives.

The Ever-Living Saviour.

Return through the Holy Spirit. A Saviour in heaven. Ever abiding with his people. Coming again in his kingdom, a universal king; the world redeemed.

THE APOSTLES AND THEIR HISTORY.

	NAME.	SURNAME.	PARENTS.	HOME.	BUSINESS.	WRITINGS.	WORK.	DEATH.
1	SIMON.	Peter Cephas } = *Rock.*	Jonah.	*Early Life:* Bethsaida. *Later:* Capernaum.	Fisherman.	1 Peter. 2 Peter. (Mark?).	A missionary among the Jews, as far as Babylon, 1 Pet. 5 : 13. Probably = Rome.	*Trad.:* Crucified head downward, at Rome.
2	ANDREW.		Jonah.	*Early Life:* Bethsaida. *Later:* Capernaum.	Fisherman.		*Tradition.* Preached in Scythia, Greece, and Asia Minor.	*Trad.:* Crucified on St. Andrew's cross (×).
3	JAMES the greater or elder.	Boanerges, or *Sons of Thunder.*	Zebedee and Salome.	Bethsaida and afterward in Jerusalem.	Fisherman.		Preached in Jerusalem and Judea.	Beheaded by Herod, A.D. 44, at Jerusalem.
4	JOHN, the beloved disciple.				Fisherman.	Gospel. 3 Epistles. Revelation.	Labored among the churches of Asia Minor, especially Ephesus.	Banished to Patmos, A.D. 95. Recalled. Died a natural death. *Trad.*
5	JAMES the less or younger.		Alpheus or Cleophas and Mary.	Galilee.		(Epistle of James ?).	Preached in Palestine and Egypt. Bishop of Jerusalem (?)	*Trad.:* Crucified in Egypt; or thrown from a pinnacle.
6	JUDE.	Same as Thaddeus and Lebbeus.		Galilee.		Epistle	Preached in Assyria and Persia. *Trad.*	Martyred in Persia. *Trad.*
7	PHILIP.			Bethsaida.			Preached in Phrygia.	Died martyr at Hierapolis in Phrygia. *Trad.*
8	BARTHOLOMEW.	Nathaniel.		Cana of Galilee.				Flayed to death. *Trad.*
9	MATTHEW.	Levi.	Alpheus.	Capernaum.	Tax-collector.	Gospel.		*Trad.:* Died a martyr in Ethiopia.
10	THOMAS.	Didymus.		Galilee.			Claimed by the Syrian Christians as the founder of their church; perhaps also in Persia and India.	*Trad.:* Shot by arrows while at prayer.
11	SIMON.	The Cananæan, or *Zelotes.*		Galilee.				*Trad.:* Crucified.
12	JUDAS.	Iscariot.		Kerioth of Judea.				Suicide.

CHRONOLOGY OF THE ACTS.

ACTS.	EVENTS.	PLACE.	DATE A.D.*	CONTEMPORARY HISTORY.
1: 1-3	Resurrection days	Galilee	30. April, May	Tiberius, emperor, 14-37 A.D.
1: 4-12	Commission to Apostles and Ascension	Bethany	30. May 18	Pontius Pilate, procurator, 26-36.
1:13, 14	Waiting for the promise of the Father	Jerusalem, in an upper room.	30	PAUL enters public life, A.D. 29, aged 30.
1:15-26	Election of Matthias to take the place of Judas	"	....	
2: 1-13	Pentecost: the Gift of Tongues	Jerusalem	....	Seneca. 4 B.C.-65 A.D.
2:14-36	Peter's address	"	....	Essays and Tragedies.
2:37-41	The first converts: 3000	"	....	
2:42-47	The early church	"	....	
3: 1-10	The lame man healed	Temple courts	....	Gamaliel. 30-40 A.D.
3:11-26	Second address by Peter	"	....	
4: 1-22	The first persecution: Peter and John imprisoned	Jerusalem	....	Philo Judæus. 20 B.C.—after 40 A.D.
4:23-37	A fresh baptism of the Spirit	"	....	
5: 1-11	Ananias and Sapphira	"	30	
5:12-16	Spread of Gospel in Jerusalem	"	to	
5:17-42	Second persecution: Sanhedrin	"	34	
6: 1-7	Appointment of deacons	"	35	
6: 8-15	Preaching of Stephen	"	35 to 36	Deposition of Pontius Pilate. 36.
7: 1-60	Martyrdom of Stephen	"	36	
8: 1-4	General persecution	....	....	Sent to Rome for trial.
8: 5-25	Philip the Evangelist in	Samaria	....	Vitellius takes his place as governor.
8:26-40	Philip and the Ethiopian	Road to Gaza	....	
9: 1-22	Conversion of Saul of Tarsus	Near Damascus	....	PAUL, aged 37.
(Gal. 1:17)	Saul in Arabia	....	....	Death of Tiberius, 16 March, 37.
9:23-27	St. Paul persecuted; escapes	Damascus	38	
9:28-29	St. Paul preaches in Jerusalem	Jerusalem	....	Accession of Caligula.
9:30	St. Paul goes to Cilicia	Tarsus, etc	38-40	Release of Herod Agrippa I.
9:31-35	St. Peter cures Æneas	Lydda	....	
9:36-42	Dorcas restored to life	Joppa	....	Banishment of Antipas, 39.
10: 1-48	Cornelius the Centurion converted	Cæsarea	41	Caligula orders his statue to be set up at Jerusalem.
11: 1-18	The question of admitting the Gentiles	Jerusalem	....	Claudius Emperor, Jan. 24, 41, to Oct. 13, 54.
11:19-21	First Gentile church	Antioch	38-41	
	Herod Agrippa I, King of Judea	....	41	Seneca in exile, 41-49.
11:22, 23	Barnabas at Antioch	Antioch	42, 43	
11:25, 26	Paul called from Tarsus to Antioch	"	42, 43	Romans in Britain, 43.
12: 1, 2	Martyrdom of St. James	Jerusalem	44. Spring	
12: 3-18	Imprisonment and deliverance of St. Peter	"	44. Spring	Death of Herod Agrippa I, 44.
12:19-23	Death of Herod Agrippa I	Cæsarea	44. Early Summer	London founded, 47.
11:27-30	Famine. Relief sent to Jerusalem by Barnabas and Saul	....	44-46	
12:24, 25	Return of Saul and Barnabas with John Mark to	Antioch	46	Expulsion of Jews from Rome, 48 (?)
13: 1-14:28	**First Missionary Journey** by Saul and Barnabas.	Asia Minor	March 47 to 49	
13: 1-3	Ordained as missionaries	Antioch	....	
13: 4-52	In Cyprus and Antioch of Pisidia.	Asia Minor	....	
14: 1-20	In Iconium, Lystra, Derbe	"	....	
14:21-25	Revisiting the churches	"	49	
14:26-28	Report to home church	Antioch	49	Caractacus defeated in Britain.
15: 1-35	Council at Jerusalem	Jerusalem	50	
15:40-18:22	**Second Missionary Journey** by St. Paul and Silas	Asia Minor and Greece	50-52	
16: 1-5	Revisiting the churches	Asia Minor	50-52	
16: 6-11	St. Paul enters Europe	Macedonia	50-52	
16:12-40	St. Paul at Philippi; Lydia; conversion of jailer	Philippi	50-52	
17: 1-14	St. Paul in Thessalonica and Berea.	Macedonia	....	Gallio pro-consul at Corinth.
17:15-34	St. Paul at Athens	Greece	51-52	

NOTE I. The dates in this column are the prevalent ones, and are sufficiently accurate for understanding the course of the history. Almost every writer on Acts differs slightly from them, but only slightly.

CHRONOLOGY OF THE ACTS (*Continued*).

Acts.	Events.	Place.	Date A.D.	Contemporary History.
18: 1-18	St. Paul at Corinth. Crispus....	Greece..........	51-52	
	1 and 2 Thessalonians....	....	....	
18:18-22	Returns home via Ephesus and Cæsarea to..............	Antioch.........	51-52	Felix, procurator, 52-59.
18:22	Brief visit to Jerusalem.........	Jerusalem.........	....	
18:22,23	St. Paul in Antioch..............	Syria...........	52	Nero, emperor, 54 68.
	Galatians..............	....	....	
18:23-21:16	**Third Missionary Journey** by Paul.	Asia Minor and Greece.........	53-57	Birth of Tacitus, 55.
18:24-28	Apollos at Ephesus..............	Asia Minor.....	....	St. Peter at Corinth, 55 or 56.
19: 1-11	St. Paul nearly three years at...	Ephesus........	53-56	
	1 Corinthians..............	"	56	
19:12-20	Sceva the Exorcist..............	"	....	
19:21-41	Riot at Ephesus. Diana.........	"	....	
20: 1-5	St. Paul revisits Macedonia.....	Macedonia.....	57	
	2 Corinthians	"	....	
	St. Paul three months at Corinth.	Greece..........	....	
	Romans..............	....	....	
20: 6-12	St. Paul at Troas. Eutychus....	Troas..........	....	
20:13-16	Sails to Miletus..............	....	....	
20:17-38	Address to Ephesian elders at...	Miletus..........	57	
21: 1-16	Journey by Tyre and Cæsarea to	Jerusalem.........	....	
21:17-20	St. Paul's reception by church..	Jerusalem.........	....	
21:21-40	St. Paul's arrest in Temple......	"	....	
22: 1-23:11	St. Paul a prisoner in Castle of Antonia..............	"	....	
23:12-22	Theconspiracyagainst Paul's life.	"	....	
23:23-35	St. Paul sent secretly to.........	Cæsarea..........	....	
24: 1-22	St. Paul's trial before Felix.....	"	....	
24:23-27	St. Paul in prison two years at..	"	57	Festus, procurator, 59-63.
25: 1-12	St. Paul accused to Festus. He appeals to Cæsar..............	"	59	*St. Luke's Gospel* probably written.
25:13-26:32	St. Paul before Festus and Agrippa..............	"	....	
27: 1-44	St. Paul's voyage and shipwreck.	Mediterranean.	Sept. 59	
28: 1-10	St. Paul on the Island of Malta..	"	60	Nero murders Agrippina.
28:11-29	St. Paul at Rome: Conference with the Jews..............	Rome..........	....	
28:30,31	Paul a prisoner in his own hired house at..............	"	61, 62	
	Colossians, Philemon, Ephesians..............	"	....	Rebellion of Boadicea in Britain.
	Philippians..............	"	....	
	Close of the history in the *Acts*..	....	....	Boadicea defeated by Suetonius about 62.
	*Probable composition of *Acts*...	Rome..........	62-68	
	First trial. Release..............	"	63	
	James..............	....	62 or earlier	Great earthquake at Pompeii.
	Hebrews (?)..............	....	....	
	Goes to Asia by way of Macedonia.	....	....	
	Sails with Titus to Crete and returns to Ephesus..............	....	....	Great Fire of Rome, ascribed by Nero to the Christians, July 19, 64.
	Leaving Timothy goes by Philippi to Corinth..............	....	....	
	1, 2, Peter..............	....	58-64	
	1 Timothy. Titus..............	....	....	
	Journey to Spain (?)..............	....	....	
	Winters at Nicopolis..............	....	....	
	Journey to Dalmatia (?) and through Macedonia to Troas...	....	....	
	Martyrdom of St. Peter..............	....	65	
	St. Paul's second arrest. Sent to Rome..............	....	66	
	Trial before Emperor..............	....	....	Jewish war begins.
	2 Timothy..............	Rome..........	....	Massacre by Florus at Jerusalem.
	Martyrdom of St. Paul..............	"	66 or 67	
	Destruction of Jerusalem..............	....	Aug. 70	Repulse of Cestius Gallus.
	Jude. 1, 2, 3, John..............	....	....	

NOTE II. What follows in this column is based chiefly on tradition and probability. But authorities vary both as to dates and fact. The events after this point refer to St. Paul's life when not definitely connected with another.

ENGLISH VERSIONS OF THE BIBLE.

Translations of the Psalter, Gospels and other portions of the Scriptures were made into Anglo-Saxon as early as the eighth century, and into English of the thirteenth century. These translations had no traceable effect on the English Bible.

WYCLIF'S VERSION (1380). — Wyclif, with some of his followers, translated the entire Bible into English from the Latin Vulgate. Being accomplished before the days of printing, it existed only in MS. form up until 1848 or 1850, when it was published in type.

TINDALE'S NEW TESTAMENT (1525). — William Tindale began the publication of his translation of the New Testament in Cologne in 1525. Being compelled to flee, he finished the publication in Worms. Three thousand copies of quarto size were printed. These Testaments began to reach England in 1526, and were burned by order of the bishops, who bought the whole edition for that purpose. Tindale used this money to print his new edition in 1534.

TINDALE'S PENTATEUCH (1530). —This was published in Mardeburg, Hesse.

TINDALE'S NEW TESTAMENT (1534). — Tindale's New Testament, carefully revised throughout by the translator, was printed at Antwerp and paid for with the money paid for the older edition.

COVERDALE'S BIBLE (1535). — This was the first version of the entire Bible published in English.

MATTHEW'S BIBLE (1537). —This was made up of Tindale's Pentateuch and New Testament, and completed from Coverdale for the rest of the Old Testament and Apocrypha, the whole edited by John Rogers. It was probably printed at Antwerp, but was published in London with the license of King Henry VIII, thus becoming the first "authorized version."

TAVERNER'S BIBLE (1539). — An edition of Matthew's Bible, edited by Taverner.

THE GREAT BIBLE (1539). —This was a new edition of Matthew's Bible, revised and compared with the Hebrew by Coverdale, and published in England under the sanction of Thomas Cromwell in 1539.

THE GENEVA BIBLE (1560). — Two years after the accession of Elizabeth an entirely new edition of the Bible was printed at Geneva. Three men out of a company of English refugees and reformers at Geneva began this work, in January, 1558, and finished it in April, 1560. This was the most scholarly English Bible that had yet appeared. It was of handy size and clear Roman type. It became for a period of seventy-five years *the* Bible of the English people. Because of the rendering in Gen. 3. 7, it became known as the "Breeches" Bible.

THE BISHOPS' BIBLE (1568). —The rapid popularity of the Geneva Bible was not acceptable to Elizabeth and her bishops, who did not sympathize with Genevan church views and polity. Therefore, a revision of the Great Bible was made, at the suggestion of Archbishop Parker, by fifteen theologians, eight of whom were bishops. A second edition of the Bishops' Bible appeared in 1572.

REIMS NEW TESTAMENT (1582). — This translation was made from the Latin Vulgate, and was published in 1583 at Reims. At the same time and place the New Testament portion of the Douay, or Roman Catholic, version appeared.

AUTHORIZED VERSION (1611). —There is no evidence that this version was authorized in any special way. It won its place, under royal and ecclesiastical patronage, by its merits. The work had its inception at Hampton Court Conference in 1604, and was promoted by James I, who approved a list of fifty-four scholars to be assigned to the undertaking. Of these but forty-seven appear to have taken part.

The central thought was "not to make a new translation, nor yet to make of a bad one a good one, but to make a good one better." The A. V. was, therefore, not a new translation, but a thorough and scholarly revision of an already good version.

THE REVISED VERSION (1881–85). — The King James or Authorized Version stood practically untouched for 270 years. True, many small changes had been introduced into the text by successive printers, but no authoritative revision had taken place. It began to be felt that revision was needed.

Accordingly, in 1870, the English Houses of Convocation appointed two bodies of revisers, consisting of twenty-five for the Old Testament and twenty-five for the New. Among other rules adopted for their guidance, they were to introduce as few changes as possible into the A. V. text; adopt no text except the evidence in favor of it greatly preponderated; make or retain no change in the text on final revision except two-thirds of those present approved.

Two similar companies of American scholars cooperated in the work. The Revised New Testament was issued in 1881, and the Revised Bible in 1885. The work as completed was a decidedly forward step in English Biblical scholarship.

THE AMERICAN STANDARD VERSION of 1901. — The American Committee of the Revisers of the 1881 Revision dissented from some of the decisions of their English associates, a partial list of which was placed in the Appendix. But the American company retained their organization, and for 20 years worked upon a new Revision which was issued in 1901 by the Nelsons of Edinburgh. "In details it shows but slight and infrequent deviations from its predecessor." But it retains largely the solid paragraphing which made the 1881 Revision so difficult to use by ordinary readers. Still in many details it is superior to the former Revision.

Yet with all the aid afforded by the Revised Version to the Bible reader and student, the Authorized Version still retains its wonted place in the popular heart.

THE DATE OF EASTER.

EASTER is the first Sunday after the full moon that occurs on or next after March 21; and if the full moon fall on Sunday, Easter is the next Sunday. Of course, if the date were the same each year, the day would be Sunday only once in six years. Some of the early Christians did fix the date in this way, while others used the present way. But in the year 325 the matter was brought by Constantine before the Council of Nice, and it was evidently thought best that the anniversary of the event which they thought changed the Sabbath from the seventh day of the week to the first day, should always fall upon the first day; for they, deciding between the two ways then in use, selected for the whole church the method which would bring Easter always on Sunday.

Since that decision, Easter cannot fall earlier than March 22, nor later than April 25, in any year. These dates are called the "Easter Limits."

The most of the other holy days of the church depend for their dates upon the date of Easter.

LENT begins 46 days before Easter, with *Ash Wednesday*. Sundays being always feast days, not fast days, this gives 40 days of fasting.

Palm Sunday is the Sunday before Easter.

Good Friday is the Friday before Easter.

Passion Week is the week ending with Palm Sunday.

Holy Week is the week ending with Easter.

WHITSUNDAY or *Pentecost* is 7 weeks after Easter.

THE DAYS ON WHICH EASTER WILL FALL FROM 1985-2020

1985	April 7	1997	Mar. 30	2009	April 12
1986	Mar. 30	1998	April 12	2010	April 4
1987	April 19	1999	April 4	2011	April 24
*1988	April 3	*2000	April 23	*2012	April 8
1989	Mar. 26	2001	April 15	2013	Mar. 31
1990	April 15	2002	Mar. 31	2014	April 20
1991	Mar. 31	2003	April 20	2015	April 5
*1992	April 19	*2004	April 11	*2016	Mar. 27
1993	April 11	2005	Mar. 27	2017	April 16
1994	April 3	2006	April 16	2018	April 1
1995	April 16	2007	April 8	2019	April 21
*1996	April 7	*2008	Mar. 23	*2020	April 12

*Leap Year

JEWISH SECTS AND PARTIES.

The following is a list of the main distinctions in Biblical times: —

1. Pharisees
2. Sadducees
3. Essenes

} Distinctions chiefly religious.

4. Herodians
5. Zealots
6. Galilæans
7. Assassins

} Distinctions chiefly political.

Subordinate terms connected with the above.

8. Scribes.
9. Lawyers.
10. Nazarites.
11. Proselytes.
12. Publicans.
13. Samaritans.
14. Sanhedrin.
15. Synagogue.

ITINERARY OF THE ISRAELITES TO THE LAND OF CANAAN.

The Itinerary of the Israelites, given in full in Num. 33., may be divided into four parts: —

A. From Goshen to the Red Sea.	
1. At Rameses.	Ex. 12. 37. Num. 33. 3.
2. Succoth.	Ex. 12. 37-39.
3. Etham.	Ex. 13. 20.
4. Pi-hahiroth.	Ex. 14. 1-9. 1 Cor. 10. 1, 2.
Crossing the Red Sea. Destruction of Pharaoh's host.	
B. From the Red Sea to Sinai.	
1. Marah (*'Ain-Hawârah*).	Ex. 15. 23-25.
2. Elim (*Wady Gharandel*).	Ex. 15. 27.
3. The Wilderness of Sin.	Ex. 16. John 6. 31, 49. Rev. 2. 17.
4. Rephidim in the Horeb.	Ex. 17. 1-8. 1 Cor. 10. 4. Ex. 17. 13.
5. The Wilderness of Sinai Mount of God (*Jebel Mûsa*).	Ex. 19. 1. Ex. 18. 5. Ex. 20. Ex. 32. 1 Cor. 10. 7. Ex. 40.
Giving of the Law from Mt. Sinai. Building of the Tabernacle.	
C. From Sinai to Kadesh-Barnea.	
After a stay of nearly a year at Sinai, on the twentieth day of the second month of the second year, they move three days' journey to	Ex. 19. 1. Num. 10. 11, 12. Num. 10. 33.
1. Taberah (*burning*).	Num. 11. 1-3.
2. Kibroth-hattaavah (*the graves of lust*).	Num. 11. 1-34.
3. Hazeroth (*Hudherah*).	Num. 11. 35.
4. Kadesh-barnea (? *Ain-el-Weibeh*).	Num. 13. 26. Num. 14. 1-39. 1 Cor. 10. 10. Num. 16.
Thirty-eight years in the wilderness.	
D. The new start. From Kadesh-Barnea to the border of the Jordan.	
At the close of the wanderings they return to	Num. 33.
1. Kadesh-barnea.	Num. 20. 14-21. Num. 27. 14.
2. Mount Hor, near Selah or Petra (Jos. *Ant.* iv. 4. 7).	Num. 20. 24-29.
3. The Arabah by way of Elath and Ezion-geber.	Deu. 2. 8 (R.V.). Num. 21. 5-9. John 3. 14. 1 Cor. 10. 9.
4. Zared (*the brook*), and Beer-Elim (*the well of heroes*).	Num. 21. 12, 16, 18.
5. Jahaz, they defeat Sihon, king of the Amorites, and at	Num. 21. 23, 24.
6. Edrei, Og, the king of Bashan. These two victories give to Israel, possession of the whole country east of Jordan. They next go to	Num. 21. 33.
7. Abel-Shittim (*the meadow* or *oasis of the acacias*), the modern *Ghor es Seiseban*, over against Jericho.	Num. 33. 49. Num. 22. 4. Num. 23. 24. Num. 25. 1 Cor. 10. 9. Num. 31.
8. Plains of Moab, opposite Jericho.	Deu. 32. Deu. 34. 6.
Moses' last charge and death. Crossing the Jordan into the Promised Land.	

PROPHECIES RELATING TO CHRIST.

1. His First Advent.
The fact, Gen. 3. 15; Deut. 18. 15; Ps. 89. 20; Isa. 2. 2; 28. 16; 32. 1; 35. 4; 42. 6; 49. 1; 55. 4; Ezek. 34. 24; Dan. 2. 44; Mic. 4. 1; Zech. 3. 8.
The time, Gen. 49. 10; Num. 24. 17; Dan. 9. 24; Mal. 3. 1.
His Divinity, Ps. 2. 7, 11; 45. 6, 7, 11; 72. 8; 102. 24-27; 89. 26, 27; 110. 1; Isa. 9. 6; 25. 9; 40. 10; Jer. 23. 6; Mic. 5. 2; Mal. 3. 1.
Human Generation, Gen. 12. 3; 18. 18; 21. 12; 22. 18; 26. 4; 28. 14; 49. 10; 2 Sam. 7. 14; Ps. 18. 4-6, 50; 22. 22, 23; 89. 4, 29, 36; 132. 11; Isa. 11. 1; Jer. 23. 5; 33. 15.

2. His Forerunner.
Isa. 40. 3; Mal. 3. 1; 4. 5.

3. His Nativity and Early Years.
The fact, Gen. 3. 15; Isa. 7. 14; Jer. 31. 22.
The place, Num. 24. 17, 19; Mic. 5. 2.
Adoration by Magi, Ps. 72. 10, 15; Isa. 60. 3, 6.
Descent into Egypt, Hos. 11. 1.
Massacre of Innocents, Jer. 31. 15.

4. His Mission and Office.
Mission, Gen. 12. 3; 49. 10; Num. 24. 19; Deut. 18. 18; Ps. 21. 1; Isa. 59. 20; Jer. 33. 16.
Priest like Melchizedek, Ps. 110. 4.

PROPHECIES RELATING TO CHRIST (*Continued*).

Prophet like Moses, Deut. 18. 15.
Conversion of Gentiles, Isa. 11. 10; Deut. 32. 43; Ps. 18. 49; 19. 4; 117. 1; Isa. 42. 1; 45. 23; 49. 6; Hos. 1. 10; 2. 23; Joel 2. 32.
Galilee, ministry in, Isa. 9. 1, 2.
Miracles, Isa. 35. 5, 6; 42. 7; 53. 4.
Spiritual graces, Ps. 45. 7; Isa. 11. 2; 42. 1; 53. 9; 61. 1, 2.
Preaching, Ps. 2. 7; 78. 2; Isa. 2. 3; 61. 1; Mic. 4. 2.
Purification of Temple, Ps. 69. 9.

5. His Passion.
Rejection by Jews and Gentiles, Ps. 2. 1; 22. 12; 41. 5; 56. 5; 69. 8; 118. 22, 23; Isa. 6. 9, 10; 8. 14; 29. 13; 53. 1; 65. 2.
Persecution, Ps. 22. 6; 35. 7, 12; 56. 5; 71. 10; 109. 2; Isa. 49. 7; 53. 3.
Triumphal entry into Jerusalem, Ps. 8. 2; 118. 25, 26; Zech. 9. 9.
Betrayal by own friend, Ps. 41. 9; 55. 13; Zech. 13. 6.
Betrayal for thirty pieces, Zech. 11. 12.
Betrayer's death, Ps. 55. 15, 23; 109. 17.
Purchase of potter's field, Zech. 11. 13.
Desertion by disciples, Zech. 13. 7.
False accusation, Ps. 27. 12; 35. 11; 109. 2; Ps. 2. 1, 2.
Silence under accusation, Ps. 38. 13; Isa. 53. 7.
Mocking, Ps. 22. 7, 8, 16; 109. 25.
Insult, buffeting, spitting, scourging, Ps. 35. 15, 21; Isa. 50. 6.
Patience under suffering, Isa. 53. 7-9.
Crucifixion, Ps. 22. 14, 17.
Gall and vinegar, offer of, Ps. 69. 21.
Prayer for enemies, Ps. 109. 4.
Cries upon the cross, Ps. 22. 1; 31. 5.
Death in prime of life, Ps. 89. 45; 102. 24.
Death with malefactors, Ps. 53. 9, 12.
Death attested by convulsions of nature, Amos 5. 20; Zech. 14. 4, 6.
Casting lots for vesture, Ps. 22. 18.
Bone not to be broken, Ps. 34. 20.
Piercing, Ps. 22. 16; Zech. 12. 10; 13. 6.
Voluntary death, Ps. 40. 6–8.
Vicarious suffering, Isa. 53. 4-6, 12; Dan. 9. 26.
Burial with the rich, Isa. 53. 9.

6. His Resurrection.
Ps. 16. 8–10; 30. 3; 41. 10; 118. 17; Hos. 6. 2.

7. His Ascension.
Ps. 16. 11; 24. 7; 68. 18; 110. 1; 118. 19.
Dominion universal and everlasting, 1 Chron. 17. 11–14; Ps. 72. 8; Isa. 9. 7; Dan. 7. 14; Ps. 2. 6–8; 8. 6; 110. 1–3; 45. 6, 7.

8. His Second Advent.
Ps. 50. 3–6; Isa. 9. 6, 7; 66. 18; Dan. 7. 13, 14; Zech. 12. 10; 14. 4–8.

MIRACLES OF THE OLD TESTAMENT.

IN EGYPT.	
Aaron's rod turned to serpent..	Ex. 7. 10–12.
The plagues: —	
1. Water made blood.........	" 7. 20–25.
2. Frogs....................	" 8. 5–14.
3. Lice	" 8. 16–18.
4. Flies....................	" 8. 20–24.
5. Murrain..................	" 9. 3–6.
6. Boils and blains.........	" 9. 8–11.
7. Thunder and hail.........	" 9. 22–26.
8. Locusts..................	" 10. 12–19.
9. Darkness.................	" 10. 21–23.
10. Slaying of firstborn....	" 12. 29, 30.
Parting of Red Sea..........	" 14. 21–31.
IN THE WILDERNESS.	
Curing of waters of Marah....	Ex. 15. 23–25.
Sending of manna............	" 16. 14–35.
Water from the rock.........	" 17. 5–7.
Death of Nadab and Abihu.....	Lev. 10. 1, 2.
Burning of the congregation...	Num. 11. 1–3.
Death of Korah, etc.........	" 16. 31–35.
Budding of Aaron's rod.......	" 17. 8.
Water at Meribah............	" 20. 7–11.
The brazen serpent..........	" 21. 8, 9.
Stoppage of Jordan..........	Josh. 3. 14–17.
IN CANAAN.	
Fall of Jericho.............	Josh. 6. 6–25.
Staying of sun and moon......	" 10. 12–14.
UNDER THE KINGS.	
Death of Uzzah..............	2 Sam. 6. 7.
Withering of Jeroboam's hand.	1 K. 13. 4–6.
BY ELIJAH.	
Staying of oil and meal.........	1 K. 17. 14–16.
Raising of widow's son.........	" 17. 17–24.
Burning of the sacrifice at Carmel........................	" 18. 30–38.
Burning of the captains........	2 K. 1. 10–12.
Dividing of Jordan.............	" 2. 7, 8.
BY ELISHA.	
Dividing of Jordan.............	2 K. 2. 14.
Cure of Jericho waters.........	" 2. 21, 22.
Destruction of mocking children	" 2. 23, 24.
Supply of waters to armies	" 3. 16–20.
Increase of widow's oil........	" 4. 2–7.
Raising Shunammite's son.....	" 4. 32–37.
Healing the poison pottage.....	" 4. 38–41.
Twenty loaves for 100 men......	" 4. 42–44.
Cure of Naaman's leprosy......	" 5. 10–27.
Making the axe swim..........	" 6. 5–7.
Smiting the Syrian army.......	" 6. 18–20.
Revival of the dead...........	" 13. 21.
MENTIONED BY ISAIAH.	
Destruction of Assyrians.......	2 K. 19. 35.
Return of sun on dial..........	" 20. 9–11.
DURING CAPTIVITY.	
Deliverance from fiery furnace.	Dan. 3. 19–27.
Deliverance from lion's den....	" 6. 16–23.
IN GENERAL.	
Smiting of Philistines.........	1 Sam. 5. 3–12.
Leprosy of Uzziah.............	2 Chr. 26. 16–21.
Deliverance of Jonah..........	Jonah 2. 1–10.

PARABLES AND FABLES OF THE OLD TESTAMENT.

PARABLES.	BY WHOM DELIVERED.	REFERENCE.
The ewe lamb..................	Nathan to David..............	2 Sam. 12. 1–4.
The two brethren and avengers of blood.	Widow of Tekoah..............	" 14. 1–11.
The escaped captive...........	A man of the prophets to Ahab..........	1 K. 20. 35–40.
The vineyard and grapes.......	Isaiah to Judah and Jerusalem..........	Is. 5. 1–7.
The eagles and the vine.......	Ezekiel to Israel............	Ezek. 17. 3–10.
The lion's whelps.............	" "	" 19. 2–9.
The boiling pot...............	" "	" 24. 3–5.
FABLES.		
Trees choosing a king.........	Jotham to Shechemites........	Judg. 9. 7–15.
Vision of Micaiah.............	Micaiah to Jehoshaphat.......	1 K. 22. 19–23.
The thistle and cedar.........	Jehoash to Amaziah...........	2 K. 14. 9.

MIRACLES OF OUR LORD.

MIRACLES.	MAT	MARK.	LUKE.	JOHN.
I. *Narrated in one Gospel only.*				
Two blind men healed	9. 27			
A dumb demoniac healed	9. 32			
Stater in the mouth of the fish	17. 24			
The deaf and dumb man healed		7. 31		
A blind man healed		8. 22		
When Christ passed unseen through the multitude			4. 30	
Draught of fishes			5. 1	
Raising the widow's son			7. 11	
Healing the crooked woman			13. 11	
Healing the man with the dropsy			14. 1	
Healing the ten lepers			17. 11	
Healing the ear of Malchus, servant of the high priest			22. 50	
Turning water into wine				2. 1
Healing the nobleman's son (of fever)				4. 46
Healing the impotent man at Bethesda				5. 1
Healing the man born blind				9. 1
Raising of Lazarus				11. 43
Draught of fishes				21. 1
II. *Narrated in two Gospels.*				
Demoniac in synagogue cured		1. 23	4. 33	
Healing centurion's servant (of palsy)	8. 5		7. 1	
The blind and dumb demoniac	12. 22		11. 14	
Healing the daughter of the Syrophenician	15. 21	7. 24		
Feeding the four thousand	15. 32	8. 1		
Cursing the fig tree	21. 18	11. 12		
III. *Narrated in three Gospels.*				
Healing the leper	8. 2	1. 40	5. 12	
Healing Peter's mother-in-law	8. 14	1. 30	4. 38	
Stilling the storm	8. 26	4. 37	8. 22	
The legion of devils entering swine	8. 28	5. 1	8. 27	
Healing the man sick of the palsy	9. 2	2. 3	5. 18	
Healing woman with issue of blood	9. 20	5. 25	8. 43	
Raising of Jairus' daughter	9. 23	5. 38	8. 49	
Healing the man with a withered hand	12. 10	3. 1	6. 6	
Walking on the sea	14. 25	6. 48		6. 19
Curing demoniac child	17. 14	9. 17	9. 38	
Curing blind Bartimæus (two blind men, Mat. 20)	20. 30	10. 46	18. 35	
IV. *Narrated in four Gospels.*				
Feeding the five thousand	14. 19	6. 35	9. 12	6. 5

NOTE. The above list names only those miracles which are described in the Gospels; but the Gospels state that he wrought great numbers of other miracles of healing.

MIRACLES OF THE EARLY CHURCH.

MIRACLES.	REFERENCES.
Gift of tongues at Pentecost	Acts 2. 1-14
Healing of the lame man at the Temple gate by Peter and John	" 3. 1-11
Death of Ananias and Sapphira at the word of Peter	" 5. 1-11
Numerous acts of healing at Jerusalem by all the apostles	" 5. 12-16
Opening of the prison doors to the apostles	" 5. 17-25
Cases of healing in Samaria by Philip the Deacon	" 8. 6,7,13
Cure of Aeneas at Lydda by Peter	" 9. 32-35
Raising of Dorcas at Joppa by Peter	" 9. 36-41
Deliverance of Peter from prison in Jerusalem	" 12. 5-17
Blindness of Elymas, at Cyprus, at the word of Paul	" 13. 9-11
Healing of impotent man at Lystra by Paul	" 14. 8-12
Cure of possessed girl at Philippi by Paul	" 16. 16-18
Numerous miracles of healing by Paul	" 19. 11,12
Raising of Eutychus at Troas by Paul	" 20. 7-12
Cure of Publius and others at Malta by Paul	" 28. 7-10

PARABLES OF OUR LORD.

PARABLES.	MAT.	MARK.	LUKE.	LEADING LESSONS.
I. *Recorded in one Gospel only.*				
The tares	13. 24			Good and evil in life and judgment.
The hid treasure	13. 44			Value of the gospel.
The goodly pearl	13. 45			The seeker finding salvation.
The draw-net	13. 47			Visible Church a mixed body.
The unmerciful servant	18. 23			Duty of forgiveness.
The labourers in the vineyard	20. 1			Precedence in service gives no claim for priority in reward.
The two sons	21. 28			Insincerity and repentance.
The marriage of the king's son	22. 2			Necessity of the robe of righteousness.
The ten virgins	25. 1			Watchful preparation and careless security.
The talents	25. 14			Use of advantages.
The sheep and goats	25. 31			Love the test of life.
The seed growing secretly		4. 26		The law of growth in religion.
The householder		13. 34		Watchfulness.
The two debtors			7. 41	Gratitude for pardon.
The good Samaritan			10. 30	Active benevolence.
The importunate friend			11. 5	Perseverance in prayer.
The rich fool			12. 16	Worldly-mindedness.
Servants watching			12. 35	Expectancy of the Second Coming.
The wise steward			12. 42	Conscientiousness in trust.
The barren fig tree			13. 6	Unprofitableness under grace.
The great supper			14. 16	Universality of the Divine call.
Building tower; king going to war			14. 28	Prudence and self-denial.
The piece of money			15. 8	Joy over penitence.
The prodigal son			15. 11	Fatherly love to returning sinner.
The unjust steward			16. 1	Faithfulness to trust.
The rich man and Lazarus			16. 19	Hopeless future of the unfaithful.
Unprofitable servants			17. 7	God's claim on all our service.
The unjust judge			18. 2	Advantage of persevering prayer.
The Pharisee and publican			18. 10	Self-righteousness and humility.
The pounds			19. 12	Diligence rewarded, sloth punished.
II. *Recorded in two Gospels.*				
House on rock, and on the sand	7. 24		6. 47	Consistent and false profession.
The leaven	13. 33		13. 20	Pervading influence of religion.
The lost sheep	18. 12		15. 4	Joy over penitent.
III. *Recorded in three Gospels.*				
Candle under a bushel	5. 15	4. 21	[11. 33 8. 16;	Dissemination of truth.
New cloth on old garment	9. 16	2. 21	5. 36	New doctrine on old prejudices.
New wine in old bottles	9. 17	2. 22	5. 37	New spirit in unregenerate heart.
The sower	13. 3	4. 3	8. 5	Hearers divided into classes.
The mustard-seed	13. 31	4. 30	13. 18	Spread of the gospel.
The wicked husbandmen	21. 33	12. 1	20. 9	Rejection of Christ by the Jews.
The fig tree and all the trees	24. 32	13. 28	21. 29	Indications of Second Advent.

NOTE. These Parables are those which are given in detail; but there are quite a number of others, brief similitudes, which are sometimes counted as parables.

DISCOURSES OF JESUS.

CHRONOLOGICALLY ARRANGED.

DISCOURSE.	PLACE.	REFERENCE.
With Nicodemus	Jerusalem.	John 3. 1-21.
With woman of Samaria	Sychar	" 4. 1-42.
In the synagogue	Nazareth	Luke 4. 16-31.
Sermon on the Mount	"	Mat. 5-7.
Apostles instructed	Galilee	" 10.
Chorazin denounced	"	" 11. 20-24.
On healing the infirm	Jerusalem.	John 5.
On plucking of corn	Judea	Mat. 12. 1-8.
On working miracles	Capernaum	" 12. 22-37.
The bread of life	"	John 6.
On internal purity	"	Mat. 15. 1-20.
On forgiveness	"	" 18.
At Feast of Tabernacles	Jerusalem.	John 7.
The adulteress	Jerusalem.	John 8. 3-11.
Sheep and shepherd	"	" 10.
Against the Pharisees	Peræa	Luke 11. 29-54.
On humility	Galilee	" 14. 7-14.
Obtaining heaven	Peræa	Mat. 19. 16-30.
Concerning sufferings	Jerusalem.	" 20. 17-19.
Against Pharisees	"	" 23.
Destruction of Jerusalem	"	" 24.
Farewell discourses in the Upper Room	"	John 13-16.
On the way to Olivet	"	Mat. 26. 31-35.
On Olivet after his resurrection	"	" 28. 18-20.

THE ITINERARY OF ST. PAUL'S MISSIONARY JOURNEYS.

PLACES.	ACTS.
I. First Missionary Journey With Barnabas and John Mark.	13: 1-14: 28
Two or more years, from 47 to 49 A.D.	
Sent forth, from	
SYRIA, the region north of Palestine.	
Antioch, the capital and home church...	13: 1-3
Seleucia, the seaport..............	13: 4
Traveled and preached in	
CYPRUS, off the coast of Syria.	
Salamis..............	13: 4,5
Paphos, where was Elymas the sorcerer.	13: 6-12
PAMPHYLIA, on southern coast of *Asia Minor*.	
Perga, where John Mark left them......	13: 13
PISIDIA, north of Pamphylia.	
Antioch, on the border of Phrygia.......	13: 14-51
LYCAONIA, east of Pisidia.	
Iconium, the capital, the modern Konia, where they were threatened with stoning..............	13: 51-14: 6
Lystra, southeast of Iconium, where Paul cured the impotent man, and the apostles were taken for Jupiter and Mercury.	14: 6-20
Derbe, southeast of Lystra, the farthest point they reached..............	14: 20, 21
On Return, preached in	
Lystra..............	14: 21-23
Iconium..............	14: 21-23
Antioch in Pisidia..............	14. 21-20
Perga..............	14: 24-25
Attalia, the modern *Adalia*, from which they sailed to..............	14: 25, 26
ANTIOCH IN SYRIA..............	14: 26-28
II. Second Missionary Journey with Silas.	15: 36-18: 22
Three or more years from 50-52 A.D.	
SYRIA,	
Antioch, the home church..............	15: 36-40
Towns to the north of Antioch..............	15: 41
CILICIA, the southeastern corner of Asia Minor, probably passing near the modern missionary towns of Aintab, Marash, Adana, Tarsus..............	15: 41
LYCAONIA, towards the northwest.	
Derbe..............	16: 1, 4, 5
Lystra, where he found Timothy........	16: 1-5
Iconium..............	16: 1-5
PHRYGIA, a large province west of Pamphylia and Pisidia	16: 6
GALATIA, So. Galatia, which really includes the cities of Derbe, Lystra and Iconium..............	16: 6
They then planned to travel in	
Mysia, a country near Phrygia............	16: 7, 8
Bithynia, the province on the Black Sea and Sea of Marmora, across the Bosphorus from Constantinople..............	16: 7
This plan they were not allowed to carry out.	
They then went to	
Troas, on the shore of the Ægean, where Paul had the vision of the man from Macedonia..............	16: 7-11
MACEDONIA, north of Greece.	
Neapolis, the port of Philippi, the modern *Kavalla*	16: 11
Philippi, where Paul cured the possessed girl..............	16: 12-40
Thessalonica, modern *Salonica*, where Jason, their host, was threatened by a mob..............	17: 1-10
Berea, the modern *Verria*, west of Thessalonica..............	17: 10-14
GREECE.	
Athens, the Capital..............	17: 15-34
Corinth, where the incident of Gallio occurred..............	18: 1-18
Cenchræa, the eastern harbor of Corinth.	18: 18
On Return	
Sailed from *Cenchræa* to..............	18: 18

PLACES.	ACTS.
Ephesus, on the coast of Asia Minor a little south of modern Smyrna..........	18: 19-21
Cæsarea, on the coast of Palestine, north of Joppa..............	18: 22
Jerusalem..............	18: 22
ANTIOCH IN SYRIA..............	18: 22
III. Third Missionary Journey with Timothy and others.	18: 23-21: 17
Three or four years, 53-56 A.D.	
SYRIA: **Antioch**, the home church.	18: 23
GALATIA and its churches, visited in the previous journey..............	18: 23
PHRYGIA, the churches visited before....	18: 23
ASIA, the Roman province so-called on the shore of the Ægean.	
Ephesus and vicinity; nearly 3 yrs. Here occurred the incidents of John's disciples, the "reasoning" in the school of Tyrannus, the burning of the books of magic, and the riot of the silversmiths.	18: 24-20: 1
MACEDONIA. Revisiting the churches...	20: 1
GREECE. Revisiting the churches........	20: 2, 3
On Return	
Philippi..............	20: 6
Troas, where occurred the death and raising of Eutychus..............	20: 6-13
Assos, where Paul took ship..............	20: 14
Mitylene, on the island of Lesbos in the Ægean..............	20: 14
Miletus, on the coast of the Ægean, where he met the elders of the church at Ephesus..............	20: 15-21: 1
Patara, on the southern coast of Asia Minor..............	21: 1, 2
Tyre, in Phœnicia, where he met many disciples..............	21: 3-7
Ptolemais = Acre, seaport, south of Tyre.	21: 7
Cæsarea, where Agabus prophesied.....	21: 8-15
Jerusalem..............	21: 15-17
IV. St. Paul's Journey to Rome	
With St. Luke, Aristarchus, and certain prisoners under charge of Julius, a Centurion of the Augustan Cohort, A.D. 59 & 60..............	27: 1-28: 31
Sailed from	
Cæsarea..............	27: 1, 2
Sidon, on coast of Phœnicia north of Tyre. Here Paul saw his friends.......	27: 3
Cyprus..............	27: 4
Myra, in Lycia, in the extreme south of Asia Minor..............	27: 5-6
Cnidus, on a promontory of Asia Minor just beyond Rhodes..............	27: 7
Salmone, the east point of the island of *Crete*..............	27: 7, 8
Fair Havens, a harbor on the southern coast of Crete..............	27: 8-13
Starting out from here for a better harbor for the winter they were struck by the storm and driven to..............	27: 13-15
Cauda, or *Clauda*, a small island west of Crete..............	27: 16
And after two weeks of tossing and danger, were finally shipwrecked on the coast of..............	27: 17-27
Malta, an island south of the eastern point of Sicily, where they spent the winter.	27: 27-28: 11
In the spring they sailed to	
Syracuse, on the eastern coast of Sicily.	28: 12
Rhegium, in Italy on the Straits of Messina. Now *Reggio*..............	28: 13
Puteoli, now *Pozzuoli* in the harbor of Naples. Here he rested seven days....	28: 13, 14
Appii Forum, a station on the Appian Way, near modern *Treponti*, 43 miles from Rome. Here the Roman Christians met him..............	28: 15
Three Taverns, another station on the Appian Way, near the modern *Cisterna*.	28: 15
ROME.............. Where he lived at the close of the history in the Acts, two years later.	28: 16-31

MEASURES OF CAPACITY.

I. Liquid.

The *Standard* or *Unit of Measure* was the **Bath** = the **Ephah** of Dry Measure.

	Earlier. Litres.	Earlier. Gallons.	Earlier. Quarts.	Earlier. Pints.	Later. Litres.	Later. Gallons.	Later. Quarts.	Later. Pints.	Approximate. Gallons.	Approximate. Quarts.	Approximate. Pints.
Log = Roman *Sextarius*	0.51	....	....	0.90	0.56	....	....	0.99	....	½	1
4 " = **Cab**	2.05	....	1	1.60	2.24	....	1	1.96	....	2	....
12 " = 3 " = **Hin**	6.12	1	1	0.80	6.75	1	1	1.80	1½	6	....
72 " = 18 " = 6 " = **Bath** or *Ephah*	36.92	8	0	1.0	40.50	8	3	1.28	9	36	....
720 " = 180 " = 60 " = 10 " = **Homer** or *Cor*	369.2	81	4	0	405.0	89	0	0.80	90	....	....

The **Bath,** the standard unit = the cube of one half a cubit. = 2500 cubic inches Greek measure, or 2300 Jewish measure. = The Greek *Metretes.*

The standards varied in different countries, and at different times; and in translating them into modern equivalents there are equal or greater variations in English measures. See *Encyc. Britannica, Eleventh Ed.* There are, for instance, four different quarts named in the Century Dictionary, as in use in this country. Hence all the numbers given are only approximate.

A Litre, the Unit of Capacity in the Metric System, used in all scientific calculations, is the volume of one kilogram of water = one cubic decimetre = 0.88 of an imperial quart, or 1.056 United States quarts.

"Measure" (Ps. 80:5; Isa. 40:12) = ⅓ Bath = 1 Seah of Dry Measure, = 11 qts.

"Measure" (Luke 16:6) = Bath = about 9 gals.

"Firkin" (John 2:6) = Gk. *Mĕtrētēs* = Bath = about 9 gals.

"Pot" (Mk. 7:4) = Rom. *Sextarius* = about one pint.

II. Dry.

The *Unit* of Measure was the **Ephah.**

	Earlier. Litres.	Earlier. Bushels.	Earlier. Pecks.	Earlier. Quarts.	Earlier. Pints.	Later. Litres.	Later. Bushels.	Later. Pecks.	Later. Quarts.	Later. Pints.	Approximate. Bushels.	Approximate. Pecks.	Approximate. Quarts.	Approximate. Pints.
Log = Roman *Sextarius*	0.51	..	..	..	0.90	0.56	..	..	..	0.99	..	..	..	1
4 " = **Cab**	2.05	..	..	1	1.60	2.25	..	..	1	1.96	..	..	2	..
7.2 " = 1.8 " = **Omer**	3.70	..	..	3	0.50	4.05	..	..	3	1.13	..	..	..	7
24 " = 6 " = 3½ " = **Seah**	12.30	..	1	2	1.6	13.5	..	1	3	1.76	..	1½	..	..
72 " = 18 " = 10 " = 3 " = **Ephah**	36.92	1	0	0	1	40.5	1	0	3	1.28	1	..	..	..
720 " = 180 " = 100 " = 30 " = 10 " = **Homer** or *Cor*	369.2	10	0	5	0	405.0	11	0	4	0.8	11	..	..	..

"Measure" (Rev. 6:6) = Gk. *Choinix* = nearly one quart (.96).

"Measure" (1 Kin. 4:22; 2 Chr. 2:10) = homer

"Bushel" (Mat. 5:15) = Rom. *Modius* = nearly a peck (.96).

The Ephah was the Unit of Dry Measure as the Bath was of Liquid.

According to the careful calculations of Lieut.-Gen. Sir Charles Warren, an Ephah or Bath contained 2333.3 cubic inches. A Log contained 32.4 cubic inches, or a cube each of whose sides = 3.185 inches.

The foregoing tables will explain many texts in the Bible. Take, for instance, Isa. 5:10, "For 10 acres of vineyard shall yield one bath (nearly 9 gallons; or 3½ quarts to an acre), and a homer of seed (10 or 11 bushels) shall yield but an Ephah" (1 bush. 3 qts.) or about $\frac{1}{10}$ as much as the seed sown.

MEASURES OF LENGTH.

I. Smaller.

The *Unit* or standard of Measure was the **Cubit**.					Roman and Attic. Metres.	Roman and Attic. Feet.	Roman and Attic. Inches.	Talmudic. Metres.	Talmudic. Feet.	Talmudic. Inches.
Digit — "finger's breadth"					0.0185	0	0.728	0.023	0	0.91
4 " =	**Palm** — "hand breadth"				0.074	0	2.912	0.092	0	3.64
12 " =	3 " =	**Span**			0.222	0	8.737	0.277	0	10.93
24 " =	6 " =	2 " =	**Cubit**		0 444	1	5.48	0.555	1	9.85
144 " —	36 " —	12 " =	6 " =	**Reed**	2.664	8	8.87	3.330	10	11.10
168 " =	42 " =	14 " =	7 " =	**Ezekiel's Reed**	3.108	10	2.30	3.885	12	8.95

The standard of measures of length was the Cubit, which was originally the length of the human arm from the elbow to the tip of the middle finger. The Span is the extent between the tips of the thumb and the little finger when stretched out. The English span is 9 inches.

From this origin of the measures it is easy to see the reason why these measures, and all derived from them, vary very much in length, because the hand and arm of different persons and different races have different lengths.

The cubit varies from 17.6 inches (the Siloam inscription at Jerusalem and the Greek Olympic cubit) to nearly 22 inches.

The cubit is given, approximately, as *a foot and a half*, and is now generally reckoned as 18 inches, except where especial exactness is required. The length of the foot varied in different periods and countries. See Harper's *Classical Dictionary*, article "Cubitus," and the tables in the Appendix, and the *Encyc. Brit.*

But though the standards vary, the relations of the measures one to another are always the same as given in the tables.

According to Lieut.-Gen. Sir Charles Warren, K.C.B., F.R.S., the length of the cubit regulated everything connected with weights and measures, and even the weight of the gold, silver, and copper coinage; as the Metre is of the whole metric system.

The *metre* is 39.37 English inches.

The *Fathom* of Acts 27:28 is a Greek and Roman measure, of approximately 6 feet.

II. Land and Distance.

The *Unit* of Measure is the **Cubit**.					English Standard. Metres.	English Standard. Miles.	English Standard. Feet.	English Standard. Inches.
Foot	= Roman *Pes*				0.296	....	0	11.65
1½	= **Cubit** = nearly 18 inches				0.444	....	1	5.48
5	= 3⅓	= **Pace** = *Passus*			1.480	....	4	10.27
600	= 400	= 120	= **Furlong** = Stadium		177.60	0.11	582	8.40
5000	= 3333⅓	= 1000	= 8	= **Mile** = *Mille Passuum*	1480.00	0.92	4856	0
5000	= 3333⅓	= 1000	= 8	= **"Sabbath Day's Journey"**	1480.00	0.92	4856	0

A pace (the stretch of the leg in walking) varies from 2½ ft. (the military pace) to 3 ft The Roman *passus* was a double pace, from the back of the foot at the start to the position of the same foot at the end of the movement. It was 5 Roman feet.

A furlong is often spoken of roughly as 600 ft.

The relations of the measures to one another are correct, but the standards vary slightly; the Roman Stadium, or furlong, being 185 metres, the Attic 177, the Olympic 192.

The Roman mile was a little more than nine-tenths of an English mile.

A metre, 39.37 English inches. The English foot is .3048 of a metre.

WEIGHTS.

The *Unit* of Weight was the **Shekel** or ½ oz. of ordinary weight.

	Heavy Weight.			Light Weight.		
	Grains.	Pounds.	Oz.	Grains.	Pounds.	Oz.
Gerah = "grain"	11.2	....	....	5.6	....	....
5 = **Rebah** = "quarter" = ¼ shekel.	56.0	....	....	28.0	....	....
10 = 2 = **Bekah** = "half" = ½ shekel	112.0	....	....	56.0	....	....
20 = 4 = 2 = **Shekel**	224.5	....	½	112.0	....	¼
400 = 80 = 40 = 20 = **Libra** = Greek *Litra* "Pound" (John 12: 4)	5,050.	....	Avoir. 11⅓	....	....	....
1000 = 200 = 100 = 50 = 2½ = **Mina** or *Maneh* "Pound" of Luke	11,225.	Troy = 2 Avoir. = 1	0 8	5612.	Troy = 1 Avoir. = 0	0 12
60,000 = 12,000 = 6,000 = 3,000 = – = 60 = **Talent** (silver)	673,500.	Troy = 117 Avoir. = 96	0 5⅓	336,750.	Troy = 58 Avoir. = 48	5+ 0
Talent (gold)	758,000.	Troy = 131 Avoir. = 108	0 0	379,000.	Troy = 65 Avoir. = 54	5+ 0

The above table is in accord with the article by A. R. S. Kennedy, D.D., in Hastings' *Bible Dictionary*, and with the weights given in the Tables of Money.

But there was a great variation in those times as there is now in different countries and at different times in the same country.

The pound in Luke 19:13 = Mina, the Attic or light weight, = 12 oz. avoir. or 1 lb. Troy.

The pound in John 12:3 and 19:39 = Libra = 11 oz.

The pound avoir. = 7000 grains.

The pound Troy = 5760 grains.

RECKONING OF DAY AND NIGHT, — WATCHES AND HOURS.

The Ciail Day began at sunset and ended at sunset of the next day, instead of from midnight to midnight with us.

The Natural Day was from sunrise to sunset.

The Natural Night was from sunset to sunrise.

Whatever the length of the day from sunrise to sunset, it was divided into twelve equal parts; so that in Palestine each hour in December, when the days were 10 of our hours long, would be only 50 minutes, while in July, the days being 14 hours and 18 minutes, their hour would be one hour and ten minutes of our reckoning. The sixth hour was always 12 o'clock. At the time of the crucifixion, day and night being equal, the hours were the same length as ours.

Night (*Ancient*).

First Watch (Lam. 2: 19) till midnight.
Middle Watch (Jud. 7: 19) till 3 A.M.
Morning Watch (Ex. 14: 24) till 6 A.M.

Day (*Ancient*).

Morning till about 10 A.M.
Heat of day till about 2 P.M.
Cool of day till about 6 P.M.

Night (*New Testament*).

First Watch, *evening* = 6 to 9 P.M.
Second Watch, *midnight* = 9 to 12 P.M.
Third Watch, *cock-crow* = 12 to 3 A.M.
Fourth Watch, *morning* = 3 to 6 A.M.

Day (*New Testament*).

Third hour = 9 A.M.
Sixth hour = 12 midday.
Ninth hour = 3 P.M.
Twelfth hour = 6 P.M.

MONEY VALUES IN THE OLD TESTAMENT.

I. Silver.

The *Unit* of Value was the **Shekel**.	Heavy *or* Common Standard.			Light Standard.		
	Weights in Grains Troy.	$	Cts.	Weights in Grains Troy.	$	Cts.
Shekel = 4 Roman *Denarii* or *Drachmas*	224½	0	64.6	112¼	0	32.3
50 = **Mina**	11,225	32	30	5,612½	16	15
3000 = 60 = **Talent**	673,500= 96½ lbs. Avoir.	1940 nearly	00	336,750	970 nearly	00

II. Gold.

The *Unit* of Value was the **Shekel**.	Heavy *or* Common Standard.			Light Standard.		
	Weights in Grains Troy.	$	Cts.	Weights in Grains Troy.	$	Cts.
Shekel = 15 silver shekels....................	252⅔	9	69	126⅓	4	85
50 = **Mina**..................................	12,630	484	75	6,315	242	38
3000 = 60 = **Talent**.........................	758,000= 108 lbs. Avoir.	29,085	00	379,000	14,542	00
Dram (A.V.) or **Daric** (R.V.) } Ezra 8:27; Neh. 7:22. A gold Persian coin	130	5	60			

The *shekel* was the unit of value in common use.

The value of the silver shekel varied at different times. The best specimens now extant weigh from 218 to 220 grains. Hastings reckons it as weighing 224½ grains, as above. Harper's *Classical Dictionary* makes it 240 grains.

The reason for the different weights of the silver and gold shekels and their multiples lay in the fact that the ratio of silver to gold was 13.3 to 1, a very inconvenient ratio. Therefore the weight of the gold shekel was increased so that its value equalled 15 silver shekels.

There are no coins mentioned in the Bible before the Exile, and only one, the gold daric, in the O. T. There were, however, ingots or bars of gold and silver of definite weight for convenience of trade.

These tables were computed by the present editor from a careful comparison of Harper's *Classical Dictionary*, and Hastings' *Bible Dictionary*, and a further consultation of a number of other authorities, including the *Jewish Cyclopedia*.

One pound avoirdupois contains 7,000 grains. One pound troy contains 5,760 grains.

MONEY VALUES IN THE NEW TESTAMENT.

					Weight in grains.		$	Cts.
I. Copper or Brass.								
Mite				= Greek *lepton*. Matt. 12:2; Lu. 12:59; 21:2	......	(⅓ farthing Eng.)	......	⅛
2				= **Farthing** = Greek *kodrantes;* Rom. *quadrans.* Matt. 5:16; Mk. 12:42	......	(⅝ farthing Eng).	......	¼
8	= 4			= **Farthing** = *Assarion* = *As.* Matt. 10:29; Luke 12:6	4	......	......	1
32	= 16	= 4		= **Sestertius** (Roman)	......		......	4
128	= 64	= 16	= 4	= **Denarius** (Silver)	60	56	......	16
II. Silver.								
Denarius (Roman) or **Drachma** (Greek)				The silver penny; the ordinary day's wage. Matt. 20:10; Luke 15:8; 20:24; Acts 19:19	60	56	......	16
?	= **Didrachma** (Roman) or **Half-Shekel** (Jewish)			"Tribute money" Matt. 17:24; 22:19	120	112½	....	32⅓
4	= 2			= **Stater** (Roman) or **Shekel** (Jewish) — Matt. 17:27. The same as *argurion*, "piece of silver" (Matt. 26:15)	240	224½	......	64⅔
100	= 50	= 25		= **Mina** = *maneh* = "pound" of Luke 19	6000	5612	16	15
6000	= 3000	= 1500	= 601	= **Talent** of Matt. 25	360,000	333,750	970	00
25				= **Aureus** = the only *gold* coin in Palestine in the time of Augustus. Nearly ¼ *Mina*. Matt. 10:9	126	120.3	5 nearly	00

The *Denarius* was the standard coin of Roman, as the *Shekel* was of Jewish, currency. The coin was about the size of an English half crown, and a little larger than a half dollar.

Since in all our coins there is an appreciable amount of alloy, the calculations of the equivalents in English money are based upon the price at which the Royal Mint buys pure gold (in 1902) viz.: £3, 17s. 10½d., per oz. of 480 grains.

The equivalents in dollars and cents are based upon the amount of pure silver in the standard dollar of 416 grs. = 371¼ grs. Silver and gold are estimated at the proportion of 16 to 1.

The variations in the values are very perplexing. No one standard was maintained in any country during different periods; and standards varied greatly at the same period in different countries. The tables therefore are approximate, or average. But with all due allowances for variations of value of both the ancient and modern coins, it is exact enough for all practical purposes.

These tables of money values will explain many parables and incidents in the Bible where money is mentioned. For example, we can understand why Naaman (2 Kings 5:23) considered two servants necessary for carrying two talents of silver and a few garments, — the talents weighed 50-100 pounds each, according to the standard used. The "30 pieces of silver" received by Judas as the reward of his treachery amounted to $24, or, according to the value of money at that time, the wage of a common laborer for about six months. The poor widow commended by Christ gave only ¼ of a cent — but it was all she had. The man who was given but one talent, in the parable, received at the lowest calculation nearly $1,000, or an amount it would have taken a laboring man twenty years to earn.

COINS IN USE IN PALESTINE.

THE PERSIAN (or golden) DARIC.

(Ezra 8 : 27.) Worth about $5.60. A.V. = "Dram."

JEWISH HALF-SHEKEL.

The coin in which the Temple tax was paid. The *tribute money* of Matt. 17 : 27. Value, 32 cents = Greek *didrachma.*

SILVER DENARIUS

of Tiberius. Coined in the time of Christ. The *Penny* of Matt. 18 : 28, etc. Value = 16 cents. An ordinary day's wage.

BRONZE COIN OF TITUS

commemorating the capture of Jerusalem, A.D. 70. The coins thus struck were of different values, gold, silver, and bronze.

JEWISH SHEKEL.

The unit of Jewish coinage = Roman stater. Value about 64 cents.

SILVER STATER

of Augustus = Tetradrachm of Antioch (Matt. 17 : 27). Same value as Jewish shekel.

BRONZE ASSARION.

The *Farthing* of Matt. 10 : 29. Value about one cent. Equals 4 Quadrans.

BRONZE QUADRANS

of Pontius Pilate. Coined in the time of Christ. The *Farthing* (Mark 12 : 42). Value ¼ cent. Equal to the widow's "two mites which make a farthing."